second edition

INTRODUCTION TO LITERATURE
Reading, Analyzing, and Writing

OROTHY U. SEYLER

ICHARD A. WILAN

rthern Virginia Community College

PRENTICE HALL, Englewood Cliffs, New Jersey 07632

Library of Congress Cataloging-in-Publication Data

Seyler, Dorothy U.
  Introduction to literature : reading, analyzing, and writing /
Dorothy U. Seyler and Richard A. Wilan.—2nd ed.
    p.   cm.
  Includes bibliographical references.
  ISBN 0-13-488123-0
  1. Rhetoric. 2. Literature—Collections. I. Wilan, Richard A.
    II. Title.
PN191.S49 1990
808'.0427—dc20   89-22982
                                                      CIP

Editorial/production supervision and
  interior design: Patricia V. Amoroso
Cover design: Bruce Kenselaar
Manufacturing buyers: Ray Keating and Mike Woerner
Photo researcher: Kay Dellosa
Cover illustration: Renoir, *The Reader*.
  c. 1874. Musée d'Orsay, Paris.

Credits and copyright acknowledgments begin on page 900, which constitutes an
extension of the copyright page.

Printed in the United States of America

10 9 8 7 6 5 4 3 2 1

ISBN 0-13-488123-0

PRENTICE-HALL INTERNATIONAL (UK) LIMITED, *London*
PRENTICE-HALL OF AUSTRALIA PTY. LIMITED, *Sydney*
PRENTICE-HALL CANADA INC., *Toronto*
PRENTICE-HALL HISPANOAMERICANA, S.A., *Mexico*
PRENTICE-HALL OF INDIA PRIVATE LIMITED, *New Delhi*
PRENTICE-HALL OF JAPAN, INC., *Tokyo*
SIMON & SCHUSTER ASIA PTE. LTD., *Singapore*
EDITORA PRENTICE-HALL DO BRASIL, LTDA., *Rio de Janeiro*

Contents

Contents

7   THE LANGUAGE OF STYLE   *193*

8   THE LANGUAGE OF TONE   *224*

9   THE EXTENSION OF MEANING: SYMBOL   *272*

10   THE EXTENSION OF MEANING: THEME   *303*

11   READING THE CRITICS AND DOCUMENTING RESEARCH   *354*

PART II: A COLLECTION OF SHORT STORIES, POEMS, AND PLAYS

SHORT STORIES   *411*

POEMS *561*

PLAYS 611

APPENDIX A: AN EXPLANATION OF METRICAL TERMS 887

APPENDIX B: MANUSCRIPT FORM AND STYLE 889

GLOSSARY 894

INDEX 904

Preface to the Second Edition

We first wrote *Introduction to Literature* to provide a text that integrated the processes of reading, analyzing, and writing about literature, an integration we did not find among existing texts, whether organized by genre or by theme. In the years since the publication of the first edition, several texts have added a writing component to their discussion of literature while others have focused on writing by reducing or eliminating a discussion of the literature. Thus there is still a need for a text that teaches students about literature *and* about writing. We are happy that Prentice Hall saw this need and asked us to prepare a second edition.

Introduction to Literature: Reading, Analyzing, and Writing begins where students must begin, with the basic processes of reading and writing about literature. Chapters 1 and 2 start with the questions that students need to ask first: Why study literature? What is the role of the reader of literature? What is literary analysis, and how is it useful? These chapters then demonstrate how relating evidence to conclusion is essential to literary analysis. Because most students do not begin their introductory courses knowing how to write skillfully about literature, we introduce writing instruction early. Chapter 2 explains paraphrase and summary, pointing out both the proper uses and the limitations of these techniques. Chapter 3, applying analysis to writing about literature, demonstrates a step-by-step process of composing an essay and concludes with a sample student paper.

Chapters 4 through 10 explain and illustrate basic literary elements: structure, character, point of view, style, tone, symbol, and theme. These chapters progress from concepts students grasp most easily to those that they find more difficult. Most readers can begin comfortably with the organization of a story and the personality of a character before moving on to point of view and the subtleties of tone. After gaining confidence from experience with analysis, students can study more sophisticated forms of structure and character and examine the role of point of view and language choice in shaping those forms. We have placed symbol and theme last because these elements, dependent upon the other elements of a work, are the most difficult for students to analyze. Chapter 11, the final chapter, returns to the uses of professional criticism briefly introduced in Chapter 1. By examining the controversy over the ending of Hemingway's "The Short Happy Life of Francis Macomber," students can again study the role of the critic and the nature of literary interpretation. Also in Chapter 11, and new to the second edition, students are guided through the process of preparing and documenting a literary research essay. At the end, as at the beginning, we stress the importance of close reading and the evaluation of evidence in building a convincing interpretation.

The integration of writing about literature with literary analysis continues throughout Chapters 4 through 10. Each of these chapters contains a sample student essay and guidelines for writing that focus on specific problems students have. Students will write more successfully if they can study student essays for assignments similar to their own. The *Selections for Further Study* sections at the end of each chapter provide additional works for class discussion and writing.

The readings in each instructional chapter can be supplemented by Part II, an anthology of short stories, poems, and plays. Readers will find an inviting blend of works—some light, some serious; some old, some new. Although we have provided a variety of styles and authors, some favorite pieces with some surprises, all selections have been chosen because they work well in the classroom. To aid in choosing additional readings, we have organized the anthology by genre, and within each genre by date.

In writing *Introduction to Literature*, we have sought as much flexibility for instructors as possible within the basic framework that integrates reading and writing about literature. More advanced classes might be assigned Chapters 1 and 2 for review only and begin with Chapter 4 (Structure), using Chapter 3 as a reference guide for writing essays. If the instructor wishes, a modified genre approach may be followed by emphasizing the short story for Chapters 4–6, poetry for Chapters 7–9, and the drama for Chapter 10. The sample student essays follow this pattern.

We believe that much can be gained in an introductory course by stressing that the process of recognizing, analyzing, and writing about literary concepts remains the same for all forms of literature. We have found, for example, that students who have discussed the unreliable narrator in Lardner's story "Haircut" are better able to understand the unreliable speaker in Browning's poem "My Last Duchess." We have used the shifting levels of consciousness in Thurber's "The Secret Life of Walter Mitty" as a preparation for the more complex shifting in Eliot's "The Love Song of J. Alfred Prufrock." The study of the tone of a dramatic speaker in a poem has helped our students to an awareness of tone in the dialogue of a story or the lines of a play. In short, stressing elements rather than genre leads students to a fuller understanding of those elements and more control of them when they analyze and write about literature. That has been our experience, an experience we invite you to share.

In preparing this edition, we have become indebted to many colleagues and students. We want to thank all of our colleagues who answered questions about the first edition and offered advice for the second, most especially Brian Hansen, who shared many student papers with us. We are also happy to acknowledge the constructive criticism of the following reviewers: Vivian Brown, Laredo Junior College, Therese Brychta, Truckee Meadows Community College, Kathleen Shine Cain, Merrimack College, Gary N. Christensen, Macomb Community College, Helen Bridge, Chabot College, Betty Hughes, Beaufort Community College. Finally, we wish to thank all of our students who eagerly followed the progress of revision and acknowledge the help of student Louis Martinez, who brought Faulkner's "Mayday" to our attention. A special thanks must go to those who have given us permission to use their essays. They are justly proud of their efforts, and we are proud of them.

DOROTHY U. SEYLER

RICHARD A. WILAN

part I

READING AND WRITING ABOUT LITERATURE

chapter 1

Literature
and the Reader

Pablo Picasso. *The Studio*. 1927–28. Oil on canvas, 59″ × 7′7″. Collection, The Museum of Modern Art, New York. Gift of Walter P. Chrysler, Jr.

WHY STUDY LITERATURE?

Most of us turn to literature for enjoyment. A friend recommends an exciting mystery. An intriguing title draws us to a story in a magazine. We do not read poetry, fiction, or drama to learn how to tune an engine, what pressure points will stop bleeding, or why the upper ozone layer may be damaged by fluorocarbons. Often, we read a book for relaxation, as an escape from work or study. Beginning a course in literature, then, probably raises some expectations of pleasure but also some questions about purpose. How will literature be relevant to other studies? To training for a career? To personal growth?

As teachers of literature we hope to share with you the enthusiasm we feel for our subject. Enjoyment ought to continue to be a major purpose of reading. Still, there are other reasons, important practical reasons, for the study you are about to begin.

In studying literature you will be learning how to read and write better, to communicate better. Good literature provides an especially valuable basis for such learning because creative writers are themselves so deeply involved in language, constantly reaching towards the best word, the right phrase, the appropriate form. As you become more aware of these careful choices, you should begin to experience what you read more fully. You should also begin to see the possibilities of additional choices in your own writing.

Literature, moreover, goes beyond technique to an imaginative vision that can enlarge our world, deepen our emotional responses, and alter our usual way of perceiving. With Ernest Hemingway (pp. 357–82) we come face to face with the lions of East Africa; with Albert Camus (pp. 480–90) the desolate plateau of northern Africa presses on us. When we read Eudora Welty's "A Worn Path" (pp. 42–48), we become sympathetically involved in an old woman's walk across miles of countryside to obtain medicine for her grandson. Or, in reading W. H. Auden's "The Unknown Citizen" (pp. 235–36), we are forced by the satirical portrayal of the speaker to reevaluate some commonly held notions of a successful life. Through literature we can live more lives than one, and on the power of a deeply felt literary experience our hearts and minds can soar. For literature is subversive. It carries us to a new vantage point from which we question our habitual views of the world. What is important, though, is not that we trade in old values for new but that we gain the ability to consider other views with understanding and tolerance.

The process that leads to new awareness is itself important to your education. This process is logical thinking: proceeding from careful observing to discovering relationships to drawing conclusions. These are the steps to follow, both as a reader and as a writer, so that you can convincingly express your experience with literature. When you write about literature, you are explaining an insight or arguing a point just as you would be if you were teaching a beginning swimmer to relax in the water or taking a stand on a nuclear freeze. Although you will now be dealing with the facts of the fictional world of literature, your present study should help you to think more clearly about many other subjects.

YOUR ROLE AS A STUDENT OF LITERATURE

Professional readers of literature are called literary critics; what they write is called literary criticism. Although the term *criticism*, as used in connection with literature, sounds negative, it usually isn't. Some critics do review new works, and they sometimes do find fault. But evaluating is only one of the roles that a critic plays. Criticism extends to any examination of literature—even of other areas, such as history or philosophy, as they relate to literature. Many approaches are valid. A work may be seen, for example, not only as an artistic creation but also as a moral treatise, a social document, or a psychological case study. You may as a student have already engaged in some forms of literary criticism. You may have used biographical criticism to explore how Ernest Hemingway drew upon his war experiences in Italy to write *A Farewell to Arms*. You may have used historical criticism in relating your study of the French Revolution to the Charles Dickens novel *A Tale of Two Cities*. Whenever you have been involved in a response to literature through reading, research, discussion, or writing, you have been in some way a literary critic.

As a critic you can play different roles. You may be intrigued by the thoughts and personality of the writer. You may be curious about the way literature sheds light on the world around us. You may read to arouse feelings, such as amusement or sympathy. Or you may enjoy the intellectual challenge of examining how literature works.

All of these approaches have value. But we can hardly see through to the author's personality or picture of the world without a reading of the work itself that is accurate and complete. Without such a reading, even our emotional responses may be more a matter of what we bring to the work than of what we discover. Your first role, then, should be that of a reader who is conscious of the specific elements of a work such as organization and word choice. That means you need to become an effective user of literary analysis.

THE ADVANTAGE OF ANALYSIS

Your initial reaction to the term *analysis* may be some version of "I don't want to tear literature apart." You may feel that we are about to wheel a poem or story into a classroom operating theater for dissection. Maybe we will be able to put the pieces back together. Maybe the patient will recover. But you would just as soon let well enough alone, content with your personal appreciation of what you have read.

Although analysis does entail dividing something into its component parts, the purpose is to understand, not to destroy. We isolate elements such as plot structure or style to discover the patterns that govern our reading. Analysis should lead to an enrichment rather than to a loss of pleasure.

We might compare a reader of literature to a spectator at a college basketball game. A spectator who has never played basketball or followed the game may share with the crowd the excitement of a close score and wonder at the skill of an agile "dunk" or a gracefully arched jump shot from twenty feet out. But what about the tension that mounts as a play must materialize before the forty-five second clock runs out? What about the strategy behind a coaching decision to shift from a man-to-man defense to a zone defense? The game will be more interesting for the fan who is aware of such elements in basketball. It should also be clear that the fan who knows the sport will have witnessed a different game in some respects from that watched by the casual spectator.

As another example, we might think of students in an art appreciation course. If appreciation meant only likes and dislikes, the final exam might be a series of slides flashed on a screen to which you respond with an "ooh," and "ah," or an "ugh." Your grade would then be determined on the percentage of "correct" emotional reactions. But what determines a correct reaction? For you to communicate with your art instructor you must go back to the basis for each response in the painting or sculpture—to color, form, texture. Then the instructor can be sure that your "ooh" to Cezanne's "Fruit Bowl, Glass, and Apples" was not just a sudden craving for a snack. Your instructor can be sure, too, that you understand why Cezanne's works are highly regarded, even though you may respond more fervently to Van Gogh's "Starry Night."

Analysis can lead us to an awareness of the creative artist's own conception of the work. One of our assumptions about writers, whether they are students writing about literature or the literary authors themselves, is that they make conscious choices. That is, a writer is being *selective* in choosing a title, beginning at a particular moment, repeating over and over an apparently unimportant phrase. This selectivity is there to be observed, to guide us. There are also, as all of us who have tried any form of writing know, subconscious choices, a double meaning or a connection that surprises us on a second reading but then strikes us as what we wanted all along.

An author's selectivity is what makes analysis possible by initiating the patterns and relationships that we discover. But the writer's choices will have little effect without a reader alert to them. The effectiveness of a work depends on the quality of the reader as well as the quality of the writer. Training in analysis will help you become the sensitive reader that good literature presupposes.

THE ANALYTICAL APPROACH

Analysis is part of a process that begins with observation and leads to interpretation. You need to understand how this process works and what the differences are between observation, analysis, and interpretation.

Observation

Even in works of imagination there are facts. Some of these facts are as much a part of our physical world as is the height of Mt. Rainier. A particular poem, for example, will have fourteen lines; a story's division into five sections may be indicated by Roman numerals. Other facts in literature are accepted as such because we agree that they are part of the created world of the work. If a poem begins "The sea is calm tonight, / The tide is full, the moon lies fair," your first assumption should be that it *is* night and that it *is* high tide. Students too often search for "hidden meanings" without first observing the obvious. If you misread a word, skip a line, or fail to stop at a period, you will soon find yourself reading a work created by your own imagination. Give the author a chance. The author wants to communicate, not to hide something. Close reading for observable data is the necessary preparation for analysis.

Analysis

Analysis begins when you start discovering patterns and relationships. You notice that a character keeps repeating an unusual gesture or that an object is being described as if it were a person. As you analyze, you will gradually become aware of such connections or even of an apparent lack of connection, such as a title that seems completely wrong. In later chapters you will learn about elements of literature, such as structure, tone, and point of view, that will help you direct your investigation by dividing the problem of reading into more easily handled parts. You will also learn about the need to ask questions as an important part of the process.

Interpretation

At some stage of your analysis you will begin to draw conclusions with which other readers may disagree. You may decide that character X secretly admires character Y or that the description of a spring day suggests a new life beginning for character Z. You will then be engaging in interpretation. Of course, the reading process does not always follow neatly the pattern of observation, analysis, and then interpretation. Sometimes we draw conclusions as we read and then need to analyze to see how the writer brought us to those conclusions. Sometimes we can't seem to make one part of the work fit into our analysis, so we have to reread and recheck our understanding of the facts. Still, as students of literature we can benefit from an awareness of these three elements of the analytic approach and from withholding complex interpretations until they can be firmly grounded in observation and analysis.

Some readers think that all discussion of literature is interpretive and that, therefore, any comment is "just a matter of interpretation." But you will find that the process of observation and analysis will eventually lead to agreement on a great many points. You will also become more confident about questioning conclusions, no matter what the source, that are not supported by evidence. The opposite extreme to an "anything goes" attitude is the acceptance of an opinion as final simply because it has found its way into print. You must judge, and be judged, on the basis of the entire analytic process that leads to and supports interpretation.

A discussion of the folowing poem by Robert Frost will serve to demonstrate the method.

ROBERT FROST   (1874–1963)

The Road Not Taken

Two roads diverged in a yellow wood,
And sorry I could not travel both
And be one traveler, long I stood
And looked down one as far as I could
To where it bent in the undergrowth;   5

Then took the other, as just as fair,
And having perhaps the better claim,
Because it was grassy and wanted wear;
Though as for that, the passing there
Had worn them really about the same,   10

And both that morning equally lay
In leaves no step had trodden black.
Oh, I kept the first for another day!
Yet knowing how way leads on to way,
I doubted if I should ever come back.   15

I shall be telling this with a sigh
Somewhere ages and ages hence:
Two roads diverged in a wood, and I—
I took the one less traveled by,
And that has made all the difference.   20

In reading "The Road Not Taken," you probably started with a visual impression of the scene, then became aware of a voice speaking to you, and finally sensed that something significant was being said. Now let us go back for a second, more detailed reading.

First we will look for the facts. We know that someone was walking in a wood and, as the road divided into two, stopped to decide which to take. We see the "yellow" color of the wood, the "undergrowth" where one of the roads disappeared from sight. We see that both roads were "grassy" and covered with leaves. We are told that the time of day was morning. We might also notice that the last eight lines present only the speaker's thoughts. We learn that our walker chose what seemed the less frequently used road.

By now we may have spotted a problem. The speaker is not consistent. In line 8 one road "was grassy and wanted wear," therefore having the "better claim" to be chosen. The speaker repeats this idea in line 19: "I took the one less traveled by." But in line 10 the two roads are described as worn "really about the same," and in lines 11–12 we learn thay they were "equally" covered by untrodden leaves. We have begun analysis by discovering this puzzling pattern.

Our discovery of the shifting pattern of thought leads us to examine the speaker's attitude. One element seems to be sadness, more precisely, perhaps, regret. The speaker was "sorry" not to have been able to choose both roads and will be telling about the choice "with a sigh" in the distant future, "ages and ages hence." The emphasis on "ages and ages" is increased by the last line: "And that has made all the difference." What must seem to us a rather simple, unimportant choice appears to have significance for the speaker. Why?

That question brings us to interpretation. Suppose someone suggests the following: "The traveler was attacked by bandits, hiding in the undergrowth, who stole all of the money he was going to invest in a new business." For a moment there is silence. A classmate responds: "But there's nothing in the poem about bandits, and we don't know the traveler's a he." A student in the second row suggests: "Maybe the choice of one road over the other represents to the speaker any wrong choice we make in life. That's where the sadness comes in." The class agrees, and we seem to have reached a reasonable interpretation. But we remember our earlier observation that the two roads were really alike, grass worn the same and the same untrodden leaves. If the roads were, after all, the same, why should one be thought of as wrong? Perhaps the roads represent two equally good choices, or two choices that only seemed different to the speaker at the time. The regret, then, would be for the inability to "travel both," for the unavoidable loss of something no matter what choice is made. These ideas remind one student of a discussion in her high school class, and she asks: "Didn't Frost write the poem to ridicule a friend of his who couldn't make a decision?" The student's reminder to the class of this biographical detail from Frost's life raises the question of the poet's attitude toward the traveler. Should we understand the words "with a sigh" and "ages and ages hence" as exaggerated responses to decision making? Is Frost poking fun at us when we inflate the importance of some choices? Can the poem be both serious and whimsical? By proceeding from observation through analysis to a consideration of several interpretations, we have gained a rich reading experience and a basis for intelligent dialogue.

You should now be ready to apply this approach to another Frost poem. Read it slowly, listing as many facts as possible.

ROBERT FROST   (1874–1963)

Stopping by Woods on a Snowy Evening

Whose woods these are I think I know.
His house is in the village, though;
He will not see me stopping here
To watch his woods fill up with snow.

My little horse must think it queer   5
To stop without a farmhouse near
Between the woods and frozen lake
The darkest evening of the year.

He gives his harness bells a shake
To ask if there is some mistake.   10
The only other sound's the sweep
Of easy wind and downy flake.

The woods are lovely, dark, and deep,
But I have promises to keep,
And miles to go before I sleep,   15
And miles to go before I sleep.

QUESTIONS

1. Where is the speaker? What is the speaker doing?
2. Has the speaker ever been here before?

3. What is the weather? Be precise.
4. What time of year is it? Can we determine the date?
5. What contrast exists between the speaker and the horse?
6. Does the repetition in the last two lines suggest any conclusions?
7. In answering the preceding questions, what facts did you refer to? What conclusions did you draw? Were there any conclusions about which there might be disagreement?

EXERCISE

Now that you have read, responded, and given thought to "Stopping by Woods on a Snowy Evening," consider these brief selections from critics. Note that the conclusions reached differ. Because they are arrived at by professional critics does not mean that the conclusions are equally valid. These conclusions should be evaluated, finally, in the context of the support presented in the longer discussions from which they are taken. Still, enough has been excerpted to give you an idea of where each critic stands. Try reconstructing some of the evidence that might have led to their interpretations. Feel free to be skeptical, to question.

A Sampling of Critical Commentary on "Stopping by Woods on a Snowy Evening"

1. Reginald Cook (quoting Frost's own spoken comments):

   He once remarked that "Stopping by Woods on a Snowy Evening" was the kind of poem he'd like to print on one page, to be followed with "forty pages of footnotes."

   ....

   "Stopping by Woods on a Snowy Evening" contains "all I ever knew."

   Can you explain the apparent discrepancy between these two quotations? How serious is the tone of the first Frost quotation? Of the second?

   "That one I've been more bothered with than anybody has ever been with any poem in just pressing it for more than it should be pressed for. It means enough without its being pressed." And, in a biting tone, he adds, "I don't say that somebody shouldn't press it, but I don't want to be there." Often he has spoken out against the "pressers" and over-readers. "You don't want the music outraged." And of "Stopping by Woods" he says that all it means is "it's all very nice but I must be getting along, getting home." Yet no true reader leaves the discussion there. He knows as well as the poet does that what is important is how the poet played with "the constant symbol" implicit in the making of the poem. "Everything is hinting," Frost reminds us.

How is Cook defining the "true reader"? Do you agree? Disagree?

2. J. McBride Dabbs:

On first reading I valued it for its excellent fusion of freshness and richness, its complete and accurate picture of the humorous shy poet, the pony giving his harness bells a shake, and "The darkest evening of the year." Now I value it for this, and for something else. For the portrait of Robert Frost himself, with those inimitable last lines. . . .

How does Dabbs see Frost's relationship to the poem? Can you think of possible problems with this approach to literature?

3. Lawrence Thompson:

The poem is a dramatic lyric which breaks into the middle of an incident, so that there is a drama-in-miniature revealed with setting and lighting and actors and properties complete. At the beginning, the reader finds the curtain going up on a little action which approaches the climax of an experience, real or imagined; that is, an experience which happened to the poet or one which came to the mind of the poet as possible. A rural traveler is the actor whose brief soliloquy describes the circumstances under which he has stopped his horse-drawn sleigh to enjoy, in spite of cold and loneliness, the strange beauty of white snowflakes falling against a background of dark trees. There are many reasons why he should not stop; common-sense reasons which seem to occur even to the traveler's little horse. But the spell of the moment is so strong that the traveler is reluctant to leave, regardless of the winter night and the cold storm. He is impelled to move on by the realization of duties and distances; those "promises" which he must keep and the "miles to go" before he completes his journey.

··

There is even a slightly tragic implication suggested by "the coldest evening of the year." Yet within this bitter cold occurs an elementary revelation of beauty which lays claim on us as existing nowhere else. Regardless of the dark and cold, we are prone to tarry quite irrationally because of this paradoxically somber excitement and recompense. The reluctance to leave becomes an expression of the endless hunger for holding and making permanent a dark moment of pleasurable discovery in a transient experience. But we are impelled forward and away by other and inevitable commitments. There are the "promises" which we have made to ourselves and to others, or which others have made for us. And there are the "miles" we travel through other kinds of experience before we yield to that final and inevitable commitment: sleep in death.

How is Thompson's approach different from that of Dabbs? How much is fact? How much is opinion?

4. Leonard Unger and William Van O'Connor:

The woods are symbolic of beauty in general, of esthetic value. This symbolism is enforced by the word "*but*" in the second line [of the last stanza]. It it were not for the promises and the miles, what would the speaker do? He might watch the woods indefinitely—he might devote his life to the experience of esthetic value. Or he might enter the woods, for it is their interior, their darkness and depth, which is lovely, and which thus suggests the peacefulness of death. In their fullest symbolic potentiality, then, the woods equate death with an exclusive commitment to esthetic value. The final lines of the poem have implications which are in accord with this interpretation. The speaker feels the urge to escape into loveliness, into the peacefulness of death, but he also acknowledges the fact that there are other values and other urges. He is committed to life, in all its diversity and complexity, and he wants to go on living, to fulfill that commitment, for death will come in time—"And miles to go before I sleep." The repetition of this last line, while it successfully closes the formal pattern of the poem, also emphasizes the symbolic function of the statement.

You do not have the whole presentation that leads to these conclusions. You do, however, have at least two facts offered as evidence. What are they? Do you consider their use valid? What would you call interpretation in this excerpt? Why?

5. Nicholas Tannenbaum:

Frost's poem effectively portrays a moment of reflection in the annual journey of the archetypal figure of Santa Claus during the rite of Christmas Eve. The Christmas season is presented by the setting: the snow and the frozen lake, the fact that it is "The darkest evening of the year." One can even hear the ringing of Santa's bells, we are told. Probably, although the poem only suggests the inference, the woods belong to the family of a little boy to whom Santa is bringing toys (perhaps a rocking horse?) without, of course, the boy's seeing him no matter how hard he may peer into the darkness. At the end of the poem, Frost makes it clear that Santa is meant, because the speaker remembers the "promises to keep" to the boy and all those other children to be reached over those "miles to go" Santa has ahead of him before he sleeps. Only a poet with the humanity of a Robert Frost could offer us such a sympathetic insight into a character too often taken for granted. Even Santa must have nodded.[1]

Evaluate Tannenbaum's interpretation.

[1] For an earlier version of this interesting reading see Herbert R. Coursen, Jr., "The Ghost of Christmas Past: 'Stopping by Woods on a Snowy Evening,'" *College English*, 24 (December 1962), 236–238.

chapter 2

The Process
of Critical Reading

Raphael. *Study for the Parnassus: Apollo.* 1508–?. Musée Wicar, Lille.

Perhaps you have been asked to read an assignment for your next class meeting, and you expect that in class there will be a discussion, or a lecture, or maybe both. How do you prepare? Reading the assignment once through for enjoyment and a general response is a good beginning. But just finishing the assignment on time is not enough. For you to become involved in a discussion or to understand a lecture, you need to have thought about your reading. That means returning to the work at least a second time for a slower, more directed examination. This chapter will introduce you to some methods for making your preliminary study productive.

READING WHAT IS ON THE PAGE

The student who brought bandits into the discussion of Frost's "The Road Not Taken" in Chapter 1 was basing conclusions on nonexistent evidence. Although literature invites you to use your imagination, you should begin your reading with what is on the page. Adding or changing details can lead to a misreading.

Just as important is not overlooking significant details. Skimming across the page may speed up your reading, but you may miss some vital information. Ernest Hemingway's story "The Short Happy Life of Francis Macomber" (pp. 357–82) provides an example. The story opens with Macomber's return from a lion hunt. Later, he lies on his cot remembering:

> It had started the night before when he had wakened and heard the lion roaring somewhere up along the river. It was a deep sound and at the end there were sort of coughing grunts that made him seem just outside the tent, and when Francis Macomber woke in the night to hear it he was afraid.

Readers who skim this passage sometimes miss the key phrase "had started the night before" and incorrectly assume that the description which follows of the lion hunt involves a new hunt rather than the memory of what already has taken place.

Sometimes even a single word can be crucial. Consider the last three lines of Matthew Arnold's "Dover Beach" (p. 573):

> And we are here as on a darkling plain
> Swept with confused alarms of struggle and flight,
> Where ignorant armies clash by night.

In this poem the speaker has called another person to a window to look out at the English Channel and share some thoughts. However, some readers conclude that the speaker is in the middle of a battlefield. They have missed the "as" in the first of these three lines. "As" sets up a comparison between the speaker's feelings about a loss of faith and the confusion of a war. No war is actually taking place.

You can avoid such problems by concentrating on slower, more observant reading rather than on speed. Reading slowly will help you to notice stage directions in a play, to catch a shift in dialogue from one character to another in a story, to consider not only line endings but also sentence endings in a poem. You will become more alert to punctuation, to shifts in tense, to pronoun reference. One technique for slowing down is reading aloud. In addition to bringing out sound and rhythm, reading aloud will make you more conscious of sentence structure and emphasis. Another technique is marking key passages and making notes in the margin. Any method you can devise for heightening your awareness of the specifics of the work will prove valuable.

You will read more accurately if you avoid expecting a work always to fit your own attitudes. A writer may want you to bring some preconceptions to your reading: an association of the bursting forth of life in the spring with renewal, an aversion to cruelty. But an author also wants you to be open to the adventure of new responses. If there were only one response to such subjects as love or death, all literature on these topics would aim at the same effect. As is illustrated by the following poem on a mother, such is not the case.

GEORGE BARKER　(b. 1913)

To My Mother

Most near, most dear, most loved and most far,
Under the window where I often found her
Sitting as huge as Asia, seismic with laughter,
Gin and chicken helpless in her Irish hand,
Irresistible as Rabelais, but most tender for   5
The lame dogs and hurt birds that surround her,—

She is a procession no one can follow after
But be like a little dog following a brass band.

She will not glance up at the bomber, or condescend
To drop her gin and scuttle to a cellar,   10
But lean on the mahogany table like a mountain
Whom only faith can move, and so I send
O all my faith, and all my love to tell her
That she will move from mourning into morning.

QUESTIONS

1. What words in this poem are those we expect to be applied to a mother?
2. What words are not the sort we expect to be applied to a mother?
3. What preconceived image of mothers might lead some readers to consider this description unfavorable?
4. Is it unfavorable?

LOOKING UP WHAT IS UNFAMILIAR

When you were reading Barker's "To My Mother," at least two words may have caused you difficulty: "seismic" and "Rabelais." Looking up these words—and any others that are unfamiliar—in a current, college-level dictionary is essential to full understanding. *Seismic*, your dictionary study will reveal, is an adjective for the vibrations caused by an earthquake. A laugh that is "seismic" must be quite a laugh! Looking up *Rabelais*, the name of a French author of the sixteenth century, may pose a problem. If you cannot find the name in a dictionary (many have a separate biographical section), you will probably find the adjective *Rabelaisian* and learn that Rabelais is associated with coarse, robust, extravagant humor. A literary encyclopedia would inform you that what is "Rabelaisian" is decidedly not prim and proper but is certainly enjoyable. The character of the mother in Barker's poem should now be clearer.

The reference to Rabelais is an example of an *allusion*, a brief reference to a well-known quotation, person, or event from literature or history. (Can you spot an allusion in lines 11–12?) The advantage of such a reference lies in the richness that can so concisely be added to the writer's expression. A reader who is familiar with the writings of Rabelais will bring to Barker's poem all of that reading experience. The disadvantage is that an allusion can block communication, particularly if it requires a knowledge that many readers no longer possess. Some allusions are topical, referring to events taking place during the time in which the work was written. Other allusions assume a background that is no longer widely shared, such as a knowledge of classical mythology. The way to add to your background information is to identify allusions when you come to them in your reading. Keep in mind that not looking up unfamiliar words and phrases will deprive you of valuable information and may make understanding impossible.

READING CRITICALLY

Armed with definitions of "seismic" and "Rabelais," you can now reread "To My Mother," interacting more fully with the text. The best approach is to support your reading with writing. In the margin of your text or in your notebook, write out the definitions you have found, your reactions to the poem, the questions you have. Here is the poem again, with marginal notes an active reader might make.

GEORGE BARKER

To My Mother

Mother is loved

big woman; large laugh loud? forceful?

Most near, most dear, most loved and most far,
Under the window where I often found her
Sitting as huge as Asia, seismic with laughter,
Gin and chicken helpless in her Irish hand,
Irresistible as Rabelais, but most tender for   5
The lame dogs and hurt birds that surround her,—
She is a procession no one can follow after

How both near and far? Past tense; not there now

But gentle too

He felt little, insignificant?

But he like a little dog following a brass band.
She will not glance up at the bomber, or condescend
To drop her gin and scuttle to a cellar,   10

War? why the cellar?

again,
her size

Still, he
loves her

> But lean on the mahogany table (like a mountain)
> Whom only faith can move, and so I send
> O all my faith, and (all my love) to tell her
> That she will move from <u>mourning</u> into <u>morning</u>.

Has
someone
died? or
a new day
coming?

UNDERSTANDING THE BASIC SITUATION

Whether writing a story, a poem, or a play, an author must establish a point of departure. Maybe a love story is beginning, or a trip into the subconscious, or an exploration of language. Whatever is taking place, we must have some sense of the basic situation we are in. Out of all the possibilities of human thought and experience, where has the writer chosen to begin and why?

To understand the basic situation, include in your critical reading the asking of some key questions. Who are the characters? Where are they? What is happening? When is the action taking place? In describing the basic situation, stay as close as possible to the facts. The speaker in "To My Mother" sends his love to his mother, who is both "near" and "far"; evidently she is separated from him geographically but "near" in his thoughts. The speaker recalls his mother sitting at the table, eating and drinking, an image from the time he was a boy. But since the past tense and adult language are used, the speaker is no longer a boy. Where is he? Why are they separated? These are key questions. Determining more of the basic situation in this poem will be difficult unless you can connect "the bomber" to the bombing of Barker's native Britain during World War II. If you bring the bomber into your examination of the situation, even if you don't know which war to be thinking of, you can at least conclude that the speaker is sending "faith" and "love" to a mother who is physically "most far" during a time of war.

SUMMARY AND PARAPHRASE

One of the best ways to train yourself to read accurately is to write a summary or a paraphrase. In a *summary* you condense the work, in your own words, into its main ideas or events. In a *paraphrase* you restate the work, in your own words, line by line or sentence by sentence. A paraphrase, since its purpose is rephrasing rather than condensing, will be close in length to the original number of words. For that reason you are likely to be assigned a summary of a longer work, such as a story or a play, and a paraphrase of a short passage or poem. The challenge of these writing exercises will be to use your own expression and at the same time to clarify the words of the writer without distorting them.

Some guidelines you should follow in writing a summary or a paraphrase are: (1) use your own words, (2) be accurate, (3) do not go beyond facts to conclusions, and (4) in summary, organize selectively around what is most important. The following story with sample summary and poem with sample paraphrase will serve as examples.

KATE CHOPIN   (1851–1904)

The Story of an Hour

Knowing that Mrs. Mallard was afflicted with a heart trouble, great care was taken to break to her as gently as possible the news of her husband's death.

It was her sister Josephine who told her, in broken sentences; veiled hints that revealed in half concealing. Her husband's friend Richards was there, too, near her. It was he who had been in the newspaper office when intelligence of the railroad disaster was received, with Brently Mallard's name leading the list of "killed." He had only taken the time to assure himself of its truth by a second telegram, and had hastened to forestall any less careful, less tender friend in bearing the sad message.

She did not hear the story as many women have heard the same, with a paralyzed inability to accept its significance. She wept at once, with sudden, wild abandonment, in her sister's arms. When the storm of grief had spent itself she went away to her room alone. She would have no one follow her.

There stood, facing the open window, a comfortable, roomy armchair. Into this she sank, pressed down by a physical exhaustion that haunted her body and seemed to reach into her soul.

She could see in the open square before her house the tops of trees that were all aquiver with the new spring life. The delicious breath of rain was in the air. In the street below a peddler was crying his wares. The notes of a distant song which some one was singing reached her faintly, and countless sparrows were twittering in the eaves.

There were patches of blue sky showing here and there through the clouds that had met and piled one above the other in the west facing her window.

She sat with her head thrown back upon the cushion of the chair, quite motionless, except when a sob came up into her throat and shook her, as a child who has cried itself to sleep continues to sob in its dreams.

She was young, with a fair, calm face, whose lines bespoke repression and even a certain strength. But now there was a dull stare in her eyes, whose gaze was fixed away off yonder on one of those patches of blue sky. It was not a glance of reflection, but rather indicated a suspension of intelligent thought.

There was something coming to her and she was waiting for it, fearfully. What was it? She did not know; it was too subtle and elusive to name. But she felt it, creeping out of the sky, reaching toward her through the sounds, the scents, the color that filled the air.

Now her bosom rose and fell tumultuously. She was beginning to recognize this thing that was approaching to possess her, and she was striving to beat it back with her will—as powerless as her two white slender hands would have been.

When she abandoned herself a little whispered word escaped her slightly parted lips. She said it over and over under her breath: "free, free, free!" The vacant stare and the look of terror that had followed it went from her eyes. They stayed keen and bright. Her pulse beat fast, and the coursing blood warmed and relaxed every inch of her body.

She did not stop to ask if it were or were not a monstrous joy that held her. A clear and exalted perception enabled her to dismiss the suggestion as trivial.

She knew that she would weep again when she saw the kind, tender hands folded in death; the face that had never looked save with love upon her, fixed and gray and dead. But she saw beyond that bitter moment a long procession of years to come that would belong to her absolutely. And she opened and spread her arms out to them in welcome.

There would be no one to live for her during those coming years; she would live for herself. There would be no powerful will bending hers in that blind persistence with which men and women believe they have a right to impose a private will upon a fellow-creature. A kind intention or a cruel intention made the act seem no less a crime as she looked upon it in that brief moment of illumination.

And yet she had loved him—sometimes. Often she had not. What did it matter! What could love, the unsolved mystery, count for in face of this possession of self-assertion which she suddenly recognized as the strongest impulse of her being!

"Free! Body and soul free!" she kept whispering.

Josephine was kneeling before the closed door with her lips to the keyhole, imploring for admission. "Louise, open the door! I beg; open the door—you will make yourself ill. What are you doing, Louise? For heaven's sake open the door."

"Go away. I am not making myself ill." No; she was drinking in a very elixir of life through that open window.

Her fancy was running riot along those days ahead of her. Spring days, and summer days, and all sorts of days that would be her own. She breathed a quick prayer that life might be long. It was only yesterday she had thought with a shudder that life might be long.

She arose at length and opened the door to her sister's importunities. There was a feverish triumph in her eyes, and she carried herself unwittingly like a goddess of Victory. She clasped her sister's waist, and together they descended the stairs. Richards stood waiting for them at the bottom.

Some one was opening the front door with a latchkey. It was Brently Mallard who entered, a little travel-stained, composedly carrying his grip-sack and umbrella. He had been far from the scene of accident, and did not even know there had been one. He stood amazed at Josephine's piercing cry; at Richards' quick motion to screen him from the view of his wife.

But Richards was too late.

When the doctors came they said she had died of heart disease—of joy that kills.

Here is a 154-word summary of "The Story of an Hour":

In Kate Chopin's "The Story of an Hour" Mrs. Mallard, a woman with a heart condition, learns that the name of her husband, Brently Mallard, is on the list of those killed in a railroad accident. She immediately bursts into tears and then goes to her room where she sits alone, looking out the window at the spring day and occasionally crying. Gradually, she begins to feel an overwhelming sense of freedom that she cannot control. Though she knows she will weep again when she sees her dead husband, she now looks forward to years of freedom to be herself. When her sister Josephine asks Mrs. Mallard to open her door, she does so, looking like "a goddess of

Victory," and goes down the stairs. Then the front door opens and Brently Mallard, who has not actually been in the accident, walks in. Mrs. Mallard dies "of heart disease" according to the doctors.

Notice that the work and author are fully identified as are the main characters. Present tense is used throughout for what takes place during the action of the story. Except for two important phrases, placed in quotation, the summary stays away from the language of the original. The less important details, such as the second telegram and the peddler, are omitted. The organization is around the important stages for Mrs. Mallard—the news, the reaction, the feeling of freedom, the shock of Brently's return. The statements are accurate. A statement, for example, that at the opening of the story Mr. Mallard has died would be inaccurate, even though all of the characters believe that to be the case. No conclusions are drawn. The temptation to say that Mrs. Mallard dies at the end because she realizes she has lost her new-found freedom has been resisted as inappropriate in a summary. The significance of her death is a matter for interpretation supported by evidence.

Now for a poem.

WILLIAM SHAKESPEARE   (1564–1616)

Sonnet 18

Shall I compare thee to a summer's day?
Thou art more lovely and more temperate:
Rough winds do shake the darling buds of May,
And summer's lease hath all too short a date:
Sometimes too hot the eye of heaven shines,   5
And often is his gold complexion dimmed;
And every fair from fair sometime declines,
By chance, or nature's changing course untrimmed;
But thy eternal summer shall not fade,

Nor lose possession of that fair thou owest;   10
Nor shall death brag thou wander'st in his shade,
When in eternal lines to time thou growest.
   So long as men can breathe, or eyes can see,
   So long lives this, and this gives life to thee.

Here is a paraphrase of "Sonnet 18":

> The speaker of Shakespeare's "Sonnet 18" raises the question of
> whether the person being addressed should be compared to a day
> in summer. The speaker answers by saying that the "thou" being
> described is more beautiful and less excessive. For example, in May
> the buds are blown about by the wind, summer doesn't last long
> enough, the sun produces too much heat and is not always bright.
> In fact, all that is beautiful in nature changes for the worse. But the
> person addressed is like a summer that continues forever without
> losing its beauty. Moreover, the person cannot die as long as these
> lines of poetry exist, because they will keep the memory of the person
> alive.

The above paraphrase is a statement in different words (and in
prose) of the lines of Shakespeare's sonnet. The purpose is to clarify
the sense of these lines. No conclusions are drawn. The paraphrase
is useful because it helps us to follow the pattern of thought that
might be initially obscured by the language and sentence structure
of the original. For example, the line "Nor lose possession of that
fair thou owest" is more simply and clearly stated as "continues
forever without losing its beauty." The paraphrase, however, makes
its statement with less economy (117 words in the paraphrase, 114
in the poem) and, more importantly, lacks the quality of the speaker's
emotion.

   When you write essays about your reading, you will make a
more limited use of paraphrase and summary. You may use these
techniques either to identify the part of the work you are focusing
on or to present facts in support of your conclusions. For example,
in discussing "The Story of an Hour," you might write:

> After hearing the news of her husband's apparent death, Mrs. Mallard
> immediately bursts into tears and then goes to her room where she
> sits alone [summary providing location in the story and evidence].

Thus we can see that, at least initially, she is filled with grief [conclusion based on summary].

Perhaps you want to demonstrate that one theme of "Sonnet 18" is the power of poetry to overcome time. You might support this point by combining paraphrase with a brief quotation:

> The power of poetry to create an "eternal summer" for the person addressed in "Sonnet 18" [conclusion] is brought out in the closing statement that as long as these lines of poetry exist, they will keep the person's memory alive [paraphrase used to present evidence].

DECIDING ON THE UNANSWERED QUESTIONS

Even a thorough preliminary study of a work will leave questions unanswered. You may have looked up the meaning of an unfamiliar word and still not know why that word was chosen. You may see clearly what actions take place and still not be certain of their significance. The final step in critical reading is to identify any unanswered questions.

Asking the right question is often just as important as coming up with an answer. For example, in reading "The Story of an Hour," you may have noticed that attention is given to what Mrs. Mallard sees through her window. Why has Chopin introduced and emphasized what Mrs. Mallard sees? If you write down the question to return to it later or to bring it up in class, you may open the way to a thoughtful answer. You may realize later that the peddler's cry, the "twittering" of the sparrows, and the blue sky are in the story to prepare us for Mrs. Mallard's new sense of freedom.

All readers will at times encounter works that puzzle them. Details here and there are clear, but the work as a whole seems to make no sense. When you are faced with such a situation, you need to establish exactly what is confusing. Raising key questions can help to define the problem and will often lead to an answer.

The following poem will serve as an example. Read it actively, making your own notes and questions. Then read the sample notes and queries that follow the poem and see how many of the key questions you also have in your notes, and then how many of them you can answer.

EDWIN ARLINGTON ROBINSON   (1869–1935)

How Annandale Went Out

"They called it Annandale—and I was there
To flourish, to find words, and to attend:
Liar, physician, hypocrite, and friend,
I watched him; and the sight was not so fair
As one or two that I have seen elsewhere: 5
An apparatus not for me to mend—
A wreck, with hell between him and the end,
Remained of Annandale; and I was there.

"I knew the ruin as I knew the man;
So put the two together, if you can,   10
Remembering the worst you know of me.
Now view yourself as I was, on the spot—
With a slight kind of engine. Do you see?
Like this . . . You wouldn't hang me? I thought not."

This poem is sometimes difficult for readers because we are given only partial information about what has happened. For example, at the end of the poem the speaker asks, "Do you see?" But we don't, for the only description of what we are supposed to see is "Like this. . . ." The speaker appears to be talking to a person—or persons—having some knowledge we don't have. The speaker also is described in a somewhat contradictory fashion as "Liar, physician, hypocrite, and friend." How does it make sense for the speaker to be a "liar" and a "hypocrite" as well as a "friend" and a "physician"? We can note at least two other intriguing questions. Annandale is referred to in line 1 as "it." But the "him" of line 7 seems clearly to refer to Annandale also. Why would a person be referred to as "it"? Another question is raised by the last line. Why is the speaker worried about being hanged? No hanging offense has specifically been mentioned.

How many of these observations and questions did you identify from your reading of the poem? Can you resolve some of these confusing issues? The following questions may further help you make sense of this difficult poem.

QUESTIONS

1. What are the meanings of *flourish*, *apparatus*, and *engine*?
2. Why might a doctor who is a friend to a seriously ill man be a "liar" and a "hypocrite"?
3. What might the speaker have done in order to be threatened with hanging?
4. What response has the speaker evidently received to the question about being hanged? What might have been the basis for this response?

SELECTIONS FOR FURTHER STUDY

JOHN KEATS (1795–1821)

On First Looking into Chapman's Homer

Much have I traveled in the realms of gold,
And many goodly states and kingdoms seen;
Round many western islands have I been
Which bards in fealty to Apollo hold.
Oft of one wide expanse had I been told   5
That deep-browed Homer ruled as his demesne;
Yet did I never breathe its pure serene
Till I heard Chapman speak out loud and bold:
Then felt I like some watcher of the skies
When a new planet swims into his ken;   10
Or like stout Cortez when with eagle eyes
He stared at the Pacific—and all his men
Looked at each other with a wild surmise—
Silent, upon a peak in Darien.

QUESTIONS

1. What does the title tell us about the basic situation?
   Look up the names *Chapman* and *Homer*. What is the connection between Chapman and Homer?
2. Check your dictionary for *bards*, *Apollo*, *fealty*, *demesne*, and *serene*.

3. Considering what the title indicates about the basic situation, what is puzzling about lines 1–8? What questions need to be answered before these lines make sense?

4. How is the comparison in lines 9–10 similar to the comparison in lines 11–14?

5. What mistake has Keats made about Cortez? How are we able to understand the allusion despite this mistake?

THEODORE ROETHKE   (1908–1963)

My Papa's Waltz

The whiskey on your breath
Could make a small boy dizzy;
But I hung on like death:
Such waltzing was not easy.

We romped until the pans   5
Slid from the kitchen shelf;
My mother's countenance
Could not unfrown itself.

The hand that held my wrist
Was battered on one knuckle;   10
At every step you missed
My right ear scraped a buckle.

You beat time on my head
With a palm caked hard by dirt,
Then waltzed me off to bed   15
Still clinging to your shirt.

QUESTIONS

1. Is the speaker male or female? What evidence is there for your conclusion?

2. Write a paraphrase of "My Papa's Waltz." Be accurate, use your own words, and draw no conclusions.

3. What differences do you notice between your paraphrase and the poem?

4. What cultural values might lead a reader to see this poem as unfavorable to the father? Is it unfavorable?

LANGSTON HUGHES (1906–1967)

Early Autumn

When Bill was very young, they had been in love. Many nights they had spent walking, talking together. Then something not very important had come between them, and they didn't speak. Impulsively, she had married a man she thought she loved. Bill went away, bitter about women.

Yesterday, walking across Washington Square, she saw him for the first time in years.

"Bill Walker," she said.

He stopped. At first he did not recognize her, to him she looked so old.

"Mary! Where did you come from?"

Unconsciously, she lifted her face as though wanting a kiss, but he held out his hand. She took it.

"I live in New York now," she said.

"Oh"—smiling politely. Then a little frown came quickly between his eyes.

"Always wondered what happened to you, Bill."

"I'm a lawyer. Nice firm, way downtown."

"Married yet?"

"Sure. Two kids."

"Oh," she said.

A great many people went past them through the park. People they didn't know. It was late afternoon. Nearly sunset. Cold.

"And your husband?" he asked her.

"We have three children. I work in the bursar's office at Columbia."

"You're looking very . . ." (he wanted to say *old*) ". . . well," he said.

She understood. Under the trees in Washington Square, she found herself desperately reaching back into the past. She had been older than he then in Ohio. Now she was not young at all. Bill was still young.

"We live on Central Park West," she said. "Come and see us sometime."

"Sure," he replied. "You and your husband must have dinner with my family some night. Any night. Lucille and I'd love to have you."

The leaves fell slowly from the trees in the Square. Fell without wind. Autumn dusk. She felt a little sick.

"We'd love it," she answered.

"You ought to see my kids." He grinned.

Suddenly the lights came on up the whole length of Fifth Avenue, chains of misty brilliance in the blue air.

"There's my bus," she said.

He held out his hand, "Good-by."

"When . . ." she wanted to say, but the bus was ready to pull off. The lights on the avenue blurred, twinkled, blurred. And she was afraid to open her mouth as she entered the bus. Afraid it would be impossible to utter a word.

Suddenly she shrieked very loudly, "Good-by!" But the bus door had closed.

The bus started. People came between them outside, people crossing the street, people they didn't know. Space and people. She lost sight of Bill. Then she remembered she had forgotten to give him her address— or to ask him for his—or tell him that her youngest boy was named Bill, too.

QUESTIONS

1. Write a summary of "Early Autumn." Use your own words, be accurate, be selective, and draw no conclusions.

2. What differences do you notice between your summary and the story?

3. One question not answered in a summary of this story is why Hughes chose the title "Early Autumn." What facts are relevant to this question? What is the answer?

4. What other facts are there? What conclusions about the characters do they lead to?

5. Formulate at least one question that you think would benefit class discussion of this story.

DORIS LESSING   (b. 1919)

A Woman on a Roof

It was during the week of hot sun, that June.

Three men were at work on the roof, where the leads got so hot they had the idea of throwing water on to cool them. But the water steamed, then sizzled; and they made jokes about getting an egg from some woman in the flats under them, to poach it for their dinner. By two it was not possible to touch the guttering they were replacing, and they speculated about what workmen did in regularly hot countries. Perhaps they should borrow kitchen gloves with the egg? They were all a bit dizzy, not used to the heat; and they shed their coats and stood side by side squeezing themselves into a foot-wide patch of shade against a chimney, careful to keep their feet in the thick socks and boots out of the sun. There was a fine view across several acres of roofs. Not far off a man sat in a deck chair reading the newspapers. Then they saw her, between chimneys, about fifty yards away. She lay face down on a brown blanket. They could see the top part of her: black hair, a flushed solid back, arms spread out.

"She's stark naked," said Stanley, sounding annoyed.

Harry, the oldest, a man of about forty-five, said: "Looks like it."

Young Tom, seventeen, said nothing, but he was excited and grinning.

Stanley said: "Someone'll report her if she doesn't watch out."

"She thinks no one can see," said Tom, craning his head all ways to see more.

At this point the woman, still lying prone, brought her two hands up behind her shoulders with the ends of a scarf in them, tied it behind her back, and sat up. She wore a red scarf tied around her breasts and brief red bikini pants. This being the first day of the sun she was white, flushing red. She sat smoking, and did not look up when Stanley let out a wolf whistle. Harry said: "Small things amuse small minds," leading the way back to their part of the roof, but it was scorching. Harry said: "Wait, I'm going to rig up some shade," and disappeared down the skylight into the building. Now that he'd gone, Stanley and Tom went to the farthest point they could to peer at the woman. She had moved, and all they could see were two pink legs stretched on the blanket. They whistled and shouted but the legs did not move. Harry came back with a blanket and shouted: "Come on, then." He sounded irritated with them. They clambered back to him and he said to Stanley: "What about your missus?" Stanley was newly married, about three months. Stanley said, jeering: "What about my missus?"—preserving his independence. Tom said nothing, but his mind was full of the nearly naked woman. Harry slung the blanket, which he had borrowed from a friendly woman downstairs, from the stem of a television aerial to a row of chimney pots. This shade fell across the piece of gutter they had to replace. But the shade kept moving, they had to adjust the blanket, and not much progress was made. At last some of the heat left the roof, and they worked fast, making up for lost time. First Stanley, then Tom, made a trip to the end of the roof to see the woman. "She's on her back," Stanley said, adding a jest which made Tom snicker, and the older man smile tolerantly. Tom's report was that she hadn't moved, but it was a lie. He wanted to keep what he had seen to himself: he had caught her in the act of rolling down the little red pants over her hips, till they were no more than a small triangle. She was on her back, fully visible, glistening with oil.

Next morning, as soon as they came up, they went to look. She was already there, face down. arms spread out, naked except for the little red pants. She had turned brown in the night. Yesterday she was a scarlet and white woman, today she was a brown woman. Stanley let out a whistle. She lifted her head, startled, as if she'd been asleep, and looked straight over at them. The sun was in her eyes, she blinked and stared, then she dropped her head again. At this gesture of indifference, they all three, Stanley, Tom, and old Harry, let out whistles and yells. Harry was doing it in parody of the younger men, making fun of them, but he was also angry. They were all angry because of her utter indifference to the three men watching her.

"Bitch," said Stanley.

"She should ask us over," said Tom, snickering.

Harry recovered himself and reminded Stanley: "If she's married, her old man wouldn't like that."

"Christ," said Stanley virtuously, "if my wife lay about like that, for everyone to see, I'd soon stop her."

Harry said, smiling: "How do you know, perhaps she's sunning herself at this very moment?"

"Not a chance, not on our roof." The safety of his wife put Stanley into a good humour, and they went to work. But today it was hotter than yesterday; and several times one or the other suggested they should tell Matthew, the foreman, and ask to leave the roof until the heat wave was over. But they didn't. There was work to be done in the basement of the big block of flats, but up here they felt free, on a different level from ordinary humanity shut in the streets or the buildings. A lot more people came out onto the roofs that day, for an hour at midday. Some married couples sat side by side in deck chairs, the women's legs stockingless and scarlet, the men in vests with reddening shoulders.

The woman stayed on her blanket, turning herself over and over. She ignored them, no matter what they did. When Harry went off to fetch more screws, Stanley said: "Come on." Her roof belonged to a different system of roofs, separated from theirs at one point by about twenty feet. It meant a scrambling climb from one level to another, edging along parapets, clinging to chimneys, while their big boots slipped and slithered, but at last they stood on a small square projecting roof looking straight down at her, close. She sat smoking, reading a book. Tom thought she looked like a poster, or a magazine cover, with the blue sky behind her and her legs stretched out. Behind her a great crane at work on a new building in Oxford Street swung its black arm across the roofs in a great arc. Tom imagined himself at work on the crane, adjusting the arm to swing over and pick her up and swing her back across the sky to drop her near him.

They whistled. She looked up at them, cool and remote, then went on reading. Again, they were furious. Or rather, Stanley was. His sun-heated face was screwed into rage as he whistled again and again, trying to make her look up. Young Tom stopped whistling. He stood beside Stanley, excited, grinning; but he felt as if he were saying to the woman: "Don't associate me with *him*," for his grin was apologetic. Last night he had thought of the unknown woman before he slept, and she had been tender with him. This tenderness he was remembering as he shifted his feet by the jeering, whistling Stanley, and watched the indifferent healthy brown woman a few feet off, with the gap that plunged to the street between them. Tom thought it was romantic, it was like being high on two hilltops. But there was a shout from Harry, and they clambered back. Stanley's face was hard, really angry. The boy kept looking at him and wondered why he hated the woman so much, for by now he loved her.

The played their little games with the blanket, trying to trap shade to work under; but again it was not until nearly four that they could work seriously, and they were exhausted, all three of them. They were grumbling about the weather, by now. Stanley was in a thoroughly bad humour. When they made their routine trip to see the woman before they packed up for the day, she was apparently asleep, face down, her back naked save for the scarlet triangle on her buttocks. "I've got a good mind to report her to the police," said Stanley, and Harry said: "What's eating you? What harm's she doing?"

"I tell you, if she was my wife!"

"But she isn't, is she?" Tom knew that Harry, like himself, was uneasy at Stanley's reaction. He was normally a sharp young man, quick at his work, making a lot of jokes, good company.

"Perhaps it will be cooler tomorrow," said Harry.

But it wasn't, it was hotter, if anything, and the weather forecast said the good weather would last. As soon as they were on the roof, Harry went over to see if the woman were there, and Tom knew it was to prevent Stanley going, to put off his bad humour. Harry had grown-up children, a boy the same age as Tom, and the youth trusted and looked up to him.

Harry came back and said: "She's not there."

"I bet her old man has put his foot down," said Stanley, and Harry and Tom caught each other's eye and smiled behind the young married man's back.

Harry suggested they should get permission to work in the basement, and they did, that day. But before packing up Stanley said: "Let's have a breath of fresh air." Again Harry and Tom smiled at each other as they followed Stanley up to the roof, Tom in the devout conviction that he was there to protect the woman from Stanley. It was about five-thirty, and a calm, full sunlight lay over the roofs. The great crane still swung its black arm from Oxford Street to above their heads. She was not there. Then there was a flutter of white from behind a parapet, and she stood up, in a belted, white dressing gown. She had been there all day, probably, but on a different patch of roof, to hide from them. Stanley did not whistle, he said nothing, but watched the woman bend to collect papers, books, cigarettes, then fold the blanket over her arm. Tom was thinking: If they weren't here, I'd go over and say . . . what? But he knew from his nightly dreams of her that she was kind and friendly. Perhaps she would ask him down to her flat? Perhaps. . . . He stood watching her disappear down the skylight. As she went, Stanley let out a shrill derisive yell; she started, and it seemed as if she nearly fell. She clutched to save herself, they could hear things falling. She looked straight at them, angry. Harry said, facetiously: "Better be careful on those slippery ladders, love." Tom knew he said it to save her from Stanley, but she could not know it. She vanished, frowning. Tom was full of a secret delight, because he knew her anger was for the others, not for him.

"Roll on some rain," said Stanley, bitter, looking at the blue evening sky.

Next day was cloudless, and they decided to finish the work in the basement. They felt excluded, shut in the grey cement basement fitting pipes, from the holiday atmosphere of London in a heat wave. At lunchtime they came up for some air, but while the married couples, and the men in shirt-sleeves or vests, were there, she was not there, either on her usual patch of roof or where she had been yesterday. They all, even Harry, clambered about, between chimney pots, over parapets, the hot leads stinging their fingers. There was not a sign of her. They took off their shirts and vests and exposed their chests, feeling their feet sweaty and hot. They did not mention the woman. But Tom felt alone again. Last night she had asked him into her flat: it was big and had fitted white carpets and a bed with a padded white leather headtop. She wore a black filmy negligée and her kindness to Tom thickened his throat as he remembered it. He felt she had betrayed him by not being there.

And again after work they climbed up, but still there was nothing to be seen of her. Stanley kept repeating that if it was as hot as this tomorrow he wasn't going to work and that's all there was to it. But they were all there next day. By ten the temperature was in the middle seventies, and it was eighty long before noon. Harry went to the foreman to say it was impossible to work on the leads in that heat; but the foreman said there was nothing else he could put them on, and they'd have to. At midday they stood, silent, watching the skylight on her roof open, and then she slowly emerged in her white gown, holding a bundle of blanket. She looked at them, gravely, then went to the part of the roof where she was hidden from them. Tom was pleased. He felt she was more his when the other men couldn't see her. They had taken off their shirts and vests, but now they put them back again, for they felt the sun bruising their flesh. "She must have the hide of a rhino," said Stanley, tugging at guttering and swearing. They stopped work, and sat in the shade, moving around behind chimney stacks. A woman came to water a yellow window box just opposite them. She was middle-aged, wearing a flowered summer dress. Stanley said to her: "We need a drink more than them." She smiled and said: "Better drop down to the pub quick, it'll be closing in a minute." They exchanged pleasantries, and she left them with a smile and a wave.

"Not like Lady Godiva," said Stanley. "She can give us a bit of a chat and a smile."

"You didn't whistle at *her*," said Tom, reproving.

"Listen to him," said Stanley, "you didn't whistle, then?"

But the boy felt as if he hadn't whistled, as if only Harry and Stanley had. He was making plans, when it was time to knock off work, to get left behind and somehow make his way over to the woman. The weather report said the hot spell was due to break, so he had to move quickly. But there was no chance of being left. The other two decided to knock off work at four, because they were exhausted. As they went down, Tom quickly climbed a parapet and hoisted himself higher by pulling his weight up a chimney. He caught a glimpse of her lying on her back, her knees up, eyes closed, a brown woman lolling in the sun. He slipped and clattered down, as Stanley looked for information: "She's gone down," he said. He felt as if he had protected her from Stanley, and that she must be grateful to him. He could feel the bond between the woman and himself.

Next day, they stood around on the landing below the roof, reluctant to climb up into the heat. The woman who had lent Harry the blanket came out and offered them a cup of tea. They accepted gratefully, and sat round Mrs. Pritchett's kitchen an hour or so, chatting. She was married to an airline pilot. A smart blonde, of about thirty, she had an eye for the handsome sharpfaced Stanley; and the two teased each other while Harry sat in a corner, watching, indulgent, though his expression reminded Stanley that he was married. And young Tom felt envious of Stanley's ease in badinage; felt, too, that Stanley's getting off with Mrs. Pritchett left his romance with the woman on the roof safe and intact.

"I thought they said the heat wave'd break," said Stanley, sullen, as the time approched when they really would have to climb up into the sunlight.

"You don't like it then?" asked Mrs. Pritchett.

"All right for some," said Stanley. "Nothing to do but lie about as if it was a beach up there. Do you ever go up?"

"Went up once," said Mrs. Pritchett. "But it's a dirty place up there, and it's too hot."

"Quite right too," said Stanley.

Then they went up, leaving the cool neat little flat and the friendly Mrs. Pritchett.

As soon as they were up they saw her. The three men looked at her, resentful at her ease in this punishing sun. Then Harry said, because of the expression on Stanley's face: "Come on, we've got to pretend to work, at least."

They had to wrench another length of guttering that ran beside a parapet out of its bed, so that they could replace it. Stanley took it in his two hands, tugged, swore, stood up. "Fuck it," he said, and sat down under a chimney. He lit a cigarette. "Fuck them," he said. "What do they think we are, lizards? I've got blisters all over my hands." Then he jumped up and climbed over the roofs and stood with his back to them. He put his fingers either side of his mouth and let out a shrill whistle. Tom and Harry squatted, not looking at each other, watching him. They could just see the woman's head, the beginnings of her brown shoulders. Stanley whistled again. Then he began stamping with his feet, and whistled and yelled and screamed at the woman, his face getting scarlet. He seemed quite mad, as he stamped and whistled, while the woman did not move, she did not move a muscle.

"Barmy," said Tom.

"Yes," said Harry, disapproving.

Suddenly the older man came to a decision. It was, Tom knew, to save some sort of scandal or real trouble over the woman. Harry stood up and began packing tools into a length of oily cloth. "Stanley," he said, commanding. At first Stanley took no notice, but Harry said: "Stanley, we're packing it in, I'll tell Matthew."

Stanley came back, cheeks mottled, eyes glaring.

"Can't go on like this," said Harry. "It'll break in a day or so. I'm going to tell Matthew we've got sunstroke, and if he doesn't like it, it's too bad." Even Harry sounded aggrieved, Tom noted. The small, competent man, the family man with his grey hair, who was never at a loss, sounded really off balance. "Come on," he said, angry. He fitted himself into the open square in the roof, and went down, watching his feet on the ladder. Then Stanley went, with not a glance at the woman. Then Tom who, his throat beating with excitement, silently promised her in a backward glance: Wait for me, wait, I'm coming.

On the pavement Stanley said: "I'm going home." He looked white now, so perhaps he really did have sunstroke. Harry went off to find the foreman who was at work on the plumbing of some flats down the street. Tom slipped back, not into the building they had been working on, but the building on whose roof the woman lay. He went straight up, no one stopping him. The skylight stood open, with an iron ladder leading up.

He emerged onto the roof a couple of yards from her. She sat up, pushing back her black hair with both hands. The scarf across her breasts bound them tight, and brown flesh bulged around it. Her legs were brown and smooth. She stared at him in silence. The boy stood grinning, foolish, claiming the tenderness he expected from her.

"What do you want?" she asked.

"I ... I came to ... make your acquaintance," he stammered, grinning, pleading with her.

They looked at each other, the slight, scarlet-faced excited boy, and the serious, nearly naked woman. Then, without a word, she lay down on her brown blanket, ignoring him.

"You like the sun, do you?" he enquired of her glistening back.

Not a word. He felt panic, thinking of how she had held him in her arms, stroked his hair, brought him where he sat, lordly, in her bed, a glass of some exhilarating liquor he had never tasted in life. He felt that if he knelt down, stroked her shoulders, her hair, she would turn and clasp him in her arms.

He said: "The sun's all right for you, isn't it?"

She raised her head, set her chin on two small fists. "Go away," she said. He did not move. "Listen," she said, in a slow reasonable voice, where anger was kept in check, though with difficulty; looking at him, her face weary with anger: "If you get a kick out of seeing women in bikinis, why don't you take a sixpenny bus ride to the Lido? You'd see dozens of them, without all this mountaineering."

She hadn't understood him. He felt her unfairness pale him. He stammered: "But I like you, I've been watching you and ..."

"Thanks," she said, and dropped her face again, turned away from him.

She lay there. He stood there. She said nothing. She had simply shut him out. He stood, saying nothing at all, for some minutes. He thought: She'll have to say something if I stay. But the minutes went past, with no sign of them in her, except in the tension of her back, her thighs, her arms—the tension of waiting for him to go.

He looked up at the sky, where the sun seemed to spin in heat; and over the roofs where he and his mates had been earlier. He could see the heat quivering where they had worked. "And they expect us to work in these conditions!" he thought, filled with righteous indignation. The woman hadn't moved. A bit of hot wind blew her black hair softly, it shone, and was iridescent. He remembered how he had stroked it last night.

Resentment of her at last moved him off and away down the ladder, through the building, into the street. He got drunk then, in hatred of her.

Next day when he woke the sky was grey. He looked at the wet grey and thought, vicious: "Well, that's fixed you, hasn't it now? That's fixed you good and proper."

The three men were at work early on the cool leads, surrounded by damp drizzling roofs where no one came to sun themselves, black roofs, slimy with rain. Because it was cool now, they would finish the job that day, if they hurried.

QUESTIONS

1. Describe the opening situation.
2. Write a summary of "A Woman on a Roof." Organize around the important events, use your own words, be accurate, and draw no conclusions.
3. Does Tom make love to the woman who is sunbathing? What evidence might lead to that conclusion? Evaluate that evidence.
4. Practice active reading. Write down some of your reactions, make some comments on each character, point out anything that intrigues or puzzles you.
5. What do you consider the most important question to ask about this story? Why?

chapter 3

Writing Essays
about Literature

Jean Pucelle. Page from the *Belleville Breviary*, illuminated manuscript.
c. 1325. Approx. 9½″ × 6¾″. Bibliothèque Nationale, Paris.

Chapters 1 and 2 introduced you to the methods of literary analysis. This chapter reviews a procedure for developing an essay and applies that procedure to the task of literary analysis. Subsequent chapters provide further guidelines for handling specific writing problems. Although many methods for writing essays can be found, what follows is a standard process that has helped many to write successful papers. The following story, "A Worn Path" by Eudora Welty, and the sample student essay on the story will serve as examples and so should be read first.

EUDORA WELTY   (b. 1909)

A Worn Path

It was December—a bright frozen day in the early morning. Far out in the country there was an old Negro woman with her head tied in a red rag, coming along a path through the pinewoods. Her name was Phoenix Jackson. She was very old and small and she walked slowly in the dark pine shadows, moving a little from side to side in her steps, with the balanced heaviness and lightness of a pendulum in a grandfather clock. She carried a thin, small cane made from an umbrella, and with this she kept tapping the frozen earth in front of her. This made a grave and persistent noise in the still air, that seemed meditative like the chirping of a solitary little bird.

She wore a dark striped dress reaching down to her shoe tops, and an equally long apron of bleached sugar sacks, with a full pocket: all neat and tidy, but every time she took a step she might have fallen over her shoelaces, which dragged from her unlaced shoes. She looked straight ahead. Her eyes were blue with age. Her skin had a pattern all its own of numberless branching wrinkles and as though a whole little tree stood in the middle of her forehead, but a golden color ran underneath, and the two knobs of her cheeks were illumined by a yellow burning under the dark. Under the red rag her hair came down on her neck in the frailest of ringlets, still black, and with an odor like copper.

Now and then there was a quivering in the thicket. Old Phoenix said, "Out of my way, all you foxes, owls, beetles, jack rabbits, coons and wild animals! . . . Keep out from under these feet, little bobwhites. . . . Keep the big wild hogs out of my path. Don't let none of those come running my direction. I got a long way." Under her small black-freckled hand her cane, limber as a buggy whip, would switch at the brush as if to rouse up any hiding things.

On she went. The woods were deep and still. The sun made the pine needles almost too bright to look at, up where the wind rocked. The cones dropped as light as feathers. Down in the hollow was the mourning dove—it was not too late for him.

The path ran up a hill. "Seem like there is chains about my feet, time I get this far," she said, in the voice of argument old people keep to use with themselves. "Something always take a hold of me on this hill— pleads I should stay."

After she got to the top she turned and gave a full, severe look behind her where she had come. "Up through pines," she said at length. "Now down through oaks."

Her eyes opened their widest, and she started down gently. But before she got to the bottom of the hill a bush caught her dress.

Her fingers were busy and intent, but her skirts were full and long, so that before she could pull them free in one place they were caught in another. It was not possible to allow the dress to tear. "I in the thorny bush," she said. "Thorns, you doing your appointed work. Never want to let folks pass, no sir. Old eyes thought you was a pretty little *green* bush."

Finally, trembling all over, she stood free, and after a moment dared to stoop for her cane.

"Sun so high!" she cried, leaning back and looking, while the thick tears went over her eyes. "The time getting all gone here."

At the foot of this hill was a place where a log was laid across the creek.

"Now comes the trial," said Phoenix.

Putting her right foot out, she mounted the log and shut her eyes. Lifting her skirt, leveling her cane fiercely before her, like a festival figure in some parade, she began to march across. Then she opened her eyes and she was safe on the other side.

"I wasn't as old as I thought," she said.

But she sat down to rest. She spread her skirts on the bank around her and folded her hands over her knees. Up above her was a tree in a pearly cloud of mistletoe. She did not dare to close her eyes, and when a little boy brought her a plate with a slice of marble-cake on it she spoke to him. "That would be acceptable," she said. But when she went to take it there was just her own hand in the air.

So she left that tree, and had to go through a barbed-wire fence. There she had to creep and crawl, spreading her knees and stretching her fingers like a baby trying to climb the steps. But she talked loudly to herself: she could not let her dress be torn now, so late in the day, and she could not pay for having her arm or her leg sawed off if she got caught fast where she was.

At last she was safe through the fence and risen up out in the clearing. Big dead trees, like black men with one arm, were standing in the purple stalks of the withered cotton field. There sat a buzzard.

"Who you watching?"

In the furrow she made her way along.

"Glad this not the season for bulls," she said, looking sideways, "and the good Lord made his snakes to curl up and sleep in the winter. A pleasure I don't see no two-headed snake coming around that tree, where it come once. It took a while to get by him, back in the summer."

She passed through the old cotton and went into a field of dead corn. It whispered and shook and was taller than her head. "Through the maze now," she said, for there was no path.

Then there was something tall, black, and skinny there, moving before her.

At first she took it for a man. It could have been a man dancing in the field. But she stood still and listened, and it did not make a sound. It was silent as a ghost.

"Ghost," she said sharply, "who be you the ghost of? For I have heard of nary death close by."

But there was no answer—only the ragged dancing in the wind.

She shut her eyes, reached out her hand, and touched a sleeve. She found a coat and inside that an emptiness, cold as ice.

"You scarecrow," she said. Her face lighted. "I ought to be shut up for good," she said with laughter. "My senses is gone. I too old. I the oldest people I ever know. Dance, old scarecrow," she said, "while I dancing with you."

She kicked her foot over the furrow, and with mouth drawn down, shook her head once or twice in a little strutting way. Some husks blew down and whirled in streamers about her skirts.

Then she went on, parting her way from side to side with the cane, through the whispering field. At last she came to the end, to a wagon track where the silver grass blew between the red ruts. The quail were walking around like pullets, seeming all dainty and unseen.

"Walk pretty," she said. "This the easy place. This the easy going."

She followed the track, swaying through the quiet bare fields, through the little strings of trees silver in their dead leaves, past cabins silver from weather, with the doors and windows boarded shut, all like old women under a spell sitting there. "I walking in their sleep," she said, nodding her head vigorously.

In a ravine she went where a spring was silently flowing through a hollow log. Old Phoenix bent and drank. "Sweet-gum makes the water sweet," she said, and drank more. "Nobody know who made this well, for it was here when I was born."

The track crossed a swampy part where the moss hung as white as lace from every limb. "Sleep on, alligators, and blow your bubbles." Then the track went into the road.

Deep, deep the road went down between the high green-colored banks. Overhead the live-oaks met, and it was as dark as a cave.

A black dog with a lolling tongue came up out of the weeds by the ditch. She was meditating, and not ready, and when he came at her she only hit him a little with her cane. Over she went in the ditch, like a little puff of milkweed.

Down there, her senses drifted away. A dream visited her, and she reached her hand up, but nothing reached down and gave her a pull. So she lay there and presently went to talking. "Old woman," she said to herself, "that black dog come up out of the weeds to stall you off, and now there he sitting on his fine tail, smiling at you."

A white man finally came along and found her—a hunter, a young man, with his dog on a chain.

"Well, Granny!" he laughed. "What are you doing there?"

"Lying on my back like a June-bug waiting to be turned over, mister," she said, reaching up her hand.

He lifted her up, gave her a swing in the air, and set her down. "Anything broken, Granny?"

"No sir, them old dead weeds is springy enough," said Phoenix, when she had got her breath. "I thank you for your trouble."

"Where do you live, Granny?" he asked, while the two dogs were growling at each other.

"Away back yonder, sir, behind the ridge. You can't even see it from here."

"On your way home?"

"No sir, I going to town."

"Why, that's too far! That's as far as I walk when I come out myself, and I get something for my trouble." He patted the stuffed bag he carried, and there hung down a little closed claw. It was one of the bob-whites, with its beak hooked bitterly to show it was dead. "Now you go on home, Granny!"

"I bound to go to town, mister," said Phoenix. "The time come around."

He gave another laugh, filling the whole landscape. "I know you old colored people! Wouldn't miss going to town to see Santa Claus!"

But something held old Phoenix very still. The deep lines in her face went into a fierce and different radiation. Without warning, she had seen with her own eyes a flashing nickel fall out of the man's pocket onto the ground.

"How old are you, Granny?" he was saying.

"There is no telling, mister," she said, "no telling."

Then she gave a little cry and clapped her hands and said, "Git on away from here, dog! Look! Look at that dog!" She laughed as if in admiration. "He ain't scared of nobody. He a big black dog." She whispered, "Sic him!"

"Watch me get rid of that cur," said the man, "Sic him, Pete! Sic him!"

Phoenix heard the dogs fighting, and heard the man running and throwing sticks. She even heard a gunshot. But she was slowly bending forward by that time, further and further forward, the lids stretched down over her eyes, as if she were doing this in her sleep. Her chin was lowered almost to her knees. The yellow palm of her hand came out from the fold of her apron. Her fingers slid down and along the ground under the piece of money with the grace and care they would have in lifting an egg from under a setting hen. Then she slowly straightened up, she stood erect, and the nickel was in her apron pocket. A bird flew by. Her lips moved. "God watching me the whole time. I come to stealing."

The man came back, and his own dog panted about them. "Well, I scared him off that time," he said, and then he laughed and lifted his gun and pointed it at Phoenix.

She stood straight and faced him.

"Doesn't the gun scare you?" he said, still pointing it.

"No, sir, I seen plenty go off closer by, in my day, and for less than what I done," she said, holding utterly still.

He smiled, and shouldered the gun. "Well, Granny," he said, "you must be a hundred years old, and scared of nothing. I'd give you a dime if I had any money with me. But you take my advice and stay home, and nothing will happen to you."

"I bound to go on my way, mister," said Phoenix. She inclined her head in the red rag. Then they went in different directions, but she could hear the gun shooting again and again over the hill.

She walked on. The shadows hung from the oak trees to the road like curtains. Then she smelled wood-smoke, and smelled the river, and she saw a steeple and the cabins on their steep steps. Dozens of little black children whirled around her. There ahead was Natchez shining. Bells were ringing. She walked on.

In the paved city it was Christmas time. There were red and green electric lights strung and crisscrossed everywhere, and all turned on in the daytime. Old Phoenix would have been lost if she had not distrusted her eyesight and depended on her feet to know where to take her.

She paused quietly on the sidewalk where people were passing by. A lady came along in the crowd, carrying an armful of red-, green- and silver-wrapped presents; she gave off perfume like the red roses in hot summer, and Phoenix stopped her.

"Please, missy, will you lace up my shoe?" She held up her foot.

"What do you want, Grandma?"

"See my shoe," said Phoenix. "Do all right for out in the country, but wouldn't look right to go in a big building."

"Stand still then, Grandma," said the lady. She put her packages down on the sidewalk beside her and laced and tied both shoes tightly.

"Can't lace 'em with a cane," said Phoenix. "Thank you, missy. I doesn't mind asking a nice lady to tie up my shoe, when I gets out on the street."

Moving slowly and from side to side, she went into the big building, and into a tower of steps, where she walked up and around and around until her feet knew to stop.

She entered a door, and there she saw nailed up on the wall the document that had been stamped with the gold seal and framed in the gold frame, which matched the dream that was hung up in her head.

"Here I be," she said. There was a fixed and ceremonial stiffness over her body.

"A charity case, I suppose," said an attendant who sat at the desk before her.

But Phoenix only looked above her head. There was sweat on her face, the wrinkles in her skin shone like a bright net.

"Speak up, Grandma," the woman said. "What's your name? We must have your history, you know. Have you been here before? What seems to be the trouble with you?"

Old Phoenix only gave a twitch to her face as if a fly were bothering her.

"Are you deaf?" cried the attendant.

But then the nurse came in.

"Oh, that's just old Aunt Phoenix," she said. "She doesn't come for herself—she has a little grandson. She makes these trips just as regular as clockwork. She lives away back off the Old Natchez Trace." She bent down. "Well, Aunt Phoenix, why don't you just take a seat? We won't keep you standing after your long trip." She pointed.

The old woman sat down, bolt upright in the chair.

"Now, how is the boy?" asked the nurse.

Old Phoenix did not speak.

"I said, how is the boy?"

But Phoenix only waited and stared straight ahead, her face very solemn and withdrawn into rigidity.

"Is his throat any better?" asked the nurse. "Aunt Phoenix, don't you hear me? Is your grandson's throat any better since the last time you came for the medicine?"

With her hands on her knees, the old woman waited, silent, erect and motionless, just as if she were in armor.

"You mustn't take up our time this way, Aunt Phoenix," the nurse said. "Tell us quickly about your grandson, and get it over. He isn't dead, is he?"

At last there came a flicker and then a flame of comprehension across her face, and she spoke.

"My grandson. It was my memory had left me. There I sat and forgot why I made my long trip."

"Forgot?" The nurse frowned. "After you came so far?"

Then Phoenix was like an old woman begging a dignified forgiveness for waking up frightened in the night. I never did go to school, I was too old at the Surrender," she said in a soft voice. "I'm an old woman without an education. It was my memory fail me. My little grandson, he is just the same, and I forgot it in the coming."

"Throat never heals, does it?" said the nurse, speaking in a loud, sure voice to old Phoenix. By now she had a card with something written on it, a little list. "Yes. Swallowed lye. When was it?—January—two, three years ago—"

Phoenix spoke unasked now. "No, missy, he not dead, he just the same. Every little while his throat begin to close up again, and he not able to swallow. He not get his breath. He not able to help himself. So the time come around, and I go on another trip for the soothing medicine."

"All right. The doctor said as long as you came to get it, you could have it," said the nurse. "But it's an obstinate case."

"My little grandson, he sit up there in the house all wrapped up, waiting by himself," Phoenix went on. "We is the only two left in the world. He suffer and it don't seem to put him back at all. He got a sweet look. He going to last. He wear a little patch quilt and peep out holding his mouth open like a little bird. I remembers so plain now. I not going to forget him again, no, the whole enduring time. I could tell him from all the others in creation."

"All right." The nurse was trying to hush her now. She brought her a bottle of medicine. "Charity," she said, making a check mark in a book.

Old Phoenix held the bottle close to her eyes, and then carefully put it into her pocket.

"I thank you," she said.

"It's Christmas time, Grandma," said the attendant. "Could I give you a few pennies out of my purse?"

"Five pennies is a nickel," said Phoenix stiffly.

"Here's a nickel," said the attendant.

Phoenix rose carefully and held out her hand. She received the nickel and then fished the other nickel out of her pocket and laid it beside the new one. She stared at her palm closely, with her head on one side.

Then she gave a tap with her cane on the floor.

"This is what come to me to do," she said. "I going to the store and buy my child a little windmill they sells, made out of paper. He going to find it hard to believe there such a thing in the world. I'll march myself back where he waiting, holding it straight up in this hand."

She lifted her free hand, gave a little nod, turned around, and walked out of the doctor's office. Then her slow step began on the stairs, going down.

STUDENT ESSAY

The Strong Character of Phoenix

James Ferguson

In "A Worn Path" Eudora Welty takes us on a journey of love and
hope. The aging Phoenix Jackson has to overcome many obstacles that
arise during a journey she must make to town to get medicine for her
ailing grandson. The way she overcomes these obstacles is important
in understanding her dominant character traits, for she is a woman of
determination who will not allow anything to stand between her and the
much needed medicine. Phoenix Jackson is a woman of strong and uncompromising character who surmounts all of the obstacles that could prevent
her from completing her journey.

Phoenix must overcome a number of physical barriers during the
course of her journey. A creek crossing must be accomplished via a log
that is laid across it, and by Phoenix's own admission this is one of
the most difficult parts of her journey, which she addresses by saying,
"Now comes the trial," and with leveled cane and eyes closed, she proceeds
to cross. Phoenix's willpower and determination become evident when
she comes upon a barbed-wire fence which she crawls through on her hands
and knees, and when she must leave the marked trail and enter a cornfield
through which there is no visible path, but driven on by her unfailing
devotion to her quest, Phoenix pushes on.

A number of obstacles are created by Phoenix's own limitations.
She is old, with failing eyesight that causes her to mistake a scarecrow
for a ghost, but she reacts to this obstacle with the same bravery that
characterized the creek crossing: "She shut her eyes, reached out her
hand and touched a sleeve." Phoenix also has a memory lapse, due undoubt-

STUDENT ESSAY

edly to her age, at which time she cannot remember why she has made the
long journey into town, and it is only after repeated questioning by
the nurse in the doctor's office that she remembers the purpose of her
journey. Phoenix's age requires her to walk with a cane, and when she
falls into a ditch she has to be helped out by a passing hunter, who
comments on the distance that she has left to go. But, undaunted, Phoenix
replies, "I bound to go to town, Mister." Although Phoenix is an old
woman with failing eyesight and intermittent losses of memory, she will
not allow any challenge to stand between her and her goal.

Phoenix has definite scruples which at times threaten to impede
her journey. Her value against stealing becomes evident during the encounter with the hunter when she picks up a nickel that has fallen out
of the man's pocket. With the nickel safely secured in her apron, Phoenix
questions the moral implications of her action: "God watching me the
whole time. I come to stealing." Phoenix's pride keeps her from answering the questions of an attendant in the clinic, who on first encountering
Phoenix responds to her by saying, "A charity case, I suppose." During
this time Phoenix remains oblivious to any thoughts except those concerning
the object of her journey, the medicine, and although at first the nurse
seems reluctant to give Phoenix the medicine, she finally concedes and
says, "All right, the doctor said as long as you came to get it, you could
have it." Even though the nurse states that "it's an obstinate case,"
Phoenix refuses to give up hope, accepts the medicine and places it carefully in her pocket.

With half the journey completed and the cherished medicine safely
secured, Phoenix's thoughts turn to a Christmas gift for her grandson.
After overcoming all of the obstacles in her way and obtaining the object
of her journey, Phoenix still thinks not of herself but of others. It

STUDENT ESSAY

is interesting to note that in Egyptian mythology, the phoenix was an
indestructible bird that rose after death by fire to new life. Phoenix
Jackson is also indestructible: a woman, energized by love, of uncompromising faith and determination.

ESTABLISHING PURPOSE

We write essays to present a clear, full development of a central idea (or thesis) so that readers both understand and are convinced of the reasonableness of our points. Whether we are explaining the challenge of white water canoeing or arguing for a pass/fail grading system, our goal will be to lead readers to the point of agreeing that indeed white water canoeing is challenging or that a pass/fail system has merit. When writing about literature, our general purpose will be the same: to explain our ideas and convince readers of their value. To demonstrate the challenge of white water canoeing, we would provide specific details from knowledge and experience. To support our assertions about a literary work, we need to provide specific details—evidence—drawn from an analysis of the work. Although we probably could not write well on the challenge of white water canoeing if we disliked the activity, we know that just saying that we enjoy the sport is not sufficient to produce an effective essay. The same holds true for writing about literature. You can use your particular preferences as a basis for selecting among topics, but you can't rely entirely on your likes and dislikes to provide a purpose for writing. Effective essays on any topic need to interest, inform, and convince readers.

We can also note more specific purposes for writing about literature. Some critics, for instance, choose to study literary works in relation to information external to the work. A critic may wish to establish a connection between biography and the work. With this purpose in mind, a critic might study the poems of Walt Whitman to explain Whitman's personality, or Whitman's poems could be interpreted in light of facts in his life. Other critics may be interested in studying a work's place in history or analyzing a work from a particular political ideology. These approaches to literature, because they require a knowledge of several fields other than literature, are not expected in introductory courses.

More characteristic of the specific purposes for your essays will be those that have in common a consideration of particular elements in the work itself. Your writing will express an understanding of the literature without drawing upon materials beyond a close reading of the work (except for a dictionary and basic reference books).

The most common assignments in introductory courses establish analysis as your purpose and approach. If you are asked to choose your topic, select one element in a literary work to analyze. The following are assignments that call for an analytic essay:

1. Analyze the dominant character traits of Phoenix Jackson in "A Worn Path."
2. Discuss the effect of Welty's use of setting in "A Worn Path." What does it contribute to the story?
3. Examine Welty's use of color imagery in "A Worn Path" and explain how it contributes to the story's theme.

Notice that only one assignment uses the word *analyze*. When an assignment asks you to "examine," "explore," or "discuss," you are still being asked to analyze. Notice, too, that not one assignment asks for your feelings about the work or for your judgment of the quality of the work; in each case you are asked to explain the meaning or functioning of one element in the literature: character, setting, or imagery.

Some assignments call for a personal response to a literary work. A student writing a personal response to "A Worn Path" could develop this thesis: *Reading "A Worn Path" helped me to appreciate the values of courage and endurance.* Although the thesis asserts that the story examines the values of courage and endurance, the specific purpose of the paper is to explain the student's response to those values. Assignments of this sort are often more difficult than they may seem. An essay on "A Worn Path," for instance, should not be used as a basis for tossing out some scattered views on courage. Good essays presenting a personal response to a work are those grounded in the process of analysis.

Even more demanding is fulfilling the purpose of evaluation. An evaluative essay may be limited to the judgment of a particular skill of the author's (the ability to create believable characters), or it may judge the work's significance as a literary endeavor. But remember that it is easy to make judgments; it is more difficult to make good judgments, ones that can be defended in a paper. To write a convincing evaluation, you need to base your judgment on an understanding of the work that grows out of skillful analysis and interpretation. If asked to write an evaluative essay, you should narrow the context of the assignment by judging the work in relation to others you have read in the course. Then you will be offering a judgment within a framework of knowledge.

The first step, then, in composing a literary essay, is defining your specific purpose: analysis/interpretation, personal response, or evaluation. Because analysis is a part of literary essays regardless of specific purpose, this chapter will illustrate the process of writing an analytic essay.

AUDIENCE AWARENESS

Unless you are writing a diary, you write to someone other than yourself; you have an audience. For your writing to be effective, you must be aware of the kind of reader you are addressing. You would not prepare the same talk on photography for a fifth grade art class that you would prepare for an advanced adult class. Before writing an essay, you need to plan the level of diction and the degree of explanation based upon an assessment of the reader's knowledge and sophistication.

When writing papers for class, students often forget to consider audience, perhaps because they place themselves (understandably) in a testing rather than a writing situation. In most cases, though, your instructor will expect you to produce a complete essay that can be understood by an interested reader who is not aware of a particular assignment. Thus it would be inappropriate to title your essay "Question #2" and to begin with the words: "She uses setting. . . ." Only the teacher audience would know who "she" is. Try to imagine that you are writing to readers who do not know that you are responding to an assigned topic.

If you are an expert writing on photography for a general audience, you can make the necessary adjustments to communicate to those who do not share your expertise. When you write about literature, what should you expect your audience to know? The usual assumption is that your audience has read the literature being discussed but will not have the work beside them and therefore will need to be reminded of selected details from the work that support your thesis. Unless you are given other instructions, also assume a knowledge of the basic terms and concepts of literary analysis. Thus a summary of the story or paraphrase of the poem will not be appropriate (your audience has this information from their own reading). Neither will you stop to define common literary terms such as setting or theme. But you will need to show how you are applying the terms to the work. Do not assume that your audience knows your proposed topic; state the title and author of the work and the topic and focus of your paper in the first paragraph.

LIMITING THE TOPIC

Once you have polished your skills in literary analysis, you will realize that much can be written about even the shortest poems. One cannot, in a 500-word essay, analyze every element in a complex literary work. If you are given a general assignment, you need to limit the topic to one you can cover adequately within the desired length of the essay. The first step to limiting your topic is to select one purpose—personal response, evaluation, or analysis. If you have decided to analyze, or if the assignment requires analysis, then choose one element in the work to examine. You might choose to write about the element that interests you most, such as the author's development of character or use of fantasy. Another guideline for limiting a topic is to focus on what seems most significant in the work. The color imagery in "A Worn Path" is important in developing the story's theme and thus would be a good topic choice. If your instructor gives a choice among several topics, these same considerations for selecting and limiting your topic can apply.

FORMULATING A PRECISE THESIS

At times, in our haste to get started (or to get finished), we would like to believe that once we have chosen and limited a topic we can begin to write. But choosing a topic is only the first step to planning an essay; still to come are formulating a thesis, selecting details to support the thesis, and ordering them into a meaningful pattern. Remember that a topic only identifies a subject area, whereas a thesis makes an assertion about the topic that must be developed and supported.

One of the best ways to move from a statement of subject to a thesis is to ask yourself questions about the subject. The answers should generate one or more appropriate thesis statements. What are Phoenix Jackson's characteristics? Which are most significant? Which relate to the meaning of the story? We can begin by listing observations about Phoenix.

1. She is old.
2. She has determination.
3. She loves her grandson.
4. She is optimistic.
5. She steals.
6. She is superstitious.

First, which are personality traits (generalizations about character) and which are facts that need little or no discussion? Statements one and five are facts, not traits. Second, which one or two statements convey what is central to the meaning of the story? Is this a story of old people, of theft, of superstition? No. What begins to stand out is Phoenix's determination, motivated by love for her grandson, which carries her through her difficult trip. By listing our observations and thinking about them in relation to what is central in the story, we can eliminate some and move toward a thesis that is worth examination because it focuses on what is significant: *Phoenix Jackson is a strong and determined woman.*

Although a good beginning, our tentative thesis can be made more precise and complete when we answer the questions that are generated by it: What is meant by strong? How is this quality revealed in the story? Not physically strong, Phoenix is uncompromising in her commitment to complete her journey successfully, a trait that is demonstrated in the story by the many obstacles she overcomes along the way. With this more complete understanding of Phoenix's character in hand, we can formulate the following thesis: *Phoenix Jackson is a woman of strong and uncompromising character who surmounts all of the obstacles that could prevent her from completing her journey.*

This is the thesis of the student essay on "A Worn Path." Did the student develop his thesis by listing a few statements about

Phoenix, drafting a tentative thesis, and then answering some questions? We don't know. What we do know is that people do not follow the same thought processes to reach an understanding of what they read. Some readers can make generalizations quickly and then need to examine the work again for evidence to support their assertions. Others work best by listing evidence relevant to the topic and then studying the evidence to see what generalizations emerge from the specific details. The key is to know which way works best for you, for the result is what matters: a coherent essay which develops and supports a thesis that makes a significant statement about the work.

GATHERING EVIDENCE
AND ORGANIZING AN APPROACH

Assuming, then, that your thinking about "A Worn Path" has produced the previously stated thesis, you need to examine the story for details that will support your thesis and then group those details into an order for your reader. Much of your contribution to your reader's understanding grows out of the way you ask that reader to look at the story, the perspective you provide by the structure you select. In most cases you should avoid using the organization of the work as the structure of your essay. Following the order of the work can lead to summarizing or paraphrasing rather than analyzing. The good essay provides more than a list of details to support the thesis; it organizes those details into a structure that is logically connected to the thesis.

Chart 3.1 gives an example of both steps: the gathering of evidence and the organization of that evidence into a logical pattern. Given our thesis, the two questions to be answered are: What are the obstacles that Phoenix overcomes and what types of obstacles does she face? The left column lists the obstacles in the order of their occurrence in the story. The list is a record of what we observe from reading. The three categories on the right reflect the student's recognition of a logical grouping of the obstacles. The categories result from the student's search for common elements in the diverse list of events; they are the product of analysis.

ORGANIZING EVIDENCE INTO PARAGRAPHS

Now that the student has identified three kinds of obstacles faced by Phoenix and understood that it is her ability to overcome all

---

CHART 3.1

Obstacles faced by Phoenix	*Types of obstacles*
1. age—stiff legs, walks with cane	I. Obstacles along the path—physical barriers
2. climbing the hill	2. climbing the hill
3. caught by thorny bush	3. caught by thorny bush
4. crossing creek on log	4. crossing creek on log
5. age—weariness, need to rest, afraid to close eyes	6. getting under fence
6. getting under barbed-wire fence	7. walking through cornfield
7. walking through pathless cornfield	II. Phoenix's limitation as a result of her age
8. afraid of scarecrow—does not see well	1. stiff legs, walks with cane
9. age—falls down when she hits dog and can't get up	5. weariness
10. steals nickel—gun pointed at her—says she's not afraid	8. does not see well
11. needs someone to tie her shoes	9. falls down when she hits dog
12. loses memory in clinic	11. needs someone to tie her shoes
13. nurse calls illness an obstinate case	12. loses memory in clinic
14. takes nickel (charity) from attendant	III. Values and attitudes that could stop Phoenix—scruples, pride, loss of hope
	10. steals nickel
	11. needs someone to tie shoes—pride as well as sign of age
	13. obstinate case—doesn't lose hope
	14. takes nickel from attendant—love over pride

---

kinds of barriers to success that demonstrates her strength of character, he is almost ready to write. His evidence can be organized into three paragraphs, one devoted to each kind of obstacle. It may not be necessary to give all of the examples listed on the chart; one can choose several of the most important, or most dramatic, examples to illustrate each type of obstacle. But to produce unified paragraphs, the examples of each type of obstacle must be grouped together. An introductory and a concluding paragraph will complete the plan.

The last decision to be made is the ordering of the three paragraphs comprising the body of the paper. If you are developing a thesis by examining three points that relate to the thesis but not to one another in any special way, then the best choice is to put the most important point last. Sometimes the three (or four or six, depending on the particular paper) points to be examined have a relationship to one another: chronological, spatial, causal, logical. If so, then use that relationship as the basis for ordering. If point two follows logically from point one, then convince your reader of point one first. In the student analysis of "A Worn Path," there is a spatial pattern of sorts in the three types of obstacles Phoenix must overcome. The student chose to begin with physical barriers, those obstacles that are imposed upon Phoenix from without, then to move to her own physical or physiological limitations, and then to place last those potential obstacles that are most "within" Phoenix: her values and attitudes. One could argue that the physical barriers pose the greatest threat to Phoenix, given her age. If you wanted to emphasize that point, then the order of the paragraphs should be reversed. Probably the least effective order would be one that placed the paragraph on physical barriers between the two paragraphs devoted to obstacles connected to Phoenix herself.

WRITING DEVELOPMENT PARAGRAPHS

Paragraphs that comprise the body of your essay need to contain more than just a list of details from the literature. Each paragraph should perform three functions: it should make an assertion (the topic sentence) that is related to the thesis; it should provide details to support the topic sentence; and it should explain how those details support the topic sentence and hence support the thesis. At times a paragraph will examine a concept or present a sequence of ideas. Even so, you have not finished your task until you have shown how that concept or those ideas explain the topic sentence and thus connect to the essay's thesis. The distinction is between *unity* and *coherence*. The writer who groups related details will have a unified paragraph, but only the writer who explains the related details will have both unity and coherence. Compare the paragraphs in Chart 3.2. On the right is the paragraph on physical barriers from the student paper. The words explaining the significance of the details are in boldface for emphasis. On the left is a paragraph that contains the same topic sentence and three details, but no explanation.

CHART 3.2

Without explanation	*With explanation*
Phoenix must overcome a number of physical barriers during the course of her journey. She must cross a creek via a log that is laid across it. She also crawls through a barbed-wire fence and enters a cornfield through which there is no visible path.	Phoenix must overcome a number of physical barriers during the course of her journey. A creek crossing must be made via a log that is laid across it, **and by Phoenix's own admission this is one of the most difficult parts of her journey, which she addresses by saying, "Now comes the trial," and with leveled cane and eyes closed, she proceeds to cross. Phoenix's will power and determination become evident** when she comes upon a barbed-wire fence which she crawls through on her hands and knees, and when she must leave the marked trail and enter into a cornfield through which there is no visible path, **but guided by her unfailing devotion to her quest, Phoenix pushes on.**

The paragraph on the left is only a list; it does not show the reader how the surmounting of these obstacles demonstrates Phoenix's strong character.

Here is another example, a paragraph that develops one point about the Duke in Browning's poem "My Last Duchess" (see p. 178). The student, Maureen O'Connor, has asserted in her thesis, at the end of paragraph 1, that "arrogance, jealousy, and materialism are his [the Duke's] most conspicuous personality traits." The following annotation of the second paragraph highlights the three parts of a good paragraph: topic sentence, evidence, and explanation.

The duke's arrogance is first recognized when he says "as if she ranked / My gift of a nine-hundred-years' old name / With anybody's gift."	topic sentence for paragraph: first trait mentioned in the thesis
Here he elevates himself through his heritage. He believes that the duchess should have felt privileged to be his wife and share his name.	textual evidence #1 (Note smooth blend of student's writing and quote)
He does not understand why she seemed to be pleased by men who, as far as he can perceive, have no worth. Because of his arrogance, he does not understand that many men have more to offer than prestige. The duchess probably enjoyed their kindness or humor or some other warm human trait that the duke lacks.	explanation of how lines show arrogance
Another example of the duke's arrogance is displayed when he says "I choose / Never to stoop."	textual evidence #2
He wants to remain on this elevated position he has established in his own mind and not lower himself. It also implies that he would have to stoop to be at the same level as his	explanation
own wife. When he says "to make your will / Quite clear to such an one, and say, 'Just this / Or that in you disgusts me; here you miss / Or there	textual evidence #3

exceed the mark,'" he has created in his mind ⎤
a model of how one should behave. He believes   ⎬ — explanation
that he fits the model but the duchess did not. ⎦

INTRODUCTORY AND CONCLUDING PARAGRAPHS

The same guidelines for beginning and ending essays on nonliterary topics apply to essays on literary works. An introductory paragraph should engage the reader's attention, state the topic for discussion (including the author and title of the work) to set the focus and limits of the paper, and usually, present the thesis. Here is Maureen O'Connor's opening paragraph on "My Last Duchess."

Would you like to marry a duke? Prob- ⎤ — personal question used as
ably not the duke in Robert Browning's "My ⎦   atttention-getter

Last Duchess." Browning successfully exposes ⎤
the personality of the duke through what the
duke says about himself, through his actions,   ⎬ — transitional explanation
and through his interpretations of earlier
incidents. ⎦

Arrogance, jealousy, and materialism ⎤
are his most conspicuous personality traits. ⎦ — thesis

Although the "thesis and support" essay format is the easiest to construct and the one most frequently taught in introductory writing courses, other formats can provide successful structures to literary essays. Instead of presenting the thesis in the opening paragraph, you can begin by asking a question that the rest of the essay answers or by posing a problem that the rest of the essay solves. You could, for instance, begin an essay on the theme of "A Woman on the Roof" by asking the key question: Why do the men become so angry over the woman's indifference? You can also begin a paper by stating a critical opinion that your essay will challenge. (Perhaps your class has debated several interpretations of a work, or you have disagreed with the thesis of a literary analysis.) This beginning establishes a debate environment; you will state your thesis in the concluding paragraph after you have presented evidence to prove it.

In establishing your topic you may need to remind readers of those elements in the work that you perceive to be significant, but do not pad your first paragraph with unnecessary summary or paraphrase. For example, the first sentence of this chapter's student paper, in addition to giving author and title, provides a brief summary that focuses the reader's attention on the student's approach to analyzing Phoenix's character: "Phoenix Jackson has to overcome many obstacles that arise during a journey she must make to town to get medicine for her ailing grandson." This is not summary to get warmed up; the student asks the reader to view Phoenix's journey as a series of obstacles to be overcome. By contrast, if the student had written, "Phoenix Jackson makes a journey to town to get medicine for her grandson," he would be summarizing without focusing attention on his topic.

Remember, too, that opening paragraphs must stand independent of the essay's title. If the title of the literary work appears as part of your title, you must still repeat the title in your first paragraph. (The title of the work alone is an ineffective one for your essay, and "Analysis of 'A Worn Path'" isn't much better. Strive for some interest in your titles.) Finally, avoid announcing what you intend to do. If you can't create a clever opening, then just get started with author, title, and topic. "In Eudora Welty's 'A Worn Path' Phoenix Jackson must . . ." is much better than "In this essay I will examine the character traits of Phoenix Jackson. . . ."

What about conclusions? A review of main points is unnecessary in a short essay, and equally ineffective is a one-sentence paragraph that repeats the thesis. Further, you do not want to end with an apology or a final plea for understanding. Consider this brief concluding paragraph:

> Edwin Arlington Robinson wrote "Richard Cory" to bring out a point. Hopefully the reader can see it and learn something from it.

What point is brought out? What will the reader "hopefully" learn? Not an effective conclusion. Still, if you simply stop after presenting the last example, your paper will seem unfinished.

Here are some suggestions for concluding. If your essay

develops logically connected points so that your final development paragraph completes your argument, then show, in a couple of sentences, how the last point confirms your thesis. If your essay is organized by classifying details, you can rephrase, not repeat, the thesis to guide your reader to a new level of insight. Note that the student writing on Phoenix saves for the final paragraph an explanation of the allusion in her name; in this way he can give a final emphasis to her indestructability. If your paper is an analysis of one element of the work, then conclude by showing how an understanding of that element helps us understand the meaning of the work as a whole. One student concluded a paper on Dylan Thomas's "Do Not Go Gentle into That Good Night" (see p. 590) this way:

> Although the speaker in the poem is addressing only his father, the theme is for all people in all times: Do not accept death passively and let go of life easily; resist death to the very end.

chapter 4

Structure

Belvedere. 1958. Lithograph, 461 × 295 (18⅛ × 11⅝"). Signed and dated: MCEV-'58. Book 1967, no. 74; Cat. 1968, no. 120. c. M. C. Escher Heirs and Cordon Art-Baarn-Holland.

All works of art—poems, paintings, musical scores—have a shape, a pattern, a *structure*. An artist selects both a subject and a pattern or arrangement of parts for that subject. If several artists were each asked to paint a still life using only oranges, apples, and cherries, they would create different paintings, because they would select different arrangements of the same fruit. Will the bowl contain only a few pieces of fruit carefully separated by type, or will it be a jumble of fruits piled high and overflowing the sides, inviting us to reach out for some? The choice of pattern is as important to the effect of the work as the choice of subject.

We take pleasure in order, in the sense of completeness that results from the wedding of subject and structure, in the feeling that to remove one cherry from the bowl would ruin the painting or that any rearrangement of words would destroy the power of the poem. Developing, then, skill in recognizing the various structural devices of a poem or story provides another dimension to the enjoyment of literature: you will see more than the unskilled reader sees. Because choice of arrangement is as important as the choice of subject in conveying the artist's vision, skill in analyzing structure is also essential to understanding the work's meaning. The terms and concepts related to analyzing structure are not ends in themselves but means to increased understanding of a literary work.

NARRATIVE STRUCTURE

"Once upon a time. . . ." So begins the traditional fairy tale. The tale, the story, the narrative, whether in prose or poetic form, recounts a sequence of events. *Plot*, or plot structure, refers to the author's arrangement of those events. Some critics use the terms *story* and *plot* interchangeably to refer to "what happens," but many reserve plot (or plot structure) for the particular order given to "what happens" by an author. As we shall see in this chapter, the same basic narrative can be shaped into different plots by different writers.

Chronology

We have said that a narrative recounts a sequence of events. The key word is sequence. The recognition of time sequence, or chronological order, is at least as old as the beginning of story telling. Although arranging a story chronologically seems simple, each author must still make important choices. First, a writer chooses a point in time to begin a story and a later point to end. Second, a writer can choose to devote considerable space to some parts of a story while quickly passing over other parts. The result of this variation is increased emphasis on those parts of the story treated at length. The following ballad will serve as the basis for discussion.

ANONYMOUS

The Demon Lover

"O where have you been, my long, long love,
   This long seven years and mair°?"   *more*
"O I'm come to seek my former vows
   Ye granted me before."

"O hold your tongue of your former vows   5
   For they will breed sad strife;
O hold your tongue of your former vows,
   For I am become a wife."

He turned him right and round about,
   And the tear blinded his ee°:   *eye* 10
"I wad never hae trodden on Irish ground,
   If it had not been for thee.

"I might have had a king's daughter,
   Far, far beyond the sea;
I might have had a king's daughter,   15
   Had it not been for love o thee."

"If ye might have had a king's daughter,
   Yer sel ye had to blame:
Ye might have taken the king's daughter,
   For ye kend° that I was nane.   *knew* 20

"If I was to leave my husband dear,
   And my two babes also,
O what have you to take me to,
If with you I should go?"

"I hae seven ships upon the sea—   25
   The eighth brought me to land—
With four-and-twenty bold mariners,
   And music on every hand."

She has taken up her two little babes,
   Kissed them baith cheek and chin: 30
"O fair ye weel, my ain two babes,
   For I'll never see you again."

She set her foot upon the ship,
   No mariners could she behold;
But the sails were o the taffetie,   35
   And the masts o the beaten gold.

They had not sailed a league, a league,
   A league but barely three,
When dismal grew his countenance,
   And drumlie° grew his ee.   *gloomy*   40

They had not sailed a league, a league,
   A league but barely three,
Until she espied his cloven foot,
   And she wept right bitterlie.

"O hold your tongue of your weeping," says he,   45
   "Of your weeping now let me be;
I will shew you how the lilies grow
   On the banks of Italy."

"O what hills are yon, yon pleasant hills,
   That the sun shines sweetly on?"   50
"O yon are the hills of heaven," he said,
   "Where you will never win°."   *gain, achieve*

"O whaten mountain is yon," she said,
   "All so dreary wi frost and snow?"
"O yon is the mountain of hell," he cried,   55
   "Where you and I will go."

He strack the tap-mast wi his hand,
   The fore-mast wi his knee,
And he brake that gallant ship in twain,
   And sank her in the sea.   60

    Reading first for what happens, we can summarize the story told in this narrative poem:

A man returns after seven years to marry his betrothed only to learn that she is married and has two children. When he tells her he has seven ships she kisses her children good-bye and goes on a ship with him. She becomes despondent. He shows her a pleasant hill and then a dreary mountain. The ship sinks into the sea.

Moving from summary to analysis, we observe that the ballad has the form of most stories in that it combines *narration* (when we listen to the storyteller) and *dialogue* (when we listen to the woman and her returned lover speak). We recognize as well the use of time sequence: the sailor returns and then she goes with him and then the ship sinks. By studying this ballad in comparison with the original story, we can observe even more of the ballad's structure.

"The Demon Lover" reproduced above is a nineteenth-century British version of an older story. Near the end of this chapter is Elizabeth Bowen's modern prose version of this old tale. The story, in its oldest form, can be told as follows: James Harris is betrothed to Jane Reynolds when he is sent to sea. When, three years later, he is reported dead, Jane marries a ship carpenter with whom she lives for four years and has two children. Then the ghost of James returns to claim his betrothed, who goes with him when he tells her he can support her. She is never seen again, and her husband hangs himself.

We now observe that the author of the ballad version is using only a part of the total time sequence of the original story. The balladeer begins with the lover's return, ends with the ship's disappearance, and provides background indirectly through dialogue. Is it correct to say that this author does not begin at the story's beginning? Is the real beginning when they exchange vows? When they first meet? Surely the real beginning (or ending) of any story is that which the writer selects for a particular story. As observant readers our concern is to understand the impact of the author's selection and ordering of events. What is the effect in "The Demon Lover" of the author's choice? First, unity is achieved by focusing entirely on the woman's destruction by her demon lover. Further, the limitation to two key moments in time, each presented through dialogue, results in a more dramatic story.

Now that we have looked more closely at the selection and ordering of events, read the poem again to analyze the impact of the relative space given to the several episodes. How many lines are given to their meeting again? What happens between stanzas 7 and 8? Between stanzas 12 and 13? What has been achieved by devoting almost half of the poem to their meeting and no words at all to the two events that take place between stanzas?

A writer can also provide variation of time sequence by using *flashback*, presenting events that actually took place at an earlier time. A flashback can be presented by a narrator who stops the story to recount earlier events; but more often, in modern stories, the flashback is presented through a character's thoughts. Mrs. Drover, in Bowen's version, takes us back to an earlier time when she recalls her strange courtship with the returning lover. Quite often an early event in a story will serve as a warning of a significant event to come later; this is called *foreshadowing*. Foreshadowing alerts a reader to the direction the story will take; more often we recognize the significance of the early events only after we finish reading and begin to analyze structure. A good example is one line in Bowen's "The Demon Lover": "No human eye watched Mrs. Drover's return"—no *human* eye indeed.

Conflict

Narratives that employ only a chronological ordering of events are said to have *episodic* plots; events unfold in time sequence, and further unity is achieved because the events (or episodes) involve a central character. But many narratives employ, in addition to chronology, an ordering that develops and finally resolves a central *conflict*, a battle of opposing forces. The principle of causation, of one event producing the next event, unites the sequence of episodes. Such a plot is described as *organic* because one event grows out of the previous event. Organic plots generally follow a standard arrangement of parts that have been given the following labels: *exposition, conflict, complication, climax*, and *resolution*.

Exposition refers to background information, to the context in which the story takes place. Although some information about characters or previous significant events may not emerge until we are well into a story (one technique for creating suspense), a writer usually presents at least some of the exposition at or near the beginning. Exposition includes both setting ("Towards the end of her day in London" from Bowen's "The Demon Lover") and information about characters (Mrs. Mallard's heart condition in "The Story of an Hour"). (In the ballad "The Demon Lover" we learn from the opening dialogue that the two speakers had exchanged vows seven years previously.)

Interest in a narrative is produced by the tension created when a *conflict* arises or when an existing situation is disturbed in some way (*complication*). In some stories an event takes place that becomes a complication in the main character's life and produces a conflict for the character. Presumably the woman in "The Demon Lover" has been content with her life before the former lover returns. His reappearance complicates her life, producing a conflict, because now she must decide whether or not to go with him. In other stories, the conflict exists first and the episodes in the story result in one or more complications for the main character because of the existing conflict. In either case, we become increasingly involved as the struggle moves to the *climax*, the point of greatest tension, a point that often involves the most critical decision which the central character must make and which will determine the *resolution* of the conflict in some manner. The simplest version of this plot structure can be diagramed as illustrated in Figure 4.1.

In some narratives, a character will make a decision to resolve the complication that has developed only to discover that this decision results in a second and perhaps a third complication, each one becoming more serious than the one before. The plot structure for such a story would look like that in Figure 4.2.

The term *resolution* can cause some difficulty if readers expect a detailed explanation of the consequences of the main character's decisions. In many stories, the resolution is presented in one or two sentences and may not therefore seem like a resolution. The only resolution may be a moment of insight, of new understanding, on the part of the main character. Thus "no" resolution can be one kind of resolution; the author's point may be that the character's life will be an endless series of complications because the character

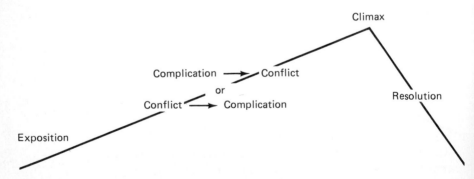

FIGURE 4.1   A simple plot structure diagramed.

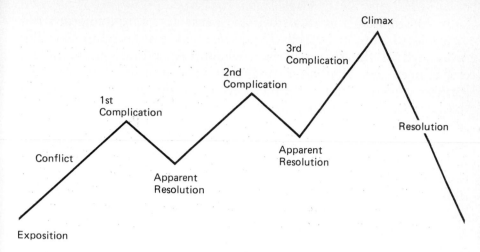

FIGURE 4.2   *A more complex plot structure.*

cannot or will not resolve the central conflict. For illustration of plot structure, look at this brief but complete story by Somerset Maugham.

W. SOMERSET MAUGHAM   (1874–1965)

Appointment in Samarra

There was a merchant in Bagdad who sent his servant to market to buy provisions, and in a little while the servant came back, white and trembling, and said, "Master, just now when I was in the market-place I was jostled by a woman in the crowd and when I turned I saw it was Death that jostled me. She looked at me and made a threatening gesture; now, lend me your horse, and I will ride away from this city and avoid my fate. I will go to Samarra and there Death will not find me." The merchant lent him his horse, and the servant mounted it, and he dug his spurs in its flanks and as fast as the horse could gallop he went. Then the merchant went down to the market-place and he saw Death standing in the crowd and he came to Death and said, "Why did you make a threatening gesture to my servant when you saw him this morning?" "That was not a threatening gesture," Death said, "It was only a start of surprise. I was astonished to see him in Bagdad, for I had an appointment with him tonight in Samarra."

The episodes in this story are presented chronologically but are related causally as well. The exposition, presented in less than one-third of the first sentence, establishes setting (Bagdad) and introduces two characters (the merchant and his servant). An ordinary event becomes complicated when the servant meets Death because Death creates a conflict for him. Since the servant wants to continue living, he attempts to resolve his conflict with Death by fleeing to Samarra. The story's climax occurs when the merchant asks Death why her gesture that morning had been a threatening one. This is the point of greatest tension, for Death's answer will tell us the servant's fate. Death's response is the resolution, but not that expected by the servant.

Much of the effect of this story is achieved by the use of *irony of situation* (see p. 230). In seeking to resolve his conflict with Death, the servant chooses a course of action that turns out to be exactly the wrong choice. Maugham drives home his point—no one can escape his appointment with Death—by creating a plot structure that turns on the contrast between what seems to be and what actually is. An analysis of structure, then, allows us not only to separate and label the various parts of the work but to see, by that process, how structure is used to establish the work's meaning.

DRAMATIC STRUCTURE

Plays differ from narratives in that they lack a storyteller or narrator. Although a playwright must also select points in time to begin and end, the passing of time must be shown by a change in scene or costume or revealed through dialogue, not provided by a narrator. Most playwrights use the conventional structure of scene and act divisions, but only readers are fully aware of this structure, for in a live performance of most plays not all scene divisions are marked by an empty stage or dropped curtain. In spite of structural devices characteristic only of the drama, plays are like stories in that most have a plot structure that can be analyzed into the component parts of exposition, conflict/complication, climax, and resolution. Exposition must, like the passing of time, be revealed through dialogue, with the help of props to locate setting. Presenting exposition through dialogue, whether in fiction or in the drama, is a demanding task since characters must speak "in character" and also provide the audience with needed information.

When you look beyond the most obvious elements of dramatic form—dialogue and scene divisions—to examine plot structure, you discover that the plot structure is, to a large degree, the result of the type of play you are reading or watching. The drama is rich in conventional or traditional forms. Almost all plays written prior to 1860 can be classified into one of four categories: comedy, tragedy, melodrama, and farce. *Farce* is really a subcategory of comedy and can best be defined as physical comedy, comedy based more on situation than on character. *Melodramas* are characterized by sensational plots and a resolution that provides for the triumph of virtuous characters over evil characters and over the most bizarre complications. The antics of Laurel and Hardy or the Keystone cops are farcical; TV soaps are examples of melodramas. The more important traditional forms are comedy and tragedy.

There are several types of *comedy*, but we can begin with a general definition: a play depicting human foibles or weaknesses (usually of a social rather than a personal nature) and resulting in a happy ending when the weaknesses are removed. The most basic plot structure for comedy, thus, is harmony → disharmony → renewed harmony. Put another way, something happens to disrupt a previously existing (social) harmony, but the complication is resolved, reuniting the characters and either reestablishing the previous harmony or, in some comedies, establishing an even better social order.

In *romantic comedy*, lovers must overcome some obstacle, foolish parents perhaps, or in plots with several pairs of lovers, a failure to perceive what the right pairings are. But "all's well that ends well," to borrow a title from Shakespeare, and all will end well if the play is a comedy. The right lovers are united, and the play ends with the social order restored and perpetuating itself into the next generation. In *satiric comedy*, the human weaknesses that are ridiculed to be corrected by laughter are often more serious, but the structure remains the same as the hypocrite, for example, is reformed and becomes a better member of the group. *Rogue* or *picaresque comedy*, depicting society's underdogs triumphing over their social betters, delights us as we identify with the clever underdogs and imagine that we, too, could outwit our bosses or parents. Comic situations may begin as probable, and the human limitations may appear all too real, but since the comic plot structure demands a happy ending, in some plays characters may have to make abrupt changes in behavior or belief. But when you are watching a comedy, the happy ending, however achieved, is (from Shakespeare again) "as you like it."

Tragedy depicts a serious struggle between the *protagonist* (the main character, the tragic hero) and the *antagonist* (the character or forces in conflict with the tragic hero), resulting in the loss of power or position and, usually, the life of the tragic hero. The tragic plot structure looks like a pyramid, as you can see in Figure 4.3.

In most ancient Greek and Elizabethan (sixteenth century) tragedies, the increasing misfortunes of the tragic hero also involve several other characters so that by the end of the play as many as five or six characters may be destroyed by the sequence of events. In spite of these losses, most readers/viewers find tragedy to be optimistic because the tragic hero is noble or heroic in aspirations, if not in all traits and accomplishments. In striving to assert his or her will, the tragic hero affirms life and human values.

The causes of the tragic hero's downfall have been debated by critics since the Greek philosopher Aristotle wrote his *Poetics*. In ancient Greek tragedy, fate, often bringing a curse to several generations of family members, is presented as a cause. Still, in many Greek plays we sense that the hero's own character is part of the cause for the tragic outcome. Aristotle suggests that the tragic ending is the result of the hero's tragic flaw (Gr. *hamartia*) which is often pride (Gr. *hybris*) but can be simply a mistake, sometimes the mistake that comes from limited knowledge.

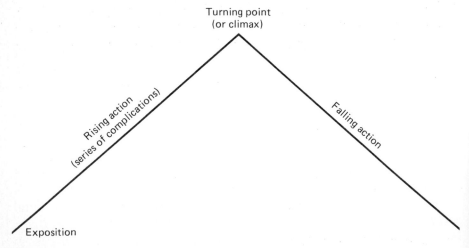

FIGURE 4.3   *Plot structure for tragedy.*

Medieval tragedies depict the hero's downfall as a result either of the wheel of fortune or of a punishment for sin, but Elizabethan tragedies, especially the plays of Shakespeare, renew the emphasis on character, together with the pressures of time, as the causes of tragedy. Often the very traits that make the hero admirable— assertiveness, largeness of heart—are the traits that bring destruction. The tragic hero may acquire new knowledge and self-awareness but the insight comes too late to stem the tragic flow of events.

Many modern plays, such as Ibsen's *A Doll's House* (pp. 740– 800), require a new category: the *problem play*. Neither comedies nor tragedies, these are serious plays examining social or psychological issues. Their plot structures can be analyzed into the same parts as those found in fiction, and their endings are often similar to those of modern short stories: open, ambiguous, providing a resolution that is "no" resolution. Problem plays tend to be realistic, with recognizable settings, probable events, and psychologically sound motivations for the behavior of characters. While most plays written from the 1860s to the 1920s were either comedies or problem plays, in the last fifty years several new types of plays, characterized by a lack of realism, have been produced. Some have realistic settings but a sequence of events that is neither probable nor predictable. Often the unrealistic plot structure is designed to reject the concept of causality in human events. Put another way, the apparent lack of structure is chosen to reinforce the play's theme.

POETIC STRUCTURES

Lyric poems express thoughts and emotions, and dramatic poems develop characters in a particular situation. These poems may create a brief scene, but only narrative poems present a sequence of events. Thus, neither lyric nor dramatic poems use a plot structure. Still, each poem has patterns or an organization that helps convey the poem's meaning. Some of the verbal and visual patterns that are analyzed as elements of a dramatist's or fiction writer's style become the dominant structures of lyric and dramatic poems. We can divide poetic structures into two categories: (1) those fixed forms and visual forms that provide an external pattern, and (2) all those verbal, logical, and psychological patterns that are part of the way we put words and sentences together to convey meaning.

External Structures: Fixed Forms

Poets expect us to recognize conventional poetic forms and to anticipate the repetitions and/or variations necessary to complete the selected form. Here are some fixed forms you need to be able to recognize and describe. (If the terminology used to discuss a poem's meter is unfamiliar to you, study the explanation provided in Appendix A.)

Blank verse, the dominant form of Shakespeare's plays, is always comprised of continuous lines of unrhymed iambic pentameter:

> To be, or not to be: that is the question.
> Whether 'tis nobler in the mind to suffer
> The slings and arrows of outrageous fortune,
> Or to take arms against a sea of troubles,
> And by opposing end them. To die; to sleep;
>
> *Hamlet*

Couplets are continuous lines with the same meter and rhyming *aabbcc*, and so on:

> Had we but world enough, and time,
> This coyness, lady, were no crime.
> We would sit down, and think which way
> To walk, and pass our long love's day;
>
> "To His Coy Mistress" (pp. 242–43)

Quatrains are four-line units with a repeated meter and rhyme scheme:

> That time of year thou mayst in me behold
> When yellow leaves, or none, or few, do hang
> Upon those boughs which shake against the cold,
> Bare ruined choirs where late the sweet birds sang.
>
> "Sonnet 73" (p. 565)

Stanzas are lines grouped into units that repeat the same number of lines, the same meter, and the same rhyme scheme, and that are separated from one another by additional spacing. One traditional stanza form is the *ballad stanza*, a four-line stanza of alternating iambic tetrameter and iambic trimeter, with the second and fourth lines rhyming:

He strack the tap-mast wi his hand,
   The fore-mast wi his knee,
And he brake that gallant ship in twain,
   And sank her in the sea.

   "The Demon Lover" (pp. 66–67)

Once we read the first stanza of a poem, or recognize that we are reading blank verse, we know how the rest of the poem will be shaped, externally. We do not know, though, when the poem will end, for poems can have any number of stanzas or any number of lines. But some fixed forms establish an exact external structure for the entire poem. Examples include the epigram, the limerick, and, probably best known, the sonnet. A glance at the poem you are about to read will tell you immediately if it is a sonnet, for a *sonnet* is always fourteen lines of iambic pentameter with a specific rhyme scheme. The *English* or *Shakespearean* sonnet (see "Sonnet 18," p. 25) has a rhyme scheme of *abab cdcd, efef, gg*, a pattern that suggests an organization of lines into three quatrains and a concluding couplet. The skilled poet will use the external form as an organizing principle. Often the English sonnet will present three examples, or images, one in each quatrain, with the concluding couplet summing up the point of the examples.

The *Italian* or *Petrarchan* sonnet has an even more demanding rhyme scheme because it uses fewer rhyming sounds. The rhyme scheme establishes a structural break between the first eight lines or *octave*, which rhyme *abbaabba*, and the last six lines or *sestet*, which usually rhyme *cdcdcd* or *cdecde*. A good example of the Italian sonnet is Keats's "On First Looking into Chapman's Homer" (p. 29). The poem's development corresponds to the two-part structure that is further emphasized by a space separating the octave and sestet.

External Structures: The Visual Patterns of Free Verse and Concrete Poetry

Many poems have been written with less external structure than that provided by stanza form, or with an external structure that is primarily visual. Some poems, such as Matthew Arnold's "Dover Beach" (p. 573), have a regular meter but no regularity of line length and no rhyme scheme; they are often divided into *verse paragraphs*, groups of lines with internal structure but not the repeated patterns of stanza forms. Poems without any regular meter are classified as *free verse*. Whitman gives us an example.

WALT WHITMAN   (1819–1892)

A Noiseless Patient Spider

A noiseless patient spider,
I mark'd where on a little promontory it stood isolated,
Mark'd how to explore the vacant vast surrounding,
It launch'd forth filament, filament, filament, out of itself,
Ever unreeling them, ever tirelessly speeding them.   5

And you O my soul where you stand,
Surrounded, detached, in measureless oceans of space,
Ceaselessly musing, venturing, throwing, seeking the spheres to connect
    them,
Till the bridge you will need be form'd, till the ductile anchor hold,
Till the gossamer thread you fling catch somewhere, O my soul.   10

Although each unit of this poem contains five lines, the considerable difference in line length tells you that this poem is composed of two verse paragraphs, not stanzas. Scanning the poem would reveal no prevailing metrical pattern; thus we conclude that this is free verse. Whitman's use of repetition of words and of a series pattern ("musing, venturing, throwing . . .") provides a rhythm, but equally important in the reader's sense of rhythm is the visual effect of the arrangement of lines on the printed page. Even more dependent on visual effect is the following poem.

IAN HAMILTON FINLAY   (b. 1925)

The Horizon of Holland

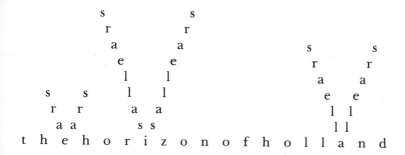

Can you find the words to complete the statement beginning "the horizon of holland"? Finlay's poem is an example of *concrete poetry*, a type of modern poetry that places emphasis on visual as well as verbal communication, on typography rather than on internal structure. Some critics do not consider such poems to be serious literary works, but they do demonstrate the role that visual patterns play in some poems—and they are fun to make and to see.

Internal Structures: Larger Patterns

There are as many internal poetic structures as there are ways to put units of thought together because (to state the obvious that the mystery and magic of poetry sometimes make us forget) poems are made up of sentences, or parts of sentences. Still, we can describe various types of structures used repeatedly by poets, indeed by all writers. A poet can describe, or explain, or argue. But since descriptive details cannot be given all at once, the parts must be placed in some order. The details that create Keats's description of autumn ("To Autumn," p. 211) are organized into three stanzas according to time sequence. In the following poem Herrick uses a spatial order.

ROBERT HERRICK   (1591–1674)

Delight in Disorder

A sweet disorder in the dress
Kindles in clothes a wantonness.
A lawn° about the shoulders thrown   *linen scarf*
Into a fine distraction;
An erring lace, which here and there   5
Enthralls the crimson stomacher°;   *waistband*
A cuff neglectful, and thereby
Ribbons to flow confusedly;
A winning wave, deserving note,
In the tempestuous petticoat;   10
A careless shoestring, in whose tie
I see a wild civility;
Do more bewitch me than when art
Is too precise in every part.

To make a comment about what is beautiful, or artistic, Herrick provides a list of details about a woman's clothes, but notice that the list is organized from shoulders to feet—or top to bottom.

Many poems attempt to clarify an idea or feeling, to explain what love is, or beauty, for example. Such a poem may present a list: love is not a, b, or c, but rather 1, 2, and 3. Or the poet can use a question and answer structure. Langston Hughes employs a variation of this pattern in "Dream Deferred" (p. 216); he answers his initial question with a series of questions. Sometimes poets use an argumentative structure that we can spot by the appearance of such connecting words as "however," "thus," or "therefore." Probably the most famous use of an argument structure in poetry is Andrew Marvell's poem, "To His Coy Mistress" (pp. 242–43). Further, a poet can develop a particular example or recreate a concrete experience. In some poems, the point of the example is not stated; the poet expects us to state it ourselves from the specifics provided. If the poet presents a conclusion, or general point, we can describe the poem's structure as a movement from the particular to the general. Consider the following poem.

ROBERT HERRICK   (1591–1674)

To Daffodils

Fair daffodils, we weep to see
  You haste away so soon;
As yet the early-rising sun
  Has not attained his noon.
     Stay, stay,   5
    Until the hasting day
     Has run
    But to the even-song;
And, having prayed together, we
    Will go with you along.   10

We have short time to stay, as you;
  We have as short a spring,
As quick a growth to meet decay,
  As you, or anything.
     We die   15
    As your hours do, and dry
     Away
    Like to the summer's rain,
Or as the pearls of morning's dew,
    Ne'er to be found again.   20

This poem, with an interesting stanza form, comments on the shortness of life. How is the poem's meaning developed? In the first stanza, the speaker, using "we" to include us all, speaks directly to the daffodil, lamenting its short life. In the second stanza the speaker makes a connection between daffodils and humans; we, too, "haste away so soon." The pattern is associative; it moves from observation of a particular experience to a general application.

Internal Structure: Verbal Patterns

In addition to selecting some kind of external form and some internal structure, poets further unify their works and reinforce meaning through verbal patterns. Whatever the particular verbal patterns selected, the general principle is one of repetition plus variation, as the following poem illustrates.

A. E. HOUSEMAN   (1859–1936)

In the Morning, In the Morning

In the morning, in the morning,
  In the happy field of hay,
Oh they looked at one another
  By the light of day.

In the blue and silver morning
  On the haycock as they lay,
Oh they looked at one another
  And they looked away.

The choice of stanza form with second and fourth lines rhyming provides one type of repetitive pattern. Further repetition is achieved by the repetition of line 3 in line 7, the repetition of initial words in lines 1 and 5, and the repetition of initial sounds in the corresponding words "happy" (line 2) and "haycock" (line 6) and "light" (line 4) and "looked" (line 8). What is the effect of these verbal patterns? The singing quality of the simple verses and the extensive use of repetition establish the expectation of a "happy" ending to the idyllic scene. The power of the last line to shock us is increased because it is in sharp contrast to the expectations created by the previous seven lines.

STRUCTURE AS COHERENT ORGANIZATION

We analyze structure with the assumption that structure and meaning are unified, that the chosen form conveys the artist's vision. We also bring certain expectations to our reading. For example, the analysis of an organic plot structure in stories and plays invariably raises the issue of plausibility. In a story that presents itself as realistic, we expect characters to behave in a believable way in response to the situations they find themselves in, and we expect events that occur to be probable outcomes of previous events, given the characters shaping those events. We may be willing to accept some coincidence, particularly in the initial situation, because we find chance or coincidence in our lives, but we would not accept a conclusion that seems completely unrelated to the pattern of events that has been developing.

On the other hand, our expectations as intelligent readers should be appropriate for the world created by the writer. Not all stories and plays are designed to depict a realistic world. Some works take us into a *fantasy* world of magical powers and strange events. We should be willing to enter the fantasy world created by the writer for the purpose of telling a story, but once we accept the basics of the fantasy we can demand an internal logic or consistency. Witches must behave wickedly, and a fairy godmother must reward the good Cinderella, not her evil stepsisters.

WRITING ABOUT STRUCTURE

As an outside assignment or class exercise, you might be asked to write a brief analysis of the structure of a poem, story, or play. But since analysis is ultimately an aid to interpretation, one rarely finds a full essay that only describes a work's structure. For longer papers you will probably be asked to relate structure to meaning, to show the effect of a writer's choice of structure. You might, for example, take a fixed-form poem and show how the poet uses the given characteristics of the form to develop meaning, or how the conventional pattern is varied to achieve special effects. Your essay would take the form of comparison or contrast. It would begin by establishing the characteristics of the fixed form and then show how the particular poem matches the fixed form, or show the ways in which the particular poem differs from the expected pattern and the effect of those variations.

You can also analyze plot structure to show that a recognition of the component parts leads one to understand the story or play's meaning or central theme. You would probably organize a paper on this topic around the parts of the plot, examining each one in order. Thus your essay would follow an organization similar to that of the story. The chief danger with such an organization lies in the tendency to summarize events rather than analyze structure. To avoid lapsing into summary, make sure that your thesis states a connection between structure and meaning, and make sure that each paragraph has a topic sentence that connects to the thesis. Then select only the significant details of the story or play to illustrate your points. The student essay on "The Necklace" (p. 92) is an analysis of that story's basic plot structure. To highlight the student's organization, terms used to analyze plot have been italicized. You should read "The Necklace" first, answering the questions following it, and then read the student essay.

GUY DE MAUPASSANT   (1850–1893)

The Necklace

She was one of those pretty and charming girls who are sometimes, as if by a mistake of destiny, born in a family of clerks. She had no dowry, no expectations, no means of being known, understood, loved, wedded, by any rich and distinguished man; and she let herself be married to a little clerk at the Ministry of Public Instruction.

She dressed plainly because she could not dress well, but she was as unhappy as though she had really fallen from her proper station; since with women there is neither caste nor rank; and beauty, grace, and charm act instead of family and birth. Natural fineness, instinct for what is elegant, suppleness of wit, are the sole hierarchy, and make from women of the people the equals of the very greatest ladies.

She suffered ceaselessly, feeling herself born for all the delicacies and all the luxuries. She suffered from the poverty of her dwelling, from the wretched look of the walls, from the worn-out chairs, from the ugliness of the curtains. All those things, of which another woman of her rank would never even have been conscious, tortured her and made her angry. The sight of the little Breton peasant who did her humble house-work aroused in her regrets which were despairing, and distracted dreams. She thought of the silent antechambers hung with Oriental tapestry, lit by tall bronze candelabra, and of the two great footmen in knee-breeches who sleep in the big arm-chairs, made drowsy by the heavy warmth of the hot-air stove. She thought of the long *salons* fitted up with ancient silk, of the delicate furniture carrying priceless curiosities, and of the coquettish perfumed boudoirs made for talks at five o'clock with intimate friends, with men famous and sought after, whom all women envy and whose attention they all desire.

When she sat down to dinner, before the round table covered with a table-cloth three days old, opposite her husband, who uncovered the soup-tureen and declared with an enchanted air, "Ah, the good *pot-au-feu!* I don't know anything better than that," she thought of dainty dinners, of shining silverware, of tapestry which peopled the walls with ancient personages and with strange birds flying in the midst of a fairy forest; and she thought of delicious dishes served on marvellous plates, and of the whispered gallantries which you listen to with a sphinx-like smile, while you are eating the pink flesh of a trout or the wings of a quail.

She had no dresses, no jewels, nothing. And she loved nothing but that; she felt made for that. She would so have liked to please, to be envied, to be charming, to be sought after.

She had a friend, a former school-mate at the convent, who was rich, and whom she did not like to go and see any more, because she suffered so much when she came back.

But, one evening, her husband returned home with a triumphant air, and holding a large envelope in his hand.

"There," said he, "here is something for you."

She tore the paper sharply, and drew out a printed card which bore these words:

"The Minister of Public Instruction and Mme. Georges Ramponneau request the honor of M. and Mme. Loisel's company at the palace of the Ministry on Monday evening, January 18th."

Instead of being delighted, as her husband hoped, she threw the invitation on the table with disdain, murmuring:

"What do you want me to do with that?"

"But, my dear, I thought you would be glad. You never go out, and this is such a fine opportunity. I had awful trouble to get it. Every one wants to go; it is very select, and they are not giving many invitations to clerks. The whole official world will be there."

She looked at him with an irritated eye and she said, impatiently:

"And what do you want me to put on my back?"

He had not thought of that; he stammered:

"Why, the dress you go to the theatre in. It looks very well, to me."

He stopped, distracted, seeing that his wife was crying. Two great tears descended slowly from the corners of her eyes towards the corners of her mouth. He stuttered:

"What's the matter? What's the matter?"

But, by a violent effort, she had conquered her grief, and she replied, with a calm voice, while she wiped her wet cheeks:

"Nothing. Only I have no dress, and therefore I can't go to this ball. Give your card to some colleague whose wife is better equipped than I."

He was in despair. He resumed:

"Come, let us see, Mathilde. How much would it cost, a suitable dress, which you could use on other occasions, something very simple?"

She reflected several seconds, making her calculations and wondering also what sum she could ask without drawing on herself an immediate refusal and a frightened exclamation from the economical clerk.

Finally, she replied, hesitatingly:

"I don't know exactly, but I think I could manage it with four hundred francs."

He had grown a little pale, because he was laying aside just that amount to buy a gun and treat himself to a little shooting next summer on the plain of Nanterre, with several friends who went to shoot larks down there, of a Sunday.

But he said:

"All right. I will give you four hundred francs. And try to have a pretty dress."

The day of the ball drew near, and Mme. Loisel seemed sad, uneasy, anxious. Her dress was ready, however. Her husband said to her one evening:

"What is the matter? Come, you've been so queer these last three days."

And she answered:

"It annoys me not to have a single jewel, not a single stone, nothing to put on. I shall look like distress. I should almost rather not go at all."

He resumed:

"You might wear natural flowers. It's very stylish at this time of the year. For ten francs you can get two or three magnificent roses."

She was not convinced.

"No; there's nothing more humiliating than to look poor among other women who are rich."

But her husband cried:

"How stupid you are! Go look up your friend Mme. Forestier, and ask her to lend you some jewels. You're quite thick enough with her to do that."

She uttered a cry of joy:

"It's true. I never thought of it."

The next day she went to her friend and told of her distress.

Mme. Forestier went to a wardrobe with a glass door, took out a large jewel-box, brought it back, opened it, and said to Mme. Loisel:

"Choose, my dear."

She saw first of all some bracelets, then a pearl necklace, then a Venetian cross, gold and precious stones of admirable workmanship. She tried on the ornaments before the glass, hesitated, could not make up her mind to part with them, to give them back. She kept asking:

"Haven't you any more?"

"Why, yes. Look. I don't know what you like."

All of a sudden she discovered, in a black satin box, a superb necklace of diamonds and her heart began to beat with an immoderate desire. Her hands trembled as she took it. She fastened it around her throat, outside her high-necked dress, and remained lost in ectasy at the sight of herself.

Then she asked, hesitating, filled with anguish:

"Can you lend me that, only that?"

"Why, yes, certainly."

She sprang upon the neck of her friend, kissed her passionately, then fled with her treasure.

The day of the ball arrived. Mme. Loisel made a great success. She was prettier than them all, elegant, gracious, smiling, and crazy with joy. All the men looked at her, asked her name, endeavored to be introduced. All the attachés of the Cabinet wanted to waltz with her. She was remarked by the minister himself.

She danced with intoxication, with passion, made drunk by pleasure, forgetting all, in the triumph of her beauty, in the glory of her success, in a sort of cloud of happiness composed of all this homage, of all this admiration, of all these awakened desires, and of that sense of complete victory which is so sweet to woman's heart.

She went away about four o'clock in the morning. Her husband had been sleeping since midnight, in a little deserted anteroom, with three other gentlemen whose wives were having a very good time.

He thew over her shoulders the wraps which he had brought, modest wraps of common life, whose poverty contrasted with the elegance of the ball dress. She felt this and wanted to escape so as not to be remarked by the other women, who were enveloping themselves in costly furs.

Loisel held her back.

"Wait a bit. You will catch cold outside. I will go and call a cab."

But she did not listen to him, and rapidly descended the stairs. When they were in the street they did not find a carriage; and they began to look for one, shouting after the cabmen whom they saw passing by at a distance.

They went down towards the Seine, in despair, shivering with cold. At last they found on the quay one of those ancient noctambulant coupés which, exactly as if they were ashamed to show their misery during the day, are never seen round Paris until after nightfall.

It took them to their door in the Rue des Martyrs, and once more, sadly, they climbed up homeward. All was ended, for her. And as to him, he reflected that he must be at the Ministry at ten o'clock.

She removed the wraps, which covered her shoulders, before the glass, so as once more to see herself in all her glory. But suddenly she uttered a cry. She had no longer the necklace around her neck!

Her husband, already half-undressed, demanded:

"What is the matter with you?"

She turned madly towards him:

"I have—I have—I've lost Mme. Forestier's necklace."

He stood up, distracted.

"What!—how?—Impossible!"

And they looked in the folds of her dress, in the folds of her cloak, in her pockets, everywhere. They did not find it.

He asked:

"You're sure you had it on when you left the ball?"

"Yes, I felt it in the vestibule of the palace."

"But if you had lost it in the street we should have heard it fall. It must be in the cab."

"Yes. Probably. Did you take his number?"

"No. And you, didn't you notice it?"

"No."

They looked, thunderstruck, at one another. At last Loisel put on his clothes.

"I shall go back on foot," said he, "over the whole route which we have taken, to see if I can't find it."

And he went out. She sat waiting on a chair in her ball dress, without strength to go to bed, overwhelmed, without fire, without a thought.

Her husband came back about seven o'clock. He had found nothing.

He went to Police Headquarters, to the newspaper offices, to offer a reward; he went to the cab companies—everywhere, in fact, whither he was urged by the least suspicion of hope.

She waited all day, in the same condition of mad fear before this terrible calamity.

Loisel returned at night with a hollow, pale face; he had discovered nothing.

"You must write to your friend," said he, "that you have broken the clasp of her necklace and that you are having it mended. That will give us time to turn round."

She wrote at his dictation.

At the end of a week they had lost all hope.

And Loisel, who had aged five years, declared:

"We must consider how to replace that ornament."

The next day they took the box which had contained it, and they went to the jeweller whose name was found within. He consulted his books.

"It was not I, madame, who sold that necklace; I must simply have furnished the case."

Then they went from jeweller to jeweller, searching for a necklace like the other, consulting their memories, sick both of them with chagrin and with anguish.

They found, in a shop at the Palais Royal, a string of diamonds which seemed to them exactly like the one they looked for. It was worth forty thousand francs. They could have it for thirty-six.

So they begged the jeweller not to sell it for three days yet. And they made a bargain that he should buy it back for thirty-four thousand francs, in case they found the other one before the end of February.

Loisel possessed eighteen thousand francs which his father had left him. He would borrow the rest.

He did borrow, asking a thousand francs of one, five hundred of another, five louis here, three louis there. He gave notes, took up ruinous obligations, dealt with usurers, and all the race of lenders. He compromised all the rest of his life, risked his signature without even knowing if he could meet it; and, frightened by the pains yet to come, by the black misery which was about to fall upon him, by the prospect of all the physical privations and of all the moral tortures which he was to suffer, he went to get the new necklace, putting down upon the merchant's counter thirty-six thousand francs.

When Mme. Loisel took back the necklace, Mme. Forestier said to her, with a chilly manner:

"You should have returned it sooner, I might have needed it."

She did not open the case, as her friend had so much feared. If she had detected the substitution, what would she have thought, what would she have said? Would she not have taken Mme. Loisel for a thief?

Mme. Loisel now knew the horrible existence of the needy. She took her part, moreover, all on a sudden, with heroism. That dreadful debt must be paid. She would pay it. They dismissed their servant; they changed their lodgings; they rented a garret under the roof.

She came to know what heavy housework meant and the odious cares of the kitchen. She washed the dishes, using her rosy nails on the greasy pots and pans. She washed the dirty linen, the shirts, and the dish-cloths, which she dried upon a line; she carried the slops down to the street every morning, and carried up the water, stopping for breath at every landing. And, dressed like a woman of the people, she went to the fruiterer, the grocer, the butcher, her basket on her arm, bargaining, insulted, defending her miserable money sou by sou.

Each month they had to meet some notes, renew others, obtain more time.

Her husband worked in the evening making a fair copy of some tradesman's accounts, and late at night he often copied manuscript for five sous a page.

And this life lasted ten years.

At the end of ten years they had paid everything, everything, with the rates of usury, and the accumulations of the compound interest.

Mme. Loisel looked old now. She had become the woman of

impoverished households—strong and hard and rough. With frowsy hair, skirts askew, and red hands, she talked loud while washing the floor with great swishes of water. But sometimes, when her husband was at the office, she sat down near the window, and she thought of that gay evening of long ago, of that ball where she had been so beautiful and so feted.

What would have happened if she had not lost that necklace? Who knows? who knows? How life is strange and changeful! How little a thing is needed for us to be lost or to be saved!

But, one Sunday, having gone to take a walk in the Champs Élysées to refresh herself from the labors of the week, she suddenly perceived a woman who was leading a child. It was Mme. Forestier, still young, still beautiful, still charming.

Mme. Loisel felt moved. Was she going to speak to her? Yes, certainly. And now that she had paid, she was going to tell her all about it. Why not?

She went up.

"Good-day, Jeanne."

The other, astonished to be familiarly addressed by this plain good-wife, did not recognize her at all, and stammered:

"But—madame!— I do not know—You must have mistaken."

"No. I am Mathilde Loisel."

Her friend uttered a cry.

"O, my poor Mathilde! How you are changed!"

"Yes, I have had days hard enough, since I have seen you, days wretched enough—and that because of you!"

"Of me! How so?"

"Do you remember that diamond necklace which you lent me to wear at the ministerial ball?"

"Yes. Well?"

"Well, I lost it."

"What do you mean? You brought it back."

"I brought you back another just like it. And for this we have been ten years paying. You can understand that it was not easy for us, us who had nothing. At last it is ended, and I am very glad."

Mme. Forestier had stopped.

"You say that you bought a necklace of diamonds to replace mine?"

"Yes. You never noticed it, then! They were very like."

And she smiled with a joy which was proud and naive at once.

Mme. Forestier, strongly moved, took her two hands.

"Oh, my poor Mathilde! Why, my necklace was paste. It was worth at most five hundred francs!"

QUESTIONS

1. Analyze the plot structure. Note each complication and its apparent resolution that precedes the climax and final resolution.

2. Mme. Loisel's conflict is within her; state the opposing forces of her conflict as precisely as you can.

3. Examine Maupassant's handling of chronology. Which events are treated at length? How does he expand parts of the story: by narration or dramatic scene?

4. Mme. Loisel is proud of her ten years of drudgery. Her friend's final words come as a complete shock to her. What term is used to describe this type of ending?

STUDENT ESSAY

"The Necklace": Diamond or Paste?

Patricia Carpenter

In Guy de Maupassant's short story "The Necklace," Maupassant
develops his plot through several related complications. Like the pieces
of a jig-saw puzzle, each complication contributes to a more complete
picture of Mme. Loisel's internal conflict and leads us to the story's
final irony. The plot structure develops, through its ironic ending,
the story's main theme: the need to know true values from false ones.

The exposition, presented at the beginning of the story, explains
Mme. Loisel's situation and her attitude toward it. Mme. Loisel is a
beautiful, charming woman who is dissatisfied with her station in life.
She wishes for all the luxuries money can buy: dresses, jewels, servants,
a fine home, and ornate furnishings. She feels cheated out of these possessions by her low birth to a family of clerks and by her subsequent
marriage to a clerk. The exposition establishes Mme. Loisel's conflict.
Her desire for a glittering life rages against the reality of her middle
class existence and blinds her to any happiness she could have with her
kind, generous husband.

The first complication appears with the invitation to the palace
ball. Instead of being pleased with the invitation, she tearfully complains to her husband that she cannot go because she has no suitable dress.
M. Loisel believes he has solved the problem by providing his wife with
money for a new dress only to have her assert once more that she cannot
go because she has no jewels to wear with the new dress. This complication
seems finally resolved when he suggests that she borrow some jewels from
her rich friend, Mme. Forestier. Mme. Loisel does borrow from her friend

STUDENT ESSAY

and is finally ready for the ball. Unfortunately, in choosing what she thinks is a magnificent diamond necklace she is trying to be something she is not, and her choice, as we learn later, shows her lack of knowledge of what is real, or truly valuable.

Mme. Loisel is a success at the ball, but before the night is over the major complication of the story develops, the loss of the necklace. Mme. Loisel is feted by all the men, who find her beautiful and charming. Perhaps some of her attractiveness is due to her self-confidence about being well dressed and finely jeweled. But when it is time to leave, Mme. Loisel's conflict makes her reject her husband's suggestion that she wait inside until he gets a carriage. She leaves with him because she is too proud to wait inside in her old wrap. We can suspect that if she had waited inside, she would not have lost her friend's necklace.

It is interesting to note some of the irony in "The Necklace." We discover that the Loisels live on Rue des Martyrs, "Street of Martyrs." Indeed, it is with the attitude of a martyr that Mme. Loisel arrives home. She feels that "all has ended"; her one shining moment is gone. She expects to live the rest of her life with nothing but memories of an evening of quality spent with rich people. Her expectations will be fulfilled in a way that she does not imagine as she travels home from the ball.

How will Mme. Loisel respond to the complication of the lost necklace? When she agrees to write to her friend that the clasp has to be repaired, her lie to borrow time to try to find the necklace is a hint of the climax that follows shortly. The additional time does not result in their finding the necklace. Her decision to replace the necklace rather than to tell her friend the truth constitutes the story's climax. The decision, which will put the Loisels into debt for ten years, is consistent with Mme. Loisel's values that we have seen throughout the story. She

STUDENT ESSAY

lies to save face with her wealthy friend, to protect a false image.

The <u>resolution</u> of the story is long but prepares us for the final irony. The Loisels toil ten years, and the years are not kind to Mme. Loisel. Ironically the pride that led her to choose the magnificent "diamond" necklace results in her loss of beauty, of which she was very proud. The story ends with the final irony when Mme. Loisel learns from her friend that the diamond necklace was only paste, worth a mere five hundred francs. By replacing the necklace Mme. Loisel lost her youth, beauty, and possessions, but she gained pride in her sacrifice. When she learns that the sacrifice was meaningless, she no longer has anything to be proud of. She has lost everything--for nothing.

SELECTIONS FOR FURTHER STUDY

E. E. CUMMINGS   (1894–1962)

the hours rise up putting off stars and it is

the hours rise up putting off stars and it is
dawn
into the street of the sky light walks scattering poems

on earth a candle is
extinguished   the city   5
wakes
with a song upon her
mouth having death in her eyes

and it is dawn
the world   10
goes forth to murder dreams. . . .

i see in the street where strong
men are digging bread
and i see the brutal faces of
people contented hideous hopeless cruel happy   15

and it is day,

in the mirror
i see a frail
man
dreaming   20
dreams
dreams in the mirror

and it
is dusk   on earth

a candle is lighted   25
and it is dark.
the people are in their houses
the frail man is in his bed
the city

sleeps with death upon her mouth having a song in her eyes   30
the hours descend,
putting on stars. . . .

in the street of the sky night walks scattering poems

QUESTIONS

1. What happens when it is dawn? During the day? When it is night?
2. Look at the poem carefully. Why is the word "mirror" repeated in the middle
   of the poem? How is the poem organized? Note all the similarities and
   differences in language and actions.
3. What are two meanings of the word "scattering"? What might the scattered
   "poems" refer to?

EDNA ST. VINCENT MILLAY (1892–1950)

Love Is Not All

xxx

Love is not all: it is not meat nor drink
Nor slumber nor a roof against the rain;
Nor yet a floating spar to men that sink
And rise and sink and rise and sink again;
Love can not fill the thickened lung with breath, 5
Nor clean the blood, nor set the fractured bone;
Yet many a man is making friends with death
Even as I speak, for lack of love alone.
It well may be that in a difficult hour,
Pinned down by pain and moaning for release, 10
Or nagged by want past resolution's power,
I might be driven to sell your love for peace,
Or trade the memory of this night for food.
It well may be. I do not think I would.

QUESTIONS

1. Using letters, indicate the poem's rhyme scheme. What type of sonnet is this?
2. Where does the logical structural break come in this type of sonnet? How does Millay use this structural device in developing the poem's meaning?
3. What is Millay's attitude toward love? Which statement best sums up the poem's meaning:
   a. Love is not essential to life because there are many things that love cannot do.
   b. Although love cannot minister directly to the body's needs, it is essential to make life worth living.

ELIZABETH BOWEN   (1899–1973)

The Demon Lover

Towards the end of her day in London Mrs Drover went round to her shut-up house to look for several things she wanted to take away. Some belonged to herself, some to her family, who were by now used to their country life. It was late August; it had been a steamy, showery day: at the moment the trees down the pavement glittered in an escape of humid yellow afternoon sun. Against the next batch of clouds, already piling up ink-dark, broken chimneys and parapets stood out. In her once familiar street, as in any unused channel, an unfamiliar queerness had silted up; a cat wove itself in and out of railings, but no human eye watched Mrs Drover's return. Shifting some parcels under her arm, she slowly forced round her latchkey in an unwilling lock, then gave the door, which had warped, a push with her knee. Dead air came out to meet her as she went in.

The staircase window having been boarded up, no light came down into the hall. But one door, she could just see, stood ajar, so she went quickly through into the room and unshuttered the big window in there. Now the prosaic woman, looking about her, was more perplexed than she knew by everything that she saw, by traces of her long former habit of life—the yellow smoke-stain up the white marble mantelpiece, the ring left by a vase on the top of the escritoire; the bruise in the wallpaper where, on the door being thrown open widely, the china handle had always hit the wall. The piano, having gone away to be stored, had left what looked like claw-marks on its part of the parquet. Though not much dust had seeped in, each object wore a film of another kind; and, the only ventilation being the chimney, the whole drawing-room smelled of the cold hearth. Mrs Drover put down her parcels on the escritoire and left the room to proceed upstairs; the things she wanted were in a bedroom chest.

She had been anxious to see how the house was—the part-time caretaker she shared with some neighbours was away this week on his holiday, known to be not yet back. At the best of times he did not look in often, and she was never sure that she trusted him. There were some cracks in the structure, left by the last bombing, on which she was anxious to keep an eye. Not that one could do anything—

A shaft of refracted daylight now lay across the hall. She stopped dead and stared at the hall table—on this lay a letter addressed to her.

She thought first—then the caretaker *must* be back. All the same, who, seeing the house shuttered, would have dropped a letter in at the box? It was not a circular, it was not a bill. And the post office redirected, to the address in the country, everything for her that came through the post. The caretaker (even if he *were* back) did not know she was due in London today—her call here had been planned to be a surprise—so his negligence in the manner of this letter, leaving it to wait in the dusk and the dust, annoyed her. Annoyed, she picked up the letter, which bore no stamp. But it cannot be important, or they would know . . . She took the letter rapidly upstairs with her, without a stop to look at the writing till she reached what had been her bedroom, where she let in light. The room looked over the garden and other gardens: the sun had gone in; as the clouds sharpened and lowered, the trees and rank lawns seemed already to smoke with dark. Her reluctance to look again at the letter came from the fact that she felt intruded upon—and by someone contemptuous of her ways. However, in the tenseness preceding the fall of rain she read it: it was a few lines.

> Dear Kathleen: You will not have forgotten that today is our anniversary, and the day we said. The years have gone by at once slowly and fast. In view of the fact that nothing has changed, I shall rely upon you to keep your promise. I was sorry to see you leave London, but was satisfied that you would be back in time. You may expect me, therefore, at the hour arranged. Until then . . .
>
> K.

Mrs Drover looked for the date: it was today's. She dropped the letter on to the bed-springs, then picked it up to see the writing again—her lips, beneath the remains of lipstick, beginning to go white. She felt so much the change in her own face that she went to the mirror, polished a clear patch in it and looked at once urgently and stealthily in. She was confronted by a woman of forty-four, with eyes starting out under a hat-brim that had been rather carelessly pulled down. She had not put on any more powder since she left the shop where she ate her solitary tea. The pearls her husband had given her on their marriage hung loose round her now rather thinner throat, slipping in the V of the pink wool jumper her sister knitted last autumn as they sat round the fire. Mrs Drover's most normal expression was one of controlled worry, but of assent. Since the birth of the third of her little boys, attended by a quite serious illness, she had had an intermittent muscular flicker to the left of her mouth, but in spite of this she could always sustain a manner that was at once energetic and calm.

Turning from her own face as precipitately as she had gone to meet it, she went to the chest where the things were, unlocked it, threw up the lid and knelt to search. But as rain began to come crashing down she could not keep from looking over her shoulder at the stripped bed on which the letter lay. Behind the blanket of rain the clock of the church that still stood struck six—with rapidly heightening apprehension she counted each of the slow strokes. 'The hour arranged . . . My God,' she said, '*what* hour? How should I . . . ? After twenty-five years . . .'

The young girl talking to the soldier in the garden had not ever completely seen his face. It was dark; they were saying goodbye under a tree. Now and then—for it felt, from not seeing him at this intense moment, as though she had never seen him at all—she verified his presence for these few moments longer by putting out a hand, which he each time pressed, without very much kindness, and painfully, on to one of the breast buttons of his uniform. That cut of the button on the palm of her hand was, principally what she was to carry away. This was so near the end of a leave from France that she could only wish him already gone. It was August 1916. Being not kissed, being drawn away from and looked at intimidated Kathleen till she imagined spectral glitters in the place of his eyes. Turning away and looking back up the lawn she saw, through branches of trees, the drawing-room window alight: she caught a breath for the moment when she could go running back there into the safe arms of her mother and sister, and cry: 'What shall I do, what shall I do? He has gone.'

Hearing her catch her breath, her fiancé said, without feeling: 'Cold?'

'You're going away such a long way.'

'Not so far as you think.'

'I don't understand?'

'You don't have to,' he said. 'You will. You know what we said.'

'But that was—suppose you—I mean, suppose.'

'I shall be with you,' he said, 'sooner or later. You won't forget that. You need do nothing but wait.'

Only a little more than a minute later she was free to run up the silent lawn. Looking in through the window at her mother and sister, who did not for the moment perceive her, she already felt that unnatural promise drive down between her and the rest of all human kind. No other way of having given herself could have made her feel so apart, lost and foresworn. She could not have plighted a more sinister troth.

Kathleen behaved well when, some months later, her fiancé was reported missing, presumed killed. Her family not only supported her but were able to praise her courage without stint because they could not regret, as a husband for her, the man they knew almost nothing about. They hoped she would, in a year or two, console herself—and had it been only a question of consolation things might have gone much straighter ahead. But her trouble, behind just a little grief, was a complete dislocation from everything. She did not reject other lovers, for these failed to appear: for years she failed to attract men—and with the approach of her 'thirties she became natural enough to share her family's anxiousness on this score.

She began to put herself out, to wonder; and at thirty-two she was very greatly relieved to find herself being courted by William Drover. She married him, and the two of them settled down in this quiet, arboreal part of Kensington: in this house the years piled up, her children were born and they all lived till they were driven out by the bombs of the next war. Her movements as Mrs Drover were circumscribed, and she dismissed any idea that they were still watched.

As things were—dead or living the letter-writer sent her only a threat. Unable, for some minutes, to go on kneeling with her back exposed to the empty room, Mrs Drover rose from the chest to sit on an upright chair whose back was firmly against the wall. The desuetude of her former bedroom, her married London home's whole air of being a cracked cup from which memory, with its reassuring power, had either evaporated or leaked away, made a crisis—and at just this crisis the letter-writer had, knowledgeably, struck. The hollowness of the house this evening cancelled years on years of voices, habits and steps. Through the shut windows she only heard rain fall on the roofs around. To rally herself, she said she was in a mood—and for two or three seconds shutting her eyes, told herself that she had imagined the letter. But she opened them—there it lay on the bed.

On the supernatural side of the letter's entrance she was not permitting her mind to dwell. Who, in London, knew she meant to call at the house today? Evidently, however, this had been known. The caretaker, *had* he come back, had had no cause to expect her: he would have taken the letter in his pocket, to forward it, at his own time, through the post. There was no other sign that the caretaker had been in—but, if not? Letters dropped in at doors of deserted houses do not fly or walk to tables in halls. They do not sit on the dust of empty tables with the air of certainty that they will be found. There is needed some human hand— but nobody but the caretaker had a key. Under circumstances she did not care to consider, a house can be entered without a key. It was possible that she was not alone now. She might be being waited for, downstairs. Waited for—until when? Until 'the hour arranged'. At least that was not six o'clock: six has struck.

She rose from the chair and went over and locked the door.

The thing was, to get out. To fly? No, not that: she had to catch her train. As a woman whose utter dependability was the keystone of her family life she was not willing to return to the country, to her husband, her little boys and her sister, without the objects she had come up to fetch. Resuming work at the chest she set about making up a number of parcels in a rapid, fumbling-decisive way. These, with her shopping parcels, would be too much to carry; these meant a taxi—at the thought of the taxi her heart went up and her normal breathing resumed. I will ring up the taxi now; the taxi cannot come too soon: I shall hear the taxi out there running its engine, till I walk calmly down to it through the hall. I'll ring up—But no: the telephone is cut off . . . She tugged at a knot she had tied wrong.

The idea of flight . . . He was never kind to me, not really. I don't remember him kind at all. Mother said he never considered me. He was set on me, that was what it was—not love. Not love, not meaning a person well. What did he do, to make me promise like that? I can't remember— But she found that she could.

She remembered with such dreadful acuteness that the twenty-five years since then dissolved like smoke and she instinctively looked for the weal left by the button on the palm of her hand. She remembered not only all that he said and did but the complete suspension of *her* existence during that August week. I was not myself—they all told me so at the time. She remembered—but with one white burning blank as where acid has dropped on photograph: *under no conditions* could she remember his face.

So, wherever he may be waiting, I shall not know him. You have no time to run from a face you do not expect.

The thing was to get to the taxi before any clock struck what could be the hour. She would slip down the street and round the side of the square to where the square gave on the main road. She would return in the taxi, safe, to her own door, and bring the solid driver into the house with her to pick up the parcels from room to room. The idea of the taxi driver made her decisive, bold: she unlocked her door, went to the top of the staircase and listened down.

She heard nothing—but while she was hearing nothing the *passé* air of the staircase was disturbed by a draught that travelled up to her face. It emanated from the basement: down there a door or window was being opened by someone who chose this moment to leave the house.

The rain had stopped; the pavements steamily shone as Mrs Drover let herself out by inches from her own front door into the empty street. The unoccupied houses opposite continued to meet her look with their damaged stare. Making towards the thoroughfare and the taxi, she tried not to keep looking behind. Indeed, the silence was so intense—one of those creeks of London silence exaggerated this summer by the damage of war—that no tread could have gained on hers unheard. Where her street debouched on the square where people went on living, she grew conscious of, and checked, her unnatural pace. Across the open end of the square two buses impassively passed each other: women, a perambulator, cyclists, a man wheeling a barrow signalized, once again, the ordinary flow of life. At the square's most populous corner should be—and was— the short taxi rank. This evening, only one taxi—but this, although it presented its blank rump, appeared already to be alertly waiting for her. Indeed, without looking round the driver started his engine as she panted up from behind and put her hand on the door. As she did so, the clock struck seven. The taxi faced the main road: to make the trip back to her house it would have to turn—she had settled back on the seat and the taxi *had* turned before she, surprised by its knowing movement, recollected that she had not 'said where'. She leaned forward to scratch at the glass panel that divided the driver's head from her own.

The driver braked to what was almost a stop, turned round and slid the glass panel back: the jolt of this flung Mrs Drover forward till her face was almost into the glass. Through the aperture driver and passenger, not six inches between them, remained for an eternity eye to eye. Mrs Drover's mouth hung open for some seconds before she could issue her first scream. After that she continued to scream freely and to beat with her gloved hands on the glass all round as the taxi, accelerating without mercy, made off with her into the hinterland of deserted streets.

QUESTIONS

1. Analyze the plot structure, making sure to state the conflict as opposing forces. Does the conflict follow or precede the complication?

2. Examine the writer's use of chronology. What is the effect of Bowen's choice of when to begin and when to end the story? What is gained by her use of flashback?

3. What clues to the demonic nature of the relationship and situation are provided?

4. What characteristics of Mrs. Drover's personality contribute to the story's outcome?

5. Within a framework of fantasy or the supernatural, is the story plausible? Can the story also be read as a realistic psychological study? Which way seems most sensible to you? Why?

DOUGLAS TURNER WARD   (b. 1930)

Happy Ending

CAST OF CHARACTERS

Ellie
Vi
Junie
Arthur

TIME: *The present, an early weekday evening around five or six* P.M.

PLACE: *The spotless kitchen of a Harlem tenement apartment. At stage-left is a closed door providing entry to the outside hallway. On the opposite side of the stage is another door leading into the interior of the railroad flat. Sandwiched between this door and a window facing the brick walls of the apartment's inner shaft is a giant, dazzling white refrigerator. Positioned center-stage is a gleaming, porcelain-topped oval table. Directly behind is a modern stove-range. To the left of the stove, another window looks out upon a backyard court. The window is flanked on its left by a kitchen sink. Adjacent to the refrigerator, upstage-right, a bathroom door completes the setting.*

As curtain rises, waning rays of daylight can be seen streaming through the courtyard window. Two handsome women, both in their late thirties or early forties, are sitting at opposite ends of the kitchen table. They are dressed as if recently entered from work. Hats and coats are still worn, handbags lie on floor propped against legs of respective chairs. They remain in dejected poses, weeping noiselessly.

ELLIE.   Let me have your handkerchief, Vi. . . . (*Vi hands it to her absently. Ellie daubs eyes, then rests hankie on table. It lies there until Vi motions for it to be handed back.*)
VI.   What we go'n' do, Ellie?
ELLIE.   Don' know. . . . Don't seem like there's much more we kin do. . . .
VI.   This time it really might happen. . . .
ELLIE.   I know. . . .
VI.   Persons kin go but just so far. . . .
ELLIE.   Lord, this may be the limit. . . .
VI.   End of the line. . . .
ELLIE.   Hear us, Savior!
VI.   . . . Think it might help if I prayed a novena to him first thing tomorrow morning?
ELLIE.   . . . Certainly couldn't do no harm. . . . (*They lapse into silence*

once again, passing hankie back and forth on request. Suddenly, JUNIE, a tall, slender, sharply handsome, tastefully dressed youth in his early twenties, bursts upon the scene, rushing through hallway door.)

JUNIE. *(Rapidly crossing, shedding coat in transit.)* Hey, Vi, Ellie . . . *(Exits through interior door, talking offstage.)* Ellie, do I have any more pleated shirts clean . . . ? Gotta make fast impression on new chick tonight. . . . *(Thrusting head back into view.)* One of them foxy, black "Four-Hundred" debutantes, you dig! All class and manners, but nothing underneath but a luscious, V-8 chassis!—Which is A-O-reeet wit' me since that's all I'm after. You hear me talking to ya! Now, tell me what I say! Hah, hah, hah! *(Withdraws head back offstage.)* . . . Sure got them petty tyrants straight at the unemployment office today. *(Dripping contempt.)* Wanted me to snatch-up one of them jive jobs they try to palm off on ya. I told 'em no, thanks!—SHOVE IT! *(Reentering, busily buttoning elegantly pleated shirt.)* If they can't find me something in my field, up to my standards, forgit it! . . . Damn, act like they paying you money out their own pockets. . . . Watcha got to eat, Ellie? . . . I'm scarfy as a bear. In fact—with little salt 'n' pepper, I could devour one of you—or both between a double-decker! *(Descends upon them to illustrate playfully. Pulls up short on noticing their tears for the first time.)* Hey? . . . What'sa matter . . . ? What's up? *(They fail to respond.)* Is it the kids? *(They shake heads negatively.)* Somebody sick down home? *(Fearfully.)* Nothing's wrong wit' mother?!!! *(They shake heads again.)* Roy or Jim in jail? . . . Arthur or Ben lose their jobs? *(Another double headshake.)* Tell me, I wanta know! Everything was fine this morning. Som'um musta happened since. Come on, what is it?!

ELLIE.   Should we tell him, Vi?

VI.   I don't know. . . . No use gitting him worried and upset. . . .

ELLIE.   *(Sighing heavily.)* Maybe we better. He's got to find out sooner or later.

JUNIE.   What are you crying for?

ELLIE.   . . . Our bosses—Mr. and Mrs. Harrison, Junie. . . .

JUNIE.   ???Mr. and Mrs. Harrison . . . ? *(Suddenly relieved, amused and sardonic.)* What happened? They escaped from a car wreck—UNHURT?

ELLIE.   *(Failing to grasp sarcasm.)* No.

JUNIE.   *(Returning to shirt-buttoning.)* Did you just git disappointing news flashes they go'n' live forever?

VI.   *(Also misreading him.)* No, Junie.

JUNIE.   Well, what then? . . . I don't get it.

ELLIE.   They's getting a divorce. . . .

JUNIE.   ???A what—?

VI.   A divorce.

JUNIE.   ???Why?

ELLIE.   'Cause Mr. Harrison caught her wit' a man.

JUNIE.   Well, it's not the first time 'cording to you.

ELLIE. The other times wasn't wit' his best friend.

JUNIE. His best friend?! WHEEE! Boy, she really did it up this time. . . . Her previous excursions were restricted to his casual acquaintances! . . . But why the hell should he be so upset? He's put up wit' all the rest. This only means she's gitting closer to home. Maybe next time it'll be him, ha, ha, ha. . . .

ELLIE. (*Reprimandingly.*) It's no joke, Junie.

JUNIE. (*Exiting into bathroom.*) How'd it happen?

ELLIE. (*Flaring at the memory.*) Just walked in and caught 'em in his own bedroom!

VI. (*Even more outraged.*) Was that dirty dog, Mr. Heller, lives on the nineteenth floor of the same building!

ELLIE. (*Anger mounting.*) I warned her to be careful when she first started messing with him. I told her Mr. Harrison was really gon' kick her out if he found out, but she'd have the snake sneak in sometimes soon as Mr. Harrison left! Even had nerve to invite him to chaperone his wife back later in the evening for a li'l' after-dinner snack!

JUNIE. (*Reentering, merrily.*) What's a little exchange of pleasantries among rich friends, bosom buddies? Now, all Harrison has to do is return the favor and even things up.

VI. She really cooked her goose this time.

JUNIE. Good for her.

ELLIE. Good . . . ?

JUNIE. Sure—what'd she 'spect? To wait 'till she hauled some cat into bed right next to her old man befo' he got the message?

VI. They is gitting a *divorce*, Junie!

JUNIE. (*Sauntering over to fruit bowl atop refrigerator.*) That's all? . . . I'm surprised I didn't read headlines 'bout a double murder and one suicide. . . . But I forgot!—that's our colored folk's method of clearing up little gummy problems like that—that is, MINUS the suicide bit.

ELLIE. *They's breaking up their home, Junie!*

JUNIE. (*Biting into apple selected from bowl.*) They'll learn to live wit' it. . . . Might even git to like the idea.

VI. And the chillun?

JUNIE. Delicate li'l' boobies will receive nice fat allowances to ease the pain until they grow up to take over the world.

ELLIE. ???Is that all you feel at a time like this, boy?

VI. Disastrous, that's what it is!

ELLIE. Tragicull 'n' unfair!

JUNIE. Is this what you boohooing 'bout?!!!

ELLIE. Could you think of anything worser?

JUNIE. But, why?! (*Exits into interior.*)

ELLIE. 'Cause this time we KNOW HE MEANS BUSINESS, JUNIE! Ain't no false alarm like them other times. We were there, right there!

. . . Had a feeling somp'um was go'n' happen soon as I answered the door and let Mr. Heller in! Like chilly pneumonia on top a breeze. . . . Miss Harrison tole me she didn't wanta be disturbed for the rest of the afternoon. Well, she was disturbed all right! They musta fell asleep 'cause Mr. Harrison even got home late and still caught 'em. . . .

JUNIE.   (*Returns with tie, etc., to continue dressing.*) Couldn't you have interrupted their togetherness and sounded a timely danger warning?

ELLIE.   We didn't hear him. I was in the kitchen, Vi down in basement ironing. I didn't know Mr. Harrison had come in 'till I heard screaming from the bedroom. But soon as I did, I called Vi and me and her tipped down the hall and heard Mr. Harrison order Mr. Heller to put his clothes back on and stop considering hisself a friend for the rest of his life! "'N' you—slut! Pack up and git out soon as you find a suitable apartment." . . . Then he invited me and Vi into the room and told us he was divorcing her. . . . That man was hurt, Junie, hurt deep! Could see it in his eyes. . . . Like a little boy, so sad he made you wanta grab hold his head and rock him in your arms like a baby.

VI.   Miss Harrison looked a sight herself, po' thing! Like a li'l' girl caught stealing crackers out the cookie jar.

ELLIE.   I almost crowned ole back-stabber Heller! Come brushing up 'gainst *me* on his way out!

JUNIE.   (*almost cracking up with laughter.*) Shoulda pinned medal on him as he flew by. Escaping wit' head still on shoulder and no bullet-holes dotting through his chest.

ELLIE.   (*Once again taking him literally.*) The skunk really left us all too high and dry for that, Junie. . . . Oh, don't think it wouldn't broke your heart, too, nephew. . . . Sneaky rascal gone, rest of us in sorrow, tears pouring down our faces 'n' me and Vi jist begging and begging. . . . (*As if to* HARRISONS.) "Y'all please think twice befo' you do anything you'll be sorry for. You love each other—and who's in better position than Vi and me to know how much you love each other—" (*JUNIE ceases dressing to listen closely.*)

VI.   'Course she love him, just can't help herself.

ELLIE.   "—When two hearts love each other as much as we know y'all do, they better take whole lots of time befo' doing something so awful as breaking up a marriage—even if it ain't hunert-percent perfect. Think about your reputation and the scandal this will cause Mr. Harrison. Jist 'bout kill your po' mother—her wit' her blood pressure, arthritis, gout, heart tickle 'n' everything. But most of all, don't orphan the kids! Kids come first. Dear li'l' angels! Just innocents looking on gitting hurt in ways they can't understand."

JUNIE.   (*Incredulous.*) You told 'em this, Ellie?

ELLIE.   Love conquers all, Junie!

JUNIE.   Wit' your assistance, Vi?

VI.   As much as I could deliver, Junie.

JUNIE. And what impression did your tender concern have on the bereaved couple?

ELLIE. Mr. Harrison said he understood 'n' appreciated our feelings and was very grateful for our kindly advice—but he was sorry, his mind was made up. She'd gone too far and he couldn't forgive her—not EVER! . . . We might judge him a harsh, vindicty man, he said, but he couldn't bring hisself to do it. Even apologized to us for being so cruel.

JUNIE. (*Continuing his slow boil.*) You accepted his apology, Vi?

VI. I should say not. I pleaded wit' him agin to think it over for sake of home, family and good name!

JUNIE. Well of all the goddamn things I ever heard!

ELLIE. (*Heartened by his misread support.*) I'm telling ya!

VI. I knew it was go'n' happen if she kept on like she did!

ELLIE. Just wouldn't listen!

JUNIE. It's a disgrace!

ELLIE. Ain't the word!

VI. Lot worse than that!

JUNIE. Did you both plop down on your knees begging him to give her another chance?

VI. NO!—But we woulda if we'd thought about it! Why didn't we, Ellie?!

ELLIE. Things happened so fast—

JUNIE. Never have I been so humiliated in all my life—!

VI. (*Self-disgusted by their glaring omission.*) No excuse not thinking 'bout it, Ellie!

ELLIE. Certainly ain't.

JUNIE. What about your pride—!?

VI. You right! Musta been false pride kept us from dropping to our knees!

JUNIE. Acting like imbeciles! Crying your heart out 'cause Massa and Mistress are go'n' break up housekeeping!!! Maybe I oughta go beat up the adulterous rat crawling in between the sheets!!! (*Pacing up and down in angry indignation as they sit stunned.*) Here we are—Africa rising to its place in the sun wit' prime ministers and other dignitaries taking seats around the international conference table—us here fighting for our rights like never before, changing the whole image, dumping stereotypes behind us and replacing 'em wit' new images of dignity and dimension—and I come home and find my own aunts, sisters of my mother, daughters of my grandpa who never took crap off no cracker even though he did live on a plantation—DROWNING themselves in tears jist 'cause boss man is gonna kick bosslady out on her nose . . . !!! Maybe *Gone With The Wind* was accurate! Maybe we jist can't help "Miss Scarrrrrrlet-ing" and "Oh Lawdying" every time mistress white gets a splinter in her pinky. That's what *I'm* talking about.

VI. Ain't you got no feelings, boy?

JUNIE.   Feelings?!!! . . . So you work every day in their kitchen, Ellie, and every Thursday you wash their stinky clothes, Vi. But that don't mean they're paying you to bleed from their scratches! . . . Look—don't get me wrong—I'm not blaming you for being domestics. It's an honorable job. It's the only kind available sometimes, and it carries no stigma in itself—but that's all it is, A JOB! An exchange of work for pay! BAD PAY AT THAT! Which is all the more reason why you shouldn't give a damn whether the Harrisons kick, kill or mangle each other!

ELLIE.   You gotta care, Junie—

JUNIE.   "Breaking up home and family!"—Why, I've seen both of you ditch two husbands apiece and itching to send third ones packing if they don't toe the line. You don't even cry over that!

ELLIE.   Don't have time to—

JUNIE.   Boy, if some gray cat was peeping in on you, he'da sprinted back home and wrote five Uncle Tom Cabins and ten Old Black Joes!

ELLIE.   Wait a minute, now—

JUNIE.   I never heard you shedding such tragic tears when your own li'l' crumbcrushers suffered through fatherless periods! All you grumbled was "good riddance, they better off wit'out the sonsabitches!" . . . Maybe Harrison tots will make out just as well. They got puny li'l' advantages of millions of dollars and slightly less parched skins!

VI.   Show some tenderness, boy. Ain't human not to trouble over our bosses' sorrows—

JUNIE.   That's what shames me. I gave you credit for more integrity. Didn't figger you had chalk streaks in ya. You oughta be shamed for *yourselves*!

ELLIE.   And done what?

JUNIE.   NOTHING!—Shoulda told 'em their sticky mess is their own mud puddle. You neutrals. Just work there. Aren't interested in what they do!

ELLIE.   That wouldn't be expressing our deepest sentiments—

JUNIE.   I'm ashamed you even had any "sentiments!" . . . Look, it's hopeless, I'm not getting anywhere trying to make you understand. . . . I'm going out for a whiff of fresh air! (*Rushes to exit.*)

ELLIE.   COME BACK HERE, BOY!

JUNIE.   (*Stopping at door.*) What? To watch you blubber over Massa? No, thanks!

ELLIE.   I said come here, you hear me talking to you!

VI.   You still ain't too big to git yourself slapped down!

ELLIE.   Your ma gave us right any time we saw fit! (*He returns reluctantly. Stands aside. An uneasy silence prevails. They commence a sweet, sly, needling attack.*) . . . Better git yourself somp'um to eat. (*Rises, taking off coat.*)

JUNIE.   (*Sulking.*) I lost my appetite.

ELLIE.   (*Hanging coat up.*) What you want?

JUNIE.   I told you I'm not hungry anymore.

VI.   *We* made you lose your appetite . . . ? (*He doesn't reply.*)

ELLIE.   What did you crave befo' you lost it?

JUNIE.   Anything you had cooked. Didn't have anything special in mind. . . .

ELLIE.   (*Off-handedly.*) Steak? . . . T-Bone? . . . Porterhouse? . . . Filet . . . ?

JUNIE.   No. . . . I didn't particularly have steak in mind.

VI.   Been eating too many lately, huh? (*Stands at table exchanging goods from ELLIE's shopping bag into her own.*)

JUNIE.   Just kinda tired of 'em, that's all.

ELLIE.   How 'bout some chicken then . . . ? Roast beef? . . . Lobster? . . . Squab? Duck, or something?

JUNIE.   (*Nettled.*) All I wanted was some food, Ellie! . . . In fact, I really had a hankering for some plain ole collard greens, neck bones or ham hocks. . . .

ELLIE.   Good eatin', boy. Glad to hear that. Means that high-class digestion hasn't spoiled your taste buds yet. . . . But if you want that rich, choice food, you welcome to it—

JUNIE.   I know that, Ellie!

ELLIE.   It's in the freezer for you, go and look.

JUNIE.   I don't hafta, Ellie, I know—

ELLIE.   Go look anyway.

JUNIE.   (*Goes and opens refrigerator door.*) It's there, Ellie, I didn't need look.

VI.   Come here for a second, Junie, got something on your pants leg. (*He obeys. She picks a piece of lint off trousers, then rubs material admiringly.*) Pants to your suit, ain't they? . . . Sure is a fine suit to be trotting off to the unemployment office. . . . Which one-'r the other you gon' wear tonight when you try to con that girl out her virginity—if she still got it?—The gray one? Brown one? The tweed? Or maybe you go'n' git sporty and strut that snazzy plaid jacket and them tight light pants? If not— which jacket and which pants?

ELLIE.   Slept good last night, nephew? Or maybe you gitting tired of that foam rubber mattress and sheep-fur blanket?

VI.   How do them fine college queens and snooty office girls like the furniture they half-see when you sneak 'em in here late at night? Surprised to see such fancy stuff in a beat-up ole flat, ain't they? But it helps you put 'em at ease, don't it? I bet even those sweet li'l' white ones are impressed by your class?

JUNIE.   (*Indignantly.*) That's not fair, Vi—

ELLIE.   When last time you bought any food in this house, boy?

JUNIE.   Ellie, you know—

ELLIE.   When Junie?

JUNIE.   Not since I been here, but—

VI.   And your last piece of clothes?

JUNIE.   (*More indignant.*) I bought some underwear last week, Vi!

VI.   I mean clothes you wear on top, Junie. Shirts, pants, jackets, coats?

JUNIE.   (*Squirming.*) You—you know I haven't, Vi—

ELLIE.   (*Resits.*) Buy anything else in your room besides that tiny, midget frame for your ma's picture?

JUNIE.   All right. I know I'm indebted to ya. You don't have to rub it in. I'll make it up to you when I git on my feet and *fulfill* my potential. . . . But that's not the point!

ELLIE.   You ain't indebted to us, Junie.

JUNIE.   Yes, I am, I know it, I thank you for it.

ELLIE.   Don't hafta thank us—

JUNIE.   But that's not the issue! Despite your benevolence, I refuse to let you blackmail my principle, slapping me in the face wit' how good you been to me during my temporary outta work period! I'm talking to you now, 'bout something above our personal relationship. Pride—Race—Dignity—

ELLIE.   What's go'n' happen to me and Vi's dignity if Mr. Harrison throws Mrs. Harrison out on her nose as you put it?

JUNIE.   Git another job! You not dependent on them. You young, healthy, in the prime of life. . . . In fact—I've always wondered why you stagnate as domestics when you're trained and qualified to do something better and more dignified.

ELLIE.   Glad you brought that up. Know why I'm not breaking my back as a practical nurse and Vi's not frying hair—'cept on the side? . . . 'Cause the work's too hard, the money ain't worth it and there's not much room for advancement—

JUNIE.   Where kin you advance as a domestic? From kitchen to closet?! (*VI has moved to fridge to deposit meats, etc.*)

ELLIE.   (*Refusing to be provoked, continuing evenly.*) Besides, when I started working for the Harrisons, Junie, Mr. Harrison vowed that he would support me for life if I stayed with 'em until his daughter Sandy, his oldest child, reached ten years old.

JUNIE.   Bully for him! He'll build ya a little cottage backs the penthouse garage!

ELLIE.   (*Still unruffled.*) Mr. Harrison is strictly a man of his word, Junie. Which means that even if I left one day after Sandy made ten, he owes me some money every week or every month as long as I live. . . . Sandy is *nine*, Junie, EN-EYE-EN-EE! If I don't last another year, the deal is off.

JUNIE.   Don't need no handouts! Even hearing you say you want any, makes me shame!

ELLIE. Done used that word quite a lot, boy. You shamed of us?
. . . Well, git slapped in the face wit' this? How shame you go'n' be when
you hafta git outta here and hustle yourself a job!—ANY JOB?!!!

JUNIE. Huh?

ELLIE. How shame you go'n' be when you start gitting raggedy and
all them foxy girls are no longer impressed 'bout how slick, smooth and
pretty you look? When you stop being one-'r the best-dressed black boys
in New York City?

JUNIE. Don't get you, Ellie?

ELLIE. I know you went to college for a coupler years, boy, but I
thought you still had some sense, or I woulda told you. . . .

VI. (*Standing at JUNIE's right as ELLIE sits to his left.*) Every time you
bite into one of them big tender juicy steaks and chaw it down into your
belly, ever think where it's coming from?

ELLIE. The Harrisons.

VI. Every time you lay one of them young gals down in that plush
soft bed of yours and hear her sigh in luxury, ever think 'bout who you
owe it to?

ELLIE. The Harrisons.

VI. When you swoop down home to that rundown house your ma
and pa rent, latch eyes on all that fine furniture there, you ever think
who's responsible?

ELLIE. The Harrisons.

VI. You ain't bought a suit or piece of clothes in five years and
none of the other four men in this family have. . . . Why not?

ELLIE. Mr. Harrison.

VI. Junie, you is a fine, choice hunk of chocolate pigmeat, pretty
as a new-minted penny and slick 'nuff to suck sugar outta gingerbread
wit'out it losing its flavor—but the Harrisons ain't hardly elected you no
favorite pin-up boy to introduce to Santa Claus. Took a heap of pow'ful
coaxing to win you such splendid sponsorship and wealthy commissions,
'cause waiting for the Harrisons to voluntarily *donate* their Christian charity
is the sure way of landing head-first in the poor-house dungeon. . . . Who
runs the Harrisons' house, Junie? (*Moves to sit at table.*)

JUNIE. ??? . . . Ellie . . . I guess . . . ?

ELLIE. *From top to bottom.* I cook the food, scrub the floor, open the
doors, serve the tables, answer the phones, dust the furniture, raise the
children, lay out the clothes, greet the guests, fix the drinks and dump
the garbage—all for bad pay as you said. . . . You right, Junie, money I
git in my envelope ain't worth the time 'n' the headache. . . . *But—God
Helps Those Who Help Themselves.* . . . I also ORDER the food, estimate the
credit, PAY the bills and BALANCE the budget. Which means that each
steak I order for them, befo' butcher carves cow, I done reserved TWO
for myself. Miss Harrison wouldn't know how much steak cost and Mr.
Harrison so loaded, he writes me a check wit'out even looking. . . . Every

once in a full moon they git so good-hearted and tell me take some left-overs home, but by that time my freezer and pantry is already fuller than theirs. . . . Every one of them high price suits I lay on you haven't been worn more than once and some of 'em not at all. You lucky to be same size as Mr. Harrison, Junie. He don't know how much clothes he got in his wardrobe, which is why *yours* is as big as *his*. Jim, Roy, Arthur and Ben can't even fit into the man's clothes, but that still don't stop 'em from cutting, shortening, altering, and stretching 'em to fit. Roy almost ruined his feet trying to wear the man's shoes. . . . Now, I've had a perfect record keeping y'all elegantly dressed and stylishly-fashion-plated—'cept that time Mr. Harrison caught me off-guard asking: Ellie, where's my brown suit?" "In the cleaners," I told him and had to snatch it off your hanger and smuggle it back—temporarily.

Vı.   If y'all warn't so lucky and Mrs. Harrison so tacky flashy Ellie and I would also be best dressed domestics of the year.

Ellie.   Which, if you didn't notice, is what your Aunt Doris was—rest her soul—when we laid her in her grave, decked out in the costliest, ritziest, most expensest nightgown the good Lord ever waited to feast his eyes on. . . . As for furniture, we could move out his whole house in one day if we had to.

Vı.   Which is what we did when they moved from the old penthouse and we hired us a moving van to haul 'nuff pieces to furnish both our own apartments and still had enough to ship a living room set down to your ma. Mr. Harrison told us to donate the stuff to charity. We did—US!

Ellie.   Add all *our* I add on to *their* bills—Jim even tried to git me to sneak in his car note, but that was going too far—all the deluxe plane tickets your ma jets up here on every year, weekly prescriptions filled on their tab, tons of laundry cleaned along wit' theirs and a thousand other services and I'm earning me quite a bonus along with my bad pay. It's the BONUS that counts, Junie. Total it up for nine years and I'd be losing money on any other job. Now Vi and I, after cutting cane, picking rice and shucking corn befo' we could braid our hair in pigtails, figure we just gitting back what's owed us. . . . But, if Mr. Harrison boots Mrs. Harrison out on her tocus, the party's over. He's not go'n' need us. Miss Harrison ain't got a copper cent of her own. Anyway, the set-up won't be as ripe for picking. My bonus is suddenly cut off and out the window go my pension.

Vı.   Suppose we did git us another job wit' one-'r them pennypinch-ing old misers hiding behind cupboards watching whether you stealing sugar cubes? Wit' our fringe benefits choked off, we'd fall down so quick to a style of living we ain't been used to for a long time, it would make your head swim. I don't think we could stand it. . . . Could you?

Ellie.   So when me and Vi saw our pigeons scampering out the window for good today, tears started flowing like rain. The first tear trickle out my eyes had a roast in it.

VI. Mine was a chicken.

ELLIE. Second had a crate of eggs.

VI. Mine a whole pig.

ELLIE. Third an oriental rug.

VI. A continental couch.

ELLIE. An overcoat for Arthur.

VI. A bathrobe for Ben.

ELLIE. My gas, electric and telephone bills in it.

VI. Three months' rent, Lord!

ELLIE. The faster the stream started gushing, the faster them nightmares crowded my eyes until I coulda flooded 'em 'nuff water to swim in. Every time I pleaded "Think of your love!—"

VI. She meant think 'bout our bills.

ELLIE. Every time I begged "Don't crack up the home!—"

VI. It meant please keep *ours* cemented together!

ELLIE. "Don't victim the chillun!—"

VI. By all means insure the happiness of *our* li'l' darlings!

ELLIE. They didn't know 'bout these eyeball visions—they only see what they see 'n' hear what they hear—and that's okey-doke wit' me—but I was gitting these watery pictures in my mind 'n' feeling a giant-size sickness in my gut! Few seconds longer and I woulda been down on my knees wit'out even thinking 'bout it!

VI. If I didn't beat ya to the floor!

ELLIE. Junie—maybe we shoulda given a little more thought to that—watchamacallit?—"image" of yours. Maybe we did dishonor Africa, embarrass the NAACP, are hopelessly behind time and scandalously outdated. But we didn't have too much time to think. . . . Now that you know the whole truth, you have a right to disown us. We hardly worthy of your respect. . . . But when I thought 'bout that new topcoat wit' the velvet-trimmed collar I just packed to bring you . . . (*Tears begin to re-form.*) . . . coupler new cashmere sweaters, brand-new slacks, a shiny new attache case for your appointments, and a scrumptous new collapsible swimming pool I promised your ma for her backyard—I couldn't help but cry. (*VI has joined her in a double torrent.*)

JUNIE. (*Who has been standing stoically throughout, says.*) . . . Vi?

VI. . . . What?

JUNIE. . . . Pass me the handkerchief. . . . (*He receives it and joins the table—a moist-faced trio. ARTHUR, ELLIE's husband, walks in, finding them thus.*)

ARTHUR. (*Beelining for bathroom.*) Even', everybody. . . . (*Hearing no response, stops before entering john.*) Hey, what's the matter? What you three looking like somebody died for?

ELLIE. It's the Harrisons, Arthur. Mr. Harrison gitting a divorce.

ARTHUR.   Aww, not ag'in!

VI.   He really means it this time, Arthur.

ARTHUR.   ... He does?

ELLIE.   Yes, Jesus.

ARTHUR.   You sure?

VI.   Caught her dead to rights.

ARTHUR.   (*Indignant.*) But he can't do that!

VI.   He is.

ARTHUR.   What 'bout us?!

JUNIE.   What you think we grieving 'bout?

ARTHUR.   Well, just don't sit there! What we go'n' do?

ELLIE.   Done it, didn't work.

ARTHUR.   Not at all?

ELLIE.   Nope.

ARTHUR.   Not even a little bit?

ELLIE.   Not one lousy inch.

ARTHUR.   (*Crestfallen.*) Make room for me. (*They provide space. He sits, completing the depressed quartet.*)

JUNIE.   (*Suddenly jolted with an idea.*) Ellie! Wait! Why don't you tell him to take her on a private ocean cruise, just the two of 'em, so they kin recapture the thrill for one another!

ELLIE.   He did that already, until somebody told him she was cuddling up with the ship stoker in the engine room.

JUNIE.   (*Undaunted.*) Advise him to spend less time wit' his business and more with her. She wouldn't need look outside for satisfaction!

ELLIE.   Tried that too, but his business like to fell apart and he caught her making eyes at the messenger bringing him the news.

JUNIE.   (*Desperate.*) Convince him she's sick! It's not her fault, he should send her to a psychiatrist!

ELLIE.   Already did ... till he found out she was doing more than talking on the couch.

JUNIE.   What 'bout a twenty-four hour guard on her? That won't give her so many opportunities?!

ELLIE.   What about guards? They men, too.

JUNIE.   (*In angry frustration.*) Well, damn, git her a chastity belt and lock her up!

ELLIE.   Locks, also, have been known to be picked.

ARTHUR.   (*Inspired by a brilliant solution.*) WAIT! *I GOT IT! I GOT IT!* ... Tell him you know of some steady-ready goofer dust ... or jooger-mooger saltpeter to cool her down. And you'll slip it in her food every day!

ELLIE.   Wouldn't work. ... Way her glands function, probably jazz her up like a Spanish fly.

VI.   Let's face it, it's all over. We just gotta tuck in our belts, stare the future square in the eye and git ready for a depression. It's not go'n' do us no good to whine over spilt clabber. . . . You jist better start scrounging 'round for that job, Junie. Befo' you git chance to sneeze, we will have had it. And call up—NO! Write your ma and tell her not to come up this year.

ELLIE. Arthur, best you scrape up another job to moonlight wit' the one you got. We facing some scuffling days 'head us.

VI. Well. . . . I better git out of here and go warn my own crew 'bout Satan's retribution. . . . Well . . . it was good while it lasted, Ellie. . . .

ELLIE. Real good. (*They glance at each other and another deluge starts. The phone interrupts, but no one bothers to answer. Finally, ARTHUR rises and exits in the direction of peals. During his absence, the disconsolate trio remains silent.*)

ARTHUR. (*Reentering slowly, treading each step with the deliberateness of a man fearful of cracking eggs.*) That—was—Mr. Harrison—he said—thank both of you for desperately trying to—shock him to his senses—pry open his eyes to the light—and rescue his house from collapsing—he and Mrs. Harrison, after stren'ous consideration, are gonna stick it out together! (*A stunned moment of absolute silence prevails, finally broken by an earsplitting, exultant whoop which erupts simultaneously from each member of the quartet. They spring to feet, embracing and prancing around the room, crying through laughter. ARTHUR simmers down first, shhushes to recapture their attention.*) ELLIE . . . Ellie, Mr. Harrison requests if it's not too much trouble, he'd like for you to come over and stay wit' Sandy and Snookie while he and Mrs. Harrison go out and celebrate their reunion and it's too late to git a baby-sitter.

ELLIE. If it's all right?!!!! . . . Tell him I'm climbing on a broomstick, then shuttling to a jet! (*ARTHUR starts to exit.*) Wait a minute! Waaaait a minute! Hold on!—I must be crazy! Don't tell him that. . . . Tell him he knows very well it's after my working hours and I'm not paid to baby-sit and since I've already made plans for the evening, I'll be glad to do it for double-overtime, two extra days' pay and triple-time off to recuperate from the imposition. . . . And, Arthur! . . . Kinda suggest that *you* is a little peeved 'cause he's interrupting me from taking care of something important for you. He might toss in a day for your suffering.

ARTHUR. He'll swear he was snatching you away from my death-bed, guarding my door 'gainst Lucifer busting through! (*Exits.*)

ELLIE. I'd better throw on some more clothes. (*Exits.*)

JUNIE. Vi, what you s'pose grandpa would say 'bout his chillun if he got a breathing-spell in between dodging pitchforks and sidestepping the fiery flames?

VI. Shame on you, boy, Papa ain't near'bouts doing no ducking 'n' dodging. Why, he's right up there plunked down safe, snuggled up tight beside the good Lord's righteous throne.

ARTHUR. (*Reentering.*) He was real sorry. "If it wasn't such a special occasion, he wouldn't bother us!" (*They guffaw heartily.*)

JUNIE.   This IS a special occasion! . . . (*Grandly.*) Arthur, break out a flagon of the latest champagne Ellie brought us.

ARTHUR.   At your service, massa Junie.

JUNIE.   The nineteen-forty-seven! That was a good year. Not the fifty, which was bad!

ARTHUR.   No kidding?! (*ARTHUR moves to refrigerator. ELLIE returns, ready to depart.*)

JUNIE.   Wait for a drink, auntie. We've gotta celebrate OUR resurrection. A Toast of Deliverance. (*ARTHUR presents JUNIE with champagne, points out '47 label, then gets goblets from shelf. JUNIE pours, they lift goblets.*) First! . . . To the victors and the vanquished, top-dog and the bottom-dog! Sometimes it's hard to tell which is which . . . !

VI.   If nothing else, boy, education did teach you how to sling around some GAB.

ARTHUR.   Ain't hardly the way I heard the slinging described. (*They all laugh.*)

JUNIE.   Second! . . . To my two cagey aunts. May they continue to prevail in times of distress!

ARTHUR.   May they!

JUNIE.   . . . Third! . . . To the Harrisons! . . . May they endure forever in marital bliss! Cheers to 'em! (*All cheer. After finishing drink, ELLIE moves to exit through hallway door. JUNIE stops her.*) Oh, Ellie . . . why don't you start fattening Mr. Harrison up? Please slip some more potatoes and starch onto his menu. I've gained a few pounds and the clothes are gitting a little tight. Don't you think it's time for him to plumpen up a bit, stick on a little weight? . . .

ELLIE.   Would ten pounds do?

JUNIE.   Perfect! (*Another round of laughter. Again she moves to exit.*) . . . AND ELLIE! . . . Kinda hint 'round to him that fashions is changing. I wouldn't want him to fall behind in the latest styles. . . .

VI.   (*Lifting goblet, along with ARTHUR and ELLIE, in a final toast.*) There's hope, Junie. You'll make it, boy, you'll make it. . . . (*Laughter rings as lights fade.*)

QUESTIONS

1. What two types of comedy are combined in *Happy Ending*?
2. Analyze the plot structure.
3. At what point in the play do you realize that you are reading a comedy?
4. What visual comic effects does Ward use? Imagine a live performance; what would be visually funny?
5. How does Ward want us to see Junie and his aunts? The Harrisons? Are we to judge any of the characters?

chapter 5

Character

Leonardo Da Vinci. *Mona-Lisa. c.* 1503–05. Oil on panel, Approx. 30" × 21".
Louvre Museum, Paris.

"What is character but the determination of incident? What is incident but the illustration of character?" The words of the writer Henry James remind us of the interaction of character and events. Things happen to people; people shape events. Conflicts force characters to react, to do something. If a complication develops, the character's response will shape the subsequent events, even if the character's response is to do nothing. In this process of action and reaction, characters reveal their attitudes toward themselves and others, their values, their typical patterns of behavior.

Although character and action are interrelated, it is easier to know what characters do than to understand their personalities. Insight into character takes close reading and skillful weighing of evidence. Everyone who has read Shakespeare's *Othello* can tell you what actions Iago takes to further the plot development. But for a long time critics have argued over Iago's *character*,* over the traits that make up his personality and motivate him to behave as he does.

FORMS OF CHARACTER

Characters come to us in all sizes, ages, and types. The *type*, or stereotype, character is one we recognize quickly and label as a representative figure because of a single, dominant quality. Type characters embody or represent a single characteristic; they are the handsome soldier, the bully, the miser, the outlaw. Because type characters are shaped by only one quality, they are easiest to create and easiest to understand, but they are also the least realistic. Life is not a TV western pitting villains against heroes, or a TV soap contrasting a pure Crystal against a scheming Alexis.

Still, some of the most memorable characters of literature are type characters. More than one eternal optimist who is sure that some good can be found in the worst circumstances has been called a "Pollyanna," and more than one old skinflint has been unkindly labeled a "Scrooge." These characters live on in our culture because they show us the essence of optimism and miserliness. Type characters often appear in satires, their one quality exaggerated for the purpose of ridicule. Type characters have their places in literature.

* The term *character* is used in two ways: (1) to refer to the fictional being (the character Iago) and (2) to refer to the traits and attitudes of the fictional being (Iago's character) that make up his or her personality.

In his study of fiction, *Aspects of the Novel*, E. M. Forster gives us two concepts for analyzing character. Forster suggests that there are flat characters and round characters in literature. The *flat character* is briefly drawn, given only a few traits. The *round character* is fully drawn, a complex, three-dimensional personality.

These terms represent either end of a scale rather than totally separate categories. The flattest characters have only one characteristic or function. In James Joyce's "Counterparts" (pp. 128–36), we find a good example in O'Halloran. He is one of Farrington's companions; we know nothing else about him. Slightly more developed is Farrington's boss Mr. Alleyne. The only developed character in the story is Farrington. He should be called a round character, although we recognize that within the limits of a short story we can expect only a glimpse of his complex personality.

We said in Chapter 4 that what happens in a narrative must have plausibility. Closely connected to plausibility in plot are consistency in character and adequate motivation for actions. A writer must give us enough clues to a character's personality to make that character's actions believable. Actions will be believable when we perceive motivation for them, when we understand that characters with certain values and behavior traits will act as they do. And actions will be believable when they are consistent. Consistency does not mean sameness; a character who behaves in exactly the same way throughout a work would be very dull. Different situations lead to different responses from a complex character, but those different responses must be plausible, given our knowledge of the character's personality. Mme. Loisel ("The Necklace," pp. 84–90), a woman who loves expensive things, chooses to spend ten years of her life in poverty to pay off a debt. Is this choice consistent? Yes, it is consistent with the false values that she displays earlier in the story. She would rather suffer hardship than lose face with her rich friend.

Consistency does not mean predictability either. The actions of characters may surprise us initially. Surprise heightens our interest in a work, but after our surprise we should be able, upon reflection, to be convinced that the character's actions are consistent with that character's traits. Most readers of "The Story of an Hour" (pp. 22–24) do not expect Mrs. Mallard's new sense of freedom; we expect the conventional response of grief to news of a spouse's death. But when we think about a wife's limited role at the time Chopin wrote, we can understand that the presumed death of Mr.

Mallard meant the removal of the controlling force in Mrs. Mallard's life.

Characters can also be viewed as either *static* or *changing*. Complex, developed characters have the capacity to change, to shape themselves in new ways or reach new insights, but not all of them do change, and there is no requirement that a character change. A changing character does not make a work better, only different. A good example of a static character is Farrington, an angry, bitter man caught in a web of conflicting forces from which he cannot break free. Sometimes authors create static characters because they are interested in showing us a particular kind of personality. Other times the unchanging character relates closely to the work's theme. The author chooses to assert that forces in life—environment, family—condition people and make it hard for them to change.

Changing characters can alter themselves—or be altered by circumstances—in one of two ways. They can change their way of life: get a different job, retire from working. Or they can change their way of thinking: develop a new awareness, reach a new understanding about themselves and about life. In some works the new understanding comes in a brief moment of awareness. James Joyce, author of "Counterparts," called the sudden moment of revelation an *epiphany*. Such an experience occurs in "The Story of an Hour" when Mrs. Mallard, sitting in her room, comes to a new sense of life's possibilities.

CHARACTER CONFLICT

In Chapter 4 we defined conflict as a struggle or tension between opposing forces, and we examined its function in plot structure. Now we need to look at the concept more fully as a way to understand the values and attitudes that motivate characters to act as they do in stories and plays or to speak as they do in dramatic poems. To analyze character conflict, you need to decide what the opposing forces are, what is in conflict, remembering that there can be several sets of opposing forces in one work. Then you need to state the two sides of each conflict as precisely as possible.

We can group character conflicts into three categories. First, a character can be in conflict with *outside forces*, with forces in the environment or in society. Stories about the hardships of early pioneers depict a human struggle for survival against an unknown, often inhospitable environment. In "Appointment at Sammara" (p. 71), the servant's conflict with death is a conflict with outside forces. Even though Death, in this story, is presented as a character, the character represents an outside force. Characters can also be in conflict with society or with a particular segment of society; they may be pressured to conform to the expectations of a neighborhood or organization of which they are a part. Generally, the social forces in conflict with a character are represented by other characters in the work, but the author makes us aware that these characters are significant because of the positions they hold, or the roles they play, not as individuals.

A character can have a *personal* conflict, a conflict with other characters as individuals. In Lessing's "A Woman on a Roof" (pp. 32–40) Harry, Stanley, and Tom are in conflict with *the* woman on the roof, not with a representative woman but with this particular woman for the very fact that she does not act the way the men expect women to act. Lessing establishes the conflict as personal by showing the pleasant response of the men to other women in the story. By contrast, Junie's aunts (*Happy Ending*, pp. 103–16) are not in a personal struggle with the Harrisons. We never see the Harrisons on stage, and the aunts show no resentment to them. Rather, the aunts are in conflict with a social system represented by the Harrisons, a system that places the aunts at the bottom socially and forces them to use their wits to survive.

Finally, characters can be in a struggle with themselves; their conflict can be *internal*. An internal conflict is a struggle between two values, goals, or beliefs that the character holds; or it may be a struggle between what the character would like to be or do and the reality that thwarts his or her desires. Farrington's internal conflict is between his view of himself and the reality of his position in the world. The chart in Figure 5.1 summarizes the types of character conflict.

When the central conflict in a work is an internal one, often that conflict is a part of the character as the story begins and leads to the first complication. Farrington's internal conflict results in his becoming increasingly frustrated by the events in his day. On the other hand, a character's conflict with others or with opposing forces usually develops from a complicating situation. The servant in "Appointment at Sammara" (p. 71) is not in turmoil until Death approaches him at the market. Analyzing plot structure to see which

Type of conflict	Example
With outside forces Environmental	American pioneer versus undeveloped west
Social	A newcomer versus the town's expectations of conformity
With other individuals	One woman versus another woman because both love the same man
With oneself (internal)	One boy's dreams of success versus the reality of his failure

FIGURE 5.1   *Types of character conflict.*

comes first, the conflict or the complication, may help you decide what type of conflict dominates the story and what issues of character are important to the author.

WAYS AN AUTHOR CONVEYS CHARACTER

Analyzing character is always a challenge because we must infer and then describe a unified personality from a few words, gestures, and actions. We know, too, that we cannot believe everything characters say about themselves, about other characters, or to other characters because we know that literary creations, like people, lie to others and to themselves. Understanding character becomes easier when we know the various techniques authors use to portray character.

Direct Statement

An author can convey character by telling us, in a direct statement, about a character's traits, feelings, values. A dramatist can tell us in the stage directions that the main character is frightened. The narrator of "Counterparts" tells us that "all the indignities of his [Farrington's] life enraged him." Because these are direct statements by the authors, we can say with confidence that the main character of the play is frightened and that Farrington is enraged. All direct statements by authors should be noted; these assertions are the easiest way to learn about character.

Remember, though, that while stage directions are usually direct statements by the playwright (editors add them to some early plays), statements about character in a story or dramatic poem are often made by other characters and therefore may not be accurate. These assertions reveal the speaker's opinion but are not necessarily the way the author wants us to view the character being described. Do not assume, without good evidence, that any particular character speaks for the author. Characters speak "in character," even a character who may be telling the story. What one character says about another may tell us more about the character speaking than about the character under discussion.

Description

Writers often use description to portray a character's personality traits and way of life. Age, physical appearance, dress, ways of walking and speaking are important clues to a character's personality. Consider the following description of Farrington:

> When he stood up he was tall and of great bulk. He had a hanging face, dark wine-colored, with fair eyebrows and moustache; his eyes bulged forward slightly and the whites of them were dirty.

Our introduction to Farrington gives us not only a physical impression of him but a suggestion of his lifestyle as well. We notice that, although a fair-haired person, Farrington has a dark complexion; further, his face is not tanned but a dark red. He could have a sunburn, but more likely, given his bloodshot eyes, he is a heavy drinker. His behavior later in the story confirms what is suggested by the narrator's description. We need to study these longer descriptions of character, but we also need to be alert for the scattered words and phrases that contribute to our total image of the person. We should consider, for example, why Farrington leaves his office with a "heavy step."

Dramatic Scenes

One interesting method for conveying character is the dramatic scene. Instead of having a narrator tell us about characters, the author chooses to have them show us their typical patterns of behavior and their values in the choices they make and the way they interact with others. The dramatist must of course rely primarily upon dramatic scenes to portray characters, but you will find that the greater portion of many short stories will be dialogue, creating the impression of a dramatic scene, rather than narration. Consider the exchange between the curate and Farrington after Farrington is beaten in arm wrestling:

> —Ah! That's the knack!
> —What the hell do you know about it? said Farrington fiercely, turning on the man. What do you put in your gab for?

In this scene Joyce shows us Farrington's quick temper. Often the most significant moments in the story are presented in a dramatic scene rather than narrated. Joyce does not merely tell us that Farrington beat his son; instead, he shows us a hulking man cutting the boy's thigh with a walking stick.

Comparison and Contrast with Other Characters

An author can reveal a character's personality by comparison with other characters. One of the chief functions of minor characters is to provide contrast to the main character, thereby helping to convey the main character's traits. The doctor's desire to befriend and help the boy in "Haircut" (pp. 165–74) shows us, by contrast, the barber's insensitivity to the feelings of others. In a variation of this technique, we understand Walter Mitty's character by observing the contrast between his "real" behavior on the shopping trip and the imagined behavior of his dream self. All of the imagined versions of Mitty the victorious provide a contrast to Mitty the ineffectual.

Dramatists seem especially partial to this technique for portraying character. Critics of the drama use the term *foil character* to describe the minor character who illuminates the main character by reflecting some of the main character's traits and contrasting with others. Often a foil character suggests, because he or she is like the main character in some important ways, what the main character might have been, if it were not for the significant differences between the two.

Associations with Other Elements in the Work

Writers can convey character through a variety of indirect, sometimes subtle techniques. Some characters are given significant names. *Faith* and *Hope* are obvious, and so is *Phoenix* Jackson ("A Worn Path"), if you recognize Welty's allusion to the mythological phoenix bird. Less immediately obvious, but revealing, are the names of the three men in "A Woman on a Roof": *Harry, Stanley,* and *Tom.* The three names are common ones, not individualized by last names; we can make the association with "Tom, Dick, and Harry," any three men.

Associations with colors and with objects can also help to portray character traits. White is often associated with purity and innocence and black with evil or the devil. The colors of Christmas—red, green, silver—are associated with Phoenix Jackson in "A Worn Path." The red rag on her head, the thorny bush which she hoped was a "pretty, little *green* bush," the frozen ground and silver grass she walks on parallel the "armful of red-, green- and silver-wrapped presents" carried by the woman in town. They remind us of the love and hope of the Christmas season that motivate Phoenix to make her long journey. In Ibsen's *A Doll's House*, Nora, the doll-like wife, loves macaroons and eats them when her husband is not present, although he has forbidden her to do so. The bag of macaroons helps to reveal both Nora's childishness and her repressed independent will. When you read "The Secret Life of Walter Mitty," think about the two items Mitty must purchase: overshoes and puppy biscuits. How do you associate these objects with Mitty's character?

Setting can help to convey character. Think, for example, of your room. What do your choices in furniture style and colors reveal about your personality? What would the worn sneakers and tennis racket by the door tell someone about your interests? Joyce uses three settings—the office, the bars, and the cold, empty house—to portray Farrington's character. Farrington is not comfortable in the office; as he "listened to the clicking of the machine . . . his mind wandered away to the glare and rattle of the public-house." When he is forced to start home, having spent all of his money, "he longed to be back again in the hot reeking public-house." Farrington needs heat, noise, people, activity to feel content.

While we can analyze character conflict to see how it shapes plot structure, we can also analyze structure to see how it conveys character. In "A Worn Path," for instance, the series of complications that test Phoenix bring out her personality—her commitment and endurance. When you read "The Secret Life of Walter Mitty," consider how the dominant structure helps to reveal Mitty's character.

WRITING ABOUT CHARACTER

When you write about character, you should be guided by the principle that a character has only those traits and qualities given by the author and that the character's life is limited to that portion portrayed in the work. Let's use Farrington as our illustration. We are not told how Farrington's internal conflict developed; we have no way to trace the early causes of his violent behavior. We should not, then, speculate about Farrington's childhood and suggest that he beats his child because his parents beat him. We can analyze his personality only as it is portrayed by Joyce within the world of the story.

Further, any value judgments about a character's traits or behavior should be limited to those suggested by the author's portrayal of character. Joyce shows us a character who is happy only when he is in noisy pubs. We should not get side-tracked on the "evils" of drinking too much or the "immorality" of bars because Joyce does not examine these issues in his story. What we can explore and want to understand is the anguish in Farrington that he seeks relief from in the crowded pub.

When writing an analysis of character, you will need to guard against the pitfall of summary. What a character does should be used as evidence of what a character is, but the focus of analysis should be on the character's traits, not on actions. The following paragraph illustrates the problem.

Action [When Farrington arrives at his home, he

Feels angry [is even more angry because he has had time to ponder the events of the evening. He becomes furious when he learns his wife

Action [is at chapel and has left him no dinner. He begins to take his frustrations out on his son. He rolls up his sleeves and goes after the boy with a walking-stick.

What point about Farrington's character is the student making in this paragraph? We can't be sure because the paragraph does not contain an assertion about Farrington's personality. It restates what Farrington does at the end of the story and reminds us that he is very angry. This writing problem can be avoided if you organize around points about character, not around what happens.

One typical assignment on character is an analysis of a character's dominant traits. Your essay will answer the question: what kind of person is character A? This is the purpose of the student essay on Phoenix Jackson in Chapter 3. (You may wish to reread that essay and the guidelines for planning such a paper.)

Another possible topic on character is the analysis of character conflict. Your purpose would be to identify the type of conflict and describe the opposing forces in detail, providing evidence from the work to support your analysis. To complete this assignment you need to state the terms of the opposing forces as precisely as possible. Usually internal conflicts are the most difficult to describe. Characters cannot be said to have conflicts between their values and themselves because their values are a part of them. Thus an internal conflict has to be between one's perceptions and reality. We can say, for example, that Farrington's internal conflict is between reality and illusion, but those terms are too general to help us understand Farrington's character. The purpose of an essay on character conflict is to establish the precise terms needed to reveal the character under discussion.

An analysis of character often takes us to the heart of a work's meaning or themes. Thus another essay topic can be the relation of character to theme. The purpose of your essay would be to show that a work's dominant theme can be understood through an understanding of character. This approach would be effective with Strindberg's play *The Stronger*, a work in which Strindberg illustrates his concept of a strong person. To write on this topic you would have to decide which character is presented as the stronger and why. In other words, what are the qualities that Strindberg defines as genuine strength?

You might also write an analysis of an author's portrayal of character. Your purpose would be to show the techniques used in a particular work to convey the main character's personality. But rather than cataloging all of the methods used, you probably should select one particularly interesting or significant method. You could, for instance, analyze Joyce's use of setting to reveal Farrington's character. The student paper following "Counterparts" analyzes Joyce's descriptive language. Note that the student has organized her evidence and explained the significance of Joyce's word choice.

JAMES JOYCE   (1882–1941)

Counterparts

The bell rang furiously and, when Miss Parker went to the tube, a furious voice called out in a piercing North of Ireland accent:

—Send Farrington here!

Miss Parker returned to her machine, saying to a man who was writing at a desk:

—Mr Alleyne wants you upstairs.

The man muttered *Blast him!* under his breath and pushed back his chair to stand up. When he stood up he was tall and of great bulk. He had a hanging face, dark wine-coloured, with fair eyebrows and moustache: his eyes bulged forward slightly and the whites of them were dirty. He lifted up the counter and, passing by the clients, went out of the office with a heavy step.

He went heavily upstairs until he came to the second landing, where a door bore a brass plate with the inscription *Mr Alleyne.* Here he halted, puffing with labour and vexation, and knocked. The shrill voice cried:

—Come in!

The man entered Mr Alleyne's room. Simultaneously Mr Alleyne, a little man wearing gold-rimmed glasses on a clean-shaven face, shot his head up over a pile of documents. The head itself was so pink and hairless that it seemed like a large egg reposing on the papers. Mr Alleyne did not lose a moment:

—Farrington? What is the meaning of this? Why have I always to complain of you? May I ask you why you haven't made a copy of that contract between Bodley and Kirwan? I told you it must be ready by four o'clock.

—But Mr Shelley said, sir—

—*Mr Shelley said, sir.* . . . Kindly attend to what I say and not to what

Mr Shelley says, sir. You have always some excuse or another for shirking work. Let me tell you that if the contract is not copied before this evening I'll lay the matter before Mr Crosbie. . . . Do you hear me now?

—Yes, sir.

—Do you hear me now? . . . Ay and another little matter! I might as well be talking to the wall as talking to you. Understand once for all that you get a half an hour for your lunch and not an hour and a half. How many courses do you want, I'd like to know. . . . Do you mind me, now?

—Yes, sir.

Mr Alleyne bent his head again upon his pile of papers. The man stared fixedly at the polished skull which directed the affairs of Crosbie & Alleyne, gauging its fragility. A spasm of rage gripped his throat for a few moments and then passed, leaving after it a sharp sensation of thirst. The man recognised the sensation and felt that he must have a good night's drinking. The middle of the month was passed and, if he could get the copy done in time, Mr Alleyne might give him an order on the cashier. He stood still, gazing fixedly at the head upon the pile of papers. Suddenly Mr Alleyne began to upset all the papers, searching for something. Then, as if he had been unaware of the man's presence till that moment, he shot up his head again, saying:

—Eh? Are you going to stand there all day? Upon my word, Farrington, you take things easy!

—I was waiting to see . . .

—Very good, you needn't wait to see. Go downstairs and do your work.

The man walked heavily towards the door and, as he went out of the room, he heard Mr Alleyne cry after him that if the contract was not copied by evening Mr Crosbie would hear of the matter.

He returned to his desk in the lower office and counted the sheets which remained to be copied. He took up his pen and dipped it in the ink but he continued to stare stupidly at the last words he had written: *In no case shall the said Bernard Bodley be* . . . The evening was falling and in a few minutes they would be lighting the gas: then he could write. He felt that he must slake the thirst in his throat. He stood up from his desk and, lifting the counter as before, passed out of the office. As he was passing out the chief clerk looked at him inquiringly.

—It's all right, Mr Shelley, said the man, pointing with his finger to indicate the objective of his journey.

The chief clerk glanced at the hat-rack but, seeing the row complete, offered no remark. As soon as he was on the landing the man pulled a shepherd's plaid cap out of his pocket, put it on his head and ran quickly down the rickety stairs. From the street door he walked on furtively on the inner side of the path towards the corner and all at once dived into a doorway. He was now safe in the dark snug of O'Neill's shop, and, filling up the little window that looked into the bar with his inflamed face, the colour of dark wine or dark meat, he called out:

—Here, Pat, give us a g.p., like a good fellow.

The curate brought him a glass of plain porter. The man drank it at a gulp and asked for a caraway seed. He put his penny on the counter and, leaving the curate to grope for it in the gloom, retreated out of the snug as furtively as he had entered it.

Darkness, accompanied by a thick fog, was gaining upon the dusk of February and the lamps in Eustace Street had been lit. The man went up by the houses until he reached the door of the office, wondering whether he could finish his copy in time. On the stairs a moist pungent odour of perfumes saluted his nose: evidently Miss Delacour had come while he was out in O'Neill's. He crammed his cap back again into his pocket and re-entered the office, assuming an air of absent-mindedness.

—Mr Alleyne has been calling for you, said the chief clerk severely. Where were you?

The man glanced at the two clients who were standing at the counter as if to intimate that their presence prevented him from answering. As the clients were both male the chief clerk allowed himself a laugh.

—I know that game, he said. Five times in one day is a little bit. . . . Well, you better look sharp and get a copy of our correspondence in the Delacour case for Mr Alleyne.

This address in the presence of the public, his run upstairs and the porter he had gulped down so hastily confused the man and, as he sat down at his desk to get what was required, he realised how hopeless was the task of finishing his copy of the contract before half past five. The dark damp night was coming and he longed to spend it in the bars, drinking with his friends amid the glare of gas and the clatter of glasses. He got out the Delacour correspondence and passed out of the office. He hoped Mr Alleyne would not discover that the last two letters were missing.

The moist pungent perfume lay all the way up to Mr Alleyne's room. Miss Delacour was a middle-aged woman of Jewish appearance. Mr Alleyne was said to be sweet on her or on her money. She came to the office often and stayed a long time when she came. She was sitting beside his desk now in an aroma of perfumes, smoothing the handle of her umbrella and nodding the great black feather in her hat. Mr Alleyne had swivelled his chair round to face her and thrown his right foot jauntily upon his left knee. The man put the correspondence on the desk and bowed respectfully but neither Mr Alleyne nor Miss Delacour took any notice of his bow. Mr Alleyne tapped a finger on the correspondence and then flicked it towards him as if to say: *That's all right: you can go.*

The man returned to the lower office and sat down again at his desk. He stared intently at the incomplete phrase: *In no case shall the said Bernard Bodley be* . . . and thought how strange it was that the last three words began with the same letter. The chief clerk began to hurry Miss Parker, saying she would never have the letters typed in time for post. The man listened to the clicking of the machine for a few minutes and then set to work to finish his copy. But his head was not clear and his mind wandered away to the glare and rattle of the public-house. It was a night for hot punches. He struggled on with his copy, but when the clock struck five he had still fourteen pages to write. Blast it! He couldn't finish it in time. He longed to execrate aloud, to bring his fist down on something violently. He was so enraged that he wrote *Bernard Bernard* instead of *Bernard Bodley* and had to begin again on a clean sheet.

He felt strong enough to clear out the whole office single-handed. His body ached to do something, to rush out and revel in violence. All the indignities of his life enraged him. . . . Could he ask the cashier privately for an advance? No, the cashier was no good, no damn good: he wouldn't give an advance. . . . He knew where he would meet the boys: Leonard and O'Halloran and Nosey Flynn. The barometer of his emotional nature was set for a spell of riot.

His imagination had so abstracted him that his name was called twice before he answered. Mr Alleyne and Miss Delacour were standing outside the counter and all the clerks had turned round in anticipation of something. The man got up from his desk. Mr Alleyne began a tirade of abuse, saying that two letters were missing. The man answered that he knew nothing about them, that he had made a faithful copy. The tirade continued: it was so bitter and violent that the man could hardly restrain his fist from descending upon the head of the manikin before him.

—I know nothing about any other two letters, he said stupidly.

—*You—know—nothing.* Of course you know nothing, said Mr Alleyne. Tell me, he added, glancing first for approval to the lady beside him, do you take me for a fool? Do you think me an utter fool?

The man glanced from the lady's face to the little egg-shaped head and back again; and, almost before he was aware of it, his tongue had found a felicitous moment:

—I don't think, sir, he said, that that's a fair question to put to me.

There was a pause in the very breathing of the clerks. Everyone was astounded (the author of the witticism no less than his neighbours) and Miss Delacour, who was a stout amiable person, began to smile broadly. Mr Alleyne flushed to the hue of a wild rose and his mouth twitched with a dwarf's passion. He shook his fist in the man's face till it seemed to vibrate like the knob of some electric machine:

—You impertinent ruffian! You impertinent ruffian! I'll make short work of you! Wait till you see! You'll apologise to me for your impertinence or you'll quit the office instanter! You'll quit this, I'm telling you, or you'll apologise to me!

....

He stood in a doorway opposite the office watching to see if the cashier would come out alone. All the clerks passed out and finally the cashier came out with the chief clerk. It was no use trying to say a word to him when he was with the chief clerk. The man felt that his position was bad enough. He had been obliged to offer an abject apology to Mr Alleyne for his impertinence but he knew what a hornet's nest the office would be for him. He could remember the way in which Mr Alleyne had hounded little Peake out of the office in order to make room for his own nephew. He felt savage and thirsty and revengeful, annoyed with himself and with everyone else. Mr Alleyne would never give him an hour's rest; his life would be a hell to him. He had made a proper fool of himself this time. Could he not keep his tongue in his cheek? But they had never pulled together from the first, he and Mr Alleyne, ever since the day Mr Alleyne had overheard him mimicking his North of Ireland accent to amuse Higgins and Miss Parker: that had been the beginning of it. He might have tried Higgins for the money, but sure Higgins never had anything for himself. A man with two establishments to keep up, of course he couldn't. . . .

He felt his great body again aching for the comfort of the public-house. The fog had begun to chill him and he wondered could he touch Pat in O'Neill's. He could not touch him for more than a bob—and a bob was no use. Yet he must get money somewhere or other: he had spent his last penny for the g.p. and soon it would be too late for getting money anywhere. Suddenly, as he was fingering his watch-chain, he thought of Terry Kelly's pawn-office in Fleet Street. That was the dart! Why didn't he think of it sooner?

He went through the narrow alley of Temple Bar quickly, muttering to himself that they could all go to hell because he was going to have a good night of it. The clerk in Terry Kelly's said *A crown!* but the consignor held out for six shillings; and in the end the six shillings was allowed him literally. He came out of the pawn-office joyfully, making a little cylinder of the coins between his thumb and fingers. In Westmoreland Street the footpaths were crowded with young men and women returning from business and ragged urchins ran here and there yelling out the names of the evening editions. The man passed through the crowd, looking on the spectacle generally with proud satisfaction and staring masterfully at the office-girls. His head was full of the noises of tram-gongs and swishing trolleys and his nose already sniffed the curling fumes of punch. As he walked on he preconsidered the terms in which he would narrate the incident to the boys:

—So, I just looked at him—coolly, you know, and looked at her. Then I looked back at him again—taking my time, you know. *I don't think that that's a fair question to put to me*, says I.

Nosey Flynn was sitting up in his usual corner of Davy Byrne's and, when he heard the story, he stood Farrington a half-one, saying it was as smart a thing as ever he heard. Farrington stood a drink in his turn. After a while O'Halloran and Paddy Leonard came in and the story was repeated to them. O'Halloran stood tailors of malt, hot, all round and told the story of the retort he had made to the chief clerk when he was in Callan's of Fownes's Street; but, as the retort was after the manner of the liberal shepherds in the eclogues, he had to admit that it was not so clever as Farrington's retort. At this Farrington told the boys to polish off that and have another.

Just as they were naming their poisons who should come in but Higgins! Of course he had to join in with the others. The men asked him to give his version of it, and he did so with great vivacity for the sight of five small hot whiskies was very exhilarating. Everyone roared laughing when he showed the way in which Mr Alleyne shook his fist in Farrington's face. Then he imitated Farrington, saying, *And here was my nabs, as cool as you please*, while Farrington looked at the company out of his heavy dirty eyes, smiling and at times drawing forth stray drops of liquor from his moustache with the aid of his lower lip.

When that round was over there was a pause. O'Halloran had money but neither of the other two seemed to have any; so the whole party left the shop somewhat regretfully. At the corner of Duke Street Higgins and Nosey Flynn bevelled off to the left while the other three turned back towards the city. Rain was drizzling down on the cold streets and, when they reached the Ballast Office, Farrington suggested the Scotch House. The bar was full of men and loud with the noise of tongues and glasses. The three men pushed past the whining match-sellers at the door and formed a little party at the corner of the counter. They began to exchange stories. Leonard introduced them to a young fellow named Weathers who was performing at the Tivoli as an acrobat and knock-about *artiste*. Farrington stood a drink all round. Weathers said he would take a small Irish and Apollinaris. Farrington, who had definite notions of what was what, asked the boys would they have an Apollinaris too; but the boys told Tim to make theirs hot. The talk became theatrical. O'Halloran stood a round and then Farrington stood another round, Weathers protesting that the hospitality was too Irish. He promised to get them in behind the scenes and introduce them to some nice girls. O'Halloran said that he and Leonard would go but that Farrington wouldn't go because he was a married man; and Farrington's heavy dirty eyes leered at the company in token that he understood he was being chaffed. Weathers made them all have just one little tincture at his expense and promised to meet them later on at Mulligan's in Poolbeg Street.

When the Scotch House closed they went round to Mulligan's. They went into the parlour at the back and O'Halloran ordered small hot specials all round. They were all beginning to feel mellow. Farrington was just standing another round when Weathers came back. Much to Farrington's relief he drank a glass of bitter this time. Funds were running low but they had enough to keep them going. Presently two young women with big hats and a young man in a check suit came in and sat at a table close by. Weathers saluted them and told the company that they were out of the Tivoli. Farrington's eyes wandered at every moment in the direction of one of the young women. There was something striking in her appearance. An immense scarf of peacock-blue muslin was wound round her hat and knotted in a great bow under her chin; and she wore bright yellow gloves, reaching to the elbow. Farrington gazed admiringly at the plump arm which she moved very often and with much grace; and when, after a little time, she answered his gaze he admired still more her large dark brown eyes. The oblique staring expression in them fascinated him. She glanced at him once or twice and, when the party was leaving the room, she brushed against his chair and said O, pardon! in a London accent. He watched her leave the room in the hope that she would look back at him, but he was disappointed. He cursed his want of money and cursed all the rounds he had stood, particularly all the whiskies and Apollinaris which he had stood to Weathers. If there was one thing that he hated it was a sponge. He was so angry that he lost count of the conversation of his friends.

When Paddy Leonard called him he found that they were talking about feats of strength. Weathers was showing his biceps muscle to the company and boasting so much that the other two had called on Farrington to uphold the national honour. Farrington pulled up his sleeve accordingly and showed his biceps muscle to the company. The two arms were examined and compared and finally it was agreed to have a trial of strength. The table was cleared and the two men rested their elbows on it, clasping hands. When Paddy Leonard said Go! each was to try to bring down the other's hand on the table. Farrington looked very serious and determined.

The trial began. After about thirty seconds Weathers brought his opponent's hand slowly down on to the table. Farrington's dark wine-coloured face flushed darker still with anger and humiliation at having been defeated by such a stripling.

—You're not to put the weight of your body behind it. Play fair, he said.

—Who's not playing fair? said the other.

—Come on again. The two best out of three.

The trial began again. The veins stood out on Farrington's forehead, and the pallor of Weathers' complexion changed to peony. Their hands and arms trembled under the stress. After a long struggle Weathers again brought his opponent's hand slowly on to the table. There was a murmur of applause from the spectators. The curate, who was standing beside the table, nodded his red head towards the victor and said with loutish familiarity:

—Ah! that's the knack!

—What the hell do you know about it? said Farrington fiercely, turning on the man. What do you put in your gab for?

—Sh, sh! said O'Halloran, observing the violent expression of Farrington's face. Pony up, boys. We'll have just one little smahan more and then we'll be off.

A very sullen-faced man stood at the corner of O'Connell Bridge waiting for the little Sandymount tram to take him home. He was full of smouldering anger and revengefulness. He felt humiliated and discontented; he did not even feel drunk; and he had only twopence in his pocket. He cursed everything. He had done for himself in the office, pawned his watch, spent all his money; and he had not even got drunk. He began to feel thirsty again and he longed to be back again in the hot reeking public-house. He had lost his reputation as a strong man, having been defeated twice by a mere boy. His heart swelled with fury and, when he thought of the woman in the big hat who had brushed against him and said *Pardon!* his fury nearly choked him.

His tram let him down at Shelbourne Road and he steered his great body along in the shadow of the wall of the barracks. He loathed returning to his home. When he went in by the side-door he found the kitchen empty and the kitchen fire nearly out. He bawled upstairs:

—Ada! Ada!

His wife was a little sharp-faced woman who bullied her husband when he was sober and was bullied by him when he was drunk. They had five children. A little boy came running down the stairs.

—Who is that? said the man, peering through the darkness.

—Me, pa.

—Who are you? Charlie?

—No, pa. Tom.

—Where's your mother?

—She's out at the chapel.

—That's right. . . . Did she think of leaving any dinner for me?

—Yes, pa. I—

—Light the lamp. What do you mean by having the place in darkness? Are the other children in bed?

The man sat down heavily on one of the chairs while the little boy lit the lamp. He began to mimic his son's flat accent, saying half to himself: *At the chapel. At the chapel, if you please!* When the lamp was lit he banged his fist on the table and shouted:

—What's for my dinner?

—I'm going . . . to cook it, pa, said the little boy.

The man jumped up furiously and pointed to the fire.

—On that fire! You let the fire out! By God, I'll teach you to do that again!

He took a step to the door and seized the walking-stick which was standing behind it.

—I'll teach you to let the fire out! he said, rolling up his sleeve in order to give his arm free play.

The little boy cried *O, pa!* and ran whimpering round the table, but the man followed him and caught him by the coat. The little boy looked about him wildly but, seeing no way of escape, fell upon his knees.

—Now, you'll let the fire out the next time! said the man, striking at him viciously with the stick. Take that, you little whelp!

The boy uttered a squeal of pain as the stick cut his thigh. He clasped his hands together in the air and his voice shook with fright.

—O, pa! he cried. Don't beat me, pa! And I'll . . . I'll say a *Hail Mary* for you. . . . I'll say a *Hail Mary* for you, pa, if you don't beat me. . . . I'll say a *Hail Mary*. . . .

QUESTIONS

1. Analyze the plot structure, using the terms presented in Chapter 4. Where does the story's climax occur?
2. You are not told the town in which the story takes place or the time of the story. What can you infer about setting from details in the story?
3. State the terms of Farrington's internal conflict as precisely as possible.
4. List and find examples of all the techniques Joyce uses to portray character. What technique seems most effective? Why?

STUDENT ESSAY

Joyce's Use of Description

Patricia Carpenter

Farrington, the central character in James Joyce's story "Counterparts," is an angry, vengeful person. These traits result from an internal conflict between his desire for the respect of others (which would encourage a positive self-image) and the reality of his humiliating existence (which produces a negative self-image). Joyce effectively uses several techniques to develop his main character, including the contrasts of setting and Farrington's contrasts with minor characters. Less obvious at first, perhaps, but equally effective, is the use of description to reveal the character of Farrington. The connotations of descriptive words chosen by Joyce show: Farrington's world as humiliating, his escape into alcohol as comforting, his apparent resignation as burdensome, and his resultant character as angry and vengeful.

Joyce conveys the humiliation of Farrington in the words used to characterize interactions between the main character and the minor characters. Mr. Alleyne doesn't ask Farrington to come up to his office; a bell rings "furiously," he calls for Farrington in a "furious voice," and he ushers him in in a "shrill voice." When offended, Alleyne doesn't issue a reprimand or even discharge Farrington from service (these terms portray no diminution of dignity); instead Alleyne begins "a tirade of abuse." Alleyne refers to Farrington as an "impertinent ruffian," and the chief clerk speaks to him "severely." These terms shout contempt and humiliation. The verb used to describe the interaction between Farrington and his wife is "bullied"; she bullied him when he was sober and he bullied her when he was drunk. "Bullied," denoting tyrannizing

STUDENT ESSAY

of the strong over the weak, speaks volumes for their humiliating relationship.

Joyce illustrates Farrington's secretive escape from his humiliating world by saying that Farrington walked "furtively" to O'Neill's
shop and also exited "furtively." Descriptive phrases such as "safe in
the dark snug" tell us that escape into alcohol is a comfort to Farrington.
The warmth and conviviality missing in his work and home world are suggested in the "glare of gas and the clatter of glasses" and in references
to "hot whiskies" and "the hot reeking public-house." By contrast, the
night is damp with a chilling fog, the streets are cold, and his kitchen
is without light or fire. The pub environment, where he hopes to meet
friends and be accepted, is always alluded to in warm, comforting terms;
the humiliating world is alluded to in cold, dreary terms.

Joyce shows Farrington's apparent resignation to his life through
phrases describing his movements. Not only does Farrington leave the
office with "a heavy step"; he also "went heavily upstairs," "walked
heavily towards the door," and "sat down heavily." We feel the burdensome
weight of resignation in each "heavy" used. Joyce's description of
Farrington's facial expressions further reveals his attempted resignation.
Farrington is described as "glaring fixedly," staring "stupidly," and
"very sullen-faced." These words depict a steady, resigned plodding,
an attempt to close out the world, to place a barrier or blank wall between
himself and what causes him pain.

The fact that Farrington is an angry, vengeful man is made clear
by Joyce's precise language describing Farrington's thoughts and reactions.
For example, Joyce writes that Farrington's "fury nearly choked him."
Phrases announcing Farrington's "spasm of rage," desire to "revel in violence," and longing "to bring his fist down on something violently" are

STUDENT ESSAY

found in the early pages of the story, while he is still at the office.
They are a foreshadowing of the violence to come. Farrington's attempts
to hide (in alcohol, a resigned step, and a blank face) from "all the
indignities of his life" which "enraged him" will not succeed in containing
the anger brewing inside.

Farrington's inner struggle is accurately defined through Joyce's
word choice. We accept the shattering of his veneer of resignation
because Joyce has built an expectation of violence throughout the story.
We are prepared for the inevitable emotional explosion by the steady
accumulation of words with connotations of violence. Through descriptive
language Joyce reveals Farrington's humiliation building to anger and
finally erupting into violence.

SELECTIONS FOR FURTHER STUDY

JAMES THURBER   (1894–1961)

The Secret Life of Walter Mitty

"We're going through!" The Commander's voice was like thin ice breaking.
He wore his full-dress uniform, with the heavily braided white cap pulled
down rakishly over one cold gray eye. "We can't make it, sir. It's spoiling
for a hurricane, if you ask me." "I'm not asking you, Lieutenant Berg,"
said the Commander. "Throw on the power lights! Rev her up to 8,500!
We're going through!" The pounding of the cylinders increased: ta-
pocketa-pocketa-pocketa-*pocketa-pocketa*. The Commander stared at the ice
forming on the pilot window. He walked over and twisted a row of
complicated dials. "Switch on No. 8 auxiliary!" he shouted. "Switch on
No. 8 auxiliary!" repeated Lieutenant Berg. "Full strength in No. 3 turret!"
shouted the Commander. "Full strength in No. 3 turret!" The crew,
bending to their various tasks in the huge, hurtling eight-engined Navy

hydroplane, looked at each other and grinned. "The Old Man'll get us through," they said to one another. "The Old Man ain't afraid of Hell!" . . .

"Not so fast! You're driving too fast!" said Mrs. Mitty. "What are you driving so fast for?"

"Hmm?" said Walter Mitty. He looked at his wife, in the seat beside him, with shocked astonishment. She seemed grossly unfamiliar, like a strange woman who had yelled at him in a crowd. "You were up to fifty-five," she said. "You know I don't like to go more than forty. You were up to fifty-five." Walter Mitty drove on toward Waterbury in silence, the roaring of the SN202 through the worst storm in twenty years of Navy flying fading in the remote, intimate airways of his mind. "You're tensed up again," said Mrs. Mitty. "It's one of your days. I wish you'd let Dr. Renshaw look you over."

Walter Mitty stopped the car in front of the building where his wife went to have her hair done. "Remember to get those overshoes while I'm having my hair done," she said. "I don't need overshoes," said Mitty. She put her mirror back into her bag. "We've been all through that," she said, getting out of the car. "You're not a young man any longer." He raced the engine a little. "Why don't you wear your gloves? Have you lost your gloves?" Walter Mitty reached in a pocket and brought out the gloves. He put them on, but after she had turned and gone into the building and he had driven on to a red light, he took them off again. "Pick it up, brother!" snapped a cop as the light changed, and Mitty hastily pulled on his gloves and lurched ahead. He drove around the streets aimlessly for a time, and then he drove past the hospital on his way to the parking lot.

. . . "It's the millionaire banker, Wellington McMillan," said the pretty nurse. "Yes?" said Walter Mitty, removing his gloves slowly. "Who has the case?" "Dr. Renshaw and Dr. Benbow, but there are two specialists here, Dr. Remington from New York and Mr. Pritchard-Mitford from London. He flew over." A door opened down a long, cool corridor and Dr. Renshaw came out. He looked distraught and haggard. "Hello, Mitty," he said "We're having the devil's own time with McMillan, the millionaire banker and close personal friend of Roosevelt. Obstreosis of the ductal tract. Tertiary. Wish you'd take a look at him." "Glad to," said Mitty.

In the operating room there were whispered introductions: "Dr. Remington, Dr. Mitty. Mr. Pritchard-Mitford, Dr. Mitty." "I've read your book on streptothricosis," said Pritchard-Mitford, shaking hands. "A brilliant performance, sir." "Thank you," said Walter Mitty. "Didn't know you were in the States, Mitty," grumbled Remington. "Coals to Newcastle, bringing Mitford and me up here for a tertiary." "You are very kind," said Mitty. A huge, complicated machine, connected to the operating table, with many tubes and wires, began at this moment to go pocketa-pocketa-pocketa. "The new anesthetizer is giving way!" shouted an interne. "There is no one in the East who knows how to fix it!" "Quiet, man!" said

Mitty, in a low, cool voice. He sprang to the machine, which was now going pocketa-pocketa-queep-pocketa-queep. He began fingering delicately a row of glistening dials. "Give me a fountain pen!" he snapped. Someone handed him a fountain pen. He pulled a faulty piston out of the machine and inserted the pen in its place. "That will hold for ten minutes," he said. "Get on with the operation." A nurse hurried over and whispered to Renshaw, and Mitty saw the man turn pale. "Coreopsis has set in," said Renshaw nervously. "If you would take over, Mitty?" Mitty looked at him and at the craven figure of Benbow, who drank, and at the grave, uncertain faces of the two great specialists. "If you wish," he said. They slipped a white gown on him; he adjusted a mask and drew on thin gloves; nurses handed him shining . . .

"Back it up, Mac! Look out for that Buick!" Walter Mitty jammed on the brakes. "Wrong lane, Mac," said the parking-lot attendant, looking at Mitty closely. "Gee. Yeh," muttered Mitty. He began cautiously to back out of the lane marked "Exit Only." "Leave her sit there," said the attendant. "I'll put her away." Mitty got out of the car. "Hey, better leave the key." "Oh," said Mitty, handing the man the ignition key. The attendant vaulted into the car, backed it up with insolent skill, and put it where it belonged.

They're so damn cocky, thought Walter Mitty, walking along Main Street; they think they know everything. Once he had tried to take his chains off, outside New Milford, and he had got them wound around the axles. A man had had to come out in a wrecking car and unwind them, a young, grinning garageman. Since then Mrs. Mitty always made him drive to a garage to have the chains taken off. The next time, he thought, I'll wear my right arm in a sling; they won't grin at me then. I'll have my right arm in a sling and they'll see I couldn't possibly take the chains off myself. He kicked at the slush on the sidewalk. "Overshoes," he said to himself, and he began looking for a shoe store.

When he came out into the street again, with the overshoes in a box under his arm, Walter Mitty began to wonder what the other thing was his wife had told him to get. She had told him, twice, before they set out from their house for Waterbury. In a way he hated these weekly trips to town—he was always getting something wrong. Kleenex, he thought, Squibb's, razor blades? No. Toothpaste, toothbrush, bicarbonate, carborundum, initiative and referendum? He gave it up. But she would remember it. "Where's the what's-its-name?" she would ask. "Don't tell me you forgot the what's-its-name." A newsboy went by shouting something about the Waterbury trial.

. . . "Perhaps this will refresh your memory." The District Attorney suddenly thrust a heavy automatic at the quiet figure on the witness stand. "Have you ever seen this before?" Walter Mitty took the gun and examined it expertly. "This is my Webley-Vickers 50.80," he said calmly. An excited buzz ran around the courtroom. The Judge rapped for order. "You are a crack shot with any sort of firearms, I believe?" said the District Attorney, insinuatingly. "Objection!" shouted Mitty's attorney. "We have shown that the defendant could not have fired the shot. We have shown that he wore his right arm in a sling on the night of the fourteenth of July." Walter Mitty raised his hand briefly and the bickering attorneys were stilled. "With any known make of gun," he said evenly, "I could have killed Gregory Fitzhurst at three hundred feet *with my left hand.*" Pandemonium broke loose in the courtroom. A woman's scream rose above the bedlam and suddenly a lovely, dark-haired girl was in Walter Mitty's arms. The District Attorney struck at her savagely. Without rising from his chair, Mitty let the man have it on the point of the chin. "You miserable cur!" . . .

"Puppy biscuit," said Walter Mitty. He stopped walking and the buildings of Waterbury rose up out of the misty courtroom and surrounded him again. A woman who was passing laughed. "He said 'Puppy biscuit,'" she said to her companion. "That man said 'Puppy biscuit' to himself." Walter Mitty hurried on. He went into an A. & P., not the first one he came to but a smaller one farther up the street. "I want some biscuit for small, young dogs," he said to the clerk. "Any special brand, sir?" The greatest pistol shot in the world thought a moment. "It says 'Puppies Bark for It' on the box," said Walter Mitty.

His wife would be through at the hairdresser's in fifteen minutes, Mitty saw in looking at his watch, unless they had trouble drying it; sometimes they had trouble drying it. She didn't like to get to the hotel first; she would want him to be there waiting for her as usual. He found a big leather chair in the lobby, facing a window, and he put the overshoes and the puppy biscuit on the floor beside it. He picked up an old copy of *Liberty* and sank down into the chair. "Can Germany Conquer the World Through the Air?" Walter Mitty looked at the pictures of bombing planes and of ruined streets.

. . . "The cannonading has got the wind up in young Raleigh, sir," said the sergeant. Captain Mitty looked up at him through touseled hair. "Get him to bed," he said wearily. "With the others. I'll fly alone." "But you can't, sir," said the sergeant anxiously. "It takes two men to handle that bomber and the Archies are pounding hell out of the air. Von Richtman's circus is between here and Saulier." "Somebody's got to get that ammunition dump," said Mitty. "I'm going over. Spot of brandy?" He poured a drink for the sergeant and one for himself. War thundered and whined around the dugout and battered at the door. There was a rending of wood and splinters flew through the room. "A bit of a near thing," said Captain Mitty carelessly. "The box barrage is closing in," said the sergeant. "We only live once, Sergeant," said Mitty, with his faint, fleeting smile. "Or do we?" He poured another brandy and tossed it off.

"I never see a man could hold his brandy like you, sir," said the sergeant. "Begging your pardon, sir." Captain Mitty stood up and strapped on his huge Webley-Vickers automatic. "It's forty kilometers through hell, sir," said the sergeant. Mitty finished one last brandy. "After all," he said softly, "what isn't?" The pounding of the cannon increased; there was the rat-rat-tatting of machine guns, and from somewhere came the menacing pocketa-pocketa-pocketa of the new flame-throwers. Walter Mitty walked to the door of the dugout humming "Auprés de Ma Blonde." He turned and waved to the sergeant. "Cheerio!" he said. . . .

Something struck his shoulder. "I've been looking all over this hotel for you," said Mrs. Mitty. "Why do you have to hide in this old chair? How did you expect me to find you?" "Things close in," said Walter Mitty vaguely. "What?" Mrs. Mitty said. "Did you get the what's-its-name? The puppy biscuit? What's in that box?" "Overshoes," said Mitty. "Couldn't you have put them on in the store?" "I was thinking," said Walter Mitty. "Does it ever occur to you that I am sometimes thinking?" She looked at him. "I'm going to take your temperature when I get you home," she said.

They went out through the revolving doors that made a faintly derisive whistling sound when you pushed them. It was two blocks to the parking lot. At the drugstore on the corner she said, "Wait here for me. I forgot something. I won't be a minute." She was more than a minute. Walter Mitty lighted a cigarette. It began to rain, rain with sleet in it. He stood up against the wall of the drugstore, smoking. . . . He put his shoulders back and his heels together. "To hell with the handkerchief," said Walter Mitty scornfully. He took one last drag on his cigarette and snapped it away. Then, with that faint, fleeting smile playing about his lips, he faced the firing squad; erect and motionless, proud and disdainful, Walter Mitty the Undefeated, inscrutable to the last.

QUESTIONS

1. Does this story have a typical plot structure? What other structure shapes the story?

2. What type of character conflict dominates the story? State the terms of the dominant conflict. What other types of character conflict can be found in the story?

3. Is Mitty flat or round? Static or changing? How would you characterize Mrs. Mitty?

4. By what techniques does Thurber convey Mitty's character? Find examples of each technique.

5. What do the dream situations have in common? What do they tell us about Mitty?

6. How are Mitty and Farrington similar? How different? In your view, is one
character more admirable than the other? If so, why? How does each author
want us to feel about his character?

ROBERT FROST   (1874–1963)

Home Burial

He saw her from the bottom of the stairs
Before she saw him. She was starting down,
Looking back over her shoulder at some fear.
She took a doubtful step and then undid it
To raise herself and look again. He spoke   5
Advancing toward her: 'What is it you see
From up there always—for I want to know.'
She turned and sank upon her skirts at that,
And her face changed from terrified to dull.
He said to gain time: 'What is it you see,'   10
Mounting until she cowered under him.
'I will find out now—you must tell me, dear.'
She, in her place, refused him any help
With the least stiffening of her neck and silence.
She let him look, sure that he wouldn't see,   15
Blind creature; and awhile he didn't see.
But at last he murmured, 'Oh,' and again, 'Oh.'

'What is it—what?' she said.
                          'Just that I see.'

'You don't,' she challenged. 'Tell me what it is.'

'The wonder is I didn't see at once.   20
I never noticed it from here before.
I must be wonted to it—that's the reason.
The little graveyard where my people are!
So small the window frames the whole of it.
Not so much larger than a bedroom, is it?   25
There are three stones of slate and one of marble,
Broad-shouldered little slabs there in the sunlight
On the sidehill. We haven't to mind *those*.
But I understand: it is not the stones,
But the child's mound—'
                          'Don't, don't, don't, don't, she cried.   30

She withdrew shrinking from beneath his arm
That rested on the bannister, and slid downstairs;
And turned on him with such a daunting look,
He said twice over before he knew himself:
'Can't a man speak of his own child he's lost?'   35

'Not you! Oh, where's my hat? Oh, I don't need it!
I must get out of here. I must get air.
I don't know rightly whether any man can.'

'Amy! Don't go to someone else this time.
Listen to me. I won't come down the stairs.'   40
He sat and fixed his chin between his fists.
'There's something I should like to ask you, dear.'

You don't know how to ask it.'

                     'Help me, then.'

Her fingers moved the latch for all reply.

'My words are nearly always an offense.   45
I don't know how to speak of anything
So as to please you. But I might be taught
I should suppose. I can't say I see how.
A man must partly give up being a man
With women-folk. We could have some arrangement   50
By which I'd bind myself to keep hands off
Anything special you're a-mind to name.
Though I don't like such things 'twixt those that love.
Two that don't love can't live together without them.
But two that do can't live together with them.'   55
She moved the latch a little. 'Don't—don't go.
Don't carry it to someone else this time.
Tell me about it if it's something human.
Let me into your grief. I'm not so much
Unlike other folks as your standing there   60
Apart would make me out. Give me my chance.
I do think, though, you overdo it a little.
What was it brought you up to think it the thing
To take your mother-loss of a first child
So inconsolably—in the face of love.   65
You'd think his memory might be satisfied—'

'There you go sneering now!'
                     'I'm not, I'm not!'

You make me angry. I'll come down to you.
God, what a woman! And it's come to this,
A man can't speak of his own child that's dead.'   70

'You can't because you don't know how to speak.
If you had any feelings, you that dug
With your own hand—how could you?—his little grave;
I saw you from that very window there,
Making the gravel leap and leap in air,   75
Leap up, like that, like that, and land so lightly
And roll back down the mound beside the hole.
I thought, Who is that man? I didn't know you.
And I crept down the stairs and up the stairs
To look again, and still your spade kept lifting.   80
Then you came in. I heard your rumbling voice
Out in the kitchen, and I don't know why,
But I went near to see with my own eyes.
You could sit there with the stains on your shoes
Of the fresh earth from your own baby's grave   85
And talk about your everyday concerns.
You had stood the spade up against the wall
Outside there in the entry, for I saw it.'

'I shall laugh the worst laugh I ever laughed.
I'm cursed. God, if I don't believe I'm cursed.'   90

'I can repeat the very words you were saying.
'Three foggy mornings and one rainy day
Will rot the best birch fence a man can build.'
Think of it, talk like that at such a time!
What had how long it takes a birch to rot   95
To do with what was in the darkened parlor.
You *couldn't* care! The nearest friends can go
With anyone to death, comes so far short
They might as well not try to go at all
No, from the time when one is sick to death,   100
One is alone, and he dies more alone.
Friends make pretense of following to the grave,
But before one is in it, their minds are turned
And making the best of their way back to life
And living people, and things they understand.   105
But the world's evil. I won't have grief so
If I can change it. Oh, I won't. I won't!'

'There, you have said it all and you feel better.
You won't go now. You're crying. Close the door.
The heart's gone out of it: why keep it up.   110
Amy! There's someone coming down the road!'

'*You*—oh, you think the talk is all. I must go—
Somewhere out of this house. How can I make you—'

'If—you—do!' She was opening the door wider.
'Where do you mean to go? First tell me that.   115
I'll follow and bring you back by force. I *will!*—'

QUESTIONS

1. Who is speaking to whom? What are the circumstances?
2. What conflict is revealed? What type of conflict is it, and what are the terms of the conflict? What distresses Amy? What does her husband worry about?
3. How would you characterize their relationship? What is the result of the conflict?
4. What techniques does Frost use to portray character?
5. How does Frost suggest that the conflict between Amy and her husband stems from differences between most men and women? Do Frost's views seem dated to you? Why or why not?

AUGUST STRINDBERG   (1849–1912)

The Stronger

CHARACTERS

Mrs. X. *actress, married*
Miss Y., *actress, unmarried*
A Waitress

SCENE: *A corner of a ladies' café* (*in Stockholm in the eighteen eighties*). *Two small wrought-iron tables, a red plush settee and a few chairs.*

MISS Y. *is sitting with a half-empty bottle of beer on the table before her, reading an illustrated weekly which from time to time she exchanges for another.*

MRS. X. *enters, wearing a winter hat and coat and carrying a decorative Japanese basket.*

MRS. X.   Why, Millie, my dear, how are you? Sitting here all alone on Christmas Eve like some poor bachelor.
MISS Y.   *looks up from her magazine, nods, and continues to read.*
MRS. X.   You know it makes me feel really sad to see you. Alone.

NOTE: Translator's addition to scene bracketed. First mention of Miss Y. and Mrs. X. reversed.

Alone in a café and on Christmas Eve of all times. It makes me feel as sad as when once in Paris I saw a wedding party at a restaurant. The bride was reading a comic paper and the bridegroom playing billiards with the witnesses. Ah me, I said to myself, with such a beginning how will it go, and how will it end? He was playing billiards on his wedding day? And she, you were going to say, was reading a comic paper on hers. But that's not quite the same.

A WAITRESS brings a cup of chocolate to MRS. X. and goes out.

MRS. X.   Do you know, Amelia, I really believe now you would have done better to stick to him. Don't forget I was the first who told you to forgive him. Do you remember? Then you would be married now and have a home. Think how happy you were that Christmas when you stayed with your fiancé's people in the country. How warmly you spoke of domestic happiness! You really quite longed to be out of the theatre. Yes, Amelia dear, home is best—next best to the stage, and as for children— but you couldn't know anything about that.

MISS Y.'s expression is disdainful. MRS X. sips a few spoonfuls of chocolate, then opens her basket and displays some Christmas presents.

MRS. X.   Now you must see what I have bought for my little chicks. *Takes out a doll.* Look at this. That's for Lisa. Do you see how she can roll her eyes and turn her head. Isn't she lovely? And here's a toy pistol for Maja.° *She loads the pistol and shoots it at MISS Y. who appears frightened.*

MRS. X.   Were you scared? Did you think I was going to shoot you? Really, I didn't think you'd believe that of me. Now if *you* were to shoot *me* it wouldn't be so surprising, for after all I did get in your way, and I know you never forget it—although I was entirely innocent. You still think I intrigued to get you out of the Grand Theatre, but I didn't. I didn't, however much you think I did. Well, it's no good talking, you will believe it was me . . . *Takes out a pair of embroidered slippers.* And these are for my old man, with tulips on them that I embroidered myself. As a matter of fact I hate tulips, but he has to have tulips on everything.

MISS Y. looks up, irony and curiosity in her face.

MRS. X.   *putting one hand in each slipper.* Look what small feet Bob has, hasn't he? And you ought to see the charming way he walks—you've never seen him in slippers, have you?

MISS Y. laughs.

MRS. X.   Look, I'll show you. *She makes the slippers walk across the table, and MISS Y. laughs again.*

Maja: pronounced Maya.

MRS. X.   But when he gets angry, look, he stamps his foot like this. "Those damn girls who can never learn how to make coffee! Blast! That silly idiot hasn't trimmed the lamp properly!" Then there's a draught under the door and his feet get cold. "Hell, it's freezing, and the damn fools can't even keep the stove going!" *She rubs the sole of one slipper against the instep of the other. MISS Y. roars with laughter.*

MRS. X.   And then he comes home and has to hunt for his slippers, which Mary has pushed under the bureau . . . Well, perhaps it's not right to make fun of one's husband like this. He's sweet anyhow, and a good, dear husband. You ought to have had a husband like him, Amelia. What are you laughing at? What is it? Eh? And, you see, I know he is faithful to me. Yes, I know it. He told me himself—what *are* you giggling at?— that while I was on tour in Norway that horrible Frederica came and tried to seduce him. Can you imagine anything more abominable? *Pause.* I'd have scratched her eyes out if she had come around while I was at home. *Pause.* I'm glad Bob told me about it himself, so I didn't just hear it from gossip. *Pause.* And, as a matter of fact, Frederica wasn't the only one. I can't think why, but all the women in the Company° seem to be crazy about my husband. They must think his position gives him some say in who is engaged at the Theatre. Perhaps you have run after him yourself? I don't trust you very far, but I know he has never been attracted by you, and you always seemed to have some sort of grudge against him, or so I felt. *Pause. They look at one another guardedly.*

MRS. X.   Do come and spend Christmas Eve with us tonight, Amelia—just to show that you're not offended with us, or anyhow not with me. I don't know why, but it seems specially unpleasant not to be friends with you. Perhaps it's because I did get in your way that time . . . *slowly* or—I don't know—really, I don't know at all why it is.

Pause. MISS Y. gazes curiously at MRS. X.

MRS X., *thoughtfully.* It was so strange when we were getting to know one another. Do you know, when we first met, I was frightened of you, so frightened I didn't dare let you out of my sight. I arranged all my goings and comings to be near you. I dared not be your enemy, so I became your friend. But when you came to our home, I always had an uneasy feeling, because I saw my husband didn't like you, and that irritated me—like when a dress doesn't fit. I did all I could to make him be nice to you, but it was no good—until you went and got engaged. Then you became such tremendous friends that at first it looked as if you only dared show your real feelings then—when you were safe. And then, let me see, how was it after that? I wasn't jealous—that's queer. And I remember at

in the Company: translator's addition.

the christening, when you were the godmother, I told him to kiss you. He did, and you were so upset . . . As a matter of fact I didn't notice that then . . . I didn't think about it afterwards either . . . I've never thought about it—until *now! Rises abruptly.* Why don't you say something? You haven't said a word all this time. You've just let me go on talking. You have sat there with your eyes drawing all these thoughts out of me—they were there in me like silk in a cocoon—thoughts . . . Mistaken thoughts? Let me think. Why did you break off your engagement? Why did you never come to our house after that? Why don't you want to come to us tonight?

Miss Y. makes a motion, as if about to speak.

MRS. X.   No. You don't need to say anything, for now I see it all. That was why—and why—and why. Yes. Yes, that's why it was. Yes, yes, all the pieces fit together now. That's it. I won't sit at the same table as you. *Moves her things to the other table.* That's why I have to embroider tulips, which I loathe, on his slippers—because you liked tulips. *Throws the slippers on the floor.* That's why we have to spend the summer on the lake—because you couldn't bear the seaside. That's why my son had to be called Eskil—because it was your father's name. That's why I had to wear your colours, read your books, eat the dishes you liked, drink your drinks—your chocolate, for instance. That's why—oh my God, its terrible to think of, terrible! Everything, everything came to me from you—even your passions. Your soul bored into mine like a worm into an apple, and ate and ate and burrowed and burrowed, till nothing was left but the skin and a little black mould. I wanted to fly from you, but I couldn't. You were there like a snake, your black eyes fascinating me. When I spread my wings, they only dragged me down. I lay in the water with my feet tied together, and the harder I worked my arms, the deeper I sank—down, down, till I reached the bottom, where you lay in waiting like a giant crab to catch me in your claws—and now here I am. Oh how I hate you! I hate you, I hate you! And you just go on sitting there, silent, calm, indifferent, not caring whether the moon is new or full, if it's Christmas or New Year, if other people are happy or unhappy. You don't know how to hate or to love. You just sit there without moving—like a cat° at a mouse-hole. You can't drag your prey out, you can't chase it, but you can out-stay it. Here you sit in your corner—you know they call it the rat-trap after you—reading the papers to see if anyone's ruined or wretched or been thrown out of the Company. Here you sit sizing up your victims and weighing your chances—like a pilot his shipwrecks for the salvage. *Pause.* Poor Amelia! Do you know, I couldn't be more sorry for you. I know you are miserable, miserable like some wounded creature, and vicious because

---

cat: in Swedish, "stork."

you are wounded. I can't be angry with you. I should like to be, but after all you are the small one—and as for your affair with Bob, that doesn't worry me in the least. Why should it matter to me? And if you, or somebody else taught me to drink chocolate, what's the difference? *Drinks a spoonful. Smugly.* Chocolate is very wholesome anyhow. And if I learnt from you how to dress, *tant mieux!*—that only gave me a stronger hold over my husband, and you have lost what I gained. Yes, to judge from various signs, I think you have now lost him. Of course, you meant me to walk out, as you once did, and which you're now regretting. But I won't do that, you may be sure. One shouldn't be narrow-minded, you know. And why should nobody else want what I have? *Pause.* Perhaps, my dear, taking everything into consideration, at this moment it is I who am the stronger. You never got anything from me, you just gave away—from yourself. And now, like the thief in the night, when you woke up I had what you had lost. Why was it then that everything you touched became worthless and sterile? You couldn't keep a man's love—for all your tulips and your passions—but I could. You couldn't learn the art of living from your books—but I learnt it. You bore no little Eskil, although that was your father's name. *Pause.* And why is it you are silent—everywhere, always silent? Yes, I used to think this was strength, but perhaps it was because you hadn't anything to say, because you couldn't think of anything. *Rises and picks up the slippers.* Now I am going home, taking the tulips with me—*your* tulips. You couldn't learn from others, you couldn't bend, and so you broke like a dry stick. I did not. Thank you, Amelia, for all your good lessons. Thank you for teaching my husband how to love. Now I am going home—to love him.

Exit.

QUESTIONS

1. What type of character conflict dominates the play? What are the terms of that conflict? Is there more than one type of conflict operating?
2. What techniques does Strindberg use to portray character?
3. What do we learn about Mrs. X.? About Miss Y.? What does Mrs. X. learn?
4. Would you describe Mrs. X. as flat or round? Static or changing?
5. The setting is a cafe on Christmas Eve; how is the date significant?
6. Who is the stronger? Explain your answer.

chapter 6

Point of View

Theo Van Doesburg, *Card Players*. 1917. Gemeentemuseum, The Hague.

Johnny, age four, is sulking in the corner of his room. No matter how hard you try to communicate, he won't say what is wrong. Deciding on an imaginative approach, you get out a hand puppet of Winnie the Pooh. "Hi, Christopher Robin," you say. "This is your friend Pooh. Let's have a talk." Johnny smiles with the pleasure of the game, and a dialogue begins. A similar dialogue is at the heart of all literature. An author selects a speaker, gives that speaker words, and directs the words toward an audience. As readers, we experience the results on the printed page. We might vizualize the process as in Figure 6.1.

Notice that the author addresses us indirectly through a created voice. Someone must tell the story, react to a sunset, argue for love. The perspective established by the selection of the voice that presents the work is called *point of view.*

The author begins to establish point of view with one of three basic choices: (1) a storyteller addressing assumed readers or listeners, (2) a character thinking, or (3) a character speaking to one or more other characters. Then come other decisions about point of view. How close will the speaker's attitude be to that of the author? What kind of personality will the speaker have? A story told by a narrator deeply involved in the action will not be presented as objectively as a story told by an uninvolved bystander. A love poem with a speaker in love for the first time will be quite different from a love poem with a speaker wise in the ways of romance.

Point of view can also include vantage point in space and time. How does the speaker's location affect what we see and hear? How does the distance in time of the speaker from the event affect the presentation? In Eudora Welty's "A Worn Path" (pp. 42–48) we

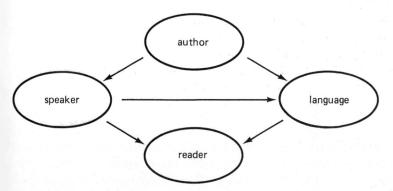

FIGURE 6.1 *Author-to-reader communication.*

follow Phoenix Jackson along the path to town. Any shift of point of view in either space or time from that path would detract from our involvement in the single-minded determination of Phoenix.

Point of view is significant in all forms of literature. However, the problems of analyzing point of view differ enough for fiction, poetry, and drama that we will examine each genre separately.

POINT OF VIEW IN FICTION

So important is point of view in short stories and novels that a widely accepted set of terms for point of view in prose fiction has been developed. The voice that tells us a story is called the *narrator*. The narrator may be either *first person* (I, we) or *third person* (he, she, it, they). Third-person narrators are further divided into *omniscient* (all knowing), *limited omniscient*, and *objective*.

First-Person Narrator

A first-person narrator recounts events in which he or she has been involved either as a major or a minor participant. Because an "I" narrator must stay in character, she (assuming a female character) is restricted in what she knows, how she can interpret, and how she can express herself. Sometimes this restriction raises a question of reliability. We tend to accept a first-person narrator who is likable, perceptive, and intelligent as a reliable reporter. But the author may, in fact, want us to view the narrator negatively. In Ring Lardner's "Haircut" (pp. 165–174), we are listening to a barber who is both imperceptive and insensitive. Although we can accept the barber's account of who did what, Lardner leads us to reject the barber's opinions about Jim's jokes and the shooting incident.

Why should an author create such problems in the first place? The reason is that a first-person narrator offers some advantages. An "I" narrator who is a major character can give us insight into that character's thoughts and emotions, perhaps enable us to understand some inner transformation. Sometimes we can be drawn into an understanding that goes beyond the narrator's limitations. This technique is effective for creating humor or irony. One variety of first-person narrator used in this way is the *innocent eye*, a narrator who is naive—a child or a not very perceptive adult. In the first-person version of Frank O'Connor's "First Confession" (pp. 185–

192) much of the humor is produced by our knowing more than does the seven-year-old narrator, Jackie. Further, an unreliable or naive narrator corresponds to our experience with those who tell us what happened in class or at last Friday's party or in a recent car accident. To judge the accuracy of the story, we must judge the storyteller's reliability.

Third-Person Narrator

The three types of third-person narrator range from an almost complete freedom of movement and knowledge to a strict limitation of what can be seen and heard in a particular place at a particular time.

The *omniscient narrator* is all-knowing. He (assuming a male narrator) is able to go anywhere, see anything, enter into the minds of any of the characters, and make comments on the story. He is clearly not a character but an author representative telling a story in which he himself is not a participant. For example, the omniscient narrator of Maupassant's "The Necklace" (pp. 84–90) opens the story with the editorial comment that Mme. Loisel's birth "into a family of clerks" was "as if by a mistake of destiny." During the narration he goes into the minds of both Mathilde, who "suffered ceaselessly," and of her husband, who was "frightened by the pains yet to come."

Selection of an omniscient narrator gives the author a considerable amount of freedom, but many authors choose to narrow that omniscience until it zeros in on the thoughts and experiences of a single character, creating what we call the *limited (selective) omniscient narrator.* We seem to stand, unseen, at the shoulder of this character—Tom, for example, in "A Woman on the Roof." We view the events and the other characters through what he sees, hears, and thinks. At the same time, the author retains two advantages of omniscient narration: the ability to understand the character's experience more fully than could the character and the ability to use language that the character would not use.

These capabilities give the author flexibility, but they can cause a reading difficulty. We may be required to distinguish between two voices—the voice expressing the thoughts of the character and the voice expressing the comment of the narrator. Take, for example, two statements from the limited omniscient version of

O'Connor's "First Confession" (pp. 180–185). Both involve the attitude of the boy, Jackie, towards his sister, Nora:

> Nora emerged. Jackie rose and looked at her with a hatred which was inappropriate to the occasion and the place.
>
> ....
>
> Ah women! Women! It was all women and girls and their silly talk. They had no real knowledge of the world.

The first statement contains an evaluation of the appropriateness of Jackie's hatred that goes beyond Jackie's current understanding. The second expresses Jackie's feelings only. To conclude that O'Connor thinks girls have "no real knowledge of the world" would be a mistake.

Sometimes a writer will take us even further into a character's mind so that the pattern becomes the seemingly disorganized flow of various levels of consciousness, not necessarily limited by time, space, or logic. This technique, called *stream of consciousness*, is most often used as an extension of limited omniscient narration but can also be used for a first-person narrator.

The third-person narrator that we call the *objective (dramatic) narrator* is often described as a combination tape recorder and camera. We are not taken into the mind of any character. We are given only what could be recorded and photographed—dialogue, setting, actions. We are presented with facts, but we must draw all of the inferences ourselves. The author seems to have disappeared, but that is an illusion. *Objective* in this narrator's label does not mean *without judgment*, for the author is in control, editing the tape and directing the camera. The limited omniscient version of "First Confession" has, towards the end, shifted to an objective point of view. The story concludes with dialogue—no comments, no inner thoughts. But the dialogue has been edited, and the camera director must shout "cut" at precisely the right moment. O'Connor has chosen to end with Nora's comment on being a sinner. We are left to ask ourselves why.

Although knowledge of the basic categories of point of view is useful, you should remember that one type of point of view may merge with another and that each work is a special case. Labeling the narrator is only the first step. You should go on to explore how the handling of point of view interacts with other elements to affect your understanding of the story.

To see more clearly the difference that selection of point of view can make, let us apply four different points of view to the same situation—a married couple, Harry and Alice, sitting at the breakfast table.

1. First Person

I knew as I watched Harry mindlessly burrowing into the sports section of the *News* that the moment had come to make a break for freedom. I had to say it. I had to say "Goodbye." He asked me to pass the jam, and I mechanically obliged. Had he noticed that my hand was trembling? Had he noticed my suitcase packed and beckoning in the hallway? Suddenly I pushed back my chair, choked out a rather faint "So long, Harry" through a last mouthful of toast, stumbled to my suitcase and out the door. As I drove away from the curb, I gave the house one last glance—just in time to see a sudden gust of wind hurl the still open door shut.

2. Limited Omniscient

Harry glanced quickly at the Cubs score only to be disappointed by another loss. They were already writing "wait till next year." It was just another bit of depression to add to his worries about the McVeigh contract. He wanted to tell Alice that his job was in danger, but all he could manage was a feeble "Pass me the jam." He didn't notice Alice's trembling hand or hear something faint she uttered. And when the door suddenly slammed he looked up, wondering who could be dropping by at seven in the morning. "Now where is that woman," he thought, as he trudged over, annoyed, to open the door. But the emptiness had already entered, drifting by him unnoticed, into the furthest reaches of the house.

3. Objective

A man and a woman sat at opposite sides of a chrome and vinyl dinette table. In the center of the table were a pot of coffee, a plate of toast, some butter, and some jam. Near the door stood a suitcase. The man was half hidden by the sports section of the morning paper. The woman was sitting tensely, staring at what she could see of her husband. "Pass the jam," he said. She passed him the jam, her hand trembling. Suddenly, she pushed back her chair, saying almost inaudibly, "So long,

Harry." She walked quickly to the suitcase, picked it up, and went out the door, leaving it open. A sudden gust of wind slammed it shut as Harry looked up with a puzzled expression on his face.

4. Omniscient

Sitting that morning at breakfast, Harry and Alice seemed perfectly matched, but in reality, they merely maintained marital harmony by avoiding bringing up anything unpleasant. Thus it was that Harry had not told Alice he was in danger of being fired, and Alice had not told Harry that she felt it necessary to go off on her own awhile to find out who she really was. As he glanced at the Cubs score, Harry thought, "Damn! Even baseball's getting depressing. They lost again. I wish I could manage to tell Alice about my losing the McVeigh contract—and just maybe my job!" Instead, he said, simply, "Pass the jam." As Alice complied, she saw that her hand was trembling. She wondered if Harry had noticed. "No matter," she thought, "This is it—the moment of goodbye, the break for freedom." She stood up and, with a half-whispered "So long, Harry," she walked to the suitcase, picked it up, and went out, leaving the door open. As the wind blew the door closed, neither knew that a few words from the heart that morning would have changed the course of their lives.

EXERCISE

1. What are some of the specific differences in these presentations that are the result of point of view selection? Note what is omitted in one version and included in another.

2. Draw a picture of the Harry and Alice scene to show where each type of narrator might be located.

3. Rewrite the first-person version of the Harry and Alice story from Harry's point of view. Rewrite the limited omniscient version from Alice's point of view.

4. Describe, from each of the four points of view, something that has recently taken place in your class.

5. Discuss the way a different point of view would affect one of the stories you have read. You might start with "Early Autumn" (pp. 31–32).

6. Rewrite Maugham's brief story "Appointment in Samarra" (p. 71), using each of the four points of view illustrated above.

POINT OF VIEW IN POETRY

Point of view in poetry is closely related to whether the form of presentation is narrative, lyric, or dramatic. The voice presenting the poem can be telling a story (narrative), revealing thoughts or emotions (lyric), or speaking to another character (dramatic). When discussing lyric or dramatic poetry, we call this voice the *speaker*. For narrative poetry, in which the speaker is a detached storyteller, we use the term *narrator*. As with fiction, you need to become aware of the nature of the point of view and its effect on the work.

The *lyric speaker* (or sometimes "singer") is usually responding inwardly to something: the sights and sounds of spring, the beauty of dark, snowy woods, an exciting translation of poetry. The basic questions to ask are: Who is responding to what? How? Why? Compare the speakers of the two lyrics that follow.

WILLIAM WORDSWORTH   (1770–1850)

She Dwelt Among the Untrodden Ways

She dwelt among the untrodden ways
  Beside the springs of Dove,
A Maid whom there were none to praise
  And very few to love;

A violet by a mossy stone   5
  Half hidden from the eye!
—Fair as a star, when only one
  Is shining in the sky.

She lived unknown, and few could know
  When Lucy ceased to be;   10
But she is in her grave, and, oh,
  The difference to me!

THEODORE ROETHKE   (1908–1963)

Elegy for Jane

My Student, Thrown by a Horse

I remember the neckcurls, limp and damp as tendrils;
And her quick look, a sidelong pickerel smile;
And how, once startled into talk, the light syllables leaped for her,
And she balanced in the delight of her thought,
A wren, happy, tail into the wind,   5
Her song trembling the twigs and small branches.
The shade sang with her;
The leaves, their whispers turned to kissing;
And the mold sang in the bleached valleys under the rose.

Oh, when she was sad, she cast herself down into such a pure depth,   10
Even a father could not find her:
Scraping her cheek against straw;
Stirring the clearest water.

My sparrow, you are not here,
Waiting like a fern, making a spiny shadow.   15
The sides of wet stones cannot console me,
Nor the moss, wound with the last light.

If only I could nudge you from this sleep,
My maimed darling, my skittery pigeon.
Over this damp grave I speak the words of my love: 20
I, with no rights in this matter,
Neither father nor lover.

QUESTIONS

1. What do we know about the speaker in each poem?
2. To what is each speaker responding?
3. What feelings about the situation does the speaker in each poem reveal?

A comparison of these two poems illustrates the effect of time and space on point of view. In the Wordsworth poem, space is important in that Lucy lived in a quiet, remote area where there are few to notice her absence. There is a sense of distance between the speaker and Lucy, but we don't know where the speaker is. The time, we can say, is after Lucy's death. The strength of the emotion suggests that she has not been dead for very many years, but the reflections leading up to the emotional last line seem too calm for a death about which the speaker has just been informed. By contrast, Roethke's speaker is given a specific physical vantage point—looking down on Jane's "damp grave." We share the immediacy of the concrete details of the "wet stones" and the "wound" moss. Because the speaker is still struggling with his emotions, we feel close in time to Jane's death.

You may have identified the speakers in these two poems as Wordsworth and Roethke—poets. Roethke's poem is addressed to "my student," and the mention of Lucy in Wordsworth's poem seems to call attention to a real person. But even if the speaker seems to be using the voice of the poet, you should usually think of that voice as a *persona*, a "mask" that an author wears to create an imagined author representative. The speaker in each poem is selected to create the voice that can best express a particular feeling about a particular subject. A different voice could have been selected. What would be the difference, for example, had Roethke made the speaker Jane's riding instructor instead of her teacher?

Another voice often found in poetry is that of the *dramatic speaker*. The dramatic speaker addresses one or more other characters and speaks in character to them. Sometimes, as in Robert Frost's "Home Burial" (p. 144), we hear the words of two or more characters speaking to each other. Often, as in the following poem, we hear only one character and are expected to imagine the replies and reactions of another.

JOHN DONNE (1572–1631)

The Flea

Mark but this flea, and mark in this
How little that which thou deny'st me is;
It sucked me first, and now sucks thee,
And in this flea our two bloods mingled be;
Thou know'st that this cannot be said   5
A sin, nor shame, nor loss of maidenhead;
   Yet this enjoys before it woo,

And pampered swells with one blood made of two,
And this, alas, is more than we would do.

Oh stay, three lives in one flea spare,   10
Where we almost, yea more than married are.
This flea is you and I, and this
Our marriage bed and marriage temple is;
Though parents grudge, and you, we are met
And cloistered in these living walls of jet.   15
   Though use make you apt to kill me,
   Let not to that, self-murder added be,
   And sacrilege, three sins in killing three.

Cruel and sudden, hast thou since
Purpled thy nail in blood of innocence?   20
Wherein could this flea guilty be,
Except in that drop which it sucked from thee?
Yet thou triumph'st and say'st that thou
Find'st not thyself, nor me the weaker now.
   'Tis true. Then learn how false fears be: 25
   Just so much honor, when thou yield'st to me,
   Will waste, as this flea's death took life from thee.

QUESTIONS

1. To whom does the "thou" in line 2 refer?
2. What is the speaker doing in the first stanza?
3. What has happened between the first stanza and the second? Between the second stanza and the third?
4. Paraphrase the speaker's argument.
5. What conclusions can we draw about the character of the speaker?

    A poem with a dramatic speaker requires that you become producer, director, and actor. Imagine staging a very short play called "The Flea." What would the actress do? What would be her gestures and facial expressions? How would the actor read his lines? In answering such questions, you should realize that your relationship with the poet has become more indirect than in either a narrative or a lyric poem. You must infer what happens to the flea and how the actor says "Oh stay" in line 10. Also, you should remember to judge the reliability of the dramatic speaker as a character possessing certain traits and influenced by circumstances and by other characters.

POINT OF VIEW IN DRAMA

The preceding discussion of dramatic poetry applies also to stage drama. Since plays are written to be performed, your role as reader is to recreate mentally a possible stage performance. That means imagining how the lines would be spoken—and much more. How would the actresses and actors move and look? What about lighting and props? Will there be sound effects?

With fiction or poetry the point of view is usually created through a single narrator or speaker. In drama, as in dramatic poetry involving more than one speaker, the presentation is normally divided among several characters. The author controls the point of view in much the same way as with the objective narrator of a story, by being selective. The characters tell their own story, but they do so only through words and actions chosen by the dramatist.

A few plays actually introduce a narrator who apparently represents the playwright to the audience. In Thornton Wilder's *Our Town* The Stage Manager introduces the people in the town to the audience. In Tennessee Williams's *The Glass Menagerie*, Laura's brother Tom is both a character and a commenator who presents the play. Similarly, a *chorus*, such as that in Sophocles's *Antigone* (pp. 613–645), can both participate in the drama—in this case as citizens of Thebes—and provide background and commentary. At the opening of *Antigone*, for example, the chorus describes the outcome of the battle for the city, philosophizes about pride, and serves as the audience for Creon's first speech. Such narrators in drama can give us an additional perspective, but we should remember that, to the extent that they are participants, there remains a question of reliability.

Most of the time the presentation of drama is through dialogue. Our knowledge of what happens and of what the characters are like emerges from the alternation of spoken lines. One character says, "Don't open that door." The other says, "I have to know what you've been keeping in that closet." The drama unfolds. Sometimes, the actors themselves tell a story. In Douglas Turner Ward's *Happy Ending* (pp. 103–116) the story of the marital troubles of the Harrisons is told entirely through the conversation of Ellie and Vi with their nephew Junie. In August Strindberg's *The Stronger* (pp. 147–151) the words of Mrs. X. gradually reveal her history and her relationship to Miss Y.

One way that dramatists actually can address us directly—but only if we are readers rather than theatergoers—is through stage directions. These directions can reveal setting, actions, and even character. Since the purpose of stage directions is to help the director and actors interpret, we do not need to assume an intervening voice between us and the author.* Some dramatists develop the directions to the point that the presentation approximates that of an omniscient narrator. Arthur Miller's *The Crucible,* for example, combines discussions of historical context with stage directions that even reveal the minds of the characters:

> The door opens, and his Negro slave enters. TITUBA is in her forties. PARRIS brought her with him from Barbados, where he spent some years as a merchant before entering the ministry. She enters as one does who can no longer bear to be barred from the sight of her beloved, but she is also very frightened because her slave sense has warned her that, as always, trouble in this house eventually lands on her back.

Here we are given background, an action, descriptive detail, and inner feeling. Such information should greatly enhance our imaginative reconstruction of a performance.

WRITING ABOUT POINT OF VIEW

If you are writing about point of view you will probably be discussing either (1) the reliability of the narrator or (2) the effect of the selection of point of view.

If you discuss reliability, you will need to focus on how the speaker's point of view differs from what you perceive to be true. In "Haircut," for example, we find that the barber who is telling the story of Jim Kendall admires Jim's jokes. But we see Jim's insensitive cruelty. Our writing challenge is to show how we have come to see Jim for what he is even though we have received all our information from a narrator who does not see Jim clearly. There seem to be two main reasons for our conclusions. First, the facts about Jim as reported by the barber give us a negative picture of Jim despite Whitey's enjoyment of Jim's humor. Second, the

---

* A word of caution: editions of some plays may contain directions inserted by editors. These are usually placed in brackets and should be treated as interpretations.

barber's own lack of sensitivity to the feelings of others leads us to question his conclusions. If the barber were more perceptive, we might accept his attitudes. If he hated Jim, we might suspect him of deviously trying to make Jim look bad. In writing on this topic, you would need to evaluate all evidence and to organize around the contrast between the reader's perception of Jim and the narrator's.

You might also write about the effect of point of view selection. Such an approach to Doris Lessing's "A Woman on a Roof" (pp. 32–40) might lead to this thesis: the use of a limited omniscient point of view in "A Woman on a Roof" allows us to see clearly the inner changes in Tom. Your purpose will then be to show the specific effects on Tom. Because we can enter his mind, we see his attempts to disassociate himself from the way his fellow workers react to the woman sunbathing on the roof. We see his fantasies about the woman. Finally, we see his shift to the attitude of the other men when the woman ignores him. Were we to know the thoughts of the other characters, we could be distracted from Tom's inner change, and he would become less important. Were we restricted to Tom's way of seeing things by use of the first person, we might lose our objectivity towards his thoughts about the woman and conclude that he is right to be angry at the end. These points could form the basis for an interesting analysis of Lessing's choice and handling of point of view.

RING LARDNER   (1885–1933)

Haircut

I got another barber that comes over from Carterville and helps me out Saturdays, but the rest of the time I can get along all right alone. You can see for yourself that this ain't no New York City and besides that, the most of the boys works all day and don't have no leisure to drop in here and get themselves prettied up.

You're a newcomer, ain't you? I thought I hadn't seen you round before. I hope you like it good enough to stay. As I say, we ain't no New York City or Chicago, but we have pretty good times. Not as good, though, since Jim Kendall got killed. When he was alive, him and Hod Meyers

used to keep this town in an uproar. I bet they was more laughin' done
here than any town its size in America.

Jim was comical, and Hod was pretty near a match for him. Since
Jim's gone, Hod tries to hold his end up just the same as ever, but it's
tough goin' when you ain't got nobody to kind of work with.

They used to be plenty fun in here Saturdays. This place is jam-
packed Saturdays, from four o'clock on. Jim and Hod would show up
right after their supper, round six o'clock. Jim would set himself down in
that big chair, nearest the blue spittoon. Whoever had been settin' in that
chair, why they'd get up when Jim come in and give it to him.

You'd of thought it was a reserved seat like they have sometimes in
a theayter. Hod would generally always stand or walk up and down, or
some Saturdays, of course, he'd be settin' in this chair part of the time,
gettin' a haircut.

Well, Jim would set there a w'ile without openin' his mouth only to
spit, and then finally he'd say to me, "Whitey,"—my right name, that is,
my right first name, is Dick, but everybody round here calls me Whitey—
Jim would say. "Whitey, your nose looks like a rosebud tonight. You must
of been drinkin' some of your aw de cologne."

So I'd say, "No, Jim, but you look like you'd been drinkin' somethin'
of that kind or somethin' worse."

Jim would have to laugh at that, but then he'd speak up and say,
"No. I ain't had nothin' to drink, but that ain't sayin' I wouldn't like
somethin.' I wouldn't even mind if it was wood alcohol."

Then Hod Meyers would say, "Neither would your wife." That would
set everybody to laughin' because Jim and his wife wasn't on very good
terms. She'd of divorced him only they wasn't no chance to get alimony
and she didn't have no way to take care of herself and the kids. She
couldn't never understand Jim. He *was* kind of rough, but a good fella at
heart.

Him and Hod had all kinds of sport with Milt Sheppard. I don't
suppose you've seen Milt. Well, he's got an Adam's apple that looks more
like a mushmelon. So I'd be shavin' Milt and when I'd start to shave down
here on his neck, Hod would holler, "Hey, Whitey, wait a minute! Before
you cut into it, let's make up a pool and see who can guess closest to the
number of seeds."

And Jim would say, "If Milt hadn't of been so hoggish, he'd of
ordered a half a cantaloupe instead of a whole one and it might not of
stuck in his throat."

All the boys would roar at this and Milt himself would force a smile,
though the joke was on him. Jim certainly was a card!

There's his shavin' mug, settin' on the shelf, right next to Charley
Vail's. "Charles M. Vail." That's the druggist. He comes in regular for his
shave, three times a week. And Jim's is the cup next to Charley's. "James

H. Kendall." Jim won't need no shavin' mug no more, but I'll leave it there just the same for old time's sake. Jim certainly was a character!

Years ago, Jim used to travel for a canned goods concern over in Carterville. They sold canned goods. Jim had the whole northern half of the State and was on the road five days out of every week. He'd drop in here Saturdays and tell his experiences for that week. It was rich.

I guess he paid more attention to playin' jokes than makin' sales. Finally the concern let him out and he come right home here and told everybody he'd been fired instead of sayin' he'd resigned like most fellas would of.

It was a Saturday and the shop was full and Jim got up out of that chair and says, "Gentlemen, I got an important announcement to make. I been fired from my job."

Well, they asked him if he was in earnest and he said he was and nobody could think of nothin' to say till Jim finally broke the ice himself. He says, "I been sellin' canned goods and now I'm canned goods myself."

You see, the concern he'd been workin' for was a factory that made canned goods. Over in Carterville. And now Jim said he was canned himself. He was certainly a card!

Jim had a great trick that he used to play w'ile he was travelin.' For instance, he'd be ridin' on a train and they'd come to some little town like, well like, we'll say, like Benton. Jim would look out the train window and read the signs on the stores.

For instance, they'd be a sign, "Henry Smith, Dry Goods." Well, Jim would write down the name and the name of the town and when he got to wherever he was goin' he'd mail back a postal card to Henry Smith at Benton and not sign no name to it, but he'd write on the card, well, somethin' like "Ask your wife about that book agent that spent the afternoon last week," or "Ask your Missus who kept her from gettin' lonesome the last time you was in Carterville." And he's sign the card, "A Friend."

Of course, he never knew what really come of none of these jokes, but he could picture what *probably* happened and that was enough.

Jim didn't work very steady after he lost his position with the Carterville people. What he did earn, doin' odd jobs round town, why he spent pretty near all of it on gin and his family might of starved if the stores hadn't of carried them along. Jim's wife tried her hand at dress-makin', but they ain't nobody goin' to get rich makin' dresses in this town.

As I say, she'd of divorced Jim, only she seen that she couldn't support herself and the kids and she was always hopin' that some day Jim would cut out his habits and give her more than two or three dollars a week.

They was a time when she would go to whoever he was workin' for and ask them to give her his wages, but after she done this once or twice, he beat her to it by borrowin' most of his pay in advance. He told it all round town, how he had outfoxed his Missus. He certainly was a caution!

But he wasn't satisfied with just outwittin' her. He was sore the way she had acted, tryin' to grab off his pay. And he made up his mind he'd get even. Well, he waited till Evans's Circus was advertised to come to town. Then he told his wife and two kiddies that he was goin' to take them to the circus. The day of the circus, he told them he would get the tickets and meet them outside the entrance to the tent.

Well, he didn't have no intentions of bein' there or buyin' tickets or nothin'. He got full of gin and laid round Wright's poolroom all day. His wife and the kids waited and waited and of course he didn't show up. His wife didn't have a dime with her, or nowhere else, I guess. So she finally had to tell the kids it was all off and they cried like they wasn't never goin' to stop.

Well, it seems, w'ile they was cryin', Doc Stair came along and he asked what was the matter, but Mrs. Kendall was stubborn and wouldn't tell him, but the kids told him and he insisted on takin' them and their mother in the show. Jim found this out afterwards and it was one reason why he had it in for Doc Stair.

Doc Stair come here about a year and a half ago. He's a mighty handsome young fella and his clothes always look like he has them made to order. He goes to Detroit two or three times a year and w'ile he's there he must have a tailor take his measure and then make him a suit to order. They cost pretty near twice as much, but they fit a whole lot better than if you just bought them in a store.

For a w'ile everybody was wonderin' why a young doctor like Doc Stair should come to a town like this where we already got old Doc Gamble and Doc Foote that's both been here for years and all the practice in town was always divided between the two of them.

Then they was a story got round that Doc Stair's gal had throwed him over, a gal up in the Northern Peninsula somewheres, and the reason he come here was to hide himself away and forget it. He said himself that he thought they wasn't nothin' like general practice in a place like ours to fit a man to be a good all round doctor. And that's why he'd came.

Anyways, it wasn't long before he was makin' enough to live on, though they tell me that he never dunned nobody for what they owed him, and the folks here certainly has got the owin' habit, even in my business. If I had all that was comin' to me for just shaves alone, I could go to Carterville and put up at the Mercer for a week and see a different picture every night. For instance, they's old George Purdy—but I guess I shouldn't ought to be gossipin'.

Well, last year, our coroner died, died of the flu. Ken Beatty, that was his name. He was the coroner. So they had to choose another man to be coroner in his place and they picked Doc Stair. He laughed at first and said he didn't want it, but they made him take it. It ain't no job that anybody would fight for and what a man makes out of it in a year would just about buy seeds for their garden. Doc's the kind, though, that can't say no to nothin' if you keep at him long enough.

But I was goin' to tell you about a poor boy we got here in town— Paul Dickson. He fell out of a tree when he was about ten years old. Lit on his head and it done somethin' to him and he ain't never been right. No harm in him, but just silly. Jim Kendall used to call him cuckoo; that's a name Jim had for anybody that was off their head, only he called people's head their bean. That was another of his gags, callin' head bean and callin' crazy people cuckoo. Only poor Paul ain't crazy, but just silly.

You can imagine that Jim used to have all kinds of fun with Paul. He'd send him to the White Front Garage for a left-handed monkey wrench. Of course they ain't no such a thing as a left-handed monkey wrench.

And once we had a kind of a fair here and they was a baseball game between the fats and the leans and before the game started Jim called Paul over and sent him way down to Schrader's hardware store to get a key for the pitcher's box.

They wasn't nothin' in the way of gags that Jim couldn't think up, when he put his mind to it.

Poor Paul was always kind of suspicious of people, maybe on account of how Jim had kept foolin' him. Paul wouldn't have much to do with anybody only his own mother and Doc Stair and a girl here in town named Julie Gregg. That is, she ain't a girl no more, but pretty near thirty or over.

When Doc first come to town, Paul seemed to feel like here was a real friend and he hung around Doc's office most of the w'ile; the only time he wasn't there was when he'd go home to eat or sleep or when he seen Julie Gregg doin' her shoppin'.

When he looked out Doc's window and seen her, he'd run downstairs and join her and tag along with her to the different stores. The poor boy was crazy about Julie and she always treated him mighty nice and made him feel like he was welcome, though of course it wasn't nothin' but pity on her side.

Doc done all he could to improve Paul's mind and he told me once that he really thought the boy was gettin' better, that they was times when he was as bright and sensible as anybody else.

But I was goin' to tell you about Julie Gregg. Old Man Gregg was in the lumber business, but got to drinkin' and lost the most of his money and when he died, he didn't leave nothin' but the house and just enough insurance for the girl to skimp along on.

Her mother was a kind of a half invalid and didn't hardly ever leave the house. Julie wanted to sell the place and move somewheres else after the old man died, but the mother said she was born here and would die here. It was tough on Julie, as the young people round this town— well, she's too good for them.

She's been away to school and Chicago and New York and different places and they ain't no subject she can't talk on, where you take the rest of the young folks here and you mention anything to them outside of Gloria Swanson or Tommy Meighan and they think you're delirious. Did you see Gloria in Wages of Virtue? You missed somethin'!

Well, Doc Stair hadn't been here more than a week when he come in one day to get shaved and I recognized who he was as he had been pointed out to me, so I told him about my old lady. She's been ailin' for a couple of years and either Doc Gamble or Doc Foote, neither one, seemed to be helpin' her. So he said he would come out and see her, but if she was able to get out herself, it would be better to bring her to his office where he could make a completer examination.

So I took her to his office and w'ile I was waitin' for her in the reception room, in come Julie Gregg. When somebody comes in Doc Stair's office, they's a bell that rings in his inside office so as he can tell they's somebody to see him.

So he left my old lady inside and come out to the front office and that's the first time him and Julie met and I guess it was what they call love at first sight. But it wasn't fifty-fifty. This young fella was the slickest lookin' fella she'd ever seen in this town and she went wild over him. To him she was just a young lady that wanted to see the doctor.

She'd came on about the same business I had. Her mother had been doctorin' for years with Doc Gamble and Doc Foote and without no results. So she'd heard they was a new doc in town and decided to give him a try. He promised to call and see her mother that same day.

I said a minute ago that it was love at first sight on her part. I'm not only judgin' by how she acted afterwards but how she looked at him that first day in his office. I ain't no mind reader, but it was wrote all over her face that she was gone.

Now Jim Kendall, besides bein' a jokesmith and a pretty good drinker, well, Jim was quite a lady-killer. I guess he run pretty wild durin' the time he was on the road for them Carterville people, and besides that, he'd had a couple little affairs of the heart right here in town. As I say, his wife could of divorced him, only she couldn't.

But Jim was like the majority of men, and women, too, I guess. He wanted what he couldn't get. He wanted Julie Gregg and worked his head off tryin' to land her. Only he'd of said bean instead of head.

Well, Jim's habits and his jokes didn't appeal to Julie and of course he was a married man, so he didn't have no more chance than, well, than a rabbit. That's an expression of Jim's himself. When somebody didn't have no chance to get elected or somethin', Jim would always say they didn't have no more chance than a rabbit.

He didn't make no bones about how he felt. Right in here, more than once, in front of the whole crowd, he said he was stuck on Julie and anybody that could get her for him was welcome to his house and his wife and kids included. But she wouldn't have nothin' to do with him; wouldn't even speak to him on the street. He finally seen he wasn't gettin' nowheres with his usual line so he decided to try the rough stuff. He went right up to her house one evenin' and when she opened the door he forced his way in and grabbed her. But she broke loose and before he could stop her, she run in the next room and locked the door and phoned to Joe Barnes. Joe's the marshal. Jim could hear who she was phonin' to and he beat it before Joe got there.

Joe was an old friend of Julie's pa. Joe went to Jim the next day and told him what would happen if he ever done it again.

I don't know how the news of this little affair leaked out. Chances is that Joe Barnes told his wife and she told somebody else's wife and they told their husband. Anyways, it did leak out and Hod Meyers had the nerve to kid Jim about it, right here in this shop. Jim didn't deny nothin' and kind of laughed it off and said for us all to wait; that lots of people had tried to make a monkey out of him, but he always got even.

Meanw'ile everybody in town was wise to Julie's bein' wild mad over the Doc. I don't suppose she had any idear how her face changed when him and her was together; of course she couldn't of, or she'd of kept away from him. And she didn't know that we was all noticin' how many times she made excuses to go up to his office or pass it on the other side of the street and look up in his window to see if he was there. I felt sorry for her and so did most other people.

Hod Meyers kept rubbin' it into Jim about how the Doc had cut him out. Jim didn't pay no attention to the kiddin' and you could see he was plannin' one of his jokes.

One trick Jim had was the knack of changin' his voice. He could make you think he was a girl talkin' and he could mimic any man's voice. To show you how good he was along this line, I'll tell you the joke he played on me once.

You know, in most towns of any size, when a man is dead and needs a shave, why the barber that shaves him soaks him five dollars for the job; that is, he don't soak *him*, but whoever ordered the shave. I just charge three dollars because personally I don't mind much shavin' a dead person. They lay a whole lot stiller than live customers. The only thing is that you don't feel like talkin' to them and you get kind of lonesome.

Well, about the coldest day we ever had here, two years ago last winter, the phone rung at the house w'ile I was home to dinner and I answered the phone and it was a woman's voice and she said she was Mrs. John Scott and her husband was dead and would I come out and shave him.

Old John had always been a good customer of mine. But they live seven miles out in the country, on the Streeter road. Still I didn't see how I could say no.

So I said I would be there, but would have to come in a jitney and it might cost three or four dollars besides the price of the shave. So she, or the voice, it said that was all right, so I got Frank Abott to drive me out to the place and when I got there, who should open the door but old John himself! He wasn't no more dead than, well, than a rabbit.

It didn't take no private detective to figure out who had played me this little joke. Nobody could of thought it up but Jim Kendall. He certainly was a card!

I tell you this incident just to show you how he could disguise his voice and make you believe it was somebody else talkin'. I'd of swore it was Mrs. Scott had called me. Anyways, some woman.

Well, Jim waited till he had Doc Stair's voice down pat; then he went after revenge.

He called Julie up on a night when he knew Doc was over in Carterville. She never questioned but what it was Doc's voice. Jim said he must see her that night; he couldn't wait no longer to tell her somethin'. She was all excited and told him to come to the house. But he said he was expectin' an important long distance call and wouldn't she please forget her manners for once and come to his office. He said they couldn't nothin' hurt her and nobody would see her and he just *must* talk to her a little w'ile. Well, poor Julie fell for it.

Doc always keeps a night light in his office, so it looked to Julie like they was somebody there.

Meanw'ile Jim Kendall had went to Wright's poolroom, where they was a whole gang amusin' themselves. The most of them had drank plenty of gin, and they was a rough bunch even when sober. They was always strong for Jim's jokes and when he told them to come with him and see some fun they give up their card games and pool games and followed along.

Doc's office is on the second floor. Right outside his door they's a flight of stairs leadin' to the floor above. Jim and his gang hid in the dark behind these stairs.

Well, Julie come up to Doc's door and rung the bell and they was nothin' doin'. She rung it again and rung it seven or eight times. Then she tried the door and found it locked. Then Jim made some kind of a noise and she heard it and waited a minute, and then she says, "Is that you, Ralph?" Ralph is Doc's first name.

They was no answer and it must of came to her all of a sudden that she'd been bunked. She pretty near fell downstairs and the whole gang after her. They chased her all the way home, hollerin', "Is that you, Ralph?" and "Oh, Ralphie, dear, is that you?" Jim says he couldn't holler it himself, as he was laughin' too hard.

Poor Julie! She didn't show up here on Main Street for a long, long time afterward.

And of course Jim and his gang told everybody in town, everybody but Doc Stair. They was scared to tell him, and he might of never knowed only for Paul Dickson. The poor cuckoo, as Jim called him, he was here in the shop one night when Jim was still gloatin' yet over what he'd done to Julie. And Paul took in as much of it as he could understand and he run to Doc with the story.

It's a cinch Doc went up in the air and swore he'd make Jim suffer. But it was a kind of a delicate thing, because if it got out that he had beat Jim up, Julie was bound to hear of it and then she'd know that Doc knew and of course knowin' that he knew would make it worse for her than ever. He was goin' to do somethin', but it took a lot of figurin'.

Well, it was a couple days later when Jim was here in the shop again, and so was the cuckoo. Jim was goin' duck-shootin' the next day and had came in lookin' for Hod Meyers to go with him. I happened to know that Hod had went over to Carterville and wouldn't be home till the end of the week. So Jim sad he hated to go alone and he guessed he would call it off. Then poor Paul spoke up and said if Jim would take him he would go along. Jim thought a w'ile and then he said, well, he guessed a half-wit was better than nothin'.

I suppose he was plottin' to get Paul out in the boat and play some joke on him, like pushin' him in the water. Anyways, he said Paul could go. He asked him had he ever shot a duck and Paul said no, he'd never even had a gun in his hands. So Jim said he could set in the boat and watch him and if he behaved himself, he might lend him his gun for a couple of shots. They made a date to meet in the mornin' and that's the last I seen of Jim alive.

Next mornin', I hadn't been open more than ten minutes when Doc Stair come in. He looked kind of nervous. He asked me had I seen Paul Dickson. I said no, but I knew where he was, out duck-shootin' with Jim Kendall. So Doc says that's what he had heard, and he couldn't understand it because Paul had told him he wouldn't never have no more to do with Jim as long as he lived.

He said Paul had told him about the joke Jim had played on Julie: He said Paul had asked him what he thought of the joke and the Doc had told him that anybody that would do a thing like that ought not to be let live.

I said it had been a kind of a raw thing, but Jim just couldn't resist no kind of a joke, no matter how raw. I said I thought he was all right at heart, but just bubblin' over with mischief. Doc turned and walked out.

At noon he got a phone call from old John Scott. The lake where Jim and Paul had went shootin' is on John's place. Paul had come runnin' up to the house a few minutes before and said they'd been an accident.

Jim had shot a few ducks and then give the gun to Paul and told him to try his luck. Paul hadn't never handled a gun and he was nervous. He was shakin' so hard that he couldn't control the gun. He let fire and Jim sunk back in the boat, dead.

Doc Stair, bein' the coroner, jumped in Frank Abbott's flivver and rushed out to Scott's farm. Paul and old John was down on the shore of the lake. Paul had rowed the boat to shore, but they'd left the body in it, waitin' for Doc to come.

Doc examined the body and said they might as well fetch it back to town. They was no use leavin' it there or callin' a jury, as it was a plain case of accidental shootin'.

Personally I wouldn't leave a person shoot a gun in the same boat I was in unless I was sure they knew somethin' about guns. Jim was a sucker to leave a new beginner have his gun, let alone a half-wit. It probably served Jim right, what he got. But still we miss him round here. He certainly was a card!

Comb it wet or dry?

QUESTIONS

1. How does the barber's language affect our response to what he tells us?

2. How do our feelings about the minor characters (Doc Stair, Julie, Paul, Hod) affect our response to the barber and to Jim?

3. How has the barber received his information? How much is firsthand? How much secondhand? Has all of the information come to him in the barber shop?

4. Assume that you are conducting an inquiry into the death of Jim. How would you evaluate the barber's testimony?

5. What do we learn about the town and its inhabitants?

6. What do we learn about the barber's values and interests?

STUDENT ESSAY

A Barber's Chair Perspective

Mark Yatsko

We are all familiar with the small town prater whose recounting of events great or small is surely open to endless interpretation. In his story "Haircut," Ring Lardner gives an account of one such person, the town barber, Whitey. The barber's recollection of the circumstances of Jim Kendall's death leads us to question Whitey's reliability. Is his narration objective, or does he slant the story? How does Lardner use Whitey to reveal Whitey's true personality and his attitude towards the other characters?

We initially have reservations about Whitey due to his colloquial speech. Throughout the story his diction and grammar are poor, leading often to barely comprehensible sentences. "It's tough goin' when you ain't got nobody to kind of work with" and "then they was a good story got round that Doc Stair's gal had throwed him over" indicate the low intellectual level of Whitey. Not only his language, but the way he empha- sizes obvious points to the newcomer reveals his ignorance. Jim's canned goods joke about being fired requires no explanation, but we get one from Whitey anyway.

We also question Whitey's tendency to make biased generalizations about people. The barber twists the statements and actions of the major characters. He says that if Julie Gregg knew how her face changed when she and Doc Stair were together, then "she'd of kept away from," but he never mentions conversing with Julie to see if she really cared that her face changed. Later he states that "it's a cinch Doc Stair went up in the air and swore he'd make Jim suffer." Again, Whitey cites no evidence

STUDENT ESSAY

that this was truly Doc Stair's reaction. Whitey also misreads Julie's friendship for Paul as "nothin' but pity."

These misinterpretations by Whitey lead us to a central conflict in the story. Whitey denigrates the characters of Doc Stair, Julie Gregg, and Paul Dickson, while admiring that of Jim Kendall. He does this because he recognizes traits in Kendall that he wishes he possessed. Thus, while slyly hinting at the failings of the other three, he is unable to criticize the appalling actions of Jim. Doc Stair is in the town because he was jilted by his girl in the Northern Peninsula and has come to hide and forget the past. Paul Dickson is always "Poor Paul" who "ain't never been right." Julie Gregg "ain't a girl no more, but pretty near thirty or over." These references convey a contempt for the actions of Paul, Julie, and Doc.

On the other hand, every explanation of Jim's behavior shows Whitey to be unknowingly projecting himself into Kendall's "adventures." Admiration is demonstrated when the barber leaves Jim's shaving mug on the shelf "for old time's sake." Whitey aspires to Kendall's boldness, cleverness, and sexual exploits. Jim's coming into the barber shop to say that he had been fired, instead of announcing that he resigned, is proof to Whitey of Jim's fearlessness towards others' opinions. Conversely, Whitey is very sensitive to others' opinions. Otherwise, he wouldn't go to such lengths to clarify all his statements about everyone to the newcomer. The numerous anecdotes, such as the one about Jim's instructions to Paul to fetch a left-handed monkey wrench, as well as Whitey's defense of Jim in every situation, serve to exhibit his idolization. He thoroughly enjoys talking about Kendall's "affairs of the heart" on the road (and in town). Further evidence of his awe for Kendall is Whitey's copying of Jim's manner of speech. Whitey remembers to use

STUDENT ESSAY

"bean," not "head," and, when relating the grotesque story of shaving the dead, he uses one of Jim's expressions in saying that old John "wasn't no more dead than, well, than a rabbit." He consistently contradicts himself about Jim's behavior. For instance, Whitey admits that it was "kind of a raw thing" to play the joke on Julie at Doc's office, but Jim was "all right at heart, just bubblin' over with mischief." Right to the end of the story we see Whitey's affinity for Jim as he repeats: "He certainly was a card."

Whitey's undiscerning mind fails to grasp the plain fact that Paul intentionally killed Jim Kendall. The reader sees the situation objectively (so Lardner hopes) and will conclude that Whitey is short-sighted in his account of the incident. Lardner makes effective use of the barber's narration to divulge the callous attitude in Whitey as typical of people in this type of rural, small-town environment. Whitey reveals more of his character to the newcomer (reader) than he realizes. We see how he is projecting Jim's adventures into his own life to overcome his inadequacies. There are two reasons for Lardner's choice of Whitey as the speaker best suited for his exposé of character. First, the barber has no personal involvement in the incident; more importantly, though, is the purpose to unmask society's commonplace and cruel toleration of inhumanity. Lardner shows his outrage through Whitey. Kendall is a vicious character, but Whitey, as a reflection of his community, refuses to acknowledge the crudeness of Kendall's behavior, even though the evidence is obvious. Through Whitey's narration, Lardner adds force and realism to his indictment of a society that produces people like Whitey and Jim. Another point of view would have lessened the impact of Whitey's irrationality because we would not have had access to Whitey's psyche.

STUDENT ESSAY

The reader views the functioning of Whitey's mind and sees why he has such distorted values. We are required to make the judgments Whitey won't make.

Thus Lardner's exposé of character flaws in Whitey is achieved by the technique of point of view in which the main character is unwittingly revealing his shortcomings throughout his narration. The strong emotional reactions by readers to this story demonstrate the effectiveness of this technique. Lardner has convincingly shown his contempt for the deplorable condition of segments of American society in his era.

SELECTIONS FOR FURTHER STUDY

ROBERT BROWNING   (1812–1889)

My Last Duchess

Ferrara

That's my last Duchess painted on the wall,
Looking as if she were alive. I call
That piece a wonder, now; Frà Pandolf's° hands
Worked busily a day, and there she stands.
Will 't please you sit and look at her? I said   5
"Frà Pandolf" by design, for never read
Strangers like you that pictured countenance,
The depth and passion of its earnest glance,
But to myself they turned (since none puts by
The curtain I have drawn for you, but I)   10
And seemed as they would ask me, if they durst,
How such a glance came there; so, not the first
Are you to turn and ask thus. Sir, 'twas not
Her husband's presence only, called that spot

---

3. *Frà Pandolf*: fictitious painter.

Of joy into the Duchess' cheek; perhaps   15
Frà Pandolf chanced to say, "Her mantle laps
Over my lady's wrist too much," or "Paint
Must never hope to reproduce the faint
Half-flush that dies along her throat." Such stuff
Was courtesy, she thought, and cause enough   20
For calling up that spot of joy. She had
A heart—how shall I say?—too soon made glad,
Too easily impressed; she liked whate'er
She looked on, and her looks went everywhere.
Sir, 'twas all one! My favor at her breast,   25
The dropping of the daylight in the West,
The bough of cherries some officious fool
Broke in the orchard for her, the white mule
She rode with round the terrace—all and each
Would draw from her alike the approving speech,   30
Or blush, at least. She thanked men—good! but thanked
Somehow—I know not how—as if she ranked
My gift of a nine-hundred-years' old name
With anybody's gift. Who'd stoop to blame
This sort of trifling? Even had you skill   35
In speech—which I have not—to make your will
Quite clear to such an one, and say "Just this
Or that in you disgusts me; here you miss,
Or there exceed the mark"—and if she let
Herself be lessoned so, nor plainly set   40
Her wits to yours, forsooth, and made excuse—
E'en then would be some stooping; and I choose
Never to stoop. Oh, sir, she smiled, no doubt,
Whene'er I passed her; but who passed without
Much the same smile? This grew; I gave commands;   45
Then all smiles stopped together. There she stands
As if alive. Will 't please you rise? We'll meet
The company below, then. I repeat,
The Count your master's known munificence
Is ample warrant that no just pretense   50
Of mine for dowry will be disallowed;
Though his fair daughter's self, as I avowed
At starting, is my object. Nay, we'll go
Together down, sir. Notice Neptune, though,
Taming a sea-horse, thought a rarity,   55
Which Claus of Innsbruck° cast in bronze for me!

56. *Claus of Innsbruck*: fictitious sculptor.

QUESTIONS

1. Who is speaking? To whom? Where? What has brought them together?
2. What is the attitude of the Duke toward his last Duchess?
3. What does the way the Duke expresses his attitude tell us about him? List the Duke's dominant character traits.
4. What are the facts we learn about the Duchess? Do we interpret them in the same say the Duke does?
5. Why has Browning chosen to begin and end this poem with the Duke pointing to a work of art?
6. How is the problem of reliability similar in this poem to that in "Haircut"? What literary technique is used?

FRANK O'CONNOR   (1903–1966)

First Confession (limited omniscient version)

It was a Saturday afternoon in early spring. A small boy whose face looked as though it had been but newly scrubbed was being led by the hand by his sister through a crowded street. The little boy showed a marked reluctance to proceed; he affected to be very interested in the shop-windows. Equally, his sister seemed to pay no attention to them. She tried to hurry him; he resisted. When she dragged him he began to bawl. The hatred with which she viewed him was almost diabolical, but when she spoke her words and tone were full of passionate sympathy.

"Ah, sha, God help us!" she intoned into his ear in a whine of commiseration.

"Leave me go!" he said, digging his heels into the pavement. "I don't want to go. I want to go home."

"But, sure, you can't go home, Jackie. You'll have to go. The parish priest will be up to the house with a stick."

"I don't care. I won't go."

"Oh, Sacred Heart, isn't it a terrible pity you weren't a good boy? Oh, Jackie, me heart bleeds for you! I don't know what they'll do to you at all, Jackie, me poor child. And all the trouble you caused your poor old nanny, and the way you wouldn't eat in the same room with her, and the time you kicked her on the shins, and the time you went for me with the bread knife under the table. I don't know will he ever listen to you at all, Jackie. I think meself he might sind you to the bishop. Oh, Jackie, how will you think of all your sins?"

Half stupefied with terror, Jackie allowed himself to be led through the sunny streets to the very gates of the church. It was an old one with two grim iron gates and a long, low, shapeless stone front. At the gates he stuck, but it was already too late. She dragged him behind her across the yard, and the commiserating whine with which she had tried to madden him gave place to a yelp of triumph.

"Now you're caught! Now, you're caught. And I hope he'll give you the pinitintial psalms! That'll cure you, you suppurating little caffler!"

Jackie gave himself up for lost. Within the old church there was no stained glass; it was cold and dark and desolate, and in the silence, the trees in the yard knocked hollowly at the tall windows. He allowed himself to be led through the vaulted silence, the intense and magical silence which seemed to have frozen within the ancient walls, buttressing them and shouldering the high wooden roof. In the street outside, yet seeming a million miles away, a ballad singer was drawling a ballad.

Nora sat in front of him beside the confession box. There were a few old women before her, and later a thin, sad-looking man with long hair came and sat beside Jackie. In the intense silence of the church that seemed to grow deeper from the plaintive moaning of the ballad singer, he could hear the buzz-buzz-buzz of a woman's voice in the box, and then the husky ba-ba-ba of the priest's. Lastly the soft thud of something that signalled the end of the confession, and out came the woman, head lowered, hands joined, looking neither to right nor left, and tiptoed up to the altar to say her penance.

It seemed only a matter of seconds till Nora rose and with a whispered injunction disappeared from his sight. He was all alone. Alone and next to be heard and the fear of damnation in his soul. He looked at the sadfaced man. He was gazing at the roof, his hands joined in prayer. A woman in a red blouse and black shawl had taken her place below him. She uncovered her head, fluffed her hair out roughly with her hand, brushed it sharply back, then, bowing, caught it in a knot and pinned it on her neck. Nora emerged. Jackie rose and looked at her with a hatred which was inappropriate to the occasion and the place. Her hands were joined on her stomach, her eyes modestly lowered, and her face had an expression of the most rapt and tender recollection. With death in his heart he crept into the compartment she left open and drew the door shut behind him.

He was in pitch darkness. He could see no priest nor anything else. And anything he had heard of confession got all muddled up in his mind. He knelt to the right-hand wall and said: "Bless me, father, for I have sinned. This is my first confession." Nothing happened. He repeated it louder. Still it gave no answer. He turned to the opposite wall, genuflected first, then again went on his knees and repeated the charm. This time he was certain he would receive a reply, but none came. He repeated the process with the remaining wall without effect. He had the feeling of someone with an unfamiliar machine, of pressing buttons at random. And finally the thought struck him that God knew. God knew about the bad confession he intended to make and had made him deaf and blind so that he could neither hear nor see the priest.

Then as his eyes grew accustomed to the blackness, he perceived something he had not noticed previously: a sort of shelf at about the height of his head. The purpose of this eluded him for a moment. Then he understood. It was for kneeling on.

He had always prided himself upon his powers of climbing, but this took it out of him. There was no foothold. He slipped twice before he succeeded in getting his knee on it, and the strain of drawing the rest of his body up was almost more than he was capable of. However, he did at last get his two knees on it, there was just room for those, but his legs hung down uncomfortably and the edge of the shelf bruised his shins. He joined his hands and pressed the last remaining button. "Bless me, father, for I have sinned. This is my first confession."

At the same moment the slide was pushed back and a dim light streamed into the little box. There was an uncomfortable silence, and then an alarmed voice asked "Who's there?" Jackie found it almost impossible to speak into the grille which was on a level with his knees, but he got a firm grip of the molding above it, bent his head down and sideways, and as though he were hanging by his feet like a monkey found himself looking almost upside down at the priest. But the priest was looking sideways at him, and Jackie, whose knees were being tortured by this new position, felt it was a queer way to hear confessions.

"'Tis me, father," he piped, and then, running all his words together in excitement, he rattled off, "Bless me, father, for I have sinned. This is my first confession."

"What?" exclaimed a deep and angry voice, and the sombre soutane figure stood bolt upright, disappearing almost entirely from Jackie's view. "What does this mean? What are you doing there? Who are you?"

And with the shock Jackie felt his hands lose their grip and his legs their balance. He discovered himself tumbling into space, and, falling, he knocked his head against the door, which shot open and permitted him to thump right into the center of the aisle. Straight on this came a small, dark-haired priest with a biretta well forward on his head. At the same time Nora came skeltering madly down the church.

"Lord God!" she cried. "The snivelling little caffler! I knew he'd do it! I knew he'd disgrace me!"

Jackie received a clout over the ear which reminded him that for some strange reason he had not yet begun to cry and that people might possibly think he wasn't hurt at all. Nora slapped him again.

"What's this? What's this?" cried the priest. "Don't attempt to beat the child, you little vixen!"

"I can't do me pinance with him," cried Nora shrilly, cocking a shocked eye on the priest. "He have me driven mad. Stop your crying, you dirty scut! Stop it now or I'll make you cry at the other side of your ugly puss!"

"Run away out of this, you little jade!" growled the priest. He suddenly began to laugh, took out a pocket handkerchief, and wiped Jackie's nose. "You're not hurt, sure you're not. Show us the ould head. . . . Ah, 'tis nothing. 'Twill be better before you're twice married. . . . So you were coming to confession?"

"I was, father."

"A big fellow like you should have terrible sins. Is it your first?"

"'Tis, father."

"Oh, my, worse and worse! Here, sit down there and wait till I get rid of these ould ones and we'll have a long chat. Never mind that sister of yours."

With a feeling of importance that glowed through his tears Jackie waited. Nora stuck out her tongue at him, but he didn't even bother to reply. A great feeling of relief was welling up in him. The sense of oppression that had been weighing him down for a week, the knowledge that he was about to make a bad confession, disappeared. Bad confession, indeed! He had made friends, made friends with the priest, and the priest expected, even demanded terrible sins. Oh, women! Women! It was all women and girls and their silly talk. They had no real knowledge of the world!

And when the time came for him to make his confession he did not beat about the bush. He may have clenched his hands and lowered his eyes, but wouldn't anyone?

"Father," he said huskily, "I made it up to kill me grandmother."

There was a moment's pause. Jackie did not dare to look up, but he could feel the priest's eyes on him. The priest's voice also seemed a trifle husky.

"Your grandmother?" he asked, but he didn't after all sound very angry.

"Yes, father."

"Does she live with you?"

"She do, father."

"And why did you want to kill her?"

"Oh, God, father, she's a horrible woman!"

"Is she now?"

"She is, father."

"What way is she horrible?"

Jackie paused to think. It was hard to explain.

"She takes snuff, father."

"Oh, my!"

"And she goes round in her bare feet, father."

"Tut-tut-tut!"

"She's a horrible woman, father," said Jackie with sudden earnestness. "She takes porter. And she ates the potatoes off the table with her hands. And me mother do be out working most days, and since that one came 'tis she gives us our dinner and I can't ate the dinner." He found himself sniffling. "And she gives pinnies to Nora and she doesn't give no pinnies to me because she knows I can't stand her. And me father sides with her, father, and he bates me, and me heart is broken and wan night in bed I made it up the way I'd kill her."

Jackie began to sob again, rubbing his nose with his sleeve, as he remembered his wrongs.

"And what way were you going to kill her?" asked the priest smoothly.

"With a hatchet, father."

"When she was in bed?"

"No, father."

"How, so?"

"When she ates the potatoes and drinks the porter she falls asleep, father."

"And you'd hit her then?"

"Yes, father."

"Wouldn't a knife be better?"

"'Twould, father, only I'd be afraid of the blood."

"Oh, of course. I never thought of the blood."

"I'd be afraid of that, father. I was near hitting Nora with the bread knife one time she came after me under the table, only I was afraid."

"You're a terrible child," said the priest with awe.

"I am, father," said Jackie noncommittally, sniffling back his tears.

"And what would you do with the body?"

"How, father?"

"Wouldn't someone see her and tell?"

"I was going to cut her up with a knife and take away the pieces and bury them. I could get an orange box for threepence and make a cart to take them away."

"My, my," said the priest. "You had it all well planned."

"Ah, I tried that," said Jackie with mounting confidence. "I borrowed a cart and practised it by meself one night after dark."

"And weren't you afraid?"

"Ah, no," said Jackie half-heartedly. "Only a bit."

"You have terrible courage," said the priest. "There's a lot of people I want to get rid of, but I'm not like you. I'd never have the courage. And hanging is an awful death."

"Is it?" asked Jackie, responding to the brightness of a new theme.

"Oh, an awful blooming death!"

"Did you ever see a fellow hanged?"

"Dozens of them, and they all died roaring."

"Jay!" said Jackie.

"They do be swinging out of them for hours and the poor fellows lepping and roaring, like bells in a belfry, and then they put lime on them to burn them up. Of course, they pretend they're dead but sure, they don't be dead at all."

"Jay!" said Jackie again.

"So if I were you I'd take my time and think about it. In my opinion 'tisn't worth it, not even to get rid of a grandmother. I asked dozens of fellows like you that killed their grandmothers about it, and they all said, no, 'twasn't worth it . . ."

Nora was waiting in the yard. The sunlight struck down on her across the high wall and its brightness made his eyes dazzle. "Well?" she asked. "What did he give you?"

"Three Hail Marys."

"You mustn't have told him anything."

"I told him everything," said Jackie confidently.

"What did you tell him?"

"Things you don't know."

"Bah! He gave you three Hail Marys because you were a cry baby!"

Jackie didn't mind. He felt the world was very good. He began to whistle as well as the hindrance in his jaw permitted.

"What are you sucking?"

"Bull's eyes."

"Was it he gave them to you?"

"'Twas."

"Almighty God!" said Nora. "Some people have all the luck. I might as well be a sinner like you. There's no use in being good."

FRANK O'CONNOR   (1903–1966)

First Confession (first-person version)

All the trouble began when my grandfather died and my grandmother— my father's mother—came to live with us. Relations in the one house are a strain at the best of times, but, to make matters worse, my grandmother was a real old countrywoman and quite unsuited to the life in town. She had a fat, wrinkled old face, and, to Mother's great indignation, went round the house in bare feet—the boots had her crippled, she said. For dinner she had a jug of porter and a pot of potatoes with—sometimes—

a bit of salt fish, and she poured out the potatoes on the table and ate them slowly, with great relish, using her fingers by way of a fork.

Now, girls are supposed to be fastidious, but I was the one who suffered most from this. Nora, my sister, just sucked up to the old woman for the penny she got every Friday out of the old-age pension, a thing I could not do. I was too honest, that was my trouble; and when I was playing with Bill Connell, the sergeant-major's son, and saw my grandmother steering up the path with the jug of porter sticking out from beneath her shawl I was mortified. I made excuses not to let him come into the house, because I could never be sure what she would be up to when we went in.

When Mother was at work and my grandmother made the dinner I wouldn't touch it. Nora once tried to make me, but I hid under the table from her and took the bread-knife with me for protection. Nora let on to be very indignant (she wasn't, of course, but she knew Mother saw through her, so she sided with Gran) and came after me. I lashed out at her with the bread-knife, and after that she left me alone. I stayed there till Mother came in from work and made my dinner, but when Father came in later Nora said in a shocked voice: "Oh, Dadda, do you know what Jackie did at dinnertime?" Then, of course, it all came out; Father gave me a flaking; Mother interfered, and for days after that he didn't speak to me and Mother barely spoke to Nora. And all because of that old woman! God knows, I was heart-scalded.

Then, to crown my misfortunes, I had to make my first confession and communion. It was an old woman called Ryan who prepared us for these. She was about the one age with Gran; she was well-to-do, lived in a big house on Montenotte, wore a black cloak and bonnet, and came every day to school at three o'clock when we should have been going home, and talked to us of hell. She may have mentioned the other place as well, but that could only have been by accident, for hell had the first place in her heart.

She lit a candle, took out a new half-crown, and offered it to the first boy who would hold one finger—only one finger!—in the flame for five minutes by the school clock. Being always very ambitious I was tempted to volunteer, but I thought it might look greedy. Then she asked were we afraid of holding one finger—only one finger!—in a little candle flame for five minutes and not afraid of burning all over in roasting hot furnaces for all eternity. "All eternity! Just think of that! A whole lifetime goes by and it's nothing, not even a drop in the ocean of your sufferings." The woman was really interesting about hell, but my attention was all fixed on the half-crown. At the end of the lesson she put it back in her purse. It was a great disappointment; a religious woman like that, you wouldn't think she'd bother about a thing like a half-crown.

Another day she said she knew a priest who woke one night to find a fellow he didn't recognize leaning over the end of his bed. The priest was a bit frightened—naturally enough—but he asked the fellow what he wanted, and the fellow said in a deep, husky voice that he wanted to go to confession. The priest said it was an awkward time and wouldn't it do in the morning, but the fellow said that last time he went to confession, there was one sin he kept back, being ashamed to mention it, and now it was always on his mind. Then the priest knew it was a bad case, because the fellow was after making a bad confession and committing a mortal sin. He got up to dress, and just then the cock crew in the yard outside, and—lo and behold!—when the priest looked round there was no sign of the fellow, only a smell of burning timber, and when the priest looked at his bed didn't he see the print of two hands burned in it? That was because the fellow had made a bad confession. This story made a shocking impression on me.

But the worst of all was when she showed us how to examine our conscience. Did we take the name of the Lord, our God, in vain? Did we honour our father and our mother? (I asked her did this include grandmothers and she said it did.) Did we love our neighbours as ourselves? Did we covet our neighbour's goods? (I thought of the way I felt about the penny that Nora got every Friday.) I decided that, between one thing and another, I must have broken the whole ten commandments, all on account of that old woman, and so far as I could see, so long as she remained in the house I had no hope of ever doing anything else.

I was scared to death of confession. The day the whole class went I let on to have a toothache, hoping my absence wouldn't be noticed; but at three o'clock, just as I was feeling safe, along comes a chap with a message from Mrs. Ryan that I was to go to confession myself on Saturday and be at the chapel for communion with the rest. To make it worse, Mother couldn't come with me and sent Nora instead.

Now, that girl had ways of tormenting me that Mother never knew of. She held my hand as we went down the hill, smiling sadly and saying how sorry she was for me, as if she were bringing me to the hospital for an operation.

"Oh, God help us!" she moaned. "Isn't it a terrible pity you weren't a good boy? Oh, Jackie, my heart bleeds for you! How will you ever think of all your sins? Don't forget you have to tell him about the time you kicked Gran on the shin."

"Lemme go!" I said, trying to drag myself free of her. "I don't want to go to confession at all."

"But sure, you'll have to go to confession, Jackie," she replied in the same regretful tone. "Sure, if you didn't, the parish priest would be up to the house, looking for you. 'Tisn't, God knows, that I'm not sorry for you. Do you remember the time you tried to kill me with the bread-knife under the table? And the language you used to me? I don't know what he'll do with you at all, Jackie. He might have to send you up to the bishop."

I remember thinking bitterly that she didn't know the half of what

I had to tell—if I told it. I knew I couldn't tell it, and understood perfectly why the fellow in Mrs Ryan's story made a bad confession; it seemed to me a great shame that people wouldn't stop criticizing him. I remember that steep hill down to the church, and the sunlit hillsides beyond the valley of the river, which I saw in the gaps between the houses like Adam's last glimpse of Paradise.

Then, when she had manoeuvred me down the long flight of steps to the chapel yard, Nora suddenly changed her tone. She became the raging malicious devil she really was.

"There you are!" she said with a yelp of triumph, hurling me through the church door. "And I hope he'll give you the penitential psalms, you dirty little caffler."

I knew then I was lost, given up to eternal justice. The door with the coloured-glass panels swung shut behind me, the sunlight went out and gave place to deep shadow, and the wind whistled outside so that the silence within seemed to crackle like ice under my feet. Nora sat in front of me by the confession box. There were a couple of old women ahead of her, and then a miserable-looking poor devil came and wedged me in at the other side, so that I couldn't escape even if I had the courage. He joined his hands and rolled his eyes in the direction of the roof, muttering aspirations in an anguished tone, and I wondered had he a grandmother too. Only a grandmother could account for a fellow behaving in that heartbroken way, but he was better off than I, for he at least could go and confess his sins; while I would make a bad confession and then die in the night and be continually coming back and burning people's furniture.

Nora's turn came, and I heard the sound of something slamming, and then her voice as if butter wouldn't melt in her mouth, and then another slam, and out she came. God, the hypocrisy of women! Her eyes were lowered, her head was bowed, and her hands were joined very low down on her stomach, and she walked up the aisle to the side altar looking like a saint. You never saw such an exhibition of devotion; and I remembered the devilish malice with which she had tormented me all the way from our door, and wondered were all religious people like that, really. It was my turn now. With the fear of damnation in my soul I went in, and the confessional door closed of itself behind me.

It was pitch-dark and I couldn't see priest or anything else. Then I really began to be frightened. In the darkness it was a matter between God and me, and He had all the odds. He knew what my intentions were before I even started; I had no chance. All I had ever been told about confession got mixed up in my mind, and I knelt to one wall and said: "Bless me, father, for I have sinned; this is my first confession." I waited for a few minutes, but nothing happened, so I tried it on the other wall. Nothing happened there either. He had me spotted all right.

It must have been then that I noticed the shelf at about one height with my head. It was really a place for grown-up people to rest their elbows, but in my distracted state I thought it was probably the place you were supposed to kneel. Of course, it was on the high side and not very deep, but I was always good at climbing and managed to get up all right. Staying up was the trouble. There was room only for my knees, and nothing you could get a grip on but a sort of wooden moulding a bit above it. I held on to the moulding and repeated the words a little louder, and this time something happened all right. A slide was slammed back; a little light entered the box, and a man's voice said: "Who's there?"

"'Tis me, father," I said for fear he mightn't see me and go away again. I couldn't see him at all. The place the voice came from was under the moulding, about level with my knees, so I took a good grip of the moulding and swung myself down till I saw the astonished face of a young priest looking up at me. He had to put his head on one side to see me, and I had to put mine on one side to see him, so we were more or less talking to one another upside-down. It struck me as a queer way of hearing confessions, but I didn't feel it my place to criticize.

"Bless me, father, for I have sinned; this is my first confession," I rattled off all in one breath, and swung myself down the least shade more to make it easier for him.

"What are you doing up there?" he shouted in an angry voice, and the strain the politeness was putting on my hold of the moulding, and the shock of being addressed in such an uncivil tone, were too much for me. I lost my grip, tumbled, and hit the door an unmerciful wallop before I found myself flat on my back in the middle of the aisle. The people who had been waiting stood up with their mouths open. The priest opened the door of the middle box and came out, pushing his biretta back from his forehead; he looked something terrible. Then Nora came scampering down the aisle.

"Oh, you dirty little caffler!" she said. "I might have known you'd do it. I might have known you'd disgrace me. I can't leave you out of my sight for one minute."

Before I could even get to my feet to defend myself she bent down and gave me a clip across the ear. This reminded me that I was so stunned I had even forgotten to cry, so that people might think I wasn't hurt at all, when in fact I was probably maimed for life. I gave a roar out of me.

"What's all this about?" the priest hissed, getting angrier than ever and pushing Nora off me. "How dare you hit the child like that, you little vixen?"

"But I can't do my penance with him, father," Nora cried, cocking an outraged eye up at him.

"Well, go and do it, or I'll give you some more to do," he said, giving me a hand up. "Was it coming to confession you were, my poor man?" he asked me.

"'Twas, father," said I with a sob.

"Oh," he said respectfully, "a big hefty fellow like you must have terrible sins. Is this your first?"

"'Tis, father," said I.

"Worse and worse," he said gloomily. "The crimes of a lifetime. I don't know will I get rid of you at all today. You'd better wait now till I'm finished with these old ones. You can see by the looks of them they haven't much to tell."

"I will, father," I said with something approaching joy.

The relief of it was really enormous. Nora stuck out her tongue at me from behind his back, but I couldn't even be bothered retorting. I knew from the very moment that man opened his mouth that he was intelligent above the ordinary. When I had time to think, I saw how right I was. It only stood to reason that a fellow confessing after seven years would have more to tell than people that went every week. The crimes of a lifetime, exactly as he said. It was only what he expected, and the rest was the cackle of old women and girls with their talk of hell, the bishop, and the penitential psalms. That was all they knew. I started to make my examination of conscience, and barring the one bad business of my grandmother it didn't seem so bad.

The next time, the priest steered me into the confession box himself and left the shutter back the way I could see him get in and sit down at the further side of the grille from me.

"Well, now," he said, "what do they call you?"

"Jackie, father," said I.

"And what's a-trouble to you, Jackie?"

"Father," I said, feeling I might as well get it over while I had him in good humour, "I had it all arranged to kill my grandmother."

He seemed a bit shaken by that, all right, because he said nothing for quite a while.

"My goodness," he said at last, "that'd be a shocking thing to do. What put that into your head?"

"Father," I said, feeling very sorry for myself, "she's an awful woman."

"Is she?" he asked. "What way is she awful?"

"She takes porter, father," I said, knowing well from the way Mother talked of it that this was a mortal sin, and hoping it would make the priest take a more favourable view of my case.

"Oh, my!" he said, and I could see he was impressed.

"And snuff, father," said I.

"That's a bad case, sure enough, Jackie," he said.

"And she goes round in her bare feet, father," I went on in a rush of self-pity, "and she know I don't like her, and she gives pennies to Nora and none to me, and my da sides with her and flakes me, and one night I was so heart-scalded I made up my mind I'd have to kill her."

"And what would you do with the body?" he asked with great interest.

"I was thinking I could chop that up and carry it away in a barrow I have," I said.

"Begor, Jackie," he said, "do you know you're a terrible child?"

"I know, father," I said, for I was just thinking the same thing myself. "I tried to kill Nora too with a bread-knife under the table, only I missed her."

"Is that the little girl that was beating you just now?" he asked.

"'Tis, father."

"Someone will go for her with a bread-knife one day, and he won't miss her," he said rather cryptically. "You must have great courage. Between ourselves, there's a lot of people I'd like to do the same to but I'd never have the nerve. Hanging is an awful death."

"Is it, father?" I asked with the deepest interest—I was always very keen on hanging. "Did you ever see a fellow hanged?"

"Dozens of them," he said solemnly. "And they all died roaring."

"Jay!" I said.

"Oh, a horrible death!" he said with great satisfaction. "Lots of the fellows I saw killed their grandmothers too, but they all said 'twas never worth it."

He had me there for a full ten minutes talking, and then walked out the chapel yard with me. I was genuinely sorry to part with him, because he was the most entertaining character I'd ever met in the religious line. Outside, after the shadow of the church, the sunlight was like the roaring of waves on a beach; it dazzled me; and when the frozen silence melted and I heard the screech of trams on the road my heart soared. I knew now I wouldn't die in the night and come back, leaving marks on my mother's furniture. It would be a great worry to her, and the poor soul had enough.

Nora was sitting on the railing, waiting for me, and she put on a very sour puss when she saw the priest with me. She was mad jealous because a priest had never come out of the church with her.

"Well," she asked coldly, after he left me, "what did he give you?"

"Three Hail Marys," I said.

"Three Hail Marys," she repeated incredulously. "You mustn't have told him anything."

"I told him everything," I said confidently.

"About Gran and all?"

"About Gran and all."

(All she wanted was to be able to go home and say I'd made a bad confession.)

"Did you tell him you went for me with the bread-knife?" she asked with a frown.

"I did to be sure."

"And he only gave you three Hail Marys?"

"That's all."

She slowly got down from the railing with a baffled air. Clearly, this was beyond her. As we mounted the steps back to the main road she looked at me suspiciously.

"What are you sucking?" she asked.

"Bullseyes."

"Was it the priest gave them to you?"

"'Twas."

"Lord God," she wailed bitterly, "some people have all the luck! 'Tis no advantage to anybody trying to be good. I might just as well be a sinner like you."

"First Confession" was originally published in *Lovat Dickson's Magazine* (January 1935) under the title "Repentance." It then appeared with its present title in *Harper's Bazaar* (March 1, 1939). This version, included in *The Best British Short Stories of 1940*, is the limited omniscient version we have reprinted. In *Traveler's Samples* (Knopf, 1951) the point of view shifted to a first-person narrator. O'Connor's final, preferred version, which we have reprinted from *The Stories of Frank O'Connor* (Knopf, 1952), makes further changes but retains the first-person point of view. Examining the same story written from different narrative points of view presents an unusual opportunity to observe the effects of the selections a writer makes. The following questions will help you focus on these effects.

QUESTIONS

1. With what point of view does the first version begin? Where does this point of view shift toward objective?

2. What overall differences are caused by the use of a first-person narrator in the second version? Why, for instance, is the second version longer?

3. Compare the two versions of the scene inside the confessional booth. Do you find one version clearer? Funnier? Why?

4. What is the difference in the moment in time with which each version opens? What is the effect of this difference?

5. The endings are almost the same, but there is a difference. What is it? What is the effect of the difference?

6. What would happen if the story were told from Nora's point of view?

chapter 7

The Language of Style

Gerhard Marcks. *Cats*. 1921. Woodcut, 9 ½″ × 15 ¼″. Philadelphia Museum of Art, Print Club Permanent Collection.

Whenever we express an idea, we make choices about language, choices that may create widely differing effects:

> The sun rose at 6:52 A.M.
>
> Early that morning, over the silent lake, rose the blood-red sun.

Although both of these statements inform us that the sun rose, the first sounds like part of a weather report, the second more like the opening of a romantic novel. The variations in word choice and arrangement that determine such differences in expression are called *style*.

Style might be termed the texture of writing. A writer interweaves various qualities of language to create a blend that is both meaningful and unique. The words may be concrete or abstract. They may be simple and straightforward, or they may be highly imaginative, involving unusual vocabulary and complex comparisons. There may be striking rhythms and sounds. Sentences may be long or short, simple or complex. Whatever fabric of language emerges will be much more than surface decoration. It will significantly affect our understanding of the work.

SYNTAX

Syntax is the arrangement of individual words in grammatical patterns. As we write, we decide whether to coordinate or subordinate ideas, where to add modifiers, how to order our words. Gradually a style begins to emerge. A series of sentences or of lines of poetry beginning with participles (running, jumping, sliding) gives a sense of continuous motion. Parallel structure (I came, I saw, I conquered) creates balance and emphasis.

Compare the following passages from two of the most influential prose stylists of twentieth-century American literature:

> I had coffee and the papers in bed and then dressed and took my bathingsuit down to the beach. Everything was fresh and cool and damp in the early morning. Nurses in uniform and in peasant costume walked under the trees with children. The Spanish children were beautiful. Some bootblacks sat together under a tree talking to

a soldier. The soldier had only one arm. The tide was in and there was a good breeze and a surf on the beach.

Ernest Hemingway, The Sun Also Rises

We had listened to it for years: the long legend of corncribs rifled, of shotes and grown pigs and even calves carried bodily into the woods and devoured, of traps and deadfalls overthrown and dogs mangled and slain, and shotgun and even rifle charges delivered at point-blank range and with no more effect than so many peas blown through a tube by a boy—a corridor of wreckage and destruction beginning back before he was born, through which sped, not fast but rather with the ruthless and irresistible deliberation of a loco-motive, the shaggy tremendous shape.

William Faulkner, "The Bear"

As you observe these two excerpts, one difference should catch your attention almost at once. Although Faulkner's is the longer of the two, it is made up of a single sentence, whereas the shorter Hemingway excerpt contains seven. Further examination of syntax reveals that Hemingway uses no subordination except for the participial phrase "talking to a soldier." In the Faulkner sentence, after the opening main clause ("He had listened to it for years . . ."), everything is subordinated so as to modify the "long legend," culminating in the bear's description, withheld to the very last, as the "shaggy tremendous shape."

Identifying grammatical patterns is not in itself enough. If all we can say about Hemingway's sentences is that they are short and choppy and all we can say about Faulkner's is that they go on and on, we will not have gained much insight. We might even conclude that these writers are guilty of "primer" style in one case and excessive subordination in the other, but to form such a conclusion is to ignore the fact that style is the result of choice. Good writers control style for the purpose of bringing out meaning. *The Sun Also Rises* is a novel about members of a "lost generation," disillusioned just after World War I and roaming aimlessly about Europe. Hemingway's sometimes seemingly incoherent stringing together of short sentences without transitions ("The soldier has only one arm. The tide was in . . .") helps us to experience the dislocation felt by these characters. Faulkner's sentence, spinning out modifier after modifier, gives us the sense of the "irresistible" power of the old bear.

RHYTHM AND SOUND

Two additional elements of style we observe—or rather hear—in the Hemingway and Faulkner passages are *rhythm* and *sound*. If you read the passage aloud, you will hear the lilting rhythm of Hemingway's "was fresh and cool in the early morning" and the sound of a train in Faulkner's "the ruthless and irresistible deliberation of a locomotive."

Rhythm and sound are present in all literature, but they are especially important in poetry. Consider this example:

EMILY DICKINSON   (1830–1886)

A Bird Came down the Walk

(J328)

A Bird came down the Walk—
He did not know I saw—
He bit an Angleworm in halves
And ate the fellow, raw,

And then he drank a Dew   5
From a convenient Grass—
And then hopped sidewise to the Wall
To let a Beetle pass—

He glanced with rapid eyes
That hurried all around—   10
They looked like frightened Beads, I thought—
He stirred his Velvet Head

Like one in danger, Cautious,
I offered him a Crumb
And he unrolled his feathers   15
And rowed him softer home—

Than Oars divide the Ocean,
Too silver for a seam—

Or Butterflies, off Banks of Noon
Leap, plashless as they swim.   20

QUESTIONS

1. Read this poem aloud. Try varying the syllables you stress and the pace with
   which you read. Where does the poem place some constraints on you? Where
   might stress and pace be open to debate?

2. Who is the "one in danger" (line 13)? How does whether or not you pause
   after line 12 determine the answer to this question? Should you pause?

3. Paraphrase the poem. Note three sentences in your paraphrase that seem
   different from the poem primarily because of difference in style. Explain how
   the styles differ.

   In poetry the combinations of stressed and unstressed syllables
that produce rhythm are often regularized into metrical patterns.
(See Appendix A for a fuller discussion of meter.) Meter establishes
a structure that helps to control rhythm, but meter is not the same
as rhythm. As in prose—and in some verse—rhythm can exist
without meter. If we force a poem into a singsong, evenly paced
stress pattern, we run the risk of losing the poem's spirit. Line 2 of
Dickinson's poem, for example, could be scanned regularly (Hĕ
díd | nŏt knŏw | Ĭ sáw—"). But the speaker's amused,
curious nature is better conveyed by our also stressing the "not"
(Hĕ díd | nót knŏw | Ĭ sáw—"). Rhythm not only varies
meter but also is more subtle. Words such as "angleworm" create
syncopation by quickening the tempo. (Other words will have the
opposite effect of slowing down a line.) When the speaker says,
"He glanced with rapid eyes," we must speed up at "rapid"—an
effect that parallels the glancing movement of the bird's eyes. In
the last six lines the pace slows, causing a counterpoint against the
bird's flight similar to the effect of slow motion in a film.
   Sound reinforces the effects of rhythm. In the last six lines
both the illusion of slow motion and a feeling of wonder are
enhanced by *assonance*, the repetition of similar sounding vowels.
Especially marked is the use of the *o* sound of "unr*o*lled," "r*o*wed,"
"h*o*me," and "*O*cean"; of "*so*fter," "*O*ars," and "*o*ff"; of "T*oo*" and
"N*oo*n." *Alliteration*, the repetition of similar consonant sounds
present in phrases such as "*d*rank a *D*ew" and "*T*oo *s*ilver for a
*s*eam—," affects rhythm also, because alliterative words gain emphasis.

DICTION

Another major element of style is *diction*, or word choice. We all have different ways of selecting from the range of our vocabularies. We might say simply and directly, "That was a good meal." We might be more formal: "It was an excellent dinner." Or we might be informal, exclaiming, "What a swell supper!" Our word choice will depend partly on our characteristic way of expressing ourselves and partly on situation and audience.

The same is true in writing. If we read several works by an author, we become aware of certain tendencies in word choice. Even in the brief passages from "The Bear" and from *The Sun Also Rises*, you may have noticed that Faulkner's language seems somewhat literary ("corridor of wreckage and destruction"), Hemingway's more like ordinary speech ("there was a good breeze"). Further reading in the works of these two authors would show these qualities to be characteristic. Try examining several examples of your own writing. Can you make any generalizations about your word choice?

Even more important than characteristic diction in writing is specific application of language. For instance, Dickinson's abrupt shift to the informal "raw" at the end of line 4, although typical of her style, is also a means of giving the poem's speaker a sense of humor appropriate to both the speaker's character and the situation. In our reading and our writing, we want to be sensitive to such special effects of word selection.

The humor in the Dickinson poem and the matter-of-fact expression in the Hemingway passage remind us that authors do not always use elevated language expressing profound thoughts. Shakespeare, for example, is admired for the endless variety of his language. Consider these three speeches of Romeo from *Romeo and Juliet*:

> Feather of lead, bright smoke, cold fire, sick health!
> Still-waking sleep, that is not what it is!
> This love feel I, that feel no love in this.
> *(I.i.186–188)*

> Sleep dwell upon thine eyes, peace in thy breast!
> Would I were sleep and peace, so sweet to rest!
> *(II.ii.187–188)*

> Well, Juliet, I will lie with thee tonight.
> *(V.i.34)*

The diction of these speeches is not identical. Rather, there are language changes that reflect a gradual character development in Romeo. In the first Romeo is madly—and foolishly—in love with a girl named Rosaline. The paired opposites such as "cold fire" and "sick health" are instances of *oxymoron*, a stylistic device overused in love poetry at the time *Romeo and Juliet* was written. Shakespeare is making fun both of the device and of an immature Romeo, in love with love. The second speech occurs at the end of the balcony scene in which Romeo and Juliet have spoken their love for each other. The language is still elaborately poetic, but it is less artificial. Romeo remains in love with love, but this time we feel that he means what he says. The third speech follows Romeo's hearing the news that Juliet—as all believe—is dead. Here we find the simple, direct sorrow of a love that has matured.

IMAGES

To achieve concreteness in writing, we often turn to *images*—words or phrases that appeal to the senses of seeing, hearing, touching, tasting, and smelling. Images as they appear collectively in a work of literature are called *imagery*. Imagery is important to communication because it helps to re-create in words the way we experience events through our senses. Note the use of images in this passage from James Joyce's "Counterparts" (p. 134):

> There was something striking in her appearance. An immense scarf of peacock-blue muslin was wound around her hat and knotted in a great bow under her chin; and she wore bright yellow gloves, reaching to the elbow. Farrington gazed admiringly at the plump arm which she moved very often and with much grace; and when, after a little time, she answered his gaze he admired still more her large dark brown eyes. The oblique staring expression in them fascinated him.

Joyce is here demonstrating concretely the sensual attraction Farrington feels for women. Without specific images such as "bright yellow gloves," Joyce could convey the general meaning that the woman's appearance was "striking," but we would lose the individual quality of Farrington's perception. Observe the use of images in the poem that follows.

WALT WHITMAN   (1819–1892)

Cavalry Crossing a Ford

A line in long array where they wind betwixt green islands,
They take a serpentine course, their arms flash in the sun—hark to the
     musical clank,
Behold the silvery river, in it the splashing horses loitering stop to
     drink,
Behold the brown-faced men, each group, each person a picture, the
     negligent rest on the saddles,
Some emerge on the opposite bank, others are just entering the ford—
     while,   5
Scarlet and blue and snowy white,
The guidon flags flutter gayly in the wind.

QUESTIONS

1. Which words appeal to the sense of sight?
2. Which words appeal to the sense of sound?
3. Where does Whitman place the reader to view the scene?
4. What are the effects of the rhythm and sound of the lines?
5. Make a precise statement of your impression of this scene. Using this statement
   as your topic sentence, develop a paragraph built on specific references to the
   images in the poem.

     Now compare "Cavalry Crossing a Ford" with another poem
about soldiers.

WILFRED OWEN   (1893–1918)

Dulce et Decorum Est

Bent double, like old beggars under sacks,
Knock-kneed, coughing like hags, we cursed through sludge,
Till on the haunting flares we turned our backs
And towards our distant rest began to trudge.
Men marched asleep. Many had lost their boots   5

But limped on, blood-shod. All went lame; all blind;
Drunk with fatigue; deaf even to the hoots
Of tired, outstripped Five-Nines that dropped behind.

Gas! Gas! Quick, boys!—An ecstasy of fumbling,
Fitting the clumsy helmets just in time;   10
But someone still was yelling out and stumbling
And flound'ring like a man in fire or lime . . .
Dim, through the misty panes and thick green light,
As under a green sea, I saw him drowning.

In all my dreams, before my helpless sight,   15
He plunges at me, guttering, choking, drowning.

If in some smothering dreams you too could pace
Behind the wagon that we flung him in,
And watch the white eyes writhing in his face,
His hanging face, like a devil's sick of sin;   20
If you could hear, at every jolt, the blood
Come gargling from the froth-corrupted lungs,
Obscene as cancer, bitter as the cud
Of vile, incurable sores on innocent tongues,—
My friend, you would not tell with such high zest   25
To children ardent for some desperate glory,
The old Lie: Dulce et decorum est
Pro patria mori.

QUESTIONS

1. What is the situation? Who is the speaker?
2. What images are especially concrete and vivid? Why?
3. What is the effect of placing three participles in a row at the end of line 16?
4. List examples of alliteration and assonance in line 19. What is gained by these techniques?
5. How is the effect of the colors green and white different than in "Cavalry Crossing a Ford"?
6. How is the poem's structure based, in part, on grammatical point of view ("we," "I," "you")? What is the effect of this structure?
7. The "old Lie" that is the basis for both the title and the conclusion is a Latin quotation from the Roman poet Horace which translates: "Sweet and befitting it is to die for one's country." Why did Owen select this quotation? How is it a "lie"?

    "Dulce et Decorum Est" presents a much different picture of soldiers than does the Whitman poem. Here the soldiers "trudge" rather than "wind" between islands. Instead of healthy appearing "brown-faced" men, we have a face that is "hanging." The images in Owen's poem convey the ugliness of war; those in Whitman's poem portray a picturesque scene.

Images that are combined, or *clustered*, to create a dominant impression are called *patterns of imagery*. Shakespeare, for example, uses blood imagery in *Macbeth* to reinforce the atmosphere of horror. In Ray Bradbury's "August 2026" (pp. 217–220), images of nature are contrasted with images of technology. Owen uses images of decrepitude, drowning, and sickness to ironically contradict the Latin word *dulce* (sweet). Such patterning of images contributes to mood, structure, and ultimately to meaning.

FIGURATIVE LANGUAGE: COMPARISONS

In addition to appealing to our senses with images, authors also appeal to our intellectual ability to connect the *literal* meanings of language (what the dictionary definitions add up to) with imagined, or *figurative* meanings. An apparent expression of one thing intended to mean another is called a *figure of speech*. For example, a literal statement that you have even more happiness than you had expected could be stated: "My cup runneth over." You don't expect someone to dash for a paper towel; you are only using a figure of speech. Similarly, if someone says, "You should have seen how Charlie fought like a lion," you don't picture him roaring, clawing, and biting. You recognize the figurative connection between the fierceness and strength of a lion and Charlie.

We are constantly using figurative comparisons even in our ordinary conversation. We fall for someone's magnetic charm like a ton of bricks, are on pins and needles, then feel like a million when the love affair clicks. Taken literally, such language is madness. Understood as figurative and used freshly, it can be intriguing, expressive, forceful. We delight in the cleverness of the comparison and gain insight into the writer's perceptions.

Simile and Metaphor

Much of the power of the images in "Dulce et Decorum Est" arises from Owen's use of *simile*, a comparison stated explicitly through a connector such as *like, as, resembles,* or *seems*. In line 1 the soldiers, literally described as "bent double," are figuratively compared by means of a simile to the image of "old beggars under sacks." In line 2 they are compared to "hags." Neither hags nor beggars are really there. But these comparisons help us to see the men as the speaker sees them. There are other similes in lines 14, 20, and 23–24. Note what is being compared to what and how the comparisons communicate the speaker's reactions.

When a comparison is stated without explicit connectors, it is called a *metaphor*. The speaker of Owen's poem, in saying that "many had lost their boots / But limped on, blood shod," is making a grim comparison between wearing boots and being "shod" in blood. The blood on the feet of those who have "lost their boots" is likened to the missing boots. But there is no *like* or *as* to tell us that.

Whenever you encounter apparently mad language that makes no literal sense (even after you have looked up all the unfamiliar words), try to discover the two terms, literal and figurative, of a comparison—the X and Y of an equation. Thus blood (X—literal) = boots (Y—figurative). If only one of the terms is present, there is an *implied* metaphor. If "boots" were not mentioned, the comparison would still be there—implied by the word "shod." The chart in Figure 7.1 illustrates the different uses of an image (flame) in creating simile or metaphor.

Image	The oaken logs were glowing with orange and yellow flame.
Simile	My love for you is like an inextinguishable flame.
Metaphor (both terms stated)	My love for you is an all-consuming flame.
Metaphor (figurative term implied)	My love for you burns brightly still.
Metaphor (literal term implied)	The bright flame within me blazes for you alone.

FIGURE 7.1   Uses of image in creating simile or metaphor.

The following poem is built around a metaphor that is an example of an *extended comparison*, one developed through several lines.

ARCHIBALD MACLEISH   (1892–1982)

Seafarer

And learn O voyager to walk
The roll of earth, the pitch and fall
That swings across these trees those stars:
That swings the sunlight up the wall.

And learn upon these narrow beds   5
To sleep in spite of sea, in spite
Of sound the rushing planet makes:
And learn to sleep against this ground.

QUESTIONS

1. To what is the earth being compared?
2. How does the title help you to recognize the comparison?
3. Which words apply both to earth and to the other term of the metaphor?
4. Where and how is the rhythm appropriate to the comparison? (Read the lines aloud.)
5. A seafarer might be expected to have to "learn" to sleep on "narrow beds." But who needs to "learn to sleep against this ground"?

Personification and Apostrophe

Another type of comparison is *personification*, in which human qualities are given to something nonhuman—to an abstract idea, an object, an animal. Personification is actually a particular form of metaphor in which the imagined term is always a person. If you say, "My car has decided to quit on me," you are personifying your car. Often associated with personification is *apostrophe*, the direct addressing of something inanimate, or of someone absent or dead. If you say, "Feet, get a move on" or "Abe Lincoln, where are you now that we need you?" you are using apostrophe. Because we normally talk only to people, the use of apostrophe often personifies an object or abstraction being addressed, as in the following poem.

EDMUND WALLER   (1606–1687)

Song

Go, lovely rose,
Tell her that wastes her time and me,
   That now she knows,
When I resemble her to thee,
   How sweet and fair she seems to be.   5

Tell her that's young,
And shuns to have her graces spied,
   That hadst thou sprung
In deserts where no men abide,
   Thou must have uncommended died.   10

Small is the worth
Of beauty from the light retired:
   Bid her come forth,
Suffer her self to be desired,
   And not blush so to be admired.   15

Then die, that she
The common fate of all things rare
   May read in thee,
How small a part of time they share,
   That are so wondrous sweet and fair.   20

QUESTIONS

1. What are the meanings of *resemble, uncommended, suffer, rare*?
2. Who is the speaker and what is the situation?
3. Identify the use of apostrophe.
4. What is personified and how?
5. What is the double meaning of "wastes" (line 2)?
6. What type of figurative language does "resemble" in line 4 indicate the speaker has been using to describe the woman?
7. "Read" in line 18 implies a metaphor. To what is the rose compared?

Metonymy

Another form of figurative language is illustrated by the well-known statement: "the pen is mightier than the sword." One would not literally picture a confrontation between a flashing sword and a waving pen. It is the association of the pen with something more general, writing, and of the sword with war that enables us to understand the meaning: words have more power than military force. The use of a part or detail to stand for something is called *metonymy*.* When we say, "Wait a second," we really mean wait a short period of time of which that second is only a part. The single second stands for several minutes of actual time. When we say "The White House made no comment on the proposed bill," we are not personifying the president's residence; we are referring to the president and the staff of the executive branch associated with the White House.

DYLAN THOMAS   (1914–1953)

The Hand That Signed the Paper

The hand that signed the paper felled a city;
Five sovereign fingers taxed the breath,
Doubled the globe of dead and halved a country;
These five kings did a king to death.

The mighty hand leads to a sloping shoulder,   5
The finger joints are cramped with chalk;
A goose's quill has put an end to murder
That put an end to talk.

The hand that signed the treaty bred a fever,
And famine grew, and locusts came;   10
Great is the hand that holds dominion over
Man by a scribbled name.

The five kings count the dead but do not soften
The crusted wound nor stroke the brow;
A hand rules pity as a hand rules heaven;   15
Hands have no tears to flow.

---

* Technically, *metonymy* is reserved for an association between something and a detail or quality closely related to it ("White House"), and another term, *synecdoche*, is used for a part representing the whole ("a second"). It seems more practical to follow the lead of some texts and use metonymy as the term for both.

QUESTIONS

1. What is the metonymy that forms the basis for the poem?
2. What other metonymies are there?
3. What is the effect of the repetition and parallel structure?
4. What are the effects of the following word choices: "cramped" (line 6), "scribbled" (line 12), and "stroke" (line 14)?
5. What proper (and literal) use of hands is suggested in lines 13–14?
6. How would you paraphrase the last line? What is lost in emotional impact when you eliminate the metonymy?

EXERCISE

Identify the examples of simile, metaphor, personification, apostrophe, and metonymy in the following quotations. Then explain each one by stating the items being compared and the point of the comparison.

1. O my luve is like a red, red rose,
     That's newly sprung in June.

> *Robert Burns*

Sample answer: A simile. The speaker compares a woman, his "luve," to a rose that has just bloomed in June. He thereby associates her with the rose's qualities of freshness and beauty.

2. O my luve is like the melodie
     That's sweetly played in tune.

> *Robert Burns*

3. Flow on, river! flow with the flood-tide, and ebb with the ebb-tide!

> *Walt Whitman*

4. The best mirror is an old friend.

> *George Herbert*

5. Death stands above me, whispering low
     I know not what into my ear;

Of his strange language all I know
  Is, there is not a word of fear.
          Walter Savage Landor

6. This bud of love, by summer's ripening breath,
  May prove a beauteous flower when next we meet.
          William Shakespeare

7. she woke sometimes to feel the daylight coming
  like a relentless milkman up the stairs.
          Adrienne Rich

8.   Scepter and crown
     Must tumble down
  And in the dust be equal made
  With the poor crooked scythe and spade.
          James Shirley

9. Our two souls therefore, which are one,
    Though I must go, endure not yet
  A breach, but an expansion,
    Like gold to airy thinness beat.
          John Donne

10. I have measured out my life with coffee spoons.
          T. S. Eliot

11. Life's but a walking shadow, a poor player
  That struts and frets his hour upon the stage
  And then is heard no more. . . .
          William Shakespeare

12. The great Pullman was whirling onward with such dignity of motion that a glance from the window seemed simply to prove that the plains of Texas were pouring eastward. Vast flats of green grass, dull-hued spaces of mesquite and cactus, little groups of frame houses, woods of light and tender trees, all

were sweeping into the east, sweeping over the horizon, a precipice.

Stephen Crane

WRITING ABOUT STYLE

When you write about style, you will be drawing conclusions from the author's use of language. You will therefore need an abundance of specific references to the text. You may need to quote words, phrases, and brief passages to show diction, sentence structure, rhythm, sound, or imagery. You may also need to carry out some analysis of syntax—of subordination, coordination, parallel structure. Or it might be necessary to identify and explain figurative language. Your generalizations will not be convincing without such specific support. On the other hand, a stylistic analysis can become cluttered with examples that are just presented rather than explained. It is not enough merely to list ten instances of sentences that begin with participial phrases or to point out a series of metaphors unless you go on to explain the effect of using these devices. You should be certain to construct your essay around a thesis that makes a connection between style and meaning. An example of such a connection for Hemingway's *The Sun Also Rises* might read: "Hemingway's use of short sentences lacking transitions magnifies the fragmented, dislocated view that the main characters have of their place in the world." Here the technique of style ("short sentences lacking transitions") is related to meaning ("fragmented, dislocated view").

In approaching your topic, you will probably be discussing an author's style in general, the style of a particular work, or style in a specific passage. Even if you are discussing only a brief passage, you should try to find a further limitation of topic. Jot down as many observations of style as you can. Try to isolate groups of observations that go together. Let us say you have noticed that references to light are consistently contrasted with references to darkness. You further discover that the author employs light imagery only when presenting the positive side of the main character and imagery of darkness only when presenting the negative side. You could then focus your thesis on this specific relation of image patterns to the portrayal of character. You could either organize your essay around the two types of imagery or around the effects on character.

Resist the urge to organize your essay according to the structure of the work. By building around a thesis and grouping elements of style into unified paragraphs, you can avoid a directionless sentence-by-sentence or line-by-line analysis. Each paragraph should develop a topic sentence or main point with specific supporting evidence, and each topic sentence needs to connect to your thesis. The advice in Chapter 3 to list evidence and then classify or group by some principle is especially valuable when writing about style.

One special problem in writing about the language of style is clear explanation of figurative language. Too often students point out the existence of a simile or metaphor without explaining how it works or why it is appropriate. Lack of clear explanation of figures of speech can be a problem both in writing papers and taking tests. Suppose you are being tested on "To Autumn," by John Keats, through a series of questions on language, each to be answered in a few sentences. First read the poem, which follows this discussion. Then assume you are asked to explain the metaphor created by "bloom" in line 25: "While barred clouds bloom the soft-dying day." To carry out this explanation well, you should: (1) point out the comparison, (2) explain how the comparison works, and (3) comment on the effect. Here is a possible response:

> The choice of "bloom" in line 25 implies a comparison between clouds and flowers. The coloring of the clouds by the sunset is likened to the blossoming of flowers. This comparison adds to autumn some of the fresh beauty normally associated with spring and thereby adds to Keats's reasons to praise the autumn season.

JOHN KEATS (1795–1821)

To Autumn

I

Seaons of mists and mellow fruitfulness,
  Close bosom-friend of the maturing sun;
Conspiring with him how to load and bless
  With fruit the vines that round the thatch-eves run;
To bend with apples the mossed cottage-trees,   5
  And fill all fruit with ripeness to the core;
    To swell the gourd, and plump the hazel shells
With a sweet kernel; to set budding more
  And still more, later flowers for the bees,
  Until they think warm days will never cease,   10
    For summer has o'er-brimmed their clammy cells.

II

Who hath not seen thee oft amid thy store?
  Sometimes whoever seeks abroad may find
Thee sitting careless on a granary floor,
  Thy hair soft-lifted by the winnowing wind;   15
Or on a half-reaped furrow sound asleep,
  Drowsed with the fume of poppies, while thy hook
    Spares the next swath and all its twined flowers:
And sometime like a gleaner thou dost keep
  Steady thy laden head across a brook;   20
  Or by a cider-press, with patient look,
    Thou watchest the last oozings hours by hours.

III

Where are the songs of Spring? Ay, where are they?
  Think not of them, thou hast thy music too,—
While barred clouds bloom the soft-dying day,   25
  And touch the stubble-plains with rosy hue;
Then in a wailful choir the small gnats mourn
  Among the river sallows, borne aloft
    Or sinking as the light wind lives or dies;
And full-grown lambs loud bleat from hilly bourn;   30
  Hedge-crickets sing; and now with treble soft
  The red-breast whistles from a garden-croft;
    And gathering swallows twitter in the skies.

QUESTIONS

1. What are the meanings of *thatch-eves, plump, granary, gleaner, swallows, bourn,* and *garden-croft?*
2. To whom or what does "him" refer in line 3? Who is "conspiring" with whom? What figure of speech is being used?
3. List examples of images appealing to each of the five senses.
4. What image patterns can be found in each stanza? How do these patterns provide structure?
5. How is apostrophe central to the poem?
6. What is the effect of the use of personification in stanza 2?
7. What is Keats's attitude toward the autumn season?

STUDENT ESSAY

Keats's Autumn: A Sensuous Season

Mark Yatsko

In his poem "To Autumn," John Keats extols the delights of the season of autumn. Through vivid imagery, Keats unfolds for us the spectacle of the harvest season. The chronological arrangement of the three stages of fall effectively presents the speaker's attitude about the season. The different stages are tied together by the quiet amazement at the bounty of the season as the provider of food and scenic beauty. The poem's division is analogous to a single day—the first stanza representing the morning, or preparation; the second the afternoon, or work; and the third the evening, or rest. Each stanza is developed through an appropriate pattern of images.

The first stanza is introduced as the dawn of the day, with the "season of mists" evoking thoughts of the morning dew upon the "mellow fruitfulness" of vines around "thatch-eves" and apples on "mossed cottage-trees." We also perceive the rich warmth of the September morning when the land is bursting with the sights and smells of nature's abundance. The "conspiring" of sun and earth to produce the crops is, for the speaker, an awe-inspiring event. The images in this passage suggest earthiness, a feeling of being close to the soil that heightens our sense of warmth, and the fullness of the reproductive process. The "maturing sun" has swelled "the gourd" and produced a "ripeness to the core." Nature's munificence is reinforced in the last line of this stanza when we see that summer has "o'er-brimmed" the bees' honeycombs. This line prepares for the transition to the actual harvesting to take place in the next stanza.

In the second stanza, autumn is personified as someone who is

STUDENT ESSAY

gathering the harvest. This is an allusion to Greek mythology, in which each season is represented by a woman who performs tasks associated with that particular season. Autumn carries a fruit basket and a scythe, thus the reference to the "hook" sparing "the next swath." The images in this stanza create a mood of steady yet relaxed energy. The image of autumn's "hair soft-lifted by the winnowing wind" enables us to envision the chaff from the harvested wheat spreading throughout the land. The references to autumn as "sound asleep" and "drowsed with the fume of poppies" picture the rest that follows work and fullness. The "patient look" given to the "last oozings" of the cider press leads us away from the harvest time and into the final stanza where the fading glory of the fall is explored.

The final stanza of the poem is the most evocative. The speaker perceives late autumn as a haunting evening, the calm before the roar of winter. The speaker is imploring us to stop and enjoy the sights and sounds instead of already looking ahead to spring. This enjoyment is transmitted through images of the "music" of autumn. We are invited to listen to the "wailful choir" of gnats or bleats from "full-grown lambs." Perhaps the most serene musical expression is that of the "treble soft" whistle of the robin, or the graceful "twitter" of swallows heading south. These last lines convey the fading of life and energy as the winter approaches. The precision of the images in striking the core of human feeling is splendid. We leave the poem with a peaceful feeling, sharing the speaker's belief that the autumn season has its virtues, too.

In "To Autumn" Keats has crafted a poem that moves, from stanza to stanza, through the season's stages. We can see the continuation from the beginning of the season, with its warmth and plenty, to the reaping during harvest, to, finally, the forlorn days of late autumn that have their own joyful song.

SELECTIONS FOR FURTHER STUDY

Pieter Breughel. *The Peasant Dance, c.* 1567. Oil on panel, 44 ¾" × 64 ½". Kunsthistorisches Museum, Vienna/Art Resource.

WILLIAM CARLOS WILLIAMS (1883–1963)

The Dance

In Breughel's great picture, The Kermess,
the dancers go round, they go round and
around, the squeal and the blare and the
tweedle of bagpipes, a bugle and fiddles
tipping their bellies (round as the thick-   5
sided glasses whose wash they impound)
their hips and their bellies off balance
to turn them. Kicking and rolling about
the Fair Grounds, swinging their butts, those
shanks must be sound to bear up under such   10
rollicking measures, prance as they dance
in Breughel's great picture, The Kermess.

QUESTIONS

1. Consult a biographical dictionary for information about Pieter Breughel.
2. A Kermess is an outdoor fair. After observing the visual images in this poem, what can you say about Breughel's picture of the fair?
3. What stylistic devices does Williams use to create sound effects?
4. What is the pace of the poem? How fast should it be read? Are there any points at which we speed up or slow down?
5. What is the purpose of repeating the first line at the end?
6. What is Williams's purpose in the poem?

LANGSTON HUGHES   (1902–1967)

Dream Deferred

What happens to a dream deferred?

    Does it dry up
    like a raisin in the sun?
    Or fester like a sore—
    And then run?   5
    Does it stink like rotten meat?
    Or crust and sugar over—
    like a syrupy sweet?

    Maybe it just sags
    like a heavy load.   10

    Or does it explode?

QUESTIONS

1. Identify and explain each simile. Where is there an implied metaphor? Complete the comparison. How is it appropriate?
2. What similarities are there in the images?
3. What is the effect of the coordinate sentence structure that is used throughout the poem?
4. What is Hughes's attitude toward deferred dreams?
5. Consult a biographical dictionary for information about Langston Hughes. How does the information enhance your understanding of the poem's possible meanings?

SYLVIA PLATH   (1932–1963)

Metaphors

I'm a riddle in nine syllables,
An elephant, a ponderous house,
A melon strolling on two tendrils.
O red fruit, ivory, fine timbers!
This loaf's big with its yeasty rising.   5
Money's new-minted in this fat purse.
I'm a means, a stage, a cow in calf.
I've eaten a bag of green apples,
Boarded the train there's no getting off.

QUESTIONS

1. The assertion "I'm a . . ." produces a series of comparisons. What are they?
2. What images are similar to other images? How?
3. The number "nine" is mentioned in line 1. How is this number applicable to the poem?
4. Explain the last line.
5. How did you know when you had solved the "riddle" of this poem? Was the class able to agree on the solution? If so, how?
6. Tell the class a riddle and let them solve it. What process was involved in solving the riddle?

RAY BRADBURY   (b. 1920)

August 2026: There Will Come Soft Rains

In the living room the voice-clock sang, *Tick-tock, seven o'clock, time to get up, time to get up, seven o'clock!* as if it were afraid that nobody would. The morning house lay empty. The clock ticked on, repeating and repeating its sounds into the emptiness. *Seven-nine, breakfast time, seven-nine!*

In the kitchen the breakfast stove gave a hissing sigh and ejected from its warm interior eight pieces of perfectly browned toast, eight eggs sunnyside up, sixteen slices of bacon, two coffees, and two cool glasses of milk.

"Today is August 4, 2026," said a second voice from the kitchen ceiling, "in the city of Allendale, California." It repeated the date three times for memory's sake. "Today is Mr. Featherstone's birthday. Today is the anniversary of Tilita's marriage. Insurance is payable, as are the water, gas, and light bills."

Somewhere in the walls, relays clicked, memory tapes glided under electric eyes.

Eight-one, tick-tock, eight-one o'clock, off to school, off to work, run, run, eight-one! But no doors slammed, no carpets took the soft tread of rubber heels. It was raining outside. The weather box on the front door sang quietly: "Rain, rain, go away; rubbers, raincoats for today . . ." And the rain tapped on the empty house, echoing.

Outside, the garage chimed and lifted its door to reveal the waiting car. After a long wait the door swung down again.

At eight-thirty the eggs were shriveled and the toast was like stone. An aluminum wedge scraped them into the sink, where hot water whirled them down a metal throat which digested and flushed them away to the distant sea. The dirty dishes were dropped into a hot washer and emerged twinkling dry.

Nine-fifteen, sang the clock, time to clean.

Out of warrens in the wall, tiny robot mice darted. The rooms were acrawl with the small cleaning animals, all rubber and metal. They thudded against chairs, whirling their mustached runners, kneading the rug nap, sucking gently at hidden dust. Then, like mysterious invaders, they popped into their burrows. Their pink electric eyes faded. The house was clean.

Ten o'clock. The sun came out from behind the rain. The house stood alone in a city of rubble and ashes. This was the one house left standing. At night the ruined city gave off a radioactive glow which could be seen for miles.

Ten-fifteen. The garden sprinklers whirled up in golden founts, filling the soft morning air with scatterings of brightness. The water pelted windowpanes, running down the charred west side where the house had been burned evenly free of its white paint. The entire west face of the house was black, save for five places. Here the silhouette in paint of a man mowing a lawn. Here, as in a photograph, a woman bent to pick flowers. Still farther over, their images burned on wood in one titanic instant, a small boy, hands flung into the air; higher up, the image of a thrown ball, and opposite him a girl, hands raised to catch a ball which never came down.

The five spots of paint—the man, the woman, the children, the ball—remained. The rest was a thin charcoaled layer.

The gentle sprinker rain filled the garden with falling light.

Until this day, how well the house had kept its peace. How carefully it had inquired, "Who goes there? What's the password?" and, getting no answer from lonely foxes and whining cats, it had shut up its windows and drawn shades in an old-maidenly preoccupation with self-protection which bordered on a mechanical paranoia.

It quivered at each sound, the house did. If a sparrow brushed a window, the shade snapped up. The bird, startled, flew off! No, not even a bird must touch the house!

The house was an altar with ten thousand attendants, big, small, servicing, attending, in choirs. But the gods had gone away, and the ritual of the religion continued senselessly, uselessly.

Twelve noon.

A dog whined, shivering, on the front porch.

The front door recognized the dog voice and opened. The dog, once huge and fleshy, but now gone to bone and covered with sores, moved in and through the house, tracking mud. Behind it whirred angry mice, angry at having to pick up mud, angry at inconvenience.

For not a leaf fragment blew under the door but what the wall panels flipped open and the copper scrap rats flashed swiftly out. The offending dust, hair, or paper, seized in miniature steel jaws, was raced back to the burrows. There, down tubes which fed into the cellar, it was dropped into the sighing vent of an incinerator which sat like evil Baal in a dark corner.

The dog ran upstairs, hysterically yelping to each door, at last realizing, as the house realized, that only silence was here.

It sniffed the air and scratched the kitchen door. Behind the door, the stove was making pancakes which filled the house with a rich baked odor and the scent of maple syrup.

The dog frothed at the mouth, lying at the door, sniffing, its eyes turned to fire. It ran wildly in circles, biting at its tail, spun in a frenzy, and died. It lay in the parlor for an hour.

Two o'clock, sang a voice.

Delicately sensing decay at last, the regiments of mice hummed out as softly as blown gray leaves in an electrical wind.

Two-fifteen.

The dog was gone.

In the cellar, the incinerator glowed suddenly and a whirl of sparks leaped up the chimney.

Two thirty-five.

Bridge tables sprouted from patio walls. Playing cards fluttered onto pads in a shower of pips. Martinis manifested on an oaken bench with egg-salad sandwiches. Music played.

But the tables were silent and the cards untouched.

At four o'clock the tables folded like great butterflies back through the paneled walls.

Four-thirty.

The nursery walls glowed.

Animals took shape: yellow giraffes, blue lions, pink antelopes, lilac panthers cavorting in crystal substance. The walls were glass. They looked out upon color and fantasy. Hidden films clocked through well-oiled sprockets, and the walls lived. The nursery floor was woven to resemble a crisp, cereal meadow. Over this ran aluminum roaches and iron crickets, and in the hot still air butterflies of delicate red tissue wavered among the sharp aroma of animal spoors! There was the sound like a great matted yellow hive of bees within a dark bellows, the lazy bumble of a purring lion. And there was the patter of okapi feet and the murmur of a fresh jungle rain, like other hoofs, falling upon the summer-starched grass. Now the walls dissolved into distances of parched weed, mile on mile, and warm endless sky. The animals drew away into thorn brakes and water holes.

It was the children's hour.

Five o'clock. The bath filled with clear hot water.

Six, seven, eight o'clock. The dinner dishes manipulated like magic tricks, and in the study a click. In the metal stand opposite the hearth where a fire now blazed up warmly, a cigar popped out, half an inch of soft gray ash on it, smoking, waiting.

Nine o'clock. The beds warmed their hidden circuits, for nights were cool here.

Nine-five. A voice spoke from the study ceiling:

"Mrs. McClellan, which poem would you like this evening?"

The house was silent.

The voice said at last, "Since you express no preference, I shall select a poem at random." Quiet music rose to back the voice. "Sara Teasdale. As I recall, your favorite. . . .

"There will come soft rains and the smell of the ground,
And swallows circling with their shimmering sound;

And frogs in the pools singing at night,
And wild plum trees in tremulous white;

Robins will wear their feathery fire,
Whistling their whims on a low fence-wire;

And not one will know of the war, not one
Will care at last when it is done.

Not one would mind, neither bird nor tree,
If mankind perished utterly;

And Spring herself, when she woke at dawn
Would scarely know that we were gone."

The fire burned on the stone hearth and the cigar fell away into a mound of quiet ash on its tray. The empty chairs faced each other between the silent walls, and the music played.

At ten o'clock the house began to die.

The wind blew. A falling tree bough crashed through the kitchen window. Cleaning solvent, bottled, shattered over the stove. The room was ablaze in an instant!

"Fire!" screamed a voice. The house lights flashed, water pumps shot water from the ceilings. But the solvent spread on the linoleum, licking, eating, under the kitchen door, while the voices took it up in chorus: "Fire, fire, fire!"

The house tried to save itself. Doors sprang tightly shut, but the windows were broken by the heat and the wind blew and sucked upon the fire.

The house gave ground as the fire in ten billion angry sparks moved with flaming ease from room to room and then up the stairs. While scurrying water rats squeaked from the walls, pistoled their water, and ran for more. And the wall sprays let down showers of mechanical rain.

But too late. Somewhere, sighing, a pump shrugged to a stop. The quenching rain ceased. The reserve water supply which had filled baths and washed dishes for many quiet days was gone.

The fire crackled up the stairs. It fed upon Picassos and Matisses in the upper halls, like delicacies, baking off the oily flesh, tenderly crisping the canvases into black shavings.

Now the fire lay in beds, stood in windows, changed the colors of drapes!

And then, reinforcements.

From attic trapdoors, blind robot faces peered down with faucet mouths gushing green chemical.

The fire backed off, as even an elephant must at the sight of a dead snake. Now there were twenty snakes whipping over the floor, killing the fire with a clear cold venom of green froth.

But the fire was clever. It had sent flame outside the house, up through the attic to the pumps there. An explosion! The attic brain which directed the pumps was shattered into bronze shrapnel on the beams.

The fire rushed back into every closet and felt of the clothes hung there.

The house shuddered, oak bone on bone, its bared skeleton cringing from the heat, its wire, its nerves revealed as if a surgeon had torn the skin off to let the red veins and capillaries quiver in the scalded air. Help, help! Fire! Run, run! Heat snapped mirrors like the first brittle winter ice. And the voices wailed Fire, fire, run, run, like a tragic nursery rhyme, a dozen voices, high, low, like children dying in a forest, alone, alone. And the voices fading as the wires popped their sheathings like hot chestnuts. One, two, three, four, five voices died.

In the nursery the jungle burned. Blue lions roared, purple giraffes bounded off. The panthers ran in circles, changing color, and ten million animals, running before the fire, vanished off toward a distant steaming river. . . .

Ten more voices died. In the last instant under the fire avalanche, other choruses, oblivious, could be heard announcing the time, playing music, cutting the lawn by remote-control mower, or setting an umbrella frantically out and in the slamming and opening front door, a thousand things happening, like a clock shop when each clock strikes the hour insanely before or after the other, a scene of maniac confusion, yet unity; singing, screaming, a few last cleaning mice darting bravely out to carry the horrid ashes away! And one voice, with sublime disregard for the situation, read poetry aloud in the fiery study, until all the film spools burned, until all the wires withered and the circuits cracked.

The fire burst the house and let it slam flat down, puffing out skirts of spark and smoke.

In the kitchen, an instant before the rain of fire and timber, the stove could be seen making breakfasts at a psychopathic rate, ten dozen eggs, six loaves of toast, twenty dozen bacon strips, which, eaten by fire, started the stove working again, hysterically hissing!

The crash. The attic smashing into kitchen and parlor. The parlor into cellar, cellar into sub-cellar. Deep freeze, armchair, film tapes, circuits, beds, and all like skeletons thrown in a cluttered mound deep under.

Smoke and silence. A great quantity of smoke.

Dawn showed faintly in the east. Among the ruins, one wall stood alone. Within the wall, a last voice said, over and over again and again, even as the sun rose to shine upon the heaped rubble and steam:

"Today is August 5, 2026, today is August 5, 2026, today is . . ."

QUESTIONS

1. What is the situation as the story opens?
2. Does the story have a main character? If so, who or what is it?
3. From what point of view is the story told? Why is the selection of this point of view appropriate?
4. List examples of simile, metaphor, and personification.

5. One type of figurative language is found throughout much of the story. Which type is it? How is its use especially appropriate in this story?

6. How is the Teasdale poem (p. 220) relevant in both imagery and theme?

7. What significance emerges from the contrast between images of nature and images of technology?

chapter 8

The Language of Tone

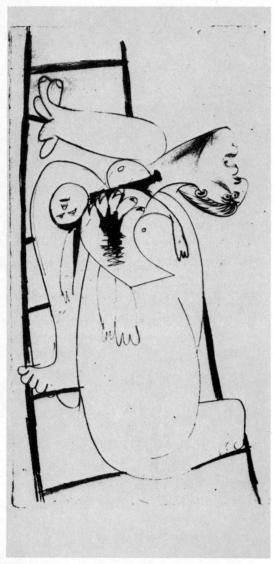

Pablo Picasso. *Mother with Dead Child on Ladder.*
1937. Pencil on white paper. 17⅞" × 9½". On
extended loan to The Museum of Modern Art,
New York, from the estate of the artist.

Suppose you are a supervisor with the difficult task of pointing out that a worker is putting in too little effort on the job. How you choose your words will determine how you come across to the worker—angry, sarcastic, surprised, friendly. "You had better stop loafing or you'll be fired" seems too threatening. Since you don't want to create an antagonistic relationship, you try: "I've noticed that your work recently has not been quite as good as it usually is. Is there anything wrong? Is there any way I can be of help?" Chances are that the worker will get the point about lack of effort and still think of you as sympathetic. The way your negative attitude toward the worker's efforts is expressed (sympathetic rather than threatening) is called *tone.*

Most of us readily catch the tone of voice of someone who is speaking to us. But tone in writing is harder to spot. Writers lack the advantages of body language and of sound effects such as pitch and volume. When speaking, we can arch an eyebrow, smile, sit on a desk. We can talk slowly with great emphasis, pause, interject a laugh. What if the lagging worker responds initially with a "Well . . ."? Because you can see and hear the worker, you will probably identify the tone—indignant, reluctant, thoughtful—even before you hear any additional words. But that same "Well . . ." on the printed page does not tell us, by itself, how to read its tone.

How, then, do we recognize tone in our reading? Sometimes an author tells us directly: "Margaret replied bitterly, choking back her resentment." Usually, though, tone is conveyed indirectly, embodied in all of the elements that comprise the work. We may need to answer several questions before we can arrive at a sound conclusion about the tone of a particular word, phrase, or passage. What kind of character is speaking? In what situation? Choosing what words?

OBSERVING THE TONE INDICATORS

One of the most important indicators of tone is *context,* the circumstances and language that surround words. The situational context, what is happening, helps us to understand what the speaker is reacting to. The verbal context, what has already been said and what will be said, helps us to see the overall pattern of the speaker's expression. Try to determine the effect of context on the tone of the poem that follows.

WALT WHITMAN   (1819–1892)

When I Heard the Learn'd Astronomer

When I heard the learn'd astronomer,
When the proofs, the figures, were ranged in columns before me,
When I was shown the charts and diagrams, to add, divide, and
    measure them,
When I sitting heard the astronomer where he lectured with much
    applause in the lecture-room,
How soon unaccountable I became tired and sick,   5
Till rising and gliding out I wandered off by myself,
In the mystical moist night-air, and from time to time,
Looked up in perfect silence at the stars.

QUESTIONS

1. What attitude seems to be conveyed the first time you read line 1? How would
   you characterize the attitude in this line once you have read the entire poem?
2. What word in line 1 would you now read differently? What would be the
   difference?
3. How does the contrast between "sitting" (line 4) and "rising" (line 6) contribute
   to a difference in tone?

At first the speaker in this poem seems to be admiringly and humbly describing an informational lecture on astronomy. However, the poem as a whole leads us to a different conclusion. We learn from lines 5 and 6 that the speaker walked out on the lecture (situational context). The speaker's words (verbal context) gradually reveal a negative reaction. The main clause that all of the subordinate *when* clauses have been leading up to is the statement: "I became tired and sick." We now read the tone of lines 1 through 4 differently—as skeptical and bored. Another effect of verbal context on tone is the contrast in diction between lines 1 through 4 and lines 6 through 8. Although appropriate to the study, "figures" and "diagrams" seem dry and insignificant when compared to the wondrous "mystical moist night-air" outside the lecture hall.

The shift in tone in Whitman's poem from skepticism to wonder is achieved through a *shift in diction*, another important tone indicator. The language selected for lines 1–4 is scientific, whereas the language of lines 5–8 is emotional. Especially effective in conveying tone are changes in the level of diction (as from formal to colloquial). In Donald Barthelme's story "Report" (pp. 244–48), the appalling quality of the chief engineer's delight in producing new forms of destruction is conveyed by the unexpected interjection of the informal word "dandies":

> We have hypodermic darts capable of piebalding the enemy's pigmentation. We have rots, blights, and rusts capable of attacking his alphabet. Those are dandies.

The suggestive, asociative quality of a word is called its *connotation*, as opposed to its dictionary definitions or *denotation*. Whitman probably ended his poem with "stars" because the word *star* suggests a beauty far beyond the ordinary concerns of people—even of astronomers. A dictionary might call a star a luminous, gaseous celestial body, but when Oscar Wilde said, "We are all in the gutter, but some of us are looking at the stars," he meant more than we would find in a dictionary definition. He was relying on our association of "gutter" with degradation and of "stars" with elevation of spirit. Selecting words with strong connotations is one of an author's most effective means for creating tone.

DISTINGUISHING BETWEEN AUTHOR AND SPEAKER

In Whitman's "When I Heard the Learn'd Astronomer," the speaker's attitude is shared by the author. Whitman presents a speaker who is not so buried in astronomical charts as to miss the beauty of the night sky; the poet invites the reader to leave the lecture, as the speaker does, and experience nature directly. But, as we learned in Chapter 6 on point of view, a speaker (or narrator) is not always a reliable representative of the author. The barber who narrates Ring Lardner's "Haircut" (pp. 165–74) recalls Jim Kendall's jokes with amusement. He is delighted by Jim's cleverness and expresses an approving attitude toward Jim, concluding that Kendall was "a card." Lardner's attitude, however, is quite different. He wants readers to share with him, and with the other characters in the story, a contempt for Jim's insensitive cruelty.

The differing views of author and speaker are revealed by

the author's use of various elements that shape tone and convey attitude. In the following poem we need to distinguish between the speaker's tone and that of the poet. A reader missing the difference would miss the point of the poem.

THOMAS HARDY   (1840–1928)

The Man He Killed

"Had he and I but met
By some old ancient inn,
We should have sat us down to wet
Right many a nipperkin!

"But ranged as infantry,   5
And staring face to face,
I shot at him as he at me
And killed him in his place.

"I shot him dead because—
Because he was my foe,   10
Just so: my foe of course he was;
That's clear enough; although

"He thought he'd 'list, perhaps,
Off-hand like—just as I—
Was out of work—had sold his traps—   15
No other reason why.

"Yes; quaint and curious war is!
You shoot a fellow down
You'd treat if met where any bar is,
Or help to half-a-crown."   20

The speaker of "The Man He Killed" is a soldier in battle who has killed someone, presumably for the first time. He is thinking how the soldier he shot might have been his friend had they met under other circumstances. The speaker wonders why, then, he killed the man, but without a satisfactory explanation dismisses the problem by calling war "quaint" and "curious." But Hardy does not want us to dismiss it so easily. Instead, we are drawn into an awareness of the irrationality of war. Thus the attitude of the author (war is absurd and divisive) is not the same as the attitude of the speaker (surely there is a good reason for this killing). The speaker's tone can be described as puzzled and, then, resigned, whereas the author is dismayed at the senseless killing and the repression of natural feelings of brotherhood.

We discover this difference in tone and attitude by observing the poet's selection of language. The repetition of "because" in lines 9 and 12, the hesitant "although" that hangs suspended at the end of line 12, and the dashes in lines 9, 14, and 15 cause the thought pattern to sound disjointed. The effect is to call our attention to the speaker's circular reasoning. Why did he kill his enemy? Because that enemy was his "foe." The speaker labels this answer as "clear enough," but we are expected to label it illogical. The poet leads us to question the speaker's conclusion and to recognize that the more appropriate response would be: "Yes, cruel and senseless war is!"

IRONY

We could also describe the tone of "The Man He Killed" as ironic. *Irony* is created by bringing together what only appears to be true with what is actually true. Appearance and reality are placed side by side to lead us, through contrast, to a new perception of truth. In Hardy's poem the difference between the speaker's tone and that of the poet helps us to see that, ironically, the speaker's attempt to face the question of why he has killed his enemy merely leads to a rationalization that enables him to avoid the issue.

Irony is usually divided into three categories: verbal irony, irony of situation, and dramatic irony. In each of these there exists some form of contradiction.

Verbal Irony

In verbal irony the contradiction is between what the words say and what the speaker means. A parent might tell a child all dressed up for an important formal occasion, "You certainly look wonderful!" If the tone is sincere, it will convey the admiring praise that we would expect from these words. But what if the child has just finished running through some briars after playing in the mud? Depending on the situation between parent and child at that moment, the same four words might sound dismayed, amused, or sarcastic. These tones, since they contradict what the words themselves seem to mean, create verbal irony.

Irony of Situation

In irony of situation the contradiction is between what we would expect to happen and what actually does happen. We move to a house surrounded by woods to be close to nature. Two months later the bulldozers arrive and level the trees to make way for a shopping center. A racing driver decides on one last race before retiring. He crashes and dies. The person spreading false rumors about us turns out to be our best friend. Maupassant's story "The Necklace" (pp. 84–90) contains several instances of irony of situation. Mme. Loisel's moment of greatest social triumph, the ministerial ball, leads to her loss of the necklace and the resulting years of poverty. She is a woman who feels herself "born for all the delicacies and all the luxuries," yet she ends up "washing the floor with great swishes of water." The borrowed necklace that the Loisels replace at the cost of 36,000 francs and ten years of drudgery turns out to have been false, worth only about 500 francs.

Dramatic Irony

In *dramatic irony* the contradiction is between what is understood by an audience or by readers and what is understood by a character. We see the irony because we know more than the character. An early use of dramatic irony was in ancient Greek tragedy. Since the plots of Greek tragedies were based on familiar legends, audiences would generally know beforehand the outcome of the action. When in Sophocles's *Oedipus Rex* Oedipus curses the murderer of King Laius and swears to avenge his death as a son would, the audience knows that, ironically, Oedipus is unknowingly both the king's murderer and his son. He is cursing himself.

We also find dramatic irony when we are aware of a contradiction between the author's attitude and the speaker's attitude as in Hardy's "The Man He Killed" or Lardner's "Haircut." Near the end of "Haircut," after the shooting, the barber says: "Jim was a sucker to leave a new beginner have his gun, let alone the half-wit. It probably served Jim right, what he got. But still we miss him around here." The barber thinks the shooting "served Jim right" because Jim had been foolish; Lardner has led us to see that it "served Jim right" because of his despicable actions. This discrepancy between what the barber means and what we understand creates dramatic irony.

Understatement, Overstatement, and Paradox

Three figures of speech related to irony, in that they all express contradictions, are understatement, overstatement, and paradox. All three figures add emphasis and have a significant effect on tone.

Understatement is a form of verbal irony in which less is stated than is meant. Hurricane Alfred has just hit the shoreline with 100 mph winds, and torrents of rain are cascading from the darkening skies. You turn to your friend on the street corner and comment: "Looks like we're in for a shower." You are understating your reaction to the storm. *Overstatement* (or *hyperbole*) says more than is meant. We exaggerate to create overstatement when we say "Uncle Jack is eating us out of house and home" or "I waited an eternity for this bus." Overstatement can be used either to heighten a sincere feeling or to create irony. The effect will depend on the situational context. Take, for example, "She's the fastest swimmer who ever lived!" If the swimmer is winning a race, we have an honest emotion being emphasized. If the swimmer is trailing far behind, we have irony.

A *paradox* is a statement that seems contradictory but is somehow true and can be explained. You are stating a paradox if you look at your checkbook and say "I can't understand it; the more money we make the less we have." If you examine your checkbook, you may find that the truth of the matter is you have been acquiring expensive tastes more rapidly than your salary has been rising. That explains the apparent contradiction. Often, explaining a paradox requires reading part of the statement metaphorically. For example, "The child is father of the man" (Wordsworth) is a logical contradiction until we see that father is used as a metaphor. A child can be compared to the "father" of the person that child will become when mature. The meaning, then, is that what we are like as children determines what we are like as adults. Observe that the paradoxical statement is much more emphatic than the longer, undramatic explanation.

Satire

A form of literature that often employs irony is *satire*. Satire ridicules the vices and follies of humanity, usually with some improvement in mind. Sometimes satire is angry, biting; at other times it is more gently humorous. (You will want to avoid confusing the terms *satire* and *sarcasm*. A sarcastic tone may be used to create satire. One term refers to tone, the other to the writer's purpose.) The effect of satire is similar to that of a political cartoon. The cartoonist exaggerates visually, for example, by picturing a well-fed politician weighed down by money bags begging John Q. Public, an emaciated skeleton in rags, for higher taxes. Irony, with its power to bring out the contrast between appearance and reality, is an effective instrument for creating satire. You will find good examples of satire at the end of this chapter in Donald Barthelme's story "Report," Jean Giraudoux's play *The Apollo of Bellac,* and W. H. Auden's poem "The Unknown Citizen," the subject of the student essay.

EXERCISES ON TONE

1. The poems "Crossing the Bar" (p. 568) and "Do Not Go Gentle into That Good Night" (p. 590) have the same subject but different attitudes toward that subject. Analyze each poem and then prepare a comparative chart that states, for each: the poem's subject, the poem's tone, and your evidence—the key words and passages that create the tone. For each piece of evidence, state the literary technique used to shape tone.

2. For each of the following passages name the literary technique used and then explain the passage.

   a. One short sleep past, we wake eternally,
      And Death shall be no more; Death thou shalt die.

      John Donne

   b. He has "the strength of twenty men."

      William Shakespeare

   c. But the most wonderful love, the Love of all loves,
      Even greater than the love for Mother,

Is the infinite, tenderest, passionate love
Of one dead drunk for another.

Anonymous

d. Treason doth never prosper: what's the reason?
For if it prosper, none dare call it treason.

John Harrington

e. Nature, to be commanded, must be obeyed.

Francis Bacon

f. Do not weep, maiden, for war is kind.
Because your lover threw wild hands toward the sky
And the affrighted steed ran on alone,
Do not weep.
War is kind.

Stephen Crane

g. Becoming a father is easy enough,
But being one can be rough.

Wilhelm Busch

h. Give me a kiss, and to that kiss a score;
Then to that twenty, add a hundred more:
A thousand to that hundred: so kiss on,
To make that thousand up a million.
Treble that million, and when that is done,
Let's kiss afresh, as when we first begun.

Robert Herrick

i. JULIET. My only love sprung from my only hate!
Too early seen unknown, and known too late!
Prodigious birth of love it is to me
That I must love a loathed enemy.

William Shakespeare

WRITING ABOUT TONE

What was said in Chapter 7 (see pp. 209–10) about stylistic analysis
applies equally to writing about tone. You will still be relying on a

close reading of the author's use of language. Brief quotations of the words and phrases that illustrate this use will again be an important part of your evidence. Watch for the word chosen for its connotation, the phrase interjected to create a shift in diction. Quote only the language relevant to your point; then make the connection. The words "quaint" and "curious" in Hardy's "The Man He Killed" are good examples of significant word choices. As you read the student essay on "The Unknown Citizen," note the selective use of quoted evidence.

You may also need to discuss character and situation. That the speaker in "The Man He Killed" is an ordinary fellow who has killed a man for the first time is important to tone. Were he a weary veteran of many battles, we might read his tone as bitter resignation rather than puzzlement. What is happening to what kind of speaker interacts with the words spoken to help determine the tone.

If you are assigned an essay on tone, you should first determine a general approach. Will you be writing about the tone of the work as a whole or focusing on a specific passage? Will you be examining the author's tone, that of a particular speaker, or the difference between author and speaker? The student essay on "The Unknown Citizen" centers on the contrast in attitude between speaker and poet to reveal the poem's meaning. An example of a topic on a specific passage would be an analysis of how particular lines should be spoken, for instance in the meeting of Agnes and Therese in *The Apollo of Bellac*. (Some assignments calling for the analysis of a specific passage lead to a short paper demonstrating the ability to perform close reading, but other assignments call for relating a specific passage to the work as a whole. When faced with the second assignment, make sure that you connect the analyzed passage to the rest of the work.)

Once you have determined your general approach, you will need a word or phrase that describes the tone you want to write about and evidence from the work of techniques that create the tone. If you have trouble describing the work's tone, then begin by listing evidence: significant words, an ironic line, a paradox, with its meaning explained. Then try again to generalize about tone. Finding precise words for tone is not easy. You may need to press your vocabulary to its limits to bring to mind that perfect adjective that keeps eluding you. But the effort is both necessary and rewarding. Don't settle for a general *negative* when you can use a specific *scornful*. You should also consider modifying your tone describers.

Overbearingly jubilant carries a meaning impossible to state in one word. A tone of *bitter scorn* is more intense than scorn alone. Here is a list of some of the words that can be used for tone. See how many more you can add.

angry, bitter, scornful, outraged, _____

friendly, sympathetic, encouraging, jovial, _____

sad, peevish, disconsolate, mournful, _____

happy, humorous, comic, joyous, _____

loving, adoring, seductive, passionate, _____

Having described the tone precisely, you can then formulate a thesis relating that tone to the way it is created in the work. As you begin to read the student essay on "The Unknown Citizen," note how the opening paragraph sets up such a thesis: ironic, satirical tone is related to the contrast of language and attitude.

W. H. Auden (1907–1973)

The Unknown Citizen

> *(To JS/07/M/378*
> *This Marble Monument*
> *Is Erected by the State)*

He was found by the Bureau of Statistics to be
One against whom there was no official complaint,
And all the reports on his conduct agree
That, in the modern sense of an old-fashioned word, he was a saint,
For in everything he did he served the Greater Community.   5
Except for the War till the day he retired
He worked in a factory and never got fired,
But satisfied his employers, Fudge Motors Inc.
Yet he wasn't a scab or odd in his views,
For his Union reports that he paid his dues,   10
(Our report on his Union shows it was sound)
And our Social Psychology workers found
That he was popular with his mates and liked a drink.

The Press are convinced that he bought a paper every day
And that his reactions to advertisements were normal in every way.   15
Policies taken out in his name prove that he was fully insured,
And his Health-card shows he was once in hospital but left it cured.
Both Producers Research and High-Grade Living declare
He was fully sensible to the advantages of the Instalment Plan
And had everything necessary to the Modern Man,   20
A phonograph, a radio, a car and a frigidaire.
Our researchers into Public Opinion are content
That he held the proper opinions for the time of year;
When there was peace, he was for peace; when there was war, he went.
He was married and added five children to the population,   25
Which our Eugenist says was the right number for a parent of his
    generation,
And our teachers report that he never interfered with their education.
Was he free? Was he happy? The question is absurd:
Had anything been wrong, we should certainly have heard.

QUESTIONS

1. Who is speaking? What is the occasion?
2. What is the first rhyme in the poem? (Read the poem aloud if necessary to find the rhyme.) What does Auden accomplish by this first rhyme?
3. What do we know about the citizen? What don't we know?
4. How is the rhythm at times (as in lines 6–7 or 9–10) inappropriate to the occasion? What is the effect?
5. What is the effect of the name "Fudge Motors Inc."?
6. What word rhymes with "drink" (line 13)? What does Auden accomplish by this rhyme?
7. What might Auden change in line 21 were he writing this poem today? Would the point remain the same? What is the point?
8. What is the speaker's tone? What is the poet's attitude toward his subject?

STUDENT ESSAY

The Use of Tone in Auden's "The Unknown Citizen"

Mark Popvichal

The speaker of W.H. Auden's poem "The Unknown Citizen" praises a nameless citizen who to the state was a "saint," but Auden satirizes the speaker and his values by making it clear that the citizen, by devoting himself entirely to serving the "Greater Community," had lost his identity. Auden accomplishes his satire through clever word choice that brings out an ironic contrast between the language of the speaker who delivers the eulogy and the attitude of the poet.

Although the speaker commends the citizen, his word choice reveals a patronizing tone. He talks about the citizen as though the citizen were a good little boy and the speaker an elementary school principal. First we are told that the "reports on his conduct" agree that the citizen was a "saint." To support this elevation to sainthood, the speaker informs us that the citizen "satisfied his employers," that public opinion analysts were "content" his opinions were "proper," that he contributed "the right number of children" to the population, and that he "never interfered" with his children's education. The speaker is clearly pleased with what he considers exemplary behavior on the part of the citizen, but the poem leads us to question the standards by which the citizen is being judged.

A clue to Auden's attitude toward the speaker's values comes in the last two lines of the poem through the connotation of "free" and "happy" and the suggestive ambiguity of "absurd" and "wrong":

Was he free? Was he happy? The question is absurd:

Had anything been wrong, we should certainly have heard.

STUDENT ESSAY

Now, in America, land of the free and home of the brave pursuers of happiness, we take "free" and "happy" to be nice words. The two questions in the second-to-last line could have been penned by old T. Jefferson himself. Yet the speaker immediately follows the questions with the remark about their absurdity. The colon indicates that "absurd" refers to the idea of the last line that if the citizen had not been free or happy the speaker would have known. But he could also be suggesting that it is absurd even to consider such questions. To show us we are on the right track, Auden immediately follows this ambiguity with still another. In the last line, "wrong" could mean either that the speaker would have heard if something were "wrong" in the sense that the citizen wasn't free or happy, or that he would have heard if something were "wrong" in the sense that he was free or happy. Auden has planted in our minds the question of whether the speaker's values encompass a negative view of freedom and happiness.

Having been thus led to question the values held by the speaker, let's examine the speaker's language as a reflection of his values. The level of diction is consistently formal and remote, almost computerized. The citizen isn't described as "having five kids and raising a family"; instead, he "added five children to the population." The curious use of capital letters throughout the poem reveals a pattern: all capitalized words relate to the concept of people as groups: "Greater Community," "Union," "Health Card," "Eugenist." By associating "Modern Man" with various social groups, the speaker indicates he sees humankind as just another unit of the state. Even the speaker's own identity is submerged as he hides behind the third person plural ("our" and "we") and his reliance on the experts.

The technique used by Auden to satirize such values is irony; through dramatic irony we find how Auden and the speaker differ in attitude

STUDENT ESSAY

toward the citizen. The speaker praises the citizen because "Our researchers into Public Opinion are content / That he held the proper opinions for the time of year," but Auden's implication is that the citizen didn't think for himself. The speaker says that "He wasn't a scab or odd in his views," but the connotation of "odd" is negative, showing us that the speaker admires lack of independent thought. The speaker praises the citizen because "he bought a paper every day / And . . . his reactions to advertisements were normal in every way." Auden, by associating the citizen's daily purchase of the newspaper with his reactions to the ads, is suggesting that the citizen's reading of the papers was superficial and mechanical.

We can now see that Auden's choice of words for the title is carefully calculated to express the irony that, despite the vast accumulation of statistics about the citizen, we really know nothing about his personal life. There is a direct parallel between the citizen and the Unknown Soldier who unselfishly sacrificed himself for the country, giving up his own personal needs without personal recognition, glory, or reward. The citizen, however, instead of dying for his country, "served the Greater Community" and in doing so became just a number, "JS/07/M/378," living by the "experts'" ideals of what a person should be and do. He thought the right thoughts, bought the right products, and had the right number of children. In other words, he subjugated his individuality in order to fit, belong, and serve. The soldier sacrificed his life; the citizen sacrificed his soul.

SELECTIONS FOR FURTHER STUDY

ROBERT GRAVES   (1895–1985)

The Naked and the Nude

For me, the naked and the nude
(By lexicographers construed
As synonyms that should express
The same deficiency of dress
Or shelter) stand as wide apart   5
As love from lies, or truth from art.

Lovers without reproach will gaze
On bodies naked and ablaze;
The Hippocratic eye will see
In nakedness, anatomy;
And naked shines the Goddess when   10
She mounts her lion among men.

The nude are bold, the nude are sly
To hold each treasonable eye.
While draping by a showman's trick   15
Their dishabille in rhetoric,
They grin a mock-religious grin
Of scorn at those of naked skin.

The naked, therefore, who compete
Against the nude may know defeat;   20
Yet when they both together tread
The briary pastures of the dead,
By Gorgons with long whips pursued,
How naked go the sometime nude!

QUESTIONS

1. Check the denotations of *lexicographers* (line 2), *construed* (line 2), *hippocratic* (line 9), *dishabille* (line 16), and *Gorgons* (line 23). Then paraphrase the poem, turning each stanza into one or two sentences.

2. What do the three examples of "the naked" presented in stanza 2 have in common?

3. Substitute synonyms for *gaze* (line 7), *bold* (line 13), *sly* (line 13), and *grin* (line 17). What are the effects of the substitutions? What does this tell you about the connotations of the four words Graves chose?

4. Explain the metaphor in line 16.

5. Why might "the naked" experience "defeat"?

6. What, then, is the difference in connotation between the words *naked* and *nude*, according to Graves?

7. Graves's distinction between *naked* and *nude* does not account for all uses of these words. How appropriate, for example, would be the Graves version of *nude* for the following: a pamphlet written for nudists, an advertisement for a strip show, an article in *Art News* on painting the human figure?

E. E. Cummings   (1894–1963)

next to of course god america i

"next to of course god america i
love you land of the pilgrims' and so forth oh
say can you see by the dawn's early my
country 'tis of centuries come and go
and are no more what of it we should worry   5
in every language even deafanddumb
thy sons acclaim your glorious name by gorry
by jingo by gee by gosh by gum
why talk of beauty what could be more beautiful than these heroic happy dead   10
who rushed like lions to the roaring slaughter
they did not stop to think they died instead
then shall the voice of liberty be mute?"

He spoke. And drank rapidly a glass of water

QUESTIONS

1. One characteristic of Cummings's style is the lack of capitalization and punctuation. What is the effect of that lack in this poem? What is the effect of the limited amount of capitalization and punctuation that does occur?

2. What is the situation in the poem? Who speaks lines 1–13? Who speaks line 14? How do the speakers differ?

3. What different kinds of diction can you find? What phrases have you heard
   before? Where?
4. Look up *jingoism*. What is the double meaning of "by jingo" in line 8?
5. What tone does the word *rapidly* give to line 14?
6. What is Cummings satirizing?

ANDREW MARVELL   (1621–1678)

To His Coy Mistress

Had we but world enough, and time,
This coyness, lady, were no crime.
We would sit down, and think which way
To walk, and pass our long love's day.
Thou by the Indian Ganges' side   5
Shouldst rubies find; I by the tide
Of Humber would complain. I would
Love you ten years before the Flood,
And you should, if you please, refuse   10
Till the conversion of the Jews.
My vegetable° love should grow   *slowly vegetative*
Vaster than empires, and more slow;
An hundred years should go to praise
Thine eyes, and on thy forehead gaze;
Two hundred to adore each breast,   15
But thirty thousand to the rest;
An age at least to every part,
And the last age should show your heart.
For, lady, you deserve this state,
Nor would I love at lower rate.   20
    But at my back I always hear
Time's wingèd chariot hurrying near;
And yonder all before us lie
Deserts of vast eternity.
Thy beauty shall no more be found,   25
Nor in thy marble vault shall sound
My echoing song; then worms shall try
That long preserved virginity,
And your quaint honor turn to dust,
And into ashes all my lust.   30

The grave's a fine and private place,
But none, I think, do there embrace.
    Now therefore, while the youthful hue
Sits on thy skin like morning dew,
And while thy willing soul tránspires   35
At evey pore with instant fires,
Now let us sport us while we may,
And now, like amorous birds of prey,
Rather at once our time devour
Than languish in his slow-chapped power.   40
Let us roll all our strength and all
Our sweetness up into one ball,
And tear our pleasures with rough strife
Thorough° the iron gates of life.   *through*   45
Thus, though we cannot make our sun
Stand still, yet we will make him run.

QUESTIONS

1. Who is speaking to whom, and what is the situation?
2. Summarize the speaker's argument using the logical structure *if, but, therefore.*
3. What figure of speech do we find throughout the first verse paragraph? What is its effect on the speaker's tone?
4. Find examples of irony of situation and understatement in the second verse paragraph.
5. How does the tone shift in the second section?
6. Explain the personification in line 22.
7. Explain the metaphor in line 30.
8. Explain the metonymy in line 45.
9. What is the paradox of the last two lines? How can it be explained?

JOHN DONNE   (1572–1631)

Batter My Heart, Three-Personed God

Batter my heart, three-personed God, for you
As yet but knock, breathe, shine, and seek to mend;
That I may rise and stand, o'erthrow me; and bend
Your force to break, blow, burn, and make me new.

I, like an usurped town, to another due,   5
Labor to admit you, but oh, to no end;
Reason, your viceroy in me, me should defend
But is captived, and proves weak or untrue.
Yet dearly I love you and would be loved fain,
But am betrothed unto your enemy;   10
Divorce me, untie or break that knot again,
Take me to you, imprison me, for I
Except you enthrall me, never shall be free,
Nor ever chaste, except you ravish me.

QUESTIONS

1. What meanings do you find in the dictionary for *fain* (line 9), *enthrall* (line 13), and *ravish* (line 14)?
2. Why is the speaker addressing God?
3. What is the implied metaphor in "Batter my heart"?
4. What is the effect of rhythm on the speaker's tone?
5. How is the speaker "like an usurped town"? Who is the "enemy" (line 10)?
6. Explain the religious paradox "three-personed God."
7. Identify and explain the paradoxes in line 3, lines 12–13, and line 14.
8. What does the speaker say? Restate the speaker's prayer more simply—in your own words.

DONALD BARTHELME (b. 1932)

Report

Our group is against the war. But the war goes on. I was sent to Cleveland to talk to the engineers. The engineers were meeting in Cleveland. I was supposed to persuade them not to do what they are going to do. I took United's 4:45 from LaGuardia arriving in Cleveland at 6:13. Cleveland is dark blue at that hour. I went directly to the motel, where the engineers were meeting. Hundreds of engineers attended the Cleveland meeting. I noticed many fractures among the engineers, bandages, traction. I noticed what appeared to be fracture of the carpal scaphoid in six examples. I noticed numerous fractures of the humeral shaft, of the os calcis, of the pelvic gridle. I noticed a high incidence of clay-shoveller's fracture. I could not account for these fractures. The engineers were making calculations, taking measurements, sketching on the blackboard, drinking beer, throwing bread, buttonholing employers, hurling glasses into the fireplace. They were friendly.

They were friendly. They full of love and information. The chief engineer wore shades. Patella in Monk's traction, clamshell fracture by the look of it. He was standing in a slum of beer bottles and microphone cable. "Have some of this chicken à la Isambard Kingdom Brunel the Great Ingineer," he said. "And declare who you are and what we can do for you. What is your line, distinguished guest?"

"Software," I said. "In every sense. I am here representing a small group of interested parties. We are interested in your thing, which seems to be functioning. In the midst of so much dysfunction, function is interesting. Other people's things don't seem to be working. The State Department's thing doesn't seem to be working. The U.N.'s thing doesn't seem to be working. The democratic left's thing doesn't seem to be working. Buddha's thing—"

"Ask us anything about our thing, which seems to be working," the chief engineer said. "We will open our hearts and heads to you, Software Man, because we want to be understood and loved by the great lay public, and have our marvels appreciated by that public, for which we daily unsung produce tons of new marvels each more life-enhancing than the last. Ask us anything. Do you want to know about evaporated thin-film metallurgy? Monolithic and hybrid integrated-circuit processes? The algebra of inequalities? Optimization theory? Complex high-speed microminiature closed and open loop systems? Fixed variable mathematical cost searches? Epitaxial deposition of semi-conductor materials? Gross interfaced space gropes? We also have specialists in the cuckooflower, the doctorfish, and the dumdum bullet as these relate to aspects of today's expanding technology, and they do in the damnedest ways."

I spoke to him then about the war. I said the same things people always say when they speak against the war. I said that the war was wrong. I said that large countries should not burn down small countries. I said that the government had made a series of errors. I said that these errors once small and forgivable were now immense and unforgivable. I said that the government was attempting to conceal its original errors under layers of new erors. I said that the government was sick with error, giddy with it. I said that ten thousand of our soldiers had already been killed in pursuit of the government's errors. I said that tens of thousands of the enemy's soldiers and civilians had been killed because of various errors, ours and theirs. I said that we are responsible for errors made in our name. I said that the government should not be allowed to make additional errors.

"Yes, yes," the chief engineer said, "there is doubtless much truth in what you say, but we can't possibly *lose* the war, can we? And stopping is losing, isn't it? The war regarded as a process, stopping regarded as an abort? We don't know *how* to lose a war. That skill is not among our skills. Our array smashes their array, that is what we know. That is the process. That is what is.

"But let's not have any more of this dispiriting downbeat counter-productive talk. I have a few new marvels here I'd like to discuss with you just briefly. A few new marvels that are just about ready to be gaped at by the admiring layman. Consider for instance the area of realtime online computer-controlled wish evaporation. Wish evaporation is going to be crucial in meeting the rising expectations of the world's peoples, which are as you know rising entirely too fast."

I noticed then distributed about the room a great many transverse fractures of the ulna. "The development of the pseudo-ruminant stomach for underdeveloped peoples," he went on, "is one of our interesting things you should be interested in. With the pseudo-ruminant stomach they can chew cuds, that is to say, eat grass. Blue is the most popular color worldwide and for that reason we are working with certain strains of your native Kentucky *Poa pratensis,* or bluegrass, as the staple input for the p/r stomach cycle, which would also give a shot in the arm to our balance-of-payments thing don't you know. . . ." I noticed about me then a great number of metatarsal fractures in banjo splints, "The kangaroo initiative . . . eight hundred thousand harvested last year . . . highest percentage of edible protein of any herbivore yet studied . . ."

"Have new kangaroos been planted?"

The engineer looked at me.

"I intuit your hatred and jealousy of our thing," he said. "The ineffectual always hate our thing and speak of it as anti-human, which is not at all a meaningful way to speak of our thing. Nothing mechanical is alien to me," he said (amber spots making bursts of light in his shades), "because I am human, in a sense, and if I think it up, then 'it' is human too, whatever 'it' may be. Let me tell you, Software Man, we have been damned forbearing in the matter of this little war you declare yourself to be interested in. Function is the cry, and our thing is functioning like crazy. There are things we could do that we have not done. Steps we could take that we have not taken. These steps are, regarded in a certain light, the light of our enlightened self-interest, quite justifiable steps. We could, of course, get irritated. We could, of course, *lose patience.*

"We could, of course, release thousands upon thousands of self-powered crawling-along-the-ground lengths of titanium wire eighteen inches long with a diameter of .0005 centimetres (that is to say, invisible) which, scenting an enemy, climb up his trouser leg and wrap themselves around his neck. We have developed those. They are within our capabilities. We could, of course, release in the arena of the upper air our new improved pufferfish toxin which precipitates an identity crisis. No special technical problems there. That is almost laughably easy. We could, of course, place up to two million maggots in their rice within twenty-four hours. The maggots are ready, massed in secret staging areas in Alabama. We have hypodermic darts capable of piebalding the enemy's pigmentation. We have rots, blights, and rusts capable of attacking his alphabet. Those are dandies. We have a hut-shrinking chemical which penetrates the fibres of the bamboo, causing it, the hut, to strangle its occupants. This operates only after 10 P.M., when people are sleeping. Their mathematics are at the mercy of a suppurating surd we have invented. We have a family of fishes trained to attack their fishes. We have the deadly testicle-destroying telegram. The cable companies are coöperating. We have a green substance that, well, I'd rather not talk about. We have a secret word that, if pronounced, produces multiples fractures in all living things in an area the size of four football fields."

"That's why—"

"Yes. Some damned fool couldn't keep his mouth shut. The point is that the whole structure of enemy life is within our power to *rend, vitiate, devour,* and *crush.* But that's not the interesting thing."

"You recount these possibilities with uncommon relish."

"Yes I realize that there is too much relish here. But *you* must realize that these capabilities represent in and of themselves highly technical and complex and interesting problems and hurdles on which our boys have expended many thousands of hours of hard work and brilliance. And that the effects are often grossly exaggerated by irresponsible victims. And that the whole thing represents a fantastic series of triumphs for the multi-disciplined problem-solving team concept."

"I appreciate that."

"We *could* unleash all this technology at once. You can imagine what would happen then. But that's not the interesting thing."

"What is the interesting thing?"

"The interesting thing is that we have *a moral sense.* It is on punched cards, perhaps the most advanced and sensitive moral sense the world has ever known."

"Because it is on punched cards?"

"It considers all considerations in endless and subtle detail," he said. "It even quibbles. With this great new moral tool, how can we go wrong? I confidently predict that, although we *could* employ all this splendid new weaponry I've been telling you about, *we're not going to do it.*"

"We're not going to do it?"

I took United's 5:44 from Cleveland arriving at Newark at 7:19. New Jersey is bright pink at that hour. Living things move about the surface of New Jersey at that hour molesting each other only in traditional ways. I made my report to the group. I stressed the friendliness of the engineers.

I said, It's all right. I said, We have a moral sense. I said, *We're not going to do it.* They didn't believe me.

QUESTIONS

1. Why has Barthelme titled this story "Report"?
2. What does the author accomplish by the repeated use of medical terms?
3. What is "software"? What is the opposite of software? How is this contrast relevant to the story?
4. Find examples of at least two different types of jargon.
5. When the narrator asks the chief engineer, "Have new kangaroos been planted?" What is his tone? How do you know?
6. What is ironic about the chief engineer's claiming that the engineers have a "moral sense"?
7. When the chief engineer calls this sense "the interesting thing," what is his tone? What is Barthelme's tone?
8. What is Barthelme satirizing?

JEAN GIRAUDOUX   (1882–1944)

The Apollo of Bellac

Adapted by Maurice Valency from the French

CHARACTERS

   Agnes
   Therese
   The Clerk
   The Man°
   The Vice President
   Mr. Cracheton
   Mr. Lepedura
   Mr. Rasemutte
   Mr. Schultz
   The President

   ° *Note:* The reader should bear in mind that Apollo, the Greek God of Music, Poetry, Prophecy, and Medicine (later also considered the God of the Sun) was believed to be the prototype of Manly Beauty, and could therefore be regarded as the God of Beauty as well.

Chevredent
The Chairman of the Board

Scene: The reception room of the International Bureau of Inventions, S.A.

This is a large, well-appointed room on the second floor of a magnificent office building in Paris. The French windows are open and afford us a view of treetops. There is an elaborate crystal chandelier hanging from the ceiling. The morning sun plays upon it. On a pedestal large enough to conceal a man a bust of Archimedes is set. Four doors open off the room. Three of them are marked Private. These lead into the office of the President, Right, and the First Vice President rear Right, and the Directors' Conference Room rear Left. The effect is French and very elegant, perhaps a trifle oppressive in its opulence.

Behind a period desk sits the RECEPTION CLERK. *The desk has an ivory telephone and a row of signal lights. It has also a period blotter on which the clerk is writing something in an appointment book. The* CLERK *is well on in years and his face makes one think of a caricature by Daumier.*

Time: Autumn in Paris. The present or shortly before.

At Rise: The CLERK *is writing with a meticulous air. The outer door opens.*
AGNES *comes in timidly from outer door, and stands in front of the desk.*
THE CLERK *does not look up.*

AGNES. Er—
CLERK. Yes?
AGNES. Is this the International Bureau of Inventions, Incorporated?
CLERK. Yes.
AGNES. Could I please see the Chairman of the Board?
CLERK. (*looks up*) The Chairman of the Board? No one sees the Chairman of the Board.
AGNES. Oh.

(*The outer door opens again.* THERESE *sweeps into the room. She is blonde, shapely, thirty-five, dressed in expensive mink.* CLERK *rises respectfully.*)

CLERK. Good morning, Madame.
THERESE. Is the President in?
CLERK. Yes, Madame. Of course.

(THERESE *walks haughtily to* PRESIDENT'S *door.* CLERK *opens it for her and closes it behind her. He goes back to his desk where* AGNES *is waiting.*)

AGNES. Could I see the President?
CLERK. No one sees the President.
AGNES. But I have—

CLERK.   What type of invention? Major? Intermediate? Minor?

AGNES.   I beg pardon?

CLERK.   Assistant Secretary to the Third Vice President. Come back Tuesday. Name?

AGNES.   My name?

CLERK.   You have a name, I presume?

(THE MAN FROM BELLAC *appears suddenly from outer door. He is nondescript, mercurial, shabby.*)

MAN.   Yes. The young lady has a name. But what permits you to conclude that the young lady's invention is as minor as all that?

CLERK.   Who are you?

MAN.   What chiefly distinguishes the inventor is modesty. You should know that by now. Pride is the invention of noninventors.

(A STREET SINGER, *accompanied by violin and accordion, begins "La Seine" outside the windows.* CLERK *crosses to close them.*)

AGNES.   (*to the* MAN) Thanks very much, but—

MAN.   To the characteristic modesty of the inventor, the young lady adds the charming modesty of her sex—(*He smiles at* AGNES) But—

(CLERK *closes one of the windows.*)

how can you be sure, you, that she has not brought us at last the invention which is destined to transform the modern world?

CLERK.   (*closes the other window*) For world-transformations it's the Second Vice President. Mondays ten to twelve.

MAN.   Today is Tuesday.

CLERK.   Now how can I help that?

MAN.   So! While all humanity awaits with anguish the discovery which will at last utilize the moon's gravitation for the removal of corns, and when we have every reason to believe that in all likelihood Mademoiselle—Mademoiselle?

AGNES.   Agnes.

MAN.   Mademoiselle Agnes has this discovery in her handbag—You tell her to come back Monday.

CLERK.   (*nervously*) There is going to be a Director's meeting in just a few minutes. The Chairman of the Board is coming. I must beg you to be quiet.

MAN.   I will not be quiet. I am quiet Mondays.

CLERK.   Now, please. I don't want any trouble.

MAN.   And the Universal Vegetable? Five continents are languishing in the hope of the Universal Vegetable which will once and for all put an end to the ridiculous specialization of the turnip, the leek and the stringbean, which will be at one and the same time bread, meat, wine and coffee, and yield with equal facility cotton, potassium, ivory and wool. The Universal Vegetable which Paracelsus could not, and Burbank dared not, imagine! Yes, my friend. And while in this handbag, which with understandable concern she clutches to her charming bosom, the seeds of the Universal Vegetable await only the signal of your President to burst upon an expectant world, you say—come back Monday.

AGNES.   Really, sir—

CLERK.   If you wish an appointment for Monday, Mademoiselle—

MAN.   She does not wish an appointment for Monday.

CLERK.   (*shrugs*) Then she can go jump in the lake.

MAN.   What did you say?

CLERK.   I said: She can go jump in the lake. Is that clear?

MAN.   That's clear. Perfectly clear. As clear as it was to Columbus when—

(*The Buzzer sounds on the* CLERK's *desk. A Light flashes on.*)

CLERK.   Excuse me. (*He crosses to the* VICE PRESIDENT's *door, knocks and enters.*)

(MAN *smiles.* AGNES *smiles back wanly.*)

AGNES.   But I'm not the inventor of the Universal Vegetable.

MAN.   I know. I am.

AGNES.   I'm just looking for a job.

MAN.   Typist?

AGNES.   Not really.

MAN.   Stenographer?

AGNES.   Not at all.

MAN.   Copy-reader, translator, bookkeeper, editor, file-clerk—stop me when I come to it.

AGNES.   You could go on like that for years before I could stop you.

MAN.   Well then—your specialty? Charm? Coquetry, devotion, seduction, flirtation, passion, romance?

AGNES.   That's getting warmer.

MAN.   Splendid. The best career for a female is to be a woman.

AGNES.   Yes, but—men frighten me.

MAN.   Men frighten you?

AGNES.   They make me feel weak all over.

MAN.   That clerk frightens you?

AGNES.   Clerks, presidents, janitors, soldiers. All a man has to do is to look at me, and I feel like a shoplifter caught in the act.

MAN.   Caught in what act?

AGNES.   I don't know.

MAN.   Perhaps it's their clothes that frighten you. Their vests? Their trousers?

AGNES.   (*shakes her head*) I feel the same panic on the beach when they don't wear their trousers.

MAN.   Perhaps you don't like men.

AGNES.   Oh, no, I like them. I like their dog-like eyes, their hairiness, their big feet. And they have special organs which inspire tenderness in a woman—. Their Adam's apple, for instance, when they eat dinner or make speeches. But the moment they speak to me, I begin to tremble—

MAN.   (*he looks appraisingly at her a moment*) You would like to stop trembling?

AGNES.   Oh yes. But— (*She shrugs hopelessly.*)

MAN.   Would you like me to teach you the secret?

AGNES.   Secret?

MAN.   Of not trembling before men. Of getting whatever you want out of them. Of making the directors jump, the presidents kneel and offer you diamonds?

AGNES.   Are there such secrets?

MAN.   One only. It is infallible.

AGNES.   Will you really tell it to me?

MAN.   Without this secret a girl has a bad time of it on this earth. With it, she becomes Empress of the World.

AGNES.   Oh tell it to me quickly.

MAN.   (*peering about the room*) No one is listening?

AGNES.   (*whispers*) No one.

MAN.   Tell them they're handsome.

AGNES.   You mean, flatter them? Tell them they're handsome, intelligent, kind?

MAN.   No. As for the intelligence and the kindness, they can shift for themselves. Tell them they're handsome.

AGNES.   All?

MAN.   All. The foolish, the wise, the modest, the vain, the young, the old. Say it to the professor of philosophy and he will give you a diploma. Say it to the butcher and he will give you a steak. Say it to the president here, and he will give you a job.

AGNES.   But to say a thing like that, one has to know a person well—

MAN.   Not at all. Say it right off. Say it before he has a chance even to open his mouth.

AGNES.   But one doesn't say a thing like that before people.

MAN.   Before people. Before all the world. The more witnesses, the better.

AGNES.   But if they're not handsome—and for the most part they're not, you know—how can I tell them that they are?

MAN.   Surely you're not narrowminded, Agnes?

(*She shrugs, not quite sure.*)

The ugly, the pimply, the crippled, the fat. Do you wish to get on in this world? Tell them they're handsome.

AGNES.   Will they believe it?

MAN.   They will believe it because they've always known it. Every man, even the ugliest, feels in his heart a secret alliance with beauty. When you tell him he's handsome, he will simply hear outwardly the voice he has been listening to inwardly all his life. And those who believe it the least will be the most grateful. No matter how ugly they may have thought themselves, the moment they find a woman who thinks them handsome, they grapple her to their hearts with hooks of steel. For them, she is the magic glass of truth, the princess of an enchanted world. When you see a woman who can go nowhere without a staff of admirers, it is not so much because they think she is beautiful, it is because she has told them they are handsome.

AGNES.   There are women then who already know this secret?

MAN.   Yes. But they know it without really knowing it. And usually they evade the issue, they go beside the point. They tell the hunchback he is generous, the wall-eyed that he's strong. There's no profit in that. I've seen a woman throw away a cool million in diamonds and emeralds because she told a clubfooted lover that he walked swiftly, when all he wanted to hear was—you know what. And now—to work. The President is in every day to those who come to tell him he's handsome.

AGNES.   I'd better come back another day. I have to have training. I have a cousin who's not at all bad-looking—I'll practice on him tomorrow, and then the next day I'll—

MAN.   You can practice right now. On the receptionist.

AGNES.   That monster?

MAN.   The monster is perfect for your purpose. After that, the Vice President. I know him. He's even better. Then the President.

(*The* VICE PRESIDENT's *door opens. The* CLERK *comes in.*)

CLERK.   (*into the doorway*) Very good, sir.

VOICE.   And another thing—

CLERK.   (*turns*) Yes sir?

VOICE.   When the Chairman of the Board—

(CLERK *goes back in and closes the door.*)

AGNES.   No, I can't!

MAN.   (*indicating the bust of Archimedes at rear*) Begin with this bust then.

AGNES.   Whose is it?

MAN.   What does it matter? It's the bust of a man. It's all ears. Speak!

AGNES.   (*shuddering*) It has a beard.

MAN.   Begin with what you like. With this chair. With this clock.

AGNES.   They're not listening.

MAN.   This fly, then. See? He's on your glove. He's listening.

AGNES.   Is he a male?

MAN.   Yes. Speak. Tell him.

AGNES.   (*with an effort*) How handsome he is!

MAN.   No, no, no. Say it to him.

AGNES.   How handsome you are!

MAN.   You see? He's twirling his moustache. Go on. More. More. What is a fly especially vain of?

AGNES.   His wings? His eyes?

MAN.   That's it. Tell him.

AGNES.   How beautiful your wings are, beautiful fly! They sparkle in the sun like jewels. And your eyes—so large, so sad, so sensitive!

MAN.   Splendid. Shoo him away now. Here comes the clerk.

AGNES.   He won't go. He's clinging to me.

MAN.   Naturally.

AGNES.   (*to the fly*) You're bowlegged. (*she smiles*) He's gone.

MAN.   You see? And now—

(*The* VICE PRESIDENT's *door opens slowly.*) Here he comes.

AGNES.   (*in panic*) What must I say?

MAN.   "How handsome you are."

(CLERK *comes in and walks to his desk.* MAN *disappears behind the bust of Archimedes.*)

AGNES.   (*after an agony of indecision*) How handsome you are!

CLERK.   (*stops dead*) What?

AGNES.   I said, how handsome you are!

CLERK.   Do you get this way often?

AGNES.   It's the first time in my life that I've ever—

CLERK.   (*finishing the sentence for her*) Called a chimpanzee handsome? Thanks for the compliment. But—why?

AGNES.   You're right. Handsome is not the word. I should have said beautiful. Because, mind you, I never judge a face by the shape of the nose or the arch of the brow. To me, what counts is the ensemble.

CLERK.   So what you're telling me is: your features are ugly, but they go beautifully together. Is that it?

AGNES.   It serves me right. Very well—It's the first time I've ever told a man he was handsome. And it's going to be the last.

CLERK.   Now don't get excited, please. I know girls. At your age a girl doesn't calculate; she says whatever comes into her head. I know you meant it. Only—why did you say it so badly?

(MAN *sticks his head out and makes a face at* AGNES *behind the* CLERK's *back.*)

AGNES. (*to the MAN*) Did I say it badly? (*to the CLERK, who thinks it is said to him*) I thought you were handsome. I may have been wrong.

CLERK. Women are blind as bats. Even if there were something good about me, they'd never see it. What's so good about me? My face? God, no. My figure? Not at all. Only my shadow. But of course you didn't notice that.

AGNES. Is that what you think? And when you leaned over to close the window, I suppose your shadow didn't lean over with you? And when you walked into the Vice President's office, did you put your shadow away in a drawer? (*She strokes his shadow with her hand*) How could I help noticing a shadow like that?

CLERK. You notice it now because I direct your attention to it.

AGNES. Have it your way. I thought I was looking at you, but what I saw was your shadow.

CLERK. Then you shouldn't say, what a handsome man. You should say, what a handsome shadow.

(*He opens the window, the room is filled with music. It is still "La Seine."*)

AGNES. From now on, I shall say no more about it.

CLERK. (*returning to desk*) Don't be angry, my dear. It's only because I'm a man of years and I have a right to warn you. I have a daughter of your age. I know what girls are. One day they see a fine shadow, and at once their heads are turned, the silly geese, and they think the man himself is handsome. Oh, I don't deny it, it's a rare thing, a fine shadow. And believe me it lasts—you don't keep your hair, you don't keep your skin, but your shadow lasts all your life. Even longer, they say. But that's not the point. These little fools invariably insist on confusing the shadow with the man, and if the idiot lets himself be talked into it, in a moment it's all over and they've ruined their lives for nothing, the nitwits. No, my dear. Heed an old man's warning. You can't live your life among shadows.

(*MAN sticks out his head and lifts an admonishing finger.*)

AGNES. How handsome you are!

CLERK. You know why? It's because when I'm angry I show my teeth. And the fact is, they are rather good. My dentist says they're perfect. It's no credit to me—It's because I eat hard foods. And when you—

(*The buzzer sounds again.*)

Ah—the Vice President needs me again. Wait just a minute, my dear. I'll make sure that he sees you at once. I'll say it's my niece.

AGNES. (*as he bends over to close a drawer*) How beautiful it is, your shadow, when it leans over. One would say it belonged to Rodin's Thinker!

CLERK. (*delighted*) Come, now, that will do. If you were my daughter,

I'd give you a good slap on the—. Sit down a minute. I'll get him for you. (*Crosses to the* VICE PRESIDENT'S *door and goes out.*)

(MAN *comes out from behind the bust. The music stops.*)

MAN.   Well, it's a start.

AGNES.   I think I'm better with flies.

MAN.   Because in your mind the idea of beauty is inseparable from the idea of the caress. Women have no sense of the abstract—a woman admiring the sky is a woman caressing the sky. In a woman's mind beauty is something she needs to touch. And you didn't want to touch the clerk, not even his shadow.

AGNES.   No.

MAN.   With my method, it's not your hands that must speak, nor your cheek, nor your lips—. It's your brain.

AGNES.   I had a narrow squeak. I almost lost him.

MAN.   Yes, he had you there with his shadow. You're not ready to tackle a Vice President. No. Not yet.

AGNES.   But there's no time. What shall I do?

MAN.   Practice. Practice on me.

AGNES.   You expect me to tell you you're handsome?

MAN.   Is it so difficult?

AGNES.   Not at all. Only—

MAN.   Think. Think before you speak.

AGNES.   Oh, you're not bad at all, you know, when you tease one like this.

MAN.   Very feeble. Why when I tease one like this? The rest of the time, I'm not handsome?

AGNES.   Oh yes. Always. Always.

MAN.   Better. Now it's no longer your hands that are speaking.

AGNES.   With you, all the same, they murmur a little something.

MAN.   Good.

AGNES.   The mass of your body is beautiful. The outline is beautiful. The face matters little.

MAN.   What nonsense is this? My face matters little?

AGNES.   (*recovering quickly*) No more than the face of Rodin's Thinker.

MAN.   In his case, doubtless the feet have more importance. Look here, Agnes, these little allusions to famous statues are ingenious. But is Rodin's Thinker the only one you know?

AGNES.   Except for the Venus of Milo. But she wouldn't be much use to me with men.

MAN.   That remains to be seen. In any case we'd better extend your repertory. Forget The Thinker. Michelangelo's David is very good. Or his Moses. But best of all—the Apollo of Bellac—

AGNES.   The Apollo of Bellac?

MAN. It doesn't exist. It will do perfectly.

AGNES. What does it look like?

MAN. A little like me, I think. I too come from Bellac. It's a little town in Limousin. I was born there.

AGNES. But they say the men of Limousin are so ugly. How does it happen that you are so handsome?

MAN. My father was a very handsome man, and he—Oh-oh. Good for you. (*He applauds.*)

AGNES. (*pursuing her advantage*) Oh never! Not with you! You taught me the secret. With you I could be no other than honest.

MAN. At last. You understand.

(*The* VICE PRESIDENT'S *door opens.*)

Here we are. (*Goes behind the bust.*)

CLERK. (*comes in, smiling tenderly*) The Vice President will be out in a moment, my dear. No need to put yourself out. A shadow like his, you may see every day—in the zoo. (*He takes some papers from his desk and goes into where the Directors will meet.*)

AGNES. (*whispers*) Help! Help!

(MAN *thrusts his head out.*)

I feel faint!

MAN. Practice. Practice.

AGNES. (*desperately*) On whom? On what?

MAN. On anything. The telephone.

AGNES. (*she speaks to the telephone*) How handsome you are, my little telephone! (*She strokes it gently.*)

MAN. No! Not with the hands.

AGNES. But it's so much easier that way.

MAN. I know. Try the chandelier. That's one thing you can't touch.

AGNES. How handsome you are, my little, my great chandelier!

(*The music begins again. Another tune.*)

Only when you're all lit up? Oh, don't say that. Other chandeliers, yes. Street lamps, store-fixtures, yes. Not you. See—you are full of sunshine. You are the chandelier of the sun. A desk lamp needs to be lit. A planet needs to be lit. But you have radiance of your own. You are as beautiful as a galaxy of stars, even more beautiful, for a galaxy is only an imitation chandelier, a cluster of uncertain lights swinging precariously in the eternal darkenss. But you are a creature of crystal with limbs of ivory and gold, a living miracle!

(*The chandelier lights up by itself.*)

MAN. Bravo!

VICE PRESIDENT.   (*The door opens. The* VICE PRESIDENT *comes in. His manner is important. His face is that of a gargoyle*) My dear young lady, I have exactly two minutes to give you. (*He crosses to close the window.*)

AGNES.   (*whispering in awe*) Oh!

VICE PRESIDENT.   (*Stops and turns*) Why do you stare at me like that? You've seen me before?

AGNES.   (*In a tone of wonder*) No! On the contrary.

VICE PRESIDENT.   And what does that mean, no, on the contrary?

AGNES.   I was expecting to see the usual Vice President, stoop-shouldered, paunchy, bald—And all at once, I see you!

(VICE PRESIDENT *freezes in his tracks.* MAN *thrusts out his head. He raises a warning finger.*)

(*Hastily*) How handsome you are!

VICE PRESIDENT.   What? (*He turns.*)

AGNES.   Nothing. I beg your pardon.

VICE PRESIDENT.   I heard you distinctly. You said I was handsome. Don't deny it. (*He steps closer to her.*)

(*Music swells up.*)

You know, it gave me rather a shock to hear you say it. However, it can't be true. If I were really—what you said—wouldn't some woman have told me before this?

AGNES.   Oh, the fools! The fools!

VICE PRESIDENT.   Whom are you calling fools, Mademoiselle? My sister, my mother, my niece?

AGNES.   (*Giving up all at once. In a formal tone*) Mr. Vice President, the truth is I am looking for a position. And I happened to hear through a friend of one of your directors, Mr Lepedura—

(MAN *thrusts out his head.*)

VICE PRESIDENT.   Never mind Monsieur Lepedura. We are discussing me. As you probably know, I am one of the world's authorities in the fields of dreams. It is I who work with those who are able to invent only while they sleep, and I have been able to extract from their dreams such extraordinary devices as the book that reads itself and the adjustable Martini, wonders of modern science which without my help would have remained mere figments of the imagination. If you appeared to me in a dream and told me I was handsome, I should have understood at once. But we are in a waking state, or are we? One moment. (*He pinches himself*) Ow! I am awake. Permit me. (*Pinches her.*)

AGNES.   Ow!

VICE PRESIDENT.   We're not dreaming, Mademoiselle. And now, my dear—(*He takes her hand*) Why did you say I was handsome? To flatter me?—I can see you are incapable of such baseness. To make fun of me? No—your eye is gentle, your lips attract—Why did you say it, Mademoiselle?

AGNES.   I say you are handsome because you are handsome. If your mother finds you ugly that's not my concern.

VICE PRESIDENT.   I cannot permit you to form so low an opinion of my mother's taste. Even when I was a boy, my mother used to say I had the hands of an artist.

AGNES.   If your niece prefers Charles Boyer—

VICE PRESIDENT.   My niece? Only yesterday at dinner she was saying that my eyebrows could have been drawn by El Greco.

AGNES.   If your sister—

VICE PRESIDENT.   My sister has never quite admitted that I am handsome, no, but she has always said that there was something distinctive about my face. A friend of hers, a history teacher, told her it's because in certain lights, I resemble Lodovico Sforza. (*He makes a deprecating gesture.*)

AGNES.   Lodovico Sforza? Never. The Apollo of Bellac, yes.

VICE PRESIDENT.   The Apollo of Bellac?

AGNES.   Wouldn't you say? Quite objectively?

VICE PRESIDENT.   Well—if you really think so—perhaps just a little. Although Lodovico Sforza, you know—I've seen engravings—

AGNES.   When I say the Apollo of Bellac, I mean, naturally, the Apollo of Bellac in a beautifully tailored suit. You see, I am frank. I say what I think. Yes, Mr. Vice President. You have the fault of all really handsome men—you dress carelessly.

VICE PRESIDENT.   (*smiling*) What insolence! And this from a girl who tells every man she meets that he's handsome!

AGNES.   I have said that to two men only in all my life. You are the second.

(*CLERK comes in.*)

VICE PRESIDENT.   What is it? Don't you see I'm busy?

CLERK.   The Directors are on the way up, sir. It's time for the meeting.

VICE PRESIDENT.   I'll be right in.

(*CLERK goes into the Director's room.*)

I'm sorry, Mademoiselle. I must go to this meeting. But we must certainly continue this wonderful conversation. Won't you come back and lunch with me? You know, my secretary is impossible. I'm having her transferred to the sales department. Now you're a first-rate typist, I'm told—

AGNES.   I don't type. I play the piano.

VICE PRESIDENT.   Ah, that's wonderful. And you take dictation?

AGNES.   In longhand, yes.

VICE PRESIDENT.   That's much the best way. That gives one time to think. Would you like to be my secretary?

AGNES.   On one condition.

VICE PRESIDENT.   A condition?

AGNES.   On condition that you never wear this awful jacket again. When I think of these wonderful shoulders in that ill-fitting suit—!

VICE PRESIDENT.   I have a beautiful blue silk suit. But it's for summer—It's a little light for the season.

AGNES.   As you please.

VICE PRESIDENT.   I'll wear it tomorrow.

AGNES.   Goodbye.

VICE PRESIDENT.   Don't forget. Lunch.

(*He goes out, smiling, by way of the door to the Director's room. The street music stops.*)

(*MAN peers out from behind the bust.*)

AGNES.   I kept my hands behind my back the whole time. I pretended I had no hands. Now I can hardly move my fingers.

MAN.   Here come the rest of the apes. Go to work.

AGNES.   On the first?

MAN.   On all. One after the other.

AGNES.   But—

(*CLERK throws open the doors of the Director's room. The street music starts again. We have a glimpse of the Director's table with chairs pulled back ready to receive the Directors. The VICE PRESIDENT is seen inside. He is posturing in front of a bookcase in the glass door of which he sees himself reflected, and he is trying vainly to give a smartly tailored appearance to his coat. CLERK glances at him in astonishment, then he stands by the outer door to announce the Directors as they appear. They come in through the outer door and cross the length of the reception room, one by one in time to the music, which is a waltz.*)

CLERK.   Mr Cracheton.

(*MR. CRACHETON come in, a lugubrious type, stiff and melancholy.*)

AGNES.   How handsome he is!

CRACHETON.   (*He snaps his head about as if shot. His expression changes. He smiles. In a low voice*) Charming girl! (*He goes into the Director's room, looking all the while over his shoulder.*)

CLERK.   Mr. Lepedura.

LEPEDURA.   (*Appears. He has a face full of suspicion and worry. As he passes AGNES, he tips his derby perfunctorily, recognizing her*) Good morning.

AGNES.   How handsome you are!

LEPEDURA.   (*stops dead*) Who says so?

AGNES. Your wife's friend, the Baroness Chagrobis. She thinks you're wonderful.

LEPEDURA. (*a changed man, gallant and charming*) She thinks I'm wonderful? Well, well, give her my love when you see her. And tell her I mean to call her up shortly myself. She has a pretty thin time of it with the Baron, you know. We have to be nice to her. Is she still at the same address?

AGNES. Oh yes. I'll tell her you're as handsome as ever.

LEPEDURA. Now don't exaggerate, my dear. We don't want to disappoint her. (*Her gives her a radiant smile, and goes in, fully six inches taller and many pounds lighter. To the* CLERK) Delightful girl!

CLERK. Mr. Rasemutte and Mr. Schultz.

(*They enter together, Mutt and Jeff.*)

AGNES. How handsome he is!

(*Both stop as if at a signal.*)

RASEMUTTE. To which of us, Mademoiselle—
SCHULTZ. —Do you refer?
AGNES. Look at each other. You will see.

(*They look at each other anxiously, and both smile radiantly.*)

RASEMUTTE. Charming creature!
SCHULTZ. Lovely girl!

(SCHULTZ *offers* RASEMUTTE *his arm. They walk into the Director's room arm in arm like characters in "Alt Wien."* CLERK *blows* AGNES *a kiss, follows them in and closes the doors behind them.* MAN *pokes his head out from behind Archimedes. He shakes his head ruefully.*)

AGNES. I'm not doing it well? You're sad?
MAN. You're doing it much too well. I'm frightened.
AGNES. You?
MAN. Like Frankenstein.

(*The door of the Director's room is flung open.*)

CLERK. The President!

(*As the* PRESIDENT *enters the room, we catch a glimpse of the* DIRECTORS. *Each has a mirror in his hand. While one combs his hair into waves, another settles his tie. Another preens his whiskers. The* VICE PRESIDENT *has taken off his jacket.*)

PRESIDENT. So you're the cause of it all, Miss—Miss—?
AGNES. Agnes.
PRESIDENT. Miss Agnes, for fifteen years this organization has been steeped in melancholy, jealousy, and suspicion. And now suddenly this

morning, everything is changed. My reception clerk, ordinarily a species of hyena—

(*The* CLERK *smiles affably.*)

has become so affable he even bows to his own shadow on the wall—

(CLERK *contemplates his silhouette in the sunshine with a nod of approval. It nods back.*)

The First Vice President, whose reputation for stuffiness and formality has never been seriously challenged, insists on sitting at the Director's meeting in his shirt sleeves, God knows why. In the Director's room, around the table, mirrors flash like sunbeams in a forest, and my Directors gaze into them with rapture. Mr. Lepedura contemplates with joy the Adam's apple of Mr. Lepedura. Mr. Rasemutte stares with pride at the nose of Mr. Rasemutte. They are all in love with themselves and with each other. How in the world did you bring about this miracle, Miss Agnes? What was it you said to them?

> AGNES.   How handsome you are!
> PRESIDENT.   I beg your pardon?
> AGNES.   I said to them, to each of them, "How handsome you are!"
> PRESIDENT.   Ah! You conveyed it to them subtly by means of a smile, a wink, a promise—
> AGNES.   I said it in a loud clear voice. Like this: How handsome you are!

(*In the Directors' room, all heads turn suddenly.* CLERK *closes the doors.*)

> PRESIDENT.   I see. Like a child winding up a mechanical doll. Well, well! No wonder my mannikins are quivering with the joy of life.

(*There is a round of applause from the Directors' room.*)

Listen to that. It's Mr. Cracheton proposing the purchase of a new three-way mirror for the men's room. Miss Agnes, I thank you. You have made a wonderful discovery.

> AGNES.   (*modestly*) Oh, it was nothing.
> PRESIDENT.   And the President? How does it happen that you don't tell the President?
> AGNES.   How handsome he is?
> PRESIDENT.   He's not worth the trouble, is that it?

(*She looks at him with a smile full of meaning.*)

You've had enough of masculine vanity for one morning?

> AGNES.   Oh, Mr. President—you know the reason as well as I.
> PRESIDENT.   No. I assure you.

AGNES.   But—I don't need to tell *you*.   You *are* handsome.

PRESIDENT.   (*Seriously*) Would you remind repeating that?

AGNES.   You are handsome.

PRESIDENT.   Think carefully, Miss Agnes. This is a serious matter. Are you quite sure that to you I seem handsome?

AGNES.   You don't seem handsome. You are handsome.

PRESIDENT.   You would be ready to repeat that before witnesses? Think. Much depends upon your answer. I have grave decisions to make today, and the outcome depends entirely upon you. Have you thought? Are you still of the same opinion?

AGNES.   Completely.

PRESIDENT.   Thank heaven. (*He goes to his private door, opens it and calls*) Chevredent!

(*CHEVREDENT comes in. She is a thin, sour woman with an insolent air. Her nose is pinched. Her chin is high. Her hair is drawn up tightly. When she opens her mouth she appears to be about to bite.*)

CHEVREDENT.   Yes? (*She looks at AGNES and sniffs audibly.*)

PRESIDENT.   Chevredent, how long have you been my private secretary?

CHEVREDENT.   Three years and two months. Why?

PRESIDENT.   In all that time there has never been a morning when the prospect of finding you in my office has not made me shudder.

CHEVREDENT.   Thanks very much. Same to you.

PRESIDENT.   I wouldn't have put up with you for ten minutes if it had ever occurred to me that I was handsome.

CHEVREDENT.   Ha-ha.

PRESIDENT.   But because I thought I was ugly, I took your meanness for generosity. Because I thought I was ugly, I assumed that your evil temper concealed a good heart. I thought it was kind of you even to look at me. For I am ugly, am I not?

(*CHEVREDENT sneers maliciously.*)

Thank you. And now listen to me. This young lady seems to be far better equipped to see than you. Her eyelids are not red like yours, her pupils are clear, her glance is limpid. Miss Agnes, look at me. Am I ugly?

AGNES.   You are beautiful.

(*CHEVREDENT shrugs.*)

PRESIDENT.   This young lady's disinterested appraisal of my manly charms has no effect on your opinion?

CHEVREDENT.   I never heard such rubbish in my life!

PRESIDENT.   Quite so. Well, here is the problem that confronts us. I have the choice of spending my working time with an ugly old shrew who thinks I'm hideous or a delightful young girl who thinks I'm handsome. What do you advise?

CEVREDENT.   You intend to replace me with this little fool?

PRESIDENT.   At once.

CHEVREDENT.   We'll soon see about that, Mr. President. You may have forgotten, but your wife is inside in your office reading your mail. She should know about this.

PRESIDENT.   She should. Tell her.

CHEVREDENT.   With pleasure. (*She rushes into the* PRESIDENT'S *office, slamming the door after her.*)

AGNES.   I'm terribly sorry, Mr. President.

PRESIDENT.   My dear, you come like an angel from heaven at the critical moment of my life. Today is my fifteenth wedding anniversary. My wife, with whose fury Chevredent threatens us, is going to celebrate the occasion by lunching with my Directors. I am going to present her with a gift. A diamond. (*He takes out a case and opens it*) Like it?

AGNES.   How handsome it is!

PRESIDENT.   Extraordinary! You praised the diamond in exactly the same tone you used for me. Is it yellow, by any chance? Is it flawed?

AGNES.   It is beautiful. Like you.

PRESIDENT.   (*His door opens*) We are about to become less so, both of us. (*He puts the case in his pocket*) Here is my wife.

THERESE.   (THERESE, *the blonde lady, comes in with icy majesty. She looks* AGNES *up and down*) So.

PRESIDENT.   Therese, my dear, permit me to present—

THERESE.   Quite unnecessary. That will be all, Mademoiselle. You may go.

PRESIDENT.   Agnes is staying, my dear. She is replacing Chevredent.

THERESE.   Agnes! So she is already Agnes!

PRESIDENT.   Why not?

THERESE.   And why is Agnes replacing Chevredent?

PRESIDENT.   Because she thinks I'm handsome.

THERESE.   Are you mad?

PRESIDENT.   No. Handsome.

THERESE.   (*To* AGNES). You think he's handsome?

AGNES.   Oh, yes.

THERESE.   He makes you think of Galahad? Of Lancelot?

AGNES.   Oh, no. His type is classic. The Apollo of Bellac.

THERESE.   The Apollo of Bellac?

PRESIDENT.   Have you ever stopped to wonder, Therese, why the good Lord made women? Obviously they were not torn from our ribs in order to make life a torment for us. Women exist in order to tell men they are handsome. And those who say it the most are those who are most beautiful. Agnes tells me I'm handsome. It's because she's beautiful. You tell me I'm ugly. Why?

MAN.   (*Appears. He applauds*) Bravo! Bravo!

THERESE.   Who is this maniac?

MAN.   When one hears a voice which goes to the very heart of humanity, it is impossible to keep silent.

PRESIDENT.   My friend—

MAN.   From the time of Adam and Eve, of Samson and Delilah, of Antony and Cleopatra, the problem of man and woman has made an impenetrable barrier between man and woman. If, as it seems, we are able to solve this problem once and for all, it will be a work of immeasurable benefit to the human race.

THERESE.   And you think we're getting somewhere with it today, is that it?

MAN.   Oh, yes.

THERESE.   You don't think the final solution could be deferred until tomorrow?

MAN.   Till tomorrow? When the President has just posed the problem so beautifully?

AGNES.   So beautifully!

THERESE.   The beautiful man poses a beautiful problem, eh, Mademoiselle?

AGNES.   I didn't say it. But I can say it. I say what I think.

THERESE.   Little cheat!

PRESIDENT.   I forbid you to insult Agnes!

THERESE.   It's she who insults me!

PRESIDENT.   When I'm called handsome, it's an insult to you—is that it?

THERESE.   I'm no liar.

PRESIDENT.   No. You show us the bottom of your heart.

MAN.   Agnes is telling the President the truth, Madame. Just as Cleopatra told the truth, just as Isolt told the truth. The truth about men is, they are beautiful, every last one of them; and your husband is right, Madame, the woman who tells it to them never lies.

THERESE.   So I am the liar!

MAN.   (*Gently*) It's only because you don't see clearly. All you have to do to see the beauty of men is to watch as they breathe and move their limbs. Each has his special grace. His beauty of body. The heavy ones—how powerfully they hold the ground! The light ones—how well they hang from the sky! His beauty of position. A hunchback on the ridge of Notre Dame makes a masterpiece of Gothic sculpture. All you have to do is to get him up there. And, finally, his beauty of function. The steamfitter has the beauty of a steamfitter. The president has the beauty of the president. There is ugliness only when these beauties become confused—when the steamfitter has the beauty of a president, the president the beauty of a steamfitter.

AGNES.   But there is no such confusion here.

THERESE.   No. He has the beauty of a garbageman.

PRESIDENT.   Thanks very much.

THERESE.   My dear, I have known you too long to deceive you. You have many good qualities. But you're ugly.

PRESIDENT.   Quiet!

THERESE.   Yes. Yes. Ugly! This girl, whatever her motives, is just able to force her lips to whisper her lies. But with every part of me—my heart, my lungs, my arms, my eyes—I scream the truth at you. My legs! You're ugly! Do you hear?

PRESIDENT.   I've heard nothing else for years.

THERESE.   Because it's true.

MAN.   There. And at last she's confessed.

THERESE.   Confessed what? What have I confessed?

MAN.   Your crime, Madame. You have injured this man. How could you expect him to be handsome in an environment that screamed at him constantly that he was ugly?

PRESIDENT.   Ah! Now I understand!

THERESE.   What do you understand? What's the matter with you all? What have I done?

PRESIDENT.   Now I understand why I am always embarrassed not only in your presence, but in the presence of everything that belongs to you.

THERESE.   Do you know what he is talking about?

PRESIDENT.   The sight of your skirt on the back of a chair shortens my spine by three inches. Can you expect me to stand up like a man when you come in? Your stockings on the bureau tell me that I'm knock-kneed and thick-ankled. Is it any wonder if I stumble? Your nail file on my desk hisses at me that my fingers are thick and my gestures clumsy. What do you expect of me after that? And your onyx clock with the Dying Gaul on the mantelpiece—no wonder I always shiver when I go near the fire. Imagine—for fifteen years that Dying Gaul has been sneering at me in my own house, and I never realized why I was uncomfortable. Well, at last I understand. And this very evening—

THERESE.   Don't you dare!

PRESIDENT.   This very evening your Dying Gaul shall die. You will find him in the garbage with the rest of the conspiracy. Your Dresden china shepherd, your Arab sheik, your directoire chairs with their scratchy bottoms—

THERESE.   Those chairs belonged to my grandmother!

PRESIDENT.   From now on they belong to the garbage. What are your chairs covered with, Agnes?

AGNES.   Yellow satin.

PRESIDENT.   I knew it. And the statues on your table?

AGNES.   There is only a bowl of fresh flowers on my table. Today it is white carnations.

PRESIDENT.   Of course. And over your fireplace?

AGNES.   A mirror.

PRESIDENT.   Naturally.

THERESE.   I warn you, if you so much as touch my chairs, I'll leave you forever.

PRESIDENT.   As you please, my dear.

THERESE.   I see. So this is my anniversary gift after fifteen years of devotion. Very well. Only tell me, what have you to complain of? In all of these years has it ever happened that your roast was too rare? Did I ever give you your coffee too cold, too hot, too light, too sweet? Thanks to me, you are known as a man whose handkerchief is always fresh, whose socks are always new. Have you ever known what it was to have a hole in your toe? Has anyone ever seen a spot on your vest? And yet how you splash in your gravy, my friend! How you go through your socks!

PRESIDENT.   Tell me one thing. Do you say I am ugly because you think I am ugly or merely to spite me?

THERESE.   Because you are ugly.

PRESIDENT.   Thank you. Therese. Go on.

THERESE.   Then this woman appears. And at the first glance we can guess the fate of the unhappy creature who marries her. We see it all— the slippers with the inner sole curled up in a scroll. The nightly battle over the newspaper. The pajamas without buttons and always too small. The headaches without aspirin, the soup without salt, the shower without towels—

PRESIDENT.   Agnes, one question. Do you tell me I'm handsome because you think I'm handsome or only to make fun of me?

AGNES.   Because you're handsome.

PRESIDENT.   Thank you, Agnes.

THERESE.   You mean because he's rich.

AGNES.   If he were the richest man in the world, I'd still say he was handsome.

THERESE.   Very well. Marry her if she thinks you're so handsome. Well? What are you waiting for?

PRESIDENT.   Nothing.

THERESE.   Take him, you, with my compliments. After fifteen years I've had enough. If you like to hear snoring at night—

AGNES.   You snore? How wonderful!

THERESE.   If you like bony knees—

AGNES.   I like legs that have character.

THERESE.   Look at that face! Now tell me he has the brow of a Roman Senator.

AGNES.   No, Madame.

THERESE.   No?

AGNES.   The brow of a king.

THERESE.   I give up. Goodbye.

PRESIDENT.   Goodbye, my love.

(*THERESE rushes out through outer door.*)

And now, Agnes in token of a happy future, accept this diamond. For me, one life has ended, and another begins.

(*CLERK comes in and signs to him.*)

Forgive me just one moment, Agnes. I must address the directors. The Chairman of the Board is evidently not coming. I'll be right back. (*He crosses to the door. To the CLERK*) Send down to the florist. I want all the white carnations he has. Agnes, you have made me the happiest of men.

AGNES.   The handsomest.

(*The PRESIDENT goes out by his door, the CLERK by outer door,*)

MAN.   Well, there you are, my dear.
You have everything—a job, a husband and a diamond. I can leave?

AGNES.   Oh no!

(*The street music starts afresh.*)

MAN.   But what more do you want?

AGNES.   Look at me. I have changed—haven't I?

MAN.   Perhaps just a little. That can't be helped.

AGNES.   It's your fault. I have told so many lies! I must tell the truth at last or I shall burst!

MAN.   What truth do you want to tell?

AGNES.   I want to tell someone who is really beautiful that he is beautiful. I want to tell the most beautiful man in the world that he is the most beautiful man in the world.

MAN.   And to caress him, perhaps, just a little?

AGNES.   Just a little.

MAN.   There is the Apollo of Bellac.

AGNES.   He doesn't exist.

MAN.   What does it matter whether or not he exists? His beauty is the supreme beauty. Tell him.

AGNES.   I can't. Unless I touch a thing I don't see it. You know that. I have no imagination.

MAN.   Close your eyes.

AGNES.   (*Closes them*) Yes?

MAN.   Suppose, Agnes, it were the God of Beauty himself who visited you this morning. Don't be astonished. Perhaps it's true. Where else could this terrible power have come from? Or this extraordinary emotion you feel? Or this sense of oppression? And suppose that now the god reveals himself?

AGNES.   It is you?

MAN. Don't open your eyes. Suppose I stand before you now in all my truth and all my splendor.

AGNES. I see you.

MAN. Call me thou.

AGNES. I see thee.

MAN. How do I seem?

AGNES. You seem—

MAN. I am taller than mortal men. My head is small and fringed with golden ringlets. From the line of my shoulders, the geometricians derived the idea of the square. From my eyebrows the bowmen drew the concept of the arc. I am nude and this nudity inspired in the musicians the idea of harmony.

AGNES. Your heels are winged, are they not?

MAN. They are not. You are thinking of the Hermes of St. Yrieix.

AGNES. I don't see your eyes.

MAN. As for the eyes, it's as well you don't see them. The eyes of beauty are implacable. My eyeballs are silver. My pupils are graphite. From the eyes of beauty poets derived the idea of death. But the feet of beauty are enchanting. They are not feet that touch the ground. They are never soiled and never captive. The toes are slender, and from them artists derived the idea of symmetry. Do you see me now?

AGNES. You dazzle my eyes.

MAN. But your heart sees me.

AGNES. I'm not so sure. Do not count on me too much, God of Beauty. My life is small. My days are long, and when I come back to my room each evening, there are five flights to climb in the greasy twilight amid smells of cooking. These five flights mark the beginning and the end of every event of my life, and oh, if you knew, Apollo, how lonely I am! Sometimes I find a cat waiting in a doorway. I kneel and stroke it for a moment, we purr together and it fills the rest of my day with joy. Sometimes I see a milk bottle that has fallen on its side. I set it right and the gesture comforts me. If I smell gas in the hallway I run and speak to the janitor. It is so good to speak to someone about something. Between the second story and the third, the steps sag. At this turning one abandons hope. At this turning one loses one's balance, and catches at the bannister, gasping with the anguish of those more fortunate ones who clutch at the rail on the heaving deck of a ship. That is my life, Apollo, a thing of shadows and tortured flesh. That is my conscience, Apollo, a staircase full of stale odors. If I hesitate to see you as you are, O beautiful god, it is because I need so much and I have so little and I must defend myself.

MAN. But I have rescued you, Agnes. You possess the secret.

AGNES. I know. From now on, my staircase will be new and full of light, the treads carpeted in velvet and adorned with initials. But to climb it with you would be unthinkable. Go away, God of Beauty. Leave me for always.

MAN.   You wish that?

AGNES.   If you were merely a handsome man, Apollo, thick and human in your flesh, with what joy I would take you in my arms! How I would love you! But you are too brilliant and too great for my staircase. I would do better to look at my diamond. Go, Apollo. Go away. Before I open my eyes, I implore you, vanish.

MAN.   When I vanish, you will see before you an ordinary creature like yourself, covered with skin, covered with clothes.

AGNES.   That is my destiny, and I prefer it. Let me kiss your lips, Apollo. And then—

MAN.   (*he kisses her*) Open your eyes, my dear. Apollo is gone. And I am going.

AGNES.   How handsome you are!

MAN.   Dear Agnes!

AGNES.   Don't go. I will make you rich. I will order the President to buy your invention.

MAN.   Which one?

AGNES.   The Universal Vegetable. There must be a fortune in it.

MAN.   I haven't quite got the hang of it yet. The roots don't hold the earth. I'll be back the moment I've perfected it.

AGNES.   You promise?

MAN.   We shall plant it together. And now—

AGNES.   You are really leaving me? You think I shall marry the President?

MAN.   No.

AGNES.   Why not?

MAN.   He's already married. And his wife has learned a lesson. You will see.

AGNES.   Then whom shall I marry, if not the President?

CLERK.   (*Enters. He crosses to the Directors' room and throws open the door. Announces*) The Chairman of the Board! *The* CHAIRMAN *enters from outer door.*)

MAN.   (*whispers*) He is a bachelor.

AGNES.   How handsome he is!

MAN.   Yes. (*He vanishes.*)

CHAIRMAN.   Mademoiselle—

PRESIDENT.   (*The* PRESIDENT *comes in quickly in great excitement*) Agnes! Agnes! A miracle! My wife has just telephoned. I don't know what has come over her. She has thrown out the Dying Gaul and the china shepherd.

AGNES.   Give her this diamond.

PRESIDENT.   Thank you, Agnes. Thank you.

CHAIRMAN.   (*taking her hand*) And who is this charming girl who gives away diamonds?

AGNES. Her name is Agnes.

CHAIRMAN. Dear Agnes!

PRESIDENT. But what's happened to our friend? He isn't here?

AGNES. He is gone.

PRESIDENT. Call him back. He must have lunch with us. Do you know his name?

AGNES. His first name only. Apollo.

PRESIDENT. (*runs to the outer door*) Apollo! Apollo!

(*The DIRECTORS come in, all adorned with white carnations.*)

Gentlemen, gentlemen, let's call him! We can't let him go like that. Apollo!

(*They each go to a door or a window save AGNES and the CHAIRMAN who remain standing hand in hand.*)

PRESIDENT and DIRECTORS. Apollo! Apollo!

CHAIRMAN. But whom are they shouting at? Is Apollo here?

AGNES. No. He just passed by.

CURTAIN

QUESTIONS

1. How do the stage directions help us to see Giraudoux's point of view towards the characters?

2. What visual and sound effects are indicated?

3. Find an example of fanciful dialogue that would not occur in a real office. How does the unrealistic style of this dialogue contribute to the play?

4. Choose one character and describe his or her tone of voice at an important moment.

5. How would you direct the dialogue between Agnes, the President, and Therese?

6. Why is it appropriate that the statue of the Apollo of Bellac doesn't exist?

7. When the Chairman of the Board enters near the end of the play, Agnes whispers "How handsome he is," and Apollo vanishes. What might be the connection? Is her tone here sincere?

8. How does Apollo define beauty?

9. What is Giraudoux satirizing through The International Bureau of Inventions? What does he satirize in the women in the play? In the men?

10. How is it significant that, at the end of the play, the directors are wearing white carnations?

11. What is the significance of the last line of the play?

chapter 9

The Extension
of Meaning: Symbol

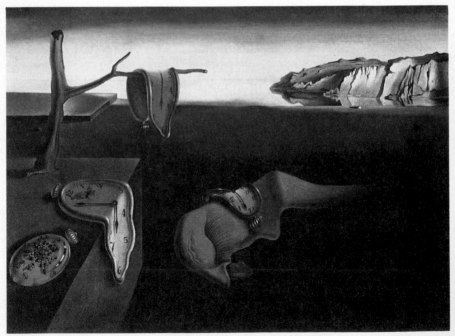

Salvador Dali. *The Persistence of Memory*. 1931. Oil on canvas. 9 ½" × 13". Collection, The
Museum of Modern Art, New York. Given anonymously.

WHAT A SYMBOL IS

When you wear a sweater to a friend's house for an evening's conversation, no one notices because your sweater is an appropriate garment for the occasion. But if a president wears a sweater instead of a dark suit and tie when he conducts a fireside chat on national television, everyone notices. Why? His sweater is more than a garment; it carries a message (I'm an informal person, just like you; let's talk together). We give his sweater significance.

Humans are always giving objects and actions special meaning. Why do men traditionally give women diamond rings when they become engaged? Why do many exchange rings at wedding ceremonies? Why does the bride traditionally wear white? The ads tell us that "diamonds are forever"; the wedding band, a circle, suggests unity, oneness; the white gown suggests innocence, purity. Because you understand the traditions of western culture, you know the meanings we give to these objects, meanings that extend beyond a particular stone, a piece of metal, or the color of a dress. When an object takes on significance beyond the object's function or worth, the object becomes symbolic. We understand and respond to symbols and are constantly creating new symbols. If we didn't, why would people drive status cars, or wear gold crosses, or, in the sixties, let their hair grow long? We should not be surprised to find writers mirroring our world by using symbols to extend meaning.

A *symbol*, then, is an object, character, or action that suggests meanings, associations, emotions beyond what is characteristic of its nature or function. A symbol is like a diamond: compact, yet many-faceted, throwing off light and picking up different colors as we turn it from side to side. Authors are attracted to symbols because they convey a rich texture of meanings without the loss of compression; they allow a writer to say—or suggest—much in a few words.

A term closely related to symbol is *allegory*. An allegory differs from a symbolic work in two ways. First, it develops a whole system of symbolic equivalents; all, or most, objects, characters, and actions in the work carry symbolic meanings. Second, the symbolic equivalents can usually be pinned down to a few specific meanings. In Book I of Spenser's *The Faerie Queene*, a sixteenth-century allegorical poem, Redcrosse Knight, seeking truth and the life of the true Christian, must slay the Dragon (the serpent, the Devil, evil), not be waylaid by Duessa (false religion) and other characters who try to impede his journey, and join finally with Una (truth, true religion).

This allegory operates on a moral level (truth is Redcrosse's quest), a religious level (true faith is his quest), and a historical level (the true Church) depicting the Reformation battle between the Roman Catholic Church and protestant churches. Most of the characters and actions in *The Faerie Queene* function consistently on three levels but, unlike symbols, do not throw off many associations beyond those we have described.

Other well-known allegories are Dante's *Divine Comedy*, Bunyan's *Pilgrim's Progress*, and Orwell's modern political allegory, *Animal Farm*. Because almost all the characters in *Animal Farm* are animals, it can also be called a beast fable, a story about animals who represent different human traits. Fables, parables (think of the parables of Jesus in the *New Testament*), and allegories are similar in that we are usually more interested in the point or moral conveyed by the characters and events than in the characters and events themselves. Allegorical figures are rarely complex characters; their significance lies in what they represent. When realism became the dominant literary mode in the nineteenth century, allegory ceased being a popular literary form. In recent years, however, fantasy techniques and medieval myths have regained popularity. In "Mayday" (see pp. 460–77), William Faulkner uses allegorical characters and a fantasy setting.

TYPES OF SYMBOLS

Before describing different types of symbols, we need to clarify the difference between symbols and *signs*. Signs carry only the meanings we agree to give them. Signs point—arbitrarily, by common agreement—to something definite. For example, the number "2" is simply a mark on the page or a sound we make. We agree to let this shape (or sound) stand for the concept of "twoness": two oranges, two books. The red light, all drivers must agree (or risk a ticket), means stop. The mathematical "symbols" π and ∞ are really signs with precise meanings. Because they are chosen arbitrarily, signs can be replaced by other signs. Symbols, on the other hand, cannot arbitrarily be changed. For instance, we can replace the American signs for "stop" and "yield" with the European pictorial signs, and American drivers will adjust. But we cannot arbitrarily replace the American eagle with the cardinal or turkey vulture. These birds do not suggest the same meanings and emotions (power, strength, freedom) as the eagle does and so cannot be substituted for the eagle as a symbol of America.

Symbols are multifaceted, less definite, and more emotion-laden than signs. At the beginning of the chapter we gave examples of one type of symbol: the cultural or conventional symbol. *Cultural or conventional symbols* are those that carry similar meanings for people who share the same culture. They include the symbols of political groups (the stars and stripes, the eagle, the elephant and donkey) and of religious groups (the star of David, the cross, baptism, the mass). We all recognize these symbols regardless of our particular political or religious preference. Many more symbols are shared by members of western culture. The red rose and the star are conventional symbols of love or the loved one. Since the writing of *Genesis*, the snake (or serpent or dragon) has been associated with evil or the devil. The chauffeur-driven limousine is a means of transportation; it is also a symbol of wealth, power, success. You might list all the cultural symbols we've mentioned so far and others you can think of; then state the ideas and emotions each one evokes.

If you compare your list with those of others in the class, you will find many of the same symbols listed, but you might also find that you have included an object that a classmate does not consider to be a symbol. There is a reason for this discrepancy. What is a sign for most members of our culture may become a symbol for some individuals, and a few may respond to a particular cultural symbol only as a sign. Both individuals and groups create new symbols when they are needed and let others die when those symbols no longer have meaning. For the student struggling in math class, the mathematical sign π may become a symbol of all the complexities of the "foreign" language that cannot be used correctly. Associated with the π sign, as it is turned into a symbol, will be all of the student's anxieties and negative feelings. Moving in the other direction, a person living in a nation but having no feelings of identification with that nation or culture could respond to that country's flag as merely a sign marking a public building—a post office or school.

Rather than picturing rigid categories of signs and various types of symbols, imagine objects clustered into groups along a continuum with the edges of each group shading into the next. Thus objects may become signs, or cultural symbols—or one of the other types of symbols we will consider next.

Contextual or *literary symbols* are those that are given symbolic significance by a writer in the context of a particular literary work. In some stories a horse is what a rancher rides to town, nothing more. In "The Horse Dealer's Daughter," because of the attention D. H. Lawrence gives the horses, and their association with the characters, the horses being led away in harness convey symbolic meanings that help reveal character. In "The Chaperone" by Henry James, a young girl decides to live with her divorced, socially rejected mother and bring her mother back into social acceptance. The girl's success is symbolically conveyed when Lady Maresfield bows to the mother and daughter. A bow is usually just a formal greeting. In James's story, the bow is more than that; it is a symbolic gesture conveying acceptance by Lady Maresfield and her group. Horses and bows do not, like the cross or a red rose, traditionally carry a rich cluster of symbolic meanings; any additional meanings attached to them are developed within a work and may vary from one work to another.

In addition to creating their own symbols in context, writers use cultural symbols. Indeed, writers are both influenced by and help to transmit the cultural symbols that are part of a literary tradition. Once a literary symbol, the rose is now a cultural symbol as well because so many writers in western culture have used the rose symbolically when writing about love and beauty. Again, we see movement along the continuum of symbolic types: cultural symbols may be used as literary symbols and literary symbols may become cultural symbols. Readers need to be careful, though, that they do not automatically apply conventional meanings to cultural symbols without seeing how they are used in a particular literary context. Sometimes authors will narrow or add to the meanings of a cultural symbol.

Some symbolic objects, characters, and actions recur so often in the writings of different cultures from different times that many critics, philosophers, anthropologists, and psychologists believe that we can call them *universal* or *natural* symbols. Water is a good example. Water is essential to life. Remember that water is used in the ritual of baptism, symbolically suggesting the new life, in a spiritual sense, experienced by the baptized person. Water can also destroy; ships can be lost at sea, and people can drown. Many literary works contain water symbolism, and writers often play with water's ambiguous symbolic qualities: destructive and life-giving. If there are universal symbols, we can expect that they would grow out of the most basic human experiences that transcend time and place.

Some important works that seem to give expression to universal human experiences are the *myths* of different cultures. Because of its several meanings, *myth* is a tricky word. It can mean not true, fictitious, as in the statement: "Santa Claus doesn't come down the chimney; that's just a myth." Used in literary studies, *myth* (from the Greek *mythos*, meaning fable, tale, speech) refers to stories about gods and legendary figures that express a group's religious beliefs and provide explanations of natural phenomena. *Mythology* refers to the collection of myths of a particular group or culture, for example, Greek mythology or Norse mythology. Most mythologies have creation myths, stories that explain how the world came into existence, myths that define the nature of the gods, the sources of evil, and the relations between humans and gods. Most mythologies also have stories about group leaders (heroes/saviors) who must take journeys to save their group from harm and many other stories in which, from culture to culture, the same types of characters and situations reappear. It is the repeated characters and situations, called *archetypes*, found in the mythologies (and folklore) of different cultures that give added weight to the argument for universal symbols. (The other major area of study providing evidence for universal symbols is psychoanalysis, most notably Sigmund Freud's study of dream symbolism.)

The term *myth* usually refers to the narrative, whereas the term *archetype*, or *archetypal pattern*, refers to the significant figure or situation in the myth. Some archetypal figures are the hero/savior, the tempter (or temptress), the magician (geni, witch doctor, fairy godmother), and the cruel mother. Archetypal patterns that appear frequently in western literature include the journey or quest (*The Faerie Queene*, the story of St. George and the Dragon), the fall from innocence or initiation into life (*Huck Finn, The Catcher in the Rye*), the Oedipal situation—the young man who wants to destroy his father and marry his mother, and the longing for paradise depicted as a beautiful, unspoiled garden (Arcadia, Eden, the "Virgin land" of early America).

Studies of the subconscious by psychologists Sigmund Freud and Carl Jung have influenced twentieth-century thinking about universal symbols and archetypes. The issue for students of literature is not whether we believe Freud and Jung but whether we can recognize their influence on twentieth-century literature and whether we can use the concepts to understand the literature we study. What is important is that you recognize that Frost's poem "The Road Not Taken" (p. 9) is not simply about choosing a path through a woods. Rather, the roads symbolically represent the road of life, the journey we all make, and the choice of a road represents the crucial choices we must make that shape the rest of our journey.

RECOGNIZING SYMBOLS

"How do you know it's a symbol?" is a question students often ask, and rightly so. When does an object cease to be only a part of the scene and begin to develop symbolic associations? Increasing your sensitivity to the role and value of symbols in our lives as well as in our literature is an important first step. Remember that a symbol is always a concrete object, character or action, never an abstract idea. A red rose may be a symbol of love, but love is not a symbol of something else. Be alert to a writer's use of cultural symbols and archetypes. Actions are often symbolic when they are part of an archetypal pattern. Thus your recognition of the archetype will help you understand the symbolic significance of the action. But be cautious about calling every object or important character or significant action a symbol; a symbol must suggest meanings beyond what is meant by the thing itself.

Being able to distinguish among *image, metaphor,* and *symbol* will help in the recognition of symbols. An image recreates a sense experience; to describe is what is intended. A metaphor states or implies a comparison between two unlike elements; it means something other than what it is. A symbol is both what it is and something more. The following will illustrate.

Image

A gigantic beauty of a stallion, fresh and responsive to my carresses,
Head high in the forehead, wide between the ears,
Limbs glossy and supple, tail dusting the ground,
Eyes full of sparking wickedness, ears finely cut, flexibly moving.

"Song of Myself," Walt Whitman

In this passage Whitman presents the image of a horse. We can see and feel the horse and sense the speaker's delight in the horse's beauty and strength.

Metaphor

There is no frigate like a book
  To take us lands away
Nor any coursers like a page
  Of prancing poetry.

"There Is No Frigate," Emily
Dickinson

Dickinson is not writing about
frigates (ships) or coursers (spir-
ited horses) at all. She is writing
about the power of poetry to
transport us. Thus certain qualities of poetry are described by
comparison to certain characteristics of ships and horses.

Symbol

The great draught-horses
swung past. They were tied
head to tail, four of them, and
they heaved along to where a
lane branched off from the
high-road, planting their great
hoofs floutingly in the fine
black mud, swinging their
great rounded haunches
sumptuously, and trotting a
few sudden steps as they were
led into the lane, round the
corner. Every movement
showed a massive, slumbrous
strength, and a stupidity which
held them in subjection. The
groom at the head looked
back, jerking the leading rope.
And the calvacade moved out
of sight up the lane, the tail of
the last horse, bobbed up tight
and stiff, held out taut from
the swinging great haunches as
they rocked behind the hedges
in a motion-like sleep. . . . Joe
watched with glazed hopeless
eyes. . . . He would marry and
go into harness. His life was
over, he would be a subject
animal now.

"The Horse Dealer's
Daughter," p. 427
D. H. Lawrence

Lawrence describes horses
being led away from the farm
that Mabel and her brothers
have lost through bankruptcy.
But Lawrence's focus on the
horses in the midst of his
description of the brothers
makes us associate the horses
with them, especially Joe. The
horses are actually part of the
story. They also symbolically
represent the animal-like
qualities of Joe. They are led
away as Joe will be led away
into a marriage of
convenience.

A symbol is not decoration added by the author as an after-thought. A symbol must function logically as a part of the scene, and its symbolic associations are developed in the work by the attention given to the symbol. An author can create symbols by *repetition*, by *emphasis*, or by *associations* that we automatically make with conventional symbols. It is this special focus that turns some-thing into a symbol we recognize and respond to in our analysis of a work. Herman Melville's focus on walls in his story "Bartleby the Scrivener" is a good example of a writer's use of repetition to turn a concrete object into a symbol. The first reference to walls is in the subtitle: "A Story of Wall Street." Further details of the setting of this story about a New York lawyer are provided early in the story when the lawyer describes his office location:

> At one end they [the lawyer's chambers] looked upon the white wall of the interior of a spacious skylight shaft, penetrating the building from top to bottom . . . the view from the other end of my chambers offered at least a contrast, if nothing more. In that direction, my windows commanded an unobstructed view of a lofty brick wall, black by age and everlasting shade, which wall requires no spyglass to bring out its lurking beauties, but, for the benefit of all nearsighted spectators, was pushed up to within ten feet of my windowpanes.

The lawyer's description emphasizes the "walled-up" nature of his office, an office lacking in life. After describing the scriveners or secretaries working for him, including the newly hired Bartleby, the lawyer describes his arrangement of the men:

> Ground-glass folding doors divided my premises into two parts, one of which was occupied by my scriveners, the other by myself. According to my humor, I threw open these doors or closed them. I resolved to assign Bartleby a corner by the folding doors . . . I placed his desk close up to a small side window in that part of the room, a window which originally had afforded a lateral view of certain grimy back yards and bricks, but which, owing to subsequent erections, commanded at present no view at all, though it gave some light. Within three feet of the panes was a wall, and the light came down from far above, between two lofty buildings. . . . I procured a high green folding screen, which might entirely isolate Bartleby from my sight.

Once again the story's setting pictures a world that physically separates people from one another. At this point, a sensitive reader might begin to suspect that these walls are more than just physical barriers. When the strange Bartleby, who refuses to work, refuses to be helped by the lawyer, refuses to leave the building, is finally removed from the office, he is taken to jail. Visiting Bartleby, the lawyer finds him "standing all alone in the quietest of the yards, his face towards a high wall." Later the lawyer discovers him in the yard whose "surrounding walls, of amazing thickness, kept off all sounds behind them." He was "strangely huddled at the base of the wall," dead. The repeated focus on walls—Wall Street, office building walls, partition walls, prison walls—does more than provide a setting or locale for the story. The setting becomes symbolic of the dehumanized world of the city that isolates people, of the isolation of "different" people such as Bartleby, and of much more.

Every story has a setting; a story must take place somewhere. In some stories details of setting are sketched in to provide the briefest of clues to locale, giving us the feeling that the story could take place almost anywhere. In other stories, the author focuses on certain elements of the setting to create atmosphere, or mood, in addition to locale. Lessing ("A Woman on a Roof") reminds us again and again of the oppressive heat that adds to the anger and frustration of the men, and Joyce ("Counterparts") makes us aware of the heat and noise of the pubs that attract Farrington. Atmosphere is created by vivid description, by adding an emotional intensity to details of setting. At some point on an intensification scale, setting provides atmosphere as well as locale. Further along the scale, setting becomes symbolic as intensification results in our attaching additional meanings to the setting. When setting is highlighted, you should judge whether the result is atmosphere (intensifying emotion) or symbol (intensifying meaning).

The repeated symbol, the object or part of the setting that appears again and again, is probably the easiest literary symbol to recognize. In contrast to the walls in "Bartleby the Scrivener," the horses in Lawrence's story appear only briefly; it is the emphasis given to their being led away that gives them symbolic significance. Here is another example.

PETER MEINKE   (b. 1932)

Advice to My Son

The trick is, to live your days
as if each one may be your last
(for they go fast, and young men lose their lives
in strange and unimaginable ways)
but at the same time, plan long range   5
(for they go slow: if you survive
the shattered windshield and the bursting shell
you will arrive
at our approximation here below
of heaven or hell).   10

To be specific, between the peony and the rose
plant squash and spinach, turnips and tomatoes;
beauty is nectar
and nectar, in a desert, saves—
but the stomach craves stronger sustenance   15
than the honied vine.

Therefore, marry a pretty girl
after seeing her mother;
show your soul to one man,
work with another;   20
and always serve bread with your wine.

But, son,
always serve wine.

QUESTIONS

1. In the poem's first section, what general advice does the speaker offer his son?
2. How is the advice seemingly contradictory? Can you reconcile the apparent contradiction?
3. What objects in the poem can be viewed symbolically? How do they parallel the "contradictory" advice at the beginning of the poem?
4. What do the objects symbolically represent?

Meinke writes specifically about planting flowers and vegetables and eating bread and wine, but these details gain significance by following more general advice about how to live one's life. The speaker literally recommends eating bread and wine, but surely he doesn't want his son to eat only bread, wine, and four vegetables. The emphasis given to these ordinary objects gives them symbolic value. What they suggest is connected to the seemingly contradictory paths the speaker advises his son to follow. Spinach and turnips seem mundane planted between beautiful flowers; similarly, bread is a basic food whereas wine adds a festive note to the meal. In both planning for the future and living for today, we balance basic needs with the joy of living that lifts the spirit. To serve bread and wine is to feed both the body and the spirit.

When writers use cultural or universal symbols, they expect their readers to attach the conventional associations to the symbol— as a starting point. But cultural symbols will also be shaped by the particular context. A writer, then, can narrow or enlarge the range of a conventional symbol by the way it is used. Consider Dunbar's handling of the red rose in the following poem.

PAUL LAWRENCE DUNBAR   (1872–1906)

Promise

I grew a rose within a garden fair,
And, tending it with more than loving care,
I thought how, with the glory of its bloom,
I should the darkness of my life illume;
And, watching, ever smiled to see the lusty bud   5
Drink freely in the summer sun to tint its blood.

My rose began to open, and its hue
Was sweet to me as to it sun and dew;
I watched it taking on its ruddy flame
Until the day of perfect blooming came,
Then hasted I with smiles to find it blushing red—   10
Too late! Some thoughtless child had plucked my rose and fled!

QUESTIONS

1. What is the situation in the poem?
2. What is the speaker's attitude toward the rose? What words convey his attitude?

3. How does the poem's ending alter the conventional symbolic meanings of a red rose? What does the rose seem to mean in this poem?

The beautiful flower is carefully nurtured into full bloom by the speaker who expects it to brighten his life. The title of the poem is significant; the rose represents great promise for the speaker who must be crushed to lose what he has nurtured and waited for. Has a rival won the speaker's loved one? A thoughtless child would not be an appropriate rival for the speaker, so it would seem that the rose is not limited to a loved person. Rather, in the context of this poem, the rose is something cherished by the speaker in anticipation of the pleasure it will bring, perhaps the promise of youth and vitality that the speaker hopes to keep for old age but loses to the young. The poet expects us to respond to the rose as something beautiful and desired, but he builds on those associations and enlarges the rose's meaning to include whatever desires and hopes we postpone only to discover that we have lost our opportunity.

WRITING ABOUT SYMBOL

Because a symbolic work conveys much of its meaning through its symbol(s), we generally write about symbol to understand a work's meaning rather than to analyze a writer's technique. You might be asked to compare the use of conventional symbols in two works, but usually you will be asked to write an analysis of symbol in one work. Your purpose will be to explain the symbol's meanings as a key to understanding the work. A successful essay on symbol, then, must not merely assert that particular objects, characters, or actions are symbolic; it must explain the meanings attached to the symbols. A weak essay on symbol usually results from one of two problems: (1) the essay demonstrates that the object is given significance so that it becomes a symbol, but the student fails to explain the symbol's meaning, or (2) the essay develops into a general discussion of meaning that is not tied to the details of the work. The second weakness can result from "symbol hunting," from deciding to write about symbol when there is little evidence that anything in the work should be viewed symbolically. You want to be alert to the possibility of the writer's use of symbol without turning every chipped teacup into a symbolic loss of social standing. When writing about symbol, you have two tasks: (1) show how the writer gives the object symbolic significance and (2) explain its symbolic associations and hence its contribution to the work's meaning.

Before reading the student essay on symbol, study Lawrence's poem "Snake" carefully. Although "Snake" is not an easy poem, you should be able to recognize that the snake is given symbolic significance by Lawrence. As the student points out, Lawrence makes us aware of the snake's symbolic quality by the language used to refer to the snake and by the conflict that the snake's presence creates in the speaker. What is difficult about "Snake" is deciding on the meanings given to the snake in this poem. In this context, as the student perceives, we cannot limit the snake's meaning to evil, but neither can we say, simply, that the snake symbolizes life. Notice, too, that the student does not let the "voices" of his "education" keep him from recognizing and considering the significance of the poem's sexual imagery. The student accomplishes the goals of a successful essay on symbol: he demonstrates that the snake should be viewed as a symbol, and he explains and supports his interpretation of the snake's symbolic meanings.

D. H. LAWRENCE   (1885–1930)

Snake

A snake came to my water-trough
On a hot, hot day, and I in pyjamas for the heat,
To drink there.

In the deep, strange-scented shade of the great dark carob-tree
I came down the steps with my pitcher   5
And must wait, must stand and wait, for there he was at the trough
    before me.

He reached down from a fissure in the earth-wall in the gloom
And trailed his yellow-brown slackness soft-bellied down, over the edge
    of the stone trough
And rested his throat upon the stone bottom,
And where the water had dripped from the tap, in a small clearness,   10
He sipped with his straight mouth,
Softly drank through his straight gums, into his slack long body,
Silently.

Someone was before me at my water-trough,
And I, like a second comer, waiting.   1

He lifted his head from his drinking, as cattle do,
And looked at me vaguely, as drinking cattle do,
And flickered his two-forked tongue from his lips, and mused a moment,
And stooped and drank a little more,
Being earth-brown, earth-golden from the burning bowels of the earth   2
On the day of Sicilian July, with Etna smoking.

The voice of my education said to me
He must be killed,
For in Sicily the black, black snakes are innocent, the gold are venomous.

And voices in me said, If you were a man
You would take a stick and break him now, and finish him off.

But must I confess how I liked him,
How glad I was he had come like a guest in quiet, to drink at my water-
    trough
And depart peaceful, pacified, and thankless,
Into the burning bowels of this earth?

Was it cowardice, that I dared not kill him?
Was it perversity, that I longed to talk to him?
Was it humility, to feel so honoured?
I felt so honoured.

And yet those voices:
If you were not afraid, you would kill him!

And truly I was afraid, I was most afraid,
But even so, honoured still more
That he should seek my hospitality
From out the dark door of the secret earth.

He drank enough
And lifted his head, dreamily, as one who has drunken,
And flickered his tongue like a forked night on the air, so black;
Seeming to lick his lips,
And looked around like a god, unseeing, into the air,
And slowly turned his head,
And slowly, very slowly, as if thrice adream,
Proceeded to draw his slow length curving round
And climb again the broken bank of my wall-face.

And as he put his head into that dreadful hole,
And as he slowly drew up, snake-easing his shoulders, and entered farther,

A sort of horror, a sort of protest against his withdrawing into that horrid
    black hole,
Deliberately going into the blackness, and slowly drawing himself after,
Overcame me now his back was turned.

I looked round, I put down my pitcher,   55
I picked up a clumsy log
And threw it at the water-trough with a clatter.

I think it did not hit him,
But suddenly that part of him that was left behind convulsed in undignified
    haste,
Writhed like lightning, and was gone   60
Into the black hole, the earth-lipped fissure in the wall-front,
At which, in the intense still noon, I stared with fascination.

And immediately I regretted it.
I thought how paltry, how vulgar, what a mean act!
I despised myself and the voices of my accursed human education.   65

And I thought of the albatross,
And I wished he would come back, my snake.

For he seemed to me again like a king,
Like a king in exile, uncrowned in the underworld,
Now due to be crowned again.   70

And so, I missed my chance with one of the lords
Of life.
And I have something to expiate;
A pettiness.

STUDENT ESSAY

The Symbolism of "Snake"

James Ferguson

The snake in D.H. Lawrence's poem "Snake" is transformed from being merely an object blocking the speaker from the water trough into a symbol representing one aspect of life. Through the language used to describe the snake's appearance and movements, Lawrence gives the snake symbolic significance such that by the end of the poem the speaker recognizes the snake as "one of the lords / Of life." To say that the snake represents life is to give it too broad a meaning (it is only <u>one</u> of the "lords / Of life") and to ignore the traditional symbolic associations of the snake with evil or the devil. Also, the snake's appearance produces a conflict for the speaker. This conflict further emphasizes the snake's symbolic significance but qualifies its meaning; it is both something positive and something threatening. The snake seems to symbolize our primitive urges and our emotions, including sexual desires, which the speaker has been taught, through his "education," not to recognize.

The way the speaker refers to the snake is one important way that Lawrence emphasizes the snake's significance and gives it symbolic meaning. During the initial confrontation, the speaker refers to the obstacle at the water trough as just "A snake," but soon the snake's actions are described in human terms: "He sipped," "He reached down." Lawrence completes the reptile's shift to the human level when he has the speaker recognize that "someone was before me at my water-trough." Later the snake shifts from being on equal terms with the speaker to being superior to the speaker, more than human. The speaker describes him as "like a god" and "Like a king in exile." The significance that the speaker

STUDENT ESSAY

gives to the snake, which leads us to see the snake as symbolic, is further
stressed when the speaker calls him "my snake." The references to a god,
a king, and, finally, a lord make clear that the snake represents
something to be valued and worshipped.

In spite of the positive references to the snake, his appearance produces
a conflict for the speaker. The speaker has to confront an inner voice
that tells him to kill the snake; we are told, "The voice of my education
said to me / He must be killed." These voices that the speaker hears are
the direct result of his being conditioned by society to repress anything
that comes from "the burning bowels of the earth." The speaker tells
us that he despised himself and "the voices of" **his** "accursed human education"
for making him afraid of the snake. Although the speaker is "most afraid"
of the snake, he also likes the snake and is honored by his visit. These
feelings tie in with the speaker's references to the snake as a king and
a lord. The speaker's inner conflict, then, seems to be between his "human
education," what society has taught him, which is to fear the snake and
send him back into the earth, and his positive feelings for what the snake
represents, the earthy or elemental desires and emotions. The snake stands
for what lies beneath the surface, in "the secret earth," that society
would have us keep hidden.

The speaker attempts to avert his problem instead of confronting
it by hastening the snake's retreat into the "horrid black hole." The
speaker feels "A sort of horror" at the snake's movement into "the earth-
lipped fissure in the wall-front." Lawrence's description of the snake's
movements and of the wall have clear sexual overtones that help to bring
out the snake's symbolic meanings. The repulsion that the speaker feels
at the snake's "deliberately going into the blackness and slowly drawing
himself after" is the result of years of repression. Although the snake

STUDENT ESSAY

poses a physical threat to the speaker, much more important is the psychological danger that arises from the speaker's problem in accepting the
passions that his conditioning has taught him to repress. In "Snake"
D.H. Lawrence has shown us what happens to modern men and women when feelings are repressed. The speaker's recognition at the end of the poem
that he has a pettiness to atone for makes clear the value Lawrence places
upon our accepting our passions.

SELECTIONS FOR FURTHER STUDY

WILLIAM BLAKE   (1757–1827)

The Sick Rose

O rose, thou art sick!
The invisible worm
That flies in the night,
In the howling storm,

Has found out thy bed   5
Of crimson joy,
And his dark secret love
Does thy life destroy.

QUESTIONS

1. What lines in the poem provide sufficiently unusual descriptions of the worm
   and rose to lead us to respond to them as symbols?
2. How can the worm and rose be associated symbolically with male and female?
3. What are the conventional symbolic associations of the worm (if seen as a
   miniature snake) and the rose?
4. Can you reconcile the worm's destructive power with its "secret love" of the
   rose?
5. How would you interpret this poem?

EDWIN MUIR   (1887–1959)

The Horses

Barely a twelvemonth after
The seven days war that put the world to sleep,
Late in the evening the strange horses came.
By then we had made our covenant with silence,
But in the first few days it was so still   5
We listened to our breathing and were afraid.
On the second day
The radios failed; we turned the knobs; no answer.
On the third day a warship passed us, heading north,
Dead bodies piled on the deck. On the sixth day   10
A plane plunged over us into the sea. Thereafter
Nothing. The radios dumb;
And still they stand in corners of our kitchens,
And stand, perhaps, turned on, in a million rooms
All over the world. But now if they should speak,   15
If on a sudden they should speak again,
If on the stroke of noon a voice should speak,
We would not listen, we would not let it bring
That old bad world that swallowed its children quick
At one great gulp. We would not have it again.   20
Sometimes we think of the nations lying asleep,
Curled blindly in impenetrable sorrow,
And then the thought confounds us with its strangeness,
The tractors lie about our fields; at evening
They look like dank sea-monsters couched and waiting.   25
We leave them where they are and let them rust:
'They'll moulder away and be like other loam'.
We make our oxen drag our rusty ploughs,
Long laid aside. We have gone back
Far past our fathers' land.
                   And then, that evening   30
Late in the summer the strange horses came.
We heard a distant tapping on the road,
A deepening drumming; it stopped, went on again
And at the corner changed to hollow thunder.
We saw the heads   35
Like a wild wave charging and were afraid.
We had sold our horses in our fathers' time
To buy new tractors. Now they were strange to us
As fabulous steeds set on an ancient shield

Or illustrations in a book of knights.   40
We did not dare go near them. Yet they waited,
Stubborn and shy, as if they had been sent
By an old command to find our whereabouts
And that long-lost archaic companionship.
In the first moment we had never a thought   45
That they were creatures to be owned and used.
Among them were some half-a-dozen colts
Dropped in some wilderness of the broken world,
Yet new as if they had come from their own Eden.
Since then they have pulled our ploughs and borne our loads   50
But that free servitude still can pierce our hearts.
Our life is changed; their coming our beginning.

QUESTIONS

1. What is significant about the "seven days war"? About the silence after the
   sixth day?
2. How are the silent, "dumb" radios an appropriate image?
3. Explain: "We have gone back / Far past our fathers' land."
4. Why does the speaker emphasize that the horses are strange to them?
5. Explain "free servitude." What figure of speech is this?
6. The speaker asserts that the horses' coming has changed their lives; how? What
   do the horses symbolize?

MARY E. WILKINS FREEMAN   (1862–1930)

A New England Nun

It was late in the afternoon, and the light was waning. There was a
difference in the look of the tree shadows out in the yard. Somewhere in
the distance cows were lowing and a little bell was tinkling; now and then
a farm-wagon tilted by, and the dust flew; some blue-shirted laborers with
shovels over their shoulders plodded past; little swarms of flies were
dancing up and down before the peoples' faces in the soft air. There
seemed to be a gentle stir arising over everything for the mere sake of
subsidence—a very premonition of rest and hush and night.

This soft diurnal commotion was over Louisa Ellis also. She had been
peacefully sewing at her sitting-room window all the afternoon. Now she

quilted her needle carefully into her work, which she folded precisely, and laid in a basket with her thimble and thread and scissors. Louisa Ellis could not remember that ever in her life she had mislaid one of these little feminine appurtenances, which had become, from long use and constant association, a very part of her personality.

Louisa tied a green apron round her waist, and got out a flat straw hat with a green ribbon. Then she went into the garden with a little blue crockery bowl, to pick some currants for her tea. After the currants were picked she sat on the back door-step and stemmed them, collecting the stems carefully in her apron, and afterwards throwing them into the hen-coop. She looked sharply at the grass beside the step to see if any had fallen there.

Louisa was slow and still in her movements; it took her a long time to prepare her tea; but when ready it was set forth with as much grace as if she had been a veritable guest to her own self. The little square table stood exactly in the centre of the kitchen, and was covered with a starched linen cloth whose border pattern of flowers glistened. Louisa had a damask napkin on her tea-tray, where were arranged a cut-glass tumbler full of teaspoons, a silver cream-pitcher, a china sugar-bowl, and one pink china cup and saucer. Louisa used china every day—something which none of her neighbors did. They whispered about it among themselves. Their daily tables were laid with common crockery, their sets of best china stayed in the parlor closet, and Louisa Ellis was no richer nor better bred than they. Still she would use the china. She had for her supper a glass dish full of sugared currants, a plate of little cakes, and one of light white biscuits. Also a leaf or two of lettuce, which she cut up daintily. Louisa was very fond of lettuce, which she raised to perfection in her little garden. She ate quite heartily, though in a delicate, pecking way; it seemed almost surprising that any considerable bulk of the food should vanish.

After tea she filled a plate with nicely baked thin corn-cakes, and carried them out into the back-yard.

"Caesar!" she called. "Caesar! Caesar!"

There was a little rush, and the clank of a chain, and a large yellow-and-white dog appeared at the door of his tiny hut, which was half hidden among the tall grasses and flowers. Louisa patted him and gave him the corn-cakes. Then she returned to the house and washed the tea-things, polishing the china carefully. The twilight had deepened; the chorus of the frogs floated in at the open window wonderfully loud and shrill, and once in a while a long sharp drone from a tree-toad pierced it. Louisa took off her green gingham apron, disclosing a shorter one of pink and white print. She lighted her lamp, and sat down again with her sewing.

In about half an hour Joe Dagget came. She heard his heavy step on the walk, and rose and took off her pink-and-white apron. Under that was still another—white linen with a little cambric edging on bottom; that was Louisa's company apron. She never wore it without her calico sewing apron over it unless she had a guest. She had barely folded the pink and white one with methodical haste and laid it in a table-drawer when the door opened and Joe Dagget entered.

He seemed to fill up the whole room. A little yellow canary that had been asleep in his green cage at the south window woke up and fluttered wildly, beating his little yellow wings against the wires. He always did so when Joe Dagget came into the room.

"Good-evening," said Louisa. She extended her hand with a kind of solemn cordiality.

"Good-evening, Louisa," returned the man, in a loud voice.

She placed a chair for him, and they sat facing each other, with the table between them. He sat bolt-upright, toeing out his heavy feet squarely, glancing with a good-humored uneasiness around the room. She sat gently erect, folding her slender hands in her white-linen lap.

"Been a pleasant day," remarked Dagget.

"Real pleasant," Louisa assented, softly. "Have you been haying?" she asked, after a little while.

"Yes, I've been haying all day, down in the ten-acre lot. Pretty hot work."

"It must be."

"Yes, it's pretty hot work in the sun."

"Is your mother well to-day?"

"Yes, mother's pretty well."

"I suppose Lily Dyer's with her now?"

Dagget colored. "Yes, she's with her," he answered, slowly.

He was not very young, but there was a boyish look about his large face. Louisa was not quite as old as he, her face was fairer and smoother, but she gave people the impression of being older.

"I suppose she's a good deal of help to your mother," she said, further.

"I guess she is; I don't know how mother'd get along without her," said Dagget, with a sort of embarrassed warmth.

"She looks like a real capable girl. She's pretty-looking too," remarked Louisa.

"Yes, she is pretty fair looking."

Presently Dagget began fingering the books on the table. There was a square red autograph album, and a Young Lady's Gift-Book which had belonged to Louisa's mother. He took them up one after the other and opened them; then laid them down again, the album on the Gift-Book.

Louisa kept eyeing them with mild uneasiness. Finally she rose and changed the position of the books, putting the album underneath. That was the way they had been arranged in the first place.

Dagget gave an awkward little laugh. "Now what difference did it make which book was on top?" said he.

Louisa looked at him with a deprecating smile. "I always keep them that way," murmured she.

"You do beat everything," said Dagget, trying to laugh again. His large face was flushed.

He remained about an hour longer, then rose to take leave. Going out, he stumbled over a rug, and trying to recover himself, hit Louisa's work-basket on the table, and knocked it on the floor.

He looked at Louisa, then at the rolling spools; he ducked himself awkwardly toward them, but she stopped him. "Never mind," said she; "I'll pick them up after you're gone."

She spoke with a mild stiffness. Either she was a little disturbed, or his nervousness affected her, and made her seem constrained in her effort to reassure him.

When Joe Daggett was outside he drew in the sweet evening air with a sigh, and felt much as an innocent and perfectly well-intentioned bear might after his exit from a china shop.

Louisa, on her part, felt much as the kind-hearted, long-suffering owner of the china shop might have done after the exit of the bear.

She tied on the pink, then the green apron, picked up all the scattered treasures and replaced them in her work-basket, and straightened the rug. Then she set the lamp on the floor, and began sharply examining the carpet. She even rubbed her fingers over it, and looked at them.

"He's tracked in a good deal of dust," she murmured. "I thought he must have."

Louisa got a dust-pan and brush, and swept Joe Dagget's track carefully.

If he could have known it, it would have increased his perplexity and uneasiness, although it would not have disturbed his loyalty in the least. He came twice a week to see Louisa Ellis, and every time, sitting there in her delicately sweet room, he felt as if surrounded by a hedge of lace. He was afraid to stir lest he should put a clumsy foot or hand through the fairy web, and he had always the consciousness that Louisa was watching fearfully lest he should.

Still the lace and Louisa commanded perforce his perfect respect and patience and loyalty. They were to be married in a month, after a singular courtship which had lasted for a matter of fifteen years. For fourteen out of the fifteen years the two had not once seen each other, and they had seldom exchanged letters. Joe had been all those years in Australia, where he had gone to make his fortune, and where he had stayed until he made it. He would have stayed fifty years if it had taken so long, and come home feeble and tottering or never come home at all, to marry Louisa.

But the fortune had been made in the fourteen years, and he had come home now to marry the woman who had been patiently and unquestioningly waiting for him all that time.

Shortly after they were engaged he had announced to Louisa his determination to strike out into new fields, and secure a competency before they should be married. She had listened and assented with the sweet serenity which never failed her, not even when her lover set forth on that long and uncertain journey. Joe, buoyed up as he was by his sturdy determination, broke down a little at the last, but Louisa kissed him with a mild blush, and said good-by.

"It won't be for long," poor Joe had said, huskily; but it was for fourteen years.

In that length of time much had happened. Louisa's mother and brother had died, and she was all alone in the world. But greatest happening of all—a subtle happening which both were too simple to understand—Louisa's feet had turned into a path, smooth maybe under a calm, serene sky, but so straight and unswerving that it could only meet a check at her grave, and so narrow that there was no room for any one at her side.

Louisa's first emotion when Joe Dagget came home (he had not apprised her of his coming) was consternation, although she would not admit it to herself, and he never dreamed of it. Fifteen years ago she had been in love with him—at least she considered herself to be. Just at that time, gently acquiescing with and falling into the natural drift of girlhood, she had seen marriage ahead as a reasonable feature and a probable desirability of life. She had listened with calm docility to her mother's views upon the subject. Her mother was remarkable for her cool sense and sweet, even temperament. She talked wisely to her daughter when Joe Daggett presented himself, and Louisa accepted him with no hesitation. He was the first lover she had ever had.

She had been faithful to him all these years. She had never dreamed of the possibility of marrying any one else. Her life, especially for the last seven years, had been full of a pleasant peace, she had never felt discontented nor impatient over her lover's absence; still she had always looked forward to his return and their marriage as the inevitable conclusion of things. However, she had fallen into a way of placing it so far in the future that it was almost equal to placing it over the boundaries of another life.

When Joe came she had been expecting him, and expecting to be married for fourteen years, but she was as much surprised and taken aback as if she had never thought of it.

Joe's consternation came later. He eyed Louisa with an instant confirmation of his old admiration. She had changed but little. She still kept her pretty manner and soft grace, and was, he considered, every whit as attractive as ever. As for himself, his stent was done; he had turned his face away from fortune-seeking, and the old winds of romance whistled as loud and sweet as ever through his ears. All the song which he had been wont to hear in them was Louisa; he had for a long time a loyal belief that he heard it still, but finally it seemed to him that although the winds sang always that one song, it had another name. But for Louisa the wind had never more than murmured; now it had gone down, and everything was still. She listened for a little while with half-wistful attention; then she turned quietly away and went to work on her wedding clothes.

Joe had made some extensive and quite magnificent alterations in his house. It was the old homestead; the newly-married couple would live there, for Joe could not desert his mother, who refused to leave her old home. So Louisa must leave hers. Every morning, rising and going about among her neat maidenly possessions, she felt as one looking her last upon the faces of dear friends. It was true that in a measure she could take them with her, but, robbed of their old environments, they would appear in such new guises that they would almost cease to be themselves. Then there were some peculiar features of her happy solitary life which she would probably be obliged to relinquish altogether. Sterner tasks than these graceful but half-needless ones would probably devolve upon her. There would be a large house to care for; there would be company to entertain; there would be Joe's rigorous and feeble old mother to wait upon; and it would be contrary to all thrifty village traditions for her to keep more than one servant. Louisa had a little still, and she used to occupy herself pleasantly in summer weather with distilling the sweet and aromatic essences from roses and peppermint and spearmint. By-and-by her still must be laid away. Her store of essences was already considerable, and there would be no time for her to distil for the mere pleasure of it. Then Joe's mother would think it foolishness; she had already hinted her opinion in the matter. Louisa dearly loved to sew a linen seam, not always for use, but for the simple, mild pleasure which she took in it. She would have been loath to confess how more than once she had ripped a seam for the mere delight of sewing it together again. Sitting at her window during long sweet afternoons, drawing her needle gently through the dainty fabric, she was peace itself. But there was small chance of such foolish comfort in the future. Joe's mother, domineering, shrewd old matron that she was even in her old age, and very likely even Joe himself, with his honest masculine rudeness, would laugh and frown down all these pretty but senseless old maiden ways.

Louisa had almost the enthusiams of an artist over the mere order and cleanliness of her solitary home. She had throbs of genuine triumph at the sight of the window-panes which she had polished until they shone like jewels. She gloated gently over her orderly bureau-drawers, with their exquisitely folded contents redolent with lavendar and sweet clover and very purity. Could she be sure of the endurance of even this? She had visions, so startling that she half repudiated them as indelicate, of coarse masculine belongings strewn about in endless litter; of dust and disorder arising necessarily from a coarse masculine presence in the midst of all this delicate harmony.

Among her forebodings of disturbance, not the least was with regard to Caesar. Caesar was a veritable hermit of a dog. For the greater part of his life he had dwelt in his secluded hut, shut out from the society of his kind and all innocent canine joys. Never had Caesar since his early youth watched at a woodchuck's hole; never had he known the delights of a stray bone at a neighbor's kitchen door. And it was all on account of a sin committed when hardly out of his puppyhood. No one knew the possible depth of remorse of which this mild-visaged, altogether innocent-looking old dog might be capable; but whether or not he had encountered remorse, he had encountered a full measure of righteous retribution. Old Caesar seldom lifted up his voice in a growl or a bark; he was fat and sleepy; there were yellow rings which looked like spectacles around his dim old eyes; but there was a neighbor who bore on his hand the imprint of several of Caesar's sharp white youthful teeth, and for that he had lived at the end of a chain, all alone in a little hut, for fourteen years. The neighbor, who was choleric and smarting with the pain of his wound, had demanded either Caesar's death or complete ostracism. So Louisa's brother, to whom the dog had belonged, had built him his little kennel and tied him up. It was now fourteen years since, in a flood of youthful spirits, he had inflicted that memorable bite, and with the exception of short excursions, always at the end of the chain, under the strict guardianship of his master or Louisa, the old dog had remained a close prisoner. It is doubtful if, with his limited ambition, he took much pride in the fact, but it is certain that he was possessed of considerable cheap fame. He was regarded by all the children in the village and by many adults as a very monster of ferocity. St. George's dragon could hardly have surpassed in evil repute Louisa Ellis's old yellow dog. Mothers charged their children with solemn emphasis not to go too near to him, and the children listened and believed greedily, with a fascinated appetite for terror, and ran by Louisa's house stealthily, with many sidelong and backward glances at the terrible dog. If perchance he sounded a hoarse bark, there was a panic. Wayfarers chancing into Louisa's yard eyed him with respect, and inquired if the chain were stout. Caesar at large might have seemed a very ordinary dog, and excited no comment whatever; chained, his reputation overshadowed him, so that he lost his own proper outlines and looked darkly vague and enormous. Joe Dagget, however, with his good-humored sense and shrewdness, saw him as he was. He strode valiantly up to him and patted him on the head, in spite of Louisa's soft clamor of warning, and even attempted to set him loose. Louisa grew so alarmed that he desisted, but kept announcing his opinion in the matter quite forcibly at intervals. "There ain't a better-natured dog in town," he would say, "and it's downright cruel to keep him tied up there. Some day I'm going to take him out."

Louisa had very little hope that he would not, one of these days, when their interests and possessions should be more completely fused in one. She pictured to herself Caesar on the rampage through the quiet and unguarded village. She saw innocent children bleeding in his path. She was herself very fond of the old dog, because he had belonged to her dead brother and he was always very gentle with her; still she had great faith in his ferocity. She always warned people not to go too near him. She fed him on ascetic fare of corn-mush and cakes, and never fired his dangerous temper with heating and sanguinary diet of flesh and bones. Louisa looked at the old dog munching his simple fare, and thought of her approaching marriage and trembled. Still no anticipation or disorder and confusion in lieu of sweet peace and harmony, no forebodings of Caesar on the rampage, no wild fluttering of her little yellow canary, were sufficient to turn her a hair's-breadth. Joe Dagget had been fond of her and working for her all these years. It was not for her, whatever came to pass, to prove untrue and break his heart. She put the exquisite little stitches into her wedding-garments, and the time went on until it was only a week before her wedding-day. It was a Tuesday evening, and the wedding was to be a week from Wednesday.

There was a full moon that night. About nine o'clock Louisa strolled down the road a little way. There were harvest-fields on either hand, bordered by low stone walls. Luxuriant clumps of bushes grew beside the wall, and trees—wild cherry and old apple-trees—at intervals. Presently Louisa sat down on the wall and looked about her with mildy sorrowful reflectiveness. Tall shrubs of blueberry and meadow-sweet, all woven together and tangled with blackberry vines and horsebriers, shut her in on either side. She had a little clear space between them. Opposite her, on the other side of the road, was a spreading tree; the moon shone between its boughs, and the leaves twinkled like silver. The road was bespread with a beautiful shifting dapple of silver and shadow; the air was full of a mysterious sweetness. "I wonder if it's wild grapes?" murmured Louisa. She sat there some time. She was just thinking of rising, when she heard footsteps and low voices, and remained quiet. It was a lonely place, and she felt a little timid. She thought she would keep still in the shadow and let the persons, whoever they might be, pass her.

But just before they reached her the voices ceased, and the footsteps. She understood that their owners had also found seats upon the stone wall. She was wondering if she could not steal away unobserved, when the voice broke the stillness. It was Joe Dagget's. She sat still and listened.

The voice was announced by a loud sigh, which was as familiar as itself. "Well," said Dagget, "you've made up your mind, then, I suppose?"

"Yes," returned another voice; "I'm going day after to-morrow."

"That's Lily Dyer," thought Louisa to herself. The voice embodied itself in her mind. She saw a girl tall and full-figured, with a firm, fair face, looking fairer and firmer in the moonlight, her strong yellow hair braided in a close knot. A girl full of a calm rustic strength and bloom, with a masterful way which might have beseemed a princess. Lily Dyer was a favorite with the village folk; she had just the qualities to arouse the admiration. She was good and handsome and smart. Louisa had often heard her praises sounded.

"Well," said Joe Dagget, "I ain't got a word to say."

"I don't know what you could say," returned Lily Dyer.

"Not a word to say," repeated Joe, drawing out the words heavily. Then there was a silence. "I ain't sorry," he began at last, "that that happened yesterday—that we kind of let on how we felt to each other. I guess it's just as well we knew. Of course I can't do anything any different. I'm going right on an' get married next week. I ain't going back on a woman that's waited for me fourteen years, an' break her heart."

"If you should jilt her to-morrow, I wouldn't have you," spoke up the girl, with sudden vehemence.

"Well, I ain't going to give you the chance," said he; "but I don't believe you would, either."

"You'd see I wouldn't. Honor's honor, an' right's right. An' I'd never think anything of any man that went against 'em for me or any other girl; you'd find that out, Joe Dagget."

"Well, you'll find out fast enough that I ain't going against 'em for you or any other girl," returned he. Their voices sounded almost as if they were angry with each other. Louisa was listening eagerly.

"I'm sorry you feel as if you must go away," said Joe, "but I don't know but it's best."

"Of course it's best. I hope you and I have got common-sense."

"Well, I suppose you're right." Suddenly Joe's voice got an undertone of tenderness. "Say, Lily," said he, "I'll get along well enough myself, but I can't bear to think—You don't suppose you're going to fret much over it?"

"I guess you'll find out I sha'nt fret much over a married man."

"Well, I hope you won't—I hope you won't, Lily. God knows I do. And—I hope—one of these days—you'll—come across somebody else—"

"I don't see any reason why I shouldn't." Suddenly her tone changed. She spoke in a sweet, clear voice, so loud that she could have been heard across the street. "No, Joe Dagget," said she, "I'll never marry any other man as long as I live. I've got good sense, an' I ain't going to break my heart nor make a fool of myself; but I'm never going to be married, you can be sure of that. I ain't that sort of a girl to feel this way twice."

Louisa heard an exclamation and a soft commotion behind the bushes; then Lily spoke again—the voice sounded as if she had risen. "This must be put a stop to," said she. "We've stayed here long enough. I'm going home."

Louisa sat there in a daze, listening to their retreating steps. After a while she got up and slunk softly home herself. The next day she did her housework methodically; that was as much a matter of course as breathing; but she did not sew on her wedding-clothes. She sat at her window and meditated. In the evening Joe came. Louisa Ellis had never known that she had any diplomacy in her, but when she came to look for it that night she found it, although meek of its kind, among her little feminine weapons. Even now she could hardly believe that she had heard aright, and that she would not do Joe a terrible injury should she break her troth-plight. She wanted to sound him without betraying too soon her own inclinations in the matter. She did it successfully, and they finally came to an understanding; but it was a difficult thing, for he was as afraid of betraying himself as she.

She never mentioned Lily Dyer. She simply said that while she had no cause of complaint against him, she had lived so long in one way that she shrank from making a change.

"Well, I never shrank, Louisa," said Dagget. "I'm going to be honest enough to say that I think maybe it's better this way; but if you'd wanted to keep on, I'd have stuck to you till my dying day. I hope you know that."

"Yes, I do," said she.

That night she and Joe parted more tenderly than they had done for a long time. Standing in the door, holding each other's hands, a last great wave of regretful memory swept over them.

"Well, this ain't the way we've thought it was all going to end, is it, Louisa?" said Joe.

She shook her head. There was a little quiver on her placid face.

"You let me know if there's ever anything I can do for you," said he. "I ain't ever going to forget you, Louisa." Then he kissed her, and went down the path.

Louisa, all alone by herself that night, wept a little, she hardly knew why; but the next morning, on waking, she felt like a queen who, after fearing lest her domain be wrested away from her, sees it firmly insured in her possession.

Now the tall weeds and grasses might cluster around Caesar's little hermit hut, the snow might fall on its roof year in and year out, but he never would go on a rampage through the unguarded village. Now the little canary might turn itself into a peaceful yellow ball night after night, and have no need to wake and flutter with wild terror against its bars. Louisa could sew linen seams, and distil roses, and dust and polish and fold away in lavender, as long as she listed. That afternoon she sat with her needle-work at the window, and felt fairly steeped in peace. Lily Dyer, tall and erect and blooming, went past; but she felt no qualm. If Louisa Ellis had sold her birthright she did not know it, the taste of the pottage was so delicious, and had been her sole satisfaction for so long.

Serenity and placid narrowness had become to her as the birthright itself. She gazed ahead through a long reach of future days strung together like pearls in a rosary, every one like the others, and all smooth and flawless and innocent, and her heart went up in thankfulness. Outside was the fervid summer afternoon; the air was filled with the sounds of the busy harvest of men and birds and bees; there were halloos, metallic clatterings, sweet calls, and long hummings. Louisa sat, prayerfully numbering her days, like an uncloistered nun.

QUESTIONS

1. What is the narrative point of view?
2. Analyze plot structure. Where is the story's climax?
3. Does the opening description of setting provide locale only? Atmosphere? Symbolic significance? Defend your choice.
4. What details of Louisa's dress and what objects can be viewed as symbols? What do they represent? How do the symbols help us to understand the story's meaning?
5. Is Louisa to be admired for her choice? Are we to pity her? What seems to be the author's attitude toward Louisa's life?

chapter 10

The Extension
of Meaning—Theme

Giorgio de Chirico. *Mystery and Melancholy of a Street.* 1914. Collection of Mr. and Mrs.
Stanley R. Resor, New Canaan, Connecticut.

WHAT IS MEANT BY THEME

> Some mice who were being chased by a cat held a meeting to discuss the problem. One mouse suggested that if the cat had a bell around its neck, the mice would hear it coming in time to run for safety. All the mice praised this idea except one who asked: "Who is going to tie the bell to the cat?"

The moral of this fable by Aesop is clear: "Good plans are easier to think up than to execute," or "a plan is good only if it can work." Fables, parables, and propaganda pieces are written to teach some truth that the writer hopes we will take to heart and act upon. But works of imaginative literature are not written primarily to teach a lesson. Rather, through the power of words, the literary artist takes us totally, emotions and imagination as well as intellect, into the world of the work. To see only a moral tag ("Crime doesn't pay") as the meaning of a complex literary work is to miss much of the pleasure of the work and to oversimplify the life experiences recreated by the writer.

But since part of our response to literature is a response of the intellect, we do legitimately ask, "What does it mean?" When we ask this question we want to know the work's central ideas, or *themes. Theme* is the critical term used to refer to the views of life or insights into human experiences that emerge from a story, poem, or play and that unify the vision of the work. (Some critics use the term *meaning* rather than theme to refer to a poem's central idea.) We express theme—or meaning—as an idea or cluster of ideas that we gain from thinking about what we have read. If someone asked you what "A Worn Path" is about, you might respond with a plot summary: it is a story of an old woman who takes a long and difficult walk to town to get medicine for her sick grandson. But, if someone asked you to explain the story's dominant theme, it would be inappropriate to mention Phoenix specifically, or any of the particular details of her journey. Instead, you would state an idea. You could say that the theme of "A Worn Path" is that love has the power to give us courage and endurance.

The central ideas or meaning of a work, whether stated briefly or explained in an essay (or book), should not be viewed as an equivalent of the work itself. Theme is an abstraction, one element in a richly textured work, but a unifying element, a central thread woven through the piece, tying it together, making it whole. Thus, being able to state a work's theme is a valuable discipline; it forces you to see how the various parts of the work fit together to form a unified, though often complex, vision.

Because recognizing and thinking about theme is only one kind of response to a literary work, most readers can respond with pleasure to works that express values they do not necessarily share. We can enjoy a poet's startling images or a dramatist's well-drawn and powerful characters without sharing either the poet's or playwright's perceptions of life. Readers who insist on reading only those works that reflect their ideas and values are restricting the pleasure that they may receive from literature and may be limiting their understanding of life. Those who choose to restrict their reading may be doing so because they bring to their reading some misconceptions about theme. Readers looking for a moral may mistakenly assume that writers approve of their "immoral" characters unless they show those characters being punished before the end of the story. Such readers become distressed over works that fail to produce happiness for the "good" and punishment for the "bad." This response often stems from the assumption that writers write to teach moral lessons when more often they are interested in exploring character or expressing emotion or showing us a part of life we might prefer to overlook.

Think back to Joyce's story "Counterparts" (pp. 128–36). There is nothing in the story to suggest that Joyce approves of Farrington's excessive drinking or the violent abuse of his son, but neither does the narrator condemn Farrington. Because Joyce is a creative artist, he explores Farrington's character without contriving his plot to have Farrington punished for his unacceptable behavior. The dominant theme of "Counterparts" is not a moral judgment; one insight the story offers can be stated as follows: people who are continually frustrated in achieving their desires may turn to violence. This is a valid observation about life; there are many frustrated people who turn to violence. Joyce does not preach to us; he reveals his insight into human motivation through the creation of a complex, believable character.

GUIDELINES FOR STATING THEME

Formulating statements about theme is not easy because it requires generalizations drawn from a knowledge of the facts, from inferences about character, from careful attention to figurative language and tone. Good readers who have learned to analyze the various elements of a work may still have trouble stating theme because drawing general points from a set of related facts and inferences is a demanding intellectual skill requiring practice. The following guidelines should help you as you develop skill in seeing how the parts of a work come together to shape the work's meaning.

First you will want to state a work's dominant theme or meaning as an idea, not as plot summary or paraphrase. Remember, too, that a statement about a main character's personality is not the same as a generalization about the work's meaning. To analyze character is to understand only one element in a story or play. You will still need to see how character traits contribute to the work's total significance. If you find yourself starting to write "the theme of 'A Worn Path' is Phoenix Jackson's endurance," you will know to stop and think again.

One way to be sure that your statement about theme is an idea is to make the statement a complete thought. "Love," "frustration," or "repression" are not statements of theme because they are not ideas. What does the work show us about love? If you find yourself thinking just of a term such as "love," ask yourself this kind of question so that you can move from the term to a complete thought about the work. If you were asked to state the central idea of Frost's poem "The Road Not Taken," your first response might be that the poem is about "making choices." That is a good beginning, but now ask yourself, "What does the poem say about making choices?" You could answer this question by formulating the following complete thought: there are choices we must make that affect the direction of the rest of our lives.

When you are analyzing theme, try to find the appropriate degree of generality justified by the work. A work's theme must emerge from the details without ignoring or distorting any of the specifics. Thus, avoid a statement so narrow that it focuses on only part of what the work reveals. To say, for example, that the theme of "A Worn Path" is that love helps us accept kindness from strangers is to narrow the scope of the story. Although Phoenix must ask for help from the hunter and the woman in town, much of her trial is one of physical endurance and of finding the courage to make the long journey. On the other hand, do not make the generalization so broad that the details of the work cannot support it. To say that the theme of "A Worn Path" is "love conquers all" is too broad a statement to be accurate. Phoenix's love for her grandson is admirable, but it probably will not bring about his recovery. In general, avoid words such as "all" and "everyone" or "never" and use words such as "some" or "may." Earlier we said that the theme of "Counterparts" is that people who are continually frustrated in achieving their desires *may* turn to violence. The story does not suggest that *all* people with thwarted dreams turn to violence, and we know that such an unqualified statement would be inaccurate. After all, Walter Mitty does not erupt into violence.

Avoid stating a work's theme as a cliché. Clichés, as in the example "love conquers all," are generally so broad that they will not be accurate statements about a specific work. Further, clichés are ways of avoiding thought, not guides to thinking. When you can find your own words to express a work's theme, you will know that you have gained insight into your reading.

A complex story, novel, or play may contain several themes. Usually they will be interrelated, or a minor theme will be developed in a subplot, a sequence of events involving minor characters. When you are asked to explain a work's theme, focus your attention first on what is central to the work. Remember: (1) a work may have several themes; (2) there is more than one way to state an idea; (3) not all readers will agree in their interpretation of a work. Remember this as well: the previous statements do not support the conclusion that any statement about a work is as accurate or insightful as any other.

THE AUTHOR'S CREATION OF THEME

If theme is the unifying vision that brings all the elements of a work into a meaningful whole, then understanding a work's theme must grow out of the entire process of literary analysis and interpretation. We can analyze a poem's images or a play's plot structure as steps to understanding their themes, but we cannot analyze theme independent of all the other parts of a work. To discuss theme fully and accurately, we need to know the facts, draw sound inferences from analysis, and develop a defensible interpretation that offers genuine insight into the work. We can demonstrate this process through discussion of the following story, "A Summer's Reading."

BERNARD MALAMUD   (1914–1987)

A Summer's Reading

George Stoyonovich was a neighborhood boy who had quit high school on an impulse when he was sixteen, run out of patience, and though he was ashamed everytime he went looking for a job, when people asked him if he had finished and he had to say no, he never went back to school. This summer was a hard time for jobs and he had none. Having so much time on his hands, George thought of going to summer school, but the kids in his classes would be too young. He also considered registering in a night high school, only he didn't like the idea of the teachers always telling him what to do. He felt they had not respected him. The result was he stayed off the streets and in his room most of the day. He was close to twenty and had needs with the neighborhood girls, but no money to spend, and he couldn't get more than an occasional few cents because his father was poor, and his sister Sophie, who resembled George, a tall bony girl of twenty-three, earned very little and what she had she kept for herself. Their mother was dead, and Sophie had to take care of the house.

Very early in the morning George's father got up to go to work in a fish market. Sophie left at about eight for her long ride in the subway to a cafeteria in the Bronx. George had his coffee by himself, then hung around in the house. When the house, a five-room railroad flat above a butcher store, got on his nerves he cleaned it up—mopped the floors with a wet mop and put things away. But most of the time he sat in his room. In the afternoons he listened to the ball game. Otherwise he had a couple of old copies of the *World Almanac* he had bought long ago, and he liked to read in them and also the magazines and newspapers that Sophie brought home, that had been left on the tables in the cafeteria. They were mostly picture magazines about movie stars and sports figures, also usually the *News* and *Mirror*. Sophie herself read whatever fell into her hands, although she sometimes read good books.

She once asked George what he did in his room all day and he said he read a lot too.

"Of what besides what I bring home? Do you ever read any worthwhile books?"

"Some," George answered, although he really didn't. He had tried to read a book or two that Sophie had in the house but found he was in no mood for them. Lately he couldn't stand made-up stories, they got on his nerves. He wished he had some hobby to work at—as a kid he was good in carpentry, but where could he work at it? Sometimes during the day he went for walks, but mostly he did his walking after the hot sun had gone down and it was cooler in the streets.

In the evening after supper George left the house and wandered in the neighborhood. During the sultry days some of the storekeepers and their wives sat in chairs on the thick, broken sidewalks in front of their shops, fanning themselves, and George walked past them and the guys hanging out on the candy store corner. A couple of them he had known his whole life, but nobody recognized each other. He had no place special to go, but generally, saving it till the last, he left the neighborhood and walked for blocks till he came to a darkly lit little park with benches and trees and an iron railing, giving it a feeling of privacy. He sat on a bench here, watching the leafy trees and the flowers blooming on the inside of the railing, thinking of a better life for himself. He thought of the jobs he had had since he had quit school—delivery boy, stock clerk, runner, lately working in a factory—and he was dissatisfied with all of them. He felt he would someday like to have a good job and live in a private house with a porch, on a street with trees. He wanted to have some dough in his pocket to buy things with, and a girl to go with, so as not to be so lonely, especially on Saturday nights. He wanted people to like and respect him. He thought about these things often but mostly when he was alone at night. Around midnight he got up and drifted back to his hot and stony neighborhood.

One time while on his walk George met Mr. Cattanzara coming home very late from work. He wondered if he was drunk but then could tell he wasn't. Mr. Cattanzara, a stocky, bald-headed man who worked in a change booth on an IRT station, lived on the next block after George's, above a shoe repair store. Nights, during the hot weather, he sat on his stoop in an undershirt, reading the *New York Times* in the light of the shoemaker's window. He read it from the first page to the last, then went up to sleep. And all the time he was reading the paper, his wife, a fat woman with a white face, leaned out of the window, gazing into the street, her thick white arms folded under her loose breast, on the window ledge.

Once in a while Mr. Cattanzara came home drunk, but it was a quiet drunk. He never made any trouble, only walked stiffly up the street and slowly climbed the stairs into the hall. Though drunk, he looked the same as always, except for his tight walk, the quietness, and that his eyes were wet. George liked Mr. Cattanzara because he remembered him giving him nickels to buy lemon ice with when he was a squirt. Mr. Cattanzara was a different type than those in the neighborhood. He asked different questions than the others when he met you, and he seemed to know what went on in all the newspapers. He read them, as his fat sick wife watched from the window.

"What are you doing with yourself this summer, George?" Mr. Cattanzara asked. "I see you walkin' around at nights."

George felt embarrassed. "I like to walk."

"What are you doin' in the day now?"

"Nothing much just right now. I'm waiting for a job." Since it shamed him to admit he wasn't working, George said, "I'm staying home—but I'm reading a lot to pick up my education."

Mr. Cattanzara looked interested. He mopped his hot face with a red handkerchief.

"What are you readin'?"

George hestiated, then said, "I got a list of books in the library once, and now I'm gonna read them this summer." He felt strange and a little unhappy saying this, but he wanted Mr. Cattanzara to respect him.

"How many books are there on it?"

"I never counted them. Maybe around a hundred."

Mr. Cattanzara whistled through his teeth.

"I figure if I did that," George went on earnestly, "it would help me in my education. I don't mean the kind they give you in high school. I want to know different things than they learn there, if you know what I mean."

The change maker nodded. "Still and all, one hundred books is a pretty big load for one summer."

"It might take longer."

"After you're finished with some, maybe you and I can shoot the breeze about them?" said Mr. Cattanzara.

"When I'm finished," George answered.

Mr. Cattanzara went home and George continued on his walk. After that, though he had the urge to, George did nothing different from usual. He still took his walks at night, ending up in the little park. But one evening the shoemaker on the next block stopped George to say he was a good boy, and George figured that Mr. Cattanzara had told him all about the books he was reading. From the shoemaker it must have gone down the street, because George saw a couple of people smiling kindly at him, though nobody spoke to him personally. He felt a little better around the neighborhood and liked it more, though not so much he would want to live in it forever. He had never exactly disliked the people in it, yet he had never liked them very much either. It was the fault of the neighborhood. To his surprise, George found out that his father and Sophie knew about his reading too. His father was too shy to say anything about it—he was never much of a talker in his whole life—but Sophie was softer to George, and she showed him in other ways she was proud of him.

As the summer went on George felt in a good mood about things. He cleaned the house every day, as a favor to Sophie, and he enjoyed the ball games more. Sophie gave him a buck a week allowance, and though it still wasn't enough and he had to use it carefully, it was a helluva lot better than just having two bits now and then. What he bought with the money—cigarettes mostly, an occasional beer or movie ticket—he got a big kick out of. Life wasn't so bad if you knew how to appreciate it. Occasionally he bought a paperback book from the newstand, but he never got around to reading it, though he was glad to have a couple of books in his room. But he read thoroughly Sophie's magazines and newspapers. And at night was the most enjoyable time, because when he passed the storekeepers sitting outside their stores, he could tell they regarded him highly. He walked erect, and though he did not say much to them, or they to him, he could feel approval on all sides. A couple of nights he felt so good that he skipped the park at the end of the evening. He just wandered in the neighborhood, where people had known him from the time he was a kid playing punchball whenever there was a game of it going; he wandered there, then came home and got undressed for bed, feeling fine.

For a few weeks he had talked only once with Mr. Cattanzara, and though the change maker had said nothing more about the books, asked no questions, his silence made George a little uneasy. For a while George didn't pass in front of Mr. Cattanzara's house anymore, until one night, forgetting himself, he approached it from a different direction than he usually did when he did. It was already past midnight. The street, except for one or two people, was deserted, and George was surprised when he saw Mr. Cattanzara still reading his newspaper by the light of the street lamp overhead. His impulse was to stop at the stoop and talk to him. He wasn't sure what he wanted to say, though he felt the words would come when he began to talk; but the more he thought about it, the more the idea scared him, and he decided he'd better not. He even considered beating it home by another street, but he was too near Mr. Cattanzara, and the change maker might see him as he ran, and get annoyed. So George unobtrusively crossed the street, trying to make it seem as if he had to look in a store window on the other side, which he did, and then went on, uncomfortable at what he was doing. He feared Mr. Cattanzara would glance up from his paper and call him a dirty rat for walking on the other side of the street, but all he did was sit there, sweating through his undershirt, his bald head shining in the dim light as he read his *Times*, and upstairs his fat wife leaned out of the window, seeming to read the paper along with him. George thought she would spy him and yell out to Mr. Cattanzara, but she never moved her eyes off her husband.

George made up his mind to stay away from the change maker until he had got some of his softback books read, but when he started them and saw they were mostly story books, he lost his interest and didn't bother to finish them. He lost his interest in reading other things too. Sophie's magazines and newspapers went unread. She saw them piling up on a chair in his room and asked why he was no longer looking at them, and George told her it was because of all the other reading he had to do. Sophie said she had guessed that was it. So for most of the day, George had the radio on, turning to music when he was sick of the human voice. He kept the house fairly neat, and Sophie said nothing on the days when he neglected it. She was still kind and gave him his extra buck, though things weren't so good for him as they had been before.

But they were good enough, considering. Also his night walks invariably picked him up, no matter how bad the day was. Then one night George saw Mr. Cattanzara coming down the street toward him. George was about to turn and run but he recognized from Mr. Cattanzara's walk that he was drunk, and if so, probably he would not even bother to notice him. So George kept on walking straight ahead until he came abreast of Mr. Cattanzara and though he felt wound up enough to pop into the sky, he was not surprised when Mr. Cattanzara passed him without a word, walking slowly, his face and body stiff. George drew a breath in relief at his narrow escape, when he heard his name called, and there stood Mr. Cattanzara at his elbow, smelling like the inside of a beer barrel. His eyes were sad as he gazed at George, and George felt so intensely uncomfortable he was tempted to shove the drunk aside and continue on his walk.

But he couldn't act that way to him, and, besides, Mr. Cattanzara took a nickel out of his pants pocket and handed it to him.

"Go buy yourself a lemon ice, Georgie."

"It's not that time anymore, Mr. Cattanzara," George said, "I am a big guy now."

"No, you ain't," said Mr. Cattanzara, to which George made no reply he could think of.

"How are all your books comin' along now?" Mr. Cattanzara asked. Though he tried to stand steady, he swayed a little.

"Fine, I guess," said George, feeling the red crawling up his face.

"You ain't sure?" The change maker smiled slyly, a way George had never seen him smile.

"Sure I'm sure. They're fine."

Though his head swayed in little arcs. Mr. Cattanzara's eyes were steady. He had small blue eyes which could hurt if you looked at them too long.

"George," he said, "name me one book on that list that you read this summer, and I will drink to your health."

"I don't want anybody drinking to me."

"Name me one so I can ask you a question on it. Who can tell, if it's a good book maybe I might wanna read it myself."

George knew he looked passable on the outside, but inside he was crumbling apart.

Unable to reply, he shut his eyes, but when—years later—he opened them, he saw that Mr. Cattanzara had, out of pity, gone away, but in his ears he still heard the words he had said when he left: "George, don't do what I did."

The next night he was afraid to leave his room, and though Sophie argued with him he wouldn't open the door.

"What are you doing in there?" she asked.

"Nothing."

"Aren't you reading?"

"No."

She was silent a minute, then asked, "Where do you keep the books you read? I never see any in your room outside of a few cheap trashy ones."

He wouldn't tell her.

"In that case you're not worth a buck of my hard-earned money. Why should I break my back for you? Go on out, you bum, and get a job."

He stayed in his room for almost a week, except to sneak into the kitchen when nobody was home. Sophie railed at him, then begged him to come out, and his old father wept, but George wouldn't budge, though the weather was terrible and his small room stifling. He found it very hard to breathe, each breath was like drawing a flame into his lungs.

One night, unable to stand the heat anymore, he burst into the street at one A.M, a shadow of himself. He hoped to sneak to the park without being seen, but there were people all over the block, wilted and listless, waiting for a breeze. George lowered his eyes and walked, in disgrace, away from them, but before long he discovered they were still friendly to him. He figured Mr. Cattanzara hadn't told on him. Maybe when he woke up out of his drunk the next morning, he had forgotten all about meeting George. George felt his confidence slowly come back to him.

That same night a man on a street corner asked him if it was true that he had finished reading so many books, and George admitted he had. The man said it was a wonderful thing for a boy his age to read so much.

"Yeah," George said, but he felt relieved. He hoped nobody would mention the books anymore, and when, after a couple of days, he accidentally met Mr. Cattanzara again, *he* didn't, though George had the idea he was the one who had started the rumor that he had finished all the books.

One evening in the fall, George ran out of his house to the library, where he hadn't been in years. There were books all over the place, wherever he looked, and though he was struggling to control an inward trembling, he easily counted off a hundred, then sat down at a table to read.

Although you will sometimes find one or two key lines in a work that can be turned, with only a little rewording, into a statement of theme, most authors create theme indirectly through all the elements in the work. Some peculiar misreadings can result from overlooking details provided by the author. To assert, for example, that the theme of "A Summer's Reading" is that liars may be rejected by family and community is to ignore some of the facts. When George won't leave his room, Sophie begs him to come out. And of course the neighbors remain friendly to George because Mr. Cattanzara chooses not to tell them that George has lied. To assert that the story's theme is that unless you read you won't amount to anything is also to misread the story. Such a misreading could result from (1) ignoring an important detail (Mr. Cattanzara reads the newspaper from cover to cover, but he hasn't amounted to much either in the world's eyes or in his own), (2) looking for a simple moral, or (3) trying to guess what an instructor might want to read. You don't want to distort the specifics of a work to arrive at a theme that merely reinforces either your—or your instructor's—values.

Recognizing what is central to a work can help to unlock theme. Recognizing the symbolic associations of the snake in Lawrence's "Snake," for example, is crucial to perceiving the speaker's conflict and hence the poem's meaning. What is dominant in "A Summer's Reading"? The answer is George—his personality, his conflict, and the resolution of his conflict—this is the story's focus. Let's examine the elements of the story more closely with this focus in mind.

First we can consider the role of setting and point of view. We are given enough details to locate the action in a working-class neighborhood in the New York City area. The heat in the small apartments over shops brings people out to the sidewalks in the summer evenings, but these details of setting seem to provide locale and plausibility for George's interaction with neighbors rather than atmosphere or symbolic significance. The limited omniscient point of view takes us into George's consciousness, tells us what George is thinking and feeling, focusing our attention on him.

Analyzing the story's plot structure and central conflict will bring us closer to an understanding of theme. The exposition, provided in the first few paragraphs, introduces George, his family, and the location of the action. George, now twenty, quit school when he was sixteen, lives with his father and sister, has had several odd jobs, but is unemployed and at home this summer. How George feels about his situation and himself is also presented. He wants respect and is afraid to return to school because his experience with teachers has been that they did not respect him. A complication develops when Mr. Cattanzara, whose newspaper reading George admires, asks George what he is doing. George, ashamed to say "nothing," says instead that he is reading a hundred books. This lie makes George feel bad. He tries to avoid Mr. Cattanzara until he has read, but the summer advances without his being able to do any serious reading. When he runs into Mr. Cattanzara one evening, the story's climax is reached. Although George cannot admit that he is not reading, he knows that Mr. Cattanzara is aware that he lied. The initial resolution is George's retreat to his room, but the final resolution occurs when, after discovering that Mr. Cattanzara has not told the neighbors, George goes to the library, takes down a hundred books, and starts to read.

What leads George to lie, to be ashamed of his lie, and yet to be unable to start reading? George has an internal conflict between his need for respect and his lack of self-respect. This conflict brings about the complications in his summer. The worse he feels about himself, the greater his anxiety, the more trapped he is by inaction. This pattern reaches its final stage in his nearly week-long retreat to his room, but when he is forced out by the heat, he is able to break the pattern and begin, painfully, to act. Perhaps we can state the story's central theme as follows: the confidence we need to take control of our lives cannot come entirely from the respect of others but must be founded on self-respect.

Let us take one more look at the story's climax. There is a significant exchange between George and Mr. Cattanzara in this scene. When George rejects the offer of a nickel saying, "I am a big guy now," Mr. Cattanzara responds by saying, "No, you ain't." Since George speaks the literal truth, we recognize that Mr. Cattanzara's reply must be the truth in another sense. His parting words are "George, don't do what I did." George's summer reading has become a summer of painful learning. George must learn that his respect for Mr. Cattanzara is as inappropriate as the neighbors' respect for George. In both cases, the respect is based on appearance only; neither one is successful, neither one has self-respect. George must learn that sitting in a park dreaming about a better life will only make him the neighborhood's next Mr. Cattanzara.

We perceive that George has learned and will change the course of his life when, at the end of the story, he leaves the secure but immature world of his room and his dreams for the frightening but grown-up world of the library. What emerges from our close look at George's conflict and the climactic scene is a recognition that the story embodies the archetypal pattern of initiation. Our earlier statement of theme is not inaccurate, but it can be expanded to convey the story's larger significance: the confidence we need to control our lives must be founded on self-respect, but that self-respect will come only when we dare to try to shape our lives and seek to become what we want to be. Notice the use of the word "dare." Malamud does not suggest that living in the adult world is easy; George has to struggle "to control an inward trembling." What Malamud shows us is that George can either struggle to shape his life or become another Mr. Cattanzara, suffering the painful existence of an unfulfilled life. Through all the elements of the work—setting, point of view, plot, character conflict—emerge some thought-provoking insights into human experience that extend beyond the specific situation of the story.

Although many works develop the initiation-into-life pattern, the themes of these works vary because what each writer sees as essential to understanding the adult world varies. But you will find that some writers, responding to key issues and attitudes of their day, or wishing to continue a literary tradition, will express the same theme. What interests these writers (and us) is their particular manner of expressing a view of life that has been expressed before. The following poem develops a popular seventeenth-century theme.

ROBERT HERRICK (1591–1674)

To the Virgins, to Make Much of Time

Gather ye rosebuds while ye may,
   Old time is still a-flying;
And this same flower that smiles today,
   Tomorrow will be dying.

The glorious lamp of heaven, the sun,   5
   The higher he's a-getting,
The sooner will his race be run,
   And nearer he's to setting.

That age is best which is the first,
   When youth and blood are warmer;   10
But being spent, the worse, and worst
   Times still succeed the former.

Then be not coy, but use your time;
   And while ye may, go marry:
For having lost but once your prime,   15
   You may forever tarry.

QUESTIONS

1. Paraphrase the argument of the poem.
2. What is the relationship between stanzas 1, 2, and 3? How is stanza 4 connected with the previous three stanzas?
3. What is the speaker's tone in addressing the virgins?
4. How would you state the poem's theme?

    Herrick's conventional theme—because life is short, you should live it to the fullest—is referred to as the *carpe diem* theme, meaning "seize the day." Marvell expresses the same theme in "To His Coy Mistress" (p. 242). Compare the two poems to see how the situation, tone, and manner of development differ.

    Herrick and Marvell develop basically the same theme in different ways. In the following two poems the poets present contrasting responses to the same issue. A popular theme in European and American literature, especially in the sixteenth century, is known as the *pastoral ideal*. The poet speaks of an ideally simple, carefree life to be found among country people that is in contrast (either stated or implied) to the bustle and vice of the city. One of the best-known expressions of the pastoral ideal is the next poem by Marlowe. Study it and then study Sir Walter Raleigh's reply.

CHRISTOPHER MARLOWE   (1564–1593)

The Passionate Shepherd to His Love

Come live with me and be my love,
And we will all the pleasures prove
That valleys, groves, hills, and fields,
Woods, or steepy mountain yields.

And we will sit upon the rocks,   5
Seeing the shepherds feed their flocks,
By shallow rivers to whose falls
Melodious birds sing madrigals.

And I will make thee beds of roses
And a thousand fragrant posies,   10
A cap of flowers, and a kirtle
Embroidered all with leaves of myrtle;

A gown made of the finest wool
Which from our pretty lambs we pull;
Fair lined slippers for the cold,   15
With buckles of the purest gold;

A belt of straw and ivy buds,
With coral clasps and amber studs:
And if these pleasures may thee move,
Come live with me, and be my love.   20

The shepherds' swains shall dance and sing
For thy delight each May morning:
If these delights thy mind may move,
Then live with me and be my love.

QUESTIONS

1. Who is speaking? To whom? What is the speaker's purpose?
2. What are the particular characteristics of the world described by the speaker?
   What is its general characteristic?
3. State the poem's central meaning or theme.

SIR WALTER RALEIGH   (*ca.* 1552–1618)

The Nymph's Reply to the Shepherd

If all the world and love were young,
And truth in every shepherd's tongue,
These pretty pleasures might me move
To live with thee and be thy love.

Time drives the flocks from field to fold   5
When rivers rage and rocks grow cold,
And Philomel becometh dumb;
The rest complains of cares to come.

The flowers do fade, and wanton fields
To wayward winter reckoning yields;   10
A honey tongue, a heart of gall,
Is fancy's spring, but sorrow's fall.

Thy gowns, thy shoes, thy beds of roses,
Thy cap, thy kirtle, and thy posies
Soon break, soon wither, soon forgotten,—   15
In folly ripe, in reason rotten.

Thy belt of straw and ivy buds,
Thy coral clasps and amber studs,
All these in me no means can move
To come to thee and be thy love.   20

But could youth last and love still breed,
Had joys no date nor age no need,
Then these delights my mind might move
To live with thee and be thy love.

QUESTIONS

1. Who is speaking? To whom? For what purpose?
2. Why does the nymph reject the shepherd's offer? List her particular reasons. What is the key point in all her reasons?
3. Would the nymph like to say yes? What is the tone of her response?
4. State the central meaning or theme of Raleigh's poem.
5. Compare Donne's "The Bait" (p. 564) to both Marlowe's and Raleigh's poems. In what way is it a reply? How does it differ in tone and attitude? How do those differences make Donne's theme different from either Marlowe's or Raleigh's?

A writer usually creates theme through the unifying effect of the particular elements of the work. Sometimes, as we have just seen, a writer creates theme in relation to other works, to a literary tradition, either by expressing a popular theme or responding to an earlier work. The more you read the more skilled you will become in recognizing recurring themes and issues as well as cultural symbols and archetypal patterns that often provide the key to theme. For many works, close reading and the process of analysis will bring you to an understanding of theme. Responding to more complex works that require building an interpretation on many inferences takes practice. Works with complex symbols suggesting many meanings, poems rich in connotative language and intentionally ambiguous lines, plays that turn on the tone in which key lines are spoken—these works will tax your alertness to language and your skill in applying the process of analysis.

WRITING ABOUT THEME

Whatever the particular approach or purpose of your essay on theme, the key to a successful paper is your ability to state the work's theme with precision. As we have pointed out, many works examine such subjects as initiation, the individual versus society, or reality versus illusion. For example, three short stories in this text— "The Necklace," "Counterparts," and "The Secret Life of Walter Mitty"—can be placed in the general category of reality versus illusion. Yet the themes of these stories are not exactly the same. You are not ready to write an essay on theme until you can state, with precision and in detail, the dominant theme of the work. Your first task in meeting a writing assignment on theme will be to go beyond a recognition of the writer's general area of concern to a precise and accurate statement of the work's central ideas.

There are several types of essays that one can develop about theme. One purpose, especially appropriate for a complex work whose theme is debatable, is to write an essay supporting your interpretation, your understanding of the work's theme. The thesis for your essay will be your statement of the work's theme: the central theme of X is. . . . You will then select and organize evidence from the work to support your thesis, much as we did in the discussion of "A Summer's Reading." (Remember: retelling the story or paraphrasing the poem will not provide support for your thesis. Instead you need to examine specific elements of the work and explain how those elements present theme.)

A second purpose, when writing about the theme of one work, is to show how a writer uses particular elements in the work to develop theme. The focus of such an essay will be as much on the author's technique as on the work's theme and can produce an interesting, effective approach when the theme is not especially debatable. A possible thesis might be: Eudora Welty, in "A Worn Path," uses setting to develop her theme of the courage, endurance, and hope that love generates. The student essay that follows (on the theme of Arrabal's *Picnic on the Battlefield*) illustrates this type of essay.

Another type of essay about theme is the contrast of two works that express essentially the same theme. The purpose of this essay would be to examine differences in manner of development, but you must first establish that the works treat the same theme. The thesis for such an essay would be: Although X and Y develop the same view that _____, they employ different _____ (structure, tone, etc.) to develop that theme. The first part of your paper will show the similarity of theme, and the second part will contrast technique. This type of essay is appropriate only for two works whose similarity of theme is apparent to most readers. If you had to prove the similarity at length, the first part of your paper would be out of balance with the second part, the contrast of technique, which should be the focus of this essay.

A fourth possibility for an essay on theme is to compare two works to show that, although they may seem quite different, they are in fact developing the same theme. The purpose of this type of essay is to establish a similarity of theme that is not readily apparent to most readers. Your thesis would have this pattern: Although stories X and Y are different in _____, both express the same view that _____. Because comparison and contrast essays are more difficult to organize, you will not want to start writing such an essay without a detailed plan. Remember that the effective critical essay not only reflects insight into the literature but also conveys that insight to a reader through a clear ordering of evidence.

FERNANDO ARRABAL   (b. 1932)

Picnic on the Battlefield

CHARACTERS

Zapo, *A soldier*
Monsieur Tépan, *The soldier's father*
Madame Tépan, *The soldier's mother*
Zépo, *An enemy soldier*
First Stretcher Bearer
Second Stretcher Bearer

Picnic on the Battlefield *premièred on April 25, 1959, in Paris, at the Théâtre de Lutèce, directed by Jean-Marie Serreau.*

A battlefield. The stage is covered with barbed wire and sandbags.

The battle is at its height. Rifle shots, exploding bombs and machine guns can be heard.

ZAPO is alone on the stage, flat on his stomach, hidden among the sandbags. He is very frightened. The sound of the fighting stops. Silence.

ZAPO takes a ball of wool and some needles out of a canvas workbag and starts knitting a pullover, which is already quite far advanced. The field telephone, which is by his side, suddenly starts ringing.

ZAPO.   Hallo, hallo . . . yes, Captain . . . yes, I'm the sentry of sector 47 . . . Nothing new, Captain . . . Excuse me, Captain, but when's the fighting going to start again? And what am I supposed to do with the hand-grenades? Do I chuck them in front of me or behind me? . . . Don't get me wrong, I didn't mean to annoy you . . . Captain, I really feel terribly lonely, couldn't you send me someone to keep me company? . . . Even if it's only a nanny-goat? [*The Captain is obviously severely reprimanding him.*] Whatever you say, Captain, whatever you say.

ZAPO hangs up. He mutters to himself. Silence. Enter MONSIEUR and MADAME TÉPAN, carrying baskets as if they are going to a picnic. They address their son, who has his back turned and doesn't see them come in.

MONS. T.   [*ceremoniously*]. Stand up, my son, and kiss your mother on the brow. [*ZAPO, surprised, gets up and kisses his mother very respectfully on the forehead. He is about to speak, but his father doesn't give him a chance.*] And now, kiss *me*.

ZAPO.   But, dear Father and dear Mother, how did you dare to come all this way, to such a dangerous place? You must leave at once.

MONS. T. So you think you've got something to teach your father about war and danger, do you? All this is just a game to me. How many times—to take the first example that comes to mind—have I got off an underground train while it was still moving.

MME. T. We thought you must be bored, so we came to pay you a little visit. This war must be a bit tedious, after all.

ZAPO. It all depends.

MONS. T. I know exactly what happens. To start with you're attracted by the novelty of it all. It's fun to kill people, and throw hand-grenades about, and wear uniforms—you feel smart, but in the end you get bored stiff. You'd have found it much more interesting in my day. Wars were much more lively, much more highly coloured. And then, the best thing was that there were horses, plenty of horses. It was a real pleasure; if the Captain ordered us to attack, there we all were immediately, on horseback, in our red uniforms. It was a sight to be seen. And then there were the charges at the gallop, sword in hand, and suddenly you found yourself face to face with the enemy, and he was equal to the occasion too—with his horses—there were always horses, lots of horses, with their well-rounded rumps—in his highly-polished boots, and his green uniform.

MME. T. No no, the enemy uniform wasn't green. It was blue. I remember distinctly that it was blue.

MONS. T. I tell you it was green.

MME. T. When I was little, how many times did I go out on to the balcony to watch the battle and say to the neighbour's little boy: 'I bet you a gum-drop the blues win.' And the blues were our enemies.

MONS. T. Oh well, you must be right, then.

MME. T. I've always liked battles. As a child I always said that when I grew up I wanted to be a Colonel of dragoons. But my mother wouldn't hear of it, you know how she will stick to her principles at all costs.

MONS. T. Your mother's just a half-wit.

ZAPO. I'm sorry, but you really must go. You can't come into a war unless you're a soldier.

MONS. T. I don't give a damn, we came here to have a picnic with you in the country and to enjoy our Sunday.

MME. T. And I've prepared an excellent meal, too. Sausage, hard-boiled eggs—you know how you like them!—ham sandwiches, red wine, salad, and cakes.

ZAPO. All right, let's have it your way. But if the Captain comes he'll be absolutely furious. Because he isn't at all keen on us having visits when we're at the front. He never stops telling us: 'Discipline and hand-grenades are what's wanted in a war, not visits.'

MONS. T. Don't worry, I'll have a few words to say to your Captain.

ZAPO. And what if we have to start fighting again?

MONS. T. You needn't think that'll frighten me, it won't be the first fighting I've seen. Now if only it was battles on horseback! Times have changed, you can't understand. [*Pause.*] We came by motor bike. No one said a word to us.

ZAPO.   They must have thought you were the referees.

MONS. T.   We had enough trouble getting through, though. What with all the tanks and jeeps.

MME. T.   And do you remember the bottle-neck that cannon caused, just when we got here?

MONS. T.   You mustn't be surprised at anything in wartime, everyone knows that.

MME. T.   Good, let's start our meal.

MONS. T.   You're quite right, I feel as hungry as a hunter. It's the smell of gunpowder.

MME. T.   We'll sit on the rug while we're eating.

ZAPO.   Can I bring my rifle witih me?

MME. T.   You leave your rifle alone. It's not good manners to bring your rifle to table with you. [*Pause.*] But you're absolutely filthy, my boy. How on earth did you get into such a state? Let's have a look at your hands.

ZAPO [*ashamed, holding out his hands*]. I had to crawl about on the ground during the manoeuvres.

MME. T.   And what about your ears?

ZAPO.   I washed them this morning.

MME. T.   Well that's all right, then. And your teeth? [*He shows them.*] Very good. Who's going to give her little boy a great big kiss for cleaning his teeth so nicely? [*To her husband*] Well, go on, kiss your son for cleaning his teeth so nicely. [M. TÉPAN *kisses his son.*] Because, you know, there's one thing I *will* not have, and that's making fighting a war an excuse for not washing.

ZAPO.   Yes, Mother.

They eat.

MONS. T.   Well, my boy, did you make a good score?

ZAPO.   When?

MONS. T.   In the last few days, of course.

ZAPO.   Where?

MONS. T.   At the moment, since you're fighting a war.

ZAPO.   No, nothing much. I didn't make a good score. Hardly ever scored a bull.

MONS. T.   Which are you best at shooting, enemy horses or soldiers?

ZAPO.   No, not horses, there aren't any horses any more.

MONS. T.   Well soldiers then?

ZAPO.   Could be.

MONS. T.   Could be? Aren't you sure?

ZAPO.   Well you see . . . I shoot without taking aim, [*pause*] and at the same time I say a Pater Noster for the chap I've shot.

MONS. T.   You must be braver than that. Like your father.

MME. T.   I'm going to put a record on.

She puts a record on the gramophone—a pasodoble. All three are sitting on the ground, listening.

MONS. T.   That really is music. Yes indeed, olé!

The music continues. Enter an enemy soldier: ZÉPO. He is dressed like ZAPO. The only difference is the colour of their uniforms. ZÉPO is in green and ZAPO is in grey. ZÉPO listens to the music openmouthed. He is behind the family so they can't see him. The record ends. As he gets up ZAPO discoveres ZÉPO. Both put their hands up. M. and MME. TÉPAN look at them in surprise.

What's going on?

ZAPO reacts—he hesitates. Finally, looking as if he's made up his mind, he points his rifle at ZÉPO.

ZAPO.   Hands up!

ZÉPO puts his hands up even higher, looking even more terrified. ZAPO doesn't know what to do. Suddenly he goes quickly over to ZÉPO and touches him gently on the shoulder, like a child playing a game of 'tag'.

Got you! [*To his father, very pleased.*] There we are ! A prisoner!

MONS. T.   Fine. And now what're you going to do with him?

ZAPO.   I don't know, but, well, could be—they might make me a corporal.

MONS. T.   In the meantime you'd better tie him up.

ZAPO.   Tie him up? Why?

MONS. T.   Prisoners always get tied up!

ZAPO.   How?

MONS. T.   Tie up his hands.

MME. T.   Yes, there's no doubt about that, you must tie up his hands, I've always seen them do that.

ZAPO.   Right. [*To the prisoner.*] Put your hands together, if you please.

ZÉPO.   Don't hurt me too much.

ZAPO.   I won't.

ZÉPO.   Ow! You're hurting me.

MONS. T.   Now now, don't maltreat your prisoner.

MME. T.   Is that the way I brought you up? How many times have I told you that we must be considerate to our fellowmen?

ZAPO.   I didn't do it on purpose. [*To ZÉPO.*] And like that, does it hurt?

ZÉPO.   No, it's all right like that.

Mons. T. Tell him straight out, say what you mean, don't mind us.

Zépo. It's all right like that.

Mons. T. Now his feet.

Zapo. His feet as well, whatever next?

Mons. T. Didn't they teach you the rules?

Zapo. Yes.

Mons. T. Well then!

Zapo [*very politely, to* Zépo]. Would you be good enough to sit on the ground, please?

Zépo. Yes, but don't hurt me.

Mme. T. You'll see, he'll take a dislike to you.

Zapo. No he won't, no he won't. I'm not hurting you, am I?

Zépo. No, that's perfect.

Zapo. Papa, why don't you take a photo of the prisoner on the ground and me with my foot on his stomach?

Mons. T. Oh yes, that'd look good.

Zépo. Oh no, not that!

Mme. T. Say yes, don't be obstinate.

Zépo. No. I said no, and no it is.

Mme. T. But just a little teeny weeny photo, what harm could that do you? And we could put it in the dining room, next to the life-saving certificate my husband won thirteen years ago.

Zépo. No—you won't shift me.

Zapo. But why won't you let us?

Zépo. I'm engaged. And if she sees the photo one day, she'll say I don't know how to fight a war properly.

Zapo. No she won't, all you'll need to say is that it isn't you, it's a panther.

Mme. T. Come on, do say yes.

Zépo. All right then. But only to please you.

Zapo. Lie down flat.

Zépo lies down. Zapo *puts a foot on his stomach and grabs his rifle with a martial air.*

Mme. T. Stick your chest out a bit further.

Zapo. Like this?

Mme. T. Yes, like that, and don't breathe.

Mons. T. Try and look like a hero.

Zapo. What d'you mean, like a hero?

Mons. T. It's quite simple; try and look like the butcher does when he's boasting about his successes with the girls.

Zapo. Like this?

Mons. T. Yes, like that.

MME. T. The most important thing is to puff your chest out and not breathe.

ZÉPO. Have you nearly finished?

MONS. T. Just be patient a moment. One . . . two . . . three.

ZAPO. I hope I'll come out well.

MME. T. Yes, you looked very martial.

MONS. T. You were fine.

MME. T. It makes me want to have my photo taken with you.

MONS. T. Now there's a good idea.

ZAPO. Right. I'll take it if you like.

MME. T. Give me your helmet to make me look like a soldier.

ZÉPO. I don't want any more photos. Even one's far too many.

ZAPO. Don't take it like that. After all, what harm can it do you?

ZÉPO. It's my last word.

MONS. T. [*to his wife*]. Don't press the point, prisoners are always very sensitive. If we go on he'll get cross and spoil our fun.

ZAPO. Right, what're we going to do with him, then?

MME. T. We could invite him to lunch. What do you say?

MONS. T. I don't see why not.

ZAPO [*to ZÉPO*]. Well, will you have lunch with us, then?

ZÉPO. Er . . .

MONS. T. We brought a good bottle with us.

ZÉPO. Oh well, all right then.

MME. T. Make yourself at home, don't be afraid to ask for anything you want.

ZÉPO. All right.

MONS. T. And what about you, did you make a good score?

ZÉPO. When?

MONS. T. In the last few days, of course.

ZÉPO. Where?

MONS. T. At the moment, since you're fighting a war.

ZÉPO. No, nothing much. I didn't make a good score, hardly ever scored a bull.

MONS. T. Which are you best at shooting? Enemy horses or soldiers?

ZÉPO. No, not horses, there aren't any horses any more.

MONS. T. Well, soldiers then?

ZÉPO. Could be.

MONS. T. Could be? Aren't your sure?

ZÉPO. Well you see . . . I shoot without taking aim [*pause*], and at the same time I say an Ave Maria for the chap I've shot.

ZAPO. An Ave Maria? I'd have thought you'd have said a Pater Noster.

ZÉPO. No, always an Ave Maria. [*Pause.*] It's shorter.

MONS. T.   Come come, my dear fellow, you must be brave.

MME. T.   [*to ZÉPO*]. We can untie you if you like.

ZÉPO.   No, don't bother, it doesn't matter.

MONS. T.   Don't start getting stand-offish with us now. If you'd like us to untie you, say so.

MME. T.   Make yourself comfortable.

ZÉPO.   Well, if that's how you feel, you can untie my feet, but it's only to please you.

MONS. T.   Zapo, untie him.

ZAPO unties him.

MME. T.   Well, do you feel better?

ZÉPO.   Yes, of course. I really am putting you to a lot of inconvenience.

MONS. T.   Not at all, just make yourself at home. And if you'd like us to untie your hands you only have to say so.

ZÉPO.   No, not my hands, I don't want to impose upon you.

MONS. T.   No no, my dear chap, no no. I tell you, it's no trouble at all.

ZÉPO.   Right . . . Well then, untie my hands too. But only for lunch, eh? I don't want you to think that you give me an inch and I take an ell.

MONS. T.   Untie his hands, son.

MME. T.   Well, since our distinguished prisoner is so charming, we're going to have a marvellous day in the country.

ZÉPO.   Don't call me your distinguished prisoner, just call me your prisoner.

MME. T.   Won't that embarrass you?

ZÉPO.   No no, not at all.

MONS. T.   Well, I must say you're modest.

Noise of aeroplanes.

ZAPO.   Aeroplanes. They're sure to be coming to bomb us.

ZAPO and ZÉPO throw themselves on the sandbags and hide.

[*To his parents*]. Take cover. The bombs will fall on you.

The noise of the aeroplanes overpowers all the other noises. Bombs immediately start to fall. Shells explode very near the stage but not on it. A deafening noise. ZAPO and ZÉPO are cowering down between the sandbags. M. TÉPAN goes on talking calmly to his wife, and she answers in the same unruffled way. We can't hear what they are saying because of the bombing. MME. TÉPAN goes over to one of the baskets and takes an umbrella out of it. She opens it. M. and MME. TÉPAN shelter under it as if it were raining. They are standing up. They shift rhythmically from one foot to the other and talk about their personal affairs.

The bombing continues.

Finally the aeroplanes go away. Silence.

M. TÉPAN stretches an arm outside the umbrella to make sure that nothing more is falling from the heavens.

MONS. T. [*to his wife*]. You can shut your umbrella.

MME. TÉPAN does so. They both go over to their son and tap him lightly on the behind with the umbrella.

Come on, out you come. The bombing's over.

ZAPO and ZÉPO come out of their hiding place.

ZAPO. Didn't you get hit?
MONS. T. What d'you think could happen to your father? [*Proudly.*] Little bombs like that! Don't make me laugh!

Enter, left, two RED CROSS SOLDIERS. They are carrying a stretcher.

1st STRETCHER BEARER. Any dead here?
ZAPO. No, no one around these parts.
1st STRETCHER BEARER. Are you sure you've looked properly?
ZAPO. Sure.
1st STRETCHER BEARER. And there isn't a single person dead?
ZAPO. I've already told you there isn't.
1st STRETCHER BEARER. No one wounded, even?
ZAPO. Not even that.
2nd STRETCHER BEARER [*to the* 1st S. B.]. Well, now we're in a mess! [*To ZAPO persuasively.*] Just look again, search everywhere, and see if you can't find us a stiff.
1st STRETCHER BEARER. Don't keep on about it, they've told you quite clearly there aren't any.
2nd STRETCHER BEARER. What a lousy trick!
ZAPO. I'm terribly sorry. I promise you I didn't do it on purpose.
2nd STRETCHER BEARER. That's what they all say. That no one's dead and that they didn't do it on purpose.
1st STRETCHER BEARER. Oh, let the chap alone!
MONS. T. [*obligingly*]. We should be only too pleased to help you. At your service.
2nd STRETCHER BEARER. Well, really, if things go on like this I don't know what the Captain will say to us.
MONS. T. But what's it all about?
2nd STRETCHER BEARER. Quite simply that the others' wrists are aching with carting so many corpses and wounded men about, and that we haven't found any yet. And it's not because we haven't looked!

Mons. T.   Well yes, that really is annoying. [*To* Zapo.] Are you quite sure no one's dead?

Zapo.   Obviously, Papa.

Mons. T.   Have you looked under all the sandbags?

Zapo.   Yes, Papa.

Mons. T.   [*angrily*]. Well then, you might as well say straight out that you don't want to lift a finger to help these gentlemen, when they're so nice, too!

1st Stretcher Bearer.   Don't be angry with him. Let him be. We must just hope we'll have more luck in another trench and that all the lot'll be dead.

Mons. T.   I should be delighted.

Mme. T.   Me too. There's nothing I like more than people who put their hearts into their work.

Mons. T.   [*indignantly, addressing his remarks to the wings*]. Then is no one going to do anything for these gentlemen?

Zapo.   If it only rested with me, it'd already be done.

Zépo.   I can say the same.

Mons. T.   But look here, is neither of you even wounded?

Zapo [*ashamed*]. No, not me.

Mons. T.   [*to* Zépo]. What about you?

Zépo [*ashamed*]. Me neither. I never have any luck.

Mme. T.   [*pleased*]. Now I remember! This morning, when I was peeling the onions, I cut my finger. Will that do you?

Mons. T.   Of course it will! [*Enthusiastically.*] They'll take you off at once!

1st Stretcher Bearer.   No, that won't work. With ladies it doesn't work.

Mons. T.   We're no further advanced, then.

1st Stretcher Bearer.   Never mind.

2nd Stretcher Bearer.   We may be able to make up for it in the other trenches.

They start to go off.

Mons. T.   Don't worry! If we find a dead man we'll keep him for you! No fear of us giving him to anyone else!

2nd Stretcher Bearer.   Thank you very much, sir.

Mons. T.   Quite all right, old chap, think nothing of it.

The two Stretcher Bearers *say goodbye. All four answer them. The* Stretcher Bearers *go out.*

Mme. T.   That's what's so pleasant about spending a Sunday in the country. You always meet such nice people. [*Pause.*] But why are you enemies?

ZÉPO. I don't know, I'm not very well educated.

MME. T. Was it by birth, or did you become enemies afterwards?

ZÉPO. I don't know, I don't know anything about it.

MONS. T. Well then, how did you come to be in the war?

ZÉPO. One day, at home, I was just mending my mother's iron, a man came and asked me: 'Are you Zépo?' 'Yes.' 'Right, you must come to the war.' And so I asked him: 'But what war?' and he said: 'Don't you read the papers then? You're just a peasant!' I told him I did read the papers but not the war bits. . . .

ZAPO. Just how it was with me—exactly how it was with me.

MONS. T. Yes, they came to fetch you too.

MME. T. No, it wasn't quite the same; that day you weren't mending an iron, you were mending the car.

MONS. T. I was talking about the rest of it. [*To ZÉPO.*] Go on, what happened then?

ZÉPO. Then I told him I had a fiancée and that if I didn't take her to the pictures on Sundays she wouldn't like it. He said that that wasn't the least bit important.

ZAPO. Just how it was with me—exactly how it was with me.

ZÉPO. And then my father came down and he said I couldn't go to the war because I didn't have a horse.

ZAPO. Just what my father said.

ZÉPO. The man said you didn't need a horse any more, and I asked him if I could take my fiancée with me. He said no. Then I asked whether I could take my aunt with me so that she could make me one of her custards on Thursdays; I'm very fond of them.

MME. T. [*realising that she'd forgotten it*]. Oh! The custard!

ZÉPO. He said no again.

ZAPO. Same as with me.

ZÉPO. And ever since then I've been alone in the trench nearly all the time.

MME. T. I think you and your distinguished prisoner might play together this afternoon, as you're so close to each other and so bored.

ZAPO. Oh no, Mother, I'm too afraid, he's an enemy.

MONS. T. Now now, you mustn't be afraid.

ZAPO. If you only knew what the General was saying about the enemy!

MME. T. What did he say?

ZAPO. He said the enemy are very nasty people. When they take prisoners they put little stones in their shoes so that it hurts them to walk.

MME. T. How awful! What barbarians!

MONS. T. [*indignantly, to ZÉPO*]. And aren't you ashamed to belong to an army of criminals?

ZÉPO. I haven't done anything. I don't do anybody any harm.

Mme. T.   He was trying to take us in, pretending to be such a little saint!

Mons. T.   We oughtn't to have untied him. You never know, we only need to turn our backs and he'll be putting a stone in our shoes.

Zépo.   Don't be so nasty to me.

Mons. T.   What d'you think we *should* be, then? I'm indignant. I know what I'll do. I'll go and find the Captain and ask him to let me fight in the war.

Zapo.   He won't let you, you're too old.

Mons. T.   Then I'll buy myself a horse and a sword and come and fight on my own account.

Mme. T.   Bravo! If I were a man I'd do the same.

Zépo.   Don't be like that with me, Madame. Anyway I'll tell you something—our General told us the same thing about you.

Mme. T.   How could he dare tell such a lie!

Zapo.   No—but the same thing really?

Zépo.   Yes, the same thing.

Mons. T.   Perhaps it was the same man who talked to you both?

Mme. T.   Well if it was the same man he might at least have said something different. That's a fine thing—saying the same thing to everyone!

Mons. T.   [*to* Zépo, *in a different tone of voice*]. Another little drink?

Mme. T.   I hope you liked our lunch?

Mons. T.   In any case, it was better than last Sunday.

Zépo.   What happened?

Mons. T.   Well, we went to the country and we put the food on the rug. While we'd got our backs turned a cow ate up all our lunch, and the napkins as well.

Zépo.   What a greedy cow!

Mons. T.   Yes, but afterwards, to get our own back, we ate the cow.

They laugh.

Zapo [*to* Zépo]. They couldn't have been very hungry after that!

Mons. T.   Cheers! [*They all drink.*]

Mme. T.   [*to* Zépo]. And what do you do to amuse yourself in the trench?

Zépo.   I spend my time making flowers out of rags, to amuse myself. I get terribly bored.

Mme. T.   And what do you do with the flowers?

Zépo.   At the beginning I used to send them to my fiancée, but one day she told me that the greehouse and the cellar were already full of them and that she didn't know what to do with them any more, and she asked me, if I didn't mind, to send her something else.

Mme. T.   And what did you do?

ZÉPO. I tried to learn to make something else, but I couldn't. So I go on making rag flowers to pass the time.

MME. T. Do you throw them away afterwards, then?

ZÉPO. No, I've found a way to use them now. I give one flower for each pal who dies. That way I know that even if I make an awful lot there'll never be enough.

MONS. T. That's a good solution you've hit on.

ZÉPO [*shyly*]. Yes.

ZAPO. Well, what I do is knit, so as not to get bored.

MME. T. But tell me, are all the soldiers as bored as you?

ZÉPO. It all depends on what they do to amuse themselves.

ZAPO. It's the same on our side.

MONS. T. Then let's stop the war.

ZÉPO. How?

MONS. T. It's very simple. [*To* ZAPO.] You just tell your pals that the enemy soldiers don't want to fight a war, and you [*to* ZÉPO] say the same to your comrades. And then everyone goes home.

ZAPO. Marvellous!

MME. T. And then you'll be able to finish mending the iron.

ZAPO. How is it that no one thought of such a good idea before?

MME. T. Your father is the only one who's capable of thinking up such ideas; don't forget he's a former student of the Ecole Normale, *and* a philatelist.

ZÉPO. But what will the sergeant-majors and corporals do?

MONS. T. We'll give them some guitars and castanets to keep them quiet!

ZÉPO. Very good idea.

MONS. T. You see how easy it is. Everything's fixed.

ZÉPO. We shall have a tremendous success.

ZAPO. My pals will be terribly pleased.

MME. T. What d'you say to putting on the pasodoble we were playing just now, to celebrate?

ZÉPO. Perfect.

ZAPO. Yes, put the record on, Mother.

MME. TÉPAN puts a record on. She turns the handle. She waits. Nothing can be heard.

MONS. T. I can't hear a thing.

MME. T. Oh, how silly of me! Instead of putting a record on I put on a beret.

She puts the record on. A gay pasodoble is heard. ZAPO dances with ZÉPO, and MME. TÉPAN with her husband. They are all very gay. The field telephone rings. None of the four hears it. They go on dancing busily. The telephone rings again. The dance continues.

The battle starts up again with a terrific din of bombs, shots and bursts of machine-gun fire. None of the four has seen anything and they go on dancing merrily. A burst of machine-gun fire mows them all down. They fall to the ground, stone dead. A shot must have grazed the gramophone; the record keeps repeating the same thing, like a scratched record. The music of the scratched record can be heard till the end of the play.

The two STRETCHER BEARERS *enter left. They are carrying the empty stretcher.*

SUDDEN CURTAIN

QUESTIONS

1. What actions of Zapo offer a comment on his military training?
2. How are Zapo and Zépo similar? What is the significance of these similarities?
3. How are the soldiers like children? How does this treatment of the soldiers contribute to theme?
4. Consider the Tépans: what are their values, their attitudes toward the war? What actions and attitudes seem inappropriate to the circumstances?
5. What is the role of the stretcher bearers?
6. How would sound effects and visual effects durng a performance of the play help to communicate theme? Consider particularly the picnic and the phonograph.
7. What is the play's theme?
8. Compare the ending of the play with the ending of "August 2026" (p. 217).
9. Compare the play with Hardy's "The Man He Killed" (p. 228). How are the themes similar? How does the manner of development differ?

STUDENT ESSAY

A Word of Advice to the World's Children:

An Analysis of Picnic on the Battlefield

Jan M. Hettenhouser

Why is war?

Fernando Arrabal's play Picnic on the Battlefield uses the theme of war as a misguided children's game to answer this question. The author demonstrates the folly and danger of never growing up, of never being held accountable for the impact of our actions. His message is that we can be responsible for the world's survival, or we can be responsible for its destruction.

Arrabal's image of the common soldier as a child becomes apparent as the play opens. The main character, Zapo, is anxiously talking on a field telephone with his commanding officer. The author uses the conversation to begin his portrayal of the war's participants as children by exposing Zapo's loneliness and confusion. He begs the captain to send him some company, as a child would plaintively cry to his parents for lack of a playmate. His uncertainty and continual questioning betray the immature uncertainty of a developing ego. The unexpected appearance of Zapo's own parents reinforces this perspective. "But you're absolutely filthy, my boy" chides **Madame** Tépan; "How on earth did you get into such a state?" Is Zapo indeed a man with a serious mission, or an errant school-child dabbling in the mud?

Other characters are also included in the author's vision of the participants as children. The stretcher bearers worry about the captain's chastisement, should they "fail" in their mission to bring back the dead and wounded. Even Madame and Monsieur Tépan are not immune from

STUDENT ESSAY

Arrabal's negative portrayal of war. What is their purpose at the battle-field but to have a picnic, calling to mind small children staging a tea party with youthful disregard for the circumstances surrounding them.

Having established the similarity of the participants' behavior to that of children, Arrabal then proceeds to liken their activities to a game of make-believe, the consequences becoming all the more tragic in the light of the unrealistic naivete of the "players." Monsieur Tépan joyfully recalls the grace and pageantry in the wars of yesteryear, wistfully describing his pleasure with the accouterments of war: "Wars were much more lively, much more highly colored. And then, the best thing was that there were horses, plenty of horses. It was a real pleasure." What remains strikingly absent from his innocent account is any sense of real harm resulting from war, any permanent result from any actions taken in its cause. This sense of naive innocence on the part of the main characters is pervasive as we see Monsieur and Madame Tépan protecting themselves from bombs with umbrellas and admonishing their son to be nice to the enemy so as not to spoil their fun. Both soldiers have a special prayer for each person they've shot, reflecting the immature belief that saying you are sorry will make it all better and erase all the consequences. One comes away with the feeling that their "game," the war, will stop shortly and all will suddenly be right with the world.

In keeping with the theme of childish games, the play makes several references to scorekeeping as though it were an innocent activity in this case, devoid of any connection with human carnage. Monsieur Tépan after asking about his son's score, casually inquires, "which are you best at shooting, enemy horses or soldiers?" The most vivid representation of scorekeeping comes in the morbidly eager stretcher bearers. Frustrated for lack of bodies to cart away, they consider taking Madame Tépan until

STUDENT ESSAY

they remember that she doesn't "count"-- women and children aren't included in the statistics to determine who's winning the war.

Arrabal uses the ending of the play to stress the necessity for individual accountability. Although the characters do finally come to the conclusion that war is pointless, they do it with the same cheerful abandon with which they fought the war, ignoring any links to unpleasant reality such as the ringing telephone. They never fully grasp the seriousness of the "game" or take responsibility for the war. Ultimately, they pay for their irresponsibility and game-playing with their lives.

SELECTIONS FOR FURTHER STUDY

EMILY DICKINSON (1830–1886)

Apparently with no surprise (J1624)

Apparently with no surprise
To any happy Flower
The Frost beheads it at its play—
In accidental power—
The blonde Assassin passes on—   5
The Sun proceeds unmoved
To measure off another Day
For an Approving God.

QUESTIONS

1. What natural event is described?
2. Who is the "blonde Assassin"? What is surprising about the combination of these words?

3. Explain the paradoxes: "accidental power" and "proceeds unmoved."

4. What general characteristic of nature is represented by the particular event described?

5. What is the poet's attitude toward that characteristic and hence toward the concept of a benevolent God?

NATHANIEL HAWTHORNE   (1804–1864)

My Kinsman, Major Molineux

After the kings of Great Britain had assumed the right of appointing the colonial governors, the measures of the latter seldom met with the ready and general approbation which had been paid to those of their predecessors, under the original charters. The people looked with most jealous scrutiny to the exercise of power which did not emanate from themselves, and they usually rewarded their rulers with slender gratitude for the compliances by which, in softening their instructions from beyond the sea, they had incurred the reprehension of those who gave them. The annals of Massachusetts Bay will inform us, that of six governors in the space of about forty years from the surrender of the old charter, under James II., two were imprisoned by a popular insurrection; a third, as Hutchinson inclines to believe, was driven from the province by the whizzing of a musket-ball; a fourth, in the opinion of the same historian, was hastened to his grave by continual bickerings with the House of Representatives; and the remaining two, as well as their successors, till the Revolution, were favored with few and brief intervals of peaceful sway. The inferior members of the court party, in times of high political excitement, led scarcely a more desirable life. These remarks may serve as a preface to the following adventures, which chanced upon a summer night, not far from a hundred years ago. The reader, in order to avoid a long and dry detail of colonial affairs, is requested to dispense with an account of the train of circumstances that had caused much temporary inflammation of the popular mind.

It was near nine o'clock of a moonlight evening, when a boat crossed the ferry with a single passenger, who had obtained his conveyance at that unusual hour by the promise of an extra fare. While he stood on the landing place, searching in either pocket for the means of fulfilling his agreement, the ferryman lifted a lantern, by the aid of which, and the newly-risen moon, he took a very accurate survey of the stranger's figure. He was a youth of barely eighteen years, evidently country-bred, and now, as it should seem, upon his first visit to town. He was clad in a coarse gray coat, well worn, but in excellent repair; his under garments were durably constructed of leather, and fitted tight to a pair of serviceable and well-shaped limbs; his stockings of blue yarn were the incontrovertible work of a mother or a sister; and on his head was a three-cornered hat, which in its better days had perhaps sheltered the graver brow of the lad's father. Under his left arm was a heavy cudgel, formed of an oak sapling, and retaining a part of the hardened root; and his equipment was completed by a wallet, not so abundantly stocked as to incommode the vigorous shoulders on which it hung. Brown, curly hair, well-shaped features, and bright, cheerful eyes, were nature's gifts, and worth all that art could have done for his adornment.

The youth, one of whose names was Robin, finally drew from his pocket the half of a little province bill of five shillings, which, in the depreciation of that sort of currency, did but satisfy the ferryman's demand, with the surplus of a sexangular piece of parchment, valued at three pence. He then walked forward into the town, with as light a step as if his day's journey had not already exceeded thirty miles, and with as eager an eye as if he were entering London city, instead of the little metropolis of a New England colony. Before Robin had proceeded far, however, it occurred to him that he knew not whither to direct his steps; so he paused, and looked up and down the narrow street, scrutinizing the small and mean wooden buildings that were scattered on either side.

"This low hovel cannot be my kinsman's dwelling," thought he, "nor yonder old house, where the moonlight enters at the broken casement; and truly I see none hereabouts that might be worthy of him. It would have been wise to inquire my way of the ferryman, and doubtless he would have gone with me, and earned a shilling from the major for his pains. But the next man I meet will do as well."

He resumed his walk, and was glad to perceive that the street now became wider, and the houses more respectable in their appearance. He soon discerned a figure moving on moderately in advance, and hastened his steps to overtake it. As Robin drew nigh, he saw that the passenger was a man in years, with a full periwig of gray hair, a wide-skirted coat of dark cloth, and silk stockings rolled above his knees. He carried a long and polished cane, which he struck down perpendicularly before him, at every step; and at regular intervals he uttered two successive hems, of a peculiarly solemn and sepulchral intonation. Having made these observations, Robin laid hold of the skirt of the old man's coat, just when the light from the open door and windows of a barber's shop fell upon both their figures.

"Good-evening to you, honored sir," said he, making a low bow, and still retaining his hold of the skirt. "I pray you tell me whereabouts is the dwelling of my kinsman, Major Molineux."

The youth's question was uttered very loudly; and one of the barbers, whose razor was descending on a well-soaped chin, and another who was dressing a Ramillies wig, left their occupations, and came to the door. The citizen, in the mean time, turned a long-favored countenance upon Robin, and answered him in a tone of excessive anger and annoyance. His two sepulchral hems, however, broke into the very centre of his rebuke, with most singular effect, like a thought of the cold grave obtruding among wrathful passions.

"Let go my garment, fellow! I tell you, I know not the man you speak of. What! I have authority, I have—hem, hem—authority; and if this be the respect you show for your betters, your feet shall be brought acquainted with the stocks by daylight, to-morrow morning!"

Robin released the old man's skirt, and hastened away, pursued by an ill-mannered roar of laughter from the barber's shop. He was at first considerably surprised by the result of his question, but, being a shrewd youth, soon thought himself able to account for the mystery.

"This is some country representative," was his conclusion, "who has never seen the inside of my kinsman's door, and lacks the breeding to answer a stranger civilly. The man is old, or verily—I might be tempted to turn back and smite him on the nose. Ah, Robin, Robin! even the barber's boys laugh at you for choosing such a guide! You will be wiser in time, friend Robin."

He now became entangled in a succession of crooked and narrow streets, which crossed each other, and meandered at no great distance from the water-side. The smell of tar was obvious to his nostrils, the masts of vessels pierced the moonlight above the tops of the buildings, and the numerous signs, which Robin paused to read, informed him that he was near the centre of business. But the streets were empty, the shops were closed, and lights were visible only in the second stories of a few dwelling-houses. At length, on the corner of a narrow lane, through which he was passing, he beheld the broad countenance of a British hero swinging before the door of an inn, whence proceeded the voices of many guests. The casement of one of the lower windows was thrown back, and a very thin curtain permitted Robin to distinguish a party at supper, round a well-furnished table. The fragrance of the good cheer steamed forth into the outer air, and the youth could not fail to recollect that the last remnant of his traveling stock of provision had yielded to his morning appetite, and that noon had found, and left him, dinnerless.

"O, that a parchment three-penny might give me a right to sit down at yonder table!" said Robin, with a sigh. "But the major will make me welcome to the best of his victuals; so I will even step boldly in, and inquire my way to his dwelling."

He entered the tavern, and was guided by the murmur of voices, and the fumes of tobacco, to the public room. It was a long and low apartment, with oaken walls, grown dark in the continual smoke, and a floor, which was thickly sanded, but of no immaculate purity. A number of persons—the larger part of whom appeared to be mariners, or in some way connected with the sea—occupied the wooden benches, or leather-bottomed chairs, conversing on various matters, and occasionally lending their attention to some topic of general interest. Three or four little groups were draining as many bowls of punch, which the West India trade had long since made a familiar drink in the colony. Others, who had the appearance of men who lived by regular and laborious handicraft, preferred the insulated bliss of an unshared potation, and became more taciturn under its influence. Nearly all, in short, evinced a predilection for the Good Creature in some of its various shapes, for this is a vice to which, as Fast-day sermons of a hundred years ago will testify, we have a long hereditary claim. The only guests to whom Robin's sympathies inclined him were two or three sheepish countrymen, who were using the inn somewhat after the fashion of a Turkish caravansary; they had gotten themselves into the darkest corner of the room, and, heedless of the Nicotian atmosphere, were supping on the bread of their own ovens, and the bacon cured in their own chimney-smoke. But though Robin felt a sort of brotherhood with these strangers, his eyes were attracted from them to a person who stood near the door, holding whispered conversation with a group of ill-dressed associates. His features were separately striking almost to grotesqueness, and the whole face left a deep impression on the memory. The forehead bulged out into a double prominence, with a vale between; the nose came boldly forth in an irregular curve, and its bridge was of more than a finger's breadth; the eyebrows were deep and shaggy, and the eyes glowed beneath them like fire in a cave.

While Robin deliberated of whom to inquire respecting his kinsman's dwelling, he was accosted by the innkeeper, a little man in a stained white apron, who had come to pay his professional welcome to the stranger. Being in the second generation from a French Protestant, he seemed to have inherited the courtesy of his parent nation; but no variety of circumstances was ever known to change his voice from the one shrill note in which he now addressed Robin.

"From the country, I presume, sir?" said he, with a profound bow. "Beg leave to congratulate you on your arrival, and trust you intend a long stay with us. Fine town here, sir, beautiful buildings, and much that may interest a stranger. May I hope for the honor of your commands in respect to supper?"

"The man sees a family likeness! the rogue has guessed that I am related to the major!" thought Robin, who had hitherto experienced little superfluous civility.

All eyes were now turned on the country lad, standing at the door, in his worn three-cornered hat, gray coat, leather breeches, and blue yarn stockings, leaning on an oaken cudgel, and bearing a wallet on his back.

Robin replied to the courteous innkeeper, with such an assumption of confidence as befitted the major's relative. "My honest friend," he said, "I shall make it a point to patronize your house on some occasion, when"—here he could not help lowering his voice—"when I may have more than a parchment three-pence in my pocket. My present business," continued he, speaking with lofty confidence, "is merely to inquire my way to the dwelling of my kinsman, Major Molineux."

There was a sudden and general movement in the room, which Robin interpreted as expressing the eagerness of each individual to become his guide. But the innkeeper turned his eyes to a written paper on the wall, which he read, or seemed to read, with occasional recurrences to the young man's figure.

"What have we here?" said he, breaking his speech into little dry fragments. "'Left the house of the subscriber, bounden servant, Hezekiah Mudge,—had on, when he went away, gray coat, leather breeches, master's third-best hat. One pound currency reward to whosoever shall lodge him in any jail of the province.' Better trudge, boy, better trudge!"

Robin had begun to draw his hand towards the lighter end of the oak cudgel, but a strange hostility in every countenance induced him to relinquish his purpose of breaking the courteous innkeeper's head. As he turned to leave the room, he encountered a sneering glance from the bold-featured personage whom he had before noticed; and no sooner was he beyond the door, than he heard a general laugh, in which the innkeeper's voice might be distinguished, like the dropping of small stones into a kettle.

"Now, is it not strange," thought Robin, with his usual shrewdness, "is it not strange, that the confession of an empty pocket should outweigh the name of my kinsman, Major Molineux? O, if I had one of those grinning rascals in the woods, where I and my oak sapling grew up together, I would teach him that my arm is heavy, though my purse be light!"

On turning the corner of the narrow lane, Robin found himself in a spacious street, with an unbroken line of lofty houses on each side, and a steepled building at the upper end, whence the ringing of a bell announced the hour of nine. The light of the moon, and the lamps from the numerous shop windows, discovered people promenading on the pavement, and amongst them Robin hoped to recognize his hitherto inscrutable relative. The result of his former inquiries made him unwilling to hazard another, in a scene of such publicity, and he determined to walk slowly and silently up the street, thrusting his face close to that of every elderly gentleman, in search of the major's lineaments. In his progress, Robin encountered many gay and gallant figures. Embroidered garments of showy colors, enormous periwigs, gold-laced hats, and silver-hilted swords, glided past him, and dazzled his optics. Travelled youths, imitators of the European fine gentlemen of the period, trod jauntily along, half-dancing to the fashionable tunes which they hummed, and making poor Robin ashamed of his quiet and natural gait. At length, after many pauses to examine the gorgeous display of goods in the shop windows, and after suffering some rebukes for the impertinence of his scrutiny into people's faces, the major's kinsman found himself near the steepled building, still unsuccessful in his search. As yet, however, he had seen only one side of the thronged street; so Robin crossed, and continued the same sort of inquisition down the opposite pavement, with stronger hopes than the philosopher seeking an honest man, but with no better fortune. He had arrived about midway towards the lower end, from which his course began, when he overheard the approach of some one, who struck down a cane on the flag-stones at every step, uttering, at regular intervals, two sepulchral hems.

"Mercy on us!" quoth Robin, recognizing the sound.

Turning a corner, which chanced to be close at his right hand, he hastened to pursue his researches in some other part of the town. His patience now was wearing low, and he seemed to feel more fatigue from his rambles since he crossed the ferry, than from his journey of several days on the other side. Hunger also pleaded loudly within him, and Robin began to balance the propriety of demanding, violently, and with lifted cudgel, the necessary guidance from the first solitary passenger whom he should meet. While a resolution to this effect was gaining strength, he entered a street of mean appearance, on either side of which a row of ill-built houses was straggling towards the harbor. The moonlight fell upon no passenger along the whole extent, but in the third domicile which Robin passed there was a half-opened door, and his keen glance detected a woman's garment within.

"My luck may be better here," said he to himself.

Accordingly, he approached the open door, and beheld it shut closer as he did so; yet an open space remained, sufficing for the fair occupant to observe the stranger, without a corresponding display on her part. All that Robin could discern was a strip of scarlet petticoat, and the occasional sparkle of an eye, as if the moonbeams were trembling on some bright thing.

"Pretty mistress," for I may call her so with a good conscience, thought the shrewd youth, since I know nothing to the contrary,—"my sweet pretty mistress, will you be kind enough to tell me whereabouts I must seek the dwelling of my kinsman, Major Molineux?"

Robin's voice was plaintive and winning, and the female, seeing nothing to be shunned in the handsome country youth, thrust open the door, and came forth into the moonlight. She was a dainty little figure, with a white neck, round arms, and a slender waist, at the extremity of which her scarlet petticoat jutted out over a hoop, as if she were standing in a balloon. Moreover, her face was oval and pretty, her hair dark beneath the little cap, and her bright eyes possessed a sly freedom, which triumphed over those of Robin.

"Major Molineux dwells here," said this fair woman.

Now, her voice was the sweetest Robin had heard that night, the airy counterpart of a stream of melted silver; yet he could not help doubting whether that sweet voice spoke Gospel truth. He looked up and down the mean street, and then surveyed the house before which they stood. It was a small, dark edifice of two stories, the second of which projected over the lower floor; and the front apartment had the aspect of a shop for petty commodities.

"Now truly I am in luck," replied Robin, cunningly, "and so indeed is my kinsman, the major, in having so pretty a housekeeper. But I prithee trouble him to step to the door; I will deliver him a message from his friends in the country, and then go back to my lodgings at the inn."

"Nay, the major has been a-bed this hour or more," said the lady of the scarlet petticoat; "and it would be to little purpose to disturb him to-night, seeing his evening draught was of the strongest. But he is a kind-hearted man, and it would be as much as my life's worth to let a kinsman of his turn away from the door. You are the good old gentleman's very picture, and I could swear that was his rainy-weather hat. Also he has garments very much resembling those leather smallclothes. But come in, I pray, for I bid you hearty welcome in his name."

So saying, the fair and hospitable dame took our hero by the hand; and the touch was light, and the force was gentleness, and though Robin read in her eyes what he did not hear in her words, yet the slender-waisted woman in the scarlet petticoat proved stronger than the athletic country youth. She had drawn his half-willing footsteps nearly to the threshold, when the opening of a door in the neighborhood startled the major's housekeeper, and, leaving the major's kinsman, she vanished speedily into her domicile. A heavy yawn preceded the appearance of a man, who, like the Moonshine of Pyramus and Thisbe, carried a lantern, needlessly aiding his sister luminary in the heavens. As he walked sleepily up the street, he turned his broad, dull face on Robin, and displayed a long staff, spiked at the end.

"Home, vagabond, home!" said the watchman, in accents that seemed to fall asleep as soon as they were uttered. "Home, or we'll set you in the stocks, by peep of day!"

"This is the second hint of the kind," thought Robin. "I wish they would end my difficulties, by setting me there to-night."

Nevertheless, the youth felt an instinctive antipathy towards the guardian of midnight order, which at first prevented him from asking his usual question. But just when the man was about to vanish behind the corner Robin resolved not to lose the opportunity, and shouted lustily after him,—

"I say, friend! will you guide me to the house of my kinsman, Major Molineux?"

The watchman made no reply, but turned the corner and was gone; yet Robin seemed to hear the sound of drowsy laughter stealing along the solitary street. At that moment, also, a pleasant titter saluted him from the open window above his head; he looked up, and caught the sparkle of a saucy eye; a round arm beckoned to him, and next he heard light footsteps descending the staircase within. But Robin, being of the household of a New England clergyman, was a good youth, as well as a shrewd one; so he resisted temptation, and fled away.

He now roamed desperately, and at random, through the town, almost ready to believe that a spell was on him, like that by which a wizard of his country had once kept three pursuers wandering, a whole winter night, within twenty paces of the cottage which they sought. The streets lay before him, strange and desolate, and the lights were extinguished in almost every house. Twice, however, little parties of men, among whom Robin distinguished individuals in outlandish attire, came hurrying along; but though on both occasions they paused to address him, such intercourse did not at all enlighten his perplexity. They did but utter a few words in some language of which Robin knew nothing, and perceiving his inability to answer, bestowed a curse upon him in plain English, and hastened away. Finally, the lad determined to knock at the door of every mansion that might appear worthy to be occupied by his kinsman, trusting that perseverance would overcome the fatality that had hitherto thwarted him. Firm in this resolve, he was passing beneath the walls of a church, which formed the corner of two streets, when, as he turned into the shade of its steeple, he encountered a bulky stranger, muffled in a cloak. The man was proceeding with the speed of earnest business, but Robin planted himself full before him, holding the oak cudgel with both hands across his body, as a bar to further passage.

"Halt, honest man, and answer me a question," said he, very resolutely. "Tell me, this instant, whereabouts is the dwelling of my kinsman, Major Molineux!"

"Keep your tongue between your teeth, fool, and let me pass!" said a deep, gruff voice, which Robin partly remembered. "Let me pass, I say, or I'll strike you to the earth!"

"No, no, neighbor!" cried Robin, flourishing his cudgel, and then thrusting its larger end close to the man's muffled face. "No, no, I'm not the fool you take me for, nor do you pass till I have an answer to my question. Whereabouts is the dwelling of my kinsman, Major Molineux?"

The stranger, instead of attempting to force his passage, stepped back into the moonlight, unmuffled his face, and stared full into that of Robin.

"Watch here an hour, and Major Molineux will pass by," said he.

Robin gazed with dismay and astonishment on the unprecedented physiognomy of the speaker. The forehead with its double prominence, the broad hooked nose, the shaggy eyebrows, and fiery eyes, were those which he had noticed at the inn, but the man's complexion had undergone a singular, or, more properly, a two-fold change. One side of the face blazed an intense red, while the other was black as midnight, the division line being in the broad bridge of the nose; and a mouth which seemed to extend from ear to ear was black or red, in contrast to the color of the cheek. The effect was as if two individual devils, a fiend of fire and a fiend of darkness, had united themselves to form this infernal visage. The stranger grinned in Robin's face, muffled his parti-colored features, and was out of sight in a moment.

"Strange things we travellers see!" ejaculated Robin.

He seated himself, however, upon the steps of the church-door, resolving to wait the appointed time for his kinsman. A few moments were consumed in philosophical speculations upon the species of man who had just left him; but having settled this point shrewdly, rationally, and satisfactorily, he was compelled to look elsewhere for his amusement. And first he threw his eyes along the street. It was of more respectable appearance than most of those into which he had wandered, and the moon, creating, like the imaginative power, a beautiful strangeness in familiar objects, gave something of romance to a scene that might not have possessed it in the light of day. The irregular and often quaint architecture of the houses, some of whose roofs were broken into numerous little peaks, while others ascended, steep and narrow, into a single point, and others again were square; the pure snow-white of some of their complexions, the aged darkness of others, and the thousand sparklings, reflected from bright substances in the walls of many; these matters engaged Robin's attention for a while, and then began to grow wearisome. Next he endeavored to define the forms of distant objects, starting away, with almost ghostly indistinctness, just as his eye appeared to grasp them; and finally he took a minute survey of an edifice which stood on the opposite side of the street, directly in front of the church-door, where he was stationed. It was a large, square mansion, distinguished from its neighbors by a balcony, which rested on tall pillars, and by an elaborate Gothic window, communicating therewith.

"Perhaps this is the very house I have been seeking," thought Robin.

Then he strove to speed away the time, by listening to a murmur which swept continually along the street, yet was scarcely audible, except to an unaccustomed ear like his; it was a low, dull, dreamy sound, compounded of many noises, each of which was at too great a distance to be separately heard. Robin marvelled at this snore of a sleeping town, and marvelled more whenever its continuity was broken by now and then a distant shout, apparently loud where it originated. But altogether it was a sleep-inspiring sound, and, to shake off its drowsy influence, Robin arose, and climbed a windowframe, that he might view the interior of the church. There the moonbeams came trembling in, and fell down upon the deserted pews, and extended along the quiet aisles. A fainter yet more awful radiance was hovering around the pulpit, and one solitary ray had dared to rest upon the opened page of the great Bible. Had nature, in that deep hour, become a worshipper in the house which man had builded? Or was that heavenly light the visible sanctity of the place,— visible because no earthly and impure feet were within the walls? The scene made Robin's heart shiver with a sensation of loneliness stronger than he had ever felt in the remotest depths of his native woods; so he turned away, and sat down again before the door. There were graves around the church, and now an uneasy thought obtruded into Robin's breast. What if the object of his search, which had been so often and so strangely thwarted, were all the time mouldering in his shroud? What if his kinsman should glide through yonder gate, and nod and smile to him in dimly passing by?

"Oh that any breathing thing were here with me!" said Robin.

Recalling his thoughts from this uncomfortable track, he sent them over forest, hill, and stream, and attempted to imagine how that evening of ambiguity and weariness had been spent by his father's household. He pictured them assembled at the door, beneath the tree, the great old tree, which had been spared for its huge twisted trunk, and venerable shade, when a thousand leafy brethren fell. There, at the going down of the summer sun, it was his father's custom to perform domestic worship, that the neighbors might come and join with him like brothers of the family, and that the wayfaring man might pause to drink at that fountain, and keep his heart pure by freshening the memory of home. Robin distinguished the seat of every individual of the little audience; he saw the good man in the midst, holding the Scriptures in the golden light that fell from the western clouds; he beheld him close the book, and all rise up to pray. He heard the old thanksgivings for daily mercies, the old supplications for their countinuance, to which he had so often listened in weariness, but which were now among his dear remembrances. He perceived the slight inequality of his father's voice when he came to speak of the absent one; he noted now his mother turned her face to the broad and knotted trunk; how his elder brother scorned, because the beard was rough upon his upper lip, to permit his features to be moved; how the younger sister drew down a low hanging branch before her eyes; and how the little one of all, whose sports had hitherto broken the decorum of the scene, understood the prayer for her playmate, and burst into clamorous grief. Then he saw them go in at the door; and when Robin would have entered also, the latch tinkled into its place, and he was excluded from his home.

"Am I here, or there?" cried Robin, starting; for all at once, when his thoughts had become visible and audible in a dream, the long, wide, solitary street shone out before him.

He aroused himself, and endeavored to fix his attention steadily upon the large edifice which he had surveyed before. But still his mind kept vibrating between fancy and reality; by turns, the pillars of the balcony lengthened into the tall, bare stems of pines, dwindled down to human figures, settled again into their true shape and size, and then commenced a new succession of changes. For a single moment, when he deemed himself awake, he could have sworn that a visage—one which he seemed to remember, yet could not absolutely name as his kinsman's—was looking towards him from the Gothic windows. A deeper sleep wrestled with and nearly overcame him, but fled at the sound of footsteps along the opposite pavement. Robin rubbed his eyes, discerned a man passing at the foot of the balcony, and addressed him in a loud, peevish, and lamentable cry.

"Hallo, friend! must I wait here all night for my kinsman, Major Molineux?"

The sleeping echoes awoke, and answered the voice; and the passenger, barely able to discern a figure sitting in the oblique shade of the steeple, traversed the street to obtain a nearer view. He was himself a gentleman in his prime, of open, intelligent, cheerful, and altogether prepossessing countenance. Perceiving a country youth, apparently homeless and without friends, he accosted him in a tone of real kindness, which had become strange to Robin's ears.

"Well, my good lad, why are you sitting here?" inquired he. "Can I be of service to you in any way?"

"I am afraid not, sir," replied Robin, despondingly; "yet I shall take it kindly, if you'll answer me a single question. I've been searching, half the night, for one Major Molineux; now, sir, is there really such a person in these parts, or am I dreaming?"

"Major Molineux! The name is not altogether strange to me," said the gentleman, smiling. "Have you any objection to telling me the nature of your business with him?"

Then Robin briefly related that his father was a clergyman, settled on a small salary, at a long distance back in the country, and that he and Major Molineux were brothers' children. The major, having inherited riches, and acquired civil and military rank, had visited his cousin, in great pomp, a year or two before; had manifested much interest in Robin and an elder brother, and, being childless himself, had thrown out hints respecting the future establishment of one of them in life. The elder brother was destined to succeed to the farm which his father cultivated in the interval of sacred duties; it was therefore determined that Robin should profit by his kinsman's generous intentions, especially as he seemed to be rather the favorite, and was thought to possess other necessary endowments.

"For I have the name of being a shrewd youth," observed Robin, in this part of his story.

"I doubt not you deserve it," replied his new friend, good-naturedly; "but pray proceed."

"Well, sir, being nearly eighteen years old, and well-grown, as you see," continued Robin, drawing himself up to his full height, "I thought it high time to begin the world. So my mother and sister put me in handsome trim, and my father gave me half the remnant of his last year's salary, and five days ago I started for this place, to pay the major a visit. But, would you believe it, sir! I crossed the ferry a little after dark, and have yet found nobody that would show me the way to his dwelling;— only, an hour or two since, I was told to wait here, and Major Molineux would pass by."

"Can you describe the man who told you this?" inquired the gentleman.

"O, he was a very ill-favored fellow, sir," replied Robin, "with two great bumps on his forehead, a hook nose, fiery eyes,—and, what struck me as the strangest, his face was of two different colors. Do you happen to know such a man, sir?"

"Not intimately," answered the stranger, "but I chanced to meet him a little time previous to your stopping me. I believe you may trust his word, and that the major will very shortly pass through this street. In the mean time, as I have a singular curiosity to witness your meeting, I will sit down here upon the steps, and bear you company."

He seated himself accordingly, and soon engaged his companion in animated discourse. It was but of brief continuance, however, for a noise of shouting, which had long been remotely audible, drew so much nearer that Robin inquired its cause.

"What may be the meaning of this uproar?" asked he. "Truly, if your town be always as noisy, I shall find little sleep, while I am an inhabitant."

"Why, indeed, friend Robin, there do appear to be three or four riotous fellows abroad to-night," replied the gentleman. "You must not expect all the stillness of your native woods, here in our streets. But the watch will shortly be at the heels of these lads, and—"

"Ay, and set them in the stocks by peep of day," interrupted Robin, recollecting his own encounter witih the drowsy lantern-bearer. "But, dear sir, if I may trust my ears, an army of watchmen would never make head against such a multitude of rioters. There were at least a thousand voices went up to make that one shout."

"May not a man have several voices, Robin, as well as two complexions?" said his friend.

"Perhaps a man may; but Heaven forbid that a woman should!" responded the shrewd youth, thinking of the seductive tones of the major's housekeeper.

The sounds of a trumpet in some neighboring street now became so evident and continual, that Robin's curiosity was strongly excited. In addition to the shouts, he heard frequent bursts from many instruments of discord, and a wild and confused laughter filled up the intervals. Robin rose from the steps, and looked wistfully towards a point whither several people seemed to be hastening.

"Surely some prodigious merry-making is going on," exclaimed he. "I have laughed very little since I left home, sir, and should be sorry to lose an opportunity. Shall we step round the corner by that darkish house, and take our share of the fun?"

"Sit down again, sit down, good Robin," replied the gentleman, laying his hand on the skirt of the gray coat. "You forget that we must wait here for your kinsman; and there is reason to believe that he will pass by, in the course of a very few moments."

The near approach of the uproar had now disturbed the neighborhood; windows flew open on all sides; and many heads, in the attire of the pillow, and confused by sleep suddenly broken, were protruded to the gaze of whoever had leisure to observe them. Eager voices hailed each other from house to house, all demanding the explanation, which not a soul could give. Half-dressed men hurried towards the unknown commotion, stumbling as they went over the stone steps, that thrust themselves into the narrow foot-walk. The shouts, the laughter, and the tuneless bray, the antipodes of music, came onwards with increasing din, till scattered individuals, and then denser bodies, began to appear round a corner at the distance of a hundred yards.

"Will you recognize your kinsman, if he passes in this crowd?" inquired the gentleman.

"Indeed, I can't warrant it, sir; but I'll take my stand here, and keep a bright look-out," answered Robin, descending to the outer edge of the pavement.

A mighty stream of people now emptied into the street, and came rolling slowly towards the church. A single horseman wheeled the corner in the midst of them, and close behind him came a band of fearful wind-instruments, sending forth a fresher discord, now that no intervening buildings kept it from the ear. Then a redder light disturbed the moonbeams, and a dense multitude of torches shone along the street, concealing, by their glare, whatever object they illuminated. The single horseman, clad in a military dress, and bearing a drawn sword, rode onward as the leader, and, by his fierce and variegated countenance, appeared like war personified: the red of one cheek was an emblem of fire and sword; the blackness of the other betokened the mourning that attends them. In his train were wild figures in the Indian dress, and many fantastic shapes without a model, giving the whole march a visionary air, as if a dream had broken forth from some feverish brain, and were sweeping visibly through the midnight streets. A mass of people, inactive, except as applauding spectators, hemmed the procession in; and several women ran along the side-walk, piercing the confusion of heavier sounds with their shrill voices of mirth or terror.

"The double-faced fellow has his eye upon me," muttered Robin, with an indefinite but an uncomfortable idea that he was himself to bear a part in the pageantry.

The leader turned himself in the saddle, and fixed his glance full upon the country youth, as the steed went slowly by. When Robin had freed his eyes from those fiery ones, the musicians were passing before him, and the torches were close at hand; but the unsteady brightness of the latter formed a veil which he could not penetrate. The rattling of wheels over the stones sometimes found its way to his ear, and confused traces of a human form appeared at intervals, and then melted into the vivid light. A moment more, and the leader thundered a command to halt: the trumpets vomited a horrid breath, and then held their peace; the shouts and laughter of the people died away, and there remained only a universal hum, allied to silence. Right before Robin's eyes was an uncovered cart. There the torches blazed the brightest, there the moon shone out like day, and there, in tar-and-feathery dignity, sat his kinsman, Major Molineux!

He was an elderly man, of large and majestic person, and strong, square features, betokening a steady soul; but steady as it was, his enemies had found means to shake it. His face was pale as death, and far more ghastly; the broad forehead was contracted in his agony, so that his eyebrows formed one grizzled line; his eyes were red and wild, and the foam hung white upon his quivering lip. His whole frame was agitated by a quick and continual tremor, which his pride strove to quell, even in those circumstances of overwhelming humiliation. But perhaps the bitterest pang of all was when his eyes met those of Robin; for he evidently knew him on the instant, as the youth stood witnessing the foul disgrace of a head grown gray in honor. They stared at each other in silence, and Robin's knees shook, and his hair bristled, with a mixture of pity and terror. Soon, however, a bewildering excitement began to seize upon his mind; the preceding adventures of the night, the unexpected appearance of the crowd, the torches, the confused din and the hush that followed, the spectre of his kinsman reviled by that great multitude,—all this, and, more than all, a perception of tremendous ridicule in the whole scene, affected him with a sort of mental inebriety. At that moment a voice of sluggish merriment saluted Robin's ears; he turned instinctively, and just behind the corner of the church stood the lantern-bearer, rubbing his eyes, and drowsily enjoying the lad's amazement. Then he heard a peal of laughter like the ringing of silvery bells; a woman twitched his arm, a saucy eye met his, and he saw the lady of the scarlet petticoat. A sharp, dry cachination appealed to his memory, and, standing on tiptoe in the crowd, with his white apron over his head, he beheld the courteous little innkeeper. And lastly, there sailed over the heads of the multitude a great, broad laugh, broken in the midst by two sepulchral hems; thus, "Haw, haw, haw,—hem, hem,—haw, haw, haw, haw!"

The sound proceeded from the balcony of the opposite edifice, and thither Robin turned his eyes. In front of the Gothic window stood the old citizen, wrapped in a wide gown, his gray periwig exchanged for a night-cap, which was thrust back from his forehead, and his silk stockings hanging about his legs. He supported himself on his polished cane in a fit of convulsive merriment, which manifested itself on his solemn old features like a funny inscription on a tomb-stone. Then Robin seemed to hear the voices of the barbers, of the guests of the inn, and of all who had made sport of him that night. The contagion was spreading among the multitude, when, all at once, it seized upon Robin, and he sent forth a shout of laughter that echoed through the street;—every man shook his sides, every man emptied his lungs, but Robin's shout was the loudest there. The cloud-spirits peeped from their silvery islands, as the congregated mirth went roaring up the sky! The Man in the Moon heard the far bellow; "Oho," quoth he, "the old earth is frolicksome to-night!"

When there was a momentary calm in that tempestuous sea of sound, the leader gave the sign, the procession resumed its march. On they went, like fiends that throng in mockery around some dead potentate, mighty no more, but majestic still in his agony. On they went, in counterfeited pomp, in senseless uproar, in frenzied merriment, trampling all on an old man's heart. On swept the tumult, and left a silent street behind.

*   *   *   *   *   *

"Well, Robin, are you dreaming?" inquired the gentleman, laying his hand on the youth's shoulder.

Robin started, and withdrew his arm from the stone post to which he had instinctively clung, as the living stream rolled by him. His cheek was somewhat pale, and his eye not quite as lively as in the earlier part of the evening.

"Will you be kind enough to show me the way to the ferry?" said he, after a moment's pause.

"You have, then, adopted a new subject of inquiry?" observed his companion, with a smile.

"Why, yes, sir," replied Robin, rather dryly. "Thanks to you, and to my other friends, I have at last met my kinsman, and he will scarce desire to see my face again. I begin to grow weary of a town life, sir. Will you show me the way to the ferry?"

"No, my good friend Robin,—not to-night, at least," said the gentleman. "Some few days hence, if you wish it, I will speed you on your journey. Or, if you prefer to remain with us, perhaps, as you are a shrewd youth, you may rise in the world without the help of your kinsman, Major Molineux."

QUESTIONS

1. From the details, what can you conclude about the time and location of the story?
2. List the various encounters that Robin has in his search for Major Molineux. What do they have in common? What are Robin's responses?
3. What are Robin's chief characteristics?
4. How is this story similar to "A Summer's Reading"?
5. How would you state the story's theme?

chapter 11

Reading the Critics
and Documenting Research

Edouard Manet. *Luncheon on the Grass*. 1863. The Louvre, Paris.

At the end of Chapter 1 you were introduced to some excerpts from professional criticism on Robert Frost's poem "Stopping by Woods on a Snowy Evening" (pp. 11–15). These excerpts suggest that some questions about this poem cannot be finally resolved. Does "sleep" in the last line represent death? Is the attraction the speaker feels towards the woods a death wish? Many pages have been written in response to these and other questions about the poem.

Although literary analysis is a process of explaining and supporting conclusions, some works provide a continuing critical controversy leading to interesting, even heated, debate. The ending of Ernest Hemingway's "The Short Happy Life of Francis Macomber," printed in this chapter, offers one such controversy. As you become involved in the story and the accompanying criticism, give some thought to the uses of professional criticism for your own reading and writing about literature.

As you study the Macomber controversy, remember that we do not read literary criticism to discover what opinions to hold. Rather, we hope to stimulate our own thinking. Since no two readers experience a work in exactly the same way, sharing the ideas of others may help us become aware of details and connections not noticed before. Carlos Baker's observation in *Hemingway: The Writer as Artist* that the shifting relationships between Macomber, Margot, and Wilson are reflected in the seating changes in the hunting car has influenced many interpretations of the story.

When reading the critics, evaluate the clarity and persuasiveness of their presentations. Do they offer adequate evidence? Are their arguments logical? What particular approach do they take to literary analysis? To avoid being overly influenced by a particular critical approach, begin with your own analysis. Then you will be prepared to read the critics critically.

Beyond stimulating your thinking, reading criticism can be a useful starting point for your writing about literature. In some literature courses, you will be asked to write analysis that incorporates secondary sources in addition to the literary work, your primary source. A discussion of the process of working with sources and preparing a documented paper and a research essay on Hemingway's story conclude this chapter.

UNDERSTANDING THE CRITICS

Edouard Manet's *Luncheon on the Grass* begins this chapter because the painting is famous for the critical responses to its first showing. Fully and formally clothed men lunching with undressed women? Some critics were intrigued; many were outraged. The outraged critics were not concerned with the painting's technical merit or its place in Manet's development; they were concerned with the painting's effect on the viewer. These three responses to the painting represent three basic starting points for the study of a literary work. Criticism can focus attention on the writer, the work, or the reader. Let's consider the work first.

Some critics believe that the primary function of criticism is to clarify our reading of a literary text and that the method appropriate to this goal is the close examination of the text itself. The poem is there, on the page. We understand it by reading it carefully, by analyzing its form, or by studying various parts that together give it its particular form—and hence meaning. This critical approach is sometimes called New Criticism, sometimes Formalism. Although no one approach has all the insights into a literary work, this approach, because of its demand that we know the text thoroughly, is a good place to start students in an introductory course. Thus, it is the primary approach of this text.

Some critics argue—quite persuasively—that a text separated from the world in which it was created is not a meaningful piece of writing. Texts do not just appear within the covers of a book; they are written by a particular person working in a specific culture, at a specific time. To ignore the environment of the text, this approach asserts, is surely to misread the text. Critics who study the writer, and the writer's world, in order to read the text can be subdivided into special emphases. Some emphasize the writer's life. We must understand the events leading up to and the circumstances surrounding Hemingway's writing of the Macomber story, for example.

Another way to emphasize the writer's life is to explore the deeper psychological influences on the writer, the influences of a pious and forceful mother on Hemingway, for instance. Still another emphasis is the sociological one. What historical events, cultural currents, and literary forces shaped Camus's existential philosophy, the sociological critic asks. In our introductions to the Greek and Elizabethan theaters that precede representative plays from those periods, we acknowledge the importance of background knowledge in the fuller understanding of a literary work.

Finally, critics who focus on the reader constitute two very different schools. The older school includes all those who stress how a work should affect readers and concern themselves with promoting "proper" works. These critics are interested in works that teach the "right" ideas. The other school's concern is psychological, not moral. These critics argue that the text does not reside in the writer's psyche or on the page; the text resides in the reader's experience. It is "created" by the reader. Although it seems worth observing that language is a shared experience (or communication is not possible), it is certainly true that no two readers experience a work in exactly the same way. When we accept the validity of several responses to Frost's "Stopping by Woods on a Snowy Evening," we take a page from this approach.

ERNEST HEMINGWAY   (1899–1961)

The Short Happy Life of Francis Macomber

It was now lunch time and they were all sitting under the double green fly of the dining tent pretending that nothing had happened.

"Will you have lime juice or lemon squash?" Macomber asked.

"I'll have a gimlet," Robert Wilson told him.

"I'll have a gimlet too. I need something," Macomber's wife said.

"I suppose it's the thing to do," Macomber agreed. "Tell him to make three gimlets."

The mess boy had started them already, lifting the bottles out of the canvas cooling bags that sweated wet in the wind that blew through the trees that shaded the tents.

"What had I ought to give them?" Macomber asked.

"A quid would be plenty," Wilson told him. "You don't want to spoil them."

"Will the headman distribute it?"

"Absolutely."

Francis Macomber had, half an hour before, been carried to his tent from the edge of the camp in triumph on the arms and shoulders of the cook, the personal boys, the skinner and the porters. The gun-bearers had taken no part in the demonstration. When the native boys put him down at the door of his tent, he had shaken all their hands, received their congratulations, and then gone into the tent and sat on the bed until his wife came in. She did not speak to him when she came in and he left the tent at once to wash his face and hands in the portable wash basin outside and go over to the dining tent to sit in a comfortable canvas chair in the breeze and the shade.

"You've got your lion," Robert Wilson said to him, "and a damned fine one too."

Mrs. Macomber looked at Wilson quickly. She was an extremely handsome and well-kept woman of the beauty and social position which had, five years before, commanded five thousand dollars as the price of endorsing, with photographs, a beauty product which she had never used. She had been married to Francis Macomber for eleven years.

"He is a good lion, isn't he?" Macomber said. His wife looked at him now. She looked at both these men as though she had never seen them before.

One, Wilson, the white hunter, she knew she had never truly seen before. He was about middle height with sandy hair, a stubby mustache, a very red face and extremely cold blue eyes with faint white wrinkles at the corners that grooved merrily when he smiled. He smiled at her now and she looked away from his face at the way his shoulders sloped in the loose tunic he wore with the four big cartridges held in loops where the left breast pocket should have been, at his big brown hands, his old slacks, his very dirty boots and back to his red face again. She noticed where the baked red of his face stopped in a white line that marked the circle left by his Stetson hat that hung now from one of the pegs of the tent pole.

"Well, here's to the lion," Robert Wilson said. He smiled at her again and, not smiling, she looked curiously at her husband.

Francis Macomber was very tall, very well built if you did not mind that length of bone, dark, his hair cropped like an oarsman, rather thin-lipped, and was considered handsome. He was dressed in the same sort of safari clothes that Wilson wore except that his were new, he was thirty-five years old, kept himself very fit, was good at court games, had a number of big-game fishing records, and had just shown himself, very publicly, to be a coward.

"Here's to the lion," he said. "I can't ever thank you for what you did."

Margaret, his wife, looked away from him and back to Wilson.

"Let's not talk about the lion," she said.

Wilson looked over at her without smiling and now she smiled at him.

"It's been a very strange day," she said. "Hadn't you ought to put your hat on even under the canvas at noon? You told me that, you know."

"Might put it on," said Wilson.

"You know you have a very red face, Mr. Wilson," she told him and smiled again.

"Drink," said Wilson.

"I don't think so," she said. "Francis drinks a great deal, but his face is never red."

"It's red today," Macomber tried a joke.

"No," said Margaret. "It's mine that's red today. But Mr. Wilson's is always red."

"Must be racial," said Wilson. "I say, you wouldn't like to drop my beauty as a topic, would you?"

"I've just started on it."

"Let's chuck it," said Wilson.

"Conversation is going to be so difficult," Margaret said.

"Don't be silly, Margot," her husband said.

"No difficulty," Wilson said. "Got a damn fine lion."

Margot looked at them both and they both saw that she was going to cry. Wilson had seen it coming for a long time and he dreaded it. Macomber was past dreading it.

"I wish it hadn't happened. Oh, I wish it hadn't happened," she said and started for her tent. She made no noise of crying but they could see that her shoulders were shaking under the rose-colored, sun-proofed shirt she wore.

"Women upset," said Wilson to the tall man. "Amounts to nothing. Strain on the nerves and one thing'n another."

"No," said Macomber. "I suppose that I rate that for the rest of my life now."

"Nonsense. Let's have a spot of the giant killer," said Wilson. "Forget the whole thing. Nothing to it anyway."

"We might try," said Macomber. "I won't forget what you did for me though."

"Nothing," said Wilson. "All nonsense."

So they sat there in the shade where the camp was pitched under some wide-topped acacia trees with a boulder-strewn cliff behind them, and a stretch of grass that ran to the bank of a boulder-filled stream in front with forest beyond it, and drank their just-cool lime drinks and avoided one another's eyes while the boys set the table for lunch. Wilson could tell that the boys all knew about it now and when he saw Macomber's personal boy looking curiously at his master while he was putting dishes on the table he snapped at him in Swahili. The boy turned away with his face blank.

"What were you telling him?" Macomber asked.

"Nothing. Told him to look alive or I'd see he got about fifteen of the best."

"What's that? Lashes?"

"It's quite illegal," Wilson said. "You're supposed to fine them."

"Do you still have them whipped?"

"Oh, yes. They could raise a row if they chose to complain. But they don't. They prefer it to the fines."

"How strange!" said Macomber.

"Not strange, really," Wilson said. "Which would you rather do? Take a good birching or lose your pay?"

Then he felt embarrassed at asking it and before Macomber could answer he went on, "We all take a beating every day, you know, one way or another."

This was no better. "Good God," he thought. "I am a diplomat, aren't I?"

"Yes, we take a beating," said Macomber, still not looking at him. "I'm awfully sorry about that lion business. It doesn't have to go any further, does it? I mean no one will hear about it, will they?"

"You mean will I tell it at the Mathaiga Club?" Wilson looked at him now coldly. He had not expected this. So he's a bloody four-letter man as well as a bloody coward, he thought. I rather liked him too until today. But how is one to know about an American?

"No," said Wilson. "I'm a professional hunter. We never talk about our clients. You can be quite easy on that. It's supposed to be bad form to ask us not to talk though."

He had decided now that to break would be much easier. He would eat, then, by himself and could read a book with his meals. They would eat by themselves. He would see them through the safari on a very formal basis—what was it the French called it? Distinguished consideration—and it would be a damn sight easier than having to go through this emotional trash. He'd insult him and make a good clean break. Then he could read a book with his meals and he'd still be drinking their whisky. That was the phrase for it when a safari went bad. You ran into another white hunter and you asked, "How is everything going?" and he answered, "Oh, I'm still drinking their whisky," and you knew everything had gone to pot.

"I'm sorry," Macomber said and looked at him with his American face that would stay adolescent until it became middle-aged, and Wilson noted his crew-cropped hair, fine eyes only faintly shifty, good nose, thin lips and handsome jaw. "I'm sorry I didn't realize that. There are lots of things I don't know."

So what could he do, Wilson thought. He was all ready to break it off quickly and neatly and here the beggar was apologizing after he had just insulted him. He made one more attempt. "Don't worry about me talking," he said. "I have a living to make. You know in Africa no woman ever misses her lion and no white man ever bolts."

"I bolted like a rabbit," Macomber said.

Now what in hell were you going to do about a man who talked like that, Wilson wondered.

Wilson looked at Macomber with his flat, blue, machine-gunner's eyes and the other smiled back at him. He had a pleasant smile if you did not notice how his eyes showed when he was hurt.

"Maybe I can fix it up on buffalo," he said. "We're after them next, aren't we?"

"In the morning if you like," Wilson told him. Perhaps he had been wrong. This was certainly the way to take it. You most certainly could not tell a damned thing about an American. He was all for Macomber again. If you could forget the morning. But, of course, you couldn't. The morning had been about as bad as they come.

"Here comes the Memsahib," he said. She was walking over from her tent looking refreshed and cheerful and quite lovely. She had a very perfect oval face, so perfect that you expected her to be stupid. But she wasn't stupid, Wilson thought, no, not stupid.

"How is the beautiful red-faced Mr. Wilson? Are you feeling better, Francis, my pearl?"

"Oh, much," said Macomber.

"I've dropped the whole thing," she said, sitting down at the table. "What importance is there to whether Francis is any good at killing lions? That's not his trade. That's Mr. Wilson's trade. Mr. Wilson is really very impressive killing anything. You do kill anything, don't you?"

"Oh, anything," said Wilson. "Simply anything." They are, he thought, the hardest in the world; the hardest, the cruelest, the most predatory and the most attractive and their men have softened or gone to pieces nervously as they have hardened. Or is it that they pick men they can handle? They can't know that much at the age they marry, he thought. He was grateful that he had gone through his education on American women before now because this was a very attractive one.

"We're going after buff in the morning," he told her.

"I'm coming," she said.

"No, you're not."

"Oh, yes, I am. Mayn't I, Francis?"

"Why not stay in camp?"

"Not for anything," she said. "I wouldn't miss something like today for anything."

When she left, Wilson was thinking, when she went off to cry, she seemed a hell of a fine woman. She seemed to understand, to realize, to be hurt for him and for herself and to know how things really stood. She is away for twenty minutes and now she is back, simply enamelled in that American female cruelty. They are the damnedest women. Really the damnedest.

"We'll put on another show for you tomorrow," Francis Macomber said.

"You're not coming," Wilson said.

"You're very mistaken," she told him. "And I want *so* to see you perform again. You were lovely this morning. That is if blowing things' heads off is lovely."

"Here's the lunch," said Wilson. "You're very merry, aren't you?"

"Why not? I didn't come out here to be dull."

"Well, it hasn't been dull," Wilson said. He could see the boulders in the river and the high bank beyond with the trees and he remembered the morning.

"Oh, no," she said. "It's been charming. And tomorrow. You don't know how I look forward to tomorrow."

"That's eland he's offering you," Wilson said.

"They're the big cowy things that jump like hares, aren't they?"

"I suppose that describes them," Wilson said.

"It's very good meat," Macomber said.

"Did you shoot it, Francis?" she asked.

"Yes."

"They're not dangerous, are they?"

"Only if they fall on you," Wilson told her.

"I'm so glad."

"Why not let up on the bitchery just a little, Margot," Macomber said, cutting the eland steak and putting some mashed potato, gravy and carrot on the down-turned fork that tined through the piece of meat.

"I suppose I could," she said, "since you put it so prettily."

"Tonight we'll have champagne for the lion," Wilson said. "It's a bit too hot at noon."

"Oh, the lion," Margot said. "I'd forgotten the lion!"

So, Robert Wilson thought to himself, she *is* giving him a ride, isn't she? Or do you suppose that's her idea of putting up a good show? How should a woman act when she discovers her husband is a bloody coward? She's damn cruel but they're all cruel. They govern, of course, and to govern one has to be cruel sometimes. Still, I've seen enough of their damn terrorism.

"Have some more eland," he said to her politely.

That afternoon, late, Wilson and Macomber went out in the motor car with the native driver and the two gun-bearers. Mrs. Macomber stayed in the camp. It was too hot to go out, she said, and she was going with them in the early morning. As they drove off Wilson saw her standing under the big tree, looking pretty rather than beautiful in her faintly rosy khaki, her dark hair drawn back off her forehead and gathered in a knot low on her neck, her face as fresh, he thought, as though she were in England. She waved to them as the car went off through the swale of high grass and curved around through the trees into the small hills of orchard bush.

In the orchard bush they found a herd of impala, and leaving the car they stalked one old ram with long, wide-spread horns and Macomber killed it with a very creditable shot that knocked the buck down at a good two hundred yards and sent the herd off bounding wildly and leaping over one another's backs in long, leg-drawn-up leaps as unbelievable and as floating as those one makes sometimes in dreams.

"That was a good shot," Wilson said. "They're a small target."

"Is it a worth-while head?" Macomber asked.

"It's excellent," Wilson told him. "You shoot like that and you'll have no trouble."

"Do you think we'll find buffalo tomorrow?"

"There's a good chance of it. They feed out early in the morning and with luck we may catch them in the open."

"I'd like to clear away that lion business," Macomber said. "It's not very pleasant to have your wife see you do something like that."

I should think it would be even more unpleasant to do it, Wilson thought, wife or no wife, or to talk about it having done it. But he said, "I wouldn't think about that any more. Any one could be upset by his first lion. That's all over."

But that night after dinner and a whisky and soda by the fire before going to bed, as Francis Macomber lay on his cot with the mosquito bar over him and listened to the night noises it was not all over. It was neither all over nor was it beginning. It was there exactly as it happened with some parts of it indelibly emphasized and he was miserably ashamed at it. But more than shame he felt cold, hollow fear in him. The fear was still there like a cold slimy hollow in all the emptiness where once his confidence had been and it made him feel sick. It was still there with him now.

It had started the night before when he had wakened and heard the lion roaring somewhere up along the river. It was a deep sound and at the end there were sort of coughing grunts that made him seem just outside the tent, and when Francis Macomber woke in the night to hear it he was afraid. He could hear his wife breathing quietly, asleep. There was no one to tell he was afraid, nor to be afraid with him, and, lying alone, he did not know the Somali proverb that says a brave man is always frightened three times by a lion; when he first sees his track, when he first hears him roar and when he first confronts him. Then while they were eating breakfast by lantern light out in the dining tent, before the sun was up, the lion roared again and Francis thought he was just at the edge of camp.

"Sounds like an old-timer," Robert Wilson said, looking up from his kippers and coffee. "Listen to him cough."

"Is he very close?"

"A mile or so up the stream."

"Will we see him?"

"We'll have a look."

"Does his roaring carry that far? It sounds as though he were right in camp."

"Carries a hell of a long way," said Robert Wilson. "It's strange the way it carries. Hope he's a shootable cat. The boys said there was a very big one about here."

"If I get a shot, where should I hit him," Macomber asked, "to stop him?"

"In the shoulders," Wilson said. "In the neck if you can make it. Shoot for bone. Break him down."

"I hope I can place it properly," Macomber said.

"You shoot very well," Wilson told him. "Take your time. Make sure of him. The first one in is the one that counts."

"What range will it be?"

"Can't tell. Lion has something to say about that. Won't shoot unless it's close enough so you can make sure."

"At under a hundred yards?" Macomber asked.

Wilson looked at him quickly.

"Hundred's about right. Might have to take him a bit under. Shouldn't chance a shot at much over that. A hundred's a decent range. You can hit him wherever you want at that. Here comes the Memsahib."

"Good morning," she said. "Are we going after that lion?"

"As soon as you deal with your breakfast," Wilson said. "How are you feeling?"

"Marvellous," she said. "I'm very excited."

"I'll just go and see that everything is ready," Wilson went off. As he left the lion roared again.

"Noisy beggar," Wilson said. "We'll put a stop to that."

"What's the matter, Francis?" his wife asked him.

"Nothing," Macomber said.

"Yes, there is," she said. "What are you upset about?"

"Nothing," he said.

"Tell me," she looked at him. "Don't you feel well?"

"It's that damned roaring," he said. "It's been going on all night, you know."

"Why didn't you wake me," she said. "I'd love to have heard it."

"I've got to kill the damned thing," Macomber said, miserably.

"Well, that's what you're out here for, isn't it?"

"Yes, But I'm nervous. Hearing the thing roar gets on my nerves."

"Well then, as Wilson said, kill him and stop his roaring."

"Yes, darling," said Francis Macomber. "It sounds easy, doesn't it?"

"You're not afraid, are you?"

"Of course not. But I'm nervous from hearing him roar all night."

"You'll kill him marvellously," she said. "I know you will. I'm awfully anxious to see it."

"Finish your breakfast and we'll be starting."

"It's not light yet," she said. "This is a ridiculous hour."

Just then the lion roared in a deep-chested moaning, suddenly guttural, ascending vibration that seemed to shake the air and ended in a sigh and a heavy, deep-chested grunt.

"He sounds almost here," Macomber's wife said.

"My God," said Macomber. "I hate that damned noise."

"It's very impressive."

"Impressive. It's frightful."

Robert Wilson came up then carrying his short, ugly, shockingly big-bored .505 Gibbs and grinning.

"Come on," he said. "Your gun-bearer has your Springfield and the big gun. Everything's in the car. Have you solids?"

"Yes."

"I'm ready," Mrs. Macomber said.

"Must make him stop that racket," Wilson said. "You get in front. The Memsahib can sit back here with me."

They climbed into the motor car and, in the gray first daylight, moved off up the river through the trees. Macomber opened the breech of his rifle and saw he had metal-cased bullets, shut the bolt and put the rifle on safety. He saw his hand was trembling. He felt in his pocket for more cartridges and moved his fingers over the cartridges in the loops of his tunic front. He turned back to where Wilson sat in the rear seat of the doorless, box-bodied motor car beside his wife, them both grinning with excitement, and Wilson leaned forward and whispered.

"See the birds dropping. Means the old boy has left his kill."

On the far bank of the stream Macomber could see, above the trees, vultures circling and plummeting down.

"Chances are he'll come to drink along here," Wilson whispered. "Before he goes to lay up. Keep an eye out."

They were driving slowly along the high bank of the stream which here cut deeply to its boulder-filled bed, and they wound in and out through big trees as they drove. Macomber was watching the opposite bank when he felt Wilson take hold of his arm. The car stopped.

"There he is," he heard the whisper. "Ahead and to the right. Get out and take him. He's a marvellous lion."

Macomber saw the lion now. He was standing almost broadside, his great head up and turned toward them. The early morning breeze that blew toward them was just stirring his dark mane, and the lion looked huge, silhouetted on the rise of bank in the gray morning light, his shoulders heavy, his barrel of a body bulking smoothly.

"How far is he?" asked Macomber, raising his rifle.

"About seventy-five. Get out and take him."

"Why not shoot from where I am?"

"You don't shoot them from cars," he heard Wilson saying in his ear. "Get out. He's not going to stay there all day."

Macomber stepped out of the curved opening at the side of the front seat, onto the step and down onto the ground. The lion still stood looking majestically and coolly toward this object that his eyes only showed in silhouette, bulking like some super-rhino. There was no man smell carried toward him and he watched the object, moving his great head a little from side to side. Then watching the object, not afraid, but hesitating before going down the bank to drink with such a thing opposite him, he saw a man figure detach itself from it and he turned his heavy head and swung away toward the cover of the trees as he heard a cracking crash and felt the slam of a .30–06 220-grain solid bullet that bit his flank and ripped in sudden hot scalding nausea through his stomach. He trotted, heavy, bigfooted, swinging wounded full-bellied, through the trees toward the tall grass and cover, and the crash came again to go past him ripping the air apart. Then it crashed again and he felt the blow as it hit his lower ribs and ripped on through, blood sudden hot and frothy in his mouth, and he galloped toward the high grass where he could crouch and not be seen and make them bring the crashing thing close enough so he could make a rush and get the man that held it.

Macomber had not thought how the lion felt as he got out of the car. He only knew his hands were shaking and as he walked away from the car it was almost impossible for him to make his legs move. They were stiff in the thighs, but he could feel the muscles fluttering. He raised the rifle, sighted on the junction of the lion's head and shoulders and pulled the trigger. Nothing happened though he pulled until he thought his finger would break. Then he knew he had the safety on and as he lowered the rifle to move the safety over he moved another frozen pace forward, and the lion seeing his silhouette now clear of the silhouette of the car, turned and started off at a trot, and, as Macomber fired, he heard a whunk that meant that the bullet was home; but the lion kept on going. Macomber shot again and every one saw the bullet throw a spout of dirt beyond the trotting lion. He shot again, remembering to lower his aim, and they all heard the bullet hit, and the lion went into a gallop and was in the tall grass before he had the bolt pushed forward.

Macomber stood there feeling sick at his stomach, his hands that held the Springfield still cocked, shaking, and his wife and Robert Wilson were standing by him. Beside him too were the two gun-bearers chattering in Wakamba.

"I hit him," Macomber said. "I hit him twice."

"You gut-shot him and you hit him somewhere forward," Wilson said without enthusiasm. The gun bearers looked very grave. They were silent now.

"You may have killed him," Wilson went on. "We'll have to wait a while before we go in to find out."

"What do you mean?"

"Let him get sick before we follow him up."

"Oh," said Macomber.

"He's a hell of a fine lion," Wilson said cheerfully. "He's gotten into a bad place though."

"Why is it bad?"

"Can't see him until you're on him."

"Oh," said Macomber.

"Come on," said Wilson. "The Memsahib can stay here in the car. We'll go to have a look at the blood spoor."

"Stay here, Margot," Macomber said to his wife. His mouth was very dry and it was hard for him to talk.

"Why?" she asked.

"Wilson says to."

"We're going to have a look," Wilson said. "You stay here. You can see even better from here."

"All right."

Wilson spoke in Swahili to the driver. He nodded and said, "Yes, Bwana."

Then they went down the steep bank and across the stream, climbing over and around the boulders and up the other bank, pulling up by some projecting roots, and along it until they found where the lion had been trotting when Macomber first shot. There was dark blood on the short grass that the gun-bearers pointed out with grass stems, and that ran away behind the river bank trees.

"What do we do?" asked Macomber.

"Not much choice," said Wilson. "We can't bring the car over. Bank's too steep. We'll let him stiffen up a bit and then you and I'll go in and have a look for him."

"Can't we set the grass on fire?" Macomber asked.

"Too green."

"Can't we send beaters?"

Wilson looked at him appraisingly. "Of course we can," he said. "But it's just a touch murderous. You see we know the lion's wounded. You can drive an unwounded lion—he'll move on ahead of a noise—but a wounded lion's going to charge. You can't see him until you're right on him. He'll make himself perfectly flat in cover you wouldn't think would hide a hare. You can't very well send boys in there to that sort of a show. Somebody bound to get mauled."

"What about the gun-bearers?"

"Oh, they'll go with us. It's their *shauri*. You see, they signed on for it. They don't look too happy though, do they?"

"I don't want to go in there," said Macomber. It was out before he knew he'd said it.

"Neither do I," said Wilson very cheerily. "Really no choice though." Then, as an afterthought, he glanced at Macomber and saw suddenly how he was trembling and the pitiful look on his face.

"You don't have to go in, of course," he said. "That's what I'm hired for, you know. That's why I'm so expensive."

"You mean you'd go in by yourself? Why not leave him there?"

Robert Wilson, whose entire occupation had been with the lion and the problem he presented, and who had not been thinking about Macomber except to note that he was rather windy, suddenly felt as though he had opened the wrong door in a hotel and seen something shameful.

"What do you mean?"

"Why not just leave him?"

"You mean pretend to ourselves he hasn't been hit?"

"No. Just drop it."

"It isn't done."

"Why not?"

"For one thing, he's certain to be suffering. For another, some one else might run onto him."

"I see."

"But you don't have to have anything to do with it."

"I'd like to," Macomber said. "I'm just scared, you know."

"I'll go ahead when we go in," Wilson said, "with Kongoni tracking. You keep behind me and a little to one side. Chances are we'll hear him growl. If we see him we'll both shoot. Don't worry about anything. I'll keep you backed up. As a matter of fact, you know, perhaps you'd better not go. It might be much better. Why don't you go over and join the Memsahib while I just get it over with?"

"No, I want to go."

"All right," said Wilson. "But don't go in if you don't want to. This is my *shauri* now, you know."

"I want to go," said Macomber.

They sat under a tree and smoked.

"Want to go back and speak to the Memsahib while we're waiting?" Wilson asked.

"No."

"I'll just step back and tell her to be patient."

"Good," said Macomber. He sat there, sweating under his arms, his mouth dry, his stomach hollow feeling, wanting to find courage to tell Wilson to go on and finish off the lion without him. He could not know that Wilson was furious because he had not noticed the state he was in earlier and sent him back to his wife. While he sat there Wilson came up. "I have your big gun," he said. "Take it. We've given him time, I think. Come on."

Macomber took the big gun and Wilson said:

"Keep behind me and about five yards to the right and do exactly as I tell you." Then he spoke in Swahili to the two gun-bearers who looked the picture of gloom.

"Let's go," he said.

"Could I have a drink of water?" Macomber asked. Wilson spoke to the older gun-bearer, who wore a canteen on his belt, and the man unbuckled it, unscrewed the top and handed it to Macomber, who took it noticing how heavy it seemed and how hairy and shoddy the felt covering was in his hand. He raised it to drink and looked ahead at the high grass with the flat-topped trees behind it. A breeze was blowing toward them and the grass rippled gently in the wind. He looked at the gun-bearer and he could see the gun-bearer was suffering too with fear.

Thirty-five yards into the grass the big lion lay flattened out along the ground. His ears were back and his only movement was a slight twitching up and down of his long, black-tufted tail. He had turned at bay as soon as he had reached this cover and he was sick with the wound through his full belly, and weakening with the wound through his lungs that brought a thin foamy red to his mouth each time he breathed. His flanks were wet and hot and flies were on the little openings the solid bullets had made in his tawny hide, and his big yellow eyes, narrowed with hate, looked straight ahead, only blinking when the pain came as he breathed, and his claws dug in the soft baked earth. All of him, pain, sickness, hatred and all of his remaining strength, was tightening into an absolute concentration for a rush. He could hear the men talking and he waited, gathering all of himself into this preparation for a charge as soon as the men would come into the grass. As he heard their voices his tail stiffened to twitch up and down, and, as they came into the edge of the grass, he made a coughing grunt and charged.

Kongoni, the old gun-bearer, in the lead watching the blood spoor, Wilson watching the grass for any movement, his big gun ready, the second gun-bearer looking ahead and listening, Macomber close to Wilson, his rifle cocked, they had just moved into the grass when Macomber heard the blood-choked coughing grunt, and saw the swishing rush in the grass. The next thing he knew he was running; running wildly, in panic in the open, running toward the stream.

He heard the *ca-ra-wong!* of Wilson's big rifle, and again in a second crashing *carawong!* and turning saw the lion, horrible-looking now, with half his head seeming to be gone, crawling toward Wilson in the edge of the tall grass while the red-faced man worked the bolt on the short ugly rifle and aimed carefully as another blasting *carawong!* came from the muzzle, and the crawling, heavy, yellow bulk of the lion stiffened and the huge, mutilated head slid forward and Macomber, standing by himself in the clearing where he had run, holding a loaded rifle, while two black men and a white man looked back at him in contempt, knew the lion was dead. He came toward Wilson, his tallness all seeming a naked reproach, and Wilson looked at him and said:

"Want to take pictures?"

"No," he said.

That was all any one had said until they reached the motor car. Then Wilson had said:

"Hell of a fine lion. Boys will skin him out. We might as well stay here in the shade."

Macomber's wife had not looked at him nor he at her and he had sat by her in the back seat with Wilson sitting in the front seat. Once he had reached over and taken his wife's hand without looking at her and she had removed her hand from his. Looking across the stream to where the gun-bearers were skinning out the lion he could see that she had been able to see the whole thing. While they sat there his wife had reached forward and put her hand on Wilson's shoulder. He turned and she had leaned forward over the low seat and kissed him on the mouth.

"Oh, I say," said Wilson, going redder than his natural baked color.

"Mr. Robert Wilson," she said. "The beautiful red-faced Mr. Robert Wilson."

Then she sat down beside Macomber again and looked away across the stream to where the lion lay, with uplifted, white-muscled, tendon-marked naked forearms, and white bloating belly, as the black men fleshed away the skin. Finally the gun-bearers brought the skin over, wet and heavy, and climbed in behind with it, rolling it up before they got in, and the motor car started. No one had said anything more until they were back in camp.

That was the story of the lion. Macomber did not know how the lion had felt before he started his rush, nor during it when the unbelievable smash of the .505 with a muzzle velocity of two tons had hit him in the mouth, nor what kept him coming after that, when the second ripping crash had smashed his hind quarters and he had come crawling on toward the crashing, blasting thing that had destroyed him. Wilson knew something about it and only expressed it by saying, "Damned fine lion," but Macomber did not know how Wilson felt about things either. He did not know how his wife felt except that she was through with him.

His wife had been through with him before but it never lasted. He was very wealthy, and would be much wealthier, and he knew she would not leave him ever now. That was one of the few things that he really knew. He knew about that, about motor cycles—that was earliest—about motor cars, about duck-shooting, about fishing, trout, salmon and big-sea, about sex in books, many books, too many books, about all court games, about dogs, not much about horses, about hanging on to his money, about most of the other things his world dealt in, and about his wife not leaving him. His wife had been a great beauty and she was still a great beauty in Africa, but she was not a great enough beauty any more at home to be able to leave him and better herself and she knew it and he knew it. She had missed the chance to leave him and he knew it. If he had been better with women she would probably have started to worry about him getting another new, beautiful wife; but she knew too much about him to worry about him either. Also, he had always had a great tolerance which seemed the nicest thing about him if it were not the most sinister.

All in all they were known as a comparatively happily married couple, one of those whose disruption is often rumored but never occurs, and as the society columnist put it, they were adding more than a spice of *adventure* to their much envied and ever-enduring *Romance* by a *Safari* in what was known as *Darkest Africa* until the Martin Johnsons lighted it on so many silver screens where they were pursuing *Old Simba* the lion, the buffalo, *Tembo* the elephant and as well collecting specimens for the Museum of Natural History. This same columnist had reported them *on the verge* as least three times in the past and they had been. But they always made it up. They had a sound basis of union. Margot was too beautiful for Macomber to divorce her and Macomber had too much money for Margot ever to leave him.

It was now about three o'clock in the morning and Francis Macomber, who had been asleep a little while after he had stopped thinking about the lion, wakened and then slept again, woke suddenly, frightened in a dream of the bloody-headed lion standing over him, and listening while his heart pounded, he realized that his wife was not in the other cot in the tent. He lay awake with that knowledge for two hours.

At the end of that time his wife came into the tent, lifted her mosquito bar and crawled cosily into bed.

"Where have you been?" Macomber asked in the darkness.

"Hello," she said. "Are you awake?"

"Where have you been?"

"I just went out to get a breath of air."

"You did, like hell."

"What do you want me to say, darling?"

"Where have you been?"

"Out to get a breath of air."

"That's a new name for it. You *are* a bitch."

"Well, you're a coward."

"All right," he said. "What of it?"

"Nothing as far as I'm concerned. But please let's not talk, darling, because I'm very sleepy."

"You think that I'll take anything."

"I know you will, sweet."

"Well, I won't."

"Please, darling, let's not talk. I'm so very sleepy."

"There wasn't going to be any of that. You promised there wouldn't be."

"Well, there is now," she said sweetly.

"You said if we made this trip that there would be none of that. You promised."

"Yes, darling. That's the way I meant it to be. But the trip was spoiled yesterday. We don't have to talk about it, do we?"

"You don't wait long when you have an advantage, do you?"

"Please let's not talk. I'm so sleepy, darling."

"I'm going to talk."

"Don't mind me then, because I'm going to sleep." And she did.

At breakfast they were all three at the table before daylight and Francis Macomber found that, of all the many men that he had hated, he hated Robert Wilson the most.

"Sleep well?" Wilson asked in his throaty voice, filling a pipe.

"Did you?"

"Topping," the white hunter told him.

You bastard, thought Macomber, you insolent bastard.

So she woke him when she came in, Wilson thought, looking at them both with his flat, cold eyes. Well, why doesn't he keep his wife where she belongs? What does he think I am, a bloody plaster saint? Let him keep her where she belongs. It's his own fault.

"Do you think we'll find buffalo?" Margot asked, pushing away a dish of apricots.

"Chance of it," Wilson said and smiled at her. "Why don't you stay in camp?"

"Not for anything," she told him.

"Why not order her to stay in camp?" Wilson said to Macomber.

"You order her," said Macomber coldly.

"Let's not have any ordering, nor," turning to Macomber, "any silliness, Francis," Margot said quite pleasantly.

"Are you ready to start?" Macomber asked.

"Any time," Wilson told him. "Do you want the Memsahib to go?"

"Does it make any difference whether I do or not?"

The hell with it, thought Robert Wilson. The utter complete hell with it. So this is what it's going to be like. Well, this is what it's going to be like, then.

"Makes no difference," he said.

"You're sure you wouldn't like to stay in camp with her yourself and let me go out and hunt the buffalo?" Macomber asked.

"Can't do that," said Wilson. "Wouldn't talk rot if I were you."

"I'm not talking rot. I'm disgusted."

"Bad word, disgusted."

"Francis, will you please try to speak sensibly?" his wife said.

"I speak too damned sensibly," Macomber said. "Did you ever eat such filthy food?"

"Something wrong with the food?" asked Wilson quietly.

"No more than with everything else."

"I'd pull yourself together, laddybuck," Wilson said very quietly. "There's a boy waits at table that understands a little English."

"The hell with him."

Wilson stood up and puffing on his pipe strolled away, speaking a few words in Swahili to one of the gun-bearers who was standing waiting for him. Macomber and his wife sat on at the table. He was staring at his coffee cup.

"If you make a scene I'll leave you, darling," Margot said quietly.

"No, you won't."

"You can try it and see."

"You won't leave me."

"No," she said. "I won't leave you and you'll behave your self."

"Behave myself? That's a way to talk. Behave myself."

"Yes. Behave yourself."

"Why don't *you* try behaving?"

"I've tried it so long. So very long."

"I hate that red-faced swine," Macomber said, "I loathe the sight of him."

"He's really *very* nice."

"Oh, *shut up*," Macomber almost shouted. Just then the car came up and stopped in front of the dining tent and the driver and the two gun-bearers got out. Wilson walked over and looked at the husband and wife sitting there at the table.

"Going shooting?" he asked.

"Yes," said Macomber, standing up. "Yes."

"Better bring a woolly. It will be cool in the car," Wilson said.

"I'll get my leather jacket," Margot said.

"The boy has it," Wilson told her. He climbed into the front with the driver and Francis Macomber and his wife sat, not speaking, in the back seat.

Hope the silly beggar doesn't take a notion to blow the back of my head off, Wilson thought to himself. Women *are* a nuisance on safari.

The car was grinding down to cross the river at a pebbly ford in the gray daylight and then climbed, angling up the steep bank, where Wilson had ordered a way shovelled out the day before so they could reach the parklike wooded rolling country on the far side.

It was a good morning, Wilson thought. There was a heavy dew and as the wheels went through the grass and low bushes he could smell the odor of the crushed fronds. It was an odor like verbena and he liked this early morning smell of the dew, the crushed bracken and the look of the tree trunks showing black through the early morning mist, as the car made its way through the untracked, parklike country. He had put the two in the back seat out of his mind now and was thinking about buffalo. The buffalo that he was after stayed in the daytime in a thick swamp where it was impossible to get a shot, but in the night they fed out into an open stretch of country and if he could come between them and their swamp with the car, Macomber would have a good chance at them in the open. He did not want to hunt buff with Macomber in thick cover. He did not want to hunt buff or anything else with Macomber at all, but he was a professional hunter and he had hunted with some rare ones in his time. If they got buff today there would only be rhino to come and the poor man would have gone through his dangerous game and things might pick up. He'd have nothing more to do with the woman and Macomber would get over that too. He must have gone through plenty of that before by the look of things. Poor beggar. He must have a way of getting over it. Well, it was the poor sod's own bloody fault.

He, Robert Wilson, carried a double size cot on safari to accommodate any windfalls he might receive. He had hunted for a certain clientele, the international, fast, sporting set, where the women did not feel they were getting their money's worth unless they had shared that cot with the white hunter. He despised them when he was away from them although he liked some of them well enough at the time, but he made his living by them; and their standards were his standards as long as they were hiring him.

They were his standards in all except the shooting. He had his own standards about the killing and they could live up to them or get some one else to hunt them. He knew, too, that they all respected him for this. This Macomber was an odd one though. Damned if he wasn't. Now the wife. Well, the wife. Yes, the wife. Hm, the wife. Well he'd dropped all that. He looked around at them. Macomber sat grim and furious. Margot smiled at him. She looked younger today, more innocent and fresher and not so professionally beautiful. What's in her heart God knows, Wilson thought. She hadn't talked much last night. At that it was a pleasure to see her.

The motor car climbed up a slight rise and went on through the trees and then out into a grassy prairie-like opening and kept in the shelter of the trees along the edge, the driver going slowly and Wilson looking carefully out across the prairie and all along its far side. He stopped the car and studied the opening with his field glasses. Then he motioned to the driver to go on and the car moved slowly along, the driver avoiding wart-hog holes and driving around the mud castles ants had built. Then, looking across the opening, Wilson suddenly turned and said,

"By God, there they are!"

And looking where he pointed, while the car jumped forward and Wilson spoke in rapid Swahili to the driver, Macomber saw three huge, black animals looking almost cylindrical in their long heaviness, like big black tank cars, moving at a gallop across the far edge of the open prairie. They moved at a stiff-necked, stiff bodied gallop and he could see the upswept wide black horns on their heads as they galloped heads out; the heads not moving.

"They're three old bulls," Wilson said. "We'll cut them off before they get to the swamp."

The car was going a wild forty-five miles an hour across the open and as Macomber watched, the buffalo got bigger and bigger until he could see the gray, hairless, scabby look of one huge bull and how his neck was a part of his shoulders and the shiny black of his horns as he galloped a little behind the others that were strung out in that steady plunging gait; and then, the car swaying as though it had just jumped a road, they drew up close and he could see the plunging hugeness of the bull, and the dust in his sparsely haired hide, the wide boss of horn and his outstretched, wide-nostrilled muzzle, and he was raising his rifle when Wilson shouted, "Not from the car, you fool!" and he had no fear, only hatred of Wilson, while the brakes clamped on and the car skidded, plowing sideways to an almost stop and Wilson was out on one side and he on the other, stumbling as his feet hit the still speeding-by of the earth, and then he was shooting at the bull as he moved away, hearing the bullets whunk into him, emptying his rifle at him as he moved steadily away, finally remembering to get his shots forward into the shoulder, and as he fumbled to re-load, he saw the bull was down. Down on his knees, his big head tossing, and seeing the other two still galloping he shot at the leader and hit him. He shot again and missed and he heard the *carawonging* roar as Wilson shot and saw the leading bull slide forward onto his nose.

"Get that other," Wilson said. "Now you're shooting!"

But the other bull was moving steadily at the same gallop and he missed, throwing a spout of dirt, and Wilson missed and the dust rose in a cloud and Wilson shouted, "Come on. He's too far!" and grabbed his arm and they were in the car again, Macomber and Wilson hanging on the sides and rocketing swayingly over the uneven ground, drawing up on the steady, plunging, heavy-necked, straight-moving gallop of the bull.

They were behind him and Macomber was filling his rifle, dropping shells onto the ground, jamming it, clearing the jam, then they were almost up with the bull when Wilson yelled "Stop," and the car skidded so that it almost swung over and Macomber fell forward onto his feet, slammed his bolt forward and fired as far forward as he could aim into the galloping, rounded black back, aimed and shot again, then again, then again, and the bullets, all of them hitting, had no effect on the buffalo that he could see. Then Wilson shot, the roar deafening him, and he could see the bull stagger. Macomber shot again, aiming carefully, and down he came, onto his knees.

"All right," Wilson said. "Nice work. That's the three."

Macomber felt a drunken elation.

"How many times did you shoot?" he asked.

"Just three," Wilson said. "You killed the first bull. The biggest one. I helped you finish the other two. Afraid they might have got into cover. You had them killed. I was just mopping up a little. You shot damn well."

"Let's go to the car," said Macomber. "I want a drink."

"Got to finish off that buff first," Wilson told him. The buffalo was on his knees and he jerked his head furiously and bellowed in pig-eyed, roaring rage as they came toward him.

"Watch he doesn't get up," Wilson said. Then, "Get a little broadside and take him in the neck just behind the ear."

Macomber aimed carefully at the center of the huge, jerking, rage-driven neck and shot. At the shot the head dropped forward.

"That does it," said Wilson. "Got the spine. They're a hell of a looking thing, aren't they?"

"Let's get the drink," said Macomber. In his life he had never felt so good.

In the car Macomber's wife sat very white faced. "You were marvellous, darling," she said to Macomber. "What a ride."

"Was it rough?" Wilson asked.

"It was frightful. I've never been more frightened in my life."

"Let's all have a drink," Macomber said.

"By all means," said Wilson. "Give it to the Memsahib." She drank the neat whisky from the flask and shuddered a little when she swallowed. She handed the flask to Macomber who handed it to Wilson.

"It was frightfully exciting," she said. "It's given me a dreadful headache. I didn't know you were allowed to shoot them from cars though.

"No one shot from cars," said Wilson coldly.

"I mean chase them from cars."

"Wouldn't ordinarily," Wilson said. "Seemed sporting enough to me though while we were doing it. Taking more chance driving that way across the plain full of holes and one thing and another than hunting on foot. Buffalo could have charged us each time we shot if he liked. Gave him every chance. Wouldn't mention it to any one though. It's illegal if that's what you mean."

"It seemed very unfair to me," Margot said, "chasing those big helpless things in a motor car."

"Did it?" said Wilson.

"What would happen if they heard about it in Nairobi?"

"I'd lose my licence for one thing. Other unpleasantnesses," Wilson said, taking a drink from the flask. "I'd be out of business."

"Really?"

"Yes, really."

"Well," said Macomber, and he smiled for the first time all day. "Now she has something on you."

"You have such a pretty way of putting things, Francis," Margot Macomber said. Wilson looked at them both. If a four-letter man carries a five-letter woman, he was thinking, what number of letters would their children be? What he said was, "We lost a gun-bearer. Did you notice it?"

"My God, no," Macomber said.

"Here he comes," Wilson said. "He's all right. He must have fallen off when we left the first bull."

Approaching them was the middle-aged gun-bearer, limping along in his knitted cap, khaki tunic, shorts and rubber sandals, gloomy-faced and disgusted looking. As he came up he called out to Wilson in Swahili and they all saw the change in the white hunter's face.

"What does he say?" asked Margot.

"He says the first bull got up and went into the bush," Wilson said with no expression in his voice.

"Oh," said Macomber blankly.

"Then it's going to be just like the lion," said Margot, full of anticipation.

"It's not going to be a damned bit like the lion," Wilson told her. "Did you want another drink, Macomber?"

"Thanks, yes," Macomber said. He expected the feeling he had had about the lion to come back but it did not. For the first time in his life he really felt wholly without fear. Instead of fear he had a feeling of definite elation.

"We'll go and have a look at the second bull," Wilson said. "I'll tell the driver to put the car in the shade."

"What are you going to do?" asked Margaret Macomber.

"Take a look at the buff," Wilson said.

"I'll come."

"Come along."

The three of them walked over to where the second buffalo bulked blackly in the open, head forward on the grass, the massive horns swung wide.

"He's a very good head," Wilson said. "That's close to a fifty-inch spread."

Macomber was looking at him with delight.

"He's hateful looking," said Margot. "Can't we go into the shade?"

"Of course," Wilson said. "Look," he said to Macomber, and pointed. "See that patch of bush?"

"Yes."

"That's where the first bull went in. The gun-bearer said when he fell off the bull was down. He was watching us helling along and the other two buff galloping. When he looked up there was the bull up and looking at him. Gun-bearer ran like hell and the bull went off slowly into that bush."

"Can we go in after him now?" asked Macomber eagerly.

Wilson looked at him appraisingly. Damned if this isn't a strange one, he thought. Yesterday he's scared sick and today he's a ruddy fire eater.

"No, we'll give him a while."

"Let's please go into the shade," Margot said. Her face was white and she looked ill.

They made their way to the car where it stood under a single, wide-spreading tree and all climbed in.

"Chances are he's dead in there," Wilson remarked. "After a little we'll have a look."

Macomber felt a wild unreasonable happiness that he had never known before.

"By God, that was a chase," he said. "I've never felt any such feeling. Wasn't it marvellous, Margot?"

"I hated it."

"Why?"

"I hated it," she said bitterly. "I loathed it."

"You know I don't think I'd ever be afraid of anything again," Macomber said to Wilson. "Something happened in me after we first saw the buff and started after him. Like a dam bursting. It was pure excitement."

"Cleans out your liver," said Wilson. "Damn funny things happen to people."

Macomber's face was shining. "You know something did happen to me," he said. "I feel absolutely different."

His wife said nothing and eyed him strangely. She was sitting far back in the seat and Macomber was sitting forward talking to Wilson who turned sideways talking over the back of the front seat.

"You know, I'd like to try another lion," Macomber said. "I'm really not afraid of them now. After all, what can they do to you?"

"That's it," said Wilson. "Worst one can do is kill you. How does it go? Shakespeare. Damned good. See if I can remember. Oh, damned good. Used to quote it to myself at one time. Let's see. 'By my troth, I care not; a man can die but once; we owe God a death and let it go which way it will he that dies this year is quit for the next.' Damned fine, eh?"

He was very embarrassed, having brought out this thing he had lived by, but he had seen men come of age before and it always moved him. It was not a matter of their twenty-first birthday.

It had taken a strange chance of hunting, a sudden precipitation into action without opportunity for worrying beforehand, to bring this about with Macomber, but regardless of how it had happened it had most certainly happened. Look at the beggar now, Wilson thought. It's that some of them stay little boys so long, Wilson thought. Sometimes all their lives. Their figures stay boyish when they're fifty. The great American boy-men. Damned strange people. But he liked this Macomber now. Damned strange fellow. Probably meant the end of cuckoldry too. Well, that would be a damned good thing. Damned good thing. Beggar had probably been afraid all his life. Don't know what started it. But over now. Hadn't had time to be afraid with the buff. That and being angry too. Motor car too. Motor cars made it familiar. Be a damn fire eater now. He'd seen it in the war work the same way. More of a change than any loss of virginity. Fear gone like an operation. Something else grew in its place. Main thing a man had. Made him into a man. Women knew it too. No bloody fear.

From the far corner of the seat Margaret Macomber looked at the two of them. There was no change in Wilson. She saw Wilson as she had seen him the day before when she had first realized what his great talent was. But she saw the change in Francis Macomber now.

"Do you have that feeling of happiness about what's going to happen?" Macomber asked, still exploring his new wealth.

"You're not supposed to mention it," Wilson said, looking in the other's face. "Much more fashionable to say you're scared. Mind you, you'll be scared too, plenty of times."

"But you *have* a feeling of happiness about action to come?"

"Yes," said Wilson. "There's that. Doesn't do to talk too much about all this. Talk the whole thing away. No pleasure in anything if you mouth it up too much."

"You're both talking rot," said Margot. "Just because you've chased some helpless animals in a motor car you talk like heroes."

"Sorry," said Wilson. "I have been gassing too much." She's worried about it already, he thought.

"If you don't know what we're talking about why not keep out of it?" Macomber asked his wife.

"You've gotten awfully brave, awfully suddenly," his wife said contemptuously, but her contempt was not secure. She was very afraid of something.

Macomber laughed, a very natural hearty laugh. "You know I *have*," he said. "I really have.'"

"Isn't it sort of late?" Margot said bitterly. Because she had done the best she could for many years back and the way they were together now was no one person's fault.

"Not for me," said Macomber.

Margot said nothing but sat back in the corner of the seat.

"Do you think we've given him time enough?" Macomber asked Wilson cheerfully.

"We might have a look," Wilson said. "Have you any solids left?"

"The gun-bearer has some."

Wilson called in Swahili and the older gun-bearer, who was skinning out one of the heads, straightened up, pulled a box of solids out of his pocket and brought them over to Macomber, who filled his magazine and put the remaining shells in his pocket.

"You might as well shoot the Springfield," Wilson said. "You're used to it. We'll leave the Mannlicher in the car with the Memsahib. Your gun-bearer can carry your heavy gun. I've this damned cannon. Now let me tell you about them." He had saved this until the last because he did not want to worry Macomber. "When a buff comes he comes with his head high and thrust straight out. The boss of the horns covers any sort of a brain shot. The only shot is straight into the nose. The only other shot is into his chest or, if you're to one side, into the neck or the shoulders. After they've been hit once they take a hell of a lot of killing. Don't try anything fancy. Take the easiest shot there is. They've finished skinning out that head now. Should we get started?"

He called to the gun-bearers, who came up wiping their hands, and the older one got into the back.

"I'll only take Kongoni," Wilson said. "The other can watch to keep the birds away."

As the car moved slowly across the open space toward the island of brushy trees that ran in a tongue of foliage along a dry water course that cut the open swale, Macomber felt his heart pounding and his mouth was dry again, but it was excitement, not fear.

"Here's where he went in," Wilson said. Then to the gun-bearer in Swahili, "Take the blood spoor."

The car was parallel to the patch of bush. Macomber, Wilson and the gun-bearer got down. Macomber, looking back, saw his wife, with the rifle by her side, looking at him. He waved to her and she did not wave back.

The brush was very thick ahead and the ground was dry. The middle-aged gun-bearer was sweating heavily and Wilson had his hat down over his eyes and his red neck showed just ahead of Macomber. Suddenly the gun-bearer said something in Swahili to Wilson and ran forward.

"He's dead in there," Wilson said. "Good work," and he turned to grip Macomber's hand and as they shook hands, grinning at each other, the gun-bearer shouted wildly and they saw him coming out of the bush sideways, fast as a crab, and the bull coming, nose out, mouth tight closed, blood dripping, massive head straight out, coming in a charge, his little pig eyes bloodshot as he looked at them. Wilson, who was ahead was kneeling shooting, and Macomber, as he fired, unhearing his shot in the roaring of Wilson's gun, saw fragments like slate burst from the huge boss of the horns, and the head jerked, he shot again at the wide nostrils and saw the horns jolt again and fragments fly, and he did not see Wilson now and, aiming carefully, shot again with the buffalo's huge bulk almost on him and his rifle almost level with the on-coming head, nose out, and he could see the little wicked eyes and the head started to lower and he felt a sudden white-hot, blinding flash explode inside his head and that was all he ever felt.

Wilson had ducked to one side to get in a shoulder shot. Macomber had stood solid and shot for the nose, shooting a touch high each time and hitting the heavy horns, splintering and chipping them like hitting a slate roof, and Mrs. Macomber, in the car, had shot at the buffalo with the 6.5 Mannlicher as it seemed about to gore Macomber and had hit her husband about two inches up and a little to one side of the base of his skull.

Francis Macomber lay now, face down, not two yards from where the buffalo lay on his side and his wife knelt over him with Wilson beside her.

"I wouldn't turn him over," Wilson said.

The woman was crying hysterically.

"I'd get back in the car," Wilson said. "Where's the rifle?"

She shook her head, her face contorted. The gun-bearer picked up the rifle.

"Leave it as it is," said Wilson. Then, "Go get Abdulla so that he may witness the manner of the accident."

He knelt down, took a handkerchief from his pocket, and spread it over Francis Macomber's crew-cropped head where it lay. The blood sank into the dry, loose earth.

Wilson stood up and saw the buffalo on his side, his legs out, his thinly-haired belly crawling with ticks. "Hell of a good bull," his brain registered automatically. "A good fifty inches, or better. Better." He called to the driver and told him to spread a blanket over the body and stay by it. Then he walked over to the motor car where the woman sat crying in the corner.

"That was a pretty thing to do," he said in a toneless voice. "He *would* have left you too."

"Stop it," she said.

"Of course it's an accident," he said. "I know that."

"Stop it," she said.

"Don't worry," he said. "There will be a certain amount of unpleasantness but I will have some photographs taken that will be very useful at the inquest. There's the testimony of the gun-bearers and the driver too. You're perfectly all right."

"Stop it," she said.

"There's a hell of a lot to be done," he said. "And I'll have to send a truck off to the lake to wireless for a plane to take the three of us into Nairobi. Why didn't you poison him? That's what they do in England."

"Stop it. Stop it. Stop it," the woman cried.

Wilson looked at her with his flat blue eyes.

"I'm through now," he said. "I was a little angry. I'd begun to like your husband."

"Oh, please stop it," she said. "Please, please stop it."

"That's better," Wilson said. "Please is much better. Now I'll stop."

QUESTIONS

1. Macomber is thirty-five when he dies. Does that explain Hemingway's choice of title? Where in the title would a comma normally be used? How would adding a comma change the meaning?

2. The chronological structure of the story is broken up by a flashback. Where does this flashback occur, and how long does it last?

3. How does our not knowing the information given in the flashback affect our reading of the opening scene?

4. What has been the relationship between Margot and Francis prior to the African safari?

5. What is Macomber's internal conflict?

6. How does Hemingway control point of view?

7. How is tone important in Margot's dialogue? Give at least one example.

8. How would you state the story's dominant theme? What archetypal pattern helps to convey the theme?

The Critical Problem of the Ending of "The Short Happy Life of Francis Macomber"

The interpretation of the ending of "The Short Happy Life of Francis Macomber" remains an unresolved critical question. Did Margot murder her husband or try to save him? If she killed him intentionally, was the killing premeditated? As they might in a court of law, the arguments center around the observable facts, the reliability of Wilson (the "witness"), and Margot's motivation. The following excerpts from literary critics will give you a sense of the nature of the controversy. A brief bibliography is provided for those who wish to read further criticism on this subject.

A. Samuel Shaw presents two sides:

> The most popular reading of the story concludes, as Wilson concludes, that Margot shot her husband because she knew that a courageous Macomber would leave her. The courage to face a charging buffalo is presumably the courage to face anything. In this approach, no allowance is made for the possibility that Margot intended to help her husband in his peril and accidentally killed him. It is a good reading, including as it does the complex interplay between the beautiful woman and the wealthy man whose eleven-year marriage has been on the verge of dissolution several times, a marriage that seems to have survived because each partner thinks he may not be able to do better. The marriage is held together by fear and insecurity rather than anything positive.
>
> ....
>
> Another reading is made possible by calling into question the moral authority of Wilson. It is usually assumed that Wilson represents the viewpoint that Hemingway intended the reader to be guided by, but a careful reading raises some doubt. First, Wilson sees nothing wrong in cuckolding Macomber. He carries a double size cot on safari so that he can take advantage of windfalls. He adopts the moral standards of his clientele in all except hunting, a neat trick.
>
> It is Wilson who labels Margot an out and out bitch and, in effect, charges her with the murder of her husband. The evidence in the story itself is far from conclusive on that point. It should be noted, too, that when Margot charges him with breaking the game laws by pursuing the buffalo from the car, he, like Macomber earlier, asks her not to report the incident, since it would cost him his license. Macomber smiles and remarks to Wilson, "Now she has something on you."
>
> When Wilson becomes aware that Macomber knows of his liaison with Margot, he hopes that "the silly beggar doesn't take a notion to blow the back of my head off." A pretty strong case can be made for Wilson's moral limitations. His attitude to women is extremely cynical: the only way to handle them is to dominate completely.

B. Warren Beck argues that Margot was trying to save her husband:

> Two further points claim notice. One is the passage describing the shooting. Macomber is indubitably brave; no longer seeing Wilson or depending on him, he is doing it on his own, coolly, "aiming carefully" as he shoots once more "with the buffalo's huge bulk almost on him," so close that "he could see the little wicked eyes,"

and he sees too that "the head started to lower," his last shot has taken effect. Then in that triumphant moment the bullet his wife has fired kills him instantly. Wilson's assumption at this point, however, must be weighed specifically in relation to what the text says: "Mrs. Macomber . . . had shot at the buffalo . . . as it seemed about to gore Macomber." The danger was indeed acute; the animal fell "not two yards" from him. In that proximity and under such excitement Mrs. Macomber, who has not been shown as an experienced shot or even a participant in the previous hunting, might indeed have killed her husband accidentally. And of chief significance is that the buffalo "seemed about to gore Macomber." This is what she sees, not that Francis, having learned to be brave, probably will leave her, but that in his bravery he is about to be killed. If she wanted him dead, she could have left it to the buffalo, as it "seemed" at that moment. Certainly the passage, with what has gone before, can be read to suggest that she wanted to save him and that she, who had tried so often before, might well have felt he had never been so worthy of her whole effort as he was now.

Furthermore, not only does the story supply throughout insights about Mrs. Macomber which transcend Wilson's view; it is Ernest Hemingway who writes that she "shot at the buffalo." Hemingway is, of course, a highly implicative artist, but he is not notably given to double-talk or passing the buck. Either his statement that she shot at the buffalo must be accepted or else the whistle must be blown and that narrative play discredited as being technically off-side. It is indeed surprising that such a painful doubt about so scrupulous a writer has not moved more of Hemingway's admirers to question whether, after all, we can take Wilson's word for what happened.

C. Mark Spilka, arguing against Beck's position, contends that Margot committed unpremeditated murder:

In the end Beck rests his case upon a single line, from which he seems to draw enormous confidence: "and Mrs. Macomber, in the car, had shot at the buffalo with the 6.5 Mannlicher as it seemed about to gore Macomber and had hit her husband about two inches up and a little to one side of the base of his skull." Beck writes of this line, that Hemingway "is not notably given to double-talk or passing the buck. Either his statement that she shot at the buffalo must be accepted or else the whistle must be blown and that narrative play discredited as being technically off-side. It is indeed surprising that such a painful doubt about so scrupulous a writer has not moved more of Hemingway's admirers to question whether, after all, we can take Wilson's word for what happened." Actually the line in question is weak for the load of meaning it has to bear, whether from Beck or Hemingway; but Hemingway's admirers have made it out, rather simply, by accepting Wilson's view and applying it to Margot's hidden heart. Perhaps unconscious is a better word than heart. In any case, consider these lines from "The Undefeated": "'Two hundred and fifty pesetas,' Retana said. He had thought of five hundred, but when he opened his mouth it said two hundred and fifty." Perhaps Margot did begin with a generous impulse, like Retana; but her controlling impulse came from hidden and more rigid sources, which said "murder." Or, consider this line from the Macomber story; "the next thing he knew he was running; running wildly, in panic, in the open, running toward the stream." The running man is Macomber; as the story begins, he is seized and betrayed by inner impulse; as the story ends, his wife is also moved from within. There are even elaborate signs of mounting hostility, which account for inner seizure; but since Beck will only allow for deliberate murder, he ignores this possibility. The imperceptive Wilson is more flexible: "Of course, it's an accident," he says, referring to Margot's initial surface impulse; but the murder charges he applies to that deep compulsion which, in the last analysis, controlled her.

Bibliography

Baker, Carlos. *Hemingway: The Writer as Artist.*

Princeton: Princeton UP, 1952.

Beck, Warren. "The Shorter Happy Life of Mrs.

Macomber." *Modern Fiction Studies* 1 (1955):

28-37. Rpt. in *Hemingway's African Stories:*

The Stories, Their Sources, Their Critics.

Ed. John M. Howell. New York: Scribner's,

1969. 119-28.

Greco, Anne. "Margot Macomber: 'Bitch Goddess,'

Exonerated." *Fitzgerald/Hemingway Annual*

1972. Eds. Matthew J. Bruccoli and C. E.

Frazer Clark, Jr. Washington: N.C.R.

Microcard Editions, 1973. 273-80.

Hutton, Virgil. "The Short Happy Life of

Macomber." *The University Review* 30 (1964):

253-63. Rpt. in *The Short Stories of Ernest*

Hemingway: Critical Essays. Ed. Jackson J.

Benson. Durham: Duke UP, 1975. 239-50.

Shaw, Samuel. *Ernest Hemingway.* New York: Ungar,

1973.

Spilka, Mark. "The Necessary Stylist: A New

Critical Revision." *Modern Fiction Studies* 6

(1960-61): 283-97.

THE LITERARY RESEARCH ESSAY

Since you have probably written some type of research or library paper before, you have a general understanding of the process and of the format for the finished paper. You know that you will need to pick a topic, find sources in the library, and write a paper that includes formal documentation of the sources used. This discussion, then, will concentrate on the steps to researching and writing about literature that differ from the process of writing on other topics.

Understanding the nature of your assignment seems especially important since there are many approaches to literature and ways to use criticism. Specialists distinguish between literary scholarship and literary criticism, using scholarship to refer to such tasks as finding the story Shakespeare used for one of his plays, determining the editor of an anonymous early edition of Marlowe's plays, or editing the letters of Edith Wharton. Using this distinction, we can say that scholarship provides new knowledge whereas criticism provides new understanding: a new reading of the Shakespeare play in the light of the uncovered source, a new interpretation of *Ethan Frome* based on comments about the story made in several of Wharton's letters. Whether you are writing about one piece of literature or several, and whether your library study is primarily in biography or critical essays, your goal is to offer some new understanding of the literature.

One type of assignment you might be given that would not offer new understanding of a work would be to study a critical controversy and report on the dominant issues in that controversy. You could, for example, study the controversy over the ending of "The Short Happy Life of Francis Macomber." Your task, then, would be to read the major sources on this topic and summarize the key positions and explain the arguments for each position. Your goal: to clarify the various sides of a controversy. When this kind of report is clear and thorough it provides a useful first step to a new understanding of a work.

If your assignment does not call for a report on criticism, then the focus of your attention needs to be on the literary work (or works), not on the criticism you read. Reading the critics can sharpen your focus on a topic and provide background information. You might choose to develop some critic's position further, or you might refer to a critic's position in order to disagree. But in either case, you will then need to go on to develop and defend your own thesis. Remember that since critics disagree, citing one critic's opinion will not automatically prove your point. The task of defending your thesis remains yours.

Selecting a Topic

Although many instructors give rather specific research paper assignments (usually based on emphases in the course and the availability of library materials), sometimes you will have to devise your own subject for study. Even when topics are provided, you will need to choose among them and then develop your own focus and approach. You may find this task easier if you can classify a possible topic as one of several general approaches. Most critical studies fit into one of the following types.

1. A study of one work that contains a problem in reading, a controversy over interpretation. Your goal is to explain and defend your reading of the work. An essay on the ending of "The Short Happy Life of Francis Macomber" fits into this category.

2. A study of several works by one author to examine recurring themes or techniques. In the sample research essay in this chapter, the student takes the concept of the Hemingway hero, a concept usually applied to several characters in his novels, and applies it to the Macomber short story.

3. A comparison of two or more writers or works to examine similar themes or techniques. Many possibilities fit into this category, including long studies of the modern political novel or surrealist drama, but also including more narrow studies such as the relationship of a derivative poem (Donne's "The Bait") to its original (Marlowe's "Come Live with Me"). Of course, these studies could also establish contrast. One could argue, for instance, that Chekhov's play *The Seagull* is best understood not as influenced in a serious way by Ibsen's *The Wild Duck* but as a satire of Ibsen's play. A word of caution may be in order, though, for students selecting this type of paper. To select two very different works that are connected only because they are both "about love" or "about death" is to risk writing an essay on love or death rather than on the literary works.

4. A study of an influence (biographical, historical, philosophical) on a work or author. Topics of this sort are especially good choices for undergraduate research essays because they depend more on a broad range of secondary sources, not on critical articles only. Even small libraries can usually provide the needed reference materials, and the application of background information to the reading of a particular work requires original thinking and organizing from students. Camus's "The Guest" as a statement of existential philosophy would be a topic in this category.

Developing a Thesis

If you have chosen a topic as a result of reading already completed and analyzed, then you can establish a tentative thesis or research question to guide your selection and reading of sources. If you remember, for example, a high school teacher discussing the

Hemingway hero concept and you have read "The Short Happy Life of Francis Macomber" in your current course, you can then formulate the research question: is Macomber a Hemingway hero? Or, in your class discussion of "The Guest," you learn that Camus was an existentialist. You've heard other references to this philosophy but realize that you don't know very much about it, so you decide to use the research assignment as an opportunity to learn about both Camus and existentialism. Your research question: How does "The Guest" reflect Camus's existential philosophy? If, however, you have selected a work or author you like but have no ideas for a topic, then you will have to start in the library sampling the critics to find an issue or problem to study. You should understand, though, that this second approach is dangerous because it can lead to mere copying from the critics rather than the development of your own ideas.

Preparing a Bibliography

Some instructors like to monitor their students' progress through a research assignment and thus will ask to see bibliography cards and, later, note cards. But even if you do not need to show cards to an instructor, you are wise to use $3'' \times 5''$ index cards for your bibliography and larger cards for taking notes. Trying to sort through notebook pages containing a mix of notes and bibliographic citations can lead to confusion when you are ready to write and, worse, to errors in presenting or documenting source material (plagiarism). If you practice good habits during research, then writing and documenting will not be complicated by needless difficulties.

Your search for appropriate sources will begin with your library's listing of books. You may need to read additional works by your author (e.g., several Hemingway novels) and books, both biographical and critical, about the writer (e.g., Carlos Baker's *Hemingway: The Writer as Artist*). If you are writing about Camus, you will want to read some of his philosophical essays and a general study of existentialism.

Small libraries will not have many books about writers or about literary or philosophical movements, so you will also need to use the reference collection for background information. The reference collection will contain literary histories, histories of philosophy, and guides or handbooks on philosophy and literary terms and movements. The reference collection also contains useful biographical dictionaries, the best place to start your study even if the focus of your paper is not biographical. Knowing the specifics of a writer's life and work can keep you from some embarrassing inaccuracy in your essay. Three biographical dictionaries you should get to know are: the *Dictionary of American Biography* (lengthy biographical/critical articles on Americans no longer living), the *Dictionary of National Biography* (on important Englishmen no longer living), and *Contemporary Authors* (major living writers from all countries).

Finally, you will need to use the various guides to articles about literature. The first guides to turn to are the ones already in your hands: the books you have located, many of which contain extensive bibliographies of books and articles on your topic. The index to articles you probably know best, *The Reader's Guide to Periodical Literature*, will not help you much with a literary essay. Remember that *The Reader's Guide* indexes popular articles, not articles in scholarly journals. *The Reader's Guide*, along with *The Book Review Digest*, will be helpful for book and play reviews. The most important index to articles on literature is the annual *MLA International Bibliography*. This is the most complete index of books and articles published in the last thirty years. It is organized by country (American), by period (Twentieth Century), and then by author (Hemingway). Thus Hemingway can be found under American Literature, Twentieth Century, Camus under French Literature, Twentieth Century. The titles of journals are abbreviated, as in other indexes, but full titles are provided in a list at the front of each volume.

When you are preparing your working bibliography, you should list all possible sources, one work to a card, that you find in the catalog of books and the MLA bibliography. It's faster to complete many cards at one sitting than it is to have to return to search again for new sources. Of course you will skip over titles that are clearly not on your particular topic and, if your library is small, you can also ignore articles published in foreign journals. But copy the rest, for some of them will turn out to be unavailable or not useful to your study.

Take time to copy accurately and put bibliographical information in the correct format according to the Modern Language Association style, the appropriate style for literary research papers.

Each citation contains author, title, and facts of publication. A bibliographic citation for a book looks like this.

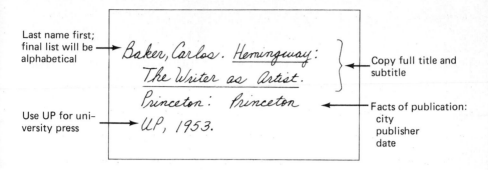

A bibliographic citation for an article in a scholarly journal looks like this.

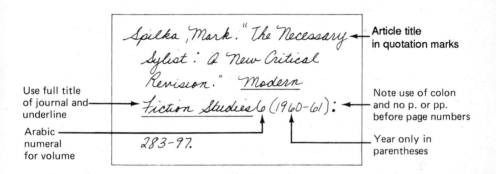

Here are several more sample citations common to literary research. The new MLA style manual provides for some changes to streamline citations, so study the samples carefully and use them as models for preparing your bibliography.

1. An essay, previously published, in a collection:

Beck, Warren, "The Shorter Happy Life of Mrs.

Macomber." <u>Modern Fiction Studies</u> 1 (1955):

28-37. Rpt. in <u>Hemingway's African Stories:</u>

The Stories, Their Sources, Their Critics.

Ed. John M. Howell. New York: Scribner's,

1969. 119–28.

(Give the complete original facts of publication and then the facts of publication for the collection. The final numbers are inclusive page numbers for the entire article.)

2. A book with more than two authors or editors and in a second or subsequent edition.

Spiller, Robert E., et al. LHUS. 3rd ed. London:

Macmillan, 1969.

(*LHUS* stands for *Literary History of the United States,* a well-known reference book that is regularly abbreviated in citations. Also abbreviate *PMLA, Publication of the Modern Language Association.*)

3. A work in an anthology:

Donne, John. "The Bait." Poetry of the English

Renaissance. Ed. J. William Hebel and Hoyt H.

Hudson. New York: Appleton, 1929. 459–460.

(The publisher Appleton-Century-Crofts should be shortened to the first name only.)

4. An encyclopedia or handbook article:

W[arnke], F[rank] J. "Metaphysical Poetry."

Princeton Encyclopedia of Poetry and Poetics.

Ed. Alex Preminger. Princeton: Princeton UP,

1974.

(If the article is initialed and a list of contributors is provided, complete the author's name, using square brackets around added letters.)

5. An article from the *Dictionary of American Biography*:

```
V[an] D[oren], C[arl]. "Nathaniel Hawthorne." DAB.

     1931.
```

(For standard dictionaries and multivolume encyclopedias without a single editor and with entries arranged alphabetically, the date, or edition and date, is sufficient for the facts of publication.)

6. A book in a series:

```
Cross, K. G. W. F. Scott Fitzgerald. Writers and

     Critics. New York: Capricorn, 1964.
```

(Provide the series title, but do not underline it. Shorten Capricorn Books to Capricorn and eliminate all similar words such as "House" or "Press" from other publishers' names.)

Taking Notes and Planning Your Paper

Just as you want to use index cards to prepare a bibliography for the flexibility cards offer, so you want to use cards for note-taking. Little is gained from cards, however, if all your "notes" are lengthy summaries of each article. The value of cards is achieved only if you can discipline yourself to record one idea or cluster of details on each card. Thus, one article important to your paper may generate five or six note cards, whereas you may take only one note from a book on philosophy—because you need that source for only one key definition. In short, as you read and take notes, keep the purpose of *your* paper in mind. Note-taking should not be an old-fashioned xeroxing technique; it should represent a purposeful selection of the information you need to develop your paper.

If you are thinking as you read, then possibilities for organizing your paper should emerge. Be sure to record your ideas as you go.

Similarly, don't just take a note on a critical view you plan to dispute; make a note, on the bottom of the card, that you plan to dispute the critic's view—better yet, make a note indicating how you plan to dispute it.

Your note cards always need at least three pieces of information, as the following sample illustrates.

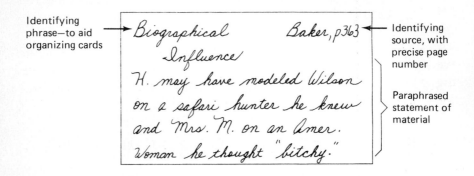

Identifying phrase—to aid organizing cards

Identifying source, with precise page number

Paraphrased statement of material

Biographical Influence
Baker, p363
H. may have modeled Wilson on a safari hunter he knew and Mrs. M. on an Amer. Woman he thought "bitchy."

The first information to record—so that you never forget—is the source and page number for the borrowed information. If you have only one Baker in your bibliography, then his last name is sufficient to identify the book. The precise page from which the note comes is necessary for documentation. If you add a note to yourself on the card, just draw a line to separate your idea from the source material.

For several good reasons, most of your notes should be paraphrased rather than direct quotations. First, the idea of research is to learn about your topic, to become a bit of an expert. If you have to quote a definition of existentialism, for example, you are not demonstrating a grasp of your subject. Second, your paper should be in your words and style, not in a mosaic of others' styles. If you paraphrase your notes and rewrite them again as you incorporate the ideas into your paper, you should be free from imitating the style of your sources. And finally, you will probably need to quote from your primary source, the literature itself. If you quote extensively from secondary sources as well, your essay will be a "cut-and-paste" paper indeed. So begin at the note-taking stage to start learning about your subject and to start finding your own words. Remember, though, that any use of ideas from sources must be acknowledged, whether quoted or paraphrased, so *all* note cards need to record the source and page number.

If you are writing about one or more long works of literature, you may also want to use note cards to record the passages you will discuss or quote from in your paper. But, if you can find the key sections easily in your well-marked copy, taking notes is not necessary. Don't forget, though, to include all works of literature in your final "Works Cited" list, because you will be citing lines from the poem or passages from the novel you are analyzing.

When your study seems complete, reexamine the thoughts you have had regarding your tentative thesis and your ideas for organizing the paper. Decide, finally, on your thesis and organization, review your notes, grouping cards according to your outline and discarding those that turn out not to fit your refined plans for the essay. You may discover that you need to go back to one source because a note card is not clear or return to the library to check another reference source. Some retracing of steps is common in processes as complex as research and writing. Finally, though, with literary texts and note cards stacked on your desk, you are ready to draft your paper.

Completing the Essay and Documenting Sources

You know all the good advice about skipping your opening paragraph if you are having trouble getting started, leaving time for revision, and proofreading your final version with care. The writing problems special to the literary research paper are the related tasks of introducing material from sources and documenting sources properly. Since you have been practicing techniques for presenting evidence from the literary text in your previous essays, you have studied the text's sample essays and the guidelines for handling direct quotations in Appendix B. Just remember to:

1. give sufficient context for a quoted or paraphrased passage
2. avoid long passages of direct quotation
3. combine paraphrase with brief quotations whenever possible
4. work quoted material smoothly into your sentences
5. comment on quoted passages to explain how they serve as evidence

    6. represent the critics' views accurately and fairly, avoiding sarcasm when you disagree

The new MLA guidelines for documenting research essays require parenthetical acknowledgment within the text accompanied by an alphabetical list of all cited sources, in the new streamlined form we have already reviewed. If you have used parenthetical documentation before, you know that, once learned, it is much simpler than footnotes. In addition, the format encourages writers to introduce, to provide a context for, both quoted and paraphrased material from sources. Models for parenthetical documentation follow, but first here are several important guidelines to note.

1. Parenthetical documentation requires specific page references to sources, just as for footnotes.

2. Borrowed information and ideas, whether paraphrased or quoted, must be documented, just as for footnotes.

3. Parenthetical references can be as brief as author last name and page number because *all* clearly connect to a full bibliographic citation in the list of works cited.

4. Parenthetical references in the text should be as brief as possible consistent with accuracy and clarity.

The Basic Pattern of Parenthetical Documentation

When you know the author of the source, and the source is the only one you use by that author, then document with one of these patterns:

1. Place the author's last name and the relevant page number(s) immediately after the borrowed material.

    Wilson may have been modeled on a hunter whom Hemingway knew and admired (Baker 363).

2. Give the author's name in the text of your paper and place only the page number in parentheses after the borrowed material.

    According to Carlos Baker, Wilson may have been modeled on a hunter whom Hemingway knew and admired (363).

3. If a quoted passage is long enough to require display form, place the parenthetical reference at the end of the passage, *after* the final period.

When Macomber shoots the buffalo, a change comes over him, and his good feeling is not dispelled when he learns that a wounded buffalo has escaped into the bush:

> He expected the feeling he had had about the lion to come back but it did not. For the first time in his life he really felt wholly without fear. Instead of fear he had a feeling of definite elation. (31)

Each of these parenthetical references is complete *only* when a full citation of the source is placed in the Works Cited, thus:

Baker, Carlos. Hemingway: A Life Story. New York:

    Scribner's, 1968.

Hemingway, Ernest. "The Short Happy Life of

    Francis Macomber." The Short Stories of

    Ernest Hemingway. New York: Scribner's 1927.

    3-37.

Other Patterns of Parenthetical Documentation

1. A work by two authors.

The "lost generation" of the Twenties was never really "lost" creatively; the decade produced some of America's finest writers (Horton and Edwards 322).

or

As Horton and Edwards explain, the "lost generation" of the Twenties was never "lost" creatively; the decade produced some of America's finest writers (322).

Works Cited

Horton, Rod W. and Herbert W. Edwards. Backgrounds

    of American Literary Thought. New York:

    Appleton, 1952.

2. A book in two or more volumes.

>   Sewall examines the role of Judge Lord in Dickinson's life (2:642–647).

or

>   Judge Lord was another one of Dickinson's preceptors (Sewall 2:642–647).

Works Cited

Sewall, Richard B. The Life of Emily Dickinson. 2

>   vols. New York: Farrar, 1974.

3. Two or more works in one parenthetical reference.

>   Several critics have argued that Hemingway's characters derive their code of conduct intuitively (Chase 160; Halliday 299).

Works Cited

Chase, Richard. The American Novel and Its

>   Tradition. Garden City: Doubleday, 1957.

Halliday, E. M. "Hemingway's Ambiguity: Symbolism

>   and Irony." American Literature 28 (1956):

>   1–22. Rpt. Interpretations of American

>   Literature. Eds. Charles Feidelson, Jr. and

>   Paul Brodtkorb, Jr. New York: Oxford, 1959.

4. Two or more works by the same author.

>   During the 1920s, "not only the drinks were mixed, but the company as well" (Allen, Only Yesterday 82).

or

>   According to Frederick Lewis Allen, the early 1900s were a period of complacency in America (The Big Change 4–5).

or

In <u>The Big Change</u>, Allen asserts that the early 1900s were a period of complacency (4–5).

Works Cited

Allen, Frederick Lewis. <u>The Big Change</u>. New York:

Harper, 1952.

---. <u>Only Yesterday: An Informal History of the</u>

<u>Nineteen-Twenties</u>. New York: Harper, 1931.

Study the following sample paper carefully for its organized development of a clear thesis, for its use of evidence from the literary work and restrained use of the critics, and for its clear introduction and documentation of borrowed material.

STUDENT ESSAY

The Hero in "The Short Happy Life of Francis Macomber"

by

Norman Blume

English Composition II, Section 23

Dr. Wilan

October 20, 1988

STUDENT ESSAY

The Hero in "The Short Happy Life of Francis Macomber"

Whenever the fiction of Ernest Hemingway is the subject of a literature class, the professor is sure to bring up the concept of the famous Hemingway hero, the hero who finds limited meaning in a meaningless world by living according to a personal code. In his introduction to Hemingway's novel A Farewell to Arms, Robert Penn Warren describes such heroes as "tough men, experienced in the hard worlds they inhabit, and not obviously given to emotional display" (xi). They have the courage to live by their code in the face of the "great nada," death (xvii).

Other critics have further defined two basic Hemingway "heroes." Philip Young in Ernest Hemingway: A Reconsideration distinguishes between the "Hemingway hero," a wounded hero—often both in the physical and psychological sense—who needs to learn about life (41) and the "code hero" who, by exhibiting what Hemingway called "grace under pressure" in terms of a code, "presents a solution to the problems . . . of the true 'Hemingway hero'" (63-64). These two heroes can come together in an "apprentice" and "exemplary" relationship in which the code hero becomes a teacher who initiates the Hemingway hero into the code (Waldhorn 23).

Just such a relationship seems to exist in Hemingway's story "The Short Happy Life of Francis Macomber," a story with an ending that has long been a puzzle for readers and a source of debate for critics. The story portrays an American couple, Francis and Margot Macomber, on a safari in Africa with a British hunting guide, Robert Wilson. The three characters are developed through their reactions to Francis Macomber's cowardice in running from a charging, wounded lion. The short happy life occurs as Francis learns courage from Wilson on a subsequent hunt, this

STUDENT ESSAY

2

time for buffalo, only to have his life abruptly ended by a bullet from
a rifle fired by Margot. The ambiguity arises from a contradiction between
the apparently omniscient narrator and Wilson. The narrator reports that
Margot "had shot at the buffalo . . . as it seemed about to gore Macomber."
Wilson, however, suggests murder by telling the sobbing Margot, "He would
have left you too" and asking her why she didn't poison her husband (36–
37). The question therefore arises: did Margot murder her husband or
try to save him from being gored by the buffalo?

Clearly the credibility of Robert Wilson becomes crucial to an
interpretation of the ending. And whether or not Wilson is Hemingway's
hero has a direct bearing on that credibility. If he really is the teacher
who initiates Francis into the courage of the hunter, then both men become
Hemingway heroes, Margot is left out in the cold, and the accusation of
murder is much more likely to represent Hemingway's own point of view.

Several critics support the conclusion that Wilson is a code
hero. Young, for example, says that Wilson teaches the code to Francis
(69). Arthur Waldhorn goes as far as to say that Wilson speaks for
Hemingway (149). Macomber is often seen as the initiate who, in the words
of Robert Penn Warren, "at last learns the lesson that the code of the
hunter demands that he go into the bush after an animal he has wounded"
(xii). Yet Wilson's character has been questioned, and Margot is seen
by some as a tragic figure. The role that each character plays in relation
to the Hemingway hero concept can help explain the question raised by
the story's ending.

If we return to the distinction between "Hemingway hero" and
"code hero," Francis Macomber seems to fit the former, playing the role
of apprentice to the "exemplary" initiate, Wilson. As the story opens

STUDENT ESSAY

3

Francis has certainly been wounded psychologically. He has run from the lion, showing a lack of courage in the face of danger. In his flashback as he lies on his cot he forces himself to confront his cowardice, describing himself as "running wildly in panic," in the aftermath Wilson's "tallness all seeming a naked reproach" (20). Furthermore, there is a suggestion of sexual problems, the psychological equivalent of the physical wound creating impotence in Jake Barnes, the "Hemingway hero" of The Sun Also Rises. Francis knows "about sex in books, many books, too many books," and he is described as not very good with women (21).

Yet Francis seems to want to prove himself even though he has been unsuccessful so far. He has tried a variety of sports—cars, shooting, fishing. The safari seems to be a self-imposed test, a way to define his manhood. If that is so, then he has failed in running from the lion. In addition, he doesn't know how to conduct himself, in Wilson's terms, in the face of failure. As Young points out, he continues to make mistakes. He asks Wilson not to report the cowardice. He apologizes. He is unable to control Margot. He asks to send the African "boys" after the lion. Worst of all, he suggests leaving the wounded lion to suffer in the grass (71-72). It is clear that he has much to learn from Wilson.

The initiation that the apprentice hero must go through takes place during the buffalo hunt. During this hunt the thirty-five-year-old "boy-man" grows up. As Jackson J. Benson points out, Francis demonstrates that he accepts Wilson's values when he faces the charging buffalo (146). Macomber and Wilson, who has now fulfilled the code hero's role as model, have become as one, and they share a few short happy moments of mutual admiration. Francis, his face "shining," tells his guide he

STUDENT ESSAY

4

feels "absolutely different" and would "like to try another lion" (32).
Wilson muses on the change—"Fear gone like an operation" (33)—and begins
to like Macomber and his newly found manhood.

The qualifications of Wilson as code hero have, however, been
challenged by some critics. Samuel Shaw, in describing the various
approaches normally taken to the story, notes a possible reading that
involves "calling into question the moral authority of Wilson." Wilson,
he comments, "sees nothing wrong in cuckolding Macomber" and "adopts
the moral standards of his clientele in all except hunting, a neat trick"
(84). Some critics feel that Hemingway is, in fact, satirizing Wilson.
One sees a critique of colonialism in the insensitive treatment of the
safari attendants (Stein). Virgil Hutton, in an extensive analysis of
Wilson's shortcomings, is especially harsh:

> behind Wilson's red face leers the red face of Molière's
> archetypal hypocrite, Tartuffe, who, like Wilson, passes
> puritanical judgments on others' actions but pleads the
> frailty of flesh and blood to excuse his own lust for his
> friend's wife. (250)

Others see Wilson in a more positive light. Mark Spilka, for
example, cites Wilson's understanding of the lion's feelings, his use
of his own standards for the hunt, and his conscious choice in facing
death (292). Philip Young, while admitting Wilson has shortcomings,
credits him with courage and honor (74). The code hero, after all, does
not have to be perfect. Manuel in "The Undefeated" has become a bad bull-
fighter. But he continues to fight with courage and without violating
his principles. Although Wilson does adopt the often decadent standards
of his clients, when it comes to the shooting he is his own man.

STUDENT ESSAY

5

Wilson's role as code hero is most clearly shown by his having come to terms with death. It is, after all, the fear of death that panics Macomber when facing the lion. And it is the two men's common acceptance of that fear which causes Wilson to share with some embarrassment (Hemingway heroes downplay their underlying sensitivity) the Shakespeare quotation by which he has lived: "By my troth I care not; a man can die but once; we owe God a death and let it go which way it will he that dies this year is quit for the next" (32). Hutton argues that, since these words from 2 Henry IV are spoken by a clown, one Francis Feeble, Wilson is being made fun of. To Carlos Baker, however, the quotation represents what Wilson really believes (Hemingway: The Writer as Artist 190). That Hemingway was, in fact, ridiculing Wilson seems unlikely, for Hemingway himself told how a British officer in 1917 taught him courage with the very same quotation (Young 73).

If Wilson has initiated Macomber into the code during the buffalo hunt, where does that leave Margot? Virgil Hutton sees Margot Macomber as a tragic heroine, because she is the only one who has insight into the situation that kills Macomber (248). Warren Beck, in arguing that the shooting was an accident, suggests that Margot tried to save Francis because, with his newfound courage, she "felt he had never been as worthy of her whole effort as he was now" (36). Wilson himself has a somewhat ambiguous attitude towards Margot. When Margot cries in response to her husband's cowardice, Wilson remarks that then "she seemed to understand, to realize, to be hurt for him" even though she is now "enamelled in that American female cruelty" (9). We are told by the narrator in a rare glimpse into Margot's mind that "she had done the best she could for many years back and the way they were together now was no one person's fault"

STUDENT ESSAY

6

(34). Perhaps, then, we have a Hemingway heroine. Catherine Barkley in A Farewell to Arms is such a heroine as she shares courage with Frederick Henry in the shadow of death. Wilson himself might agree with Catherine's sentiment: "The brave dies perhaps two thousand deaths if he's intelligent. He simply doesn't mention them" (146).

Hemingway's own testimony on Margot, though, is not very positive. He reported that he "invented her complete with handles from the worst bitch he knew, and when he first knew her she'd been lovely" (Baker, Ernest Hemingway: A Life Story 363). Although authors may dramatically change their real life models, the similarity here to Wilson's view of Margot is clear.

Also significant is Margot's reaction to Macomber's initiation into the code of courage. She turns pale and looks ill. Having seen the change in Francis and listening to the two men sharing their conquest of fear, she accuses them of "talking rot" (33). She is described as being "very afraid of something" (34). Perhaps what she fears is being the odd person out. Unlike Catherine Barkley, she cannot become one with the Hemingway hero through love. She can only hold over Wilson's head his violation of the legal code about not chasing animals in cars, a code he has not accepted as one of his personal standards. Ironically, it is Margot who violates the code that Wilson does accept, not to shoot from the car, as she fires the 6.5 Mannlicher and kills her husband.

Whether or not that action is murder will surely continue to be debated. However, we must take Wilson's testimony seriously, for the short happy life of the buffalo hunt presents Francis Macomber as the Hemingway hero with his psychological wound of cowardice being transformed into the hunter's courage of Wilson, the code hero.

STUDENT ESSAY

7

List of Works Cited

Baker, Carlos. Hemingway: The Writer as Artist. 4th ed.

    Princeton: Princeton UP, 1952.

---. Ernest Hemingway: A Life Story. New York: Bantam, 1970.

Beck, Warren. "The Shorter Happy Life of Mrs. Macomber."

    Modern Fiction Studies 1 (1955): 28-37.

Benson, Jackson J. Hemingway: The Writer's Art of Self Defense.

    Minneapolis: U of Minnesota P, 1969.

Hemingway, Ernest. A Farewell to Arms. New York: Scribner's, 1929.

---. The Short Stories of Ernest Hemingway. 6th ed. New York:

    Scribner's, 1938.

Hutton, Virgil. "The Short Happy Life of Macomber." The University

    Review 30 (1964): 253-63. Rpt. in The Short Stories of Ernest

    Hemingway: Critical Essays. Ed. Jackson J. Benson. Durham:

    Duke UP, 1975. 239-50.

Shaw, Samuel. Ernest Hemingway. New York: Ungar, 1973.

Spilka, Mark. "The Necessary Stylist: A New Critical Revision."

    Modern Fiction Studies 6 (1960-61): 283-97.

Stein, William Bysshe. "Hemingway's 'The Short Happy Life of Francis

    Macomber.'" Explicator 19 (1961): Item 47.

Young, Philip. Ernest Hemingway: A Reconsideration. University

    Park: Pennsylvania State UP, 1966.

Waldhorn, Arthur. A Reader's Guide to Ernest Hemingway.

    New York: Farrar, 1972.

Warren, Robert Penn. Introduction. A Farewell to Arms.

    By Ernest Hemingway. New York: Scribner's, 1929. vii-xxxvi.

The Third Class Carriage. Oil. Metropolitan Museum of Art. Bequest of Mrs. H. O. Havemeyer. 1929.

part II

A COLLECTION OF SHORT STORIES, POEMS, AND PLAYS

Short Stories

EDGAR ALLAN POE   (1809–1849)

The Fall of the House of Usher

> Son coeur est un luth suspendu;
> Sitôt qu'on le touche il résonne.
>
> *De Béranger.*°

During the whole of a dull, dark, and soundless day in the autumn of the year, when the clouds hung oppressively low in the heavens, I had been passing alone, on horseback, through a singularly dreary tract of country; and at length found myself, as the shades of the evening drew on, within view of the melancholy House of Usher. I know not how it was—but, with the first glimpse of the building, a sense of insufferable gloom pervaded my spirit. I say insufferable; for the feeling was unrelieved by any of that half-pleasurable, because poetic, sentiment, with which the mind usually receives even the sternest natural images of the desolate or terrible. I looked upon the scene before me—upon the mere house, and the simple landscape features of the domain—upon the bleak walls—upon the vacant eye-like windows—upon a few rank sedges—and upon a few white trunks of decayed trees—with an utter depression of soul which I can compare to no earthly sensation more properly than to the afterdream of the reveller upon opium—the bitter lapse into everyday life—the hideous

---

° *De Béranger*: from Pierre Jean de Béranger's "Le Rufus": "His heart is a suspended lute; / No sooner touched than it resounds."

dropping off of the veil. There was an iciness, a sinking, a sickening of the heart—an unredeemed dreariness of thought which no goading of the imagination could torture into aught of the sublime. What was it—I paused to think—what was it that so unnerved me in the contemplation of the House of Usher? It was a mystery all insoluble; nor could I grapple with the shadowy fancies that crowded upon me as I pondered. I was forced to fall back upon the unsatisfactory conclusion, that while, beyond doubt, there are combinations of very simple natural objects which have the power of thus affecting us, still the analysis of this power lies among considerations beyond our depth. It was possible, I reflected, that a mere different arrangement of the particulars of the scene, of the details of the picture, would be sufficient to modify, or perhaps to annihilate its capacity for sorrowful impression; and, acting upon this idea, I reined my horse to the precipitous brink of a black and lurid tarn that lay in unruffled lustre by the dwelling, and gazed down—but with a shudder even more thrilling than before—upon the remodelled and inverted images of the gray sedge, and the ghastly tree-stems, and the vacant and eye-like windows.

Nevertheless, in this mansion of gloom I now proposed to myself a sojourn of some weeks. Its proprietor, Roderick Usher, had been one of my boon companions in boyhood; but many years had elapsed since our last meeting. A letter, however, had lately reached me in a distant part of the country—a letter from him—which, in its wildly importunate nature, had admitted of no other than a personal reply. The MS. gave evidence of nervous agitation. The writer spoke of acute bodily illness—of a mental disorder which oppressed him—and of an earnest desire to see me, as his best, and indeed his only personal friend, with a view of attempting, by the cheerfulness of my society, some alleviation of his malady. It was the manner in which all this, and much more, was said—it was the apparent *heart* that went with his request—which allowed me no room for hesitation; and I accordingly obeyed forthwith what I still considered a very singular summons.

Although, as boys, we had been even intimate associates, yet I really knew little of my friend. His reserve had been always excessive and habitual. I was aware, however, that his very ancient family had been noted, time out of mind, for a peculiar sensibility of temperament, displaying itself, through long ages, in many works of exalted art, and manifested, of late, in repeated deeds of munificent yet unobstrusive charity, as well as in a passionate devotion to the intricacies, perhaps even more than to the orthodox and easily recognisable beauties, of musical science. I had learned, too, the very remarkable fact, that the stem of the Usher race, all time-honored as it was, had put forth, at no period, any enduring branch; in other words, that the entire family lay in the direct line of descent, and had always, with very trifling and very temporary variation, so lain. It was this deficiency, I considered, while running over in thought the perfect keeping of the character of the premises with the accredited character of the people, and while speculating upon the possible influence which the one, in the long lapse of centuries, might have exercised upon the other—it was this deficiency, perhaps, of collateral issue, and the consequent undeviating transmission, from sire to son, of the patrimony with the name, which had, at length, so identified the two as to merge the original title of the estate in the quaint and equivocal appellation of the "House of Usher"—an appellation which seemed to include, in the minds of the peasantry who used it, both the family and the family mansion.

I have said that the sole effect of my somewhat childish experiment— that of looking down within the tarn—had been to deepen the first singular impression. There can be no doubt that the consciousness of the rapid increase of my superstition—for why should I not so term it?— served mainly to accelerate the increase itself. Such, I have long known, is the paradoxical law of all sentiments having terror as a basis. And it might have been for this reason only, that, when I again uplifted my eyes to the house itself, from its image in the pool, there grew in my mind a strange fancy—a fancy so ridiculous, indeed, that I but mention it to show the vivid force of the sensations which oppressed me. I had so worked upon my imagination as really to believe that about the whole mansion and domain there hung an atmosphere peculiar to themselves and their immediate vicinity—an atmosphere which had no affinity with the air of heaven, but which had reeked up from the decayed trees, and the gray wall and the silent tarn—a pestilent and mystic vapor, dull, sluggish, faintly discernible, and leaden-hued.

Shaking off from my spirit what *must* have been a dream, I scanned more narrowly the real aspect of the building. Its principal feature seemed to be that of an excessive antiquity. The discoloration of ages had been great. Minute fungi overspread the whole exterior, hanging in a fine tangled web-work from the eaves. Yet all this was apart from any extraordinary dilapidation. No portion of the mansonry had fallen; and there appeared to be a wild inconsistency between its still perfect adaptation of parts, and the crumbling condition of the individual stones. In this there was much that reminded me of the specious totality of old woodwork which has rotted for long years in some neglected vault, with no disturbance from the breath of the external air. Beyond this indication of extensive decay, however, the fabric gave little token of instability. Perhaps the eye of a scrutinizing observer might have discovered a barely perceptible fissure, which, extending from the roof of the building in front, made its way down the wall in a zigzag direction, until it became lost in the sullen waters of the tarn.

Noticing these things, I rode over a short causeway to the house. A servant in waiting took my horse, and I entered the Gothic archway of the hall. A valet, of stealthy step, thence conducted me, in silence, through many dark and intricate passages in my progress to the *studio* of his master. Much that I encountered on the way contributed, I know not how, to heighten the vague sentiments of which I have already spoken. While the objects around me—while the carvings of the ceilings, the sombre tapestries of the walls, the ebon blackness of the floors, and the phantas-magoric armorial trophies which rattled as I strode, were but matters to which, or to such as which, I had been accustomed from my infancy—while I hesitated not to acknowledge how familiar was all this—I still wondered to find how unfamiliar were the fancies which ordinary images were stirring up. On one of the staircases, I met the physician of the family. His countenance, I thought, wore a mingled expression of low cunning and perplexity. He accosted me with trepidation and passed on. The valet now threw open a door and ushered me into the presence of his master.

The room in which I found myself was very large and lofty. The windows were long, narrow, and pointed, and at so vast a distance from the black oaken floor as to be altogether inaccessible from within. Feeble gleams of encrimsoned light made their way through the trellised panes, and served to render sufficiently distinct the more prominent objects around; the eye, however, struggled in vain to reach the remoter angles of the chamber, or the recesses of the vaulted and fretted ceiling. Dark draperies hung upon the walls. The general furniture was profuse, comfortless, antique, and tattered. Many books and musical instruments lay scattered about, but failed to give any vitality to the scene. I felt that I breathed an atmosphere of sorrow. An air of stern, deep, and irredeemable gloom hung over and pervaded all.

Upon my entrance, Usher arose from a sofa on which he had been lying at full length, and greeted me with a vivacious warmth which had much in it, I at first thought, of an overdone cordiality—of the constrained effort of the *ennuyé* man of the world. A glance, however, at his counte-nance, convinced me of his perfect sincerity. We sat down; and for some moments, while he spoke not, I gazed upon him with a feeling half of pity, half of awe. Surely, man had never before so terribly altered, in so brief a period, as had Roderick Usher! It was with difficulty that I could bring myself to admit the identity of the wan being before me with the companion of my early boyhood. Yet the character of his face had been at all times remarkable. A cadaverousness of complexion; an eye large, liquid, and luminous beyond comparison; lips somewhat thin and very pallid, but of a surpassingly beautiful curve; a nose of a delicate Hebrew model, but with a breadth of nostril unusual in similar formations; a finely moulded chin, speaking, in its want of prominence, of a want of moral energy; hair of a more than web-like softness and tenuity; these features, with an inordinate expansion above the regions of the temple, made up altogether a countenance not easily to be forgotten. And now in the mere exaggeration of the prevailing character of these features, and of the expression they were wont to convey, lay so much of change that I doubted to whom I spoke. The now ghastly pallor of the skin, and the now miraculous lustre of the eye, above all things startled and even awed me. The silken hair, too, had been suffered to grow all unheeded, and as, in its wild gossamer texture, it floated rather than fell about the face, I could not, even with effort, connect its Arabesque expression with any idea of simple humanity.

In the manner of my friend I was at once struck with an incoherence— an inconsistency; and I soon found this to arise from a series of feeble and futile struggles to overcome an habitual trepidancy—an excessive nervous agitation. For something of this nature I had indeed been prepared, no less by his letter, than by reminiscences of certain boyish traits, and by conclusions deduced from his peculiar physical conformation and temperament. His action was alternately vivacious and sullen. His voice varied rapidly from a tremulous indecision (when the animal spirtis seemed utterly in abeyance) to that species of energetic concision—that abrupt, weighty, unhurried, and hollow-sounding enunciation—that leaden, self-balanced and perfectly modulated guttural utterance, which may be observed in the lost drunkard, or the irreclaimable eater of opium, during the periods of his most intense excitement.

It was thus that he spoke of the object of my visit, of his earnest desire to see me, and of the solace he expected me to afford him. He entered, at some length, into what he conceived to be the nature of his malady. It was, he said, a constitutional and a family evil, and one for which he despaired to find a remedy—a mere nervous affection, he immediately added, which would undoubtedly soon pass. It displayed itself in a host of unnatural sensations. Some of these, as he detailed them, interested and bewildered me; although, perhaps, the terms, and the general manner of the narration had their weight. He suffered much from a morbid acuteness of the senses; the most insipid food was alone endurable; he could wear only garments of certain texture; the odors of all flowers were oppressive; his eyes were tortured by even a faint light; and there were but peculiar sounds, and these from stringed instruments, which did not inspire him with horror.

To an anomalous species of terror I found him a bounden slave. "I shall perish," said he, "I *must* perish in this deplorable folly. Thus, thus, and not otherwise, shall I be lost. I dread the events of the future, not in themselves, but in their results. I shudder at the thought of any, even the most trivial, incident, which may operate upon this intolerable agitation of soul. I have, indeed, no abhorrence of danger, except in its absolute effect—in terror. In this unnerved—in this pitiable condition—I feel that the period will sooner or later arrive when I must abandon life and reason together, in some struggle with the grim phantasm, FEAR."

I learned, moreover, at intervals, and through broken and equivocal hints, another singular feature of his mental condition. He was enchained by certain superstitious impressions in regard to the dwelling which he tenanted, and whence, for many years, he had never ventured forth—in regard to an influence whose supposititious force was conveyed in terms too shadowy here to be re-stated—an influence which some peculiarities in the mere form and substance of his family mansion, had, by dint of long sufferance, he said, obtained over his spirt—an effect which the *physique* of the gray walls and turrets, and of the dim tarn into which they all looked down, had, at length, brought about upon the *morale* of his existence.

He admitted, however, although with hesitation, that much of the peculiar gloom which thus afflicted him could be traced to a more natural and far more palpable origin—to the severe and long-continued illness—indeed to the evidently approaching dissolution—of a tenderly beloved sister—his sole companion for long years—his last and only relative on earth. "Her decease," he said, with a bitterness which I can never forget, "would leave him (him the hopeless and the frail) the last of the ancient race of the Ushers." While he spoke, the lady Madeline (for so was she called) passed slowly through a remote portion of the apartment, and, without having noticed my presence, disappeared. I regarded her with an utter astonishment not unmingled with dread—and yet I found it impossible to account for such feelings. A sensation of stupor oppressed me, as my eyes followed her retreating steps. When a door, at length, closed upon her, my glance sought instinctively and eagerly the countenance of the brother—but he had buried his face in his hands, and I could only perceive that a far more than ordinary wanness had overspread the emaciated fingers through which trickled many passionate tears.

The disease of the lady Madeline had long baffled the skill of her physicians. A settled apathy, a gradual wasting away of the person, and frequent although transient affections of a partially cataleptical character, were the unusual diagnosis. Hitherto she had steadily borne up against the pressure of her malady, and had not betaken herself finally to bed; but, on the closing in of the evening of my arrival at the house, she succumbed (as her brother told me at night with inexpressible agitation) to the prostrating power of the destroyer; and I learned that the glimpse I had obtained of her person would thus probably be the last I should obtain—that the lady, at least while living, would be seen by me no more.

For several days ensuing, her name was unmentioned by either Usher or myself: and during this period I was busied in earnest endeavors to alleviate the melancholy of my friend. We painted and read together; or I listened, as if in a dream, to the wild improvisations of his speaking guitar. And thus, as a closer and still closer intimacy admitted me more unreservedly into the recesses of his spirit, the more bitterly did I perceive the futility of all attempt at cheering a mind from which darkness, as if an inherent positive quality, poured forth upon all objects of the moral and physical universe, in one unceasing radiation of gloom.

I shall ever bear about me a memory of the many solemn hours I thus spent alone with the master of the House of Usher. Yet I should fail in any attempt to convey an idea of the exact character of the studies, or of the occupations, in which he involved me, or led me the way. An excited and highly distempered ideality threw a sulphureous lustre over all. His long improvised dirges will ring forever in my ears. Among other things, I hold painfully in mind a certain singular perversion and amplification of the wild air of the last waltz of Von Weber.° From the paintings over which his elaborate fancy brooded, and which grew, touch by touch, into vagueness at which I shuddered the more thrillingly, because I shuddered knowing not why;—from these paintings (vivid as their images now are before me) I would in vain endeavor to educe more than a small portion which should lie within the compass of merely written words. By the utter simplicity, by the nakedness of his designs, he arrested and overawed attention. If ever mortal painted an idea, that mortal was Roderick Usher. For me at least, in the circumstances then surrounding me, there arose out of the pure abstractions which the hypochondriac contrived to throw upon his canvass, an intensity of intolerable awe, no shadow of which felt I ever yet in the contemplation of the certainly glowing yet too concrete reveries of Fuseli.°

One of the phantasmagoric conceptions of my friend, partaking not so rigidly of the spirit of abstraction, may be shadowed forth, although feebly, in words. A small picture presented the interior of an immensely long and rectangular vault or tunnel, with low walls, smooth, white, and without interruption or device. Certain accessory points of the design served well to convey the idea that this excavation lay at an exceeding depth below the surface of the earth. No outlet was observed in any portion of its vast extent, and no torch, or other artificial source of light was discernible; yet a flood of intense rays rolled throughout, and bathed the whole in a ghastly and inappropriate splendor.

I have just spoken of that morbid condition of the auditory nerve which rendered all music intolerable to the sufferer with the exception of certain effects of stringed instruments. It was, perhaps, the narrow limits to which he thus confined himself upon the guitar, which gave birth, in great measure, to the fantastic character of his performances. But the

---

° *last waltz of Von Weber*: the waltz was composed by Karl Reissiger and copied by Karl Maria, Baron von Weber; Poe is mistaken here.
° *Fuseli*: Henry Fuseli was an English romantic impressionistic painter of Swiss birth.

fervid *facility* of his *impromptus* could not be so accounted for. They must have been, and were, in the notes, as well as in the words of his wild fantasias (for he not unfrequently accompanied himself with rhymed verbal improvisations), the result of that intense mental collectedness and concentration to which I have previously alluded as observable only in particular moments of the highest artificial excitement. The words of one of these rhapsodies I have easily remembered. I was, perhaps, the more forcibly impressed with it, as he gave it, because, in the under or mystic current of its meaning, I fancied that I perceived, and for the first time, a full consciousness on the part of Usher, of the tottering of his lofty reason upon her throne. The verses, which were entitled "The Haunted Palace,"° ran very nearly, if not accurately, thus:

I

In the greenest of our valleys,
   By good angels tenanted,
Once a fair and stately palace—
   Radiant palace—reared its head.
In the monarch Thought's dominion—
   It stood there!
Never seraph spread a pinion
   Over fabric half so fair.

II

Banners yellow, glorious, golden,
   On its roof did float and flow;
(This—all this—was in the olden
   Time long ago)
And every gentle air that dallied,
   In that sweet day,
Along the ramparts plumed and pallid,
   A winged odor went away.

III

Wanderers in that happy valley
   Through two luminous windows saw
Spirits moving musically
   To a lute's well-tuned law,
Round about a throne, where sitting
   (Porphyrogene!)

° *"The Haunted Palace"*: this poem by Poe was first published in the Baltimore *American Museum of Science, Literature, and the Arts* for April 1939.

In state his glory well befitting.
  The ruler of the realm was seen.

IV

And all with pearl and ruby glowing
  Was the fair palace door,
Through which came flowing, flowing, flowing,
  And sparkling evermore,
A troop of Echoes whose sweet duty
  Was but to sing,
In voices of surpassing beauty,
  The wit and wisdom of their king.

V

But evil things, in robes of sorrow,
  Assailed the monarch's high estate;
(Ah, let us mourn, for never morrow
  Shall dawn upon him, desolate!)
And, round about his home, the glory
  That blushed and bloomed
Is but a dim-remembered story
  Of the old time entombed.

VI

And travellers now within that valley,
  Through the red-litten windows, see
Vast forms that move fantastically
  To a discordant melody;
While, like a rapid ghastly river,
  Through the pale door,
A hideous throng rush out forever,
  And laugh—but smile no more.

I well remember that suggestions arising from this ballad led us into a train of thought wherein there became manifest an opinion of Usher's which I mention not so much on account of its novelty, (for other men° have thought thus,) as on account of the pertinacity with which he maintained it. This opinion, in its general form, was that of the sentience of all vegetable things. But, in his disordered fancy, the idea had assumed

---

° *other men*: Watson, Dr. Percival, Spallanzani, and especially the Bishop of Landaff.— See "Chemical Essays," vol. v [Poe's note.]

a more daring character, and trespassed, under certain conditions, upon the kingdom of inorganization. I lack words to express the full extent, or the earnest *abandon* of his persuasion. The belief, however, was connected (as I have previously hinted) with the gray stones of the home of his forefathers. The conditions of the sentience had been here, he imagined, fulfilled in the method of collocation of these stones—in the order of their arrangement, as well as in that of the many *fungi* which overspread them, and of the decayed trees which stood around—above all, in the long undisturbed endurance of this arrangement, and in its reduplication in the still waters of the tarn. Its evidence—the evidence of the sentience—was to be seen, he said, (and I here started as he spoke,) in the gradual yet certain condensation of an atmosphere of their own about the waters and the walls. The result was discoverable, he added, in that silent, yet importunate and terrible influence which for centuries had moulded the destinies of his family, and which made *him* what I now saw him—what he was. Such opinions need no comment, and I will make none.

Our books—the books which, for years, had formed no small portion of the mental existence of the invalid—were, as might be supposed, in strict keeping with this character of phantasm. We pored together over such works as the "Ververt et Chartreuse" of Gresset; the "Belphegor" of Machiavelli; the "Heaven and Hell" of Swedenborg; the "Subterranean Voyage of Nicholas Klimm" by Holberg; the "Chiromancy" of Robert Flud, of Jean D'Indaginé, and of De la Chambre; the "Journey into the Blue Distance of Tieck"; and the "City of the Sun" of Campanella. One favorite volume was a small octavo edition of the *Directorium Inquisitorum,* by the Dominican Eymeric de Gironne; and there were passages in Pomponius Mela, about the old African satyrs and Œgipans, over which Usher would sit dreaming for hours. His chief delight, however, was found in the perusal of an exceedingly rare and curious book in quarto Gothic—the manual of a forgotten church—the *Vigiliae Mortuorum secundum Chorum Ecclesiae Maguntinae.*°

I could not help thinking of the wild ritual of this work, and of its probable influence upon the hypochondriac, when, one evening, having informed me abruptly that the lady Madeline was no more, he stated his intension of preserving her corpse for a fortnight, (previously to its final interment,) in one of the numerous valults within the main walls of the building. The worldly reason, however, assigned for this singular proceeding, was one which I did not feel at liberty to dispute. The brother had been led to his resolution (so he told me) by consideration of the unusual character of the malady of the deceased, of certain obtrusive and eager inquiries on the part of her medical men, and of the remote and exposed situation of the burial-ground of the family. I will not deny that

° All the works listed here are actual books.

when I called to mind the sinister countenance of the person whom I met upon the staircase, on the day of my arrival at the house, I had no desire to oppose what I regarded as at best but a harmless, and by no means an unnatural, precaution.

At the request of Usher, I personally aided him in the arrangements for the temporary emtombment. The body having been encoffined, we two alone bore it to its rest. The vault in which we placed it (and which had been so long unopened that our torches, half smothered in its oppressive atmosphere, gave us little opportunity for investigation) was small, damp, and entirely without means of admission for light; lying, at great depth, immediately beneath that portion of the building in which was my own sleeping apartment. It had been used, apparently, in remote feudal times, for the worst purposes of a donjon-keep, and, in later days, as a place of deposit for powder, or some other highly combustible substance, as a portion of its floor, and the whole interior of a long archway through which we reached it, were carefully sheathed with copper. The door, of massive iron, had been, also, similarly protected. Its immense weight caused an unusually sharp grating sound, as it moved upon its hinges.

Having deposited our mournful burden upon tressels within this region of horror, we partially turned aside the yet unscrewed lid of the coffin, and looked upon the face of the tenant. A striking similitude between the brother and sister now first arrested my attention; and Usher, divining, perhaps, my thoughts, murmured out some few words from which I learned that the deceased and himself had been twins, and that sympathies of a scarcely intelligible nature had always existed between them. Our glances, however, rested not long upon the dead—for we could not regard her unawed. The disease which had thus emtombed the lady in the maturity of youth, had left, as usual in all maladies of a strictly cataleptical character, the mockery of a faint blush upon the bosom and the face, and that suspiciously lingering smile upon the lip which is so terrible in death. We replaced and screwed down the lid, and, having secured the door of iron, made our way, with toil, into the scarcely less gloomy apartments of the upper portion of the house.

And now, some days of bitter grief having elapsed, an observable change came over the features of the mental disorder of my friend. His ordinary manner had vanished. His ordinary occupations were neglected or forgotten. He roamed from chamber to chamber with hurried, unequal, and objectless step. The pallor of his countenance had assumed, if possible, a more ghastly hue—but the luminousness of his eye had utterly gone out. The once occasional huskiness of his tone was heard no more; and a tremulous quaver, as if of extreme terror, habitually characterized his utterance. There were times, indeed, when I thought his unceasingly agitated mind was laboring with some oppressive secret, to divulge which he struggled for the necessary courage. At times, again, I was obliged to resolve all into the mere inexplicable vagaries of madness, for I beheld him gazing upon vacancy for long hours, in an attitude of the profoundest attention, as if listening to some imaginary sound. It was no wonder that his condition terrified—that it infected me. I felt creeping upon me, by slow yet certain degrees, the wild influences of his own fantastic yet impressive superstitions.

It was, especially, upon retiring to bed late in the night of the seventh or eighth day after the placing of the lady Madeline within the donjon, that I experienced the full power of such feelings. Sleep came not near my couch—while the hours waned and waned away. I struggled to reason off the nervousness which had dominion over me. I endeavored to believe that much, if not all of what I felt, was due to the bewildering influence of the gloomy furniture of the room—of the dark and tattered draperies, which, tortured into motion by the breath of a rising tempest, swayed fitfully to and fro upon the walls, and rustled uneasily about the decorations of the bed. But my efforts were fruitless. An irrepressible tremor gradually pervaded my frame; and, at length, there sat upon my very heart an incubus of utterly causeless alarm. Shaking this off with a gasp and a struggle, I uplifted myself upon the pillows, and, peering earnestly within the intense darkness of the chamber, harkened—I know not why, except that an instinctive spirit prompted me—to certain low and indefinite sounds which came, through the pauses of the storm, at long intervals, I knew not whence. Overpowered by an intense sentiment of horror, unaccountable yet unendurable, I threw on my clothes with haste (for I felt that I should sleep no more during the night), and endeavored to arouse myself from the pitiable condition into which I had fallen, by pacing rapidly to and fro through the apartment.

I had taken but few turns in this manner, when a light step on an adjoining staircase arrested my attention. I presently recognised it as that of Usher. In an instant afterward he rapped, with a gentle touch, at my door, and entered, bearing a lamp. His countenance was, as usual, cadaverously wan—but, moreover, there was a species of mad hilarity in his eyes—an evidently restrained *hysteria* in his whole demeanor. His air appalled me—but anything was preferable to the solitude which I had so long endured, and I even welcomed his presence as a relief.

"And you have not seen it?" he said abruptly, after having stared about him for some moments in silence—"you have not then seen it?—but, stay! you shall." Thus speaking, and having carefully shaded his lamp, he hurried to one of the casements, and threw it freely open to the storm.

The impetuous fury of the entering gust nearly lifted us from our feet. It was, indeed, a tempestuous yet sternly beautiful night, and one wildly singular in its terror and its beauty. A whirlwind had apparently collected its force in our vicinity; for there were frequent and violent alterations in the direction of the wind; and the exceeding density of the clouds (which hung so low as to press upon the turrets of the house) did not prevent our perceiving the life-like velocity with which they flew careering from all points against each other, without passing away into the distance. I say that even their exceeding density did not prevent our perceiving this—yet we had no glimpse of the moon or stars—nor was there any flashing forth of the lightning. But the under surfaces of the huge masses of agitated vapor, as well as terrestrial objects immediately around us, were glowing in the unnatural light of a faintly luminous and distinctly visible gaseous exhalation which hung about and enshrouded the mansion.

"You must not—you shall not behold this!" said I, shudderingly, to Usher, as I led him, with a gentle violence, from the window to a seat. "These appearances, which bewilder you, are merely electrical phenomena not uncommon—or it may be that they have their ghastly origin in the rank miasma of the tarn. Let us close this casement;—the air is chilling and dangerous to your frame. Here is one of your favorite romances. I will read, and you shall listen;—and so we will pass away this terrible night together."

The antique volume which I had taken up was the *Mad Trist of Sir Launcelot Canning*;° but I had called it a favorite of Usher's more in sad jest than in earnest; for, in truth, there is little in its uncouth and unimaginative prolixity which could have had interest for the lofty and spiritual ideality of my friend. It was, however, the only book immediately at hand; and I indulged a vague hope that the excitement which now agitated the hypochrondriac, might find relief (for the history of mental disorder is full of similar anomalies) even in the extremeness of the folly which I should read. Could I have judged, indeed, by the wild overstrained air of vivacity with which he harkened, or apparently harkened, to the words of the tale, I might well have congratulated myself upon the success of my design.

I had arrived at that well-known portion of the story where Ethelred, the hero of the Trist, having sought in vain for peaceable admission into the dwelling of the hermit, proceeds to make good an entrance by force. Here, it will be remembered, the words of the narrative run thus:

"And Ethelred, who was by nature of a doughty heart, and who was now mighty withal, on account of the powerfulness of the wine which he had drunken, waited no longer to hold parley with the hermit, who, in sooth, was of an obstinate and maliceful turn, but, feeling the rain upon his shoulders, and fearing the rising of the tempest, uplifted his mace outright, and, with blows, made quickly room in the plankings of the door

---

° *Mad Trist* . . .: this book has never been identified by scholars; it was probably invented by Poe.

for his gauntleted hand; and now pulling therewith sturdily, he so cracked, and ripped, and tore all asunder, that the noise of the dry and hollow-sounding wood alarummed and reverberated throughout the forest."

At the termination of this sentence I started, and for a moment, paused; for it appeared to me (although I at once concluded that my excited fancy had deceived me)—it appeared to me that, from some very remote portion of the mansion, there came, indistinctly, to my ears, what might have been, in its exact similarity of character, the echo (but a stifled and dull one certainly) of the very cracking and ripping sound which Sir Launcelot had so particularly described. It was, beyond doubt, the coincidence alone which had arrested my attention; for, amid the rattling of the sashes of the casements, and the ordinary commingled noises of the still increasing storm, the sound, in itself, had nothing, surely, which should have interested or disturbed me. I continued the story:

"But the good champion Ethelred, now entering within the door, was sore enraged and amazed to perceive no signal of the maliceful hermit; but, in the stead thereof, a dragon of a scaly and prodigious demeanor, and of a fiery tongue, which sate in guard before a palace of gold, with a floor of silver; and upon the wall there hung a shield of shining brass with this legend enwritten—

Who entereth herein, a conqueror hath bin;
Who slayeth the dragon, the shield he shall win;

And Ethelred uplifted his mace, and struck upon the head of the dragon, which fell before him, and gave up his pesty breath, with a shriek so horrid and harsh, and withal so piercing, that Ethelred had fain to close his ears with his hands against the dreadful noise of it, the like whereof was never before heard."

Here again I paused abruptly, and now with a feeling of wild amazement—for there could be no doubt whatever that, in this instance, I did actually hear (although from what direction it proceeded I found it impossible to say) a low and apparently distant, but harsh, protracted, and most unusual screaming or grating sound—the exact counterpart of what my fancy had already conjured up for the dragon's unnatural shriek as described by the romancer.

Oppressed, as I certainly was, upon the occurrence of this second and most extraordinary coincidence, by a thousand conflicting sensations, in which wonder and extreme terror were predominant, I still retained sufficient presence of mind to avoid exciting, by any observation, the sensitive nervousness of my companion. I was by no means certain that he had noticed the sounds in question; although, assuredly, a strange alteration had, during the last few minutes, taken place in his demeanor. From a position fronting my own, he had gradually brought round his chair, so as to sit with his face to the door of the chamber; and thus I could but partially perceive his features, although I saw that his lips trembled as if he were murmuring inaudibly. His head had dropped upon his breast—yet I knew that he was not asleep, from the wide and rigid opening of the eye as I caught a glance of it in profile. The motion of his body, too, was at variance with this idea—for he rocked from side to side with a gentle yet constant and uniform sway. Having rapidly taken notice of all this, I resumed the narrative of Sir Launcelot, which thus proceeded:

"And now, the champion, having escaped from the terrible fury of the dragon, bethinking himself of the brazen shield, and of the breaking up of the enchantment which was upon it, removed the carcass from out of the way before him, and approached valorously over the silver pavement of the castle to where the shield was upon the wall; which in sooth tarried not for his full coming, but fell down at his feet upon the silver floor, with a mighty great and terrible ringing sound."

No sooner had these syllables passed my lips, than—as if a shield of brass had indeed, at the moment, fallen heavily upon a floor of silver—I became aware of a distinct, hollow, metallic, and clangorous, yet apparently muffled reverberation. Completely unnerved, I leaped to my feet; but the measured rocking movement of Usher was undisturbed. I rushed to the chair in which he sat. His eyes were bent fixedly before him, and throughout his whole countenance there reigned a stony rigidity. But, as I placed my hand upon his shoulder, there came a strong shudder over his whole person; a sickly smile quivered about his lips; and I saw that he spoke in a low, hurried, and gibbering murmur, as if unconscious of my presence. Bending closely over him, I at length drank in the hideous import of his words.

"Not hear it?—yes, I hear it, and *have* heard it. Long—long—long— many minutes, many hours, many days, have I heard it—yet I dared not—oh, pity me, miserable wretch that I am!—I dared not—I *dared* not speak! *We have put her living in the tomb!* Said I not that my senses were acute? I *now* tell you that I heard her first feeble movements in the hollow coffin. I heard them—many, many days ago—yet I dared not—*I dared not speak!* And now—to-night—Ethelred—ha! ha!—the breaking of the hermit's door, and the death-cry of the dragon, and the clangor of the shield!—say, rather, the rending of her coffin, and the grating of the iron hinges of her prison, and her struggles within the coppered archway of the vault! Oh whither shall I fly? Will she not be here anon? Is she not hurrying to upbraid me for my haste? Have I not heard her footstep on the stair? Do I not distinguish that heavy and horrible beating of her heart? Madman!"—here he sprang furiously to his feet, and shrieked out his syllables, as if in the effort he were giving up his soul—*"Madman! I tell you that she now stands without the door!"*

As if in the superhuman energy of his utterance there had been found the potency of a spell—the huge antique pannels to which the speaker pointed, threw slowly back, upon the instant, their ponderous and ebony jaws. It was the work of the rushing gust—but then without those doors there *did* stand the lofty and enshrouded figure of the lady Madeline of Usher. There was blood upon her white robes, and the evidence of some bitter struggle upon every portion of her emaciated frame. For a moment she remained trembling and reeling to and fro upon the threshold—then, with a low moaning cry, fell heavily inward upon the person of her brother, and in her violent and now final death-agonies, bore him to the floor a corpse, and a victim to the terrors he had anticipated.

From the chamber, and from that mansion, I fled aghast. The storm was still abroad in all its wrath as I found myself crossing the old causeway. Suddenly there shot along the path a wild light, and I turned to see whence a gleam so unusual could have issued; for the vast house and its shawdows were alone behind me. The radiance was that of the full, setting, and blood-red moon, which now shone vividly through that once barely-discernible fissure, of which I have before spoken as extending from the roof of the building, in a zigzag direction, to the base. While I gazed, this fissure rapidly widened—there came a fierce breath of the whirlwind—the entire orb of the satellite burst at once upon my sight—my brain reeled as I saw the mighty walls rushing asunder—there was a long tumultuous shouting sound like the voice of a thousand waters—and the deep and dank tarn at my feet closed sullenly and silently over the fragments of the *"House of Usher."*

D. H. LAWRENCE   (1885–1930)

The Horse Dealer's Daughter

"Well, Mabel, and what are you going to do with yourself?" asked Joe, with foolish flippancy. He felt quite safe himself. Without listening for an answer, he turned aside, worked a grain of tobacco to the tip of his tongue, and spat it out. He did not care about anything, since he felt safe himself.

The three brothers and the sister sat round the desolate breakfast-table, attempting some sort of desultory consultation. The morning's post had given the final tap to the family fortunes, and all was over. The dreary dining-room itself, with is heavy mahogany furniture, looked as if it were waiting to be done away with.

But the consultation amounted to nothing. There was a strange air of ineffectuality about the three men, as they sprawled at table, smoking and reflecting vaguely on their own condition. The girl was alone, a rather short, sullen-looking young woman of twenty-seven. She did not share the same life as her brothers. She would have been good-looking, save for the impressive fixity of her face, 'bull-dog', as her brothers called it.

There was a confused tramping of horses' feet outside. The three men all sprawled round in their chairs to watch. Beyond the dark holly bushes that separated the strip of lawn from the high-road, they could see a cavalcade of shire horses swinging out of their own yard, being taken for exercise. This was the last time. These were the last horses that would go through their hands. The young men watched with critical, callous look. They were all frightened at the collapse of their lives, and the sense of disaster in which they were involved left them no inner freedom.

Yet they were three fine, well-set fellows enough. Joe, the eldest, was a man of thirty-three, broad and handsome in a hot, flushed way. His face was red, he twisted his black moustache over a thick finger, his eyes were shallow and restless. He had a sensual way of uncovering his teeth when he laughed, and his bearing was stupid. Now he watched the horses with a glazed look of helplessness in his eyes, a certain stupor of downfall.

The great draught-horses swung past. They were tied head to tail, four of them, and they heaved along to where a lane branched off from the high-road, planting their great hoofs floutingly in the fine black mud, swinging their great rounded haunches sumptuously, and trotting a few sudden steps as they were led into the lane, round the corner. Every movement showed a massive, slumbrous strength, and a stupidity which held them in subjection. The groom at the head looked back, jerking the leading rope. And the cavalcade moved out of sight up the lane, the tail of the last horse, bobbed up right and stiff, held out taut from the swinging great haunches as they rocked behind the hedges in a motion-like sleep.

Joe watched with glazed hopeless eyes. The horses were almost like his own body to him. He felt he was done for now. Luckily he was engaged to a woman as old as himself, and therefore her father, who was steward of a neighbouring estate, would provide him with a job. He would marry and go into harness. His life was over, he would be a subject animal now.

He turned uneasily aside, the retreating steps of the horses echoing in his ears. Then, with foolish restlessness, he reached for the scraps of bacon-rind from the plates, and making a faint whistling sound, flung them to the terrier that lay against the fender. He watched the dog swallow them, and waited till the creature looked into his eyes. Then a faint grin came on his face, and in a high, foolish voice he said:

"You won't get much more bacon, shall you, you little b———?"

The dog faintly and dismally wagged its tail, then lowered its haunches, circled round, and lay down again.

There was another helpless silence at the table. Joe sprawled uneasily in his seat, not willing to go till the family conclave was dissolved. Fred

Henry, the second brother, was erect, clean-limbed, alert. He had watched the passing of the horses with more *sang-froid*. If he was an animal, like Joe, he was an animal which controls, not one which is controlled. He was master of any horse, and he carried himself with a well-tempered air of mastery. But he was not master of the situations of life. He pushed his coarse brown moustache upwards, off his lip, and glanced irritably at his sister, who sat impassive and inscrutable.

"You'll go and stop with Lucy for a bit, shan't you?" he asked. The girl did not answer.

"I don't see what else you can do," persisted Fred Henry.

"Go as a skivvy," Joe interpolated laconically.

The girl did not move a muscle.

"If I was her, I should go in for training for a nurse," said Malcolm, the youngest of them all. He was the baby of the family, a young man of twenty-two, with a fresh, jaunty *museau*.

But Mabel did not take any notice of him. They had talked at her and round her for so many years, that she hardly heard them at all.

The marble clock on the mantelpiece softly chimed the half-hour, the dog rose uneasily from the hearth-rug and looked at the party at the breakfast-table. But still they sat on in ineffectual conclave.

"Oh, all right," said Joe suddenly, apropos of nothing. "I'll get a move on."

He pushed back his chair, straddled his knees with a downward jerk, to get them free, in horsey fashion, and went to the fire. Still he did not go out of the room; he was curious to know what the others would do or say. He began to charge his pipe, looking down at the dog and saying in a high, affected voice:

"Going wi' me? Going wi' me are ter? Tha'rt goin' further than tha counts on just now, dost hear?"

The dog faintly wagged its tail, the man stuck out his jaw and covered his pipe with his hands, and puffed intently, losing himself in the tobacco, looking down all the while at the dog with an absent brown eye. The dog looked up at him in mournful distrust. Joe stood with his knees stuck out, in real horsey fashion.

"Have you had a letter from Lucy?" Fred Henry asked of his sister.

"Last week," came the neutral reply.

"And what does she say?"

There was no answer.

"Does she *ask* you to go and stop there?" persisted Fred Henry.

"She says I can if I like."

"Well, then, you'd better. Tell her you'll come on Monday."

This was received in silence.

"That's what you'll do then, is it?" said Fred Henry, in some exasperation.

But she made no answer. There was a silence of futility and irritation in the room. Malcolm grinned fatuously.

"You'll have to make up your mind between now and next Wednesday," said Joe loudly, "or else find yourself lodgings on the kerbstone."

The face of the young woman darkened, but she sat on immutable.

"Here's Jack Ferguson!" exclaimed Malcolm, who was looking aimlessly out of the window.

"Where?" exclaimed Joe loudly.

"Just gone past."

"Coming in?"

Malcolm craned his neck to see the gate.

"Yes," he said.

There was a silence. Mabel sat on like one condemned, at the head of the table. Then a whistle was heard from the kitchen. The dog got up and barked sharply. Joe opened the door and shouted:

"Come on."

After a moment a young man entered. He was muffled up in overcoat and a purple woollen scarf, and his tweed cap, which he did not remove, was pulled down on his head. He was of medium height, his face was rather long and pale, his eyes looked tired.

"Hello, Jack! Well, Jack!" exclaimed Malcolm and Joe. Fred Henry merely said: "Jack."

"What's doing?" asked the newcomer, evidently addressing Fred Henry.

"Same. We've got to be out by Wednesday. Got a cold?"

"I have—got it bad, too."

"Why don't you stop in?"

"*Me* stop in? When I can't stand on my legs, perhaps I shall have a chance." The young man spoke huskily. He had a slight Scotch accent.

"It's a knock-out, isn't it," said Joe, boisterously, "if a doctor goes round croaking with a cold. Looks bad for the patients, doesn't it?"

The young doctor looked at him slowly.

"Anything the matter with *you*, then?" he asked sarcastically.

"Not as I know of. Damn your eyes, I hope not. Why?"

"I thought you were very concerned about the patients, wondered if you might be one yourself."

"Damn it, no, I've never been patient to no flaming doctor, and hope I never shall be," returned Joe.

At this point Mabel rose from the table, and they all seemed to become aware of her existence. She began putting the dishes together. The young doctor looked at her, but did not address her. He had not greeted her. She went out of the room with the tray, her face impassive and unchanged.

"When are you off then, all of you?" asked the doctor.

"I'm catching the eleven-forty," replied Malcolm. "Are you goin' down wi' th' trap, Joe?"

"Yes, I've told you I'm going down wi' th' trap, haven't I?"

"We'd better be getting her in then. So long, Jack, if I don't see you before I go," said Malcolm, shaking hands.

He went out, followed by Joe, who seemed to have his tail between his legs.

"Well, this is the devil's own," exclaimed the doctor, when he was left alone with Fred Henry. "Going before Wednesday, are you?"

"That's the orders," replied the other.

"Where, to Northampton?"

"That's it."

"The devil!" exclaimed Ferguson, with quiet chagrin.

And there was silence between the two.

"All settled up, are you?" asked Ferguson.

"About."

There was another pause.

"Well, I shall miss yer, Freddy, boy," said the young doctor.

"And I shall miss thee, Jack," returned the other.

"Miss you like hell," mused the doctor.

Fred Henry turned aside. There was nothing to say. Mabel came in again, to finish clearing the table.

"What are *you* going to do, then, Miss Pervin?" asked Fergusson. "Going to your sister's, are you?"

Mabel looked at him with her steady, dangerous eyes, that always made him uncomfortable, unsettling his superficial ease.

"No," she said.

"Well, what in the name of fortune *are* you going to do? Say what you mean to do," cried Fred Henry, with futile intensity.

But she only averted her head, and continued her work. She folded the white table-cloth, and put on the chenille cloth.

"The sulkiest bitch that ever trod!" muttered her brother.

But she finished her task with perfectly impassive face, the young doctor watching her interestedly all the while. Then she went out.

Fred Henry stared after her, clenching his lips, his blue eyes fixing in sharp antagonism, as he made a grimace of sour exasperation.

"You could bray her into bits, and that's all you'd get out of her," he said, in a small, narrowed tone.

The doctor smiled faintly.

"What's she *going* to do, then?" he asked.

"Strike me if *I* know!" returned the other.

There was a pause. Then the doctor stirred.

"I'll be seeing you to-night, shall I?" he said to his friend.

"Ay—where's it to be? Are we going over to Jessdale?"

"I don't know. I've got such a cold on me. I'll come round to the 'Moon and Stars', anyway."

"Let Lizzie and May miss their night for once, eh?"

"That's it—if I feel as I do now."

"All's one————"

The two young men went through the passage and down to the back door together. The house was large, but it was servantless now, and desolate. At the back was a small bricked houseyard and beyond that a big square, gravelled fine and red, and having stables on two sides. Sloping, dank, winter-dark fields stretched away on the open sides.

But the stables were empty. Joseph Pervin, the father of the family, had been a man of no education, who had become a fairly large horse dealer. The stables had been full of horses, there was a great turmoil and come-and-go of horses and of dealers and grooms. Then the kitchen was full of servants. But of late things had declined. The old man had married a second time, to retrieve his fortunes. Now he was dead and everything was gone to the dogs, there was nothing but debt and threatening.

For months, Mabel had been servantless in the big house, keeping the home together in penury for her ineffectual brothers. She had kept house for ten years. But previously it was with unstinted means. Then, however brutal and coarse everything was, the sense of money had kept her proud, confident. The men might be foul-mouthed, the women in the kitchen might have bad reputations, her brothers might have illegitimate children. But so long as there was money, the girl felt herself established, and brutally proud, reserved.

No company came to the house, save dealers and coarse men. Mabel had no associates of her own sex, after her sister went away. But she did not mind. She went regularly to church, she attended to her father. And she lived in the memory of her mother, who had died when she was fourteen, and whom she had loved. She had loved her father, too, in a different way, depending upon him, and feeling secure in him, until at the age of fifty-four he married again. And then she had set hard against him. Now he had died and left them all hopelessly in debt.

She had suffered badly during the period of poverty. Nothing, however, could shake the curious, sullen, animal pride that dominated each member of the family. Now, for Mabel, the end had come. Still she would not cast about her. She would follow her own way just the same. She would always hold the keys of her own situation. Mindless and persistent, she endured from day to day. Why should she think? Why should she answer anybody? It was enough that this was the end, and there was no way out. She need not pass any more darkly along the main street of the small town, avoiding every eye. She need not demean herself any more, going into the shops and buying the cheapest food. This was at an end. She thought of nobody, not even of herself. Mindless and persistent, she seemed in a sort of ecstasy to be coming nearer to her fulfilment, her own glorification, approaching her dead mother, who was glorified.

In the afternoon she took a little bag, with shears and sponge and a small scrubbing-brush, and went out. It was a grey, wintry day, with saddened, dark green fields and an atmosphere blackened by the smoke of foundries not far off. She went quickly, darkly along the causeway, heeding nobody, through the town to the churchyard.

There she always felt secure, as if no one could see her, although as a matter of fact she was exposed to the stare of everyone who passed along under the churchyard wall. Nevertheless, once under the shadow of the great looming church, among the graves, she felt immune from the world, reserved within the thick churchyard wall as in another country.

Carefully she clipped the grass from the grave, and arranged the pinky white, small chrysanthemums in the tin cross. When this was done, she took an empty jar from a neighbouring grave, brought water, and carefully, most scrupulously sponged the marble headstone and the coping-stone.

It gave her sincere satisfaction to do this. She felt in immediate contact with the world of her mother. She took minute pains, went through the park in a state bordering on pure happiness, as if in performing this task she came into a subtle, intimate connection with her mother. For the life she followed here in the world was far less real than the world of death she inherited from her mother.

The doctor's house was just by the church. Fergusson, being a mere hired assistant, was slave to the country-side. As he hurried now to attend to the out-patients in the surgery, glancing across the graveyard with his quick eye, he saw the girl at her task at the grave. She seemed so intent and remote, it was like looking into another world. Some mystical element was touched in him. He slowed down as he walked, watching her as if spellbound.

She lifted her eyes, feeling him looking. Their eyes met. And each looked again at once, each feeling, in some way, found out by the other. He lifted his cap and passed on down the road. There remained distinct in his consciousness, like a vision, the memory of her face, lifted from the tombstone in the churchyard, and looking at him with slow, large, portentous eyes. It *was* portentous, her face. It seemed to mesmerise him. There was a heavy power in her eyes which laid hold of his whole being, as if he had drunk some powerful drug. He had been feeling weak and done before. Now the life came back into him, he felt delivered from his own fretted, daily self.

He finished his duties at the surgery as quickly as might be, hastily filling up the bottles of the waiting people with cheap drugs. Then, in perpetual haste, he set off again to visit several cases in another part of his round, before tea-time. At all times he preferred to walk if he could, but particularly when he was not well. He fancied the motion restored him.

The afternoon was falling. It was grey, deadened, and wintry, with a slow, moist, heavy coldness sinking in and deadening all the faculties. But why should he think or notice? He hastily climbed the hill and turned across the dark green fields, following the black cinder-track. In the distance, across a shallow dip in the country, the small town was clustered like smouldering ash, a tower, a spire, a heap of low, raw, extinct houses. And on the nearest fringe of the town, sloping into the dip, was Oldmeadow, the Pervins' house. He could see the stables and the outbuildings distinctly, as they lay towards him on the slope. Well, he would not go there many more times! Another resource would be lost to him, another place gone: the only company he cared for in the alien, ugly little town he was losing. Nothing but work, drudgery, constant hastening from dwelling to dwelling among the colliers and the iron-workers. It wore him out, but at the same time he had a craving for it. It was a stimulant to him to be in the homes of the working people, moving, as it were, through the innermost body of their life. His nerves were excited and gratified. He could come so near, into the very lives of the rough, inarticulate, powerfully emotional men and women. He grumbled, he said he hated the hellish hole. But as a matter of fact it excited him, the contact with the rough, strongly-feeling people was a stimulant applied direct to his nerves.

Below Oldmeadow, in the green, shallow, soddened hollow of fields, lay a square, deep pond. Roving across the landscape, the doctor's quick eye detected a figure in black passing through the gate of the field, down towards the pond. He looked again. It would be Mabel Pervin. His mind suddenly became alive and attentive.

Why was she going down there? He pulled up on the path on the slope above, and stood staring. He could just make sure of the small black figure moving in the hollow of the failing day. He seemed to see her in the midst of such obscurity, that he was like a clairvoyant, seeing rather with the mind's eye than with ordinary sight. Yet he could see her positively enough, whilst he kept his eye attentive. He felt, if he looked away from her, in the thick, ugly falling dusk, he would lose her altogether.

He followed her minutely as she moved, direct and intent, like something transmitted rather than stirring in voluntary activity, straight down the field towards the pond. There she stood on the bank for a moment. She never raised her head. Then she waded slowly into the water.

He stood motionless as the small black figure walked slowly and deliberately towards the centre of the pond, very slowly, gradually moving deeper into the motionless water, and still moving forward as the water got up to her breast. Then he could see her no more in the dusk of the dead afternoon.

"There!" he exclaimed. "Would you believe it?"

And he hastened straight down, running over the wet, soddened fields, pushing through the hedges, down into the depression of callous wintry obscurity. It took him several minutes to come to the pond. He stood on the bank, breathing heavily. He could see nothing. His eyes seemed to penetrate the dead water. Yes, perhaps that was the dark shadow of her black clothing beneath the surface of the water.

He slowly ventured into the pond. The bottom was deep, soft clay, he sank in, and the water clasped dead cold round his legs. As he stirred he could smell the cold, rotten clay that fouled up into the water. It was objectionable in his lungs. Still, repelled and yet not heeding, he moved deeper into the pond. The cold water rose over his thighs, over his loins, upon his abdomen. The lower part of his body was all sunk in the hideous cold element. And the bottom was so deeply soft and uncertain, he was afraid of pitching with his mouth underneath. He could not swim, and was afraid.

He crouched a little, spreading his hands under the water and moving them round, trying to feel for her. The dead cold pond swayed upon his chest. He moved again, a little deeper, and again, with his hands underneath, he felt all around under the water. And he touched her clothing. But it evaded his fingers. He made a desperate effort to grasp it.

And so doing he lost his balance and went under, horribly, suffocating in the foul earthy water, struggling madly for a few moments. At last, after what seemed an eternity, he got his footing, rose again into the air and looked around. He gasped, and knew he was in the world. Then he looked at the water. She had risen near him. He grasped her clothing, and drawing her nearer, turned to take his way to land again.

He went very slowly, carefully, absorbed in the slow progress. He rose higher, climbing out of the pond. The water was now only about his legs; he was thankful, full of relief to be out of the clutches of the pond. He lifted her and staggered on to the bank, out of the horror of wet, grey clay.

He laid her down on the bank. She was quite unconscious and running with water. He made the water come from her mouth, he worked to restore her. He did not have to work very long before he could feel the breathing begin again in her; she was breathing naturally. He worked a little longer. He could feel her live beneath his hands; she was coming back. He wiped her face, wrapped her in his overcoat, looked round into the dim, dark grey world, then lifted her and staggered down the bank and across the fields.

It seemed an unthinkably long way, and his burden so heavy he felt he would never get to the house. But at last he was in the stable-yard, and then in the house-yard. He opened the door and went into the house. In the kitchen he laid her down on the hearth-rug and called. The house was empty. But the fire was burning in the grate.

Then again he kneeled to attend to her. She was breathing regularly, her eyes were wide open and as if conscious, but there seemed something missing in her look. She was conscious in herself, but unconscious of her surroundings.

He ran upstairs, took blankets from a bed, and put them before the fire to warm. Then he removed her saturated, earthy-smelling clothing, rubbed her dry with a towel, and wrapped her naked in the blankets. Then he went into the dining-room, to look for spirits. There was a little whisky. He drank a gulp himself, and put some into her mouth.

The effect was instantaneous. She looked full into his face, as if she had been seeing him for some time, and yet had only just become conscious of him.

"Dr. Fergusson?" she said.

"What?" he answered.

He was divesting himself of his coat, intending to find some dry clothing upstairs. He could not bear the smell of the dead, clayey water, and he was mortally afraid for his own health.

"What did I do?" she asked.

"Walked into the pond," he replied. He had begun to shudder like one sick, and could hardly attend to her. Her eyes remained full on him, he seemed to be going dark in his mind, looking back at her helplessly. The shuddering became quieter in him, his life came back to him, dark and unknowing, but strong again.

"Was I out of my mind?" she asked, while her eyes were fixed on him all the time.

"Maybe, for the moment," he replied. He felt quiet, because his strength had come back. The strange fretful strain had left him.

"Am I out of my mind now?" she asked.

"Are you?" he reflected a moment. "No," he answered truthfully, "I don't see that you are." He turned his face aside. He was afraid now, because he felt dazed, and felt dimly that her power was stronger than his, in this issue. And she continued to look at him fixedly all the time. "Can you tell me where I shall find some dry things to put on?" he asked.

"Did you dive into the pond for me?" she asked.

"No," he answered. "I walked in. But I went in overhead as well."

There was silence for a moment. He hesitated. He very much wanted to go upstairs to get into dry clothing. But there was another desire in him. And she seemed to hold him. His will seemed to have gone to sleep, and left him, standing there slack before her. But he felt warm inside himself. He did not shudder at all, though his clothes were sodden on him.

"Why did you?" she asked.

"Because I didn't want you to do such a foolish thing," he said.

"It wasn't foolish," she said, still gazing at him as she lay on the floor, with a sofa cushion under her head. "It was the right thing to do. I knew best, then."

"I'll go and shift these wet things," he said. But still he had not the power to move out of her presence, until she sent him. It was as if she had the life of his body in her hands, and he could not extricate himself. Or perhaps he did not want to.

Suddenly she sat up. Then she became aware of her own immediate condition. She felt the blankets about her, she knew her own limbs. For a moment it seemed as if her reason were going. She looked round, with wild eye, as if seeking something. He stood still with fear. She saw her clothing lying scattered.

"Who undressed me?" she asked, her eyes resting full and inevitable on his face.

"I did," he replied, "to bring you round."

For some moments she sat and gazed at him awfully, her lips parted.

"Do you love me, then?" she asked.

He only stood and stared at her, fascinated. His soul seemed to melt.

She shuffled forward on her knees, and put her arms round him, round his legs, as he stood there, pressing her breasts against his knees and thighs, clutching him with strange, convulsive certainty, pressing his thighs against her, drawing him to her face, her throat, as she looked up at him with flaring, humble eyes of transfiguration, triumphant in first possession.

"You love me," she murmured, in strange transport, yearning and triumphant and confident. "You love me. I know you love me, I know."

And she was passionately kissing his knees, through the wet clothing, passionately and indiscriminately kissing his knees, his legs, as if unaware of everything.

He looked down at the tangled wet hair, the wild, bare, animal shoulders. He was amazed, bewildered, and afraid. He had never thought of loving her. He had never wanted to love her. When he rescued her and restored her, he was a doctor, and she was a patient. He had had no single personal thought of her. Nay, this introduction of the personal element was very distasteful to him, a violation of his professional honour. It was horrible to have her there embracing his knees. It was horrible. He revolted from it, violently. And yet—and yet—he had not the power to break away.

She looked at him again, with the same supplication of powerful love, and that same transcendent, frightening light of triumph. In view of the delicate flame which seemed to come from her face like a light, he was powerless. And yet he had never intended to love her. He had never intended. And something stubborn in him could not give way.

"You love me," she repeated, in a murmur of deep, rhapsodic assurance. "You love me."

Her hands were drawing him, drawing him down to her. He was afraid, even a little horrified. For he had, really, no intention of loving her. Yet her hands were drawing him towards her. He put out his hand quickly to steady himself, and grasped her bare shoulder. A flame seemed to burn the hand that grasped her soft shoulder. He had no intention of loving her: his whole will was against his yielding. It was horrible. And yet wonderful was the touch of her shoulders, beautiful the shining of her face. Was she perhaps mad? He had a horror of yielding to her. Yet something in him ached also.

He had been staring away at the door, away from her. But his hand remained on her shoulder. She had gone suddenly very still. He looked down at her. Her eyes were now wide with fear, with doubt, the light was dying from her face, a shadow of terrible greyness was returning. He could not bear the touch of her eyes' question upon him, and the look of death behind the question.

With an inward groan he gave way, and let his heart yield towards her. A sudden gentle smile came on his face. And her eyes, which never left his face, slowly, slowly filled with tears. He watched the strange water rise in her eyes, like some slow fountain coming up. And his heart seemed to burn and melt away in his breast.

He could not bear to look at her any more. He dropped on his knees and caught her head with his arms and pressed her face against his throat. She was very still. His heart, which seemed to have broken, was burning with a kind of agony in his breast. And he felt her slow, hot tears wetting his throat. But he could not move.

He felt the hot tears wet his neck and the hollows of his neck, and he remained motionless, suspended through one of man's eternities. Only now it had become indispensable to him to have her face pressed close to him; he could never let her go again. He could never let her head go away from the close clutch of his arm. He wanted to remain like that for ever, with his heart hurting him in a pain that was also life to him. Without knowing, he was looking down on her damp, soft brown hair.

Then, as it were suddenly, he smelt the horrid stagnant smell of that water. And at the same moment she drew away from him and looked at him. Her eyes were wistful and unfathomable. He was afraid of them, and he fell to kissing her, not knowing what he was doing. He wanted her eyes not to have that terrible, wistful, unfathomable look.

When she turned her face to him again, a faint delicate flush was glowing, and there was again dawning that terrible shining of joy in her eyes, which really terrified him, and yet which he now wanted to see, because he feared the look of doubt still more.

"You love me?" she said, rather faltering.

"Yes." The word cost him a painful effort. Not because it wasn't true. But because it was too newly true, the *saying* seemed to tear open again his newly-torn heart. And he hardly wanted it to be true, even now.

She lifted her face to him, and he bent forward and kissed her on the mouth, gently, with the one kiss that is an eternal pledge. And as he kissed her his heart strained again in his breast. He never intended to love her. But now it was over. He had crossed over the gulf to her, and all that he had left behind had shrivelled and become void.

After the kiss, her eyes again slowly filled with tears. She sat still, away from him, with her face drooped aside, and her hands folded in her lap. The tears fell very slowly. There was complete silence. He too sat there motionless and silent on the hearth-rug. The strange pain of his heart that was broken seemed to consume him. That he should love her? That this was love! That he should be ripped open in this way! Him, a doctor! How they would all jeer if they knew! It was agony to him to think they might know.

In the curious naked pain of the thought he looked again to her. She was sitting there drooped into a muse. He saw a tear fall, and his heart flared hot. He saw for the first time that one of her shoulders was quite uncovered, one arm bare, he could see one of her small breasts; dimly, because it had become almost dark in the room.

"Why are you crying?" he asked, in an altered voice.

She looked up at him, and behind her tears the consciousness of her situation for the first time brought a dark look of shame to her eyes.

"I'm not crying, really," she said, watching him, half frightened.

He reached his hand, and softly closed it on her bare arm.

"I love you! I love you!" he said in a soft, low vibrating voice, unlike himself.

She shrank, and dropped her head. The soft, penetrating grip of his hand on her arm distressed her. She looked up at him.

"I want to go," she said. "I want to go and get you some dry things."

"Why?" he said. "I'm all right."

"But I want to go," she said. "And I want you to change your things."

He released her arm, and she wrapped herself in the blanket, looking at him rather frightened. And still she did not rise.

"Kiss me," she said wistfully.

He kissed her, but briefly, half in anger.

Then, after a second, she rose nervously, all mixed up in the blanket. He watched her in her confusion as she tried to extricate herself and wrap herself up so that she could walk. He watched her relentlessly, as she knew. And as she went, the blanket trailing, and as he saw a glimpse of her feet and her white leg, he tried to remember her as she was when he had wrapped her in the blanket. But then he didn't want to remember, because she had been nothing to him then, and his nature revolted from remembering her as she was when she was nothing to him.

A tumbling, muffled noise from within the dark house startled him. Then he heard her voice: "There are clothes." He rose and went to the foot of the stairs, and gathered up the garments she had thrown down. Then he came back to the fire, to rub himself down and dress. He grinned at his own appearance when he had finished.

The fire was sinking, so he put on coal. The house was now quite dark, save for the light of a street-lamp that shone in faintly from beyond the holly trees. He lit the gas with matches he found on the mantelpiece. Then he emptied the pockets of his own clothes, and threw all his wet things in a heap into the scullery. After which he gathered up her sodden clothes, gently, and put them in a separate heap on the coppertop in the scullery.

It was six o'clock on the clock. His own watch had stopped. He ought to go back to the surgery. He waited, and still she did not come down. So he went to the foot of the stairs and called:

"I shall have to go."

Almost immediately he heard her coming down. She had on her best dress of black voile, and her hair was tidy, but still damp. She looked at him—and in spite of herself, smiled.

"I don't like you in those clothes," she said.

"Do I look a sight?" he answered.

They were shy of one another.

"I'll make you some tea," she said.

"No, I must go."

"Must you?" And she looked at him again with the wide, strained, doubtful eyes. And again, from the pain of his breast, he knew how he loved her. He went and bent to kiss her, gently, passionately, with his heart's painful kiss.

"And my hair smells so horrible," she murmured in distraction. "And I'm so awful, I'm so awful! Oh no, I'm too awful." And she broke into bitter, heart-broken sobbing. "You can't want to love me, I'm horrible."

"Don't be silly, don't be silly," he said, trying to comfort her, kissing her, holding her in his arms. "I want you, I want to marry you, we're going to be married, quickly, quickly—to-morrow if I can."

But she only sobbed terribly, and cried:

"I feel awful. I feel awful. I feel I'm horrible to you."

"No, I want you, I want you," was all he answered, blindly, with that terrible intonation which frightened her almost more than her horror lest he should *not* want her.

KATHERINE MANSFIELD   (1888–1918)

Miss Brill

Although it was so brilliantly fine—the blue sky powdered with gold and great spots of light like white wine splashed over the Jardins Publiques— Miss Brill was glad that she had decided on her fur. The air was motionless, but when you opened your mouth there was just a faint chill, like a chill from a glass of iced water before you sip, and now and again a leaf came drifting—from nowhere, from the sky. Miss Brill put up her hand and touched her fur. Dear little thing! It was nice to feel it again. She had taken it out of its box that afternoon, shaken out the moth-powder, given it a good brush, and rubbed the life back into the dim little eyes. "What has been happening to me?" said the sad little eyes. Oh, how sweet it was to see them snap at her again from the red eiderdown! . . . But the nose, which was of some black composition, wasn't at all firm. It must have had a knock, somehow. Never mind—a little dab of black sealing-wax when the time came—when it was absolutely necessary. . . . Little rogue! Yes, she really felt like that about it. Little rogue biting its tail just by her left ear. She could have taken it off and laid it on her lap and stroked it. She felt a tingling in her hands and arms, but that came from walking, she supposed. And when she breathed, something light and sad—no, not sad, exactly—something gentle seemed to move in her bosom.

There were a number of people out this afternoon, far more than last Sunday. And the band sounded louder and gayer. That was because the Season had begun. For although the band played all the year round on Sundays, out of season it was never the same. It was like some one playing with only the family to listen; it didn't care how it played if there weren't any strangers present. Wasn't the conductor wearing a new coat, too? She was sure it was new. He scraped with his foot and flapped his arms like a rooster about to crow, and the bandsmen sitting in the green rotunda blew out their cheeks and glared at the music. Now there came a little "flutey" bit—very pretty!—a little chain of bright drops. She was sure it would be repeated. It was; she lifted her head and smiled.

Only two people shared her "special" seat: a fine old man in a velvet coat, his hands clasped over a huge carved walking-stick, and a big old woman, sitting upright, with a roll of knitting on her embroidered apron. They did not speak. This was disappointing, for Miss Brill always looked forward to the conversation. She had become really quite expert, she thought, at listening as though she didn't listen, at sitting in other people's lives just for a minute while they talked round her.

She glanced, sideways, at the old couple. Perhaps they would go soon. Last Sunday, too, hadn't been as interesting as usual. An Englishman and his wife, he wearing a dreadful Panama hat and she button boots. And she'd gone on the whole time about how she ought to wear spectacles; she knew she needed them; but that it was no good getting any; they'd be sure to break and they'd never keep on. And he'd been so patient. He'd suggested everything—gold rims, the kind that curved round your ears, little pads inside the bridge. No, nothing would please her. "They'll always be sliding down my nose!" Miss Brill had wanted to shake her.

The old people sat on the bench, still as statues. Never mind, there was always the crowd to watch. To and fro, in front of the flower-beds and the band rotunda, the couples and groups paraded, stopped to talk, to greet, to buy a handful of flowers from the old beggar who had his tray fixed to the railings. Little children ran among them, swooping and laughing; little boys with big white silk bows under their chins, little girls, little French dolls, dressed up in velvet and lace. And sometimes a tiny staggerer came suddenly rocking into the open from under the trees, stopped, stared, as suddenly sat down "flop," until its small high-stepping mother, like a young hen, rushed scolding to its rescue. Other people sat on the benches and green chairs, but they were nearly always the same, Sunday after Sunday, and—Miss Brill had often noticed—there was something funny about nearly all of them. They were odd, silent, nearly all old, and from the way they stared they looked as though they'd just come from dark little rooms or even—even cupboards!

Behind the rotunda the slender trees with yellow leaves down drooping, and through them just a line of sea, and beyond the blue sky with gold-veined clouds.

Tum-tum-tum tiddle-um! tiddle-um! tum tiddley-um tum ta! blew the band.

Two young girls in red came by and two young soldiers in blue met them, and they laughed and paired and went off arm-in-arm. Two peasant women with funny straw hats passed, gravely, leading beautiful smoke-coloured donkeys. A cold, pale nun hurried by. A beautiful woman came along and dropped her bunch of violets, and a little boy ran after to hand them to her, and she took them and threw them away as if they'd been poisoned. Dear me! Miss Brill didn't know whether to admire that or not! And now an ermine toque and a gentleman in grey met just in front of her. He was tall, stiff, dignified, and she was wearing the ermine toque she'd bought when her hair was yellow. Now everything, her hair, her face, even her eyes, was the same colour as the shabby ermine, and her hand, in its cleaned glove, lifted to dab her lips, was a tiny yellowish paw. Oh, she was so pleased to see him—delighted! She rather thought they were going to meet that afternoon. She described where she'd been—everywhere, here, there, along by the sea. The day was so charming—didn't he agree? And wouldn't he, perhaps? . . . But he shook his head, lighted a cigarette, slowly breathed a great deep puff into her face, and, even while she was still talking and laughing, flicked the match away and walked on. The ermine toque was alone; she smiled more brightly than ever. But even the band seemed to know what she was feeling and played more softly, played tenderly, and the drum beat, "The Brute! The Brute!" over and over. What would she do? What was going to happen now? But as Miss Brill wondered, the ermine toque turned, raised her hand as though she'd seen someone else, much nicer, just over there, and pattered away. And the band changed again and played more quickly, more gaily than ever, and the old couple on Miss Brill's seat got up and marched away, and such a funny old man with long whiskers hobbled along in time to the music and was nearly knocked over by four girls walking abreast.

Oh, how fascinating it was! How she enjoyed it! How she loved sitting here, watching it all! It was like a play. It was exactly like a play. Who could believe the sky at the back wasn't painted? But it wasn't till a little brown dog trotted on solemn and then slowly trotted off, like a little "theatre" dog, a little dog that had been drugged, that Miss Brill discovered what it was that made it so exciting. They were all on the stage. They weren't only the audience, not only looking on; they were acting. Even she had a part and came every Sunday. No doubt somebody would have noticed if she hadn't been there; she was part of the performance after all. How strange she'd never thought of it like that before! And yet it explained why she made such a point of starting from home at just the same time each week—so as not to be late for the performance—and it also explained why she had quite a queer, shy feeling at telling her English pupils how she spent her Sunday afternoons. No wonder! Miss Brill nearly laughed out loud. She was on the stage. She thought of the old invalid gentleman to whom she read the newspaper four afternoons a week while he slept in the garden. She had got quite used to the frail head on the cotton pillow, the hollowed eyes, the open mouth and the high pinched nose. If he'd been dead she mightn't have noticed for weeks; she wouldn't have minded. But suddenly he knew he was having the paper read to him by an actress! "An actress!" The old head lifted; two points of light quivered in the old eyes. "An actress—are ye?" And Miss Brill smoothed the newspaper as though it were the manuscript of her part and said gently: "Yes, I have been an actress for a long time."

The band had been having a rest. Now they started again. And what they played was warm, sunny, yet there was just a faint chill—a something, what was it?—not sadness—no, not sadness—a something that made you want to sing. The tune lifted, lifted, the light shone; and it seemed to Miss Brill that in another moment all of them, all the whole company, would begin singing. The young ones, the laughing ones who were moving together, they would begin, and the men's voices, very resolute and brave, would join them. And then she too, she too, and the others on the benches—they would come in with a kind of accompaniment—something low, that scarcely rose or fell, something so beautiful—moving. . . . And

Miss Brill's eyes filled with tears and she looked smiling at all the other members of the company. Yes, we understand, we understand, she thought—though what they understood she didn't know.

Just at that moment a boy and a girl came and sat down where the old couple had been. They were beautifully dressed; they were in love. The hero and heroine, of course, just arrived from his father's yacht. And still soundlessly singing, still with that trembling smile, Miss Brill prepared to listen.

"No, not now," said the girl. "Not here, I can't."

"But why? Because of that stupid old thing at the end there?" asked the boy. "Why does she come here at all—who wants her? Why doesn't she keep her silly old mug at home?"

"It's her fu-fur which is so funny," giggled the girl. "It's exactly like a fried whiting."

"Ah, be off with you!" said the boy in an angry whisper. Then: "Tell me, ma petite chérie—"

"No, not here," said the girl. "Not *yet*."

On her way home she usually bought a slice of honey-cake at the baker's. It was her Sunday treat. Sometimes there was an almond in her slice, sometimes not. It made a great difference. If there was an almond it was like carrying home a tiny present—a surprise—something that might very well not have been there. She hurried on the almond Sundays and struck the match for the kettle in quite a dashing way.

But to-day she passed the baker's by, climbed the stairs, went into the little dark room—her room like a cupboard—and sat down on the red eiderdown. She sat there for a long time. The box that the fur came out of was on the bed. She unclasped the necklet quickly; quickly, without looking, laid it inside. But when she put the lid on she thought she heard something crying.

PÄR LAGERKVIST (1891–1974)

The Children's Campaign

Translated by Alan Blair

Even the children at that time received military training, were assembled in army units and exercised just as though on active service, had their own headquarters and annual manoeuvres when everything was conducted as in a real state of war. The grown-ups had nothing directly to do with this training; the children actually exercised themselves and all command was entrusted to them. The only use made of adult experience was to arrange officers' training courses for specially suitable boys, who were chosen with the greatest care and who were then put in charge of the military education of their comrades in the ranks.

These schools were of high standing and there was hardly a boy throughout the land who did not dream of going to them. But the entrance tests were particularly hard; not only a perfect physique was required but also a highly developed intelligence and character. The age of admission was six to seven years and the small cadets then received an excellent training, both purely military and in all other respects, chiefly the further moulding of character. It was also greatly to one's credit in after life to have passed through one of these schools. It was really on the splendid foundation laid here that the quality, organization and efficiency of the child army rested.

Thereafter, as already mentioned, the grown-ups in no way interfered but everything was entrusted to the children themselves. No adult might meddle in the command, in organizational details or matters of promotion. Everything was managed and supervised by the children; all decisions, even the most vital, being reached by their own little general staff. No one over fourteen was allowed. The boys then passed automatically into the first age-group of the regular troops with no mean military training already behind them.

The large child army, which was the object of the whole nation's love and admiration, amounted to three army corps of four divisions: infantry, light field artillery, medical and service corps. All physically fit boys were enrolled in it and a large number of girls belonged to it as nurses, all volunteers.

Now it so happened that a smaller, quite insignificant nation behaved in a high-handed and unseemly way toward its powerful neighbour, and the insult was all the greater since this nation was by no means an equal. Indignation was great and general and, since people's feelings were running high, it was necessary to rebuke the malapert and at the same time take the chance to subjugate the country in question. In this situation the child army came forward and through its high command asked to be charged with the crushing and subduing of the foe. The news of this caused a sensation and a wave of fervour throughout the country. The proposal was given serious consideration in supreme quarters and as a result the commission was given, with some hesitation, to the children. It was in fact a task well suited to this army, and the people's obvious wishes in the matter had also to be met, if possible.

The Foreign Office therefore sent the defiant country an unacceptable ultimatum and, pending the reply, the child army was mobilized within twenty-four hours. The reply was found to be unsatisfactory and war was declared immediately.

Unparalleled enthusiasm marked the departure for the front. The intrepid little youngsters had green sprigs in the barrels of their rifles and were pelted with flowers. As is so often the case, the campaign was begun in the spring, and this time the general opinion was that there was something symbolic in it. In the capital the little commander-in-chief and chief of general staff, in the presence of huge crowds, made a passionate speech to the troops in which he expressed the gravity of the hour and his conviction of their unswerving valour and willingness to offer their lives for their country.

The speech, made in a strong voice, aroused the greatest ecstasy. The boy—who had a brilliant career behind him and had reached his exalted position at the age of only twelve and a half—was acclaimed with wild rejoicing and from this moment was the avowed hero of the entire nation. There was not a dry eye, and those of the many mothers especially shone with pride and happiness. For them it was the greatest day in their lives. The troops marched past below fluttering banners, each regiment with its music corps at the head. It was an unforgettable spectacle.

There were also many touching incidents, evincing a proud patriotism, as when a little four-year-old, who had been lifted up on his mother's arm so that he could see, howled with despair and shouted, "I want to go, too. I want to go, too!" while his mother tried to hush him, explaining that he was too small. "Small am I, eh?" he exclaimed, punching her face so that her nose bled. The evening papers were full of such episodes showing the mood of the people and of the troops who were so sure of victory. The big march past was broadcast and the C.-in-C's speech, which had been recorded, was broadcast every evening during the days that followed, at 7.15 P.M.

Military operations had already begun, however, and reports of victory began to come in at once from the front. The children had quickly taken the offensive and on one sector of the front had inflicted a heavy defeat on the enemy, seven hundred dead and wounded and over twelve hundred prisoners, while their own losses amounted to only a hundred or so fallen. The victory was celebrated at home with indescribable rejoicing and with thanksgiving services in the churches. The newspapers were filled with accounts of individual instances of valour and pictures several columns wide of the high command, of which the leading personalities, later so well-known, began to appear now for the first time. In their joy, mothers and aunts sent so much chocolate and other sweets to the army that headquarters had to issue a strict order that all such parcels were, for the time being at any rate, forbidden, since they had made whole regiments unfit for battle and these in their turn had nearly been surrounded by the enemy.

For the child army was already far inside enemy territory and still managed to keep the initiative. The advance sector did retreat slightly in order to establish contact with its wings, but only improved its positions by so doing. A stalemate ensued in the theatre of war for some time after this.

During July, however, troops were concentrated for a big attack along the whole line and huge reserves—the child army's, in comparison with those of its opponent, were almost inexhaustible—were mustered to the front. The new offensive, which lasted for several weeks, resulted, too, in an almost decisive victory for the whole army, even though casualties were high. The children defeated the enemy all along the line, but did not manage to pursue him and thereby exploit their success to the full, because he was greatly favoured by the fact that his legs were so much longer, an advantage of which he made good use. By dint of forced marches, however, the children finally succeeded in cutting the enemy's right flank to pieces. They were now in the very heart of the country and their outposts were only a few days' march from the capital.

It was a pitched battle on a big scale and the newspapers had enormous headlines every day which depicted the dramatic course of events. At set hours the radio broadcast the gunfire and a résumé of the position. The war correspondents described in rapturous words and vivid colours the state of affairs at the front—the children's incredible feats, their indomitable courage and self-sacrifice, the whole morale of the army. It was no exaggeration. The youngsters showed the greatest bravery; they really behaved like heroes. One only had to see their discipline and contempt of death during an attack, as though they had been grownup men at least.

It was an unforgettable sight to see them storm ahead under murderous machine-gun fire and the small medical orderlies dart nimbly forward and pick them up as they fell. Or the wounded and dying who were moved behind the front, those who had had a leg shot away or their bellies ripped open by a bayonet so that their entrails hung out—but without one sound of complaint crossing their small lips. The hand-to-hand fighting had been very fierce and a great number of children fell in this, while they were superior in the actual firing. Losses were estimated at 4000 on the enemy side and 7000 among the children, according to the secret reports. The victory had been hard won but all the more complete.

This battle became very famous and was also of far greater importance than any previously. It was now clear beyond all doubt that the children were incomparably superior in tactics, discipline and individual courage. At the same time, however, it was admitted by experts that the enemy's head-long retreat was very skillfully carried out, that his strength was evidently in defence and that he should not be underrated too much. Toward the end, also, he had unexpectedly made a stubborn resistance which had prevented any further penetration.

This observation was not without truth. In actual fact the enemy was anything but a warlike nation, and indeed his forces found it very difficult to hold their own. Nevertheless, they improved with practice during the fighting and became more efficient as time went on. This meant that they caused the children a good deal of trouble in each succeeding battle. They also had certain advantages on their side. As their opponents were so small, for instance, it was possible after a little practice to spit several of them on the bayonet at once, and often a kick was enough to fell them to the ground.

But against this, the children were so much more numerous and also braver. They were everywhere. They swarmed over one and in between one's legs and the unwarlike people were nearly demented by all these small monsters who fought like fiends. Little fiends was also what they were generally called—not without reason—and this name was even adopted in the children's homeland, but there it was a mark of honour and a pet name. The enemy troops had all their work cut out merely defending themselves. At last, however, they were able to check the other's advance and even venture on one or two counter-attacks. Everything then came to a standstill for a while and there was a breathing-space.

The children were now in possession of a large part of the country. But this was not always so easy. The population did not particularly like them and proved not to be very fond of children. It was alleged that snipers fired on the boys from houses and that they were ambushed when they moved in small detachments. Children had even been found impaled on stakes or with their eyes gouged out, so it was said. And in many cases these stories were no doubt true. The population had quite lost their heads, were obviously goaded into a frenzy, and as they were of little use as a warlike nation and their cruelty could therefore find no natural outlet, they tried to revenge themselves by atrocities. They felt overrun by all the foreign children as by troublesome vermin and, being at their wits' end, they simply killed whenever they had the chance. In order to put an end to these outrages the children burned one village after the other and shot hundreds of people daily, but this did not improve matters. The despicable deeds of these craven guerrillas caused them endless trouble.

At home, the accounts of all this naturally aroused the most bitter resentment. People's blood boiled to think that their small soldiers were treated in this way by those who had nothing to do with the war, by barbarous civilians who had no notion of established and judicial forms. Even greater indignation was caused, however, by an incident that occurred inside the occupied area some time after the big summer battle just mentioned.

A lieutenant who was walking in the countryside came to a stream where a large, fat woman knelt washing clothes. He asked her the way to a village close by. The woman, who probably suspected him of evil intent, retorted, "What are you doing here? You ought to be at home with your mother." Whereupon the lieutenant drew his sabre to kill her, but the woman grabbed hold of him and, putting him over her knee, thwacked him black and blue with her washboard so that he was unable to sit down for several days afterward. He was so taken aback that he did nothing, armed though he was to the teeth. Luckily no one saw the incident, but there were orders that all outrages on the part of the population were to be reported to headquarters. The lieutenant therefore duly reported what had happened to him. True, it gave him little satisfaction, but as he had to obey orders he had no choice. And so it all came out.

The incident aroused a storm of rage, particularly among those at home. The infamous deed was a humiliation for the country, an insult which nothing could wipe out. It implied a deliberate violation by this militarily ignorant people of the simplest rules of warfare. Everywhere, in the press, in propaganda speeches, in ordinary conversation, the deepest contempt and disgust for the deed was expressed. The lieutenant who had so flagrantly shamed the army had his officer's epaulettes ripped off in front of the assembled troops and was declared unworthy to serve any longer in the field. He was instantly sent home to his parents, who belonged to one of the most noted families but who now had to retire into obscurity in a remote part of the country.

The woman, on the other hand, became a heroic figure among her people and the object of their rapturous admiration. During the whole of the war she and her deed were a rallying national symbol which people looked up to and which spurred them on to further effort. She subsequently became a favourite motif in the profuse literature about their desperate struggle for freedom; a vastly popular figure, brought to life again and again as time passed, now in a rugged, everyday way which appealed to the man in the street, now in heroic female form on a grandiose scale, to become gradually more and more legendary, wreathed in saga and myth. In some versions she was shot by the enemy; in others she lived to a ripe old age, loved and revered by her people.

This incident, more than anything else, helped to increase the bad feelings between the two countries and to make them wage the war with ever greater ruthlessness. In the late summer, before the autumn rains began, both armies, ignorant of each other's plans, simultaneously launched a violent offensive, which devastated both sides. On large sectors of the front the troops completely annihilated each other so that there was not a single survivor left. Any peaceful inhabitants thereabouts who were still alive and ventured out of their cellars thought that the war was over, because all were slain.

But soon new detachments came up and began fighting again. Great confusion arose in other quarters from the fact that in the heat of attack men ran past each other and had to turn around in order to go on fighting; and that some parts of the line rushed ahead while others came behind, so that the troops were both in front of and behind where they should have been and time and again attacked each other in the rear. The battle raged in this way with extreme violence and shots were fired from all directions at once.

When at last the fighting ceased and stock was taken of the situation, it apppeared that no one had won. On both sides there was an equal number of fallen, 12,924, and after all attacks and retreats the position of the armies was exactly the same as at the start of the battle. It was agreed that both should claim the victory. Thereafter the rain set in and the armies went to earth in trenches and put up barbed-wire entanglements.

The children were the first to finish their trenches, since they had had more to do with that kind of thing, and settled down in them as best they could. They soon felt at home. Filthy and lousy, they lived there in the darkness as though they had never done anything else. With the adaptability of children they quickly got into the way of it. The enemy found this more difficult; he felt miserable and home-sick for the life above ground to which he was accustomed. Not so the children. When one saw them in their small grey uniforms, which were caked thick with mud, and their small gas masks, one could easily think they had been born to this existence. The crept in and out of the holes down into the earth and scampered about the passages like mice. When their burrows were attacked they were instantly up on the parapet and snapped back in blind fury. As the months passed, this hopeless, harrowing life put endurance to an increasingly severe test. But they never lost courage or the will to fight.

For the enemy the strain was often too much; the glaring pointlessness of it all made many completely apathetic. But the little ones did not react like this. Children are really more fitted for war and take more pleasure in it, while grown-ups tire of it after a while and think it is boring. The boys continued to find the whole thing exciting and they wanted to go on living as they were now. They also had a more natural herd instinct; their unit and camaraderies helped them a great deal, made it easier to hold out.

But, of course, even they suffered great hardship. Especially when winter set in with its incessant rain, a cold sleet which made everything sodden and filled the trenches with mud. It was enough to unman anyone. But it would never have entered their heads to complain. However bad things were, nothing could have made them admit it. At home everyone was very proud of them. All the cinemas showed parades behind the front and the little C.-in-C. and his generals pinning medals for bravery on their soldiers' breasts. People thought of them a great deal out there, of their little fiends, realizing that they must be having a hard time.

At Christmas, in particular, thoughts went out to them, to the lighted

Christmas trees and all the sparkling childish eyes out in the trenches; in every home people sat wondering how they were faring. But the children did not think of home. They were soldiers out and out, absorbed by their duty and their new life. They attacked in several places on the morning of Christmas Eve, inflicting fairly big losses on the enemy in killed and wounded, and did not stop until it was time to open their parcels. They had the real fighting spirit which might have been a lesson even to adults.

There was nothing sentimental about them. The war had hardened and developed them, made them men. It did happen that one poor little chap burst into tears when the Christmas tree was lighted, but he was made the laughing-stock of them all. "Are you homesick for your mummy, you bastard?" they said, and kept on jeering at him all evening. He was the object of their scorn all through Christmas; he behaved suspiciously and tried to keep to himself. Once he walked a hundred yards away from the post and, because he might well have been thinking of flight, he was seized and court-martialled. He could give no reason for having absented himself, and since he had obviously intended to desert he was shot.

If those at home had been fully aware of the morale out there, they need not have worried. As it was, they wondered if the children could really hold their ground and half-regretted having entrusted them with the campaign, now that it was dragging on so long because of this nerve-racking stationary warfare. After the New Year help was even offered in secret, but it was rejected with proud indignation.

The morale of the enemy, on the other hand, was not so high. They did intend to fight to the last man, but the certainty of a complete victory was not so general as it should have been. They could not help thinking, either, how hopeless their fight really was; that in the long run they could not hold their own against these people who were armed to the very milk teeth, and this often dampened their courage.

Hardly had nature begun to come to life and seethe with the newly awakened forces of spring before the children started with incredible intensity to prepare for the decisive battle. Heavy mechanized artillery was brought up and placed in strong positions; huge troop movements went on night and day; all available fighting forces were concentrated in the very front lines. After murderous gunfire which lasted for six days, an attack was launched with great force and extreme skill. Individual bravery was, if possible, more dazzling then ever. The whole army was also a year older, and that means much at that age. But their opponents, too, were determined to do their utmost. They had assembled all their reserves, and their spirits, now that the rain had stopped and the weather was fine, were full of hope.

It was a terrible battle. The hospital trains immediately started going back from both sides packed with wounded and dying. Machine guns, tanks and gas played fearful havoc. For several days the outcome was impossible to foresee, since both armies appeared equally strong and the tide of battle constantly changed. The position gradually cleared, however. The enemy had expected the main attack in the centre, but the child army turned out to be weakest there. Use was made of this, especially because they themselves were best prepared at this very point, and this part of the children's front was soon made to waver and was forced farther and farther back by repeated attack. Advantage was also taken of an ideal evening breeze from just the right quarter to gas the children in thousands. Encouraged by their victory, the troops pursued the offensive with all their might and with equal success.

The child army's retreat, however, turned out to be a stratagem, brilliantly conceived and carried out. Its centre gave way more and more and the enemy, giving all his attention to this, forgot that at the same time he himself was wavering at both wings. In this way he ran his head into a noose. When the children considered that they had retreated far enough they halted, while the troops on the outermost wings, already far ahead, advanced swiftly until they met behind the enemy's back. The latter's entire army was thereby surrounded and in the grip of an iron hand. All the children's army had to do now was to draw the noose tighter. At last the gallant defenders had to surrender and let themselves be taken prisoner, which in fact they already were. It was the most disastrous defeat in history; not a single one escaped other than by death.

This victory became much more famous than any of the others and was eagerly studied at all military academies on account of its brilliantly executed, doubly effective encircling movement. The great general Sludelsnorp borrowed its tactics outright seventy years later at his victory over the Slivokvarks in the year 2048.

The war could not go on any longer now, because there was nothing left to fight, and the children marched to the capital with the imprisoned army between them to dictate the peace terms. These were handed over by the little commander-in-chief in the hall of mirrors in the stately old palace at a historic scene which was to be immortalized time and again in art and even now was reproduced everywhere in the weekly press. The film cameras whirred, the flashlights hissed and the radio broadcast the great moment to the world. The commander-in-chief, with austere and haughty mien and one foot slightly in front of the other, delivered the historic document with his right hand. The first and most important condition was the complete cession of the country, besides which the expenses of its capture were to be borne by the enemy, who thus had to pay the cost of the war on both sides, and the last clause on account of the fact that he had been the challenging party and, according to his own admission, the cause of the war. The document was signed in dead silence, the only sound was the scratching of the fountain pen, which, according to the commentator's whisper, was solid gold and undoubtedly a future museum piece.

With this, everything was settled and the children's army returned to its own country, where it was received with indescribable rapture. Everywhere along the roads the troops were greeted with wild rejoicing; their homecoming was one long victory parade. The march into the capital and the dismissal there of the troops, which took place before vast crowds, were especially impressive. People waved and shouted in the streets as they passed, were beside themselves with enthusiasm, bands played, eyes were filled with tears of joy. Some of the loudest cheering was for the small invalids at the rear of the procession, blind and with limbs amputated, who had sacrificed themselves for their country. Many of them had already got small artificial arms and legs so that they looked just the same as before. The victory salute thundered, bayonets flashed in the sun. It was an unforgettable spectacle.

A strange, new leaf was written in the great book of history which would be read with admiration in time to come. The nation had seen many illustrious deeds performed, but never anything as proud as this. What these children had done in their devotion and fervent patriotism could never be forgotten.

Nor was it. Each spring, on the day of victory, school children marched out with flags in their hands to the cemeteries with all the small graves where the heroes rested under their small white crosses. The mounds were strewn with flowers and passionate speeches were made, reminding everyone of the glorious past, their imperishable honour and youthful, heroic spirit of self-sacrifice. The flags floated in the sun and the voices rang out clear as they sang their rousing songs, radiant childish eyes looking ahead to new deeds of glory.

KATHERINE ANNE PORTER   (1894–1980)

He

Life was very hard for the Whipples. It was hard to feed all the hungry mouths, it was hard to keep the children in flannels during the winter, short as it was: "God knows what would become of us if we lived north," they would say: keeping them decently clean was hard. "It looks like our luck won't never let up on us," said Mr. Whipple, but Mrs. Whipple was all for taking what was sent and calling it good, anyhow when the neighbors were in earshot. "Don't ever let a soul hear us complain," she kept saying to her husband. She couldn't stand to be pitied. "No, not if it comes to it that we have to live in a wagon and pick cotton around the country," she said, "nobody's going to get a chance to look down on us."

Mrs. Whipple loved her second son, the simple-minded one, better than she loved the other two children put together. She was forever saying so, and when she talked with certain of her neighbors, she would even throw in her husband and her mother for good measure.

"You needn't keep on saying it around," said Mr. Whipple, "you'll make people think nobody else has any feelings about Him but you."

It's natural for a mother," Mrs. Whipple would remind him. "You know yourself it's more natural for a mother to be that way. People don't expect so much of fathers, some way."

This didn't keep the neighbors from talking plainly among themselves. "A Lord's pure mercy if He should die," they said. "It's the sins of the fathers," they agreed among themselves. "There's bad blood and bad doings somewhere, you can bet on that." This behind the Whipples' backs. To their faces everybody said, "He's not so bad off. He'll be all right yet. Look how He grows!"

Mrs. Whipple hated to talk about it, she tried to keep her mind off it, but every time anybody set foot in the house, the subject always came up, and she had to talk about Him first, before she could get on to anything else. It seemed to ease her mind. "I wouldn't have anything happen to Him for all the world, but it just looks like I can't keep Him out of mischief. He's so strong and active, He's always into everything; He was like that since He could walk. It's actually funny sometimes, the way He can do anything; it's laughable to see Him up to His tricks. Emly has more accidents; I'm forever tying up her bruises, and Adna can't fall a foot without cracking a bone. But He can do anything and not get a scratch. The preacher said such a nice thing once when he was here. He said, and I'll remember it to my dying day, 'The innocent walk with God—that's why He don't get hurt.'" Whenever Mrs. Whipple repeated these words, she always felt a warm pool spread in her breast, and the tears would fill her eyes, and then she could talk about something else.

He did grow and He never got hurt. A plank blew off the chicken house and struck Him on the head and He never seemed to know it. He had learned a few words, and after this He forgot them. He didn't whine for food as the other children did, but waited until it was given Him; He ate squatting in the corner, smacking and mumbling. Rolls of fat covered Him like an overcoat, and He could carry twice as much wood and water as Adna. Emly had a cold in the head most of the time—"she takes that after me," said Mrs. Whipple—so in bad weather they gave her the extra blanket off His cot. He never seemed to mind the cold.

Just the same, Mrs. Whipple's life was a torment for fear something might happen to Him. He climbed the peach trees much better than Adna and went skittering along the branches like a monkey, just a regular monkey. "Oh, Mrs. Whipple, you hadn't ought to let Him do that. He'll lose His balance sometime. He can't rightly know what He's doing."

Mrs. Whipple almost screamed out at the neighbor. "He *does* know what He's doing! He's as able as any other child! Come down out of there, you!" When He finally reached the ground she could hardly keep her hands off Him for acting like that before people, a grin all over His face and her worried sick about Him all the time.

"It's the neighbors," said Mrs. Whipple to her husband. "Oh, I do mortally wish they would keep out of our business. I can't afford to let Him do anything for fear they'll come nosing around about it. Look at the bees, now. Adna can't handle them, they sting him up so; I haven't got time to do everything, and now I don't dare let Him. But if He gets a sting He don't really mind."

"It's just because He ain't got sense enough to be scared of anything," said Mr. Whipple.

"You ought to be ashamed of yourself," said Mrs. Whipple, "talking that way about your own child. Who's to take up for Him if we don't, I'd like to know? He sees a lot that goes on, He listens to things all the time. And anything I tell Him to do He does it. Don't never let anybody hear you say such things. They'd think you favored the other children over Him."

"Well, now I don't, and you know it, and what's the use of getting all worked up about it? You always think the worst of everything. Just let Him alone, He'll get along somehow. He gets plenty to eat and wear, don't He?" Mr. Whipple suddenly felt tired out. "Anyhow, it can't be helped now."

Mrs. Whipple felt tired too, she complained in a tired voice. "What's done can't never be undone, I know that good as anybody; but He's my child, and I'm not going to have people say anything. I get sick of people coming around saying things all the time."

In the early fall Mrs. Whipple got a letter from her brother saying he and his wife and two children were coming over for a little visit next Sunday week. "Put the big pot in the little one," he wrote at the end. Mrs. Whipple read this part out loud twice, she was so pleased. Her brother was a great one for saying funny things. "We'll just show him that's no joke," she said, "we'll just butcher one of the sucking pigs."

"It's a waste and I don't hold with waste the way we are now," said Mr. Whipple. "That pig'll be worth money by Christmas."

"It's a shame and a pity we can't have a decent meal's vittles once in a while when my own family comes to see us," said Mrs. Whipple. "I'd hate for his wife to go back and say there wasn't a thing in the house to eat. My God, it's better than buying up a great chance of meat in town. There's where you'd spend the money!"

"All right, do it yourself then," said Mr. Whipple. "Christamighty, no wonder we can't get ahead!"

The question was how to get the little pig away from his ma, a great fighter, worse than a Jersey cow. Adna wouldn't try it: "That sow'd rip my insides out all over the pen." "All right, old fraidy," said Mrs. Whipple, "*He's* not scared. Watch *Him* do it." And she laughed as though it was all a good joke and gave Him a little push towards the pen. He sneaked up and snatched the pig right away from the teat and galloped back and was over the fence with the sow raging at His heels. The little black squirming thing was screeching like a baby in a tantrum, stiffening its back and stretching its mouth to the ears. Mrs. Whipple took the pig with her face stiff and sliced its throat with one stroke. When He saw the blood He gave a great jolting breath and ran away. "But He'll forget and eat plenty, just the same," thought Mrs. Whipple. Whenever she was thinking, her lips moved making words. "He'd eat it all if I didn't stop Him. He'd eat up every mouthful from the other two if I'd let Him."

She felt badly about it. He was ten years old now and a third again as large as Adna, who was going on fourteen. "It's a shame, a shame," she kept saying under her breath, "and Adna with so much brains!"

She kept on feeling badly about all sorts of things. In the first place it was the man's work to butcher; the sight of the pig scraped pink and naked made her sick. He was too fat and soft and pitiful-looking. It was simply a shame the way things had to happen. By the time she had finished it up, she almost wished her brother would stay at home.

Early Sunday morning Mrs. Whipple dropped everything to get Him all cleaned up. In an hour He was dirty again, with crawling under fences after a possum, and straddling along the rafters of the barn looking for eggs in the hayloft. "My Lord, look at you now after all my trying! And here's Adna and Emly staying so quiet. I get tired trying to keep you decent. Get off that shirt and put on another, people will say I don't half dress you!" And she boxed Him on the ears, hard. He blinked and blinked and rubbed His head, and His face hurt Mrs. Whipple's feelings. Her knees began to tremble, she had to sit down while she buttoned His shirt. "I'm just all gone before the day starts."

The brother came with his plump healthy wife and two great roaring hungry boys. They had a grand dinner, with the pig roasted to a crackling in the middle of the table, full of dressing, a pickled peach in his mouth and plenty of gravy for the sweet potatoes.

"This looks like prosperity all right," said the brother; "you're going to have to roll me home like I was a barrel when I'm done."

Everybody laughed out loud; it was fine to hear them laughing all at once around the table. Mrs. Whipple felt warm and good about it. "Oh, we've got six more of these; I say it's as little as we can do when you come to see us so seldom."

He wouldn't come into the dining room, and Mrs. Whipple passed it off very well. "He's timider than my other two," she said, "He'll just have to get used to you. There isn't everybody He'll make up with, you know how it is with some children, even cousins." Nobody said anything out of the way.

"Just like my Alfy here," said the brother's wife. "I sometimes got to lick him to make him shake hands with his own grand-mammy."

So that was over, and Mrs. Whipple loaded up a big plate for Him first, before everybody. "I always say He ain't to be slighted, no matter who else goes without," she said, and carried it to Him herself.

"He can chin Himself on the top of the door," said Emly, helping along.

"That's fine, He's getting along fine," said the brother.

They went away after supper. Mrs. Whipple rounded up the dishes, and sent the children to bed and sat down and unlaced her shoes. "You see?" she said to Mr. Whipple. "That's the way my whole family is. Nice and considerate about everything. No out-of-the-way remarks—they *have* got refinement. I get awfully sick of people's remarks. Wasn't that pig good?"

Mr. Whipple said, "Yes, we're out three hundred pounds of pork, that's all. It's easy to be polite when you come to eat. Who knows what they had in their minds all along?"

"Yes, that's like you," said Mrs. Whipple. "I don't expect anything else from you. You'll be telling me next that my own brother will be saying around that we made Him eat in the kitchen! Oh, my God!" She rocked her head in her hands, a hard pain started in the very middle of her forehead. "Now it's all spoiled, and everything was so nice and easy. All right, you don't like them and you never did—all right, they'll not come here again soon, never you mind! But they *can't* say He wasn't dressed every lick as good as Adna—oh, honest, sometimes I wish I was dead!"

"I wish you'd let up," said Mr. Whipple. "It's bad enough as it is."

It was a hard winter. It seemed to Mrs. Whipple that they hadn't ever known anything but hard times, and now to cap it all a winter like this. The crops were about half of what they had a right to expect; after the cotton was in it didn't do much more than cover the grocery bill. They swapped off one of the plow horses, and got cheated, for the new one died of the heaves. Mrs. Whipple kept thinking all the time it was terrible to have a man you couldn't depend on not to get cheated. They cut down on everything, but Mrs. Whipple kept saying there are things you can't cut down on, and they cost money. It took a lot of warm clothes for Adna and Emly, who walked four miles to school during the three-months session. "He sets around the fire a lot, He won't need so much," said Mr.

Whipple. "That's so," said Mrs. Whipple, "and when He does the outdoor chores He can wear your tarpaullion coat. I can't do no better, that's all."

In February He was taken sick, and lay curled up under His blanket looking very blue in the face and acting as if He would choke. Mr. and Mrs. Whipple did everything they could for Him for two days, and then they were scared and sent for the doctor. The doctor told them they must keep Him warm and give Him plenty of milk and eggs. "He isn't as stout as He looks, I'm afraid," said the doctor. "You've got to watch them when they're like that. You must put more cover onto Him, too."

"I just took off His big blanket to wash," said Mrs. Whipple, ashamed. "I can't stand dirt."

"Well, you'd better put it back on the minute it's dry," said the doctor, "or He'll have pneumonia."

Mr. and Mrs. Whipple took a blanket off their own bed and put His cot in by the fire. "They can't say we didn't do everything for Him," she said, "even to sleeping cold ourselves on His account."

When the winter broke He seemed to be well again, but He walked as if His feet hurt Him. He was able to run a cotton planter during the season.

"I got it all fixed up with Jim Ferguson about breeding the cow next time," said Mr. Whipple. "I'll pasture the bull this summer and give Jim some fodder in the fall. That's better than paying out money when you haven't got it."

"I hope you didn't say such a thing before Jim Ferguson," said Mrs. Whipple. "You oughtn't to let him know we're so down as all that."

"Godamighty, that ain't saying we're down. A man is got to look ahead sometimes. *He* can lead the bull over today. I need Adna on the place."

At first Mrs. Whipple felt easy in her mind about sending Him for the bull. Adna was too jumpy and couldn't be trusted. You've got to be steady around animals. After He was gone she started thinking, and after a while she could hardly bear it any longer. She stood in the lane and watched for Him. It was nearly three miles to go and a hot day, but He oughtn't to be so long about it. She shaded her eyes and stared until colored bubbles floated in her eyeballs. It was just like everything else in life, she must always worry and never know a moment's peace about anything. After a long time she saw Him turn into the side lane, limping. He came on very slowly, leading the big hulk of an animal by a ring in the nose, twirling a little stick in His hand, never looking back or sideways, but coming on like a sleepwalker with His eyes half shut.

Mrs. Whipple was scared sick of bulls; she had heard awful stories about how they followed on quietly enough, and then suddenly pitched on with a bellow and pawed and gored a body to pieces. Any second now that black monster would come down on Him, my God, He'd never have sense enough to run.

She mustn't make a sound nor a move; she mustn't get the bull started. The bull heaved his head aside and horned the air at a fly. Her voice burst out of her in a shriek, and she screamed at Him to come on, for God's sake. He didn't seem to hear her clamor, but kept on twirling His switch and limping on, and the bull lumbered along behind him as gently as a calf. Mrs. Whipple stopped calling and ran towards the house, praying under her breath: "Lord, don't let anything happen to Him. Lord, you *know* people will say we oughtn't to have sent Him. You *know* they'll say we didn't take care of Him. Oh, get Him home, safe home, safe home, and I'll look out for Him better! Amen."

She watched from the window while He led the beast in, and tied him up in the barn. It was no use trying to keep up, Mrs. Whipple couldn't bear another thing. She sat down and rocked and cried with her apron over her head.

From year to year the Whipples were growing poorer and poorer. The place just seemed to run down of itself, no matter how hard they worked. "We're losing our hold," said Mrs. Whipple. "Why can't we do like other people and watch for our best chances? They'll be calling us poor white trash next."

"When I get to be sixteen I'm going to leave," said Adna. "I'm going to get a job in Powell's grocery store. There's money in that. No more farm for me."

"I'm going to be a schoolteacher," said Emly. "But I've got to finish the eighth grade, anyhow. Then I can live in town. I don't see any chances here."

"Emly takes after my family," said Mrs. Whipple. "Ambitious every last one of them, and they don't take second place for anybody."

When fall came Emly got a chance to wait on table in the railroad eating-house in the town near by, and it seemed such a shame not to take it when the wages were good and she could get her food too, that Mrs. Whipple decided to let her take it, and not bother with school until the next session. "You've got plenty of time," she said. "You're young and smart as a whip."

With Adna gone too, Mr. Whipple tried to run the farm with just Him to help. He seemed to get along fine, doing His work and part of Adna's without noticing it. They did well enough until Christmas time, when one morning He slipped on the ice coming up from the barn. Instead of getting up He thrashed round and round, and when Mr. Whipple got to Him, He was having some sort of fit.

They brought Him inside and tried to make Him sit up, but He blubbered and rolled, so they put Him to bed and Mr. Whipple rode to town for the doctor. All the way there and back he worried about where the money was to come from: it sure did look like he had about all the troubles he could carry.

From then on He stayed in bed. His legs swelled up double their size, and the fits kept coming back. After four months, the doctor said, "It's no use, I think you'd better put Him in the County Home for treatment right away. I'll see about it for you. He'll have good care there and be off your hands."

"We don't begrudge Him any care, and I won't let Him out of my sight," said Mrs. Whipple. "I won't have it said I sent my sick child off among strangers."

"I know how you feel," said the doctor. "You can't tell me anything about that, Mrs. Whipple. I've got a boy of my own. But you'd better listen to me. I can't do anything more for Him, that's the truth."

Mr. and Mrs. Whipple talked it over a long time that night after they went to bed. "It's just charity," said Mrs. Whipple, "that's what we've come to, charity! I certainly never looked for this."

"We pay taxes to help support the place just like everybody else," said Mr. Whipple, "and I don't call that taking charity. I think it would be fine to have Him where He'd get the best of everything . . . and besides, I can't keep up with these doctor bills any longer."

"Maybe that's why the doctor wants us to send Him—he's scared he won't get his money," said Mrs. Whipple.

"Don't talke like that," said Mr. Whipple, feeling pretty sick, "or we won't be able to send Him."

"Oh, but we won't keep Him there long," said Mrs. Whipple. "Soon's He's better, we'll bring Him right back home."

"The doctor has told you and told you time and again He can't ever get better, and you might as well stop talking," said Mr. Whipple.

"Doctors don't know everything," said Mrs. Whipple, feeling almost happy. "But anyhow, in the summer Emly can come home for a vacation, and Adna can get down for Sundays: we'll all work together and get on our feet again, and the children will feel they've got a place to come to."

All at once she saw it full summer again, with the garden going fine, and new white roller shades up all over the house, and Adna and Emly home, so full of life, all of them happy together. Oh, it could happen, things would ease up on them.

They didn't talk before Him much, but they never knew just how much He understood. Finally the doctor set the day and a neighbor who owned a double-seated carryall offered to drive them over. The hospital would have sent an ambulance, but Mrs. Whipple couldn't stand to see Him going away looking so sick as all that. They wrapped Him in blankets, and the neighbor and Mr. Whipple lifted Him into the back seat of the carryall beside Mrs. Whipple, who had on her black shirtwaist. She couldn't stand to go looking like charity.

"You'll be all right, I guess I'll stay behind," said Mr. Whipple. "It don't look like everybody ought to leave the place at once."

"Besides, it ain't as if He was going to stay forever," said Mrs. Whipple to the neighbor. "This is only for a little while."

They started away, Mrs. Whipple holding to the edges of the blankets to keep Him from sagging sideways. He sat there blinking and blinking. He worked His hands out and began rubbing His nose with His knuckles, and then with the end of the blanket. Mrs. Whipple couldn't believe what she saw; He was scrubbing away big tears that rolled out of the corners of His eyes. He sniveled and made a gulping noise. Mrs. Whipple kept saying, "Oh, honey, you don't feel so bad, do you? You don't feel so bad, do you?" for He seemed to be accusing her of something. Maybe He remembered that time she boxed His ears, maybe He had been scared that day with the bull, maybe He had slept cold and couldn't tell her about it; maybe He knew they were sending Him away for good and all because they were too poor to keep Him. Whatever it was, Mrs. Whipple couldn't bear to think of it. She began to cry, frightfully, and wrapped her arms tight around Him. His head rolled on her shoulder: she had loved Him as much as she possibly could, there were Adna and Emly who had to be thought of too, there was nothing she could do to make up to Him for His life. Oh, what a mortal pity He was ever born.

They came in sight of the hospital, with the neighbor driving very fast, not daring to look behind him.

WILLIAM FAULKNER   (1897–1962)

Mayday

And the tale tells how at last one came to him. Dawn had already come without, flushing up the high small window so that this high small window which had been throughout the night only a frame for slow and scornful stars became now as a rose unfolding on the dark wall of the chapel. The song of birds came up on the dawn, and the young spring waking freshly, golden and white and troubling: flowers were birdcries about meadows unseen and birdcries were flowers necklaced about the trees. Then the sun like a swordblade touched his own stainless long sword, his morion and hauberk and greaves, and his spurs like twin golden lightnings where they rested beneath the calm sorrowful gaze of the Young Compassionate One, touching his own young face where he had knelt all night on a stone floor, waiting for day.

And it was as though he had passed through a valley between shelving vague hills where the air was gray and smelled of spring, and had come at last upon a dark hurrying stream which, as he watched, became filled suddenly with atoms of color like darting small fish, and the water was no longer dark.

"What does this signify?" he asked of a small green design with a hundred prehensile mouths which stood at his right hand, and the small green design was called Hunger.

"Wait," replied Hunger. And the darting small fish began to coalesce and to assume familiar forms. First the dark ones segregated and the light ones segregated and became stabilized and began to follow each other in measured regular succession.

"What does this signify?" he asked of a small red design with a hundred restless hands, which stood at his left hand, and the small red design was called Pain.

"Wait," replied Pain. And in the water there appeared a face which was vaguely familiar, as the green design on his right hand and the red design at his left were familiar, and then other faces; and he leaned nearer above the waters and Hunger and Pain drew closer and he knew that he was not ever to lose them. The stream was now like an endless tapestry unfolding before him. All the faces he had known and loved and hated were there, impersonal now and dispassionate; and familiar places— cottages and castles, battlements and walled towers; and forests and meads, all familiar but small, much smaller than he had remembered.

"What does this signify?" he repeated, and Hunger and Pain drew subtly nearer and said together:

"Wait."

The tapestry unrolled endlessly. It now seemed on the point of assuming a definite pattern, what he did not know, but Hunger and Pain drew subtly nearer. Here was now in the dark hurrying water a stark thin face more beautiful than death, and it was Fortitude; and a tall bright one like a pillar of silver fire, and this one was Ambition; and knights in gold and silver armour and armour of steel, bearing lances with scarlet pennons passed remote and slow and majestic as clouds across a sunset that was as blown trumpets at evening. Himself appeared at last, tiny in mock battle with quarter staff and blunt lance and sword, and Hunger lay in his belly like fire and Pain lay in all his limbs. Then Hunger touched him and said Look! and there in the hurrying dark waters was a face all young and red and white, and with long shining hair like a column of fair sunny water; and he thought of young hyacinths in the spring, and honey and sunlight. He looked upon the face for a long while, and the hundred prehensile mouths of Hunger and the hundred restless hands of Pain were upon him.

Near the stream was a tree covered with bright never-still leaves of a thousand unimaginable colors, and the tree spoke and when the tree spoke the leaves whirled into the air and spun about it. The tree was an old man with a long shining beard like a silver cuirass and the leaves were birds of a thousand kinds and colors. And he replied to the tree, saying: "What sayest thou, good Saint Francis?"

But the good Saint Francis answered only: "Wait, it is not yet time."

Then Pain touched him and he looked again into the waters. The face in the waters was the face of a girl, and Pain and Hunger lay in all his limbs and body so that he burned like fire. And the girl in the dark hurrying stream raised her white arms to him and he would have gone to her, but Pain drew him one way and Hunger drew him another way so that he could not move as she sank away from him into the dark stream that was filled with darting fragments of sound and color. Soon these too became indistinct and then the water was once more opaque and silent and hurrying, filling the world about him until he was as one kneeling on a stone floor in a dark place, waiting for day.

And the tale tells how, in a while, one came to him, saying: "Rise, Sir Galwyn, be faithful, fortunate and brave." So he rose up and put on his polished armour and the golden spurs like twin lightnings, and his bright hair was like a sun hidden by the cloudy silver of his plumed helm, and he took up his bright unscarred shield and his stainless long sword and young Sir Galwyn went out therefrom.

His horse was caparisoned in scarlet and cloth of gold and he mounted and rode forth. Trumpets saluted him, and pennons flapped out on a breeze like liquid silver, beneath a golden morning like the first morning of the world, and young Sir Galwyn's charger marched slow and stately with pride, and young Sir Galwyn looked not back whence he had come.

In a while they came to a forest. This was a certain enchanted forest and the trees in this forest were more ancient than any could remember; for it was beneath these trees that, in the olden time, one Sir Morvidus, Earl Warwick, had slain a giant which had assaulted Sir Morvidus with the trunk of a tree torn bodily from the earth; and Sir Morvidus to commemorate this encounter assumed the ragged staff for the cognizance which his descendants still bear. The trees of this forest were not as ordinary trees, for each bough bore a living eye and these eyes stared without winking at young Sir Galwyn as he rode beneath them. These boughs were never still, but writhed always as though in agony, and where one bough touched another they made desolate moaning. But young Sir Galwyn minded them not. His bright smooth face whereon naught was as yet written, shone serene beneath his plumed morion, and his beautiful blank shield whereon naught was as yet written, swung flashing from his saddlebow, while his stainless long sword made a martial clashing against his greaves and his golden spurs like twin lightnings. And Hunger and Pain rode always at his right hand and his left hand, and his shadow circled tireless before and beneath and behind him.

For seven days they rode through this forest where enchantments were as thick as mayflowers, and as they rode young Sir Galwyn conversed with Pain and Hunger, and because he was young he gained from them much information but no wisdom. On the seventh day, having pursued and slain a small dragon of an inferior and cowardly type which had evidently strayed prematurely from its den (so that this encounter is scarcely worth recording—indeed, as Hunger later reminded him, he had much better have slain a fallow deer) young Sir Galwyn and his two companions came upon a small ivycovered stone dwelling, upon the door of which young Sir Galwyn thundered stoutly with his axe helve. One appeared in reply to this summons and stood regarding young Sir Galwyn contemplatively, tickling its nose with a feather, and sneezing at intervals.

"Give you god-den, young master," said this one civilly.

Now this was civil enough, and sensible; but young Sir Galwyn was young and hasty, and being somewhat new at the trade of errantry and having expected a giant, or at least a dragon to answer his summons, knew not exactly what was expected of him here, the regulations of knighthood having no formula covering such a situation. Whereupon young Sir Galwyn, in righteous displeasure and with admirable presence of mind, thundered in return:

"What, varlét? what, minion! Would'st address a belted knight as young master? Hast no manners, knave?"

"Why now, as for that," replies the other gravely, "during all the years I have served the people it has ever been my policy to address all men as they would be addressed, king and cook, poet and hind. But, sir belted knight, before craving pardon of you I wish to remind you that we philosophers who, so to speak, live lives of retirement, cannot be expected to keep abreast of the latest quirks and fantasies of fashion regarding the approach by a stranger of a private dwelling and so forth; an we both be but as the other judge him, then by'r lady, there are two of us here without manners."

"Ah, yes: you refer to these two staring gentlemen riding beside me. But they are friends: I vouch for them both."

"Ay, I know them," replied the other, smiling a little, "I have seen both these gaudy staring gentlemen before. In fact, but for them no one would ever ride into this enchanted wood."

Young Sir Galwyn looked doubtful and a trifle bewildered at this, then his stainless long sword clashed against his greaves and reminded him that he was Sir Galwyn. So young Sir Galwyn said:

"But enough of this: we are wasting time."

"On the contrary," rejoins the other courteously, "I assure you that you are causing me no inconvenience whatever. In fact, and I do not say it to flatter you, I find our conversation most salutary."

"I am afraid, friend," says young Sir Galwyn haughtily, "that I do not follow you."

"Why, you just remarked that you were wasting time, and I do assure you that I am suffering no inconvenience whatever from this rencontre."

Then says young Sir Galwyn: "There is something wrong here: one of the two of us is laboring under a delusion. I have been led by those who should know to believe that Time is an old gentleman with a long white beard; and now you who are not old and who certainly have no long white beard, set yourself up to be Time. How can this be?"

"Well," replies the other, "as for my personal appearance: in this enlightened day when, as any standard magazine will inform you, one's appearance depends purely on one's inclination or disinclination to change it, what reason could I possibly have for wishing to look older than I feel? Then my wife (who, I am desolated to inform you, is away for the weekend, visiting her parents) my wife thinks that it does not look well for a man in my business to resemble a doddering centenarian, particularly as my new system of doing business eliminates the middle man from all dealings with my customers."

"Ah," says young Sir Galwyn, "you also have reorganized your business then? This was done recently?"

"Fairly so," agrees the other. "Yesterday it was. Though translated into your temporal currency it boils up into quite an imposing mess. Let me see—something like two million years, though I cannot give the exact date off hand."

"Oh. . . ." Young Sir Galwyn ponders briefly while Pain and Hunger sat their steeds sedately on his right hand and his left hand. Then young Sir Galwyn says: "Certainly this is spoken glibly enough, but how can I know that you are really Time?"

The other shrugged. "You materialists! You are like crows, with a single cry for all occasions: 'Proof! Proof!' Well, then; take for example the proverb Time and tide wait for no man. Do you believe in the soundness of this proverb?"

"Surely: I have demonstrated this truth to my complete satisfaction. And it seems to me that you who, by your own account, have spent your life serving mankind in this wood, convict yourself."

"Very well. Let us begin by asking these two gentlemen who have ridden with you for some time and who should know, what you are." He turned to young sir Galwyn's two companions and said: "Sir Green Design and Sir Red Design, what is this thing calling itself Sir Galwyn of Arthgyl?"

Whereupon the green design called Hunger and the red design called Pain answered together: "He is but a handful of damp clay which we draw hither and yon at will until the moisture is gone completely out of him, as two adverse winds toy with a feather; and when the moisture is all gone out of him he will be as any other pinch of dust, and we will not be concerned with him any longer."

"Why, really," says young Sir Galwyn, somewhat taken aback, "I had no idea that two travellers with whom one has shared hunger and hardship could have such an uncomplimentary opinion of one, let alone expressing it in such a bald manner. But, heigh ho, gentlemen! I see that I am but wasting my youth talking with two shadows and a doddering fool who would convince me that I am not even a shadow—a thing which I, who am Sir Galwyn of Arthgyl, know to be false just as I know that beyond the boundaries of this enchanted wood Fame awaits me with a little pain and some bloodshed, and at last much pleasure. For there I shall find and deliver from captivity a young princess whom I have seen in a dream and who reminds me of young hyacinths in spring. And which of you, who are two shadows and a doddering imbecile, can know or tell me differently?"

The green design which was called Hunger and the red design called Pain sat quietly in the intermittent shadows of young leaves, but the other raised his sad dark eyes and gazed upon young Sir Galwyn's bright empty face with envious admiration. "Ah, Sir Galwyn, Sir Galwyn," said this one, "what would I not give to be also young and heedless, yet with your sublime faith in your ability to control that destiny which some invisible and rather unimaginative practical joker has devised for you! Ah, but I too would then find this mad world an uncomplex place of light and shadow and good earth on which to disport me. Still, everyone to his taste. And certainly the taking of prodigious pains to overtake a fate which it is already written will inevitably find me, is not mine. So there is naught left but for each to follow that path which seems—no, not good: rather let us say, less evil—to him; and I who am immortal find it in my heart to envy you who are mortal and who inherited with the doubtful privilege of breathing a legacy of pain and sorrow and, at last, oblivion. Therefore, young Sir Galwyn of Arthgyl, in what way can I serve you?"

"Why, in what way save by directing me to the castle where a certain princess whose hair is like a column of fair sunny water is held captive?"

"Now your description, I am sure, is most comprehensive, and it is impossible that it fit any other princess than she who reminds you, as you have previously told me, of young hyacinths in spring. But has it not occurred to you that every young knight who rides into this enchanted wood seeks a maiden whose hair is like bright water and who reminds him of young hyacinths, or perhaps of narcissi, or of cherry bloom? So I repeat, though your description of her is most happily conceived, I must ask you to bear in mind the fact that I am an old man and that it has been many a day since a girl has clung in my heart as unforgettable as a branch of apple bloom (though my wife, I do assure you, is a matchless woman and I would not for the world have it thought that I do not appreciate her) so I fear it will be necessary for me to have something a bit more tangible than an emotional reaction to understand just what captive princess you refer to."

"Is this particular wood," says young Sir Galwyn, "so full of captive princesses that you cannot tell me which one I seek?"

"Now I do not intimate that every turret you are likely to see contains a sighing virgin playing the lute and languishing for deliverance and honorable wedlock; but certainly there are enough of them whose rank and beauty will please the most exacting taste. For instance, to the westward, not far from where the sun lies down at evening there languishes in a castle of green stone the Princess Elys, daughter of Sethynnen ap Seydnn Seidi called the Drunkard, King of Wales, and her shining sleek head is the evening star in the sky above the sunset. Or to the eastward, where the sun rises from the yellow morning, there languishes in a castle of yellow stone the Princess Aelia daughter of Aelian, prince among the Merovingians and Crown Marshal of Arles, and her shining sleek head is the morning star above the dawn. Now which of these two ladies most appeals to you? You cannot go wrong (though 'tis said the Princess Elys is rather given to tears and that the Princess Aelia being of a—well, lively disposition, left some talk behind her in Provence, not all of which was flattering. In fact, one hears that old Aelian himself had more to do with his daughter's deplorable capture than people generally know. But that is all as may be: is beside the point) Which ever one you choose, these two princes are well able to set a son-in-law up in any business he wishes."

"Ah, I do not know," says young Sir Galwyn. "How can I know which of these maidens is her whom I saw in a dream? Who is there who can tell me, since you admit that you cannot? Though I am sorry that these two princesses should pine in captivity, I cannot spend my youth chasing here and there, releasing captive maidens who for all I know are much happier in durance than they would be freed again and who might object to my meddling, for I must seek her who reminds me of honey and sunlight; and so—" young Sir Galwyn turns politely to the green design called Hunger and the red design called Pain "—and so, if you gentlemen are ready, we had better take leave of this puzzling incomprehensible stranger and get onward."

And the tale tells how young Sir Galwyn of Arthgyl rode on through this enchanted forest with Hunger at his right hand and Pain at his left hand while the hermit stood staring after young Sir Galwyn's retreating back with envious admiration. Then he shook his head and turned, and entered his hut again.

The border of the wood broke suddenly before him as a wave breaks, shattering into a froth of sunlight. Beyond him, up to the horizon and beyond it until his eyes felt like two falcons straining in their sockets, down and heath flowed in a long swooping flight to a rumourous blue haze. This was the sea.

A river cut the center of this plain, and young Sir Galwyn bore toward it. The stream was hidden beyond twinkling aspen and alder, and slender white birches like poised dancing girls; and one with a spear rose from the path, saying "Halt!"

Young Sir Galwyn regarded this green jerkined yeoman haughtily. "Stand aside, knave, and let me pass."

But the man-at-arms held his ground. "In the King's name, Lord, stop ye; else I must thrust my spear into this goodly steed, for none must pass hither on pain of my life."

"In the name of what king do you cry halt to a traveller on the public road, and to a belted knight at that? Stand aside: dost think to provoke my stainless long sword against thy scurvy carcase?"

"In the name of my master, Mark, King of Cornwall, do I bid all travellers halt at this point, for in yonder stream the princess Yseult is bathing; and no man, be he knight or varlet, may look upon the naked body of the bride of a king."

"Now, certainly," says young Sir Galwyn, "this is most strange. Who is your master, that he sends his bride gallivanting about the country, bathing in rivers, in charge of a man-at-arms?"

"It is not I who am in charge of this princess: it is King Mark's nephew, Tristram, whom you will find (were I to let you pass) lying in yonder shade and writhing with love for the maiden whom he has sworn a knightly oath to bring untarnished to the bed of his uncle. And it is my opinion that the sooner this maiden is delivered to King Mark the better for us all, for I do not like the look of this expedition. I am a family man and must take care of the appearance of things."

So young Sir Galwyn, without a backward glance at that thing which had been a Cornish man-at-arms, rode on down a shaded path towards a muted rumourous flashing of hidden water. One clad in armour rose and barred his way. "Halt, or die!" spoke this one in a terrible voice.

"Who bids Sir Galwyn of Arthgyl to halt?" rejoins young Sir Galwyn in cold displeasure, as they paused eyeing each other like two young wolf hounds. They were so much alike, from their bright young faces (though to be sure the other's face was not empty, being terrible with jealousy and passion) to their mailed feet, that it was not strange that they should hate each other on sight.

"It is Tristram of Lyonness, by the grace of God and Uther Pendragon, knight; and he who would dispute this passage will be unshriven carrion beneath this sunset."

Now certainly, thinks young sir Galwyn, I shall waste no time arguing with this unmannerly brute whose face is the color of thunder. And a would-be adulterer, also! Faith, and his vow of knighthood rests but lightly upon him who would make a Menelaus of his own uncle. But minstrels do sing of this Yseult, telling that she is as the morning star, and before her unguarded bosom's rich surprise men are maddened and their faces grow sharp as the spears of an assault. I am inclined to think it would be the part of wisdom to see this paragon of a maid while I have the opportunity, if only to tell my grandchildren of it in the years. "Ho, friend," he spake, "cannot one draw near enough to look upon this ward of thine?"

Without a word the other drew his sword and furiously attacked young Sir Galwyn, so young Sir Galwyn slew this one, and tethered his horse to a near-by tree. At the end of the glade was a screen of willow and aspen; beyond this screen, young Sir Galwyn knew, would be water. So young Sir Galwyn drew near and parted the slender willows and the tire- and waiting-women of the Princess Yseult scurried with shrill cries, like plump partridges. And the Princess Yseult, who stood like a young birch tree in the water, screamed delicately, putting her two hands before her eyes.

"Ah, Tristram, Tristram!" says she, "wouldst violate thine own uncle's bed? Mother Mary, protect me from this ravisher!" then spreading her fingers a little more: "Why, this is not Sir Tristram! Who is this strange young man who dares approach the bride of a king in her bath? Help, wenches: protect me!"

"No, lady," replies young Sir Galwyn, "I am Galwyn of Arthgyl, knight at the hand of the Constable du Boisgeclin, who, having heard the beauty of the Princess Yseult sung by many a minstrel in many a banquetting hall, must needs dare all things to see her; and who, now that he has gazed upon her, finds that all his life before this moment was a stale thing, and that all the beautiful faces upon which he has looked are as leaves in a wind; and that you who are like honey and sunlight and young hyacinths have robbed him of peace and contentment as a gale strips the leaves from a tree; and because you are the promised bride of a king there is no help for it anywhere."

Well, really, thinks the princess on hearing these words, such a nice-spoken young man would hardly have the courage to harm anyone. . . . I am afraid. Then aloud: "Who are you, and how have you managed to pass Sir Tristram, who swore that none should draw near?"

"Ah, lady," rejoins young Sir Galwyn, "what boots it who I am, who have now found all beauty and despair and all delight in an inaccessible place to which living I can never attain and which dead I can never forget? As for your Sir Tristram of Lyonness: I do not know him, unless he be one I have recently slain in yonder glade."

"Do you really think I am beautiful?" says the Princess Yseult in pleased surprise, "You say it so convincingly that I must believe you have said it before—I am sure you have said that to other girls. Now, haven't you? But I am sorry you saw me with my hair done this way. It does not suit me at all. . . . So you have killed that impossible Sir Tristram. Really I am not at all sorry: I have stood in this cold water until, as you can see—" blushing delightfully "—that my skin is completely covered with goose bumps, and I made that stupid young man promise three times that none should approach me. It is a shame that one as handsome as he should be so impossibly dull. . . . I am distressed you should have seen me with my hair done like this, but then you know what maids are in these degenerate days."

And the tale tells how the Princess Yseult came naked out of the water and she and young sir Galwyn sojourned in the shade of a tree discussing various things, and how young Sir Galwyn's glib tongue wove such a magic that the Princess Yseult purred like a kitten. And afterwards they talked some more and the Princess Yseult told young Sir Galwyn all about herself and Sir Tristram and King Mark, and so forth and so on. But after a while young Sir Galwyn began to be restlessly aware that young hyacinths were no longer fresh, once you had picked them. So breaking into the middle of the plans the Princess Yseult was comfortably making for hers and young Sir Galwyn's future, young Sir Galwyn said:

"Lady, though the sound of your voice is as that of lute strings touched sweetly among tapers in a windless dusk and therefore I will never tire of hearing it, and though your body is as a narrow pool of fair water in this twilight, do you not think—" diffidently "—that it would be wise to call your women and put something on it beside the green veils of this twilight? You know how difficult a spring cold can be."

"Why, how thoughtful of you, Galwyn! But, really now, there is no hurry, is there? Surely we cannot go anywhere this late. But then, perhaps you are right about my getting into some clothes: someone might drop in. I blush to think of it, but for some reason—though it is not at all like myself—I feel no sense of immodesty whatever in being naked with you, for you are different from other men: you really understand me. However, perhaps you are right. Do you wait here quietly for me: I shall not be long. Now, promise not to follow me, not to move."

So young Sir Galwyn promised and the Princess Yseult kissed him and closed his eyes with her finger tips and kissed his eyelids and made him promise not to open them until she was out of sight, and retired. Young Sir Galwyn was too much of a gentleman to open them or to tell the Princess Yseult that he preferred seeing her back to her front, naked or otherwise, so he sat until the Princess Yseult had had ample time to collect her women, whereupon young Sir Galwyn rose and with furtive nonchalance betook him to the tree where his horse was tethered, and where the green design called Hunger and the red design called Pain waited him courteously; and they mounted and rode away from that place. And young Sir Galwyn at last drew a deep breath.

"By my faith, sir," spoke Hunger, "that was surely no sigh of a lover reft recently of his mistress? It struck me as being rather more a sigh of relief."

"To be frank with you, friend, I do not know myself exactly what that exhalation signified. Surely, one cannot find in this world one fairer than her whom I have recently left, and it seemed to me that all life must halt while I gazed upon her body like a young birch tree in the dusk, or felt the texture of her hair like a column of sunny water; still. . . ."

"—still, this maid who is fairer than a man may hope to find more than once in a lifetime, must fain interpose between you that less fair but more tireless virtue which lives behind her little white teeth," the green design called Hunger completed for him.

"Exactly. And I now know that she is no different from all the other girls I have known, be they plain or be they beautiful. It occurs to me," young Sir Galwyn continued profoundly, "that it is not the thing itself that man wants, so much as the wanting of it. But ah, it is sharper than swords to know that she who is fairer than music could not content me for even a day."

"But that, Sir Galwyn, is what life is: a ceaseless fretting to gain shadows to which there is no substance. To my notion man is a buzzing fly blundering through a strange world, seeking something he can neither name nor recognize and probably will not want. Still, you are young and you have a certain number of years to get through some how, so better luck next time."

So they rode on beneath squadrons of high pale stars, westward where the sky was like transparent oiled green silk upon a full and glowing breast, and a single star like a silver rose pinned to it. There was a faint greenish glow about them, and fireflies were like blown sparks from invisible fires. Suddenly a milk white doe bounded into the glade before them and kneeling before young Sir Galwyn, begged him to pierce her with his sword. Young Sir Galwyn did so, and lo! there knelt before him Elys, daughter of the King of Wales. She wore a green robe and a silver girdle studded with sapphires and she took young Sir Galwyn by the hand and led him deeper into the forest to a tent of lilac colored silk and ivory poles, and a bed of rushes. And young Sir Galwyn looked into the west and he saw that the evening star was no longer there.

And the tale tells how after a while young Sir Galwyn waked and raised himself to his elbow. The Princess Elys yet slept and young Sir Galwyn looked upon her in a vague sadness, and he kissed her sleeping mouth with a feeling of pity for her and of no particular pride in himself, and he rose quietly and passed without the tent. So he mounted his horse again.

The east was becoming light: high above him the morning star swam immaculately in a river of space. He heard faint horns triumphant as flung banners, and the horns grew louder. Then all at once he was surrounded by heralds with trumpets, and sarabands of dancing girls circled about him: their breasts were stained with gold and lipped with vermilion, and pages in scarlet lept among them. Then came a chariot of gold with a canopy of amythest on scarlet poles; nine white dolphins drew the chariot and in the chariot was the Princess Aelia, daughter of Aelius the Merovingian, dressed in a yellow robe and a girdle of sapphires, and the Princess Aelia stopped and leaned toward him.

"Come, Sir Galwyn of Arthgyl. I have long awaited you."

"Ah, lady," says young Sir Galwyn, "I am as one who has thirsted in a desert, and who sees before him in a dream a region of all beauty and despair and of all delight."

The Princess Aelia was pleased at this. "What a charming speech! I have heard of you, Sir Galwyn, but I had not thought to find such a nice spoken young man, or one so handsome. So come, and please to enter my chariot, and let us be going."

So young Sir Galwyn entered, and the trumpets flourished, and the nine white dolphins which drew the chariot moved like the wind. And looking upward young Sir Galwyn saw that the morning star was gone.

"Now then," says the Princess Aelia, "we can talk comfortably. So tell me about yourself."

"What can he tell you, Princess," replies young Sir Galwyn, "who has sought the whole earth over for one he has seen in a dream, who reminds him of honey and sunlight and young hyacinths; and who at last finds her in the person of an immortal whom he may only cry after as an infant in darkness, and whom he dare not touch? And because she is fairer than the song of birds at dawn or the feet of the Loves that make light in the air like doves' wings, he may never get her out of his heart, and because she is an immortal and a princess, there is no help for it anywhere."

"Why, do you really think that I am beautiful?" says the Princess Aelia in pleased surprise. "I am sorry you saw me in this rag. I hate yellow: it makes me look—oh—fat, and I am not fat. But you say that rather glibly—" giving him a glance of bright suspicion "—how many girls have you told that to, Sir Galwyn?"

"Well," says young Sir Galwyn, slightly ill at ease, "there was a certain Yseult, going to wed with the King of Cornwall, whom I paused out of curiosity to watch bathing in a pool and who insisted on my stopping to talk with her (which I could not refuse out of sheer politeness) I think I said something of this nature to her; and there was the Princess Elys who stopped me in a forest and who insisted that I accompany her to her tent to pass the night, and this too politeness forbade my refusing. And I may have said something like this to her."

"If that isn't just like a man!" exclaimed the Princess Aelia incomprehensibly. Then she stared at young Sir Galwyn with curiosity and some respect. "But I really must say, you are certainly a fast worker, as well as a discreet young man. . . . the Princess Elys! that yellow haired hussy! Heavens, what abysmal taste! Oh, men are such children: any toy for the moment. Really, I cannot see how you could have the nerve to repeat to me the same speeches you have made to a girl who roams forests at night and accosts strange young men. She is very evidently no better than she should be." The Princess Aelia stared away into space for a while. The chariot had left earth far behind and was now rushing through the sky, crashing through silver clouds like a swift ship among breakers, while falcons on planing rigid wings and with eyes like red and yellow jewels whirled about it, screaming.

The Princess Aelia continued: "To leave a creature like that, and come to me! With the same words on your lips! Ah, you have no respect for me," she wailed, "associating my name with a creature like that!" She burst into tears. "No, no, don't try to justify yourself! To think that I have come off alone with a man like you! What will my good name be worth now? How can I hold my head up ever again? Oh, I hate you, I hate you!"

"Now certainly, lady," says young Sir Galwyn, "you cannot blame me for this situation: it was on your invitation that I first entered this golden chariot."

This was sound logic, and had its usual result. "Don't talk to me!" wept the Princess Aelia, "it is just as I expected from a man like you: to injure me irreparably, and then try to justify yourself in my eyes."

"Well, this may be remedied by taking me back to earth. I am sure that I had no intention of doing anyone an injury. In fact, I cannot see that I have accomplished any hurt to you."

"But how can taking you back to earth remedy things? You will sit around low taverns and simply tear my reputation to shreds. Oh, I know you men! What am I to do?"

"Then," says young Sir Galwyn, "if you won't take me back to earth, I'll go back alone." And young Sir Galwyn threw his leg over the side of the chariot.

The Princess Aelia shrieked and threw her arms about him. "No, no! you'll be killed!"

"Then will you promise to stop crying and blaming me for something I have not done?"

"Yes." So young Sir Galwyn drew in his leg and the Princess Aelia dried her eyes on her sleeve. "Really, Galwyn, you are too stupid for words. But it did hurt me to find that, after all the nice things you said to me, or led me believe, that I am no more to you than that—" and the Princess Aelia used a shocking word.

Young Sir Galwyn was properly shocked. "Really, Princess, I must object to such terms being applied to my friends. Besides, a lady would never know such a word, let alone repeat it."

"Oh, your ladies and your friends! Pooh, what do I care for either? But, tell me truly," clinging to him, "don't you think I am better looking than she?"

"Why, now," begins young Sir Galwyn lamely.

"Oh, you brute, I hate you! Why did I ever come away with such a beast! I wish I were dead!"

"Yes, yes!" young Sir Galwyn almost shouted, "anything if you won't cry again!"

"Ah, Galwyn, Galwyn, why are you so abysmally truthful? If you knew anything about women, you'd have learned better. But how can you have learned anything about women, poor dear, having been so successful with them? Anyway, you shouldn't have taken up with that nasty little Elys. But I'll show you what love is, Sir Galwyn; ah, I'll show you something you'll not soon forget!"

She spoke to the nine white dolphins in a strange tongue, and they turned earthward and flew at a dizzying speed. Young Sir Galwyn would have screamed with fear but the Princess Aelia's mouth was on his and young Sir Galwyn could not scream; and time and eternity swirled up and vortexed about the rush of their falling and the earth was but a spinning bit of dust in a maelstrom of blue space. The falcons planed plummetting beside the chariot and the wind screamed through the feathers of their wings, and the red and yellow jewels of their eyes were like coals of fire fanned to a heat unbearable. Young Sir Galwyn was no longer afraid: never had his heart known such ecstasy! he was a god and a falling star, consuming the whole world in a single long swooping rush through measureless regions of horror and delight down down, leaving behind him no change of light nor any sound.

And the tale tells how, in a while, young Sir Galwyn waked in a forest. Near him was his tethered steed browsing on the tender leaves of a young poplar, and beside it on two more horses sat the green design that was called Hunger and the red design called Pain, gravely and sedately waiting. So young sir Galwyn rose and mounted, and the three of them rode away from that place. And young Sir Galwyn drew a deep breath.

"By my faith, sir," quoth Hunger, "that was surely no sigh of a lover reft recently of his mistress? It struck me as being rather more a sigh of relief."

"To be frank with you, friend, I do not myself know exactly what that exhalation signified. Surely, a man is not to find in this world three fairer ladies than I have found in as many days; and yet. . . ."

"Ay, Sir Galwyn, and yet and yet. You have known the bride of a king before ever her husband looked upon her, you have possessed, in the persons of the daughters of the two most important minor princes in Christendom, the morning and the evening stars, and yet you have gained nothing save a hunger which gives you no ease. I remember to have remarked once that man is a buzzing insect blundering through a strange world, seeking something he can neither name nor recognize, and probably will not want. I think now that I shall refine this aphorism to: Man is a buzzing fly beneath the inverted glass tumbler of his illusions." Hunger fell silent and the three of them paced steadily on amid the dappled intermittent shadows. Flowers were about the glades merrily, and birds sang every where, and the sun shone full on young Sir Galwyn's face on which was at last something written although it was not a thing of which young Sir Galwyn was especially proud, and his shield swung from his saddlebow and it did not flash quite as brightly as it once did, for there was something written on it also that young Sir Galwyn was not particularly proud of, and young Sir Galwyn's long sword had stained through its scabbard and so young Sir Galwyn drew the skirt of his cloak over his sword.

Hunger spoke again in a while: "There is still one more girl I may show you, and I guarantee that she will smoothe that look of hunger from your face. What say you, young Sir Galwyn? Shall we seek this maid?"

And young sir Galwyn said: "Who is this maid who can smoothe all hunger and remembering from my face?"

And the other replied: "It is my sister."

And young sir Galwyn said: "Lead on."

So the three of them rode onward into the west from which the last light was ebbing as from a smooth beach.

This place, too, was familiar. That is, it seemed to young Sir Galwyn that soon there would appear something that he had seen and known long since, that here would be reenacted a scene that he had once looked upon or taken part in. So they rode on through a valley between shelving vague hills where the air was gray and smelled of spring. At last, at young Sir Galwyn's feet lay a dark hurrying stream and beside the stream stood a tree covered with leaves of a thousand different colors, and near the tree was a paunchy little man neither standing nor lying, with a beautiful white high brow and eyes of no particular color, resembling nothing so much as water wherein a great many things had been drowned. And young Sir Galwyn stopped at the brink of the stream and Hunger and Pain paused obediently near him, and as he gazed into the dark hurrying waters he knew that he had stood here before, and he wondered if his restless seeking through the world had been only a devious unnecessary way of returning to a place he need never have left.

In a while he of the calm beautiful brow drew near to young Sir Galwyn and he made a gesture with his long pale hand. Whereupon

Hunger and Pain withdrew, and they were in a desolate place. And he with the high white brow said to young Sir Galwyn:

"Choose."

And young sir Galwyn asked: "What shall I choose?"

But the other only replied: "Look, and see."

So they stood side by side, staring into the dark waters. And as they watched the waters were no longer dark but were filled with formless fragments of color and sound like darting small fish which, as young Sir Galwyn watched, began to coalesce into a regular measured succession of light and dark.

"Now," said the paunchy little man who looked as though standing up was very uncomfortable for him, "you, who have crossed this stream once without being wetted, must now choose one of two things. In this hurrying dark flood will appear the various phases of all life, from the beginning of time down to this moment, left in this stream by those who have preceded you here and whose memories have been washed clean and blank and smooth as a marble surface after rain. And now, having completed the cycle I have allowed you, you may choose any one of these phases to live over again. And though you will be but a shadow among shades it will seem to you that this which is now transpiring was but a dark dream which you had dreamed and that you are a palpable thing directing your destiny in a palpable world.

"Or you may choose to be submerged in these waters. Then you will remember nothing, not even this conversation or this choosing; and all your petty victories, your loving and hating, all the actions you have achieved will be washed from your mind to linger in these hurrying dark waters like darting small fish for those who are to come here after you to gaze upon; and this is Fame. But once these waters have closed above you, your memory will be as a smooth surface after rain, and you will remember nothing at all."

"What, then," says young Sir Galwyn, "will I be?"

"You will not be anything."

"Not even a shadow?"

"Not even a shadow."

"And if I choose to cross this stream, how may I do so without being wetted?"

The other moved his pale smooth hand and there appeared from out the mist beyond the dark hurrying water a gray man in a gray boat without oars. The boat touched the shore at their feet and the gray man stood with his head bent, staring into the water, and his gray garment hung from his lean figure in formal motionless folds.

"And if I choose to cross this stream?" repeated young Sir Galwyn.

"As I have already told you, you will be a shadow subject to all shadowy ills—hunger and pain and bodily discomforts, and love and hate and hope and despair. And you will know no better how to combat them than you did on your last journey through the world, for my emigration laws prohibit Experience leaving my domains. And besides, man should beware of Experience as he should beware of all women, for with her or without her he will be miserable, but without her he will not be dangerous."

"Then I will no longer be that thing men call Sir Galwyn of Arthgyl?"

"You will no longer be that thing men call Sir Galwyn of Arthgyl."

"But, if I am a shadow, how can I know hunger and pain?"

The other raised his head. His eyes were the color of sleep and he regarded young sir Galwyn wearily. "Have not Hunger and Pain been beside you since before you could remember? have they not ridden at your right hand and your left hand in all your journeys and battles? were they not closer to you than the young Yseult and Elys and Aelia could ever attain, or any of them who reminded you of honey and sunlight and young hyacinths in spring?"

"Yes, that is true. . . ." young Sir Galwyn admitted slowly. "But," he said suddenly, "I was not a shadow then."

"How do you know you were not a shadow?"

Young Sir Galwyn thought a while, and it was as though a cold wind had blown upon him. Then he said: "Who are you, who bids me choose one of two alternatives, neither of which is particularly pleasing to me?"

"I am the Lord of Sleep."

And young sir Galwyn regarded the paunchy little man with the beautiful high brow and eyes the color of sleep, and young Sir Galwyn was silent. In a while the other said:

"Look."

And young Sir Galwyn looked as he was bid, and in the hurrying dark waters were three faces. The Princess Yseult, now Queen of Cornwall, returned his gaze, haughty with power and offended pride, and passed on; the face of the Princess Elys, daughter of the King of Wales, whom he had abandoned in the enchanted forest looked at him in reproach and sorrow. Her face was blurred as with weeping, and she raised her delicate young arms to him as she sank away into the dark stream. The third was the glittering passionate face of Aelia, princess of the Merovingians; she gave him a fierce glance and her mouth was a thin red scorn and she too passed onward with the other glittering wreckage in the water, and Pain and Hunger drawing near again said together:

"Look."

And Hunger and Pain drew subtly nearer, and there in the water was one all young and white, and with long shining hair like a column of fair sunny water, and young Sir Galwyn thought of young hyacinths in spring, and honey and sunlight. Young Sir Galwyn looked upon this face and he was as one sinking from a fever into a soft and bottomless sleep; and he stepped forward into the water and Hunger and Pain went away from him, and as the water touched him it seemed to him that he knelt in a dark room waiting for day and that one like a quiet soft shining came to him, saying: "Rise, Sir Galwyn; be faithful, fortunate, and brave."

And the tree covered with leaves of a thousand different colours spoke, and all the leaves whirled up into the air and spun about it; and the tree was an old man with a shining white beard like a silver cuirass, and the leaves were birds.

What sayest thou, good Saint Francis?

"Little sister Death," said the good Saint Francis.

Thus it was in the old days.

ANAIS NIN   (1903–1977)

Ragtime

The city was asleep on its right side and shaking with violent nightmares. Long puffs of snoring came out of the chimneys. Its feet were sticking out because the clouds did not cover it altogether. There was a hole in them and the white feathers were falling out. The city had untied all the bridges like so many buttons to feel at ease. Wherever there was a lamplight the city scratched itself until it went out.

Trees, houses, telegraph poles, lay on their side. The ragpicker walked among the roots, the cellars, the breathing sewers, the open pipe works, looking for odds and ends, for remnants, for rags, broken bottles, paper, tin and old bread. The ragpicker walked in and out of the pockets of the sleeping city with his ragpicker's pick. In and out of the pockets over the watch chain on its belly, in and out of the sleeves, around its dusty collar, through the wands of its hair, picking the broken strands. The broken strands to repair mandolins. The fringe on the sleeve, the crumbs of bread, the broken watch face, the grains of tobacco, the subway ticket, the string, the stamp. The ragpicker worked in silence among the stains and smells.

His bag was swelling.

The city turned slowly on its left side, but the eyes of the houses remained closed, and the bridges unclasped. The ragpicker worked in silence and never looked at anything that was whole. His eyes sought the broken, the worn, the faded, the fragmented. A complete object made him sad. What could one do with a complete object? Put it in a museum. Not touch it. But a torn paper, a shoelace without its double, a cup without saucer, that was stirring. They could be transformed, melted into something else. A twisted piece of pipe. Wonderful, this basket without a handle. Wonderful, this bottle without a stopper. Wonderful, the box without a key. Wonderful, half a dress, the ribbon off a hat, a fan with a feather missing. Wonderful, the camera plate without the camera, the lone bicycle wheel, half a phonograph disk. Fragments, incompleted worlds, rags, detritus, the end of objects, and the beginning of transmutations.

The ragpicker shook his head with pleasure. He had found an object without a name. It shone. It was round. It was inexplicable. The ragpicker was happy. He would stop searching. The city would be waking up with the smell of bread. His bag was full. There were even fleas in it, pirouetting. The tail of a dead cat for luck.

His shadow walked after him, bent, twice as long. The bag on the shadow was the hump of a camel. The beard the camel's muzzle. The camel's walk, up and down the sand dunes. The camel's walk, up and down. I sat on the camel's hump.

It took me to the edge of the city. No trees. No bridge. No pavement. Earth. Plain earth trodden dead. Shacks of smoke-stained wood from demolished buildings. Between the shacks gypsy carts. Between the shacks and the carts a path so narrow that one must walk Indian file. Around the shacks palisades. Inside the shack rags. Rags for beds. Rags for chairs. Rags for tables. On the rags men, women, brats. Inside the women more brats. Fleas. Elbows resting on an old shoe. Head resting on a stuffed deer whose eyes hung loose on a string. The ragpicker gives the woman the object without a name. The woman picks it up and looks at the blank disk, then behind it. She hears tick, tick, tick, tick, tick. She says it is a clock. The ragpicker puts it to his ear and agrees it ticks like a clock but since its face is blank they will never know the time. Tick, tick, tick, the beat of time and no hour showing.

The tip of the shack is pointed like an Arab tent. The windows oblique like oriental eyes. On the sill a flower pot. Flowers made of beads and iron stems, which fell from a tomb. The woman waters them and the stems are rusty.

The brats sitting in the mud are trying to make an old shoe float like a boat. The woman cuts her thread with half a scissor. The ragpicker reads the newspaper with broken specs. The children go to the fountain with leaky pails. When they come back the pails are empty. The ragpickers crouch around the contents of their bags. Nails fall out. A roof tile. A signpost with letters missing.

Out of the gypsy cart behind them comes a torso. A torso on stilts, with his head twisted to one side. What had he done with his legs and arms? Were they under the pile of rags? Had he been thrown out of a window? A fragment of a man found at dawn.

Through the cracks in the shacks came the strum of a mandolin with one string.

The ragpicker looks at me with his one leaking eye. I pick a basket without bottom. The rim of a hat. The lining of a coat. Touch myself. Am I complete? Arms? Legs? Hair? Eyes? Where is the sole of my foot? I take off my shoe to see, to feel. Laugh. Glued to my sole is a blue rag. Ragged but blue like cobalt dust.

The rain falls. I pick up the skeleton of an umbrella. Sit on a hill of corks perfumed by the smell of wine. A ragpicker passes, the handle of a knife in his hand. With it he points to a path of dead oysters. At the end of the path is my blue dress. I had wept over its death. I had danced in it when I was seventeen, danced until it fell into pieces. I try to put it on and come out the other side. I cannot stay inside of it. Here I am, and there the dress, and I forever out of the blue dress I had loved, and I dance right through air, and fall on the floor because one of my heels came off, the heel I lost on a rainy night walking up a hill kissing my loved one deliriously.

Where are all the other things, I say, where are all the things I thought dead?

The ragpicker gave me a wisdom tooth, and my long hair which I had cut off. Then he sinks into a pile of rags and when I try to pick him up I find a scarecrow in my hands with sleeves full of straw and a high top hat with a bullet hole through it.

The ragpickers are sitting around a fire made of broken shutters, window frames, artificial beards, chestnuts, horse's tails, last year's holy palm leaves. The cripple sits on the stump of his torso, with his stilts beside him. Out of the shacks and the gypsy carts come the women and the brats.

Can't one throw anything away forever? I asked.

The ragpicker laughs out of the corner of his mouth, half a laugh, a fragment of a laugh, and they all begin to sing.

First came the breath of garlic which they hang like little red Chinese lanterns in their shacks, the breath of garlic followed by a serpentine song:

Nothing is lost but it changes
into the new string old string
in the new bag old bag
in the new pan old tin
in the new shoe old leather
in the new silk old hair
in the new hat old straw
in the new man the child
and the new not new
the new not new
the new not new

All night the ragpicker sang the new not new the new not new until I fell asleep and they picked me up and put me in a bag.

ALBERT CAMUS   (1913–1960)

The Guest

Translated by Justin O'Brien

The schoolmaster was watching the two men climb toward him. One was on horseback, the other on foot. They had not yet tackled the abrupt rise leading to the schoolhouse built on the hillside. They were toiling onward, making slow progress in the snow, among the stones, on the vast expanse of the high, deserted plateau. From time to time the horse stumbled. Without hearing anything yet, he could see the breath issuing from the horse's nostrils. One of the men, at least, knew the region. They were following the trail although it had disappeared days ago under a layer of dirty white snow. The schoolmaster calculated that it would take them half an hour to get onto the hill. It was cold; he went back into the school to get a sweater.

He crossed the empty, frigid classroom. On the blackboard the four rivers of France, drawn with four different colored chalks, had been flowing toward their estuaries for the past three days. Snow had suddenly fallen in mid-October after eight months of drought without the transition of rain, and the twenty pupils, more or less, who lived in the villages scattered over the plateau had stopped coming. With fair weather they would return. Daru now heated only the single room that was his lodging, adjoining the classroom and giving also onto the plateau to the east. Like the class windows, his window looked to the south too. On that side the school was a few kilometers from the point where the plateau began to slope toward the south. In clear weather could be seen the purple mass of the mountain range where the gap opened onto the desert.

Somewhat warmed, Daru returned to the window from which he had first seen the two men. They were no longer visible. Hence they must have tackled the rise. The sky was not so dark, for the snow had stopped falling during the night. The morning had opened with a dirty light which had scarcely become brighter as the ceiling of clouds lifted. At two in the afternoon it seemed as if the day were merely beginning. But still this was better than those three days when the thick snow was falling amidst unbroken darkness with little gusts of wind that rattled the double door of the classroom. Then Daru had spent long hours in his room, leaving it only to go to the shed and feed the chickens or get some coal. Fortunately the delivery truck from Tadjid, the nearest village to the north, had brought his supplies two days before the blizzard. It would return in forty-eight hours.

Besides, he had enough to resist a siege, for the little room was cluttered with bags of wheat that the administration left as a stock to distribute to those of his pupils whose families had suffered from the drought. Actually they had all been victims because they were all poor. Every day Daru would distribute a ration to the children. They had missed it, he knew, during these bad days. Possibly one of the fathers or big brothers would come this afternoon and he could supply them with grain. It was just a matter of carrying them over to the next harvest. Now shiploads of wheat were arriving from France and the worst was over. But it would be hard to forget that poverty, that army of ragged ghosts wandering in the sunlight, the plateaus burned to a cinder month after month, the earth shriveled up little by little, literally scorched, every stone bursting into dust under one's foot. The sheep had died then by thousands and even a few men, here and there, sometimes without anyone's knowing.

In contrast with such poverty, he who lived almost like a monk in his remote schoolhouse, nonetheless satisfied with the little he had and with the rough life, had felt like a lord with his whitewashed walls, his narrow couch, his unpainted shelves, his well, and his weekly provision of water and food. And suddenly this snow, without warning, without the foretaste of rain. This is the way the region was, cruel to live in, even without men—who didn't help matters either. But Daru had been born here. Everywhere else, he felt exiled.

He stepped out onto the terrace in front of the schoolhouse. The two men were now halfway up the slope. He recognized the horseman as Balducci, the old gendarme he had known for a long time. Balducci was holding on the end of a rope an Arab who was walking behind him with his hands bound and head lowered. The Gendarme waved a greeting to which Daru did not reply, lost as he was in contemplation of the Arab dressed in a faded blue jellaba, his feet in sandals but covered with socks of heavy raw wool, his head surmounted by a narrow, short *chèche*. They were approaching. Balducci was holding back his horse in order not to hurt the Arab, and the group was advancing slowly.

Within earshot, Balducci shouted: "One hour to do the three kilometers from El Ameur!" Daru did not answer. Short and square in his thick sweater, he watched them climb. Not once had the Arab raised his head. "Hello," said Daru when they got up onto the terrace. "Come in and warm up." Balducci painfully got down from his horse without letting go the rope. From under his bristling mustache he smiled at the schoolmaster. His little dark eyes, deep-set under a tanned forehead, and his mouth surrounded with wrinkles made him look attentive and studious. Daru took the bridle, led the horse to the shed, and came back to the two men, who were now waiting for him in the school. He led them into his room. "I am going to heat up the classroom," he said. "We'll be more comfortable there." When he entered the room again, Balducci was on the couch. He had undone the rope tying him to the Arab, who had squatted near the stove. His hands still bound, the *chéche* pushed back on his head, he was looking toward the window. At first Daru noticed only his huge lips, fat, smooth, almost Negroid; yet his nose was straight, his eyes were dark and full of fever. The *chéche* revealed an obstinate forehead and, under the weathered skin now rather discolored by the cold, the whole face had a restless and rebellious look that struck Daru when the Arab, turning his face toward him, looked him straight in the eyes. "Go into the other room," said the schoolmaster, "and I'll make you some mint tea." "Thanks," Balducci said. "What a chore! How I long for retirement." And addressing his prisoner in Arabic: "Come on, you." The Arab got up and, slowly, holding his bound wrists in front of him, went into the classroom.

With the tea, Daru brought a chair. But Balducci was already enthroned on the nearest pupil's desk and the Arab had squatted against the teacher's platform facing the stove, which stood between the desk and the window. When he held out the glass of tea to the prisoner, Daru hesitated at the sight of his bound hands. "He might perhaps be untied." "Sure," said Balducci. "That was for the trip." He started to get to his feet. But Daru, setting the glass on the floor, had knelt beside the Arab. Without saying anything, the Arab watched him with his feverish eyes. Once his hands were free, he rubbed his swollen wrists against each other, took the glass of tea, and sucked up the burning liquid in swift little sips.

"Good," said Daru. "And where are you headed?"

Balducci withdrew his mustache from the tea. "Here, son."

"Odd pupils! And you're spending the night?"

"No. I'm going back to El Ameur. And you will deliver this fellow to Tinguit. He is expected at police headquarters."

Balducci was looking at Daru with a friendly little smile.

"What's this story?" asked the schoolmaster. "Are you pulling my leg?"

"No, son. Those are the orders."

"The orders? I'm not . . ." Daru hesitated, not wanting to hurt the old Corsican. "I mean, that's not my job."

"What! What's the meaning of that? In wartime people do all kinds of jobs."

"Then I'll wait for the declaration of war!"

Balducci nodded.

"O.K. But the orders exist and they concern you too. Things are brewing, it appears. There is talk of a forthcoming revolt. We are mobilized, in a way."

Daru still had his obstinate look.

"Listen, son," Balducci said. "I like you and you must understand. There's only a dozen of us at El Ameur to patrol throughout the whole territory of a small department and I must get back in a hurry. I was told to hand this guy over to you and return without delay. He couldn't be kept there. His village was beginning to stir; they wanted to take him back. You must take him to Tinguit tomorrow before the day is over. Twenty kilometers shouldn't faze a husky fellow like you. After that, all will be over. You'll come back to your pupils and your comfortable life."

Behind the wall the horse could be heard snorting and pawing the earth. Daru was looking out the window. Decidedly, the weather was clearing and the light was increasing over the snowy plateau. When all the snow was melted, the sun would take over again and once more would burn the fields of stone. For days, still, the unchanging sky would shed its dry light on the solitary expanse where nothing had any connection with man.

"After all," he said, turning around toward Balducci, "what did he do?" And, before the gendarme had opened his mouth, he asked: "Does he speak French?"

"No, not a word. We had been looking for him for a month, but they were hiding him. He killed his cousin."

"Is he against us?"

"I don't think so. But you can never be sure."

"Why did he kill?"

"A family squabble, I think. One owed the other grain, it seems. It's not at all clear. In short, he killed his cousin with a billhook. You know, like a sheep, *kreezk!*" Balducci made the gesture of drawing a blade across his throat and the Arab, his attention attracted, watched him with a sort of anxiety. Daru felt a sudden wrath against the man, against all men with their rotten spite, their tireless hates, their blood lust.

But the kettle was singing on the stove. He served Balducci more tea, hesitated, then served the Arab again, who, a second time, drank avidly. His raised arms made the jellaba fall open and the schoolmaster saw his thin, muscular chest.

"Thanks, kid," Balducci said. "And now, I'm off."

He got up and went toward the Arab, taking a small rope from his pocket.

"What are you doing?" Daru asked dryly.

Balducci, disconcerted, showed him the rope.

"Don't bother."

The old gendarme hesitated. "It's up to you. Of course, you are armed?"

"I have my shotgun."

"Where?"

"In the trunk."

"You ought to have it near your bed."

"Why? I have nothing to fear."

"You're crazy, son. If there's an uprising, no one is safe, we're all in the same boat."

"I'll defend myself. I'll have time to see them coming."

Balducci began to laugh, then suddenly the mustache covered the white teeth.

"You'll have time? O.K. That's just what I was saying. You have always been a little cracked. That's why I like you, my son was like that."

At the same time he took out his revolver and put it on the desk.

"Keep it; I don't need two weapons from here to El Ameur."

The revolver shone against the black paint of the table. When the gendarme turned toward him, the schoolmaster caught the smell of leather and horseflesh.

"Listen, Balducci," Daru said suddenly, "every bit of this disgusts me, and first of all your fellow here. But I won't hand him over. Fight, yes, if I have to. But not that."

The old gendarme stood in front of him and looked at him severely.

"You're being a fool," he said slowly. "I don't like it either. You don't get used to putting a rope on a man even after years of it, and you're even ashamed—yes, ashamed. But you can't let them have their way."

"I won't hand him over," Daru said again.

"It's an order, son, and I repeat it."

"That's right. Repeat to them what I've said to you: I won't hand him over."

Balducci made a visible effort to reflect. He looked at the Arab and at Daru. At last he decided.

"No, I won't tell them anything. If you want to drop us, go ahead; I'll not denounce you. I have an order to deliver the prisoner and I'm doing so. And now you'll just sign this paper for me."

"There's no need. I'll not deny that you left him with me."

Don't be mean with me. I know you'll tell the truth. You're from hereabouts and you are a man. But you must sign, that's the rule."

Daru opened his drawer, took out a little square bottle of purple ink, the red wooden penholder with the "sergeant-major" pen he used for making models of penmanship, and signed. The gendarme carefully folded the paper and put it into his wallet. Then he moved toward the door.

"I'll see you off," Daru said.

"No," said Balducci. "There's no use being polite. You insulted me."

He looked at the Arab, motionless in the same spot, sniffed peevishly, and turned away toward the door. "Good-by, son," he said. The door shut behind him. Balducci appeared suddenly outside the window and then disappeared. His footsteps were muffled by the snow. The horse stirred on the other side of the wall and several chickens fluttered in fright. A moment later Balducci reappeared outside the window leading the horse by the bridle. He walked toward the little rise without turning around and disappeared from sight with the horse following him. A big stone could be heard bouncing down. Daru walked back toward the prisoner, who, without stirring, never took his eyes off him. "Wait," the schoolmaster said in Arabic and went toward the bedroom. As he was going through the door, he had a second thought, went to the desk, took the revolver, and stuck it in his pocket. Then, without looking back, he went into his room.

For some time he lay on his couch watching the sky gradually close over, listening to the silence. It was this silence that had seemed painful to him during the first days here, after the war. He had requested a post in a little town at the base of the foothills separating the upper plateaus from the desert. There, rocky walls, green and black to the north, pink and lavender to the south, marked the frontier of eternal summer. He had been named to a post farther north, on the plateau itself. In the beginning, the solitude and the silence had been hard for him on these wastelands peopled only by stones. Occasionally, furrows suggested cultivation, but they had been dug to uncover a certain kind of stone good for building. The only plowing here was to harvest rocks. Elsewhere a thin layer of soil accumulated in the hollows would be scraped out to enrich paltry village gardens. This is the way it was: bare rock covered three quarters of the region. Towns sprang up, flourished, then disappeared; men came by, loved one another or fought bitterly, then died. No one in this desert, neither he nor his guest, mattered. And yet, outside this desert neither of them, Daru knew, could have really lived.

When he got up, no noise came from the classroom. He was amazed at the unmixed joy he derived from the mere thought that the Arab might have fled and that he would be alone with no decision to make. But the prisoner was there. He had merely stretched out between the stove and the desk. With eyes open, he was staring at the ceiling. In that position, his thick lips were particularly noticeable, giving him a pouting look. "Come," said Daru. The Arab got up and followed him. In the bedroom, the schoolmaster pointed to a chair near the table under the window. The Arab sat down without taking his eyes off Daru.

"Are you hungry?"

"Yes," the prisoner said.

Daru set the table for two. He took flour and oil, shaped a cake in a frying-pan, and lighted the little stove that functioned on bottled gas. While the cake was cooking, he went out to the shed to get cheese, eggs, dates, and condensed milk. When the cake was done he set it on the window sill to cool, heated some condensed milk diluted with water, and beat up the eggs into an omelette. In one of his motions he knocked against the revolver stuck in his right pocket. He set the bowl down, went into the classroom, and put the revolver in his desk drawer. When he came back to the room, night was falling. He put on the light and served the Arab. "Eat," he said. The Arab took a piece of the cake, lifted it eagerly to his mouth, and stopped short.

"And you?" he asked.

"After you. I'll eat too."

The thick lips opened slightly. The Arab hesitated, then bit into the cake determinedly.

The meal over, the Arab looked at the schoolmaster. "Are you the judge?"

"No, I'm simply keeping you until tomorrow."

"Why do you eat with me?"

"I'm hungry."

The Arab fell silent. Daru got up and went out. He brought back a folding bed from the shed, set it up between the table and the stove, perpendicular to his own bed. From a large suitcase which, upright in a corner, served as a shelf for papers, he took two blankets and arranged them on the camp bed. Then he stopped, felt useless, and sat down on his bed. There was nothing more to do or to get ready. He had to look at this man. He looked at him, therefore, trying to imagine his face bursting with rage. He couldn't do so. He could see nothing but the dark yet shining eyes and the animal mouth.

"Why did you kill him?" he asked in a voice whose hostile tone surprised him.

The Arab looked away.

"He ran away. I ran after him."

He raised his eyes to Daru again and they were full of a sort of woeful interrogation. "Now what will they do to me?"

"Are you afraid?"

He stiffened, turning his eyes away.

"Are you sorry?"

The Arab stared at him openmouthed. Obviously he did not understand. Daru's annoyance was growing. At the same time he felt awkward and self-conscious with his big body wedged between the two beds.

"Lie down there," he said impatiently. "That's your bed."

The Arab didn't move. He called to Daru:

"Tell me."

The schoolmaster looked at him.

"Is the gendarme coming back tomorrow?"

"I don't know."

"Are you coming with us?"

"I don't know. Why?"

The prisoner got up and stretched out on top of the blankets, his feet toward the window. The light from the electric bulb shone straight into his eyes and he closed them at once.

"Why?" Daru repeated, standing beside the bed.

The Arab opened his eyes under the blinding light and looked at him, trying not to blink.

"Come with us," he said.

In the middle of the night, Daru was still not asleep. He had gone to bed after undressing completely; he generally slept naked. But when he suddenly realized that he had nothing on, he hesitated. He felt vulnerable and the temptation came to put his clothes back on. Then he shrugged his shoulders; after all, he wasn't a child and, if need be, he could break his adversary in two. From his bed he could observe him, lying on his back, still motionless with his eyes closed under the harsh light. When Daru turned out the light, the darkness seemed to coagulate all of a sudden. Little by little, the night came back to life in the window where the starless sky was stirring gently. The schoolmaster soon made out the body lying at his feet. The Arab still did not move, but his eyes seemed open. A faint wind was prowling around the schoolhouse. Perhaps it would drive away the clouds and the sun would reappear.

During the night the wind increased. The hens fluttered a little and then were silent. The Arab turned over on his side with his back to Daru, who thought he heard him moan. Then he listened for his guest's breathing, become heavier and more regular. He listened to that breath so close to him and mused without being able to go to sleep. In this room where he had been sleeping alone for a year, this presence bothered him. But it bothered him also by imposing on him a sort of brotherhood he knew well but refused to accept in the present circumstances. Men who share the same rooms, soldiers or prisoners, develop a strange alliance as if, having cast off their armor with their clothing, they fraternized every evening, over and above their differences, in the ancient community of dream and fatigue. But Daru shook himself; he didn't like such musings, and it was essential to sleep.

A little later, however, when the Arab stirred slightly, the schoolmaster was still not asleep. When the prisoner made a second move, he stiffened, on the alert. The Arab was lifting himself slowly on his arms with almost the motion of a sleep-walker. Seated upright in his bed, he waited motionless without turning his head toward Daru, as if he were listening attentively. Daru did not stir; it had just occurred to him that the revolver was still in the drawer of his desk. It was better to act at once. Yet he continued to observe the prisoner, who, with the same slithery motion, put his feet on the ground, waited again, then began to stand up slowly. Daru was about to call out to him when the Arab began to walk, in a quite natural but extraordinarily silent way. He was heading toward the door at the end of the room that opened into the shed. He lifted the latch with precaution and went out, pushing the door behind him but without shutting it. Daru had not stirred. "He is running away," he merely thought. "Good riddance!" Yet he listened attentively. The hens were not fluttering; the guest must be on the plateau. A faint sound of water reached him, and he didn't know what it was until the Arab again stood framed in the doorway, closed the door carefully, and came back to bed without a sound. Then Daru turned his back on him and fell asleep. Still later he seemed, from the depths of his sleep, to hear furtive steps around the schoolhouse. "I'm dreaming! I'm dreaming!" he repeated to himself. And he went on sleeping.

When he awoke, the sky was clear; the loose window let in a cold, pure air. The Arab was asleep, hunched up under the blankets now, his mouth open, utterly relaxed. But when Daru shook him, he started dreadfully, staring at Daru with wild eyes as if he had never seen him and such a frightened expression that the schoolmaster stepped back. "Don't be afraid. It's me. You must eat." The Arab nodded his head and said yes. Calm had returned to his face, but his expression was vacant and listless.

The coffee was ready. They drank it seated together on the folding bed as they munched their pieces of the cake. Then Daru led the Arab under the shed and showed him the faucet where he washed. He went back into the room, folded the blankets and the bed, made his own bed and put the room in order. Then he went through the classroom and out onto the terrace. The sun was already rising in the blue sky; a soft, bright light was bathing the deserted plateau. On the ridge the snow was melting in spots. The stones were about to reappear. Crouched on the edge of the plateau, the schoolmaster looked at the deserted expanse. He thought of Balducci. He had hurt him, for he had sent him off in a way as if he didn't want to be associated with him. He could still hear the gendarme's farewell and, without knowing why, he felt strangely empty and vulnerable. At that moment, from the other side of the schoolhouse, the prisoner coughed. Daru listened to him almost despite himself and then, furious, threw a pebble that whistled through the air before sinking into the snow. That man's stupid crime revolted him, but to hand him over was contrary to honor. Merely thinking of it made him smart with humiliation. And he cursed at one and the same time his own people who had sent him this Arab and the Arab too who had dared to kill and not managed to get away. Daru got up, walked in a circle on the terrace, waited motionless, and then went back into the schoolhouse.

The Arab, leaning over the cement floor of the shed, was washing his teeth with two fingers. Daru looked at him and said: "Come." He went back into the room ahead of the prisoner. He slipped a hunting-jacket on over his sweater and put on walking-shoes. Standing, he waited until the Arab had put on his *chèche* and sandals. They went into the classroom and the schoolmaster pointed to the exit, saying: "Go ahead." The fellow didn't budge. "I'm coming," said Daru. The Arab went out. Daru went back into the room and made a package of pieces of rusk, dates, and sugar. In the classroom, before going out, he hesitated a second in front of his desk, then crossed the threshold and locked the door. "That's the way," he said. He started toward the east, followed by the prisoner. But, a short distance from the schoolhouse, he thought he heard a slight sound behind them. He retraced his steps and examined the surroundings of the house; there was no one there. The Arab watched him without seeming to understand. "Come on," said Daru.

They walked for an hour and rested beside a sharp peak of limestone. The snow was melting faster and faster and the sun was drinking up the puddles at once, rapidly cleaning the plateau, which gradually dried and vibrated like the air itself. When they resumed walking, the ground rang under their feet. From time to time a bird rent the space in front of them with a joyful cry. Daru breathed in deeply the fresh morning light. He felt a sort of rapture before the vast familiar expanse, now almost entirely yellow under its dome of blue sky. They walked an hour more, descending toward the south. They reached a level height made up of crumbly rocks. From there on, the plateau sloped down, eastward, toward a low plain where there were a few spindly trees and, to the south, toward outcroppings of rock that gave the landscape a chaotic look.

Daru surveyed the two directions. There was nothing but the sky on the horizon. Not a man could be seen. He turned toward the Arab, who was looking at him blankly. Daru held out the package to him. "Take it," he said. "There are dates, bread, and sugar. You can hold out for two days. Here are a thousand francs too." The Arab took the package and the money but kept his full hands at chest level as if he didn't know what to do with what was being given him. "Now look," the schoolmaster said as he pointed in the direction of the east, "there's the way to Tinguit. You have a two-hour walk. At Tinguit you'll find the administration and the police. They are expecting you." The Arab looked toward the east, still holding the package and the money against his chest. Daru took his elbow and turned him rather roughly toward the south. At the foot of the height on which they stood could be seen a faint path. "That's the trail across the plateau. In the day's walk from here you'll find pasturelands and the first nomads. They'll take you in and shelter you according to their law." The Arab had now turned toward Daru and a sort of panic was visible in his expression. "Listen," he said. Daru shook his head: "No, be quiet. Now I'm leaving you." He turned his back on him, took two long steps in the direction of the school, looked hesitantly at the motionless Arab, and started off again. For a few minutes he heard nothing but his own step resounding on the cold ground and did not turn his head. A moment later, however, he turned around. The Arab was still there on the edge of the hill, his arms hanging now, and he was looking at the schoolmaster. Daru felt something rise in his throat. But he swore with impatience, waved vaguely, and started off again. He had already gone some distance when he again stopped and looked. There was no longer anyone on the hill.

Daru hesitated. The sun was now rather high in the sky and was beginning to beat down on his head. The schoolmaster retraced his steps, at first somewhat uncertainly, then with decision. When he reached the little hill, he was bathed in sweat. He climbed it as fast as he could and stopped, out of breath, at the top. The rock-fields to the south stood out sharply against the blue sky, but on the plain to the east a steamy heat was already rising. And in that slight haze, Daru, with heavy heart, made out the Arab walking slowly on the road to prison.

A little later, standing before the window of the classroom, the schoolmaster was watching the clear light bathing the whole surface of the plateau, but he hardly saw it. Behind him on the blackboard, among the winding French rivers, sprawled the clumsily chalked-up words he had just read: "You handed over our brother. You will pay for this." Daru looked at the sky, the plateau, and, beyond, the invisible lands stretching all the way to the sea. In this vast landscape he had loved so much, he was alone.

SHIRLEY JACKSON   (1919–1965)

Flower Garden

After living in an old Vermont manor house together for almost eleven years, the two Mrs. Winnings, mother and daughter-in-law, had grown to look a good deal alike, as women will who live intimately together, and work in the same kitchen and get things done around the house in the same manner. Although young Mrs. Winning had been a Talbot, and had dark hair which she wore cut short, she was now officially a Winning, a member of the oldest family in town and her hair was beginning to grey where her mother-in-law's hair had greyed first, at the temples; they both had thin sharp-featured faces and eloquent hands, and sometimes when they were washing dishes or shelling peas or polishing silverware together, their hands, moving so quickly and similarly, communicated more easily and sympathetically than their minds ever could. Young Mrs. Winning thought sometimes, when she sat at the breakfast table next to her mother-in-law, with her baby girl in the high-chair close by, that they must resemble some stylized block print for a New England wallpaper; mother, daughter, and granddaughter, with perhaps Plymouth Rock or Concord Bridge in the background.

On this, as on other cold mornings, they lingered over their coffee, unwilling to leave the big kitchen with the coal stove and the pleasant atmosphere of food and cleanliness, and they sat together silently sometimes until the baby had long finished her breakfast and was playing quietly in the special baby corner, where uncounted Winning children had played with almost identical toys from the same heavy wooden box.

"It seems as though spring would never come," young Mrs. Winning said. "I get so tired of the cold."

"Got to be cold some of the time," her mother-in-law said. She began to move suddenly and quickly, stacking plates, indicating that the time for sitting was over and the time for working had begun. Young Mrs. Winning, rising immediately to help, thought for the thousandth time that her mother-in-law would never relinquish the position of authority in her own house until she was too old to move before anyone else.

"And I wish someone would move into the old cottage," young Mrs. Winning added. She stopped halfway to the pantry with the table napkins and said longingly, "If only *someone* would move in before spring." Young Mrs. Winning had wanted, long ago, to buy the cottage herself, for her husband to make with his own hands into a home where they could live with their children, but now, accustomed as she was to the big old house at the top of the hill where her husband's family had lived for generations, she had only a great kindness left toward the little cottage, and a wistful anxiety to see some happy young people living there. When she heard it was sold, as all the old houses were being sold in these days when no one could seem to find a newer place to live, she had allowed herself to watch daily for a sign that someone new was coming; every morning she glanced down from the back porch to see if there was smoke coming out of the cottage chimney, and every day going down the hill on her way to the store she hesitated past the cottage, watching carefully for the least movement within. The cottage had been sold in January and now, nearly two months later, even though it seemed prettier and less worn with the snow gently covering the overgrown garden and icicles in front of the blank windows, it was still forlorn and empty, despised since the day long ago when Mrs. Winning had given up all hope of ever living there.

Mrs. Winning deposited the napkins in the pantry and turned to tear the leaf off the kitchen calendar before selecting a dish towel and joining her mother-in-law at the sink. "March already," she said despondently.

"They *did* tell me down at the store yesterday," her mother-in-law said, "that they were going to start painting the cottage this week."

"Then that *must* mean someone's coming!"

"Can't take more than a couple of weeks to paint inside that little house," old Mrs. Winning said.

It was almost April, however, before the new people moved in. The snow had almost melted and was running down the street in icy, half-solid rivers. The ground was slushy and miserable to walk on, the skies grey and dull. In another month the first amazing green would start in the trees and on the ground, but for the better part of April there would be cold rain and perhaps more snow. The cottage had been painted inside, and new paper put on the walls. The front steps had been repaired and new glass put into the broken windows. In spite of the grey sky and the patches of dirty snow the cottage looked neater and firmer, and the painters were coming back to do the outside when the weather cleared. Mrs. Winning, standing at the foot of the cottage walk, tried to picture the cottage as it stood now, against the picture of the cottage she had made years ago, when she had hoped to live there herself. She had wanted roses by the porch; that could be done, and the neat colorful garden she had planned. She would have painted the outside white, and that too might still be done. Since the cottage had been sold she had not gone inside, but she remembered the little rooms, with the windows over the garden that could be so bright with gay curtains and window boxes, the small kitchen she would have painted yellow, the two bedrooms upstairs with slanting ceilings under the eaves. Mrs. Winning looked at the cottage for a long time, standing on the wet walk, and then went slowly on down to the store.

The first news she had of the new people came, at last, from the grocer a few days later. As he was tieing the string around the three pounds of hamburger the large Winning family would consume in one meal, he asked cheerfully, "Seen your new neighbors yet?"

"Have they moved in?" Mrs. Winning asked. "The people in the cottage?"

"Lady in here this morning," the grocer said. "Lady and a little boy, seem like nice people. They say her husband's dead. Nice-looking lady."

Mrs. Winning had been born in the town and the grocer's father had given her jawbreakers and licorice in the grocery store while the present grocer was still in high school. For a while, when she was twelve and the grocer's son was twenty, Mrs. Winning had hoped secretly that he would want to marry her. He was fleshy now, and middle-aged, and although he still called her Helen and she still called him Tom, she belonged now to the Winning family and had to speak critically to him, no matter how unwillingly, if the meat were tough or the butter price too high. She knew that when he spoke of the new neighbor as a "lady" he meant something different than if he had spoken of her as a "woman" or a "person." Mrs. Winning knew that he spoke of the two Mrs. Winnings to his other customers as "ladies." She hesitated and then asked, "Have they really moved in to stay?"

"She'll have to stay for a while," the grocer said drily. "Bought a week's worth of groceries."

Going back up the hill with her package Mrs. Winning watched all the way to detect some sign of the new people in the cottage. When she reached the cottage walk she slowed down and tried to watch not too obviously. There was no smoke coming from the chimney, and no sign of furniture near the house, as there might have been if people were still moving in, but there was a middle-aged car parked in the street before the cottage and Mrs. Winning thought she could see figures moving past the windows. On a sudden irresistible impulse she turned and went up the walk to the front porch, and then, after debating for a moment, on up the steps to the door. She knocked, holding her bag of groceries in one arm, and then the door opened and she looked down on a little boy, about the same age, she thought happily, as her own son.

"Hello," Mrs. Winning said.

"Hello," the boy said. He regarded her soberly.

"Is your mother here?" Mrs. Winning asked. "I came to see if I could help her move in."

"We're all moved in," the boy said. He was about to close the door, but a woman's voice said from somewhere in the house, "Davey? Are you talking to someone?"

"That's my mommy," the little boy said. The woman came up behind him and opened the door a little wider. "Yes?" she said.

Mrs. Winning said, "I'm Helen Winning. I live about three houses up the street, and I thought perhaps I might be able to help you."

"Thank you," the woman said doubtfully. She's younger than I am, Mrs. Winning thought, she's about thirty. And pretty. For a clear minute Mrs. Winning saw why the grocer had called her a lady.

"It's so nice to have someone living in this house," Mrs. Winning said shyly. Past the other woman's head she could see the small hallway, with the larger living-room beyond and the door on the left going into the kitchen, the stairs on the right, with the delicate stair-rail newly painted; they had done the hall in light green, and Mrs. Winning smiled with friendship at the woman in the doorway, thinking, She *has* done it right; this is the way it should look after all, she knows about pretty houses.

After a minute the other woman smiled back, and said, "Will you come in?"

As she stepped back to let Mrs. Winning in, Mrs. Winning wondered with a suddenly stricken conscience if perhaps she had not been too forward, almost pushing herself in. . . . "I hope I'm not making a nuisance of myself," she said unexpectedly, turning to the other woman. "It's just that I've been wanting to live here myself for so long." Why did I say that, she wondered; it had been a very long time since young Mrs. Winning had said the first thing that came into her head.

"Come see *my* room," the little boy said urgently, and Mrs. Winning smiled down at him.

"I have a little boy just about your age," she said. "What's your name?"

"Davey," the little boy said, moving closer to his mother. "Davey William MacLane."

"My little boy," Mrs. Winning said soberly, "is named Howard Talbot Winning.

The little boy looked up at his mother uncertainly, and Mrs. Winning, who felt ill at ease and awkward in this little house she so longed for, said, "How old are you? My little boy is five."

"I'm five," the little boy said, as though realizing it for the first time. He looked again at his mother and she said graciously, "Will you come in and see what we've done to the house?"

Mrs. Winning put her bag of groceries down on the slim-legged table in the green hall, and followed Mrs. MacLane into the living-room, which was L-shaped and had the windows Mrs. Winning would have fitted with gay curtains and flower-boxes. As she stepped into the room Mrs. Winning realized, with a quick wonderful relief, that it was really going to be all right, after all. Everything, from the andirons in the fireplace to the books on the table, was exactly as Mrs. Winning might have done if she were eleven years younger; a little more informal, perhaps, nothing of quite such good quality as young Mrs. Winning might have chosen, but still richly, undeniably right. There was a picture of Davey on the mantel, flanked by a picture which Mrs. Winning supposed was Davey's father; there was a glorious blue bowl on the low coffee table, and around the corner of the L stood a row of orange plates on a shelf, and a polished maple table and chairs.

"It's lovely," Mrs. Winning said. This could have been mine, she was thinking, and she stood in the doorway and said again, "It's perfectly lovely."

Mrs. MacLane crossed over to the low armchair by the fireplace and picked up the soft blue material that lay across the arm. "I'm making curtains," she said, and touched the blue bowl with the tip of one finger. "Somehow I always make my blue bowl the center of the room," she said. "I'm having the curtains the same blue, and my rug—when it comes!— will have the same blue in the design."

"It matches Davey's eyes," Mrs. Winning said, and when Mrs. MacLane smiled again she saw that it matched Mrs. MacLane's eyes too. Helpless before so much that was magic to her, Mrs. Winning said "*Have* you painted the kitchen yellow?"

"Yes," Mrs. MacLane said, surprised. "Come and see." She led the way through the L, around past the orange plates to the kitchen, which caught the late morning sun and shone with clean paint and bright aluminum; Mrs. Winning noticed the electric coffeepot, the waffle iron, the toaster, and thought, *she* couldn't have much trouble cooking, not with just the two of them.

"When I have a garden," Mrs. MacLane said, "we'll be able to see it from almost all the windows." She gestured to the broad kitchen windows, and added, "I love gardens. I imagine I'll spend most of my time working in this one, as soon as the weather is nice."

"It's a good house for a garden," Mrs. Winning said. "I've heard that it used to be one of the prettiest gardens on the block."

"I thought so too," Mrs. MacLane said. "I'm going to have flowers on all four sides of the house. With a cottage like this you can, you know."

Oh, I know, I know, Mrs. Winning thought wistfully, remembering the neat charming garden she could have had, instead of the row of nasturtiums along the side of the Winning house, which she tended so carefully; no flowers would grow well around the Winning house, because of the heavy old maple trees which shaded all the yard and which had been tall when the house was built.

Mrs. MacLane had had the bathroom upstairs done in yellow, too, and the two small bedrooms with overhanging eaves were painted green and rose. "All garden colors," she told Mrs. Winning gaily, and Mrs. Winning, thinking of the oddly-matched, austere bedrooms in the big Winning house, sighed and admitted that it would be wonderful to have window seats under the eaved windows. Davey's bedroom was the green one, and his small bed was close to the window. "This morning," he told Mrs. Winning solemnly, "I looked out and there were four icicles hanging by my bed."

Mrs. Winning stayed in the cottage longer than she should have; she felt certain, although Mrs. MacLane was pleasant and cordial, that her visit was extended past courtesy and into curiosity. Even so, it was only her sudden guilt about the three pounds of hamburger and dinner for the Winning men that drove her away. When she left, waving good-bye to Mrs. MacLane and Davey as they stood in the cottage doorway, she had invited Davey up to play with Howard, Mrs. MacLane up for tea, both of them to come for lunch some day, and all without the permission of her mother-in-law.

Reluctantly she came to the big house and turned past the bolted front door to go up the walk to the back door, which all the family used in the winter. Her mother-in-law looked up as she came into the kitchen and said irritably, "I called the store and Tom said you left an hour ago."

"I stopped off at the old cottage," Mrs. Winning said. She put the package of groceries down on the table and began to take things out quickly, to get the doughnuts on to a plate and the hamburger into the pan before too much time was lost. With her coat still on and her scarf over her head she moved as fast as she could while her mother-in-law, slicing bread at the kitchen table, watched her silently.

"Take your coat off," her mother-in-law said finally. "Your husband will be home in a minute."

By twelve o'clock the house was noisy and full of mud tracked across the kitchen floor. The oldest Howard, Mrs. Winning's father-in-law, came in from the farm and went silently to hang his hat and coat in the dark hall before speaking to his wife and daughter-in-law; the younger Howard, Mrs. Winning's husband, came in from the barn after putting the truck away and nodded to his wife and kissed his mother; and the youngest Howard, Mrs. Winning's son, crashed into the kitchen, home from kindergarten, shouting, "Where's dinner?"

The baby, anticipating food, banged on her high-chair with the silver cup which had first been used by the oldest Howard Winning's mother. Mrs. Winning and her mother-in-law put plates down on the table swiftly, knowing after many years the exact pause between the latest arrival and the serving of food, and with a minimum of time three generations of the Winning family were eating silently and efficiently, all anxious to be back about their work: the farm, the mill, the electric train; the dishes, the sewing, the nap. Mrs. Winning, feeding the baby, trying to anticipate her mother-in-law's gestures of serving, thought, today more poignantly than ever before, that she had at least given them another Howard, with the Winning eyes and mouth, in exchange for her food and her bed.

After dinner, after the men had gone back to work and the children were in bed, the baby for her nap and Howard resting with crayons and coloring book, Mrs. Winning sat down with her mother-in-law over their sewing and tried to describe the cottage.

"It's just perfect," she said helplessly. "Everything is so pretty. She invited us to come down some day and see it when it's all finished, the curtains and everything."

"I was talking to Mrs. Blake," the elder Mrs. Winning said, as though in agreement. "She says the husband was killed in an automobile accident. *She* had some money in her own name and I guess she decided to settle down in the country for the boy's health. Mrs. Blake said he looked peakish."

"She loves gardens," Mrs. Winning said, her needle still in her hand for a moment. "She's going to have a big garden all around the house."

"She'll need help," the elder woman said humorlessly, "that's a mighty big garden she'll have."

"She has the *most* beautiful blue bowl, Mother Winning. You'd love it, it's almost like silver."

"Probably," the elder Mrs. Winning said after a pause, "probably her people came from around here a ways back, and *that's* why she's settled in these parts."

The next day Mrs. Winning walked slowly past the cottage, and slowly the next, and the day after, and the day after that. On the second day she saw Mrs. MacLane at the window, and waved, and on the third day she met Davey on the sidewalk. "When are you coming to visit my little boy?" she asked him, and he stared at her solemnly and said, "Tomorrow."

Mrs. Burton, next-door to the MacLanes, ran over on the third day they were there with a fresh apple pie, and then told all the neighbors about the yellow kitchen and the bright electric utensils. Another neighbor, whose husband had helped Mrs. MacLane start her furnace, explained that Mrs. MacLane was only very recently widowed. One or another of the townspeople called on the MacLanes almost daily, and frequently, as young Mrs. Winning passed, she saw familiar faces at the windows, measuring the blue curtains with Mrs. MacLane, or she waved to acquaintances who stood chatting with Mrs. MacLane on the now firm front steps. After the MacLanes had been in the cottage for about a week Mrs. Winning met them one day in the grocery and they walked up the hill together, and talked about putting Davey into the kindergarten. Mrs. MacLane wanted to keep him home as long as possible, and Mrs. Winning asked her, "Don't you feel terribly tied down, having him with you all the time?"

"I like it," Mrs. MacLane said cheerfully, "we keep each other company," and Mrs. Winning felt clumsy and ill-mannered, remembering Mrs. MacLane's widowhood.

As the weather grew warmer and the first signs of green showed on the trees and on the wet ground, Mrs. Winning and Mrs. MacLane became better friends. They met almost daily at the grocery and walked up the hill together, and twice Davey came up to play with Howard's electric train, and once Mrs. MacLane came up to get him and stayed for a cup of coffee in the great kitchen while the boys raced round and round the table and Mrs. Winning's mother-in-law was visiting a neighbor.

"It's such an old house," Mrs. MacLane said, looking up at the dark ceiling. "I love old houses; they feel so secure and warm, as though lots of people had been perfectly satisfied with them and they *knew* how useful they were. You don't get that feeling with a new house."

"This dreary old place," Mrs. Winning said. Mrs. MacLane, with a rose-colored sweater and her bright soft hair, was a spot of color in the kitchen that Mrs. Winning knew she could never duplicate. "I'd give anything in the world to live in your house," Mrs. Winning said.

"*I* love it," Mrs. MacLane said. "I don't think I've ever been so happy. Everyone around here is so nice, and the house is so pretty, and I planted a lot of bulbs yesterday." She laughed. "I used to sit in that apartment in New York and dream about planting bulbs again."

Mrs. Winning looked at the boys, thinking how Howard was half-a-head taller, and stronger, and how Davey was small and weak and loved his mother adoringly. "It's been good for Davey already," she said. "There's color in his cheeks."

"Davey loves it," Mrs. MacLane agreed. Hearing his name Davey came over and put his head in her lap and she touched his hair, bright like her own. "We'd better be getting on home, Davey boy," she said.

"Maybe our flowers have grown some since yesterday," said Davey.

Gradually the days became miraculously long and warm, and Mrs. MacLane's garden began to show colors and became an ordered thing, still very young and unsure, but promising rich brilliance for the end of the summer, and the next summer, and summers ten years from now.

"It's even better than I hoped," Mrs. MacLane said to Mrs. Winning, standing at the garden gate. "Things grow so much better here than almost anywhere else."

Davey and Howard played daily after the school was out for the summer, and Howard was free all day. Sometimes Howard stayed at Davey's house for lunch, and they planted a vegetable patch together in the MacLane back yard. Mrs. Winning stopped for Mrs. MacLane on her way to the store in the mornings and Davey and Howard frolicked ahead of them down the street. They picked up their mail together and read it walking back up the hill, and Mrs. Winning went more cheerfully back to the big Winning house after walking most of the way home with Mrs. MacLane.

One afternoon Mrs. Winning put the baby in Howard's wagon and with the two boys they went for a long walk in the country. Mrs. MacLane picked Queen Anne's lace and put it into the wagon with the baby, and the boys found a garter snake and tried to bring it home. On the way up the hill Mrs. MacLane helped pull the wagon with the baby and the Queen Anne's lace, and they stopped halfway to rest and Mrs. MacLane said, "Look, I believe you can see my garden all the way from here."

It was a spot of color almost at the top of the hill and they stood looking at it while the baby threw the Queen Anne's lace out of the wagon. Mrs. MacLane said, "I always want to stop here to look at it," and then, "Who is that *beautiful* child?"

Mrs. Winning looked, and then laughed. "He *is* attractive, isn't he," she said. "It's Billy Jones." She looked at him herself, carefully, trying to see him as Mrs. MacLane would. He was a boy about twelve, sitting quietly on a wall across the street, with his chin in his hands, silently watching Davey and Howard.

"He's like a young statue," Mrs. MacLane said. "So brown, and will you look at that face?" She started to walk again to see him more clearly, and Mrs. Winning followed her. "Do I know his mother and fath—?"

"The Jones children are half-Negro," Mrs. Winning said hastily. "But they're all beautiful children; you should see the girl. They live just outside town."

Howard's voice reached them clearly across the summer air. "Nigger," he was saying, "nigger, nigger boy."

"Nigger," Davey repeated, giggling.

Mrs. MacLane gasped, and then said, *"Davey,"* in a voice that made Davey turn his head apprehensively; Mrs. Winning had never heard her friend use such a voice, and she too watched Mrs. MacLane.

"Davey," Mrs. MacLane said again, and Davey approached slowly. "What did I hear you say?"

"Howard," Mrs. Winning said, "leave Billy alone."

"Go tell that boy you're sorry," Mrs. MacLane said. "Go at once and tell him you're sorry."

Davey blinked tearfully at his mother and then went to the curb and called across the street, "I'm sorry."

Howard and Mrs. Winning waited uneasily, and Billy Jones across the street raised his head from his hands and looked at Davey and then, for a long time, at Mrs. MacLane. Then he put his chin on his hands again.

Suddenly Mrs. MacLane called, "Young man—Will you come here a minute, please?"

Mrs. Winning was surprised, and stared at Mrs. MacLane, but when the boy across the street did not move Mrs. Winning said sharply, "Billy! Billy Jones! Come here at once!"

The boy raised his head and looked at them, and then slid slowly down from the wall and started across the street. When he was across the street and about five feet from them he stopped, waiting.

"Hello," Mrs. MacLane said gently, "what's your name?"

The boy looked at her for a minute and then at Mrs. Winning, and Mrs. Winning said, "He's Billy Jones. Answer when you're spoken to, Billy."

"Billy," Mrs. MacLane said, "I'm sorry my little boy called you a name, but he's very little and he doesn't always know what he's saying. But he's sorry, too."

"Okay," Billy said, still watching Mrs. Winning. He was wearing an old pair of blue jeans and a torn white shirt, and he was barefoot. His skin and hair were the same color, the golden shade of a very heavy tan, and his hair curled lightly; he had the look of a garden statue.

"Billy," Mrs. MacLane said, "how would you like to come and work for me? Earn some money?"

"Sure," Billy said.

"Do you like gardening?" Mrs. MacLane asked. Billy nodded soberly. "Because," Mrs. MacLane went on enthusiastically, "I've been needing someone to help me with my garden, and it would be just the thing for you to do." She waited a minute and then said, "Do you know where I live?"

"Sure," Billy said. He turned his eyes away from Mrs. Winning and for a minute looked at Mrs. MacLane, his brown eyes expressionless. Then he looked back at Mrs. Winning, who was watching Howard up the street.

"Fine," Mrs. MacLane said. "Will you come tomorrow?"

"Sure," Billy said. He waited for a minute, looking from Mrs. MacLane to Mrs. Winning, and then ran back across the street and vaulted over the wall where he had been sitting. Mrs. MacLane watched him admiringly. Then she smiled at Mrs. Winning and gave the wagon a tug to start it up the hill again. They were nearly at the MacLane cottage before Mrs. MacLane finally spoke. "I just can't stand that," she said, "to hear children attacking people for things they can't help."

"They're strange people, the Joneses," Mrs. Winning said readily. "The father works around as a handyman; maybe you've seen him. You see—" she dropped her voice—"the mother was white, a girl from around here. A local girl," she said again, to make it more clear to a foreigner. "She left the whole litter of them when Billy was about two, and went off with a white man."

"Poor children," Mrs. MacLane said.

"*They're* all right," Mrs. Winning said. "The church takes care of them, of course, and people are always giving them things. The girl's old enough to work now, too. She's sixteen, but. . . ."

"But what?" Mrs. MacLane said, when Mrs. Winning hesitated.

"Well, people talk about her a lot, you know," Mrs. Winning said. "Think of her mother, after all. And there's another boy, couple of years older than Billy."

They stopped in front of the MacLane cottage and Mrs. MacLane touched Davey's hair. "Poor unfortunate child," she said.

"Chilren *will* call names," Mrs. Winning said. "There's not much you can do."

"Well . . ." Mrs. MacLane said. "Poor child."

The next day, after the dinner dishes were washed, and while Mrs. Winning and her mother-in-law were putting them away, the elder Mrs. Winning said casually, "Mrs. Blake tells me your friend Mrs. MacLane was asking around the neighbors how to get hold of the Jones boy."

"She wants someone to help in the garden, I think," Mrs. Winning said weakly. "She needs help in that big garden."

"Not *that* kind of help," the elder Mrs. Winning said. "You tell her about them?"

"She seemed to feel sorry for them," Mrs. Winning said, from the depths of the pantry. She took a long time settling the plates in even stacks in order to neaten her mind. She *shouldn't* have done it, she was thinking, but her mind refused to tell her why. She should have asked me first, though, she thought finally.

The next day Mrs. Winning stopped off at the cottage with Mrs. MacLane after coming up the hill from the store. They sat in the yellow kitchen and drank coffee, while the boys played in the back yard. While they were discussing the possibilities of hammocks between the apple trees there was a knock at the kitchen door and when Mrs. MacLane opened it she found a man standing there, so that she said, "Yes?" politely, and waited.

"Good morning," the man said. He took off his hat and nodded his head at Mrs. MacLane. "Billy told me you was looking for someone to work your garden," he said.

"Why . . ." Mrs. MacLane began, glancing sideways uneasily at Mrs. Winning.

"I'm Billy's father," the man said. He nodded his head toward the back yard and Mrs. MacLane saw Billy Jones sitting under one of the apple trees, his arms folded in front of him, his eyes on the grass at his feet.

"How do you do," Mrs. MacLane said inadequately.

"Billy told me you said for him to come work your garden," the man said. "Well, now, I think maybe a summer job's too much for a boy his age, he ought to be out playing in the good weather. And that's the kind of work I do anyway, so's I thought I'd just come over and see if you found anyone yet."

He was a big man, very much like Billy, except that where Billy's hair curled only a little, his father's hair curled tightly, with a line around his head where his hat stayed constantly and where Billy's skin was a golden tan, his father's skin was darker, almost bronze. When he moved, it was gracefully, like Billy, and his eyes were the same fathomless brown. "Like to work this garden," Mr. Jones said, looking around. "Could be a mighty nice place."

"You were very nice to come," Mrs. MacLane said. "I certainly do need help."

Mrs. Winning sat silently, not wanting to speak in front of Mr. Jones. She was thinking, I wish she'd ask me first, this is impossible . . . and Mr. Jones stood silently, listening courteously, with his dark eyes on Mrs. MacLane while she spoke. "I guess a lot of the work would be too much for a boy like Billy," she said. "There are a lot of things I can't even do myself, and I was sort of hoping I could get someone to give me a hand."

"That's fine, then," Mr. Jones said. "Guess I can manage most of it," he said, and smiled.

"Well," Mrs. MacLane said, "I guess that's all settled, then. When do you want to start?"

"How about right now?" he said.

"Grand," Mrs. MacLane said enthusiastically, and then, "Excuse me for a minute," to Mrs. Winning over her shoulder. She took down her gardening gloves and wide straw hat from the shelf by the door. "Isn't it a lovely day?" she asked Mr. Jones as she stepped out into the garden while he stood back to let her pass.

"You go along home now, Bill," Mr. Jones called as they went toward the side of the house.

"Oh, why not let him stay?" Mrs. MacLane said. Mrs. Winning heard her voice going on as they went out of sight. "He can play around the garden, and he'd probably enjoy . . ."

For a minute Mrs. Winning sat looking at the garden, at the corner around which Mr. Jones had followed Mrs. MacLane, and then Howard's face appeared around the side of the door and he said, "Hi, is it nearly time to eat?"

"Howard," Mrs. Winning said quietly, and he came in through the door and came over to her. "It's time for you to run along home," Mrs. Winning said. "I'll be along in a minute."

Howard started to protest, but she added, "I want you to go right away. Take my bag of groceries if you think you can carry it."

Howard was impressed by her conception of his strength, and he lifted down the bag of groceries; his shoulders, already broad out of proportion, like his father's and his grandfather's, strained under the weight, and then he steadied on his feet. "Aren't I strong?" he asked exultantly.

"*Very* strong," Mrs. Winning said. "Tell Grandma I'll be right up. I'll just say good-bye to Mrs. MacLane."

Howard disappeared through the house; Mrs. Winning heard him walking heavily under the groceries, out through the open front door and down the steps. Mrs. Winning rose and was standing by the kitchen door when Mrs. MacLane came back.

"You're not ready to go?" Mrs. MacLane exclaimed when she saw Mrs. Winning with her jacket on. "Without finishing your coffee?"

"I'd better catch Howard," Mrs. Winning said. "He ran along ahead."

"I'm sorry I left you like that," Mrs. MacLane said. She stood in the doorway beside Mrs. Winning, looking out into the garden. "How *wonderful* it all is," she said, and laughed happily.

They walked together through the house; the blue curtains were up by now, and the rug with the touch of blue in the design was on the floor.

"Good-bye," Mrs. Winning said on the front steps.

Mrs. MacLane was smiling, and following her look Mrs. Winning turned and saw Mr. Jones, his shirt off and his strong back shining in the sun as he bent with a scythe over the long grass at the side of the house. Billy lay nearby, under the shade of the bushes; he was playing with a grey kitten. "I'm going to have the finest garden in town," Mrs. MacLane said proudly.

"You won't have him working here past today, will you?" Mrs. Winning asked. "Of course you won't have him any longer than just today?"

"But surely—" Mrs. MacLane began, with a tolerant smile, and Mrs. Winning, after looking at her for an incredulous minute, turned and started, indignant and embarrassed, up the hill.

Howard had brought the groceries safely home and her mother-in-law was already setting the table.

"Howard says you sent him home from MacLane's," her mother-in-law said, and Mrs. Winning answered briefly, "I thought it was getting late."

The next morning when Mrs. Winning reached the cottage on her way down to the store she saw Mr. Jones swinging the scythe expertly against the side of the house, and Billy Jones and Davey sitting on the front steps watching him. "Good morning, Davey," Mrs. Winning called, "is your mother ready to go downstreet?"

"Where's Howard?" Davey asked, not moving.

"He stayed home with his grandma today," Mrs. Winning said brightly. "Is your mother ready?"

"She's making lemonade for Billy and me," Davey said. "We're going to have it in the garden."

"Then tell her," Mrs. Winning said quickly, "tell her that I said I was in a hurry and that I had to go on ahead. I'll see her later." She hurried on down the hill.

In the store she met Mrs. Harris, a lady whose mother had worked for the elder Mrs. Winning nearly forty years before. "Helen," Mrs. Harris said, "you get greyer every year. You ought to stop all this running around."

Mrs. Winning, in the store without Mrs. MacLane for the first time in weeks, smiled shyly and said that she guessed she needed a vacation.

"Vacation!" Mrs. Harris said. "Let that husband of yours do the housework for a change. He doesn't have nuthin' else to do."

She laughed richly, and shook her head. "Nuthin' else to do," she said. "The Winnings!"

Before Mrs. Winning could step away Mrs. Harris added, her laughter penetrated by a sudden sharp curiosity: "Where's that dressed-up friend of yours get to? Usually downstreet together, ain't you?"

Mrs. Winning smiled courteously, and Mrs. Harris said, laughing again, "Just couldn't believe those shoes of hers, first time I seen them. Them shoes!"

While she was laughing Mrs. Winning escaped to the meat counter and began to discuss the potentialities of pork shoulder earnestly with the grocer. Mrs. Harris only says what everyone else says, she was thinking, are they talking like that about Mrs. MacLane? Are they laughing at her? When she thought of Mrs. MacLane she thought of the quiet house, the soft colors, the mother and son in the garden; Mrs. MacLane's shoes were green and yellow platform sandals, odd-looking certainly next to Mrs. Winning's solid white oxfords, but so inevitably right for Mrs. MacLane's house, and her garden. . . . Mrs. Harris came up behind her and said, laughing again, "What's she got, that Jones fellow working for her now?"

When Mrs. Winning reached home, after hurrying up the hill past the cottage, where she saw no one, her mother-in-law was waiting for her in front of the house, watching her come the last few yards. "Early enough today," her mother-in-law said. "MacLane out of town?"

Resentful, Mrs. Winning said only, "Mrs. Harris nearly drove me out of the store, with her jokes."

"Nothing wrong with Lucy Harris getting away from that man of hers wouldn't cure," the elder Mrs. Winning said. Together, they began to walk around the house to the back door. Mrs. Winning, as they walked, noticed that the grass under the trees had greened up nicely, and that the nasturtiums beside the house were bright.

"I've got something to say to you, Helen," the elder Mrs. Winning said finally.

"Yes?" her daughter-in-law said.

"It's the MacLane girl, about her, I mean. You know her so well, you ought to talk to her about that colored man working there."

"I suppose so," Mrs. Winning said.

"You *sure* you told her? You told her about those people?"

"I told her," Mrs. Winning said.

"He's there every blessed day," her mother-in-law said. "and working out there without his shirt on. He goes in the house."

And that evening Mr. Burton, next-door neighbor to Mrs. MacLane, dropped in to see the Howard Winnings about getting a new lot of shingles at the mill; he turned, suddenly, to Mrs. Winning, who was sitting sewing next to her mother-in-law at the table in the front room, and raised his voice a little when he said, "Helen, I wish you'd tell your friend Mrs. MacLane to keep that kid of hers out of my vegetables."

"Davey?" Mrs. Winning said involuntarily.

"No," Mr. Burton said, while all the Winnings looked at the younger Mrs. Winning, "no, the other one, the colored boy. He's been running loose through our back yard. Makes me sort of mad, that kid coming in spoiling other people's property. You know," he added, turning to the Howard Winnings, "you know, that does make a person mad." There was a silence, and then Mr. Burton added, rising heavily, "Guess I'll say good-night to you people."

They all attended him to the door and came back to their work in silence. I've got to do something, Mrs. Winning was thinking, pretty soon they'll stop coming to me first, they'll tell someone else to speak to *me*. She looked up, found her mother-in-law looking at her, and they both looked down quickly.

Consequently Mrs. Winning went to the store the next morning earlier than usual, and she and Howard crossed the street just above the MacLane house, and went down the hill on the other side.

"Aren't we going to see Davey?" Howard asked once, and Mrs. Winning said carelessly, "Not today, Howard. Maybe your father will take you out to the mill this afternoon."

She avoided looking across the street at the MacLane house, and hurried to keep up with Howard.

Mrs. Winning met Mrs. MacLane occasionally after that at the store or the post office, and they spoke pleasantly. When Mrs. Winning passed the cottage after the first week or so, she was no longer embarrassed about going by, and even looked at it frankly once or twice. The garden was going beautifully; Mr. Jones's broad back was usually visible through the bushes, and Billy Jones sat on the steps or lay on the grass with Davey.

One morning on her way down the hill Mrs. Winning heard a conversation between Davey MacLane and Billy Jones; they were in the bushes together and she heard Davey's high familiar voice saying, "Billy, you want to build a house with me today?"

"Okay," Billy said. Mrs. Winning slowed her steps a little to hear.

"We'll build a big house out of branches," Davey said excitedly, "and when it's finished we'll ask my mommy if we can have lunch out there."

"You can't build a house just out of branches," Billy said. "You ought to have wood, and boards."

"And chairs and tables and dishes," Davey agreed. "And walls."

"Ask your mommy can we have two chairs out here," Billy said. "Then we can pretend the whole garden is our house."

"And I'll get us some cookies, too," Davey said. "And we'll ask my mommy and your daddy to come in our house." Mrs. Winning heard them shouting as she went down along the sidewalk.

You have to admit, she told herself as though she were being strictly just, you have to admit that he's doing a lot with that garden; it's the prettiest garden on the street. And Billy acts as though he had as much right there as Davey.

As the summer wore on into long hot days undistinguishable one from another, so that it was impossible to tell with any real accuracy whether the light shower had been yesterday or the day before, the Winnings moved out into their yard to sit after supper, and in the warm darkness Mrs. Winning sometimes found an opportunity of sitting next to her husband so that she could touch his arm; she was never able to teach Howard to run to her and put his head in her lap, or inspire him with other than the perfunctory Winning affection, but she consoled herself with the thought that at least they were a family, a solid respectable thing.

The hot weather kept up, and Mrs. Winning began to spend more time in the store, postponing the long aching walk up the hill in the sun. She stopped and chatted with the grocer, with other young mothers in the town, with older friends of her mother-in-law's, talking about the weather, the reluctance of the town to put in a decent swimming pool, the work that had to be done before school started in the fall, chickenpox, the P.T.A. One morning she met Mrs. Burton in the store, and they spoke of their husbands, the heat, and the hot-weather occupations of their children before Mrs. Burton said: "By the way, Johnny will be six on Saturday and he's having a birthday party; can Howard come?"

"Wonderful," Mrs. Winning said, thinking, His good white shorts, the dark blue shirt, a carefully-wrapped present.

"Just about eight children," Mrs. Burton said, with the loving carelessness mothers use in planning the birthday parties of their children. "They'll stay for supper, of course—send Howard down about three-thirty."

"That sounds so nice," Mrs. Winning said. "He'll be delighted when I tell him."

"I thought I'd have them all play outdoors most of the time," Mrs. Burton said. "In this weather. And then perhaps a few games indoors, and supper. Keep it simple—*you* know." She hesitated, running her finger around and around the top rim of a can of coffee. "Look," she said, "I hope you won't mind me asking, but would it be all right with you if I didn't invite the MacLane boy?"

Mrs. Winning felt sick for a minute, and had to wait for her voice to even out before she said lightly, "It's all right with me if it's all right with *you*; why do you have to ask *me*?"

Mrs. Burton laughed. "I just thought you might mind if he didn't come."

Mrs. Winning was thinking. Something bad has happened, somehow people think they know something about me that they won't say, they all pretend it's nothing, but this never happened to me before; I live with the Winnings, don't I? "Really," she said, putting the weight of the old Winning house into her voice, "why in the *world* would it bother me?" Did I take it too seriously, she was wondering, did I seem too anxious, should I have let it go?

Mrs. Burton was embarrassed, and she set the can of coffee down on the shelf and began to examine the other shelves studiously. "I'm sorry I mentioned it at all," she said.

Mrs. Winning felt that she had to say something further, something to state her position with finality, so that no longer would Mrs. Burton, at least, dare to use such a tone to a Winning, presume to preface a question with "I hope you don't mind me asking." "After all," Mrs. Winning said carefully, weighing the words, "she's like a second mother to Billy."

Mrs. Burton, turning to look at Mrs. Winning for confirmation, grimaced and said, "Good Lord, Helen!"

Mrs. Winning shrugged and then smiled and Mrs. Burton smiled and then Mrs. Winning said, "I do feel so sorry for the little boy, though."

Mrs. Burton said, "Such a sweet little thing, too."

Mrs. Winning had just said, "He and Billy are together *all* the time now," when she looked up and saw Mrs. MacLane regarding her from the end of the aisle of shelves; it was impossible to tell whether she had heard them or not. For a minute Mrs. Winning looked steadily back at Mrs. MacLane, and then she said, with just the right note of cordiality, "Good morning, Mrs. MacLane. Where is your little boy this morning?"

"Good morning, Mrs. Winning," Mrs. MacLane said, and moved on past the aisle of shelves, and Mrs. Burton caught Mrs. Winning's arm and made a desperate gesture of hiding her face and, unable to help themselves, both she and Mrs. Winning began to laugh.

Soon after that, although the grass in the Winning yard under the maple trees stayed smooth and green, Mrs. Winning began to notice in her daily trips past the cottage that Mrs. MacLane's garden was suffering from the heat. The flowers wilted under the morning sun, and no longer stood up fresh and bright; the grass was browning slightly and the rose bushes Mrs. MacLane had put in so optimistically were noticeably dying. Mr. Jones seemed always cool, working steadily; sometimes bent down with his hands in the earth, sometimes tall against the side of the house, setting up a trellis or pruning a tree, but the blue curtains hung lifelessly at the windows. Mrs. MacLane still smiled at Mrs. Winning in the store, and then one day they met at the gate of Mrs. MacLane's garden and, after hesitating for a minute, Mrs. MacLane said, "Can you come in for a few minutes? I'd like to have a talk, if you have time."

"Surely," Mrs. Winning said courteously, and followed Mrs. MacLane up the walk, still luxuriously bordered with flowering bushes, but somehow disenchanted, as though the summer heat had baked away the vivacity from the ground. In the familiar living-room Mrs. Winning sat down on a straight chair, holding herself politely stiff, while Mrs. MacLane sat as usual in her armchair.

"How is Davey?" Mrs. Winning asked finally, since Mrs. MacLane did not seem disposed to start any conversation.

"He's very well," Mrs. MacLane said, and smiled as she always did when speaking of Davey. "He's out back with Billy."

There was a quiet minute, and then Mrs. MacLane said, staring at the blue bowl on the coffee table, "What I wanted to ask you is, what on earth is gone wrong?"

Mrs. Winning had been holding herself stiff in readiness for some such question, and when she said, "I don't know what you mean," she thought, I sound exactly like Mother Winning, and realized, I'm enjoying this, just as *she* would; and no matter what she thought of herself she was unable to keep from adding, "*Is* something wrong?"

"Of course," Mrs. MacLane said. She stared at the blue bowl, and said slowly, "When I first came, everyone was so nice, and they seemed to like Davey and me and want to help us."

That's wrong, Mrs. Winning was thinking, you mustn't ever talk about whether people like you, that's bad taste.

"And the garden was going so well," Mrs. MacLane said helplessly. "And now, no one ever does more than just speak to us—I used to say 'Good morning' over the fence to Mrs. Burton, and she'd come to the fence and we'd talk about the garden, and now she just says 'Morning' and goes in the house—and no one ever smiles, or anything."

This is dreadful, Mrs. Winning thought, this is childish, this is complaining. People treat you as you treat them, she thought; she wanted desperately to go over and take Mrs. MacLane's hand and ask her to come back and be one of the nice people again; but she only sat straighter in the chair and said, "I'm sure you must be mistaken. I've never heard anyone speak of it."

"*Are* you sure?" Mrs. MacLane turned and looked at her. "Are you sure it isn't because of Mr. Jones working here?"

Mrs. Winning lifted her chin a little higher and said, "Why on earth would anyone around here be rude to you because of Jones?"

Mrs. MacLane came with her to the door, both of them planning vigorously for the days some time next week, when they would all go swimming, when they would have a picnic, and Mrs. Winning went down the hill thinking, The nerve of her, trying to blame the colored folks.

Toward the end of the summer there was a bad thunderstorm, breaking up the prolonged hot spell. It raged with heavy wind and rain over the town all night, sweeping without pity through the trees, pulling up young bushes and flowers ruthlessly; a barn was struck on one side of town, the wires pulled down on another. In the morning Mrs. Winning opened the back door to find the Winning yard littered with small branches from the maples, the grass bent almost flat to the ground.

Her mother-in-law came to the door behind her. "Quite a storm," she said, "did it wake you?"

"I woke up once and went to look at the children," Mrs. Winning said. "It must have been about three o'clock."

"I was up later," her mother-in-law said. "I looked at the children too; they were both asleep."

They turned together and went in to start breakfast.

Later in the day Mrs. Winning started down to the store; she had almost reached the MacLane cottage when she saw Mrs. MacLane standing in the front garden with Mr. Jones standing beside her and Billy Jones with Davey in the shadows of the front porch. They were all looking silently at a great branch from one of the Burtons' trees that lay across the center of the garden, crushing most of the flowering bushes and pinning down what was to have been a glorious tulip bed. As Mrs. Winning stopped, watching, Mrs. Burton came out on to her front porch to survey the storm-damage, and Mrs. MacLane called to her, "Good morning, Mrs. Burton, it looks like we have part of your tree over here."

"Looks so," Mrs. Burton said, and she went back into her house and closed the door flatly.

Mrs. Winning watched while Mrs. MacLane stood quietly for a minute. Then she looked up at Mr. Jones almost hopefully and she and Mr. Jones looked at one another for a long time. Then Mrs. MacLane said, her clear voice carrying lightly across the air washed clean by the storm: "Do you think I ought to give it up, Mr. Jones? Go back to the city where I'll never have to see another garden?"

Mr. Jones shook his head despondently, and Mrs. MacLane, her shoulders tired, went slowly over and sat on her front steps and Davey came and sat next to her. Mr. Jones took hold of the great branch angrily and tried to move it, shaking it and pulling until his shoulders tensed with the strength he was bringing to bear, but the branch only gave slightly and stayed, clinging to the garden.

"Leave it alone, Mr. Jones," Mrs. MacLane said finally. "Leave it for the next people to move!"

But still Mr. Jones pulled against the branch, and then suddenly Davey stood up and cried out, "There's Mrs. Winning! Hi, Mrs. Winning!"

Mrs. MacLane and Mr. Jones both turned, and Mrs. MacLane waved and called out, "Hello!"

Mrs. Winning swung around without speaking and started, with great dignity, back up the hill toward the old Winning house.

MILAN KUNDERA   (b. 1929)

The Hitchhiking Game

Translated by Suzanne Rappaport

1

The needle on the gas gauge suddenly dipped toward empty and the young driver of the sports car declared that it was maddening how much gas the car ate up. "See that we don't run out of gas again," protested the girl (about twenty-two), and reminded the driver of several places where this had already happened to them. The young man replied that he wasn't worried, because whatever he went through with her had the charm of adventure for him. The girl objected; whenever they had run out of gas on the highway it had, she said, always been an adventure only for her. The young man had hidden and she had had to make ill use of her charms by thumbing a ride and letting herself be driven to the nearest gas station, then thumbing a ride back with a can of gas. The young man asked the girl whether the drivers who had given her a ride had been unpleasant, since she spoke as if her task had been a hardship. She replied (with awkward flirtatiousness) that sometimes they had been *very* pleasant but that it hadn't done her any good as she had been burdened with the can and had had to leave them before she could get anything going. "Pig," said the young man. The girl protested that she wasn't a pig, but that he really was. God knows how many girls stopped him on the highway, when he was driving the car alone! Still driving, the young man put his arm around the girl's shoulders and kissed her gently on the forehead. He knew that she loved him and that she was jealous. Jealousy isn't a pleasant quality, but if it isn't overdone (and if it's combined with modesty), apart from its inconvenience there's even something touching about it. At least that's what the young man thought. Because he was only twenty-eight, it seemed to him that he was old and knew everything that a man could know about women. In the girl sitting beside him he valued precisely what, until now, he had met with least in women: purity.

The needle was already on empty, when to the right the young man caught sight of a sign, announcing that the station was a quarter of a mile ahead. The girl hardly had time to say how relieved she was before the young man was signaling left and driving into a space in front of the pumps. However, he had to stop a little way off, because beside the pumps was a huge gasoline truck with a large metal tank and a bulky hose, which was refilling the pumps. "We'll have to wait," said the young man to the girl and got out of the car. "How long will it take?" he shouted to the man in overalls. "Only a moment," replied the attendant, and the young man said: "I've heard that one before." He wanted to go back and sit in the car, but he saw that the girl had gotten out the other side. "I'll take a little walk in the meantime," she said. "Where to?" the young man asked on purpose, wanting to see the girl's embarrassment. He had known her for a year now but she would still get shy in front of him. He enjoyed her moments of shyness, partly because they distinguished her from the women he'd met before, partly because he was aware of the law of universal transience, which made even his girl's shyness a precious thing to him.

2

The girl really didn't like it when during the trip (the young man would drive for several hours without stopping) she had to ask him to stop for a moment somewhere near a clump of trees. She always got angry when, with feigned surprise, he asked her why he should stop. She knew that her shyness was ridiculous and old-fashioned. Many times at work she had noticed that they laughed at her on account of it and deliberately provoked her. She always got shy in advance at the thought of how she was going to get shy. She often longed to feel free and easy about her body, the way most of the women around her did. She had even invented a special course in self-persuasion: she would repeat to herself that at birth every human being received one out of the millions of available bodies, as one would receive an allotted room out of the millions of rooms in an enormous hotel; that, consequently, the body was fortuitous and impersonal, only a ready-made, borrowed thing. She would repeat this to herself in different ways, but she could never manage to feel it. This mind-body dualism was alien to her. She was too much one with her body; that is why she always felt such anxiety about it.

She experienced this same anxiety even in her relations with the young man, whom she had known for a year and with whom she was happy, perhaps because he never separated her body from her soul and she could live with him *wholly*. In this unity there was happiness, but right behind the happiness lurked suspicion, and the girl was full of that. For instance, it often occurred to her that the other women (those who weren't anxious) were more attractive and more seductive and that the young man, who did not conceal the fact that he knew this kind of woman well, would someday leave her for a woman like that. (True, the young man declared that he'd had enough of them to last his whole life, but she knew that he was still much younger than he thought.) She wanted him to be completely hers and she to be completely his, but it often seemed to her that the more she tried to give him everything, the more she denied him something: the very thing that a light and superficial love or a flirtation gives to a person. It worried her that she was not able to combine seriousness with lightheartedness.

But now she wasn't worrying and any such thoughts were far from her mind. She felt good. It was the first day of their vacation (of their two-week vacation, about which she had been dreaming for a whole year), the sky was blue (the whole year she had been worrying about whether the sky would really be blue), and he was beside her. At his, "Where to?" she blushed, and left the car without a word. She walked around the gas station, which was situated beside the highway in total isolation, surrounded by fields. About a hundred yards away (in the direction in which they were traveling), a wood began. She set off for it, vanished behind a little bush, and gave herself up to her good mood. (In solitude it was possible for her to get the greatest enjoyment from the presence of the man she loved. If his presence had been continuous, it would have kept on disappearing. Only when alone was she able to *hold on* to it.)

When she came out of the wood onto the highway, the gas station was visible. The large gasoline truck was already pulling out and the sports car moved forward toward the red turret of the pump. The girl walked on along the highway and only at times looked back to see if the sports car was coming. At last she caught sight of it. She stopped and began to wave at it like a hitchhiker waving at a stranger's car. The sports car slowed down and stopped close to the girl. The young man leaned toward the window, rolled it down, smiled, and asked, "Where are you headed, miss?" "Are you going to Bystritsa?" asked the girl, smiling flirtatiously at him. "Yes, please get in," said the young man, opening the door. The girl got in and the car took off.

3

The young man was always glad when his girl friend was gay. This didn't happen too often; she had a quite tiresome job in an unpleasant environment, many hours of overtime without compensatory leisure and, at home, a sick mother. So she often felt tired. She didn't have either particularly good nerves or self-confidence and easily fell into a state of anxiety and fear. For this reason he welcomed every manifestation of her gaiety with the tender solicitude of a foster parent. He smiled at her and said: "I'm lucky today. I've been driving for five years, but I've never given a ride to such a pretty hitchhiker."

The girl was grateful to the young man for every bit of flattery; she wanted to linger for a moment in its warmth and so she said, "You're very good at lying."

"Do I look like a liar?"

"You look like you enjoy lying to women," said the girl, and into her words there crept unawares a touch of the old anxiety, because she really did believe that her young man enjoyed lying to women.

The girl's jealousy often irritated the young man, but this time he could easily overlook it for, after all, her words didn't apply to him but to the unknown driver. And so he just casually inquired, "Does it bother you?"

"If I were going with you, then it would bother me," said the girl and her words contained a subtle, instructive message for the young man; but the end of her sentence applied only to the unknown driver, "but I don't know you, so it doesn't bother me."

"Things about her own man always bother a woman more than things about a stranger" (this was now the young man's subtle, instructive message to the girl), "so seeing that we are strangers, we could get on well together."

The girl purposely didn't want to understand the implied meaning of his message, and so she now addressed the unknown driver exclusively: "What does it matter, since we'll part company in a little while?"

"Why?" asked the young man.

"Well, I'm getting out at Bystritsa."

"And what if I get out with you?"

At these words the girl looked up at him and found that he looked exactly as she imagined him in her most agonizing hours of jealousy. She was alarmed at how he was flattering her and flirting with her (an unknown hitchhiker), and *how becoming it was to him*. Therefore she responded with defiant provocativeness, "What would *you* do with me, I wonder?"

"I wouldn't have to think too hard about what to do with such a beautiful woman," said the young man gallantly and at this moment he was once again speaking far more to his own girl than to the figure of the hitchhiker.

But this flattering sentence made the girl feel as if she had caught him at something, as if she had wheedled a confession out of him with a fraudulent trick. She felt toward him a brief flash of intense hatred and said, "Aren't you rather too sure of yourself?"

The young man looked at the girl. Her defiant face appeared to him to be completely convulsed. He felt sorry for her and longed for her usual, familiar expression (which he used to call childish and simple). He leaned toward her, put his arm around her shoulders, and softly spoke the name with which he usually addressed her and with which he now wanted to stop the game.

But the girl released herself and said: "You're going a bit too fast!"

At this rebuff the young man said: "Excuse me, miss," and looked silently in front of him at the highway.

4

The girl's pitiful jealousy, however, left her as quickly as it had come over her. After all, she was sensible and knew perfectly well that all this was merely a game; now it even struck her as a little ridiculous that she had repulsed her man out of jealous rage; it wouldn't be pleasant for her if he found out why she had done it. Fortunately she had the miraculous ability to change the meaning of her actions after the event. Using this ability, she decided that she had repulsed him not out of anger but so that she could go on with the game, which, with its whimsicality, so well suited the first day of their vacation.

So again she was the hitchhiker, who had just repulsed the overenterprising driver, but only so as to slow down his conquest and make it more exciting. She half turned toward the young man and said caressingly:

"I didn't mean to offend you, mister!"

"Excuse me, I won't touch you again," said the young man.

He was furious with the girl for not listening to him and refusing to be herself when that was what he wanted. And since the girl insisted on continuing in her role, he transferred his anger to the unknown hitchhiker whom she was portraying. And all at once he discovered the character of his own part: he stopped making the gallant remarks with which he had wanted to flatter his girl in a roundabout way, and began to play the tough guy who treats women to the coarser aspects of his masculinity: willfulness, sarcasm, self-assurance.

This role was a complete contradiction of the young man's habitually solicitous approach to the girl. True, before he had met her, he had in fact behaved roughly rather than gently toward women. But he had never resembled a heartless tough guy, because he had never demonstrated either a particularly strong will or ruthlessness. However, if he did not resemble such a man, nonetheless he had *longed* to at one time. Of course it was a quite naive desire, but there it was. Childish desires withstand all the snares of the adult mind and often survive into ripe old age. And this childish desire quickly took advantage of the opportunity to embody itself in the proffered role.

The young man's sarcastic reserve suited the girl very well—it freed her from herself. For she herself was, above all, the epitome of jealousy. The moment she stopped seeing the gallantly seductive young man beside her and saw only his inaccessible face, her jealousy subsided. The girl could forget herself and give herself up to her role.

Her role? What was her role? It was a role out of trashy literature. The hitchhiker stopped the car not to get a ride, but to seduce the man who was driving the car. She was an artful seductress, cleverly knowing how to use her charms. The girl slipped into this silly, romantic part with an ease that astonished her and held her spellbound.

5

There was nothing the young man missed in his life more than light-heartedness. The main road of his life was drawn with implacable precision: his job didn't use up merely eight hours a day, it also infiltrated the remaining time with the compulsory boredom of meetings and home study, and, by means of the attentiveness of his countless male and female colleagues, it infiltrated the wretchedly little time he had left for his private life as well; this private life never remained secret and sometimes even became the subject of gossip and public discussion. Even two weeks' vacation didn't give him a feeling of liberation and adventure; the gray shadow of precise planning lay even here. The scarcity of summer accommodations in our country compelled him to book a room in the Tatras six months in advance, and since for that he needed a recommendation from his office, its omnipresent brain thus did not cease knowing about him even for an instant.

He had become reconciled to all this, yet all the same from time to time the terrible thought of the straight road would overcome him—a road along which he was being pursued, where he was visible to everyone, and from which he could not turn aside. At this moment that thought returned to him. Through an odd and brief conjunction of ideas the figurative road became identified with the real highway along which he was driving—and this led him suddenly to do a crazy thing.

"Where did you say you wanted to go?" he asked the girl.

"To Banska Bystritsa," she replied.

"And what are you going to do there?"

"I have a date there."

"Who with?"

"With a certain gentleman."

The car was just coming to a large crossroads. The driver slowed down so he could read the road signs, then turned off to the right.

"What will happen if you don't arrive for that date?"

"It would be your fault and you would have to take care of me."

"You obviously didn't notice that I turned off in the direction of Nove Zamky."

"Is that true? You've gone crazy!"

"Don't be afraid, I'll take care of you," said the young man.

So they drove and chatted thus—the driver and the hitchhiker who did not know each other.

The game all at once went into a higher gear. The sports car was moving away not only from the imaginary goal of Banska Bystritsa, but also from the real goal, toward which it had been heading in the morning: the Tatras and the room that had been booked. Fiction was suddenly making an assault upon real life. The young man was moving away from himself and from the implacable straight road, from which he had never strayed until now.

"But you said you were going to the Low Tatras!" The girl was surprised.

"I am going, miss, wherever I feel like going. I'm a free man and I do what I want and what it pleases me to do."

6

When they drove into Nove Zamky it was already getting dark.

The young man had never been here before and it took him a while to orient himself. Several times he stopped the car and asked the passersby directions to the hotel. Several streets had been dug up, so that the drive to the hotel, even though it was quite close by (as all those who had been asked asserted), necessitated so many detours and roundabout routes that it was almost a quarter of an hour before they finally stopped in front of it. The hotel looked unprepossessing, but it was the only one in town and the young man didn't feel like driving on. So he said to the girl, "Wait here," and got out of the car.

Out of the car he was, of course, himself again. And it was upsetting for him to find himself in the evening somewhere completely different from his intended destination—the more so because no one had forced him to do it and as a matter of fact he hadn't even really wanted to. He blamed himself for this piece of folly, but then became reconciled to it. The room in the Tatras could wait until tomorrow and it wouldn't do any harm if they celebrated the first day of their vacation with something unexpected.

He walked through the restaurant—smoky, noisy, and crowded—and asked for the reception desk. They sent him to the back of the lobby near the staircase, where behind a glass panel a superannuated blonde was sitting beneath a board full of keys. With difficulty, he obtained the key to the only room left.

The girl, when she found herself alone, also threw off her role. She didn't feel ill-humored, though, at finding herself in an unexpected town. She was so devoted to the young man that she never had doubts about anything he did, and confidently entrusted every moment of her life to him. On the other hand the idea once again popped into her mind that perhaps—just as she was now doing—other women had waited for her man in his car, those women whom he met on business trips. But surprisingly enough this idea didn't upset her at all now; in fact, she smiled at the thought of how nice it was that today she was this other woman, this irresponsible, indecent other woman, one of those women of whom she was so jealous; it seemed to her that she was cutting them all out, that she had learned how to use their weapons; how to give the young man what until now she had not known how to give him: lightheartedness, shamelessness, and dissoluteness; a curious feeling of satisfaction filled her, because she alone had the ability to be all women and in this way (she alone) could completely captivate her lover and hold his interest.

The young man opened the car door and led the girl into the restaurant. Amid the din, the dirt, and the smoke he found a single, unoccupied table in a corner.

7

"So how are you going to take care of me now?" asked the girl provocatively.

"What would you like for an aperitif?"

The girl wasn't too fond of alcohol, still she drank a little wine and liked vermouth fairly well. Now, however, she purposely said: "Vodka."

"Fine," said the young man. "I hope you won't get drunk on me."

"And if I do?" said the girl.

The young man did not reply but called over a waiter and ordered two vodkas and two steak dinners. In a moment the waiter brought a tray with two small glasses and placed it in front of them.

The man raised his glass, "To you!"

"Can't you think of a wittier toast?"

Something was beginning to irritate him about the girl's game; now sitting face to face with her, he realized that it wasn't just the *words* which were turning her into a stranger, but that her *whole persona* had changed, the movements of her body and her facial expression, and that she unpalatably and faithfully resembled that type of woman whom he knew so well and for whom he felt some aversion.

And so (holding his glass in his raised hand), he corrected his toast: "O.K., then I won't drink to you, but to your kind, in which are combined so successfully the better qualities of the animal and the worse aspects of the human being."

"By 'kind' do you mean all women?" asked the girl.

"No, I mean only those who are like you."

"Anyway it doesn't seem very witty to me to compare a woman with an animal."

"O.K.," the young man was still holding his glass aloft, "then I won't drink to your kind, but to your soul. Agreed? To your soul, which lights up when it descends from your head into your belly, and which goes out when it rises back up to your head."

The girl raised her glass. "O.K., to my soul, which descends into my belly."

"I'll correct myself once more," said the young man. "To your belly, into which your soul descends."

"To my belly," said the girl, and her belly (now that they had named it specifically), as it were, responded to the call; she felt every inch of it.

Then the waiter brought their steaks and the young man ordered them another vodka and some soda water (this time they drank to the girl's breasts), and the conversation continued in this peculiar, frivolous tone. It irritated the young man more and more how *well able* the girl was to become the lascivious miss; if she was able to do it so well, he thought, it meant that she really *was* like that; after all, no alien soul had entered into her from somewhere in space; what she was acting now was she herself; perhaps it was that part of her being which had formerly been locked up and which the pretext of the game had let out of its cage. Perhaps the girl supposed that by means of the game she was *disowning* herself, but wasn't it the other way around? wasn't she becoming herself only through the game? wasn't she freeing herself through the game? no, opposite him was not sitting a strange woman in his girl's body; it was his girl, herself, no one else. He looked at her and felt growing aversion toward her.

However, it was not only aversion. The more the girl withdrew from him *psychically*, the more he longed for her *physically*; the alienation of her soul drew attention to her body; yes it turned her body into a body; as if until now it had been hidden from the young man within clouds of compassion, tenderness, concern, love, and emotion, as if it had been lost in these clouds (yes, as if this body had been *lost!*). It seemed to the young man that today he was *seeing* his girl's body for the first time.

After her third vodka and soda the girl got up and said flirtatiously, "Excuse me."

The young man said, "May I ask you where you are going, miss?"

"To piss, if you'll permit me," said the girl and walked off between the tables back toward the plush screen.

8

She was pleased with the way she had astounded the young man with this word, which—in spite of all its innocence—he had never heard from her; nothing seemed to her truer to the character of the woman she was playing than this flirtatious emphasis placed on the word in question; yes, she was pleased, she was in the best of moods; the game captivated her. It allowed her to feel what she had not felt till now: *a feeling of happy-go-lucky irresponsibility*.

She, who was always uneasy in advance about her every next step, suddenly felt completely relaxed. The alien life in which she had become involved was a life without shame, without biographical specifications, without past or future, without obligations; it was a life that was extraordinarily free. The girl, as a hitchhiker, could do anything: *everything was permitted her*; she could say, do, and feel whatever she liked.

She walked through the room and was aware that people were watching her from all the tables; it was also a new sensation, one she didn't recognize: *indecent joy caused by her body.* Until now she had never been able to get rid of the fourteen-year-old girl within herself who was ashamed of her breasts and had the disagreeable feeling that she was indecent, because they stuck out from her body and were visible. Even though she was proud of being pretty and having a good figure, this feeling of pride was always immediately curtailed by shame; she rightly suspected that feminine beauty functioned above all as sexual provocation and she found this distasteful; she longed for her body to relate only to the man she loved; when men stared at her breasts in the street it seemed to her that they were invading a piece of her most secret privacy which should belong only to herself and her lover. But now she was the hitchhiker, the woman without a destiny. In this role she was relieved of the tender bonds of her love and began to be intensely aware of her body; and her body became more aroused the more alien the eyes watching it.

She was walking past the last table when an intoxicated man, wanting to show off his worldliness, addressed her in French: *"Combien, mademoiselle?"*

The girl understood. She thrust out her breasts and fully experienced every movement of her hips, then disappeared behind the screen.

9

It was a curious game. This curiousness was evidenced, for example, in the fact that the young man, even though he himself was playing the unknown driver remarkably well, did not for a moment stop seeing his girl in the hitchhiker. And it was precisely this that was tormenting; he saw his girl seducing a strange man, and had the bitter privilege of being present, of seeing at close quarters how she looked and of hearing what she said when she was cheating on him (when she had cheated on him, when she would cheat on him); he had the paradoxical honor of being himself the pretext for her unfaithfulness.

This was all the worse because he worshipped rather than loved her; it had always seemed to him that her inward nature was *real* only within the bounds of fidelity and purity, and that beyond these bounds it simply didn't exist; beyond these bounds she would cease to be herself, as water ceases to be water beyond the boiling point. When he now saw her crossing this horrifying boundary with nonchalant elegance, he was filled with anger.

The girl came back from the rest room and complained: "A guy over there asked me: *Combien, mademoiselle?*"

"You shouldn't be surprised," said the young man, "after all, you look like a whore."

"Do you know that it doesn't bother me in the least?"

"Then you should go with the gentleman!"

"But I have you."

"You can go with him after me. Go and work out something with him."

"I don't find him attractive."

"But in principle you have nothing against it, having several men in one night."

"Why not, if they're good-looking."

"Do you prefer them one after the other or at the same time?"

"Either way," said the girl.

The conversation was proceeding to still greater extremes of rudeness; it shocked the girl slightly but she couldn't protest. Even in a game there lurks a lack of freedom; even a game is a trap for the players. If this had not been a game and they had really been two strangers, the hitchhiker could long ago have taken offense and left. But there's no escape from a game. A team cannot flee from the playing field before the end of the match, chess pieces cannot desert the chessboard: the boundaries of the playing field are fixed. The girl knew that she had to accept whatever form the game might take, just because it was a game. She knew that the more extreme the game became, the more it would be a game and the more obediently she would have to play it. And it was futile to evoke good sense and warn her dazed soul that she must keep her distance from the game and not take it seriously. Just because it was only a game her soul was not afraid, did not oppose the game, and narcotically sank deeper into it.

The young man called the waiter and paid. Then he got up and said to the girl, "We're going."

"Where to?" The girl feigned surprise.

"Don't ask, just come on," said the young man.

"What sort of way is that to talk to me?"

"The way I talk to whores," said the young man.

10

They went up the badly lit staircase. On the landing below the second floor a group of intoxicated men was standing near the rest room. The young man caught hold of the girl from behind so that he was holding her breast with his hand. The men by the rest room saw this and began to call out. The girl wanted to break away, but the young man yelled at her: "Keep still!" The men greeted this with general ribaldry and addressed several dirty remarks to the girl. The young man and the girl reached the second floor. He opened the door of their room and switched on the light.

It was a narrow room with two beds, a small table, a chair, and a washbasin. The young man locked the door and turned to the girl. She was standing facing him in a defiant pose with insolent sensuality in her eyes. He looked at her and tried to discover behind her lascivious expression the familiar features which he loved tenderly. It was as if he were looking at two images through the same lens, at two images superimposed one upon the other with the one showing through the other. These two images showing through each other were telling him that *everything* was in the girl, that her soul was terrifyingly amorphous, that it held faithfulness and unfaithfulness, treachery and innocence, flirtatiousness and chastity. This disorderly jumble seemed disgusting to him, like the variety to be found in a pile of garbage. Both images continued to show through each other and the young man understood that the girl differed only on the surface from other women, but deep down was the same as they: full of all possible thoughts, feelings, and vices, which justified all his secret misgivings and fits of jealousy. The impression that certain outlines delineated her as an individual was only a delusion to which the other person, the one who was looking, was subject—namely himself. It seemed to him that the girl he loved was a creation of his desire, his thoughts, and his faith and that the *real* girl now standing in front of him was hopelessly *alien*, hopelessly *ambiguous*. He hated her.

"What are you waiting for? Strip," he said.

The girl flirtatiously bent her head and said, "Is it necessary?"

The tone in which she said this seemed to him very familiar; it seemed to him that once long ago some other woman had said this to him, only he no longer knew which one. He longed to humiliate her. Not the hitchhiker, but his own girl. The game merged with life. The game of humiliating the hitchhiker became only a pretext for humiliating his girl. The young man had forgotten that he was playing a game. He simply hated the woman standing in front of him. He stared at her and took a fifty-crown bill from his wallet. He offered it to the girl. "Is that enough?"

The girl took the fifty crowns and said: "You don't think I'm worth much."

The young man said: "You aren't worth more."

The girl nestled up against the young man. "You can't get around me like that! You must try a different approach, you must work a little!"

She put her arms around him and moved her mouth toward his. He put his fingers on her mouth and gently pushed her away. He said: "I only kiss women I love."

"And you don't love me?"

"No."

"Whom do you love?"

"What's that got to do with you? Strip!"

11

She had never undressed like this before. The shyness, the feeling of inner panic, the dizziness, all that she had always felt when undressing in front of the young man (and she couldn't hide in the darkness), all this was gone. She was standing in front of him self-confident, insolent, bathed in light, and astonished at where she had all of a sudden discovered the gestures, heretofore unknown to her, of a slow, provocative striptease. She took in his glances, slipping off each piece of clothing with a caressing movement and enjoying each individual stage of this exposure.

But then suddenly she was standing in front of him completely naked and at this moment it flashed through her head that now the whole game would end, that since she had stripped off her clothes, she had also stripped away her dissimulation, and that being naked meant that she was now herself and the young man ought to come up to her now and make a gesture with which he would wipe out everything and after which would follow only their most intimate love-making. So she stood naked in front of the young man and at this moment stopped playing the game. She felt embarrassed and on her face appeared the smile which really belonged to her: a shy and confused smile.

But the young man didn't come to her and didn't end the game. He didn't notice the familiar smile; he saw before him only the beautiful, alien body of his own girl, whom he hated. Hatred cleansed his sensuality of any sentimental coating. She wanted to come to him, but he said: "Stay where you are, I want to have a good look at you." Now he longed only to treat her as a whore. But the young man had never had a whore and the ideas he had about them came from literature and hearsay. So he turned to these ideas and the first thing he recalled was the image of a woman in black underwear (and black stockings) dancing on the shiny top of a piano. In the little hotel room there was no piano, there was only a small table covered with a linen cloth leaning against the wall. He ordered the girl to climb up on it. The girl made a pleading gesture, but the young man said, "You've been paid."

When she saw the look of unshakable obsession in the young man's eyes, she tried to go on with the game, even though she no longer could and no longer knew how. With tears in her eyes she climbed onto the table. The top was scarcely three feet square and one leg was a little bit shorter than the others so that standing on it the girl felt unsteady.

But the young man was pleased with the naked figure, now towering above him, and the girl's shy insecurity merely inflamed his imperiousness. He wanted to see her body in all positions and from all sides, as he imagined other men had seen it and would see it. He was vulgar and lascivious. He used words that she had never heard from him in her life. She wanted to refuse, she wanted to be released from the game. She called him by his first name, but he immediately yelled at her that she had no right to address him so intimately. And so eventually in confusion and on the verge of tears, she obeyed, she bent forward and squatted according to the young man's wishes, saluted, and then wiggled her hips as she did the Twist for him; during a slightly more violent movement, when the cloth slipped beneath her feet and she nearly fell, the young man caught her and dragged her to the bed.

He had intercourse with her. She was glad that at least now finally the unfortunate game would end and they would again be the two people they had been before and would love each other. She wanted to press her mouth against his. But the young man pushed her head away and repeated that he only kissed women he loved. She burst into loud sobs. But she wasn't even allowed to cry, because the young man's furious passion gradually won over her body, which then silenced the complaint of her soul. On the bed there were soon two bodies in perfect harmony, two sensual bodies, alien to each other. This was exactly what the girl had most dreaded all her life and had scrupulously avoided till now: love-making without emotion or love. She knew that she had crossed the forbidden boundary, but she proceeded across it without objections and as a full participant; only somewhere, far off in a corner of her consciousness, did she feel horror at the thought that she had never known such pleasure, never so much pleasure as at this moment—beyond that boundary.

12

Then it was all over. The young man got up off the girl and, reaching out for the long cord hanging over the bed, switched off the light. He didn't want to see the girl's face. He knew that the game was over, but didn't feel like returning to their customary relationship; he feared this return. He lay beside the girl in the dark in such a way that their bodies would not touch.

After a moment he heard her sobbing quietly; the girl's hand diffidently, childishly touched his; it touched, withdrew, then touched again, and then a pleading, sobbing voice broke the silence, calling him by his name and saying, "I am me, I am me . . ."

The young man was silent, he didn't move, and he was aware of the sad emptiness of the girl's assertion, in which the unknown was defined by the same unknown.

And the girl soon passed from sobbing to loud crying and went on endlessly repeating this pitiful tautology: "I am me, I am me, I am me . . ."

The young man began to call compassion to his aid (he had to call it from afar, because it was nowhere near at hand), so as to be able to calm the girl. There were still thirteen days' vacation before them.

JOYCE CAROL OATES   (b. 1938)

Where Are You Going, Where Have You Been?

For Bob Dylan

Her name was Connie. She was fifteen and she had a quick, nervous giggling habit of craning her neck to glance into mirrors or checking other people's faces to make sure her own was all right. Her mother, who noticed everything and knew everything and who hadn't much reason any longer to look at her own face, always scolded Connie about it. "Stop gawking at yourself. Who are you? You think you're so pretty?" she would say. Connie would raise her eyebrows at these familiar old complaints and look right through her mother, into a shadowy vision of herself as she was right at that moment: she knew she was pretty and that was everything. Her mother had been pretty once too, if you could believe those old snapshots in the album, but now her looks were gone and that was why she was always after Connie.

"Why don't you keep your room clean like your sister? How've you got your hair fixed—what the hell stinks? Hair spray? You don't see your sister using that junk."

Her sister June was twenty-four and still lived at home. She was a secretary in the high school Connie attended, and if that wasn't bad enough—with her in the same building—she was so plain and chunky and steady that Connie had to hear her praised all the time by her mother and her mother's sisters. June did this, June did that, she saved money and helped clean the house and cooked and Connie couldn't do a thing, her mind was all filled with trashy daydreams. Their father was away at work most of the time and when he came home he wanted supper and he read the newspaper at supper and after supper he went to bed. He didn't bother talking much to them, but around his bent head Connie's mother kept picking at her until Connie wished her mother was dead and she herself was dead and it was all over. "She makes me want to throw up sometimes," she complained to her friends. She had a high, breathless, amused voice that made everything she said sound a little forced, whether it was sincere or not.

There was one good thing: June went places with girl friends of hers, girls who were just as plain and steady as she, and so when Connie wanted to do that her mother had no objections. The father of Connie's best girl friend drove the girls the three miles to town and left them at a shopping plaza so they could walk through the stores or go to a movie, and when he came to pick them up again at eleven he never bothered to ask what they had done.

They must have been familiar sights, walking around the shopping plaza in their shorts and flat ballerina slippers that always scuffed on the sidewalk, with charm bracelets jingling on their thin wrists; they would lean together to whisper and laugh secretly if someone passed who amused or interested them. Connie had long dark blond hair that drew anyone's eye to it, and she wore part of it pulled up on her head and puffed out and the rest of it she let fall down her back. She wore a pull-over jersey blouse that looked one way when she was at home and another way when she was away from home. Everything about her had two sides to it, one for home and one for anywhere that was not home: her walk, which could be childlike and bobbing, or languid enough to make anyone think she was hearing music in her head; her mouth, which was pale and smirking most of the time, but bright and pink on these evenings out; her laugh, which was cynical and drawling at home—"Ha, ha, very funny,"—but highpitched and nervous anywhere else, like the jingling of the charms on her bracelet.

Sometimes they did go shopping or to a movie, but sometimes they went across the highway, ducking fast across the busy road, to a drive-in restaurant where older kids hung out. The restaurant was shaped like a big bottle, though squatter than a real bottle, and on its cap was a revolving figure of a grinning boy holding a hamburger aloft. One night in midsummer they ran across, breathless with daring, and right away someone leaned out a car window and invited them over, but it was just a boy from high school they didn't like. It made them feel good to be able to ignore him. They went up through the maze of parked and cruising cars to the bright-lit, fly-infested restaurant, their faces pleased and expectant as if they were entering a sacred building that loomed up out of the night to give them what haven and blessing they yearned for. They sat at the counter and crossed their legs at the ankles, their thin shoulders rigid with excitement, and listened to the music that made everything so good: the music was always in the background, like music at a church service; it was something to depend upon.

A boy named Eddie came in to talk with them. He sat backwards on his stool, turning himself jerkily around in semicircles and then stopping and turning back again, and after a while he asked Connie if she would like something to eat. She said she would and so she tapped her friend's arm on her way out—her friend pulled her face up into a brave, droll look—and Connie said she would meet her at eleven, across the way. "I just hate to leave her like that," Connie said earnestly, but the boy said that she wouldn't be alone for long. So they went out to his car, and on the way Connie couldn't help but let her eyes wander over the windshields and faces all around her, her face gleaming with a joy that had nothing to do with Eddie or even this place; it might have been the music. She drew her shoulders up and sucked in her breath with the pure pleasure of being alive, and just at that moment she happened to glance at a face just a few feet away from hers. It was a boy with shaggy black hair, in a convertible jalopy painted gold. He stared at her and then his lips widened into a grin. Connie slit her eyes at him and turned away, but she couldn't help glancing back and there he was, still watching her. He wagged a finger and laughed and said, "Gonna get you, baby," and Connie turned away again without Eddie noticing anything.

She spent three hours with him, at the restaurant where they ate hamburgers and drank Cokes in wax cups that were always sweating, and then down an alley a mile or so away, and when he left her off at five to eleven only the movie house was still open at the plaza. Her girl friend was there, talking with a boy. When Connie came up, the two girls smiled at each other and Connie said, "How was the movie?" and the girl said, "*You* should know." They rode off with the girl's father, sleepy and pleased, and Connie couldn't help but look back at the darkened shopping plaza with its big empty parking lot and its signs that were faded and ghostly now, and over at the drive-in restaurant where cars were still circling tirelessly. She couldn't hear the music at this distance.

Next morning June asked her how the movie was and Connie said, "So-so."

She and that girl and occasionally another girl went out several times a week, and the rest of the time Connie spent around the house—it was summer vacation—getting in her mother's way and thinking, dreaming about the boys she met. But all the boys fell back and dissolved into a single face that was not even a face but an idea, a feeling, mixed up with the urgent insistent pounding of the music and the humid night air of July. Connie's mother kept dragging her back to the daylight by finding things for her to do or saying suddenly, "What's this about the Pettinger girl?"

And Connie would say nervously, "Oh, her. That dope." She always drew thick clear lines between herself and such girls, and her mother was simple and kind enough to believe it. Her mother was so simple, Connie thought, that it was maybe cruel to fool her so much. Her mother went scuffling around the house in old bedroom slippers and complained over the telephone to one sister about the other, then the other called up and the two of them complained about the third one. If June's name was mentioned her mother's tone was approving, and if Connie's name was mentioned it was disapproving. This did not really mean she disliked Connie, and actually Connie thought that her mother preferred her to June just because she was prettier, but the two of them kept up a pretense of exasperation, a sense that they were tugging and struggling over something of little value to either of them. Sometimes, over coffee, they were almost friends, but something would come up—some vexation that was like a fly buzzing suddenly around their heads—and their faces went hard with contempt.

One Sunday Connie got up at eleven—none of them bothered with church—and washed her hair so that it could dry all day long in the sun. Her parents and sister were going to a barbecue at an aunt's house and Connie said no, she wasn't interested, rolling her eyes to let her mother know just what she thought of it. "Stay home alone then," her mother said sharply. Connie sat out back in a lawn chair and watched them drive away, her father quiet and bald, hunched around so that he could back the car out, her mother with a look that was still angry and not at all softened through the windshield, and in the back seat poor old June, all dressed up as if she didn't know what a barbecue was, with all the running yelling kids and the flies. Connie sat with her eyes closed in the sun, dreaming and dazed with the warmth about her as if this were a kind of love, the caresses of love, and her mind slipped over onto thoughts of the boy she had been with the night before and how nice he had been, how sweet it always was, not the way someone like June would suppose but sweet, gentle, the way it was in movies and promised in songs; and when she opened her eyes she hardly knew where she was, the back yard ran off into weeds and a fence-like line of trees and behind it the sky was perfectly blue and still. The asbestos "ranch house" that was now three years old startled her—it looked small. She shook her head as if to get awake.

It was too hot. She went inside the house and turned on the radio to drown out the quiet. She sat on the edge of her bed, barefoot, and listened for an hour and a half, to a program called XYZ Sunday Jamboree, record after record of hard, fast, shrieking songs she sang along with, interspersed by exclamations from "Bobby King": "An' look here, you girls at Napoleon's—Son and Charley want you to pay real close attention to this song coming up!"

And Connie paid close attention herself, bathed in a glow of slow-pulsed joy that seemed to rise mysteriously out of the music itself and lay languidly about the airless little room, breathed in and breathed out with each gentle rise and fall of her chest.

After a while she heard a car coming up the drive. She sat up at once, startled, beacacuse it couldn't be her father so soon. The gravel kept crunching all the way in from the road—the driveway was long—and Connie ran to the window. It was a car she didn't know. It was an open jalopy, painted a bright gold that caught the sunlight opaquely. Her heart began to pound and her fingers snatched at her hair, checking it, and she whispered, "Christ, Christ," wondering how she looked. The car came to a stop at the side door and the horn sounded four short taps, as if this were a signal Connie knew.

She went into the kitchen and approached the door slowly, then hung out the screen door, her bare toes curling down off the step. There were two boys in the car and now she recognized the driver: he had shaggy, shabby black hair that looked crazy as a wig and he was grinning at her.

"I ain't late, am I?" he said.

"Who the hell do you think you are?" Connie said.

"Toldja I'd be out, didn't I?"

"I don't even know who you are."

She spoke sullenly, careful to show no interest or pleasure, and he spoke in a fast, bright monotone. Connie looked past him to the other boy, taking her time. He had fair brown hair, with a lock that fell onto his forehead. His sideburns gave him a fierce, embarrassed look, but so far he hadn't even bothered to glance at her. Both boys wore sunglasses. The driver's glasses were metallic and mirrored everything in miniature.

"You wanta come for a ride?" he said.

Connie smirked and let her hair fall loose over one shoulder.

"Don'tcha like my car? New paint job," he said. "Hey."

"What?"

"You're cute."

She pretended to fidget, chasing flies away from the door.

"Don'tcha believe me, or what?" he said.

"Look, I don't even know who you are," Connie said in disgust.

"Hey, Ellie's got a radio, see. Mine broke down." He lifted his friend's arm and showed her the little transistor radio the boy was holding, and now Connie began to hear the music. It was the same program that was playing inside the house.

"Bobby King?" she said.

"I listen to him all the time. I think he's great."

"He's kind of great," Connie said reluctantly.

"Listen, that guy's *great*. He knows where the action is."

Connie blushed a little, because the glasses made it impossible for her to see just what this boy was looking at. She couldn't decide if she liked him or if he was a jerk, and so she dawdled in the doorway and wouldn't come down or go back inside. She said, "What's all that stuff painted on your car?"

"Can'tcha read it?" He opened the door very carefully, as if he were afraid it might fall off. He slid out just as carefully, planting his feet firmly on the ground, the tiny metallic world in his glasses slowing down like gelatine hardening, and in the midst of it Connie's bright green blouse. "This here is my name, to begin with," he said. ARNOLD FRIEND was written in tarlike black letters on the side, with a drawing of a round, grinning face that reminded Connie of a pumpkin, except it wore sunglasses. "I wanta introduce myself. I'm Arnold Friend and that's my real name and I'm gonna be your friend, honey, and inside the car's Ellie Oscar, he's kinda shy." Ellie brought his transistor radio up to his shoulder and balanced it there. "Now, these numbers are a secret code, honey," Arnold

Friend explained. He read off the numbers 33, 19, 17 and raised his eyebrows at her to see what she thought of that, but she didn't think much of it. The left rear fender had been smashed and around it was written, on the gleaming gold background: DONE BY CRAZY WOMAN DRIVER. Connie had to laugh at that. Arnold Friend was pleased at her laughter and looked up at her. "Around the other side's a lot more—you wanta come and see them?"

"No."

"Why not?"

"Why should I?"

"Don'tcha wanta see what's on the car? Don'tcha wanta go for a ride?"

"I don't know."

"Why not?"

"I got things to do."

"Like what?"

"Things."

He laughed as if she had said something funny. He slapped his thighs. He was standing in a strange way, leaning back against the car as if he were balancing himself. He wasn't tall, only an inch or so taller than she would be if she came down to him. Connie liked the way he was dressed, which was the way all of them dressed: tight faded jeans stuffed into black, scuffed boots, a belt that pulled his waist in and showed how lean he was, and a white pull-over shirt that was a little soiled and showed the hard small muscles of his arms and shoulders. He looked as if he probably did hard work, lifting and carrying things. Even his neck looked muscular. And his face was a familiar face, somehow; the jaw and chin and cheeks slightly darkened because he hadn't shaved for a day or two, and the nose long and hawklike, sniffing as if she were a treat he was going to gobble up and it was all a joke.

"Connie, you ain't telling the truth. This is your day set aside for a ride with me and you know it," he said, still laughing. The way he straightened and recovered from his fit of laughing showed that it had been all fake.

"How do you know what my name is?" she said suspiciously.

"It's Connie."

"Maybe and maybe not."

"I know my Connie," he said, wagging his finger. Now she remembered him even better, back at the restaurant, and her cheeks warmed at the thought of how she had sucked in her breath just at the moment she passed him—how she must have looked to him. And he had remembered her. "Ellie and I come out here especially for you," he said. "Ellie can sit in back. How about it?"

"Where?"

"Where what?"

"Where're we going?"

He looked at her. He took off the sunglasses and she saw how pale the skin around his eyes was, like holes that were not in shadow but instead in light. His eyes were like chips of broken glass that catch the light in an amiable way. He smiled. It was as if the idea of going for a ride somewhere, to someplace, was a new idea to him.

"Just for a ride, Connie sweetheart."

"I never said my name was Connie," she said.

"But I know what it is. I know your name and all about you, lots of things," Arnold Friend said. He had not moved yet but stood still leaning back against the side of his jalopy. "I took a special interest in you, such a pretty girl, and found out all about you—like I know your parents and sister are gone somewheres and I know where and how long they're going to be gone, and I know who you were with last night, and your best friend's name is Betty. Right?"

He spoke in a simple lilting voice, exactly as if he were reciting the words to a song. His smile assured her that everything was fine. In the car Ellie turned up the volume on his radio and did not bother to look around at them.

"Ellie can sit in the back seat," Arnold Friend said. He indicated his friend with a casual jerk of his chin, as if Ellie did not count and she should not bother with him.

"How'd you find out all that stuff?" Connie said.

"Listen: Betty Schultz and Tony Fitch and Jimmy Pettinger and Nancy Pettinger," he said in a chant. "Raymond Stanley and Bob Hutter—"

"Do you know all those kids?"

"I know everybody."

"Look, you're kidding. You're not from around here."

"Sure."

"But—how come we never saw you before?"

"Sure you saw me before," he said. He looked down at his boots, as if he were a little offended. "You just don't remember."

"I guess I'd remember you," Connie said.

"Yeah?" He looked up at this, beaming. He was pleased. He began to mark time with the music from Ellie's radio, tapping his fists lightly together. Connie looked away from his smile to the car, which was painted so bright it almost hurt her eyes to look at it. She looked at that name, ARNOLD FRIEND. And up at the front fender was an expression that was familiar—MAN THE FLYING SAUCERS. It was an expression kids had used the year before but didn't use this year. She looked at it for a while as if the words meant something to her that she did not yet know.

"What're you thinking about? Huh?" Arnold Friend demanded. "Not worried about your hair blowing around in the car, are you?"

"No."

"Think I maybe can't drive good?"

"How do I know?"

"You're a hard girl to handle. How come?" he said. "Don't you know I'm your friend? Didn't you see me put my sign in the air when you walked by?"

"What sign?"

"My sign." And he drew an X in the air, leaning out toward her. They were maybe ten feet apart. After his hand fell back to his side the X was still in the air, almost visible. Connie let the screen door close and stood perfectly still inside it, listening to the music from her radio and the boy's blend together. She stared at Arnold Friend. He stood there so stiffly relaxed, pretending to be relaxed, with one hand idly on the door handle as if he were keeping himself up that way and had no intention of ever moving again. She recognized most things about him, the tight jeans that showed his thighs and buttocks and the greasy leather boots and the tight shirt, and even that slippery friendly smile of his, that sleepy dreamy smile that all the boys used to get across ideas they didn't want to put into words. She recognized all this and also the singsong way he talked, slightly mocking, kidding, but serious and a little melancholy, and she recognized the way he tapped one fist against the other in homage to the perpetual music behind him. But all these things did not come together.

She said suddenly, "Hey, how old are you?"

His smiled faded. She could see then that he wasn't a kid, he was much older—thirty, maybe more. At this knowledge her heart began to pound faster.

"That's a crazy thing to ask. Can'tcha see I'm your own age?"

"Like hell you are."

"Or maybe a coupla years older. I'm eighteen."

"Eighteen?" she said doubtfully.

He grinned to reassure her and lines appeared at the corners of his mouth. His teeth were big and white. He grinned so broadly his eyes became slits and she saw how thick the lashes were, thick and black as if painted with a black tarlike material. Then, abruptly, he seemed to become embarrassed and looked over his shoulder at Ellie. "*Him*, he's crazy," he said. "Ain't he a riot? He's a nut, a real character." Ellie was still listening to the music. His sunglasses told nothing about what he was thinking. He wore a bright orange shirt unbuttoned halfway to show his chest, which was a pale, bluish chest and not muscular like Arnold Friend's. His shirt collar was turned up all around and the very tips of the collar pointed out past his chin as if they were protecting him. He was pressing the transistor radio up against his ear and sat there in a kind of daze, right in the sun.

"He's kinda strange," Connie said.

"Hey, she says you're kinda strange! Kinda strange!" Arnold Friend cried. He pounded on the car to get Ellie's attention. Ellie turned for the first time and Connie saw with shock that he wasn't a kid either—he had a fair, hairless face, cheeks reddened slightly as if the veins grew too close to the surface of his skin, the face of a forty-year-old baby. Connie felt a wave of dizziness rise in her at this sight and she stared at him as if waiting for something to change the shock of the moment, make it all right again. Ellie's lips kept shaping words, mumbling along with the words blasting in his ear.

"Maybe you two better go away," Connie said faintly.

"What? How come?" Arnold Friend cried. "We come out here to take you for a ride. It's Sunday." He had the voice of the man on the radio now. It was the same voice, Connie thought. "Don'tcha know it's Sunday all day? And honey, no matter who you were with last night, today you're with Arnold Friend and don't you forget it! Maybe you better step out here," he said, and this last was in a different voice. It was a little flatter, as if the heat was finally getting to him.

"No. I got things to do."

"Hey."

"You two better leave."

"We ain't leaving until you come with us."

"Like hell I am—"

"Connie, don't fool around with me. I mean—I mean, don't fool *around*," he said, shaking his head. He laughed incredulously. He placed his sunglasses on top of his head, carefully, as if he were indeed wearing a wig, and brought the stems down behind his ears. Connie stared at him, another wave of dizziness and fear rising in her so that for a moment he wasn't even in focus but was just a blur standing there against his gold car, and she had the idea that he had driven up the driveway all right but had come from nowhere before that and belonged nowhere and that everything about him and even about the music that was so familiar to her was only half real.

"If my father comes and sees you—"

"He ain't coming. He's at a barbecue."

"How do you know that?"

"Aunt Tillie's. Right now they're—uh—they're drinking. Sitting around," he said vaguely, squinting as if he were staring all the way to town and over to Aunt Tillie's back yard. Then the vision seemed to get clear and he nodded energetically. "Yeah. Sitting around. There's your sister in a blue dress, huh? And high heels, the poor sad bitch—nothing like you, sweetheart! And your mother's helping some fat woman with the corn, they're cleaning the corn—husking the corn—"

"What fat woman?" Connie cried.

"How do I know what fat woman, I don't know every goddamn fat woman in the world!" Arnold Friend laughed.

"Oh, that's Mrs. Hornsby. . . . Who invited her?" Connie said. She felt a little lightheaded. Her breath was coming quickly.

"She's too fat. I don't like them fat. I like them the way you are, honey," he said, smiling sleepily at her. They stared at each other for a while through the screen door. He said softly, "Now, what you're going to do is this: you're going to come out that door. You're going to sit up front with me and Ellie's going to sit in the back, the hell with Ellie, right? This isn't Ellie's date. You're my date. I'm your lover, honey."

"What? You're crazy—"

"Yes. I'm your lover. You don't know what that is but you will," he said. "I know that too. I know all about you. But look: it's real nice and you couldn't ask for nobody better than me, or more polite. I always keep my word. I'll tell you how it is, I'm always nice at first, the first time. I'll hold you so tight you won't think you have to try to get away or pretend anything because you'll know you can't. And I'll come inside you where it's all secret and you'll give in to me and you'll love me—"

"Shut up! You're crazy!" Connie said. She backed away from the door. She put her hands up against her ears as if she'd heard something terrible, something not meant for her. "People don't talk like that, you're crazy," she muttered. Her heart was almost too big now for her chest and its pumping made sweat break out all over her. She looked out to see Arnold Friend pause and then take a step toward the porch, lurching. He almost fell. But, like a clever drunken man, he managed to catch his balance. He wobbled in his high boots and grabbed hold of one of the porch posts.

"Honey?" he said. "You still listening?"

"Get the hell out of here!"

"Be nice, honey. Listen."

"I'm going to call the police—"

He wobbled again and out of the side of his mouth came a fast spat curse, an aside not meant for her to hear. But even this "Christ!" sounded forced. Then he began to smile again. She watched this smile come, awkward as if he were smiling from inside a mask. His whole face was a mask, she thought wildly, tanned down to his throat but then running out as if he had plastered makeup on his face but had forgotten about his throat.

"Honey—? Listen, here's how it is. I always tell the truth and I promise you this: I ain't coming in that house after you."

"You better not! I'm going to call the police if you—if you don't—"

"Honey," he said, talking right through her voice, "honey. I'm not coming in there but you are coming out here. You know why?"

She was panting. The kitchen looked like a place she had never seen before, some room she had run inside but that wasn't good enough, wasn't going to help her. The kitchen window had never had a curtain, after three years, and there were dishes in the sink for her to do—probably— and if you ran your hand across the table you'd probably feel something stick there.

"You listening, honey? Hey?"

"—going to call the police—"

"Soon as you touch the phone I don't need to keep my promise and can come inside. You won't want that."

She rushed forward and tried to lock the door. Her fingers were shaking. "But why lock it," Arnold Friend said gently, talking right into her face. "It's just a screen door. It's just nothing." One of his boots was at a strange angle, as if his foot wasn't in it. It pointed out to the left, bent at the ankle. "I mean, anybody can break through a screen door and glass and wood and iron or anything else if he needs to, anybody at all, and specially Arnold Friend. If the place got lit up with a fire, honey, you'd come runnin' out into my arms, right into my arms an' safe at home— like you knew I was your lover and'd stopped fooling around. I don't mind a nice shy girl but I don't like no fooling around." Part of those words were spoken with a slight rhythmic lilt, and Connie somehow recognized them—the echo of a song from last year, about a girl rushing into her boy friend's arms and coming home again—

Connie stood barefoot on the linoleum floor, staring at him. "What do you want?" she whispered.

"I want you," he said.

"What?"

"Seen you that night and thought, that's the one, yes sir. I never needed to look anymore."

"But my father's coming back. He's coming to get me. I had to wash my hair first—" She spoke in a dry, rapid voice, hardly raising it for him to hear.

"No, your daddy is not coming and yes, you had to wash your hair and you washed it for me. It's nice and shining and all for me. I thank you sweetheart," he said with a mock bow, but again he almost lost his balance. He had to bend and adjust his boots. Evidently his feet did not go all the way down; the boots must have been stuffed with something so that he would seem taller. Connie stared out at him and behind him at Ellie in the car, who seemed to be looking off toward Connie's right, into nothing. This Ellie said, pulling the words out of the air one after another as if he were just discovering them, "You want me to pull out the phone?"

"Shut your mouth and keep it shut," Arnold Friend said, his face red from bending over or maybe from embarrassment because Connie had seen his boots. "This ain't none of your business."

"What—what are you doing? What do you want?" Connie said. "If I call the police they'll get you, they'll arrest you—"

"Promise was not to come in unless you touch that phone, and I'll keep that promise," he said. He resumed his erect position and tried to force his shoulders back. He sounded like a hero in a movie, declaring something important. But he spoke too loudly and it was as if he were speaking to someone behind Connie. "I ain't made plans for coming in that house where I don't belong but just for you to come out to me, the way you should. Don't you know who I am?"

"You're crazy," she whispered. She backed away from the door but did not want to go into another part of the house, as if this would give him permission to come through the door. "What do you . . . you're crazy, you. . . ."

"Huh? What're you saying, honey?"

Her eyes darted everywhere in the kitchen. She could not remember what it was, this room.

"This is how it is, honey: you come out and we'll drive away, have a nice ride. But if you don't come out we're gonna wait till your people come home and then they're all going to get it."

"You want that telephone pulled out?" Ellie said. He held the radio away from his ear and grimaced, as if without the radio the air was too much for him.

"I toldja shut up, Ellie," Arnold Friend said, "you're deaf, get a hearing aid, right? Fix yourself up. This little girl's no trouble and's gonna be nice to me, so Ellie keep to yourself, this ain't your date—right? Don't hem in on me, don't hog, don't crush, don't bird dog, don't trail me," he said in a rapid, meaningless voice, as if he were running through all the expressions he'd learned but was no longer sure which of them was in style, then rushing on to new ones, making them up with his eyes closed. "Don't crawl under my fence, don't squeeze in my chipmunk hole, don't sniff my glue, suck my popsicle, keep your own greasy fingers on yourself!" He shaded his eyes and peered in at Connie, who was backed against the kitchen table. "Don't mind him, honey, he's just a creep. He's a dope. Right? I'm the boy for you and like I said, you come out here nice like a lady and give me your hand, and nobody else gets hurt, I mean, your nice old bald-headed daddy and your mummy and your sister in her high heels. Because listen: why bring them in this?"

"Leave me alone," Connie whispered.

"Hey, you know that old woman down the road, the one with the chickens and stuff—you know her?"

"She's dead!"

"Dead? What? You know her?" Arnold Friend said.

"She's dead—"

"Don't you like her?"

"She's dead—she's—she isn't here any more—"

"But don't you like her, I mean, you got something against her?

Some grudge or something?" Then his voice dipped as if he were conscious of a rudeness. He touched the sunglasses perched up on top of his head as if to make sure they were still there. "Now, you be a good girl."

"What are you going to do?"

"Just two things, or maybe three," Arnold Friend said. "But I promise it won't last long and you'll like me the way you get to like people you're close to. You will. It's all over for you here, so come on out. You don't want your people in any trouble, do you?"

She turned and bumped against a chair or something, hurting her leg, but she ran into the back room and picked up the telephone. Something roared in her ear, a tiny roaring, and she was so sick with fear that she could do nothing but listen to it—the telephone was clammy and very heavy and her fingers groped down to the dial but were too weak to touch it. She began to scream into the phone, into the roaring. She cried out, she cried for her mother, she felt her breath start jerking back and forth in her lungs as if it were something Arnold Friend was stabbing her with again and again with no tenderness. A noisy sorrowful wailing rose all about her and she was locked inside it the way she was locked inside this house.

After a while she could hear again. She was sitting on the floor with her wet back against the wall.

Arnold Friend was saying from the door, "That's a good girl. Put the phone back."

She kicked the phone away from her.

"No, honey. Pick it up. Put it back right."

She picked it up and put it back. The dial tone stopped.

"That's a good girl. Now, you come outside."

She was hollow with what had been fear but what was now just an emptiness. All that screaming had blasted it out of her. She sat, one leg cramped under her, and deep inside her brain was something like a pinpoint of light that kept going and would not let her relax. She thought, I'm not going to see my mother again. She thought, I'm not going to sleep in my bed again. Her bright green blouse was all wet.

Arnold Friend said, in a gentle-loud voice that was like a stage voice, "The place where you came from ain't there any more, and where you had in mind to go is cancelled out. This place you are now—inside your daddy's house—is nothing but a cardboard box I can knock down any time. You know that and always did know it. You hear me?"

She thought, I have got to think. I have got to know what to do.

"We'll go out to a nice field, out in the country here where it smells so nice and it's sunny," Arnold Friend said. 'I'll have my arms tight around you so you won't need to try to get away and I'll show you what love is like, what it does. The hell with this house! It looks solid all right," he said. He ran his fingernail down the screen and the noise did not make

Connie shiver, as it would have the day before. "Now, put your hand on your heart, honey. Feel that? That feels solid too but we know better. Be nice to me, be sweet like you can because what else is there for a girl like you but to be sweet and pretty and give in?—and get away before her people get back?"

She felt her pounding heart. Her hand seemed to enclose it. She thought for the first time in her life that it was nothing that was hers, that belonged to her, but just a pounding, living thing inside this body that wasn't really hers either.

"You don't want them to get hurt," Arnold Friend went on. "Now, get up, honey. Get up all by yourself."

She stood.

"Now, turn this way. That's right. Come over here to me.—Ellie, put that away, didn't I tell you? You dope. You miserable creepy dope," Arnold Friend said. His words were not angry but only part of an incantation. The incantation was kindly. "Now, come out through the kitchen to me, honey, and let's see a smile, try it, you're a brave, sweet little girl and now they're eating corn and hot dogs cooked to bursting over an outdoor fire, and they don't know one thing about you and never did and honey, you're better than them because not a one of them would have done this for you."

Connie felt the linoleum under her feet; it was cool. She brushed her hair back out of her eyes. Arnold Friend let go of the post tentatively and opened his arms for her, his elbows pointing in toward each other and his wrists limp, to show that this was an embarrassed embrace and a little mocking, he didn't want to make her self-conscious.

She put out her hand against the screen. She watched herself push the door slowly open as if she were back safe somewhere in the other doorway, watching this body and this head of long hair moving out into the sunlight where Arnold Friend waited.

"My sweet little blue-eyed girl," he said in a half-sung sigh that had nothing to do with her brown eyes but was taken up just the same by the vast sunlit reaches of the land behind him and on all sides of him—so much land that Connie had never seen before and did not recognize except to know that she was going to it.

RICHARD BAUSCH   (b. 1945)

Wise Men at Their End

Theodore Weathers would probably have let things lapse after his son—
the only one with whom he had any relations at all—passed away, but his
daughter-in-law had adopted him. "You're all the family I've got left," she
told him, and the irony was that he had never really liked her very much
in the first place. He'd always thought she was a little empty-headed and
gossipy—one of those people who had to manage everything, were always
too ready to give advice, or suggest a course of action, or give an outright
order. She was fifty-two years old and looked ten years older than that,
but she called him Dad, and she had the energy of six people. She came
by to see him every day—she seemed to think this was something they'd
arranged—and she would go through his house as if it were hers, setting
everything in order, she said, so they could relax and talk. Mostly this
meant that she would be telling him what she thought he could do to
improve his life, as if at eighty-three there were anything much he could
do one way or the other.

   She thought he spent too much time watching television, that he
should be more active; she didn't like his drinking, or the fact that he
wasn't eating the healthiest foods; it wasn't right for a person to take such
poor care of himself, to be so negligent of his own well-being, and there
were matters other than diet or drink that concerned her: the city was
dangerous, she said, and he didn't have good locks on his doors or
windows; he'd developed bad habits all around; he left the house lights
burning through the night; he'd let the dishes go. He never dusted or
tidied up enough to suit her. He was unshaven. He needed a haircut. It
was like having another wife, he told her, and she took this as praise. She
never seemed to hear things as they were meant, and it was clear that in
her mind she was being quite wonderful—cheerful and sweet and witty
in the face of his irascibility and pigheadedness. She said he was entitled
to some measure of ill temper, having lived so long; and she took everything
he said and did with a kind of proprietary irony, as if another person
were there to note how unmanageable and troublesome he could be. At
times it seemed that any moment she might turn and speak to some
unseen auditor: "You see, don't you? You see what I have to go through
with this guy?"

   He had never considered himself to be the type of man who liked
to hurt other people's feelings, but he was getting truly tired of all this,
and he was thinking of telling her so in terms that would make her
understand he meant business.

   Lately, it had been the fact that he was living alone. There was a retirement community right down the street: a room of his own; games, movies, company, trips to other cities, book clubs, hobbies, someone to get the meals. She went on and on about it, and Theodore would close his eyes and clap his hands over his ears and recite Keats, loudly, so he couldn't hear her. "'My head aches, and a drousy numbness pains my sense,'" he would shout, "'As though of hemlock I had drunk.' As though of hemlock, Judy. Hemlock, get it? Hemlock."

"All right," she would say, "All right, all right," and she would move about the house picking things up and putting them down, her mouth set in a determined straight line.

But of course there was always the next round, and when her temper had cooled she seemed to enjoy getting back into it—she hadn't spent a lifetime telling other people what to do without having developed a certain species of hope or confidence in her ability to bend someone else's will to her own. He had watched her lead her husband around like a puppy most of his poor, cut-short life, and he told her so.

"John was happy with me, which is more than I can say for his mother when she was with you," she said. "He had a good, rich, full life."

"Sixty-six years is not a rich full life in my book."

"No, it wouldn't be, in your book."

"Maybe Margaret wasn't happy with me because I wouldn't let her lead me around like a damn puppy dog all the time."

"No, and she wouldn't let you lead her around, either."

"It was twenty years ago—who can remember who led who?"

"Speaking of remembering things, you have two sons still living in Vermont, and time isn't standing still. Don't you think it would be a good thing for you to reopen lines of communication? Maybe get on a plane and go see them. I thought you might make things up at John's funeral, and I was very sad to see that you didn't. John would've liked it if you had. Why don't you go visit them in their homes—see what their lives are like. They have children you've never seen, wives you haven't met."

"I knew their first wives."

"Is that why they fell from grace? Because they had divorces?"

"They fell from grace, as you put it, because they were messy and selfish about their lives and because they never had a thought for me or their mother."

"Do you know what John thought about the whole thing?"

"I don't care what John thought about the whole thing."

"He thought we stayed in your good graces because we kept everything about ourselves a secret—you never knew what trouble we had."

She was a registered nurse specializing in pediatrics, and she was mostly on morning shifts, so he would say he liked that time the best: he would leave the phone off the hook and lie in bed reading the newspapers until his eyes hurt. Then he would get up and fix himself an egg, a piece of toast. By this time the sun would be high. He would pour himself a tumblerful of whiskey and take it out on the front porch to sit in his wicker chair in the warmth and sip the whiskey until it was gone. The sun warmed his skin; the whiskey warmed his bones. Before him was the street, what traffic there was; it all looked as though it moved behind smoked glass. If he was really relaxed, he might doze off. It would be shady now, past noon. He would drift, and dream, and in the dreams he was always doing something quite ordinary, like working in the yard, or sitting in the shade of a porch, dreaming. When he woke up he would have a little more of the whiskey, to get ready, he told himself, for her arrival.

Today he went out back to talk over the fence, as he sometimes did, to his one acquaintance in the neighborhood, who was twenty years his junior, and a very bad hypochondriac. It made him feel good talking to this poor man, so beaten down by his own dire expectations. And it was good to know that Judy wouldn't find him on the porch, half asleep, out of dignity for the day, an old, dozing man. He looked at the mess in the kitchen on his way through, and felt a little rush of glee as if this were part of a game he was winning. His neighbor sat in a lawn chair with a newspaper in his lap; *he* was dozing, and this was how he spent *his* afternoons. Theodore called to him from the fence, and he stirred, walked over. The two of them stood there in the sun talking about the hot weather. When Judy arrived, she sang hello to Theodore from behind the back-door screen and said she would make some iced tea.

Then she said, "I'll get your straw hat, Dad. The sun's so bright!"

"The way she worries about me," Theodore said to his neighbor. "Jesus."

The neighbor said, "I got severe abdominal cramps, lately."

"Pay no attention to it," Theodore said.

"It's quite bad sometimes—it radiates into my shoulder. I'm afraid it's my pancreas."

"What the hell is that?"

"The pancreas is something you have to have or you die."

"Well, then I guess we got ours."

"You mean to tell me you don't know what the pancreas is?"

"Sure, I know what it is," Theodore said, "I just don't think about it a lot. I bet I haven't spent five minutes thinking about my pancreas in my whole life."

"I believe mine hurts," said his neighbor.

"Maybe it hurts because you're thinking about it. Stand around and think about your lungs for a while, maybe it'll go away and your lungs will start to hurt."

"You noticed something funny about my breathing."

"I thought we were talking about your pancreas."

Judy came out of the house, carrying a tray with iced tea on it, and wearing Theodore's wide-brimmed straw hat at a crooked angle. "If you're going to stand out in the sun you ought to have a hat on," she said to him. She put the tray down on the umbrella table and came over and put the hat on his head. Then she opened the gate and invited the neighbor to come have a glass of iced tea. The neighbor, whose name was Benjamin Hawkins, was obviously a little confused at first, since in the five or six years that they had been meeting to talk over this fence neither of the two men had ever suggested that things turn into a full-fledged visit—not at this time of day, just before supper. It just wasn't in their pattern, though sometimes in the evenings they watched baseball together, and once in a while they might stroll down to the corner, to the tavern there, for a beer. Talking over the fence was reserved for those times when one or the other or both of them didn't feel much like doing anything else.

And so the invitation was not a very good idea, and Theodore let Judy know it with a look—though she ignored it and went right on talking to Ben Hawkins about what a nice thing it was to have a cool drink in the shade on a hot summer day. It was as if she were hurrying through everything she said, her voice rising with emphasis, as she took Ben's arm and started him in the direction of the umbrella table. In only a moment, Theodore understood what was happening, for he had turned and he could see that someone, a woman, not young, was standing in the back door.

"Well," Ben was saying, "you make it sound so good, Mrs. Weathers."

"What the hell," Theodore said to his daughter-in-law.

She squeezed his elbow, and asked for kindness. "This is a nice lady I work with sometimes at the hospital. She's a volunteer—and she's a doll."

"I don't remember asking you to introduce me to people."

"Dad—please. She's already nervous about meeting you."

"I don't remember saying a thing about being introduced to anyone."

"She was a mathematics teacher, Dad—like you. And she loves poetry and books. She's a wonderful talker."

"So, put her on Johnny Carson."

"This is what I have to deal with," she said to Ben.

"This is what she has to deal with in my house," Theodore said.

"Dad, I swear I'll never forgive you."

She took Ben by the elbow again, and walked with him across the yard, and Theodore followed, lagging behind. The old woman opened the back door and stepped out on the small porch there, already apologizing for having intruded, speaking so low that you had to strain to hear her, while Judy forged on with the introductions, as if this were the beginning of a party. She hustled and got them all seated at the umbrella table and then she poured the iced tea, and nobody had a thing to say until Ben asked the woman, whose name was Alice Karnes, if she ever had any trouble with caffeine in her system.

"Pardon me?" Alice Karnes said.

"Well, I guess I was wondering if any of us are allergic to caffeine. It does funny things to me—"

"That's your nerves," Judy said.

"I've read that caffeine raises your blood pressure," said Ben. "I only allow myself two cups of coffee a day, and I've had my two cups—so this tea is cheating."

There was a pause in which everyone seemed to consider this, and finally Judy remarked that the tea was decaffeinated. "Oh, well," Ben said, and laughed. Theodore stared off at the fenced yards in their even rows down the block, and left his glass untouched; Judy knew very well that he didn't like sweet drinks. He would have preferred a touch of whiskey, and apparently the thought produced the words, because now Judy had fixed him with her eyes.

"Did I speak out of turn?" he said.

Judy seemed about to scold, but then her guest spoke: "Actually, I think I'd like a touch of whiskey myself."

Theodore looked at her. "What was your name again?"

"I'm Alice Karnes."

"Where you from, Alice."

"Why, I'm from Ohio."

"And I bet they drink good whiskey in Ohio, don't they."

"I never thought about it, but I guess they do."

"Would you like a touch of Virginia bourbon whiskey?"

She looked a trifle uncertain, glancing at Judy. Then she nodded. "I believe I would, yes."

"I never met anybody that a little whiskey wouldn't improve," Theodore said.

"It kills brain cells," said Judy.

"But we have millions of those," Ben Hawkins said.

Theodore had already got to his feet, and was going into the house. He had some of today's bottle left, and since Judy had moved in on his life he kept a stash in the basement, behind a brick in the wall at the base of the stairs, where for thirty-two years he had hid pint bottles of whiskey from his wife, Margaret. Margaret had been a very religious woman with a strong inclination to worry, whose father had stupidly drunk himself into ruin. Theodore had managed to convince her that one drink was all right—was even beneficial—and so he would have his one drink in the evenings, and then if he wanted more (he almost always wanted at least a little bit more) he would sneak it. Margaret had gone to her grave convinced of the moderate habits of her husband, who, often enough in the thirty-two years, came to bed late, and slept more deeply than he ever did when there *was* no inducement to sleep coursing through his blood. In the last few weeks he had gone back to keeping the stash, partly as a defense against the meddling of his daugher-in-law—the idea had come from that—but also, now, because it brought back a sense of his life in better times.

Except that this time of all times, all the thousands of times he'd descended these stairs with the thought of a drink of whiskey . . . this time something gave way in his leg, near the knee.

It might have been simply a false step. But something that had always been there before wasn't there for a crucial, awful instant, and he was airborne, tumbling into the dark. He hit twice, and was conscious enough to hear the terrible clatter he made—his leg snapped as he struck bottom. It sounded like an old stick. Nothing quite hurt yet, though. What he felt more than anything was surprise. He lay there at the bottom of the stairs, still in his straw hat, waiting for someone to get to him, and then the pain began to seep into his leg; it made him nauseous. "Goddamn," he said, or thought he said. Then Judy was on the stairs, thumping partway down. He believed he heard her cry of alarm, and he wanted to tell her to calm down and shut up, a woman more than fifty years old crying and screaming like a little girl. He wanted to tell her to please get someone, and to hurry, but he couldn't speak, couldn't draw in enough air. Somewhere far away Benjamin Hawkins was crying out for God, his voice shaking, seeming to shrink somehow, and Theodore strained to keep hearing it, feeling himself start downward, floating downward and into some other place, a place none of them could be now. It was quiet, and he knew he was gone, he was aware of it, and he turned in himself and looked at it—a man knocked out and staring at his own unconsciousness. Then it was all confused, he was talking to his sons, it was decades ago—they were gathered around him, like a congregation, and he was speaking to them, only what he was saying made no sense; it was just numbers and theorems and equations, as if this were one of the thousands of math classes he had taught. There had been so many times when he had constructed in his mind exactly what he would say to them if he could have got them together like this— all their slights and their carelessness and their use of him, and their use of their mother, all the things he wanted them to know they had done, and here he was with math coming out of his mouth.

He woke up in a bright hospital room with a television set suspended in the air above his head, and a window to his left looking out on a soot-stained brick wall. Sitting in one of two chairs by his bed was a woman he did not at first remember having seen before.

"Who are *you*," he said.

"Alice Karnes."

He looked along the length of his body. His leg was in an ugly brace, and there was a pin sticking through his knee. It went into the violet, bruised skin there like something stuck through rubber. There were pulleys and gears attached to an apparatus at the foot of the bed, looking like instruments of torture. He lay back and closed his eyes, and remembered his dream of talking, and thought of death. It came to him like a chilly little breath at the base of his neck, and he opened his eyes to look at Alice Karnes.

"Does it hurt very bad?" she asked.

"What're you doing here," he said.

"Judy asked me to come. I'm sorry."

"How long have I been here."

"Just a day. I'm sorry—last night and today."

"What is Judy doing?"

"She went to get something to eat. She wanted me to stay in case you woke up. You've been in and out, sort of."

"I don't remember a thing." He looked at her. She had very light blue eyes, a small, thin mouth. Her hair was arranged in a tight little bun on top of her head. She sat there with her hands folded tightly in her lap, smiling at him as if someone had just said something embarrassing or off-color. "What're we supposed to do now," he said.

"Well, I don't think we'll do any calisthenics," she said. Then she blushed. "I guess that's a bad joke, isn't it."

"It's hilarious. I'm chuckling on the inside."

"I'm sorry."

"You're trying to be kind, is that it?"

"Judy didn't want you to wake up alone—"

"Maybe I want to be alone."

"That's your privilege." She sat there.

"And what do *you* want?"

"Oh, I wouldn't be able to say."

"Why not?"

She shrugged. "Judy wanted me to sit with her. I felt bad about what happened to you."

"I've never been in a hospital as a patient in my life," he said. "Not in eighty-three years."

"I guess there's a time for everything."

"I guess there is."

"Do you want me to leave?" she asked him.

He closed his eyes again. It had come to him that he might never leave the hospital. He breathed slowly, feeling himself begin to shake deep in his bones.

"Of course, I don't mind staying," she said.

"Why?" His voice had been steady; he'd heard how steady it was.

"I'm the volunteer type," she said.

"I don't want any damned charity," he said, trying to glare at her.

"Oh, it's not charity."

"Charity begins at home. Go home and give it to your own people."

She said something about distances, and times; other lives. he didn't quite catch it. A sudden pain had throbbed through his knee, on up the thigh; it made him realize how badly he'd been hurt, how deep the aches were in his hips and lower back and shoulders. When he touched his own cheek, he felt a lump as big as an ice cube, and it was a moment before he realized that it was a bandage over a bruise or laceration.

"Well, I don't want anything," he heard himself say.

"I'm calling the nurse for you," she said, "Then if you want I'll go."

"Don't go."

"Whatever you say."

"This is awful," he said.

"I'm so sorry," she told him.

"Don't talk to me about sorry. I don't want to hear sorry."

"I'm sorry."

"Jesus."

"I didn't mean that—is there anything I can do to make you more comfortable?"

The pain had let up some, but he was still shaking inside. He took a deep breath. "You could put me out of my misery," he said.

"I've pushed the button for the nurse. She ought to be here."

A moment later, wanting talk, he said "How old are you?"

"Oh, you shouldn't ask a lady her age."

"I'm eight-three," he said, "goddammit. How old are you?"

"Seventy-eight."

"A baby," he said.

"That's very kind of you."

A moment later, he said, "I remember when I was your age."

She smiled.

"Got any children?" he asked. then he said, "Come on, talk."

"I had two children—they live in Tennessee—"

"They ever come to see you?"

"I go to see them. Christmases and holidays. And for a while in summer."

The pain had mostly subsided now. He sighed, breathed, tried to remain perfectly still for a moment. Then he turned his head and looked straight at her. "Are you lonely?"

"That's not a proper question to ask someone like me."

"You're lonely as hell," he said.

"And you?" she asked, her eyes flashing.

"I don't think about if if I'm allowed not to."

She looked down at her hands.

"I got a daughter-in-law that insists on reminding me of it—and now she's trying to match us up. You know that, don't you?"

"I wish you wouldn't say such things. She told me I'd like you, as a matter of fact—she said you were interesting and that I'd like you. I found the whole thing very embarrassing."

"You found me a little blunt for you—a little rough, maybe."

"Is that the way you see yourself?"

"Suppose it is?"

"It seems to me that if you knew you were being too blunt or rough you'd do something about it."

"Right," he said, "I should remember to be charming. Can I get you anything?"

"Do you want me to leave? Just say so."

He didn't want her to leave; he didn't want to be alone. He said, "Tell me about your children."

"There's not much to tell—*they* have children. I think I need a frame of reference, you know—a—a context." She pulled the edge of her dress down over her knees. "What about you? Tell me about your children."

"My children are mostly gone now. The ones who survive hate me."

'I'm sure that's not so."

"Don't say crap like that when I tell you something," he said, "I'm telling you something. I know what I'm talking about. There's no love lost, you know? Maybe I just don't have anything else to do right now but tell the truth. And to tell you the truth, I never much liked my children. I never had much talent for people in general, if you want to know the truth about it."

"I think I might've gleaned that," she said.

"Well, then," he told her, "Good for you." The pain had come back, this time with a powerful jolt to his chest and abdomen: it felt like a sudden fright, and he turned his head on the pillow, looking at the room. There was another bed, empty, and with the sheets gone. Someone had put a pitcher of water and a glass on the night table. He closed his eyes again, going down in the pain. Somewhere in the middle of it, he was sure, was his death, and knowing this made him want to say something, as if there were matters that must be cleared up before he let go. But when he searched his mind there was nothing.

"Where is everybody," he said.

"I've been ringing for the nurse. Do you want me to go get one?"

"No. Stay."

"I think that's the first friendly thing you've said."

"Pay no attention to it," he said.

"It was a slip of the tongue?" she asked.

"Exactly."

"I'll disregard it, then."

"Do."

She smiled. "I don't think you're as mean as you think you are."

"I'm dying," he said.

"You have a broken leg, some cuts and bruises."

"I'll probably never get out of this bed."

"Your mind's made up," she said.

"Don't be cute. I hate that—do me a favor and don't be the life-affirming visitor with me, okay?"

"Your mind *is* made up, isn't it?"

They were quiet. A doctor came in and looked into his eyes with a bright light, and touched his knee where the metal pin went in. The doctor was very young and blond and his hair was blow-dried, his nails perfectly manicured. He introduced himself as Doctor German or Garman or something; Theodore wasn't listening. The doctor was a kid, no more than thirty. He smelled like rubbing alcohol and he sounded like somebody doing a television quiz show when he talked, his voice lilting like that, full of empty good cheer and smiles. When he was gone, Alice Karnes said "You can see how alarmed the young man is at your condition."

"What does he care?"

"He's obviously certain you'll never get up."

"I don't need sarcasm now either, thank you."

"Poor man," she said.

He said nothing for a moment, and then the aching in his bones brought a moan up out of him.

"I *am* sorry," she said.

"Sorry for what."

"For being sarcastic."

"I can't figure out what you're doing here at all."

"I asked if you wanted me to leave."

"Yes, you did—and I said no. I remember that clearly. But I still don't know what you're doing here in the first place."

"Well it certainly isn't for romance, is it."

"Why not?" he said. "Let's have a whirlwind courtship."

"I don't drink whiskey," she told him.

He looked at her.

"I don't—I've never even tasted whiskey," she said. "I asked for whiskey, remember? You went in to get it and this happened—and I don't even drink it. I was just trying to be—friendly, I guess."

He stared at her.

"We—we were always very strict Baptists. We never did anything like drinking alcohol—especially whiskey."

"You—" he began.

"I feel responsible," she said.

A nurse came into the room—a woman not much younger than they were. She took his temperature and his pulse and blood pressure, and then she, too, touched his knee where the pin was.

"Nurse," he said, "give me something for the pain."

She put some cold solution on the skin around the opening in the knee, using a Q-tip.

"Nurse."

She looked at her watch. "I'm afraid you're not due for another hour." Her voice was grandmotherly and sweet, and she put her hand on his forehead and smoothed the thin hair back; her fingers were cool and dry.

When Theodore moaned, Alice Karnes said, "Can't you do something for him?"

"We're doing everything we can, Mrs. Weathers." The nurse studied Theodore and then nodded. "Just hold on for another fifteen minutes or so and we'll cheat a little—how's that?"

"What's fifteen minutes, for God's sake," Theodore said, "I'm dying here."

"Just fifteen minutes," the nurse said, turning. She walked out of the room without a word or gesture of leave-taking, as if she had been in the room alone.

"Did you hear what she called me?" Alice Karnes said.

He couldn't think. He said, "Tell me."

"She called me Mrs. Weathers."

"She did, did she?"

"The assumptions people make."

"Maybe we could kill her for it," Theodore said.

She smiled at this, and then she reached over and put her hand on his arm. For a long moment she left it there, without saying anything, and then she took it away, sat back, still smiling.

"Well," he said.

She said, "Try to sleep now."

"You got me all excited," he said.

Her smile changed slightly, and she looked away out the window.

He was in the hospital for almost a month. They put his leg in a cast, and they showed him how to use crutches, and they all talked about how strong he was, a man who ought to live to be a hundred and twenty; they congratulated him for his quick adjustment to the new situation. They showed him why he would always have to use a cane. They laughed at his ill temper and his gruff ways and his jokes, and when they sent him home a group of the nurses and therapists chipped in and bought him a large basket of fruit and a card with a picture of the Phantom of the Opera on the front of it and an inscription that read, "Why did she turn away when I tried to kiss her?" The card was signed by everyone, including the young blond doctor, Doctor Garman—who called him Dad, just as Judy did, with the same proprietary irony. He didn't mind, particularly. He was just glad to be going home. Judy had come to see him almost every day, and he made jokes about having nothing to put between himself and her except feigned sleep. She brought Alice Karnes along with her now and then, but rarely left them alone. In Judy's presence, the older woman was often too mortified to speak: Judy kept talking at and through her, obviously trying to get Theodore to see her many fine qualities—how resourceful she was, and self-reliant; how good her stories were and how well she told them; her wit and her generosity and what good friends they had become. The whole thing was like a talk show, except the unfortunate guest never got to really speak for herself.

"You should hear Alice do Keats," Judy said. "She's got you beat, Dad. She know all of Keats."

"Well," Alice said, "one poem."

"Yes, but every word of it, and it's a long poem."

"I took a speech class," Alice said. "It's nothing. Everybody had to do it."

"Go ahead, give it to us," Judy said.

"Oh—now, you don't want to hear that."

"We do—don't we, Dad."

Alice looked at Theodore. "Your daughter-in-law just mentioned that you liked to recite Keats aloud, and I told her I knew the one poem."

"Did she tell you just when and how I recite Keats?"

Judy said, "We want to hear you recite your poem, Alice."

"Sure, why not?" Theodore said. He lay there and listened to Alice try to remember the "Ode on a Grecian Urn," her face crimson with embarrassment. It was interesting to watch her thin lips frame the words, and in fact she had a very pleasant voice. He caught himself wondering if Alice Karnes, for all her apparent unease, hadn't planned everything out with Judy. Once, in the first week of his stay in the hospital, he had awakened to find the two of them whispering to each other on the other side of the room; it was clear that something was in contention between them, until Judy saw that he was awake, and immediately changed her demeanor as though to warn the other woman that they were being watched.

Before he got out of the hospital he decided that they were in fact conspiring together about something—they had, after all, become friends, as Judy put it. They were more like sisters, in fact. It was evident enough that Judy wanted to see a romance develop, and Theodore found that he rather liked the idea that the two woman were in cahoots about it; it flattered him of course. But there was something else, too—some element of pleasure in simply divining what they were up to. He felt oddly as if in his recent suffering there had been a sharpening of his senses somehow, as though a new kind of apprehension were possible that hadn't been possible before. He might have expressed it in this way if he'd wanted anyone to know about it. The good thing was that no one did: to Judy he was, of course, the same. He gave the same cantankerous or sarcastic answers to her questions, made the same faces at her, the same mugged expressions; he even continued to recite Keats over her talk when he was tired of listening to her, and he still insisted on his whiskey and his bad habits, though of course, under the circumstances, he had to insist on these things in theory.

But now he was going home. He could get around, however laboriously, on his own. He was almost eighty-four and he had suffered a bad fall, and he was strong enough, after three and a half weeks, to get around on crutches. Of this he was very proud. When Judy came to the hospital to take him home, she naturally brought Alice along, and as the three of them worked together to get him safely into the car, he had a bad moment of remembering the little chilly puff of air he had felt on the base of his neck when he'd first awakened in the hospital bed; he was convinced now that it had been death. He tried to put it out of his mind, but it left its cold little residue, and he was abruptly quite irritable. When Alice Karnes reached into the car to put his shirt collar down—it had come up as he settled himself in the front seat—he took her wrist and said, as roughly as he could, "I'll get it."

"Of course," she said softly.

He sat with his arms folded, hunched down in the seat. He didn't want their talk now or their cheerfulness, their hopes for him. When Judy started the car up he turned to her and said, "I don't want any company today."

"You're going to have it today," she said, as if she were proud of him, "you old goat."

They said nothing all the way to the house. Alice Karnes sat in the back seat and stared out the window. The few times that Theodore looked at her, he felt again the sense of a new nerve of perception, except that it all seemed to bend itself into the shape of this aggravation—as though he could read her thoughts, and each thought irritated him further.

At home, they showed him how they'd fixed everything up for him; they'd waxed the floors and organized the books; they'd washed all the curtains and dusted and cleaned, and everything looked new or bleached or worn away with scrubbing.

"Look here," Judy said, and showed him a half-gallon of bourbon that they had set into the bookcase, like a bookend. "But you can't have any of it now. Not while you're on the antibiotics."

He went out onto the porch to sit in his wicker chair in what was left of the morning's sun there. They helped him. Judy got him a hassock to rest his leg on. It took a long time getting him settled, and they bustled around him, nervous for his unsteadiness. But he was sure of himself. He sat in the chair and took a deep breath, and they stood on either side of him. "Don't loom over me," he said.

Alice Karnes went back into the house.

"There's a new element to your bad temper, Dad. A meanness. And I don't like it."

"I don't know what you're talking about," he said. "You're in my sun."

"I know," said his daughter-in-law, "you just want to be left alone."

Ben Hawkins came walking around the house and up onto the porch. "I saw the car come down the block," he said. "I was watching for you."

"You found me," Theodore said.

"You look okay," said Ben.

"I'm fine."

"He's been such a dear," Judy said, and turned to go back into the house. Ben Hawkins offered a polite bow, which she didn't see, then settled himself into the chair next to Theodore's. He sat there quietly.

"Well," Theodore said.

The other man stirred, almost as if startled. "Yes, sir," he said, "I guess you made it through all right."

"I guess I did," Theodore said.

"I been getting some palpitations, but other than that, okay."

"Palpitations," Theodore said.

"Heart—you know."

"But nothing serious."

"Oh, no. Other than that, okay."

"You been to a doctor?"

"They don't know what they're looking at. I looked it up, though— palpitations are almost always okay."

"There's machines that measure the heartbeat and everything," Theodore said.

"Other than a little palpitation now and then I'm okay, though."

"You'll probably die, don't you think, Ben? It's a distinct possibility, isn't it?"

"I'm feeling better," Ben said.

They were quiet. After a while they exchanged a few remarks about the brightness of the sun, the coolness of the air when the wind stirred. The women came back out, and Ben Hawkins stood up and bowed to them and, after shaking Theodore's hand, took his leave. He went down the steps and walked back around the house, and once again the two women were with Theodore there on the porch. The sunlight had traversed that side of the house; they were in the shade now. It was cool, and quiet. Theodore had watched Ben Hawkins walk away, and the sun had caught a wisp of the man's sparse hair, had shown Theodore somehow the defeat and bafflement in his stride—in the way his back was bent and in the bowed slant of his head. Theodore had seen it, and his newfound acuity had without warning presented him with a sense of having failed the other man. He tried to reject it, but it blew through him like a soul, and then it opened wide, fanning out in him, such an abysmal feeling of utter dereliction that he gripped the arms of the wicker chair as if to keep from being swept away. And now Judy was talking to him again, telling him about some prior arrangements.

"What?" he said into her talk. "What?"

Alice Karnes had again gone back into the house.

Judy was talking. "I said I got Alice to agree to stay here with you while I go to work, although God knows we ought to just let you fend for yourself—but she still feels bad about your fall. So you are going to let her stay here until I come back from work."

He nodded.

"She's been very kind to you," Judy said, "So please. Remember your manners."

"Yes," Theodore said, not really hearing himself. "Yes."

He watched her walk off the porch and out to her car. She waved, before she drove off, and he held his hand up; but she was waving at Alice, who stood in the doorway behind him, and now cleared her throat as if to announce her presence.

Theodore said, "Well, you going to stand there all day?"

"I thought you might want to be alone," she said.

He heard himself say, "No." Then, "Do you need an invitation?"

He breathed, and breathed again. Judy had driven herself away, and now he felt her absence with something like grief. He couldn't believe it. Alice Karnes stepped out and took the rocking chair across from him. She rested one arm on the porch rail and looked out at the yard.

"I'm only staying as long as Judy continues to feel she needs me," she said.

"You want something to drink?" Theodore managed.

She leaned back and closed her eyes, and breathed a sigh. The sunlight was on her hair, and she looked younger. "I'll fix you something cold," she said.

"Anything," said Theodore.

But they sat there in the shade of the porch. They looked like a couple long married, still in the habit of love.

ALICE WALKER (b. 1944)

"Really, Doesn't *Crime Pay?"*

(Myrna)

SEPTEMBER, 1961

PAGE 118

I sit here by the window in a house with a thirty-year mortgage, writing in this notebook, looking down at my Helena Rubenstein hands . . . and why not? Since I am not a serious writer my nails need not be bitten off, my cuticles need not have jagged edges. I can indulge myself—my hands— in Herbessence nail-soak, polish, lotions, and creams. The result is a truly beautiful pair of hands: sweet-smelling, small, and soft. . . .

I lift them from the page where I have written the line "Really, *Doesn't* Crime Pay?" and send them seeking up my shirt front (it is a white and frilly shirt) and smoothly up the column of my throat, where gardenia scent floats beneath my hairline. If I should spread my arms and legs or whirl, just for an instant, the sweet smell of my body would be more than I could bear. But I fit into my new surroundings perfectly; like a jar of cold cream melting on a mirrored vanity shelf.

PAGE 119

"I have a surprise for you," Ruel said, the first time he brought me here. And you know how sick he makes me now when he grins.

"What is it?" I asked, not caring in the least.

And that is how we drove up to the house. Four bedrooms and two toilets and a half.

"Isn't it a beauty?" he said, not touching me, but urging me out of the car with the phony enthusiasm of his voice.

"Yes," I said. It is "a beauty." Like new Southern houses everywhere. The bricks resemble cubes of raw meat; the roof presses down, a field hat made of iron. The windows are narrow, beady eyes; the aluminum glints. The yard is a long undressed wound, the few trees as bereft of foliage as hairpins stuck in a mud cake.

"Yes," I say, "it sure is a beauty." He beams, in his chill and reassured way. I am startled that he doesn't still wear some kind of military uniform. But no. He came home from Korea a hero, and a glutton for sweet smells.

"Here we can forget the past," he says.

PAGE 120

We have moved in and bought new furniture. The place reeks of newness, the green walls turn me bilious. He stands behind me, his hands touching the edges of my hair. I pick up my hairbrush and brush his hands away. I have sweetened my body to such an extent that even he (especially he) may no longer touch it.

I do not want to forget the past; but I say "Yes," like a parrot. "We can forget the past here."

The past of course is Mordecai Rich, the man who, Ruel claims, caused my breakdown. The past is the night I tried to murder Ruel with one of his chain saws.

MAY, 1958

PAGE 2

Mordecai Rich

Mordecai does not believe Ruel Johnson is my husband. "*That* old man," he says, in a mocking, cruel way.

"Ruel is not old," I say. "Looking old is just his way." Just as, I thought, looking young is your way, although you're probably not much younger than Ruel.

Maybe it is just that Mordecai is a vagabond, scribbling down impressions of the South, from no solid place, going to none . . . and Ruel has never left Hancock County, except once, when he gallantly went off to war. He claims travel broadened him, especially his two months of European leave. He married me because although my skin is brown he thinks I look like a Frenchwoman. Sometimes he tells me I look Oriental: Korean or Japanese. I console myself with this thought: My family tends to darken and darken as we get older. One day he may wake up in bed with a complete stranger.

"He works in the store," I say. "He also raises a hundred acres of peanuts." Which is surely success.

"That many," muses Mordecai.

It is not pride that makes me tell him what my husband does, is. It is a way I can tell him about myself.

PAGE 4

Today Mordecai is back. He tells a funny/sad story about a man in town who could not move his wife. "He huffed and puffed," laughed Mordecai, "to no avail." Then one night as he was sneaking up to her bedroom he heard joyous cries. Rushing in he found his wife in the arms of another woman! The wife calmly dressed and began to pack her bags.

The husband begged and pleaded. "Anything you want," he promised. "What *do* you want?" he pleaded. The wife began to chuckle and, laughing, left the house with her friend.

Now the husband gets drunk every day and wants an ordinance passed. He cannot say what the ordinance will be against, but that is what he buttonholes people to say: "I want a goddam ordinance passed!" People who know the story make jokes about him. They pity him and give him enough money to keep him drunk.

PAGE 5

I think Mordecai Rich has about as much heart as a dirt-eating toad. Even when he makes me laugh I know that nobody ought to look on other people's confusion with that cold an eye.

"But that's what I am," he says, flipping through the pages of his scribble pad. "A cold eye. An eye looking for Beauty. An eye looking for Truth."

"Why don't you look for other things?" I want to know. "Like neither Truth nor Beauty, but places in people's lives where things have just slipped a good bit off the track."

"That's too vague," said Mordecai, frowning.

"So is Truth," I said. "Not to mention Beauty."

PAGE 10

Ruel wants to know why "the skinny black tramp"—as he calls Mordecai—keeps hanging around. I made the mistake of telling him Mordecai is thinking of using our house as the setting for one of his Southern country stories.

"Mordecai is from the North," I said. "He never saw a wooden house with a toilet in the yard."

"Well, maybe he better go back where he from," said Ruel, "and shit the way he's used to."

It's Ruel's pride that is hurt. He's ashamed of this house that seems perfectly adequate to me. One day we'll have a new house, he says, of brick, with a Japanese bath. How should I know why?

PAGE 11

When I told Mordecai what Ruel said he smiled in that snake-eyed way he has and said, "Do *you* mind me hanging around?"

I didn't know what to say. I stammered something. Not because of his question but because he put his hand point-blank on my left nipple. He settled his other hand deep in my hair.

"I am married more thoroughly than a young boy like you could guess," I told him. But I don't expect that to stop him. Especially since the day he found out I wanted to be a writer myself.

It happened this way: I was writing in the grape arbor, on the ledge by the creek that is hidden from the house by trees. He was right in front of me before I could put my notebook away. He snatched it from me and began to read. What is worse, he read aloud. I was embarrassed to death.

"No wife of mine is going to embarrass me with a lot of foolish, vulgar stuff," Mordecai read. (This is Ruel's opinion of my writing.) *Every time he tells me how peculiar I am for wanting to write stories he brings up having a baby or going shopping, as if these things are the same. Just something to occupy my time.*

"If you have time on your hands," he said today, "why don't you go shopping in that new store in town."

I went. I bought six kinds of face cream, two eyebrow pencils, five nightgowns and a longhaired wig. Two contour sticks and a pot of gloss for my lips.

And all the while I was grieving over my last story. Outlined—which is as far as I take stories now—but dead in embryo. My hand stilled by cowardice, my heart the heart of a slave.

PAGE 14

Of course Mordecai wanted to see the story. What did I have to lose?

"Flip over a few pages," I said. "It is the very skeleton of a story, but one that maybe someday I will write."

"The One-Legged Woman," Mordecai began to read aloud, then continued silently.

The characters are poor dairy farmers. One morning the husband is too hung over to do the milking. His wife does it and when she has finished the cows are frightened by thunder and stampede, trampling her. She is also hooked severely in one leg. Her husband is asleep and does not hear her cry out. Finally she drags herself home and wakes him up. He washes her wounds and begs her to forgive him. He does not go for a doctor because he is afraid the doctor will accuse him of being lazy and a drunk, undeserving of his good wife. He wants the doctor to respect him. The wife, understanding, goes along with this.

However, gangrene sets in and the doctor comes. He lectures the husband and amputates the leg of the wife. The wife lives and tries to forgive her husband for his weakness.

While she is ill the husband tries to show he loves her, but cannot look at the missing leg. When she is well he finds he can no longer make love to her. The wife, sensing his revulsion, understands her sacrifice was for nothing. She drags herself to the barn and hangs herself.

The husband, ashamed that anyone should know he was married to a one-legged woman, buries her himself and later tells everyone that she is visiting her mother.

While Mordecai was reading the story I looked out over the fields. If he says one good thing about what I've written, I promised myself, I will go to bed with him. (How else could I repay him? All I owned in any supply were my jars of cold cream!) As if he read my mind he sank down on the seat beside me and looked at me strangely.

"*You* think about things like this?" he asked.

He took me in his arms, right there in the grape arbor. "You sure do have a lot of heavy, sexy hair," he said, placing me gently on the ground. After that, a miracle happened. Under Mordecai's fingers my body opened like a flower and carefully bloomed. And it was strange as well as wonderful. For I don't think love had anything to do with this at all.

PAGE 17

After that, Mordecai praised me for my intelligence, my sensitivity, the depth of the work he had seen—and naturally I showed him everything I had: old journals from high school, notebooks I kept hidden under tarpaulin in the barn, stories written on paper bags, on table napkins, even on shelf paper from over the sink. I am amazed—even more amazed than Mordecai—by the amount of stuff I have written. It is over twenty years' worth, and would fill, easily, a small shed.

"You must give these to me," Mordecai said finally, holding three notebooks he selected from the rather messy pile. "I will see if something can't be done with them. You could be another Zora Hurston—" he smiled—"another Simone de Beauvoir!"

Of course I am flattered. "Take it! Take it! I cry. Already I see myself as he sees me. A famous authoress, miles away from Ruel, miles away from anybody. I am dressed in dungarees, my hands are a mess. I smell of sweat. I glow with happiness.

"How could such pretty brown fingers write such ugly, deep stuff?" Modecai asks, kissing them.

PAGE 20

For a week we deny each other nothing. If Ruel knows (how could he not know? His sheets are never fresh), he says nothing. I realize now that he never considered Mordecai a threat. Because Mordecai seems to have nothing to offer but his skinny self and his funny talk. I gloat over this knowledge. Now Ruel will find that I am not a womb without a brain that can be bought with Japanese bathtubs and shopping sprees. The moment of my deliverance is at hand!

PAGE 24

Mordecai did not come today. I sit in the arbor writing down those words and my throat begins to close up. I am nearly strangled by my fear.

PAGE 56

I have not noticed anything for weeks. Not Ruel, not the house. Everything whispers to me that Mordecai has forgotten me. Yesterday Ruel told me not to go into town and I said I wouldn't, for I have been hunting Mordecai up and down the streets. People look at me strangely, their glances slide off me in a peculiar way. It is as if they see something on my face that embarrasses them. Does everyone know about Mordecai and me? Does good loving show so soon? . . . But it is not soon. He has been gone already longer than I have known him.

PAGE 61

Ruel tells me I act like my mind's asleep. It is asleep, of course. Nothing will wake it but a letter from Mordecai telling me to pack my bags and fly to New York.

PAGE 65

If I could have read Mordecai's scribble pad I would know exactly what he thought of me. But now I realize he never once offered to show it to me, though he had a chance to read every serious thought I ever had. I'm afraid to know what he thought. I feel crippled, deformed. But if he ever wrote it down, that would make it true.

PAGE 66

Today Ruel brought me in from the grape arbor, out of the rain. I didn't know it was raining. "Old folks like us might catch rheumatism if we don't be careful," he joked. I don't know what he means. I am thirty-two. He is forty. I never felt old before this month.

PAGE 79

Ruel came up to bed last night and actually cried in my arms! He would give anything for a child, he says.

"Do you think we could have one?" he said.

"Sure," I said. "Why not?"

He began to kiss me and carry on about my goodness. I began to laugh. He became very angry, but finished what he started. He really does intend to have a child.

PAGE 80

I must really think of something better to do than kill myself.

PAGE 81

Ruel wants me to see a doctor about speeding up conception of the child.

"Will you go, honey?" he asks, like a beggar.

"Sure," I say. "Why not?"

PAGE 82

Today at the doctor's office the magazine I was reading fell open at a story about a one-legged woman. They had a picture of her, drawn by someone who painted the cows orange and green, and painted the woman white, like a white cracker, with little slit-blue eyes. Not black and heavy like she was in the story I had in mind. But it is still my story, filled out and switched about as things are. The author is said to be Mordecai Rich. They show a little picture of him on a back page. He looks severe and has grown a beard. And underneath his picture there is that same statement he made to me about going around looking for Truth.

They say his next book will be called "The Black Woman's Resistance to Creativity in the Arts."

PAGE 86

Last night while Ruel snored on his side of the bed I washed the prints of his hands off my body. Then I plugged in one of his chain saws and tried to slice off his head. This failed because of the noise. Ruel woke up right in the nick of time.

PAGE 95

The days pass in a haze that is not unpleasant. The doctors and nurses do not take me seriously. They fill me full of drugs and never even bother to lock the door. When I think of Ruel I think of the song the British sing: "Ruel Britannia"! I can even whistle it, or drum it with my fingers.

SEPTEMBER, 1961

PAGE 218

People tell my husband all the time that I do not look crazy. I have been out for almost a year and he is beginning to believe them. Nights, he climbs on me with his slobber and his hope, cursing Mordecai Rich for messing up his life. I wonder if he feels our wills clashing in the dark. Sometimes I see the sparks fly inside my head. It is amazing how normal everything is.

PAGE 223

The house still does not awaken to the pitter-patter of sweet little feet, because I religiously use the Pill. It is the only spot of humor in my entire day, when I am gulping that little yellow tablet and washing it down with soda pop or tea. Ruel spends long hours at the store and in the peanut field. He comes in sweaty, dirty, tired, and I wait for him smelling of Arpège, My Sin, Wind Song, and Jungle Gardenia. The women of the community feel sorry for him, to be married to such a fluff of nothing.

I wait, beautiful and perfect in every limb, cooking supper as if my life depended on it. Lying unresisting on his bed like a drowned body washed to shore. But he is not happy. For he knows now that I intend to do nothing but say yes until he is completely exhausted.

I go to the new shopping mall twice a day now; once in the morning and once in the afternoon, or at night. I buy hats I would not dream of wearing, or even owning. Dresses that are already on their way to Goodwill. Shoes that will go to mold and mildew in the cellar. And I keep the bottles of perfume, the skin softeners, the pots of gloss and eye shadow. I amuse myself painting my own face.

When he is quite, quite tired of me I will tell him how long I've relied on the security of the Pill. When I am quite, quite tired of the sweet, sweet smell of my body and the softness of these Helena Rubenstein hands I will leave him and this house. Leave them forever without once looking back.

Poems

Hina Tefatu, *The Moon and the Earth*. 1893. Oil on burlap,
45″ × 24½″. Collection, The Museum of Modern Art,
New York, Lillie P. Bliss Collection.

ANONYMOUS

Edward

"Why dois° your brand° sae drap wi bluid,   *does; sword*
                 Edward, Edward,
Why dois your brand sae drap wi bluid,
     And why sae sad gang° yee O?"   *go*
"O I hae killed my hauke sae guid,
                 Mither, mither,
O I hae killed my hauke sae guid,
     And I had nai mair° bot° hee O."   *more; but*

"Your haukis bluid was nevir sae reid,
                 Edward, Edward,
Your haukis bluid was nevir sae reid,
     My deir son I tell thee O."
"O I hae killed my reid roan steid,
                 Mither, mither,
O I hae killed my reid-roan steid,
     That erst° was sae fair and frie° O."   *once; spirited*

"Your steid was auld, and ye hae got mair,
                 Edward, Edward,
Your steid was auld, and ye hae got mair,
     Sum other dule° ye drie° O."   *grief; suffer*
"O I hae killed my fadir deir,
                 Mither, mither,
O I hae killed my fadir deir,
     Alas, and wae is mee O!"

"And whatten penance wul ye drie for that,
                 Edward, Edward,
And whatten penance wul ye drie for that?
     My deir son, now tell me O."
"Ile set my feit in yonder boat,
                 Mither, mither,
Ile set my feit in yonder boat,
     And Ile fare ovir the sea O."

"And what wul ye doe wi your towirs and your ha,°   *hall*
                 Edward, Edward,
And what wul ye doe wi your towirs and your ha,
     That were sae fair to see O?"

"Ile let thame stand tul they doun fa,°   *fall*
      Mither, mither,
Ile let thame stand tul they doun fa,
For here nevir mair maun° I bee O."   *must*   40

"And what wul ye leive to your bairns° and your wife,   *children*
      Edward, Edward,
And what wul ye leive to your bairns and your wife,
  Whan ye gang ovir the sea O?"
"The warldis° room, late them beg thrae° life,   *world's; through*   45
      Mither, mither,
The warldis room, late them beg thrae life,
  For thame nevir mair wul I see O."

"And what wul ye leive to your ain mither deir,
      Edward, Edward?   50
And what wul ye leive to your ain mither deir?
  My deir son, now tell me O."
"The curse of hell frae me sall ye beir,
      Mither, mither,
The curse of hell frae me sall ye beir,   55
  Sic° counseils ye gave to me O."   *Such*

ANONYMOUS

The Limerick

There was a young man from Japan
Whose limericks never would scan;
  When they said it was so,
  He replied, "Yes, I know,
But I always try to get as many words into the last line as ever I possibly
  can."   5

ANONYMOUS

Not Just for the Ride

There was a young lady of Niger
Who smiled as she rode on a tiger:
   They came back from the ride
   With the lady inside
And the smile on the face of the tiger.

ANONYMOUS

Relativity

There was a young lady named Bright,
Who traveled much faster than light,
   She started one day
   In the relative way,
And returned on the previous night.

SIR PHILIP SIDNEY   (1554–1586)

With How Sad Steps, O Moon

With how sad steps, O Moon, thou climb'st the skies!
   How silently, and with how wan a face!
   What! may it be that even in heavenly place
That busy archer° his sharp arrows tries?   *Cupid*
Sure, if that long-with-love-acquainted eyes
   Can judge of love, thou feel'st a lover's case.
   I read it in thy looks; thy languished grace
To me, that feel the like, thy state descries.
   Then, even of fellowship, O Moon, tell me:
Is constant love deemed there but want of wit?
Are beauties there as proud as here they be?
Do they above love to be loved, and yet
   Those lovers scorn whom that love doth possess?
   Do they call virtue there ungratefulness?

WILLIAM SHAKESPEARE (1564–1616)

Sonnet 73

That time of year thou mayst in me behold
When yellow leaves, or none, or few, do hang
Upon those boughs which shake against the cold,
Bare ruined choirs where late the sweet birds sang.
In me thou see'st the twilight of such day   5
As after sunset fadeth in the west,
Which by and by black night doth take away,
Death's second self, that seals up all in rest.
In me thou see'st the glowing of such fire
That on the ashes of his youth doth lie,   10
As the deathbed whereon it must expire,
Consumed with that which it was nourished by.
   This thou perceivest, which makes thy love more strong,
   To love that well which thou must leave ere long.

WILLIAM SHAKESPEARE (1564–1616)

Sonnet 116

Let me not to the marriage of true minds
Admit impediments. Love is not love
Which alters when it alteration finds,
Or bends with the remover to remove.
O no! it is an ever fixed mark   5
That looks on tempests and is never shaken;
It is the star to every wandering bark,
Whose worth's unknown, although his height be taken.
Love's not Time's fool, though rosy lips and cheeks
Within his bending sickle's compass come;   10
Love alters not with his brief hours and weeks,
But bears it out even to the edge of doom.
   If this be error and upon me proved,
   I never writ, nor no man ever loved.

JOHN DONNE   (1572–1631)

The Bait[1]

Come live with me and be my love,
And we will some new pleasures prove,
Of golden sands and crystal brooks,
With silken lines and silver hooks.

There will the river whispering run,
Warmed by thy eyes more than the sun;
And there the enamored fish will stay,
Begging themselves they may betray.

When thou wilt swim in that live bath,
Each fish, which every channel hath,
Will amorously to thee swim,
Gladder to catch thee, than thou him.

If thou to be so seen be'st loath,
By sun or moon, thou dark'nest both;
And if myself have leave to see,
I need not their light, having thee.

Let others freeze with angling reeds,
And cut their legs with shells and weeds,
Or treacherously poor fish beset
With strangling snare or windowy net.

Let coarse bold hands from slimy nest
The bedded fish in banks out-wrest,
Or curious traitors, sleave-silk flies,
Bewitch poor fishes' wand'ring eyes.

For thee, thou need'st no such deceit,
For thou thyself art thine own bait;
That fish that is not catched thereby,
Alas, is wiser far than I.

---

[1] See Christopher Marlowe, "The Passionate Shepherd to His Love" (p. 317).

JOHN DONNE   (1572–1631)

The Sun Rising

   Busy old fool, unruly Sun,
   Why dost thou thus
Through windows and through curtains call on us?
Must to thy motions lovers' seasons run?
   Saucy pedantic wretch, go chide   5
   Late schoolboys and sour prentices°,   *apprentices*
  Go tell court-huntsmen that the king will ride,
  Call country ants to harvest offices;
Love, all alike, no season knows, nor clime,
Nor hours, days, months, which are the rags of time.   10

   Thy beams so reverend and strong
   Why shouldst thou think?
I could eclipse and cloud them with a wink,
But that I would not lose her sight so long;
   If her eyes have not blinded thine,   15
   Look, and tomorrow late tell me,
  Whether both th'Indias° of spice and mine   *East and West Indies*
  Be where thou left'st them, or lie here with me.
Ask for those kings whom thou saw'st yesterday,
And thou shalt hear, all here in one bed lay.   20

   She's all states, and all princes I;
   Nothing else is.
Princes do but play us; compared to this,
All honor's mimic, all wealth alchemy.
   Thou, Sun, art half as happy as we,   25
   In that the world's contracted thus;
  Thine age asks ease, and since thy duties be
  To warm the world, that's done in warming us.
Shine here to us, and thou art everywhere;
This bed thy center is, these walls thy sphere.   30

JOHN MILTON (1608–1674)

When I Consider How My Light Is Spent[1]

When I consider how my light is spent
   Ere half my days, in this dark world and wide,
   And that one talent[2] which is death to hide
   Lodged with me useless, though my soul more bent
To serve therewith my Maker, and present
   My true account, lest he returning chide,
   "Doth God exact day-labor, light denied?"
   I fondly° ask. But Patience, to prevent   *foolishly*
That murmur, soon replies, "God doth not need
   Either man's work or his own gifts. Who best
   Bear his mild yoke, they serve him best. His state
Is kingly: thousands at his bidding speed,
   And post o'er land and ocean without rest;
   They also serve who only stand and wait."

WILLIAM BLAKE (1757–1827)

The Chimney Sweeper

When my mother died I was very young,
And my father sold me while yet my tongue
Could scarcely cry "'weep! 'weep! 'weep! 'weep!"
So your chimneys I sweep, and in soot I sleep.

There's little Tom Dacre, who cried when his head,
That curled like a lamb's back, was shaved; so I said,
"Hush, Tom! never mind it, for, when your head's bare,
You know that the soot cannot spoil your white hair."

And so he was quiet, and that very night,
As Tom was asleeping, he had such a sight!
That thousands of sweepers, Dick, Joe, Ned, and Jack,
Were all of them locked up in coffins of black.

And by came an Angel who had a bright key,
And he opened the coffins and set them all free;

---

[1] Milton was blind before he was fifty.

[2] A pun on Milton's talent as a poet and Christ's Parable of the Talents (Matthew 25:14–30).

Then down a green plain leaping, laughing, they run,   15
And wash in a river, and shine in the sun.

Then naked and white, all their bags left behind,
They rise upon clouds and sport in the wind;
And the Angel told Tom, if he'd be a good boy,
He'd have God for his father, and never want joy.   20

And so Tom awoke, and we rose in the dark,
And got with our bags and our brushes to work.
Though the morning was cold, Tom was happy and warm;
So if all do their duty they need not fear harm.

WILLIAM WORDSWORTH   (1770–1850)

I Wandered Lonely as a Cloud

I wandered lonely as a cloud
That floats on high o'er vales and hills,
When all at once I saw a crowd,
A host, of golden daffodils;
Beside the lake, beneath the trees,   5
Fluttering and dancing in the breeze.

Continuous as the stars that shine
And twinkle on the milky way,
They stretched in never-ending line
Along the margin of a bay: 10
Ten thousand saw I at a glance,
Tossing their heads in sprightly dance.

The waves beside them danced; but they
Outdid the sparkling waves in glee;
A poet could not but be gay,   15
In such a jocund company;
I gazed—and gazed—but little thought
What wealth the show to me had brought:

For oft, when on my couch I lie
In vacant or in pensive mood,   20
They flash upon that inward eye
Which is the bliss of solitude;
And then my heart with pleasure fills,
And dances with the daffodils.

PERCY BYSSHE SHELLEY   (1792–1822)

Ozymandias

I met a traveller from an antique land
Who said: Two vast and trunkless legs of stone
Stand in the desert . . . Near them, on the sand,
Half sunk, a shattered visage lies, whose frown,
And wrinkled lip, and sneer of cold command,
Tell that its sculptor well those passions read
Which yet survive, stamped on these lifeless things,
The hand that mocked them, and the heart that fed:
And on the pedestal these words appear:
"My name is Ozymandias, king of kings:
Look on my works, ye Mighty, and despair!"
Nothing beside remains. Round the decay
Of that colossal wreck, boundless and bare
The lone and level sands stretch far away.

ALFRED, LORD TENNYSON   (1809–1892)

Crossing the Bar

Sunset and evening star,
  And one clear call for me!
And may there be no moaning of the bar,
  When I put out to sea,

But such a tide as moving seems asleep,
  Too full for sound and foam,
When that which drew from out the boundless deep
  Turns again home.

Twilight and evening bell,
  And after that the dark!
And may there be no sadness of farewell,
  When I embark;

For tho' from out our bourne of Time and Place
  The flood may bear me far,
I hope to see my Pilot face to face
  When I have crost the bar.

ALFRED, LORD TENNYSON   (1809–1892)

Ulysses[1]

It little profits that an idle king,
By this still hearth, among these barren crags,
Matched with an agèd wife, I mete and dole
Unequal laws unto a savage race,
That hoard, and sleep, and feed, and know not me.   5
I cannot rest from travel; I will drink
Life to the lees. All times I have enjoyed
Greatly, have suffered greatly, both with those
That loved me, and alone; on shore, and when
Through scudding drifts the rainy Hyades   10
Vext the dim sea. I am become a name;
For always roaming with a hungry heart
Much have I seen and known,—cities of men
And manners, climates, councils, governments,
Myself not least, but honored of them all;   15
And drunk delight of battle with my peers,
Far on the ringing plains of windy Troy.
I am a part of all that I have met,
Yet all experience is an arch wherethrough
Gleams that untraveled world, whose margin fades   20
For ever and for ever when I move.
How dull it is to pause, to make an end,
To rust unburnished, not to shine in use!
As though to breathe were life! Life piled on life
Were all too little, and of one to me   25
Little remains; but every hour is saved
From that eternal silence, something more,
A bringer of new things; and vile it were
For some three suns to store and hoard myself,
And this grey spirit yearning in desire   30
To follow knowledge like a sinking star,
Beyond the utmost bound of human thought.

This is my son, mine own Telemachus,
To whom I leave the scepter and the isle—
Well-loved of me, discerning to fulfil   35

---

[1] *Ulysses* (Odysseus): a hero in Homer's *Iliad* and *Odyssey*. In the *Odyssey*, he goes through ten years of adventurous trials to return home to his wife Penelope and his son Telemachus. The story of a final journey after this return comes from Dante's *Inferno* (Canto XXVI).

This labor, by slow prudence to make mild
A rugged people, and through soft degrees
Subdue them to the useful and the good.
Most blameless is he, centered in the sphere
Of common duties, decent not to fail   4
In offices of tenderness, and pay
Meet adoration to my household gods,
When I am gone. He works his work, I mine.

There lies the port; the vessel puffs her sail:
There gloom the dark, broad seas. My mariners,   4
Souls that have toiled, and wrought, and thought with me—
That ever with a frolic welcome took
The thunder and the sunshine, and opposed
Free hearts, free foreheads,—you and I are old;
Old age hath yet his honor and his toil.   5
Death closes all; but something ere the end,
Some work of noble note, may yet be done,
Not unbecoming men that strove with Gods.
The lights begin to twinkle from the rocks;
The long day wanes; the slow moon climbs; the deep
Moans round with many voices. Come, my friends,
'Tis not too late to seek a newer world.
Push off, and sitting well in order smite
The sounding furrows; for my purpose holds
To sail beyond the sunset, and the baths
Of all the western stars, until I die.
It may be that the gulfs will wash us down;
It may be we shall touch the Happy Isles,[2]
And see the great Achilles, whom we knew.
Though much is taken, much abides; and though
We are not now that strength which in old days
Moved earth and heaven, that which we are, we are:
One equal temper of heroic hearts,
Made weak by time and fate, but strong in will
To strive, to seek, to find, and not to yield.

---

[2] The Elysian Fields, Greek paradise where Achilles, hero of the *Iliad*, would be.

MATTHEW ARNOLD (1822–1888)

Dover Beach

The sea is calm tonight,
The tide is full, the moon lies fair
Upon the straits;—on the French coast the light
Gleams and is gone; the cliffs of England stand,
Glimmering and vast, out in the tranquil bay.   5
Come to the window, sweet is the night-air!
Only, from the long line of spray
Where the sea meets the moon-blanched land,
Listen! you hear the grating roar
Of pebbles which the waves draw back, and fling,   10
At their return, up the high strand,
Begin, and cease, and then again begin,
With tremulous cadence slow, and bring
The eternal note of sadness in.

Sophocles long ago   15
Heard it on the Aegean, and it brought
Into his mind the turbid ebb and flow
Of human misery; we
Find also in the sound a thought,
Hearing it by this distant northern sea.   20

The Sea of Faith
Was once, too, at the full, and round earth's shore
Lay like the folds of a bright girdle furled.
But now I only hear
Its melancholy, long, withdrawing roar,   25
Retreating, to the breath
Of the night-wind, down the vast edges drear
And naked shingles° of the world.   *pebbled beaches*

Ah, love, let us be true
To one another! for the world, which seems   30
To lie before us like a land of dreams,
So various, so beautiful, so new,
Hath really neither joy, nor love, nor light,
Nor certitude, nor peace, nor help for pain;
And we are here as on a darkling plain   35
Swept with confused alarms of struggle and flight,
Where ignorant armies clash by night.

EMILY DICKINSON (1830–1886)

After Great Pain, a Formal Feeling Comes (J341)

After great pain, a formal feeling comes—
The Nerves sit ceremonious, like Tombs—
The stiff Heart questions was it He, that bore,
And Yesterday, or Centuries before?

The Feet, mechanical, go round—
Of Ground, or Air, or Ought—
A Wooden way
Regardless grown,
A Quartz contentment, like a stone—

This is the Hour of Lead—
Remembered, if outlived,
As Freezing persons, recollect the Snow—
First—Chill—then Stupor—then the letting go—

EMILY DICKINSON (1830–1886)

A Narrow Fellow in the Grass (J986)

A narrow Fellow in the Grass
Occasionally rides—
You may have met Him—did you not
His notice sudden is—

The Grass divides as with a Comb—
A spotted shaft is seen—
And then it closes at your feet
And opens further on—

He likes a Boggy Acre
A Floor too cool for Corn—
Yet when a Boy, and Barefoot—
I more than once at Noon
Have passed, I thought, a Whip lash
Unbraiding in the Sun
When stooping to secure it
It wrinkled, and was gone—

Several of Nature's People
I know, and they know me—
I feel for them a transport
Of cordiality—   20

But never met this Fellow
Attended, or alone
Without a tighter breathing
And Zero at the Bone—

EMILY DICKINSON   (1830–1886)

Where Ships of Purple—Gently Toss (J265)

Where Ships of Purple—gently toss—
On Seas of Daffodil—
Fantastic Sailors—mingle—
And then—the Wharf is still!

A. E. HOUSMAN   (1859–1936)

Is My Team Ploughing

"Is my team ploughing,
   That I was used to drive
And hear the harness jingle
   When I was man alive?"

Ay, the horses trample,   5
   The harness jingles now;
No change though you lie under
   The land you used to plough.

"Is football playing
   Along the river shore,   10
With lads to chase the leather,
   Now I stand up no more?"

Ay, the ball is flying,
　　The lads play heart and soul;
The goal stands up, the keeper　　　　　　　　　　　　　　15
　　Stands up to keep the goal.

"Is my girl happy,
　　That I thought hard to leave,
And has she tired of weeping　　　　　　　　　　　　　　2
　　As she lies down at eve?"

Ay, she lies down lightly,
　　She lies not down to weep:
Your girl is well contented.
　　Be still, my lad, and sleep.

"Is my friend hearty,　　　　　　　　　　　　　　　　　2
　　Now I am thin and pine,
And has he found to sleep in
　　A better bed than mine?"

Yes, lad, I lie easy,
　　I lie as lads would choose;　　　　　　　　　　　　　3
I cheer a dead man's sweetheart,
　　Never ask me whose.

WILLIAM BUTLER YEATS   (1865–1939)

Sailing to Byzantium[1]

I

That[2] is no country for old men. The young
In one another's arms, birds in the trees
—Those dying generations—at their song,
The salmon-falls, the mackerel-crowded seas,
Fish, flesh, or fowl, commend all summer long
Whatever is begotten, born, and dies.
Caught in that sensual music all neglect
Monuments of unageing intellect.

---

　[1] Byzantium (now Istanbul) was the ancient eastern capital of Christendom, symbolic
to Yeats of timeless spiritual perfection achieved through art.
　[2] Ireland, here associated with the temporal, sensuous world.

II

An aged man is but a paltry thing,
A tattered coat upon a stick, unless   10
Soul clap its hands and sing, and louder sing
For every tatter in its mortal dress,
Nor is there singing school but studying
Monuments of its own magnificence;
And therefore I have sailed the seas and come   15
To the holy city of Byzantium.

III

O sages standing in God's holy fire
As in the gold mosaic of a wall,
Come from the holy fire, perne° in a gyre,°   *whirl; spiral*
And be the singing-masters of my soul.   20
Consume my heart away; sick with desire
And fastened to a dying animal
It knows not what it is; and gather me
Into the artifice of eternity.

IV

Once out of nature I shall never take   25
My bodily form from any natural thing,
But such a form as Grecian goldsmiths make
Of hammered gold and gold enamelling
To keep a drowsy Emperor awake;[3]
Or set upon a golden bough to sing   30
To lords and ladies of Byzantium
Of what is past, or passing, or to come.

EDWIN ARLINGTON ROBINSON (1869–1935)

Richard Cory

Whenever Richard Cory went down town,
We people on the pavement looked at him:
He was a gentleman from sole to crown,
Clean favored, and imperially slim.

---

[3] Yeats's note: "I have read somewhere that in the Emperor's palace at Byzantium was a tree made of gold and silver, and artificial birds that sang."

And he was always quietly arrayed,   5
And he was always human when he talked;
But still he fluttered pulses when he said,
"Good-morning," and he glittered when he walked.

And he was rich—yes, richer than a king—
And admirably schooled in every grace: 1(
In fine, we thought that he was everything
To make us wish that we were in his place.

So on we worked, and waited for the light,
And went without the meat, and cursed the bread;
And Richard Cory, one calm summer night,   1.
Went home and put a bullet through his head.

AMY LOWELL   (1874–1925)

Patterns

I walk down the garden paths,
And all the daffodils
Are blowing, and the bright blue squills.
I walk down the patterned garden-paths
In my stiff, brocaded gown.
With my powdered hair and jewelled fan,
I too am a rare
Pattern. As I wander down
The garden paths.

My dress is richly figured,
And the train
Makes a pink and silver stain
On the gravel, and the thrift
Of the borders.
Just a plate of current fashion
Tripping by in high-heeled, ribboned shoes.
Not a softness anywhere about me,
Only whalebone and brocade.
And I sink on a seat in the shade
Of a lime tree. For my passion
Wars against the stiff brocade.
The daffodils and squills

Flutter in the breeze
As they please.
And I weep;   25
For the lime-tree is in blossom
And one small flower has dropped upon my bosom.

And the plashing of waterdrops
In the marble fountain
Comes down the garden-paths.   30
The dripping never stops.
Underneath my stiffened gown
Is the softness of a woman bathing in a marble basin,
A basin in the midst of hedges grown
So thick, she cannot see her lover hiding,   35
But she guesses he is near,
And the sliding of the water
Seems the stroking of a dear
Hand upon her.
What is Summer in a fine brocaded gown!   40
I should like to see it lying in a heap upon the ground.
All the pink and silver crumpled up on the ground.

I would be the pink and silver as I ran along the paths,
And he would stumble after,
Bewildered by my laughter.   45
I should see the sun flashing from his sword-hilt and buckles on his
    shoes.
I would choose
To lead him in a maze along the patterned paths,
A bright and laughing maze for my heavy-booted lover.
Till he caught me in the shade,   50
And the buttons of his waistcoat bruised my body as he clasped me,
Aching, melting, unafraid.
With the shadows of the leaves and the sundrops,
And the plopping of the waterdrops,
All about us in the open afternoon—   55
I am very like to swoon
With the weight of this brocade,
For the sun sifts through the shade.

Underneath the fallen blossom
In my bosom,   60
Is a letter I have hid.
It was brought to me this morning by a rider from the Duke.
"Madam, we regret to inform you that Lord Hartwell

Died in action Thursday se'nnight."
As I read it in the white, morning sunlight,   65
The letters squirmed like snakes.
"Any answer, Madam," said my footman.
"No," I told him.
"See that the messenger takes some refreshment.
No, no answer."   70
And I walked into the garden,
Up and down the patterned paths,
In my stiff, correct brocade.

The blue and yellow flowers stood up proudly in the sun,
Each one.   75
I stood upright too,
Held rigid to the pattern
By the stiffness of my gown.
Up and down I walked.
Up and down.   80

In a month he would have been my husband.
In a month, here, underneath this lime,
We would have broken the pattern;
He for me, and I for him,
He as Colonel, I as Lady,
On this shady seat.
He had a whim
That sunlight carried blessing.
And I answered, "It shall be as you have said."
Now he is dead.

In Summer and in Winter I shall walk
Up and down
The patterned garden-paths
In my stiff, brocaded gown.
The squills and daffodils
Will give place to pillared roses, and to asters, and to snow.
I shall go
Up and down,
In my gown.
Gorgeously arrayed,
Boned and stayed.
And the softness of my body will be guarded from embrace
By each button, hook, and lace.
For the man who should loose me is dead,
Fighting with the Duke in Flanders,
In a pattern called a war.
Christ! What are patterns for?

AMY LOWELL   (1874–1925)

Taxi

When I go away from you
The world beats dead
Like a slackened drum.
I call out for you against the jutted stars
And shout into the ridges of the wind.   5
Streets coming fast,
One after the other,
Wedge you away from me,
And the lamps of the city prick my eyes
So that I can no longer see your face.   10
Why should I leave you,
To wound myself upon the sharp edges of the night?

ROBERT FROST   (1874–1963)

After Apple Picking

My long two-pointed ladder's sticking through a tree
Toward heaven still,
And there's a barrel that I didn't fill
Beside it, and there may be two or three
Apples I didn't pick upon some bough.   5
But I am done with apple-picking now.
Essence of winter sleep is on the night,
The scent of apples: I am drowsing off.
I cannot rub the strangeness from my sight
I got from looking through a pane of glass   10
I skimmed this morning from the drinking trough
And held against the world of hoary grass.
It melted, and I let it fall and break.
But I was well
Upon my way to sleep before it fell,   15
And I could tell
What form my dreaming was about to take.
Magnified apples appear and disappear,
Stem end and blossom end,

And every fleck of russet showing clear.   20
My instep arch not only keeps the ache,
It keeps the pressure of a ladder-round.
I feel the ladder sway as the boughs bend.
And I keep hearing from the cellar bin
The rumbling sound   25
Of load on load of apples coming in.
For I have had too much
Of apple-picking: I am overtired
Of the great harvest I myself desired.
There were ten thousand thousand fruit to touch,   30
Cherish in hand, lift down, and not let fall.
For all
That struck the earth,
No matter if not bruised or spiked with stubble,
Went surely to the cider-apple heap   35
As of no worth.
One can see what will trouble
This sleep of mine, whatever sleep it is.
Were he not gone,
The woodchuck could say whether it's like his   4
Long sleep, as I describe its coming on,
Or just some human sleep.

ROBERT FROST   (1874–1963)

Fire and Ice

Some say the world will end in fire,
Some say in ice.
From what I've tasted of desire
I hold with those who favor fire.
But if it had to perish twice,
I think I know enough of hate
To say that for destruction ice
Is also great
And would suffice.

SIEGFRIED SASSON   (1886–1967)

Base Details

If I were fierce, and bald, and short of breath,
    I'd live with scarlet Majors at the Base,
And speed glum heroes up the line to death.
    You'd see me with my puffy petulant face,
Guzzling and gulping in the best hotel,   5
    Reading the Roll of Honour. "Poor young chap,"
I'd say—"I used to know his father well;
    Yes, we've lost heavily in this last scrap."
And when the war is done and youth stone dead,
I'd toddle safely home and die—in bed.   10

T. S. ELIOT   (1888–1965)

The Love Song of J. Alfred Prufrock

S'io credesse che mia risposta fosse
A persona che mai tornasse al mondo,
Questa fiamma staria senza piu scosse.
Ma perciocche giammai di questo fondo
Non torno vivo alcun, s'i'odo il vero,
Senza tema d'infamia ti rispondo.[1]

Let us go then, you and I,
When the evening is spread out against the sky
Like a patient etherised upon a table;
Let us go, through certain half-deserted streets,
The muttering retreats   5
Of restless nights in one-night cheap hotels
And sawdust restaurants with oyster-shells:
Streets that follow like a tedious argument
Of insidious intent

---

[1] Dante's Inferno (Canto XXVII, lines 61–66): "If I believed that my reply were to someone who would ever go back to earth, this flame would quiver no more. But since from this depth no one ever returns alive, if I hear true, without fear of infamy I respond to you." These words are spoken by Count Guido da Montefeltro, in Hell as one of the False Counselors punished by being wrapped in flame. Dante has just asked to hear his story.

To lead you to an overwhelming question . . .   10
Oh, do not ask, "What is it?"
Let us go and make our visit.

In the room the women come and go
Talking of Michelangelo.

The yellow fog that rubs its back upon the window-panes,   15
The yellow smoke that rubs its muzzle on the window-panes
Licked its tongue into the corners of the evening,
Lingered upon the pools that stand in drains,
Let fall upon its back the soot that falls from chimneys,
Slipped by the terrace, made a sudden leap,   20
And seeing that it was a soft October night,
Curled once about the house, and fell asleep.

And indeed there will be time
For the yellow smoke that slides along the street,
Rubbing its back upon the window-panes;   2⁵
There will be time, there will be time
To prepare a face to meet the faces that you meet;
There will be time to murder and create,
And time for all the works and days[2] of hands
That lift and drop a question on your plate;   ³⁰
Time for you and time for me,
And time yet for a hundred indecisions,
And for a hundred visions and revisions,
Before the taking of a toast and tea.

In the room the women come and go   ³⁵
Talking of Michelangelo.

And indeed there will be time
To wonder, "Do I dare?" and, "Do I dare?"
Time to turn back and descend the stair,
With a bald spot in the middle of my hair—
[They will say: "How his hair is growing thin!"]
My morning coat, my collar mounting firmly to the chin,
My necktie rich and modest, but asserted by a simple pin—
[They will say: "But how his arms and legs are thin!"]
Do I dare
Disturb the universe?
In a minute there is time
For decisions and revisions which a minute will reverse.

---

[2] An allusion to *Works and Days*, a poem by Hesiod (Eighth century B.C.) celebrating farm life.

For I have known them all already, known them all:—
Have known the evenings, mornings, afternoons,   50
I have measured out my life with coffee spoons;
I know the voices dying with a dying fall
Beneath the music from a farther room.
    So how should I presume?

And I have known the eyes already, known them all—   55
The eyes that fix you in a formulated phrase,
And when I am formulated, sprawling on a pin,
When I am pinned and wriggling on the wall,
Then how should I begin
To spit out all the butt-ends of my days and ways?   60
    And how should I presume?

And I have known the arms already, known them all—
Arms that are braceleted and white and bare
[But in the lamplight, downed with light brown hair!]
Is it perfume from a dress   65
That makes me so digress?
Arms that lie along a table, or wrap about a shawl.
    And should I then presume?
    And how should I begin?

                    .   .   .   .   .

Shall I say, I have gone at dusk through narrow streets   70
And watched the smoke that rises from the pipes
Of lonely men in shirt-sleeves, leaning out of windows? . . .

    I should have been a pair of ragged claws
Scuttling across the floors of silent seas.

                    .   .   .   .   .

And the afternoon, the evening, sleeps so peacefully!   75
Smoothed by long fingers,
Asleep . . . tired . . . or it malingers,
Stretched on the floor, here beside you and me.
Should I, after tea and cakes and ices,
Have the strength to force the moment to its crisis?   80
But though I have wept and fasted, wept and prayed,
Though I have seen my head [grown slightly bald] brought in upon a
    platter,[3]
I am no prophet—and here's no great matter;

[3] See Matthew 14:3–11. Upon the request of Salome, Herod had John the Baptist
beheaded and the head presented to her on a platter.

I have seen the moment of my greatness flicker,
And I have seen the eternal Footman hold my coat, and snicker,   85
And in short, I was afraid.

   And would it have been worth it, after all,
After the cups, the marmalade, the tea,
Among the porcelain, among some talk of you and me,
Would it have been worth while,   90
To have bitten off the matter with a smile,
To have squeezed the universe into a ball[4]
To roll it toward some overwhelming question,
To say: "I am Lazarus,[5] come from the dead,
Come back to tell you all, I shall tell you all"—   95
If one, settling a pillow by her head,
   Should say: "That is not what I meant at all.
   That is not it, at all."

   And would it have been worth it, after all,
Would it have been worth while,   100
After the sunsets and the dooryards and the sprinkled streets,
After the novels, after the teacups, after the skirts that trail along the
   floor—
And this, and so much more?—
It is impossible to say just what I mean!
But as if a magic lantern threw the nerves in patterns on a screen: 105
Would it have been worth while
If one, settling a pillow or throwing off a shawl,
And turning toward the window, should say:
   "That is not it at all,
   That is not what I meant, at all."   110

      .   .   .   .

No! I am not Prince Hamlet, nor was meant to be;
Am an attendant lord, one that will do
To swell a progress, start a scene or two,
Advise the prince; no doubt, an easy tool,
Deferential, glad to be of use,
Politic, cautious, and meticulous;
Full of high sentence, but a bit obtuse;
At times, indeed, almost ridiculous—
Almost, at times, the Fool.

[4] See Andrew Marvell, "To His Coy Mistress" (p. 242).
[5] Probably the Lazarus Christ raised from the dead (John 11:1–44) or possibly the beggar Lazarus who was not allowed to leave Heaven to help the rich man in Hell or to warn his brothers of Hell (Luke 16:19–31).

I grow old . . . I grow old . . .   120
I shall wear the bottoms of my trousers rolled.

Shall I part my hair behind? Do I dare to eat a peach?
I shall wear white flannel trousers, and walk upon the beach.
I have heard the mermaids singing, each to each.

I do not think that they will sing to me.   125

I have seen them riding seaward on the waves
Combing the white hair of the waves blown back
When the wind blows the water white and black.

We have lingered in the chambers of the sea
By sea-girls wreathed with seaweed red and brown   130
Till human voices wake us, and we drown.

JOHN CROWE RANSON   (1888–1974)

Piazza Piece

—I am a gentleman in a dustcoat trying
To make you hear. Your ears are soft and small
And listen to an old man not at all,
They want the young men's whispering and sighing.
But see the roses on your trellis dying   5
And hear the spectral singing of the moon;
For I must have my lovely lady soon,
I am a gentleman in a dustcoat trying.

—I am a lady young in beauty waiting
Until my truelove comes, and then we kiss.   10
But what grey man among the vines is this
Whose words are dry and faint as in a dream?
Back from my trellis, Sir, before I scream!
I am a lady young in beauty waiting.

ARCHIBALD MACLEISH   (1892–1982)

You, Andrew Marvell[1]

And here face down beneath the sun
And here upon earth's noonward height
To feel the always coming on
The always rising of the night:

To feel creep up the curving east
The earthy chill of dusk and slow
Upon those under lands the vast
And ever climbing shadow grow

And strange at Ecbatan the trees
Take leaf by leaf the evening strange
The flooding dark about their knees
The mountains over Persia change

And now at Kermanshah the gate
Dark empty and the withered grass
And through the twilight now the late
Few travelers in the westward pass

And Baghdad darken and the bridge
Across the silent river gone
And through Arabia the edge
Of evening widen and steal on

And deepen on Palmyra's street
The wheel rut in the ruined stone
And Lebanon fade out and Crete
High through the clouds and overblown

And over Sicily the air
Still flashing with the landward gulls
And loom and slowly disappear
The sails above the shadowy hulls

And Spain go under and the shore
Of Africa the gilded sand
And evening vanish and no more
The low pale light across that land

---

[1] See Andrew Marvell, "To His Coy Mistress" (p. 242).

Nor now the long light on the sea:
And here face downward in the sun
To feel how swift how secretly   35
The shadow of the night comes on . . .

JEAN TOOMER   (1894–1967)

Her Lips Are Copper Wire

whisper of yellow globes
gleaming on lamp-posts that sway
like bootleg licker drinkers in the fog

and let your breath be moist against me
like bright beads on yellow globes   5

telephone the power-house
that the main wires are insulate

(her words play softly up and down
dewy corridors of billboards)

then with your tongue remove the tape   10
and press your lips to mine
till they are incandescent

LOUISE BOGAN   (1897–1970)

The Dream

O God, in the dream the terrible horse began
To paw at the air, and make for me with his blows.
Fear kept for thirty-five years poured through his mane,
And retribution equally old, or nearly, breathed through his nose.

Coward complete, I lay and wept on the ground   5
When some strong creature appeared, and leapt for the rein.
Another woman, as I lay half in a swound,
Leapt in the air, and clutched at the leather and chain.

Give him, she said, something of yours as a charm.
Throw him, she said, some poor thing you alone claim.   10
No, no, I cried, he hates me; he's out for harm,
And whether I yield or not, it is all the same.

But, like a lion in a legend, when I flung the glove
Pulled from my sweating, my cold right hand,
The terrible beast, that no one may understand,   1
Came to my side, and put down his head in love.

OGDEN NASH   (1902–1972)

Love Under the Republicans (or Democrats)[1]

Come live with me and be my love
And we will all the pleasures prove
Of a marriage conducted with economy
In the Twentieth Century Anno Donomy.
We'll live in a dear little walk-up flat
With practically room to swing a cat
And a potted cactus to give it hauteur
And a bathtub equipped with dark brown water.
We'll eat, without undue discouragement
Foods low in cost but high in nouragement
And quaff with pleasure, while chatting wittily,
The peculiar wine of Little Italy.
We'll remind each other it's smart to be thrifty
And buy our clothes for something-fifty.
We'll stand in line on holidays
For seats at unpopular matinees,
And every Sunday we'll have a lark
And take a walk in Central Park.
And one of these days not too remote
I'll probably up and cut your throat.

---

[1] See Christopher Marlowe, "The Passionate Shepherd to His Love" (p. 317).

PABLO NERUDA   (b. 1904)

The United Fruit Co.

Translated by Robert Bly

When the trumpet sounded, it was
all prepared on the earth,
and Jehovah parceled out the earth
to Coca-Cola, Inc., Anaconda,
Ford Motors, and other entities: 5
The Fruit Company, Inc.
reserved for itself the most succulent,
the central coast of my own land,
the delicate waist of America.
It rechristened its territories   10
as the "Banana Republics"
and over the sleeping dead,
over the restless heroes
who brought about the greatness,
the liberty and the flags,   15
it established the comic opera:
abolished the independencies,
presented crowns of Caesar,
unsheathed envy, attracted
the dictatorship of the flies,   20
Trujillo flies, Tacho flies,
Carias flies, Martinez flies,
Ubico flies, damp flies
of modest blood and marmalade,
drunken flies who zoom   25
over the ordinary graves,
circus flies, wise flies
well trained in tryanny.

Among the bloodthirsty flies
the Fruit Company lands its ships,   30
taking off the coffee and the fruit;
the treasure of our submerged
territories flows as though
on plates into the ships.

Meanwhile Indians are falling   35
into the sugared chasms
of the harbors, wrapped
for burial in the mist of the dawn:
a body rolls, a thing
that has no name, a fallen cipher,   4●
a cluster of dead fruit
thrown down the dump.

DYLAN THOMAS   (1914–1953)

Do Not Go Gentle into That Good Night

Do not go gentle into that good night,
Old age should burn and rave at close of day;
Rage, rage against the dying of the light.

Though wise men at their end know dark is right,
Because their words had forked no lightning they
Do not go gentle into that good night.

Good men, the last wave by, crying how bright
Their frail deeds might have danced in a green bay,
Rage, rage against the dying of the light.

Wild men who caught and sang the sun in flight,
And learn, too late, they grieved it on its way,
Do not go gentle into that good night.

Grave men, near death, who see with blinding sight
Blind eyes could blaze like meteors and be gay,
Rage, rage against the dying of the light.

And you, my father, there on the sad height,
Curse, bless, me now with your fierce tears, I pray.
Do not go gentle into that good night.
Rage, rage against the dying of the light.

RANDALL JARRELL (1914–1965)

The Death of the Ball Turret Gunner

From my mother's sleep I fell into the State,
And I hunched in its belly till my wet fur froze.
Six miles from earth, loosed from its dream of life,
I woke to black flak and the nightmare fighters.
When I died they washed me out of the turret with a hose.   5

GWENDOLYN BROOKS (b. 1917)

The Life of Lincoln West

Ugliest little boy
that everyone ever saw.
That is what everyone said.

Even to his mother it was apparent—
when the blue-aproned nurse came into the   5
northeast end of the maternity ward
bearing his squeals and plump bottom
looped up in a scant receiving blanket,
bending, to pass the bundle carefully
into the waiting mother-hands—that this   10
was no cute little ugliness, no sly baby waywardness
that was going to inch away
as would baby fat, baby curl, and
baby spot-rash. The pendulous lip, the
branching ears, the eyes so wide and wild,   15
the vague unvibrant brown of the skin,
and, most disturbing, the great head.
These components of That Look bespoke
the sure fibre. The deep grain.

His father could not bear the sight of him.   20
His mother high-piled her pretty dyed hair and
put him among her hairpins and sweethearts,
dance slippers, torn paper roses.
He was not less than these,
he was not more.   25

As the little Lincoln grew,
uglily upward and out, he began
to understand that something was
wrong. His little ways of trying
to please his father, the bringing
of matches, the jumping aside at
warning sound of oh-so-large and
rushing stride, the smile that gave
and gave and gave—Unsuccessful!

Even Christmases and Easters were spoiled.
He would be sitting at the
family feasting table, really
delighting in the displays of mashed potatoes
and the rich golden
fat-crust of the ham or the festive
fowl, when he would look up and find
somebody feeling indignant about him.

What a pity what a pity. No love
for one so loving. The little Lincoln
loved Everybody. Ants. The changing
caterpillar. His much-missing mother.
His kindergarten teacher.

His kindergarten teacher—whose
concern for him was composed of one
part sympathy and two parts repulsion.
The others ran up with their little drawings.
He ran up with his.
She
tried to be as pleasant with him as
with others, but it was difficult.
For she was all pretty! all daintiness,
all tiny vanilla, with blue eyes and fluffy
sun-hair. One afternoon she
saw him in the hall looking bleak against
the wall. It was strange because the
bell had long since rung and no other
child was in sight. Pity flooded her.
She buttoned her gloves and suggested
cheerfully that she walk him home. She
started out bravely, holding him by the
hand. But she had not walked far before
she regretted it. The little monkey.

Must everyone look? And clutching her
hand like that . . . Literally pinching
it . . .

70

At seven, the little Lincoln loved
the brother and sister who
moved next door. Handsome. Well—
dressed. Charitable, often, to him. They
enjoyed him because he was
resourceful, made up
games, told stories. But when
their More Acceptable friends came they turned
their handsome backs on him. He
hated himself for his feeling
of well-being when with them despite—
Everything.

75

80

He spent much time looking at himself
in mirrors. What could be done?
But there was no
shrinking his head. There was no
binding his ears.

85

"Don't touch me!" cried the little
fairy-like being in the playground.

her name was Nerissa. The many
children were playing tag, but when
he caught her, she recoiled, jerked free
and ran. It was like all the
rainbow that ever was, going off
forever, all, all the sparklings in
the sunset west.

90

95

One day, while he was yet seven,
a thing happened. In the down-town movies
with his mother a white
man in the seat beside him whispered
loudly to a companion, and pointed at
the little Linc.
"THERE! That's the kind I've been wanting
to show you! One of the best
examples of the specie. Not like
those diluted Negroes you see so much of on
the streets these days, but the
real thing.

100

105

Black, ugly, and odd. You
can see the savagery. The blunt   110
blankness. That is the real
thing."

His mother—her hair had never looked so
red around the dark brown
velvet of her face—jumped up,   115
shrieked "Go to—" She did not finish.
She yanked to his feet the little
Lincoln, who was sitting there
staring in fascination at his assessor. At the author of his
new idea.   12⦁

All the way home he was happy. Of course,
he had not liked the word
"ugly."
But, after all, should he not
be used to that by now? What had   12
struck him, among words and meanings
he could little understand, was the phrase
"the real thing."
He didn't know quite why,
but he liked that.   1
He liked that very much.

When he was hurt, too much
stared at—
too much
left alone—he   ⦁
thought about that. He told himself
"After all, I'm
the real thing."

It comforted him.

LAWRENCE FERLINGHETTI   (b. 1919)

Constantly Risking Absurdity

    Constantly risking absurdity
                    and death
       whenever he performs
              above the heads
                    of his audience

```
            the poet like an acrobat
                        climbs on rime
                                    to a high wire of his own making
and balancing on eyebeams
                                    above a sea of faces                                    10
            paces his way
                        to the other side of day
      performing entrechats
                              and sleight-of-foot tricks
and other high theatrics                                                                    15
                        and all without mistaking
                  any thing
                              for what it may not be

      For he's the super realist
                        who must perforce perceive                                          20
            taut truth
                        before the taking of each stance or step
in his supposed advance

                              toward that still higher perch
            where Beauty stands and waits                                                   25
                              with gravity
                                    to start her death-defying leap

            And he
                  a little charleychaplin man
                              who may or may not catch                                      30
                  her fair eternal form
                                    spreadeagled in the empty air
                  of existence
```

HOWARD NEMEROV   (b. 1920)

Boom!

Sees Boom in Religion, Too

Atlantic City, June 23, 1957 (AP).—President Eisenhower's pastor said to-
night that Americans are living in a period of "unprecedented religious ac-
tivity" caused partially by paid vacations, the eight-hour day and modern
conveniences.

"These fruits of material progress," said the Rev. Edward L. R. Elson
of the National Presbyterian Church, Washington, "have provided the lei-
sure, the energy, and the means for a level of human and spiritual values
never before reached."

Here at the Vespasian-Carlton,[1] it's just one
religious activity after another; the sky
is constantly being crossed by cruciform
airplanes, in which nobody disbelieves
for a second, and the tide, the tide
of spiritual progress and prosperity
miraculously keeps rising, to a level
never before attained. The churches are full,
the beaches are full, and the filling-stations
are full, God's great ocean is full
of paid vacationers praying an eight-hour day
to the human and spiritual values, the fruits,
the leisure, the energy, and the means, Lord,
the means for the level, the unprecedented level,
and the modern conveniences, which also are full.
Never before, O Lord, have the prayers and praises
from belfry and phonebooth, from ballpark and barbecue
the sacrifices, so endlessly ascended.

It was not thus when Job in Palestine
sat in the dust and cried, cried bitterly;[2]
when Damien kissed the lepers on their wounds[3]
it was not thus; it was not thus
when Francis worked a fourteen-hour day
strictly for the birds;[4] when Dante took
a week's vacation without pay and it rained
part of the time,[5] O Lord, it was not thus.

But now the gears mesh and the tires burn
and the ice chatters in the shaker and the priest
in the pulpit, and Thy Name, O Lord,
is kept before the public, while the fruits

---

[1] Vespasian was an emperor of Rome (70–79 A.D.).
[2] In the *Book of Job*, Job's faith was tested through loss of possessions and family and through bodily affliction.
[3] Father Damien (1840–1889) was a Belgian missionary who worked with lepers on the Hawaiian island of Molokai.
[4] St. Francis of Assisi (1181–1226), noted for his closeness to all living creatures.
[5] In Dante's *Inferno*, Dante travels through Hell. In the third circle he comes upon the gluttons, who are pelted by a cold, dirty rain.

ripen and religion booms and the level rises
and every modern convenience runneth over,
that it may never be with us as it hath been
with Athens and Karnak and Nagasaki,
nor Thy sun for one instant refrain from shining   35
on the rainbow Buick by the breezeway
or the Chris Craft with the uplift life raft;
that we may continue to be the just folks we are,
plain people with ordinary superliners and
disposable diaperliners, people of the stop'n'shop   40
'n'pray as you go, of hotel, motel, boatel,
the humble pilgrims of no deposit no return
and please adjust thy clothing, who will give to Thee,
if Thee will keep us going, our annual
Miss Universe, for Thy Name's Sake, Amen.   45

RICHARD WILBUR   (b. 1921)

A Simile for Her Smile

Your smiling, or the hope, the thought of it,
Makes in my mind such pause and abrupt ease
As when the highway bridgegates fall,
Balking the hasty traffic, which must sit
On each side massed and staring, while   5
Deliberately the drawbridge starts to rise:

Then horns are hushed, the oilsmoke rarefies,
Above the idling motors one can tell
The packet's smooth approach, the slip,
Slip of the silken river past the sides,   10
The ringing of clear bells, the dip
And slow cascading of the paddle wheel.

MARI EVANS   (b. 19–)

Status Symbol

         i
Have Arrived
         i
   am the
New Negro

         i
am the result of
President Lincoln
World War I
and Paris
the
Red Ball Express
white drinking fountains
sitdowns and
sit-ins
Federal Troops
Marches on Washington
and
prayer meetings
today
They hired me

it
is a status
job . . .

along
with my papers
They
gave me my
Status Symbol

the
key
to the
White . . . Locked . . .
John

ALASTAIR REID   (b. 1926)

Curiosity

may have killed the cat. More likely,
the cat was just unlucky, or else curious
to see what death was like, having no cause
to go on licking paws, or fathering
litter on litter of kittens, predictably.   5

Nevertheless, to be curious
is dangerous enough. To distrust
what is always said, what seems,
to ask odd questions, interfere in dreams,
smell rats, leave home, have hunches,   10
does not endear cats to those doggy circles
where well-smelt baskets, suitable wives, good lunches
are the order of things, and where prevails
much wagging of incurious heads and tails.

Face it. Curiosity   15
will not cause us to die—
only lack of it will.
Never to want to see
the other side of the hill
or that improbable country   20
where living is an idyll
(although a probable hell)
would kill us all.
Only the curious
have if they live a tale   25
worth telling at all.

Dogs say cats love too much, are irresponsible,
are dangerous, marry too many wives,
desert their children, chill all dinner tables
with tales of their nine lives.   30
Well, they are lucky. Let them be
nine-lived and contradictory,
curious enough to change, prepared to pay
the cat-price, which is to die
and die again and again,   35

each time with no less pain.
A cat-minority of one
is all that can be counted on
to tell the truth; and what cats have to tell
on each return from hell   4
is this: that dying is what the living do,
that dying is what the loving do,
and that dead dogs are those who never know
that dying is what, to live, each has to do.

ANNE SEXTON   (1928–1974)

Cinderella

You always read about it:
the plumber with twelve children
who wins the Irish Sweepstakes.
From toilets to riches.
That story.

Or the nursemaid,
some luscious sweet from Denmark
who captures the oldest son's heart.
From diapers to Dior.
That story.

Or a milkman who serves the wealthy,
eggs, cream, butter, yogurt, milk,
the white truck like an ambulance
who goes into real estate
and makes a pile.
From homogenized to martinis at lunch.

Or the charwoman
who is on the bus when it cracks up
and collects enough from the insurance.
From mops to Bonwit Teller.
That story.

Once
the wife of a rich man was on her deathbed
and she said to her daughter Cinderella:

Be devout. Be good. Then I will smile 25
down from heaven in the seam of a cloud.
The man took another wife who had
two daughters, pretty enough
but with hearts like blackjacks.
Cinderella was their maid. 30
She slept on the sooty hearth each night
and walked around looking like Al Jolson.
Her father brought presents home from town,
jewels and gowns for the other women
but the twig of a tree for Cinderella. 35
She planted that twig on her mother's grave
and it grew to a tree where a white dove sat.
Whenever she wished for anything the dove
would drop it like an egg upon the ground.
The bird is important, my dears, so heed him. 40

Next came the ball, as you all know.
It was a marriage market.
The prince was looking for a wife.
All but Cinderella were preparing
and gussying up for the big event. 45
Cinderella begged to go too.
Her stepmother threw a dish of lentils
into the cinders and said: Pick them
up in an hour and you shall go.
The white dove brought all his friends; 50
all the warm wings of the fatherland came,
and picked up the lentils in a jiffy.
No, Cinderella, said the stepmother,
you have no clothes and cannot dance.
That's the way with stepmothers. 55

Cinderella went to the tree at the grave
and cried forth like a gospel singer:
Mama! Mama! My turtledove,
send me to the prince's ball!
The bird dropped down a golden dress 60
and delicate little gold slippers.
Rather a large package for a simple bird.
So she went. Which is no surprise.
Her stepmother and sisters didn't
recognize her without her cinder face 65
and the prince took her hand on the spot
and danced with no other the whole day.

As nightfall came she thought she'd better
get home. The prince walked her home
and she disappeared into the pigeon house 7(
and although the prince took an axe and broke
it open she was gone. Back to her cinders.
These events repeated themselves for three days.
However on the third day the prince
covered the palace steps with cobbler's wax 7
and Cinderella's gold shoe stuck upon it.

Now he would find whom the shoe fit
and find his strange dancing girl for keeps.
He went to their house and the two sisters
were delighted because they had lovely feet. 8
The eldest went into a room to try the slipper on
but her big toe got in the way so she simply
sliced it off and put on the slipper.
The prince rode away with her until the white dove
told him to look at the blood pouring forth. 8
That is the way with amputations.
They don't just heal up like a wish.
The other sister cut off her heel
— but the blood told as blood will.
The prince was getting tired.
He began to feel like a shoe salesman.
But he gave it one last try.
This time Cinderella fit into the shoe
like a love letter into its envelope.

At the wedding ceremony
the two sisters came to curry favor
and the white dove pecked their eyes out.
Two hollow spots were left
like soup spoons.

Cinderella and the prince
lived, they say, happily ever after,
like two dolls in a museum case
never bothered by diapers or dust,
never arguing over the timing of an egg,
never telling the same story twice,
never getting a middle-aged spread,
their darling smiles pasted on for eternity.
Regular Bobbsey Twins.
That story.

ADRIENNE RICH (b. 1929)

Living in Sin

She had thought the studio would keep itself;
no dust upon the furniture of love.
Half heresy, to wish the taps less vocal,
the panes relieved of grime. A plate of pears,
a piano with a Persian shawl, a cat   5
stalking the picturesque amusing mouse
had risen at his urging.
Not that at five each separate stair would writhe
under the milkman's tramp; that morning light
so coldly would delineate the scraps   10
of last night's cheese and three sepulchral bottles;
that on the kitchen shelf among the saucers
a pair of beetle-eyes would fix her own—
envoy from some village in the moldings . . .
Meanwhile, he, with a yawn,   15
sounded a dozen notes upon the keyboard,
declared it out of tune, shrugged at the mirror,
rubbed at his beard, went out for cigarettes;
while she, jeered by the minor demons,
pulled back the sheets and made the bed and found   20
a towel to dust the table-top,
and let the coffee-pot boil over on the stove.
By evening she was back in love again,
though not so wholly but throughout the night
she woke sometimes to feel the daylight coming   25
like a relentless milkman up the stairs.

LINDA PASTAN (b. 1932)

Marks

My husband gives me an A
for last night's supper,
an incomplete for my ironing,
a B plus in bed.

My son says I am average,   5
an average mother, but if
I put my mind to it
I could improve.
My daughter believes
in Pass/Fail and tells me   10
I pass. Wait 'til they learn
I'm dropping out.

ETHERIDGE KNIGHT   (b. 1933)

For Black Poets Who Think of Suicide

Black Poets should live—not leap
From steel bridges (Like the white boys do.
Black Poets should *live*—not lay
Their necks on railroad tracks (like the white boys do.
Black Poets should seek—but not search too much
In sweet dark caves, nor hunt for snipe
Down psychic trails (like the white boys do.

For Black Poets belong to Black People. Are
The Flutes of Black Lovers. Are
The Organs of Black Sorrows. Are   1
The Trumpets of Black Warriors.
Let All Black Poets die as trumpets,
And be buried in the dust of marching feet.

RICHARD BRAUTIGAN   (b. 1935)

Romeo and Juliet

If you will die for me,
I will die for you

and our graves will
be like two lovers washing
their clothes together
in a laundromat.

If you will bring the soap,
I will bring the bleach.

ROGER MCGOUGH   (b. 1937)

40—Love

middle	aged
couple	playing
ten	nis
when	the
game	ends
and	they
go	home
the	net
will	still
be	be
tween	them

BOB DYLAN   (b. 1941)

It's All Over Now, Baby Blue

You must leave now take what you need, you think will last
But whatever you wish to keep, you better grab it fast.
Yonder stands your orphan, with his gun
Crying like a fire in the sun.
Look out the Saints are coming through   5
And it's all over now, baby blue.

The highway is for gamblers, better use your sins
Take what you have gathered from coincidence
The empty handed painter from your streets
Is drawing crazy patterns on your sheets   10
This sky too, is folding under you
And it's all over now, baby blue.

All your seasick sailors, they are rowing home
All your reindeer armies, are all going home

The lover who just walked out your door
Has taken all his blankets from the floor
The carpet too, is moving under you
And it's all over now, baby blue.

Leave your stepping stones behind, something calls for you
Forget the dead you've left, they will not follow you
The vagabond who's rapping at your door
Is standing in the clothes that you once wore
Strike another match, go start anew
And it's all over now, baby blue.

HENRY TAYLOR   (b. 1942)

At the Swings

      Midafternoon in Norfolk,
late July. I am taking our two sons for a walk
  away from their grandparents' house; we have
  directions to a miniature playground,
    and I have plans to wear them down
      toward a nap at five,

      when my wife and I
will leave them awhile with her father. A few blocks
  south of here, my wife's mother drifts from us
  beneath hospital sheets, her small strength bent
    to the poisons and the rays they use
      against a spreading cancer.

      In their house now, deep love
is studying to live with deepening impatience
  as each day gives our hopes a different form
  and household tasks rise like a powdery mist
    of restless fatigue. Still, at five,
      my wife and I will dress

      and take the boulevard
across the river to a church where two dear friends
  will marry; rings will be blessed, promises kept
  and made, and while our sons lie down to sleep,
    the groom's niece, as the flower girl,
      will almost steal the show.

But here the boys have made   25
an endless procession on the slides, shrieking down
    slick steel almost too hot to touch; and now
    they charge the swings. I push them from the front,
        one with each hand, until at last
            the rhythm, and the sunlight   30

        that splashes through live oak
and crape myrtle, dappling dead leaves on the ground,
    lull me away from this world toward a state
    still and remote as an old photograph
        in which I am standing somewhere   35
            I may have been before:

        there was this air, this light,
a day of thorough and forgetful happiness;
    where was it, or how long ago? I try
    to place it, but it has gone for good,   40
        to leave me gazing at these swings,
            thinking of something else

        I may have recognized—
an irrecoverable certainty that now,
    and now, this perfect afternoon, while friends   45
    are struggling to put on their cutaways
        or bridal gowns, and my wife's mother,
            dearer still, is dozing

        after her medicine,
or turning a small thing in her mind, like someone   50
    worrying a ring of keys to make small sounds
    against great silence, and while these two boys
        swing back and forth against my hand,
            time's crosshairs quarter me

        no matter where I turn.   55
Now it is time to go. The boys are tired enough,
    and my wife and I must dress and go to church.
    Because I love our friends, and ceremony,
        the usual words will make me weep:
            hearing the human prayers   60

        for holy permanence
will remind me that a life is much to ask
    of anyone, yet not too much to give
    to love. And once or twice, as I stand there,

that dappled moment at the swings   6
  will rise between the lines,

  when I beheld our sons
as, in the way of things, they will not be again,
  though even years from now their hair may lift
  a little in the breeze, as if they stood   7
    somewhere along their way from us,
      poised for a steep return.

Plays

Francisco Goya. *The Sleep of Reason Produces Monsters*, from *The Caprices*.
1793–98. The Metropolitan Museum of Art, New York. Gift of M. Knoedler & Co.

A NOTE ON THE GREEK THEATER

Plays are written primarily to be performed, not read, and the condition under which they are produced will influence a playwright's work. Certainly the circumstances surrounding the presentation of the early Greek plays did much to shape the plays written by Sophocles and others who created Greek drama in the fifth century B.C.

To stage *Antigone* in your mind, picture a football stadium rather than a modern auditorium. Greek plays were presented in large outdoor arenas capable of seating many thousand spectators. Unlike the performers in a modern rock concert, however, the Greek actors did not have amplifying equipment. Their movements and gestures therefore needed to be simple and stylized, and they generally spoke behind large masks not only to show a happy or a sad face but to help project the actor's voice throughout the arena. Acoustics were further aided by the tiered seats of the audience creating a bowl effect, and by the *skene* (scene building) that contained dressing rooms and served as a backdrop to the *orchestra*, or dancing place, where the chorus performed. Later a wooden platform (the modern stage) was added between the scene building and orchestra. The scene building allowed for entrances and exits, could suggest the setting of a temple or palace, and aided acoustics.

The role of the chorus in *Antigone* reflects the probable origin of Greek drama in religious ritual. The chorus chanted the lines of their odes in unison, moving first in one direction and then the other. These odes are interspersed between the dramatic episodes. The idea of individualized characters, that is, of drama itself, may have developed from religious music (choral dances) performed by a chorus with some solo parts. This connection between ritual and the early drama accounts for a play of dialogue with action taking place offstage and reported by a messenger.

Finally, we need to remember that Sophocles could assume an audience acquainted with the stories his plays presented—with, for instance, the story of Oedipus. Knowing how the story will end allows us to understand that, ironically, when Oedipus condemns the person who has brought the plague upon Thebes, he is condemning himself—the man who unknowingly has married his mother and killed his father.

SOPHOCLES (496?–406 B.C.)

Antigone

Translated by Dudley Fitts and Robert Fitzgerald

PERSONS REPRESENTED

Antigone
Ismene
Eurydice
Creon
Haimon
Teiresias
A Sentry
A Messenger
Chorus

SCENE: *Before the palace of* CREON, *King of Thebes. A central double door, and two lateral doors. A platform extends the length of the façade, and from this platform three steps lead down into the "orchestra," or chorus-ground.* TIME: *dawn of the day after the repulse of the Argive army from the assault on Thebes.*

PROLOGUE[1]

> [ANTIGONE *and* ISMENE *enter from the*
> *central door of the Palace.*

ANTIGONE.   Ismenê, dear sister,
   You would think that we had already suffered enough
   For the curse on Oedipus:
   I cannot imagine any grief

---

[1] Greek audiences knew the story of Oedipus, which led to the situation at the beginning of this play. Oedipus, warned by the Delphic oracle that he would kill his father and marry his mother, fled from the home of his presumed parents in Corinth. On the road to Thebes, Oedipus kills Laios, king of Thebes, solves the riddle of the monster Sphinx who had plagued Thebes, and becomes King of Thebes, marrying the Queen Iocastê. They have two sons, Eteoclês and Polyneicês, and two daughters, Antigonê and Ismenê. When Oedipus learns that he has fulfilled the oracle's prophesy, he blinds himself and banishes himself from Thebes. Eteoclês and Polyneicês were to share the throne, but Polyneicês was driven out, only to return with the Argive army to reclaim his share of the throne. The two brothers kill each other in single combat, and Creon, their uncle, becomes king.

That you and I have not gone through. And now—
Have they told you of the new decree of our King Creon?
ISMENE.   I have heard nothing: I know
That two sisters lost two brothers, a double death
In a single hour; and I know that the Argive army
Fled in the night; but beyond this, nothing.   10
ANTIGONE.   I thought so. And that is why I wanted you
To come out here with me. There is something we must do.
ISMENE.   Why do you speak so strangely?
ANTIGONE.   Listen, Ismenê:
Creon buried our brother Eteoclês
With military honors, gave him a soldier's funeral,
And it was right that he should; but Polyneicês,
Who fought as bravely and died as miserably,—
They say that Creon has sworn
No one shall bury him, no one mourn for him,   2(
But his body must lie in the fields, a sweet treasure
For carrion birds to find as they search for food.
That is what they say, and our good Creon is coming here
To announce it publicly; and the penalty—
Stoning to death in the public square!
                                                    There it is,
And now you can prove what you are:
A true sister, or a traitor to your family.
ISMENE.   Antigonê, you are mad! What could I possibly do?
ANTIGONE.   You must decide whether you will help me or not.
ISMENE.   I do not understand you. Help you in what?   ≤
ANTIGONE.   Ismenê, I am going to bury him. Will you come?
ISMENE.   Bury him! You have just said the new law forbids it.
ANTIGONE.   He is my brother. And he is your brother, too.
ISMENE.   But think of the danger! Think what Creon will do!
ANTIGONE.   Creon is not strong enough to stand in my way.
ISMENE.   Ah sister!
Oedipus died, everyone hating him
For what his own search brought to light, his eyes
Ripped out by his own hand; and Iocastê died,
His mother and wife at once: she twisted the cords
That strangled her life; and our two brothers died,
Each killed by the other's sword. And we are left:
But oh, Antigonê,
Think how much more terrible than these
Our own death would be if we should go against Creon
And do what he has forbidden! We are only women,
We cannot fight with men, Antigonê!

The law is strong, we must give in to the law
In this thing, and in worse. I beg the Dead
To forgive me, but I am helpless: I must yield   50
To those in authority. And I think it is dangerous business
To be always meddling.
ANTIGONE.   If that is what you think,
I should not want you, even if you asked to come.
You have made your choice, you can be what you want to be.
But I will bury him; and if I must die,
I say that this crime is holy: I shall lie down
With him in death, and I shall be as dear
To him as he to me.
                    It is the dead,
Not the living, who make the longest demands:
We die for ever . . .
                    You may do as you like,   60
Since apparently the laws of the gods mean nothing to you.
ISMENE.   They mean a great deal to me; but I have no strength
To break laws that were made for the public good.
ANTIGONE.   That must be your excuse, I suppose. But as for me,
I will bury the brother I love.
ISMENE.   Antigonê,
I am so afraid for you!
ANTIGONE.   You need not be:
You have yourself to consider, after all.
ISMENE.   But no one must hear of this, you must tell no one!
I will keep it a secret, I promise!
ANTIGONE.   Oh tell it! Tell everyone!
Think how they'll hate you when it all comes out   70
If they learn that you knew about it all the time!
ISMENE.   So fiery! You should be cold with fear.
ANTIGONE.   Perhaps. But I am doing only what I must.
ISMENE.   But can you do it? I say that you cannot.
ANTIGONE.   Very well: when my strength gives out, I shall do no more.
ISMENE.   Impossible things should not be tried at all.
ANTIGONE.   Go away, Ismenê:
I shall be hating you soon, and the dead will too,
For your words are hateful. Leave me my foolish plan:
I am not afraid of the danger; if it means death,   80
It will not be the worst of deaths—death without honor.
ISMENE.   Go then, if you feel that you must.
You are unwise,
But a loyal friend indeed to those who love you.

> *[Exit into the Palace. ANTIGONE goes off,*
> *L. Enter the CHORUS.*

PÁRODOS[2]

[*Strophe 1*

CHORUS.   Now the long blade of the sun, lying
    Level east to west, touches with glory
    Thebes of the Seven Gates. Open, unlidded
    Eye of golden day! O marching light
    Across the eddy and rush of Dircê's stream,[3]
    Striking the white shields of the enemy
    Thrown headlong backward from the blaze of morning!
CHORAGOS.[4]   Polyneicês their commander
    Roused them with windy phrases,
    He the wild eagle screaming
    Insults above our land,
    His wings their shields of snow,
    His crest their marshalled helms.

1

[*Antistrophe 1*

CHORUS.   Against our seven gates in a yawning ring
    The famished spears came onward in the night;
    But before his jaws were sated with our blood,
    Or pinefire took the garland of our towers,
    He was thrown back; and as he turned, great Thebes—
    No tender victim for his noisy power—
    Rose like a dragon behind him, shouting war.
CHORAGOS.   For God hates utterly
    The bray of bragging tongues;
    And when he beheld their smiling,
    Their swagger of golden helms,
    The frown of his thunder blasted
    Their first man from our walls.

[*Strophe 2*

CHORUS.   We heard his shout of triumph high in the air
    Turn to a scream; far out in a flaming arc
    He fell with his windy torch, and the earth struck him.
    And others storming in fury no less than his
    Found shock of death in the dusty joy of battle.
CHORAGOS.   Seven captains at seven gates
    Yielded their clanging arms to the god

---

[2] *Párodos*, first song chanted by the Chorus as it enters the stage.
[3] *Dircê's stream*, river west of Thebes.
[4] *Choragos*, chorus leader.

That bends the battle-line and breaks it.
These two only, brothers in blood,
Face to face in matchless rage,
Mirroring each the other's death,
Clashed in long combat.

[*Antistrophe 2*

CHORUS.   But now in the beautiful morning of victory
    Let Thebes of the many chariots sing for joy!   40
    With hearts for dancing we'll take leave of war:
    Our temples shall be sweet with hymns of praise,
    And the long night shall echo with our chorus.

SCENE I

CHORAGOS.   But now at last our new King is coming:
    Creon of Thebes, Menoikeus' son.
    In this auspicious dawn of his reign
    What are the new complexities
    That shifting Fate has woven for him?
    What is his counsel? Why has he summoned
    The old men to hear him?

[*Enter* CREON *from the Palace, C. He addresses the* CHORUS *from the top step.*

CREON.   Gentlemen: I have the honor to inform you that our Ship of
State, which recent storms have threated to destroy, has come safely
to harbor at last, guided by the merciful wisdom of Heaven. I have   10
summoned you here this morning because I know that I can depend
upon you: your devotion to King Laïos was absolute; you never
hesitated in your duty to our late ruler Oedipus; and when Oedipus
died, your loyalty was transferred to his children. Unfortunately, as
you know, his two sons, the princes Eteoclês and Polyneicês, have
killed each other in battle; and I, as the next in blood, have succeeded
to the full power of the throne.
  I am aware, of course, that no Ruler can expect complete loyalty from
his subjects until he has been tested in office. Nevertheless, I say to
you at the very outset that I have nothing but contempt for the kind   20
of Governor who is afraid, for whatever reason, to follow the course
that he knows is best for the State; and as for the man who sets
private friendship above the public welfare,—I have no use for him,
either. I call God to witness that if I saw my country headed for

ruin, I should not be afraid to speak out plainly; and I need hardly remind you that I would never have any dealings with an enemy of the people. No one values friendship more highly than I; but we must remember that friends made at the risk of wrecking our Ship are not real friends at all.

These are my principles, at any rate, and that is why I have made the following decision concerning the sons of Oedipus: Eteoclês, who died as a man should die, fighting for his country, is to be buried with full military honors, with all the ceremony that is usual when the greatest heroes die; but his brother Polyneicês, who broke his exile to come back with fire and sword against his native city and the shrines of his fathers' gods, whose one idea was to spill the blood of his blood and sell his own people into slavery—Polyneicês, I say, is to have no burial: no man is to touch him or say the least prayer for him; he shall lie on the plain, unburied; and the birds and the scavenging dogs can do with him whatever they like.

This is my command, and you can see the wisdom behind it. As long as I am King, no traitor is going to be honored with the loyal man. But whoever shows by word and deed that he is on the side of the State, —he shall have my respect while he is living, and my reverence when he is dead.

CHORAGOS.   If that is your will, Creon son of Menoikeus,
You have the right to enforce it: we are yours.

CREON.   That is my will. Take care that you do your part.

CHORAGOS.   We are old men: let the younger ones carry it out.

CREON.   I do not mean that: the sentries have been appointed.

CHORAGOS: Then what is it that you would have us do?

CREON.   You will give no support to whoever breaks this law.

CHORAGOS.   Only a crazy man is in love with death!

CREON.   And death it is; yet money talks, and the wisest
Have sometimes been known to count a few coins too many.

[Enter SENTRY from L.

SENTRY.   I'll not say that I'm out of breath from running, King, because every time I stopped to think about what I have to tell you, I felt like going back. And all the time a voice kept saying, "You fool, don't you know you're walking straight into trouble?"; and then another voice: "Yes, but if you let somebody else get the news to Creon first, it will be even worse than that for you!" But good sense won out, at least I hope it was good sense, and here I am with a story that makes no sense at all; but I'll tell it anyhow, because, as they say, what's going to happen's going to happen, and—

CREON.   Come to the point. What have you to say?

SENTRY.   I did not do it. I did not see who did it. You must not punish
    me for what someone else has done.
CREON.   A comprehensive defense! More effective, perhaps,
    If I knew its purpose. Come: what is it?
SENTRY.   A dreadful thing . . . I don't know how to put it—   70
CREON.   Out with it!
SENTRY.

                Well, then;
  The dead man—
           Polyneicês—

                    [Pause. The SENTRY is overcome, fumbles
                      for words. CREON waits impassively.

              out there—
                      someone,—
  New dust on the slimy flesh!

                    [Pause. No sign from CREON

  Someone has given it burial that way, and
  Gone . . .

                [Long pause. CREON finally speaks with
                          deadly control:

CREON.   And the man who dared do this?
SENTRY.   I swear I
  Do not know! You must believe me!
                     Listen:
  The ground was dry, not a sign of digging, no,
  Not a wheeltrack in the dust, no trace of anyone.
  It was when they relieved us this morning: and one of them,   80
  The corporal, pointed to it.
                  There it was,
  The strangest—
         Look:
  The body, just mounded over with light dust: you see?
  Not buried really, but as if they'd covered it
  Just enough for the ghost's peace. And no sign
  Of dogs or any wild animal that had been there.
  And then what a scene there was! Every man of us
  Accusing the other: we all proved the other man did it,
  We all had proof that we could not have done it.
  We were ready to take hot iron in our hands,   90
  Walk through fire, swear by all the gods,

It was not I!
I do not know who it was, but it was not I!

> [CREON'S *rage has been mounting steadily,*
> *but the* SENTRY *is too intent upon his story*
> *to notice it*

And then, when this came to nothing, someone said
A thing that silenced us and made us stare
Down at the ground: you had to be told the news,
And one of us had to do it! We threw the dice,
And the bad luck fell to me. So here I am,
No happier to be here than you are to have me:
Nobody likes the man who brings bad news.   10

CHORAGOS.   I have been wondering, King: can it be that the gods have
      done this?

> [*Furiously*

CREON.   Stop!
  Must you doddering wrecks
Go out of your heads entirely? "The gods!"
Intolerable!
The gods favor this corpse? Why? How had he served them?
Tried to loot their temples, burn their images,
Yes, and the whole State, and its laws with it!
Is it your senile opinion that the gods love to honor bad men?
A pious thought!—
                No, from the very beginning   1
There have been those who have whispered together,
Stiff-necked anarchists, putting their heads together,
Scheming against me in alleys. These are the men,
And they have bribed my own guard to do this thing.

> [*Sententiously*

Money!
There's nothing in the world so demoralizing as money.
Down go your cities,
Homes gone, men gone, honest hearts corrupted,
Crookedness of all kinds, and all for money!

> [*To* SENTRY

              But you—!
I swear by God and by the throne of God,
The man who has done this thing shall pay for it!
Find that man, bring him here to me, or your death

Will be the least of your problems: I'll string you up
Alive, and there will be certain ways to make you
Discover your employer before you die;
And the process may teach you a lesson you seem to have missed:
The dearest profit is sometimes all too dear:
That depends on the source. Do you understand me?
A fortune won is often misfortune.

SENTRY.   King, may I speak?
CREON.   Your very voice distresses me.   130
SENTRY.   Are you sure that it is my voice, and not your conscience?
CREON.   By God, he wants to analyze me now!
SENTRY.   It is not what I say, but what has been done, that hurts you.
CREON.   You talk too much.
SENTRY.   Maybe; but I've done nothing.
CREON.   Sold your soul for some silver: that's all you've done.
SENTRY.   How dreadful it is when the right judge judges wrong!
CREON.   Your figures of speech
May entertain you now; but unless you bring me the man,
You will get little profit from them in the end.

> [*Exit* CREON *into the Palace.*

SENTRY.   "Bring me the man"—!   140
I'd like nothing better than bringing him the man!
But bring him or not, you have seen the last of me here.
At any rate, I am safe!

> [*Exit* SENTRY

ODE I

> [*Strophe 1*

CHORUS.   Numberless are the world's wonders, but none
More wonderful than man; the stormgray sea
Yields to his prows, the huge crests bear him high;
Earth, holy and inexhaustible, is graven
With shining furrows where his plows have gone
Year after year, the timeless labor of stallions.

> [*Antistrophe 1*

The lightboned birds and beasts that cling to cover,
The lithe fish lighting their reaches of dim water,
All are taken, tamed in the net of his mind;
The lion on the hill, the wild horse windy-maned,   10

Resign to him; and his blunt yoke has broken
The sultry shoulders of the mountain bull.

[*Strophe 2*

Words also, and thought as rapid as air,
He fashions to his good use; statecraft is his,
And his the skill that deflects the arrows of snow,
The spears of winter rain: from every wind
He has made himself secure—from all but one:
In the late wind of death he cannot stand.

[*Antistrophe 2*

O clear intelligence, force beyond all measure!
O fate of man, working both good and evil!
When the laws are kept, how proudly his city stands!
When the laws are broken, what of his city then?
Never may the anárchic man find rest at my hearth,
Never be it said that my thoughts are his thoughts.

SCENE II

[*Re-enter* SENTRY *leading* ANTIGONE.

CHORAGOS.   What does this mean? Surely this captive woman
    Is the Princess, Antigonê. Why should she be taken?
SENTRY.   Here is the one who did it! We caught her
    In the very act of burying him.—Where is Creon?
CHORAGOS.   Just coming from the house.

Enter CREON, *C.*

CREON.   What has happened?
    Why have you come back so soon?

[*Expansively*

SENTRY.   O King,
    A man should never be too sure of anything:
    I would have sworn
    That you'd not see me here again: your anger
    Frightened me so, and the things you threatened me with;
    But how could I tell then
    That I'd be able to solve the case so soon?

No dice-throwing this time: I was only too glad to come!

Here is this woman. She is the guilty one:
We found her trying to bury him.
Take her, then; question her; judge her as you will.
I am through with the whole thing now, and glád óf it.
CREON.   But this is Antigonê! Why have you brought her here?
SENTRY.   She was burying him, I tell you!

[*Severely*

CREON.   Is this the truth?
SENTRY.   I saw her with my own eyes. Can I say more?   20
CREON.   The details: come, tell me quickly!
SENTRY.   It was like this:
After those terrible threats of yours, King,
We went back and brushed the dust away from the body.
The flesh was soft by now, and stinking,
So we sat on a hill to windward and kept guard.
No napping this time! We kept each other awake.
But nothing happened until the white round sun
Whirled in the center of the round sky over us:
Then, suddenly,
A storm of dust roared up from the earth, and the sky   30
Went out, the plain vanished with all its trees
In the stinging dark. We closed our eyes and endured it.
The whirlwind lasted a long time, but it passed;
And then we looked, and there was Antigonê!
I have seen
A mother bird come back to a stripped nest, heard
Her crying bitterly a broken note or two
For the young ones stolen. Just so, when this girl
Found the bare corpse, and all her love's work wasted,
She wept, and cried on heaven to damn the hands   40
That had done this thing.
                         And then she brought more dust
And sprinkled wine three times for her brother's ghost.

We ran and took her at once. She was not afraid,
Not even when we charged her with what she had done.
She denied nothing.
                    And this was a comfort to me,
And some uneasiness: for it is a good thing
To escape from death, but it is no great pleasure
To bring death to a friend.
                         Yet I always say
There is nothing so comfortable as your own safe skin!

[*Slowly, dangerously*

CREON.   And you, Antigonê,   50
    You with your head hanging,—do you confess this thing?
ANTIGONE.   I do. I deny nothing.

                                                              [*To* SENTRY:

CREON.   You may go.

                                                              [*Exit* SENTRY
                                                              [*To* ANTIGONE:

    Tell me, tell me briefly:
    Had you heard my proclamation touching this matter?
ANTIGONE.   It was public. Could I help hearing it?
CREON.   And yet you dared defy the law.
ANTIGONE.   I dared.
    It was not God's proclamation. That final Justice
    That rules the world below makes no such laws.

    Your edict, King, was strong,
    But all your strength is weakness itself against   ε
    The immortal unrecorded laws of God.
    They are not merely now: they were, and shall be,
    Operative for ever, beyond man utterly.

    I knew I must die, even without your decree:
    I am only mortal. And if I must die
    Now, before it is my time to die,
    Surely this is no hardship: can anyone
    Living, as I live, with evil all about me,
    Think Death less than a friend? This death of mine
    Is of no importance; but if I had left my brother
    Lying in death unburied, I should have suffered.
    Now I do not.
                        You smile at me. Ah Creon,
    Think me a fool, if you like; but it may well be
    That a fool convicts me of folly.
CHORAGOS.   Like father, like daughter: both headstrong, deaf to reason!
    She has never learned to yield.
CREON.   She has much to learn.
    The inflexible heart breaks first, the toughest iron
    Cracks first, and the wildest horses bend their necks
    At the pull of the smallest curb.
                                    Pride? In a slave?
    This girl is guilty of a double insolence,
    Breaking the given laws and boasting of it.
    Who is the man here,
    She or I, if this crime goes unpunished?

Sister's child, or more than sister's child,
Or closer yet in blood—she and her sister
Win bitter death for this!

                                         [*To servants:*

                        Go, some of you,
Arrest Ismenê. I accuse her equally.
Bring her: you will find her sniffling in the house there.

Her mind's a traitor: crimes kept in the dark
Cry for light, and the guardian brain shudders;   90
But how much worse than this
Is brazen boasting of barefaced anarchy!
ANTIGONE.   Creon, what more do you want than my death?
CREON: Nothing.
    That gives me everything.
ANTIGONE.   Then I beg you: kill me.
This talking is a great weariness: your words
Are distasteful to me, and I am sure that mine
Seem so to you. And yet they should not seem so:
I should have praise and honor for what I have done.
All these men here would praise me
Were their lips not frozen shut with fear of you.   100

                                           [*Bitterly*

Ah the good fortune of kings,
Licensed to say and do whatever they please!
CREON.   You are alone here in that opinion.
ANTIGONE.   No, they are with me. But they keep their tongues in leash.
CREON.   Maybe. But you are guilty, and they are not.
ANTIGONE.   There is no guilt in reverence for the dead.
CREON.   But Eteoclês—was he not your brother too?
ANTIGONE.   My brother too.
CREON.   And you insult his memory?

                                           [*Softly*

ANTIGONE.   The dead man would not say that I insult it.
CREON.   He would: for you honor a traitor as much as him.   110
ANTIGONE.   His own brother, traitor or not, and equal in blood.
CREON.   He made war on his country. Eteoclês defended it.
ANTIGONE.   Nevertheless, there are honors due all the dead.
CREON.   But not the same for the wicked as for the just.
ANTIGONE.   Ah Creon, Creon,
    Which of us can say what the gods hold wicked?
CREON.   An enemy is an enemy, even dead.

ANTIGONE.   It is my nature to join in love, not hate.

[*Finally losing patience*

CREON.   Go join them, then; if you must have your love,
Find it in hell!   12

CHORAGOS.   But see, Ismenê comes:

[*Enter* ISMENE, *guarded*

Those tears are sisterly, the cloud
That shadows her eyes rains down gentle sorrow.

CREON.   You too, Ismenê,
Snake in my ordered house, sucking my blood
Stealthily—and all the time I never knew
That these two sisters were aiming at my throne!

Ismenê,

Do you confess your share in this crime, or deny it?
Answer me.

ISMENE.   Yes, if she will let me say so. I am guilty.   1:

[*Coldly*

ANTIGONE.   No, Ismenê. You have no right to say so.
You would not help me, and I will not have you help me.

ISMENE.   But now I know what you meant; and I am here
To join you, to take my share of punishment.

ANTIGONE.   The dead man and the gods who rule the dead
Know whose act this was. Words are not friends.

ISMENE.   Do you refuse me, Antigonê? I want to die with you:
I too have a duty that I must discharge to the dead.

ANTIGONE.   You shall not lessen my death by sharing it.

ISMENE.   What do I care for life when you are dead?

ANTIGONE.   Ask Creon. You're always hanging on his opinions.

ISMENE.   You are laughing at me. Why, Antigonê?

ANTIGONE.   It's a joyless laughter, Ismenê.

ISMENE.   But can I do nothing?

ANTIGONE.   Yes. Save yourself. I shall not envy you.
There are those who will praise you; I shall have honor, too.

ISMENE.   But we are equally guilty!

ANTIGONE.   No more, Ismenê.
You are alive, but I belong to Death.

[*To the* CHORUS:

CREON.   Gentlemen, I beg you to observe these girls:
One has just now lost her mind; the other,
It seems, has never had a mind at all.

ISMENE.   Grief teaches the steadiest minds to waver, King.
CREON.   Yours certainly did, when you assumed guilt with the guilty!
ISMENE.   But how could I go on living without her?
CREON.   You are.
    She is already dead.
ISMENE.   But your own son's bride!
CREON.   There are places enough for him to push his plow.
    I want no wicked women for my sons!
ISMENE.   O dearest Haimon, how your father wrongs you!
CREON.   I've had enough of your childish talk of marriage!
CHORAGOS.   Do you really intend to steal this girl from your son?
CREON.   No; Death will do that for me.
CHORAGOS.   Then she must die?   160

                                                      [*Ironically*

CREON.   You dazzle me.
                    —But enough of this talk!

                                                      [*To* GUARDS:

You, there, take them away and guard them well:
For they are but women, and even brave men run
When they see Death coming.

                              [*Exeunt* ISMENE, ANTIGONE, *and* GUARDS

ODE II

                                                      [*Strophe 1*
CHORUS.   Fortunate is the man who has never tasted God's vengeance!
    Where once the anger of heaven has struck, that house is shaken
    For ever: damnation rises behind each child
    Like a wave cresting out of the black northeast,
    When the long darkness under sea roars up
    And bursts drumming death upon the windwhipped sand.

                                                      [*Antistrophe 1*

    I have seen this gathering sorrow from time long past
    Loom upon Oedipus' children: generation from generation
    Takes the compulsive rage of the enemy god.
    So lately this last flower of Oedipus' line   10
    Drank the sunlight! but now a passionate word
    And a handful of dust have closed up all its beauty.

                                                      [*Strophe 2*

What mortal arrogance
Transcends the wrath of Zeus?
Sleep cannot lull him, nor the effortless long months
Of the timeless gods: but he is young for ever,
And his house is the shining day of high Olympos.
All that is and shall be,
And all the past, is his.
No pride on earth is free of the curse of heaven.   2

[*Antistrophe 2*

The straying dreams of men
May bring them ghosts of joy:
But as they drowse, the waking embers burn them;
Or they walk with fíxed éyes, as blind men walk.
But the ancient wisdom speaks for our own time:
Fate works most for woe
With Folly's fairest show.
Man's little pleasure is the spring of sorrow.

SCENE III

CHORAGOS.   But here is Haimon, King, the last of all your sons.
Is it grief for Antigonê that brings him here,
And bitterness at being robbed of his bride?

[*Enter* HAIMON

CREON.   We shall soon see, and no need of diviners.
—Son,
You have heard my final judgment on that girl:
Have you come here hating me, or have you come
With deference and with love, whatever I do?
HAIMON.   I am your son, father. You are my guide.
You make things clear for me, and I obey you.
No marriage means more to me than your continuing wisdom.
CREON.   Good. That is the way to behave: subordinate
Everything else, my son, to your father's will.
This is what a man prays for, that he may get
Sons attentive and dutiful in his house,
Each one hating his father's enemies,
Honoring his father's friends. But if his sons
Fail him, if they turn out unprofitably,
What has he fathered but trouble for himself
And amusement for the malicious?
So you are right
Not to lose your head over this woman.

Your pleasure with her would soon grow cold, Haimon,
And then you'd have a hellcat in bed and elsewhere.
Let her find her husband in Hell!
Of all the people in this city, only she
Has had contempt for my law and broken it.

Do you want me to show myself weak before the people?
Or to break my sworn word? No, and I will not.
The woman dies.
I suppose she'll plead "family ties." Well, let her.
If I permit my own family to rebel,   30
How shall I earn the world's obedience?
Show me the man who keeps his house in hand,
He's fit for public authority.
                             I'll have no dealings
With law-breakers, critics of the government:
Whoever is chosen to govern should be obeyed—
Must be obeyed, in all things, great and small,
Just and unjust! O Haimon,
The man who knows how to obey, and that man only,
Knows how to give commands when the time comes.
You can depend on him, no matter how fast   40
The spears come: he's a good soldier, he'll stick it out.

Anarchy, anarchy! Show me a greater evil!
This is why cities tumble and the great houses rain down,
This is what scatters armies!

No, no: good lives are made so by discipline.
We keep the laws then, and the lawmakers,
And no woman shall seduce us. If we must lose,
Let's lose to a man, at least! Is a woman stronger than we?
CHORAGOS.   Unless time has rusted my wits,
What you say, King, is said with point and dignity.   50

                                        [*Boyishly earnest*

HAIMON.   Father:
    Reason is God's crowning gift to man, and you are right
    To warn me against losing mine. I cannot say—
    I hope that I shall never want to say!—that you
    Have reasoned badly. Yet there are other men
    Who can reason, too; and their opinions might be helpful.
    You are not in a position to know everything
    That people say or do, or what they feel:
    Your temper terrifies them—everyone
    Will tell you only what you like to hear.   60
    But I, at any rate, can listen; and I have heard them

Muttering and whispering in the dark about this girl.
They say no woman has ever, so unreasonably,
Died so shameful a death for a generous act:
"She covered her brother's body. Is this indecent?
She kept him from dogs and vultures. Is this a crime?
Death?—She should have all the honor that we can give her!"

This is the way they talk out there in the city.

You must believe me:
Nothing is closer to me than your happiness.
What could be closer? Must not any son
Value his father's fortune as his father does his?
I beg you, do not be unchangeable:
Do not believe that you alone can be right.
The man who thinks that,
The man who maintains that only he has the power
To reason correctly, the gift to speak, the soul—

A man like that, when you know him, turns out empty.

It is not reason never to yield to reason!
In flood time you can see how some trees bend,
And because they bend, even their twigs are safe,
While stubborn trees are torn up, roots and all.
And the same thing happens in sailing:
Make your sheet fast, never slacken,—and over you go,
Head over heels and under: and there's your voyage.
Forget you are angry! Let yourself be moved!
I know I am young; but please let me say this:
The ideal condition
Would be, I admit, that men should be right by instinct;
But since we are all too likely to go astray,
The reasonable thing is to learn from those who can teach.

CHORAGOS: You will do well to listen to him, King,
   If what he says is sensible. And you, Haimon,
   Must listen to your father.—Both speak well.
CREON.   You consider it right for a man of my years and experience
   To go to school to a boy?
HAIMON.   It is not right
   If I am wrong. But if I am young, and right,
   What does my age matter?
CREON.   You think it right to stand up for an anarchist?
HAIMON.   Not at all. I pay no respect to criminals.
CREON.   Then she is not a criminal?
HAIMON.   The City would deny it, to a man.
CREON.   And the City proposes to teach me how to rule?

HAIMON.   Ah. Who is it that's talking like a boy now?
CREON.   My voice is the one voice giving orders in this City!
HAIMON.   It is no City if it takes orders from one voice.
CREON.   The State is the King!
HAIMON.   Yes, if the State is a desert.

[Pause

CREON.   This boy, it seems, has sold out to a woman.
HAIMON.   If you are a woman: my concern is only for you.
CREON.   So? Your "concern"! In a public brawl with your father!   110
HAIMON.   How about you, in a public brawl with justice?
CREON.   With justice, when all that I do is within my rights?
HAIMON.   You have no right to trample on God's right.

[Completely out of control

CREON.   Fool, adolescent fool! Taken in by a woman!
HAIMON.   You'll never see me taken in by anything vile.
CREON.   Every word you say is for her!

[Quietly, darkly

HAIMON.   And for you.
And for me. And for the gods under the earth.
CREON.   You'll never marry her while she lives.
HAIMON.   Then she must die.—But her death will cause another.
CREON.   Another?   120
Have you lost your senses? Is this an open threat?
HAIMON.   There is no threat in speaking to emptiness.
CREON.   I swear you'll regret this superior tone of yours!
You are the empty one!
HAIMON.   If you were not my father,
I'd say you were perverse.
CREON.   You girlstruck fool, don't play at words with me!
HAIMON.   I am sorry. You prefer silence.
CREON: Now, by God—!
I swear, by all the gods in heaven above us,
You'll watch it, I swear you shall!

[To the SERVANTS:
Bring her out!
Bring the woman out! Let her die before his eyes!   130
Here, this instant, with her bridegroom beside her!
HAIMON.   Not here, no; she will not die here, King.
And you will never see my face again.
Go on raving as long as you've a friend to endure you.

[Exit HAIMON

CHORAGOS.   Gone, gone.
    Creon, a young man in a rage is dangerous!
CREON.   Let him do, or dream to do, more than a man can.
    He shall not save these girls from death.
CHORAGOS.   These girls?
    You have sentenced them both?
CREON.   No, you are right.
    I will not kill the one whose hands are clean.   1.
CHORAGOS.   But Antigonê?

[*Somberly*

CREON.   I will carry her far away
    Out there in the wilderness, and lock her
    Living in a vault of stone. She shall have food,
    As the custom is, to absolve the State of her death.
    And there let her pray to the gods of hell:
    They are her only gods:
    Perhaps they will show her an escape from death,
    Or she may learn,
              though late,
    That piety shown the dead is pity in vain.

[*Exit* CREON

ODE III

[*Strophe*

CHORUS.   Love, unconquerable
    Waster of rich men, keeper
    Of warm lights and all-night vigil
    In the soft face of a girl:
    Sea-wanderer, forest-visitor!
    Even the pure Immortals cannot escape you,
    And mortal man, in his one day's dusk,
    Trembles before your glory.

[*Antistrophe*

    Surely you swerve upon ruin
    The just man's consenting heart,
    As here you have made bright anger
    Strike between father and son—
    And none has conquered but Love!
    A girl's glánce wórking the will of heaven:

Pleasure to her alone who mocks us,
Merciless Aphroditê.[5]

SCENE IV

[*As* ANTIGONE *enters guarded*

CHORAGOS.   But I can no longer stand in awe of this,
Nor, seeing what I see, keep back my tears.
Here is Antigonê, passing to that chamber
Where all find sleep at last.

[*Strophe 1*

ANTIGONE.   Look upon me, friends, and pity me
Turning back at the night's edge to say
Good-by to the sun that shines for me no longer;
Now sleepy Death
Summons me down to Acheron,[6] that cold shore:
There is no bridesong there, nor any music.   10
CHORUS.   Yet not unpraised, not without a kind of honor,
You walk at last into the underworld;
Untouched by sickness, broken by no sword.
What woman has ever found your way to death?

[*Antistrophe 1*

ANTIGONE.   How often I have heard the story of Niobê,[7]
Tantalos' wretched daughter, how the stone
Clung fast about her, ivy-close: and they say
The rain falls endlessly
And sifting soft snow; her tears are never done.
I feel the loneliness of her death in mine.   20
CHORUS.   But she was born of heaven, and you
Are woman, woman-born. If her death is yours,
A mortal woman's, is this not for you
Glory in our world and in the world beyond?

[*Strophe 2*

ANTIGONE.   You laugh at me. Ah, friends, friends,
Can you not wait until I am dead? O Thebes,

---

[5] *Aphroditê*, goddess of love.
[6] *Acheron*, river of the Greek underworld.
[7] *Niobê*. Because Niobê boasted of her twelve children, two gods, angered by her insult, killed them. When she wept, Zeus turned her into a weeping stone statue.

O men many-charioted, in love with Fortune,
Dear springs of Dircê, sacred Theban grove,
Be witnesses for me, denied all pity,
Unjustly judged! and think a word of love
For her whose path turns
Under dark earth, where there are no more tears.

CHORUS.   You have passed beyond human daring and come at last
Into a place of stone where Justice sits.
I cannot tell
What shape of your father's guilt appears in this.

[Antistrophe 2

ANTIGONE.   You have touched it at last: that bridal bed
Unspeakable, horror of son and mother mingling:
Their crime, infection of all our family!
O Oedipus, father and brother!
Your marriage strikes from the grave to murder mine.
I have been a stranger here in my own land:
All my life
The blasphemy of my birth has followed me.

CHORUS.   Reverence is a virtue, but strength
Lives in established law: that must prevail.
You have made your choice,
Your death is the doing of your conscious hand.

[Epode[8]

ANTIGONE.   Then let me go, since all your words are bitter,
And the very light of the sun is cold to me.
Lead me to my vigil, where I must have
Neither love nor lamentation; no song, but silence.

[CREON interrupts impatiently

CREON.   If dirges and planned lamentations could put off death,
Men would be singing for ever.

[To the SERVANTS:

Take her, go!
You know your orders: take her to the vault
And leave her alone there. And if she lives or dies,
That's her affair, not ours: our hands are clean.

ANTIGONE.   O tomb, vaulted bride-bed in eternal rock,
Soon I shall be with my own again

[8] *Epode*, third section of a three-part ode.

Where Persephonê[9] welcomes the thin ghosts underground: 60
And I shall see my father again, and you, mother,
And dearest Polyneicês—
                    dearest indeed
To me, since it was my hand
That washed him clean and poured the ritual wine:
And my reward is death before my time!

And yet, as men's hearts know, I have done no wrong,
I have not sinned before God. Or if I have,
I shall know the truth in death. But if the guilt
Lies upon Creon who judged me, then, I pray,
May his punishment equal my own.
CHORAGOS.   O passionate heart,   70
    Unyielding, tormented still by the same winds!
CREON.   Her guards shall have good cause to regret their delaying.
ANTIGONE.   Ah! That voice is like the voice of death!
CREON.   I can give you no reason to think you are mistaken.
ANTIGONE.   Thebes, and you my fathers' gods,
    And rulers of Thebes, you see me now, the last
    Unhappy daughter of a line of kings,
    Your kings, led away to death. You will remember
    What things I suffer, and at what men's hands,
    Because I would not transgress the laws of heaven.   80

[*To the* GUARDS, *simply:*

Come: let us wait no longer.

[*Exit* ANTIGONE, *L., guarded*

ODE IV

[*Strophe 1*

CHORUS.   All Danaê's[10] beauty was locked away
    In a brazen cell where the sunlight could not come:
    A small room, still as any grave, enclosed her.
    Yet she was a princess too,
    And Zeus in a rain of gold poured love upon her.

---

[9] *Persephonê*, queen of the underworld.
[10] *Danaê*. When an oracle told Danaê's father that his grandson would kill him, he locked Danaê in a bronze chamber to keep her from having a child. But Zeus, disguised as a shower of gold, impregnated her and she had a son, Perseus, who years later killed his grandfather.

O child, child,
No power in wealth or war
Or tough sea-blackened ships
Can prevail against untiring Destiny!

[*Antistrophe 1*

And Dryas' son[11] also, that furious king,   1(
Bore the god's prisoning anger for his pride:
Sealed up by Dionysos in deaf stone,
His madness died among echoes.
So at the last he learned what dreadful power
His tongue had mocked:
For he had profaned the revels,
And fired the wrath of the nine
Implacable Sisters[12] that love the sound of the flute.

[*Strophe 2*

And old men tell a half-remembered tale
Of horror done where a dark ledge splits the sea   2
And a double surf beats on the gráy shóres:
How a king's new woman,[13] sick
With hatred for the queen he had imprisoned,
Ripped out his two sons' eyes with her bloody hands
While grinning Arês[14] watched the shuttle plunge
Four times: four blind wounds crying for revenge,

[*Antistrophe 2*

Crying, tears and blood mingled. —Piteously born,
Those sons whose mother was of heavenly birth!
Her father was the god of the North Wind
And she was cradled by gales,
She raced with young colts on the glittering hills
And walked untrammeled in the open light:
But in her marriage deathless Fate found means
To build a tomb like yours for all her joy.

[11] *Dryas' son*, Lycurgus, King of Thrace, who was driven insane by Dionysos, god of revelry.
[12] *Sisters*, the Muses.
[13] *King's new woman*, Eidothea, second wife of King Phineus, blinded her stepsons.
[14] *Arês*, god of war.

SCENE V

> [*Enter blind* TEIRESIAS,[15] *led by a boy. The opening speeches of* TEIRESIAS *should be in singsong contrast to the realistic lines of* CREON.

TEIRESIAS.   This is the way the blind man comes, Princes, Princes,
  Lock-step, two heads lit by the eyes of one.
CREON.   What new thing have you to tell us, Old Teiresias?
TEIRESIAS.   I have much to tell you: listen to the prophet, Creon.
CREON.   I am not aware that I have ever failed to listen.
TEIRESIAS.   Then you have done wisely, King, and ruled well.
CREON.   I admit my debt to you. But what have you to say?
TEIRESIAS.   This, Creon: you stand once more on the edge of fate.
CREON.   What do you mean? Your words are a kind of dread.
TEIRESIAS.   Listen, Creon: 10
  I was sitting in my chair of augury, at the place
  Where the birds gather about me. They were all a-chatter,
  As is their habit, when suddenly I heard
  A strange note in their jangling, a scream, a
  Whirring fury; I knew that they were fighting,
  Tearing each other, dying
  In a whirlwind of wings clashing. And I was afraid.
  I began the rites of burnt-offering at the altar,
  But Hephaistos[16] failed me: instead of bright flame,
  There was only the sputtering slime of the fat thigh-flesh   20
  Melting: the entrails dissolved in gray smoke,
  The bare bone burst from the welter. And no blaze!
  This was a sign from heaven. My boy described it,
  Seeing for me as I see for others.

  I tell you, Creon, you yourself have brought
  This new calamity upon us. Our hearths and altars
  Are stained with the corruption of dogs and carrion birds
  That glut themselves on the corpse of Oedipus' son.
  The gods are deaf when we pray to them, their fire
  Recoils from our offering, their birds of omen   30
  Have no cry of comfort, for they are gorged
  With the thick blood of the dead.
                          O my son,
  These are no trifles! Think: all men make mistakes,

---

[15] *Teiresias*. Athena blinded him, but then gave him the gift of prophesy to compensate.
[16] *Hephaistos*, god of fire.

But a good man yields when he knows his course is wrong,
And repairs the evil. The only crime is pride.

Give in to the dead man, then: do not fight with a corpse—
What glory is it to kill a man who is dead?
Think, I beg you:
It is for your own good that I speak as I do.
You should be able to yield for your own good.   40

CREON.   It seems that prophets have made me their especial province.
All my life long
I have been a kind of butt for the dull arrows
Of doddering fortune-tellers!
                         No, Teiresias:
If your birds—if the great eagles of God himself
Should carry him stinking bit by bit to heaven,
I would not yield. I am not afraid of pollution:
No man can defile the gods.
                         Do what you will,
Go into business, make money, speculate
In India gold or that synthetic gold from Sardis,   5
Get rich otherwise than by my consent to bury him.
Teiresias, it is a sorry thing when a wise man
Sells his wisdom, lets out his words for hire!

TEIRESIAS.   Ah Creon! Is there no man left in the world—

CREON.   To do what?—Come, let's have the aphorism!

TEIRESIAS.   No man who knows that wisdom outweighs any wealth?

CREON.   As surely as bribes are baser than any baseness.

TEIRESIAS.   You are sick, Creon! You are deathly sick!

CREON.   As you say: it is not my place to challenge a prophet.

TEIRESIAS.   Yet you have said my prophecy is for sale.   6

CREON.   The generation of prophets has always loved gold.

TEIRESIAS.   The generation of kings has always loved brass.

CREON.   You forget yourself! You are speaking to your King.

TEIRESIAS.   I know it. You are a king because of me.

CREON.   You have a certain skill; but you have sold out.

TEIRESIAS.   King, you will drive me to words that—

CREON.   Say them, say them!
Only remember: I will not pay you for them.

TEIRESIAS.   No, you will find them too costly.

CREON.   No doubt. Speak:
Whatever you say, you will not change my will.

TEIRESIAS.   Then take this, and take it to heart!
The time is not far off when you shall pay back
Corpse for corpse, flesh of your own flesh.
You have thrust the child of this world into living night,

You have kept from the gods below the child that is theirs:
The one in a grave before her death, the other,
Dead, denied the grave. This is your crime:
And the Furies[17] and the dark gods of Hell
Are swift with terrible punishment for you.

Do you want to buy me now, Creon?

                           Not many days,
And your house will be full of men and women weeping,   80
And curses will be hurled at you from far
Cities grieving for sons unburied, left to rot
Before the walls of Thebes.

These are my arrows, Creon: they are all for you.

                                   [*To* Boy:

But come, child: lead me home.
Let him waste his fine anger upon younger men.
Maybe he will learn at last
To control a wiser tongue in a better head.

                              [*Exit* Teiresias

CHORAGOS. The old man has gone, King, but his words
    Remain to plague us. I am old, too,   90
    But I cannot remember that he was ever false.
CREON. That is true. . . . It troubles me.
    Oh it is hard to give in! but it is worse
    To risk everything for stubborn pride.
CHORAGOS. Creon: take my advice.
CREON.   What shall I do?
CHORAGOS. Go quickly: free Antigonê from her vault
    And build a tomb for the body of Polyneicês.
CREON. You would have me do this?
CHORAGOS.   Creon, yes!
    And it must be done at once: God moves
    Swiftly to cancel the folly of stubborn men.   100
CREON. It is hard to deny the heart! But I
    Will do it: I will not fight with destiny.
CHORAGOS. You must go yourself, you cannot leave it to others.
CREON. I will go.
          —Bring axes, servants:
    Come with me to the tomb. I buried her, I
    Will set her free.

---

[17] *Furies*, three avenging spirits.

                    Oh quickly!
My mind misgives—
The laws of the gods are mighty, and a man must serve them
To the last day of his life!

                                        [*Exit* CREON

PÆAN[18]

                                            [*Strophe 1*

CHORAGOS.   God of many names
CHORUS.   O Iacchos[19]
                                        son
     of Kadmeian Sémelê
                     O born of the Thunder!
     Guardian of the West
                        Regent
     of Eleusis'[20] plain
                     O Prince of maenad Thebes
     and the Dragon Field by rippling Ismenos:[21]

                                        [*Antistrophe 1*

CHORAGOS.   God of many names
CHORUS.   the flame of torches
     flares on our hills
                     the nymphs of Iacchos
     dance at the spring of Castalia:[22]
     from the vine-close mountain
                             come ah come in ivy:
     Evohé evohé! sings through the streets of Thebes

CHORAGOS.   God of many names   [*Strophe 2*
CHORUS.   Iacchos of Thebes
     heavenly Child
                     of Sémelê bride of the Thunderer!
     The shadow of plague is upon us:
                         come

---

[18] *Paean*, hymn sung to the gods.
[19] *Iacchos*, also known as Dionysos, god of wine.
[20] *Eleusis*, town near Athens containing a temple to Demeter and Dionysos.
[21] *Ismenos*, river near Thebes where presumably the ancestors of Thebes sprang from sown dragon's teeth.
[22] *Castalia*, spring on Mount Parnasos, home of Apollo.

with clement feet
   oh come from Parnasos
 down the long slopes
    across the lamenting water

            [Antistrophe 2

CHORAGOS. Iô Fire! Chorister of the throbbing stars!
 O purest among the voices of the night!
 Thou son of god, blaze for us!
CHORUS. Come with choric rapture of circling Maenads
 Who cry *Iô Iacche!*
    God of many names!   20

ÉXODOS[23]

           [Enter MESSENGER, *L.*

MESSENGER. Men of the line of Kadmos,[24] you who live
 Near Amphion's citadel.[25]
        I cannot say
Of any condition of human life "This is fixed,
This is clearly good, or bad". Fate raises up,
And Fate casts down the happy and unhappy alike:
No man can foretell his Fate.
        Take the case of Creon:
Creon was happy once, as I count happiness:
Victorious in battle, sole governor of the land,
Fortunate father of children nobly born.
And now it has all gone from him! Who can say   10
That a man is still alive when his life's joy fails?
He is a walking dead man. Grant him rich,
Let him live like a king in his great house:
If his pleasure is gone, I would not give
So much as the shadow of smoke for all he owns.
CHORAGOS. Your words hint at sorrow: what is your news for us?
MESSENGER. They are dead. The living are guilty of their death.
CHORAGOS. Who is guilty? Who is dead? Speak!
MESSENGER.   Haimon.
 Haimon is dead; and the hand that killed him
 Is his own hand.

---

[23] *Éxodos*, last scene of the play, coming after the final ode.
[24] *Kadmos*, founder of Thebes.
[25] *Amphion's citadel*. Amphion played his lyre so sweetly that he charmed stones into a fortification around Thebes.

CHORAGOS.   His father's? or his own?   20
MESSENGER.   His own, driven mad by the murder his father had done.
CHORAGOS.   Teiresias, Teiresias, how clearly you saw it all!
MESSENGER.   This is my news: you must draw what conclusions you can
      from it.
CHORAGOS.   But look: Eurydicê, Our Queen:
    Has she overheard us?

> [*Enter* EURYDICE *from the Palace, C.*

EURYDICE.   I have heard something, friends:
    As I was unlocking the gate of Pallas'[26] shrine,
    For I needed her help today, I heard a voice
    Telling of some new sorrow. And I fainted
    There at the temple with all my maidens about me.   30
    But speak again: whatever it is, I can bear it:
    Grief and I are no strangers.
MESSENGER.   Dearest Lady,
    I will tell you plainly all that I have seen.
    I shall not try to comfort you: what is the use,
    Since comfort could lie only in what is not true?
    The truth is always best.
                   I went with Creon
    To the outer plain where Polyneicês was lying,
    No friend to pity him, his body shredded by dogs.
    We made our prayers in that place to Hecatê[27]
    And Pluto,[28] that they would be merciful. And we bathed   40
    The corpse with holy water, and we brought
    Fresh-broken branches to burn what was left of it,
    And upon the urn we heaped up a towering barrow
    Of the earth of his own land.
                 When we were done, we ran
    To the vault where Antigonê lay on her couch of stone.
    One of the servants had gone ahead,
    And while he was yet far off he heard a voice
    Grieving within the chamber, and he came back
    And told Creon. And as the King went closer,
    The air was full of wailing, the words lost,   50
    And he begged us to make all haste. "Am I a prophet?"
    He said, weeping, "And must I walk this road,
    The saddest of all that I have gone before?

---

[26] *Pallas*, Pallas Athene, goodess of wisdom.
[27] *Hecatê*, a goddess of the underworld.
[28] *Pluto*, chief god of the underworld.

My son's voice calls me on. Oh quickly, quickly!
Look through the crevice there, and tell me
If it is Haimon, or some deception of the gods!"

We obeyed; and in the cavern's farthest corner
We saw her lying:
She had made a noose of her fine linen veil
And hanged herself. Haimon lay beside her,   60
His arms about her waist, lamenting her,
His love lost under ground, crying out
That his father had stolen her away from him.

When Creon saw him the tears rushed to his eyes
And he called to him: "What have you done, child? Speak to me.
What are you thinking that makes your eyes so strange?
O my son, my son, I come to you on my knees!"
But Haimon spat in his face. He said not a word,
Staring—
            And suddenly drew his sword
And lunged. Creon shrank back, the blade missed; and the boy,   70
Desperate against himself, drove it half its length
Into his own side, and fell. And as he died
He gathered Antigonê close in his arms again,
Choking, his blood bright red on her white cheek.
And now he lies dead with the dead, and she is his
At last, his bride in the houses of the dead.

> [*Exit EURYDICE into the Palace*

CHORAGOS.   She has left us without a word. What can this mean?
MESSENGER.   It troubles me, too; yet she knows what is best,
    Her grief is too great for public lamentation,
    And doubtless she has gone to her chamber to weep   80
    For her dead son, leading her maidens in his dirge.
CHORAGOS.   It may be so: but I fear this deep silence.

> [*Pause*

MESSENGER.   I will see what she is doing. I will go in.

> [*Exit MESSENGER into the Palace*

> [*Enter CREON with attendants, bearing*
> *HAIMON'S body*

CHORAGOS.   But here is the King himself: oh look at him,
    Bearing his own damnation in his arms.
CREON.   Nothing you say can touch me any more.
    My own blind heart has brought me

From darkness to final darkness. Here you see
The father murdering, the murdered son—
And all my civic wisdom!   90

Haimon my son, so young, so young to die,
I was the fool, not you; and you died for me.
CHORAGOS.   That is the truth; but you were late in learning it.
CREON.   This truth is hard to bear. Surely a god
Has crushed me beneath the hugest weight of heaven,
And driven me headlong a barbaric way
To trample out the thing I held most dear.

The pains that men will take to come to pain!

[*Enter* MESSENGER *from the Palace*

MESSENGER.   The burden you carry in your hands is heavy,
But it is not all: you will find more in your house.   10
CREON.   What burden worse than this shall I find there?
MESSENGER.   The Queen is dead.
CREON.   O port of death, deaf world,
Is there no pity for me? And you, Angel of evil,
I was dead, and your words are death again.
Is it true, boy? Can it be true?
Is my wife dead? Has death bred death?
MESSENGER.   You can see for yourself.

[*The doors are opened, and the body of*
EURYDICE *is disclosed within.*

CREON.   Oh pity!
All true, all true, and more than I can bear!   1
O my wife, my son!
MESSENGER.   She stood before the altar, and her heart
Welcomed the knife her own hand guided,
And a great cry burst from her lips for Megareus[29] dead,
And for Haimon dead, her sons; and her last breath
Was a curse for their father, the murderer of her sons.
And she fell, and the dark flowed in through her closing eyes.
CREON.   O God, I am sick with fear.
Are there no swords here? Has no one a blow for me?
MESSENGER.   Her curse is upon you for the deaths of both.
CREON.   It is right that it should be. I alone am guilty.
I know it, and I say it. Lead me in,
Quickly, friends.

---

[29] *Megareus*, a son of Creon and Eurydicê who gave his life trying to spare Thebes
from the Argive army.

I have neither life nor substance. Lead me in.
CHORAGOS.   You are right, if there can be right in so much wrong.
The briefest way is best in a world of sorrow.
CREON.   Let it come,
Let death come quickly, and be kind to me.
I would not ever see the sun again.
CHORAGOS.   All that will come when it will; but we, meanwhile,   130
Have much to do. Leave the future to itself.
CREON.   All my heart was in that prayer!
CHORAGOS.   Then do not pray any more: the sky is deaf.
CREON.   Lead me away. I have been rash and foolish.
I have killed my son and my wife.
I look for comfort; my comfort lies here dead.
Whatever my hands have touched has come to nothing.
Fate has brought all my pride to a thought of dust.

> [*As* CREON *is being led into the house, the*
> CHORAGOS *advances and speaks directly to*
> *the audience*

CHORAGOS.   There is no happiness where there is no wisdom;
No wisdom but in submission to the gods.   140
Big words are always punished,
And proud men in old age learn to be wise.

A NOTE ON THE ELIZABETHAN THEATER

Performances of the plays of Shakespeare and his contemporaries
in sixteenth-century England were quite different from the presentations of early Greek plays in large amphitheaters. The theater
buildings constructed on the outskirts of London were smaller,
partially enclosed, and certainly more intimate than an outdoor
stadium. From records of the acting companies and letters of visitors
to England, we can conclude that the theater buildings were round
or polygonal wooden structures consisting of a platform stage
extending, from one side, out into an open, unroofed area where
part of the audience stood (the cheapest "seats") that was then
surrounded by tiered and roofed galleries for those willing to pay
more. At the back of the stage was a curtained inner area for
intimate scenes (or eavesdropping). Juliet's balcony would have been
found above the inner room, and the outer wooden stage floor
contained a trapdoor from which ghosts or devils could emerge.

Although the more complex Elizabethan theater allowed for more stage action than the Greek stadium, still there were few scenery props and no outer curtain to allow stagehands to alter scenery. Apparently, then, there were no breaks between scenes, and new locations had to be established by what the characters said. Plays were performed in the afternoon while it was still light, so night scenes were also established by the characters' remarks. (In the hands of a Shakespeare, the need to mark the day and nighttime scenes in *Romeo and Juliet* resulted in both beautiful and significant light and dark imagery.)

From reading the plays of the Elizabethan period, we can imagine that Elizabethan acting was still more stylized than today, generating broad gestures and a rapid delivery of lines. Still, the audience was close enough to allow for asides and intimate love scenes. In contrast to the Greek drama, there was much more stage business: sound effects, crowd scenes, sword duels, and poisoned characters collapsing on stage. Above all, the dramatists employed the varied possibilities of the English language—from puns and bawdy jokes to some of the most exquisite lines of poetry ever written.

WILLIAM SHAKESPEARE   (1564–1616)

Othello

Edited by Hardin Craig and David Bevington

THE NAMES OF THE ACTORS

> Othello, *the Moor.*
> Brabantio, [*a senator,*] *father to Desdemona.*
> Cassio, *an honourable lieutenant* [*to Othello*].
> Iago, [*Othello's ancient,*] *a villain.*
> Roderigo, *a gulled gentleman.*
> Duke of Venice.
> Senators [*of Venice*].
> Montano, *governor of Cyprus.*
> Lodovico *and* Gratiano, [*kinsmen to Brabantio,*] *two noble Venetians.*
> Sailors.

Clown.
Desdemona, [*daughter to Brabantio and*] *wife to Othello.*
Emilia, *wife to Iago.*
Bianca, *a courtezan* [*and mistress to Cassio*].

[Messenger, Herald, Officers, Gentlemen, Musicians, *and* Attendants.]

[SCENE: *Venice: a Sea-port in Cyprus.*]

ACT I.

Scene I. [*Venice. A street.*]

Enter RODERIGO *and* IAGO.

ROD.   Tush! never tell me; I take it much unkindly
    That thou, Iago, who hast had my purse
    As if the strings were thine, shouldst know of this.
IAGO.   'Sblood,° but you'll not hear me:
    If ever I did dream of such a matter,
    Abhor me.
ROD.   Thou told'st me thou didst hold him in thy hate.
IAGO.   Despise me, if I do not. Three great ones of the city,°
    In personal suit to make me his lieutenant,
    Off-capp'd to him:° and, by the faith of man,   10
    I know my price, I am worth no worse a place:
    But he, as loving his own pride and purposes,
    Evades them, with a bombast circumstance
    Horribly stuff'd with epithets of war;
    And, in conclusion,
    Nonsuits° my mediators; for, 'Certes,' says he,
    'I have already chose my officer.'
    And what was he?
    Forsooth, a great arithmetician,°
    One Michael Cassio, a Florentine,   20
    A fellow almost damn'd in a fair wife;°
    That never set a squadron in the field,
    Nor the division° of a battle knows

---

4. *'Sblood:* an oath, "by God's blood."   8. *great ones of the city:* Iago means to indicate his importance in the community; this is suggested also by his use of the word *worth* in line 11.   10. *him:* Othello.   16. *Nonsuits:* rejects.   19. *arithmetician:* a man whose military knowledge was merely theoretical, based on books of tactics.   21. *a . . . wife:* Cassio does not seem to be married, but his counterpart in Shakespeare's source did have a wife.   23. *division,* disposition of a battle line.

More than a spinster; unless the bookish theoric,°
Wherein the toged° consuls can propose°
As masterly as he: mere prattle, without practice,
Is all his soldiership. But he, sir, had th' election:
And I, of whom his eyes had seen the proof
At Rhodes, at Cyprus° and on other grounds
Christian and heathen, must be be-lee'd and calm'd   30
By debitor and creditor: this counter-caster,°
He, in good time,° must his lieutenant be,
And I—God bless the mark!°—his Moorship's ancient.°

Rod.   By heaven, I rather would have been his hangman.

Iago.   Why, there's no remedy; 'tis the curse of service,
Preferment goes by letter and affection,
And not by old gradation,° where each second
Stood heir to th' first. Now, sir, be judge yourself,
Whether I in any just term am affin'd°
To love the Moor.

Rod.   I would not follow him then.   40

Iago.   O, sir, content you;
I follow him to serve my turn upon him:
We cannot all be masters, nor all masters
Cannot be truly follow'd. You shall mark
Many a duteous and knee-crooking knave,
That, doting on his own obsequious bondage,
Wears out his time, much like his master's ass,
For nought but provender, and when he's old, cashier'd:
Whip me such honest knaves. Others there are
Who, trimm'd in forms and visages of duty,   5
Keep yet their hearts attending on themselves,
And, throwing but shows of service on their lords,
Do well thrive by them and when they have lin'd their coats
Do themselves homage: these fellows have some soul;
And such a one do I profess myself. For, sir,
It is as sure as you are Roderigo,
Were I the Moor, I would not be Iago:°
In following him, I follow but myself;
Heaven is my judge, not I for love and duty,
But seeming so, for my peculiar end:

24. *theoric,* theory.   25. *toged,* wearing the toga. *propose,* discuss.   29. *Rhodes, Cyprus,* islands in the Mediterranean south of Asia Minor, long subject to contention between the Venetians and the Turks.   31. *counter-caster,* a sort of bookkeeper; contemptuous term.   32. *in good time,* forsooth.   33. *God bless the mark,* anciently a pious interjection to avert evil omens. *ancient,* standardbearer, ensign.   37. *old gradation,* seniority. Iago here expresses a characteristic prejudice of professional soldiers.   39. *affin'd,* bound.   57. *Were . . . Iago.* Were I in the position of the Moor, I should not feel as Iago feels.

For when my outward action doth demonstrate
The native act and figure of my heart
In compliment extern,° 'tis not long after
But I will wear my heart upon my sleeve
For daws to peck at: I am not what I am.

Rod.   What a full fortune does the thick-lips° owe,
If he can carry't thus!

Iago.   Call up her father,
Rouse him: make after him, poison his delight,
Proclaim him in the streets; incense her kinsmen,
And, though he in a fertile climate dwell,   70
Plague him with flies: though that his joy be joy,
Yet throw such changes of vexation on't,
As it may lose some colour.

Rod.   Here is her father's house; I'll call aloud.

Iago.   Do, with like timorous° accent and dire yell
As when, by night and negligence, the fire
Is spied in populous cities.

Rod.   What, ho, Brabantio! Signior Brabantio, ho!

Iago.   Awake! what, ho, Brabantio! thieves! thieves! thieves!
Look to your house, your daughter and your bags!   80
Thieves! thieves!

Brabantio [appears] above [at a window].

Bra.   What is the reason of this terrible summons?
What is the matter there?

Rod.   Signior, is all your family within?

Iago.   Are your doors lock'd?

Bra.   Why, wherefore ask you this?

Iago.   'Zounds, sir y' are robb'd; for shame, put on your gown;
Your heart is burst, you have lost half your soul;
Even now, now, very now, an old black ram
Is tupping your white ewe. Arise, arise;
Awake the snorting° citizens with the bell,   90
Or else the devil will make a grandsire of you:
Arise, I say.

Bra.   What, have you lost your wits?

Rod.   Most reverend signior, do you know my voice?

Bra.   Not I: what are you?

Rod.   My name is Roderigo.

---

63. *compliment extern*, outward civility.   66. *thick-lips:* Elizabethans often applied the term
"Moor" to blacks.   75. *timorous*, frightening.   90. *snorting*, snoring.

BRA.   The worser welcome:
I have charg'd thee not to haunt about my doors:
In honest plainness thou hast heard me say
My daughter is not for thee; and now, in madness,
Being full of supper and distemp'ring draughts,
Upon malicious bravery,° dost thou come   100
To start° my quiet.

ROD.   Sir, sir, sir,—

BRA.   But thou must needs be sure
My spirit and my place have in them power
To make this bitter to thee.

ROD.   Patience, good sir.

BRA.   What tell'st thou me of robbing? this is Venice;
My house is not a grange.°

ROD.   Most grave Brabantio,
In simple and pure soul I come to you.

IAGO.   'Zounds, sir, you are one of those that will not serve God, if the
devil bid you. Because we come to do you service and you think we
are ruffians, you'll have your daughter covered with a Barbary horse;   11
you'll have your nephews° neigh to you; you'll have coursers for
    cousins and gennets° for germans.°

BRA.   What profane wretch art thou?

IAGO.   I am one, sir, that comes to tell you your daughter and the Moor
are now making the beast with two backs.

BRA.   Thou art a villain.

IAGO.   You are—a senator.

BRA.   This thou shalt answer; I know thee, Roderigo.

ROD.   Sir, I will answer any thing. But, I beseech you,
If't be your pleasure and most wise consent,
As partly I find it is, that your fair daughter,   1
At this odd-even° and dull watch o' th' night,
Transported, with no worse nor better guard
But with a knave of common hire, a gondolier,
To the gross clasps of a lascivious Moor,—
If this be known to you and your allowance,°
We then have done you bold and saucy wrongs;
But if you know not this, my manners tell me
We have your wrong rebuke. Do not believe
That, from° the sense of all civility,
I thus would play and trifle with your reverence:
Your daughter, if you have not given her leave,

---

100. *bravery,* defiance, bravado.   101. *start,* disrupt.   106. *grange,* isolated farmhouse.   111. *nephews,* grandsons.   112. *gennets,* small Spanish horses.   113. *germans,*
near relatives.   121. *odd-even,* between night and morning.   125. *allowance,* permission.   129. *from,* contrary to.

I say again, hath made a gross revolt;
Tying her duty, beauty, wit and fortunes
In an extravagant° and wheeling° stranger
Of here and every where. Straight satisfy yourself:
If she be in her chamber or your house,
Let loose on me the justice of the state
For thus deluding you.

BRA.   Strike on the tinder,° ho!
Give me a taper! call up all my people!
This accident° is not unlike my dream: 140
Belief of it oppresses me already.
Light, I say! light!

                                                                     Exit [above].

IAGO.   Farewell; for I must leave you:
It seems not meet, nor wholesome to my place,
To be produc'd—as, if I stay, I shall—
Against the Moor: for, I do know, the state,
However this may gall him with some check,°
Cannot with safety cast° him, for he's embark'd
With such loud reason to the Cyprus wars,
Which even now stand in act,° that, for their souls,
Another of his fathom° they have none,   150
To lead their business: in which regard,
Though I do hate him as I do hell-pains,
Yet, for necessity of present life,
I must show out a flag and sign of love,
Which is indeed but sign. That you shall surely find him,
Lead to the Sagittary° the raised search:
And there will I be with him. So, farewell.

                                                                           Exit.

Enter [below] BRABANTIO, *with* SERVANTS *and torches.*

BRA.   It is too true an evil: gone she is;
And what's to come of my despised time
Is nought but bitterness. Now, Roderigo,   160
Where didst thou see her? O unhappy girl!
With the Moor, say'st thou? Who would be a father!
How didst thou know 'twas she? O, she deceives me
Past thought! What said she to you? Get moe° tapers:
Raise all my kindred. Are they married, think you?

---

134. *extravagant*, wandering. *wheeling*, vagabond.   138. *tinder*, charred linen kept in a metal
box and ignited by a spark from flint and steel.   140. *accident*, occurrence, event.   146.
check, rebuke.   147. *cast*, dismiss.   149. *stand in act*, are going on.   150. *fathom*, ability.   156. *Sagittary*, probably an inn.   164. *moe*, more.

Rod. Truly, I think they are.

Bra. O heaven! How got she out? O treason of the blood!
Fathers, from hence trust not your daughters' minds
By what you see them act. Is° there not charms
By which the property° of youth and maidhood   170
May be abus'd? Have you not read, Roderigo,
Of some such thing?

Rod.   Yes sir, I have indeed.

Bra. Call up my brother. O, would you° had had her!
Some one way, some another. Do you know
Where we may apprehend her and the Moor?

Rod. I think I can discover him, if you please
To get good guard and go along with me.

Bra. Pray you, lead on. At every house I'll call;
I may command at most. Get weapons, ho!
And raise some special officers of night.°   18

On, good Roderigo: I will deserve your pains.

Exeunt.

Scene II. [*Another street.*]

Enter OTHELLO, IAGO, ATTENDANTS *with torches.*

Iago. Though in the trade of war I have slain men,
Yet do I hold it very stuff o' th' conscience
To do no contriv'd murder: I lack iniquity
Sometime to do me service: nine or ten times
I had thought t' have yerk'd° him here under the ribs.

Oth. 'Tis better as it is.

Iago.   Nay, but he prated,
And spoke such scurvy and provoking terms
Against your honour
That, with the little godliness I have,
I did full hard forbear him. But, I pray you, sir,
Are you fast married? Be assur'd of this,
That the magnifico° is much belov'd,
And hath in his effect° a voice potential°
As double° as the duke's: he will divorce you;
Or put upon you what restraint and grievance
The law, with all his might to enforce it on,
Will give him cable.

---

169. *Is,* are.   170. *property,* special quality.   173. *you,* Roderigo.   180. *officers of night,*
police.   5. *yerk'd,* stabbed.   12. *magnifico,* Venetian grandee (i.e., Brabantio).   13.
effect, influence. *potential,* powerful.   14. *double,* twice as influential as most men's.

OTH.   Let him do his spite;
My services which I have done the signiory°
Shall out-tongue his complaints. 'Tis yet to know,—
Which, when I know that boasting is an honour,   20
I shall promulgate—I fetch my life and being
From men of royal siege,° and my demerits°
May speak unbonneted° to as proud a fortune
As this that I have reach'd: for know, Iago,
But that I love the gentle Desdemona,
I would not my unhoused free condition
Put into circumscription and confine
For the sea's worth. But, look! what lights come yond?
IAGO.   Those are the raised father and his friends:
You were best go in.
OTH.   Not I; I must be found: 30
My parts, my title and my perfect soul°
Shall manifest me rightly. Is it they?
IAGO.   By Janus, I think no.

Enter CASSIO *[and certain* OFFICERS*] with torches.*

OTH.   The servants of the duke, and my lieutenant.
The goodness of the night upon you, friends!
What is the news?
CAS.   The duke does greet you, general,
And he requires your haste-post-haste appearance,
Even on the instant.
OTH.   What is the matter, think you?
CAS.   Something from Cyprus, as I may divine:
It is a business of some heat: the galleys   40
Have sent a dozen sequent° messengers
This very night at one another's heels,
And many of the consuls,° rais'd and met,
Are at the duke's already: you have been hotly call'd for;
When, being not at your lodging to be found,
The senate hath sent about three several° quests
To search you out.
OTH.   'Tis well I am found by you.
I will but spend a word here in the house,
And go with you.

                                                                  [Exit.]

CAS.   Ancient, what makes he here?

18. *signiory,* Venetian government.   22. *siege,* rank. *demerits,* deserts.   23. *unbonneted,* on equal terms.   31. *perfect soul,* unflawed conscience.   41. *sequent,* successive.   43. *consuls,* senators.   46. *several,* separate.

IAGO.   'Faith, he to-night hath boarded a land carack:°   50
    If it prove lawful prize, he's made for ever.
CAS.   I do not understand.
IAGO.   He's married.
CAS.   To who?

[Enter OTHELLO.]

IAGO.   Marry, to—Come, captain, will you go?
OTH.   Have with you.
CAS.   Here comes another troop to seek for you.

Enter BRABANTIO, RODERIGO, with OFFICERS and torches.

IAGO.   It is Brabantio. General, be advis'd;
    He comes to bad intent.
OTH.   Holla! stand there!
ROD.   Signior, it is the Moor.
BRA.   Down with him, thief!

                        [They draw on both sides.]

IAGO.   You, Roderigo! come, sir, I am for you.
OTH.   Keep up your bright swords, for the dew will rust them.
    Good signior, you shall more command with years
    Than with your weapons.
BRA.   O thou foul thief, where hast thou stow'd my daughter?
    Damn'd as thou art, thou hast enchanted her;
    For I'll refer me to all things of sense,°
    If she in chains of magic were not bound,
    Whether a maid so tender, fair and happy,
    So opposite to marriage that she shunn'd
    The wealthy curled darlings of our nation,
    Would ever have, t' incur a general mock,
    Run from her guardage° to the sooty bosom
    Of such a thing as thou, to fear, not to delight.
    Judge me the world, if 'tis not gross in sense°
    That thou hast practis'd on her with foul charms,
    Abus'd her delicate youth with drugs or minerals°
    That weaken motion:° I'll have't disputed on;°
    'Tis probable and palpable to thinking.
    I therefore apprehend and do attach thee
    For an abuser of the world,° a practiser

---

50. *carack,* large merchant ship.   64. *things of sense,* common-sense understandings of the natural order.   70. *guardage,* guardianship.   72. *gross in sense,* easily discernible in apprehension or perception.   74. *minerals,* medicine, poison.   75. *motion,* thought, reason. *disputed on,* argued in court by professional counsel.   78. *abuser of the world,* corrupter of society.

Of arts inhibited° and out of warrant
Lay hold upon him; if he do resist, 80
Subdue him at his peril.

OTH.   Hold your hands,
Both you of my inclining,° and the rest:
Were it my cue to fight, I should have known it
Without a prompter. Wither will you that I go
To answer this your charge?

BRA.   To prison, till fit time
Of law and course of direct session°
Call thee to answer.

OTH.   What if I do obey?
How may the duke be therewith satisfied,
Whose messengers are here about my side,
Upon some present business of the state 90
To bring me to him?

FIRST OFF.   'Tis true, most worthy signior;
The duke's in council, and your noble self,
I am sure, is sent for.

BRA.   How! the duke in council!
In this time of the night! Bring him away:
Mine's not an idle cause: the duke himself,
Or any of my brothers of the state,
Cannot but feel this wrong as 'twere their own;
For if such actions may have passage free,
Bond-slaves and pagans° shall our statesmen be.

                                Exeunt.

Scene III. [*A council-chamber.*]

Enter DUKE, SENATORS, *and* OFFICERS *[set at a table, with lights and* ATTENDANTS*]*.

DUKE.   There is no composition in these news
That gives them credit.

FIRST SEN.   Indeed, they are disproportion'd;°
My letters say a hundred and seven galleys.

DUKE.   And mine, a hundred forty.

SEC. SEN.   And mine, two hundred:
But though they jump° not on a just account,—
As in these cases, where the aim° reports,

---

79. *inhibited,* prohibited.   82. *inclining,* following, party.   86. *course of direct session,* regular legal proceedings.   99. *Bond-slaves and pagans,* contemptuous reference to Othello's past history.   2. *disproportion'd,* inconsistent.   5. *jump,* agree.   6. *aim,* conjecture.

'Tis oft with difference—yet do they all confirm
A Turkish fleet, and bearing up to Cyprus.
DUKE.   Nay, it is possible enough to judgment:
I do not so secure me° in the error,
But the main article° I do approve
In fearful sense.
SAILOR.   *(Within)* What, ho! what, ho! what, ho!
FIRST OFF.   A messenger from the galleys.

Enter SAILOR.

DUKE.   Now, what's the business?
SAIL.   The Turkish preparation makes for Rhodes;
So was I bid report here to the state
By Signior Angelo.
DUKE.   How say you by this change?
FIRST SEN.   This cannot be,
By no assay° of reason: 'tis a pageant,
To keep us in false gaze. When we consider
Th' importancy of Cyprus to the Turk,
And let ourselves again but understand,
That as it more concerns the Turk than Rhodes,
So may he with more facile question° bear it,
For that it stands not in such warlike brace.°
But altogether lacks th' abilities
That Rhodes is dress'd in: if we make thought of this,
We must not think the Turk is so unskillful
To leave that latest which concerns him first,
Neglecting an attempt of ease and gain,
To wake and wage a danger profitless.
DUKE.   Nay, in all confidence, he's not for Rhodes.
FIRST OFF.   Here is more news.

Enter a MESSENGER.

MESS.   The Ottomites, reverend and gracious,
Steering with due course toward the isle of Rhodes,
Have there injointed them with an after fleet.
FIRST SEN.   Ay, so I thought. How many, as you guess?
MESS.   Of thirty sail: and now they do re-stem°
Their backward course, bearing with frank appearance
Their purposes toward Cyprus. Signior Montano,

10. *secure me*, feel myself secure.   11. *main article*, i.e., that the Turkish fleet is threatening.   18. *assay*, test.   23. *more facile question*, greater facility of effort.   24. *brace*, state of defense.   37. *re-stem*, steer again.

Your trusty and most valiant servitor,   40
    With his free duty recommends you thus,
    And prays you to believe him.
DUKE.   'Tis certain, then, for Cyprus.
    Marcus Luccicos, is not he in town?
FIRST SEN.   He's now in Florence.
DUKE.   Write from us to him; post-post-haste dispatch.
FIRST SEN.   Here comes Brabantio and the valiant Moor.

Enter BRABANTIO, OTHELLO, CASSIO, IAGO, RODERIGO, *and* OFFICERS.

DUKE.   Valiant Othello, we must straight employ you
    Against the general enemy Ottoman.
    [*To* BRABANTIO] I did not see you; welcome, gentle signior;   50
    We lack'd your counsel and your help to-night.
BRA.   So did I yours. Good your grace, pardon me;
    Neither my place nor aught I heard of business
    Hath rais'd me from my bed, nor doth the general care
    Take hold on me, for my particular grief
    Is of so flood-gate and o'erbearing nature
    That it engluts° and swallows other sorrows
    And it is still itself.
DUKE.   Why, what's the matter?
BRA.   My daughter! O, my daughter!
DUKE and SEN.   Dead?
BRA.   Ay, to me;
    She is abus'd, stol'n from me, and corrupted   60
    By spells and medicines bought of mountebanks;
    For nature so preposterously to err,
    Being not deficient, blind, or lame of sense,
    Sans witchcraft could not.
DUKE.   Whoe'er he be that in this foul proceeding
    Hath thus beguil'd your daughter of herself
    And you of her, the bloody book of law
    You shall yourself read in the bitter letter
    After your own sense, yea, though our proper son
    Stood in your action.°
BRA.   Humbly I thank your grace.   70
    Here is the man, this Moor, whom now, it seems,
    Your special mandate for the state-affairs
    Hath hither brought.
DUKE and SEN.   We are very sorry for 't.
DUKE.   [*To* OTHELLO] What, in your own part, can you say to this?

57. *engluts,* engulfs.   70. *Stood . . . action,* was under your accusation.

BRA.   Nothing, but this is so.

OTH.   Most potent, grave, and reverend signiors,
My very noble and approv'd good masters,
That I have ta'en away this old man's daughter,
It is most true; true, I have married her:
The very head and front of my offending
Hath this extent, no more. Rude am I in my speech,
And little bless'd with the soft phrase of peace;
For since these arms of mine had seven years' pith,°
Till now some nine moons wasted, they have us'd
Their dearest action in the tented field,
And little of this great world can I speak,
More than pertains to feats of broil and battle,
And therefore little shall I grace my cause
In speaking for myself. Yet, by your gracious patience,°
I will a round unvarnish'd tale deliver
Of my whole course of love; what drugs, what charms,
What conjuration and what mighty magic,
For such proceeding I am charg'd withal,
I won his daughter.

BRA.   A maiden never bold;
Of spirit so still and quiet, that her motion
Blush'd at herself;° and she, in spite of nature,
Of years, of country, credit, every thing,
To fall in love with what she fear'd to look on!
It is a judgement maim'd and most imperfect
That will confess perfection so could err
Against all rules of nature, and must be driven
To find out practices of cunning hell,
Why this should be. I therefore vouch° again
That with some mixtures pow'rful o'er the blood,
Or with some dram conjur'd to this effect,
He wrought upon her.

DUKE.   To vouch this, is no proof,
Without more wider and more overt test
Than these thin habits and poor likelihoods
Of modern seeming do prefer against him.

FIRST SEN.   But, Othello, speak:
Did you by indirect and forced courses
Subdue and poison this young maid's affections?
Or came it by request and such fair question
As soul to soul affordeth?

OTH.   I do beseech you,

83. *pith,* strength, vigor.   89. *patience,* sufferance, permission.   95–96. *motion . . . herself,*
inward impulses blushed at themselves.   103. *vouch,* assert.

84 (margin)

Send for the lady to the Sagittary,
And let her speak of me before her father:
If you do find me foul in her report,
The trust, the office I do hold of you,
Not only take away, but let your sentence
Even fall upon my life.

DUKE.   Fetch Desdemona hither.   120
OTH.   Ancient, conduct them; you best know the place.

                    [*Exeunt IAGO and ATTENDANTS.*]

And, till she come, as truly as to heaven
I do confess the vices of my blood,
So justly to your grave ears I'll present
How I did thrive in this fair lady's love,
And she in mine.

DUKE.   Say it, Othello.
OTH.   Her father lov'd me; oft invited me;
Still question'd me the story of my life,
From year to year, the battles, sieges, fortunes,   130
That I have pass'd.
I ran it through, even from my boyish days,
To th' very moment that he bade me tell it;
Wherein I spake of most disastrous chances,
Of moving accidents by flood and field,
Of hair-breadth scapes i' th' imminent° deadly breach,
Of being taken by the insolent foe
And sold to slavery, of my redemption thence
And portance° in my travels' history:
Wherein of antres° vast and deserts idle,°   140
Rough quarries, rocks and hills whose heads touch heaven,
It was my hint° to speak,—such was the process;
And of the Cannibals that each other eat,°
The Anthropophagi° and men whose heads
Do grow beneath their shoulders. This to hear
Would Desdemona seriously incline:
But still the house-affairs would draw her thence:
Which ever as she could with haste dispatch,
She 'ld come again, and with a greedy ear
Devour up my discourse: which I observing,   150
Took once a pliant hour, and found good means
To draw from her a prayer of earnest heart
That I would all my pilgrimage dilate,°

---

136. *imminent*, i.e., impending parts when a gap has been made in a fortification.   139.
portance, conduct.   140. *antres*, caverns. *idle*, barren, unprofitable.   142. *hint*, occasion.   143. *eat*, ate.   144. *Anthropophagi*, man-eaters.   153. *dilate*, relate in detail.

Whereof by parcels she had something heard,
But not intentively:° I did consent,
And often did beguile her of her tears,
When I did speak of some distressful stroke
That my youth suffer'd. My story being done,
She gave me for my pains a world of sighs:
She swore, in faith, 'twas strange, 'twas passing strange,   160
'Twas pitiful, 'twas wondrous pitiful:
She wish'd she had not heard it, yet she wish'd
That heaven had made her such a man: she thank'd me,
And bade me, if I had a friend that lov'd her,
I should but teach him how to tell my story,
And that would woo her. Upon this hint I spake:
She lov'd me for the dangers I had pass'd,
And I lov'd her that she did pity them.
This only is the witchcraft I have us'd:
Here comes the lady; let her witness it.   17

Enter DESDEMONA, IAGO, *[and]* ATTENDANTS.

DUKE.   I think this tale would win my daughter too.
    Good Brabantio,
    Take up this mangled matter at the best:
    Men do their broken weapons rather use
    Than their bare hands.
BRA.   I pray you, hear her speak:
    If she confess that she was half the wooer,
    Destruction on my head, if my bad blame
    Light on the man! Come hither, gentle mistress:
    Do you perceive in all this noble company
    Where most you owe obedience?
DES.   My noble father,
    I do perceive here a divided duty:°
    To you I am bound for life and education;
    My life and education both do learn me
    How to respect you; you are the lord of duty;
    I am hitherto your daughter: but here's my husband,
    And so much duty as my mother show'd
    To you, preferring you before her father,
    So much I challenge that I may profess
    Due to the Moor my lord.
BRA.   God be with you! I have done.
    Please it your grace, on to° the state-affairs:

---

155. *intentively,* with full attention.   181. *divided duty.* Desdemona recognizes that she still
owes a duty to her father even after marriage.   190. *on to,* i.e., proceed with.

I had rather to adopt a child than get° it.
Come hither, Moor:
I here do give thee that with all my heart
Which, but thou hast already, with all my heart
I would keep from thee. For your sake,° jewel,
I am glad at soul I have no other child;
For thy escape would teach me tyranny,
To hang clogs on them. I have done, my lord.

DUKE.   Let me speak like yourself,° and lay a sentence,°
Which, as a grise° or step, may help these lovers   200
Into your favour.
When remedies are past, the griefs are ended
By seeing the worst, which late on hopes depended,
To mourn a mischief that is past and gone
Is the next° way to draw new mischief on.
What cannot be preserv'd when fortune takes,
Patience her injury a mock'ry makes.
The robb'd that smiles steals something from the thief;
He robs himself that spends a bootless grief.

BRA.   So let the Turk of Cyprus us beguile;   210
We lose it not, so long as we can smile.
He bears the sentence well that nothing bears
But the free comfort° which from thence he hears,
But he bears both the sentence and the sorrow
That, to pay grief, must of poor patience borrow.
These sentences, to sugar, or to gall,
Being strong on both sides, are equivocal:
But words are words; I never yet did hear
That the bruis'd heart was pierced through the ear.
I humbly beseech you, proceed to th' affairs of state.   220

DUKE.   The Turk with a most mighty preparation makes for Cyprus.
Othello, the fortitude° of the place is best known to you; and though
we have there a substitute of most allowed° sufficiency, yet opinion,
a sovereign mistress of effects, throws a more safer voice on you:°
you must therefore be content to slubber° the gloss of your new
fortunes with this more stubborn and boisterous expedition.

OTH.   The tyrant custom, most grave senators,
Hath made the flinty and steel couch of war
My thrice-driven° bed of down: I do agnize°

---

191. *get*, beget.   195. *For your sake*, on your account.   199. *like yourself*, i.e., as you would,
in your proper temper. *sentence*, maxim.   200. *grise*, step.   205. *next*, nearest.   213.
comfort, i.e., the consolation that it may be borne with patience.   222. *fortitude*,
strength.   223. *allowed*, acknowledged.   223–224. *opinion . . . on you*, public opinion, an
important determiner of affairs, chooses you as the best man.   225. *slubber*, soil,
sully.   229. *thrice-driven*, thrice sifted. *agnize*, know in myself.

A natural and prompt alacrity   23(
I find in hardness,° and do undertake
These present wars against the Ottomites.
Most humbly therefore bending to your state,
I crave fit disposition for my wife,
Due reference of place and exhibition,°
With such accommodation and besort°
As levels with her breeding.

DUKE.   If you please,
Be 't at her father's.

BRA.   I'll not have it so.

OTH.   Nor I.

DES.   Nor I; I would not there reside,
To put my father in impatient thoughts   24
By being in his eye. Most gracious duke,
To my unfolding lend your prosperous° ear;
And let me find a charter° in your voice,
T' assist my simpleness.°

DUKE.   What would you, Desdemona?

DES.   That I did love the Moor to live with him,
My downright violence and storm of fortunes
May trumpet to the world: my heart's subdu'd
Even to the very quality of my lord:
I saw Othello's visage in his mind,   2
And to his honours and his valiant parts
Did I my soul and fortunes consecrate.
So that, dear lords, if I be left behind,
A moth of peace, and he go to the war,
The rites for why I love him are bereft me,
And I a heavy interim shall support
By his dear absence. Let me go with him.

OTH.   Let her have your voices.
Vouch with me, heaven, I therefore beg it not,
To please the palate of my appetite,
Nor to comply with heat—the young affects°
In me defunct—and proper satisfaction,
But to be free and bounteous to her mind:
And heaven defend your good souls, that you think
I will your serious and great business scant
When she is with me: no, when light-wing'd toys
Of feather'd Cupid seel° with wanton dullness

231. *hardness,* hardship.   235. *exhibition,* allowance.   236. *besort,* suitable company.   242. *prosperous,* propitious.   243. *charter,* privilege.   244. *simpleness,* simplicity.   261. *affects,* inclination, desires.   267. *seel,* in falconry, to make blind by sewing up
the eyes of the hawk in training.

My speculative and offic'd instruments,°
That° my disports° corrupt and taint° my business,
Let housewives make a skillet of my helm,   270
And all indign° and base adversities
Make head against my estimation!°
DUKE.   Be it as you shall privately determine,
Either for her stay or going: th' affair cries haste,
And speed must answer it.
FIRST SEN.   You must away to-night.
OTH.   With all my heart.
DUKE.   At nine i' th' morning here we'll meet again.
Othello, leave some officer behind,
And he shall our commission bring to you;
With such things else of quality and respect   280
As doth import° you.
OTH.   So please your grace, my ancient;
A man he is of honesty and trust:
To his conveyance I assign my wife,
With what else needful your good grace shall think
To be sent after me.
DUKE.   Let it be so.
Good night to every one. [*To* BRAB.] And, noble signior,
If virtue no delighted° beauty lack,
Your son-in-law is far more fair than black.
FIRST SEN.   Adieu, brave Moor; use Desdemona well.
BRA.   Look to her, Moor, if thou hast eyes to see: 290
She has deceiv'd her father, and may thee.

                *Exeunt [*DUKE, SENATORS, OFFICERS, *& c.].*

OTH.   My life upon her faith! Honest Iago,°
My Desdemona must I leave to thee:
I prithee, let thy wife attend on her;
And bring them after in the best advantage.
Come, Desdemona; I have but an hour
Of love, of worldly matters and direction,
To spend with thee: we must obey the time.

                        Exit [with DESDEMONA].

ROD.   Iago,—
IAGO.   What say'st thou, noble heart?   300

---

268. *speculative . . . instruments*, ability to see and reason clearly.   269. *That*, so that. *disports*, pastime. *taint*, impair.   271. *indign*, unworthy, shameful.   272. *estimation*, reputation.   281. *import*, concern.   287. *delighted*, delightful.   292. *Honest Iago*, an evidence of Iago's carefully built reputation.

Rod. What will I do, thinkest thou?

Iag. Why, go to bed, and sleep.

Rod. I will incontinently° drown myself.

Iago. If thou dost, I shall never love thee after.
Why, thou silly gentleman!

Rod. It is silliness to live when to live is torment; and then have we a
prescription to die when death is our physician.   30

Iago. O villanous! I have looked upon the world for four times seven
years; and since I could distinguish betwixt a benefit and an injury,
I never found man that knew how to love himself. Ere I would say,
I would drown myself for the love of a guinea-hen, I would change
my humanity with a baboon.   3|

Rod. What should I do? I confess it is my shame to be so fond; but it is
not in my virtue° to amend it.

Iago. Virtue! a fig! 'tis in ourselves that we are thus or thus. Our bodies
are our gardens, to the which our wills are gardeners; so that if we
will plant nettles, or sow lettuce, set hyssop° and weed up thyme,
supply it with one gender° of herbs, or distract it with many, either
to have it sterile with idleness,° or manured with industry, why, the
power and corrigible authority° of this lies in our wills. If the balance
of our lives had not one scale of reason to poise another of sensuality,
the blood and baseness of our natures would conduct us to most
preposterous conclusions: but we have reason to cool our raging
motions,° our carnal strings, our unbitted° lusts, whereof I take this
that you call love to be a sect° or scion.   ?

Rod. It cannot be.

Iago. It is merely a lust of the blood and a permission of the will. Come,
be a man. Drown thyself! drown cats and blind puppies. I have
professed me thy friend and I confess me knit to thy deserving with
cables of perdurable° toughness; I could never better stead thee than
now. Put money in thy purse; follow thou the wars; defeat thy
favour° with an usurped beard; I say, put money in thy purse. It
cannot be that Desdemona should long continue her love to the
Moor,—put money in thy purse,—nor he his to her: it was a violent
commencement in her, and thou shalt see an answerable sequestration:°—put but money in thy purse. These Moors are changeable in

---

303. *incontinently*, immediately.   314. *virtue*, strength.   317. *hyssop*, an herb of the mint
family.   318. *gender*, kind.   319. *idleness*, want of cultivation.   320. *corrigible authority*,
the power to correct.   321–324. *reason . . . motions.* Iago understands the warfare between
reason and sensuality, but his ethics are totally inverted; reason works in him not good, as it
should according to natural law, but evil, which he has chosen for his good.   324. *motions*,
appetites. *unbitted*, uncontrolled.   325. *sect*, cutting.   330. *perdurable*, very dura-
ble.   332. *defeat thy favour*, disguise and disfigure thy face.   336. *answerable sequestration*,
a separation corresponding.

their wills:—fill thy purse with money:—the food that to him now
is as luscious as locusts,° shall be to him shortly as bitter as coloquintida.° She must change for youth: when she is sated with his body,
she will find the error of her choice: she must have change, she
must: therefore put money in thy purse. If thou wilt needs damn
thyself, do it a more delicate way than drowning. Make all the money
thou canst: if sanctimony and a frail vow betwixt an erring° barbarian
and a super-subtle Venetian be not too hard for my wits and all the
tribe of hell, thou shalt enjoy her; therefore make money. A pox of
drowning thyself! it is clean out of the way: seek thou rather to be
hanged in compassing thy joy than to be drowned and go without
her.   348

Rod.   Wilt thou be fast to my hopes, if I depend on the issue?

Iago.   Thou art sure of me:—go, make money:—I have told thee often,
and I re-tell thee again and again, I hate the Moor: my cause is
hearted;° thine hath no less reason. Let us be conjunctive° in our
revenge against him; if thou canst cuckold him, thou dost thyself a
pleasure, me a sport. There are many events in the womb of time
which will be delivered. Traverse!° go, provide thy money. We will
have more of this to-morrow. Adieu.   356

Rod.   Where shall we meet i' the morning?

Iago.   At my lodging.

Rod.   I'll be with thee betimes.

Iago.   Go to; farewell. Do you hear, Roderigo?   360

Rod.   What say you?

Iago.   No more of drowning, do you hear?

Rod.   I am changed: I'll go sell all my land.

Exit.

Iago.   Thus do I ever make my fool my purse;
    For I mine own gain'd knowledge should profane,
    If I would time expend with such a snipe,°
    But for my sport and profit. I hate the Moor;
    And it is thought abroad, that 'twixt my sheets
    H'as done my office: I know not if't be true;
    But I, for mere suspicion in that kind,   370
    Will do as if for surety. He holds me well;
    The better shall my purpose work on him.
    Cassio's a proper man: let me see now:
    To get his place and to plume up° my will

---

338. *locusts*, of doubtful meaning; defined as fruit of the carob tree, as honeysuckle, and as
lollipops or sugar sticks.   339. *coloquintida*, colocynth, or bitter apple, a purgative.   343.
erring, wandering.   352. *hearted*, fixed in the heart. *conjunctive*, united.   355. *Traverse*,
go (military term).   366. *snipe*, gull, fool.   374. *plume up*, glorify, gratify.

In double knavery—How, how?—Let's see:—
After some time, to abuse Othello's ears
That he° is too familiar with his wife.
He hath a person and a smooth dispose°
To be suspected, fram'd to make women false.
The Moor is of a free° and open nature,
That thinks men honest that but seem to be so,
And will as tenderly be led by th' nose
As asses are.
I have't. It is engend'red. Hell and night
Must bring this monstrous birth to the world's light.

38

                                                        [*Exit.*]

ACT II.

Scene I. [*A Sea-port in Cyprus. An open place near the Quay.*]

Enter MONTANO *and two* GENTLEMEN.

MON.   What from the cape can you discern at sea?
FIRST GENT.   Nothing at all: it is a high-wrought flood;
        I cannot, 'twixt the heaven and the main,
        Descry a sail.
MON.   Methinks the wind hath spoke aloud at land;
        A fuller blast ne'er shook our battlements:
        If it hath ruffian'd° so upon the sea,
        What ribs of oak, when mountains melt on them,
        Can hold the mortise?° What shall we hear of this?
SEC. GENT.   A segregation° of the Turkish fleet:
        For do but stand upon the foaming shore,
        The chidden billow seems to pelt the clouds:
        The wind-shak'd surge, with high and monstrous mane,
        Seems to cast water on the burning bear,°
        And quench the guards° of th' ever-fixed pole:
        I never did like molestation view
        On the enchafed° flood.

---

377. *he*, i.e., Cassio.   378. *dispose*, external manner.   380. *free*, frank.   7. *ruffian'd*, raged.   9. *mortise*, the socket hollowed out in fitting timbers.   10. *segregation*, dispersion.   14. *bear*, a constellation.   15. *quench the guards*, overwhelm the stars near the polestar.   17. *enchafed*, angry.

MON.   If that the Turkish fleet
 Be not enshelter'd and embay'd, they are drown'd;
 It is impossible they bear it out.

Enter a [third] GENTLEMAN.

THIRD GENT. News, lads! our wars are done.   20
 The desperate tempest hath so bang'd the Turks,
 That their designment° halts: a noble ship of Venice
 Hath seen a grievous wrack and sufferance°
 On most part of their fleet.
MON. How! is this true?
THIRD GENT.   The ship is here put in,
 A Veronesa; Michael Cassio,
 Lieutenant to the warlike Moor Othello,
 Is come on shore: the Moor himself at sea,
 And is in full commission here for Cyprus.
MON. I am glad on't; 'tis a worthy governor.   30
THIRD GENT. But this same Cassio, though he speak of comfort
 Touching the Turkish loss, yet he looks sadly,
 And prays the Moor be safe; for they were parted
 With foul and violent tempest.
MON.   Pray heavens he be;
 For I have serv'd him, and the man commands
 Like a full° soldier. Let's to the seaside, ho!
 As well to see the vessel that's come in
 As to throw out our eyes for brave Othello,
 Even till we make the main and th' aerial blue
 An indistinct regard.°
THIRD GENT.   Come, let's do so;   40
 For every minute is expectancy
 Of more arrivance.°

Enter CASSIO.

CAS. Thanks, you the valiant of this warlike isle,
 That so approve the Moor! O, let the heavens
 Give him defence against the elements,
 For I have lost him on a dangerous sea.
MON. Is he well shipp'd?
CAS. His bark is stoutly timber'd and his pilot
 Of very expert and approv'd allowance;°

---

22. *designment,* enterprise. 23. *sufferance,* disaster. 36. *full,* perfect. 39–40. *make . . . regard,* cause the blue of the sea and the air to grow indistinguishable in our view. 42. *arrivance,* arrival. 49. *allowance,* reputation.

Therefore my hopes, not surfeited to death, 50
Stand in bold cure. [*A cry*] *within* 'A sail, a sail, a sail!'

[Enter a fourth GENTLEMAN.*]*

CAS. What noise?
FOURTH GENT. The town is empty; on the brow o' th' sea
 Stand ranks of people, and they cry 'A sail!'
CAS. My hopes do shape him for the governor.

 [Guns heard.]

SEC. GENT. They do discharge their shot of courtesy:
 Our friends at least.
CAS. I pray you, sir, go forth,
 And give us truth who 'tis that is arriv'd.
SEC. GENT. I shall.

 Exit.

MON. But good lieutenant, is your general wiv'd? 6
CAS. Most fortunately: he hath achiev'd a maid
 That paragons° description and wild fame;
 One that excells the quirks° of blazoning° pens,
 And in th' essential vesture of creation°
 Does tire the ingener.°

 Enter [second] GENTLEMAN.

 How now! who has put in?
SEC. GENT. 'Tis one Iago, ancient to the general.
CAS. Has had most favourable and happy speed:
 Tempests themselves, high seas and howling winds,
 The gutter'd° rocks and congregated sands,—
 Traitors ensteep'd° to clog the guiltless keel,—
 As having sense of beauty, do omit
 Their mortal° natures, letting go safely by
 The divine Desdemona.
MON. What is she?
CAS. She that I spake of, our great captain's captain,
 Left in the conduct of the bold Iago,
 Whose footing here anticipates our thoughts
 A se'nnight's° speed. Great Jove, Othello guard,

---

62. *paragons*, surpasses. 63. *quirks*, witty conceits. *blazoning*, setting forth honorably in words. 64. *vesture of creation*, the real qualities with which creation has invested her. 65. *ingener*, inventor, praiser. 69. *gutter'd*, jagged, trenched. 70. *ensteep'd*, lying under water. 72. *mortal*, deadly. 77. *se'nnight's*, week's.

And swell his sail with thine own pow'rful breath,
That he may bless this bay with his tall ship,
Make love's quick pants in Desdemona's arms,   80
Give renew'd fire to our extincted spirits,
And bring all Cyprus comfort!

> *Enter* DESDEMONA, IAGO, RODERIGO, *and* EMILIA,
> *[with* ATTENDANTS*].*

         O, behold,
The riches of the ship is come on shore!
You men of Cyprus, let her have your knees.
Hail to thee, lady! and the grace of heaven,
Before, behind thee and on every hand,
Enwheel thee round!
DES.   I thank you, valiant Cassio.
 What tidings can you tell me of my lord?
CAS. He is not yet arriv'd: nor know I aught
 But that he's well and will be shortly here.   90
DES. O, but I fear—How lost you company?
CAS. The great contention of the sea and skies
 Parted our fellowship—But, hark! a sail.
      (*Within*) 'A sail, a sail!'

              [*Guns heard.*]

SEC GENT. They give their greeting to the citadel:
 This likewise is a friend.
CAS.   See for the news.

          [*Exit* GENTLEMAN.]

Good ancient, you are welcome. [*To* EMILIA] Welcome, mistress:
Let it not gall your patience, good Iago,
That I extend my manners; 'tis my breeding.
That gives me this bold show of courtesy.   100

           [*Kissing her.*]

IAGO. Sir, would she give you so much of her lips
 As of her tongue she oft bestows on me,
 You would have enough.
DES.   Alas, she has no speech.
IAGO. In faith, too much;
 I find it still, when I have list to sleep:
 Marry, before your ladyship, I grant,
 She puts her tongue a little in her heart,

And chides with thinking.

EMIL.   You have little cause to say so.

IAGO.   Come on, come on; you are pictures out of doors,   110
Bells in your parlours, wild-cats in your kitchens,
Saints in your injuries, devils being offended,
Players in your housewifery, and housewives° in your beds.

DES.   O, fie upon thee, slanderer!

IAGO.   Nay, it is true, or else I am a Turk:
You rise to play and go to bed to work.

EMIL.   You shall not write my praise.

IAGO.   No, let me not.

DES.   What wouldst thou write of me, if thou shouldst praise me?

IAGO.   O gentle lady, do not put me to 't;
For I am nothing, if not critical.°   120

DES.   Come on, assay. There's one gone to the harbour?

IAGO.   Ay, madam.

DES.   I am not merry; but I do beguile
The thing I am, by seeming otherwise.
Come, how wouldst thou praise me?

IAGO.   I am about it; but indeed my invention
Comes from my pate as birdlime° does from frieze;°
It plucks out brains and all: but my Muse labours,
And thus she is deliver'd.
If she be fair and wise, fairness and wit,   130
The one's for use, the other useth it.

DES.   Well praised! How if she be black and witty?

IAGO.   If she be black, and thereto have a wit,
She'll find a white° that shall her blackness fit.

DES.   Worse and worse.

EMIL.   How if fair and foolish?

IAGO.   She never yet was foolish that was fair;
For even her folly help'd her to an heir.

DES.   These are old fond° paradoxes to make fools laugh i' the alehouse.
What miserable praise hast thou for her that's foul and foolish?

IAGO.   There's none so foul and foolish thereunto,   1
But does foul pranks which fair and wise ones do.

DES.   O heavy ignorance! thou praisest the worst best. But what praise
couldst thou bestow on a deserving woman indeed, one that, in the
authority of her merit, did justly put on the vouch° of very malice
itself?

---

113. *housewives*, hussies.   120. *critical*, censorious.   127. *birdlime*, sticky substance smeared
on twigs to catch small birds. *frieze*, coarse woolen cloth.   134. *white*, a fair person, with a
wordplay on "wight."   139. *fond*, foolish.   145. *put on the vouch*, compel the approval.

IAGO.   She that was ever fair and never proud,
Had tongue at will and yet was never loud,
Never lack'd gold and yet went never gay,
Fled from her wish and yet said 'Now I may,'   150
She that being ang'red, her revenge being nigh,
Bade her wrong stay and her displeasure fly,
She that in wisdom never was so frail
To change the cod's head for the salmon's tail,°
She that could think and ne'er disclose her mind,
See suitors following and not look behind,
She was a wight, if ever such wight were,—
DES.   To do what?
IAGO.   To suckle fools and chronicle small beer.°
DES.   O most lame and impotent conclusion! Do not learn of him, Emilia,
though he be thy husband. How say you, Cassio? is he not a most
profane and liberal° counsellor?   162
CAS.   He speaks home,° madam: you may relish him more in the soldier
than in the scholar.
IAGO.   [*Aside*] He takes her by the palm: ay, well said, whisper: with as
little a web as this will I ensnare as great a fly as Cassio. Ay, smile
upon her, do; I will gyve° thee in thine own courtship.° You say true;
'tis so, indeed: if such tricks as these strip you out of your lieutenantry,
it had been better you had not kissed your three fingers° so oft,
which now again you are most apt to play the sir° in. Very good;
well kissed! an excellent courtesy! 'tis so, indeed. Yet again your
fingers to your lips? would they were clyster-pipes° for your sake!
[*Trumpet within.*] The Moor! I know his trumpet.   173
CAS.   'Tis truly so.
DES.   Let's meet him and receive him.
CAS.   Lo, where he comes!

Enter OTHELLO and ATTENDANTS.

OTH.   O my fair warrior!
DES.   My dear Othello!
OTH.   It gives me wonder great as my content
To see you here before me. O my soul's joy!
If after every tempest come such calms,   180
May the winds blow till they have waken'd death!
And let the labouring bark climb hills of seas

---

154. *To change . . . tail*, to exchange a delicacy for mere refuse.   159. *chronical small beer*,
keep petty household accounts.   162. *liberal*, licentious.   163. *speaks home*, i.e., without
reserve.   167. *gyve*, fetter, shackle. *courtship*, courtesy.   169. *kissed your three fingers*. He
kisses his own hand as a token of reverence.   170. *the sir*, i.e., the fine gentleman.   172.
clyster-pipes, tubes used for enemas.

Olympus-high and duck again as low
As hell's from heaven! If it were now to die,
'Twere now to be most happy; for, I fear,
My soul hath her content so absolute
That not another comfort like to this
Succeeds in unknown fate.

DES.　　　　　　　　　　The heavens forbid
But that our loves and comforts should increase,
Even as our days do grow!

OTH.　　　　　　　　　　Amen to that, sweet powers!　　　　190
I cannot speak enough of this content;
It stops me here; it is too much of joy:
And this, and this, the greatest discords be　　　[*Kissing her.*]
That e'er our hearts shall make!

IAGO.　　　　　　　　　　[*Aside*] O, you are well tun'd now!
But I'll set down the pegs° that make this music,
As honest as I am.

OTH.　　　　　　　Come, let us to the castle.
News, friends; our wars are done, the Turks are drown'd.
How does my old acquaintance of this isle?
Honey, you shall be well desir'd in Cyprus;
I have found great love amongst them. O my sweet,　　　20
I prattle out of fashion, and I dote
In mine own comforts. I prithee, good Iago,
Go to the bay and disembark my coffers:
Bring thou the master to the citadel;
He is a good one, and his worthiness
Does challenge much respect. Come, Desdemona,
Once more, well met at Cyprus.

Exeunt OTHELLO *and* DESDEMONA *[and all but* IAGO *and* RODERIGO*].*

IAGO.　[*To an* ATTENDANT] Do thou meet me presently at the harbour.
[*To* ROD.] Come hither. If thou be'st valiant,—as, they say, base men
being in love have then a nobility in their natures more than is native
to them,—list me. The lieutenant tonight watches on the court of
guard:°—first, I must tell thee this—Desdemona is directly in love
with him.　　　　　　　　　　　　　　　　　　　　　　　　　2

ROD.　With him! why, 'tis not possible.

IAGO.　Lay thy finger thus, and let thy soul be instructed. Mark me with
what violence she first loved the Moor, but for bragging and telling
her fantastical lies: and will she love him still for prating? let not thy
discreet heart think it. Her eye must be fed; and what delight shall

195. *set down the pegs,* lower the pitch of the strings, i.e., disturb the harmony.
212. *court of guard,* guardhouse.

she have to look on the devil? When the blood is made dull with the act of sport, there should be, again to inflame it and to give satiety a fresh appetite, loveliness in favour, sympathy° in years, manners and beauties; all which the Moor is defective in: now, for want of these required conveniences, her delicate tenderness will find itself abused, begin to heave the gorge, disrelish and abhor the Moor; very nature will instruct her in it and compel her to some second choice. Now, sir, this granted,—as it is a most pregnant and unforced position—who stands so eminent in the degree of this fortune as Cassio does? a knave very voluble; no further conscionable° than in putting on the mere form of civil and humane seeming, for the better compassing of his salt° and most hidden loose affection? why, none; why, none: a slipper° and subtle knave, a finder of occasions, that has an eye can stamp and counterfeit advantages, though true advantage never present itself; a devilish knave. Besides, the knave is handsome, young, and hath all those requisites in him that folly and green minds look after: a pestilent complete knave; and the woman hath found him already.   236

Rod.   I cannot believe that in her; she's full of most blessed condition.

Iago.   Blessed fig's-end! the wine she drinks is made of grapes: if she had been blessed, she would never have loved the Moor. Blessed pudding! Didst thou not see her paddle with the palm of his hand? didst not mark that?   241

Rod.   Yes, that I did; but that was but courtesy.

Iago.   Lechery, by this hand; an index and obscure prologue to the history of lust and foul thoughts. They met so near with their lips that their breaths embraced together. Villanous thoughts, Roderigo! when these mutualities so marshal the way, hard at hand comes the master and main exercise, the incorporate conclusion, Pish! But, sir, be you ruled by me: I have brought you from Venice. Watch you to-night; for the command, I'll lay't upon you. Cassio knows you not. I'll not be far from you: do you find some occasion to anger Cassio, either by speaking too loud, or tainting° his discipline; or from what other course you please, which the time shall more favourably minister.   253

Rod.   Well.

Iago.   Sir, he is rash and very sudden in choler, and haply may strike at you: provoke him, that he may; for even out of that will I cause these of Cyprus to mutiny; whose qualification° shall come into no true taste again but by the displanting of Cassio. So shall you have a shorter journey to your desires by the means I shall then have to

---

228. *conscionable*, conscientious.   230. *salt*, licentious.   231. *slipper*, slippery.   251. *tainting*, disparaging.   257. *qualification*, appeasement.

prefer them; and the impediment most profitably removed, without
the which there were no expectation of our prosperity.   261

Rod.   I will do this, if I can bring it to any opportunity.

Iago.   I warrant thee. Meet me by and by° at the citadel: I must fetch
his necessaries ashore. Farewell.

Exit.

Rod.   Adieu.

Iago.   That Cassio loves her, I do well believe 't;
That she loves him, 'tis apt° and of great credit:°
The Moor, howbeit that I endure him not,
Is of a constant, loving, noble nature,
And I dare think he'll prove to Desdemona   270
A most dear husband. Now, I do love her too;
Not out of absolute lust, though peradventure
I stand accountant for as great a sin,
But partly led to diet my revenge,
For that I do suspect the lusty Moor
Hath leap'd into my seat; the thought whereof
Doth, like a poisonous mineral, gnaw my inwards;
And nothing can or shall content my soul
Till I am even'd with him, wife for wife,
Or failing so, yet that I put the Moor   28
At least into a jealousy so strong
That judgement cannot cure. Which thing to do,
If this poor trash° of Venice, whom I trash°
For his quick hunting, stand the putting on,°
I'll have our Michael Cassio on the hip,°
Abuse him to the Moor in the rank garb—
For I fear Cassio with my night-cap too—
Make the Moor thank me, love me and reward me,
For making him egregiously an ass
And practising upon hs peace and quiet   2
Even to madness. 'Tis here, but yet confus'd:
Knavery's plain face is never seen till us'd.

Exit.

---

263. *by and by,* immediately.   267. *apt,* probable. *credit,* credibility.   283. *trash,* worthless
thing (Roderigo). *trash,* hold in check.   284. *putting on,* incitement to quarrel.   285. *on
the hip,* at my mercy (wrestling term).

Scene II. [*A street.*]

Enter OTHELLO'S HERALD with a proclamation.

HER. It is Othello's pleasure, our noble and valiant general, that, upon
certain tidings now arrived, importing the mere perdition° of the
Turkish fleet, every man put himself into triumph; some to dance,
some to make bonfires, each man to what sport and revels his
addiction leads him: for, besides these beneficial news, it is the
celebration of his nuptial. So much was his pleasure should be
proclaimed. All offices° are open, and there is full liberty of feasting
from this present hour of five till the bell have told eleven. Heaven
bless the isle of Cyprus and our noble general Othello!

Exit.

[**Scene III.** *A hall in the castle.*]

Enter OTHELLO, DESDEMONA, CASSIO, and ATTENDANTS.

OTH. Good Michael, look you to the guard to-night:
Let's teach ourselves that honourable stop,°
Not to outsport discretion.
CAS. Iago hath direction what to do;
But notwithstanding, with my personal eye
Will I look to 't.
OTH.   Iago is most honest.
Michael, good night: to-morrow with your earliest
Let me have speech with you. [*To DESDEMONA*] Come, my dear love,
The purchase made, the fruits are to ensue;
That profit 's yet to come 'tween me and you.   10
Good night.

Exit [*OTHELLO, with DESDEMONA and ATTENDANTS*].

Enter IAGO.

CAS. Welcome, Iago; we must to the watch.
IAGO. Not this hour, lieutenant; 'tis not yet ten o' the clock. Our general
cast° us thus early for the love of his Desdemona; who let us not
therefore blame: he hath not yet made wanton the night with her;
and she is sport for Jove.
CAS. She's a most exquisite lady.
IAGO. And, I'll warrant her, full of game.

---

2. *mere perdition*, complete destruction.   7. *offices*, rooms where food and drink were
kept.   2. *stop*, restraint.   14. *cast*, dismissed.

CAS.   Indeed, she's a most fresh and delicate creature.

IAGO.   What an eye she has! methinks it sounds a parley of provocation.

CAS.   An inviting eye; and yet methinks right modest.   21

IAGO.   And when she speaks, is it not an alarum to love?

CAS.   She is indeed perfection.

IAGO.   Well, happiness to their sheets! Come, lieutenant, I have a stoup°
of wine; and here without are a brace of Cyprus gallants that would
fain have a measure to the health of black Othello.

CAS.   Not to-night, good Iago: I have very poor and unhappy brains for
drinking: I could well wish courtesy would invent some other custom
of entertainment.

IAGO.   O, they are our friends; but one cup: I'll drink for you.   30

CAS.   I have drunk but one cup to-night, and that was craftily qualified°
too, and, behold, what innovation° it makes here:° I am unfortunate
in the infirmity, and dare not task my weakness with any more.

IAGO.   What, man! 'tis a night of revels: the gallants desire it.

CAS.   Where are they?

IAGO.   Here at the door; I pray you, call them in.

CAS.   I'll do 't; but it dislikes me.

                                                                    Exit.

IAGO.   If I can fasten but one cup upon him,
With that which he hath drunk to-night already,
He'll be as full of quarrel and offence   4
As my young mistress' dog. Now, my sick fool Roderigo,
Whom love hath turn'd almost the wrong side out,
To Desdemona hath to-night carous'd
Potations pottle-deep;° and he's to watch:
Three lads of Cyprus, noble swelling spirits,
That hold their honours in a wary distance,°
The very elements° of this warlike isle,
Have I to-night fluster'd with flowing cups,
And they watch° too. Now, 'mongst this flock of drunkards,
Am I to put our Cassio in some action
That may offend the isle.—But here they come:

Enter CASSIO, MONTANO, *and* GENTLEMEN *[; servants following with wine].*

If consequence do but approve° my dream,
My boat sail freely, both with wind and stream.

CAS.   'Fore God, they have given me a rouse° already.

---

24. *stoup,* measure of liquor, two quarts.   31. *qualified,* diluted.   32. *innovation,* disturbance. *here,* i.e., in Cassio's head.   44. *pottle-deep,* to the bottom of the tankard.   46. *hold
. . . distance,* i.e. are extremely sensitive of their honor.   47. *very elements,* true representatives.   49. *watch,* are members of the guard.   52. *approve,* confirm.   54. *rouse,* full
draft of liquor.

MON.   Good faith, a little one; not past a pint, as I am a soldier.
IAGO.   Some wine, ho!
      [*Sings*] And let me the canakin° clink, clink;
      And let me the canakin clink:
         A soldier's a man;
         A life's but a span;   60
      Why, then, let a soldier drink.
      Some wine, boys!
CAS.   'Fore God, an excellent song.
IAGO.   I learned it in England, where, indeed, they are most potent in
    potting: your Dane, your German, and your swag-bellied Hol-
    lander—Drink, ho!—are nothing to your English.
CAS.   Is your Englishman so expert in his drinking?
IAGO.   Why, he drinks you, with facility, your Dane dead drunk; he
    sweats not to overthrow your Almain;° he gives your Hollander a
    vomit, ere the next pottle can be filled.   70
CAS.   To the health of our general!
MON.   I am for it, lieutenant; and I'll do you justice.°
IAGO.   O sweet England [*Sings.*]
      King Stephen was a worthy peer,
         His breeches cost him but a crown;
      He held them sixpence all too dear,
         With that he call'd the tailor lown.°

      He was a wight of high renown,
         And thou art but of low degree:
      Tis pride that pulls the country down;   80
         Then take thine auld cloak about thee.
      Some wine, ho!
CAS.   Why, this is a more exquisite song than the other.
IAGO.   Will you hear 't again?
CAS.   No; for I hold him to be unworthy of his place that does those
    things. Well, God's above all; and there be souls must be saved, and
    there be souls must not be saved.
IAGO.   It's true, good lieutenant.
CAS.   For mine own part,—no offence to the general, nor any man of
    quality,—I hope to be saved.   90
IAGO.   And so do I too, lieutenant.
CAS.   Ay, but, by your leave, not before me; the lieutenant is to be saved
    before the ancient. Let's have no more of this; let's to our affairs.—

---

57. *canakin,* small drinking vessel.   69. *Almain,* German.   72. *I'll . . . justice,* i.e., drink as
much as you.   77. *lown,* lout, loon.

God forgive us our sins!—Gentlemen, let's look to our business. Do not think, gentlemen, I am drunk: this is my ancient; this is my right hand, and this is my left: I am not drunk now; I can stand well enough, and speak well enough.

ALL.   Excellent well.

CAS.   Why, very well then; you must not think then that I am drunk.

Exit.

MON.   To th' platform, masters; come, let's set the watch.   100

IAGO.   You see this fellow that is gone before;
    He's a soldier fit to stand by Cæsar
    And give direction: and do but see his vice;
    'Tis to his virtue a just equinox,°
    The one as long as th' other: 'tis pity of him.
    I fear the trust Othello puts him in,
    On some odd time of his infirmity,
    Will shake this island.

MON.   But is he often thus?

IAGO.   'Tis evermore the prologue to his sleep:
    He'll watch the horologe° a double set,°   11
    If drink rock not his cradle.

MON.   It were well
    The general were put in mind of it.
    Perhaps he sees it not; or his good nature
    Prizes the virtue that appears in Cassio,
    And looks not on his evils: is not this true?

Enter RODERIGO.

IAGO.   [*Aside to him*] How now. Roderigo!
    I pray you, after the lieutenant; go.

[*Exit RODERIGO.*]

MON.   And 'tis great pity that the noble Moor
    Should hazard such a place as his own second
    With one of an ingraft° infirmity: 1
    It were an honest action to say
    So to the Moor.

IAGO.   Not I, for this fair island:
    I do love Cassio well; and would do much
    To cure him of this evil—But, hark! what noise?

[*Cry within:* 'Help! Help!']

104. *equinox,* equal length of days and nights; used figuratively to mean "counterpart."   110.
horologe, clock. *double set,* twice around.   120. *ingraft,* ingrafted, inveterate.

Enter CASSIO, *pursuing* RODERIGO.

CAS. 'Zounds, you rogue! you rascal!
MON.   What's the matter, lieutenant?
CAS. A knave teach me my duty!
    I'll beat the knave into a twiggen° bottle.
ROD. Beat me!
CAS. Dost thou prate, rogue?

[*Striking* RODERIGO.]

MON.   Nay, good lieutenant;

[*Staying him.*]

    I pray you, sir, hold your hand.
CAS.   Let me go, sir,   130
    Or I'll knock you o'er the mazzard.°
MON.   Come, come, you're drunk.
CAS. Drunk!

[*They fight.*]

IAGO. [*Aside to* RODERIGO] Away, I say; go out and cry a mutiny.

[*Exit* RODERIGO.]

    Nay, good lieutenant,—God's will, gentlemen;—
    Help, ho!—Lieutenant,—sir,—Montano,—sir;—
    Help, masters!—Here's a goodly watch indeed!

[*Bells rings.*]

    Who's that which rings the bell?—Diablo,° ho!
    The town will rise:° God's will, lieutenant, hold!
    You'll be asham'd for ever.

Enter OTHELLO *and* ATTENDANTS.

OTH.   What is the matter here?
MON. 'Zounds, I bleed still; I am hurt to th' death.   140
    He dies!

[*Thrusts at* CASSIO.]

OTH. Hold, for your lives!
IAGO. Hold, ho! Lieutenant,—sir,—Montano,—gentlemen,—
    Have you forgot all sense of place and duty?
    Hold! the general speaks to you; hold, for shame!

127. *twiggen*, covered with woven twigs.   131. *mazzard*. head.   137. *Diablo*, the
Devil.   138. *rise*, grow riotous.

OTH.   Why, how now, ho! from whence ariseth this?
        Are we turn'd Turks,° and to ourselves do that
        Which heaven hath forbid the Ottomites?
        For Christian shame, put by this barbarous brawl:
        He that stirs next to carve for° his own rage   150
        Holds his soul light; he dies upon his motion.
        Silence that dreadful bell: it frights the isle
        From her propriety.° What is the matter, masters?
        Honest Iago, that looks dead with grieving,
        Speak, who began this? on thy love, I charge thee.
IAGO.   I do not know: friends all but now, even now,
        In quarter,° and in terms like bride and groom
        Devesting them for bed; and then, but now—
        As if some planet had unwitted men—
        Swords out, and tilting one at other's breast,   160
        In opposition bloody. I cannot speak
        Any beginning to this peevish odds;°
        And would in action glorious I had lost
        Those legs that brought me to a part of it!
OTH.   How comes it, Michael, you are thus forgot?
CAS.   I pray you, pardon me; I cannot speak.
OTH.   Worthy Montano, you were wont be civil;
        The gravity and stillness of your youth
        The world hath noted, and your name is great
        In mouths of wisest censure:° what's the matter,   17
        That you unlace° your reputation thus
        And spend your rich opinion for the name
        Of a night-brawler? give me answer to it.
MON.   Worthy Othello, I am hurt to danger:
        Your officer, Iago, can inform you,—
        While I spare speech, which something now offends me,—
        Of all that I do know: nor know I aught
        By me that's said or done amiss this night;
        Unless self-charity be sometimes a vice,
        And to defend ourselves it be a sin   1
        When violence assails us.
OTH.   Now, by heaven,
        My blood begins my safer guides to rule;
        And passion, having my best judgment collied,°
        Assays to lead the way: if I once stir,

---

147. *turn'd Turks*, changed completely for the worse; proverbial.   150. *carve for*, indulge.   153. *propriety*, proper state or condition.   157. *In quarter*, on terms.   162. *peevish odds*, childish quarrel.   170. *censure*, judgment.   171. *unlace*, degrade.   183. *collied*, darkened.

Or do but lift this arm, the best of you
Shall sink in my rebuke. Give me to know
How this foul rout began, who set it on;
And he that is approv'd in° this offence,
Though he had twinn'd with me, both at a birth,
Shall lose me. What! in a town of war,   190
Yet wild, the people's hearts brimful of fear,
To manage private and domestic quarrel,
In night, and on the court and guard° of safety!
'Tis monstrous. Iago, who began 't?
MON.   If partially affin'd,° or leagu'd in office,
Thou dost deliver more or less than truth,
Thou art no soldier.
IAGO.   Touch me not so near:
I had rather have this tongue cut from my mouth
Than it should do offence to Michael Cassio;
Yet, I persuade myself to speak the truth   200
Shall nothing wrong him. Thus it is, general.
Montano and myself being in speech,
There comes a fellow crying out for help;
And Cassio following him with determin'd sword,
To execute° upon him. Sir, this gentleman
Steps in to Cassio, and entreats his pause:
Myself the crying fellow did pursue,
Lest by his clamour—as it so fell out—
The town might fall in fright: he, swift of foot,
Outran my purpose; and I return'd the rather   210
For that I heard the clink and fall of swords,
And Cassio high in oath; which till to-night
I ne'er might say before. When I came back—
For this was brief—I found them close together,
At blow and thrust; even as again they were
When you yourself did part them.
More of this matter cannot I report:
But men are men; the best sometimes forget:
Though Cassio did some little wrong to him,
As men in rage strike those that wish them best,   220
Yet surely Cassio, I believe, receiv'd
From him that fled some strange indignity,
Which patience could not pass.
OTH.   I know, Iago,

---

188. *approv'd in*, found guilty of.   193. *court and guard*, spot and guarding place, i.e., the
main guardhouse.   195. *affin'd*, bound by a tie.   205. *execute*, give effect to (his anger).

Thy honesty and love doth mince this matter,
Making it light to Cassio. Cassio, I love thee;
But never more be officer of mine.

Enter DESDEMONA, *attended.*

Look, if my gentle love be not rais'd up!
I'll make thee an example.
DES.   What's the matter?
OTH.   All's well now, sweeting; come away to bed.
Sir, for your hurts, myself will be your surgeon: 230
Lead him off.

                                    [*To* MONTANO, *who is led off.*]

Iago, look with care about the town,
And silence those whom this vile brawl distracted.
Come, Desdemona: 'tis the soldiers' life
To have their balmy slumbers wak'd with strife.

                              Exit [*with all but* IAGO *and* CASSIO].

IAGO.   What, are you hurt, lieutenant?
CAS.   Ay, past all surgery.
IAGO.   Marry, God forbid!
CAS.   Reputation, reputation, reputation! O, I have lost my reputation! I
have lost the immortal part of myself, and what remains is bestial.
My reputation, Iago, my reputation!   24
IAGO.   As I am an honest man, I thought you had received some bodily
wound; there is more sense in that than in reputation. Reputation is
an idle and most false imposition; oft got without merit, and lost
without deserving: you have lost no reputation at all, unless you
repute yourself such a loser. What, man! there are ways to recover
the general again: you are but now cast in his mood, a punishment
more in policy than in malice; even so as one would beat his offenceless
dog to affright an imperious lion: sue to him again, and he's yours.
CAS.   I will rather sue to be despised than to deceive so good a commander
with so slight, so drunken, and so indiscreet an officer. Drunk? and
speak parrot?° and squabble? swagger? swear? and discourse fustian°
with one's own shadow? O thou invisible spirit of wine, if thou hast
no name to be known by, let us call thee devil!   2
IAGO.   What was he that you followed with your sword? What had he
done to you?
CAS.   I know not.
IAGO.   Is't possible?
CAS.   I remember a mass of things, but nothing distinctly; a quarrel, but

252. *speak parrot,* talk nonsense. *discourse fustian,* talk nonsense.

nothing wherefore. O God, that men should put an enemy in their mouths to steal away their brains! that we should, with joy, pleasance, revel and applause, transform ourselves into beasts!   262

IAGO.   Why, but you are now well enough: how came you thus recovered?

CAS.   It hath pleased the devil drunkenness to give place to the devil wrath: one unperfectness° shows me another, to make me frankly despise myself.

IAGO.   Come, you are too severe a moraler: as the time, the place, and the condition of this country stands, I could heartily wish this had not befallen; but, since it is as it is, mend it for your own good.   269

CAS.   I will ask him for my place again; he shall tell me I am a drunkard! Had I as many mouths as Hydra,° such an answer would stop them all. To be now a sensible man, by and by a fool, and presently a beast! O strange! Every inordinate cup is unblessed and the ingredient is a devil.

IAGO.   Come, come, good wine is a good familiar creature, if it be well used: exclaim no more against it. And, good lieutenant, I think you think I love you.   277

CAS.   I have well approved° it, sir. I drunk!

IAGO.   You or any man living may be drunk at a time, man. I'll tell you what you shall do. Our general's wife is now the general: I may say so in this respect, for that he hath devoted and given up himself to the contemplation, mark, and denotement° of her parts and graces: confess yourself freely to her; importune her help to put you in your place again: she is of so free, so kind, so apt, so blessed a disposition, she holds it a vice in her goodness not to do more than she is requested: this broken joint between you and her husband entreat her to splinter;° and, my fortunes against any lay° worth naming, this crack of your love shall grow stronger than it was before.

CAS.   You advise me well.

IAGO.   I protest, in the sincerity of love and honest kindness.   290

CAS.   I think it freely; and betimes in the morning I will beseech the virtuous Desdemona to undertake for me: I am desperate of my fortunes if they check° me here.

IAGO.   You are in the right. Good night, lieutenant; I must to the watch.

CAS.   Good night, honest Iago.

Exit CASSIO.

IAGO.   And what's he then that says I play the villain?
        When this advice is free I give and honest,

---

265. *unperfectness,* imperfection.   271. *Hydra,* a monster with many heads, slain by Hercules as the second of his twleve labors.   278. *approved,* proved.   282. *denotement,* observation.   287. *splinter,* bind with splints. *lay,* stake, wager.   293. *check,* repulse.

Probal° to thinking and indeed the course
To win the Moor again? For 'tis most easy
Th' inclining° Desdemona to subdue°   300
In any honest suit: she's fram'd as fruitful
As the free elements. And then for her
To win the Moor—were't to renounce his baptism,
All seals and symbols of redeemed sin,
His soul is so enfetter'd to her love,
That she may make, unmake, do what she list,
Even as her appetitie shall play the god
With his weak function. How am I then a villain
To counsel Cassio to this parallel° course,
Directly to his good? Divinity of hell!   31
When devils will the blackest sins put on,°
They do suggest° at first with heavenly shows,
As I do now: for whiles this honest fool
Plies Desdemona to repair his fortunes
And she for him pleads strongly to the Moor,
I'll pour this pestilence into his ear,
That she repeals him° for her body's lust;
And by how much she strives to do him good,
She shall undo her credit with the Moor.
So will I turn her virtue into pitch,   3
And out of her own goodness make the net
That shall enmesh them all.

                                        Enter RODERIGO.

                    How now, Roderigo!
ROD.   I do follow here in the chase, not like a hound that hunts, but one
       that fills up the cry.° My money is almost spent; I have been to-night
       exceedingly well cudgelled; and I think the issue will be, I shall have
       so much experience for my pains, and so, with no money at all and
       a little more wit, return again to Venice.
IAGO.   How poor are they that have not patience!
       What wound did ever heal but by degrees?
       Thou know'st we work by wit, and not by witchcraft;
       And wit depends on dilatory time.
       Does't not go well? Cassio hath beaten thee,
       And thou, by that small hurt, hast cashier'd° Cassio:
       Though other things grow fair against the sun,

---

298. *Probal*, probable.   300. *inclining*, favorably disposed. *subdue*, persuade.   309. *parallel*,
probably, corresponding to his best interest.   311. *put on*, further.   312. *suggest*,
tempt.   317. *repeals him*, i.e., attempts to get him restored.   324. *cry*, pack.   333.
cashier'd, dismissed from service.

Yet fruits that blossom first will first be ripe:
Content thyself awhile. By th' mass, 'tis morning;
Pleasure and action make the hours seem short.
Retire thee; go where thou art billeted:
Away, I say; thou shalt know more hereafter:
Nay, get thee gone.

Exit RODERIGO.

Two things are to be done: 340
My wife must move for Cassio to her mistress;
I'll set her on;
Myself the while to draw the Moor apart,
And bring him jump° when he may Cassio find
Soliciting his wife: ay, that's the way:
Dull not device by coldness and delay.

Exit.

ACT III.

Scene I. [*Before the castle.*]

Enter CASSIO *[and]* MUSICIANS.

CAS. Masters, play here; I will content° your pains;
    Something that's brief; and bid 'Good morrow, general.'

[*They play.*]

[*Enter*] CLOWN.

CLO. Why, masters, have your instruments been in Naples, that they
    speak i' the nose° thus?
FIRST MUS. How, sir, how!
CLO. Are these, I pray you, wind-instruments?
FIRST MUS. Ay, marry, are they, sir.
CLO. O, thereby hangs a tail.
FIRST MUS. Whereby hangs a tale,° sir?   9
CLO. Marry, sir, by many a wind-instrument that I know. But, masters,
    here's money for you: and the general so likes your music, that he
    desires you, for love's sake, to make no more noise with it.
FIRST MUS. Well, sir, we will not.

---

344. *jump,* precisely.   1. *content,* reward.   4. *speak i' the nose,* i.e., like Neapolitans, who spoke a nasal dialect (with a joke on syphilis, which attacks the nose).   9. *tale,* pun on *tail,* a wind instrument of sorts.

CLO. If you have any music that may not be heard, to 't again: but, as they say, to hear music the general does not greatly care.

FIRST MUS. We have none such, sir.

CLO. Then put up your pipes in your bag, for I'll away: go; vanish into air; away!

Exeunt MUSICIANS.

CAS. Dost thou hear, my honest friend?

CLO. No, I hear not your honest friend; I hear you.

CAS. Prithee, keep up thy quillets. There 's a poor piece of gold for thee: if the gentlewoman that attends the general's wife be stirring, tell her there's one Cassio entreats her a little favour of speech: wilt thou do this?

CLO. She is stirring, sir: if she will stir hither, I shall seem to notify unto her.

CAS. Do, good my friend.

Exit CLOWN.

Enter IAGO.

In happy time, Iago.

IAGO. You have not been a-bed, then?

CAS. Why, no; the day had broke
Before we parted. I have made bold, Iago,
To send in to your wife: my suit to her
Is, that she will to virtuous Desdemona
Procure me some access.

IAGO.   I'll send her to you presently;
And I'll devise a mean to draw the Moor
Out of the way, that your converse and business
May be more free.

CAS. I humbly thank you for 't.

Exit [IAGO].

I never knew
A Florentine more kind and honest.

Enter EMILIA.

EMIL. Good morrow, good lieutenant: I am sorry
For your displeasure; but all will sure be well.
The general and his wife are talking of it;
And she speaks for you stoutly: the Moor replies,
That he you hurt is of great fame in Cyprus
And great affinity° and that in wholesome wisdom

---

44. *affinity*, kindred, family connection.

He might not but refuse you, but he protests he loves you
And needs no other suitor but his likings
To take the safest occasion by the front°
To bring you in again.

Cas.   Yet, I beseech you,
If you think fit, or that it may be done,
Give me advantage of some brief discourse   50
With Desdemona alone.

Emil.   Pray you, come in:
I will bestow you where you shall have time
To speak your bosom freely.

Cas.   I am much bound to you.

                                                    [*Exeunt.*]

Scene II. [*A room in the castle.*]

Enter OTHELLO, IAGO, and GENTLEMEN.

Oth.   These letters give, Iago, to the pilot;
And by him do my duties to the senate:
That done, I will be walking on the works;°
Repair there to me.

Iago.   Well, my good lord, I'll do 't.

Oth.   This fortification, gentlemen, shall we see 't?

Gent.   We'll wait upon your lordship.

                                                    Exeunt.

Scene III. [*The garden of the castle.*]

Enter DESDEMONA, CASSIO, and EMILIA.

Des.   Be thou assur'd, good Cassio, I will do
All my abilities in thy behalf.

Emil.   Good madam, do: I warrant it grieves my husband,
As if the case were his.

Des.   O, that's an honest fellow. Do not doubt, Cassio,
But I will have my lord and you again
As friendly as you were.

Cas.   Bounteous madam,
Whatever shall become of Michael Cassio,
He's never any thing but your true servant.

Des.   I know't; I thank you. You do love my lord: 10
You have known him long; and be you well assur'd

---

47. *by the front*, i.e., by the forelock.   3. *works*, earthworks, fortifications.

> He shall in strangeness° stand no farther off
> Than in a politic distance.

CAS.   Ay, but, lady,
> That policy may either last so long,
> Or feed upon such nice and waterish diet,
> Or breed itself so out of circumstance,°
> That, I being absent and my place supplied,
> My general will forget my love and service.

DES.   Do not doubt° that; before Emilia here
> I give thee warrant of thy place: assure thee,
> If I do vow a friendship, I'll perform it
> To the last article: my lord shall never rest;
> I'll watch him tame° and talk him out of patience;
> His bed shall seem a school, his board a shrift;°
> I'll intermingle every thing he does
> With Cassio's suit: therefore be merry, Cassio;
> For thy solicitor shall rather die
> Than give thy cause away.°

Enter OTHELLO *and* IAGO *[at a distance].*

EMIL.   Madam, here comes my lord.

CAS.   Madam, I'll take my leave.

DES.   Why, stay, and hear me speak.

CAS.   Madam, not now: I am very ill at ease,
> Unfit for mine own purposes.

DES.   Well, do your discretion.

Exit CASSIO.

IAGO.   Ha! I like not that.

OTH.   What dost thou say?

IAGO.   Nothing, my lord: or if—I know not what.

OTH.   Was not that Cassio parted from my wife?

IAGO.   Cassio, my lord! No, sure, I cannot think it,
> That he would steal away so guilty-like,
> Seeing you coming.

OTH.   I do believe 'twas he.

DES.   How now, my lord!
> I have been talking with a suitor here,
> A man that languishes in your displeasure.

OTH.   Who is 't you mean?

---

12. *strangeness*, distant behavior.   16. *breed . . . circumstance*, increase itself so on account of accidents.   19. *doubt*, fear.   23. *watch him tame*, tame him by keeping him from sleeping (a term from falconry).   24. *shrift*, confessional.   28. *away*, up.

DES.   Why, your lieutenant, Cassio. Good my lord,
    If I have any grace or power to move you,
    His present reconciliation take;
    For if he be not one that truly loves you,
    That errs in ignorance and not in cunning,
    I have no judgement in an honest face: 50
    I prithee, call him back.
OTH.   Went he hence now?
DES.   Ay, sooth; so humbled
    That he hath left part of his grief with me.
    To suffer with him. Good love, call him back.
OTH.   Not now, sweet Desdemon; some other time.
DES.   But shall't be shortly?
OTH.   The sooner, sweet, for you.
DES.   Shall't be to-night at supper?
OTH.   No, not to-night.
DES.   To-morrow dinner, then?
OTH.   I shall not dine at home;
    I meet the captains at the citadel.
DES.   Why, then, to-morrow night; or Tuesday morn;   60
    On Tuesday noon, or night; on Wednesday morn:
    I prithee, name the time, but let it not
    Exceed three days: in faith, he's penitent;
    And yet his trespass, in our common reason°—
    Save that, they say, the wars must make examples
    Out of their best—is not almost a fault
    T' incur a private check. When shall he come?
    Tell me, Othello: I wonder in my soul,
    What you would ask me, that I should deny,
    Or stand so mamm'ring° on. What! Michael Cassio,   70
    That came a-wooing with you, and so many a time,
    When I have spoke of you dispraisingly,
    Hath ta'en your part; to have so much to do
    To bring him in! Trust me, I could do much,—
OTH.   Prithee, no more: let him come when he will;
    I will deny thee nothing.
DES.   Why, this is not a boon;
    'Tis as I should entreat you wear your gloves,
    Or feed on nourishing dishes, or keep you warm,
    Or sue to you to do a peculiar profit
    To your own person: nay, when I have a suit   80
    Wherein I mean to touch your love indeed,

---

64. *common reason*, everyday judgments.   70. *mamm'ring on*, wavering.

It shall be full of poise° and difficult weight
And fearful to be granted.

OTH.   I will deny thee nothing:
Whereon, I do beseech thee, grant me this,
To leave me but a little to myself.

DES.   Shall I deny you? no: farewell, my lord.

OTH.   Farewell, my Desdemona: I'll come to thee straight.

DES.   Emilia, come. Be as your fancies teach you;
Whate'er you be, I am obedient.

Exit [with EMILIA].

OTH.   Excellent wretch!° Perdition catch my soul,
But I do love thee! and when I love thee not,
Chaos is come again.

IAGO.   My noble lord,—

OTH.   What doest thou say, Iago?

IAGO.   Did Michael Cassio, when you woo'd my lady,
Know of your love?

OTH.   He did, from first to last: why dost thou ask?

IAGO.   But for a satisfaction of my thought;
No further harm.

OTH.   Why of thy thought, Iago?

IAGO.   I did not think he had been acquainted with her.

OTH.   O, yes; and went between us very oft.

IAGO.   Indeed!

OTH.   Indeed! ay, indeed: discern'st thou aught in that?
Is he not honest?

IAGO.   Honest, my lord!

OTH.   Honest! ay, honest.

IAGO.   My lord, for aught I know.

OTH.   What dost thou think?

IAGO.   Think, my lord!

OTH.   Think, my lord!
By heaven, he echoes me,
As if there were some monster in his thought
Too hideous to be shown. Thou dost mean something:
I heard thee say even now, thou lik'st not that,
When Cassio left my wife: what didst not like?
And when I told thee he was of my counsel
In my whole course of wooing, thou criedst 'Indeed!'
And didst contract and purse thy brow together,

---

82. *poise*, weight, heaviness.   90. *wretch*, term of affectionate endearment with a connotation of pity.

As if thou then hadst shut up in thy brain
Some horrible conceit: if thou dost love me,
Show me thy thought.
IAGO.   My lord, you know I love you.
OTH.   I think thou dost;
And, for I know thou 'rt full of love and honesty,
And weigh'st thy words before thou giv'st them breath,
Therefore these stops of thine fright me the more: 120
For such things in a false disloyal knave
Are tricks of custom, but in a man that's just
They're close delations,° working from the heart
That passion cannot rule.
IAGO.   For Michael Cassio,
I dare be sworn I think that he is honest.
OTH.   I think so too.
IAGO.   Men should be what they seem;
Or those that be not, would they might seem none!
OTH.   Certain, men should be what they seem.
IAGO.   Why, then, I think Cassio's an honest man.
OTH.   Nay, yet there's more in this: 130
I prithee, speak to me as to thy thinkings,
As thou dost ruminate, and give thy worst of thoughts
The worst of words.
IAGO.   Good my lord, pardon me:
Though I am bound to every act of duty,
I am not bound to that all slaves are free to.
Utter my thoughts? Why, say they are vile and false;
As where's that palace whereinto foul things
Sometimes intrude not? who has a breast so pure,
But some uncleanly apprehensions
Keep leets° and law-days° and in sessions sit   140
With meditations lawful?
OTH.   Thou dost conspire against thy friend, Iago,
If thou but think'st him wrong'd and mak'st his ear
A stranger to thy thoughts.
IAGO.   I do beseech you—
Though I perchance am vicious° in my guess,
As I confess, it is my nature's plague
To spy into abuses, and oft my jealousy°
Shapes faults that are not—that your wisdom yet,
From one that so imperfectly conceits,°

---

123. *close delations*, secret or involuntary accusations.   140. *Keep leets*, hold courts. *law-days*,
court-days.   145. *vicious*, wrong.   147. *jealousy*, suspicion of evil.   149. *conceits*, judges.

Would take no notice, nor build yourself a trouble 15(
Out of his scattering and unsure observance.
It were not for your quiet nor your good,
Nor for my manhood, honesty, or wisdom,
To let you know my thoughts.

OTH.   What dost thou mean?

IAGO.   Good name in man and woman, dear my lord,
Is the immediate jewel of their souls:
Who steals my purse steals trash; 'tis something, nothing;
'Twas mine, 'tis his, and has been slave to thousands;
But he that filches from me my good name
Robs me of that which not enriches him 1(
And makes me poor indeed.

OTH.   By heaven, I'll know thy thoughts.

IAGO.   You cannot, if my heart were in your hand;
Nor shall not, whilst 'tis in my custody.

OTH.   Ha!

IAGO.   O, beware, my lord, of jealousy;
It is the green-ey'd monster which doth mock
The meat it feeds on: that cuckold lives in bliss
Who, certain of his fate, loves not his wronger;
But, O, what damned minutes tells he o'er
Who dotes, yet doubts, suspects, yet strongly loves!

OTH.   O misery!

IAGO.   Poor and content is rich and rich enough,
But riches fineless° is as poor as winter
To him that ever fears he shall be poor.
Good God, the souls of all my tribe defend
From jealousy!

OTH.   Why, why is this?
Think'st thou I'ld make a life of jealousy,
To follow still the changes of the moon
With fresh suspicions? No; to be once in doubt
Is once to be resolv'd: exchange me for a goat,
When I shall turn the business of my soul
To such exsufflicate and blown° surmises,
Matching thy inference. 'Tis not to make me jealous
To say my wife is fair, feeds well, loves company,
Is free of speech, sings, plays and dances well;
Where virtue is, these are more virtuous:
Nor from mine own weak merits will I draw
The smallest fear or doubt of her revolt;

---

173. *fineless*, boundless.   182. *exsufflicate and blown*, unsubstantial and inflated, flyblown.

For she had eyes, and chose me. No, Iago;
I'll see before I doubt; when I doubt, prove;   190
And on the proof, there is no more but this,—
Away at once with love or jealousy!

IAGO. I am glad of this; for now I shall have reason
To show the love and duty that I bear you
With franker spirit: therefore, as I am bound,
Receive it from me. I speak not yet of proof.
Look to your wife; observe her well with Cassio;
Wear your eye thus, not jealous nor secure:°
I would not have your free and noble nature,
Out of self-bounty,° be abus'd; look to 't: 200
I know our country disposition well;
In Venice they do let heaven see the pranks
They dare not show their husbands; their best conscience
Is not to leave't undone, but keep't unknown.

OTH. Dost thou say so?

IAGO. She did deceive her father, marrying you;
And when she seem'd to shake and fear your looks,
She lov'd them most,

OTH.   And so she did.

IAGO.   Why, go to then;
She that, so young, could give out such a seeming,°
To seel° her father's eyes up close as oak—   210
He thought 'twas witchcraft—but I am much to blame;
I humbly do beseech you of your pardon
For too much loving you.

OTH.   I am bound to thee for ever.

IAGO. I see this hath a little dash'd your spirits.

OTH. Not a jot, not a jot.

IAGO.   I' faith, I fear it has.
I hope you will consider what is spoke
Comes from my love. But I do see y' are mov'd:
I am to pray you not to strain my speech
To grosser issues nor to larger reach°
Than to suspicion.   220

OTH. I will not.

IAGO.   Should you do so, my lord,
My speech should fall into such vile success
As my thoughts aim not at. Cassio's my worthy friend—
My lord, I see y' are mov'd.

---

198. *secure*, free from uneasiness.   200. *self-bounty*, inherent or natural goodness.   209.
seeming, false appearance.   210. *seel*, blind (a term from falconry).   219. *reach*, meaning.

OTH.   No, not much mov'd:
    I do not think but Desdemona's honest.
IAGO.   Long live she so! and long live you to think so!
OTH.   And yet, how nature erring from itself,—
IAGO.   Ay, there's the point: as—to be bold with you—
    Not to affect many proposed matches
    Of her own clime, complexion, and degree,   23
    Whereto we see in all things nature tends—
    Foh! one may smell in such a will° most rank,
    Foul disproportion,° thoughts unnatural.
    But pardon me; I do not in position°
    Distinctly speak of her; though I may fear
    Her will, recoiling to° her better judgement,
    May fall to match you with her country forms°
    And happily repent.°
OTH.   Farewell, farewell:
    If more thou dost perceive, let me know more;
    Set on thy wife to observe: leave me, Iago.   2
IAGO.   [Going] My lord, I take my leave.
OTH.   Why did I marry? This honest creature doubtless
    Sees and knows more, much more, than he unfolds.
IAGO.   [Returning] My Lord, I would I might entreat your honour
    To scan this thing no farther; leave it to time:
    Although 'tis fit that Cassio have his place,
    For, sure, he fills it up with great ability,
    Yet, if you please to hold him off awhile,
    You shall by that perceive him and his means:
    Note, if your lady strain his entertainment°
    With any strong or vehement importunity;
    Much will be seen in that. In the mean time,
    Let me be thought too busy in my fears—
    As worthy cause I have to fear I am—
    And hold her free,° I do beseech your honour.
OTH.   Fear not my government.°
IAGO.   I once more take my leave.

                                                              Exit.

OTH.   This fellow's of exceeding honesty,
    And knows all qualities, with a learned spirit,
    Of human dealings. If I do prove her haggard,°

232. *will,* sensuality.   233. *disproportion,* abnormality.   234. *position,* general argument.   236. *recoiling to,* falling back upon, or recoiling against.   237. *fall ... forms,*
happen to compare you with Venetian norms of handsomeness.   238. *repent,* i.e., of her
marriage.   250. *strain his entertainment,* urge his reinstatement.   255. *hold her free,* regard
her as innocent.   256. *government,* self-control.   260. *haggard,* a wild female duck.

Though that her jesses° were my dear heartstrings,
I'ld whistle her off and let her down the wind,
To prey at fortune.° Haply, for I am black
And have not those soft parts of conversation
That chamberers° have, or for I am declin'd
Into the vale of years,—yet that's not much—
She's gone. I am abus'd: and my relief
Must be to loathe her. O curse of marriage,
That we can call these delicate creatures ours,
And not their appetites! I had rather be a toad,   270
And live upon the vapour of a dungeon,
Than keep a corner in the thing I love
For others' uses. Yet, 'tis the plague of great ones;
Prerogativ'd° are they less than the base;
'Tis destiny unshunnable, like death:
Even then this forked° plague is fated to us
When we do quicken.° Look where she comes:

          Enter DESDEMONA and EMILIA.

    If she be false, O, then heaven mocks itself!
    I'll not believe 't.
DES.   How now, my dear Othello!
    Your dinner, and the generous° islanders   280
    By you invited, do attend your presence.
OTH.   I am to blame.
DES.   Why do you speak so faintly?
    Are you not well?
OTH.   I have a pain upon my forehead here.
DES.   'Faith, that's with watching;° 'twill away again:
    Let me but bind it hard, within this hour
    It will be well.
OTH.   Your napkin is too little:

          [He puts the handkerchief from him; and it drops.]

    Let it alone. Come, I'll go in with you.
DES.   I am very sorry that you are not well.

          Exit [with OTHELLO].

EMIL.   I am glad I have found this napkin:
    This was her first remembrance from the Moor: 290

---

261. *jesses*, straps fastened around the legs of a trained hawk.   263. *at fortune*, at random.   265. *chamberers*, gallants.   274. *Prerogativ'd*, privileged.   276. *forked*, an allusion to the horns of the cuckhold.   277. *quicken*, receive life.   280. *generous*, noble.   285. *watching*, working late.

My wayward husband hath a hundred times
Woo'd me to steal it; but she so loves the token,
For he conjur'd her she should ever keep it,
That she reserves it evermore about her
To kiss and talk to. I'll have the work ta'en out,°
And give 't Iago: what he will do with it
Heaven knows, not I;
I nothing but to please his fantasy.

Enter IAGO.

IAGO.   How now! what do you here alone?   3(
EMIL.   Do not you chide; I have a thing for you.
IAGO.   A thing for me? it is a common thing°—
EMIL.   Ha!
IAGO.   To have a foolish wife.
EMIL.   O, is that all? What will you give me now
    For that same handkerchief?
IAGO.   What handkerchief?
EMIL.   What handkerchief!
    Why, that the Moor first gave to Desdemona;
    That which so often you did bid me steal.
IAGO.   Hast stol'n it from her?   9
EMIL.   No. 'faith: she let it drop by negligence,
    And, to th' advantage, I, being here, took 't up.
    Look, here it is.
IAGO.   A good wench; give it me.
EMIL.   What will you do with 't, that you have been so earnest
    To have me filch it?
IAGO.   [*Snatching it*] Why, what is that to you?
EMIL.   If it be not for some purpose of import,
    Give 't me again: poor lady, she'll run mad
    When she shall lack it.
IAGO.   Be not acknown on 't;° I have use for it.
    Go, leave me.

Exit EMILIA.

I will in Cassio's lodging lose this napkin,
And let him find it. Trifles light as air
Are to the jealous confirmations strong
As proofs of holy writ: this may do something.
The Moor already changes with my poison:

296. *work ta'en out*, design copied.   302. *common thing* (with bawdy suggestion).   319. *Be*
. . . *on't*, do not confess knowledge of it.

Dangerous conceits are, in their natures, poisons,
Which at the first are scarce found to distaste,
But with a little act° upon the blood,
Burn like the mines of sulphur. I did say so:

Enter OTHELLO.

Look, where he comes! Not poppy, nor mandragora,   330
Nor all the drowsy syrups of the world,
Shall ever medicine thee to that sweet sleep
Which thou owedst yesterday.

OTH.   Ha! ha! false to me?

IAGO.   Why, how now, general! no more of that.

OTH.   Avaunt! be gone! thou hast set me on the rack;
    I swear 'tis better to be much abus'd
    Than but to know 't a little.

IAGO.   How now, my lord!

OTH.   What sense had I of her stol'n hours of lust?
    I saw 't not, thought it not, it harm'd not me:
    I slept the next night well, fed well, was free and merry;   340
    I found not Cassio's kisses on her lips:
    He that is robb'd, not wanting what is stol'n,
    Let him not know 't, and he's not robb'd at all.

IAGO.   I am sorry to hear this.

OTH.   I had been happy, if the general camp,
    Pioners° and all, had tasted her sweet body,
    So I had nothing known. O, now, for ever
    Farewell the tranquil mind! farewell content!
    Farewell the plumed troop, and the big wars,
    That make ambition virtue! O, farewell!   350
    Farewell the neighing steed, and the shrill trump,
    The spirit-stirring drum, th' ear-piercing fife,
    The royal banner, and all quality,
    Pride, pomp and circumstance° of glorious war!
    And, O you mortal engines,° whose rude throats
    Th' immortal Jove's dread clamours counterfeit,
    Farewell! Othello's occupation's gone!

IAGO.   Is't possible, my lord?

OTH.   Villain, be sure thou prove my love a whore,
    Be sure of it; give me the ocular proof;   360
    Or, by the worth of mine eternal soul,

---

328. *act*, action, working.   346. *Pioners*, sappers, a low grade of soldiers.   354. *circumstance*, attendant fact; here, formal display.   355. *mortal engines*, i.e., cannon.

     Thou hadst been better have been born a dog
     Than answer my wak'd wrath!
IAGO.   Is't come to this?
OTH.   Make me to see't; or, at the least, so prove it,
     That the probation bear no hinge nor loop
     To hang a doubt on; or woe upon thy life!
IAGO.   My noble lord,—
OTH.   If thou dost slander her and torture me,
     Never pray more; abandon all remorse;
     On horror's head horrors° accumulate;   37
     Do deeds to make heaven weep, all earth amaz'd;
     For nothing canst thou to damnation add
     Greater than that.
IAGO.   O grace! O heaven forgive me!
     Are you a man? have you a soul or sense?
     God be wi' you; take mine office. O wretched fool,
     That liv'st to make thine honesty a vice!
     O monstrous world! Take note, take note, O world,
     To be direct and honest is not safe.
     I thank you for this profit; and from hence
     I'll love no friend, sith love breeds such offence.   3
OTH.   Nay, stay: thou shouldst be honest.
IAGO.   I should be wise, for honesty's a fool
     And loses that it works for.
OTH.   By the world,
     I think my wife be honest and think she is not;
     I think that thou art just and think thou art not.
     I'll have some proof. Her name, that was as fresh
     As Dian's visage, is now begrim'd and black
     As mine own face. If there be cords, or knives,
     Poison, or fire, or suffocating streams,
     I'll not endure it. Would I were satisfied!
IAGO.   I see, sir, you are eaten up with passion:
     I do repent me that I put it to you.
     You would be satisfied?
OTH.   Would! nay, I will.
IAGO.   And may: but, how? how satisfied, my lord?
     Would you, the supervisor, grossly gape on—
     Behold her topp'd?
OTH.   Death and damnation! O!
IAGO.   It were a tedious difficulty, I think,
     To bring them to that prospect: damn them then,
     If ever mortal eyes do see them bolster°

---

370. *horrors*, object of *accumulate*.   399. *bolster*, lie together.

More than their own! What then? how then?   400
What shall I say? Where's satisfaction?
It is impossible you should see this,
Were they as prime as goats, as hot as monkeys,
As salt° as wolves in pride, and fools as gross
As ignorance made drunk. But yet, I say,
If imputation° and strong circumstances,
Which lead directly to the door of truth,
Will give you satisfaction, you may have 't.

OTH. Give me a living reason she's disloyal.

IAGO. I do not like the office: 410
But sith I am ent'red in this cause so far,
Prick'd to 't by foolish honesty and love,
I will go on. I lay with Cassio lately;
And, being troubled with a raging tooth,
I could not sleep.
There are a kind of men so loose of soul,
That in their sleeps will mutter their affairs:
One of this kind is Cassio:
In sleep I heard him say 'Sweet Desdemona,
Let us be wary, let us hide our loves;'   420
And then, sir, would he gripe and wring my hand,
Cry 'O sweet creature!' and then kiss me hard,
As if he pluck'd up kisses by the roots
That grew upon my lips: then laid his leg
Over my thigh, and sigh'd, and kiss'd; and then
Cried 'Cursed fate that gave thee to the Moor!'

OTH. O monstrous! monstrous!

IAGO.   Nay, this was but his dream.

OTH. But this denoted a foregone conclusion:°
'Tis a shrewd doubt, though it be but a dream.

IAGO. And this may help to thicken other proofs   430
That do demonstrate thinly.

OTH.   I'll tear her all to pieces.

IAGO. Nay, but be wise: yet we see nothing done;
She may be honest yet. Tell me but this,
Have you not sometimes seen a handkerchief
Spotted with strawberries in your wife's hand?

OTH. I gave her such a one; 'twas my first gift.

IAGO. I know not that: but such a handkerchief—
I am sure it was your wife's—did I to-day
See Cassio wipe his beard with.

---

404. *salt*, wanton, sensual.   406. *imputation*, i.e., opinion founded on strong circumstantial evidence.   428. *foregone conclusion*, previous trial or experience (not used in our sense).

OTH.   If it be that,—
IAGO.   If it be that, or any that was hers,   44(
    It speaks against her with the other proofs.
OTH.   O, that the slave had forty thousand lives!
    One is too poor, too weak for my revenge.
    Now do I see 'tis true. Look here, Iago;
    All my fond love thus do I blow to heaven.
    'Tis gone.
    Arise, black vengeance, from the hollow hell!
    Yield up, O love, thy crown and hearted° throne
    To tyrannous hate! Swell, bosom, with thy fraught,°
    For 'tis of aspics'° tongues!
IAGO.   Yet be content.   45
OTH.   O, blood, blood, blood!
IAGO.   Patience, I say; your mind perhaps may change.
OTH.   Never, Iago, Like to the Pontic sea,
    Whose icy current and compulsive course
    Ne'er feels retiring ebb, but keeps due on
    To the Propontic and the Hellespont,
    Even so my bloody thoughts, with violent pace,
    Shall ne'er look back, ne'er ebb to humble love,
    Till that a capable and wide revenge
    Swallow them up. Now, by yond marble° heaven,   4
    [*Kneels*] In the due reverence of a sacred vow
    I here engage my words.
IAGO.   Do not rise yet.
    [*Kneels*] Witness, you ever-burning lights above,
    You elements that clip us round about,
    Witness that here Iago doth give up
    The execution° of his wit, hands, heart,
    To wrong'd Othello's service! Let him command,
    And to obey shall be in me remorse,°
    What bloody business ever.

                                        [*They rise.*]

OTH.   I greet thy love,
    Not with vain thanks, but with acceptance bounteous,
    And will upon the instant put thee to 't:
    Within these three days let me hear thee say
    That Cassio's not alive.

---

448. *hearted*, fixed in the heart.   449. *fraught*, freight, burden.   450. *aspics'*, venomous serpents'.   460. *marble*, i.e., gleaming like marble.   466. *execution*, exercise.   468. *remorse*, pity for Othello's wrong.

Iago. My friend is dead; 'tis done at your request:
  But let her live.
Oth. Damn her, lewd minx! O, damn her! damn her!
  Come, go with me apart; I will withdraw,
  To furnish me with some swift means of death
  For the fair devil. Now art thou my lieutenant.
Iago. I am your own for ever.   480

Exeunt.

Scene IV. [*Before the castle.*]

Enter DESDEMONA, EMILIA, and CLOWN.

Des. Do you know, sirrah, where Lieutenant Cassio lies?
Clo. I dare not say he lies anywhere.
Des. Why, man?
Clo. He's a soldier, and for one to say a soldier lies, is stabbing.
Des. Go to: where lodges he?
Clo. To tell you where he lodges, is to tell you where I lie.
Des. Can any thing be made of this?
Clo. I know not where he lodges, and for me to devise a lodging and
  say he lies here or he lies there, were to lie in mine own throat.
Des. Can you inquire him out, and be edified by report?   10
Clo. I will catechize the world for him; that is, make questions, and by
  them answer.
Des. Seek him, bid him come hither: tell him I have moved my lord on
  his behalf, and hope all will be well.
Clo. To do this is within the compass of man's wit; and therefore I will
  attempt the doing it.

Exit CLO.

Des. Where should I lose that handkerchief, Emilia?
Emil. I know not, madam.
Des. Believe me, I had rather have lost my purse
  Full of crusadoes:° and, but my noble Moor   20
  Is true of mind and made of no such baseness
  As jealous creatures are, it were enough
  To put him to ill thinking.
Emil.   Is he not jealous?
Des. Who, he? I think the sun where he was born
  Drew all such humours from him.
Emil.   Look, where he comes.

---

20. *crusadoes*, Portuguese gold coins.

Enter OTHELLO.

DES.   I will not leave him now till Cassio
        Be call'd to him.—How is 't with you, my lord?
OTH.   Well, my good lady. [*Aside*] O, hardness to dissemble!—
        How do you, Desdemona?
DES.   Well, my good lord.
OTH.   Give me your hand: this hand is moist, my lady.   3C
DES.   It yet hath felt no age nor known no sorrow.
OTH.   This argues fruitfulness and liberal heart:
        Hot, hot, and moist: this hand of yours requires
        A sequester° from liberty, fasting and prayer,
        Much castigation, exercise devout;
        For here's a young and sweating devil here,
        That commonly rebels. 'Tis a good hand,
        A frank one.
DES.   You may, indeed, say so;
        For 'twas that hand that gave away my heart.
OTH.   A liberal hand: the hearts of old gave hands;   4
        But our new heraldry is hands, not hearts.°
DES.   I cannot speak of this. Come now, your promise.
OTH.   What promise, chuck?
DES.   I have sent to bid Cassio come speak with you.
OTH.   I have a salt and sorry rheum° offends me;
        Lend me thy handkerchief.
DES.   Here, my lord.
OTH.   That which I gave you.
DES.   I have it not about me.
OTH.   Not?
DES.   No, indeed, my lord.
OTH.   That's a fault.
        That handkerchief
        Did an Egyptian° to my mother give;
        She was a charmer, and could almost read
        The thoughts of people: she told her, while she kept it,
        'Twould make her amiable and subdue my father
        Entirely to her love, but if she lost it
        Or made a gift of it, my father's eye
        Should hold her loathed and his spirits should hunt
        After new fancies: she, dying, gave it me;
        And bid me, when my fate would have me wive,

---

34. *sequester*, separation, sequestration.   41. *new . . . hearts*, a current expression referring
to marriages in which there is a joining of hands without the giving of hearts.   45. *sorry
rheum*, distressful head cold.   50. *Egyptian*, gypsy.

To give it her. I did so: and take heed on 't;
Make it a darling like your precious eye;   60
To lose 't or give 't away were such perdition
As nothing else could match.
DES.   Is't possible?
OTH.   'Tis true: there's magic in the web of it:
A sibyl, that had numb'red in the world
The sun to course two hundred compasses,
In her prophetic fury sew'd the work:
The worms were hallow'd that did breed the silk;
And it was dy'd in mummy° which the skillful
Conserv'd of° maidens' hearts.
DES.   Indeed! is 't true?
OTH.   Most veritable; therefore look to 't well.   70
DES.   Then would to God that I had never seen 't!
OTH.   Ha! wherefore?
DES.   Why do you speak so startingly and rash?
OTH.   Is 't lost? is 't gone? speak, is it out o' th' way?
DES.   Heaven bless us!
OTH.   Say you?
DES.   It is not lost; but what an if it were?
OTH.   How!
DES.   I say, it is not lost.
OTH.   Fetch 't, let me see 't.
DES.   Why, so I can, sir, but I will not now.   80
This is a trick to put me from my suit:
Pray you, let Cassio be receiv'd again.
OTH.   Fetch me the handkerchief: my mind misgives.
DES.   Come, come;
You'll never meet a more sufficient man.
OTH.   The handkerchief!
DES.   I pray, talk me of Cassio.
OTH.   The handkerchief!   90
DES.   A man that all his time
Hath founded his good fortunes on your love,
Shar'd dangers with you,—
OTH.   The handkerchief!
DES.   In sooth, you are to blame.
OTH.   Away!

                                        Exit OTHELLO.

EMIL.   Is not this man jealous?

---

68. *mummy*, medicinal or magical preparation drained from the flesh of mummified bodies.   69. *Conserv'd of*, preserved out of.

DES.   I ne'er saw this before.
 Sure, there's some wonder in this handkerchief:
 I am most unhappy in the loss of it.
EMIL.   'Tis not a year or two shows us a man:
 They are all but stomachs, and we all but food;
 They eat us hungerly, and when they are full,
 They belch us.

Enter IAGO and CASSIO.

 Look you, Cassio and my husband!   100
IAGO.   There is no other way; 'tis she must do 't:
 And, lo, the happiness! go, and importune her.
DES.   How now, good Cassio! what's the news with you?
CAS.   Madam, my former suit: I do beseech you
 That by your virtuous means I may again
 Exist, and be a member of his love
 Whom I with all the office of my heart
 Entirely honour: I would not be delay'd.
 If my offence be of such mortal kind
 That nor my service past, nor present sorrows,   11
 Nor purpos'd merit in futurity,
 Can ransom me into his love again,
 But to know so must be my benefit;°
 So shall I clothe me in a forc'd content,
 And shut myself up in some other course,
 To fortune's alms.
DES.   Alas, thrice-gentle Cassio!
 My advocation° is not now in tune;
 My lord is not my lord; nor should I know him,
 Were he in favour as in humour alter'd.
 So help me every spirit sanctified,   1?
 As I have spoken for you all my best
 And stood within the blank° of his displeasure
 For my free speech! you must awhile be patient:
 What I can do I will; and more I will
 Than for myself I dare: let that suffice you.
IAGO.   Is my lord angry?
EMIL.   He went hence but now,
 And certainly in strange unquietness.
IAGO.   Can he be angry? I have seen the cannon,
 When it hath blown his ranks into the air,

---

113. *to know . . . benefit,* to know that my case is hopeless will end my vain endeavor.   117.
advocation, advocacy.   122. *blank,* white spot in the center of a target; here, range.

And, like the devil, from his very arm   130
Puff'd his own brother:—and can he be angry?
Something of moment then: I will go meet him:
There's matter in 't indeed, if he be angry.

DES. I prithee, do so.

*Exit [*IAGO*].*

               Something, sure, of state,
Either from Venice, or some unhatch'd practice
Made demonstrable here in Cyprus to him,
Hath puddled° his clear spirit; and in such cases
Men's natures wrangle with inferior things,
Though great ones are their object. 'Tis even so;
For let our finger ache, and it indues°   140
Our other healthful members even to a sense
Of pain: nay, we must think men are not gods,
Nor of them look for such observancy
As fits the bridal. Beshrew me much, Emilia,
I was, unhandsome° warrior as I am,
Arraigning his unkindness with my soul;
But now I find I had suborn'd the witness,
And he's indicted falsely.

EMIL. Pray heaven it be state-matters, as you think,
And no conception° nor no jealous toy   150
Concerning you.

DES. Alas the day I never gave him cause.

EMIL. But jealous souls will not be answer'd so;
They are not ever jealous for the cause,
But jealous for they are jealous: 'tis a monster
Begot upon itself, born on itself.

DES. Heaven keep that monster from Othello's mind!

EMIL. Lady, amen.

DES. I will go seek him. Cassio, walk here about:
If I do find him fit, I'll move your suit   160
And seek to effect it to my uttermost.

CAS. I humbly thank your ladyship.

*Exit [*DESDEMONA *with* EMILIA]*

Enter BIANCA.

BIAN. Save you, friend Cassio!

CAS.   What make you from home?

---

137. *puddled,* sullied the purity of.   140. *indues,* brings to the same condition.   145.
unhandsome, unfair.   150. *conception,* mere fancy.

How is't with you, my most fair Bianca?
I' faith, sweet love, I was coming to your house.
BIAN.   And I was going to your lodging, Cassio.
What, keep a week away? seven days and nights?
Eight score eight hours? and lovers' absent hours,
More tedious than the dial eight score times?
O weary reck'ning!
CAS.   Pardon me, Bianca: 170
I have this while with leaden thoughts been press'd;
But I shall, in a more continuate° time,
Strike off this score of absence. Sweet Bianca,

                [*Giving her* DESDEMONA'S *handkerchief.*]

Take me this work out.°
BIAN.   O Cassio, whence came this?
This is some token from a newer friend:
To the felt absence now I feel a cause:
Is 't come to this? Well, well.
CAS.   Go to, woman!
Throw your vile guesses in the devil's teeth,
From whence you have them. You are jealous now
That this is from some mistress, some remembrance: 18
No, in good troth, Bianca.
BIAN.   Why, whose is it?
CAS.   I know not, sweet: I found it in my chamber.
I like the work well: ere it be demanded—
As like enough it will—I would have it copied:
Take it, and do 't; and leave me for this time.
BIAN.   Leave you! wherefore?
CAS.   I do attend here on the general;
And think it no addition, nor my wish,
To have him see me woman'd.
BIAN.   Why, I pray you?
CAS.   Not that I love you not.
BIAN.   But that you do not love me.   1
I pray you, bring me on the way a little,
And say if I shall see you soon at night.
CAS.   'Tis but a little way that I can bring you;
For I attend here: but I'll see you soon.
BIAN.   'Tis very good; I must be circumstanc'd.°

                                    Exeunt omnes.

---

172. *continuate*, uninterrupted.   174. *Take . . . out*, i.e., copy this embroidery for me.   195.
circumstanc'd, governed by circumstances.

ACT IV.

Scene I. [*Cyprus. Before the castle.*]

Enter OTHELLO and IAGO.

IAGO. Will you think so?
OTH.   Think so, Iago!
IAGO.   What,
   To kiss in private?
OTH.   An unauthoriz'd kiss.
IAGO. Or to be naked with her friend in bed
   An hour or more, not meaning any harm?
OTH. Naked in bed, Iago, and not mean harm!
   It is hypocrisy against the devil:
   They that mean virtuously, and yet do so,
   The devil their virtue tempts, and they tempt heaven.
IAGO. So° they do nothing, 'tis a venial slip:
   But if I give my wife a handkerchief,—   10
OTH. What then?
IAGO. Why, then, 'tis hers, my lord; and, being hers,
   She may, I think, bestow 't on any man.
      OTH. She is protectress of her honour too:
   May she give that?
IAGO. Her honour is an essence that's not seen;
   They have it very oft that have it not:
   But, for the handkerchief,—
OTH. By heaven, I would most gladly have forgot it.
   Thou said'st—O, it comes o'er my memory,   20
   As doth the raven o'er the infected house,°
   Boding to all—he had my handkerchief.
IAGO. Ay, what of that?
OTH.   That's not so good now.
IAGO.   What,
   If I had said I had seen him do you wrong?
   Or heard him say,—as knaves be such abroad,
   Who having, by their own importunate suit,
   Or voluntary dotage of some mistress,
   Convinced or supplied° them, cannot choose
   But they must blab—
OTH.   Hath he said any thing?

---

9. *So*, so long as.   21. *raven . . . house*, allusion to the belief that the raven hovered over a
house of sickness or infection.   28. *Convinced or supplied*, i.e., mistresses gained by impor-
tunity and those who doted voluntarily.

IAGO.   He hath, my lord; but be you well assur'd,   30
    No more than he'll unswear.
OTH.   What hath he said?
IAGO.   'Faith, that he did—I know not what he did.
OTH.   What? What?
IAGO.   Lie—
OTH.   With her?
IAGO.   With her, on her; what you will.
OTH.   Lie with her! lie on her! We say lie on her, when they belie her.
    Lie with her! that's fulsome.— Handkerchief—confessions—hand-
    kerchief!—To confess, and be hanged for his labour;—first, to be
    hanged, and then to confess.—I tremble at it. Nature would not
    invest herself in such shadowing passion without some instruction.°
    It is not words that shakes me thus. Pish! Noses, ears, and lips.—
    Is't possible?—Confess—handkerchief!—O devil! *Falls in a trance.*

IAGO.   Work on,   4.
    My medicine, work! Thus credulous fools are caught;
    And many worthy and chaste dames even thus,
    All guiltless, meet reproach. What, ho! my lord!
    My lord, I say! Othello!

Enter CASSIO.

                    How now, Cassio!
CAS.   What's the matter?
IAGO.   My lord is fall'n into an epilepsy:
    This is his second fit; he had one yesterday.
CAS.   Rub him about the temples.
IAGO.   No, forbear;   5
    The lethargy° must have his quiet course:
    If not, he foams at mouth and by and by
    Breaks out to savage madness. Look, he stirs:
    Do you withdraw yourself a little while,
    He will recover straight: when he is gone,
    I would on great occasion speak with you.

                              [*Exit CASSIO*].

    How is it, general? have you not hurt your head?
OTH.   Dost thou mock me?
IAGO.   I mock you! no, by heaven.
    Would you would bear your fortune like a man!
OTH.   A horned man 's a monster and a beast.

38–39. *Nature ... instruction,* i.e., my jealousy cannot be merely the result of natural imagination, but must have some foundation in fact.   51. *lethargy,* unconscious condition.

IAGO.   There 's many a beast then in a populous city,
    And many a civil° monster.
OTH.   Did he confess it?
IAGO.   Good sir, be a man:
    Think every bearded fellow that 's but yok'd
    May draw with you:° there 's millions now alive
    That nightly lie in those unproper° beds
    Which they dare swear peculiar:° your case is better.
    O, 'tis the spite of hell, the fiend's arch-mock,
    To lip a wanton in a secure couch,
    And to suppose her chaste! No, let me know;   70
    And knowing what I am, I know what she shall be.
OTH.   O, thou art wise; 'tis certain.
IAGO.   Stand you awhile apart;
    Confine yourself but in a patient list.°
    Whilst you were here o'erwhelmed with your grief—
    A passion most unsuiting such a man—
    Cassio came hither: I shifted him away,
    And laid good 'scuse upon your ecstasy,
    Bade him anon return and here speak with me;
    The which he promis'd. Do but encave° yourself,
    And mark the fleers,° the gibes, and notable scorns,   80
    That dwell in every region of his face;
    For I will make him tell the tale anew,
    Where, how, how oft, how long ago, and when
    He hath, and is again to cope your wife:
    I say, but mark his gesture. Marry, patience;
    Or I shall say y' are all in all in spleen,
    And nothing of a man.
OTH.   Dost thou hear, Iago?
    I will be found most cunning in my patience;
    But—dost thou hear?—most bloody.
IAGO.   That's not amiss;
    But yet keep time° in all. Will you withdraw?   90

                         [OTHELLO retires.]

    Now will I question Cassio of Bianca,
    A housewife that by selling her desires
    Buys herself bread and clothes: it is a creature
    That dotes on Cassio; as 'tis the strumpet's plague

---

62. *civil*, i.e., in civilized society.   65. *draw with you*, i.e., share your fate as cuckold.   66.
unproper, not belonging exclusively to an individual.   67. *peculiar*, private, one's own.   73.
patient list, within the bounds of patience.   79. *encave*, conceal.   80. *fleers*, sneers.   90.
keep time, use judgment and order.

To beguile many and be beguil'd by one:
He, when he hears of her, cannot refrain
From the excess of laughter. Here he comes:

Enter CASSIO.

As he shall smile, Othello shall go mad;
And his unbookish° jealousy must conster°
Poor Cassio's smiles, gestures and light behaviour,   100
Quite in the wrong. How do you now, lieutenant?
CAS.   The worser that you give me the addition°
Whose want even kills me.
IAGO.   Ply Desdemona well, and you are sure on 't.
    [*Speaking lower*] Now, if this suit lay in Bianca's power,
How quickly should you speed!
CAS.   Alas, poor caitiff!
OTH.   Look, how he laughs already!
IAGO.   I never knew woman love man so.
CAS.   Alas, poor rogue! I think, i' faith, she loves me.
OTH.   Now he denies it faintly, and laughs it out.   11
IAGO.   Do you hear, Cassio?
OTH.   Now he importunes him
    To tell it o'er: go to; well said, well said.
IAGO.   She gives it out that you shall marry her:
Do you intend it?
CAS.   Ha, ha, ha!
OTH.   Do you triumph, Roman?° do you triumph?
CAS.   I marry her! what? a customer!° Prithee, bear some charity to my
    wit; do not think it so unwholesome. Ha, ha, ha!
OTH.   So, so, so, so: they laugh that win.
IAGO.   'Faith, the cry goes that you shall marry her.   1
CAS.   Prithee, say true.
IAGO.   I am a very villain else.
OTH.   Have you scored me?° Well.
CAS.   This is the monkey's own giving out: she is persuaded I will marry
    her, out of her own love and flattery, not out of my promise.
OTH.   Iago beckons me; now he beings the story.
CAS.   She was here even now; she haunts me in every place. I was the
    other day talking on the seabank with certain Venetians; and thither
    comes the bauble,° and, by this hand, she falls me thus about my
    neck—

---

99. *unbookish,* uninstructed. *conster,* construe.   102. *addition,* title.   116. *Roman,* The
epithet arises from the association of the Romans with the idea of triumph.   117. *customer,*
prostitute.   123. *scored me,* made up my reckoning, or branded me.   129. *bauble,*
plaything.

OTH. Crying, 'O dear Cassio!' as it were: his gesture imports it.

CAS. So hangs, and lolls, and weeps upon me; so shakes, and pulls me: ha, ha, ha!

OTH. Now he tells how she plucked him to my chamber. O, I see that nose of yours, but not that dog I shall throw it to.

CAS. Well, I must leave her company.

IAGO. Before me!° look, where she comes.

Enter BIANCA.

CAS. 'Tis such another fitchew!° marry, a perfumed one.—What do you mean by this haunting of me?   139

BIAN. Let the devil and his dam haunt you! What did you mean by that same handkerchief you gave me even now? I was a fine fool to take it. I must take out the work?—A likely piece of work, that you should find it in your chamber, and not know who left it there! This is some minx's token, and I must take out the work? There; give it your hobby-horse:° wheresoever you had it, I'll take out no work on 't.

CAS. How now, my sweet Bianca! how now! how now!

OTH. By heaven, that should be my handkerchief!

BIAN. An you'll come to supper to-night, you may; an you will not, come when you are next prepared for.

Exit.

IAGO. After her, after her.   150

CAS. 'Faith, I must; she'll rail in the street else.

IAGO. Will you sup there?

CAS. Yes, I intend so.

IAGO. Well, I may chance to see you; for I would very fain speak with you.

CAS. Prithee, come; will you?

IAGO. Go to; say no more.

[Exit CASSIO.]

OTH. [*Advancing*] How shall I murder him, Iago?

IAGO. Did you perceive how he laughed at his vice?

OTH. O Iago!   160

IAGO. And did you see the handkerchief?

OTH. Was that mine?

IAGO. Yours, by this hand: and to see how he prizes the foolish woman your wife! she gave it him, and he hath given it his whore.

OTH. I would have him nine years a-killing. A fine woman! a fair woman! a sweet woman!

137. *Before me!* On my soul!   138. *fitchew*, polecat (because of her strong perfume; also, slang for prostitute).   145. *hobby-horse*, harlot.

IAGO.   Nay, you must forget that.

OTH.   Ay, let her rot, and perish, and be damned to-night; for she shall
not live: no, my heart is turned to stone; I strike it, and it hurts my
hand. O, the world hath not a sweeter creature: she might lie by an
emperor's side and command him tasks.   171

IAGO.   Nay, that's not your way.°

OTH.   Hang her! I do but say what she is: so delicate with her needle:
an admirable musician: O! she will sing the savageness out of a bear:
of so high and plenteous wit and invention:—

IAGO.   She's the worse for all this.

OTH.   O, a thousand thousand times: and then, of so gentle a condition!

IAGO.   Ay, too gentle.

OTH.   Nay, that's certain: but yet the pity of it, Iago! O Iago, the pity of
it, Iago!   18●

IAGO.   If you are so fond over her iniquity, give her patent° to offend;
for, if it touch not you, it comes near nobody.

OTH.   I will chop her into messes:° cuckold me!

IAGO.   O, 'tis foul in her.

OTH.   With mine officer!

IAGO.   That's fouler.

OTH.   Get me some poison, Iago; this night: I'll not expostulate with her,
lest her body and beauty unprovide° my mind again: this night, Iago.

IAGO.   Do it not with poison, strangle her in her bed, even the bed she
hath contaminated.   19

OTH.   Good, good: the justice of it pleases: very good.

IAGO.   And for Cassio, let me be his undertaker:° you shall hear more by
midnight.

OTH.   Excellent good. [*A trumpet within.*] What trumpet is that same?

IAGO.   I warrant something from Venice.

Enter LODOVICO, DESDEMONA, *and* ATTENDANTS.

                    'Tis Lodovico.
This comes from the duke: and, see, your wife's with him.

LOD.   God save you, worthy general!

OTH.   With all my heart, sir.

LOD.   The duke and the senators of Venice greet you.

                                     [*Gives him a letter.*]

OTH.   I kiss the instrument of their pleasures.

                               [*Opens the letter, and reads.*]

---

172. *your way,* i.e., the way you should think of her.   181. *patent,* license.   183. *messes,*
dishes of food.   188. *unprovide,* weaken, unfit.   192. *let . . . undertaker,* i.e., let me settle
with him.

DES.   And what's the news, good cousin Lodovico?   200
IAGO.   I am very glad to see you, signior;
    Welcome to Cyprus.
LOD.   I thank you. How does Lieutenant Cassio?
IAGO.   Lives, sir.
DES.   Cousin, there 's fall'n between him and my lord
    An unkind breach: but you shall make all well.
OTH.   Are you sure of that?
DES.   My lord?
OTH.   [*Reads*] 'This fail you not to do, as you will—'
LOD.   He did not call; he's busy in the paper.   210
    Is there division 'twixt my lord and Cassio?
DES.   A most unhappy one: I would do much
    T' attone them, for the love I bear to Cassio.
OTH.   Fire and brimstone!
DES.   My lord?
OTH.   Are you wise?
DES.   What, is he angry?
LOD.   May be the letter mov'd him;
    For, as I think, they do command him home,
    Deputing Cassio in his government.°
DES.   Trust me, I am glad on 't.
OTH.   Indeed!
DES.   My lord?
OTH.   I am glad to see you mad.
DES.   Why, sweet Othello,—
OTH.   [*Striking her*] Devil!   220
DES.   I have not deserv'd this.
LOD.   My lord, this would not be believ'd in Venice,
    Though I should swear I saw 't: 'tis very much:
    Make her amends; she weeps.
OTH.   O devil, devil!
    If that the earth could teem with woman's tears,
    Each drop she falls would prove a crocodile.°
    Out of my sight!
DES.   I will not stay to offend you. [*Going*].
LOD.   Truly, an obedient lady:
    I do beseech your lordship, call her back.
OTH.   Mistress!
DES.   My lord?
OTH.   What would you with her, sir?   230
LOD.   Who, I, my lord?

---

217. *government*, office.   226. *prove a crocodile*, i.e., by weeping crocodile tears; it was
believed the crocodile shed tears over the body of the man he was eating.

OTH.   Ay; you did wish that I would make her turn:
Sir, she can turn, and turn, and yet go on,
And turn again; and she can weep, sir, weep;
And she's obedient, as you say, obedient,
Very obedient. Proceed you in your tears.
Concerning this, sir,—O well-painted passion!°—
I am commanded home. Get you away:
I'll send for you anon. Sir, I obey the mandate,
And will return to Venice. Hence, avaunt!   240

[*Exit* DESDEMONA.]

Cassio shall have my place. And, sir, to-night,
I do entreat that we may sup together:
You are welcome, sir, to Cyprus.—Goats and monkeys!

Exit.

LOD.   Is this the noble Moor whom our full senate
Call all in all sufficient? Is this the nature
Whom passion could not shake? whose solid virtue
The shot of accident, nor dart of chance,
Could neither graze nor pierce?
IAGO.   He is much chang'd.
LOD.   Are his wits safe? is he not light of brain?
IAGO.   He's that he is: I may not breathe my censure   25
What he might be: if what he might he is not,
I would to heaven he were!
LOD.   What, strike his wife!
IAGO.   'Faith, that was not so well; yet would I knew
That stroke would prove the worst!
LOD.   Is it his use?
Or did the letters work upon his blood,
And new-create this fault?
IAGO.   Alas, alas!
It is not honesty in me to speak
What I have seen and known. You shall observe him,
And his own courses will denote him so
That I may save my speech: do but go after,
And mark how he continues.
LOD.   I am sorry that I am deceiv'd in him.

Exeunt.

---

237. *well-painted passion*, well-simulated emotion.

Scene II. [*A room in the castle.*]

Enter OTHELLO and EMILIA.

OTH. You have seen nothing then?
EMIL. Nor ever heard, nor ever did suspect.
OTH. Yes, you have seen Cassio and she together.
EMIL. But then I saw no harm, and then I heard
        Each syllable that breath made up between them.
OTH. What, did they never whisper?
EMIL.   Never, my lord.
OTH. Nor send you out o' th' way?
EMIL. Never.
OTH. To fetch her fan, her gloves, her mask, nor nothing?
EMIL. Never, my lord.   10
OTH. That's strange.
EMIL. I durst, my lord, to wager she is honest,
        Lay down my soul at stake: if you think other,
        Remove your thought; it doth abuse your bosom.
        If any wretch have put this in your head,
        Let heaven requite it with the serpent's curse!
        For, if she be not honest, chaste, and true,
        There's no man happy; the purest of their wives
        Is foul as slander.
OTH.   Bid her come hither: go.

                                            Exit EMILIA.

        She says enough; yet she's a simple bawd   20
        That cannot say as much. This is a subtle whore,
        A closet lock and key° of villanous secrets:
        And yet she'll kneel and pray; I have seen her do 't.

Enter DESDEMONA and EMILIA.

DES. My lord, what is your will?
OTH.   Pray, chuck, come hither.
DES. What is your pleasure?
OTH.   Let me see your eyes;
        Look in my face.
DES.   What horrible fancy 's this?
OTH. [*To EMILIA*] Some of your function,° mistress;
        Leave procreants° alone and shut the door;

---

22. *closet lock and key*, complete storeroom.   27. *Some . . . function*, i.e., set to work in your
chosen profession, that of bawd.   28. *procreants*, mating couples.

Cough, or cry 'hem', if any body come:
Your mystery, your mystery:° nay, dispatch.   3(

Exit EMILIA.

DES.   Upon my knees, what doth your speech import?
I understand a fury in your words,
But not the words.

OTH.   Why, what art thou?

DES.   Your wife, my lord; your true
And loyal wife.

OTH.   Come, swear it, damn thyself;
Lest, being like one of heaven, the devils themselves
Should fear to seize thee: therefore be double damn'd:
Swear thou art honest.

DES.   Heaven doth truly know it.

OTH.   Heaven truly knows that thou art false as hell.

DES.   To whom, my lord? with whom? how am I false?

OTH.   O Desdemon! away! away! away!

DES.   Alas the heavy day! Why do you weep?
Am I the motive of these tears, my lord?
If haply you my father do suspect
An instrument of this your calling back,
Lay not your blame on me: if you have lost him,
Why, I have lost him too.

OTH.   Had it pleas'd heaven
To try me with affliction; had they° rain'd
All kinds of sores and shames on my bare head,
Steep'd me in poverty to the very lips,
Given to captivity me and my utmost hopes,
I should have found in some place of my soul
A drop of patience: but, alas, to make me
A fixed figure for the time of scorn
To point his slow unmoving finger at!°
Yet could I bear that too; well, very well:
But there, where I have garner'd up my heart,
Where either I must live, or bear no life;
The fountain from the which my current runs,
Or else dries up; to be discarded thence!
Or keep it as a cistern for foul toads
To knot and gender° in! Turn thy complexion° there,

---

30. *mystery*, trade, occupation.   48. *they*, heavenly powers.   54–55. *A . . . at*. Othello
possibly thinks of himself as a man set in a pillory at whom the scornful world points in
mockery. There seems to be a comparison with the sundial, whose gnomon, or indicator,
becomes the finger of scornful time.   62. *gender*, engender. *Turn thy complexion*, grow pale.

Patience, thou young and rose-lipp'd cherubin,—
Ay, there, look grim as hell!

DES. I hope my noble lord esteems me honest.

OTH. O, ay; as summer flies are in the shambles,°
That quicken° even with blowing. O thou weed,
Who art so lovely fair and smell'st so sweet
That the sense aches at thee, would thou hadst ne'er been born!

DES. Alas, what ignorant sin have I committed? 70

OTH. Was this fair paper, this most goodly book,
Made to write 'whore' upon? What committed!
Committed! O thou public commoner!°
I should make very forges of my cheeks,
That would to cinders burn up modesty,
Did I but speak thy deeds. What committed!
Heaven stops the nose at it and the moon winks,
The bawdy wind that kisses all it meets
Is hush'd within the hollow mine of earth,
And will not hear it. What committed! 80
Impudent strumpet!

DES.   By heaven, you do me wrong.

OTH. Are not you a strumpet?

DES.   No, as I am a Christian:
If to preserve this vessel° for my lord
From any other foul unlawful touch
Be not to be a strumpet, I am none.

OTH. What, not a whore?

DES.   No, as I shall be sav'd.

OTH. Is 't possible?

DES. O, heaven forgive us!

OTH.   I cry you mercy, then:
I took you for that cunning whore of Venice
That married with Othello. [*Raising his voice*] You, mistress, 90
That have the office opposite to Saint Peter,
And keep the gate of hell!

Enter EMILIA.

You, you, ay you!
We have done our course; there's money for your pains:
I pray you, turn the key and keep our counsel.

Exit.

---

66. *shambles*, slaughterhouse.   67. *quicken*, come to life.   73. *commoner*, prostitute.   83.
vessel, body.

EMIL.   Alas, what does this gentleman conceive?
    How do you, madam? how do you, my good lady?
DES.   'Faith, half asleep.
EMIL.   Good madam, what's the matter with my lord?
DES.   With who?
EMIL.   Why, with my lord, madam.   10(
DES.   Who is thy lord?
EMIL.   He that is yours, sweet lady.
DES.   I have none: do not talk to me, Emilia:
    I cannot weep; nor answers have I none,
    But what should go by water.° Prithee, tonight
    Lay on my bed my wedding sheets: remember;
    And call thy husband hither.
EMIL.   Here's a change indeed!

                                           Exit.

DES.   'Tis meet I should be us'd so, very meet.
    How have I been behav'd, that he might stick
    The small'st opinion on my least misuse?°

                        Enter IAGO *and* EMILIA.

IAGO.   What is your pleasure, madam? How is 't with you?   1
DES.   I cannot tell. Those that do teach young babes
    Do it with gentle means and easy tasks:
    He might have chid me so; for, in good faith,
    I am a child to chiding.
IAGO.   What is the matter, lady?
EMIL.   Alas, Iago, my lord hath so bewhor'd her,
    Thrown such despite° and heavy terms upon her,
    As true hearts cannot bear.
DES.   Am I that name, Iago?
IAGO.   What name, fair lady?
DES.   Such as she said my lord did say I was.
EMIL.   He call'd her whore: a beggar in his drink
    Could not have laid such terms upon his callet.°
IAGO.   Why did he so?
DES.   I do not know; I am sure I am none such.
IAGO.   Do not weep, do no weep. Alas the day!
EMIL.   Hath she forsook so many noble matches,
    Her father and her country and her friends,
    To be call'd whore? would it not make one weep?

---

104. *go by water*, be expressed by tears.   109. *misuse*, evil conduct.   116. *despite*, contempt,
scorn.   121. *callet*, lewd woman.

DES.   It is my wretched fortune.

IAGO.   Beshrew him for 't!
    How comes this trick upon him?

DES.   Nay, heaven doth know.

EMIL.   I will be hang'd, if some eternal villain,   130
    Some busy and insinuating rogue,
    Some cogging,° cozening slave, to get some office,
    Have not devis'd this slander; I will be hang'd else.

IAGO.   Fie, there is no such man; it is impossible.

DES.   If any such there be, heaven pardon him!

EMIL.   A halter pardon him! and hell gnaw his bones!
    Why should he call her whore? who keeps her company?
    What place? what time? what form? what likelihood?
    The Moor 's abus'd by some most villanous knave,
    Some base notorious knave, some scurvy fellow.   140
    O heaven, that such companions thou 'ldst unfold,
    And put in every honest hand a whip
    To lash the rascals naked through the world
    Even from the east to th' west!

IAGO.   Speak within door.°

EMIL.   O, fie upon them! Some such squire he was
    That turn'd your wit the seamy side without,
    And made you to suspect me with the Moor.

IAGO.   You are a fool; go to.

DES.   Alas, Iago,
    What shall I do to win my lord again?
    Good friend, go to him; for, by this light of heaven,   150
    I know not how I lost him. Here I kneel:
    If e'er my will did trespass 'gainst his love,
    Either in discourse of thought or actual deed,
    Or that mine eyes, mine ears, or any sense,
    Delighted them in any other form;
    Or that I do not yet, and ever did,
    And ever will—though he do shake me off
    To beggarly divorcement—love him dearly,
    Comfort forswear me! Unkindness may do much;
    And his unkindness may defeat my life,   160
    But never taint my love. I cannot say 'whore:'
    It doth abhor me now I speak the word;
    To do the act that might the addition° earn
    Not the world's mass of vanity could make me.

IAGO.   I pray you, be content; 'tis but his humour:

---

132. *cogging*, cheating.   144. *Speak within door*, i.e., not so.   163. *addition*, title.

The business of the state does him offence,
And he does chide with you.
DES.   If 'twere no other,—
IAGO.   'Tis but so, I warrant.

[*Trumpets within.*]

Hark, how these instruments summon to supper!
The messengers of Venice stay the meat:°   17
Go in, and weep not; all things shall be well.

Exeunt DESDEMONA *and* EMILIA.

Enter RODERIGO.

How now, Roderigo!
ROD.   I do not find that thou dealest justly with me.
IAGO.   What in the contrary?
ROD.   Every day thou daffest me° with some device, Iago; and rather, as
it seems to me now, keepest from me all conveniency° than suppliest
me with the least advantage of hope. I will indeed no longer endure
it, nor am I yet persuaded to put up° in peace what already I have
foolishly suffered.
IAGO.   Will you hear me, Roderigo?   1
ROD.   'Faith, I have heard too much, for your words and performances
are no kin together.
IAGO.   You charge me most unjustly.
ROD.   With nought but truth. I have wasted myself out of my means.
The jewels you have had from me to deliver to Desdemona would
half have corrupted a votarist:° you have told me she hath received
them and returned me expectations and comforts of sudden respect
and acquaintance, but I find none.
IAGO.   Well; go to; very well.
ROD.   Very well! go to! I cannot go to, man; nor 'tis not very well: nay, I
think it is scurvy, and begin to find myself fopped° in it.
IAGO.   Very well.
ROD.   I tell you 'tis not very well. I will make myself known to Desdemona:
if she will return me my jewels, I will give over my suit and repent
my unlawful solicitation; if not, assure yourself I will seek satisfaction
of you.
IAGO.   You have said now.°
ROD.   Ay, and said nothing but what I protest intendment° of doing.
IAGO.   Why, now I see there's mettle in thee, and even from this instant

170. *stay the meat*, are waiting for supper.   175. *daffest me*, puttest me off with an excuse.   176. *conveniency*, advantage, opportunity.   178. *put up*, submit to.   186. *votarist*,
nun.   191. *fopped*, fooled.   197. *You have said now*, well said, quite right.   198. *intend-
ment*, purpose, intention.

do build on thee a better opinion than ever before. Give me thy hand, Roderigo: thou hast taken against me a most just exception; but yet, I protest, I have dealt most directly in thy affair.

ROD. It hath not appeared. 203

IAGO. I grant indeed it hath not appeared, and your suspicion is not without wit and judgment. But, Roderigo, if thou hast that in thee indeed, which I have greater reason to believe now than ever, I mean purpose, courage and valour, this night show it: if thou the next night following enjoy not Desdemona, take me from this world with treachery and devise engines for° my life.

ROD. Well, what is it? is it within reason and compass? 210

IAGO. Sir, there is especial commision come from Venice to depute Cassio in Othello's place.

ROD. Is that true? why, then Othello and Desdemona return again to Venice.

IAGO. O, no; he goes into Mauritania° and takes away with him the fair Desdemona, unless his abode be lingered here by some accident: wherein none can be so determinate° as the removing of Cassio.

ROD. How do you mean, removing of him?

IAGO. Why, by making him uncapable of Othello's place; knocking out his brains. 220

ROD. And that you would have me to do?

IAGO. Ay, if you dare do yourself a profit and a right. He sups to-night with a harlotry,° and thither will I go to him: he knows not yet of his honourable fortune. If you will watch his going thence, which I will fashion to fall out between twelve and one, you may take him at your pleasure: I will be near to second your attempt, and he shall fall between us. Come, stand not amazed at it, but go along with me; I will show you such a necessity in his death that you shall think yourself bound to put it on him. It is now high° supper-time, and the night grows to waste: about it. 230

ROD. I will hear further reason for this.

IAGO. And you shall be satisfied.

Exeunt.

Scene III. [*Another room in the castle.*]

Enter OTHELLO, LODOVICO, DESDEMONA, EMILIA, and ATTENDANTS.

LOD. I do beseech you, sir, trouble yourself no further.

OTH. O, pardon me; 'twill do me good to walk.

---

209. *engines for*, plots against.   215. *Mauritania*, Roman name of northwest Africa, supposed land of the moors.   217. *determinate*, decisive.   223. *harlotry*, courtesan.   229. *high*, quite.

LOD.   Madam, good night; I humbly thank your ladyship.
DES.   Your honour is most welcome.
OTH.   Will you walk, sir?
        O,—Desdemona,—
DES.   My lord?
OTH.   Get you to bed on th' instant; I will be returned forthwith; dismiss
        your attendant there: look 't be done.
DES.   I will, my lord.

                        Exit [OTHELLO, *with* LODOVICO *and* ATTENDANTS].

EMIL.   How goes it now? he looks gentler than he did.
DES.   He says he will return incontinent:°
        He hath commanded me to go to bed,
        And bade me to dismiss you.
EMIL.   Dismiss me!
DES.   It was his bidding; therefore, good Emilia,
        Give me my nightly wearing, and adieu:
        We must not now displease him.
EMIL.   I would you had never seen him!
DES.   So would not I: my love doth so approve him,
        That even his stubbornness,° his checks,° his frowns,—
        Prithee, unpin me,—have grace and favour in them.
EMIL.   I have laid those sheets you bade me on the bed.
DES.   All's one. Good faith, how foolish are our minds!
        If I do die before thee, prithee, shroud me
        In one of those same sheets.
EMIL.   Come, come you talk.
DES.   My mother had a maid call'd Barbary:
        She was in love, and he she lov'd prov'd mad
        And did forsake her: she had a song of 'willow;'
        An old thing 'twas, but it express'd her fortune,
        And she died singing it: that song to-night
        Will not go from my mind; I have much to do,
        But to° go hang my head all at one side,
        And sing it like poor Barbary. Prithee, dispatch.
EMIL.   Shall I go fetch your night-gown?°
DES.   No, unpin me here.
        This Lodovico is a proper man.
EMIL.   A very handsome man.
DES.   He speaks well.
EMIL.   I know a lady in Venice would have walked barefoot to Palestine
        for a touch of his nether lip.

---

11. *incontinent*, immediately.   19. *stubbornness*, harshness. *checks*, rebukes.   31. *But to*, not
to.   33. *night-gown*, dressing gown.

DES.   [*Singing*] The poor soul sat sighing by a sycamore tree,
   Sing all a green willow;   40
  Her hand on her bosom, her head on her knee,
   Sing willow, willow, willow:
  The fresh streams ran by her, and murmur'd her moans;
   Sing willow, willow, willow;
  Her salt tears fell from her, and soft'ned the stones;—
Lay by these:—
[*Singing*] Sing willow, willow, willow;
Prithee, hie thee; he'll come anon:—
[*Singing*] Sing all a green willow must be my garland.
  Let nobody blame him; his scorn I approve,—   50
Nay, that's not next.—Hark! who is't that knocks?
EMIL.   It's the wind.
DES. [*Singing*] I call'd my love false love; but what said he then?
   Sing willow, willow, willow:
  If I court moe women, you'll couch with moe men.—
So, get thee gone; good night. Mine eyes do itch;
Doth that bode weeping?
EMIL.   'Tis neither here nor there.
DES.   I have heard it said so. O, these men, these men!
Dost thou in conscience think,—tell me, Emilia,—
That there be women do abuse their husbands   60
In such gross kind?
EMIL.   There be some such, no question.
DES.   Wouldst thou do such a deed for all the world?
EMIL.   Why, would not you?
DES.   No, by this heavenly light!
EMIL.   Nor I neither by this heavenly light; I might do 't as well i' the
dark.
DES.   Wouldst thou do such a deed for all the world?
EMIL.   The world's a huge thing: it is a great price
For a small vice.
DES.   In troth, I think thou wouldst not.   69
EMIL.   In troth, I think I should; and undo 't when I had done. Marry,
I would not do such a thing for a joint-ring,° nor for measures of
lawn, nor for gowns, petticoats, nor caps, nor any petty exhibition;°
but, for all the whole world,—why, who would not make her husband
a cuckold to make him a monarch? I should venture purgatory for
't.
DES.   Beshrew me, if I would do such a wrong
For the whole world.

71. *joint-ring*, a ring made in separable halves as a lover's token.
72. *exhibition*, gift, present.

EMIL.   Why, the wrong is but a wrong i' the world; and having the world
for your labour, 'tis a wrong in your own world, and you might
quickly make it right.   8

DES.   I do not think there is any such woman.

EMIL.   Yes, a dozen; and as many to the vantage° as would store the
world they played for.
But I do think it is their husbands' faults
If wives do fall: say that they slack their duties,
And pour our treasures into foreign laps,°
Or else break out in peevish jealousies,
Throwing restraint upon us; or say they strike us,
Or scant our former having in despite;°
Why, we have galls,° and though we have some grace,°   ⊊
Yet have we some revenge. Let husbands know
Their wives have sense like them: they see and smell
And have their palates both for sweet and sour,
As husbands have. What is it that they do
When they change us for others? Is it sport?
I think it is: and doth affection breed it?
I think it doth: is't frailty that thus errs?
It is so too: and have not we affections,
Desires for sport, and frailty, as men have?
Then let them use us well: else let them know,   1
The ills we do, their ills instruct us so.

DES.   Good night, good night: heaven me such uses send,
Not to pick bad from bad, but by bad mend!

Exeunt.

ACT V.

Scene I. [*Cyprus. A street.*]

Enter IAGO and RODERIGO.

IAGO.   Here stand behind this bulk;° straight will he come:
Wear thy good rapier bare, and put it home:
Quick, quick; fear nothing; I'll be at thy elbow:
It makes us, or it mars us; think on that,
And fix most firm thy resolution.

---

82. *to the vantage*, in addition.   86. *pour . . . laps*, i.e., are unfaithful.   89. *scant . . . despite*,
reduce our allowance to spite us.   90. *have galls*, are capable of resenting injury and insult.
grace, i.e., to forgive.   1. *bulk*, framework projecting from the front of a shop.

Rod. Be near at hand; I may miscarry in 't.
Iago.   Here, at thy hand: be bold, and take thy stand.

[Retires.]

Rod.   I have no great devotion to the deed;
    And yet he hath given me satisfying reasons:
    'Tis but a man gone. Forth, my sword: he dies.   10
Iago.   I have rubb'd this young quat° almost to the sense,°
    And he grows angry. Now, whether he kill Cassio,
    Or Cassio him, or each do kill the other,
    Every way makes my gain: live Roderigo,
    He calls me to a restitution large
    Of gold and jewels that I bobb'd° from him,
    As gifts to Desdemona;
    It must not be: if Cassio do remain,
    He hath a daily beauty in his life
    That makes me ugly; and, besides, the Moor   20
    May unfold me to him; there stand I in much peril:
    No, he must die. But so: I hear him coming.

Enter Cassio.

Rod.   I know his gait, 'tis he.—Villain, thou diest!

[Makes a pass at Cassio.]

Cas.   That thrust had been mine enemy indeed,
    But that my coat° is better than thou know'st:
    I will make proof of thine.

[Draws, and wounds Roderigo.]

Rod.   O, I am slain!

[Iago from behind wounds Cassio in the leg, and exit.]

Cas.   I am maim'd for ever. Help, ho! murder! murder!

[Falls.]

Enter Othello.

Oth.   The voice of Cassio: Iago keeps his word.
Rod.   O, villain that I am!
Oth.   It is even so.
Cas.   O, help, ho! light! a surgeon!   30
Oth.   'Tis he:—O brave Iago, honest and just,

---

11. *quat,* pimple, pustule; used contemptuously. *to the sense,* to the quick.   16. *bobb'd,* filched cunningly.   25. *coat,* coat of mail.

That hast such noble sense of thy friend's wrong!
Thou teachest me. Minion, your dear lies dead,
And your unblest fate hies: strumpet, I come.
Forth of my heart those charms, thine eyes, are blotted;
Thy bed, lust-stain'd, shall with lust's blood be spotted.

Exit OTHELLO.

Enter LODOVICO *and* GRATIANO.

CAS.   What, ho! no watch? no passage?° murder! murder!
GRA.   'Tis some mischance; the cry is very direful.
CAS.   O, help!
LOD.   Hark!   4
ROD.   O wretched villain!
LOD.   Two or three groan: it is a heavy° night:
       These may be counterfeits: let's think 't unsafe
       To come in to the cry without more help.
ROD.   Nobody come? then shall I bleed to death.
LOD.   Hark!

Enter IAGO [*with a light*].

CAS.   Here's one comes in his shirt, with light and weapons.
IAGO.   Who's there? whose noise is this that cries on° murder?
LOD.   We do not know.
IAGO.   Did not you hear a cry?
CAS.   Here, here! for heaven's sake, help me!
IAGO.   What's the matter?
GRA.   This is Othello's ancient, as I take it.
LOD.   The same indeed; a very valiant fellow.
IAGO.   What are you here that cry so grievously?
CAS.   Iago? O, I am spoil'd, undone by villains!
       Give me some help.
IAGO.   O me, lieutenant! what villains have done this?
CAS.   I think that one of them is hereabout,
       And cannot make away.
IAGO.   O treacherous villains!
       What are you there? come in, and give some help.

[*To* LODOVICO *and* GRATIANO.]

ROD.   O, help me here!
CAS.   That's one of them.
IAGO.   O murd'rous slave! O villain!

[*Stabs* RODERIGO.]

37. *passage*, people passing.   42. *heavy*, thick, cloudy.   48. *cries on*, cries out.

Rod. O damn'd Iago! O inhuman dog!
Iago. Kill men i' th' dark!—Where be these bloody thieves?—
    How silent is this town!—Ho! murder! murder!—
    What° may you be? are you of good or evil?
Lod. As you shall prove us, praise us.
Iago. Signior Lodovico?
Lod. He, sir.
Iago. I cry you mercy. Here's Cassio hurt by villains.
Gra. Cassio!   70
Iago. How is 't, brother!
Cas. My leg is cut in two.
Iago.   Marry, heaven forbid!
    Light, gentlemen: I'll bind it with my shirt.

Enter BIANCA.

Bian. What is the matter, ho? who is 't that cried?
Iago. Who is 't that cried?
Bian. O my dear Cassio! my sweet Cassio!
    O Cassio, Cassio, Cassio!
Iago. O notable strumpet? Cassio, may you suspect
    Who they should be that have thus mangled you?
Cas. No.   80
Gra. I am sorry to find you thus: I have been to seek you.
Iago. Lend me a garter. So. O, for a chair,°
    To bear him easily hence!
Bian. Alas, he faints! O Cassio, Cassio, Cassio!
Iago. Gentlemen all, I do suspect this trash°
    To be a party in this injury.
    Patience awhile, good Cassio. Come, come;
    Lend me a light. Know we this face or no?
    Alas, my friend and my dear countryman
    Roderigo! no:—yes, sure:—O heaven! Roderigo.   90
Gra. What, of Venice?
Iago. Even he, sir: did you know him?
Gra.   Know him! ay.
Iago. Signior Gratiano? I cry you gentle pardon;
    These bloody accidents must excuse my manners,
    That so neglected you.
Gra.   I am glad to see you.
Iago. How do you, Cassio? O, a chair, a chair!
Gra. Roderigo!
Iago. He, he, 'tis he. [*A chair brought in.*] O, that's well said; the chair.
    Some good man bear him carefully from hence;

---

65. *What,* who.   82. *chair,* sedan chair.   85. *trash,* worthless thing, i.e., Bianca.

I'll fetch the general's surgeon. [*To* BIANCA] For you, mistress,   100
Save you your labour. He that lies slain here, Cassio,
Was my dear friend: what malice was between you?
CAS.   None in the world; nor do I know the man.
IAGO.   [*To* BIAN] What, look you pale? O, bear him out o' th' air.

[CASSIO *and* RODERIGO *are borne off.*]

Stay you, good gentlemen. Look you pale, mistress?
Do you perceive the gastness° of her eye?
Nay, if you stare, we shall hear more anon.
Behold her well; I pray you, look upon her:
Do you see, gentlemen? nay, guiltiness will speak,
Though tongues were out of use.   11

[*Enter* EMILIA.]

EMIL.   'Las, what's the matter? what's the matter, husband?
IAGO.   Cassio hath here been set on in the dark
By Roderigo and fellows that are scap'd:
He's almost slain, and Roderigo dead.
EMIL.   Alas, good gentleman! alas, good Cassio!
IAGO.   This is the fruit of whoring. Prithee, Emilia,
Go know of Cassio where he supp'd to-night.
[*To* BIANCA] What, do you shake at that?
BIAN.   He supp'd at my house; but I therefore shake not.
IAGO.   O, did he so? I charge you, go with me.   1!
EMIL.   Fie, fie upon thee, strumpet!
BIAN.   I am no strumpet; but of life as honest
As you that thus abuse me.
EMIL.   As I! foh! fie upon thee!
IAGO.   Kind gentlemen, let's go see poor Cassio dress'd.
Come, mistress, you must tell 's another tale.
Emilia, run you to the citadel,
And tell my lord and lady what hath happ'd.
Will you go on afore? [*Aside*] This is the night
That either makes me or fordoes° me quite.

                                                          Exeunt.

Scene II. [*A bedchamber in the castle.*]

Enter OTHELLO [*with a light*]; DESDEMONA *in her bed.*

OTH.   It is the cause,° it is the cause, my soul,—
Let me not name it to you, you chaste stars!—

---

106. *gastness*, terror, ghastliness.   129. *foredoes*, undoes, ruins.   1. *It is the cause*, i.e., the cause of justice on which Othello must act, Desdemona's deed, which is too unmentionable to be named to the chaste stars.

It is the cause. Yet I'll not shed her blood;
Nor scar that whiter skin of hers than snow,
And smooth as monumental alabaster.
Yet she must die, else she'll betray more men.
Put out the light, and then put out the light:
If I quench thee, thou flaming minister,
I can again thy former light restore,
Should I repent me: but once put out thy light,   10
Thou cunning'st pattern of excelling nature,
I know not where is that Promethean heat°
That can thy light relume.° When I have pluck'd the rose,
I cannot give it vital growth again,
It needs must wither: I'll smell thee on the tree.

                                        [*Kissing her.*]

O balmy breath, that dost almost persuade
Justice to break her sword! One more, one more.
Be thus when thou art dead, and I will kill thee,
And love thee after. One more, and that's the last:
So sweet was ne'er so fatal. I must weep,   20
But they are cruel tears: this sorrow's heavenly;°
It strikes where it doth love. She wakes.
DES. Who's there? Othello?
OTH.   Ay, Desdemona.
DES. Will you come to bed, my lord?
OTH.   Have you pray'd to-night, Desdemon?
DES.   Ay, my lord.
OTH.   If you bethink yourself of any crime
Unreconcil'd as yet to heaven and grace,
Solicit for it straight.
DES. Alack, my lord, what may you mean by that?
OTH.   Well, do it, and be brief; I will walk by: 30
I would not kill thy unprepared spirit;
No; heaven forfend! I would not kill thy soul.
DES. Talk you of killing?
OTH.   Ay, I do.
DES.   Then heaven
Have mercy on me!
OTH.   Amen, with all my heart!
DES. If you say so, I hope you will not kill me.
OTH. Hum!
DES. And yet I fear you; for you're fatal then

---

12. *Promethean heat*, divine fire; allusion to the theft of fire from heaven by Prometheus.   13.
relume, rekindle.   21. *this sorrow's heavenly*, this tenderness, with which I lament the
punishment which justice compels me to inflict, is a holy passion.

When your eyes roll so: why I should fear I know not,
Since guiltiness I know not; but yet I feel I fear.

OTH.   Think on thy sins.

DES.   They are loves I bear to you.

OTH.   Ay, and for that thou diest.

DES.   That death 's unnatural that kills for loving.
Alas, why gnaw you so your nether lip?
Some bloody passion shakes your very frame:
These are portents; but yet I hope, I hope,
They do not point on me.

OTH.   Peace, and be still!

DES.   I will so. What's the matter?

OTH.   That handkerchief which I so lov'd and gave thee
Thou gav'st to Cassio.

DES.   No, by my life and soul!
Send for the man and ask him.

OTH.   Sweet soul, take heed,
Take heed of perjury; thou art on thy deathbed.

DES.   Ay, but not yet to die.

OTH.   Yes, presently:
Therefore confess thee freely of thy sin;
For to deny each article with oath
Cannot remove nor choke the strong conception°
That I do groan withal. Thou art to die.

DES.   Then Lord have mercy on me!

OTH.   I say, amen.

DES.   And have you mercy too! I never did
Offend you in my life; never lov'd Cassio
But with such general warranty of heaven
As I might love; I never gave him token.

OTH.   By heaven, I saw my handkerchief in 's hand.
O perjur'd woman! thou dost stone° my heart,
And makes me call what I intend to do
A murder, which I thought a sacrifice:
I saw the handkerchief.

DES.   He found it then;
I never gave it him: send for him hither;
Let him confess a truth.

OTH.   He hath confess'd.

DES.   What, my lord?

OTH.   That he hath us'd thee.

---

55. *conception*, plan, intention.   63. *stone*, turn to stone, harden; Othello means that he will
be tempted to kill her in sheer anger because of her perjury.

DES.   How? unlawfully?
OTH.   Ay.   70
DES.   He will not say so.
OTH.   No, his mouth is stopp'd;
    Honest Iago hath ta'en order° for 't.
DES.   O! my fear interprets: what, is he dead?
OTH.   Had all his hairs been lives, my great revenge
    Had stomach for them all.
DES.   Alas! he is betray'd and I undone.
OTH.   Out, strumpet! weep'st thou for him to my face?
DES.   O banish me, my lord, but kill me not!
OTH.   Down, strumpet!
DES.   Kill me to-morrow: let me live to-night!   80
OTH.   Nay, if you strive,—
DE.   But half an hour!
OTH.   Being done, there is no pause.°
DES.   But while I say one prayer!
OTH.   It is too late.

                                                Smothers her.

EMIL.   *(At the door)* My lord, my lord! what, ho! my lord, my lord!
OTH.   What noise is this? Not dead? not yet quite dead?
    I that am cruel am yet merciful;
    I would not have thee linger in thy pain:
    So, so.
EMIL.   *(Within)* What, ho! my lord, my lord!
OTH.   Who's there?
EMIL.   [*Within*] O, good my lord, I would speak a word with you!   90
OTH.   Yes: 'tis Emilia. By and by. She's dead.
    'Tis like she comes to speak of Cassio's death.—
    The noise was here. Ha! no more moving?
    Still as the grave. Shall she come in? were 't good?—
    I think she stirs again:—no. What 's best to do?
    If she come in, she'll sure speak to my wife:
    My wife! my wife! what wife? I have no wife.
    O, insupportable! O heavy hour!
    Methinks it should be now a huge eclipse
    Of sun and moon, and that th' affrighted globe   100
    Should yawn° at alteration.°
EMIL.   [*Within*] I do beseech you
    That I may speak with you, O, good my lord!

---

72. *ta'en order*, taken measures.   82. *Being . . . pause*, i.e., when the execution of the deed
has once begun, there is no stopping.   101. *yawn*, gape in amazement. *at alteration*, at the
change.

OTH.   I had forgot thee: O, come in, Emilia:
    Soft; by and by. Let me the curtains draw.
    Where art thou?

                                    [*Closes bed-curtains and opens door.*]

Enter EMILIA.   What's the matter with thee now?
EMIL.   O, my good lord, yonder's foul murders done!
OTH.   What, now?
EMIL.   But now, my lord.
OTH.   It is the very error° of the moon;   11
    She comes more nearer earth than she was wont,
    And makes men mad.
EMIL.   Cassio, my lord, hath kill'd a young Venetian
    Call'd Roderigo.
OTH.   Roderigo kill'd!
    And Cassio kill'd!
EMIL.   No, Cassio is not kill'd.
OTH.   Not Cassio kill'd! then murder's out of tune,
    And sweet revenge grows harsh.
DES.   O, falsely, falsely, murder'd!
EMIL.   Alas, what cry is that?
OTH.   That! what?
EMIL.   Out, and alas! that was my lady's voice.
    Help! help, ho! help! O lady, speak again!   1?
    Sweet Desdemona! O sweet mistress, speak!
DES.   A guiltless death I die.
EMIL.   O, who hath done this deed?
DES.   Nobody: I myself. Farewell:
    Commend me to my kind lord: O, farewell!

                                                        [*Dies.*]

OTH.   Why, how should she be murd'red?
EMIL.   Alas, who knows?
OTH.   You heard her say herself, it was not I.
EMIL.   She said so: I must needs report the truth.
OTH.   She 's, like a liar, gone to burning hell:
    'Twas I that kill'd her.
EMIL.   O, the more angel she,
    And you the blacker devil!
OTH.   She turn'd to folly,° and she was a whore.
EMIL.   Thou dost belie her, and thou art a devil.
OTH.   She was false as water.
EMIL.   Thou art rash as fire, to say

---

109. *error*, irregularity.   132. *folly*, unchastity.

That she was false: O, she was heavenly true!

OTH.   Cassio did top her; ask thy husband else.
O, I were damn'd beneath all depth in hell,
But that I did proceed upon just grounds
To this extremity. Thy husband knew it all.

EMIL.   My husband!   140

OTH.   Thy husband.

EMIL.   That she was false to wedlock?

OTH.   Ay, with Cassio. Nay, had she been true,
If heaven would make me such another world
Of one entire and perfect chrysolite,°
I 'ld not have sold her for it.

EMIL.   My husband!

OTH.   Ay, 'twas he that told me first:
An honest man he is, and hates the slime
That sticks on filthy deeds.

EMIL.   My husband!

OTH.   What needs this iterance,° woman? I say thy husband.   150

EMIL.   O mistress, villany hath made mocks with° love!
My husband say that she was false!

OTH.   He, woman;
I say thy husband: dost understand the word?
My friend, thy husband, honest, honest Iago.

EMIL.   If he say so, may his pernicious soul
Rot half a grain a day! he lies to th' heart:
She was too fond of her most filthy bargain.

OTH.   Ha!

EMIL.   Do thy worst:
This deed of thine is no more worthy heaven   160
Than thou wast worthy her.

OTH.   Peace, you were best.

EMIL.   Thou hast not half that power to do me harm
As I have to be hurt.° O gull! O dolt!
As ignorant as dirt! thou hast done a deed—
I care not for thy sword: I'll make thee known,
Though I lost twenty lives.—Help! help, ho! help!
The Moor hath kill'd my mistress! Murder! murder!

Enter MONTANO, GRATIANO, and IAGO [with others].

MON.   What is the matter? How now, general!

---

145. *chrysolite*, the golden stone; a name given to various precious stones of green color.   150. *iterance*, iteration, repetition.   151. *made mocks with*, derided, made sport of.   163. *to be hurt*, i.e., to endure hurting.

EMIL.   O, are you come, Iago? you have done well,
That men must lay their murders on your neck.   170

GRA.   What is the matter?

EMIL.   Disprove this villain, if thou be'st a man:
He says thou told'st him that his wife was false:
I know thou didst not, thou 'rt not such a villain:
Speak, for my heart is full.

IAGO.   I told him what I thought, and told no more
Than what he found himself was apt° and true.

EMIL.   But did you ever tell him she was false?

IAGO.   I did.

EMIL.   You told a lie; an odious, damned lie;   18
Upon my soul, a lie, a wicked lie.
She false with Cassio!—did you say with Cassio?

IAGO.   With Cassio, mistress. Go to, charm° your tongue.

EMIL.   I will not charm my tongue; I am bound to speak:
My mistress here lies murdered in her bed,—

ALL.   O heavens forfend!

EMIL.   And your reports have set the murder on.

OTH.   Nay, stare not, masters: it is true, indeed.

GRA.   'Tis a strange truth.

MON.   O monstrous act!

EMIL.   Villany, villany, villany!   19
I think upon 't, I think: I smell 't: O villany!—
I thought so then:°—I'll kill myself for grief:—
O villany, villany!

IAGO.   What, are you mad? I charge you, get you home.

EMIL.   Good gentlemen, let me have leave to speak:
'Tis proper I obey him, but not now.
Perchance, Iago, I will ne'er go home.

OTH.   O! O! O!

[He falls on the bed.]

EMIL.   Nay, lay thee down and roar;
For thou hast kill'd the sweetest innocent
That e'er did lift up eye.

OTH.   *[Rising]* O, she was foul!   2
I scarce did know you, uncle: there lies your niece,
Whose breath, indeed, these hands have newly stopp'd:
I know this act shows horrible and grim.

GRA.   Poor Desdemon! I am glad thy father's dead:

---

177. *apt*, natural, likely.   183. *charm*, keep silent.   192. *then*, i.e., at some earlier time, probably IV, ii, 130–144, when she suspected the machination of *some eternal villain:* she did not, however, know that villain to be Iago until this moment.

Thy match was mortal to him, and pure grief
Shore° his old thread in twain: did he live now,
This sight would make him do a desperate turn,
Yea, curse his better angel from his side,
And fall to reprobation.°

OTH. 'Tis pitiful; but yet Iago knows   210
That she with Cassio hath the act of shame
A thousand times committed: Cassio confess'd it:
And she did gratify his amorous works
With that recognizance° and pledge of love
Which I first gave her; I saw it in his hand:
It was a handkerchief, an antique token
My father gave my mother.

EMIL. O heaven! O heavenly pow'rs!

IAGO. Come, hold your peace.

EMIL.   'Twill out, 'twill out: I peace!
No, I will speak as liberal as the north:°   220
Let heaven and men and devils, let them all,
All, all, cry shame against me, yet I'll speak.

IAGO. Be wise, and get you home.

EMIL.   I will not.

[IAGO offers to stab EMILIA.]

GRA.   Fie!
Your sword upon a woman?

EMIL. O thou dull Moor! that handkerchief thou speak'st of
I found by fortune° and did give my husband;
For often, with a solemn earnestness,
More than indeed belong'd to such a trifle,
He begg'd of me to steal it.

IAGO.   Villanous whore!

EMIL. She give it Cassio! no, alas! I found it,   230
And I did give 't my husband.

IAGO.   Filth, thou liest!

EMIL. By heaven, I do not, I do not, gentlemen.
O murd'rous coxcomb!° what should such a fool
Do with so good a wife?

OTH.   Are there no stones in heaven°
But what serves for the thunder? Precious villain!

[He runs at IAGO: IAGO, from behind, stabs EMILIA, and exit.]

206. *Shore*, cut. 209. *reprobation*, damnation, rejection by God. 214. *recognizance*,
token. 220 *liberal as the north*, freely as the north wind. 226. *fortune*, chance. 233.
coxcomb, fool; addressed to Othello. 234. *stones in heaven*, thunderbolts. It was supposed
that real stones fell with the thunder and caused the damage.

GRA.   The woman falls; sure, he hath kill'd his wife.
EMIL.   Ay, ay: O, lay me by my mistress' side.
GRA.   He 's gone, but his wife 's kill'd.
MON.   'Tis a notorious villain. Take you this weapon.
  Which I have here recover'd from the Moor: 24●
  Come, guard the door without; let him not pass,
  But kill him rather. I'll after that same villain,
  For 'tis a damned slave.

         Exit [*with all but* OTHELLO *and* EMILIA.]

OTH.   I am not valiant neither,
  But every puny whipster° gets my sword:
  But why should honour outlive honesty?°
  Let it go all.
EMIL.   What did thy song bode, lady?
  Hark, canst thou hear me? I will play the swan,
  And die in music. [*Singing*] Willow, willow, willow.—
  Moor, she was chaste, she lov'd thee, cruel Moor;
  So come my soul to bliss, as I speak true;   2●
  So speaking as I think, I die, I die.

              [*Dies.*]

OTH.   I have another weapon in this chamber;
  It is a sword of Spain, the ice-brook's temper:°—
  O, here it is. Uncle, I must come forth.
GRA.   [*Within*] If thou attempt it, it will cost thee dear:
  Thou has no weapon, and perforce must suffer.
OTH.   Look in upon me then and speak with me,
  Or, naked° as I am, I will assault thee.

           [*Enter* GRATIANO.]

GRA.   What is the matter?
OTH.   Behold, I have a weapon;
  A better never did itself sustain   2●
  Upon a soldier's thigh: I have seen the day,
  That, with this little arm and this good sword,
  I have made my way through more impediments
  Than twenty times your stop:° but, O vain boast!
  Who can control his fate? 'tis not so now.
  Be not afraid, though you do see me weapon'd;
  Here is my journey's end, here is my butt,°

---

244. *whipster*, contemptible fellow. 245. *honour outlive honesty*. Othello realizes that he has done a shameful deed; he asks why his reputation for valor should endure. 253. *ice-brook's temper*, usually defined as "tempered in ice-cold water." 258. *naked*, unarmed. 264. *stop*, power. 267. *butt*, mark for archery, goal, limit.

And very sea-mark° of my utmost sail.
Do you go back dismay'd? 'tis a lost fear;
Man° but a rush° against Othello's breast,   270
And he retires. Where should Othello go?
Now, how dost thou look now? O ill-starr'd wench!
Pale as thy smock! when we shall meet at compt,°
This look of thine will hurl my soul from heaven,
And fiends will snatch at it. Cold, cold, my girl!
Even like thy chastity. O cursed, cursed slave!
Whip me, ye devils,
From the possession of this heavenly sight!
Blow me about in winds! roast me in sulphur!
Wash me in steep-down gulfs of liquid fire!   280
O Desdemon! Dead Desdemon! dead!
Oh! Oh!

Enter LODOVICO, CASSIO *[carried in a chair]*, MONTANO, *and* IAGO *[prisoner], with*
OFFICERS.

LOD. Where is this rash and most unfortunate man?
OTH. That 's he that was Othello: here I am.
LOD. Where is that viper? bring the villain forth.
OTH. I look down towards his feet;° but that 's a fable.
  If that thou be'st a devil, I cannot kill thee.

[Wounds IAGO.*]*

LOD. Wrench his sword from him.
IAGO.   I bleed, sir; but not kill'd.
OTH. I am not sorry neither: I 'ld have thee live;
  For, in my sense, 'tis happiness to die.   290
LOD. O thou Othello, that wert once so good,
  Fall'n in the practice of a damned slave,
  What shall be said to thee?
OTH.   Why, any thing:
  An honourable murderer, if you will;
  For nought I did in hate, but all in honour.
LOD. This wretch hath part confess'd his villany:
  Did you and he consent in Cassio's death?
OTH. Ay.
CAS. Dear general, I never gave you cause.
OTH. I do believe it, and I ask you pardon.   300

---

268. *sea-mark*, beacon (marking his destination or limit).   270. *Man*, provide, as in manning
a gun. *rush*, reed.   273. *compt*, account, judgment day.   286. *towards his feet*, i.e., to see
if they were cloven like a devil's.

Will you, I pray, demand that demi-devil
Why he hath thus ensnar'd my soul and body?

IAGO.   Demand me nothing: what you know, you know:
From this time forth I never will speak word.

LOD.   What, not to pray?

GRA.   Torments will ope your lips.

OTH.   Well, thou dost best.

LOD.   Sir, you shall understand what hath befall'n,
Which, as I think, you know not. Here is a letter
Found in the pocket of the slain Roderigo;
And here another: the one of them imports   310
The death of Cassio to be undertook
By Roderigo.

OTH.   O villain!

CAS.   Most heathenish and most gross!

LOD.   Now here 's another discontented° paper,
Found in his pocket too; and this, it seems,
Roderigo meant t' have sent this damned villain;
But that belike Iago in the interim
Came in and satisfied him.

OTH.   O thou pernicious caitiff!°—
How came you, Cassio, by that handkerchief
That was my wife's?

CAS.   I found it in my chamber: 32
And he himself confess'd but even now
That there he dropp'd it for a special purpose
Which wrought to his desire.

OTH.   O fool! fool! fool!

CAS.   There is besides in Roderigo's letter,
How he upbraids Iago, that he made him
Brave° me upon the watch; whereon it came
That I was cast:° and even but now he spake,
After long seeming dead, Iago hurt him,
Iago set him on.

LOD.   You must forsake this room, and go with us: 33
Your power and your command is taken off,°
And Cassio rules in Cyprus. For this slave,
If there be any cunning cruelty
That can torment him much and hold him long,
It shall be his. You shall close prisoner rest,
Till that the nature of your fault be known
To the Venetian state. Come, bring him away.

---

314. *discontented*, expressing dissatisfaction.   318. *caitiff*, wretch.   326. *Brave*,
defy.   327. *cast*, dismissed.   331. *taken off*, taken away.

OTH.   Soft you; a word or two before you go.
    I have done the state some service, and they know 't.
    No more of that. I pray you, in your letters,   340
    When you shall these unlucky deeds relate,
    Speak of me as I am; nothing extenuate,°
    Nor set down aught in malice: then must you speak
    Of one that lov'd not wisely but too well;
    Of one not easily jealous, but being wrought,
    Perplex'd° in the extreme; of one whose hand,
    Like the base Judean,° threw a pearl away
    Richer than all his tribe; of one whose subdu'd eyes,
    Albeit unused to the melting mood,
    Drop tears as fast as the Arabian trees   350
    Their medicinable gum. Set you down this;
    And say besides, that in Aleppo° once,
    Where a malignant and a turban'd Turk
    Beat a Venetian and traduc'd the state,
    I took by th' throat the circumcised dog,
    And smote him, thus.

                            [Stabs himself.]

LOD.   O bloody period!°
GRA.   All that is spoke is marr'd.
OTH.   I kiss'd thee ere I kill'd thee: no way but this;
    Killing myself, to die upon a kiss.

                  [Falls on the bed, and] dies.

CAS.   This did I fear, but thought he had no weapon;   360
    For he was great of heart.
LOD.   *[To IAGO]* O Spartan dog,°
    More fell than anguish, hunger, or the sea!
    Look on the tragic loading of this bed;
    This is thy work: the object poisons sight;
    Let it be hid. Gratiano, keep the house,
    And seize upon the fortunes of the Moor,
    For they succeed on you. To you, lord governor,
    Remains the censure of this hellish villain;
    The time, the place, the torture: O, enforce it!
    Myself will straight aboard; and to the state   370
    This heavy act with heavy heart relate.

                           Exeunt.

342. *extenuate*, diminish, depreciate; the idea is contrasted with the thought of *malice* in the following line.   346. *Perplex'd*, confounded, distracted.   347. *Judean*, infidel or disbeliever.   352. *Aleppo*, a Turkish city where the Venetians had special trading privileges. It is stated that it was immediate death for a Christian to strike a Turk in Aleppo; Othello risked his life for the honor of Venice.   357. *period*, termination, conclusion.   361. *Spartan dog*, Spartan dogs were noted for their savagery.

HENRIK IBSEN   (1828–1906)

A Doll's House

Translated by R. Farquharson Sharp

DRAMATIS PERSONÆ

>   Torvald Helmer.
>   Nora, *his wife.*
>   Doctor Rank.
>   Mrs. Linde.
>   Nils Krogstad.
>   Helmer's three young children.
>   Anne, *their nurse.*
>   A Housemaid.
>   A Porter.

(The action takes place in HELMER'S *house.)*

ACT I

(SCENE.—*A room furnished comfortably and tastefully, but not extravagantly. At the back, a door to the right leads to the entrance-hall, another to the left leads to Helmer's study. Between the doors stands a piano. In the middle of the left-hand wall is a door, and beyond it a window. Near the window are a round table, arm-chairs and a small sofa. In the right-hand wall, at the farther end, another door; and on the same side, nearer the footlights, a stove, two easy chairs and a rocking-chair; between the stove and the door, a small table. Engravings on the walls; a cabinet with china and other small objects; a small book-case with well bound books. The floors are carpeted, and a fire burns in the stove. It is winter.*

A bell rings in the hall; shortly afterwards the door is heard to open. Enter NORA, *humming a tune and in high spirits. She is in out-door dress and carries a number of parcels; these she lays on the table to the right. She leaves the outer door open after her, and through it is seen a* PORTER *who is carrying a Christmas Tree and a basket, which he gives to the* MAID *who has opened the door.)*

NORA.   Hide the Christmas Tree carefully, Helen. Be sure the children do not see it till this evening, when it is dressed. (*To the* PORTER, *taking out her purse.*) How much?

PORTER. Sixpence.

NORA. There is a shilling. No, keep the change. (*The PORTER thanks her, and goes out. NORA shuts the door. She is laughing to herself, as she takes off her hat and coat. She takes a packet of macaroons from her pocket and eats one or two; then goes cautiously to her husband's door and listens.*) Yes, he is in. (*Still humming, she goes to the table on the right.*)

HELMER (*calls out from his room*). Is that my little lark twittering out there?

NORA (*busy opening some of the parcels.*) Yes, it is!

HELMER. Is it my little squirrel bustling about?

NORA. Yes!

HELMER. When did my squirrel come home?

NORA. Just now. (*Puts the bag of macaroons into her pocket and wipes her mouth.*) Come in here, Torvald, and see what I have bought.

HELMER. Don't disturb me. (*A little later, he opens the door and looks into the room, pen in hand.*) Bought, did you say? All these things? Has my little spendthrift been wasting money again?

NORA. Yes but, Torvald, this year we can really let outselves go a little. This is the first Christmas that we have not needed to economise.

HELMER. Still, you know, we can't spend money recklessly.

NORA. Yes, Torvald, we may be a wee bit more reckless now, mayn't we? Just a tiny wee bit! You are going to have a big salary and earn lots and lots of money.

HELMER. Yes, after the New Year; but then it will be a whole quarter before the salary is due.

NORA. Pooh! we can borrow till then.

HELMER. Nora! (*Goes up to her and takes her playfully by the ear.*) The same little featherhead! Suppose, now, that I borrowed fifty pounds to-day, and you spent it all in the Christmas week, and then on New Year's Eve a slate fell on my head and killed me, and—

NORA (*putting her hands over his mouth*). Oh! don't say such horrid things.

HELMER. Still, suppose that happened,—what then?

NORA. If that were to happen, I don't suppose I should care whether I owed money or not.

HELMER. Yes, but what about the people who had lent it?

NORA. They? Who would bother about them? I should not know who they were.

HELMER. That is like a woman! But seriously, Nora, you know what I think about that. No debt, no borrowing. There can be no freedom or beauty about a home life that depends on borrowing and debt. We two have kept bravely on the straight road so far, and we will go on the same way for the short time longer that there need be any struggle.

NORA (*moving towards the stove*). As you please, Torvald.

HELMER (*following her*). Come, come, my little skylark must not droop her wings. What is this! Is my little squirrel out of temper? (*Taking out his purse.*) Nora, what do you think I have got here?

NORA   (*turning round quickly*). Money!

HELMER.   There you are. (*Gives her some money.*) Do you think I don't know what a lot is wanted for housekeeping at Christmas-time?

NORA   (*counting*). Ten shillings—a pound—two pounds! Thank you, thank you, Torvald; that will keep me going for a long time.

HELMER.   Indeed it must.

NORA.   Yes, yes, it will. But come here and let me show you what I have bought. And all so cheap! Look, here is a new suit for Ivar, and a sword; and a horse and a trumpet for Bob; and a dolly and dolly's bedstead for Emmy,—they are very plain, but anyway she will soon break them in pieces. And here are dress-lengths and handkerchiefs for the maids; old Anne ought really to have something better.

HELMER.   And what is in this parcel?

NORA   (*crying out*). No, no! you mustn't see that till this evening.

HELMER.   Very well. But now tell me, you extravagant little person, what would you like for yourself?

NORA.   For myself? Oh, I am sure I don't want anything.

HELMER.   Yes, but you must. Tell me something reasonable that you would particularly like to have.

NORA.   No, I really can't think of anything—unless, Torvald—

HELMER.   Well?

NORA   (*playing with his coat buttons, and without raising her eyes to his*). If you really want to give me something, you might—you might—

HELMER.   Well, out with it!

NORA   (*speaking quickly*). You might give me money, Torvald. Only just as much as you can afford; and then one of these days I will buy something with it.

HELMER.   But, Nora—

NORA.   Oh, do! dear Torvald; please, please do! Then I will wrap it up in beautiful gilt paper and hang it on the Christmas Tree. Wouldn't that be fun?

HELMER.   What are little people called that are always wasting money?

NORA.   Spendthrifts—I know. Let us do as you suggest, Torvald, and then I shall have time to think what I am most in want of. That is a very sensible plan, isn't it?

HELMER.   (*smiling*). Indeed it is—that is to say, if you were really to save out of the money I give you, and then really buy something for yourself. But if you spend it all on the housekeeping and any number of unnecessary things, then I merely have to pay up again.

NORA.   Oh but, Torvald—

HELMER.   You can't deny it, my dear little Nora. (*Puts his arm round her waist.*) It's a sweet little spendthrift, but she uses up a deal of money. One would hardly believe how expensive such little persons are!

NORA.   It's a shame to say that. I do really save all I can.

HELMER   (*laughing*). That's very true,—all you can. But you can't save anything!

NORA   (*smiling quietly and happily*). You haven't any idea how many expenses we skylarks and squirrels have, Torvald.

HELMER.   You are an odd little soul. Very like your father. You always find some new way of wheedling money out of me, and, as soon as you have got it, it seems to melt in your hands. You never know where it has gone. Still, one must take you as you are. It is in the blood; for indeed it is true that you can inherit these things, Nora.

NORA.   Ah, I wish I had inherited many of papa's qualities.

HELMER.   And I would not wish you to be anything but just what you are, my sweet little skylark. But, do you know, it strikes me that you are looking rather—what shall I say—rather uneasy to-day?

NORA.   Do I?

HELMER.   You do, really. Look straight at me.

NORA   (*looks at him*). Well?

HELMER   (*wagging his finger at her*). Hasn't Miss Sweet-Tooth been breaking rules in town to-day?

NORA.   No; what makes you think that?

HELMER.   Hasn't she paid a visit to the confectioner's?

NORA.   No, I assure you, Torvald—

HELMER.   Not been nibbling sweets?

NORA.   No, certainly not.

HELMER.   Not even taken a bite at a macaroon or two?

NORA.   No, Torvald, I assure you really—

HELMER.   There, there, of course I was only joking.

NORA   (*going to the table on the right*). I should not think of going against your wishes.

HELMER.   No, I am sure of that; besides, you gave me your word—(*Going up to her.*) Keep your little Christmas secrets to yourself, my darling. They will all be revealed to-night when the Christmas Tree is lit, no doubt.

NORA.   Did you remember to invite Doctor Rank?

HELMER.   No. But there is no need; as a matter of course he will come to dinner with us. However, I will ask him when he comes in this morning. I have ordered some good wine. Nora, you can't think how I am looking forward to this evening.

NORA.   So am I! And how the children will enjoy themselves, Torvald!

HELMER.   It is splendid to feel that one has a perfectly safe appointment, and a big enough income. It's delightful to think of, isn't it?

NORA.   It's wonderful!

HELMER.   Do you remember last Christmas? For a full three weeks beforehand you shut yourself up every evening till long after midnight, making ornaments for the Christmas Tree, and all the other fine things that were to be a surprise to us. It was the dullest three weeks I ever spent!

NORA.   I didn't find it dull.

HELMER   (*smiling*). But there was precious little result, Nora.

NORA.   Oh, you shouldn't tease me about that again. How could I help the cat's going in and tearing everything to pieces?

HELMER.   Of course you couldn't, poor little girl. You had the best of intentions to please us all, and that's the main thing. But it is a good thing that our hard times are over.

NORA.   Yes, it is really wonderful.

HELMER.   This time I needn't sit here and be dull all alone, and you needn't ruin your dear eyes and your pretty little hands—

NORA   (*clapping her hands*). No, Torvald, I needn't any longer, need I! It's wonderfully lovely to hear you say so! (*Taking his arm.*) Now I will tell you how I have been thinking we ought to arrange things, Torvald. As soon as Christmas is over—(*A bell rings in the hall.*) There's the bell. (*She tidies the room a little.*) There's some one at the door. What a nuisance!

HELMER.   If it is a caller, remember I am not at home.

MAID   (*in the doorway*). A lady to see you, ma'am,—a stranger.

NORA.   Ask her to come in.

MAID   (*to HELMER*). The doctor came at the same time, sir.

HELMER.   Did he go straight into my room?

MAID.   Yes, sir.

(*HELMER goes into his room. The MAID ushers in MRS. LINDE, who is in travelling dress, and shuts the door.*)

MRS. LINDE (*in a dejected and timid voice*). How do you do, Nora?

NORA   (*doubtfully*). How do you do—

MRS. LINDE.   You don't recognise me, I suppose.

NORA.   No, I don't know—yes, to be sure, I seem to—(*Suddenly.*) Yes! Christine! Is it really you?

MRS. LINDE.   Yes, it is I.

NORA.   Christine! To think of my not recognising you! And yet how could I—(*In a gentle voice.*) How you have altered, Christine!

MRS. LINDE.   Yes, I have indeed. In nine, ten long years—

NORA.   Is it so long since we met? I suppose it is. The last eight years have been a happy time for me, I can tell you. And so now you have come into the town, and have taken this long journey in winter—that was plucky of you.

MRS. LINDE.   I arrived by steamer this morning.

NORA. To have some fun at Christmas-time, of course. How delightful! We will have such fun together! But take off your things. You are not cold, I hope. (*Helps her*). Now we will sit down by the stove, and be cosy. No, take this armchair; I will sit here in the rocking-chair. (*Takes her hands.*) Now you look like your old self again; it was only the first moment—You are a little paler, Christine, and perhaps a little thinner.

MRS. LINDE. And much, much older, Nora.

NORA. Perhaps a little older; very, very little; certainly not much. (*Stops suddenly and speaks seriously.*) What a thoughtless creature I am, chattering away like this. My poor, dear Christine, do forgive me.

MRS. LINDE. What do you mean, Nora?

NORA (*gently*). Poor Christine, you are a widow.

MRS. LINDE. Yes; it is three years ago now.

NORA. Yes, I knew; I saw it in the papers. I assure you, Christine, I meant ever so often to write to you at the time, but I always put it off and something always prevented me.

MRS. LINDE. I quite understand, dear.

NORA. It was very bad of me, Christine. Poor thing, how you must have suffered. And he left you nothing?

MRS. LINDE. No.

NORA. And no children?

MRS. LINDE. No.

NORA. Nothing at all, then.

MRS. LINDE. Not even any sorrow or grief to live upon.

NORA (*looking incredulously at her.*) But, Christine, is that possible?

MRS. LINDE (*smiles sadly and strokes her hair.*) It sometimes happens, Nora.

NORA. So you are quite alone. How dreadfully sad that must be. I have three lovely children. You can't see them just now, for they are out with their nurse. But now you must tell me all about it.

MRS. LINDE. No, no; I want to hear about you.

NORA. No, you must begin. I mustn't be selfish to-day; to-day I must only think of your affairs. But there is one thing I must tell you. Do you know we have just had a great piece of good luck?

MRS. LINDE. No, what is it?

NORA. Just fancy, my husband has been made manager of the Bank!

MRS. LINDE. Your husband? What good luck!

NORA. Yes, tremendous! A barrister's profession is such an uncertain thing, especially if he won't undertake unsavoury cases; and naturally Torvald has never been willing to do that, and I quite agree with him. You may imagine how pleased we are! He is to take up his work in the Bank at the New Year, and then he will have a big salary and lots of commissions. For the future we can live quite differently—we can do just as we like. I feel so relieved and so happy, Christine! It will be splendid to have heaps of money and not need to have any anxiety, won't it?

MRS. LINDE.   Yes, anyhow I think it would be delightful to have what one needs.

NORA.   No, not only what one needs, but heaps and heaps of money.

MRS. LINDE   (*smiling*). Nora, Nora, haven't you learnt sense yet? In our schooldays you were a great spendthrift.

NORA   (*laughing*). Yes, that is what Torvald says now. (*Wags her finger at her.*) But "Nora, Nora" is not so silly as you think. We have not been in a position for me to waste money. We have both had to work.

MRS. LINDE.   You too?

NORA.   Yes; odds and ends, needlework, crotchet-work, embroidery, and that kind of thing. (*Dropping her voice.*) And other things as well. You know Torvald left his office when we were married? There was no prospect of promotion there, and he had to try and earn more than before. But during the first year he over-worked himself dreadfully. You see, he had to make money every way he could, and he worked early and late; but he couldn't stand it, and fell dreadfully ill, and the doctors said it was necessary for him to go south.

MRS. LINDE.   You spent a whole year in Italy, didn't you?

NORA.   Yes. It was no easy matter to get away, I can tell you. It was just after Ivar was born; but naturally we had to go. It was a wonderfully beautiful journey, and it saved Torvald's life. But it cost a tremendous lot of money, Christine.

MRS. LINDE.   So I should think.

NORA.   It cost about two hundred and fifty pounds. That's a lot, isn't it?

MRS. LINDE.   Yes, and in emergencies like that it is lucky to have the money.

NORA.   I ought to tell you that we had it from papa.

MRS. LINDE.   Oh, I see. It was just about that time that he died, wasn't it?

NORA.   Yes; and, just think of it, I couldn't go and nurse him. I was expecting little Ivar's birth every day and I had my poor sick Torvald to look after. My dear, kind father—I never saw him again, Christine. That was the saddest time I have known since our marriage.

MRS. LINDE.   I know how fond you were of him. And then you went off to Italy?

NORA.   Yes; you see we had money then, and the doctors insisted on our going, so we started a month later.

MRS. LINDE.   And your husband came back quite well?

NORA.   As sound as a bell!

MRS. LINDE.   But—the doctor?

NORA.   What doctor?

MRS. LINDE.   I thought your maid said the gentleman who arrived here just as I did, was the doctor?

NORA.   Yes, that was Doctor Rank, but he doesn't come here professionally. He is our greatest friend, and comes in at least once every day. No, Torvald has not had an hour's illness since then, and our children are strong and healthy and so am I. (*Jumps up and claps her hands.*) Christine! Christine! it's good to be alive and happy!—But how horrid of me; I am talking of nothing but my own affairs. (*Sits on a stool near her, and rests her arms on her knees.*) You mustn't be angry with me. Tell me, is it really true that you did not love your husband? Why did you marry him?

MRS. LINDE.   My mother was alive then, and was bedridden and helpless, and I had to provide for my two younger brothers; so I did not think I was justified in refusing his offer.

NORA.   No, perhaps you were quite right. He was rich at that time, then?

MRS. LINDE.   I believe he was quite well off. But his business was a precarious one; and, when he died, it all went to pieces and there was nothing left.

NORA.   And then?—

MRS. LINDE.   Well, I had to turn my hand to anything I could find— first a small shop, then a small school, and so on. The last three years have seemed like one long working-day, with no rest. Now it is at an end, Nora. My poor mother needs me no more, for she is gone; and the boys do not need me either; they have got situations and can shift for themselves.

NORA.   What a relief you must feel it—

MRS. LINDE.   No, indeed; I only feel my life unspeakably empty. No one to live for any more. (*Gets up restlessly.*) That was why I could not stand the life in my little backwater any longer. I hope it may be easier here to find something which will busy me and occupy my thoughts. If only I could have the good luck to get some regular work—office work of some kind—

NORA.   But, Christine, that is so frightfully tiring, and you look tired out now. You had far better go away to some watering-place.

MRS. LINDE (*walking to the window*). I have no father to give me money for a journey, Nora.

NORA (*rising*). Oh, don't be angry with me.

MRS. LINDE (*going up to her*). It is you that must not be angry with me, dear. The worst of a position like mine is that it makes one so bitter. No one to work for, and yet obliged to be always on the look-out for chances. One must live, and so one becomes selfish. When you told me of the happy turn your fortunes have taken—you will hardly believe it— I was delighted not so much on your account as on my own.

NORA.   How do you mean?—Oh, I understand. You mean that perhaps Torvald could get you something to do.

MRS. LINDE.   Yes, that was what I was thinking of.

NORA.   He must, Christine. Just leave it to me; I will broach the subject very cleverly—I will think of something that will please him very much. It will make me so happy to be of some use to you.

MRS. LINDE.   How kind you are, Nora, to be so anxious to help me! It is doubly kind in you, for you know so little of the burdens and troubles of life.

NORA.   I—? I know so little of them?

MRS. LINDE (*smiling*). My dear! Small household cares and that sort of thing!—You are a child, Nora.

NORA (*tosses her head and crosses the stage*). You ought not to be so superior.

MRS. LINDE.   No?

NORA.   You are just like the others. They all think that I am incapable of anything really serious—

MRS. LINDE.   Come, come—

NORA.   —that I have gone through nothing in this world of cares.

MRS. LINDE.   But, my dear Nora, you have just told me all your troubles.

NORA.   Pooh!—those were trifles. (*Lowering her voice.*) I have not told you the important thing.

MRS. LINDE.   The important thing? What do you mean?

NORA.   You look down upon me altogether, Christine—but you ought not to. You are proud, aren't you, of having worked so hard and so long for your mother?

MRS. LINDE.   Indeed, I don't look down on any one. But it is true that I am both proud and glad to think that I was privileged to make the end of my mother's life almost free from care.

NORA.   And you are proud to think of what you have done for your brothers.

MRS. LINDE.   I think I have the right to be.

NORA.   I think so, too. But now, listen to this; I too have something to be proud and glad of.

MRS. LINDE.   I have no doubt you have. But what do you refer to?

NORA.   Speak low. Suppose Torvald were to hear! He mustn't on any account—no one in the world must know, Christine, except you.

MRS. LINDE.   But what is it?

NORA.   Come here. (*Pulls her down on the sofa beside her.*) Now I will show you that I too have something to be proud and glad of. It was I who saved Torvald's life.

MRS. LINDE.   "Saved"? How?

NORA.   I told you about our trip to Italy. Torvald would never have recovered if he had not gone there—

MRS. LINDE.   Yes, but your father gave you the necessary funds.

NORA (*smiling*). Yes, that is what Torvald and all the others think, but—

MRS. LINDE. But—

NORA. Papa didn't give us a shilling. It was I who procured the money.

MRS. LINDE. You? All that large sum?

NORA. Two hundred and fifty pounds. What do you think of that?

MRS. LINDE. But, Nora, how could you possibly do it? Did you win a prize in the Lottery?

NORA (*contemptuously*). In the Lottery? There would have been no credit in that.

MRS. LINDE. But where did you get it from, then?

NORA (*humming and smiling with an air of mystery*). Hm, hm! Aha!

MRS. LINDE. Because you couldn't have borrowed it.

NORA. Couldn't I? Why not?

MRS. LINDE. No, a wife cannot borrow without her husband's consent.

NORA (*tossing her head*). Oh, if it is a wife who has any head for business—a wife who has the wit to be a little bit clever—

MRS. LINDE. I don't understand it at all, Nora.

NORA. There is no need you should. I never said I had borrowed the money. I may have got it some other way. (*Lies back on the sofa.*) Perhaps I got it from some other admirer. When anyone is as attractive as I am—

MRS. LINDE. You are mad creature.

NORA. Now, you know you're full of curiosity, Christine.

MRS. LINDE. Listen to me, Nora dear. Haven't you been a little bit imprudent?

NORA (*sits up straight.*) Is it imprudent to save your husband's life?

MRS. LINDE. It seems to me imprudent, without his knowledge, to—

NORA. But it was absolutely necessary that he should not know! My goodness, can't you understand that? It was necessary he should have no idea what a dangerous condition he was in. It was to me that the doctors came and said that his life was in danger, and that the only thing to save him was to live in the south. Do you suppose I didn't try, first of all, to get what I wanted as if it were for myself? I told him how much I should love to travel abroad like other young wives; I tried tears and entreaties with him; I told him that he ought to remember the condition I was in, and that he ought to be kind and indulgent to me; I even hinted that he might raise a loan. That nearly made him angry, Christine. He said I was thoughtless, and that it was his duty as my husband not to indulge me in my whims and caprices—as I believe he called them. Very well, I thought, you must be saved—and that was how I came to devise a way out of the difficulty—

MRS. LINDE.   And did your husband never get to know from your father that the money had not come from him?

NORA.   No, never. Papa died just at that time. I had meant to let him into the secret and beg him never to reveal it. But he was so ill then—alas, there never was any need to tell him.

MRS. LINDE.   And since then have you never told your secret to your husband?

NORA.   Good Heavens, no! How could you think so? A man who has such strong opinions about these things! And besides, how painful and humiliating it would be for Torvald, with his manly independence, to know that he owed me anything! It would upset our mutual relations altogether; our beautiful happy home would no longer be what it is now.

MRS. LINDE.   Do you mean never to tell him about it?

NORA (*meditatively, and with a half smile*). Yes—some day, perhaps, after many years, when I am no longer as nice-looking as I am now. Don't laugh at me! I mean, of course, when Torvald is no longer as devoted to me as he is now; when my dancing and dressing-up and reciting have palled on him; then it may be a good thing to have something in reserve—(*Breaking off.*) What nonsense! The time will never come. Now, what do you think of my great secret, Christine? Do you still think I am of no use? I can tell you, too, that this affair has caused me a lot of worry. It has been by no means easy for me to meet my engagements punctually. I may tell you that there is something that is called, in business, quarterly interest, and another thing called payment in instalments, and it is always so dreadfully difficult to manage them. I have had to save a little here and there, where I could, you understand. I have not been able to put aside much from my housekeeping money, for Torvald must have a good table. I couldn't let my children be shabbily dressed; I have felt obliged to use up all he gave me for them, the sweet little darlings!

MRS. LINDE.   So it has all had to come out of your own necessaries of life, poor Nora!

NORA.   Of course. Besides, I was the one responsible for it. Whenever Torvald has given me money for new dresses and such things, I have never spent more than half of it; I have always bought the simplest and cheapest things. Thank Heaven, any clothes look well on me, and so Torvald has never noticed it. But it was often very hard on me, Christine—because it is delightful to be really well dressed, isn't it?

MRS. LINDE.   Quite so.

NORA.   Well, then I have found other ways of earning money. Last winter I was lucky enough to get a lot of copying to do; so I locked myself up and sat writing every evening until quite late at night. Many a time I was desperately tired; but all the same it was a tremendous pleasure to sit there working and earning money. It was like being a man.

MRS. LINDE.   How much have you been able to pay off in that way?

NORA.   I can't tell you exactly. You see, it is very difficult to keep an account of a business matter of that kind. I only know that I have paid every penny that I could scrape together. Many a time I was at my wits' end. (*Smiles.*) Then I used to sit here and imagine that a rich old gentleman had fallen in love with me—

MRS. LINDE.   What! Who was it?

NORA.   Be quiet!—that he had died; and that when his will was opened it contained, written in big letters, the instruction: "The lovely Mrs. Nora Helmer is to have all I possess paid over to her at once in cash."

MRS. LINDE.   But, my dear Nora who could the man be?

NORA.   Good gracious, can't you understand? There was no old gentleman at all; it was only something that I used to sit here and imagine, when I couldn't think of any way of procuring money. But it's all the same now; the tiresome old person can stay where he is, as far as I am concerned; I don't care about him or his will either, for I am free from care now. (*Jumps up.*) My goodness, it's delightful to think of, Christine! Free from care! To be able to be free from care, quite free from care; to be able to play and romp with the children; to be able to keep the house beautifully and have everything just as Torvald likes it! And, think of it, soon the spring will come and the big blue sky! Perhaps we shall be able to take a little trip—perhaps I shall see the sea again! Oh, it's a wonderful thing to be alive and be happy. (*A bell is heard in the hall.*)

MRS. LINDE   (*rising*). There is the bell; perhaps I had better go.

NORA.   No, don't go; no one will come in here; it is sure to be for Torvald.

SERVANT   (*at the hall door*). Excuse me, ma'am—there is a gentleman to see the master, and as the doctor is with him—

NORA.   Who is it?

KROGSTAD   (*at the door*). It is I, Mrs. Helmer. (*MRS. LINDE starts, trembles, and turns to the window.*)

NORA   (*takes a step towards him, and speaks in a strained, low voice*). You? What is it? What do you want to see my husband about?

KROGSTAD.   Bank business—in a way. I have a small post in the Bank, and I hear your husband is to be our chief now—

NORA.   Then it is—

KROGSTAD.   Nothing but dry business matters, Mrs. Helmer; absolutely nothing else.

NORA.   Be so good as to go into the study, then. (*She bows indifferently to him and shuts the door into the hall; then comes back and makes up the fire in the stove.*)

MRS. LINDE.   Nora—who was that man?

NORA.   A lawyer, of the name of Krogstad.

MRS. LINDE.   Then it really was he.

NORA.   Do you know the man?

MRS. LINDE.   I used to—many years ago. At one time he was a solicitor's clerk in our town.

NORA.   Yes, he was.

MRS. LINDE.   He is greatly altered.

NORA.   He made a very unhappy marriage.

MRS. LINDE.   He is a widower now, isn't he?

NORA.   With several children. There now, it is burning up. (*Shuts the door of the stove and moves the rocking-chair aside.*)

MRS. LINDE.   They say he carries on various kinds of business.

NORA.   Really! Perhaps he does; I don't know anything about it. But don't let us think of business; it is so tiresome.

DOCTOR RANK   (*comes out of HELMER'S study. Before he shuts the door he calls to him*). No, my dear fellow, I won't disturb you; I would rather go in to your wife for a little while. (*Shuts the door and sees MRS. LINDE.*) I beg your pardon; I am afraid I am disturbing you too.

NORA.   No, not at all. (*Introducing him.*) Doctor Rank, Mrs. Linde.

RANK.   I have often heard Mrs. Linde's name mentioned here. I think I passed you on the stairs when I arrived, Mrs. Linde?

MRS. LINDE.   Yes, I go up very slowly; I can't manage stairs well.

RANK.   Ah! some slight internal weakness?

MRS. LINDE.   No, the fact is I have been overworking myself.

RANK.   Nothing more than that? Then I suppose you have come to town to amuse yourself with our entertainments?

MRS. LINDE.   I have come to look for work.

RANK.   Is that a good cure for overwork?

MRS. LINDE.   One must live, Doctor Rank.

RANK.   Yes, the general opinion seems to be that it is necessary.

NORA.   Look here, Doctor Rank—you know you want to live.

RANK.   Certainly. However wretched I may feel, I want to prolong the agony as long as possible. All my patients are like that. And so are those who are morally diseased; one of them, and a bad case too, is at this very moment with Helmer—

MRS. LINDE   (*sadly*). Ah!

NORA.   Whom do you mean?

RANK.   A lawyer by the name of Krogstad, a fellow you don't know at all. He suffers from a diseased moral character, Mrs. Helmer; but even he began talking of its being highly important that he should live.

NORA.   Did he? What did he want to speak to Torvald about?

RANK.   I have no idea; I only heard that it was something about the Bank.

NORA.   I didn't know this—what's his name—Krogstad had anything to do with the Bank.

RANK.   Yes, he has some sort of appointment there. (*To MRS. LINDE.*)

I don't know whether you find also in your part of the world that there are certain people who go zealously snuffing about to smell out moral corruption, and, as soon as they have found some, put the person concerned into some lucrative position where they can keep their eye on him. Healthy natures are left out in the cold.

MRS. LINDE. Still I think the sick are those who most need taking care of.

RANK (*shrugging his shoulders*). Yes, there you are. That is the sentiment that is turning society into a sick-house.

(*NORA, who has been absorbed in her thoughts, breaks out into smothered laughter and claps her hands.*)

RANK. Why do you laugh at that? Have you any notion what Society really is?

NORA. What do I care about tiresome Society? I am laughing at something quite different, something extremely amusing. Tell me, Doctor Rank, are all the people who are employed in the Bank dependent on Torvald now?

RANK. Is that what you find so extremely amusing?

NORA (*smiling and humming*). That's my affair! (*Walking about the room.*) It's perfectly glorious to think that we have—that Torvald has so much power over so many people. (*Takes the packet from her pocket.*) Doctor Rank, what do you say to a macaroon?

RANK. What, macaroons? I thought they were forbidden here.

NORA. Yes, but these are some Christine gave me.

MRS. LINDE. What! I?—

NORA. Oh, well, don't be alarmed! You couldn't know that Torvald had forbidden them. I must tell you that he is afraid they will spoil my teeth. But, bah!—once in a way—That's so, isn't it, Doctor Rank? By your leave! (*Puts a macaroon into his mouth.*) You must have one too, Christine. And I shall have one, just a little one—or at most two. (*Walking about.*) I am tremendously happy. There is just one thing in the world now that I should dearly love to do.

RANK. Well, what is that?

NORA. It's something I should dearly love to say, if Torvald could hear me.

RANK. Well, why can't you say it?

NORA. No, I daren't; it's so shocking.

MRS. LINDE. Shocking?

RANK. Well, I should not advise you to say it. Still, with us you might. What is it you would so much like to say if Torvald could hear you?

NORA. I should just love to say—Well, I'm damned!

RANK. Are you mad?

Mrs. Linde.   Nora, dear—!

Rank.   Say it, here he is!

Nora   (*hiding the packet*). Hush! Hush! Hush! (*Helmer comes out of his room, with his coat over his arm and his hat in his hand.*)

Nora.   Well, Torvald dear, have you got rid of him?

Helmer.   Yes, he has just gone.

Nora.   Let me introduce you—this is Christine, who has come to town.

Helmer.   Christine—? Excuse me, but I don't know—

Nora.   Mrs. Linde, dear; Christine Linde.

Helmer.   Of course. A school friend of my wife's, I presume?

Mrs. Linde.   Yes, we have known each other since then.

Nora.   And just think, she has taken a long journey in order to see you.

Helmer.   What do you mean?

Mrs. Linde.   No, really, I—

Nora.   Christine is tremendously clever at book-keeping, and she is frightfully anxious to work under some clever man, so as to perfect herself—

Helmer.   Very sensible, Mrs. Linde.

Nora.   And when she heard you had been appointed manager of the Bank—the news was telegraphed, you know—she travelled here as quick as she could. Torvald, I am sure you will be able to do something for Christine, for my sake, won't you?

Helmer.   Well, it is not altogether impossible. I presume you are a widow, Mrs. Linde?

Mrs. Linde.   Yes.

Helmer.   And have had some experience of book-keeping?

Mrs. Linde.   Yes, a fair amount.

Helmer.   Ah! well, it's very likely I may be able to find something for you—

Nora   (*clapping her hands*). What did I tell you? What did I tell you?

Helmer.   You have just come at a fortunate moment, Mrs. Linde.

Mrs. Linde.   How am I to thank you?

Helmer.   There is no need. (*Puts on his coat.*) But to-day you must excuse me—

Rank.   Wait a minute; I will come with you. (*Brings his fur coat from the hall and warms it at the fire.*)

Nora.   Don't be long away, Torvald dear.

Helmer.   About an hour, not more.

Nora.   Are you going too, Christine?

Mrs. Linde   (*putting on her cloak*). Yes, I must go and look for a room.

Helmer.   Oh, well then, we can walk down the street together.

NORA (*helping her*). What a pity it is we are so short of space here; I am afraid it is impossible for us—

MRS. LINDE. Please don't think of it! Good-bye, Nora dear, and many thanks.

NORA. Good-bye for the present. Of course you will come back this evening. And you too, Dr. Rank. What do you say? If you are well enough? Oh, you must be! Wrap yourself up well. (*They go to the door all talking together. Children's voices are heard on the staircase.*)

NORA. There they are! There they are! (*She runs to open the door. The NURSE comes in with the children.*) Come in! Come in! (*Stoops and kisses them.*) Oh, you sweet blessings! Look at them, Christine! Aren't they darlings?

RANK. Don't let us stand here in the draught.

HELMER. Come along, Mrs. Linde; the place will only be bearable for a mother now!

(*RANK, HELMER, and MRS. LINDE go downstairs. The NURSE comes forward with the children; NORA shuts the hall door.*)

NORA. How fresh and well you look! Such red cheeks!—like apples and roses. (*The children all talk at once while she speaks to them.*) Have you had great fun? That's splendid! What, you pulled both Emmy and Bob along on the sledge?—both at once?—that *was* good. You are a clever boy, Ivar. Let me take her for a little, Anne. My sweet little baby doll! (*Takes the baby from the MAID and dances it up and down.*) Yes, yes, mother will dance with Bob too. What! Have you been snowballing? I wish I had been there too! No, no, I will take their things off, Anne; please let me do it, it is such fun. Go in now, you look half frozen. There is some hot coffee for you on the stove.

(*The NURSE goes into the room on the left. NORA takes off the children's things and throws them about, while they all talk to her at once.*)

NORA. Really! Did a big dog run after you? But it didn't bite you? No, dogs don't bite nice little dolly children. You mustn't look at the parcels, Ivar. What are they? Ah, I daresay you would like to know. No, no—it's something nasty! Come, let us have a game! What shall we play at? Hide and Seek? Yes, we'll play Hide and Seek. Bob shall hide first. Must I hide? Very well, I'll hide first. (*She and the children laugh and shout, and romp in and out of the room; at last NORA hides under the table, the children rush in and out for her, but do not see her; they hear her smothered laughter, run to the table, lift up the cloth and find her. Shouts of laughter. She crawls forward and pretends to frighten them. Fresh laughter. Meanwhile there has been a knock at the hall door, but none of them has noticed it. The door is half opened, and KROGSTAD appears. He waits a little; the game goes on.*)

KROGSTAD. Excuse me, Mrs. Helmer.

NORA   (*with a stifled cry, turns round and gets up on to her knees*). Ah!
what do you want?

KROGSTAD.   Excuse me, the outer door was ajar; I suppose someone
forgot to shut it.

NORA   (*rising*). My husband is out, Mr. Krogstad.

KROGSTAD.   I know that.

NORA.   What do you want here, then?

KROGSTAD.   A word with you.

NORA.   With me?—(*To the children, gently.*) Go in to nurse. What?
No, the strange man won't do mother any harm. When he has gone we
will have another game. (*She takes the children into the room on the left, and
shuts the door after them.*) You want to speak to me?

KROGSTAD.   Yes, I do.

NORA.   To-day? It is not the first of the month yet.

KROGSTAD.   No, it is Christmas Eve, and it will depend on yourself
what sort of a Christmas you will spend.

NORA.   What do you mean? To-day it is absolutely impossible for
me—

KROGSTAD.   We won't talk about that till later on. This is something
different. I presume you can give me a moment?

NORA.   Yes—yes, I can—although—

KROGSTAD.   Good. I was in Olsen's Restaurant and saw your husband
going down the street—

NORA.   Yes?

KROGSTAD.   With a lady?

NORA.   What then?

KROGSTAD.   May I make so bold as to ask it if was a Mrs. Linde?

NORA.   It was.

KROGSTAD.   Just arrived in town?

NORA.   Yes, to-day.

KROGSTAD.   She is a great friend of yours, isn't she?

NORA.   She is. But I don't see—

KROGSTAD.   I knew her too, once upon a time.

NORA.   I am aware of that.

KROGSTAD.   Are you? So you know all about it; I thought as much.
Then I can ask you, without beating about the bush—is Mrs. Linde to
have an appointment in the Bank?

NORA.   What right have you to question me, Mr. Krogstad?—You,
one of my husband's subordinates! But since you ask, you shall know.
Yes, Mrs. Linde *is* to have an appointment. And it was I who pleaded her
cause, Mr. Krogstad, let me tell you that.

KROGSTAD.   I was right in what I thought, then.

NORA   (*walking up and down the stage*). Sometimes one has a tiny bit
of influence, I should hope. Because one is a woman, it does not necessarily

follow that—. When anyone is in a subordinate position, Mr. Krogstad, they should really be careful to avoid offending anyone who—who—

KROGSTAD. Who has influence?

NORA. Exactly.

KROGSTAD (*changing his tone*). Mrs. Helmer, you will be so good as to use your influence on my behalf.

NORA. What? What do you mean?

KROGSTAD. You will be so kind as to see that I am allowed to keep my subordinate position in the Bank.

NORA. What do you mean by that? Who proposes to take your post away from you?

KROGSTAD. Oh, there is no necessity to keep up the pretence of ignorance. I can quite understand that your friend is not very anxious to expose herself to the chance of rubbing shoulders with me; and I quite understand, too, whom I have to thank for being turned off.

NORA. But I assure you—

KROGSTAD. Very likely; but, to come to the point, the time has come when I should advise you to use your influence to prevent that.

NORA. But, Mr. Krogstad, I *have* no influence.

KROGSTAD. Haven't you? I thought you said yourself just now—

NORA. Naturally I did not mean you to put that construction on it. I! What should make you think I have any influence of that kind with my husband?

KROGSTAD. Oh, I have known your husband from our student days. I don't suppose he is any more unassailable than other husbands.

NORA. If you speak slightingly of my husband, I shall turn you out of the house.

KROGSTAD. You are bold, Mrs. Helmer.

NORA. I am not afraid of you any longer. As soon as the New Year comes, I shall in a very short time be free of the whole thing.

KROGSTAD (*controlling himself*). Listen to me, Mrs. Helmer. If necessary, I am prepared to fight for my small post in the Bank as if I were fighting for my life.

NORA. So it seems.

KROGSTAD. It is not only for the sake of the money; indeed that weighs least with me in the matter. There is another reason—well, I may as well tell you. My position is this. I daresay you know, like everybody else, that once, many years ago, I was guilty of an indiscretion.

NORA. I think I have heard something of the kind.

KROGSTAD. The matter never came into court; but every way seemed to be closed to me after that. So I took to the business that you know of. I had to do something; and, honestly, I don't think I've been one of the worst. But now I must cut myself free from all that. My sons are growing up; for their sake I must try and win back as much respect as I can in the town. This post in the Bank was like the first step up for me—and now your husband is going to kick me downstairs again into the mud.

NORA.   But you must believe me, Mr. Krogstad; it is not in my power to help you at all.

KROGSTAD.   Then it is because you haven't the will; but I have the means to compel you.

NORA.   You don't mean that you will tell my husband that I owe you money?

KROGSTAD.   Hm!—suppose I were to tell him?

NORA.   It would be perfectly infamous of you. (*Sobbing.*) To think of his learning my secret, which has been my joy and pride, in such an ugly, clumsy way—that he should learn it from you! And it would put me in a horribly disagreeable position—

KROGSTAD.   Only disagreeable?

NORA   (*impetuously*). Well, do it, then!—and it will be the worse for you. My husband will see for himself what a blackguard you are, and you certainly won't keep your post then.

KROGSTAD.   I asked you if it was only a disagreeable scene at home that you were afraid of?

NORA.   If my husband does get to know of it, of course he will at once pay you what is still owing, and we shall have nothing more to do with you.

KROGSTAD   (*coming a step nearer*). Listen to me, Mrs. Helmer. Either you have a very bad memory or you know very little of business. I shall be obliged to remind you of a few details.

NORA.   What do you mean?

KROGSTAD.   When your husband was ill, you came to me to borrow two hundred and fifty pounds.

NORA.   I didn't know anyone else to go to.

KROGSTAD.   I promised to get you that amount—

NORA.   Yes, and you did so.

KROGSTAD.   I promised to get you that amount, on certain conditions. Your mind was so taken up with your husband's illness, and you were so anxious to get the money for your journey, that you seem to have paid no attention to the conditions of our bargain. Therefore it will not be amiss if I remind you of them. Now, I promised to get the money on the security of a bond which I drew up.

NORA.   Yes, and which I signed.

KROGSTAD.   Good. But below your signature there were a few lines constituting your father a surety for the money; those lines your father should have signed.

NORA.   Should? He did sign them.

KROGSTAD.   I had left the date blank; that is to say, your father should himself have inserted the date on which he signed the paper. Do you remember that?

NORA.   Yes, I think I remember—

KROGSTAD.   Then I gave you the bond to send by post to your father. Is that not so?

NORA.   Yes.

KROGSTAD.   And you naturally did so at once, because five or six days afterwards you brought me the bond with your father's signature. And then I gave you the money.

NORA.   Well, haven't I been paying it off regularly.

KROGSTAD.   Fairly so, yes. But—to come back to the matter in hand—that must have been a very trying time for you, Mrs. Helmer.

NORA.   It was, indeed.

KROGSTAD.   Your father was very ill, wasn't he?

NORA.   He was very near his end.

KROGSTAD.   And died soon afterwards?

NORA.   Yes.

KROGSTAD.   Tell me, Mrs. Helmer, can you by any chance remember what day your father died?—on what day of the month, I mean.

NORA.   Papa died on the 29th of September.

KROGSTAD.   That is correct; I have ascertained it for myself. And, as that is so, there is a discrepancy (*taking a paper from his pocket*) which I cannot account for.

NORA.   What discrepancy? I don't know—

KROGSTAD.   The discrepancy consists, Mrs. Helmer, in the fact that your father signed this bond three days after his death.

NORA.   What do you mean? I don't understand—

KROGSTAD.   Your father died on the 29th of September. But, look here; your father has dated his signature the 2nd of October. It is a discrepancy, isn't it? (*NORA is silent.*) Can you explain it to me? (*NORA is still silent.*) It is a remarkable thing, too, that the words "2nd of October," as well as the year, are not written in your father's handwriting but in one that I think I know. Well, of course it can be explained; your father may have forgotten to date his signature, and someone else may have dated it haphazard before they knew of his death. There is no harm in that. It all depends on the signature of the name; and *that* is genuine, I suppose, Mrs. Helmer? It was your father himself who signed his name here?

NORA   (*after a short pause, throws her head up and looks defiantly at him*). No, it was not. It was I that wrote papa's name.

KROGSTAD.   Are you aware that is a dangerous confession?

NORA.   In what way? You shall have your money soon.

KROGSTAD.   Let me ask you a question; why did you not send the paper to your father?

NORA.   It was impossible; papa was so ill. If I had asked him for his signature, I should have had to tell him what the money was to be used for; and when he was so ill himself I couldn't tell him that my husband's life was in danger—it was impossible.

KROGSTAD.   It would have been better for you if you had given up your trip abroad.

NORA.   No, that was impossible. That trip was to save my husband's life; I couldn't give that up.

KROGSTAD.   But did it never occur to you that you were committing a fraud on me?

NORA.   I couldn't take that into account; I didn't trouble myself about you at all. I couldn't bear you, because you put so many heartless difficulties in my way, although you knew what a dangerous condition my husband was in.

KROGSTAD.   Mrs. Helmer, you evidently do not realise clearly what it is that you have been guilty of. But I can assure you that my one false step, which lost me all my reputation, was nothing more or nothing worse than what you have done.

NORA.   You? Do you ask me to believe that you were brave enough to run a risk to save your wife's life?

KROGSTAD.   The law cares nothing about motives.

NORA.   Then it must be a very foolish law.

KROGSTAD.   Foolish or not, it is the law by which you will be judged, if I produce this paper in court.

NORA.   I don't believe it. Is a daughter not to be allowed to spare her dying father anxiety and care? Is a wife not to be allowed to save her husband's life? I don't know much about law; but I am certain that there must be laws permitting such things as that. Have you no knowledge of such laws—you who are a laywer? You must be a very poor lawyer, Mr. Krogstad.

KROGSTAD.   Maybe. But matters of business—such business as you and I have had together—do you think I don't understand that? Very well. Do as you please. But let me tell you this—if I lose my position a second time, you shall lose yours with me. (*He bows, and goes out through the hall.*)

NORA   (*appears buried in thought for a short time, then tosses her head*). Nonsense! Trying to frighten me like that!—I am not so silly as he thinks. (*Begins to busy herself putting the children's things in order.*) And yet—? No, it's impossible! I did it for love's sake.

THE CHILDREN   (*in the doorway on the left*). Mother, the stranger man has gone out through the gate.

NORA.   Yes, dears, I know. But, don't tell anyone about the stranger man. Do you hear? Not even papa.

CHILDREN.   No, mother; but will you come and play again?

NORA.   No, no,—not now.

CHILDREN.   But, mother, you promised us.

NORA.   Yes, but I can't now. Run away in; I have such a lot to do. Run away in, my sweet little darlings. (*She gets them into the room by degrees and shuts the door on them; then sits down on the sofa, takes up a piece of needlework and sews a few stitches, but soon stops.*) No! (*Throws down the work, gets up, goes to the hall door and calls out.*) Helen! bring the Tree in. (*Goes to the table on the left, opens a drawer, and stops again.*) No, no! it is quite impossible!

MAID (*coming in with the Tree*). Where shall I put it, ma'am?

NORA. Here, in the middle of the floor.

MAID. Shall I get you anything else?

NORA. No, thank you. I have all I want.

[*Exit* MAID.

NORA (*begins dressing the tree*). A candle here—and flowers here—. The horrible man! It's all nonsense—there's nothing wrong. The Tree shall be splendid! I will do everything I can think of to please you, Torvald!—I will sing for you, dance for you—(*HELMER comes in with some papers under his arm.*) Oh! are you back already?

HELMER. Yes. Has any one been here?

NORA. Here? No.

HELMER. That is strange. I saw Krogstad going out of the gate.

NORA. Did you? Oh yes, I forgot, Krogstad was here for a moment.

HELMER. Nora, I can see from your manner that he has been here begging you to say a good word for him.

NORA. Yes.

HELMER. And you were to appear to do it of your own accord; you were to conceal from me the fact of his having been here; didn't he beg that of you too?

NORA. Yes, Torvald, but—

HELMER. Nora, Nora, and you would be a party to that sort of thing? To have any talk with a man like that, and give him any sort of promise? And to tell me a lie into the bargain?

NORA. A lie—?

HELMER. Didn't you tell me no one had been here? (*Shakes his finger at her.*) My little song-bird must never do that again. A song-bird must have a clean beak to chirp with—no false notes! (*Puts his arm around her waist.*) That is so, isn't it? Yes, I am sure it is. (*Lets her go.*) We will say no more about it. (*Sits down by the stove.*) How warm and snug it is here! (*Turns over his papers.*)

NORA (*after a short pause, during which she busies herself with the Christmas Tree.*) Torvald!

HELMER. Yes.

NORA. I am looking forward tremendously to the fancy-dress ball at the Stenborgs' the day after to-morrow.

HELMER. And I am tremendously curious to see what you are going to surprise me with.

NORA. It was very silly of me to want to do that.

HELMER.   What do you mean?

NORA.   I can't hit upon anything that will do; everything I think of seems so silly and insignificant.

HELMER.   Does my little Nora acknowledge that at last?

NORA   (*standing behind his chair with her arms on the back of it*). Are you very busy, Torvald?

HELMER.   Well—

NORA.   What are all those papers?

HELMER.   Bank business.

NORA.   Already?

HELMER.   I have got authority from the retiring manager to undertake the necessary changes in the staff and in the rearrangement of the work; and I must make use of the Christmas week for that, so as to have everything in order for the new year.

NORA.   Then that was why this poor Krogstad—

HELMER.   Hm!

NORA   (*leans against the back of his chair and strokes his hair*). If you hadn't been so busy I should have asked you a tremendously big favour, Torvald.

HELMER.   What is that? Tell me.

NORA.   There is no one has such good taste as you. And I do so want to look nice at the fancy-dress ball. Torvald, couldn't you take me in hand and decide what I shall go as, and what sort of a dress I shall wear?

HELMER.   Aha! so my obstinate little woman is obliged to get someone to come to her rescue?

NORA.   Yes, Torvald, I can't get along a bit without your help.

HELMER.   Very well, I will think it over, we shall manage to hit upon something.

NORA.   That is nice of you. (*Goes to the Christmas Tree. A short pause.*) How pretty the red flowers look—. But, tell me, was it really something very bad that this Krogstad was guilty of?

HELMER.   He forged someone's name. Have you any idea what that means?

NORA.   Isn't it possible that he was driven to do it by necessity?

HELMER.   Yes; or, as in so many cases, by imprudence. I am not so heartless as to condemn a man altogether because of a single false step of that kind.

NORA.   No, you wouldn't, would you, Torvald?

HELMER.   Many a man has been able to retrieve his character, if he has openly confessed his fault and taken his punishment.

NORA.   Punishment—?

HELMER.   But Krogstad did nothing of that sort; he got himself out of it by a cunning trick, and that is why he has gone under altogether.

NORA.   But do you think it would—?

HELMER.   Just think how a guilty man like that has to lie and play the hypocrite with every one, how he has to wear a mask in the presence of those near and dear to him, even before his own wife and children. And about the children—that is the most terrible part of it all, Nora.

NORA.   How?

HELMER.   Because such an atmosphere of lies infects and poisons the whole life of a home. Each breath the children take in such a house is full of the germs of evil.

NORA   (*coming nearer him*). Are you sure of that?

HELMER.   My dear, I have often seen it in the course of my life as a lawyer. Almost everyone who has gone to the bad early in life has had a deceitful mother.

NORA.   Why do you only say—mother?

HELMER.   If seems most common to be the mother's influence, though naturally a bad father's would have the same result. Every lawyer is familiar with the fact. This Krogstad, now, has been persistently poisoning his own children with lies and dissimulation; that is why I say he has lost all moral character. (*Holds out his hands to her.*) That is why my sweet little Nora must promise me not to plead his cause. Give me your hand on it. Come, come, what is this? Give me your hand. There now, that's settled. I assure you it would be quite impossible for me to work with him; I literally feel physically ill when I am in the company of such people.

NORA   (*takes her hand out of his and goes to the opposite side of the Christmas Tree*). How hot it is in here; and I have such a lot to do.

HELMER   (*getting up and putting his papers in order*). Yes, and I must try and read through some of these before dinner; and I must think about your costume, too. And it is just possible I may have something ready in gold paper to hang up on the Tree. (*Puts his hand on her head.*) My precious little singing-bird! (*He goes into his room and shuts the door after him.*)

NORA   (*after a pause, whispers*). No, no—it isn't true. It's impossible; it must be impossible.

(*The NURSE opens the door on the left.*)

NURSE.   The little ones are begging so hard to be allowed to come in to mamma.

NORA.   No, No, No! Don't let them come in to me! You stay with them, Anne.

NURSE.   Very well, Ma'am. (*Shuts the door.*)

NORA   (*pale with terror*). Deprave my little children? Poison my home? (*A short pause. Then she tosses her head.*) It's not true. It can't possibly be true.

ACT II

(*THE SAME SCENE.—The Christmas Tree is in the corner by the piano, stripped of its ornaments and with burnt-down candle-ends on its dishevelled branches. NORA'S cloak and hat are lying on the sofa. She is alone in the room, walking about uneasily. She stops by the sofa and takes up her cloak.*)

NORA   (*drops her cloak*). Someone is coming now! (*Goes to the door and listens.*) No—it is no one. Of course, no one will come to-day. Christmas Day—nor to-morrow either. But, perhaps—(*opens the door and looks out*). No, nothing in the letter-box; it is quite empty. (*Comes forward.*) What rubbish! of course he can't be in earnest about it. Such a thing couldn't happen; it is impossible—I have three little children.

(*Enter the NURSE from the room on the left, carrying a big cardboard box.*)

NURSE.   At last I have found the box with the fancy dress.

NORA.   Thanks; put it on the table.

NURSE   (*doing so*). But it is very much in want of mending.

NORA.   I should like to tear it into a hundred thousand pieces.

NURSE.   What an idea! It can easily be put in order—just a little patience.

NORA.   Yes, I will go and get Mrs. Linde to come and help me with it.

NURSE.   What, out again? In this horrible weather? You will catch cold, ma'am, and make yourself ill.

NORA.   Well, worse than that might happen. How are the children?

NURSE.   The poor little souls are playing with their Christmas presents, but—

NORA.   Do they ask much for me?

NURSE.   You see, they are so accustomed to have their mamma with them.

NORA.   Yes, but, nurse, I shall not be able to be so much with them now as I was before.

NURSE.   Oh well, young children easily get accustomed to anything.

NORA.   Do you think so? Do you think they would forget their mother if she went away altogether?

NURSE.   Good heavens!—went away altogether?

NORA.   Nurse, I want you to tell me something I have often wondered about—how could you have the heart to put your own child out among strangers?

NURSE.   I was obliged to, if I wanted to be little Nora's nurse.

NORA.   Yes, but how could you be willing to do it?

NURSE.   What, when I was going to get such a good place by it? A poor girl who has got into trouble should be glad to. Besides, that wicked man didn't do a single thing for me.

NORA.   But I suppose your daughter has quite forgotten you.

NURSE.   No, indeed she hasn't. She wrote to me when she was confirmed, and when she was married.

NORA (*putting her arms round her neck*). Dear old Anne, you were a good mother to me when I was little.

NURSE.   Little Nora, poor dear, had no other mother but me.

NORA.   And if my little ones had no other mother, I am sure you would— What nonsense I am talking! (*Opens the box.*) Go in to them. Now I must—. You will see to-morrow how charming I shall look.

NURSE.   I am sure there will be no one at the ball so charming as you ma'am. (*Goes into the room on the left.*)

NORA (*begins to unpack the box, but soon pushes it away from her*). If only I dared go out. If only no one would come. If only I could be sure nothing would happen here in the meantime. Stuff and nonsense! No one will come. Only I mustn't think about it. I will brush my muff. What lovely, lovely gloves! Out of my thoughts, out of my thoughts! One, two, three, four, five, six— (*Screams.*) Ah! there is someone coming—. (*Makes a movement towards the door, but stands irresolute.*)

(*Enter MRS. LINDE from the hall, where she has taken off her cloak and hat.*)

NORA.   Oh, it's you, Christine. There is no one else out there, is there? How good of you to come!

MRS. LINDE.   I heard you were up asking for me.

NORA.   Yes, I was passing by. As a matter of fact, it is something you could help me with. Let us sit down here on the sofa. Look here. To-morrow evening there is to be a fancy-dress ball at the Stenborgs', who live above us; and Torvald wants me to go as a Neapolitan fisher-girl, and dance the Tarantella that I learnt at Capri.

MRS. LINDE.   I see; you are going to keep up the character.

NORA.   Yes, Torvald wants me to. Look, here is the dress; Torvald had it made for me there, but now it is all so torn, and I haven't any idea—

MRS. LINDE.   We will easily put that right. It is only some of the trimming come unsewn here and there. Needle and thread? Now then, that's all we want.

NORA.   It *is* nice of you.

MRS. LINDE (*sewing*). So you are going to be dressed up to-morrow, Nora. I will tell you what—I shall come in for a moment and see you in your fine feathers. But I have completely forgotten to thank you for a delightful evening yesterday.

NORA (*gets up, and crosses the stage*). Well, I don't think yesterday was as pleasant as usual. You ought to have come to town a little earlier, Christine. Certainly Torvald does understand how to make a house dainty and attractive.

MRS. LINDE. And so do you, it seems to me; you are not your father's daughter for nothing. But tell me, is Doctor Rank always as depressed as he was yesterday?

NORA. No; yesterday it was very noticeable. I must tell you that he suffers from a very dangerous disease. He has consumption of the spine, poor creature. His father was a horrible man who committed all sorts of excesses; and that is why his son was sickly from childhood, do you understand?

MRS. LINDE (*dropping her sewing*). But, my dearest Nora, how do you know anything about such things?

NORA (*walking about*). Pooh! When you have three children, you get visits now and then from—from married women, who know something of medical matters, and they talk about one thing and another.

MRS. LINDE (*goes on sewing. A short silence*). Does Doctor Rank come here every day?

NORA. Every day regularly. He is Torvald's most intimate friend, and a great friend of mine too. He is just like one of the family.

MRS. LINDE. But tell me this—is he perfectly sincere? I mean, isn't he the kind of man that is very anxious to make himself agreeable?

NORA. Not in the least. What makes you think that?

MRS. LINDE. When you introduced him to me yesterday, he declared he had often heard my name mentioned in this house; but afterwards I noticed that your husband hadn't the slightest idea who I was. So how could Doctor Rank—?

NORA. That is quite right, Christine. Torvald is so absurdly fond of me that he wants me absolutely to himself, as he says. At first he used to seem almost jealous if I mentioned any of the dear folk at home, so naturally I gave up doing so. But I often talk about such things with Doctor Rank, because he likes hearing about them.

MRS. LINDE. Listen to me, Nora. You are still very like a child in many things, and I am older than you in many ways and have a little more experience. Let me tell you this—you ought to make an end of it with Doctor Rank.

NORA. What ought I to make an end of?

MRS. LINDE. Of two things, I think. Yesterday you talked some nonsense about a rich admirer who was to leave you money—

NORA. An admirer who doesn't exist, unfortunately! But what then?

MRS. LINDE. Is Doctor Rank a man of means?

NORA. Yes, he is.

MRS. LINDE. And has no one to provide for?

NORA. No, no one; but—

MRS. LINDE. And comes here every day?

NORA. Yes, I told you so.

MRS. LINDE. But how can this well-bred man be so tactless?

NORA. I don't understand you at all.

MRS. LINDE. Don't prevaricate, Nora. Do you suppose I don't know who lent you the two hundred and fifty pounds?

NORA. Are you out of your senses? How can you think of such a thing! A friend of ours, who comes here every day! Do you realise what a horribly painful position that would be?

MRS. LINDE. Then it really isn't he?

NORA. No, certainly not. It would never have entered into my head for a moment. Besides, he had no money to lend then; he came into his money afterwards.

MRS. LINDE. Well, I think that was lucky for you, my dear Nora.

NORA. No, it would never have come into my head to ask Doctor Rank. Although I am quite sure that if I had asked him—

MRS. LINDE. But of course you won't.

NORA. Of course not. I have no reason to think it could possibly be necessary. But I am quite sure that if I told Doctor Rank—

MRS. LINDE. Behind your husband's back?

NORA. I must make an end of it with the other one, and that will be behind his back too. I *must* make an end of it with him.

MRS. LINDE. Yes, that is what I told you yesterday, but—

NORA (*walking up and down*). A man can put a thing like that straight much easier than a woman—

MRS. LINDE. One's husband, yes.

NORA. Nonsense! (*Standing still.*) When you pay off a debt you get your bond back, don't you?

MRS. LINDE. Yes, as a matter of course.

NORA. And can tear it into a hundred thousand pieces, and burn it up—the nasty dirty paper!

MRS. LINDE (*looks hard at her, lays down her sewing and gets up slowly*). Nora, you are concealing something from me.

NORA. Do I look as if I were?

MRS. LINDE. Something has happened to you since yesterday morning. Nora, what is it?

NORA (*going nearer to her*). Christine! (*Listens.*) Hush! there's Torvald come home. Do you mind going in to the children for the present? Torvald can't bear to see dressmaking going on. Let Anne help you.

MRS. LINDE (*gathering some of the things together*). Certainly—but I am not going away from here till we have had it out with one another. (*She goes into the room on the left, as* HELMER *comes in from the hall.*)

NORA (*going up to* HELMER). I have wanted you so much, Torvald dear.

HELMER. Was that the dressmaker?

NORA. No, it was Christine; she is helping me to put my dress in order. You will see I shall look quite smart.

HELMER.   Wasn't that a happy thought of mine, now?

NORA.   Splendid! But don't you think it is nice of me too, to do as you wish?

HELMER.   Nice?—because you do as your husband wishes? Well, well, you little rogue, I am sure you did not mean it in that way. But I am not going to disturb you; you will want to be trying on your dress, I expect.

NORA.   I suppose you are going to work.

HELMER.   Yes. (*Shows her a bundle of papers.*) Look at that. I have just been into the bank. (*Turns to go into his room.*)

NORA.   Torvald.

HELMER.   Yes.

NORA.   If your little squirrel were to ask you for something very, very prettily—?

HELMER.   What then?

NORA.   Would you do it?

HELMER.   I should like to hear what it is, first.

NORA.   Your squirrel would run about and do all her tricks if you would be nice, and do what she wants.

HELMER.   Speak plainly.

NORA.   Your skylark would chirp about in every room, with her song rising and falling—

HELMER.   Well, my skylark does that anyhow.

NORA.   I would play the fairy and dance for you in the moonlight, Torvald.

HELMER.   Nora—you surely don't mean that request you made to me this morning?

NORA   (*going near him*). Yes, Torvald, I beg you so earnestly.

HELMER.   Have you really the courage to open up that question again?

NORA.   Yes, dear, you *must* do as I ask; you *must* let Krogstad keep his post in the bank.

HELMER.   My dear Nora, it is his post that I have arranged Mrs. Linde shall have.

NORA.   Yes, you have been awfully kind about that; but you could just as well dismiss some other clerk instead of Krogstad.

HELMER.   This is simply incredible obstinacy! Because you chose to give him a thoughtless promise that you would speak for him, I am expected to—

NORA.   That isn't the reason, Torvald. It is for your own sake. This fellow writes in the most scurrilous newspapers; you have told me so yourself. He can do you an unspeakable amount of harm. I am frightened to death of him—

HELMER. Ah, I understand; it is recollections of the past that scare you.

NORA. What do you mean?

HELMER. Naturally you are thinking of your father.

NORA. Yes—yes, of course. Just recall to your mind what these malicious creatures wrote in the papers about papa, and how horribly they slandered him. I believe they would have procured his dismissal if the Department had not sent you over to inquire into it, and if you had not been so kindly disposed and helpful to him.

HELMER. My little Nora, there is an important difference between your father and me. Your father's reputation as a public official was not above suspicion. Mine is, and I hope it will continue to be so, as long as I hold my office.

NORA. You never can tell what mischief these men may contrive. We ought to be so well off, so snug and happy here in our peaceful home, and have no cares—you and I and the children, Torvald! That is why I beg you so earnestly—

HELMER. And it is just by interceding for him that you make it impossible for me to keep him. It is already known at the Bank that I mean to dismiss Krogstad. Is it to get about now that the new manager has changed his mind at his wife's bidding—

NORA. And what if it did?

HELMER. Of course!—if only this obstinate little person can get her way! Do you suppose I am going to make myself ridiculous before my whole staff, to let people think that I am a man to be swayed by all sorts of outside influence? I should very soon feel the consequences of it, I can tell you! And besides, there is one thing that makes it quite impossible for me to have Krogstad in the Bank as long as I am manager.

NORA. Whatever is that?

HELMER. His moral failings I might perhaps have overlooked, if necessary—

NORA. Yes, you could—couldn't you?

HELMER. And I hear he is a good worker, too. But I knew him when we were boys. It was one of those rash friendships that so often prove an incubus in after life. I may as well tell you plainly, we were once on very intimate terms with one another. But this tactless fellow lays no restraint on himself when other people are present. On the contrary, he thinks it gives him the right to adopt a familiar tone with me, and every minute it is "I say, Helmer, old fellow!" and that sort of thing. I assure you it is extremely painful to me. He would make my position in the Bank intolerable.

NORA. Torvald, I don't believe you mean that.

HELMER. Don't you? Why not?

NORA. Because it is such a narrow-minded way of looking at things.

HELMER. What are you saying? Narrow-minded? Do you think I am narrow-minded?

NORA. No, just the opposite, dear—and it is exactly for that reason.

HELMER. It's the same thing. You say my point of view is narrow-minded, so I must be so too. Narrow-minded! Very well—I must put an end to this. (*Goes to the hall door and calls.*) Helen!

NORA. What are you going to do?

HELMER (*looking among his papers*). Settle it. (*Enter* MAID.) Look here; take this letter and go downstairs with it at once. Find a messenger and tell him to deliver it, and be quick. The address is on it, and here is the money.

MAID Very well, sir. (*Exit with the letter.*)

HELMER (*putting hs papers together*). Now then, little Miss Obstinate.

NORA (*breathlessly*). Torvald—what was that letter?

HELMER. Krogstad's dismissal.

NORA. Call her back, Torvald! There is still time. Oh Torvald, call her back! Do it for my sake—for your own sake—for the children's sake! Do you hear me, Torvald? Call her back! You don't know what that letter can bring upon us.

HELMER. It's too late.

NORA. Yes, it's too late.

HELMER. My dear Nora, I can forgive the anxiety you are in, although really it is an insult to me. It is, indeed. Isn't it an insult to think that I should be afraid of a starving quill-driver's vengeance? But I forgive you nevertheless, because it is such eloquent witness to your great love for me. (*Takes her in his arms.*) And that is as it should be, my own darling Nora. Come what will, you may be sure I shall have both courage and strength if they be needed. You will see I am man enough to take everything upon myself.

NORA (*in a horror-stricken voice*). What do you mean by that?

HELMER. Everything I say—

NORA (*recovering herself*). You will never have to do that.

HELMER. That's right. Well, we will share it, Nora, as man and wife should. That is how it shall be. (*Caressing her.*) Are you content now? There! there!—not these frightened dove's eyes! The whole thing is only the wildest fancy!—Now, you must go and play through the Tarantella and practise with your tambourine. I shall go into the inner office and shut the door, and I shall hear nothing; you can make as much noise as you please. (*Turns back at the door.*) And when Rank comes, tell him where he will find me. (*Nods to her, takes his papers and goes into his room, and shuts the door after him.*)

NORA (*bewildered with anxiety, stands as if rooted to the spot, and whispers*).

He was capable of doing it. He will do it. He will do it in spite of everything—No, not that! Never, never! Anything rather than that! Oh, for some help, some way out of it! (*The door-bell rings.*) Doctor Rank! Anything rather than that—anything, whatever it is! (*She puts her hands over her face, pulls herself together, goes to the door and opens it. RANK is standing without, hanging up his coat. During the following dialogue it begins to grow dark.*)

NORA.   Good-day, Doctor Rank. I knew your ring. But you mustn't go in to Torvald now; I think he is busy with something.

RANK.   And you?

NORA   (*brings him in and shuts the door after him*). Oh, you know very well I always have time for you.

RANK.   Thank you. I shall make use of as much of it as I can.

NORA.   What do you mean by that? As much of it as you can?

RANK.   Well, does that alarm you?

NORA.   It was such a strange way of putting it. Is anything likely to happen?

RANK.   Nothing but what I have long been prepared for. But I certainly didn't expect it to happen so soon.

NORA   (*gripping him by the arm*). What have you found out? Doctor Rank, you must tell me.

RANK   (*sitting down by the stove*). It is all up with me. And it can't be helped.

NORA   (*with a sigh of relief*). Is it about yourself?

RANK.   Who else? It is no use lying to one's self. I am the most wretched of all my patients, Mrs. Helmer. Lately I have been taking stock of my internal economy. Bankrupt! Probably within a month I shall lie rotting in the churchyard.

NORA.   What an ugly thing to say!

RANK.   The thing itself is cursedly ugly, and the worst of it is that I shall have to face so much more that is ugly before that. I shall only make one more examination of myself; when I have done that, I shall know pretty certainly when it will be that the horrors of dissolution will begin. There is something I want to tell you. Helmer's refined nature gives him an unconquerable disgust at everything that is ugly; I won't have him in my sick-room.

NORA.   Oh, but, Doctor Rank—

RANK.   I won't have him there. Not on any account. I bar my door to him. As soon as I am quite certain that the worst has come, I shall send you my card with a black cross on it, and then you will know that the loathsome end has begun.

NORA.   You are quite absurd to-day. And I wanted you so much to be in a really good humour.

RANK.   With death stalking beside me?—To have to pay this penalty for another man's sin! Is there any justice in that? And in every single family, in one way or another, some such inexorable retribution is being exacted—

NORA   *(putting her hands over her ears)*. Rubbish! Do talk of something cheerful.

RANK.   Oh, it's a mere laughing matter, the whole thing. My poor innocent spine has to suffer for my father's youthful amusements.

NORA   *(sitting at the table on the left)*. I suppose you mean that he was too partial to asparagus and pâté de foie gras, don't you?

RANK.   Yes, and to truffles.

NORA.   Truffles, yes. And oysters too, I suppose?

RANK.   Oysters, of course, that goes without saying.

NORA.   And heaps of port and champagne. It is sad that all these nice things should take their revenge on our bones.

RANK.   Especially that they should revenge themselves on the unlucky bones of those who have not had the satisfaction of enjoying them.

NORA.   Yes, that's the saddest part of it all.

RANK   *(with a searching look at her)*. Hm!—

NORA   *(after a short pause)*. Why did you smile?

RANK.   No, it was you that laughed.

NORA.   No, it was you that smiled, Doctor Rank!

RANK   *(rising)*. You are a greater rascal than I thought.

NORA.   I am in a silly mood to-day.

RANK.   So it seems.

NORA   *(putting her hands on his shoulders)*. Dear, dear Doctor Rank, death mustn't take you away from Torvald and me.

RANK.   It is a loss you would easily recover from. Those who are gone are soon forgotten.

NORA   *(looking at him anxiously)*. Do you believe that?

RANK.   People form new ties, and then—

NORA.   Who will form new ties?

RANK.   Both you and Helmer, when I am gone. You yourself are already on the high road to it, I think. What did that Mrs. Linde want here last night?

NORA.   Oho!—you don't mean to say you are jealous of poor Christine?

RANK.   Yes, I am. She will be my successor in this house. When I am done for, this woman will—

NORA.   Hush! don't speak so loud. She is in that room.

RANK.   To-day again. There, you see.

NORA.   She has only come to sew my dress for me. Bless my soul, how unreasonable you are! *(Sits down on the sofa.)* Be nice now, Doctor Rank, and to-morrow you will see how beautifully I shall dance, and you can imagine I am doing it all for you—and for Torvald too, of course.

(*Takes various things out of the box.*) Doctor Rank, come and sit down here, and I will show you something.

RANK (*sitting down*). What is it?

NORA. Just look at those!

RANK. Silk stockings.

NORA. Flesh-coloured. Aren't they lovely? It is so dark here now, but to-morrow—. No, no, no! you must only look at the feet. Oh well, you may have leave to look at the legs too.

RANK. Hm!—

NORA. Why are you looking so critical? Don't you think they will fit me?

RANK. I have no means of forming an opinion about that.

NORA (*looks at him for a moment*). For shame! (*Hits him lightly on the ear with the stockings.*) That's to punish you. (*Folds them up again.*)

RANK. And what other nice things am I to be allowed to see?

NORA. Not a single thing more, for being so naughty. (*She looks among the things, humming to herself.*)

RANK (*after a short silence*). When I am sitting here, talking to you as intimately as this, I cannot imagine for a moment what would have become of me if I had never come into this house.

NORA (*smiling*). I believe you do feel thoroughly at home with us.

RANK (*in a lower voice, looking straight in front of him*). And to be obliged to leave it all—

NORA. Nonsense, you are not going to leave it.

RANK (*as before*). And not be able to leave behind one the slightest token of one's gratitude, scarcely even a fleeting regret—nothing but an empty place which the first comer can fill as well as any other.

NORA. And if I asked you now for a—? No!

RANK. For what?

NORA. For a big proof of your friendship—

RANK. Yes, yes!

NORA. I mean a tremendously big favour—

RANK. Would you really make me so happy for once?

NORA. Ah, but you don't know what it is yet.

RANK. No—but tell me.

NORA. I really can't, Doctor Rank. It is something out of all reason; it means advice, and help, and a favour—

RANK. The bigger a thing it is the better. I can't conceive what it is you mean. Do tell me. Haven't I your confidence?

NORA. More than any one else. I know you are my truest and best friend, and so I will tell you what it is. Well, Doctor Rank, it is something you must help me to prevent. You know how devotedly, how inexpressibly deeply Torvald loves me; he would never for a moment hesitate to give his life for me.

RANK   (*leaning towards her*). Nora—do you think he is the only one—?

NORA   (*with a slight start*). The only one—?

RANK.   The only one who would gladly give his life for your sake.

NORA   (*sadly*). Is that it?

RANK.   I was determined you should know it before I went away, and there will never be a better opportunity than this. Now you know it, Nora. And now you know, too, that you can trust me as you would trust no one else.

NORA   (*rises, deliberately and quietly.*) Let me pass.

RANK   (*makes room for her to pass him, but sits still*). Nora!

NORA   (*at the hall door*). Helen, bring in the lamp. (*Goes over to the stove.*) Dear Doctor Rank, that was really horrid of you.

RANK.   To have loved you as much as any one else does? Was that horrid?

NORA.   No, but to go and tell me so. There was really no need—

RANK.   What do you mean? Did you know—? (*MAID enters with lamp, puts it down on the table, and goes out.*) Nora—Mrs. Helmer— tell me, had you any idea of this?

NORA.   Oh, how do I know whether I had or whether I hadn't? I really can't tell you— To think you could be so clumsy, Doctor Rank! We were getting on so nicely.

RANK.   Well, at all events you know now that you can command me, body and soul. So won't you speak out?

NORA   (*looking at him*). After what happened?

RANK.   I beg you to let me know what it is.

NORA.   I can't tell you anything now.

RANK.   Yes, yes. You mustn't punish me in that way. Let me have permission to do for you whatever a man may do.

NORA.   You can do nothing for me now. Besides, I really don't need any help at all. You will find that the whole thing is merely fancy on my part. It really is so—of course it is! (*Sits down in the rocking-chair, and looks at him with a smile.*) You are a nice sort of man, Doctor Rank!—don't you feel ashamed of yourself, now the lamp has come?

RANK.   Not a bit. But perhaps I had better go—for ever?

NORA.   No, indeed, you shall not. Of course you must come here just as before. You know very well Torvald can't do without you.

RANK.   Yes, but you?

NORA.   Oh, I am always tremendously pleased when you come.

RANK.   It is just that, that put me on the wrong track. You are a riddle to me. I have often thought that you would almost as soon be in my company as in Helmer's.

NORA.   Yes—you see there are some people one loves best, and others whom one would almost always rather have as companions.

RANK.   Yes, there is something in that.

NORA. When I was at home, of course I loved papa best. But I always thought it tremendous fun if I could steal down into the maids' room, because they never moralised at all, and talked to each other about such entertaining things.

RANK. I see—it is *their* place I have taken.

NORA (*jumping up and going to him*). Oh, dear, nice Doctor Rank, I never meant that at all. But surely you can understand that being with Torvald is a little like being with papa—

(*Enter MAID from the hall.*)

MAID. If you please, ma'am. (*Whispers and hands her a card.*)

NORA (*glancing at the card*). Oh! (*Puts it in her pocket.*)

RANK. Is there anything wrong?

NORA. No, no, not in the least. It is only something—it is my new dress—

RANK. What? Your dress is lying there.

NORA. Oh, yes, that one; but this is another. I ordered it. Torvald mustn't know about it—

RANK. Oho! Then that was the great secret.

NORA. Of course. Just go in to him; he is sitting in the inner room. Keep him as long as—

RANK. Make your mind easy; I won't let him escape. (*Goes into HELMER'S room.*)

NORA (*to the MAID*). And he is standing waiting in the kitchen?

MAID. Yes; he came up the back stairs.

NORA. But didn't you tell him no one was in?

MAID. Yes, but it was no good.

NORA. He won't go away?

MAID. No; he says he won't until he has seen you, ma'am.

NORA. Well, let him come in—but quietly. Helen, you mustn't say anything about it to any one. It is a surprise for my husband.

MAID. Yes, ma'am, I quite understand.

(*Exit.*)

NORA. This dreadful thing is going to happen! It will happen in spite of me! No, no, no, it can't happen—it shan't happen! (*She bolts the door of HELMER'S room. The MAID opens the hall door for KROGSTAD and shuts it after him. He is wearing a fur coat, high boots and a fur cap.*)

NORA (*advancing towards him*). Speak low—my husband is at home.

KROGSTAD. No matter about that.

NORA. What do you want of me?

KROGSTAD. An explanation of something.

NORA. Make haste then. What is it?

KROGSTAD. You know, I suppose, that I have got my dimissal.

NORA.   I couldn't prevent it, Mr. Krogstad. I fought as hard as I could on your side, but it was no good.

KROGSTAD.   Does your husband love you so little, then? He knows what I can expose you to, and yet he ventures—

NORA.   How can you suppose that he has any knowledge of the sort?

KROGSTAD.   I didn't suppose so at all. It would not be the least like our dear Torvald Helmer to show so much courage—

NORA.   Mr. Krogstad, a little respect for my husband, please.

KROGSTAD.   Certainly—all the respect he deserves. But since you have kept the matter so carefully to yourself, I make bold to suppose that you have a little clearer idea, than you had yesterday, of what it actually is that you have done?

NORA.   More than you could ever teach me.

KROGSTAD.   Yes, such a bad lawyer as I am.

NORA.   What is it you want of me?

KROGSTAD.   Only to see how you were, Mrs. Helmer. I have been thinking about you all day long. A mere cashier, a quill-driver, a—well, a man like me—even if he has a little of what is called feeling, you know.

NORA.   Show it, then; think of my little children.

KROGSTAD.   Have you and your husband thought of mine? But never mind about that. I only wanted to tell you that you need not take this matter too seriously. In the first place there will be no accusation made on my part.

NORA.   No, of course not; I was sure of that.

KROGSTAD.   The whole thing can be arranged amicably; there is no reason why anyone should know anything about it. It will remain a secret between us three.

NORA.   My husband must never get to know anything about it.

KROGSTAD.   How will you be able to prevent it? Am I to understand that you can pay the balance that is owing?

NORA.   No, not just at present.

KROGSTAD.   Or perhaps that you have some expedient for raising the money soon?

NORA.   No expedient that I mean to make use of.

KROGSTAD.   Well, in any case, it would have been of no use to you now. If you stood there with ever so much money in your hand, I would never part with your bond.

NORA.   Tell me what purpose you mean to put it to.

KROGSTAD.   I shall only preserve it—keep it in my possession. No one who is not concerned in the matter shall have the slightest hint of it. So that if the thought of it has driven you to any desperate resolution—

NORA.   It has.

KROGSTAD.   If you had put it in your mind to run away from your home—

NORA. I had.

KROGSTAD. Or even something worse—

NORA. How could you know that?

KROGSTAD. Give up the idea.

NORA. How did you know I had thought of *that*?

KROGSTAD. Most of us think of that at first. I did, too—but I hadn't the courage.

NORA (*faintly*). No more had I.

KROGSTAD (*in a tone of relief*). No, that's it, isn't it—you hadn't the courage either?

NORA. No, I haven't—I haven't.

KROGSTAD. Besides, it would have been a great piece of folly. Once the first storm at home is over—. I have a letter for your husband in my pocket.

NORA. Telling him everything?

KROGSTAD. In as lenient a manner as I possibly could.

NORA (*quickly*). He mustn't get the letter. Tear it up. I will find some means of getting money.

KROGSTAD. Excuse me, Mrs. Helmer, but I think I told you just now—

NORA. I am not speaking of what I owe you. Tell me what sum you are asking my husband for, and I will get the money.

KROGSTAD. I am not asking your husband for a penny.

NORA. What do you want, then?

KROGSTAD. I will tell you. I want to rehabilitate myself, Mrs. Helmer; I want to get on; and in that your husband must help me. For the last year and a half I have not had a hand in anything dishonourable, and all that time I have been struggling in most restricted circumstances. I was content to work my way up step by step. Now I am turned out, and I am not going to be satisfied with merely being taken into favour again. I want to get on, I tell you. I want to get into the Bank again, in a higher position. Your husband must make a place for me—

NORA. That he will never do!

KROGSTAD. He will; I know him; he dare not protest. And as soon as I am in there again with him, then you will see! Within a year I shall be the manager's right hand. It will be Nils Krogstad and not Torvald Helmer who manages the Bank.

NORA. That's a thing you will never see!

KROGSTAD. Do you mean that you will—?

NORA. I have courage enough for it now.

KROGSTAD. Oh, you can't frighten me. A fine, spoilt lady like you—

NORA. You will see, you will see.

KROGSTAD. Under the ice, perhaps? Down into the cold, coal-black water? And then, in the spring, to float up to the surface, all horrible and unrecognisable, with your hair fallen out—

NORA.   You can't frighten me.

KROGSTAD.   Nor you me. People don't do such things, Mrs. Helmer. Besides, what use would it be? I should have him completely in my power all the same.

NORA.   Afterwards? When I am no longer—

KROGSTAD.   Have you forgotten that it is I who have the keeping of your reputation? (*NORA stands speechlessly looking at him.*) Well, now, I have warned you. Do not do anything foolish. When Helmer has had my letter, I shall expect a message from him. And be sure you remember that it is your husband himself who has forced me into such ways as this again. I will never forgive him for that. Goody-bye, Mrs. Helmer. (*Exit through the hall.*)

NORA   (*goes to the hall door, opens it slightly and listens.*) He is going. He is not putting the letter in the box. Oh no, no! that's impossible! (*Opens the door by degrees.*) What is that? He is standing outside. He is not going downstairs. Is he hesitating? Can he—? (*A letter drops into the box; then KROGSTAD'S footsteps are heard, till they die away as he goes downstairs. NORA utters a stifled cry, and runs across the room to the table by the sofa. A short pause.*)

NORA.   In the letter-box. (*Steals across to the hall door.*) There it lies— Torvald, Torvald, there is no hope for us now!

(*MRS. LINDE comes in from the room on the left, carrying the dress.*)

MRS. LINDE.   There, I can't see anything more to mend now. Would you like to try it on—?

NORA   (*in a hoarse whisper*). Christine, come here.

MRS. LINDE   (*throwing the dress down on the sofa*). What is the matter with you? You look so agitated!

NORA.   Come here. Do you see that letter? There, look—you can see it through the glass in the letter-box.

MRS. LINDE.   Yes, I see it.

NORA.   That letter is from Krogstad.

MRS. LINDE.   Nora—it was Krogstad who lent you the money!

NORA.   Yes, and now Torvald will know all about it.

MRS. LINDE.   Believe me, Nora, that's the best thing for both of you.

NORA.   You don't know all. I forged a name.

MRS. LINDE.   Good heavens—!

NORA.   I only want to say this to you, Christine— you must be my witness.

MRS. LINDE.   Your witness? What do you mean? What am I to—?

NORA.   If I should go out of my mind—and it might easily happen—

MRS. LINDE.   Nora!

NORA.   Or if anything else should happen to me—anything, for instance, that might prevent my being here—

MRS. LINDE.   Nora! Nora! you are quite out of your mind.

NORA.   And if it should happen that there were some one who wanted to take all the responsibility, all the blame, you understand—

MRS. LINDE.   Yes, yes—but how can you suppose—?

NORA.   Then you must be my witness, that it is not true, Christine. I am not out of my mind at all! I am in my right senses now, and I tell you no one else has known anything about it; I, and I alone, did the whole thing. Remember that.

MRS. LINDE.   I will, indeed. But I don't understand all this.

NORA.   How should you understand it? A wonderful thing is going to happen!

MRS. LINDE.   A wonderful thing?

NORA.   Yes, a wonderful thing!—But it is so terrible, Christine; it *mustn't* happen, not for all the world.

MRS. LINDE.   I will go at once and see Krogstad.

NORA.   Don't go to him; he will do you some harm.

MRS. LINDE.   There was a time when he would gladly do anything for my sake.

NORA.   He?

MRS. LINDE.   Where does he live?

NORA.   How should I know—? Yes (*feeling in her pocket*), here is his card. But the letter, the letter—!

HELMER   (*calls from his room, knocking at the door*). Nora!

NORA   (*cries out anxiously*). Oh, what's that? What do you want?

HELMER.   Don't be so frightened. We are not coming in; you have locked the door. Are you trying on your dress?

NORA.   Yes, that's it. I look so nice, Torvald.

MRS. LINDE   (*who has read the card*). I see he lives at the corner here.

NORA.   Yes, but it's no use. It is hopeless. The letter is lying there in the box.

MRS. LINDE.   And your husband keeps the key?

NORA.   Yes, always.

MRS. LINDE.   Krogstad must ask for his letter back unread, he must find some pretence—

NORA.   But is is just at this time that Torvald generally—

MRS. LINDE.   You must delay him. Go in to him in the meantime. I will come back as soon as I can. (*She goes out hurriedly through the hall door.*)

NORA   (*goes to* HELMER'S *door, opens it and peeps in*). Torvald!

HELMER   (*from the inner room*). Well? May I venture at last to come into my own room again? Come along, Rank, now you will see—(*Halting in the doorway.*) But what is this?

NORA.   What is what, dear?

HELMER.   Rank led me to expect a splendid transformation.

RANK   (*in the doorway*). I understood so, but evidently I was mistaken.

NORA.   Yes, nobody is to have the chance of admiring me in my dress until to-morrow.

HELMER.   But, my dear Nora, you look so worn out. Have you been practising too much?

NORA.   No, I have not practised at all.

HELMER.   But you will need to—

NORA.   Yes, indeed I shall, Torvald. But I can't get on a bit without you to help me; I have absolutely forgotten the whole thing.

HELMER.   Oh, we will soon work it up again.

NORA.   Yes, help me, Torvald. Promise that you will! I am so nervous about it—all the people—. You must give yourself up to me entirely this evening. Not the tiniest bit of business—you mustn't even take a pen in your hand. Will you promise, Torvald dear?

HELMER.   I promise. This evening I will be wholly and absolutely at your service, you helpless little mortal. Ah, by the way, first of all I will just—(*Goes towards the hall door.*)

NORA.   What are you going to do there?

HELMER.   Only see if any letters have come.

NORA.   No, no! don't do that, Torvald!

HELMER.   Why not?

NORA.   Torvald, please don't. There is nothing there.

HELMER.   Well, let me look. (*Turns to go to the letter-box. NORA, at the piano, plays the first bars of the Tarantella. HELMER stops in the doorway.*) Aha!

NORA.   I can't dance to-morrow if I don't practise with you.

HELMER   (*going up to her*). Are you really so afraid of it, dear?

NORA.   Yes, so dreadfully afraid of it. Let me practise at once; there is time now, before we go to dinner. Sit down and play for me, Torvald dear; criticise me, and correct me as you play.

HELMER.   With great pleasure, if you wish me to. (*Sits down at the piano.*)

NORA   (*takes out of the box a tambourine and a long variegated shawl. She hastily drapes the shawl round her. Then she springs to the front of the stage and calls out*). Now play for me! I am going to dance!

(*HELMER plays and NORA dances. RANK stands by the piano behind HELMER, and looks on.*)

HELMER   (*as he plays*). Slower, slower!

NORA.   I can't do it any other way.

HELMER.   Not so violently, Nora!

NORA.   This is the way.

HELMER   (*stops playing*). No, no—that is not a bit right.

NORA   (*laughing and swinging the tambourine*). Didn't I tell you so?

RANK.   Let me play for her.

HELMER   (*getting up*). Yes, do. I can correct her better then.

(*RANK sits down at the piano and plays. NORA dances more and more wildly. HELMER has taken up a position beside the stove, and during her dance gives her frequent instructions. She does not seem to hear him; her hair comes down and falls over her shoulders; she pays no attention to it, but goes on dancing. Enter* MRS. LINDE.)

MRS. LINDE (*standing as if spell-bound in the doorway.*) Oh!—

NORA (*as she dances*). Such fun, Christine!

HELMER. My dear darling Nora, you are dancing as if your life depended on it.

NORA. So it does.

HELMER. Stop, Rank; this is sheer madness. Stop, I tell you! (*RANK stops playing and* NORA *suddenly stands still.* HELMER *goes up to her.*) I could never have believed it. You have forgotten everything I taught you.

NORA (*throwing away the tambourine*). There, you see.

HELMER. You will want a lot of coaching.

NORA. Yes, you see how much I need it. You must coach me up to the last minute. Promise me that, Torvald!

HELMER. You can depend on me.

NORA. You must not think of anything but me, either to-day or to-morrow; you mustn't open a single letter—not even open the letter-box—

HELMER. Ah, you are still afraid of that fellow—

NORA. Yes, indeed I am.

HELMER. Nora, I can tell from your looks that there is a letter from him lying there.

NORA. I don't know; I think there is; but you must not read anything of that kind now. Nothing horrid must come between us till this is all over.

RANK (*whispers to* HELMER). You mustn't contradict her.

HELMER (*taking her in his arms*). The child shall have her way. But to-morrow night, after you have danced—

NORA. Then you will be free. (*The* MAID *appears in the doorway to the right.*)

MAID. Dinner is served, ma'am.

NORA. We will have champagne, Helen.

MAID. Very good, ma'am.

[*Exit.*

HELMER. Hullo!—are we going to have a banquet?

NORA. Yes, a champagne banquet till the small hours. (*Calls out.*) And a few macaroons, Helen—lots, just for once!

HELMER. Come, come, don't be so wild and nervous. Be my own little skylark, as you used.

NORA. Yes, dear, I will. But go in now and you too, Doctor Rank. Christine, you must help me to do up my hair.

RANK (*whispers to* HELMER *as they go out*). I suppose there is nothing— she is not expecting anything?

HELMER. Far from it, my dear fellow; it is simply nothing more than this childish nervousness I was telling you of. (*They go into the right-hand room.*)

NORA. Well!

MRS. LINDE. Gone out of town.

NORA. I could tell from your face.

MRS. LINDE. He is coming home to-morrow evening. I wrote a note for him.

NORA. You should have let it alone; you must prevent nothing. After all, it is splendid to be waiting for a wonderful thing to happen.

MRS. LINDE. What is it that you are waiting for?

NORA. Oh, you wouldn't understand. Go in to them, I will come in a moment. (MRS. LINDE *goes into the dining-room.* NORA *stands still for a little while, as if to compose herself. Then she looks at her watch.*) Five o'clock. Seven hours till midnight; and then four-and-twenty hours till the next midnight. Then the Tarantella will be over. Twenty-four and seven? Thirty-one hours to live.

HELMER (*from the doorway on the right*). Where's my little skylark?

NORA (*going to him with her arms outstretched*). Here she is!

ACT III

(*THE SAME SCENE.—The table has been placed in the middle of the stage, with chairs round it. A lamp is burning on the table. The door into the hall stands open. Dance music is heard in the room above. MRS. LINDE is sitting at the table idly turning over the leaves of a book; she tries to read, but does not seem able to collect her thoughts. Every now and then she listens intently for a sound at the outer door.*)

MRS. LINDE (*looking at her watch*). Not yet—and the time is nearly up. If only he does not—. (*Listens again.*) Ah, there he is. (*Goes into the hall and opens the outer door carefully. Light footsteps are heard on the stairs. She whispers.*) Come in. There is no one here.

KROGSTAD (*in the doorway*). I found a note from you at home. What does this mean?

MRS. LINDE. It is absolutely necessary that I should have a talk with you.

KROGSTAD. Really? And is it absolutely necessary that it should be here?

MRS. LINDE. It is impossible where I live; there is no private entrace to my rooms. Come in; we are quite alone. The maid is asleep, and the Helmers are at the dance upstairs.

KROGSTAD (*coming into the room*). Are the Helmers really at a dance to-night?

MRS. LINDE.   Yes, why not?

KROGSTAD.   Certainly—why not?

MRS. LINDE.   Now, Nils, let us have a talk.

KROGSTAD.   Can we two have anything to talk about?

MRS. LINDE.   We have a great deal to talk about.

KROGSTAD.   I shouldn't have thought so.

MRS. LINDE.   No, you have never properly understood me.

KROGSTAD.   Was there anything else to understand except what was obvious to all the world—a heartless woman jilts a man when a more lucrative chance turns up?

MRS. LINDE.   Do you believe I am as absolutely heartless as all that? And do you believe that I did it with a light heart?

KROGSTAD.   Didn't you?

MRS. LINDE.   Nils, did you really think that?

KROGSTAD.   If it were as you say, why did you write to me as you did at the time?

MRS. LINDE.   I could do nothing else. As I had to break with you, it was my duty also to put an end to all that you felt for me.

KROGSTAD   (*wringing his hands*). So that was it. And all this—only for the sake of money!

MRS. LINDE.   You must not forget that I had a helpless mother and two little brothers. We couldn't wait for you, Nils; your prospects seemed hopeless then.

KROGSTAD.   That may be so, but you had no right to throw me over for anyone else's sake.

MRS. LINDE.   Indeed I don't know. Many a time did I ask myself if I had the right to do it.

KROGSTAD   (*more gently*). When I lost you, it was as if all the solid ground went from under my feet. Look at me now—I am a shipwrecked man clinging to a bit of wreckage.

MRS. LINDE.   But help may be near.

KROGSTAD.   It *was* near; but then you came and stood in my way.

MRS. LINDE.   Unintentionally, Nils. It was only to-day that I learnt it was your place I was going to take in the Bank.

KROGSTAD.   I believe you, if you say so. But now that you know it, are you not going to give it up to me?

MRS. LINDE.   No, because that would not benefit you in the least.

KROGSTAD.   Oh, benefit, benefit—I would have done it whether or no.

MRS. LINDE.   I have learnt to act prudently. Life, and hard, bitter necessity have taught me that.

KROGSTAD.   And life has taught me not to believe in fine speeches.

MRS. LINDE.   Then life has taught you something very reasonable. But deeds you must believe in?

KROGSTAD.   What do you mean by that?

MRS. LINDE.   You said you were like a shipwrecked man clinging to some wreckage.

KROGSTAD.   I had good reason to say so.

MRS. LINDE.   Well, I am like a shipwrecked woman clinging to some wreckage—no one to mourn for, no one to care for.

KROGSTAD.   It was your own choice.

MRS. LINDE.   There was no other choice—then.

KROGSTAD.   Well, what now?

MRS. LINDE.   Nils, how would it be if we two shipwrecked people could join forces?

KROGSTAD.   What are you saying?

MRS. LINDE.   Two on the same piece of wreckage would stand a better chance than each on their own.

KROGSTAD.   Christine!

MRS. LINDE.   What do you suppose brought me to town?

KROGSTAD.   Do you mean that you gave me a thought?

MRS. LINDE.   I could not endure life without work. All my life, as long as I can remember, I have worked, and it has been my greatest and only pleasure. But now I am quite alone in the world—my life is so dreadfully empty and I feel so forsaken. There is not the least pleasure in working for one's self. Nils, give me someone and something to work for.

KROGSTAD.   I don't trust that. It is nothing but a woman's over-strained sense of generosity that prompts you to make such an offer of yourself.

MRS. LINDE.   Have you ever noticed anything of the sort in me?

KROGSTAD.   Could you really do it? Tell me—do you know all about my past life?

MRS. LINDE.   Yes.

KROGSTAD.   And do you know what they think of me here?

MRS. LINDE.   You seemed to me to imply that with me you might have been quite another man.

KROGSTAD.   I am certain of it.

MRS. LINDE.   Is it too late now?

KROGSTAD.   Christine, are you saying this deliberately? Yes, I am sure you are. I see it in your face. Have you really the courage, then—?

MRS. LINDE.   I want to be a mother to someone, and your children need a mother. We two need each other. Nils, I have faith in your real character—I can dare anything together with you.

KROGSTAD   (grasps her hands). Thanks, thanks, Christine! Now I shall find a way to clear myself in the eyes of the world. Ah, but I forgot—

MRS. LINDE   (listening). Hush! The Tarantella! Go, go!

KROGSTAD.   Why? What is it?

MRS. LINDE.   Do you hear them up there? When that is over, we may expect them back.

KROGSTAD.   Yes, yes—I will go. But it is all no use. Of course you are not aware what steps I have taken in the matter of the Helmers.

MRS. LINDE.   Yes, I know all about that.

KROGSTAD.   And in spite of that have you the courage to—?

MRS. LINDE.   I understand very well to what lengths a man like you might be driven by despair.

KROGSTAD.   If I could only undo what I have done!

MRS. LINDE.   You cannot. Your letter is lying in the letter-box now.

KROGSTAD.   Are you sure of that?

MRS. LINDE.   Quite sure, but—

KROGSTAD   (*with a searching look at her*). Is that what it all means?— that you want to save your friend at any cost? Tell me frankly. Is that it?

MRS. LINDE.   Nils, a woman who has once sold herself for another's sake, doesn't do it a second time.

KROGSTAD.   I will ask for my letter back.

MRS. LINDE.   No, no.

KROGSTAD.   Yes, of course I will. I will wait here till Helmer comes; I will tell him he must give me my letter back—that it only concerns my dismissal—that he is not to read it—

MRS. LINDE.   No, Nils, you must not recall your letter.

KROGSTAD.   But, tell me, wasn't it for that very purpose that you asked me to meet you here?

MRS. LINDE.   In my first moment of fright, it was. But twenty-four hours have elapsed since then, and in that time I have witnessed incredible things in this house. Helmer must know all about it. This unhappy secret must be disclosed; they must have a complete understanding between them, which is impossible with all this concealment and falsehood going on.

KROGSTAD.   Very well, if you will take the responsibility. But there is one thing I can do in any case, and I shall do it at once.

MRS. LINDE   (*listening*). You must be quick and go! The dance is over; we are not safe a moment longer.

KROGSTAD.   I will wait for you below.

MRS. LINDE.   Yes, do. You must see me back to my door.

KROGSTAD.   I have never had such an amazing piece of good fortune in my life! (*Goes out through the outer door. The door between the room and the hall remains open.*)

MRS. LINDE   (*tidying up the room and laying her hat and cloak ready*). What a difference! what a difference! Some one to work for and live for—a home to bring comfort into. That I will do, indeed. I wish they would be quick and come—(*Listens.*) Ah, there they are now. I must put on my things.

(*Takes up her hat and cloak. HELMER'S and NORA'S voices are heard outside; a key is turned, and HELMER brings NORA almost by force into the hall. She is in an*

Italian costume with a large black shawl round her; he is in evening dress, and a black domino which is flying open.)

NORA (*hanging back in the doorway, and struggling with him*). No, no, no! don't take me in. I want to go upstairs again; I don't want to leave so early.

HELMER.   But, my dearest Nora—

NORA.   Please, Torvald dear—please, *please*—only an hour more.

HELMER.   Not a single minute, my sweet Nora. You know that was our agreement. Come along into the room; you are catching cold standing there. (*He brings her gently into the room, in spite of her resistance.*)

MRS. LINDE.   Good-evening.

NORA.   Christine!

HELMER.   You here, so late, Mrs. Linde?

MRS. LINDE.   Yes, you must excuse me; I was so anxious to see Nora in her dress.

NORA.   Have you been sitting here waiting for me?

MRS. LINDE.   Yes, unfortunately I came too late, you had already gone upstairs; and I thought I couldn't go away again without having seen you.

HELMER (*taking off NORA's shawl*). Yes, take a good look at her. I think she is worth looking at. Isn't she charming, Mrs. Linde?

MRS. LINDE.   Yes, indeed she is.

HELMER.   Doesn't she look remarkably pretty? Everyone thought so at the dance. But she is terribly self-willed, this sweet little person. What are we to do with her? You will hardly believe that I had almost to bring her away by force.

NORA.   Torvald, you will repent not having let me stay, even if it were only for half an hour.

HELMER.   Listen to her. Mrs. Linde! She had danced her Tarantella, and it had been a tremendous success, as it deserved—although possibly the performance was a trifle too realistic—a little more so, I mean, than was strictly compatible with the limitations of art. But never mind about that! The chief thing is, she had made a success—she had made a tremendous success. Do you think I was going to let her remain there after that, and spoil the effect? No, indeed! I took my charming little Capri maiden—my capricious little Capri maiden, I should say—on my arm; took one quick turn round the room; a curtsey on either side, and, as they say in novels, the beautiful apparition disappeared. An exit ought always to be effective, Mrs. Linde; but that is what I cannot make Nora understand. Pooh! this room is hot. (*Throws his domino on a chair, and opens the door of his room.*) Hullo! it's all dark in here. Oh, of course—excuse me—. (*He goes in, and lights some candles.*)

NORA (*in a hurried and breathless whisper.*) Well?

MRS. LINDE   (*in a low voice*). I have had a talk with him.

NORA.   Yes, and—

MRS. LINDE.   Nora, you must tell your husband all about it.

NORA   (*in an expressionless voice*). I knew it.

MRS. LINDE.   You have nothing to be afraid of as far as Krogstad is concerned; but you must tell him.

NORA.   I won't tell him.

MRS. LINDE.   Then the letter will.

NORA.   Thank you, Christine. Now I know what I must do. Hush—!

HELMER   (*coming in again*). Well, Mrs. Linde, have you admired her?

MRS. LINDE.   Yes, and now I will say good-night.

HELMER.   What, already? Is this yours, this knitting?

MRS. LINDE   (*taking it*). Yes, thank you, I had very nearly forgotten it.

HELMER.   So you knit?

MRS. LINDE.   Of course.

HELMER.   Do you know, you ought to embroider.

MRS. LINDE.   Really? Why?

HELMER.   Yes, it's far more becoming. Let me show you. You hold the embroidery thus in your left hand, and use the needle with the right— like this—with a long, easy sweep. Do you see?

MRS. LINDE.   Yes, perhaps—

HELMER.   But in the case of knitting—that can never be anything but ungraceful; look here—the arms close together, the knitting-needles going up and down—it has a sort of Chinese effect—. That was really excellent champagne they gave us.

MRS. LINDE.   Well,—good-night, Nora, and don't be self-willed any more.

HELMER.   That's right, Mrs. Linde.

MRS. LINDE.   Good-night, Mr. Helmer.

HELMER   (*accompanying her to the door*). Good-night, good-night. I hope you will get home all right. I should be very happy to—but you haven't any great distance to go. Good-night, good-night. (*She goes out; he shuts the door after her and comes in again.*) Ah!—at last we have got rid of her. She is a frightful bore, that woman.

NORA.   Aren't you very tired, Torvald?

HELMER.   No, not in the least.

NORA.   Nor sleepy?

HELMER.   Not a bit. On the contrary, I feel extraordinarily lively. And you?—you really look both tired and sleepy.

NORA.   Yes, I am very tired. I want to go to sleep at once.

HELMER.   There, you see it was quite right of me not to let you stay there any longer.

NORA.   Everything you do is quite right, Torvald.

HELMER   (*kissing her on the forehead*). Now my little skylark is speaking reasonably. Did you notice what good spirits Rank was in this evening?

NORA.   Really? Was he? I didn't speak to him at all.

HELMER.   And I very little, but I have not for a long time seen him in such good form. (*Looks for a while at her and then goes nearer to her.*) It is delightful to be at home by ourselves again, to be all alone with you—you fascinating, charming little darling!

NORA.   Don't look at me like that, Torvald.

HELMER.   Why shouldn't I look at my dearest treasure?—at all the beauty that is mine, all my very own?

NORA   (*going to the other side of the table*). You mustn't say things like that to me to-night.

HELMER   (*following her*). You have still got the Tarantella in your blood, I see. And it makes you more captivating than ever. Listen—the guests are beginning to go now. (*In a lower voice.*) Nora—soon the whole house will be quiet.

NORA.   Yes, I hope so.

HELMER.   Yes, my own darling, Nora. Do you know, when I am out at a party with you like this, why I speak so little to you, keep away from you, and only send a stolen glance in your direction now and then?—do you know why I do that? It is because I make believe to myself that we are secretly in love, and you are my secretly promised bride, and that no one suspects there is anything between us.

NORA.   Yes, yes—I know very well your thoughts are with me all the time.

HELMER.   And when we are leaving, and I am putting the shawl over your beautiful young shoulders—on your lovely neck—then I imagine that you are my young bride and that we have just come from the wedding, and I am bringing you for the first time into our home—to be alone with you for the first time—quite alone with my shy little darling! All this evening I have longed for nothing but you. When I watched the seductive figures of the Tarantella, my blood was on fire; I could endure it no longer, and that was why I brought you down so early—

NORA.   Go away, Torvald! You must let me go. I won't—

HELMER.   What's that? You're joking, my little Nora! You won't—you won't? Am I not your husband—? (*A knock is heard at the outer door.*)

NORA   (*starting*). Did you hear—?

HELMER   (*going into the hall*). Who is it?

RANK   (*outside*). It is I. May I come in for a moment?

HELMER   (*in a fretful whisper*). Oh, what does he want now? (*Aloud.*) Wait a minute! (*Unlocks the door.*) Come, that's kind of you not to pass by our door.

RANK.   I thought I heard your voice, and felt as if I should like to look in. (*With a swift glance round.*) Ah, yes!—these dear familiar rooms. You are very happy and cosy in here, you two.

HELMER. It seems to me that you looked after yourself pretty well upstairs too.

RANK. Excellently. Why shouldn't I? Why shouldn't one enjoy everything in this world?—at any rate as much as one can, and as long as one can. The wine was capital—

HELMER. Especially the champagne.

RANK. So you noticed that too? It is almost incredible how much I managed to put away!

NORA. Torvald drank a great deal of champagne to-night too.

RANK. Did he?

NORA. Yes, and he is always in such good spirits afterwards.

RANK. Well, why should one not enjoy a merry evening after a well-spent day?

HELMER. Well spent? I am afraid I can't take credit for that.

RANK (*slapping him on the back*). But I can, you know!

NORA. Doctor Rank, you must have been occupied with some scientific investigation to-day.

RANK. Exactly.

HELMER. Just listen!—little Nora talking about scientific investigations!

NORA. And may I congratulate you on the result?

RANK. Indeed you may.

NORA. Was it favourable, then?

RANK. The best possible, for both doctor and patient—certainty.

NORA (*quickly and searchingly*). Certainty?

RANK. Absolute certainty. So wasn't I entitled to make a merry evening of it after that?

NORA. Yes, you certainly were, Doctor Rank.

HELMER. I think so too, so long as you don't have to pay for it in the morning.

RANK. Oh well, one can't have anything in this life without paying for it.

NORA. Doctor Rank—are you fond of fancy-dress balls?

RANK. Yes, if there is a fine lot of pretty costumes.

NORA. Tell me—what shall we two wear at the next?

HELMER. Little featherbrain!—are you thinking of the next already?

RANK. We two? Yes, I can tell you. You shall go as a good fairy—

HELMER. Yes, but what do you suggest as an appropriate costume for that?

RANK. Let your wife go dressed just as she is in everyday life.

HELMER. That was really very prettily turned. But can't you tell us what you will be?

RANK. Yes, my dear friend, I have quite made up my mind about that.

HELMER. Well?

RANK.   At the next fancy-dress ball I shall be invisible.

HELMER.   That's a good joke!

RANK.   There is a big black hat—have you never heard of hats that make you invisible? If you put one on, no one can see you.

HELMER (*suppressing a smile*). Yes, you are quite right.

RANK.   But I am clean forgetting what I came for. Helmer, give me a cigar—one of the dark Havanas.

HELMER.   With the greatest pleasure. (*Offers him his case.*)

RANK   (*takes a cigar and cuts off the end*). Thanks.

NORA   (*striking a match*). Let me give you a light.

RANK.   Thank you. (*She holds the match for him to light his cigar*). And now good-bye!

HELMER.   Good-bye, good-bye, dear old man!

NORA.   Sleep well, Doctor Rank.

RANK.   Thank you for that wish.

NORA.   Wish me the same.

RANK.   You? Well, if you want me to sleep well! And thanks for the light. (*He nods to them both and goes out.*)

HELMER   (*in a subdued voice*). He has drunk more than he ought.

NORA   (*absently*). Maybe. (*HELMER takes a bunch of keys out of his pocket and goes into the hall.*) Torvald! what are you going to do there?

HELMER.   Empty the letter-box; it is quite full; there will be no room to put the newspaper in to-morrow morning.

NORA.   Are you going to work to-night?

HELMER.   You know quite well I'm not. What is this? Someone has been at the lock.

NORA.   At the lock—?

HELMER.   Yes, someone has. What can it mean? I should never have thought the maid—. Here is a broken hairpin. Nora, it is one of yours.

NORA   (*quickly*). Then it must have been the children—

HELMER.   Then you must get them out of those ways. There, at last I have got it open. (*Takes out the contents of the letter-box, and calls to the kitchen.*) Helen!—Helen, put out the light over the front door. (*Goes back into the room and shuts the door into the hall. He holds out his hand full of letters.*) Look at that—look what a heap of them there are. (*Turning them over.*) What on earth is that?

NORA   (*at the window*). The letter—No! Torvald, no!

HELMER.   Two cards—of Rank's.

NORA.   Of Doctor Rank's?

HELMER (*looking at them*). Doctor Rank. They were on the top. He must have put them in when he went out.

NORA.   Is there anything written on them?

HELMER.   There is a black cross over the name. Look there—what an uncomfortable idea! It looks as if he were announcing his own death.

NORA.   It is just what he is doing.

HELMER.   What? Do you know anything about it? Has he said anything to you?

NORA.   Yes. He told me that when the cards came it would be his leave-taking from us. He means to shut himself up and die.

HELMER.   My poor old friend! Certainly I knew we should not have him very long with us. But so soon! And so he hides himself away like a wounded animal.

NORA.   If it has to happen, it is best it should be without a word—don't you think so, Torvald?

HELMER (*walking up and down*). He had so grown into our lives. I can't think of him as having gone out of them. He, with his sufferings and his loneliness, was like a cloudy background to our sunlit happiness. Well, perhaps it is best so. For him, anyway. (*Standing still.*) And perhaps for us too, Nora. We two are thrown quite upon each other now. (*Puts his arms around her.*) My darling wife, I don't feel as if I could hold you tight enough. Do you know, Nora, I have often wished that you might be threatened by some great danger, so that I might risk my life's blood, and everything, for your sake.

NORA (*disengages herself, and says firmly and decidedly*). Now you must read your letters, Torvald.

HELMER.   No, no; not to-night. I want to be with you, my darling wife.

NORA.   With the thought of your friend's death—

HELMER.   You are right, it has affected us both. Something ugly has come between us—the thought of the horrors of death. We must try and rid our minds of that. Until then—we will each go to our own room.

NORA (*hanging on his neck*). Good-night, Torvald—Good-night!

HELMER (*kissing her on the forehead*). Good-night, my little singing-bird. Sleep sound, Nora. Now I will read my letters through. (*He takes his letters and goes into his room, shutting the door after him.*)

NORA (*gropes distractedly about, seizes* HELMER'S *domino, throws it round her, while she says in quick, hoarse, spasmodic whispers*). Never to see him again. Never! Never! (*Puts her shawl over her head.*) Never to see my children again either—never again. Never! Never!—Ah! the icy, black water—the unfathomable depths—If only it were over! He has got it now—now he is reading it. Good-bye, Torvald and my children! (*She is about to rush out through the hall, when* HELMER *opens his door hurriedly and stands with an open letter in his hand.*)

HELMER.   Nora!

NORA.   Ah!—

HELMER.   What is this? Do you know what is in this letter?

NORA.   Yes, I know. Let me go! Let me get out!

HELMER (*holding her back*). Where are you going?

NORA (*trying to get free*). You shan't save me, Torvald!

HELMER (*reeling*). True? Is this true, that I read here? Horrible! No, no—it is impossible that it can be true.

NORA. It is true. I have loved you above everything else in the world.

HELMER. Oh, don't let us have any silly excuses.

NORA (*taking a step towards him*). Torvald—!

HELMER. Miserable creature—what have you done?

NORA. Let me go. You shall not suffer for my sake. You shall not take it upon yourself.

HELMER. No tragedy airs, please. (*Locks the hall door.*) Here you shall stay and give me an explanation. Do you understand what you have done? Answer me! Do you understand what you have done?

NORA (*looks steadily at him and says with a growing look of coldness in her face*). Yes, now I am beginning to understand thoroughly.

HELMER (*walking about the room*). What a horrible awakening! All these eight years—she who was my joy and pride—a hypocrite, a liar—worse, worse—a criminal! The unutterable ugliness of it all!—For shame! For shame! (*NORA is silent and looks steadily at him. He stops in front of her.*) I ought to have suspected that something of that sort would happen. I ought to have foreseen it. All your father's want of principle—be silent!—all your father's want of principle has come out in you. No religion, no morality, no sense of duty—. How I am punished for having winked at what he did! I did it for your sake, and this is how you repay me.

NORA. Yes, that's just it.

HELMER. Now you have destroyed all my happiness. You have ruined all my future. It is horrible to think of! I am in the power of an unscrupulous man; he can do what he likes with me, ask anything he likes of me, give me any orders he pleases—I dare not refuse. And I must sink to such miserable depths because of a thoughtless woman!

NORA. When I am out of the way, you will be free.

HELMER. No fine speeches, please. Your father had always plenty of those ready, too. What good would it be to me if you were out of the way, as you say? Not the slightest. He can make the affair known everywhere; and if he does, I may be falsely suspected of having been a party to your criminal action. Very likely people will think I was behind it all—that it was I who prompted you! And I have to thank you for all this—you whom I have cherished during the whole of our married life. Do you understand now what it is you have done for me?

NORA (*coldly and quietly*). Yes.

HELMER. It is so incredible that I can't take it in. But we must come to some understanding. Take off that shawl. Take it off, I tell you. I must try and appease him some way or another. The matter must be hushed up at any cost. And as for you and me, it must appear as if everything between us were just as before—but naturally only in the eyes of the world. You will still remain in my house, that is a matter of course. But I shall not allow you to bring up the children; I dare not trust them to you. To think that I should be obliged to say so to one whom I have loved so dearly, and whom I still—. No, that is all over. From this moment happiness is not the question; all that concerns us is to save the remains, the fragments, the appearance—

(*A ring is heard at the front-door bell.*)

HELMER (*with a start*). What is that? So late! Can the worst—? Can he—? Hide yourself, Nora. Say you are ill.

(NORA *stands motionless.* HELMER *goes and unlocks the hall door.*)

MAID (*half-dressed, comes to the door*). A letter for the mistress.

HELMER. Give it to me. (*Takes the letter, and shuts the door.*) Yes, it is from him. You shall not have it; I will read it myself.

NORA. Yes, read it.

HELMER (*standing by the lamp*). I scarcely have the courage to do it. It may mean ruin for both of us. No, I must know. (*Tears open the letter, runs his eye over a few lines, looks at a paper enclosed, and gives a shout of joy.*) Nora! (*She looks at him questioningly.*) Nora!—No, I must read it once again—. Yes, it is true! I am saved! Nora, I am saved!

NORA. And I?

HELMER. You too, of course; we are both saved, both you and I. Look, he sends you your bond back. He says he regrets and repents—that a happy change in his life—never mind what he says! We are saved, Nora! No one can do anything to you. Oh, Nora, Nora!—no, first I must destroy these hateful things. Let me see—. (*Takes a look at the bond.*) No, no, I won't look at it. The whole thing shall be nothing but a bad dream to me. (*Tears up the bond and both letters, throws them all into the stove, and watches them burn.*) There—now it doesn't exist any longer. He says that since Christmas Eve you—. These must have been three dreadful days for you Nora,

NORA. I have fought a hard fight these three days.

HELMER. And suffered agonies, and seen no way out but—. No, we won't call any of the horrors to mind. We will only shout with joy, and keep saying, "It's all over! It's all over!" Listen to me, Nora. You don't seem to realise that it is all over. What is this?—such a cold, set face! My poor little Nora, I quite understand; you don't feel as if you could believe that I have forgiven you. But it is true, Nora, I swear it; I have forgiven you everything. I know that what you did, you did out of love for me.

NORA. That is true.

HELMER. You have loved me as a wife ought to love her husband. Only you had not sufficient knowledge to judge of the means you used. But do you suppose you are any the less dear to me, because you don't understand how to act on your own responsibility? No, no; only lean on me; I will advise you and direct you. I should not be a man if this womanly helplessness did not just give you a double attractiveness in my eyes. You must not think any more about the hard things I said in my first moment of consternation, when I thought everything was going to overwhelm me. I have forgiven you, Nora; I swear to you I have forgiven you.

NORA.   Thank you for your forgiveness. (*She goes out through the door to the right.*)

HELMER.   No, don't go—. (*Looks in.*) What are you doing in there?

NORA (*from within*). Taking off my fancy dress.

HELMER (*standing at the open door*). Yes, do. Try and calm yourself, and make your mind easy again, my frightened little singing-bird. Be at rest, and feel secure; I have broad wings to shelter you under. (*Walks up and down by the door.*) How warm and cosy our home is, Nora. Here is shelter for you; here I will protect you like a hunted dove that I have saved from a hawk's claws; I will bring peace to your poor beating heart. It will come, little by little, Nora, believe me. To-morrow morning you will look upon it all quite differently; soon everything will be just as it was before. Very soon you won't need me to assure you that I have forgiven you; you will yourself feel the certainty that I have done so. Can you suppose I should ever think of such a thing as repudiating you, or even reproaching you? You have no idea what a true man's heart is like, Nora. There is something so indescribably sweet and satisfying, to a man, in the knowledge that he has forgiven his wife—forgiven her freely, and with all his heart. It seems as if that had made her, as it were, doubly his own; he has given her a new life, so to speak; and she has in a way become both wife and child to him. So you shall be for me after this, my little scared, helpless darling. Have no anxiety about anything, Nora; only be frank and open with me, and I will serve as will and conscience both to you—. What is this? Not gone to bed? Have you changed your things?

NORA (*in everyday dress*). Yes, Torvald, I have changed my things now.

HELMER.   But what for?—so late as this.

NORA.   I shall not sleep to-night.

HELMER.   But, my dear Nora—

NORA (*looking at her watch*). It is not so very late. Sit down here, Torvald. You and I have much to say to one another. (*She sits down at one side of the table.*)

HELMER.   Nora—what is this?—this cold, set face?

NORA.   Sit down. It will take some time; I have a lot to talk over with you.

HELMER (*sits down at the opposite side of the table*). You alarm me, Nora!—and I don't understand you.

NORA.   No, that is just it. You don't understand me, and I have never understood you either—before to-night. No, you mustn't interrupt me. You must simply listen to what I say. Torvald, this is a settling of accounts.

HELMER.   What do you mean by that?

NORA   (*After a short silence*). Isn't there one thing that strikes you as strange in our sitting here like this?

HELMER.   What is that?

NORA.   We have been married now eight years. Does it not occur to you that this is the first time we two, you and I, husband and wife, have had a serious conversation?

HELMER.   What do you mean by serious?

NORA.   In all these eight years—longer than that—from the very beginning of our acquaintance, we have never exchanged a word on any serious subject.

HELMER.   Was it likely that I would be continually and for ever telling you about worries that you could not help me to bear?

NORA.   I am not speaking about business matters. I say that we have never sat down in earnest together to try and get at the bottom of anything.

HELMER.   But, dearest Nora, would it have been any good to you?

NORA.   That is just it; you have never understood me. I have been greatly wronged, Torvald—first by papa and then by you.

HELMER.   What! By us two—by us two, who have loved you better than anyone else in the world?

NORA   (*shaking her head*). You have never loved me. You have only thought it pleasant to be in love with me.

HELMER.   Nora, what do I hear you saying?

NORA.   It is perfectly true, Torvald. When I was at home with papa, he told me his opinion about everything, and so I had the same opinions; and if I differed from him I concealed the fact, because he would not have liked it. He called me his doll-child, and he played with me just as I used to play with my dolls. And when I came to live with you—

HELMER.   What sort of an expression is that to use about our marriage?

NORA   (*undisturbed*). I mean that I was simply transferred from papa's hands into yours. You arranged everything according to your own taste, and so I got the same tastes as you—or else I pretended to, I am really not quite sure which—I think sometimes the one and sometimes the other. When I look back on it, it seems to me as if I had been living here like a poor woman—just from hand to mouth. I have existed merely to perform tricks for you, Torvald. But you would have it so. You and papa have committed a great sin against me. It is your fault that I have made nothing of my life.

HELMER.   How unreasonable and how ungrateful you are, Nora! Have you not been happy here?

NORA. No, I have never been happy. I thought I was, but it has never really been so.

HELMER. Not—not happy!

NORA. No, only merry And you have always been so kind to me. But our home has been nothing but a playroom. I have been your doll-wife, just as at home I was papa's doll-child; and here the children have been my dolls. I thought it great fun when you played with me, just as they thought it great fun when I played with them. That is what our marriage has been, Torvald.

HELMER. There is some truth in what you say—exaggerated and strained as your view of it is. But for the future it shall be different. Playtime shall be over, and lesson-time shall begin.

NORA. Whose lessons? Mine, or the children's?

HELMER. Both yours and the children's, my darling Nora.

NORA. Alas, Torvald, you are not the man to educate me into being a proper wife for you.

HELMER. And you can say that!

NORA. And I—how am I fitted to bring up the children?

HELMER. Nora!

NORA. Didn't you say so yourself a little while ago—that you dare not trust me to bring them up?

HELMER. In a moment of anger! Why do you pay any heed to that?

NORA. Indeed, you were perfectly right. I am not fit for the task. There is another task I must undertake first. I must try and educate myself—you are not the man to help me in that. I must do that for myself. And that is why I am going to leave you now.

HELMER (*springing up*). What do you say?

NORA. I must stand quite alone, if I am to understand myself and everything about me. It is for that reason that I cannot remain with you any longer.

HELMER. Nora, Nora!

NORA. I am going away from here now, at once. I am sure Christine will take me in for the night—

HELMER. You are out of your mind! I won't allow it! I forbid you!

NORA. It is no use forbidding me anything any longer. I will take with me what belongs to myself. I will take nothing from you, either now or later.

HELMER. What sort of madness is this!

NORA. To-morrow I shall go home—I mean, to my old home. It will be easiest for me to find something to do there.

HELMER. You blind, foolish woman!

NORA. I must try and get some sense, Torvald.

HELMER. To desert your home, your husband and your children! And you don't consider what people will say!

NORA. I cannot consider that at all. I only know that it is necessary for me.

HELMER. It's shocking. This is how you would neglect your most sacred duties.

NORA. What do you consider my most sacred duties?

HELMER. Do I need to tell you that? Are they not your duties to your husband and your children?

NORA. I have other duties just as sacred.

HELMER. That you have not. What duties could those be?

NORA. Duties to myself.

HELMER. Before all else, you are a wife and a mother.

NORA. I don't believe that any longer. I believe that before all else I am a reasonable human being, just as you are—or, at all events, that I must try and become one. I know quite well, Torvald, that most people would think you right, and that views of that kind are to be found in books; but I can no longer content myself with what most people say, or with what is found in books. I must think over things for myself and get to understand them.

HELMER. Can you not understand your place in your own home? Have you not a reliable guide in such matters as that?—have you no religion?

NORA. I am afraid, Torvald, I do not exactly know what religion is.

HELMER. What are you saying?

NORA. I know nothing but what the clergyman said, when I went to be confirmed. He told us that religion was this, and that, and the other. When I am away from all this, and am alone, I will look into that matter too. I will see if what the clergyman said is true, or at all events if it is true for me.

HELMER. This is unheard of in a girl of your age! But if religion cannot lead you aright, let me try and awaken your conscience. I suppose you have some moral sense? Or—answer me—am I to think you have none?

NORA. I assure you, Torvald, that is not an easy question to answer. I really don't know. The thing perplexes me altogether. I only know that you and I look at it in quite a different light. I am learning, too, that the law is quite another thing from what I supposed; but I find it impossible to convince myself that the law is right. According to it a woman has no right to spare her old dying father, or to save her husband's life. I can't believe that.

HELMER. You talk like a child. You don't understand the conditions of the world in which you live.

NORA. No, I don't. But now I am going to try. I am going to see if I can make out who is right, the world or I.

HELMER.   You are ill, Nora; you are delirious; I almost think you are out of your mind.

NORA.   I have never felt my mind so clear and certain as to-night.

HELMER.   And is it with a clear and certain mind that you forsake your husband and your children?

NORA.   Yes, it is.

HELMER.   Then there is only one possible explanation.

NORA.   What is that?

HELMER.   You do not love me any more.

NORA.   No, that is just it.

HELMER.   Nora!—and you can say that?

NORA.   It gives me great pain, Torvald, for you have always been so kind to me, but I cannot help it. I do not love you any more.

HELMER   (regaining his composure). Is that a clear and certain conviction too?

NORA.   Yes, absolutely clear and certain. That is the reason why I will not stay here any longer.

HELMER.   And can you tell me what I have done to forfeit your love?

NORA.   Yes, indeed I can. It was to-night, when the wonderful thing did not happen; then I saw you were not the man I had thought you.

HELMER.   Explain yourself better. I don't understand you.

NORA.   I have waited so patiently for eight years; for, goodness knows, I knew very well that wonderful things don't happen every day. Then this horrible misfortune came upon me; and then I felt quite certain that the wonderful thing was going to happen at last. When Krogstad's letter was lying out there, never for a moment did I imagine that you would consent to accept this man's conditions. I was so absolutely certain that you would say to him: Publish the thing to the whole world. And when that was done—

HELMER.   Yes, what then?—when I had exposed my wife to shame and disgrace?

NORA.   When that was done, I was so absolutely certain, you would come forward and take everything upon yourself, and say: I am the guilty one.

HELMER.   Nora—!

NORA.   You mean that I would never have accepted such a sacrifice on your part? No, of course not. But what would my assurances have been worth against yours? That was the wonderful thing which I hoped for and feared; and it was to prevent that, that I wanted to kill myself.

HELMER.   I would gladly work night and day for you, Nora—bear sorrow and want for your sake. But no man would sacrifice his honour for the one he loves.

NORA.   It is a thing hundreds of thousands of women have done.

HELMER. Oh, you think and talk like a heedless child.

NORA. Maybe. But you neither think nor talk like the man I could bind myself to. As soon as your fear was over—and it was not fear for what threatened me, but for what might happen to you—when the whole thing was past, as far as you were concerned it was exactly as if nothing at all had happened. Exactly as before, I was your little skylark, your doll, which you would in future treat with doubly gentle care, because it was so brittle and fragile. (*Getting up.*) Torvald—it was then it dawned upon me that for eight years I had been living here with a strange man, and had borne him three children—. Oh, I can't bear to think of it! I could tear myself into little bits!

HELMER (*sadly*). I see, I see. An abyss has opened between us—there is no denying it. But, Nora, would it not be possible to fill it up?

NORA. As I am now, I am no wife for you.

HELMER. I have it in me to become a different man.

NORA. Perhaps—if your doll is taken away from you.

HELMER. But to part!—to part from you! No, no, Nora, I can't understand that idea.

NORA (*going out to the right*). That makes it all the more certain that it must be done. (*She comes back with her cloak and hat and a small bag which she puts on a chair by the table.*)

HELMER. Nora, Nora, not now! Wait till to-morrow.

NORA (*putting on her cloak*). I cannot spend the night in a strange man's room.

HELMER. But can't we live here like brother and sister—?

NORA (*putting on her hat*). You know very well that would not last long. (*Puts the shawl around her.*) Good-bye, Torvald. I won't see the little ones. I know they are in better hands than mine. As I am now, I can be of no use to them.

HELMER. But some day, Nora—some day?

NORA. How can I tell? I have no idea what is going to become of me.

HELMER. But you are my wife, whatever becomes of you.

NORA. Listen, Torvald. I have heard that when a wife deserts her husband's house, as I am doing now, he is legally freed from all obligations towards her. In any case I set you free from all your obligations. You are not to feel yourself bound in the slightest way, any more than I shall. There must be perfect freedom on both sides. See, here is your ring back. Give me mine.

HELMER. That too?

NORA. That too.

HELMER. Here it is.

NORA. That's right. Now it is all over. I have put the keys here. The maids know all about everything in the house—better than I do. To-morrow, after I have left her, Christine will come here and pack my own things that I brought with me from home. I will have them sent after me.

HELMER.   All over! All over!—Nora, shall you never think of me again?

NORA.   I know I shall often think of you and the children and this house.

HELMER.   May I write to you, Nora?

NORA.   No—never. You must not do that.

HELMER.   But at least let me send you—

NORA.   Nothing—nothing—

HELMER.   Let me help you if you are in want.

NORA.   No. I can receive nothing from a stranger.

HELMER.   Nor—can I never be anything more than a stranger to you?

NORA   (*taking her bag*). Ah, Torvald, the most wonderful thing of all would have to happen.

HELMER.   Tell me what that would be!

NORA.   Both you and I would have to be so changed that—. Oh, Torvald, I don't believe any longer in wonderful things happening.

HELMER.   But I will believe in it. Tell me! So changed that—?

NORA.   That our life together would be a real wedlock. Good-bye. (*She goes out through the hall.*)

HELMER   (*sinks down on a chair at the door and buries his face in his hands*). Nora! Nora! (*Looks round, and rises.*) Empty. She is gone. (*A hope flashes across his mind.*) The most wonderful thing of all—?

(*The sound of a door shutting is heard from below.*)

BERNARD SHAW   (1856–1950)

Pygmalion (A Romance in Five Acts)

PREFACE TO PYGMALION
A PROFESSOR OF PHONETICS

As will be seen later on, Pygmalion needs, not a preface, but a sequel, which I have supplied in its due place.

The English have no respect for their language, and will not teach their children to speak it. They spell it so abominably that no man can teach himself what it sounds like. It is impossible for an Englishman to open his mouth without making some other Englishman hate or despise him. German and Spanish are accessible to foreigners: English is not accessible even to Englishmen. The reformer England needs today is an energetic phonetic enthusiast: that is why I have made such a one the hero of a popular play. There have been heroes of that kind crying in the wilderness for many years past. When I became interested in the subject towards the end of the eighteen-seventies, the illustrious Alexander Melville Bell, the inventor of Visible Speech, had emigrated to Canada, where his son invented the telephone; but Alexander J. Ellis was still a London patriarch, with an impressive head always covered by a velvet skull cap, for which he would apologize to public meetings in a very courtly manner. He and Tito Pagliardini, another phonetic veteran, were men whom it was impossible to dislike. Henry Sweet, then a young man, lacked their sweetness of character: he was about as conciliatory to conventional mortals as Ibsen or Samuel Butler. His great ability as a phonetician (he was, I think, the best of them all at his job) would have entitled him to high official recognition, and perhaps enabled him to popularize his subject, but for his Satanic contempt for all academic dignitaries and persons in general who thought more of Greek than of phonetics. Once, in the days when the Imperial Institute rose in South Kensington, and Joseph Chamberlain was booming the Empire, I induced the editor of a leading monthly review to commission an article from Sweet on the imperial importance of his subject. When it arrived, it contained nothing but a savagely derisive attack on a professor of language and literature whose chair Sweet regarded as proper to a phonetic expert only. The article, being libellous, had to be returned as impossible; and I had to renounce my dream of dragging its author into the limelight. When I met him afterwards, for the first time for many years, I found to my astonishment that he, who had been a quite tolerably presentable young man, had actually managed by sheer scorn to alter his personal appearance until he had become a sort of walking repudiation of Oxford and all its traditions. It must have been largely in his own despite that he was squeezed into something called a Readership of phonetics there. The future of phonetics rests probably with his pupils, who all swore by him; but nothing could bring the man himself into any sort of compliance with the university to which he nevertheless clung by divine right in an intensely Oxonian way. I daresay his papers, if he has left any, include some satires that may be published without too destructive results fifty years hence. He was, I believe, not in the least an illnatured man: very much the opposite, I should say; but he would not suffer fools gladly.

Those who knew him will recognize in my third act the allusion to the patent shorthand in which he used to write postcards, and which may be acquired from a four and sixpenny manual published by the Clarendon Press. The postcards which Mrs Higgins describes are such as I have received from Sweet. I would decipher a sound which a cockney would represent by *zerr*, and a Frenchman by *seu*, and then write demanding with some heat what on earth it meant. Sweet, with boundless contempt for my stupidity, would reply that it not only meant but obviously was the word Result, as no other word containing that sound, and capable of making sense with the context, existed in any language spoken on earth. That less expert mortals should require fuller indications was beyond Sweet's patience. Therefore, though the whole point of his current Shorthand is that it can express every sound in the language perfectly, vowels as well as consonants, and that your hand has to make no stroke except the easy and current ones with which you write m, n, and u, l, p, and q, scribbling them at whatever angle comes easiest to you, his unfortunate determination to make this remarkable and quite legible script serve also as a shorthand reduced it in his own practice to the most inscrutable of cryptograms. His true objective was the provision of a full, accurate, legible script for our noble but ill-dressed language; but he was led past that by his contempt for the popular Pitman system of shorthand, which he called the Pitfall system. The triumph of Pitman was a triumph of business organization: there was a weekly paper to persuade you to learn Pitman: there were cheap textbooks and exercise books and transcripts of speeches for you to copy, and schools where experienced teachers coached you up to the necessary proficiency. Sweet could not organize his market in that fashion. He might as well have been the Sybil who tore up the leaves of prophecy that nobody would attend to. The four and sixpenny manual, mostly in his lithographed handwriting, that was never vulgarly advertized, may perhaps some day be taken up by a syndicate and pushed upon the public as The Times pushed the Encyclopædia Britannica; but until then it will certainly not prevail against Pitman. I have bought three copies of it during my lifetime; and I am informed by the publishers that its cloistered existence is still a steady and healthy one. I actually learned the system too several times; and yet the shorthand in which I am writing these lines is Pitman's. And the reason is, that my secretary cannot transcribe Sweet, having been perforce taught in the schools of Pitman. Therefore, Sweet railed at Pitman as vainly as Thersites railed at Ajax: his raillery, however it may have eased his soul, gave no popular vogue to Current Shorthand.

Pygmalion Higgins is not a portrait of Sweet, to whom the adventure of Eliza Doolittle would have been impossible; still, as will be seen, there are touches of Sweet in the play. With Higgins's physique and temperament

Sweet might have set the Thames on fire. As it was, he impressed himself professionally on Europe to an extent that made his comparative personal obscurity, and the failure of Oxford to do justice to his eminence, a puzzle to foreign specialists in his subject. I do not blame Oxford, because I think Oxford is quite right in demanding a certain social amenity from its nurslings (heaven knows it is not exorbitant in its requirements!); for although I well know how hard it is for a man of genius with a seriously underrated subject to maintain serene and kindly relations with the men who underrate it, and who keep all the best places for less important subjects which they profess without originality and sometimes without much capacity for them, still, if he overwhelms them with wrath and disdain, he cannot expect them to heap honors on him.

Of the later generations of phoneticians I know little. Among them towers the Poet Laureate, to whom perhaps Higgins may owe his Miltonic sympathies, though here again I must disclaim all portraiture. But if the play makes the public aware that there are such people as phoneticians, and that they are among the most important people in England at present, it will serve its turn.

I wish to boast that Pygmalion has been an extremely successful play all over Europe and North America as well as at home. It is so intensely and deliberately didactic, and its subject is esteemed so dry, that I delight in throwing it at the heads of the wiseacres who repeat the parrot cry that art should never be didactic. It goes to prove my contention that art should never be anything else.

Finally, and for the encouragement of people troubled with accents that cut them off from all high employment, I may add that the change wrought by Professor Higgins in the flower-girl is neither impossible nor uncommon. The modern concierge's daughter who fulfils her ambition by playing the Queen of Spain in Ruy Blas at the Théâtre Français is only one of many thousands of men and women who have sloughed off their native dialects and acquired a new tongue. But the thing has to be done scientifically, or the last state of the aspirant may be worse than the first. An honest and natural slum dialect is more tolerable than the attempt of a phonetically untaught person to imitate the vulgar dialect of the golf club; and I am sorry to say that in spite of the efforts of our Royal Academy of Dramatic Art, there is still too much sham golfing English on our stage, and too little of the noble English of Forbes Robertson.

ACT I

Covent Garden at 11.15 P.M. Torrents of heavy summer rain. Cab whistles blowing frantically in all directions. Pedestrians running for shelter into the market and under the portico of St Paul's Church, where there are already several people, among them a lady and her daughter in evening dress. They are all peering out gloomily at the rain, except one man with his back turned to the rest, who seems wholly preoccupied with a notebook in which he is writing busily.

The church clock strikes the first quarter.

THE DAUGHTER   [*in the space between the central pillars, close to the one on her left*] I'm getting chilled to the bone. What can Freddy be doing all this time? He's been gone twenty minutes.

THE MOTHER   [*on her DAUGHTER'S right*] Not so long. But he ought to have got us a cab by this.

A BYSTANDER   [*on the lady's right*] He wont get no cab not until half-past eleven, missus, when they come back after dropping their theatre fares.

THE MOTHER.   But we must have a cab. We cant stand here until half-past eleven. It's too bad.

THE BYSTANDER.   Well, it aint my fault, missus.

THE DAUGHTER.   If Freddy had a bit of gumption, he would have got one at the theatre door.

THE MOTHER.   What could he have done, poor boy?

THE DAUGHTER.   Other people got cabs. Why couldn't he?

FREDDY rushes in out of the rain from the Southampton Street side, and comes between them closing a dripping umbrella. He is a young man of twenty, in evening dress, very wet round the ankles.

THE DAUGHTER.   Well, havnt you got a cab?

FREDDY.   Theres not one to be had for love or money.

THE MOTHER.   Oh, Freddy, there must be one. You cant have tried.

THE DAUGHTER.   It's too tiresome. Do you expect us to go and get one ourselves?

FREDDY.   I tell you theyre all engaged. The rain was so sudden: nobody was prepared; and everybody had to take a cab. Ive been to Charing Cross one way and nearly to Ludgate Circus the other; and they were all engaged.

THE MOTHER.   Did you try Trafalgar Square?

FREDDY.   There wasnt one at Trafalgar Square.

THE DAUGHTER.   Did you try?

FREDDY.   I tried as far as Charing Cross Station. Did you expect me to walk to Hammersmith?

THE DAUGHTER.   You havnt tried at all.

THE MOTHER.   You really are very helpless, Freddy. Go again; and dont come back until you have found a cab.

FREDDY.   I shall simply get soaked for nothing.

THE DAUGHTER.   And what about us? Are we to stay here all night in this draught, with next to nothing on? You selfish pig—

FREDDY.   Oh, very well: I'll go, I'll go. [*He opens his umbrella and dashes off Strandwards, but comes into collision with a* FLOWER GIRL, *who is hurrying in for shelter, knocking her basket out of her hands. A blinding flash of lightning, followed instantly by a rattling peal of thunder, orchestrates the incident*].

THE FLOWER GIRL.   Nah then, Freddy: look why' y' gowin, deah.

FREDDY.   Sorry [*he rushes off*].

THE FLOWER GIRL   [*picking up her scattered flowers and replacing them in the basket*] Theres menners f' yer? Te-oo banches o voylets trod into the mad. [*She sits down on the plinth of the column, sorting her flowers, on the lady's right. She is not at all an attractive person. She is perhaps eighteen, perhaps twenty, hardly older. She wears a little sailor hat of black straw that has long been exposed to the dust and soot of London and has seldom if ever been brushed. Her hair needs washing rather badly: its mousy color can hardly be natural. She wears a shoddy black coat that reaches nearly to her knees and is shaped to her waist. She has a brown skirt with a coarse apron. Her boots are much the worse for wear. She is no doubt as clean as she can afford to be; but compared to the ladies she is very dirty. Her features are no worse than theirs; but their condition leaves something to be desired; and she needs the services of a dentist*].

THE MOTHER.   How do you know that my son's name is Freddy, pray?

THE FLOWER GIRL.   Ow, eez ye-ooa san, is e? Wal, fewd dan y' de-ooty bawmz a mather should, eed now bettern to spawl a pore gel's flahrzn than ran awy athaht pyin. Will ye-oo py me f'them? [*Here, with apologies, this desperate attempt to represent her dialect without a phonetic alphabet must be abandoned as unintelligible outside London*].

THE DAUGHTER.   Do nothing of the sort, mother. The idea!

THE MOTHER.   Please allow me, Clara. Have you any pennies?

THE DAUGHTER.   No. Ive nothing smaller than sixpence.

THE FLOWER GIRL   [*hopefully*] I can give you change for a tanner, kind lady.

THE MOTHER   [to CLARA] Give it to me. [CLARA *parts reluctantly*]. Now [*to the girl*] this is for your flowers.

THE FLOWER GIRL.   Thank you kindly, lady.

THE DAUGHTER.   Make her give you the change. These things are only a penny a bunch.

THE MOTHER.   Do hold your tongue, Clara. [*To the girl*] You can keep the change.

THE FLOWER GIRL.   Oh, thank you, lady.

THE MOTHER.   Now tell me how you know that young gentleman's name.

THE FLOWER GIRL.   I didnt.

THE MOTHER.   I heard you call him by it. Dont try to deceive me.

THE FLOWER GIRL   [*protesting*] Who's trying to deceive you? I called him Freddy or Charlie same as you might yourself if you was talking to a stranger and wished to be pleasant. [*She sits down beside her basket*].

THE DAUGHTER.   Sixpence thrown away! Really, mamma, you might have spared Freddy that. [*She retreats in disgust behind the pillar*].

An elderly GENTLEMAN *of the amiable military type rushes into the shelter, and closes a dripping umbrella. He is in the same plight as* FREDDY, *very wet about the ankles. He is in evening dress, with a light overcoat. He takes the place left vacant by* THE DAUGHTER'S *retirement.*

THE GENTLEMAN.   Phew!

THE MOTHER   [*to the* GENTLEMAN] Oh, sir, is there any sign of its stopping?

THE GENTLEMAN.   I'm afraid not. It started worse than ever about two minutes ago [*he goes to the plinth beside the* FLOWER GIRL; *puts up his foot on it; and stoops to turn down his trouser ends*].

THE MOTHER.   Oh dear! [*She retires sadly and joins her* DAUGHTER].

THE FLOWER GIRL   [*taking advantage of the military gentleman's proximity to establish friendly relations with him*] If it's worse, it's a sign it's nearly over. So cheer up, Captain; and buy a flower off a poor girl.

THE GENTLEMAN.   I'm sorry. I havnt any change.

THE FLOWER GIRL.   I can give you change, Captain.

THE GENTLEMAN.   For a sovereign? Ive nothing less.

THE FLOWER GIRL.   Garn! Oh do buy a flower off me, Captain. I can change half-a-crown. Take this for tuppence.

THE GENTLEMAN.   Now dont be troublesome: theres a good girl. [*Trying his pockets*] I really havnt any change—Stop: heres three hapence, if thats any use to you [*he retreats to the other pillar*].

THE FLOWER GIRL   [*disappointed, but thinking three half-pence better than nothing*] Thank you, sir.

THE BYSTANDER   [*to the girl*] You be careful: give him a flower for it. Theres a bloke here behind taking down every blessed word youre saying. [*All turn to the man who is taking notes*].

THE FLOWER GIRL   [*springing up terrified*] I aint done nothing wrong by speaking to the gentleman. Ive a right to sell flowers if I keep off the kerb. [*Hysterically*] I'm a respectable girl: so help me, I never spoke to him except to ask him to buy a flower off me. [*General hubbub, mostly sympathetic to the* FLOWER GIRL, *but deprecating her excessive sensibility. Cries of* Dont start hollerin. Who's hurting you? Nobody's going to touch you. Whats the good of fussing? Steady on. Easy easy, etc., *come from the elderly staid spectators, who pat her comfortingly. Less patient ones bid her shut her head, or ask her roughly what is wrong with her. A remoter group, not knowing what the matter is, crowd in and increase the noise with question and answer:* Whats the row? Whatshe do? Where is he? A tec taking her down. What! him? Yes: him over there: Took money off the gentleman, etc. *The FLOWER GIRL, distraught and mobbed, breaks through them to the GENTLEMAN, crying wildly]* Oh, sir, dont let him charge me. You dunno what it means to me. Theyll take away my character and drive me on the streets for speaking to gentlemen. They—

THE NOTE TAKER   [*coming forward on her right, the rest crowding after him*] There, there, there, there! who's hurting you, you silly girl? What do you take me for?

THE BYSTANDER.   It's all right: he's a gentleman: look at his boots. [*Explaining to the NOTE TAKER*] She thought you was a copper's nark, sir.

THE NOTE TAKER   [with quick interest] Whats a copper's nark?

THE BYSTANDER   [*inapt at definition*] It's a—well, it's a copper's nark, as you might say. What else would you call it? A sort of informer.

THE FLOWER GIRL   [*still hysterical*] I take my Bible oath I never said a word—

THE NOTE TAKER   [*overbearing but good-humored*] Oh, shut up, shut up. Do I look like a policeman?

THE FLOWER GIRL   [*far from reassured*] Then what did you take down my words for? How do I know whether you took me down right? You just shew me what youve wrote about me. [*The NOTE TAKER opens his book and holds it steadily under her nose, though the pressure of the mob trying to read it over his shoulders would upset a weaker man*]. Whats that? That aint proper writing. I cant read that.

THE NOTE TAKER.   I can. [*reads, reproducing her pronunciation exactly*] "Cheer ap, Keptin; n' baw ya flahr orf a pore gel."

THE FLOWER GIRL   [*much distressed*] It's because I called him Captain. I meant no harm. [*To the GENTLEMAN*] Oh, sir, dont let him lay a charge agen me for a word like that. You—

THE GENTLEMAN.   Charge! I make no charge. [*To the NOTE TAKER*] Really, sir, if you are a detective, you need not begin protecting me against molestation by young women until I ask you. Anybody could see that the girl meant no harm.

THE BYSTANDERS GENERALLY   [*demonstrating against police espionage*] Course they could. What business is it of yours? You mind your own affairs. He wants promotion, he does. Taking down people's words! Girl never said a word to him. What harm if she did? Nice thing a girl cant shelter from the rain without being insulted, etc., etc., etc. [*She is conducted by the more sympathetic demonstrators back to her plinth, where she resumes her seat and struggles with her emotion*].

THE BYSTANDER.   He aint a tec. He's a blooming busybody: that's what he is. I tell you, look at his boots.

THE NOTE TAKER [*turning on him genially*] And how are all your people down at Selsey?

THE BYSTANDER [*suspiciously*] Who told you my people come from Selsey?

THE NOTE TAKER. Never you mind. They did. [*To the girl*] How do you come to be up so far east? You were born in Lisson Grove.

THE FLOWER GIRL [*appalled*] Oh, what harm is there in my leaving Lisson Grove? It wasnt fit for a pig to live in; and I had to pay four-and-six a week. [*In tears*] Oh, boo—hoo–oo–

THE NOTE TAKER. Live where you like; but stop that noise.

THE GENTLEMAN [*to the girl*] Come, come! he cant touch you: you have a right to live where you please.

A SARCASTIC BYSTANDER [*thrusting himself between the* NOTE TAKER *and the* GENTLEMAN] Park Lane, for instance. I'd like to into the Housing Question with you, I would.

THE FLOWER GIRL [*subsiding into a brooding melancholy over her basket, and talking very low-spiritedly to herself*] I'm a good girl, I am.

THE SARCASTIC BYSTANDER [*not attending to her*] Do you know where *I* come from?

THE NOTE TAKER [*promptly*] Hoxton.

Titterings. Popular interest in the NOTE TAKER'S *performance increases.*

THE SARCASTIC ONE [*amazed*] Well, who said I didnt? Bly me! You know everything, you do.

THE FLOWER GIRL [*still nursing her sense of injury*] Aint no call to meddle with me, he aint.

THE BYSTANDER [*to her*] Of course he aint. Dont you stand it from him. [*To the* NOTE TAKER] See here: what call have you to know about people what never offered to meddle with you? Wheres your warrant?

SEVERAL BYSTANDERS [*encouraged by this seeming point of law*] Yes: wheres your warrant?

THE FLOWER GIRL. Let him say what he likes. I dont want to have no truck with him.

THE BYSTANDER. You take us for dirt under your feet, dont you? Catch you taking liberties with a gentleman?

THE SARCASTIC BYSTANDER. Yes: tell him where he come from if you want to go fortune-telling.

THE NOTE TAKER. Cheltenham, Harrow, Cambridge, and India.

THE GENTLEMAN. Quite right. [*Great laughter. Reaction in the* NOTE TAKER'S *favor. Exclamations of* He knows all about it. Told him proper. Hear him tell the toff where he come from? etc.] May I ask, sir, do you do this for your living at a music hall?

THE NOTE TAKER. Ive thought of that. Perhaps I shall some day.

The rain has stopped; and the persons on the outside of the crowd begin to drop off.

THE FLOWER GIRL   [*resenting the reaction*] He's no gentleman, he aint, to interfere with a poor girl.

THE DAUGHTER   [*out of patience, pushing her way rudely to the front and displacing the GENTLEMAN, who politely retires to the other side of the pillar*] What on earth is Freddy doing? I shall get pneumonia if I stay in this draught any longer.

THE NOTE TAKER   [*to himself, hastily making a note of her pronunciation of "monia"*] Earlscourt.

THE DAUGHTER   [*violently*] Will you please keep your impertinent remarks to yourself.

THE NOTE TAKER.   Did I say that out loud? I didnt mean to. I beg your pardon. Your mother's Epsom, unmistakeably.

THE MOTHER   [*advancing between her DAUGHTER and the NOTE TAKER*] How very curious! I was brought up in Largelady Park, near Epsom.

THE NOTE TAKER   [*uproariously amused*] Ha! ha! What a devil of a name! Excuse me. [*To the DAUGHTER*] You want a cab, do you?

THE DAUGHTER.   Dont dare speak to me.

THE MOTHER.   Oh please, please, Clara. [*Her DAUGHTER repudiates her with an angry shrug and retires haughtily*]. We should be so grateful to you, sir, if you found us a cab. [*The NOTE TAKER produces a whistle*]. Oh, thank you. [*She joins her DAUGHTER*].

The NOTE TAKER blows a piercing blast.

THE SARCASTIC BYSTANDER.   There! I knowed he was a plain-clothes copper.

THE BYSTANDER.   That aint a police whistle: thats a sporting whistle.

THE FLOWER GIRL   [*still preoccupied with her wounded fellings*] He's no right to take away my character. My character is the same to me as any lady's.

THE NOTE TAKER.   I dont know whether youve noticed it; but the rain stopped about two minutes ago.

THE BYSTANDER.   So it has. Why didnt you say so before? and us losing our time listening to your silliness! [*He walks off towards the Strand*].

THE SARCASTIC BYSTANDER.   I can tell where you come from. You come from Anwell. Go back there.

THE NOTE TAKER   [*helpfully*] *H*anwell.

THE SARCASTIC BYSTANDER   [*affecting great distinction of speech*] Thenk you, teacher. Haw haw! So long [*he touches his hat with mock respect and strolls off*].

THE FLOWER GIRL.   Frightening people like that! How would he like it himself?

THE MOTHER.   It's quite fine now, Clara. We can walk to a motor bus. Come. [*She gathers her skirts above her ankles and hurries off towards the Strand*].

THE DAUGHTER.   But the cab—[*her* MOTHER *is out of hearing*]. Oh, how tiresome! [*She follows angrily*].

All the rest have gone except the NOTE TAKER, *the* GENTLEMAN, *and the* FLOWER GIRL, *who sits arranging her basket and still pitying herself in murmurs*.

THE FLOWER GIRL.   Poor girl! Hard enough for her to live without being worrited and chivied.

THE GENTLEMAN   [*returning to his former place on the* NOTE TAKER'S *left*] How do you do it, if I may ask?

THE NOTE TAKER.   Simply phonetics. The science of speech. Thats my profession: also my hobby. Happy is the man who can make a living by his hobby! You can spot an Irishman or a Yorkshireman by his brogue. *I* can place any man within six miles. I can place him within two miles in London. Sometimes within two streets.

THE FLOWER GIRL.   Ought to be ashamed of himself, unmanly coward!

THE GENTLEMAN.   But is there a living in that?

THE NOTE TAKER.   Oh yes. Quite a fat one. This is an age of upstarts. Men begin in Kentish Town with £80 a year, and end in Park Lane with a hundred thousand. They want to drop Kentish Town; but they give themselves away every time they open their mouths. Now I can teach them—

THE FLOWER GIRL.   Let him mind his own business and leave a poor girl—

THE NOTE TAKER   [*explosively*] Woman: cease this detestable boo-hooing instantly; or else seek the shelter of some other place of worship.

THE FLOWER GIRL   [*with feeble defiance*] Ive a right to be here if I like, same as you.

THE NOTE TAKER.   A woman who utters such depressing and disgusting sounds has no right to be anywhere—no right to live. Remember that you are a human being with a soul and the divine gift of articulate speech: that your native language is the language of Shakespear and Milton and The Bible: and don't sit there crooning like a bilious pigeon.

THE FLOWER GIRL   [*quite overwhelmed, looking up at him in mingled wonder and deprecation without daring to raise her head*] Ah-ah-ah-ow-ow-ow-oo!

THE NOTE TAKER   [*whipping out his book*] Heavens! what a sound! [*He writes; then holds out the book and reads, reproducing her vowels exactly*] Ah-ah-ah-ow-ow-ow-oo!

THE FLOWER GIRL [*tickled by the performance, and laughing in spite of herself*] Garn!

THE NOTE TAKER. You see this creature with her kerbstone English: the English that will keep her in the gutter to the end of her days. Well, sir, in three months I could pass that girl off as a duchess at an ambassador's garden party. I could even get her a place as lady's maid or shop assistant, which requires better English. Thats the sort of thing I do for commercial millionaires. And on the profits of it I do genuine scientific work in phonetics, and a little as a poet on Miltonic lines.

THE GENTLEMAN. I am myself a student of Indian dialects; and—

THE NOTE TAKER [*eagerly*] Are you? Do you know Colonel Pickering, the author of Spoken Sanscrit?

THE GENTLEMAN. I am Colonel Pickering. Who are you?

THE NOTE TAKER. Henry Higgins, author of Higgins's Universal Alphabet.

PICKERING [*with enthusiasm*] I came from India to meet you.

HIGGINS. I was going to India to meet you.

PICKERING. Where do you live?

HIGGINS. 27A Wimpole Street. Come and see me tomorrow.

PICKERING. I'm at the Carlton. Come with me now and lets have a jaw over some supper.

HIGGINS. Right you are.

THE FLOWER GIRL [*to PICKERING, as he passes her*] Buy a flower, kind gentleman. I'm short for my lodging.

PICKERING. I really havent any change. I'm sorry [*he goes away*].

HIGGINS [*shocked at the girl's mendacity*] Liar. You said you could change half-a-crown.

THE FLOWER GIRL [*rising in desperation*] You ought to be stuffed with nails, you ought. [*Flinging the basket at his feet*] Take the whole blooming basket for sixpence.

The church clock strikes the second quarter.

HIGGINS [*hearing in it the voice of God, rebuking him for his Pharisaic want of charity to the poor girl*] A reminder. [*He raises his hat solemnly; then throws a handful of money into the basket and follows PICKERING*].

THE FLOWER GIRL [*picking up a half-crown*] Ah-ow-ooh! [*Picking up a couple of florins*] Aaah-ow-ooh! [*Picking up several coins*] Aaaaaah-ow-ooh! [*Picking up a half-sovereign*] Aaaaaaaaaaaah-ow-ooh!!!

FREDDY [*springing out of a taxicab*] Got one at last. Hallo! [*To the girl*] Where are the two ladies that were here?

THE FLOWER GIRL. They walked to the bus when the rain stopped.

FREDDY. And left me with a cab on my hands! Damnation!

THE FLOWER GIRL [*with grandeur*] Never mind, young man. *I*'m going home in a taxi. [*She sails off to the cab. The driver puts his hand behind him and holds the door firmly shut against her. Quite understanding his mistrust, she shews him her handful of money*]. Eightpence aint no object to me, Charlie. [*He grins and opens the door*]. Angel Court, Drury Lane, round the corner of Micklejohn's oil shop. Lets see how fast you can make her hop it. [*She gets in and pulls the door to with a slam as the taxicab starts*].

FREDDY.   Well, I'm dashed!

ACT II

Next day at 11 A.M. HIGGINS's laboratory in Wimpole Street. It is a room on the first floor, looking on the street, and was meant for the drawing room. The double doors are in the middle of the back wall; and persons entering find in the corner to their right two tall file cabinets at right angles to one another against the walls. In this corner stands a flat writing-table, on which are a phonograph, a laryngoscope, a row of tiny organ pipes with bellows, a set of lamp chimneys for singing flames with burners attached to a gas plug in the wall by an indiarubber tube, several tuning-forks of different sizes, a life-size image of half a human head, shewing in section the vocal organs, and a box containing a supply of wax cylinders for the phonograph.

Further down the room, on the same side, is a fireplace, with a comfortable leather-covered easy-chair at the side of the hearth nearest the door, and a coal-scuttle. There is a clock on the mantelpiece. Between the fireplace and the phonograph table is a stand for newspapers.

On the other side of the central door, to the left of the visitor, is a cabinet of shallow drawers. On it is a telephone and the telephone directory. The corner beyond, and most of the side wall, is occupied by a grand piano, with the keyboard at the end furthest from the door, and a bench for the player extending the full length of the keyboard. On the piano is a dessert dish heaped with fruit and sweets, mostly chocolates.

The middle of the room is clear. Besides the easy-chair, the piano bench, and two chairs at the phonograph table, there is one stray chair. It stands near the fireplace. On the walls, engravings: mostly Piranesi and mezzotint portraits. No paintings.

PICKERING is seated at the table, putting down some cards and a tuning-fork which he has been using. HIGGINS is standing up near him, closing two or three file drawers which are hanging out. He appears in the morning light as a robust, vital, appetizing sort of man of forty or thereabouts, dressed in a professional-looking black frock-coat with a white linen collar and black silk tie. He is of the energetic, scientific type, heartily, even violently interested in everything that can be studied as a scientific subject, and careless about himself and other people, including their feelings. He is, in fact, but for his years and size, rather like a very impetuous baby "taking notice" eagerly and loudly , and requiring almost as much watching to keep him out of unintended mischief. His manner varies from genial bullying when he is in a good humor to stormy petulance when anything goes wrong; but he is so entirely frank and void of malice that he remains likeable even in his least reasonable moments.

HIGGINS [*as he shuts the last drawer*] Well, I think thats the whole show.

PICKERING. It's really amazing. I havnt taken half of it in, you know.

HIGGINS. Would you like to go over any of it again?

PICKERING [*rising and coming to the fireplace, where he plants himself with his back to the fire*] No, thank you; not now. I'm quite done up for this morning.

HIGGINS [*following him, and standing beside him on his left*] Tired of listening to sounds?

PICKERING. Yes. It's a fearful strain. I rather fancied myself because I can pronouce twenty-four distinct vowel sounds; but your hundred and thirty beat me. I cant hear a bit of difference between most of them.

HIGGINS [*chuckling, and going over to the piano to eat sweets*] Oh, that comes with practice. You hear no difference at first; but you keep on listening, and presently you find theyre all as different as A from B [*MRS PEARCE looks in: she is HIGGINS's housekeeper*]. Whats the matter?

MRS PEARCE [*hesitating, evidently perplexed*] A young woman wants to see you sir.

HIGGINS. A young woman! What does she want?

MRS PEARCE. Well, sir, she says youll be glad to see her when you know what she's come about. She's quite a common girl, sir. Very common indeed. I should have sent her away, only I thought perhaps you wanted her to talk into your machines. I hope Ive not done wrong; but really you see such queer people sometimes—youll excuse me, I'm sure, sir—

HIGGINS. Oh, thats all right, Mrs Pearce. Has she an interesting accent?

MRS PEARCE. Oh, something dreadful, sir, really. I dont know how you can take an interest in it.

HIGGINS [*to PICKERING*] Lets have her up. Shew her up, Mrs Pearce [*he rushes across to his working table and picks out a cylinder to use on the phonograph*].

MRS PEARCE [*only half resigned to it*] Very well sir. It's for you to say. [*She goes downstairs*].

HIGGINS. This is rather a bit of luck. I'll shew you how I make records. We'll set her talking; and I'll take it down first in Bell's visible Speech; then in broad Romic; and then we'll get her on the phonograph so that you can turn her on as often as you like with the written transcript before you.

MRS PEARCE   [*returning*] This is the young woman, sir.

The FLOWER GIRL *enters in state. She has a hat with three ostrich feathers, orange, sky-blue, and red. She has a nearly clean apron, and the shoddy coat has been tidied a little. The pathos of this deplorable figure, with its innocent vanity and consequential air, touches* PICKERING, *who has already straightened himself in the presence of* MRS PEARCE. *But as to* HIGGINS, *the only distinction he makes between men and women is that when he is neither bullying nor exclaiming to the heavens against some feather-weight cross, he coaxes women as a child coaxes its nurse when it wants to get anything out of her.*

HIGGINS   [*brusquely, recognizing her with unconcealed disappointment, and at once, babylike, making an intolerable grievance of it*] Why, this is the girl I jotted down last night. She's no use: Ive got all the records I want of the Lisson Grove lingo; and I'm not going to waste another cylinder on it. [*To the girl*] Be off with you: I dont want you.

THE FLOWER GIRL.   Dont you be so saucy. You aint heard what I come for yet. [*To* MRS PEARCE, *who is waiting at the door for further instructions*] Did you tell him I come in a taxi?

MRS PEARCE.   Nonsense, girl! what do you think a gentleman like Mr. Higgins cares what you came in?

THE FLOWER GIRL.   Oh, we are proud! He aint above giving lessons, not him: I heard him say so. Well, I aint come here to ask for any compliment; and if my money's not good enough I can go elsewhere.

HIGGINS.   Good enough for what?

THE FLOWER GIRL.   Good enough for ye-oo. Now you know, dont you? I'm come to have lessons, I am. And to pay for em too: make no mistake.

HIGGINS   [*stupent*] Well!!! [*Recovering his breath with a gasp*] What do you expect me to say to you?

THE FLOWER GIRL.   Well, if you was a gentleman, you might ask me to sit down, I think. Dont I tell you I'm bringing you business?

HIGGINS.   Pickering: shall we ask this baggage to sit down, or shall we throw her out of the window?

THE FLOWER GIRL   [*running away in terror to the piano, where she turns at bay*] Ah-ah-oh-ow-ow-ow-oo! [*Wounded and whimpering*] I wont be called a baggage when Ive offered to pay like any lady.

Motionless, the two men stare at her from the other side of the room, amazed.

PICKERING   [*gently*] What is it you want, my girl?

THE FLOWER GIRL.   I want to be a lady in a flower shop stead of selling at the corner of Tottenham Court Road. But they wont take me unless I can talk more genteel. He said he could teach me. Well, here I am ready to pay him—not asking any favor—and he treats me as if I was dirt.

Mrs Pearce. How can you be such a foolish ignorant girl as to think you could afford to pay Mr Higgins?

The Flower Girl. Why shouldnt I? I know what lessons cost as well as you do; and I'm ready to pay.

Higgins. How much?

The Flower Girl [*coming back to him, triumphant*] Now youre talking! I thought youd come off it when you saw a chance of getting back a bit of what you chucked at me last night. [*Confidentially*] Youd had a drop in, hadnt you?

Higgins [*peremptorily*] Sit down.

The Flower Girl. Oh, if youre going to make a compliment of it—

Higgins [*thundering at her*] Sit down.

Mrs Pearce [*severely*] Sit down, girl. Do as youre told. [*She places the stray chair near the hearthrug between Higgins and Pickering, and stands behind it waiting for the girl to sit down*].

The Flower Girl. Ah-ah-ah-ow-ow-oo! [*She stands, half rebellious, half bewildered*].

Pickering [*very courteous*] Wont you sit down?

Liza [*coyly*] Dont mind if I do. [*She sits down. Pickering returns to the hearthrug*].

Higgins. Whats your name?

The Flower Girl. Liza Doolittle.

Higgins [*declaiming gravely*]

Eliza, Elizabeth, Betsy and Bess,
They went to the woods to get a bird's nes':

Pickering. They found a nest with four eggs in it:

Higgins. They took one apiece, and left three in it.

They laugh heartily at their own wit.

Liza. Oh, dont be silly.

Mrs Pearce. You mustnt speak to the gentleman like that.

Liza. Well, why wont he speak sensible to me?

Higgins. Come back to business. How much do you propose to pay me for the lessons?

Liza. Oh, I know whats right. A lady friend of mine gets French lessons for eighteenpence an hour from a real French gentleman. Well, you wouldn't have the face to ask me the same for teaching me my own language as you would for French; so I wont give more than a shilling. Take it or leave it.

Higgins [*walking up and down the room, rattling his keys and his cash in his pockets*] You know, Pickering, if you consider a shilling, not as a simple shilling, but as a percentage of this girl's income, it works out as fully equivalent to sixty or seventy guineas from a millionaire.

PICKERING.   How so?

HIGGINS.   Figure it out. A millionaire has about £150 a day. She earns about half-a-crown.

LIZA   [*haughtily*] Who told you I only—

HIGGINS   [*continuing*] She offers me two-fifths of her day's income for a lesson. Two-fifths of a millionaire's income for a day would be somewhere about £60. It's handsome. By George, it's enormous! it's the biggest offer I ever had.

LIZA   [*rising, terrified*] Sixty pounds! What are you talking about? I never offered you sixty pounds. Where would I get—

HIGGINS.   Hold your tongue.

LIZA   [*weeping*] But I aint got sixty pounds. Oh—

MRS PEARCE.   Dont cry, you silly girl. Sit down. Nobody is going to touch your money.

HIGGINS.   Somebody is going to touch you, with a broomstick, if you dont stop snivelling. Sit down.

LIZA.   [*obeying slowly*] Ah-ah-ah-ow-oo-o! One would think you was my father.

HIGGINS.   If I decide to teach you, I'll be worse than two fathers to you. Here [*he offers her his silk handkerchief*]!

LIZA.   Whats this for?

HIGGINS.   To wipe your eyes. To wipe any part of your face that feels moist. Remember: thats your handkerchief; and thats your sleeve. Dont mistake the one for the other if you wish to become a lady in a shop.

Liza, utterly bewildered, stares helplessly at him.

MRS PEARCE.   It's no use talking to her like that, Mr Higgins: she doesnt understand you. Besides, youre quite wrong: she doesnt do it that way at all [*she takes the handkerchief*].

LIZA   [*snatching it*] Here! You give me that handkerchief. He give it to me, not to you.

PICKERING   [*laughing*] He did. I think it must be regarded as her property, Mrs Pearce.

MRS PEARCE   [*resigning herself*] Serve you right, Mr Higgins.

PICKERING.   Higgins: I'm interested. What about the ambassador's garden party? I'll say youre the greatest teacher alive if you make that good. I'll bet you all the expenses of the experiment you cant do it. And I'll pay for the lessons.

LIZA.   Oh, you are real good. Thank you, Captain.

HIGGINS   [*tempted, looking at her*] It's almost irresistible. She's so deliciously low—so horribly dirty—

LIZA   [*protesting extremely*] Ah-ah-ah-ah-ow-ow-oo-oo!!! I aint dirty: I washed my face and hands afore I come, I did.

PICKERING.   Youre certainly not going to turn her head with flattery, Higgins.

Mrs Pearce [*uneasy*] Oh, dont say that, sir: theres more ways than one of turning a girl's head; and nobody can do it better than Mr Higgins, though he may not always mean it. I do hope, sir, you wont encourage him to do anything foolish.

Higgins [*becoming excited as the idea grows on him*] What is life but a series of inspired follies? The difficulty is to find them to do. Never lose a chance: it doesn't come every day. I shall make a duchess of this draggletailed guttersnipe.

Liza [*strongly deprecating this view of her*] Ah-ah-ah-ow-ow-oo!

Higgins [*carried away*] Yes: in six months—in three if she has a good ear and a quick tongue—I'll take her anywhere and pass her off as anything. We'll start today: now! this moment! Take her away and clean her, Mrs Pearce. Monkey Brand, if it wont come off any other way. Is there a good fire in the kitchen?

Mrs Pearce [*protesting*] Yes; but—

Higgins [*storming on*] Take all her clothes off and burn them. Ring up Whiteley or somebody for new ones. Wrap her up in brown paper til they come.

Liza. Youre no gentleman, youre not, to talk of such things. I'm a good girl. I am; and I know what the like of you are, I do.

Higgins. We want none of your Lisson Grove prudery here, young woman. Youve got to learn to behave like a duchess. Take her away, Mrs Pearce. If she gives you any trouble, wallop her.

Liza [*springing up and running between* Pickering *and* Mrs Pearce *for protection*] No! I'll call the police, I will.

Mrs Pearce. But Ive no place to put her.

Higgins. Put her in the dustbin.

Liza. Ah-ah-ah-ow-ow-oo!

Pickering. Oh come, Higgins! be reasonable.

Mrs Pearce [*resolutely*] You must be reasonable, Mr Higgins; really you must. You cant walk over everybody like this.

Higgins, *thus scolded, subsides. The hurricane is succeeded by a zephyr of amiable surprise.*

Higgins [*with professional exquisiteness of modulation*] I walk over everybody! My dear Mrs Pearce, my dear Pickering, I never had the slightest intention of walking over anyone. All I propose is that we should be kind to this poor girl. We must help her to prepare and fit herself for her new station in life. If I did not express myself clearly it was because I did not wish to hurt her delicacy, or yours.

Liza, *reassured, steals back to her chair.*

Mrs Pearce [*to* Pickering] Well, did you ever hear anything like that, sir?

Pickering [*laughing heartily*] Never, Mrs. Pearce: never.

HIGGINS [*patiently*] Whats the matter?

MRS PEARCE.   Well, the matter is, sir, that you cant take a girl up like that as if you were picking up a pebble on the beach.

HIGGINS.   Why not?

MRS PEARCE.   Why not! But you dont know anything about her. What about her parents? She may be married.

LIZA.   Garn!

HIGGINS.   There! As the girl very properly says, Garn! Married indeed! Dont you know that a woman of that class looks a worn out drudge of fifty a year after she's married?

LIZA.   Whood marry me?

HIGGINS [*suddenly resorting to the most thrillingly beautiful low tones in his best elocutionary style*] By George, Eliza, the streets will be strewn with the bodies of men shooting themselves for your sake before Ive done with you.

MRS PEARCE.   Nonsense, sir. You mustnt talk like that to her.

LIZA [*rising and squaring herself determinedly*] I'm going away. He's off his chump, he is. I dont want no balmies teaching me.

HIGGINS [*wounded in his tenderest point by her insensibility to his elocution*] Oh, indeed! I'm mad, am I? Very well, Mrs Pearce: you neednt order the new clothes for her. Throw her out.

LIZA [*whimpering*] Nah-ow. You got no right to touch me.

MRS PEARCE.   You see now what comes of being saucy. [*Indicating the door*] This way, please.

LIZA [*almost in tears*] I didnt want no clothes. I wouldnt have taken them [*she throws away the handkerchief*]. I can buy my own clothes.

HIGGINS [*deftly retrieving the handkerchief and intercepting her on her reluctant way to the door*] Youre an ungrateful wicked girl. This is my return for offering to take you out of the gutter and dress you beautifully and make a lady of you.

MRS PEARCE.   Stop, Mr Higgins. I wont allow it. It's you that are wicked. Go home to your parents, girl; and tell them to take better care of you.

LIZA.   I aint got no parents. They told me I was big enough to earn my own living and turned me out.

MRS PEARCE.   Wheres your mother?

LIZA.   I aint got no mother. Her that turned me out was my sixth stepmother. But I done without them. And I'm a good girl, I am.

HIGGINS.   Very well, then, what on earth is all this fuss about? The girl doesnt belong to anybody—is no use to anybody but me. [*He goes to MRS PEARCE and begins coaxing*]. You can adopt her, Mrs Pearce: I'm sure a daughter would be a great amusement to you. Now dont make any more fuss. Take her downstairs; and—

MRS PEARCE.   But whats to become of her? Is she to be paid anything? Do be sensible, sir.

HIGGINS. Oh, pay her whatever is necessary: put it down in the housekeeping book. [*Impatiently*] What on earth will she want with money? She'll have her food and her clothes. She'll only drink if you give her money.

LIZA [*turning on him*] Oh you are a brute. It's a lie: nobody ever saw the sign of liquor on me. [*She goes back to her chair and plants herself there defiantly*].

PICKERING [*in good-humored remonstrance*] Does it occur to you, Higgins, that the girl has some feelings?

HIGGINS [*looking critically at her*] Oh no, I dont think so. Not any feelings that we need bother about. [*Cheerily*] Have you, Eliza?

LIZA. I got my feelings same as anyone else.

HIGGINS [*to PICKERING, reflectively*] You see the difficulty?

PICKERING. Eh? What difficulty?

HIGGINS. To get her to talk grammar. The mere pronunciation is easy enough.

LIZA. I dont want to talk grammar. I want to talk like a lady.

MRS PEARCE. Will you please keep to the point, Mr Higgins? I want to know on what terms the girl is to be here. Is she to have any wages? And what is to become of her when youve finished your teaching? You must look ahead a little.

HIGGINS [*impatiently*] Whats to become of her if I leave her in the gutter? Tell me that, Mrs Pearce.

MRS PEARCE. Thats her own business, not yours, Mr Higgins.

HIGGINS. Well, when Ive done with her, we can throw her back into the gutter; and then it will be her own business again; so thats all right.

LIZA. Oh, youve no feeling heart in you: you dont care for nothing but yourself [*she rises and takes the floor resolutely*]. Here! Ive had enough of this. I'm going [*making for the door*]. You ought to be ashamed of yourself, you ought.

HIGGINS [*snatching a chocolate cream from the piano, his eyes suddenly beginning to twinkle with mischief*] Have some chocolates, Eliza.

LIZA [*halting, tempted*] How do I know what might be in them? Ive heard of girls being drugged by the like of you.

HIGGINS whips out his penknife; cuts a chocolate in two; puts one half into his mouth and bolts it; and offers her the other half.

HIGGINS. Pledge of good faith, Eliza. I eat one half: you eat the other. [*Lisa opens her mouth to retort: he pops the half chocolate into it*]. You shall have boxes of them, barrels of them, every day. You shall live on them. Eh?

LIZA [*who has disposed of the chocolate after being nearly choked by it*] I wouldnt have ate it, only I'm too ladylike to take it out of my mouth.

HIGGINS. Listen, Eliza. I think you said you came in a taxi.

LIZA.   Well, what if I did? Ive as good a right to take a taxi as anyone else.

HIGGINS.   You have, Eliza; and in future you shall have as many taxis as you want. You shall go up and down and round the town in a taxi every day. Think of that, Eliza.

MRS PEARCE.   Mr Higgins: youre tempting the girl. It's not right. She should think of the future.

HIGGINS.   At her age! Nonsense! Time enough to think of the future when you havnt any future to think of. No, Eliza: do as this lady does: think of other people's futures; but never think of your own. Think of chocolates, and taxis, and gold, and diamonds.

LIZA.   No: I dont want no gold and no diamonds. I'm a good girl, I am. [*She sits down again, with an attempt at dignity*].

HIGGINS.   You shall remain so, Eliza, under the care of Mrs Pearce. And you shall marry an officer in the Guards, with a beautiful moustache: the son of a marquis, who will disinherit him for marrying you, but will relent when he sees your beauty and goodness—

PICKERING.   Excuse me, Higgins; but I really must interfere. Mrs Pearce is quite right. If this girl is to put herself in your hands for six months for an experiment in teaching, she must understand thoroughly what she's doing.

HIGGINS.   How can she? She's incapable of understanding anything. Besides, do any of us understand what we are doing? If we did, would we ever do it?

PICKERING.   Very clever, Higgins; but not sound sense. [*To ELIZA*] Miss Doolittle—

LIZA   [*overwhelmed*] Ah-ah-ow-oo!

HIGGINS.   There! Thats all youll get out of Eliza. Ah-ah-ow-oo! No use explaining. As a military man you ought to know that. Give her her orders: thats what she wants. Eliza: you are to live here for the next six months, learning how to speak beautifully, like a lady in a florist's shop. If youre good and do whatever youre told, you shall sleep in a proper bedroom, and have lots to eat, and money to buy chocolates and take rides in taxis. If youre naughty and idle you will sleep in the back kitchen among the black beetles, and be walloped by Mrs Pearce with a broomstick. At the end of six months you shall go to Buckingham Palace in a carriage, beautifully dressed. If the King finds out youre not a lady, you will be taken by the police to the Tower of London, where your head will be cut off as a warning to other presumptuous flower girls. If you are not found out, you shall have a present of seven-and-six-pence to start life with as a lady in a shop. If you refuse this offer you will be a most ungrateful and wicked girl; and the angels will weep for you. [*To PICKERING*] Now are you satisfied, Pickering? [*To MRS PEARCE*] Can I put it more plainly and fairly, Mrs Pearce?

MRS PEARCE [*patiently*] I think youd better let me speak to the girl properly in private. I dont know that I can take charge of her or consent to the arrangement at all. Of course I know you dont mean her any harm; but when you get what you call interested in people's accents, you never think or care what may happen to them or you. Come with me, Eliza.

HIGGINS. Thats all right. Thank you, Mrs Pearce. Bundle her off to the bath-room.

LIZA [*rising reluctantly and suspiciously*] Youre a great bully, you are. I wont stay here if I dont like. I wont let nobody wallop me. I never asked to go to Bucknam Palace, I didnt. I was never in trouble with the police, not me. I'm a good girl—

MRS PEARCE. Dont answer back, girl. You dont understand the gentleman. Come with me. [*She leads the way to the door and holds it open for* ELIZA].

LIZA [*as she goes out*] Well, what I say is right. I wont go near the King, not if I'm going to have my head cut off. If I'd known what I was letting myself in for, I wouldnt have come here. I always been a good girl; and I never offered to say a word to him; and I dont owe him nothing; and I dont care; and I wont be put upon; and I have my feelings the same as anyone else—

MRS PEARCE shuts the door; and ELIZA's *plaints are no longer audible.* PICKERING *comes from the hearth to the chair and sits astride it with his arms on the back.*

PICKERING. Excuse the straight question, Higgins. Are you a man of good character where women are concerned?

HIGGINS [*moodily*] Have you ever met a man of good character where women are concerned?

PICKERING. Yes: very frequently.

HIGGINS [*dogmatically, lifting himself on his hands to the level of the piano, and sitting on it with a bounce*] Well, I havnt. I find that the moment I let a woman make friends with me, she becomes jealous, exacting, suspicious, and a damned nuisance. I find that the moment I let myself make friends with a woman, I become selfish and tyrannical. Women upset everything. When you let them into your life, you find that the woman is driving at one thing and youre driving at another.

PICKERING. At what, for example?

HIGGINS [*coming off the piano restlessly*] Oh, Lord knows! I suppose the woman wants to live her own life; and the man wants to live his; and each tries to drag the other on to the wrong track. One wants to go north and the other south; and the result is that both have to go east, though they both hate the east wind [*He sits down on the bench at the keyboard*]. So here I am, a confirmed old bachelor, and likely to remain so.

PICKERING [*rising and standing over him gravely*] Come, Higgins! You know what I mean. If I'm to be in this business I shall feel responsible for that girl. I hope it's understood that no advantage is to be taken of her position.

HIGGINS.   What! That thing! Sacred, I assure you. [*Rising to explain*] You see, she'll be a pupil; and teaching would be impossible unless pupils were sacred. Ive taught scores of American millionairesses how to speak English: the best looking women in the world. I'm seasoned. They might as well be blocks of wood. *I* might as well be a block of wood. It's—

Mrs Pearce opens the door. She has Eliza's hat in her hand. Pickering retires to the easy-chair at the hearth and sits down.

HIGGINS   [*eagerly*] Well, Mrs Pearce: is it all right?

MRS PEARCE   [*at the door*] I just wish to trouble you with a word, if I may, Mr Higgins.

HIGGINS.   Yes, certainly. Come in. [*She comes forward*]. Dont burn that, Mrs Pearce. I'll keep it as a curiosity. [*He takes the hat*].

MRS PEARCE.   Handle it carefully, sir, please. I had to promise her not to burn it; but I had better put it in the oven for a while.

HIGGINS   [*putting it down hastily on the piano*] Oh! thank you. Well, what have you to say to me?

PICKERING.   Am I in the way?

MRS PEARCE.   Not at all, sir. Mr Higgins: will you please be very particular what you say before the girl?

HIGGINS   [*sternly*] Of course. I'm always particular about what I say. Why do you say this to me?

MRS PEARCE   [*unmoved*] No, sir: youre not at all particular when youve mislaid anything or when you get a little impatient. Now it doesnt matter before me: I'm used to it. But you really must not swear before the girl.

HIGGINS   [*indignantly*] I swear! [*Most emphatically*] I never swear. I detest the habit. What the devil do you mean?

MRS PEARCE   [*stolidly*] Thats what I mean, sir. You swear a great deal too much. I dont mind you damning and blasting, and w h a t the devil and w h e r e the devil and w h o the devil—

HIGGINS.   Mrs Pearce: this language from your lips! Really!

MRS PEARCE   [*not to be put off*]—but there is a certain word I must ask you not to use. The girl has just used it herself because the bath was too hot. It begins with the same letter as bath. She knows no better: she learnt it at her mother's knee. But she must not hear it from your lips.

HIGGINS   [*loftily*] I cannot charge myself with having ever uttered it, Mrs Pearce. [*She looks at him steadfastly. He adds, hiding an uneasy conscience with a judicial air*] Except perhaps in a moment of extreme and justifiable excitement.

MRS PEARCE.   Only this morning, sir, you applied it to your boots, to the butter, and to the brown bread.

HIGGINS. Oh, that! Mere alliteration, Mrs Pearce, natural to a poet.

MRS PEARCE. Well, sir, whatever you choose to call it, I beg you not to let the girl hear you repeat it.

HIGGINS. Oh, very well, very well. Is that all?

MRS PEARCE. No sir. We shall have to be very particular with this girl as to personal cleanliness.

HIGGINS. Certainly. Quite right. Most important.

MRS PEARCE. I mean not to be slovenly about her dress or untidy in leaving things about.

HIGGINS [*going to her solemnly*] Just so. I intended to call your attention to that. [*He passes on to* PICKERING, *who is enjoying the conversation immensely*]. It is these little things that matter, Pickering. Take care of the pence and the pounds will take care of themselves is as true of personal habits as of money. [*He comes to anchor on the hearthrug, with the air of a man in an unassailable position*].

MRS PEARCE. Yes, sir. Then might I ask you not to come down to breakfast in your dressing-gown, or at any rate not to use it as a napkin to the extent you do, sir. And if you would be so good as not to eat everything off the same plate, and to remember not to put the porridge saucepan out of your hand on the clean tablecloth, it would be a better example to the girl. You know you nearly choked yourself with a fishbone in the jam only last week.

HIGGINS [*routed from the hearthrug and drifting back to the piano*] I may do these things sometimes in absence of mind; but surely I dont do them habitually. [*Angrily*] By the way: my dressing-gown smells most damnably of benzine.

MRS PEARCE. No doubt it does, Mr Higgins. But if you will wipe your fingers—

HIGGINS [*yelling*] Oh very well, very well: I'll wipe them in my hair in future.

MRS PEARCE. I hope youre not offended, Mr Higgins.

HIGGINS [*shocked at finding himself thought capable of an unamiable sentiment*] Not at all, not at all. Youre quite right, Mrs Pearce: I shall be particularly careful before the girl. Is that all?

MRS PEARCE. No, sir. Might she use some of those Japanese dresses you brought from abroad? I really cant put her back into her old things.

HIGGINS. Certainly. Anything you like. Is that all?

MRS PEARCE. Thank you, sir. Thats all. [*She goes out*].

HIGGINS. You know, Pickering, that woman has the most extraordinary ideas about me. Here I am, a shy, diffident sort of man. Ive never been able to feel really grown-up and tremendous, like other chaps. And yet she's firmly persuaded that I'm an arbitrary overbearing bossing kind of person. I cant account for it.

MRS PEARCE returns.

MRS PEARCE.   If you please, sir, the trouble's beginning already. Theres a dustman downstairs, Alfred Doolittle, wants to see you. He says you have his daughter here.

PICKERING   [*rising*] Phew! I say [*He retreats to the hearthrug*].

HIGGINS   [*promptly*] Send the blackguard up.

MRS PEARCE.   Oh, very well, sir. [*She goes out*].

PICKERING.   He may not be a blackguard, Higgins.

HIGGINS.   Nonsense. Of course he's a blackguard.

PICKERING.   Whether he is or not, I'm afraid we shall have some trouble with him.

HIGGINS   [*confidently*] Oh no: I think not. If theres any trouble he shall have it with me, not I with him. And we are sure to get something interesting out of him.

PICKERING.   About the girl?

HIGGINS.   No. I mean his dialect.

PICKERING.   Oh!

MRS PEARCE   [*at the door*] Doolittle, sir. [*She admits DOOLITTLE and retires*].

ALFRED DOOLITTLE is an elderly but vigorous dustman, clad in the costume of his profession, including a hat with a back brim covering his neck and shoulders. He has well marked and rather interesting features, and seems equally free from fear and conscience. He has a remarkably expressive voice, the result of a habit of giving vent to his feelings without reserve. His present pose is that of wounded honor and stern resolution.

DOOLITTLE   [*at the door, uncertain which of the two gentlemen is his man*] Professor Higgins?

HIGGINS.   Here. Good morning. Sit down.

DOOLITTLE.   Morning, Governor. [*He sits down magisterially*] I come about a very serious matter, Governor.

HIGGINS   [*To PICKERING*] Brought up in Hounslow. Mother Welsh, I should think. [*DOOLITTLE opens his mouth, amazed. HIGGINS continues*] What do you want, Doolittle?

DOOLITTLE.   [*menacingly*] I want my daughter: thats what I want. See?

HIGGINS.   Of course you do. Youre her father, arnt you? You dont suppose anyone else wants her, do you? I'm glad to see you have some spark of family feeling left. She's upstairs. Take her away at once.

DOOLITTLE   [*rising, fearfully taken aback*] What!

HIGGINS.   Take her away. Do you suppose I'm going to keep your daughter for you?

DOOLITTLE   [*remonstrating*] Now, now, look here, Governor. Is this reasonable? Is it fairity to take advantage of a man like this? The girl belongs to me. You got her. Where do I come in? [*He sits down again*].

HIGGINS.   Your daughter had the audacity to come to my house and ask me to teach her how to speak properly so that she could get a place in a flower-shop. This gentleman and my housekeeper have been here all the time. [*Bullying him*] How dare you come here and attempt to blackmail me? You sent her here on purpose.

DOOLITTLE   [*protesting*] No, Governor.

HIGGINS.   You must have. How else could you possibly know that she is here?

DOOLITTLE.   Dont take a man up like that, Governor.

HIGGINS.   The police shall take you up. This is a plant—a plot to extort money by threats. I shall telephone for the police. [*He goes resolutely to the telephone and opens the directory*].

DOOLITTLE.   Have I asked you for a brass farthing? I leave it to the gentleman here: have I said a word about money?

HIGGINS   [*throwing the book aside and marching down on DOOLITTLE with a poser*] What else did you come for?

DOOLITTLE [*sweetly*] Well, what would a man come for? Be human, Governor.

HIGGINS   [*disarmed*] Alfred: did you put her up to it?

DOOLITTLE.   So help me, Governor, I never did: I take my Bible oath I aint seen the girl these two months past.

HIGGINS.   Then how did you know she was here?

DOOLITTLE   ["*most musical, most melancholy*"] I'll tell you, Governor, if youll only let me get a word in. I'm willing to tell you. I'm wanting to tell you. I'm waiting to tell you.

HIGGINS.   Pickering: this chap has a certain natural gift of rhetoric. Observe the rhythm of his native woodnotes wild. "I'm willing to tell you: I'm wanting to tell you: I'm waiting to tell you." Sentimental rhetoric! thats the Welsh strain in him. It also accounts for his mendacity and dishonesty.

PICKERING.   Oh, please, Higgins: I'm west country myself. [*To DOO-LITTLE*] How did you know the girl was here if you didnt send her?

DOOLITTLE.   It was like this, Governor. The girl took a boy in the taxi to give him a jaunt. Son of her landlady, he is. He hung about on the chance of her giving him another ride home. Well, she sent him back for her luggage when she heard you was willing for her to stop here. I met the boy at the corner of Long Acre and Endell Street.

HIGGINS.   Public house. Yes?

DOOLITTLE.   The poor man's club, Governor: why shouldnt I?

PICKERING.   Do let him tell his story, Higgins.

DOOLITTLE.   He told me what was up. And I ask you, what was my feelings and my duty as a father? I says to the boy, "You bring me the luggage," I says—

PICKERING.   Why didnt you go for it yourself?

DOOLITTLE.   Landlady wouldnt have trusted me with it, Governor. She's that kind of woman: you know. I had to give the boy a penny afore he trusted me with it, the little swine. I brought it to her just to oblige you like, and make myself agreeable. Thats all.

HIGGINS.   How much luggage?

DOOLITTLE.   Musical instrument, Governor. A few pictures, a trifle of jewelry, and a bird-cage. She said she didnt want no clothes. What was I to think from that, Governor? I ask you as a parent what was I to think?

HIGGINS.   So you came to rescue her from worse than death, eh?

DOOLITTLE [*appreciatively: relieved at being so well understood*] Just so, Governor. Thats right.

PICKERING.   But why did you bring her luggage if you intended to take her away?

DOOLITTLE.   Have I said a word about taking her away? Have I now?

HIGGINS [*determinedly*] Youre going to take her away, double quick. [*He crosses to the hearth and rings the bell*].

DOOLITTLE [*rising*] No, Governor. Dont say that. I'm not the man to stand in my girl's light. Heres a career opening for her, as you might say; and—

MRS PEARCE opens the door and awaits orders.

HIGGINS.   Mrs Pearce: this is Eliza's father. He has come to take her away. Give her to him. [*He goes back to the piano, with an air of washing his hands of the whole affair*].

DOOLITTLE.   No. This is a misunderstanding. Listen here—

MRS PEARCE.   He cant take her away, Mr Higgins: how can he? You told me to burn her clothes.

DOOLITTLE.   Thats right. I cant carry the girl through the streets like a blooming monkey, can I? I put it to you.

HIGGINS.   You have put it to me that you want your daughter. Take your daughter. If she has no clothes go out and buy her some.

DOOLITTLE [*desperate*] Wheres the clothes she come in? Did I burn them or did your missus here?

MRS PEARCE.   I am the housekeeper, if you please. I have sent for some clothes for your girl. When they come you can take her away. You can wait in the kitchen. This way, please.

DOOLITTLE, much troubled, accompanies her to the door; then hesitates; finally turns confidentially to HIGGINS.

DOOLITTLE.   Listen here, Governor. You and me is men of the world, aint we?

HIGGINS.   Oh! Men of the world, are we? Youd better go, Mrs. Pearce.

MRS PEARCE.   I think so, indeed, sir. [*She goes, with dignity*].

PICKERING.   The floor is yours, Mr Doolittle.

DOOLITTLE   [*to* PICKERING] I thank you, Governor. [*To* HIGGINS, *who takes refuge on the piano bench, a little overwhelmed by the proximity of his visitor; for* DOOLITTLE *has a professional flavor of dust about him*]. Well, the truth is, Ive taken a sort of fancy to you, Governor; and if you want the girl, I'm not so set on having her back home again but what I might be open to an arrangement. Regarded in the light of a young woman, she's a fine handsome girl. As a daughter she's not worth her keep; and so I tell you straight. All I ask is my rights as a father; and youre the last man alive to expect me to let her go for nothing; for I can see youre one of the straight sort, Governor. Well, whats a five-pound note to you? And whats Eliza to me? [*He returns to his chair and sits down judicially*].

PICKERING.   I think you ought to know, Doolittle, that Mr Higgins's intentions are entirely honorable.

DOOLITTLE.   Course they are, Governor. If I thought they wasnt, I'd ask fifty.

HIGGINS   [*revolted*] Do you mean to say, you callous rascal, that you would sell your daughter for £50?

DOOLITTLE.   Not in a general way I wouldnt; but to oblige a gentleman like you I'd do a good deal, I do assure you.

PICKERING.   Have you no morals, man?

DOOLITTLE   [*unabashed*] Cant afford them, Governor. Neither could you if you was as poor as me. Not that I mean any harm, you know. But if Liza is going to have a bit out of this, why not me too?

HIGGINS   [*troubled*] I dont know what to do, Pickering. There can be no question that as a matter of morals it's a positive crime to give this chap a farthing. And yet I feel a sort of rough justice in his claim.

DOOLITTLE.   Thats it, Governor. Thats all I say. A father's heart, as it were.

PICKERING.   Well, I know the feeling; but really it seems hardly right—

DOOLITTLE.   Dont say that, Governor. Dont look at it that way. What am I, Governors both? I ask you, what am I? I'm one of the undeserving poor: thats what I am. Think of what that means to a man. It means that he's up agen middle class morality all the time. If theres anything going, and I put in for a bit of it, it's always the same story. "Youre undeserving; so you cant have it." But my needs is as great as the most deserving widow's that ever got money out of six different charities in one week for the death of the same husband. I dont need less than a deserving man: I need more. I dont eat less hearty than him; and I drink a lot more. I want a bit of amusement, cause I'm a thinking man. I want cheerfulness and a song and a band when I feel low. Well, they charge me just the same for everything as they charge the deserving. What is middle class morality? Just an excuse for never giving me anything. Therefore, I ask you, as two gentlemen, not to play that game on me. I'm playing straight with you. I aint pretending to be deserving. I'm undeserving; and I mean to go on being undeserving. I like it; and thats the truth. Will you take advantage of a man's nature to do him out of the price of his own daughter what he's brought up and fed and clothed by the sweat of his brow until she's growed big enough to be interesting to you two gentlemen? Is five pounds unreasonable? I put it to you; and I leave it to you.

HIGGINS   [*rising, and going over to* PICKERING] Pickering: if we were to take this man in hand for three months, he could choose between a seat in the Cabinet and a popular pulpit in Wales.

PICKERING.   What do you say to that, Doolittle?

DOOLITTLE.   Not me, Governor, thank you kindly. Ive heard all the preachers and all the prime ministers—for I'm a thinking man and game for politics or religion or social reform same as all the other amusements—and I tell you it's a dog's life any way you look at it. Undeserving poverty is my line. Taking one station in society with another, it's—it's—well, it's the only one that has any ginger in it, to my taste.

HIGGINS.   I suppose we must give him a fiver.

PICKERING.   He'll make a bad use of it, I'm afraid.

DOOLITTLE.   Not me, Governor, so help me I wont. Dont you be afraid that I'll save it and spare it and live idle on it. There wont be a penny of it left by Monday: I'll have to go to work same as if I'd never had it. It wont pauperize me, you bet. Just one good spree for myself and the missus, giving pleasure to ourselves and employment to others, and satisfaction to you to think it's not been throwed away. You couldnt spend it better.

HIGGINS   [*taking out his pocket book and coming between* DOOLITTLE *and the piano*] This is irresistible. Lets give him ten. [*He offers two notes to the dustman*].

DOOLITTLE.   No, Governor. She wouldnt have the heart to spend ten; and perhaps I shouldnt neither. Ten pounds is a lot of money: it makes a man feel prudent like; and then goodbye to happiness. You give me what I ask you, Governor: not a penny more, and not a penny less.

PICKERING.   Why dont you marry that missus of yours? I rather draw the line at encouraging that sort of immorality.

DOOLITTLE.   Tell her so, Governor: tell her so. I'm willing. It's me that suffers by it. Ive no hold on her. I got to be agreeable to her. I got to give her presents. I got to buy her clothes something sinful. I'm a slave to that woman, Governor, just because I'm not her lawful husband. And she knows it too. Catch her marrying me! Take my advice, Governor: marry Eliza while she's young and dont know no better. If you dont youll be sorry for it after. If you do, she'll be sorry for it after; but better her than you, because youre a man, and she's only a woman and dont know how to be happy anyhow.

HIGGINS. Pickering: if we listen to this man another minute, we shall have no convictions left. [*To DOOLITTLE*] Five pounds I think you said.

DOOLITTLE. Thank you kindly, Governor.

HIGGINS. Youre sure you wont take ten?

DOOLITTLE. Not now. Another time, Governor.

HIGGINS [*handing him a five-pound note*] Here you are.

DOOLITTLE. Thank you Governor. Good morning. [*He hurries to the door, anxious to get away with his booty. When he opens it he is confronted with a dainty and exquisitely clean young Japanese lady in a simple blue cotton kimono printed cunningly with small white jasmine blossoms. MRS PEARCE is with her. He gets out of her way deferentially and apologizes*]. Beg pardon, miss.

THE JAPANESE LADY. Garn! Dont you know your own daughter?

DOOLITTLE ⎤ *exclaiming* ⎧ Bly me! it's Eliza!
HIGGINS ⎬ *simul-* ⎨ What's that! This!
PICKERING ⎦ *taneously* ⎩ By Jove!

LIZA. Dont I look silly?

HIGGINS. Silly?

MRS PEARCE [*at the door*] Now, Mr Higgins, please dont say anything to make the girl conceited about herself.

HIGGINS [*conscientiously*] Oh! Quite right, Mrs Pearce. [*To ELIZA*] Yes: damned silly.

MRS PEARCE. Please, sir.

HIGGINS [*correcting himself*] I mean extremely silly.

LIZA. I should look all right with my hat on. [*She takes up her hat; puts it on; and walks across the room to the fireplace with a fashionable air*].

HIGGINS. A new fashion, by George! And it ought to look horrible!

DOOLITTLE [*with fatherly pride*] Well, I never thought she'd clean up as good looking at that, Governor. She's a credit to me, aint she?

LIZA. I tell you, it's easy to clean up here. Hot and cold water on tap, just as much as you like, there is. Woolly towels, there is; and a towel horse so hot, it burns your fingers. Soft brushes to scrub yourself, and a wooden bowl of soap smelling like primroses. Now I know why ladies is so clean. Washing's a treat for them. Wish they saw what it is for the like of me!

HIGGINS. I'm glad the bathroom met with your approval.

LIZA. It didnt: not all of it; and I dont care who hears me say it. Mrs Pearce knows.

HIGGINS. What was wrong, Mrs Pearce?

MRS PEARCE [*blandly*] Oh, nothing sir. It doesn't matter.

LIZA. I had a good mind to break it. I didn't know which way to look. But I hung a towel over it, I did.

HIGGINS. Over what?

MRS PEARCE. Over the looking-glass, sir.

HIGGINS. Doolittle: you have brought your daughter up too strictly.

DOOLITTLE. Me! I never brought her up at all, except to give her a lick of a strap now and again. Dont put it on me, Governor. She aint accustomed to it, you see: thats all. But she'll soon pick up your free-and-easy ways.

LIZA.   I'm a good girl, I am; and I wont pick up no free-and-easy ways.

HIGGINS.   Eliza: if you say again that youre a good girl, your father shall take you home.

LIZA.   Not him. You dont know my father. All he come here for was to touch you for some money to get drunk on.

DOOLITTLE.   Well, what else would I want money for? To put into the plate in church, I suppose. [*She puts out her tongue at him. He is so incensed by this that PICKERING presently finds it necessary to step between them*]. Dont you give me none of your lip; and dont let me hear you giving this gentleman any of it neither, or youll hear from me about it. See?

HIGGINS.   Have you any further advice to give her before you go, Doolittle? Your blessing, for instance.

DOOLITTLE.   No, Governor: I aint such a mug as to put up my children to all I know myself. Hard enough to hold them in without that. If you want Eliza's mind improved, Governor, you do it yourself with a strap. So long, gentlemen. [*He turns to go*].

HIGGINS   [*impressively*] Stop. Youll come regularly to see your daughter. It's your duty, you know. My brother is a clergyman; and he could help you in your talks with her.

DOOLITTLE   [*evasively*] Certainly. I'll come, Governor. Not just this week, because I have a job at a distance. But later on you may depend on me. Afternoon, gentlemen. Afternoon, maam. [*He takes off his hat to MRS PEARCE, who disdains the salutation and goes out. He winks at HIGGINS, thinking him probably a fellow-sufferer from MRS PEARCE's difficult disposition, and follows her*].

LIZA.   Dont you believe the old liar. He'd as soon you set a bull-dog on him as a clergyman. You wont see him again in a hurry.

HIGGINS.   I dont want to, Eliza. Do you?

LIZA.   Not me. I dont want never to see him again, I dont. He's a disgrace to me, he is, collecting dust, instead of working at his trade.

PICKERING.   What is his trade, Eliza?

LIZA.   Taking money out of other people's pockets into his own. His proper trade's a navvy; and he works at it sometimes too—for exercise—and earns good money at it. Aint you going to call me Miss Doolittle any more?

PICKERING.   I beg your pardon, Miss Doolittle. It was a slip of the tongue.

LIZA.   Oh, I dont mind; only it sounded so genteel. I should just like to take a taxi to the corner of Tottenham Court Road and get out there and tell it to wait for me, just to put the girls in their place a bit. I wouldn't speak to them, you know.

PICKERING. Better wait til we get you something really fashionable.

HIGGINS. Besides, you shouldn't cut your old friends now that you have risen in the world. Thats what we call snobbery.

LIZA. You dont call the like of them my friends now, I should hope. Theyve took it out of me often enough with their ridicule when they had the chance; and now I mean to get a bit of my own back. But if I'm to have fashionable clothes, I'll wait. I should like to have some. Mrs Pearce says youre going to give me some to wear in bed at night different to what I wear in the daytime; but it do seem a waste of money when you could get something to shew. Besides, I never could fancy changing into cold things on a winter night.

MRS PEARCE [*coming back*] Now, Eliza. The new things have come for you to try on.

LIZA. Ah-ow-oo-ooh! [*She rushes out*].

MRS PEARCE [*following her*] Oh, dont rush about like that, girl. [*She shuts the door behind her*].

HIGGINS. Pickering: we have taken on a stiff job.

PICKERING [*with conviction*] Higgins: we have.

ACT III

It is MRS HIGGINS's *at-home day. Nobody has yet arrived. Her drawing room, in a flat on Chelsea Embankment, has three windows looking on the river; and the ceiling is not so lofty as it would be in an older house of the same pretension. The windows are open, giving access to a balcony with flowers in pots. If you stand with your face to the windows, you have the fireplace on your left and the door in the right-hand wall close to the corner nearest the windows.*

MRS HIGGINS *was brought up on Morris and Burne Jones; and her room, which is very unlike her son's room in Wimpole Street, is not crowded with furniture and little tables and nick-nacks. In the middle of the room there is a big ottoman; and this, with the carpet, the Morris wall-papers, and the Morris chintz window curtains and brocade covers of the ottoman and its cushions, supply all the ornament, and are much too handsome to be hidden by odds and ends of useless things. A few good oil-paintings from the exhibitions in the Grosvenor Gallery thirty years ago (the Burne Jones, not the Whistler side of them) are on the walls. The only landscape is a Cecil Lawson on the scale of a Rubens. There is a portrait of* MRS HIGGINS *as she was when she defied fashion in her youth in one of the beautiful Rossettian costumes which, when caricatured by people who did not understand, led to the absurdities of popular estheticism in the eighteen-seventies.*

In the corner diagonally opposite the door MRS HIGGINS, *now over sixty and long past taking the trouble to dress out of the fashion, sits writing at an elegantly simple writing-table with a bell button within reach of her hand. There is a Chippendale chair further back in the room between her and the window nearest her side.*

At the other side of the room, further forward, is an Elizabethan chair roughly carved in the taste of Inigo Jones. On the same side a piano in a decorated case. The corner between the fireplace and the window is occupied by a divan cushioned in Morris chintz.

It is between four and five in the afternoon.

The door is opened violently; and HIGGINS enters with his hat on.

MRS HIGGINS [*dismayed*] Henry [*scolding him*]! What are you doing here to-day? It is my at-home day: you promised not to come. [*As he bends to kiss her, she takes his hat off, and presents it to him*].

HIGGINS. Oh bother! [*He throws the hat down on the table*].

MRS HIGGINS. Go home at once.

HIGGINS [*kissing her*] I know, mother. I came on purpose.

MRS HIGGINS. But you mustnt. I'm serious, Henry. You offend all my friends: they stop coming whenever they meet you.

HIGGINS. Nonsense! I know I have no small talk; but people dont mind. [*He sits on the settee*].

MRS HIGGINS. Oh! dont they? Small talk indeed! What about your large talk? Really, dear, you mustnt stay.

HIGGINS. I must. Ive a job for you. A phonetic job.

MRS HIGGINS. No use, dear. I'm sorry; but I cant get round your vowels; and though I like to get pretty postcards in your patent shorthand, I always have to read the copies in ordinary writing you so thoughtfully send me.

HIGGINS. Well, this isnt a phonetic job.

MRS HIGGINS. You said it was.

HIGGINS. Not your part of it. Ive picked up a girl.

MRS HIGGINS. Does that mean that some girl has picked you up?

HIGGINS. Not at all. I dont mean a love affair.

MRS HIGGINS. What a pity!

HIGGINS. Why?

MRS HIGGINS. Well, you never fall in love with anyone under forty-five. When will you discover that there are some rather nice-looking young women about?

HIGGINS. Oh, I cant be bothered with young women. My idea of a lovable woman is something as like you as possible. I shall never get into the way of seriously liking young women: some habits lie too deep to be changed. [*Rising abruptly and walking about, jingling his money and his keys in his trouser pockets*] Besides, theyre all idiots.

MRS HIGGINS. Do you know what you would do if you really loved me, Henry?

HIGGINS. Oh bother! What? Marry, I suppose?

MRS HIGGINS. No. Stop fidgeting and take your hands out of your pockets. [*With a gesture of despair, he obeys and sits down again.*] Thats a good boy. Now tell me about the girl.

HIGGINS.   She's coming to see you.

MRS HIGGINS.   I dont remember asking her.

HIGGINS.   You didnt. *I* asked her. If youd known her you wouldnt have asked her.

MRS HIGGINS.   Indeed! Why?

HIGGINS.   Well, it's like this. She's a common flower girl. I picked her off the kerbstone.

MRS HIGGINS.   And invited her to my at-home!

HIGGINS   [*rising and coming to her to coax her*] Oh, thatll be all right. Ive taught her to speak properly; and she has strict orders as to her behavior. She's to keep to two subjects: the weather and everybody's health—Fine day and How do you do, you know—and not to let herself go on things in general. That will be safe.

MRS HIGGINS.   Safe! To talk about our health! about our insides! perhaps about our outsides! How could you be so silly, Henry?

HIGGINS   [*impatiently*] Well, she must talk about something. [*He controls himself and sits down again*]. Oh, she'll be all right: dont you fuss. Pickering is in it with me. Ive a sort of bet on that I'll pass her off as a duchess in six months. I started on her some months ago; and she's getting on like a house on fire. I shall win my bet. She has a quick ear; and she's been easier to teach than my middle-class pupils because she's had to learn a complete new language. She talks English almost as you talk French.

MRS HIGGINS.   Thats satisfactory, at all events.

HIGGINS.   Well, it is and it isnt.

MRS HIGGINS.   What does that mean?

HIGGINS.   You see, Ive got her pronunciation all right; but you have to consider not only h o w a girl pronounces, but w h a t she pronounces; and thats where—

They are interrupted by the parlor-maid, announcing guests.

THE PARLOR-MAID.   Mrs and Miss Eynsford Hill. [*She withdraws*].

HIGGINS.   Oh Lord! [*He rises; snatches his hat from the table; and makes for the door; but before he reaches it his mother introduces him*].

MRS and MISS EYNSFORD HILL are the mother and daughter who sheltered from the rain in Covent Garden. The mother is well bred, quiet, and has the habitual anxiety of straitened means. The daughter has acquired a gay air of being very much at home in society: the bravado of genteel poverty.

MRS EYNSFORD HILL   [*to MRS HIGGINS*] How do you do? [*They shake hands*].

MISS EYNSFORD HILL.   How d'you do? [*She shakes*].

MRS HIGGINS   [*introducing*] My son Henry.

MRS EYNSFORD HILL.   Your celebrated son! I have so longed to meet you, Professor Higgins.

HIGGINS [*glumly, making no movement in her direction*] Delighted. [*He backs against the piano and bows brusquely*].

MISS EYNSFORD HILL [*going to him with confident familiarity*] How do you do?

HIGGINS [*staring at her*] Ive seen you before somewhere. I havent the ghost of a notion where; but Ive heard your voice. [*Drearily*] It doesnt matter. Youd better sit down.

MRS HIGGINS. I'm sorry to say that my celebrated son has no manners. You mustnt mind him.

MISS EYNSFORD HILL [*gaily*] I dont. [*She sits in the Elizabethan chair*].

MRS EYNSFORD HILL [*a little bewildered*] Not at all. [*She sits on the ottoman between her daugher and MRS HIGGINS, who has turned her chair away from the writing-table*].

HIGGINS. Oh, have I been rude? I didnt mean to be.

He goes to the central window, through which, with his back to the company, he contemplates the river and the flowers in Battersea Park on the opposite bank as if they were a frozen desert.

The parlor-maid returns, ushering in PICKERING.

THE PARLOR-MAID. Colonel Pickering. [*She withdraws*].

PICKERING. How do you do, Mrs Higgins?

MRS HIGGINS. So glad youve come. Do you know Mrs Eynsford Hill—Miss Eynsford Hill? [*Exchange of bows. The COLONEL brings the Chippendale chair a little forward between MRS HILL and MRS HIGGINS, and sits down*].

PICKERING. Has Henry told you what weve come for?

HIGGINS [*over his shoulder*] We were interrupted: damn it!

MRS HIGGINS. Oh Henry, Henry, really!

MRS EYNSFORD HILL [*half rising*] Are we in the way?

MRS HIGGINS [*rising and making her sit down again*] No, no. You couldnt have come more fortunately: we want you to meet a friend of ours.

HIGGINS [*turning hopefully*] Yes, by George! We want two or three people. Youll do as well as anybody else.

The parlor-maid returns, ushering FREDDY.

THE PARLOR-MAID. Mr Eynsford Hill.

HIGGINS [*almost audibly, past endurance*] God of Heaven! another of them.

FREDDY [*shaking hands with MRS HIGGINS*] Ahdedo?

MRS HIGGINS. Very good of you to come. [*Introducing*] Colonel Pickering.

FREDDY [*bowing*] Ahdedo?

MRS HIGGINS. I dont think you know my son, Professor Higgins.

FREDDY [*going to HIGGINS*] Ahdedo?

HIGGINS [*looking at him much as if he were a pickpocket*] I'll take my oath Ive met y o u before somewhere. Where was it?

FREDDY. I dont think so.

HIGGINS [*resignedly*] It dont matter, anyhow. Sit down.

He shakes FREDDY's hand, and almost slings him on to the ottoman with his face to the windows; then comes round to the other side of it.

HIGGINS. Well, here we are, anyhow! [*He sits down on the ottoman next MRS EYNSFORD HILL, on her left*]. And now, what the devil are we going to talk about until Eliza comes?

MRS HIGGINS. Henry: you are the life and soul of the Royal Society's soirées; but really youre rather trying on more commonplace occasions.

HIGGINS. Am I? Very sorry. [*Beaming suddenly*] I suppose I am, you know. [*Uproariously*] Ha, ha!

MISS EYNSFORD HILL [*who considers HIGGINS quite eligible matrimonially*] I sympathize. *I* havent any small talk. If people would only be frank and say what they really think!

HIGGINS [*relapsing into gloom*] Lord forbid!

MRS EYNSFORD HILL [*taking up her daughter's cue*] But why?

HIGGINS. What they think they ought to think is bad enough, Lord knows; but what they really think would break up the whole show. Do you suppose it would be really agreeable if I were to come out now with what *I* really think?

MISS EYNSFORD HILL [*gaily*] Is it so very cynical?

HIGGINS. Cynical! Who the dickens said it was cynical? I mean it wouldnt be decent.

MRS EYNSFORD HILL [*seriously*] Oh! I'm sure you dont mean that, Mr Higgins.

HIGGINS. You see, we're all savages, more or less. We're supposed to be civilized and cultured—to know all about poetry and philosophy and art and science, and so on; but how many of us know even the meanings of these names? [*To MISS HILL*] What do you know of poetry? [*To MRS HILL*] What do you know of science? [*Indicating FREDDY*] What does he know of art or science or anything else? What the devil do you imagine I know of philosophy?

MRS HIGGINS [*warningly*] Or of manners, Henry?

THE PARLOR-MAID [*opening the door*] Miss Doolittle. [*She withdraws*].

HIGGINS [*rising hastily and running to MRS HIGGINS*] Here she is, mother. [*He stands on tiptoe and makes signs over his mother's head to ELIZA to indicate to her which lady is her hostess*].

ELIZA, who is exquisitely dressed, produces an impression of such remarkable distinction and beauty as she enters that they all rise, quite fluttered. Guided by HIGGINS's signals, she comes to MRS HIGGINS with studied grace.

LIZA [*speaking with pedantic correctness of pronunciation and great beauty of tone*] How do you do, Mrs Higgins? [*She gasps slightly in making sure of the H in Higgins, but is quite successful*]. Mr Higgins told me I might come.

MRS HIGGINS [*cordially*] Quite right: I'm very glad indeed to see you.

PICKERING.   How do you do, Miss Doolittle?

LIZA [*shaking hands with him*] Colonel Pickering, is it not?

MRS EYNSFORD HILL.   I feel sure we have met before, Miss Doolittle. I remember your eyes.

LIZA.   How do you do? [*She sits down on the ottoman gracefully in the place just left vacant by HIGGINS*].

MRS EYNSFORD HILL [*introducing*] My daughter Clara.

LIZA.   How do you do?

CLARA [*impulsively*] How do you do? [*She sits down on the ottoman beside ELIZA, devouring her with her eyes*].

FREDDY [*coming to their side of the ottoman*] Ive certainly had the pleasure.

MRS EYNSFORD HILL [*introducing*] My son Freddy.

LIZA.   How do you do?

FREDDY bows and sits down in the Elizabethan chair, infatuated.

HIGGINS [*suddenly*] By George, yes: it all comes back to me! [*They stare at him*]. Covent Garden! [*Lamentably*] What a damned thing!

MRS HIGGINS.   Henry, please! [*He is about to sit on the edge of the table*] Dont sit on my writing-table: youll break it.

HIGGINS [*sulkily*] Sorry.

He goes to the divan, stumbling into the fender and over the fire-irons on his way; extricating himself with muttered imprecations; and finishing his disastrous journey by throwing himself so impatiently on the divan that he almost breaks it. MRS HIGGINS looks at him, but controls herself and says nothing.

A long and painful pause ensues.

MRS HIGGINS [*at last, conversationally*] Will it rain, do you think?

LIZA.   The shallow depression in the west of these islands is likely to move slowly in an easterly direction. There are no indications of any great change in the barometrical situation.

FREDDY.   Ha! ha! how awfully funny!

LIZA.   What is wrong with that, young man? I bet I got it right.

FREDDY.   Killing!

MRS EYNSFORD HILL.   I'm sure I hope it wont turn cold. Theres so much influenza about. It runs right through our whole family regularly every spring.

LIZA [*darkly*] My aunt died of influenza: so they said.

MRS EYNSFORD HILL [*clicks her tongue sympathetically*]!!!

LIZA [*in the same tragic tone*] But it's my belief they done the old woman in.

MRS HIGGINS [*puzzled*] Done her in?

LIZA. Y-e-e-e-es, Lord love you! Why should s h e die of influenza? She come through diphtheria right enough the year before. I saw her with my own eyes. Fairly blue with it, she was. They all thought she was dead; but my father he kept ladling gin down her throat til she came to so sudden that she bit the bowl off the spoon.

MRS EYNSFORD HILL [*startled*] Dear me!

LIZA [*piling up the indictment*] What call would a woman with that strength in her have to die of influenza? What become of her new straw hat that should have come to me? Somebody pinched it; and what I say is, them as pinched it done her in.

MRS EYNSFORD HILL. What does doing her in mean?

HIGGINS [*hastily*] Oh, thats the new small talk. To do a person in means to kill them.

MRS EYNSFORD HILL [*To ELIZA, horrified*] You surely dont believe that your aunt was killed?

LIZA. Do I not! Them she lived with would have killed her for a hat-pin, let alone a hat.

MRS EYNSFORD HILL. But it cant have been right for your father to pour spirits down her throat like that. It might have killed her.

LIZA. Not her. Gin was mother's milk to her. Besides, he'd poured so much down his own throat that he knew the good of it.

MRS EYNSFORD HILL. Do you mean that he drank?

LIZA. Drank! My word! Something chronic.

MRS EYNSFORD HILL. How dreadful for you!

LIZA. Not a bit. It never did him no harm what I could see. But then he did not keep it up regular. [*Cheerfully*] On the burst, as you might say, from time to time. And always more agreeable when he had a drop in. When he was out of work, my mother used to give him fourpence and tell him to go out and not come back until he'd drunk himself cheerful and loving-like. Theres lots of women has to make their husbands drunk to make them fit to live with. [*Now quite at her ease*] You see, it's like this. If a man has a bit of a conscience, it always takes him when he's sober; and then it makes him low-spirited. A drop of booze just takes that off and makes him happy. [*To FREDDY, who is in convulsions of suppressed laughter*] Here! what are you sniggering at?

FREDDY. The new small talk. You do it so awfully well.

LIZA. If I was doing it proper, what was you laughing at? [*To HIGGINS*] Have I said anything I oughtnt?

MRS HIGGINS [*interposing*] Not at all, Miss Doolittle.

LIZA. Well, thats a mercy, anyhow. [*Expansively*] What I always say is—

HIGGINS [*rising and looking at his watch*] Ahem!

LIZA [*looking round at him; taking the hint; and rising*] Well: I must go. [*They all rise. FREDDY goes to the door*]. So pleased to have met you. Goodbye. [*She shakes hands with MRS HIGGINS*].

MRS HIGGINS. Goodbye.

LIZA. Goodbye, Colonel Pickering.

PICKERING. Goodbye, Miss Doolittle. [*They shake hands*].

LIZA [*nodding to the others*] Goodbye, all.

FREDDY [*opening the door for her*] Are you walking across the Park, Miss Doolittle? If so—

LIZA. Walk! Not bloody likely. [*Sensation*]. I am going in a taxi. [*She goes out*].

PICKERING *gasps and sits down.* FREDDY *goes out on the balcony to catch another glimpse of* ELIZA.

MRS EYNSFORD HILL [*suffering from shock*] Well, I really cant get used to the new ways.

CLARA [*throwing herself discontentedly into the Elizabethan chair*] Oh, it's all right, mamma, quite right. People will think we never go anywhere or see anybody if you are so old-fashioned.

MRS EYNSFORD HILL. I daresay I am very old-fashioned; but I do hope you wont begin using that expression, Clara. I have got accustomed to hear you talking about men as rotters, and calling everything filthy and beastly; though I do think it horrible and unladylike. But this last is really too much. Dont you think so, Colonel Pickering?

PICKERING. Dont ask me. Ive been away in India for several years; and manners have changed so much that I sometimes dont know whether I'm at a respectable dinner-table or in a ship's forecastle.

CLARA. It's all a matter of habit. Theres no right or wrong in it. Nobody means anything by it. And it's s o quaint, and gives such a smart emphasis to things that are not in themselves very witty. I find the new small talk delightful and quite innocent.

MRS EYNSFORD HILL [*rising*] Well, after that, I think it's time for us to go.

PICKERING *and* HIGGINS *rise.*

CLARA [*rising*] Oh yes: we have three at-homes to go to still. Goodbye, Mrs Higgins. Goodbye, Colonel Pickering. Goodbye, Professor Higgins.

HIGGINS [*coming grimly at her from the divan, and accompanying her to the door*] Goodbye. Be sure you try on that small talk at the three at-homes. Dont be nervous about it. Pitch it in strong.

CLARA [*all smiles*] I will. Goodbye. Such nonsense, all this early Victorian prudery!

HIGGINS [*tempting her*] Such damned nonsense!

CLARA. Such bloody nonsense!

MRS EYNSFORD HILL [*convulsively*] Clara!

CLARA. Ha! ha! [*She goes out radiant, conscious of being thoroughly up to date, and is heard descending the stairs in a stream of silvery laughter*].

FREDDY [*to the heavens at large*] Well, I ask you—[*He gives it up, and comes to* MRS HIGGINS]. Goodbye.

MRS HIGGINS [*shaking hands*] Goodbye. Would you like to meet Miss Doolittle again?

FREDDY [*eagerly*] Yes, I should, most awfully.

MRS HIGGINS. Well, you know my days.

FREDDY. Yes. Thanks awfully. Goodbye. [*He goes out*].

MRS EYNSFORD HILL. Goodbye, Mr Higgins.

HIGGINS. Goodbye. Goodbye.

MRS EYNSFORD HILL [*to* PICKERING] It's no use. I shall never be able to bring myself to use that word.

PICKERING. Dont. It's not compulsory, you know. Youll get on quite well without it.

MRS EYNSFORD HILL. Only, Clara is so down on me if I am not positively reeking with the latest slang. Goodbye.

PICKERING. Goodbye [*They shake hands*].

MRS EYNSFORD HILL [*To* MRS HIGGINS] You mustnt mind Clara. [PICKERING, *catching from her lowered tone that this is not meant for him to hear, discreetly joins* HIGGINS *at the window*]. We're so poor! and she gets so few parties, poor child! She doesnt quite know. [MRS HIGGINS, *seeing that her eyes are moist, takes her hand sympathetically and goes with her to the door*]. But the boy is nice. Dont you think so?

MRS HIGGINS. Oh, quite nice. I shall always be delighted to see him.

MRS EYNSFORD HILL. Thank you, dear. Goodbye. [*She goes out*].

HIGGINS [*eagerly*] Well? Is Eliza presentable? [*He swoops on his mother and drags her to the ottoman, where she sits down in* ELIZA's *place with her son on her left*].

PICKERING *returns to his chair on her right.*

MRS HIGGINS. You silly boy, of course she's not presentable. She's a triumph of your art and of her dressmaker's; but if you suppose for a moment that she doesnt give herself away in every sentence she utters, you must be perfectly cracked about her.

PICKERING. But dont you think something might be done? I mean something to eliminate the sanguinary element from her conversation.

MRS HIGGINS. Not as long as she is in Henry's hands.

HIGGINS [*aggrieved*] Do you mean that my language is improper?

MRS HIGGINS. No, dearest: it would be quite proper—say on a canal barge; but it would not be proper for her at a garden party.

HIGGINS [*deeply injured*] Well I must say—

PICKERING   [*interrupting him*] Come, Higgins: you must learn to know yourself. I havnt heard such language as yours since we used to review the volunteers in Hyde Park twenty years ago.

HIGGINS   [*sulkily*] Oh, well, y o u say so, I suppose I dont always talk like a bishop.

MRS HIGGINS   [*quieting HENRY with a touch*] Colonel Pickering: will you tell me what is the exact state of things in Wimpole Street?

PICKERING   [*cheerfully: as if this completely changed the subject*] Well, I have come to live there with Henry. We work together at my Indian Dialects; and we think it more convenient—

MRS HIGGINS.   Quite so. I know all about that: it's an excellent arrangement. But where does this girl live?

HIGGINS.   With us, of course. Where s h o u l d she live?

MRS HIGGINS.   But on what terms? Is she a servant? If not, what is she?

PICKERING   [*slowly*] I think I know what you mean, Mrs Higgins.

HIGGINS.   Well, dash me if *I* do! Ive had to work at the girl every day for months to get her to her present pitch. Besides, she's useful. She knows where my things are, and remembers my appointments and so forth.

MRS HIGGINS.   How does your housekeeper get on with her?

HIGGINS.   Mrs Pearce? Oh, she's jolly glad to get so much taken off her hands; for before Eliza came, s h e used to have to find things and remind me of my appointments. But she's got some silly bee in her bonnet about Eliza. She keeps saying "You dont think, sir": doesn't she, Pick?

PICKERING.   Yes: thats the formula. "You dont think, sir." Thats the end of every conversation about Eliza.

HIGGINS.   As if I ever stop thinking about the girl and her confounded vowels and consonants. I'm worn out, thinking about her, and watching her lips and her teeth and her tongue, not to mention her soul, which is the quaintest of the lot.

MRS HIGGINS.   You certainly are a pretty pair of babies, playing with your live doll.

HIGGINS.   Playing! The hardest job I ever tackled: make no mistake about that, mother. But you have no idea how frightfully interesting it is to take a human being and change her into a quite different human being by creating a new speech for her. It's filling up the deepest gulf that separates class from class and soul from soul.

PICKERING   [*drawing his chair closer to MRS HIGGINS and bending over to her eagerly*] Yes: it's enormously interesting. I assure you, Mrs Higgins, we take Eliza very seriously. Every week—every day almost—there is some new change. [*Closer again*] We keep records of every stage—dozens of gramophone disks and photographs—

HIGGINS   [*assailing her at the other ear*] Yes, by George: it's the most absorbing experiment I ever tackled. She regularly fills our lives up: doesnt she, Pick?

PICKERING.   We're always talking Eliza.

HIGGINS.   Teaching Eliza.

PICKERING.   Dressing Eliza.

MRS HIGGINS.   What!

HIGGINS.   Inventing new Elizas.

HIGGINS.		You know, she has the most extraordinary quickness of ear:
PICKERING.	[*speaking together*]	I assure you, my dear Mrs Higgins, that girl
HIGGINS.		just like a parrot. Ive tried her with every
PICKERING.		is a genius. She can play the piano quite beautifully.
HIGGINS.		possible sort of sound that a human being can make—
PICKERING.		We have taken her to classical concerts and to music
HIGGINS.		Continental dialects, African dialects, Hottentot
PICKERING.		halls; and it's all the same to her: she plays everything
HIGGINS.		clicks, things it took me years to get hold of; and
PICKERING.		she hears right off when she comes home, whether it's
HIGGINS.		she picks them up like a shot, right away, as if she had
PICKERING.		Beethoven and Brahms or Lehar and Lionel Monckton;
HIGGINS.		been at it all her life.
PICKERING.		though six months ago, she'd never as much as touched a piano—

MRS HIGGINS   [*putting her fingers in her ears, as they are by this time shouting one another down with an intolerable noise*] Sh-sh-sh—sh! [*They stop*].

PICKERING.   I beg your pardon. [*He draws his chair back apologetically*].

HIGGINS.   Sorry. When Pickering starts shouting nobody can get a word in edgeways.

MRS HIGGINS.   Be quiet, Henry. Colonel Pickering: dont you realize that when Eliza walked into Wimpole Street, something walked in with her?

PICKERING.   Her father did. But Henry soon got rid of him.

MRS HIGGINS.   It would have been more to the point if her mother had. But as her mother didnt something else did.

PICKERING.   But what?

MRS HIGGINS   [*unconsciously dating herself by the word*] A problem.

PICKERING.   Oh, I see. The problem of how to pass her off as a lady.

HIGGINS.   I'll solve that problem. Ive half solved it already.

MRS HIGGINS.   No, you two infinitely stupid male creatures: the problem of what is to be done with her afterwards.

HIGGINS.   I dont see anything in that. She can go her own way, with all the advantages I have given her.

MRS HIGGINS.   The advantages of that poor woman who was here just now! The manners and habits that disqualify a fine lady from earning her own living without giving her a fine lady's income! Is that what you mean?

PICKERING   [*indulgently, being rather bored*] Oh, that will be all right, Mrs Higgins. [*He rises to go*].

HIGGINS   [*rising also*] We'll find her some light employment.

PICKERING.   She's happy enough. Dont you worry about her. Goodbye. [*He shakes hands as if he were consoling a frightened child, and makes for the door*].

HIGGINS.   Anyhow, theres no good bothering now. The thing's done. Goodbye, mother. [*He kisses her, and follows PICKERING*].

PICKERING   [*turning for a final consolation*] There are plenty of openings. We'll do whats right. Goodbye.

HIGGINS   [*to PICKERING as they go out together*] Let's take her to the Shakespear exhibition at Earls Court.

PICKERING.   Yes: lets. Her remarks will be delicious.

HIGGINS.   She'll mimic all the people for us when we get home.

PICKERING.   Ripping. [*both are heard laughing as they go downstairs*].

MRS HIGGINS   [*rises with an impatient bounce, and returns to her work at the writing-table. She sweeps a littler of disarranged papers out of her way; snatches a sheet of paper from her stationery case; and tries resolutely to write. At the third line she gives it up; flings down her pen; grips the table angrily and exclaims*] Oh, men! men!! men!!!

ACT IV

The Wimpole Street laboratory. Midnight. Nobody in the room. The clock on the mantelpiece strikes twelve. The fire is not alight: it is a summer night. Presently HIGGINS and PICKERING are heard on the stairs.

HIGGINS   [*calling down to PICKERING*] I say, Pick: lock up, will you? I shant be going out again.

PICKERING.   Right. Can Mrs Pearce go to bed? We dont want anything more, do we?

HIGGINS.   Lord, no!

ELIZA opens the door and is seen on the lighted landing in opera cloak, brillant evening dress, and diamonds, with fan, flowers, and all accessories. She comes to the hearth, and switches on the electric lights there. She is tired: her pallor contrasts strongly with her dark eyes and hair; and her expression is almost tragic. She takes off her cloak; puts her fan and flowers on the piano; and sits down on the bench, brooding and silent. HIGGINS, in evening dress, with overcoat and hat, comes in, carrying a smoking jacket which he has picked up downstairs. He takes off the hat and overcoat; throws them carelessly on the newspaper stand; disposes of his coat in the same way; puts on the smoking jacket; and throws himself wearily into the easy-chair at the hearth. PICKERING, similarly attired, comes in. He also takes off his hat and overcoat, and is about to throw them on HIGGINS's when he hesitates.

HIGGINS.   I say: Mrs Pearce will row if we leave these things lying about in the drawing room.

HIGGINS.   Oh, chuck them over the bannisters into the hall. She'll find them there in the morning and put them away all right. She'll think we were drunk.

PICKERING.   We are, slightly. Are there any letters?

HIGGINS.   I didnt look. [*PICKERING takes the overcoats and hats and goes downstairs. HIGGINS begins half singing half yawning an air from La Fanciulla del Golden West. Suddenly he stops and exclaims*] I wonder where the devil my slippers are!

ELIZA looks at him darkly; then rises suddenly and leaves the room.

HIGGINS yawns again, and resumes his song.

PICKERING returns, with the contents of the letter-box in his hand.

PICKERING.   Only circulars, and this coroneted billet-doux for you. [*He throws the circulars into the fender, and posts himself on the hearthrug, with his back to the grate*].

HIGGINS   [*glancing at the billet-doux*] Money-lender. [*He throws the letter after the circulars*].

ELIZA returns with a pair of large down-at-heel slippers. She places them on the carpet before HIGGINS, and sits as before without a word.

HIGGINS   [*yawning again*] Oh Lord! What an evening! What a crew! What a silly tomfoolery![*He raises his shoe to unlace it, and catches sight of his slippers. He stops unlacing and looks at them as if they had appeared there of their own accord*]. Oh! theyre there, are they?

PICKERING   [*stretching himself*] Well, I feel a bit tired. It's been a long day. The garden party, a dinner party, and the opera! Rather too much of a good thing. But youve won your bet, Higgins. Eliza did the trick, and something to spare, eh?

HIGGINS   [*fervently*] Thank God it's over!

ELIZA flinches violently; but they take no notice of her; and she recovers herself and sits stonily as before.

PICKERING.   Were you nervous at the garden party? *I* was. Eliza didnt seem a bit nervous.

HIGGINS.   Oh, s h e wasnt nervous. I knew she'd be all right. No: it's the strain of putting the job through all these months that has told on me. It was interesting enough at first, while we were at the phonetics; but after that I got deadly sick of it. If I hadnt backed myself to do it I should have chucked the whole thing up two months ago. It was a silly notion: the whole thing has been a bore.

PICKERING.   Oh come! the garden party was frightfully exciting. My heart began beating like anything.

HIGGINS.   Yes, for the first three minutes. But when I saw we were going to win hands down, I felt like a bear in a cage, hanging about doing nothing. The dinner was worse: sitting gorging there for over an hour, with nobody but a damned fool of a fashionable woman to talk to! I tell you, Pickering, never again for me. No more artificial duchesses. The whole thing has been simple purgatory.

PICKERING.   Youve never been broken in properly to the social routine. [*Strolling over to the piano*] I rather enjoy dipping into it occasionally myself: it makes me feel young again. Anyhow, it was a great success: an immense success. I was quite frightened once or twice because Eliza was doing it so well. You see, lots of the real people cant do it at all: theyre such fools that they think style comes by nature to people in their position; and so they never learn. Theres always something professional about doing a thing superlatively well.

HIGGINS.   Yes: thats what drives me mad: the silly people dont know their own silly business. [*Rising*] However, it's over and done with; and now I can go to bed at last without dreading tomorrow.

ELIZA's beauty becomes murderous.

PICKERING.   I think I shall turn in too. Still, it's been a great occasion: a triumph for you. Goodnight. [*He goes*].

HIGGINS   [*following him*] Goodnight. [*Over his shoulder, at the door*] Put out the lights, Eliza; and tell Mrs Pearce not to make coffee for me in the morning: I'll take tea. [*He goes out*].

ELIZA tries to control herself and feel indifferent as she rises and walks across to the hearth to switch off the lights. By the time she gets there she is on the point of screaming. She sits down in HIGGINS's chair and holds on hard to the arms. Finally she gives way and flings herself furiously on the floor, raging.

HIGGINS   [*in despairing wrath outside*] What the devil have I done with my slippers? [*He appears at the door*].

LIZA [*snatching up the slippers, and hurling them at him one after the other with all her force*] There are your slippers. And there. Take your slippers; and may you never have a day's luck with them!

HIGGINS [*astounded*] What on earth—! [*He comes to her*]. Whats the matter? Get up. [*He pulls her up*]. Anything wrong?

LIZA [*breathless*] Nothing wrong—with y o u. Ive won your bet for you, havnt I? Thats enough for you. *I* dont matter, I suppose.

HIGGINS. Y o u won my bet! You! Presumptuous insect! *I* won it. What did you throw those slippers at me for?

LIZA. Because I wanted to smash your face. I'd like to kill you, you selfish brute. Why didnt you leave me where you picked me out of—in the gutter? You thank God it's all over, and that now you can throw me back again there, do you? [*She crisps her fingers frantically*].

HIGGINS [*looking at her in cool wonder*] The creature is nervous, after all.

LIZA [*gives a suffocated scream of fury, and instinctively darts her nails at his face*]!!

HIGGINS [*catching her wrists*] Ah! would you? Claws in, you cat. How dare you shew your temper to me? Sit down and be quiet. [*He throws her roughly into the easy-chair*].

LIZA [*crushed by superior strength and weight*] Whats to become of me? Whats to become of me?

HIGGINS. How the devil do I know whats to become of you? What does it matter what becomes of you?

LIZA. You dont care. I know you dont care. You wouldnt care if I was dead. I'm nothing to you—not so much as them slippers.

HIGGINS [*thundering*] T h o s e slippers.

LIZA [*with bitter submission*] Those slippers. I didnt think it made any difference now.

A pause. ELIZA *hopeless and crushed.* HIGGINS *a little uneasy.*

HIGGINS [*in his loftiest manner*] Why have you begun going on like this? May I ask whether you complain of your treatment here?

LIZA. No.

HIGGINS. Has anybody behaved badly to you? Colonel Pickering? Mrs Pearce? Any of the servants?

LIZA. No.

HIGGINS. I presume you dont pretend that *I* have treated you badly?

LIZA. No.

HIGGINS. I am glad to hear it. [*He moderates his tone*]. Perhaps youre tired after the strain of the day. Will you have a glass of champagne? [*He moves towards the door*].

LIZA. No. [*Recollecting her manners*] Thank you.

HIGGINS [*good-humored again*] This has been coming on you for some days. I suppose it was natural for you to be anxious about the garden party. But thats all over now. [*He pats her kindly on the shoulder. She writhes*]. Theres nothing more to worry about.

LIZA.   No. Nothing more for y o u to worry about. [*She suddenly rises and gets away from him by going to the piano bench, where she sits and hides her face*] Oh God! I wish I was dead.

HIGGINS [*staring after her in sincere surprise*] Why? In heaven's name, why? [*Reasonably, going to her*] Listen to me, Eliza. All this irritation is purely subjective.

LIZA.   I dont understand. I'm too ignorant.

HIGGINS.   It's only imagination. Low spirits and nothing else. Nobody's hurting you. Nothing's wrong. You go to bed like a good girl and sleep it off. Have a little cry and say your prayers: that will make you comfortable.

LIZA.   I heard your prayers. "Thank God it's all over!"

HIGGINS [*impatiently*] Well, d o n t you thank God it's all over? Now you are free and can do what you like.

LIZA [*pulling herself together in desperation*] What am I fit for? What have you left me fit for? Where am I to go? What am I to do? Whats to become of me?

HIGGINS [*enlightened, but not at all impressed*] Oh t h a t s whats worrying you, is it? [*He thrusts his hands into his pockets, and walks about in his usual manner, rattling the contents of his pockets, as if condescending to a trivial subject out of pure kindness*]. I shouldnt bother about it if I were you. I should imagine you wont have much difficulty in settling yourself somewhere or other, though I hadnt quite realized that you were gong away. [*She looks quickly at him: he does not look at her, but examines the dessert stand on the piano and decides that he will eat an apple*]. You might marry, you know. [*He bites a large piece out of the apple and munches it noisily*]. You see, Eliza, all men are not confirmed old bachelors like me and the Colonel. Most men are the marrying sort (poor devils!); and youre not bad-looking: it's quite a pleasure to look at you sometimes—not now, of course, because youre crying and looking as ugly as the very devil; but when youre all right and quite yourself, youre what I should call attractive. That is, to the people in the marrying line, you understand. You go to bed and have a good nice rest; and then get up and look at yourself in the glass; and you wont feel so cheap.

ELIZA again looks at him, speechless, and does not stir.

The look is quite lost on him: he eats his apple with a dreamy expression of happiness, as it is quite a good one.

HIGGINS [*a genial afterthought occurring to him*] I daresay my mother could find some chap or other who would do very well.

LIZA.   We were above that at the corner of Tottenham Court Road.

HIGGINS [*waking up*] What do you mean?

LIZA.   I sold flowers. I didnt sell myself. Now youve made a lady of me I'm not fit to sell anything else. I wish youd left me where you found me.

HIGGINS [*slinging the core of the apple decisively into the grate*] Tosh, Eliza. Dont you insult human relations by dragging all this cant about buying and selling into it. You neednt marry the fellow if you dont like him.

LIZA.   What else am I to do?

HIGGINS.   Oh, lots of things. What about your old idea of a florist's shop? Pickering could set you up in one: he's lots of money. [*Chuckling*] He'll have to pay for all those togs you have been wearing today; and that, with the hire of the jewellery, will make a big hole in two hundred pounds. Why, six months ago you would have thought it the millennium to have a flower shop of your own. Come! youll be all right. I must clear off to bed: I'm devilish sleepy. By the way, I came down for something: I forget what it was.

LIZA.   Your slippers.

HIGGINS.   Oh yes, of course. You shied them at me. [*He picks them up, and is going out when she rises and speaks to him*].

LIZA.   Before you go, sir—

HIGGINS [*dropping the slippers in his surprise at her calling him Sir*] Eh?

LIZA.   Do my clothes belong to me or to Colonel Pickering?

HIGGINS [*coming back into the room as if her question were the very climax of unreason*] What the devil use would they be to Pickering?

LIZA.   He might want them for the next girl you pick up to experiment on.

HIGGINS [*shocked and hurt*] Is t h a t the way you feel towards us?

LIZA.   I dont want to hear anything more about that. All I want to know is whether anything belongs to me. My own clothes were burnt.

HIGGINS.   But what does it matter? Why need you start bothering about that in the middle of the night?

LIZA.   I want to know what I may take away with me. I dont want to be accused of stealing.

HIGGINS [*now deeply wounded*] Stealing! You shouldnt have said that, Eliza. That shews a want of feeling.

LIZA.   I'm sorry. I'm only a common ignorant girl; and in my station I have to be careful. There cant be any feelings between the like of you and the like of me. Please will you tell me what belongs to me and what doesnt?

HIGGINS [*very sulky*] You may take the whole damned houseful if you like. Except the jewels. Theyre hired. Will that satisfy you? [*He turns on his heel and is about to go in extreme dudgeon*].

LIZA [*drinking in his emotion like nectar, and nagging him to provoke a further supply*] Stop, please. [*She takes off her jewels*]. Will you take these to your room and keep them safe? I dont want to run the risk of their being missing.

HIGGINS   [*furious*] Hand them over. [*She puts them into his hands*]. If these belonged to me instead of to the jeweller, I'd ram them down your ungrateful throat. [*He perfunctorily thrusts them into his pockets, unconsciously decorating himself with the protruding ends of the chains*].

LIZA   [*taking a ring off*] This ring isnt the jeweller's: it's the one you bought me in Brighton. I dont want it now. [*HIGGINS dashes the ring violently into the fireplace, and turns on her so threateningly that she crouches over the piano with her hands over her face, and exclaims*]. Dont you hit me.

HIGGINS.   Hit you! You infamous creature, how dare you accuse me of such a thing? It is you who have hit me. You have wounded me to the heart.

LIZA   [*thrilling with hidden joy*] I'm glad. Ive got a little of my own back, anyhow.

HIGGINS   [*with dignity, in his finest professional style*] You have caused me to lose my temper: a thing that has hardly ever happened to me before. I prefer to say nothing more tonight. I am going to bed.

LIZA   [*pertly*] Youd better leave a note for Mrs Pearce about the coffee; for she wont be told by me.

HIGGINS   [*formally*] Damn Mrs Pearce; and damn the coffee; and damn you; and damn my own folly in having lavished hard-earned knowledge and the treasure of my regard and intimacy on a heartless guttersnipe. [*He goes out with impressive decorum, and spoils it by slamming the door savagely*].

ELIZA smiles for the first time; expresses her feelings by a wild pantomime in which an imitation of HIGGINS's exit is confused with her own triumph; and finally goes down on her knees on the hearthrug to look for the ring.

ACT V

MRS HIGGINS's drawing room. She is at her writing-table as before. The parlor-maid comes in.

THE PARLOR-MAID   [*at the door*] Mr Henry, maam, is downstairs with Colonel Pickering.

MRS HIGGINS.   Well, shew them up.

THE PARLOR-MAID.   Theyre using the telephone, maam. Telephoning to the police, I think.

MRS HIGGINS.   What!

THE PARLOR-MAID   [*coming further in and lowering her voice*] Mr Henry is in a state, maam. I thought I'd better tell you.

Mrs Higgins.   If you had told me that Mr Henry was not in a state it would have been more surprising. Tell them to come up when theyve finished with the police. I suppose he's lost something.

The Parlor-Maid.   Yes, maam [*going*].

Mrs Higgins.   Go upstairs and tell Miss Doolittle that Mr Henry and the Colonel are here. Ask her not to come down til I send for her.

The Parlor-Maid.   Yes, maam.

Higgins bursts in. He is, as the parlor-maid has said, in a state.

Higgins.   Look here, mother: heres a confounded thing!

Mrs Higgins.   Yes, dear. Good morning. [*He checks his impatience and kisses her, whilst the parlor-maid goes out*]. What is it?

Higgins.   Eliza's bolted.

Mrs Higgins   [*calmly continuing her writing*] You must have frightened her.

Higgins.   Frightened her! nonsense! She was left last night, as usual, to turn out the lights and all that; and instead of going to bed she changed her clothes and went right off: her bed wasnt slept in. She came in a cab for her things before seven this morning; and that fool Mrs Pearce let her have them without telling me a word about it. What am I to do?

Mrs Higgins.   Do without, I'm afraid, Henry. The girl has a perfect right to leave if she chooses.

Higgins   [*wandering distractedly across the room*] But I cant find anything. I dont know what appointments Ive got. I'm —[*Pickering comes in. Mrs Higgins puts down her pen and turns away from the writing-table*].

Pickering   [*shaking hands*] Good morning, Mrs Higgins. Has Henry told you? [*He sits down on the ottoman*].

Higgins.   What does that ass of an inspector say? Have you offered a reward?

Mrs Higgins   [*rising in indignant amazement*] You dont mean to say you have set the police after Eliza.

Higgins.   Of course. What are the police for? What else could we do? [*He sits in the Elizabethan chair*].

Pickering.   The inspector made a lot of difficulties. I really think he suspected us of some improper purpose.

Mrs Higgins.   Well, of course he did. What right have you to go to the police and give the girl's name as if she were a thief, or a lost umbrella, or something? Really! [*She sits down again, deeply vexed*].

Higgins.   But we want to find her.

Pickering.   We cant let her go like this, you know, Mrs Higgins. What were we to do?

Mrs Higgins.   You have no more sense, either of you, than two children. Why—

The parlor-maid comes in and breaks off the conversation.

THE PARLOR-MAID.   Mr Henry: a gentleman wants to see you very particular. He's been sent on from Wimpole Street.

HIGGINS.   Oh, bother! I cant see anyone now. Who is it?

THE PARLOR-MAID.   A Mr Doolittle, sir.

PICKERING.   Doolittle! Do you mean the dustman?

THE PARLOR-MAID.   Dustman! Oh no, sir: a gentleman.

HIGGINS [*springing up excitedly*] By George, Pick, it's some relative of hers that she's gone to. Somebody we know nothing about. [*To the parlor-maid*] Send him up, quick.

THE PARLOR-MAID.   Yes, sir. [*She goes*].

HIGGINS [*eagerly, going to his mother*] Genteel relatives! now we shall hear something. [*He sits down in the Chippendale chair*].

MRS HIGGINS.   Do you know any of her people?

PICKERING.   Only her father: the fellow we told you about.

THE PARLOR-MAID [*announcing*] Mr Doolittle. [*She withdraws*].

DOOLITTLE enters. He is brilliantly dressed in a new fashionable frock-coat, with white waistcoat and grey trousers. A flower in his buttonhole, a dazzling silk hat, and patent leather shoes complete the effect. He is too concerned with the business he has come on to notice MRS HIGGINS. He walks straight to HIGGINS, and accosts him with vehement reproach.

DOOLITTLE [*indicating his own person*] See here! Do you see this? You done this.

HIGGINS.   Done what, man?

DOOLITTLE.   This, I tell you. Look at it. Look at this hat. Look at this coat.

PICKERING.   Has Eliza been buying you clothes?

DOOLITTLE.   Eliza! not she. Not half. Why would she buy me clothes?

MRS HIGGINS.   Good morning, Mr Doolittle. Wont you sit down?

DOOLITTLE [*taken aback as he becomes conscious that he has forgotten his hostess*] Asking your pardon, maam. [*He approaches her and shakes her proffered hand*]. Thank you. [*He sits down on the ottoman, on PICKERING's right*]. I am that full of what has happened to me that I cant think of anything else.

HIGGINS.   What the dickens has happened to you?

DOOLITTLE.   I shouldnt mind if it had only happened to me: anything might happen to anybody and nobody to blame but Providence, as you might say. But this is something that you done to me: yes, you, Henry Higgins.

HIGGINS.   Have you found Eliza? Thats the point.

DOOLITTLE.   Have you lost her?

HIGGINS.   Yes.

DOOLITTLE.   You have all the luck, you have. I aint found her; but she'll find me quick enough now after what you done to me.

MRS HIGGINS.   But what has my son done to you, Mr. Doolittle?

DOOLITTLE.   Done to me! Ruined me. Destroyed my happiness. Tied me up and delivered me into the hands of middle class morality.

HIGGINS   [*rising intolerantly and standing over* DOOLITTLE] Youre raving. Youre drunk. Youre mad. I gave you five pounds. After that I had two conversations with you, at half a-crown an hour. Ive never seen you since.

DOOLITTLE.   Oh! Drunk! am I? Mad! am I? Tell me this. Did you or did you not write a letter to an old blighter in America that was giving five millions to found Moral Reform Societies all over the world, and that wanted you to invent a universal language for him?

HIGGINS.   What! Ezra D. Wannafeller! He's dead. [*He sits down again carelessly*].

DOOLITTLE.   Yes: he's dead; and I'm done for. Now did you or did you not write a letter to him to say that the most original moralist at present in England, to the best of your knowledge, was Alfred Doolittle, a common dustman.

HIGGINS.   Oh, after your last visit I remember making some silly joke of the kind.

DOOLITTLE.   Ah! you may well call it a silly joke. It put the lid on me right enough. Just give him the chance he wanted to shew that Americans is not like us: that they recognize and respect merit in every class of life, however humble. Them words is in his blooming will, in which, Henry Higgins, thanks to your silly joking, he leaves me a share in his Pre-digested Cheese Trust worth three thousand a year on condition that I lecture for his Wannafeller Moral Reform World League as often as they ask me up to six times a year.

HIGGINS.   The devil he does! [*Brightening suddenly*] What a lark!

PICKERING.   A safe thing for you, Doolittle. They wont ask you twice.

DOOLITTLE.   It aint the lecturing I mind. I'll lecture them blue in the face, I will, and not turn a hair. It's making a gentleman of me that I object to. Who asked him to make a gentleman of me? I was happy. I was free. I touched pretty nigh everybody for money when I wanted it, same as I touched you, Henry Higgins. Now I am worrited; tied neck and heels; and everybody touches me for money. It's a fine thing for you, says my solicitor. Is it? says I. You mean it's a good thing for you, I says. When I was a poor man and had a solicitor once when they found a pram in the dust cart, he got me off, and got shut of me and got me shut of him as quick as he could. Same with the doctors: used to shove me out of the hospital before I could hardly stand on my legs, and nothing to pay. Now they finds out that I'm not a healthy man and cant live unless they looks after me twice a day. In the house I'm not let do a hand's turn for myself: somebody else must do it and touch me for it. A year ago I hadnt a relative in the world except two or three that wouldnt speak to me. Now Ive fifty, and not a decent week's wages among the lot of them. I have to live for others and not for myself: thats middle class morality. You talk of losing Eliza. Dont you be anxious: I bet she's on my doorstep by this: she that could support herself easy by selling flowers if I wasnt respectable. And the next one to touch me will be you, Henry Higgins. I'll have to learn to speak middle class language from you, instead of speaking proper English. Thats where youll come in; and I daresay thats what you done it for.

MRS HIGGINS.   But, my dear Mr Doolittle, you need not suffer all this if you are really in earnest. Nobody can force you to accept this bequest. You can repudiate it. Isnt that so, Colonel Pickering?

PICKERING.   I believe so.

DOOLITTLE   [*softening his manner in deference to her sex*] Thats the tragedy of it, maam. It's easy to say chuck it; but I havnt the nerve. Which of us has? We're all intimidated. Intimidated, maam: thats what we are. What is there for me if I chuck it but the workhouse in my old age? I have to dye my hair already to keep my job as a dustman. If I was one of the deserving poor, and had put by a bit, I could chuck it; but then why should I, acause the deserving poor might as well be millionaires for all the happiness they ever has. They dont know what happiness is. But I, as one of the undeserving poor, have nothing between me and the pauper's uniform but this here blasted three thousand a year that shoves me into the middle class. (Excuse the expression, maam: youd use it yourself if you had my provocation.) Theyve got you every way you turn: it's a choice between the Skilly of the workhouse and the Char Bydis of the middle class; and I havnt the nerve for the workhouse. Intimidated: thats what I am. Broke. Bought up. Happier men than me will call for my dust, and touch me for their tip; and I'll look on helpless, and envy them. And thats what your son has brought me to. [*He is overcome by emotion*].

MRS HIGGINS.   Well, I'm very glad youre not going to do anything foolish, Mr. Doolittle. For this solves the problem of Eliza's future. You can provide for her now.

DOOLITTLE   [*with melancholy resignation*] Yes, maam: I'm expected to provide for everyone now, out of three thousand a year.

HIGGINS   [*jumping up*] Nonsense! he cant provide for her. He shant provide for her. She doesnt belong to him. I paid him five pounds for her. Doolittle: either youre an honest man or a rogue.

DOOLITTLE   [*tolerantly*] A little of both, Henry, like the rest of us: a little of both.

HIGGINS.   Well, you took that money for the girl; and you have no right to take her as well.

MRS HIGGINS.   Henry: dont be absurd. If you want to know where Eliza is, she is upstairs.

HIGGINS   [*amazed*] Upstairs!!! Then I shall jolly soon fetch her downstairs. [*He makes resolutely for the door*].

MRS HIGGINS   [*rising and following him*] Be quiet, Henry. Sit down.

HIGGINS. I—

MRS HIGGINS. Sit down, dear; and listen to me.

HIGGINS. Oh very well, very well, very well. [*He throws himself ungraciously on the ottoman, with his face towards the windows*]. But I think you might have told us this half an hour ago.

MRS HIGGINS. Eliza came to me this morning. She passed the night partly walking about in a rage, partly trying to throw herself into the river and being afraid to, and partly in the Carlton Hotel. She told me of the brutal way you two treated her.

HIGGINS [*bounding up again*] What!

PICKERING [*rising also*] My dear Mrs Higgins, she's been telling you stories. We didnt treat her brutally. We hardly said a word to her; and we parted on particularly good terms. [*Turning on HIGGINS*]. Higgins: did you bully her after I went to bed?

HIGGINS. Just the other way about. She threw my slippers in my face. She behaved in the most outrageous way. I never gave her the slightest provocation. The slippers came bang into my face the moment I entered the room—before I had uttered a word. And used perfectly awful language.

PICKERING [*astonished*] But why? What did we do to her?

MRS HIGGINS. I think I know pretty well what you did. The girl is naturally rather affectionate, I think. Isnt she, Mr Doolittle?

DOOLITTLE. Very tender-hearted, maam. Takes after me.

MRS HIGGINS. Just so. She had become attached to you both. She worked very hard for you, Henry! I dont think you quite realize what anything in the nature of brain work means to a girl like that. Well, it seems that when the great day of trial came, and she did this wonderful thing for you without making a single mistake, you two sat there and never said a word to her, but talked together of how glad you were that it was all over and how you had been bored with the whole thing. And then you were surprised because she threw your slippers at you! *I* should have thrown the fire-irons at you.

HIGGINS. We said nothing except that we were tired and wanted to go to bed. Did we, Pick?

PICKERING [*shrugging his shoulders*] That was all.

MRS HIGGINS [*ironically*] Quite sure?

PICKERING. Absolutely. Really, that was all.

MRS HIGGINS. You didnt thank her, or pet her, or admire her, to tell her how splendid she'd been.

HIGGINS [*impatiently*] But she knew all about that. We didnt make speeches to her, if thats what you mean.

PICKERING [*conscience stricken*] Perhaps we were a little inconsiderate. Is she very angry?

MRS HIGGINS [*returning to her place at the writing-table*] Well, I'm afraid she wont go back to Wimpole Street, especially now that Mr Doolittle is able to keep up the position you have thrust on her; but she says she is quite willing to meet you on friendly terms and to let bygones be bygones.

HIGGINS   [*furious*] Is she, by George? Ho!

MRS HIGGINS.   If you promise to behave yourself, Henry, I'll ask her to come down. If not, go home; for you have taken up quite enough of my time.

HIGGINS.   Oh, all right. Very well. Pick: you behave yourself. Let us put on our best Sunday manners for this creature that we picked out of the mud. [*He flings himself sulkily into the Elizabethan chair*].

DOOLITTLE   [*remonstrating*] Now, now, Henry Higgins! have some consideration for my feelings as a middle class man.

MRS HIGGINS.   Remember your promise, Henry. [*She presses the bell-button on the writing-table*]. Mr Doolittle: will you be so good as to step out on the balcony for a moment. I dont want Eliza to have the shock of your news until she has made it up with these two gentlemen. Would you mind?

DOOLITTLE.   As you wish, lady. Anything to help Henry to keep her off my hands. [*He disappears through the window*].

The parlor-maid answers the bell. PICKERING sits down in DOOLITTLE's place.

MRS HIGGINS.   Ask Miss Doolittle to come down, please.

THE PARLOR-MAID.   Yes, maam. [*She goes out*].

MRS HIGGINS.   Now, Henry: be good.

HIGGINS.   I am behaving myself perfectly.

PICKERING.   He is doing his best, Mrs Higgins.

A pause. HIGGINS throws back his head; stretches out his legs; and begins to whistle.

MRS HIGGINS.   Henry, dearest, you dont look at all nice in that attitude.

HIGGINS   [*pulling himself together*] I was not trying to look nice, mother.

MRS HIGGINS.   It doesnt matter, dear. I only wanted to make you speak.

HIGGINS.   Why?

MRS HIGGINS.   Because you cant speak and whistle at the same time.

HIGGINS groans. Another very trying pause.

HIGGINS   [*springing up, out of patience*] Where the devil is that girl? Are we to wait here all day?

ELIZA enters, sunny, self-possessed, and giving a staggeringly convincing exhibition of ease of manner. She carries a little work-basket, and is very much at home. PICKERING is too much taken aback to rise.

LIZA.   How do you do, Professor Higgins? Are you quite well?

HIGGINS [*choking*] Am I—[*He can say no more*].

LIZA. But of course you are: you are never ill. So glad to see you again, Colonel Pickering. [*He rises hastily; and they shake hands*]. Quite chilly this morning, isnt it? [*She sits down on his left. He sits beside her*].

HIGGINS. Dont you dare try this game on me. I taught it to you; and it doesnt take me in. Get up and come home; and dont be a fool.

ELIZA takes a piece of needlework from her basket, and begins to stitch at it, without taking the least notice of this outburst.

MRS HIGGINS. Very nicely put, indeed, Henry. No woman could resist such an invitation.

HIGGINS. You let her alone, mother. Let her speak for herself. You will jolly soon see whether she has an idea that I havnt put into her head or a word that I havnt put into her mouth. I tell you I have created this thing out of the squashed cabbage leaves of Covent Garden; and now she pretends to play the fine lady with me.

MRS HIGGINS [*placidly*] Yes, dear; but youll sit down, wont you?

HIGGINS sits down again, savagely.

LIZA [*to PICKERING, taking no apparent notice of HIGGINS, and working away deftly*] Will you drop me altogether now that the experiment is over, Colonel Pickering?

PICKERING. Oh dont. You mustnt think of it as an experiment. It shocks me, somehow.

LIZA. Oh, I'm only a squashed cabbage leaf—

PICKERING [*impulsively*] No.

LIZA [*continuing quietly*]—but I owe so much to you that I should be very unhappy if you forgot me.

PICKERING. It's very kind of you to say so, Miss Doolittle.

LIZA. It's not because you paid for my dresses. I know you are generous to everybody with money. But it was from you that I learnt really nice manners; and that is what makes one a lady, isnt it? You see it was so very difficult for me with the example of Professor Higgins always before me. I was brought up to be just like him, unable to control myself, and using bad language on the slightest provocation. And I should never have known that ladies and gentlemen didnt behave like that if you hadnt been there.

HIGGINS. Well!!

PICKERING. Oh, thats only his way, you know. He doesnt mean it.

LIZA. Oh, *I* didnt mean it either, when I was a flower girl. It was only my way. But you see I did it; and thats what makes the difference after all.

PICKERING. No doubt. Still, he taught you to speak; and I couldnt have done that, you know.

LIZA   [*trivially*] Of course: that is his profession.

HIGGINS.   Damnation!

LIZA   [*continuing*] It was just like learning to dance in the fashionable way: there was nothing more than that in it. But do you know what began my real education?

PICKERING.   What?

LIZA   [*stopping her work for a moment*] Your calling me Miss Doolittle that day when I first came to Wimpole Street. That was the beginning of self-respect for me. [*She resumes her stitching*]. And there were a hundred little things you never noticed, because they came naturally to you. Things about standing up and taking off your hat and opening doors—

PICKERING.   Oh, that was nothing.

LIZA.   Yes: things that shewed you thought and felt about me as if I were something better than a scullery-maid; though of course I know you would have been just the same to a scullery-maid if she had been let into the drawing room. You never took off your boots in the dining room when I was there.

PICKERING.   You mustnt mind that. Higgins takes off his boots all over the place.

LIZA.   I know. I am not blaming him. It is his way, isnt it? But it made such a difference to me that you didnt do it. You see, really and truly, apart from the things anyone can pick up (the dressing and the proper way of speaking, and so on), the difference between a lady and a flower girl is not how she behaves, but how she's treated. I shall always be a flower girl to Professor Higgins, because he always treats me as a flower girl, and always will; but I know I can be a lady to you, because you always treat me as a lady, and always will.

MRS HIGGINS.   Please dont grind your teeth, Henry.

PICKERING.   Well, this is really very nice of you Miss Doolittle.

LIZA.   I should like you to call me Eliza, now, if you would.

PICKERING.   Thank you. Eliza, of course.

LIZA.   And I should like Professor Higgins to call me Miss Doolittle.

HIGGINS.   I'll see you damned first.

MRS HIGGINS.   Henry! Henry!

PICKERING   [*laughing*] Why dont you slang back at him? Dont stand it. It would do him a lot of good.

LIZA.   I cant. I could have done it once; but now I cant go back to it. Last night, when I was wandering about, a girl spoke to me; and I tried to get back into the old way with her; but it was no use. You told me, you know, that when a child is brought to a foreign country, it picks up the language in a few weeks, and forgets its own. Well, I am a child in your country. I have forgotten my own language, and can speak nothing but yours. Thats the real break-off with the corner of Tottenham Court Road. Leaving Wimpole Street finishes it.

PICKERING [*much alarmed*] Oh! but youre coming back to Wimpole Street, arnt you? Youll forgive Higgins?

HIGGINS [*rising*] Forgive! Will she, by George! Let her go. Let her find out how she can get on without us. She will relapse into the gutter in three weeks without me at her elbow.

DOOLITTLE appears at the centre window. With a look of dignified reproach at HIGGINS, he comes slowly and silently to his daughter, who, with her back to the window, is unconscious of his approach.

PICKERING. He's incorrigible, Eliza. You wont relapse, will you?

LIZA. No: not now. Never again. I have learnt my lesson. I dont believe I could utter one of the old sounds if I tried. [*DOOLITTLE touches her on her left shoulder. She drops her work, losing her self-possession utterly at the spectacle of her fathers splendor*] A-a-a-a-a-ah-ow-ohh!

HIGGINS [*with a crow of triumph*] Aha! Just so. A-a-a-a-ahowooh! A-a-a-a-ahowooh! A-a-a-a-ahowooh! Victory! Victory! [*He throws himself on the divan, folding his arms, and spraddling arrogantly*].

DOOLITTLE. Can you blame the girl? Dont look at me like that, Eliza. It aint my fault. Ive come into some money.

LIZA. You must have touched a millionaire this time, dad.

DOOLITTLE. I have. But I'm dressed something special today. I'm going to St George's, Hanover Square. Your stepmother is going to marry me.

LIZA [*angrily*] Youre going to let yourself down to marry that low common woman!

PICKERING [*quietly*] He ought to, Eliza. [*To DOOLITTLE*] Why has she changed her mind?

DOOLITTLE [*sadly*] Intimidated, Governor. Intimidated. Middle class morality claims its victim. Wont you put on your hat, Liza, and come and see me turned off?

LIZA. If the Colonel says I must, I—I'll [*almost sobbing*] I'll demean myself. And get insulted for my pains, like enough.

DOOLITTLE. Dont be afraid: she never comes to words with anyone now, poor woman! respectability has broke all the spirit out of her.

PICKERING [*squeezing ELIZA'S elbow gently*] Be kind to them, Eliza. Make the best of it.

LIZA [*forcing a little smile for him through her vexation*] Oh well, just to shew theres no ill feeling. I'll be back in a moment. [*She goes out*].

DOOLITTLE [*sitting down beside PICKERING*] I feel uncommon nervous about the ceremony, Colonel. I wish youd come and see me through it.

PICKERING. But youve been through it before, man. You were married to Eliza's mother.

DOOLITTLE. Who told you that, Colonel?

PICKERING. Well, nobody told me. But I concluded— naturally—

DOOLITTLE.   No: that aint the natural way, Colonel: it's only the middle class way. My way was always the undeserving way. But dont say nothing to Eliza. She dont know: I always had a delicacy about telling her.

PICKERING.   Quite right. We'll leave it so, if you dont mind.

DOOLITTLE.   And youll come to the church, Colonel, and put me through straight?

PICKERING.   With pleasure. As far as a bachelor can.

MRS HIGGINS.   May I come, Mr Doolittle? I should be very sorry to miss your wedding.

DOOLITTLE.   I should indeed be honored by your condescension, maam; and my poor old woman would take it as a tremendous compliment. She's been very low, thinking of the happy days that are no more.

MRS HIGGINS   [*rising*] I'll order the carriage and get ready. [*The men rise, except HIGGINS*]. I shant be more than fifteen minutes. [*As she goes to the door ELIZA comes in, hatted and buttoning her gloves*]. I'm going to the church to see your father married, Eliza. You had better come in the brougham with me. Colonel Pickering can go on with the bridegroom.

MRS HIGGINS goes out. ELIZA comes to the middle of the room between the centre window and the ottoman. PICKERING joins her.

DOOLITTLE.   Bridegroom! What a word! It makes a man realize his position, somehow. [*He takes up his hat and goes towards the door*].

PICKERING.   Before I go, Eliza, do forgive him and come back to us.

LIZA.   I dont think papa would allow me. Would you, dad?

DOOLITTLE   [*sad but magnanimous*] They played you off very cunning, Eliza, them two sportsmen. If it had been only one of them, you could have nailed him. But you see, there was two; and one of them chaperoned the other, as you might say. [*To PICKERING*] It was artful of you, Colonel; but I bear no malice: I should have done the same myself. I been the victim of one woman after another all my life; and I dont grudge you two getting the better of Eliza. I shant interfere. It's time for us to go, Colonel. So long, Henry. See you in St. George's, Eliza. [*He goes out*].

PICKERING   [*coaxing*] Do stay with us, Eliza. [*He follows DOOLITTLE*].

ELIZA goes out on the balcony to avoid being alone with HIGGINS. He rises and joins her there. She immediately comes back into the room and makes for the door; but he goes along the balcony quickly and gets his back to the door before she reaches it.

HIGGINS.   Well, Eliza, youve had a bit of your own back, as you call it. Have you had enough? and are you going to be reasonable? Or do you want any more?

LIZA.   You want me back only to pick up your slippers and put up with your tempers and fetch and carry for you.

HIGGINS.   I havnt said I wanted you back at all.

LIZA.   Oh, indeed. Then what are we talking about?

HIGGINS. About you, not about me. If you come back I shall treat you just as I have always treated you. I cant change my nature; and I dont intend to change my manners. My manners are exactly the same as Colonel Pickering's.

LIZA. Thats not true. He treats a flower girl as if she was a duchess.

HIGGINS. And I treat a duchess as if she was a flower girl.

LIZA. I see. [*She turns away composedly, and sits on the ottoman, facing the window*]. The same to everybody.

HIGGINS. Just so.

LIZA. Like father.

HIGGINS [*grinning, a little taken down*] Without accepting the comparison at all points, Eliza, it's quite true that your father is not a snob, and that he will be quite at home in any station of life to which his eccentric destiny may call him. [*Seriously*] The great secret, Eliza, is not having bad manners or good manners or any other particular sort of manners, but having the same manner for all human souls: in short, behaving as if you were in Heaven, where there are no third-class carriages, and one soul is as good as another.

LIZA. Amen. You are a born preacher.

HIGGINS [*irritated*] The question is not whether I treat you rudely, but whether you ever heard me treat anyone else better.

LIZA [*with sudden sincerity*] I dont care how you treat me. I dont mind your swearing at me. I dont mind a black eye: Ive had one before this. But [*standing up and facing him*] I wont be passed over.

HIGGINS. Then get out of my way; for I wont stop for you. You talk about me as if I were a motor bus.

LIZA. So you are a motor bus: all bounce and go, and no consideration for anyone. But I can do without you: dont think I cant.

HIGGINS. I know you can. I told you you could.

LIZA [*wounded, getting away from him to the other side of the ottoman with her face to the hearth*] I know you did, you brute. You wanted to get rid of me.

HIGGINS. Liar.

LIZA. Thank you. [*She sits down with dignity*].

HIGGINS. You never asked yourself, I suppose, whether *I* could do without you.

LIZA [*earnestly*] Dont you try to get round me. Youll have to do without me.

HIGGINS [*arrogant*] I can do without anybody. I have my own soul: my own spark of divine fire. But [*with sudden humility*] I shall miss you, Eliza. [*He sits down near her on the ottoman*]. I have learnt something from your idiotic notions: I confess that humbly and gratefully. And I have grown accustomed to your voice and appearance. I like them, rather.

LIZA. Well, you have both of them on your gramophone and in your book of photographs. When you feel lonely without me, you can turn the machine on. It's got no feelings to hurt.

HIGGINS.   I cant turn your soul on. Leave me those feelings; and you can take away the voice and the face. They are not you.

LIZA.   Oh, you are a devil. You can twist the heart in a girl as easy as some could twist her arms to hurt her. Mrs Pearce warned me. Time and again she has wanted to leave you; and you always got round her at the last minute. And you dont care a bit for her. And you dont care a bit for me.

HIGGINS.   I care for life, for humanity; and you are a part of it that has come my way and been built into my house. What more can you or anyone ask?

LIZA.   I wont care for anybody that doesnt care for me.

HIGGINS.   Commercial principles, Eliza. Like [*reproducing her Covent Garden pronunication with professional exactness*] s'yollin voylets [selling violets], isnt it?

LIZA.   Dont sneer at me. It's mean to sneer at me.

HIGGINS.   I have never sneered in my life. Sneering doesnt become either the human face or the human soul. I am expressing my righteous contempt for Commercialism. I dont and wont trade in affection. You call me a brute because you couldnt buy a claim on me by fetching my slippers and finding my spectacles. You were a fool: I think a woman fetching a man's slippers is a disgusting sight: did I ever fetch your slippers? I think a good deal more of you for throwing them in my face. No use slaving for me and then saying you want to be cared for: who cares for a slave? If you come back, come back for the sake of good fellowship; for youll get nothing else. Youve had a thousand times as much out of me as I have out of you; and if you dare to set up your little dog's trick of fetching and carrying slippers against my creation of a Duchess Eliza, I'll slam the door in your silly face.

LIZA.   What did you do it for if you didnt care for me?

HIGGINS   [*heartily*] Why, because it was my job.

LIZA.   You never thought of the trouble it would make for me.

HIGGINS.   Would the world ever have been made if its maker had been afraid of making trouble? Making life means making trouble. Theres only one way of escaping trouble; and thats killing things. Cowards, you notice, are always shrieking to have troublesome people killed.

LIZA.   I'm no preacher: I dont notice things like that. I notice that you dont notice me.

HIGGINS   [*jumping up and walking about intolerantly*] Eliza: youre an idiot. I waste the treasures of my Miltonic mind by spreading them before you. Once for all, understand that I go my way and do my work without caring two-pence what happens to either of us. I am not intimidated, like your father and your stepmother. So you can come back or go to the devil: which you please.

LIZA.   What am I to come back for?

HIGGINS [*bouncing up on his knees on the ottoman and leaning over it to her*] For the fun of it. Thats why I took you on.

LIZA [*with averted face*] And you may throw me out tomorrow if I dont do everything you want me to?

HIGGINS.   Yes; and you may walk out tomorrow if I dont do everything you want me to.

LIZA.   And live with my stepmother?

HIGGINS.   Yes, or sell flowers.

LIZA.   Oh! if I only could go back to my flower basket! I should be independent of both you and father and all the world! Why did you take my independence from me? Why did I give it up? I'm a slave now, for all my fine clothes.

HIGGINS.   Not a bit. I'll adopt you as my daughter and settle money on you if you like. Or would you rather marry Pickering?

LIZA [*looking fiercely round at him*] I wouldnt marry you if you asked me; and youre nearer my age than what he is.

HIGGINS [*gently*] Than he is: not "than what he is."

LIZA [*losing her temper and rising*] I'll talk as I like. Youre not my teacher now.

HIGGINS [*reflectively*] I dont suppose Pickering would, though. He's as confirmed an old bachelor as I am.

LIZA.   Thats not what I want; and dont you think it. Ive always had chaps enough wanting me that way. Freddy Hill writes to me twice and three times a day, sheets and sheets.

HIGGINS [*disagreeably surprised*] Damn his impudence! [*He recoils and finds himself sitting on his heels*].

LIZA.   He has a right to if he likes, poor lad. And he does love me.

HIGGINS [*getting off the ottoman*] You have no right to encourage him.

LIZA.   Every girl has a right to be loved.

HIGGINS.   What! By fools like that?

LIZA.   Freddy's not a fool. And if he's weak and poor and wants me, may be he'd make me happier than my betters that bully me and dont want me.

HIGGINS.   Can he make anything of you? Thats the point.

LIZA.   Perhaps I could make something of him. But I never thought of us making anything of one another; and you never think of anything else. I only want to be natural.

HIGGINS.   In short, you want me to be as infatuated about you as Freddy? Is that it?

LIZA.   No I dont. Thats not the sort of feeling I want from you. And dont you be too sure of yourself or of me. I could have been a bad girl if I'd liked. Ive seen more of some things than you, for all your learning. Girls like me can drag gentlemen down to make love to them easy enough. And they wish each other dead the next minute.

HIGGINS.   Of course they do. Then what in thunder are we quarrelling about?

LIZA   [*much troubled*] I want a little kindness. I know I'm a common ignorant girl, and you a book-learned gentleman; but I'm not dirt under your feet. What I done [*correcting herself*] what I did was not for the dresses and the taxis: I did it because we were pleasant together and I come— came—to care for you; not to want you to make love to me, and not forgetting the difference between us, but more friendly like.

HIGGINS.   Well, of course. Thats just how I feel. And how Pickering feels. Eliza: youre a fool.

LIZA.   Thats not a proper answer to give me [*she sinks on the chair at the writing-table in tears*].

HIGGINS.   It's all youll get until you stop being a common idiot. If youre going to be a lady, youll have to give up feeling neglected if the men you know dont spend half their time snivelling over you and the other half giving you black eyes. If you cant stand the coldness of my sort of life, and the strain of it, go back to the gutter. Work til you are more a brute than a human being; and then cuddle and squabble and drink til you fall asleep. Oh, it's a fine life, the life of the gutter. It's real: it's warm: it's violent: you can feel it through the thickest skin: you can taste it and smell it without any training or any work. Not like Science and Literature and Classical Music and Philosophy and Art. You find me cold, unfeeling, selfish, dont you? Very well: be off with you to the sort of people you like. Marry some sentimental hog or other with lots of money, and a thick pair of lips to kiss you with and a thick pair of boots to kick you with. If you cant appreciate what youve got, youd better get what you can appreciate.

LIZA   [*desperate*] Oh, you are a cruel tyrant. I cant talk to you: you turn everything against me: I'm always in the wrong. But you know very well all the time that youre nothing but a bully. You know I cant go back to the gutter, as you call it, and that I have no real friends in the world but you and the Colonel. You know well I couldnt bear to live with a low common man after you two; and it's wicked and cruel of you to insult me by pretending I could. You think I must go back to Wimpole Street because I have nowhere else to go but father's. But dont you be too sure that you have me under your feet to be trampled on and talked down. I'll marry Freddy, I will, as soon as he's able to support me.

HIGGINS   [*sitting down beside her*] Rubbish! you shall marry an ambassador. You shall marry the Governor-General of India or the Lord-

Lieutenant of Ireland or somebody who wants a deputy-queen. I'm not going to have my masterpiece thrown away on Freddy.

LIZA. You think I like you to say that. But I havnt forgot what you said a minute ago; and I wont be coaxed round as if I was a baby or a puppy. If I cant have kindness, I'll have independence.

HIGGINS. Independence? That middle class blasphemy. We are all dependent on one another, every soul of us on earth.

LIZA [*rising determinedly*] I'll let you see whether I'm dependent on you. If you can preach, I can teach. I'll go and be a teacher.

HIGGINS. Whatll you teach, in heaven's name?

LIZA. What you taught me. I'll teach phonetics.

HIGGINS. Ha! ha! ha!

LIZA. I'll offer myself as an assistant to Professor Nepean.

HIGGINS [*rising in a fury*] What! That impostor! that humbug! that toadying ignoramus! Teach him my methods! my discoveries! You take one step in his direction and I'll wring your neck. [*He lays hands on her*]. Do you hear?

LIZA [*defiantly non-resistant*] Wring away. What do I care? I knew youd strike me some day. [*He lets her go, stamping with rage at having forgotten himself, and recoils so hastily that he stumbles back into his seat on the ottoman*]. Aha! Now I know how to deal with you. What a fool I was not to think of it before! You cant take away the knowledge you gave me. You said I had a finer ear than you. And I can be civil and kind to people, which is more than you can. Aha! Thats done you, Henry Higgins, it has. Now I dont care that [*snapping her fingers*] for your bullying and your big talk. I'll advertize it in the papers that your duchess is only a flower girl that you taught, and that she'll teach anybody to be a duchess just the same in six months for a thousand guineas. Oh, when I think of myself crawling under your feet and being trampled on and called names, when all the time I had only to lift up my finger to be as good as you, I could just kick myself.

HIGGINS [*wondering at her*] You damned impudent slut, you! But it's better than snivelling; better than fetching slippers and finding spectacles, isnt' it? [*Rising*] By George, Eliza, I said I'd make a woman of you; and I have. I like you like this.

LIZA. Yes: you turn round and make up to me now that I'm not afraid of you, and can do without you.

HIGGINS. Of course I do, you little fool. Five minutes ago you were like a millstone round my neck. Now youre a tower of strength: a consort battleship. You and I and Pickering will be three old bachelors together instead of only two men and a silly girl.

MRS HIGGINS returns, dressed for the wedding. ELIZA instantly becomes cool and elegant.

MRS HIGGINS.   The carriage is waiting, Eliza. Are you ready?

LIZA.   Quite. Is the Professor coming?

MRS HIGGINS.   Certainly not. He cant behave himself in church. He makes remarks out loud all the time on the clergyman's pronunciation.

LIZA.   Then I shall not see you again, Professor. Good bye. [*She goes to the door*].

MRS HIGGINS   [*coming to HIGGINS*] Goodbye, dear.

HIGGINS.   Goodbye, mother. [*He is about to kiss her, when he recollects something*]. Oh, by the way, Eliza, order a ham and a Stilton cheese, will you? And buy me a pair of reindeer gloves, number eights, and a tie to match that new suit of mine, at Eale & Binman's. You can choose the color. [*His cheerful, careless, vigorous voice shows that he is incorrigible*].

LIZA   [*disdainfully*] Buy them yourself. [*She sweeps out*].

MRS HIGGINS.   I'm afraid youve spoiled that girl, Henry. But never mind, dear: I'll buy you the tie and gloves.

HIGGINS   [*sunnily*] Oh, dont bother. She'll buy em all right enough. Goodbye.

They kiss. MRS HIGGINS runs out. HIGGINS, left alone, rattles his cash in his pocket; chuckles; and disports himself in a highly self-satisfied manner.

* * * * *

The rest of the story need not be shewn in action, and indeed, would hardly need telling if our imaginations were not so enfeebled by their lazy dependence on the ready-mades and reach-me-downs of the ragshop in which Romance keeps its stock of "happy endings" to misfit all stories. Now, the history of Eliza Doolittle, though called a romance because the transfiguration it records seems exceedingly improbable, is common enough. Such transfigurations have been achieved by hundreds of resolutely ambitious young women since Nell Gwynne set them the example by playing queens and fascinating kings in the theatre in which she began by selling oranges. Nevertheless, people in all directions have assumed, for no other reason than that she became the heroine of a romance, that she must have married the hero of it. This is unbearable, not only because her little drama, if acted on such a thoughtless assumption, must be spoiled, but because the true sequel is patent to anyone with a sense of human nature in general, and of feminine instinct in particular.

Eliza, in telling Higgins she would not marry him if he asked her was not coquetting: she was announcing a well-considered decision. When a bachelor interests, and dominates, and teaches, and becomes important to a spinster, as Higgins with Eliza, she always, if she has character enough to be capable of it, considers very seriously indeed whether she will play for becoming that bachelor's wife, especially if he is so little interested in marriage that a determined and devoted woman might capture him if she set herself resolutely to do it. Her decision will depend a good deal on whether she is really free to choose; and that, again, will depend on her age and income. If she is at the end of her youth, and has no security for her livelihood, she will marry him because she must marry anybody who will provide for her. But at Eliza's age a good-looking girl does not feel that pressure: she feels free to pick and choose. She is therefore guided by her instinct in the matter. Eliza's instinct tells her not to marry Higgins. It does not tell her to give him up. It is not in the slightest doubt as to his remaining of the strongest personal interests in her life. It would be very sorely strained if there was another woman likely to supplant her with him. But as she feels sure of him on that last point, she has no doubt at all as to her course, and would not have any, even if the difference of twenty years in age, which seems so great to youth, did not exist between them.

As our own instincts are not appealed to by her conclusion, let us see whether we cannot discover some reason in it. When Higgins excused his indifference to young women on the ground that they had an irresistible rival in his mother, he gave the clue to his inveterate old-bachelordom. The case is uncommon only to the extent that remarkable mothers are uncommon. If an imaginative boy has a sufficiently rich mother who has intelligence, personal grace, dignity of character without harshness, and a cultivated sense of the best art of her time to enable her to make her house beautiful, she sets a standard for him against which very few women can struggle, besides effecting for him a disengagement of his affections, his sense of beauty, and his idealism from his specifically sexual impulses. This makes him a standing puzzle to the huge number of uncultivated people who have been brought up in tasteless homes by commonplace or disagreeable parents, and to whom, consequently, literature, painting, sculpture, music, and affectionate personal relations come as modes of sex if they come at all. The word passion means nothing else to them; and that Higgins could have a passion for phonetics and idealize his mother instead of Eliza, would seem to them absurd and unnatural. Nevertheless, when we look round and see that hardly anyone is too ugly or disagreeable to find a wife or a husband if he or she wants one, whilst many old maids and bachelors are above the average in quality and culture, we cannot help suspecting that the disentanglement of sex from the associations with which it is so commonly confused, a disentanglement which persons of genius achieve by sheer intellectual analysis, is sometimes produced or aided by parental fascination.

Now, though Eliza was incapable of thus explaining to herself Higgins's formidable powers of resistance to the charm that prostrated Freddy at the first glance, she was instinctively aware that she could never obtain a complete grip of him, or come between him and his mother (the first necessity of the married woman). To put it shortly, she knew that for some mysterious reason he had not the makings of a married man in him, according to her conception of a husband as one to whom she would be his nearest and fondest and warmest interest. Even had there been no mother-rival, she would still have refused to accept an interest in herself that was secondary to philosophic interests. Had Mrs Higgins died, there would still have been Milton and the Universal Alphabet. Landor's remark that to those who have the greatest power of loving, love is a secondary affair, would not have recommended Landor to Eliza. Put that along with her resentment of Higgins's domineering superiority, and her mistrust of his coaxing cleverness in getting round her and evading her wrath when he had gone too far with his impetuous bullying, and you will see that Eliza's instinct had good grounds for warning her not to marry her Pygmalion.

And now, whom did Eliza marry? For if Higgins was a predestinate old bachelor, she was most certainly not a predestinate old maid. Well, that can be told very shortly to those who have not guessed it from the indications she has herself given them.

Almost immediately after Eliza is stung into proclaiming her considered determination not to marry Higgins, she mentions the fact that young Mr Frederick Eynsford Hill is pouring out his love for her daily through the post. Now Freddy is young, practically twenty years younger than Higgins: he is a gentleman (or, as Eliza would qualify him, a toff), and speaks like one; he is nicely dressed, is treated by the Colonel as an equal, loves her unaffectedly, and is not her master, nor ever likely to dominate her in spite of his advantage of social standing. Eliza has no use for the foolish romantic tradition that all women love to be mastered, if not actually bullied and beaten. "When you go to women," says Nietzsche, "take your whip with you." Sensible despots have never confined that precaution to women: they have taken their whips with them when they have dealt with men, and been slavishly idealized by the men over whom they have flourished the whip much more than by women. No doubt there are slavish women as well as slavish men: and women, like men, admire those that are stronger than themselves. But to admire a strong person and to live under that strong person's thumb are two different things. The weak may not be admired and hero-worshipped; but they are by no means disliked or shunned; and they never seem to have the least difficulty in marrying people who are too good for them. They may fail in emergencies; but life is not one long emergency: it is mostly a string of situations for which no exceptional strength is needed, and with which even rather weak people can cope if they have a stronger partner to help them out. Accordingly, it is a truth everywhere in evidence that strong people, masculine or feminine, not only do not marry stronger people, but do not shew any preference for them in selecting their friends. When a lion meets another with a louder roar "the first lion thinks the last a bore." The man or woman who feels strong enough for two, seeks for every other quality in a partner than strength.

The converse is also true. Weak people want to marry strong people who do not frighten them too much; and this often leads them to make the mistake we describe metaphorically as "biting off more than they can chew." They want too much for too little; and when the bargain is unreasonable beyond all bearing, the union becomes impossible: it ends in the weaker party being either discarded or borne as a cross, which is worse. People who are not only weak, but silly or obtuse as well, are often in these difficulties.

This being the state of human affairs, what is Eliza fairly sure to do when she is placed between Freddy and Higgins? Will she look forward to a lifetime of fetching Higgins's slippers or to a lifetime of Freddy fetching hers? There can be no doubt about the answer. Unless Freddy is biologically repulsive to her, and Higgins biologically attractive to a degree that overwhelms all her other instincts, she will, if she marries either of them, marry Freddy.

And that is just what Eliza did.

Complications ensued; but they were economic, not romantic. Freddy had no money and no occupation. His mother's jointure, a last relic of the opulence of Largelady Park, had enabled her to struggle along in Earlscourt with an air of gentility, but not to procure any serious secondary education for her children, much less give the boy a profession. A clerkship at thirty shillings a week was beneath Freddy's dignity, and extremely distasteful to him besides. His prospects consisted of a hope that if he kept up appearances somebody would do something for him. The something appeared vaguely to his imagination as a private secretaryship or a sinecure of some sort. To his mother it perhaps appeared as a marriage to some lady of means who could not resist her boy's niceness. Fancy her feelings when he married a flower girl who had become déclassée under extraordinary circumstances which were now notorious!

It is true that Eliza's situation did not seem wholly inelegible. Her father, though formerly a dustman, and now fantastically disclassed, had become extremely popular in the smartest society by a social talent which triumphed over every prejudice and every disadvantage. Rejected by the middle class, which he loathed, he had shot up at once into the highest circles by his wit, his dustmanship (which he carried like a banner), and his Nietzschean transcendence of good and evil. At intimate ducal dinners he sat on the right hand of the Duchess; and in country houses he smoked in the pantry and was made much of by the butler when he was not feeding in the dining room and being consulted by cabinet ministers. But he found it almost as hard to do all this on four thousand a year as Mrs Eynsford Hill to live in Earlscourt on an income so pitiably smaller that I have not the heart to disclose its exact figure. He absolutely refused to add the last straw to his burden by contributing to Eliza's support.

Thus Freddy and Eliza, now Mr and Mrs Eynsford Hill, would have spent a penniless honeymoon but for a wedding present of £500 from the

Colonel to Eliza. It lasted a long time because Freddy did not know how to spend money, never having had any to spend, and Eliza, socially trained by a pair of old bachelors, wore her clothes as long as they held together and looked pretty, without the least regard to their being many months out of fashion. Still, £500 will not last two young people for ever; and they both knew, and Eliza felt as well, that they must shift for themselves in the end. She could quarter herself on Wimpole Street because it had come to be her home; but she was quite aware that she ought not to quarter Freddy there, and that it would not be good for his character if she did.

Not that the Wimpole Street bachelors objected. When she consulted them, Higgins declined to be bothered about her housing problem when that solution was so simple. Eliza's desire to have Freddy in the house with her seemed of no more importance than if she had wanted an extra piece of bedroom furniture. Pleas as to Freddy's character, and the moral obligation on him to earn his own living, were lost on Higgins. He denied that Freddy had any character, and declared that if he tried to do any useful work some competent person would have the trouble of undoing it: a procedure involving a net loss to the community, and great unhappiness to Freddy himself, who was obviously intended by Nature for such light work as amusing Eliza, which, Higgins declared, was a much more useful and honorable occupation than working in the city. When Eliza referred again to her project of teaching phonetics, Higgins abated not a jot of his violent opposition to it. He said she was not within ten years of being qualified to meddle with his pet subject; and as it was evident that the Colonel agreed with him, she felt she could not go against them in this grave matter, and that she had no right, without Higgins's consent, to exploit the knowledge he had given her; for his knowledge seemed to her as much his private property as his watch: Eliza was no communist. Besides, she was superstitiously devoted to them both, more entirely and frankly after her marriage than before it.

It was the Colonel who finally solved the problem, which had cost him much perplexed cogitation. He one day asked Eliza, rather shyly, whether she had quite given up her notion of keeping a flower shop. She replied that she had thought of it, but had put it out of her head, because the Colonel had said, that day at Mrs Higgins's, that it would never do. The Colonel confessed that when he said that, he had not quite recovered from the dazzling impression of the day before. They broke the matter to Higgins that evening. The sole comment vouchsafed by him very nearly led to a serious quarrel with Eliza. It was to the effect that she would have in Freddy an ideal errand boy.

Freddy himself was next sounded on the subject. He said he had been thinking of a shop himself; though it had presented itself to his pennilessness as a small place in which Eliza should sell tobacco at one counter whilst he sold newspapers at the opposite one. But he agreed that it would be extraordinarily jolly to go early every morning with Eliza to Covent Garden and buy flowers on the scene of their first meeting: a sentiment which earned him many kisses from his wife. He added that he had always been afraid to propose anything of the sort, because Clara would make an awful row about a step that must damage her matrimonial chances, and his mother could not be expected to like it after clinging for so many years to that step of the social ladder on which retail trade is impossible.

This difficulty was removed by an event highly unexpected by Freddy's mother. Clara, in the course of her incursions into those artistic circles which were the highest within her reach, discovered that her conversational qualifications were expected to include a grounding in the novels of Mr H. G. Wells. She borrowed them in various directions so energetically that she swallowed them all within two months. The result was a conversion of a kind quite common today. A modern Acts of the Apostles would fill fifty whole Bibles if anyone were capable of writing it.

Poor Clara, who appeared to Higgins and his mother as a disagreeable and ridiculous person, and to her own mother as in some inexplicable way a social failure, had never seen herself in either light; for, though to some extent ridiculed and mimicked in West Kensington like everybody else there, she was accepted as a rational and normal—or shall we say inevitable?—sort of human being. At worst they called her The Pusher; but to them no more than to herself had it ever occurred that she was pushing the air, and pushing it in a wrong direction. Still, she was not happy. She was growing desperate. Her one asset, the fact that her mother was what the Epsom greengrocer called a carriage lady, had no exchange value, apparently. It had prevented her from getting educated, because the only education she could have afforded was education with the Earlscourt greengrocer's daughter. It had led her to seek the society of her mother's class; and that class simply would not have her, because she was much poorer than the greengrocer, and, far from being able to afford a maid, could not afford even a housemaid, and had to scrape along at home with an illiberally treated general servant. Under such circumstances nothing could give her an air of being a genuine product of Largelady Park. And yet its tradition made her regard a marriage with anyone within her reach as an unbearable humiliation. Commercial people and professional people in a small way were odious to her. She ran after painters and novelists; but she did not charm them; and her bold attempts to pick up and practice artistic and literary talk irritated them. She was, in short, an utter failure, an ignorant, incompetent, pretentious, unwelcome, penniless, useless little snob; and though she did not admit these disqualifications (for nobody ever faces unpleasant truths of this kind until the possibility of a way out dawns on them) she felt their effects too keenly to be satisfied with her position.

Clara had a startling eyeopener when, on being suddenly wakened to enthusiasm by a girl of her own age who dazzled her and produced in her a gushing desire to take her for a model, and gain her friendship, she discovered that this exquisite apparition had graduated from the gutter in a few months time. It shook her so violently, that when Mr H. G. Wells lifted her on the point of his puissant pen, and placed her at the angle of view from which the life she was leading and the society to which she clung appeared in its true relation to real human needs and worthy social structure, he effected a conversion and a conviction of sin comparable to the most sensational feats of General Booth or Gypsy Smith. Clara's snobbery went bang. Life suddenly began to move with her. Without knowing how or why, she began to make friends and enemies. Some of the acquaintances to whom she had been a tedious or indifferent or ridiculous affliction, dropped her: others became cordial. To her amazement she found that some "quite nice" people were saturated with Wells, and that this accessibility to ideas was the secret of their niceness. People she had thought deeply religious, and had tried to conciliate on that tack with disastrous results, suddenly took an interest in her, and revealed a hostility to conventional religion which she had never conceived possible except among the most desperate characters. They made her read Galsworthy; and Galsworthy exposed the vanity of Largelady Park and finished her. It exasperated her to think that the dungeon in which she had languished for so many unhappy years had been unlocked all the time, and that the impulses she had so carefully struggled with and stifled for the sake of keeping well with society, were precisely those by which alone she could have come into any sort of sincere human contact. In the radiance of these discoveries, and the tumult of their reaction, she made a fool of herself as freely and conspicuously as when she so rashly adopted Eliza's expletive in Mrs Higgins's drawing room; for the new-born Wellsian had to find her bearings almost as ridiculously as a baby; but nobody hates a baby for its ineptitudes, or thinks the worse of it for trying to eat the matches; and Clara lost no friends by her follies. They laughed at her to her face this time; and she had to defend herself and fight it out as best she could.

When Freddy paid a visit to Earlscourt (which he never did when he could possibly help it) to make the desolating announcement that he and his Eliza were thinking of blackening the Largelady scutcheon by opening a shop, he found the little household already convulsed by a prior announcement from Clara that she also was going to work in an old furniture shop in Dover Street, which had been started by a fellow Wellsian. This appointment Clara owed, after all, to her old social accomplishment of Push. She had made up her mind that, cost what it might, she would see Mr Wells in the flesh; and she had achieved her end at a garden party. She had better luck than so rash an enterprise deserved. Mr Wells came up to her expectations. Age had not withered him, nor could custom stale his infinite variety in half an hour. His pleasant neatness and compactness, his small hands and feet, his teeming ready brain, his unaffected accessibility, and a certain fine apprehensiveness which stamped him as susceptible from his topmost hair to his tipmost toe, proved irresistible. Clara talked of nothing else for weeks and weeks afterwards. And as she happened to talk to the lady of the furniture shop, and that lady also desired above all things to know Mr Wells and sell pretty things to him, she offered Clara a job on the chance of achieving that end through her.

And so it came about that Eliza's luck held, and the expected opposition to the flower shop melted away. The shop is in the arcade of a railway station not very far from the Victoria and Albert Museum; and if you live in that neighborhood you may go there any day and buy a buttonhole from Eliza.

Now here is a last opportunity for romance. Would you not like to be assured that the shop was an immense success, thanks to Eliza's charms and her early business experience in Covent Garden? Alas! the truth is the truth: the shop did not pay for a long time, simply because Eliza and her Freddy did not know how to keep it. True, Eliza had not to begin at the very beginning: she knew the names and prices of the cheaper flowers; and her elation was unbounded when she found that Freddy, like all youths educated at cheap, pretentious, and thoroughly inefficient schools, knew a little Latin. It was very little, but enough to make him appear to her a Porson or Bentley, and to put him at his ease with botanical nomenclature. Unfortunately he knew nothing else; and Eliza, though she could count money up to eighteen shillings or so, and had acquired a certain familiarity with the language of Milton from her struggles to qualify herself for winning Higgins's bet, could not write out a bill without utterly disgracing the establishment. Freddy's power of stating in Latin that Balbus built a wall and that Gaul was divided into three parts did not carry with it the slightest knowledge of accounts or business: Colonel Pickering had to explain to him what a cheque book and a bank account meant. And the pair were by no means easily teachable. Freddy backed up Eliza in her obstinate refusal to believe that they could save money by engaging a bookkeeper with some knowlege of the business. How, they argued, could you possibly save money by going to extra expense when you already could not make both ends meet? But the Colonel, after making the ends meet over and over again, at last gently insisted; and Eliza, humbled to the dust by having to beg from him so often, and stung by the uproarious derision of Higgins, to whom the notion of Freddy succeeding at anything was a joke that never palled, grasped the fact that business, like phonetics, has to be learned.

On the piteous spectacle of the pair spending their evenings in shorthand schools and polytechnic classes, learning bookkeeping and typewriting with incipient junior clerks, male and female, from the elementary schools, let me not dwell. There were even classes at the London School of Economics, and a humble personal appeal to the director of that institution to recommend a course bearing on the flower business. He, being a humorist, explained to them the method of the celebrated Dickensian essay on Chinese Metaphysics by the gentleman who read an article on China and an article on Metaphysics and combined the information. He suggested that they should combine the London School with Kew Gardens. Eliza, to whom the procedure of the Dickensian gentleman seemed perfectly correct (as in fact it was) and not in the least funny (which was only her ignorance), took his advice with entire gravity. But the effort that cost her the deepest humiliation was a request to Higgins, whose pet artistic fancy, next to Milton's verse, was caligraphy, and who himself wrote a most beautiful Italian hand, that he would teach her to write. He declared that she was congenitally incapable of forming a single letter worthy of the least of Milton's words; but she persisted; and again he suddenly threw himself into the task of teaching her with a combination of stormy intensity, concentrated patience, and occasional bursts of interesting disquisition on the beauty and nobility, the august mission and destiny, of human handwriting. Eliza ended by acquiring an extremely uncommercial script which was a positive extension of her personal beauty, and spending three times as much on stationery as anyone else because certain qualities and shapes of paper became indispensable to her. She could not even address an envelope in the usual way because it made the margins all wrong.

Their commercial schooldays were a period of disgrace and despair for the young couple. They seemed to be learning nothing about flower shops. At last they gave it up as hopeless, and shook the dust of the shorthand schools, and the polytechnics, and the London School of Economics from their feet for ever. Besides, the business was in some mysterious way beginning to take care of itself. They had somehow forgotten their objections to employing other people. They came to the conclusion that their own way was the best, and that they had really a remarkable talent for business. The Colonel, who had been compelled for some years to keep a sufficient sum on current account at his bankers to make up their deficits, found that the provision was unnecessary: the young people were prospering. It is true that there was not quite fair play between them and their competitors in trade. Their week-ends in the country cost them nothing and saved them the price of their Sunday dinners; for the motor car was the Colonel's; and he and Higgins paid the hotel bills. Mr F. Hill, florist and greengrocer (they soon discovered that there was money in asparagus; and asparagus led to other vegetables), had an air which stamped the business as classy; and in private life he was still Frederick Eynsford Hill, Esquire. Not that there was any swank about him: nobody but Eliza knew that he had been christened Frederick Challoner. Eliza herself swanked like anything.

That is all. That is how it has turned out. It is astonishing how much Eliza still manages to meddle in the housekeeping at Wimpole Street in spite of the shop and her own family. And it is notable that though she never nags her husband, and frankly loves the Colonel as if she were his favorite daughter, she has never got out of the habit of nagging Higgins that was established on the fatal night when she won his bet for him. She snaps his head off on the faintest provocation, or on none. He no longer dares to tease her by assuming an abysmal inferiority of Freddy's mind to his own. He storms and bullies and derides: but she stands up to him so ruthlessly that the Colonel has to ask her from time to time to be kinder to Higgins; and it is the only request of his that brings a mulish expression into her face. Nothing but some emergency or calamity great enough to break down all likes and dislikes, and throw them both back on their common humanity—and may they be spared any such trial!—will ever alter this. She knows that Higgins does not need her, just as her father did not need her. The very scrupulousness with which he told her that day that he had become used to having her there, and dependent on her for all sorts of little services, and that he should miss her if she went away (it would never have occurred to Freddy or the Colonel to say anything of the sort) deepens her inner certainty that she is "no more to him than them slippers"; yet she has a sense, too, that his indifference is deeper than the infatuation of commoner souls. She is immensely interested in him. She has even secret mischievous moments in which she wishes she could get him alone, on a desert island, away from all ties and with nobody else in the world to consider, and just drag him off his pedestal and see him making love like any common man. We all have private imaginations of that sort. But when it comes to business, to the life that she really leads as distinguished from the life of dreams and fancies, she likes Freddy and she likes the Colonel; and she does not like Higgins and Mr Doolittle. Galatea never does quite like Pygmalion: his relation to her is too godlike to be altogether agreeable.

SUSAN GLASPELL   (1882–1948)

Trifles

CHARACTERS

> George Henderson, *County Attorney*
> Henry Peters, *Sheriff*
> Lewis Hale, *A Neighboring Farmer*
> Mrs. Peters
> Mrs. Hale

SCENE: *The kitchen in the now abandoned farmhouse of* JOHN WRIGHT, *a gloomy kitchen, and left without having been put in order—unwashed pans under the sink, a loaf of bread outside the bread-box, a dish-towel on the table—other signs of incomplete work. At the rear the outer door opens and the* SHERIFF *comes in followed by the* COUNTY ATTORNEY *and* HALE. *The* SHERIFF *and* HALE *are men in middle life, the* COUNTY ATTORNEY *is a young man; all are much bundled up and go at once to the stove. They are followed by the two women— the* SHERIFF'S *wife first; she is a slight wiry woman, a thin nervous face.* MRS. HALE *is larger and would ordinarily be called more comfortable looking, but she is disturbed now and looks fearfully about as she enters. The women have come in slowly, and stand close together near the door.*

COUNTY ATTORNEY.   [*Rubbing his hands.*] This feels good. Come up to the fire, ladies.

MRS PETERS.   [*After taking a step forward.*] I'm not—cold.

SHERIFF.   [*Unbuttoning his overcoat and stepping away from the stove as if to mark the beginning of official business.*] Now, Mr. Hale, before we move things about, you explain to Mr. Henderson just what you saw when you came here yesterday morning.

COUNTY ATTORNEY.   By the way, has anything been moved? Are things just as you left them yesterday?

SHERIFF.   [*Looking about.*] It's just the same. When it dropped below zero last night I thought I'd better send Frank out this morning to make a fire for us—no use getting pneumonia with a big case on, but I told him not to touch anything except the stove—and you know Frank.

COUNTY ATTORNEY.   Somebody should have been left here yesterday.

SHERIFF.   Oh—yesterday. When I had to send Frank to Morris Center for that man who went crazy—I want you to know I had my hands full yesterday. I knew you could get back from Omaha by today and as long as I went over everything here myself—

COUNTY ATTORNEY. Well, Mr. Hale, tell just what happened when you came here yesterday morning.

HALE. Harry and I had started to town with a load of potatoes. We came along the road from my place and as I got here I said, "I'm going to see if I can't get John Wright to go in with me on a party telephone." I spoke to Wright about it once before and he put me off, saying folks talked too much anyway, and all he asked was peace and quiet—I guess you know about how much he talked himself; but I thought maybe if I went to the house and talked about it before his wife, though I said to Harry that I didn't know as what his wife wanted made much difference to John—

COUNTY ATTORNEY. Let's talk about that later, Mr. Hale. I do want to talk about that, but tell now just what happened when you got to the house.

HALE. I didn't hear or see anything; I knocked at the door, and still it was all quiet inside. I knew they must be up, it was past eight o'clock. So I knocked again, and I thought I heard somebody say, "Come in." I wasn't sure, I'm not sure yet, but I opened the door—this door [*indicating the door by which the two women are still standing*] and there in that rocker— [*pointing to it*] sat Mrs. Wright.

[*They all look at the rocker.*]

COUNTY ATTORNEY. What—was she doing?

HALE. She was rockin' back and forth. She had her apron in her hand and was kind of—pleating it.

COUNTY ATTORNEY. And how did she—look?

HALE. Well, she looked queer.

COUNTY ATTORNEY. How do you mean—queer?

HALE. Well, as if she didn't know what she was going to do next. And kind of done up.

COUNTY ATTORNEY. How did she seem to feel about your coming?

HALE. Why, I don't think she minded—one way or other. She didn't pay much attention. I said, "How do, Mrs. Wright, it's cold ain't it?" And she said, "Is it?"—and went on kind of pleating at her apron. Well, I was surprised; she didn't ask me to come up to the stove, or to set down, but just sat there, not even looking at me, so I said, "I want to see John." And then she—laughed. I guess you would call it a laugh. I thought of Harry and the team outside, so I said a little sharp: "Can't I see John?" "No," she says, kind o' dull like. "Ain't he home?" says I. "Yes," says she, "he's home." "Then why can't I see him?" I asked her, out of patience. "'Cause he's dead," says she. *"Dead?"* says I. She just nodded her head, not getting a bit excited, but rockin' back and forth. "Why—where is he?" says I, not knowing what to say. She just pointed upstairs—like that [*himself pointing to the room above*]. I got up, with the idea of going up there. I walked from there to here—then I says, "Why, what did he die of?" "He died of a rope round his neck," says she, and just went on pleatin' at her apron. Well, I went out and called Harry. I thought I might—need help. We went upstairs and there he was lyin'—

COUNTY ATTORNEY.   I think I'd rather have you go into that upstairs, where you can point it all out. Just go on now with the rest of the story.

HALE.   Well, my first thought was to get that rope off. It looked . . . [*Stops, his face twitches*] . . . but Harry, he went up to him, and he said, "No, he's dead all right, and we'd better not touch anything." So we went back down stairs. She was still sitting that same way. "Has anybody been notified?" I asked. "No," says she, unconcerned. "Who did this, Mrs. Wright?" said Harry. He said it business-like—and she stopped pleatin' of her apron. "I don't know," she says. "You don't *know?*" says Harry. "No," says she. "Weren't you sleepin' in the bed with him?" says Harry. "Yes," says she, "but I was on the inside." "Somebody slipped a rope round his neck and strangled him and you didn't wake up?" says Harry. "I didn't wake up," she said after him. We must 'a looked as if we didn't see how that could be, for after a minute she said, "I sleep sound." Harry was going to ask her more questions but I said maybe we ought to let her tell her story first to the coroner, or the sheriff, so Harry went fast as he could to Rivers' place, where there's a telephone.

COUNTY ATTORNEY.   And what did Mrs. Wright do when she knew that you had gone for the coroner?

HALE.   She moved from that chair to this one over here [*Pointing to a small chair in the corner*] and just sat there with her hands held together and looking down. I got a feeling that I ought to make some conversation, so I said I had come in to see if John wanted to put in a telephone, and at that she started to laugh, and then she stopped and looked at me—scared. [*The COUNTY ATTORNEY, who has had his notebook out, makes a note.*] I dunno, maybe it wasn't scared. I wouldn't like to say it was. Soon Harry got back, and then Dr. Lloyd came, and you, Mr. Peters, and so I guess that's all I know that you don't.

COUNTY ATTORNEY.   [*Looking around.*] I guess we'll go upstairs first—and then out to the barn and around there. [*To the SHERIFF.*] You're convinced that there was nothing important here—nothing that would point to any motive.

SHERIFF.   Nothing here but kitchen things.

> [*The COUNTY ATTORNEY, after again looking around the kitchen, opens the door of a cupboard closet. He gets up on a chair and looks on a shelf. Pulls his hand away, sticky.*]

COUNTY ATTORNEY.   Here's a nice mess.

[*The women draw nearer.*

MRS. PETERS.   [*To the other woman.*] Oh, her fruit; it did freeze. [*To the LAWYER.*] She worried about that when it turned so cold. She said the fire'd go out and her jars would break.

SHERIFF.   Well, can you beat the women! Held for murder and worryin' about her preserves.

COUNTY ATTORNEY.   I guess before we're through she may have something more serious than preserves to worry about.

HALE.   Well, women are used to worrying over trifles.

[*The two women move a little closer together.*

COUNTY ATTORNEY.   [*With the gallantry of a young politician.*] And yet, for all their worries, what would we do without the ladies? [*The women do not unbend. He goes to the sink, takes a dipperful of water from the pail and pouring it into a basin, washes his hands. Starts to wipe them on the roller-towel, turns it for a cleaner place.*] Dirty towels! [*Kicks his foot against the pans under the sink.*] Not much of a housekeeper, would you say, ladies?

MRS. HALE.   [*Stiffly.*] There's a great deal of work to be done on a farm.

COUNTY ATTORNEY.   To be sure. And yet [*With a little bow to her*] I know there are some Dickson county farmhouses which do not have such roller towels.

[*He gives it a pull to expose its full length again.*

MRS. HALE.   Those towels get dirty awful quick. Men's hands aren't always as clean as they might be.

COUNTY ATTORNEY.   Ah, loyal to your sex, I see. But you and Mrs. Wright were neighbors. I suppose you were friends, too.

MRS. HALE.   [*Shaking her head.*] I've not seen much of her of late years. I've not been in this house—it's more than a year.

COUNTY ATTORNEY.   And why was that? You didn't like her?

MRS. HALE.   I liked her all well enough. Farmers' wives have their hands full, Mr. Henderson. And then—

COUNTY ATTORNEY.   Yes—?

MRS. HALE.   [*Looking about.*] It never seemed a very cheerful place.

COUNTY ATTORNEY.   No—it's not cheerful. I shouldn't say she had the homemaking instinct.

MRS. HALE.   Well, I don't know as Wright had, either.

COUNTY ATTORNEY.   You mean that they didn't get on very well?

MRS. HALE.   No, I don't mean anything. But I don't think a place'd be any cheerfuller for John Wright's being in it.

COUNTY ATTORNEY.   I'd like to talk more of that a little later. I want to get the lay of things upstairs now.

[*He goes to the left, where three steps lead to a stair door.*

SHERIFF.   I suppose anything Mrs. Peters does'll be all right. She was to take in some clothes for her, you know, and a few little things. We left in such a hurry yesterday.

COUNTY ATTORNEY.   Yes, but I would like to see what you take, Mrs. Peters, and keep an eye out for anything that might be of use to us.

MRS. PETERS.   Yes, Mr. Henderson.

[*The women listen to the men's steps on the stairs, then look about the kitchen.*

MRS. HALE.   I'd hate to have men coming into my kitchen, snooping around and criticising.

[*She arranges the pans under sink which the LAWYER had shoved out of place.*

MRS. PETERS.   Of course it's no more than their duty.

MRS. HALE.   Duty's all right, but I guess that deputy sheriff that came out to make the fire might have got a little of this on. [*Gives the roller towel a pull.*] Wish I'd thought of that sooner. Seems mean to talk about her for not having things slicked up when she had to come away in such a hurry.

MRS. PETERS.   [*Who has gone to a small table in the left rear corner of the room, and lifted one end of a towel that covers a pan.*] She had bread set.

[*Stands still.*

MRS. HALE.   [*Eyes fixed on a loaf of bread beside the breadbox, which is on a low shelf at the other side of the room. Moves slowly toward it.*] She was going to put this in there. [*Picks up loaf, then abruptly drops it. In a manner of returning to familiar things.*] It's a shame about her fruit. I wonder if it's all gone. [*Gets up on the chair and looks.*] I think there's some here that's all right, Mrs. Peters. Yes—here; [*Holding it toward the window*] this is cherries, too. [*Looking again.*] I declare I believe that's the only one. [*Gets down, bottle in her hand. Goes to the sink and wipes it off on the outside.*] She'll feel awful bad after all her hard work in the hot weather. I remember the afternoon I put up my cherries last summer.

[*She puts the bottle on the big kitchen table, center of the room. With a sigh, is about to sit down in the rocking-chair. Before she is seated realizes what chair it is; with a slow look at it, steps back. The chair which she has touched rocks back and forth.*]

MRS. PETERS. Well, I must get those things from the front room closet. [*She goes to the door at the right, but after looking into the room, steps back.*] You coming with me, Mrs. Hale? You could help me carry them.

[*They go in the other room; reappear, MRS. PETERS carrying a dress and skirt, MRS. HALE following with a pair of shoes.*]

MRS. PETERS. My, it's cold in there.

[*She puts the clothes on the big table, and hurries to the stove.*]

MRS. HALE. [*Examining the skirt.*] Wright was close. I think maybe that's why she kept so much to herself. She didn't even belong to the Ladies Aid. I suppose she felt she couldn't do her part, and then you don't enjoy things when you feel shabby. She used to wear pretty clothes and be lively, when she was Minnie Foster, one of the town girls singing in the choir. But that—oh, that was thirty years ago. This all you was to take in?

MRS PETERS. She said she wanted an apron. Funny thing to want, for there isn't much to get you dirty in jail, goodness knows. But I suppose just to make her feel more natural. She said they was in the top drawer in this cupboard. Yes, here. And then her little shawl that always hung behind the door. [*Opens stair door and looks.*] Yes, here it is.

[*Quickly shuts door leading upstairs.*]

MRS. HALE. [*Abruptly moving toward her.*] Mrs. Peters?
MRS. PETERS. Yes, Mrs. Hale?
MRS. HALE. Do you think she did it?
MRS. PETERS. [*In a frightened voice.*] Oh, I don't know.
MRS. HALE. Well, I don't think she did. Asking for an apron and her little shawl. Worrying about her fruit.
MRS. PETERS. [*Starts to speak, glances up, where footsteps are heard in the room above. In a low voice.*] Mr. Peters says it looks bad for her. Mr.

Henderson is awful sarcastic in a speech and he'll make fun of her sayin' she didn't wake up.

MRS. HALE.   Well, I guess John Wright didn't wake when they was slipping that rope under his neck.

MRS. PETERS.   No, it's strange. It must have been done awful crafty and still. They say it was such a—funny way to kill a man, rigging it all up like that.

MRS. HALE.   That's just what Mr. Hale said. There was a gun in the house. He says that's what he can't understand.

MRS. PETERS.   Mr. Henderson said coming out that what was needed for the case was a motive; something to show anger, or—sudden feeling.

MRS. HALE.   [*Who is standing by the table.*] Well, I don't see any signs of anger around here. [*She puts her hand on the dish towel which lies on the table, stands looking down at the table, one half of which is clean, the other half messy.*] It's wiped to here. [*Makes a move as if to finish work, then turns and looks at loaf of bread outside the breadbox. Drops towel. In that voice of coming back to familiar things.*] Wonder how they are finding things upstairs. I hope she had it a little more red-up up there. You know, it seems kind of *sneaking*. Locking her up in town and then coming out here and trying to get her own house to turn against her!

MRS. PETERS.   But Mrs. Hale, the law is the law.

MRS. HALE.   I s'pose 'tis. [*Unbuttoning her coat.*] Better loosen up your things, Mrs. Peters. You won't feel them when you go out.

> [MRS. *PETERS takes off her fur tippet, goes to hang it on hook at back of room, stands looking at the under part of the small corner table.*

MRS. PETERS.   She was piecing a quilt.

> [*She brings the large sewing basket and they look at the bright pieces.*

MRS. HALE.   It's log cabin pattern. Pretty, isn't it? I wonder if she was goin' to quilt it or just knot it?

> [*Footsteps have been heard coming down the stairs. The SHERIFF enters followed by HALE and the COUNTY ATTORNEY.*

SHERIFF.   They wonder if she was going to quilt it or just knot it!

> [*The men laugh, the women look abashed.*

COUNTY ATTORNEY.   [*Rubbing his hands over the stove.*] Frank's fire didn't do much up there, did it? Well, let's go out to the barn and get that cleared up.

[*The men go outside.*

MRS. HALE. [*Resentfully.*] I don't know as there's anything so strange, our takin' up our time with little things while we're waiting for them to get the evidence. [*She sits down at the big table smoothing out a block with decision.*] I don't see as it's anything to laugh about.

MRS. PETERS. [*Apologetically.*] Of course they've got awful important things on their minds.

[*Pulls up a chair and joins* MRS. HALE
at the table.

MRS. HALE. [*Examining another block.*] Mrs. Peters, look at this one. Here, this is the one she was working on, and look at the sewing! All the rest of it has been so nice and even. And look at this! It's all over the place! Why, it looks as if she didn't know what she was about!

[*After she has said this they look at
each other, then start to glance back
at the door. After an instant* MRS.
HALE *has pulled at a knot and ripped
the sewing.*

MRS. PETERS. Oh, what are you doing, Mrs. Hale?

MRS. HALE. [*Mildly.*] Just pulling out a stitch or two that's not sewed very good. [*Threading a needle.*] Bad sewing always made me fidgety.

MRS. PETERS. [*Nervously.*] I don't think we ought to touch things.

MRS. HALE. I'll just finish up this end. [*Suddenly stopping and leaning forward.*] Mrs. Peters?

MRS. PETERS. Yes, Mrs. Hale?

MRS. HALE. What do you suppose she was so nervous about?

MRS. PETERS. Oh—I don't know. I don't know as she was nervous. I sometimes sew awful queer when I'm just tired. [*MRS. HALE starts to say something, looks at* MRS. PETERS, *then goes on sewing.*] Well I must get these things wrapped up. They may be through sooner than we think. [*Putting apron and other things together.*] I wonder where I can find a piece of paper, and string.

MRS. HALE. In that cupboard, maybe.

MRS. PETERS. [*Looking in cupboard.*] Why, here's a bird-cage. [*Holds it up.*] Did she have a bird, Mrs. Hale?

MRS. HALE. Why, I don't know whether she did or not—I've not been here for so long. There was a man around last year selling canaries cheap, but I don't know as she took one; maybe she did. She used to sing real pretty herself.

MRS. PETERS. [*Glancing around.*] Seems funny to think of a bird here. But she must have had one, or why would she have a cage? I wonder what happened to it.

MRS. HALE. I s'pose maybe the cat got it.

MRS. PETERS. No, she didn't have a cat. She's got that feeling some people have about cats—being afraid of them. My cat got in her room and she was real upset and asked me to take it out.

MRS. HALE. My sister Bessie was like that. Queer, ain't it?

MRS. PETERS. [*Examining the cage.*] Why, look at this door. It's broke. One hinge is pulled part.

MRS. HALE. [*Looking too.*] Looks as if someone must have been rough with it.

MRS. PETERS. Why, yes.

[*She brings the cage forward and puts it on the table.*

MRS. HALE. I wish if they're going to find any evidence they'd be about it. I don't like this place.

MRS. PETERS. But I'm awful glad you came with me, Mrs. Hale. It would be lonesome for me sitting here alone.

MRS. HALE. It would, wouldn't it? [*Dropping her sewing.*] But I tell you what I do wish, Mrs. Peters. I wish I had come over sometimes when *she* was here. I—[*Looking around the room*]—wish I had.

MRS. PETERS. But of course you were awful busy, Mrs. Hale—your house and your children.

MRS. HALE. I could've come. I stayed away because it weren't cheerful—and that's why I ought to have come. I—I've never liked this place. Maybe because it's down in a hollow and you don't see the road. I dunno what it is, but it's a lonesome place and always was. I wish I had come over to see Minnie Foster sometimes. I can see now—

[*Shakes her head.*

MRS. PETERS. Well, you mustn't reproach yourself, Mrs. Hale. Somehow we just don't see how it is with other folks until—something comes up.

MRS. HALE. Not having children makes less work—but it makes a quiet house, and Wright out to work all day, and no company when he did come in. Did you know John Wright, Mrs. Peters?

MRS. PETERS. Not to know him; I've seem him in town. They say he was a good man.

MRS. HALE. Yes—good; he didn't drink, and kept his word as well as most, I guess, and paid his debts. But he was a hard man, Mrs. Peters. Just to pass the time of day with him— [*Shivers.*] Like a raw wind that gets to the bone. [*Pauses, her eye falling on the cage.*] I should think she would 'a wanted a bird. But what do you suppose went with it?

MRS. PETERS.   I don't know, unless it got sick and died.

> [*She reaches over and swings the broken door, swings it again, both women watch it.*]

MRS. HALE.   You weren't raised round here, were you? [*MRS. PETERS shakes her head.*] You didn't know—her?

MRS. PETERS.   Not till they brought her yesterday.

MRS. HALE.   She—come to think of it, she was kind of like a bird herself—real sweet and pretty, but kind of timid and—fluttery. How— she—did—change. [*Silence; then as if struck by a happy thought and relieved to get back to every day things.*] Tell you what, Mrs. Peters, why don't you take the quilt in with you? It might take up her mind.

MRS. PETERS.   Why, I think that's a real nice idea, Mrs. Hale. There couldn't possibly be any objection to it, could there? Now, just what would I take? I wonder if her patches are in here—and her things.

> [*They look in the sewing basket.*]

MRS. HALE.   Here's some red. I expect this has got sewing things in it. [*Brings out a fancy box.*] What a pretty box. Looks like something somebody would give you. Maybe her scissors are in here. [*Opens box. Suddenly puts her hand to her nose.*] Why—[*MRS. PETERS bends nearer, then turns her face away.*] There's something wrapped up in this piece of silk.

MRS. PETERS.   Why, this isn't her scissors.

MRS. HALE.   [*Lifting the silk.*] Oh, Mrs. Peters—its—

> [*MRS PETERS bends closer.*]

MRS. PETERS.   It's the bird.

MRS. HALE.   [*Jumping up.*] But, Mrs. Peters—look at it! It's neck! Look at its neck! It's all—other side *to.*

MRS. PETERS.   Somebody—wrung—its—neck.

> [*Their eyes meet. A look of growing comprehension, of horror. Steps are heard outside. MRS. HALE slips box under quilt pieces, and sinks into her chair. Enter SHERIFF and COUNTY ATTORNEY. MRS. PETERS rises.*]

COUNTY ATTORNEY.   [*As one turning from serious things to little pleasantries.*] Well, ladies, have you decided whether she was going to quilt it or knot it?

Mrs. Peters.   We think she was going to—knot it.

County Attorney.   Well, that's interesting, I'm sure. [*Seeing the birdcage*] Has the bird flown?

Mrs. Hale.   [*Putting more quilt pieces over the box.*] We think the—cat got it.

County Attorney.   [*Preoccupied.*] Is there a cat?

[*Mrs. Hale glances in a quick covert way at Mrs. Peters.*

Mrs. Peters.   Well, not *now*. They're superstitious, you know. They leave.

County Attorney.   [*To Sheriff Peters, continuing an interrupted conversation.*] No sign at all of anyone having come from the outside. Their own rope. Now let's go up again and go over it piece by piece. [*They start upstairs.*] It would have to have been someone who knew just the—

[*Mrs. Peters sits down. The two women sit there not looking at one another, but as if peering into something and at the same time holding back. When they talk now it is in the manner of feeling their way over strange ground, as if afraid of what they are saying, but as if they can not help saying it.*

Mrs. Hale.   She liked the bird. She was going to bury it in the pretty box.

Mrs. Peters.   [*In a whisper.*] When I was a girl—my kitten—there was a boy took a hatchet, and before my eyes—and before I could get there—[*Covers her face an instant.*] If they hadn't held me back I would have–[*Catches herself, looks upstairs where steps are heard, falters weakly*]—hurt him.

Mrs. Hale.   [*With a slow look around her.*] I wonder how it would seem never to have had any children around. [*Pause.*] No, Wright wouldn't like the bird—a thing that sang. She used to sing. He killed that, too.

Mrs. Peters.   [*Moving uneasily.*] We don't know who killed the bird.

Mrs. Hale.   I knew John Wright.

Mrs. Peters.   It was an awful thing was done in this house that night, Mrs. Hale. Killing a man while he slept, slipping a rope around his neck that choked the life out of him.

Mrs. Hale.   His neck. Choked the life out of him.

[*Her hand goes out and rests on the bird-cage*

MRS. PETERS. [*With rising voice.*] We don't know who killed him. We dont *know*.

MRS. HALE. [*Her own feeling not interrupted.*] If there'd been years and years of nothing, then a bird to sing to you, it would be awful—still, after the bird was still.

MRS. PETERS. [*Something within her speaking.*] I know what stillness is. When we homesteaded in Dakota, and my first baby died—after he was two years old, and me with no other then—

MRS. HALE. [*Moving.*] How soon do you suppose they'll be through, looking for the evidence?

MRS. PETERS. I know what stillness is. [*Pulling herself back.*] The law has got to punish crime, Mrs. Hale.

MRS. HALE. [*Not as if answering that.*] I wish you'd seen Minnie Foster when she wore a white dress with blue ribbons and stood up there in the choir and sang. [*A look around the room.*] Oh, I *wish* I'd come over here once in a while! That was a crime! That was a crime! Who's going to punish that?

MRS. PETERS. [*Looking upstairs.*] We mustn't—take on.

MRS. HALE. I might have known she needed help! I know how things can be—for women. I tell you, it's queer, Mrs. Peters. We live close together and we live far apart. We all go through the same things—it's all just a different kind of the same thing. [*Brushes her eyes, noticing the bottle of fruit, reaches out for it.*] If I was you I wouldn't tell her her fruit was gone. Tell her it *ain't*. Tell her it's all right. Take this in to prove it to her. She—she may never know whether it was broke or not.

MRS. PETERS. [*Takes the bottle, looks about for something to wrap it in; takes petticoat from the clothes brought from the other room, very nervously begins winding this around the bottle. In a false voice.*] My, it's a good thing the men couldn't hear us. Wouldn't they just laugh! Getting all stirred up over a little thing like a—dead canary. As if that could have anything to do with—with—wouldn't they *laugh*!

[*The men are heard coming down stairs.*]

MRS. HALE. [*Under her breath.*] Maybe they would—maybe they wouldn't.

COUNTY ATTORNEY. No, Peters, it's all perfectly clear except a reason for doing it. But you know juries when it comes to women. If there was some definite thing. Something to show—something to make a story about—a thing that would connect up with this strange way of doing it—

[*The women's eyes meet for an instant.
Enter HALE from outer door.*]

HALE. Well, I've got the team around. Pretty cold out there.

COUNTY ATTORNEY. I'm going to stay here a while by myself. [*To the* SHERIFF.] You can send Frank out for me, can't you? I want to go over everything. I'm not satisfied that we can't do better.

SHERIFF.   Do you want to see what Mrs. Peters is going to take in?

[*The* LAWYER *goes to the table, picks up the apron, laughs.*]

COUNTY ATTORNEY.   Oh, I guess they're not very dangerous things the ladies have picked out. [*Moves a few things about, disturbing the quilt pieces which cover the box. Steps back.*] No, Mrs. Peters doesn't need supervising. For that matter, a sheriff's wife is married to the law. Ever think of it that way, Mrs. Peters?

MRS. PETERS.   Not—just that way.

SHERIFF.   [*Chuckling.*] Married to the law. [*Moves toward the other room.*] I just want you to come in here a minute George. We ought to take a look at these windows.

COUNTY ATTORNEY.   [*Scoffingly.*] Oh, windows!

SHERIFF.   We'll be right out, Mr. Hale.

> [HALE *goes outside. The* SHERIFF *follows the* COUNTY ATTORNEY *into the other room. Then* MRS. HALE *rises, hands tight together, looking intensely at* MRS. PETERS, *whose eyes make a slow turn, finally meeting* MRS. HALE'S. *A moment* MRS. HALE *holds her, then her own eyes point the way to where the box is concealed. Suddenly* MRS. PETERS *throws back quilt pieces and tries to put the box in the bag she is wearing. It is too big. She opens box, starts to take bird out, cannot touch it, goes to pieces, stands there helpless. Sound of a knob turning in the other room.* MRS. HALE *snatches the box and puts it in the pocket of her big coat. Enter* COUNTY ATTORNEY *and* SHERIFF.]

COUNTY ATTORNEY.   [*Facetiously.*] Well, Henry, at least we found out that she was not going to quilt it. She was going to—what is it you call it, ladies?

HALE.   [*Her hands against her pocket.*] We call it—knot it, Mr. Henderson.

(CURTAIN)

appendix A

An Explanation of Metrical Terms

The regular patterns of stressed and unstressed syllables found in most English-language poetry are called *meter*. Analyzing and marking meter is called *scansion*. In order to scan a line of poetry, we first determine the number of syllables and the position of the stresses (or accents). Stressed and unstressed syllables are marked in the following manner: ĭn (unstressed) lóve (stressed). The basic unit of meter is the *foot*, usually one stressed syllable and one or more unstressed syllables. The basic feet are:

iamb (adj. *iambic*)—one unstressed syllable followed by one stressed syllable: abóve

trochee (adj. *trochaic*)—one stressed syllable followed by one unstressed syllable: únder

anapest (adj. *anapestic*)—two unstressed syllables followed by one stressed syllable: ĭn thĕ sky

dactyl (adj. *dactylic*)—one stressed syllable followed by two unstressed syllables: sílvĕrwăre

monosyllable (adj. *monosyllabic*)—one stressed syllable: thére

spondee (adj. *spondaic*)—two stressed syllables: súnshíne

The metrical length of a line is determined by the number of feet:

monometer—one foot

dimeter—two feet

trimeter—three feet

tetrameter—four feet

pentameter—five feet

hexameter—six feet

heptameter—seven feet

octameter—eight feet

We label the meter of a line, stanza, or poem by combining the kind of feet with the line length: iambic pentameter, anapestic tetrameter. Here is an example of an iambic pentameter line with stress indicators and vertical lines to show the division between feet:

What ŏft | wăs thoúght, | bŭt né'er | sŏ wéll | ĕxpréssed.

To indicate a caesura, a pause somewhere within the line, use double vertical lines:

What ŏft | wăs thoúght, ‖ bŭt né'er | sŏ wéll | ĕxpréssed.

Since variation is essential to rhythm, do not expect meter always to be perfectly regular. This iambic tetrameter line, for example, begins with a trochee:

Gáthĕr | yĕ róse | bŭds whíle | yĕ máy.

Not all readers agree on how to scan every foot of every line. The primary purpose of scanning is to recognize the prevailing meter and to be aware of variations.

appendix B

Manuscript Form and Style

TITLES OF LITERARY WORKS

Titles of short stories and most poems are placed within quotation marks: "The Guest," "Snake." Titles of very long poems are underlined (italicized in print): Paradise Lost. Titles of plays and novels are underlined: Othello, The Great Gatsby.

REFERENCES TO AUTHORS

First references to authors usually include the full name: Katherine Anne Porter. Subsequent references use the last name only: Porter. Do not use Mr. or Ms., and do not refer to authors by their first names.

PAPER TITLES

Create an appropriate title for your paper. Do not use only the title of the work under discussion. If the title of the work is part of your title, place it in quotation marks or underline as appropriate: The Satiric Tone of "The Unknown Citizen." Do not place *your* title in quotation marks.

HANDLING DIRECT QUOTATIONS: FORM

1. Quote accurately. Take time to compare what you have copied with the original.

2. When quoting two lines of poetry, or a part of two lines, separate the two lines with a slash (/) and reproduce the capital letter that begins the second line:

> The significance of the snake is further emphasized when the speaker calls him "one of the lords / Of life."

[Notice that "one" is not capitalized because it is not the first work in the poetic line.]

3. If quoted material runs to more than three lines in your paper, present it in *display form*: indent the quotation ten spaces from the left margin and, when typing, continue to double space. When using display form, do not use quotation marks as well. Example:

> The subject life of Mabel and her brothers is reinforced through the symbolic description of the sold horses:
>> The great draught-horses swung past. They were tied head to tail, four of them, and they heaved along. . . . Every movement showed a massive, slumbrous strength, and a stupidity which held them in subjection.

4. More than two lines of poetry should be presented in display form and reproduced exactly as they appear in the original. Line numbers are usually provided for quotations from longer poems.

> Prufrock's empty life is depicted in the directionless life of the city:

>> Let us go, through certain half-deserted streets,
>> The muttering retreats
>> Of restless nights in one-night cheap hotels

>>> (11. 4–6)

5. When quoting more than one speech from a play, use display form and reproduce the conventional pattern of indicating the speakers. Provide act and scene numbers after the quotation. For poetic drama, provide act, scene and line numbers.

> In the following exchange Iago subtly plants suspicion of Cassio in the mind of Othello:

>> Oth.   Was not that Cassio parted from my wife?
>> Iago.   Cassio, my lord! No, sure, I cannot think it,

> That he would steal away so guilty-like,
> Seeing you coming.

Oth.   I do believe 'twas he.

$$(III.iii.37{-}40)$$

Note that Othello's last remark is a continuation of line 40. His words are placed on a new line but moved to the right of "coming."

6. When quoted material from fiction and prose dramas forms only a part of a sentence, the first quoted word is not capitalized even if it was capitalized in the original, unless the quoted material follows a colon. (As we have already illustrated, first words from lines of poetry retain the initial capital letter, unless only the one word is quoted.)

> *Orig.:*   She shut her eyes, reached out her hand and touched a sleeve. (From "A Worn Path")
>
> *Ex. 1:*   Phoenix next demonstrates her bravery when "she shut[s] her eyes" and reaches out to touch the scarecrow.
>
> *Ex. 2:*   Phoenix reacts to the scarecrow with the same bravery that characterizes the creek crossing: "She shut her eyes, reached out her hand and touched a sleeve."

Note: Any additions to direct quotations must be placed in square brackets ([]). In this case, the "s" is added to maintain present tense throughout the sentence.

When quoted material comes at the end of the sentence, use only the punctuation appropriate to complete the sentence.

> *Incorrect:*   Emerson's faith in self-reliance is summed up in two words: "trust thyself:."
>
> *Correct:*   Emerson's faith in self-reliance is summed up in two words: "trust thyself."

7. When presenting direct quotations, place the commas and periods needed to punctuate your sentence *inside* the final quotation marks.

When the speaker finally recognizes the snake as "one of the lords / Of life," he feels guilty for his earlier behavior and describes that behavior as a "pettiness."

Colons and semicolons needed in your sentence are placed *outside* a final quotation mark. Note that commas are not used to introduce a direct quotation; they appear only when required by the structure of the sentence.

8. Irrelevant portions can be omitted to reduce the length of direct quotations. Indicate omitted material by using the *ellipsis* (three spaced periods: . . .). If the omitted material comes at the end of a sentence, use four periods; the first, placed without a space after the word it follows, marks the end of the sentence.

> The subject life of Mabel and her brothers is reinforced through the symbolic description of the sold horses:
>> The great draught-horses swung past. They were tied head to tail, four of them, and they heaved along. . . . Every movement showed a massive, slumbrous strength, and a stupidity which held them in subjection.

HANDLING DIRECT QUOTATIONS: STYLE

1. Quote only what is needed to support your point. Usually quoting selected single words or phrases combined with paraphrase will be more effective than quoting several lines or sentences. For example:

> The first quatrain of Shakespeare's "Sonnet 73" contains a comparison between the speaker and late autumn, when the "few" remaining leaves are "yellow" and the boughs of the trees "shake against the cold."

> *Not:* The first quatrain of Shakespeare's "Sonnet 73" contains a comparison between the speaker and late autumn:
>> That time of year thou mayst in me behold
>> When yellow leaves, or none, or few, do hang
>> Upon those boughs which shake against the cold,
>> Bare ruined choirs where late the sweet birds sang.

Long quotations such as this frustrate a reader expecting analysis.

2. Weave quotations coherently into your sentences. A quotation within one of your sentences must not distort the grammar, syntax, or logic of that sentence. Here are some typical problems:

> *Tense shift:* As Mrs. Mallard *looks* out of the window, she *feels* that "there *was* something coming to her."

Revision: As Mrs. Mallard *looks* out of the window, she *feels* that there *is* "something coming to her."

Note: Problems with tense consistency in quoting literature often arise because we use present tense to describe what happens in the work even though it may be presented in the past tense. The solution is usually, as in the above revision, to quote less and use more of your own words.

Person shift: The Duke says that "I choose / Never to stoop."

Revision: The Duke says that he chooses "Never to stoop."

Faulty structure: The speaker thinks back to coming upon "Two roads diverged in a yellow wood."

Revision: The speaker thinks back to coming upon two roads which "diverged in a yellow wood."

Glossary

Allegory Work containing a system of symbolic equivalents whose meanings can usually be rather precisely defined.

Alliteration Repetition of the initial letter or sound in a series of words, e.g., "Science, that *s*imple *s*aint."

Allusion Reference to lines or characters from literature or mythology, or to figures or events from history.

Analysis Dividing a literary work into its component parts.

Antagonist Character who opposes, or represents the forces which oppose, the main character or protagonist.

Apostrophe Direct address to an object, animal, or dead or fictitious person.

Archetype In literature, characters and situations reappearing in different times and cultures that seem to represent or appeal to basic human perceptions of the world and basic human values.

Assonance Repetition of a vowel sound in a series of words, e.g., "To f*i*t *i*ts r*i*bs."

Atmosphere The emotional quality or feeling of a work, often established by the way setting is described.

Ballad A narrative poem composed (usually) in a ballad stanza, a four-line stanza of alternating iambic tetrameter and iambic trimeter with the second and fourth lines rhyming.

Beast Fable A fable (tale with a moral) in which the characters are real or imaginary animals with human traits.

Blank Verse Continuous lines of poetry in unrhymed iambic pentameter.

Character Any person in narrative and dramatic works. Also, the personality traits that together form a person's "character."

Chorus A group of actors in a play who speak or chant in unison and comment on, rather than participate in, the action.

Chronology The sequence of events in a narrative.

Climax The point of greatest tension and interest in a narrative or play; usually the point that determines the eventual resolution.

Comedy A play depicting human weaknesses or foibles that, when overcome or laughed away, result in (usually) a happy ending.

> **Romantic Comedy** The lovers must overcome some problem, often foolish parents, but the lovers eventually triumph and are united.
>
> **Comedy of Manners** Ridicules silly "drawing-room" behavior.
>
> **Rogue or Picaresque Comedy** Society's underdogs triumph over their social betters.
>
> **Satiric Comedy** Serious human weaknesses are examined with the aim of correcting such behavior.

Complication Any development in the plot of a narrative or play that brings about or increases the conflict.

Conflict Tension between opposing forces—characters, ideas, goals; may be internal (between opposing goals of the main character), personal (between two characters), or social/environmental (between a character and society, environmental forces, or "fate").

Connotation The associations and emotional overtones conveyed by a word.

Consonance Repetition of final consonant sounds in a series of words, e.g., "the first frost."

Couplet Two continuous lines of verse alike in metrical pattern and rhyme.

Criticism The analyses, interpretations, and evaluations of literature by literary critics.

Denotation Dictionary meanings of a word.

Dialogue Words spoken by characters.

Diction A writer's word choice.

Dramatic Irony *See* Irony.

Dramatic Monologue Words delivered by a speaker to a silent listener or listeners.

English Sonnet *See* Sonnet.

Epiphany A moment of awareness or revelation experienced by a character. The term was introduced by James Joyce.

Exposition The presentation of the context in which a narrative or drama takes place, including information about the setting, the characters, and previous significant events.

Fable A narrative told to teach a lesson or moral.

Falling Action The part of the plot following the climax; usually refers to action in a tragedy.

Fantasy A work presenting strange characters or events that do not seem bound by what is considered realistic or probable.

Farce A type of comedy that features physical comedy, extreme actions, and unusual situations.

Fiction An imagined story.

Figurative Language   Language containing figures of speech that extend meaning beyond the literal.

First Person Point of View   *See* Point of View.

Flashback   A break in time sequence to present events that actually take place at an earlier time.

Flat Character   A character who is given only a few traits or characteristics; one who is not fully developed.

Foil Character   A minor character who helps to illuminate, by contrast, traits in a major character.

Folklore   Beliefs and customs transmitted, usually orally, to members of the same culture.

Foreshadowing   Using events or statements early in a work to hint of forthcoming events.

Free Verse   Verse that does not have a sustained metrical pattern, but may have rhyme.

Genre   A type or category of literature, e.g., a novel, a play.

Hyperbole   *See* Overstatement.

Image   The recreation in words of a sense experience.

Imagery   All of the images in a given work. Also, a cluster of similar images creating a dominant impression in a work, e.g., the blood imagery in *Macbeth*.

Irony   In general, the expression of some form of incongruity or discrepancy. *Verbal irony* expresses a discrepancy between what is said and what is meant. *Dramatic irony* expresses a discrepancy between what a character says or does and what we perceive to be true. *Irony of situation* develops a discrepancy between what we expect to happen and what actually happens.

Italian Sonnet   *See* Sonnet.

Limited Omniscient   *See* Point of view.

Lyric   A poem that communicates the thoughts and feelings of a speaker who may be closely identified with the poet or who may be a created character or persona.

Melodrama   A type of drama characterized by sensational incidents, representational or undeveloped characters, and the victory of good over evil.

Metaphor   A figure of speech in which a comparison is either stated or implied between two basically unlike things.

Meter   A pattern of stressed and unstressed syllables in lines of poetry. The basic metrical unit of verse in English is the foot, which normally consists of one stressed and one or more unstressed syllables.

Metonymy   A figure of speech in which a detail or related element is used to represent the complete object or experience: "The White House approved."

Mood   *See* Atmosphere.

Myth   A narrative about gods or legendary figures that expresses a group's religious beliefs and gives explanations of natural phenomena, such as the creation of the world.

Narrative   A recounting in prose or verse of a sequence of events.

Narrator   The one who tells the story by recounting a sequence of events in prose or verse.

Objective Point of View   *See* Point of View.

Octave   An eight-line unit of poetry, e.g., the first eight lines of an Italian sonnet.

Omniscient Point of View   *See* Point of View.

Overstatement (or Hyperbole)   An intentional exaggeration not meant to be taken literally: "I waited an eternity."

Parable   A story told to illustrate, point for point, a moral or lesson: e.g., the story of the prodigal son.

Paradox   A statement that seems contradictory but that nevertheless can be explained: "I could not love thee dear so much / Loved I not honor more."

Paraphrase   A restatement in different words of what is said in a work or a passage. The purpose is to clarify rather than to condense.

Persona   The created voice, or mask, through which the author speaks.

Personification   A comparison that gives human qualities to something nonhuman: "Old age hath yet his honor and his toil."

Plot   The selective ordering of events in a narrative.

Point of View   The angle of vision through which we are shown the work, determined by the author's selection of speaker. In fiction, subdivided as follows:

> **first-person point of view**   a participant in the story recounting events in his/her own voice using the first person (I, we).
>
> **omniscient point of view**   an all-knowing third person narrator, able to go anywhere, see anything, enter the minds of the characters, and make comments on the story.
>
> **limited omniscient point of view**   a third-person narrator limited to the thoughts and experiences of a single character.
>
> **objective point of view**   a third-person narrator reporting only what can be observed or overheard without any interpretive comment.

Problem Play   A serious drama examining a social or psychological issue.

Protagonist   The main character of a work. *See* Antagonist.

Quatrain   A unit of four lines of poetry.

Realism   A literary mode in which the goal is to depict recognizable settings, believable characters, and probable events.

Resolution   Following the climax, the outcome of the conflict.

Rhythm   The arrangement of stressed and unstressed syllables.

Rhyme   The repetition of the accented vowel sound and following consonants or syllables in corresponding positions in two or more lines of poetry (moon, spoon; farming, charming). Rhyme appearing at the end of lines is *end rhyme*; rhyme appearing within a line is *internal rhyme*. Rhyme in which the sounds correspond imperfectly (light, late) is *off rhyme*.

Rising Action   That part of a dramatic plot leading through complication to the climax.

Round Character   A fully developed, three-dimensional character.

Sarcasm   Bitter or cutting expression, often ironic.

Satire   Literature that ridicules the vices and follies of humanity (usually) to bring about the possibility of reform.

Sestet   A six-line unit of poetry, e.g., the last six lines of an Italian sonnet.

Setting   The physical locale in the work.

Shakespearean Sonnet   *See* Sonnet.

Simile   A comparison between two basically unlike things stated explicitly through a connector such as *like* or *as, seems* or *appears*: "My luve is like a red, red rose."

Situational Irony   *See* Irony.

Soliloquy   Lines spoken by a character either directly to an audience or to himself or herself.

Sonnet   A fourteen-line poem is iambic pentameter with a fixed rhyme scheme. The major forms are the English or Shakespearean (rhyming *abab cdcd efef gg*) and the Italian or Petrarchan (rhyming *abbaabba cdcdcd* or *cdecde*).

Speaker   The voice presenting the thoughts and feelings of a dramatic or lyric poem.

Stanza   The grouping of lines of poetry into a unit that is repeated with the same meter, rhyme, and number of lines.

Stream of Consciousness   A narrative technique reproducing the seemingly disorganized free associations in the mind at various levels of consciousness.

Structure   A meaningful pattern that organizes the work as a whole.

Style   The author's selection and arrangement of language.

Symbol   An object, character, or action that suggests meanings, associations, and emotions beyond what is characteristic of its nature or function. A rose is a flower, but symbolically a rose is associated with love and beauty.

Synecdoche   A figure of speech in which a part stands for the whole: "The hand that signed the paper felled the city."

Syntax   The arrangement of words within a phrase or sentence.

Theme   The central idea (or ideas) that the work embodies.

Tone   The expression of attitude (e.g., playful, bitter) by a speaker or by the author.

Tragedy A dramatization of serious events, usually depicting the assertion of the will of an heroic main character and the eventual loss of position, and often life, of that character.

Type Character A character who embodies or represents a single quality or characteristic.

Understatement A form of verbal irony in which less is stated than is meant. The effect is an unexpected emphasis: "The grave's a fine and private place / But none, I think, do there embrace."

Verbal Irony *See* Irony.

Credits

Index of Authors, Titles, and First Lines of Poems

(Authors are in bold type; titles are in italics; and first lines are in roman.)

Index of Critical Terms